We have
30 Luxury Weeke...

to be won in the AA Lifestyl...
Draw with the Country Club ...oup

Winners can choose from 10 fabulous Country Club Resorts in the UK.

- Redwood Lodge Hotel, Bristol
- Dalmahoy Hotel, Nr Edinburgh
- Goodwood Park Hotel, Nr.Chichester
- Meon Valley Hotel, Nr.Southampton
- Tewkesbury Park Hotel, Tewkesbury

- Broughton Park Hotel, Preston
- St.Pierre Hotel, Chepstow
- Tudor Park Hotel, Nr.Maidstone
- Breadsall Priory Hotel, Breadsall, Nr Derby
- Forest of Arden Hotel, Nr Coventry

A total of 6 Prize Draws throughout the year, with 5 winners per draw.

Draws will be made on the last day of December '95 and then February, April, June, August and October '96

For more information on Leisure and Golf Breaks with the Country Club Hotel Group, please call 01582 56 78 99

HOW TO ENTER

Just complete (in capitals, please) and send off this card or, alternatively, send your name and address on a postcard to the address overleaf (no purchase required).
No stamp is needed for entries posted in the UK.

MR/MRS/MISS/MS/OTHER, PLEASE STATE:

NAME:

ADDRESS:

POSTCODE:

TEL.NOS:

Are you an AA Member ?   Yes/No

Have you bought this or any other AA Lifestyle Guide before?   Yes/No
If yes, please indicate the year of the last edition you bought:

The AA Hotel Guide	19____
AA Best Restaurants	19____
AA Bed and Breakfast Guide	19____
AA Camping and Caravanning (Britain & Ireland)	19____
AA Camping and Caravanning (W.Country & S. England)	19____

If you do not wish to receive further information or special offers on
AA books, please tick the box   **BB 96**

Terms and Conditions

1. Five winners will be drawn for each of six prize draws to take place on 29 December 1995, 29 February, 30 April, 28 June, 30 August and 31 October 1996.

2. Closing date for receipt of entries is 1 day prior to the relevant draw date. **Final close date for receipt of entries is 30 October 1996.**

3. Entries received after any draw date will go forward into the next available draw. Entries will be placed in one draw only.

4. Winners will be notified by post within 14 days of the relevant draw date. Prizes will be valid for three months from the relevant draw date. Prizes are not transferable and there will be no cash alternative.

5. Each prize comprises of two nights with dinner, bed and breakfast and the 'Champagne Celebration Package' for two people sharing a double/twin room at any of the 10 Country Club Resorts listed overleaf. Dates are subject to availability. The prize does not include any travelling expenses. All other meals, drinks (except as stated), and extras (including golf) will be charged as taken.

6. All hotel accommodation, services and facilities are provided by the Country Club Hotel Group and AA Publishing are not party to your agreement with the Country Club Hotel Group in this regard.

7. The prize draw is open to anyone over the age of 18 other than employees of the Automobile Association or the Country Club Hotel Group, its subsidiary companies, their families or agents.

8. For a list of winners, please send a stamped self-addressed envelope to: AA Lifestyle Guide Winners, Publishing Admin., Fanum House, Basing View, Basingstoke, Hants RG21 4EA.

NO STAMP
NECESSARY
IN THE UK

AA Lifestyle Guide Prize Draw

FREEPOST BZ 343
BASINGSTOKE
HANTS RG21 2BR

AA

BED AND BREAKFAST
Guide to Britain and Ireland 1996

Produced by AA Publishing
Atlas prepared by the AA's Cartographic Department
Maps © The Automobile Association 1995

—■—

Directory generated by the AA Establishment Database,
Information Research and Control, Hotel and Touring Services

—■—

Advertisements
Head of Advertisement Sales: Christopher Heard Tel. 01256 20123 ext. 21544
Advertisement Production: Karen Weeks Tel. 01256 20123 ext. 21545

—■—

Typeset by Avonset, Midsomer Norton, Bath
Printed and bound in Great Britain by William Clowes Limited, London and Beccles

—■—

—■—

© The Automobile Association 1995
Reprinted March 1996
Reprinted June 1996

—■—

A CIP catalogue record for this book is available from the British Library

—■—

Published by AA Publishing which is a trading name of Automobile Association Developments
Limited whose registered office is Norfolk House, Basingstoke, Hampshire RG24 9NY,
Registered number 1878835

—■—

AA Ref 52922
—■—
ISBN 0 7495 1112 5

CONTENTS

Follow the Country Code

Enjoy the countryside and respect its life and work.

Guard against all risk of fire.

Fasten all gates.

Keep your dogs under close control.

Keep to public paths across farmland.

Use gates and stiles to cross fences, hedges and walls.

Leave livestock, crops and machinery alone.

Take your litter home.

Help to keep all water clean.

Protect wildlife, plants and trees.

Take special care on country roads.

Make no unnecessary noise.

Inspection and Classification

A LL ESTABLISHMENTS in the guide are inspected and assessed for the quality of what they provide. This assessment of guest houses farmhouses or inns is made by our hotel inspectors on a subjective basis, following each inspection, and indicates the quality of the accommodation and services provided by each establishment.

Each establishment receives from one to five quality symbols in ascending order of merit. Q to QQQ awards are designated 'AA Recommended' and may display this on the AA sign outside their premises. This wording, however, is not part of their entry in the directory.

Those places gaining QQQQ are designated 'AA Selected' and QQQQQ awards are designated 'AA Premier Selected'. Both may display these words on their AA signs. These have entries in the book highlighted either by a box titled 'Selected' or, for 'Premier Selected', a box with a photograph and tinted panel.

Q *Recommended*
This assessment indicates an establishment with simple accommodation and adequate bathroom facilities.

QQ *Recommended*
This assessment indicates a sound standard of accommodation offering more in terms of decor and comfort and likely to have some bedrooms with en suite bath or shower rooms.

QQQ *Recommended*
This assessment indicates well appointed accommodation and a wider range of facilities than a one or two Q establishment. Bedrooms may have en suite bath/shower rooms.

QQQQ *Selected*
This assessment indicates that the accommodation will be comfortable and well appointed, that hospitality and facilities will be of high quality, and that a reasonable proportion of bedrooms will have en suite bath or shower rooms

QQQQQ *Premier Selected*
This is the AA's highest assessment for guest houses, farmhouses or inns. It has been introduced in response to the rapidly growing number of really excellent establishments. It indicates an outstanding level of accommodation and service, with an emphasis on quality, good facilities for guests and an exceptionally friendly hospitable atmosphere.
The majority of bedrooms will have en suite bath or shower rooms.

The quality assessment is shown in the directory entry as follows:

FALMOUTH *Cornwall* Map **2** SX25
GH QQ Ram Hotel High Road XY21 1AB
☎ (015036) 4321

♥ QQQ Mr & Mrs J Smith Homestead DX8 1WY
(SX261567)
☎ (015036) 3421

This year 839 places have been awarded the distinction of a SELECTED assessment and 203 places have the highest assessment of PREMIER SELECTED. A quick reference list of the Premier Selected QQQQQ and Selected QQQQ establishments are listed at the beginning of each country. There is also a comphrehensive list of Premier Selected on pages 14-15.

HINTS FOR BOOKING YOUR STAY

THE AA INSPECTS and classifies more than 3500 small hotels, guest houses, farmhouses and inns for its 'AA Recommended', 'AA Selected' and 'AA Premier Selected' categories. The precise number of places in the guide varies slightly from year to year, and we are delighted that each year we have an increase both in the total number of establishments in the guide and – as a result of continuously improving standards – in the top two categories.

Q
QUALITY AWARDS

All the establishments listed in the directory are given awards of between one and five Q for quality. More details about the Q awards can be found in the section headed 'Quality Assessment' on page 5. Those places that have gained the two highest ratings - QQQQ and QQQQQ awards - have their entries highlighted in the directory.

For quick reference, you will find a list of the establishments awarded five Q on page 14. Establishments awarded four Q and five Q are listed at the begining of each country.

COMMON TO ALL

Whatever the type of establishment, there are certain requirements common to all, including a well-maintained exterior, clean and hygienic kitchens; good standards of furnishing; friendly and courteous service; access to the premises at reasonable times; the use of a telephone; and a full, cooked breakfast in the British or Irish tradition.

Bedrooms should be equipped with comfortable beds, a wardrobe, a bedside cabinet, a washbasin (unless there is an en suite or private bath/shower room) with soap, towel, mirror and shaver socket and at least a carpet beside the bed. There should not be an extra charge for the use of baths or lavatories, and heating should not be metered.

NB. Where the entry for an establishment shows the central heating abbreviation, it does not necessarily mean that central heating will be available all year round. Some places only use it in winter, and then it will be at at their own discretion.

STAYING AT A GUEST HOUSE

The term 'guest house' can lead to some confusion, particularly when many include the word 'hotel' in their name. For AA purposes, small and private hotels are included in this category when they cannot offer all the services required for our hotel star rating system.

The term does not imply that guest houses are inferior to hotels, just that they are different. Many, indeed, offer a very high standard of accommodation. It is not unusual to be offered en suite bathrooms, for instance, or to find a direct-dial telephone and a colour television in your room.

Some guest houses offer bed and breakfast only, so guests must go out for the evening meal. It is also wise to check when booking if there are any restrictions to your access to the house, particularly in the late morning and during the afternoon.

However, many guest houses do provide an evening meal. They may only able to offer a set meal, but many offer an interesting menu and a standard of service that one would expect in a good restaurant. You may have to arrange dinner in advance, so you should ask about the arrangements for evening meals when booking. Many places have a full license, or at least a table license and wine list.

LONDON

Guest houses in the London section of the book are all small hotels. London prices tend to be higher than outside the capital, but those that we list offer cost-conscious accommodation, although normally only bed and breakfast is provided. We have also included a few which provide a full meal service and the charges for these will naturally be higher.

STAYING AT A FARMHOUSE

Farmhouse accommodation is particularly noted for being inexpensive and cosy, with a high standard of good home-cooking. Those listed in our book are generally working farms, and some farmers are happy to allow visitors to look around, or even to help feed the animals. However, we must stress that the modern farm is a potentially dangerous place, especially where machinery and chemicals are concerned, and visitors must be prepared to exercise care, particularly if they bring children. **Never leave children unsupervised around the farm.**

Sometimes, guest accommodation is run as a separate concern from the farm, and visitors are discouraged from venturing on to the working land. In other cases, the land has been sold off and only the house remains. Although the directory entry states the acreage and the type of farming carried out, you should

check when booking to make sure that it matches your expectations.

As with guest houses, standards will vary considerably, and are often far above what one would expect. Some of our farmhouses are grand ex-manor houses furnished with antiques and offering a stylish way of life, whereas others offer more simply furnished accommodation, and in others guests may have to share the family bathroom and sitting/dining room.

OFF THE BEATEN TRACK

All of the farmhouses are listed under town or village names, but obviously many will be some distance from any other habitation. The owners will, of course, give directions when you book, and we publish a six-figure map reference against the directory entry which can be used in conjunction with Ordnance Survey large-scale maps like the 1:50 000 Landranger series.

STAYING AT AN INN

We all know what we can expect to find in a traditional inn – a cosy bar, a convivial atmosphere, good beer and pub food. Nevertheless, there are a few extra criteria which must be met for the AA classification: breakfast is a must , in a suitable breakfast room, and the inn should also serve at least light meals during licensing hours.

In this guide, a number of small, fully licensed hotels are classified as inns, and the character of the properties will vary according to whether they are traditional country inns or larger establishments in towns. Again it is important to check details before you book, and also remember to ask if you can arrive at any time of the day or only during opening hours.

BOOKING

Book as early as possible, particularly for the peak holiday period from the beginning of June to the end of September, and may also include Easter and other public holidays, In some parts of Scotland the skiing season is a peak holiday period.

Although it is possible for chance callers to find a night's accommodation, it is by no means a certainty, especially at peak holiday times and in popular areas, so it is always advisable to book as far in advance as possible. Some may only accept weekly bookings from Saturday. Some establishments will require a deposit on booking.

We have tried to provide as much information as possible about the establishments in our directory, but if you require further information, write to or telephone the establishment itself. Do remember to enclose a stamped addressed envelope, or an international reply-paid coupon if writing from overseas, and please quote this publication in any enquiry. Although we try to publish accurate and up to date information, please remember that any details, and particularly prices, are subject to change without notice and this may happen during the currency of the guide.

SMOKING REGULATIONS

'No-smoking' when used by itself in the guide indicates a total ban on smoking throughout the premises. If only certain areas are designated no-smoking (eg bedrooms, dining room) this is shown.

Although we have tried to get accurate information on this question from the establishments, you must remember that the situation may change during the currency of this edition. If the freedom to smoke or to be in a smoke-free atmosphere is important to you, please make sure about the rules before you book.

Cancellation

If you find that you must cancel a booking, let the proprietor know at once, because if the room you booked cannot be re-let, you may be held legally responsible for partial payment. Whether it is a matter of losing your deposit, or of being liable for compensation, you should seriously consider taking out cancellation insurance, such as AA Travelsure.

Complaints

Readers who have any cause to complain are urged to do so on the spot. This should provide an opportunity for the proprietor to correct matters. If a personal approach fails, readers should inform: AA Hotel Services, Basingstoke, Hants, RG21 2EA.

FIRE PRECAUTIONS

Many of the establishments listed in the Guide are subject to the requirements of the Fire Precautions Act of 1971. As far as we can discover, every establishment in this book has applied for, and not been refused, a fire certificate.

The Fire Precautions Act does not apply to Ireland (see the Contents page for the Irish Directory), the Channel Islands or the Isle of Man, which exercise their own rules regarding fire precautions for hotels.

FOOD AND DRINK

If you intend to take dinner at an establishment, note that sometimes the meal must be ordered in advance of the actual meal time. In some cases, this may be at breakfast time, or even on the previous evening. If you have booked on bed, breakfast and evening meal terms, you may find that the tariff includes only the set menu, but, if there is one, you can usually order from the à la carte menu and pay a supplement. On Sundays, many establishments serve the main meal at midday, and provide only a cold supper in the evening.

Some London establishments provide only a Continental breakfast. If a full English breakfast is available, this is indicated in their description.

In some parts of Britain, particularly in Scotland, high tea (i.e. a savoury dish followed by bread and butter, scones, cakes, etc.) is sometimes served instead of dinner, but dinner may be available as an alternative. The last time at which high tea or dinner may be ordered on weekdays is shown, but this may vary at weekends.

LICENSED PREMISES

The directory entry will show whether or not the establishment is licensed to serve alcohol. Many places in the guest house category hold a residential or restaurant license only, but all inns hold a full license. Licensed premises are not obliged to remain open throughout the permitted hours, and they may do so only when they expect reasonable trade.

Note that in establishments which have registered clubs, club membership does not come into effect, nor can a drink be bought, until 48 hours after joining.

PAYMENT

Most proprietors will only accept cheques in payment of accounts if notice is given and some form of identification (preferably a cheque card) is produced. If a hotel accepts credit or charge cards, this is shown by the appropriate credit card symbol in its directory entry (see page 13 for details).

BEST BUDGET BARGAINS

Establishments that offer bed and breakfast for £16 or under are indicated by the symbol 🛌 💷 against their entry.

MONEY-OFF VOUCHER SCHEME

At the back of this book you will find ten £1 vouchers which can be redeemed against your bill for accommodation at any of the establishments that show the £ symbol in the directory. Conditions applying to this offer are as follows:

Only one voucher is accepted per person or party per night. In the case of a joint booking for a group of people the discount will only apply to the accommodation of the person or couple presenting the guide. Use of the voucher is restricted to when payment is made before leaving the premises.

A copy of *AA Bed & Breakfast Guide 1996* must be presented with the voucher on arrival and check in at reception. You must tell the proprietor or receptionist that you wish to use the voucher when you check in at reception and show your copy of the 1996 Guide. If you do not mention the voucher until you are checking out, the proprietor is entitled to refuse to accept it because the bill may already have been made out.

The voucher is only accepted against an accommodation bill charged at full tariff rates, and is not valid if any other discount or special off-peak rates has already been applied. Vouchers cannot be used for discounts of meals or bar bills.

The voucher is not valid after 31 December 1996 nor is it redeemable for cash, No change is given.

The voucher scheme is not applicable in the Republic of Ireland

PRICES

It should be noted that daily terms quoted throughout this publication show minimum and maximum prices for both one (s) and two persons (d) and include a full breakfast. If dinner is also included this will be indicated in parenthesis (incl. dinner). Weekly terms, where available, show minimum and maximum prices per person, which take into account minimum double occupancy and maximum single occupancy, where appropriate, and may include the price of an evening meal (wklyhlf-bd).

VAT is payable in the United Kingdom and in the Isle of Man, on both basic prices and any service. VAT does not apply in the Channel Islands. With this exception, prices quoted in the Guide are inclusive of VAT (and service where applicable).

You should always confirm the current prices before making a booking. Those given in this book have been provided by proprietors in good faith, and must be accepted as indications rather than firm quotations.

UNCONFIRMED PRICES

In some cases, proprietors have been unable to provide us with their 1996 charges, but to give you a rough guide we publish the 1995 price, prefixed with an asterisk (∗). It is also a good idea to ascertain all that is included in the price. Weekly terms can vary according to the meals that are included. We cannot indicate whether or not you are able to arrive mid-week, so if this is your intention, do check when making your reservation. Where information about 1996 prices is not given, you are requested to make enquiries direct.

THE REPUBLIC OF IRELAND

Prices for the Republic of Ireland are shown in Irish punts. At the time of going to press (July 1995), the exchange rate is 0.97 Punts = £1.00 Sterling.

CODES OF PRACTICE

The Hotel Industry Voluntary Code of Booking Practice was revised in 1986, and the AA encourages its use in appropriate establishments. Its prime object is to ensure that the customer is clear about the precise services and facilities s/he is buying and what price will have to be paid, before entering into a contractually binding agreement. If the price has not been previously confirmed in writing, the guest should be handed a card at the time of registration, stipulating the total obligatory charge.

The Tourism (Sleeping Accommodation Price Display) Order 1977 compels hotels, motels, guest houses, farmhouses, inns and self-catering accommodation with four or more letting bedrooms to display in entrance halls the minimum and maximum prices charged for each category of room. This order complements the Voluntary Code of Booking Practice. The tariffs quoted in the directory of this book may be affected in the coming year by inflation, variations in the rate of VAT and many other factors.

HOW TO USE THE GUIDE

Symbols and Abbreviations

Bed and breakfast for £16 or under	xx	wkly b&b	Weekly terms, bed and breakfast, per person
Quality assessment (see p.5)	Q	wkly hllf-bd	Weekly terms bed, breakfast and evening meal, per person
Telephone number	x	alc	A la carte
Private bath and WC	bth	CTV	Colour television
Private shower and WC	shr	Etr	Easter
1995 prices	x	fmly	Family bedroom
Full central heating	Cen ht	fr	From
Special facilities for children (see p.13)	ch fac	Last d	Time last dinner can be ordered
Single room including breakfast per person per night	s	rm	Letting bedrooms in main building
		rs	Restricted service
Double room (2 persons sharing a room) including breakfast per night	d	xxxxx	Credit cards (see p.13)
		x	Voucher scheme (see p.9)

THE EXAMPLE OF an entry below is intended to help you find your way through the directory.

1 — **BRISTOL** Avon   Map 02 SX25

2 — **XX** GH **QQQ Mikes Layby** 17 City Wall   XY21 1AB   (2m W off A30)

5 — **tel** 01222 333333   FAX 01222 333334   **3**   **4**

6 — Closed 2 wks Xmas rs Jan

A lovely Victorian rectory, There is a sun lounge. Breakfast is hearty. There are also vegetarian dishes at dinner.   **7**

8 — 14 en suite (bth/shr) (1 fmly) No smoking in 4 bedrooms No smoking area of dining room CTV in all bedrooms No dogs Fishing Golf 18 Last d 6pm

9 — **PRICE GUIDE**
ROOMS: s £12.50-£15.50; d £26-£31

10 — CARDS:

SAMPLE ENTRY (fictitious)

11

1 Towns are listed in alphabetical order under each country: England, Channel Islands, Isle of Man, Scotland, Wales, Northern Ireland and the Republic of Ireland.

The town name is followed by the administrative county or region. Please note that the postal address may give a different county or region. For Scotland the old county name follows in italics.

The map reference denotes the map page number, followed by the National Grid Reference. To find the location, read the first figure across and the second figure vertically within the lettered square

2 a) ⊯⊒ This symbol indicates that the establishment expects to provide bed and breakfast for under £16 per person, per night during 1996, but remember that circumstances and prices can change during the currency of the Guide.

b) Guest houses are identified by the letters GH, Farmhouses by the symbol ❤, Inns by the symbol ◀ and Town and Country (Ireland only) by T&C – this is also the order in which they are listed beneath the town headings.

c) All establishments are rated for quality on a scale of one to five, denoted by the symbol ◖. See page 5 for a full explanation.

3 Establishment name, address, postal code When an establishment's name is shown in italics the particulars have not been confirmed by the proprietor.

Farmhouse entries only – as they are often in remote areas, we provide a six-figure map reference which can be used with Ordnance Survey maps.This Ordnance Survey map reference is shown in italics in parenthesis after the establishment name, eg (*SN191184*).

4 Directions are given wherever they have been supplied by the proprietor.

5 Telephone numbers may be changed during the currency of this book in some areas. In case of difficulty, check with the operator.

6 Opening details – unless otherwise stated, the establishments are open all year, but where dates are shown they are inclusive: e.g. 'Apr-Oct' indicates that the establishment is open from the beginning of April to the end of October.

Some places are open all year, but offer a restricted service off season. The abbreviation 'rs' indicates this. It may mean either that evening meals are not served or that other facilities listed are not available. If the text does not say what the restricted services are, you should check before booking.

7 Description of the property. Note – if there are rooms adapted for or suitable for disabled people reference may be made in the description. Further details for disabled people will be found in the AA's Guide for the Disabled Traveller available from AA shops, free to members, £3.99 to non-members. Guests with any form of disability should notify proprietors, so that arrangements can be made to minimise difficulties, particularly in the event of an emergency.

8 Accommodation details (For key to symbols and abbreviations, see page 11)

The first figure shows the number of letting bedrooms. Where rooms have en suite bath or shower, the number precedes the appropriate abbreviation. Other bedrooms may be shown in this number that have a private bathroom facility adjacent.

Annexe – bedrooms available in an annexe are shown. Their standard is acceptable, but facilities may not be the same as in the main building, and it is advisable to check the nature of the accommodation and tariff before making a reservation.

fmly – indicates family bedrooms.

No smoking – if the establishment is only partly no-smoking, the areas where smoking is not permitted are shown

all CTV – means televisions permanently in bedrooms or available on request. Colour television may also be available in the lounge.

No dogs – Establishments which do not normally accept dogs may accept guide dogs. Some establishments that accept dogs may restrict the size and breed of dogs permitted and the rooms into which they may be taken. Generally, dogs are not allowed in the dining room. Check when booking the conditions under which pets are accepted.

No children – indicatates that children cannot be accommodated. A minimum age may be specified (e.g. No children 4 yrs = no children under fours years old). Although establishments may accept children of all ages they may not necessarily be able to provide special facilities. If you have very young children, check before booking about provisions like cots and high chairs, and any reductions made.

ch fac – indicates establishments with special facilities for children, which will include baby-sitting service or baby intercom system, playroom or playground, laundry facilities, drying and ironing facilities, cots, high chairs and special meals.

No coaches – this information is published in good faith from details supplied by the establishments concerned. Inns, however, have well-defined legal obligations towards travellers, and any member with cause for complaint should take this up with the proprietor or the local licensing authority.

Additional facilities – such as lifts or any leisure activities available are listed

9 Price Guide: ROOMS – these are prices per night. **s** – Bed and breakfast per person; **d** – Bed and breakfast two persons.
Wkly b+b – indicates the cost of bed and breakfast for one week;
wkly hlf-bd – means price includes dinner. The price range indicates the minumum and maximum during the year. For a full explanation see page 9.
 Prices given have been provided by the owner in good faith, and are indications rather than firm quotations. Some establishments offer free accommodation to children provided they share the parents' room. Check current prices before booking.

10 Payment details (the following cards or discount vouchers may be accepted, but check current details when booking)

- Access/Eurocard/Mastercard
- American Express
- Barclaycard/Visa
- Diners
- Connect
- Delta
- Switch

(£) - Establishment accepts AA Money-Off Vouchers as detailed on page 9.

BRITAIN'S BEST BED & BREAKFAST PREMIER SELECTED

QQQQQ

A QUICK REFERENCE list in country and county order – England, Channel Islands, Scotland, Wales, Ireland – of all the 1996 PREMIER SELECTED QQQQQ establishments – the AA's highest rating for Guest Houses, Farmhouses and Inns

Premier Selected are highlighted in the directory with a panel and a picture

ENGLAND

AVON
Bath
Dorian House
Haydon House
Holly Lodge
Leighton House
Meadowland
Monkshill
Newbridge House Hotel
The Lodge Hotel
The Old School House

SWINEFORD
Gaites House

BERKSHIRE
Maidenhead
Beehive Manor

CHESHIRE
Chester
Redland Private Hotel
Malpas
Tilston Lodge

CO DURHAM
Fir Tree
Greenhead Hotel

**CORNWALL & THE
ISLES OF SCILLY**
Crackington Haven
Manor Farm
Trevigue Farm
Treworgie Barton

Falmouth
Prospect House

Lizard
Landewednack House

Padstow
St Petroc's House

Polperro
Trenderway Farm

St Blazey
Nanscawen House

CUMBRIA
St Hilary
Ennys Farm

Ambleside
Grey Friar Lodge Hotel

Ambleside
Rowanfield

Boltongate
The Old Rectory

Borrowdale
Hazel Bank

Buttermere
Pickett Howe

Cockermouth
Low Hall

Coniston
Coniston Lodge Hotel
Wheelgate Hotel

Grange-Over-Sands
Greenacres

Kendal
Lane Head Hotel
Low Jock Scar

Keswick
Derwent Cottage

Kirby Lonsdale
Cobwebs
Hipping Hall

Longtown
Bessiestown Farm

Lorton
New House Farm

Near Sawrey
Ees Wyke

DERBYSHIRE
Ashbourne
Biggin Mill House

Buxton
Brookfield On Longhill

Doveridge
Beeches Farmhouse

Shottle
Dannah Farm

DEVON
Bantham
Widcombe House

Bovey Tracey
Front House Lodge

Croyde
Whiteleaf At Croyde

Dartmouth
Boringdon House
Ford House

Horn's Cross
Lower Waytown

Lydford
Moor View House Hotel

Lynton
Victoria Lodge

Morchard Bishop
Wigham

Moretonhampstead
Blackaller Hotel
Gate House

Parkham
The Old Rectory

Poundsgate
Leusdon Lodge

Sidmouth
Broad Oak

South Molton
Kerscott Farm

Staverton
Kingston House

Teignmouth
Thomas Luny House

Tiverton
Hornhill Farm

Totnes
The Watermans Arms

West Down
The Long House

DORSET
Dorchester
Yalbury Cottage Hotel

Horton
Northill House

EAST SUSSEX
Arlington
Bates Green

**Hastings & St
Leonards**
Bryn-y-Mor
Parkside House

Rye
Green Hedges
Jeakes House
The Old Vicarage Hotel

GLOUCESTERSHIRE
Cheltenham
Cleeve Hill Hotel
Lypiatt House

Chipping Campden
he Malt House

Clearwell
Tudor Farmhouse Hotel

Frampton on Severn
The Old School House

Lechlade
Cottage-by-the-Church

Moreton-in-Marsh
College House

Rendcomb
Shawswell

Tetbury
Tavern House

**GREATER
MANCHESTER**
Altringham
Ash Farm

HAMPSHIRE
Brockenhurst
Thatched Cottage Hotel

Hayling Island
Cockle Warren Cottage
Hotel

Odiham
Poland Mill

Ringwood
Little Forest Lodge Hotel

Romsey
Highfield House

Sway
The Nurse's Cottage

Winchester
The Wykeham Arms

Woodfalls
The Woodfalls Inn

**HEREFORD &
WORCESTER**
Bishampton
Nightingale Hotel

Broadway
Old Rectory

Whitney-on-Wye
The Rhydspence Inn

KENT
Canterbury
The Old Rectory
Thruxted Oast

Cranbrook
Hancocks Farmhouse

Eynesford
Home Farm

Hawkhurst
Conghurst Farm

Penshurst
Swale Cottage

**Royal Tunbridge
Wells**
Danehurst House
The Old Parsonage

Sittingbourne
Hempstead House Hotel

Tonbridge
Goldhill Mill

LANCASHIRE
Carnforth
New Capernwray Farm

Harrop Fold
Hrrop Fold Farmhouse H
otel

Slaidburn
Parrock Head Farm
House Hotel

Thornton
The Victorian House

**LONDON POSTAL
DISTRICTS**
London E11
Lakeside

London NW3
Sandringham Hotel

NORTHUMBERLAND
Corbridge
The Courtyard

NORTH YORKSHIRE
Harrogate
Ruskin Hotel

Reeth
Arkleside Hotel

Richmond
Whashton Springs Farm

Starbottom
Hilltop

Whitby
Dunsley Hall

YORK
Arndale Hotel

NOTTINGHAMSHIRE
North Wheatley
The Old Plough

OXFORDSHIRE
Burford
Andrews Hotel

Oxford
Cotswold House
Fallowfields

Thame
Upper Green Farm

SHROPSHIRE
Church Stretton
Rectory Farm

SOMERSET
Beercrocombe
Frog Street Farm
Whittles Farm

Crewkerne
Broadview

Dunster
Dollons House

Kilve
Hood Arms

Langport
Hillards Farm

Norton St Philip
Monmouth Lodge

Rode
Irondale

Somerton
The Lynch

Watchet
Chidgley Hill Farm

Wells
Infield House
Littlewell Farm

Yeovil
Holywell House

STAFFORDSHIRE
Audley
Domvilles Farm

Oakamoor
Bank House

SUFFOLK
Bury St Edmonds
Twelve Angel Hill

Otley
Otley House

WARWICKSHIRE
Warwick
Shrewley House

WEST SUSSEX
Bepton
Park House Hotel

Billingshurst
Old Wharf

Bosham
Kenwood

Rogate
Mizzards Farm

Sutton
The White Horse Inn

WILTSHIRE
Alderton
Manor Farm

Bradford On Avon
Bradford Old Windmill
Burghope Manor
Fern Cottage
Widbrook Grange

Burbage
The Old Vicarage

Calne
Chilvester Hill House

Cricklade
Latton House

Lacock
At the Sign of the Angel

Little Cheverell
Little Cheverell House

Marlborough
Laurel Cottage

West Grafton
Mayfield

CHANNEL ISLANDS

GUERNSEY
St Peter Port
Midhurst House

SCOTLAND

BORDERS
Coldingham
Dunlaverock House

Jedburgh
The Spinney

CENTRAL
Brig O'Turk
Dundarroch

Callender
Arran Lodge

FIFE
Anstruther
Hermitage

Auchtermuchty
Ardchoille Farmhouse

Cupar
Todhall House

GRAMPIAN
Aberdeen
Ewood House

HIGHLAND
Boat of Garten
Heathbank The Victorian
House

Conon Bridge
Kinkell House

Dornoch
Highfield

Fort William
Ashburn House
The Grange
Torbeag House

Granton-on-Spey
Ardconnel House
Culdearn House

Inverness
Ballifeary House Hotel
Culduthel Lodge
Moyness House

LOTHIAN
Edinburgh
Drummond House5
Elmview

STRATHCLYDE
Ballantrae
Cosses

Connel
Ards House

Paisley
Myfarrclan Guest House

Tobermory
Strongarbh House

TAYSIDE
Aberfeldy
Fernbank House

Arbroth
Farmhouse Kitchen

WALES

CLWYD
Ruthin
Eyarth Station

GWYNEDD
Barmouth
Plas Bach

Betws-y-coed
Tan-y-Foel

Bontddu
Borthwnog Hall Hotel

Llanfachreth
Ty Isaf Farmhouse

Llanwnda
Pengwern Farm

POWYS
Newtown
Dyffryn Farmhouse

Penybont
Ffaldau

WEST GLAMORGAN
Neath
Green Lanterns

**NORTHERN
IRELAND**

TYRONE
Dungannon
Grange Lodge

**REPUBLIC OF
IRELAND**

CORK
Fermoy
Ballyvolane House

Kanturk
Assolas

DUBLIN
Dublin
Aberdeen Lodge
Ariel House
Cedar Lodge
The Grey Door

GALWAY
Galway
Killeen House

Past AA Landladies of the Year Finalists 1994-5

Christine Moodie,
Rovie Farm, Rogart, Sutherland (Winner 1994)

Muriel Orme,
Bank House, Oakamoor, Staffordshire (runner up)

Sylvia Knott,
Ffaldau Country House, Pen-y-Bont, Powys (runner-up)

Sîan Bisdee, Ashcombe Court, Weston-super-Mare, Avon
Norah Brown, Grange Lodge, Dungannon, Co Tyrone
Freda Burns, Chapel Uchaf Farm, Carmarthen, Dyfed
Sylvia Dobbs, Kenmore Guest House, Littlehampton, West Sussex
Joyce Fielder, Old Stable Cottage, Carew, Dyfed
Jenny Hadfield, Jeakes House, Rye, East Sussex
Jill Jenkins, Thanington Hotel, Canterbury, Kent
Ria Johnston, White Gables, Bushmills, Co Antrim
Elsie Moore, Maes-y-Gwernen, Abercraf, Swansea
Mollie Rees, Dormy House Hotel, Sarisbury Green, Hants
Anwen Roberts, Bach-y-Graig, St Asaph, Clwyd
Jen Spencer, Eyarth Station, Ruthin, Clwyd
Eileen Spray, Grasmead House, York, North Yorkshire
Ivy Stanley, Fresh Fields, Twynholm, Kirkcudbright, Dumfries & Galloway
Muriel White, Chadstone Guest House, Craven Arms, Shropshire
Sue White, Ennys Farm, Penzance, Cornwall

Past Guest House of the Year Award Winners 1994-5

England
Goldhill Mill, Tonbridge, Kent

Scotland
Culdearn House, Grantown-on-Spey, Morayshire, Highland

Wales
Tan-y-Foel, Betws-y-Coed, Gwynedd

Ireland
The Old Rectory Hotel & Restaurant, Wicklow, Co Wicklow

GUEST HOUSE
OF THE
YEAR
AWARDS
1995-6

Our team of professional AA inspectors cover the whole of the British Isles, inspecting every nook and cranny of every establishment in this guide. The *AA Bed & Breakfast Guide* is a result of their efforts to select the very best of small hotels, guest houses, farmhouses and inns. The selection system aims to help readers chose the most pleasant and comfortable accommodation, so that they may fully enjoy their holidays or short breaks. The establishments are graded from one Q to five Qs, so the quality of accommodation can be easily assessed. However, some places are exceptional in the high standards they offer. The most outstanding of these have been selected by our inspectors for the award 'Guest House of the Year' for 1996.

**ENGLAND
Channel Islands
Hotel Petit Champ,
Sark**

THIS YEAR OUR INSPECTORS have selected a winner of the Guest House of the Year from the most southerly parts of Britain. The Hotel Petit Champ on the tiny island of Sark, only three and a half miles long and a mile and a half wide, has been selected from the thousands of entries in the 1995 guide. Of the beautiful Channel Islands, Sark is the smallest and the most fascinating of the four main islands. To call this wonderful island 'Out of this world' is no exaggeration when, even at the end of the 20th century, it is unspoilt by motor cars or any of the hurly-burly of modern life.

The Hotel Petit Champ has an unrivalled, secluded position on the headlands of Sark's beautiful west coast, from which there are superb views of the sea and the islands of Herm, Jethou and Guernsey. There are scores of little bays and coves all within easy walking distance of the hotel and, with only one road on the island, even the most popular beaches are never crowded. Bicycles, boats or horsedrawn carriages can be hired for trips slightly further afield.

Originally built in the 19th-century from granite quarried from nearby, the hotel tries to preserve a 'country house' atmosphere. There is now a swimming pool in the sheltered quarry from which the stone for the house was taken. Caroline and Chris Robins are truly caring hosts and many guests return year after year.

SCOTLAND
Mardella Farmhouse
Gartocharn, Strathclyde

SET AMID SPECTACULAR scenery at the foot of Loch Lomond, Sally and Angus MacDonnell's home provides an excellent base for visiting the surrounding countryside. The brochure offers *Ceúd míle fàilte* – A hundred thousand welcomes – and visitors will be sure of such a Scottish tradition at Mardella. The three comfortable bedrooms, all with private facilities, a cosy sitting room and a hearty breakfast all ensure a pleasant stay. The large bay window of the sitting room looks over paddocks to the mountains beyond. The paddocks are filled with the MacDonnell's large collection of ducks, geese, chickens, peacocks and sheep. Feeding them provides great entertainment for children - wellies essential! There is even a welcoming committee of stone ducks on the steps up to the house.

WALES
Ffaldau Country House
Penybont, Powys

IN THE VERY HEART of Wales is Ffaldau Country House, a picturesque cruck-built, longhouse dating from 1500, which has been lovingly restored by Sylvia and Leslie Knott. The unusual interior has a high steep-sloping gable in the cosy, upstairs sitting room. As would be expected in a cottage, the bedrooms are not large, but they all have private facilities and have been decorated in an appealing cottage style. Downstairs are capacious inglenook fireplaces and the large dining room has a superb slate flagstone floor. Sylvia Knott, a runner-up in Landlady of the Year 1994/95, is a friendly hostess, keen to help with information about places to visit and scenic routes. An excellent cook, ably assisted by her daughter she offers a chance to try international and traditional Welsh dishes.

IRELAND
Assolas Country House
Kanturk, Co Cork

AN ELEGANT QUEEN ANNE-style manor house in extensive wooded grounds sloping down to lovely stream, is the fitting candidate for our Inspectors' Choice for Ireland. Assolas, the home of the Bourke family for generations, is still a family home as well as a comfortable guesthouse. There are nine bedrooms, all with en-suite facilities, as well as a magnificent sitting room and two dining rooms. The grounds, with their long wooded drive and sweeping lawns are immaculately maintained. Guests are encouraged to make good use of the lawn tennis court or croquet lawn or boating on the river. Nearby are fishing, riding and golf at some of the country's best courses, as well as easy access to sights such as the Ring of Kerry and Blarney Castle. Guests also have the opportunity of sampling Hazel Bourke's cooking - which has a fine reputation. Most of the vegetable and herbs are grown in the extensive and celebrated kitchen garden.

LANDLADY
OF THE
YEAR
AWARDS
1995-6

For the second year running, the AA Hotels Services has run its successful and popular selection of Landlady of the Year, and once again we have found many real stars among the 3,500 hard-working band of landladies. Having made thousands of beds, cooked thousands of breakfasts and cleaned endless rooms, they have still managed to maintain a cheerful smile and take an real interest in the well-being of their guests. What a feat!

BRITAIN'S TOP LANDLADIES were treated to a day out at one of London's top hotels, to find out who had won the **AA's 1995 Landlady of the Year Award,** sponsored by Caithness Glass. The 20 finalists, from bed and breakfast establishments all over the country, gathered together for the ceremony at London's Hyde Park Hotel – one of the world's most luxurious hotels.

The winner – **KathieRitchie,** runs Tilston Lodge in Malpas, Cheshire. Her prize was a weekend for two in Paris, and a

Kathie Ritchie, AA Landlady of the Year 1995–6, with her trophy outside Tilston Lodge

trophy created especially for the occasion by Caithness Glass, manufacturers of the celebrated BBC *Mastermind* trophy.

There were two runner-up prizes which were taken by Sue Jones from Dyffryn Farm, Newton, Wales and Judith Clegg of Redacre Mill, Hebden Bridge, West Yorkshire.

All AA winners
Presenting the awards, Albert Hampson, Business Manager of AA Hotel Services said 'Running a guesthouse isn't just about providing a room for the night and making breakfast the next day. It takes care, consideration, effort and dedication to be a successful landlady, and Kathie is the perfect example.

'But our Landlady of the Year Awards recognise the long hours and hard work that bed and breakfast proprietors put into their jobs, and all 20 of the finalists are AA winners in their own right.'

Cheshire champion for the Heart of England

AA Landlady of the Year, Kathie Ritchie, who runs Tilston Lodge and farm with her husband Neil, has been in the bed and breakfast business for just four years and has really loved it. She was chosen as the winner after passing a series of AA tests – including a letter, telephone calls and a weekend visit by an AA employee and her family. News of her success travelled fast, and she became an instant media star with radio interviews, television appearances and press comments about her achievements.

Kathie's bed and breakfast career has been full of surprises. One Scottish couple arrived at Tilston Lodge with their own dinner plate-sized mushroom, and asked her to cook it for their breakfast. Another guest fell in love with the Ritchie's new-born golden retriever puppies, and returned

The twenty finalists of the AA Landlady of the Year 1995-6 with Albert Hampson, Business Manager, AA Hotels

two months later to buy one. Kathie has also put up two next-door neighbours who had unknowingly booked the same weekend at her guesthouse!

AA LANDLADIES OF THE YEAR FINALISTS 1995-6

Kathie Ritchie, Tilston Lodge, Malpas, Cheshire (winner)
Sue Jones, Dyffryn Farm, Newtown, Powys (runner-up)
Judith Clegg, Redacre Mill, Hebden Bridge, West Yorks (runner-up)

Ann Addison, Old Parsonage Farm, Hanley Castle, Hereford
Anne Birbeck, Greenhead Hotel, Crook, Co Durham
Bernie Clarke, Twelve Angel Hill, Bury St Edmunds, Suffolk
Enid Davies, Low Hall, Cockermouth Cumbria

Gillian Hingston, Piggot's Mill, Thaxted, Essex
Ria Johnston, White Gables, Bushmills, County Antrim
Isobel Little, Culdearn House, Grantown-on-Spey, Morayshire
Andrea Londors, Boswell House Hotel, Chelmsford, Essex
Sally MacDonell, Mardella Farmhouse, Gartocharn, Dumbartonshire
Muriel Orme, Bank End, Oakamoor, Staffordshire

Dorota Perruzza, Green Gables, Chester, Cheshire
Theresa Quinn and Anne Waite, Powys House Estate, Corwen, Clwyd
Sandra Ridden, Westcott Hotel, Falmouth, Cornwall
Marie Rathmell, Hilltop Country Guesthouse, Skipton, North Yorks
Yvonne Thompson, Kingsdown Country Hotel, Deal, Kent
Vicky Umbers, Parrock Head Farmhouse, Clitheroe, Lancs
Jean Wilson, Manuel's Farm, Newquay, Cornwall
★★★

CONGRATULATIONS ALSO TO

Sue Jones, Dyffryn Farm
Several miles down narrow lanes brings you to a small, wooded valley in which Dyffryn Farm, a converted 300-year-old longhouse, nestles beside a stream. This is very much a working farm with cows and sheep grazing in the fields bordering the garden. Sue is an excellent cook and caters for hearty appetites stimulated by all the fresh air! She is very enthusiastic about this part of the world and involved in several schemes for promoting tourism to the area.

Judith Clegg, Redacre Mill
Judith and John Clegg converted an old industrial mill on the Rochdale Canal into a guest house. The canal is now a tourist attraction and the mill, with its warm stone walls and large windows, has made a most attractive home. Judith Clegg is a very good cook and a friendly hostess, with a real eye for what makes guests feel comfortable and welcome.

Kathie Ritchie, flanked by runners-up Sue Jones and Judith Clegg, with Albert Hampson and Pete Johnson, Managing Director, AA Commercial Services. On the right is Alistair Mair, Chairman of Caithness Glass.

If you broke down en route it would be a real emergency.

AA

TO OUR
MEMBERS WE'RE
THE 4TH
EMERGENCY
SERVICE

TO JOIN CALL 0800 91 95 95

ENGLAND

PREMIER SELECTED
QQQQQ

A QUICK-REFERENCE of establishments in England and the Channel Islands in this year's guide with a QQQQQ rating for Quality – the AA's highest rating for guest houses, farmhouses and inns.

AVON
BATH
Dorian House
Haydon House
Holly Lodge
Leighton House
Meadowland
Monkshill
Newbridge House
 Hotel
The Lodge Hotel
The Old School
 House

SWINEFORD
Gaites House

BERKSHIRE
MAIDENHEAD
Beehive Manor

CHESHIRE
CHESTER
Redland Private
 Hotel

MALPAS
Tilston Lodge

CO DURHAM
FIR TREE
Greenhead Hotel

**CORNWALL &
THE ISLES OF
SCILLY**

CRACKINGTON
HAVEN
Manor Farm
Trevigue Farm
Treworgie Barton

FALMOUTH
Prospect House

LIZARD
Landewednack House

PADSTOW
St Petroc's House

POLPERRO
Trenderway Farm

ST BLAZEY
Nanscawen House

CUMBRIA
ST HILARY
Ennys Farm

AMBLESIDE
Grey Friar Lodge
 Hotel

AMBLESIDE
Rowanfield

BOLTONGATE
The Old Rectory

BORROWDALE
Hazel Bank

BUTTERMERE
Pickett Howe

COCKERMOUTH
Low Hall

CONISTON
Coniston Lodge
 Hotel
Wheelgate Hotel

GRANGE-OVER-
SANDS
Greenacres

KENDAL
Lane Head Hotel
Low Jock Scar

KESWICK
Derwent Cottage

KIRKBY
 LONSDALE
Cobwebs
Hipping Hall

LONGTOWN
Bessiestown Farm

LORTON
New House Farm

NEAR SAWREY
Ees Wyke

DERBYSHIRE
ASHBOURNE
Biggin Mill House

BUXTON
Brookfield On
 Longhill

DOVERIDGE
Beeches Farmhouse

SHOTTLE
Dannah Farm

DEVON
BANTHAM
Widcombe House

BOVEY TRACEY
Front House Lodge

CROYDE
Whiteleaf At Croyde

DARTMOUTH
Boringdon House
Ford House

25

HORN'S CROSS
Lower Waytown

LYDFORD
Moor View House
Hotel

LYNTON
Victoria Lodge

MORCHAR
BISHOP
Wigham

MORETONHAMP-
STEAD
Blackaller Hotel
Gate House

PARKHAM
The Old Rectory

POUNDSGATE
Leusdon Lodge

SIDMOUTH
Broad Oak

SOUTH MOLTON
Kerscott Farm

STAVERTON
Kingston House

TEIGNMOUTH
Thomas Luny House

TIVERTON
Hornhill Farm

TOTNES
The Watermans Arms

WEST DOWN
The Long House

DORSET
DORCHESTER
Yalbury Cottage Hotel

HORTON
Northill House

EAST SUSSEX
ARLINGTON
Bates Green

HASTINGS & ST
LEONARDS
Bryn-y-Mor
Parkside House

RYE
Green Hedges
Jeakes House
The Old Vicarage
Hotel

**GLOUCESTER-
SHIRE**
CHELTENHAM
Cleeve Hill Hotel
Lypiatt House

CHIPPING
CAMPDEN
The Malt House

CLEARWELL
Tudor Farmhouse
Hotel

FRAMPTON ON
SEVERN
The Old School
House

LECHLADE
Cottage-by-the-
Church

MORETON-IN-
MARSH
College House

RENDCOMB
Shawswell

TETBURY
Tavern House

**GREATER
MANCHESTER**
ALTRINCHAM
Ash Farm

HAMPSHIRE
BROCKENHURST
Thatched Cottage
Hotel

HAYLING ISLAND
Cockle Warren Cottage
Hotel

ODIHAM
Poland Mill

RINGWOOD
Little Forest Lodge
Hotel

ROMSEY
Highfield House

SWAY
The Nurse's Cottage

WINCHESTER
The Wykeham Arms

WOODFALLS
The Woodfalls Inn

**HEREFORD &
WORCESTER**
BISHAMPTON
Nightingale Hotel

BROADWAY
Old Rectory

WHITNEY-ON-
WYE
The Rhydspence Inn

KENT
CANTERBURY
The Old Rectory
Thruxted Oast

CRANBROOK
Hancocks Farmhouse

EYNSFORD
Home Farm

HAWKHURST
Conghurst Farm

PENSHURST
Swale Cottage

ROYAL TUNBRIDGE
WELLS
Danehurst House
The Old Parsonage

SITTINGBOURNE
Hempstead House
Hotel

TONBRIDGE
Goldhill Mill

LANCASHIRE
CARNFORTH
New Capernwray
Farm

HARROP FOLD
Harrop Fold Farmhouse
Hotel

SLAIDBURN
Parrock Head Farm
House Hotel

THORNTON
The Victorian House

LONDON POSTAL DISTRICTS
LONDON E11
Lakeside

LONDON NW3
Sandringham Hotel

NORTHUMBER-LAND
CORBRIDGE
The Courtyard

NORTH YORKSHIRE
HARROGATE
Ruskin Hotel

REETH
Arkleside Hotel

RICHMOND
Whashton Springs Farm

STARBOTTON
Hilltop

WHITBY
Dunsley Hall

YORK
Arndale Hotel

NOTTINGHAM-SHIRE
NORTH WHEATLEY
The Old Plough

OXFORDSHIRE
BURFORD
Andrews Hotel

OXFORD
Cotswold House
Fallowfields

THAME
Upper Green Farm

SHROPSHIRE
CHURCH STRETTON
Rectory Farm

SOMERSET
BEERCROCOMBE
Frog Street Farm
Whittles Farm

CREWKERNE
Broadview

DUNSTER
Dollons House

KILVE
Hood Arms

LANGPORT
Hillards Farm

NORTON ST PHILIP
Monmouth Lodge

RODE
Irondale

SOMERTON
The Lynch

WATCHET
Chidgley Hill Farm

WELLS
Infield House
Littlewell Farm

YEOVIL
Holywell House

STAFFORDSHIRE
AUDLEY
Domvilles Farm

OAKAMOOR
Bank House

SUFFOLK
BURY ST EDMUNDS
Twelve Angel Hill

OTLEY
Otley House

WARWICKSHIRE
WARWICK
Shrewley House

WEST SUSSEX
BEPTON
Park House Hotel

BILLINGSHURST
Old Wharf

BOSHAM
Kenwood

ROGATE
Mizzards Farm

SUTTON
The White Horse Inn

WILTSHIRE
ALDERTON
Manor Farm

BRADFORD ON AVON
Bradford Old Windmill
Burghope Manor
Fern Cottage
Widbrook Grange

BURBAGE
The Old Vicarage

CALNE
Chilvester Hill House

CRICKLADE
Latton House

LACOCK
At the Sign of the Angel

LITTLE CHEVERELL
Little Cheverell House

MARLBOROUGH
Laurel Cottage

WEST GRAFTON
Mayfield

CHANNEL ISLANDS

GUERNSEY
ST PETER PORT
Midhurst House

A quick-reference of establishments in England and the Channel Islands in this year's guide with a QQQQ rating for Quality – each year more establishments in the guide rise to a very high standard which the AA recognises the award of QQQQ's.

ENGLAND

AVON
Almondsbury
Abbotts Way
Bath
Badminton Villa
Bailbrook Lodge
Blairgowrie House
Bloomfield House
Brocks
Brompton House Hotel
Cheriton House
Chesterfield Hotel
Cranleigh
Highways House
Kennard Hotel
Laura Place Hotel
Marlborough House
Oakleigh House
Paradise House Hotel
Sarnia
Somerset House Hotel
Sydney Gardens Hotel
The Bath Tasburgh
Villa Magdala Hotel
Keynsham
Grasmere Court Hotel
Old Sodbury
The Sodbury House
 Hotel
Weston-Super-Mare
Ashcombe Court
Braeside
Milton Lodge
Wychwood Hotel

BEDFORDSHIRE
Sandy
Highfield Farm

BERKSHIRE
Lambourne
Lodge Down
Windsor
Melrose

BUCKINGHAM-
 SHIRE
Aston Clinton
West Lodge Hotel
Marlow
Holly Tree House
Milton Keynes
The Old Bakery Hotel

CAMBRIDGESHIRE
Cambridge
Old School Hotel
Ely
Hill House Farm

CHESHIRE
Chester
Green Gables
Grove House
Crewe
Clayhanger Hall Farm

Hatton Heath
Golborne Manor
Knutsford
Laburnum Cottage
The Dog Inn
The Hinton
Macclesfield
Hardingland Farm
Malpas
Broughton House
Laurel Farm
Nantwich
Oakland House

CLEVELAND
Stockton-on-Tees
The Edwardian Hotel

CO DURHAM
Darlington
Clow Beck House
Durham
Hillrise

CORNWALL &
 ISLES OF SCILLY
Bodmin
Treffry Farm
Boscastle
Tolcarne House Hotel
Trerosewill Farmhouse

Bude
Cliff Hotel
Court Farm
Crackington Haven
Nancemellan
Falmouth
Penmere
Rosemary Hotel
Westcott Hotel
Fowey
Carnethic House
Helston
Halzephron Inn
Nanplough Farm
Launceston
Hurdon Farm
Lelant
The Badger Inn
Liskeard
Tregondale Farm
Looe
Coombe Farm
Harescombe Lodge
Panorama Hotel
Woodlands
Mevagissey
Kerryanna
Mevagissey House
Newquay
Degembris Farmhouse
Manuels Farm
Pendeen Hotel
Porth Enodoc
Priory Lodge Hotel
Towan Beach Hotel
Windward Hotel

Penzance
Blue Seas Hotel
Chy-an-Mor
Rose Farm
The Yacht Inn
Perranuthnoe
Ednovean Farm
Polperro
Landaviddy Manor
Lanhael House
Port Issac
Archer Farm Hotel
Portreath
Benson's
Praa Sands
Higher Trevurvas Farm
Saltash
The Crooked Inn
St Austell
Poltarrow Farm
T'Gallants
St Ives
Dean Court Hotel
Kynance
Lyonesse Hotel
Monowai Private Hotel
Regent Hotel
Trewinnard
St Just-in-Roseland
Rose-Da-Mar Hotel
St Mary's
Carnwethers
Crebinick House
St Wenn
Wenn Manor
Truro
Bissick Old Mill
Lands Vue
Rock Cottage
Trevispian Vean Farm
Tywardreath
Elmswood House
 Hotel

CUMBRIA
Amleside
Drunken Duck Inn
Rothay Garth Hotel
Borrowdale
Greenbank
Brampton
Cracrop Farm
Brampton
Oakwood Park Hotel
Brough
Augill House Farm
Carlilse
Howard House
Crosthwaite
Crosthwaite House
Far Sawrey
West Vale Country
Hawshead
Rough Close
Kendal
Burrow Hall
Higher House Farm
Keswick
Abacourt House
Acorn House Hotel
Applethwaite Hotel
Craglands
Dalegarth House
 Hotel
Greystones
Ravensworth Hotel
Kirby Thore
Bridge End Farm
Kirkoswald
Prospect Hill Hotel
Near Sawrey
The Garth
Newby Bridge
Hill Crest
Rosley
Causa Grange
Underbarrow
Tranthwaite Hall
Windermere
Blenheim Lodge Hotel
Fayrer Garden House
Fir Trees

Glencree Private Hotel
Hawksmoor
Howbeck
Kirkwood
Newstead
Parson Wyke
The Archway
The Beaumont Hotel
Woodlands

DERBYSHIRE
Alkmonton
Dairy House Farm
Ashbourne
Lichfield
Beeley
Beeley House
Belper
Shottle Hall
Buxton
Buxton Wheel House
 Hotel
Coningsby
The Grosvenor House
 Hotel
Westminster Hotel
Carsington
Henmore Grange
Hope
Underleigh House
Matlock
Hodgkinsons Hotel
Lane End House
Weston Underwood
Parkview Farm
Winster
The Dower House

DEVON
Ashburton
Gages Mill
Axminster
Millbrook Farmhouse
Barnstaple
Home Park Farm

Bickington
East Burne Farm
Bovey Tracey
Willmead Farm
Bratton Fleming
Bracken House
Buckfastleigh
Dartbridge Inn
Budleigh Salterton
Long Range Hotel
Chagford
Glendarah House
Thornworthy House
Chulmleigh
The Old Bakehouse
Cullompton
Rullands
Dartmouth
Broome Court
Captains House
Hedley House
The Seale Arms
Dawlish
Walton House
Exeter
Rydon Farm
The Edwardian
Holne
Wellpritton Farm
Holsworthy
Woodlands
Honiton
Colestocks House
The Heathfield
Ilfracombe
Varley House
Kingston
Trebles Cottage Hotel
Lustleigh
Eastwrey Barton Hotel
Lynmouth
Bonnicott House
Countisbury Lodge
 Hotel
The Heatherville
Lynton
Alford House Hotel
Hazeldene

Highcliffe House
Ingleside Hotel
Lynhurst Hotel
Mayfair Hotel
Waterloo House Hotel
Moretonhampstead
Great Sloncombe Farm
Moorcote
Mortehoe
Sunnycliffe Hotel
Newton Abbot
The Barn Owl Inn
Oakford
Newhouse Farm
Ottery St Mary
Claypits Farm
Paignton
Clennon Valley Hotel
Plymouth
Bowling Green Hotel
Netton Farm House
Salcombe
Devon Tor Hotel
Seaton
Boshill House
Shillingford
The Old Mill
Sidmouth
Number Four
Tavistock
Old Coach House
 Hotel
Teignmouth
Fonthill
Tiverton
Lower Collipriest Farm
Torquay
Barn Hayes Hotel
Blue Haze Hotel
Glenorleigh Hotel
Kingston House
Millbrook House
Mulberry House
Olivia Court
Suite Dreams
The Berburry Hotel
Westgate Hotel
Totnes

Askew Cottage
The Old Forge at
 Totnes
The Red Slipper
Whimple
Down House
Witheridge
Marchweeke Farm

DORSET
Blandford Forum
Home Farm
Bournemouth
Cliff House Hotel
Silver Trees
The Boltons Hotel
Tudor Grange Hotel
Wood Lodge Hotel
Bridport
Britmead House
Charmouth
Newlands House
Dorchester
Westwood House
 Hotel
Evershot
Rectory House
Nettlecombe
The Marquis of Lorne
Poole
Acorns
Ringstead
The Creek
Sherborne
Almshouse Farm
The Alders
The Pheasants
Wheatsheaf House
Wareham
Redcliffe Farm
Weymouth
Bay Lodge
Channel View
Cumberland Hotel

EAST SUSSEX
Battle
Brakes Coppice Farm
Brighton
Adelaide Hotel
Amblecliff Hotel
Arlanda Hotel
Eastbourne
Beachy Rise
Queens Cliff Hotel
Hartfield
Bolebroke Watermill
**Hastings & St
Leonards**
Filsham Farmhouse
Tower House Hotel
Lewes
Nightingales
Mayfield
The Rose & Crown Inn
Rushlake Green
Great Crouch's
Rye
Holloway House
Mint Lodge
Old Borough Arms
Playden Cottage
The Old Vicarage
Seaford
Avondale Hotel
Uckfield
Hooke Hall
South Paddock
Wilmington
Crossways Hotel
Winchelsea
The Country House at
 Winchelsea

ESSEX
Canvey Island
Maisonwyck
Chelmsford
Snows Oaklands Hotel
Frating
Hockley Place

Great Dunmow
The Starr
Thaxted
Piggots Mill
Wix
Dairy House Farm

**GLOUCESTER-
SHIRE**
Berkeley
Greenacres Farm
Bibury
Cotteswold House
Blockley
Lower Brook House
**Bourton-on-the-
Water**
Coombe House
The Ridge
Cheltenham
Beaumont House
 Hotel
Beechworth Lawn
 Hotel
Charlton House
Malvern View
Milton House Hotel
Stretton Lodge
Cirencester
The Eliot Arms Hotel
Laverton
Leasow House
Newland
Millend House &
 Gardens
Stow-on-the-Wold
Bretton House
Cotswold Cottage
Crestow House
Kings Head Inn
Royalist Hotel
Stroud
Hunters Lodge
Winchcombe
Wesley House

GREATER LONDON
Croydon
Hayesthorpe Hotel

GREATER MANCHESTER
Altrincham
The Old Packet House
Hyde
Needhams Farm

HAMPSHIRE
Barton-on-Sea
Bank Cottage
Cleeve House
Hotel Gainsborough
Laurel Lodge
Basingstoke
Fernbank Hotel
Bransgore
Tothill House
Wiltshire House
Brockenhurst
The Cottage Hotel
Burley
Pikes Post
Rosebay Cottage
Cadnam
Kents Farm
Walnut Cottage
Emsworth
The Crown Hotel
Fareham
Avenue House Hotel
Fordingbridge
Forest Cottage Farm
Fritham
Fritham Farm
Itchen Abbas
The Trout Inn
Lymington
Albany House
Durlston House
Efford Cottage
Our Bench
Ormonde House

Portsmouth & Southsea
Upper Mount House Hotel
Ringwood
The Nest
Romsey
Country Accommodation
Sarisbury Green
Dormy House Hotel
Southampton
Hunters Lodge Hotel
Landguard Lodge
Warsash
Solent View Private Hotel
Winchester
Leckhampton
Shawlands

HEREFORD & WORCESTER
Bredwardine
Bredwardine Hall
Broadway
Bretforton Manor
Cowley House
Cusack's Glebe
Milestone House Hotel
Orchard Grove
The Pond House
Hanley Castle
Old Parsonage Farm
Hereford
Dormington Court Hotel
Grafton Villa Farm
Hermitage Manor
Himbleton
Phepson Farm
Kidderminster
Cedars Hotel
Leominster
Hills Farm
Malvern
Wyche Keep

Ross-on-Wye
Edde Cross House
Ruckhall
The Ancient Camp Inn

HERTFORDSHIRE
Bishop's Stortford
Cottage
St Albans
Ardmore House

HUMBERSIDE
Low Catton
Derwent Lodge

ISLE OF WIGHT
Sandown
St Catherine's Hotel
Shanklin
Osborne House
The Bondi Hotel

KENT
Benenden
Crit Hall
Canterbury
Ebury Hotel
Ersham Lodge
Magnolia House
Pointers Hotel
Thanington Hotel
The Pilgrims Hotel
The White House
Waltham Court Hotel
Cranbrook
The Oast
Deal
Dunkerleys Restaurant
Faversham
Frith Farm House
Goudhurst
Mill House
Gravesend
Overcliffe Hotel

Maidstone
Conway House
Willington Court
Margate
The Greswolde Hotel
Pluckley
Elvey Farm Hotel
Shipbourne
The Chaser Inn
Sittingbourne
Saywell Farmhouse
West Malling
Scott House
Woodgate

LANCASHIRE
Blackpool
Burlees Hotel
Blackpool
Sunray
Clayton-Le-Woods
Brook House Hotel
Clitheroe
Peter Barn
Colne
Higher Wanless Farm
Longridge
Jenkinsons Farmhouse
Whitewell
The Inn at Whitewell
Yealand Conyers
The Bower

LEICESTERSHIRE
Bruntingthorpe
Knaptoft House Farm & The Greenway
Coalville
Church Lane Farm
Hinckly
Ambion Court Hotel
Uppingham
Rutland House

LINCOLNSHIRE
Conisholme
Wickham House
Horncastle
Greenfield Farm
Lincoln
Carline
D'Isney Place Hotel
Minster Lodge Hotel
Louth
Masons Arms
Marton
Black Swan Coaching
Inn
Sleaford
Carre Arms Hotel
Stamford
The Priory
Sturton by Stow
Gallows Dale Farm

LONDON POSTAL
DISTRICTS
N4
Mount View
NW3
The Langorf Hotel
SW1
Windermere Hotel
SW3
Claverley House
SW5
Henley House Hotel
SW7
Five Sumner Place
Hotel
Kensington Manor
Hotel
W1
Bryanston Court
The Regency Hotel
W2
Byron Hotel
Mornington Hotel
Norfolk Plaza Hotel
Norfolk Towers Hotel

W4
Chiswick Hotel
W7
Wellmeadow Lodge
W14
Aston Court Hotel

NORFOLK
Coltishall
The Hedges
Hunstanton
Claremont
King's Lynn
Andel House
Fairlight Lodge
Russet House Hotel
North Walsham
The Toll Barn
Sheringham
Fairlawns
Swaffham
Corfield House
Tivetshall St Mary
Old Ram Coaching Inn

NORTH YORKSHIRE
Boroghbridge
The Crown Inn
Brafferton
Brafferton Hall
Filey
Downcliffe House
Grassington
Ashfield House Hotel
Harrogate
Acacia Lodge
Alexa House & Stable
Cottages
Ashley House Hotel
Delaine Hotel
Kimberley Hotel
The Dales Hotel
Hunton
The Countryman's Inn
Ingleby Greenhow
Manor House Farm

Ingleton
Ferncliffe
Oakroyd Old Rectory
Kettlewell
Langcliffe Country
Kirbymoorside
Appletree Court
Leyburn
Park Gate House
Low Row
Peat Gate Head
Masham
Bank Villa
Patrick Brompton
Elmfield House
Pickering
Rawcliffe House Farm
Raskelf
Old Farmhouse Hotel
Scarborough
Paragon Hotel
Scotch Corner
Vintage Hotel
Thirsk
Spital Hill
Whitby
Seacliffe Hotel
Waverley Private Hotel
York
Ashbourne House
Ashbury Hotel
Curzon Lodge &
Stable Cottages
Four Seasons Hotel
Grasmead House
Hotel
Hazelwood
Holmwood House Hotel
Midway House Hotel
Priory Hotel
St Denys Hotel
The Heathers

NORTHAMPTON-
SHIRE
Northampton
Quinton Green

NORTHUMBERLAND
Alnmouth
High Buston Hall
Marine House Private
Hotel
Bellingham
Westfield House
**Berwick-Upon-
Tweed**
Dervaig
Harvone
The Old Vicarage
Haltwhistle
Ald White Craig Farm
Broomshaw Hill Farm
Hexham
Dene House
East Peterel Field Farm
Middlemarch
Kirkwhelpington
Shieldhall
Rothbury
Orchard

NOTTINGHAMSHIRE
Bingham
Bingham Court Hotel
Nottingham
Hall Farm House
Windsor Lodge Hotel

OXFORDSHIRE
Banbury
La Madonette
Burford
Elm House
Chipping Norton
The Forge House
Chislehampton
Coach & Horses Inn
Kidlington
Bowood House
Kingham
Conygree Gate
Lew
The Farmhouse Hotel

Milton-Under-Wychwood
Hillborough Hotel
Oxford
Chestnuts
Dial House
Galaxie Private Hotel
Marlborough House
Tilbury Lodge Private Hotel
Shenington
Cotman House
Woodstock
The Laurels
Woolstone
The White Horse

SHROPSHIRE
Aston Munslow
Chadstone
Church Stretton
Belvedere
Jinlye
Clun
New House Farm
Hanwood
The White House
Ironbridge
The Library House
Ludlow
Moor Hall
Number Twenty Eight
Market Drayton
Mickley House
Stoke Manor
Shrewsbury
Fieldside
Mytton Hall
Sandford House Hotel
Telford
Church Farm
Wellington
Shray Hill
Wem
Foxleigh House
Soulton Hall

SOMERSET
Bridgwater
Woodlands
Cary Fitzpaine
Cary Fitzpaine Farm
Castle Cary
The George Hotel
Chedder
Tor Farm
Dulverton
Dassels
Highercombe
Minehead
Gascony Hotel
Marston Lodge Hotel
Norton St Philip
The Plaine
Roadwater
Wood Advent Farm
Rode
Wheelbrook Mill
Spaxton
Gatesmoor
Taunton
Higher Dipford Farm
Meryan House Hotel
Washford
The Washford Inn
Waterrow
Manor Mill
Wellington
Pinksmoor Mill House
Wells
Bekynton House
Box Tree House
Southway Farm
Tor
West Bagborough
Higher House
Wheddon Cross
Rest and be Thankful Inn
Wincanton
Lower Church Farm
Wiveliscombe
Alpine House

SOUTH YORKSHIRE
Rotherham
Stonecroft Residential Hotel

STAFFORDSHIRE
Cheddleton
Choir Cottage & Choir House
Oakamoor
Ribden Farm
Stoke-on-Trent
The Old Dairy House
Stone
Whitgreave Manor

SUFFOLK
Beyton
Manorhouse
Bury St Edmunds
The Six Bells Inn
Fressingfield
Chippenhall Hall
Gislingham
The Old Guildhall
Higham
The Bauble
The Old Vicarage
Lowestoft
Abbe
Needham Market
Pipps Ford Farm
Stoke-by-Nayland
The Angel Inn

SURREY
Horley
High Trees
The Lawn
Vulcan Lodge
Redhill
Ashleigh House Hotel
Reigate
Cranleigh Hotel

TYNE & WEAR
Tynemouth
Hope House

WARWICKSHIRE
Haseley Knob
Croft
Hatton
Northleigh House
Kenilworth
Victoria Lodge Hotel
Nuneaton
Leathermill Grange
Oxhill
Nolands Farm
Stratford-Upon-Avon
Eastnor House Hotel
Gravelside Barn
Sequoia House Private Hotel
Twelfth Night
Victoria Spa Lodge
Warwick
The Old Rectory

WEST SUSSEX
Rustington
Kenmore
Selsey
St Andrews Lodge
Steyning
Springwells Hotel
Worthing
Aspen House
Delmar Hotel
Moorings

WEST YORKSHIRE
Bingley
Five Rise Locks
Hebden Bridge
Redacre Mill
Holmfirth
Holme Castle Hotel

Wakefield
Stanley View

WILTSHIRE
Box
The Hermitage
Corsham
Manor Farm
Longleat
Sturford Mead Farm
Marlborough
The Vines

Mere
Chetcombe House
 Hotel
Nettleton
Fosse Farmhouse
Hotel
Salisbury
Grasmere House
Stratford Lodge
The Old House
Swindon
Portquin
Trowbridge
The Old Manor Hotel

Whiteparish
Brickworth Farmhouse
Winterbourne Stoke
Scotland Lodge

CHANNEL ISLANDS

ALDERNEY
The Georgian House

GUERNSEY
St Peter Port
Farnborough Hotel
Les Ozouets Lodge

St Sampson
Ann-Dawn Private
 Hotel

JERSEY
Grouville
Lavender Villa Hotel
St Aubin
The Panorama
St Helier
Kaieteur Guest House
Sark
Hotel Petit Champ

Over 2,500 courses

This guide has something to suit every golfer – from the novices to the most proficient player

Packed with useful information – it gives you –

- The latest information about visitors, green fees, entry restrictions and club and refreshment facilities
- Descriptions of each course – especially the more challenging aspects.
- Full page features of twenty major Championship Courses.
- NEW for 1996 – a national directory of Driving Ranges.

ENGLAND, CHANNEL ISLES & ISLE OF MAN

ABBERLEY Hereford & Worcester Map **03** SO76

GH 🅠🅠🅠 **Whoppets Wood** WR6 6BU (1.3m from 'Shavers End' signpost off A451 between Dunley and Great Witley) ☎01299 896545
Closed Dec-1 Jan
This former farm house dates back to the late 18th century. It is remotely located on the side of a picturesque valley about half a mile south east of Abberley village. It is set in its own extensive grounds with direct access onto the Worcestershire Way and is therefore very popular with walkers. The bedrooms, which include a family suite, contain modern equipment; all have en suite facilities except one with a private bathroom nearby. There is also a room at ground floor level with its own dining area and kitchen facility which can be accessed directly from the car park. From its elevated position, the house enjoys panoramic views of the surrounding countryside.
3 rms (2 bth/shr) (2 fmly) No smoking CTV in all bedrooms Tea and coffee making facilities No dogs Cen ht No children 4yrs 6P No coaches
PRICE GUIDE
ROOMS: s £18-£20; d £32-£35✱

ABBOTS BROMLEY Staffordshire Map **07** SK02

❤🅠🅠 Mrs M K Hollins *Marsh (SK069261)* WS15 3EJ (1m N on B5013) ☎01283 840323
Closed Dec
A large modernised old farmhouse is located on the B5103 road to Uttoxeter, one mile north of the village. There are two bedrooms; one is quite spacious with modern furnishings and a shower cubicle, the other has exposed ceiling beams and is furnished with some antique pieces. Separate tables are provided in the large breakfast room, which also features exposed beams.
2 rms (1 fmly) No smoking in dining room CTV in 1 bedroom Tea and coffee making facilities Cen ht 8P 64 acres dairy

🚩🅠🅠 **Crown** Market Place WS15 3BS (on B5013, in centre of village, opposite Butter Cross) ☎01283 840227 FAX 01283 840227
This characterful Inn which overlooks the ancient Butter Cross in the centre of this attractive village, is ideally situated for exploring Staffordshire, the Potteries and Alton Towers are within easy reach. The six spacious bedrooms, which share two modern shower rooms, are bright, freshly decorated, soundly furnished and equipped with tea and coffee making facilities and televisions. A good choice of home-cooked dishes are available in the lounge bar, there is also a public bar where, which is popular with locals where real ales are served and a small, well appointed breakfast room.
6 rms (1 fmly) No smoking in 3 bedrooms CTV in all bedrooms Tea and coffee making facilities Cen ht 40P Last d 9.30pm
PRICE GUIDE
ROOMS: s £20-£25; d £40; wkly b&b £115; wkly hlf-bd £170
MEALS: Lunch £5-£14 Dinner £7.50-£14
CARDS: 🅠 💳

ACASTER MALBIS North Yorkshire Map **08** SE54

🚩🅠🅠🅠 **Ship** YO2 1JH (2m S of A64 Bypass, accessible through villages of Copmanthorpe or Bishopthorpe) ☎01904 705609 & 703888 FAX 01904 705971
The Ship is an attractive old coaching inn standing on the banks of the River Ouse. It has a warm and inviting atmosphere, with pine furnished bedrooms and a character pub, where a good range of food is offered both at lunchtime and in the evening. Other facilities include a children's playground and mooring for boats at the quay.

8 en suite (bth/shr) CTV in all bedrooms Tea and coffee making facilities Cen ht 60P Fishing Last d 9.30pm
PRICE GUIDE
ROOMS: s £29.95-£37.50; d £37.95-£65✱
MEALS: Bar Lunch £1.95-£8.95 Dinner £12.50&alc✱
CARDS: 🅠 💳

See advertisement under YORK

ADBASTON Staffordshire Map **07** SJ72

🛏🖤 ❤🅠🅠 Mrs M Hiscoe-James **Offley Grove** *(SJ760270)* ST20 0QB (4m off A519, between Shebdon and Adbaston) ☎01785 280205
Three simple but sound modern bedrooms, all no-smoking, are offered at this early 18th-century farmhouse which is set on a small mixed farm about half a mile south of Adbaston village. Separate tables are provided in the traditionally furnished dining room, and guests have the choice of two comfortable lounges, both with TV. At the time of our last visit a former farm building was being converted into self-catering accommodation.
3 rms No smoking in bedrooms No smoking in dining room Tea and coffee making facilities No dogs (ex guide dogs) Cen ht CTV P 45 acres arable sheep
PRICE GUIDE
ROOMS: s £16; d £32; wkly b&b £112

AISLABY North Yorkshire Map **08** SE78

GH 🅠🅠 **Blacksmiths Arms** Pickering YO18 8PE (on A170, 2m W of Pickering) ☎01751 472182
Closed 4-31 Jan
An attractive roadside restaurant offers pretty pine-furnished bedrooms, some with original crook beams. Parts of the building date from Elizabethan times, when it was a licensed public house; it was last used as a Smithy during World War II and many of the original Blacksmith's tools can be seen in the bar, where the old forge is now used as an open fireplace. There are beams and stone walls throughout the ground floor and the restaurant has the original bread oven in its inglenook fire place.
5 rms (1 bth 2 shr) (1 fmly) No smoking in dining room CTV in all bedrooms Tea and coffee making facilities Licensed Cen ht 35P Last d 9pm
PRICE GUIDE
ROOMS: s £20-£22; d £40-£44; wkly b&b £140-£154; wkly hlf-bd £224-£238✱
CARDS: 🅠 💳 💳 💳 💳

ALBURY Surrey Map **04** TQ04

🚩🅠🅠🅠 **Drummond Arms** The Street GU5 9AG (off main A25 between Guildford and Dorking, take A248 marked Albury, Godalming, establishment 1m on right) ☎01483 202039 FAX 01483 202039
This appealing inn at the heart of a picturesque village has an attractive garden with duck pond to its rear. Bedrooms were recently brought up to an excellent standard, with good en suite bathrooms and coordinating decor and fabrics setting off quality pine furniture. A traditional bar menu augmented by some more adventurous blackboard specials offers an alternative to the elegant restaurant's carte meals and fondue evenings.
7 en suite (bth/shr) (1 fmly) CTV in all bedrooms Tea and coffee making facilities No dogs (ex guide dogs) Cen ht No children 14yrs 70P No coaches Last d 9.30pm

➡

PRICE GUIDE
ROOMS: s £38; d £50
MEALS: Lunch £14.95 Dinner £14.95
CARDS: 🔲 🔲 🔲 🔲 🔲

ALCONBURY Cambridgeshire Map **04** TL17

🔲 **Q Q** *The Manor House Hotel* Chapel St PE17 5DY
☎01480 890423 FAX 01480 891663
Located in the centre of the village, this 16th-century former
manor farmhouse is now a popular inn. The accomodation is of a
good standard in comfortably equipped bedrooms. Public areas are
cosy with exposed beams and open fires. Guests have the option
of choosing from a bar menu with daily specials or from the
restaurant's dinner carte from Tuesday to Saturday.
4 en suite (bth/shr) (2 fmly) No smoking in area of dining room
CTV in all bedrooms Tea and coffee making facilities Cen ht
25P Last d 9pm
CARDS: 🔲 🔲 🔲 🔲 🔲

ALDERTON Wiltshire Map **03** ST88

Premier Selected

♥ **Q Q Q Q Q** Mrs V
Lippiatt **Manor Farm**
(ST840831) SN14 6NL
(follow B4040 for
Malmesbury to Luckington,
turn left and follow signs to
Alderton. Farm at N of
village near church)
☎01666 840271
This impressive gabled
farmhouse, built of local
stone in the 17th century, stands in the picturesque village of
Alderton surrounded by pretty Cotswold scenery; the ancient
towns of Malmesbury and Tetbury are close by and the farm
is ideally located for touring the counties of Wiltshire and
Avon. Victoria and Jeffrey Lippiatt and family extend a warm
welcome to guests. Three spacious bedrooms have been
tastefully decorated and comfortably furnished, and
downstairs there is an elegant dining room where breakfast
can be served either around one large table or separately. In
the lounge, colourful soft furnishings have been carefully used
to enhance the character of the original features and the
results are restful and most attractive. Whether for business or
pleasure, Manor Farm is highly recommended.
3 rms (2 bth/shr) No smoking in bedrooms CTV in all
bedrooms Tea and coffee making facilities No dogs (ex
guide dogs) Cen ht CTV No children 12yrs 8P 600 acres
arable
PRICE GUIDE
ROOMS: d £45-£50✱
(£)

ALFRETON Derbyshire Map **08** SK45

♥ **Q Q Q** Mrs K Prince **Oaktree Farm** *(SK385566)* Matlock
Rd, Oakerthorpe, Wessington DE55 7NA (from A38 follow
A615 signed Matlock and fork left at Peacock Inn under
bridge and past cottages for farmhouse on left)
☎01773 832957
Set aside the A615 in a totally rural location, this modern 1960's
farmhouse faced in local stone operates a small holding. The
accommodation is of a very high standard with co-ordinated
decor, soft furnishings and excellent modern en suites. Mrs Prince

---

cooks a hearty breakfast using home produced free range eggs,
taken in a cheerful breakfast room. The house is kept in an
immaculate condition.
3 en suite (bth/shr) No smoking CTV in all bedrooms Tea and
coffee making facilities No dogs Cen ht CTV 10P Fishing 22
acres mixed Last d 6pm
PRICE GUIDE
ROOMS: s £18-£20; d £36-£40; wkly b&b £107-£119; wkly hlf-
bd £150-£165✱
(£)

ALKMONTON Derbyshire Map **07** SK13

Selected

♥ **Q Q Q Q** Mr A Harris **Dairy House** *(SK198367)*
DE6 3DG (3m up Woody Lane after turning off A50 at
Foston) ☎01335 330359 FAX 01335 330359
This red brick, 16th-century farmhouse has a relaxed and
friendly atmosphere - thanks to the enthusiastic owners Mr
and Mrs Harris. Guests can enjoy freshly cooked farmhouse
fare at a communal table in the delightful dining room.
Bedrooms, some of them en suite, offer fresh, neat
accommodation. This is a non-smoking establishment, and is
unsuitable for young children or pets.
7 rms (1 bth 3 shr) No smoking Tea and coffee making
facilities No dogs (ex guide dogs) Licensed Cen ht CTV
No children 14yrs 8P 82 acres stock Last d 7pm
PRICE GUIDE
ROOMS: s £16-£23; d £32-£38; wkly b&b £105-£126;
wkly hlf-bd £189-£210✱

ALMONDSBURY Avon Map **03** ST68

Selected

GH **Q Q Q Q** **Abbotts Way** Gloucester Rd BS12 4JB (on
A38, 2m N of junct 16, M5)
☎01454 613134 FAX 01454 613134
This large modern house is set in twelve acres and has fine
views of the surrounding countryside. Bedrooms are
comfortable and well furnished, and the spacious
conservatory/dining room is a delightful setting in which to
enjoy the delicious breakfasts.
6 rms (5 shr) (2 fmly) No smoking in bedrooms No smoking
in dining room Tea and coffee making facilities Cen ht CTV
10P No coaches Last d breakfast
PRICE GUIDE
ROOMS: s fr £25; d fr £40; wkly b&b fr £175; wkly hlf-bd
fr £245
CARDS: 🔲 🔲 🔲
(£)

ALNMOUTH Northumberland Map **12** NU21

Selected

GH **Q Q Q Q** **High Buston Hall** High Buston NE66 3QH
(off A1068 between Alnmouth & Warkworth)
☎01665 830341 FAX 01665 830341
Closed Jan
An impressive Georgian Grade II listed country house stands
in five acres of beautiful grounds, in an elevated position with
commanding views overlooking Alnmouth and the

Northumberland coastline. The elegantly furnished house is the home of John and Alison Edwards, who are very friendly and caring hosts. Bedrooms are spacious and have been thoughtfully equipped and delightfully decorated and furnished. There is an elegant and comfortable lounge with an open fire, and home-cooked dinners are served house-party style around a large table in the attractive dining room.

3 rms (2 bth/shr) No smoking CTV in all bedrooms Tea and coffee making facilities No dogs (ex guide dogs) Licensed Cen ht 9P No coaches Last d 9am

PRICE GUIDE

ROOMS: d £50-£65; wkly b&b £150-£200

Selected

GH **QQQQ Marine House Private Hotel** 1 Marine Dr NE66 2RW ☎01665 830349

Looking out over the golf links and Alnmouth Bay, this 17th-century listed building was built as a granary and once served as a vicarage. Bedrooms vary in size, but are all attractive and stylishly decorated with eye-catching fabrics. Public areas include a traditional first-floor lounge and a cosy bar. High quality five-course dinners are served each evening.

10 en suite (bth/shr) (4 fmly) No smoking in bedrooms No smoking in dining room CTV in all bedrooms Tea and coffee making facilities Licensed Cen ht CTV No children 3yrs 12P No coaches Last d 4pm

PRICE GUIDE

ROOMS: (incl. dinner) d £78-£84; wkly hlf-bd £250-£270

CARDS: 🔳 ⬛

GH **QQQ** *Westlea* 29 Riverside Rd NE66 2SD ☎01665 830730

Closed 25-26 Dec

A family-owned guest house by the River Aln, Westlea is conveniently located for the village centre and the sandy beaches. The house is beautifully maintained and guests can be sure of a warm welcome. Bedrooms are well equipped and there is a spacious lounge with plenty of books and tourist information. Good home cooking is provided.

7 rms (6 shr) (1 fmly) CTV in all bedrooms Tea and coffee making facilities No dogs Cen ht CTV No children 2yrs 9P Last d 6pm

ALNWICK Northumberland Map **12** NU11

GH **QQQ Aln House** South Rd NE66 2NZ (on A1068) ☎01665 602265

Mar-Nov

A well maintained Victorian house surrounded by gardens is set back from the road on the southern approach to town. Most of the attractively furnished bedrooms have modern en suite bathrooms, the lounge is stylish and comfortable and the dining room is adorned with decorative plates.

7 rms (5 bth/shr) (2 fmly) No smoking in 2 bedrooms No smoking in dining room No smoking in lounges CTV in all bedrooms Tea and coffee making facilities Licensed Cen ht No children 4yrs 8P No coaches

PRICE GUIDE

ROOMS: s fr £18; d fr £38

GH **QQQ Bondgate House Hotel** Bondgate Without NE66 1PN ☎01665 602025 FAX 01665 602554

This interesting Georgian house lies on the main road on the southeast side of the town with a car park to the rear. Well

furnished throughout, bedrooms have good pine pieces and comfortable seating; there is also an attractive dining room and a comfortable lounge with lots of tourist information.

8 rms (5 shr) (3 fmly) No smoking in dining room CTV in all bedrooms Tea and coffee making facilities No dogs (ex guide dogs) Licensed Cen ht CTV 8P Last d 4.30pm

PRICE GUIDE

ROOMS: s £18-£25; d £36-£40; wkly b&b £126-£175; wkly hlf-bd £200-£249

CARDS: 🔳 ⬛

GH **QQQ Charlton House** 2 Aydon Gardens, South Rd NE66 2NT (from A1 pass Hardy's Fishing Museum on right and go straight over mini-roundabout for about 200yds) ☎01665 605185

rs Xmas

This semi-detached house lies on the main road leading into the town from the south, and has been carefully decorated and adorned with antique and period pieces to enhance its Victorian character in a most stylish manner. Stripped pine and original fireplaces feature in several bedrooms, whilst all have quality fabrics and beautiful quilts hand-made by owner Mrs Jones. One bedroom, complete with its own lounge and patio, makes up a quiet rear extension. Both the lounge and dining room echo the same theme, the black floor boards and white lace table cloths helping to give the latter a striking appearance.

5 en suite (bth/shr) (1 fmly) No smoking in bedrooms No smoking in dining room CTV in all bedrooms Tea and coffee making facilities No dogs (ex guide dogs) Cen ht CTV 3P No coaches Last d 6pm

PRICE GUIDE

ROOMS: s £18; d £32-£36; wkly b&b £112-£126; wkly hlf-bd £182-£191✱

Marine House Private Hotel

AA Selected QQQQ

ALNMOUTH, NORTHUMBERLAND NE66 2RW
Telephone: Alnmouth (01665) 830349

RUNNERS-UP FOR AA Best Family Holiday in Britain 1984 and Northumbria Tourist Board. Holiday Hosts Award 1985. Relax in the friendly atmosphere of this 200-year-old building of considerable charm, once a Granary. Overlooking the golf links and beautiful beaches. 10 individually appointed en suite bedrooms, Tester and Crown drapes, Col TVs and Teasmades. Delicious imaginative homecooking cocktail bar and spacious lounge. Children and pets welcome. Two adjacent self-catering cottages. Shiela and Gordon Inkster.
GO FOR GOLF MID SEPT TO MID MAY.
SPECIAL LOG FIRE BREAKS OCT TO APRIL INCLUSIVE

ALRESFORD Hampshire Map **04** SU53

◄ Q Q Q **Woolpack** Totford SO24 9TJ
☎01962 732101 FAX 01962 732889
Guests feel at home in the relaxed and welcoming atmosphere of this listed 16th-century inn which enjoys lovely views across the fields from its setting in a winding country lane between Basingstoke and Alresford. The bedrooms are located in a converted barn, and each offers modern en suite shower facilities together with a good standard of furniture and decor. The bar and lounges are cosy, and an extensive blackboard menu includes tempting home-made desserts.

10 en suite (shr) No smoking in 2 bedrooms No smoking in area of dining room CTV in all bedrooms Tea and coffee making facilities Direct dial from bedrooms Cen ht P Last d 9.50pm
PRICE GUIDE
ROOMS: s £36; d £46.50
MEALS: Lunch fr £5.50alc Dinner fr £5.50alc
CARDS: 🔴 ▬▬

ALTON Hampshire Map **04** SU73

◄ Q Q **White Hart** London Rd, Holybourne GU34 4EY
☎01420 87654
A sizeable pub is situated in the pretty village of Holybourne, north east of Alton. It offers simply furnished bedrooms and attracts a good local clientele who enjoy the weekly quiz night and occasional discos held in the Games Bar, which has a pool table, darts board and juke box. The garden is popular in the summer.

4 rms CTV in all bedrooms Tea and coffee making facilities No dogs (ex guide dogs) Cen ht 40P Last d 10pm
CARDS: 🔴 ▬▬

ALTRINCHAM Greater Manchester Map **07** SJ78

Premier Selected

GH Q Q Q Q Q **Ash Farm**
Park Ln, Little Bollington
WA14 4TJ (turn off A56
beside Stamford Arms)
☎0161 929 9290
Closed 22 Dec-14 Jan
This carefully restored 19th-century farmhouse is set amid National Trust land in the quiet village of Little Bollington, convenient for Manchester and the airport via the M56 and M6. Comfortable bedrooms are tastefully decorated and furnished with hand-made pine beds, chests and cupboards, while public areas include an inviting lounge/dining room where hearty breakfasts and interesting evening meals are served; a fire is lit in winter, and books and games are provided. A full-sized snooker table is also available - not surprisingly, as the owner is snooker player David Taylor!

3 rms (2 bth/shr) No smoking in 1 bedrooms CTV in all bedrooms Tea and coffee making facilities No dogs (ex guide dogs) Licensed Cen ht No children 9yrs 6P No coaches Snooker Last d 8pm
PRICE GUIDE
ROOMS: s £40-£45; d £52-£58✳
CARDS: 🔴 ▬ ▬▬ 🟦 ▬▬ ▬▬

GH Q ***Bollin Hotel*** 58 Manchester Rd WA14 4PJ (on A56)
☎0161 928 2390
This well maintained, family-run hotel is very conveniently located beside the A56, close to the town centre and within easy reach of the airport and M56 and M6 Motorways. The freshly decorated and soundly furnished bedrooms include family rooms; all are well equipped with washbasins, televisions and tea and coffee making facilities, and share two good sized bathrooms. There is an attractive breakfast room with separate tables, a large comfortably furnished lounge and an on-site car park.

10 rms (2 fmly) No smoking in dining room CTV in all bedrooms Tea and coffee making facilities Cen ht CTV 10P No coaches

Selected

◄ Q Q Q Q **The Old Packet House** Navigation Rd, Broadheath WA14 1LW (on A56 Altrincham/Sale road at junct with Navigation Road)
☎0161 929 1331 FAX 0161 929 1331
A pleasant old inn has a car park at the rear. Attractively decorated bedrooms are equipped with such modern extras as trouser presses, while public areas retain the charm and character bestowed by exposed beams and open fires.

4 en suite (bth/shr) No smoking in area of dining room CTV in all bedrooms Tea and coffee making facilities No dogs (ex guide dogs) Cen ht 10P Last d 9pm
PRICE GUIDE
ROOMS: s £29.50-£39.50; d £34-£44; wkly b&b £256✳
CARDS: 🔴 ▬▬

AMBLESIDE Cumbria Map **07** NY30

GH Q Q Q ***2 Cambridge Villas*** Church St LA22 9DL
☎015394 32142
Closed 30 Nov-1 Jan
In summer, colourful flower beds surround this attractive Victorian villa which is situated conveniently close to the town centre, with tennis courts, a bowling green and facilities for mini-golf just across the road. Bedrooms, though small, are charmingly decorated with matching wall coverings and fabrics, and there are a very comfortable guests' lounge and a good-sized dining room with separate tables.

5 rms (1 fmly) No smoking in bedrooms No smoking in dining room CTV in all bedrooms Tea and coffee making facilities No dogs Cen ht CTV No parking Last d 10.30am

GH Q Q Q **Compston House Hotel** Compston Rd LA22 9DJ (in centre of village overlooking the park) ☎015394 32305
Ideally situated close to the town centre, this small family-owned hotel is worth seeking out. The carefully tended accommodation comprises fresh bedrooms and cosy public rooms, and the owners, Mr and Mrs Smith, provide a warm welcome and friendly service.

8 en suite (shr) (1 fmly) No smoking in 1 bedrooms No smoking in dining room CTV in all bedrooms Tea and coffee making facilities No dogs (ex guide dogs) Licensed Cen ht No children 5yrs No parking No coaches Complimentary membership of leisure club Last d 10am
PRICE GUIDE
ROOMS: d £35-£55; wkly b&b £117.50-£187.50; wkly hlf-bd £240-£310
£

GH Q Q Q **Easedale** Compston Rd LA22 9DJ (on one way system going north through Ambleside - bottom of Compston Road on corner overlooking bowling & putting greens)
☎015394 32112

This comfortable guest house is situated in a central position and overlooks a small park with tennis courts and putting and bowling greens. Many of the bedrooms have been recently upgraded to a very good modern standard and, throughout, the house is very well maintained. There is a cosy lounge, a nicely appointed dining room and a small private car park.

6 rms (2 shr) (1 fmly) No smoking in bedrooms No smoking in dining room CTV in all bedrooms Tea and coffee making facilities No dogs Cen ht 8P No coaches

PRICE GUIDE
ROOMS: s £14-£20; d £28-£45; wkly b&b £93-£152.50✱

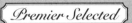

GH 🇶🇶🇶🇶🇶 **Grey Friar Lodge Country House Hotel**
Brathay LA22 9NE (1.5m W off A593) ☎015394 33158
FAX 015394 33158
Mar-Oct

Sheila and Tony Sutton have created a delightful country house from this former vicarage which lies in terraced gardens and grounds two miles from Ambleside on the road to Coniston and Langdale. They run it enthusiastically and their guests are assured of every care and attention. The house is sympathetically furnished and graced with antiques and bric-á-brac to give a warm and relaxing ➡

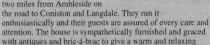
Premier Selected

atmosphere. There are two lounges and a lovely dining room with lace-covered tables and a collection of plates adorning the walls. Bedrooms come in a variety of sizes and are all individual. The larger ones retain the period style of the house, whilst other have more of a cosy cottage feel. They are thoughtfully equipped to include books and home-made sponge cake on arrival. Most of the bedrooms and all the public rooms enjoy magnificent views of the Brathay valley. Shiela's five course dinners and hearty breakfasts exemplify the very best in traditional English cooking. Tony has a great deal of experience in fell walking and will be happy to give advice on the area.

8 en suite (bth/shr) No smoking in bedrooms No smoking in dining room No smoking in 1 lounge CTV in all bedrooms Tea and coffee making facilities No dogs Licensed Cen ht No children 12yrs 12P No coaches Last d 7.30pm
PRICE GUIDE
ROOMS: d £40-£61; wkly b&b £140-£215; wkly hlf-bd £217-£290

GH 🇶🇶 **Haven Cottage** Rydal Rd LA22 9AY (on A591 opposite health centre, 250yds from the Bridge House)
☎015394 33270
Cheery owners contribute to a friendly atmosphere at this two storey guest house with small parking area to front, lying on the main road on the northern side of town. Bedrooms are bright and airy but vary in size and when busy, the small lounge area adjacent the dining room is also used for meals.

9 rms (1 bth/shr) (1 fmly) No smoking CTV in all bedrooms Tea and coffee making facilities Cen ht CTV 10P Last d am
PRICE GUIDE
ROOMS: s £16-£20; d £32-£44; wkly b&b £112-£126; wkly hlf-bd £196-£210✻

GH 🇶🇶🇶 **Lacet House** Kelsick Rd LA22 0BZ
☎015394 34342
Close to the centre of town, this small guest house is situated on a corner above a flower shop. The bedrooms are similarly styled with modern pine furniture, attractive coordinated fabrics and white walls. One room has bunk beds and is ideal for family occupation, and all have modern en suite facilities.

4 rms (3 shr) (2 fmly) CTV in all bedrooms Tea and coffee making facilities No dogs (ex guide dogs) Cen ht 1P Last d noon
PRICE GUIDE
ROOMS: d £33-£36✻

GH 🇶🇶🇶 *Lyndhurst Hotel* Wansfell Rd LA22 0EG (leave M6 at junct 36 onto A591)
☎015394 32421 FAX 015394 32421
The Lyndhurst is a small family-run hotel set in secluded gardens within easy walking distance of the town centre. The prettily decorated bedrooms are all en suite, and one has a four-poster bed. Downstairs there is a cosy lounge and a small bar. The dining room, in a recently built conservatory, is an attractive setting for dinner, served at 6.45pm.

6 en suite (shr) 2 annexe en suite (shr) No smoking in 1 bedrooms No smoking in area of dining room No smoking in 1 lounge CTV in all bedrooms Tea and coffee making facilities No dogs Licensed Cen ht No children 8P No coaches Last d 4pm

Selected

GH 🇶🇶🇶🇶 **Rothay Garth Hotel** Rothay Rd LA22 0EE (off A591 one way road approaching Ambleside from south) ☎015394 32217 FAX 015394 34400

Situated in attractive gardens on the edge of the village, this beautifully appointed family-run hotel provides a high standard of accommodation. The individually decorated bedrooms are well equipped and have either an en suite shower or bath. Elegant public rooms include the Loughrigg Restaurant, a comfortable lounge, cocktail bar and conservatory.

16 rms (14 bth/shr) (3 fmly) No smoking in 10 bedrooms No smoking in dining room No smoking in lounges CTV in all bedrooms Tea and coffee making facilities Direct dial from bedrooms Licensed Cen ht CTV 17P Last d 8.30pm
PRICE GUIDE
ROOMS: (incl. dinner) s £35.50-£45; d £71-£90; wkly hlf-bd £259-£357
CARDS:

Premier Selected

GH 🇶🇶🇶🇶🇶
Rowanfield Country House
Kirkstone Rd LA22 9ET (off
A591 at Bridge House,
signed 'Kirkstone')
☎015394 33686
Mar-Nov, Xmas & New Year

Rowanfield lies on the side of the valley high above the town on the Kirkstone road, its elevated position giving it a superb vista of the opposite hillside, mountains, the town and Lake Windermere in the distance. It has been restored with great thought, combining quality fabrics and wall coverings with lovely period pieces and stripped pine, to create a simple country farmhouse style and a relaxed atmosphere. Bedrooms are not large but they do have character; one has an upstairs bathroom and the ground-floor room has fitted bunks. The little lounge has chunky sofas, a woodburning stove and is filled with magazines. The dining room was originally the kitchen and has a flagstone floor; the three-course dinners offer a commendable choice and may start with cream of sweet potato soup, followed by chunky cod pieces tossed in butter with fennel seeds and lemon grass, with warm armagnac and prune tart with walnut pastry to finish. The house is not licensed but you are welcome to bring your own wine.

7 en suite (bth/shr) (1 fmly) No smoking CTV in all bedrooms Tea and coffee making facilities No dogs (ex guide dogs) Cen ht No children 5yrs 8P No coaches Last d 5pm
PRICE GUIDE
ROOMS: d £50-£56; wkly b&b £175-£182; wkly hlf-bd £248-£264
CARDS:

GH 🇶🇶🇶 **Rydal Lodge Hotel** LA22 9LR (2m NW A591)
☎015394 33208
Closed 3 Jan-12 Feb
This small hotel, to which the assurance of warm hospitality, friendly service and home-cooked dinners brings guests back year after year, was originally Rydal's coaching inn, and parts of it date back to the early 1600s. Most of the individually decorated, traditionally furnished bedrooms are centrally heated, and both the comfortable first-floor lounge and attractive dining room look out over pretty gardens running down to the River Rothay. There is a car park behind the hotel.

8 rms (2 shr) (1 fmly) No smoking in dining room Tea and

coffee making facilities Licensed CTV ch fac 12P Fishing Last d 7pm
PRICE GUIDE
ROOMS: s £27-£28; d £40-£44; wkly b&b £135-£140; wkly hlf-bd £190-£195
CARDS: ▣ ▤

GH ▣▣▣ **Smallwood Hotel** Compston Rd LA22 9DJ
☎015394 32330
This spacious detached Lakeland stone building stands in the heart of the village and dates back to the early 19th century. Bedrooms are well equipped and have pretty decor, and there is a pleasant residents' lounge. The tea shop next door is also owned by the hotel.
13 rms (11 bth/shr) 1 annexe en suite (bth) (4 fmly) No smoking in dining room CTV in 13 bedrooms Tea and coffee making facilities Licensed Cen ht 13P Last d 8pm
PRICE GUIDE
ROOMS: s £17-£25.50; d £34-£46; wkly b&b £110-£145; wkly hlf-bd £205-£240

Selected

▣ ▣▣▣▣ *Drunken Duck* Barngates LA22 0NG
☎015394 36347 FAX 015394 36781
This old inn is situated at a crossroads, between Ambleside and Hawkshead. For more than 300 years it was known as "Barngates Inn", but legend has it that in Victorian times the lady of the house, thinking all her ducks were dead, began to pluck them, only to find that beer had found its way into their feeding ditch and they were merely intoxicated. All rooms are en suite and have been individually furnished and decorated, some with antique furniture. Beams, prints, ladder backed chairs and log fires are a feature in the bars, where extensive meals are served as well as excellent beers and more than 60 whiskies. There is also a small residents' dining room.
8 en suite (bth) 2 annexe en suite (shr) No smoking in dining room CTV in all bedrooms Tea and coffee making facilities Direct dial from bedrooms Cen ht 40P Fishing Last d 9pm
CARDS: ▣ ▤ ▤

AMPORT Hampshire Map **04** SU34

GH ▣▣▣ **Broadwater** SP11 8AY (from A303 take turning for Hawk Conservancy/Amport. At T-junction, turn right, first road right, first cottage on right)
☎01264 772240 FAX 01264 772240
Closed 20-31 Dec
This attractive 17th-century property is situated in the village of Amport, near Andover and is an ideal base for visiting Salisbury Plain and Stonehenge. The en suite bedrooms retain many of the original features; public areas include a comfortable lounge with an inglenook fireplace and a cosy dining room where evening meals can be served on request. Baby sitting can also be arranged.
2 en suite (bth/shr) No smoking in bedrooms No smoking in dining room Tea and coffee making facilities No dogs Cen ht CTV 3P No coaches
PRICE GUIDE
ROOMS: s £20-£25; d £40; wkly b&b fr £140; wkly hlf-bd fr £210

GH ▣▣▣ **Old Barn** SP11 8AE (off A303, 3.5m W of Andover, follow signs to Hawk Conservancy and Amport, turn left at t-junction. First house past inn)
☎01264 710410 FAX 01264 710410
2 en suite (bth/shr) (1 fmly) No smoking CTV in all bedrooms Tea and coffee making facilities No dogs (ex guide dogs) Cen ht

No children 8yrs 4P No coaches
PRICE GUIDE
ROOMS: s £21-£23; d £32-£36; wkly b&b £119-£140

ANCASTER Lincolnshire Map **08** SK94

🌱 ▣ Mrs F Mival **Woodlands** *(SK966437)* West Willoughby NG32 3SH (off the A153 between Sleaford and Grantham, 1m W of Ancaster) ☎01400 230340
Etr-Dec
Woodlands Farm is a stone-built Victorian house surrounded by delightful cottage gardens and set back from the main road at West Willoughby, about a mile west of Ancaster. It offers sound accommodation with limited facilities, together with a combined lounge and breakfast room. Mrs Mival, the charming owner, always offers a warm welcome.
2 rms (1 fmly) No smoking in bedrooms Tea and coffee making facilities Cen ht CTV No children 1yr 3P 12 acres mixed Last d previous day
PRICE GUIDE
ROOMS: s £17-£18; d £30-£32✳

ANDOVER Hampshire Map **04** SU34

See also Amport

GH ▣▣▣ **Virginia Lodge** Salisbury Rd, Abbotts Ann SP11 7NX (on A343, 1m on right after Jet garage)
☎01264 710713
This attractive modern bungalow stands two miles from Andover, close to the village of Abotts Ann. Guests are warmly welcomed by Mr and Mrs Stuart who offer them tea on arrival and are able to recommend local restaurants for evening meals. Traditional English breakfasts - or vegetarian options - include home-made preserves made from fruits grown in the lovely garden. Bedrooms are prettily decorated, and there is a cosy lounge area and dining room. This is a no-smoking establishment.
3 rms (1 bth/shr) No smoking CTV in all bedrooms Tea and coffee making facilities No dogs (ex guide dogs) Cen ht CTV No children 3yrs 6P No coaches
PRICE GUIDE
ROOMS: s £20-£25; d £32-£36

APPLEBY-IN-WESTMORLAND Cumbria Map **12** NY62

GH ▣▣▣ **Bongate House** Bongate CA16 6UE (0.5m from town centre on B6542 signposted Brough) ☎017683 51245
Closed Xmas & New Year
This fine Georgian residence stands in an acre of landscaped gardens on the old main road south of town. Accommodation includes individually decorated bedrooms, a comfortable lounge and a cosy bar; the atmosphere is homely and relaxed.
8 rms (1 bth 4 shr) (4 fmly) No smoking in dining room CTV in all bedrooms Tea and coffee making facilities No dogs (ex guide dogs) Licensed Cen ht No children 7yrs 10P Croquet & putting lawn Last d 6pm
PRICE GUIDE
ROOMS: s £17; d £34-£39; wkly b&b £110-£130; wkly hlf-bd £160-£180

Factual details of establishments in this Guide are from questionnaires we send to all establishments that feature in the book.

ARLINGTON East Sussex Map **05** TQ50

Premier Selected

♥ QQQQQ Mrs C
McCutchan **Bates Green**
(TQ553077) BN26 6SH (2.5m
W of A22 towards Arlington
turn right Old Oak Inn)
☎01323 482039
Closed 22-27 Dec
Brick-built and tile-hung, this
delightful 18th-century
gamekeeper's cottage has
now been restored and
considerably enlarged to
provide accommodation in three unfussy but well equipped
bedrooms. There is a choice of lounges - one on the first floor
and the other, warmed by an open fire, downstairs. A home-
cooked three-course dinner is served at 7.30pm (by
arrangement during the winter months); guests can bring their
own wine, and service is particularly attentive and helpful.
The guest house is personally run by gardening enthusiast Mrs
Carolyn McCutchan, and its lovely gardens are regularly open
for all to enjoy under the National Gardens Scheme.
3 en suite (bth/shr) No smoking Tea and coffee making
facilities No dogs No children 10yrs 3P
Tennis (hard) 130 acres sheep turkey
PRICE GUIDE
ROOMS: d £42-£52; wkly b&b £132-£151✳

ARNSIDE Cumbria Map **07** SD47

GH QQQ **Willowfield Hotel** The Promenade, Arnside
LA5 0AD (turn off A6 at Milnthorpe traffic lights onto B5282,
right at T-junction on entering town and right again at Albion
public house) ☎01524 761354
Standing above Morecambe Bay, this attractive Victorian hotel
enjoys panoramic views of the estuary and the Lakeland hills
beyond. The comfortable, well equipped bedrooms are attractively
furnished and guests also have the use of a lounge and dining
room with spectacular views. Other facilities include a terraced
garden and a private car park. A strict no-smoking policy is
applied.
10 rms (6 shr) (2 fmly) No smoking CTV in all bedrooms Tea
and coffee making facilities Cen ht 8P No coaches Last d 2pm
PRICE GUIDE
ROOMS: s £18-£22; d £36-£44; wkly b&b £115-£135; wkly hlf-
bd £185-£200✳
CARDS: 🔲 🔲 🔲

ARUNDEL West Sussex Map **04** TQ00

GH QQQ **Arden** 4 Queens Ln BN18 9JN ☎01903 882544
This Victorian villa, dating back to 1840, is quietly situated off a
small lane approaching the town centre, and is very neat and well
maintained. Bedrooms are all furnished in the same basic modern
style; some are on the ground floor. Full English breakfast is
provided in the dining room with service personally supervised by
the resident proprietors Carol and Jeff Short.
8 rms (3 shr) CTV in all bedrooms Tea and coffee making
facilities No dogs (ex guide dogs) Cen ht No children 2yrs 4P
No coaches
PRICE GUIDE
ROOMS: s £17-£24; d £30-£36✳

GH QQQ **Bridge House** 18 Queen St BN18 9JG
☎01903 882142 & 882779 FAX 01903 883600
Closed 23-30 Dec
As its name suggests, this small hotel is located by the bridge, and
some rooms overlook the River Arun. The range of well equipped
bedrooms includes those in the adjoining 16th-century cottage,
standard ground-floor rooms and larger family rooms. Some have
recently been upgraded to a higher standard. There is a
comfortable lounge, breakfast room and bar, and the evening meal
is selected from a blackboard menu.
16 rms (12 bth/shr) 3 annexe en suite (bth/shr) (6 fmly) No
smoking in 4 bedrooms No smoking in dining room No smoking
in lounges CTV in all bedrooms Tea and coffee making facilities
Licensed Cen ht CTV 12P Last d 7.30pm
PRICE GUIDE
ROOMS: s £18-£26; d £32-£40
CARDS: 🔲 🔲 🔲 🔲 🔲

ASHBOURNE Derbyshire Map **07** SK14

See also **Stanton & Waterhouses**

Premier Selected

GH QQQQQ **Biggin
Mill House** Biggin-by-Hulland
DE6 3FN (turn off A517
signposted Millington Green,
after 1m take first turning on
left after Ford)
☎01335 370414
FAX 01335 370414
Biggin Mill nestles in the lee
of a valley amongst a cluster
of dwellings and is set in
three acres of delightful gardens which lead down to a stream
and ford beyond. The house is made up of a series of cottages
and guests' are invited into a lovely sitting room which has a
wood-burning stove, deep cushioned chairs and sofas, vases
of fresh flowers and plenty of books and magazines; its walls
and the stairs are finished with a trompe l'oeil bookcase
effect. The dining room, with its richly polished tables, is on
the first floor and has a well stocked honesty bar and it is here
that Mrs Bazeley, an accomplished cook, provides a
magnificent breakfast as well as dinner where home-made
bread cooked on her Aga is superb. The two bedrooms, one en
suite and one with exclusive use of its own bathroom, are
thoughtfully furnished and include many personal touches.
2 en suite (bth/shr) No smoking CTV in all bedrooms Tea
and coffee making facilities No dogs Licensed Cen ht No
children 4P No coaches Last d 24hrs
PRICE GUIDE
ROOMS: s £60; d £75-£80✳
CARDS: 🔲 🔲 🔲

Selected

GH QQQQ **Lichfield** Bridge View, Mayfield DE6 2HN
(from town take A52 for Leek, after 1.25m at Queens
Arms turn left, 200yds up hill on left)
☎01335 344422 FAX 01335 344422
Closed 25 & 26 Dec
Perched above the River Dove with fine views of the bridge,
waterfall and hills, this attractive old house is decorated in
character but has been thoroughly modernised. the gardens are

especially charming and colourful with a bench to take advantage of the views. The bedrooms are thoughtfully furnished and wholly coordinated. The breakfast room is timbered and furnished with individual pine scrubbed tables.
4 rms (2 shr) (1 fmly) No smoking CTV in all bedrooms Tea and coffee making facilities No dogs Cen ht CTV 10P No coaches
PRICE GUIDE
ROOMS: s £18-£20; d £37-£40; wkly b&b £112-£125✱

♥ Ⓠ Mrs J Wain **Air Cottage Farm** (*SK131351*) Ilam DE6 2BD (from Ashbourne take A515 and turn left when signposted Thorpe/Dovedale/Ilam. At Ilam turn right at the Memorial Stone to Alstonfield) ☎01335 350475
Mar-Nov
This former farm-estate cottage stands high upon the moorlands with glorious views and immediate access to Dovedale below and Tissington Spires and Thorpe Cloud beyond. The accommodation is traditional, homely, and comfortable and the two rooms share a modern bathroom. There are also a children's room, a big lounge and a breakfast room where Mrs Wain serves a hearty breakfast which includes home-made preserves and fresh oatcakes.
3 rms Tea and coffee making facilities No dogs (ex guide dogs) CTV P
PRICE GUIDE
ROOMS: s £14-£16; d £28-£32✱

♥ ⒬⒬⒬ Mrs M Hollingsworth **Collycroft** (*SK166434*) Clifton DE6 2GN (2.5m S off A515) ☎01335 342187
Mrs Hollingsworth extends a genuinely warm welcome to this farmhouse surrounded by well tended gardens amid the farm's 250 acres - all set in lovely countryside. Spacious bedrooms have very comfortable beds and are traditionally furnished with satinwood-veneered mahogany bedroom suites. The milking sheds are decked with colourful hanging baskets, and a very friendly bull and a Schnauzer are popular with guests. Wholesome, hearty breakfasts are noteworthy.
3 rms (1 shr) CTV in all bedrooms Tea and coffee making facilities P
PRICE GUIDE
ROOMS: s £15-£18; d £34-£38✱

◀ ⒬⒬⒬ **Dog and Partridge** Swinscoe DE6 2HS ☎01335 343183
Situated just a few miles from Ashbourne, handy for Alton Towers, this 17th-century coaching inn retains some popular rustic features in the bar and restaurant. The bedrooms are in weather-boarded blocks in the grounds, and these are comfortable, modern and well equipped; one block provides self-catering accommodation. The inn caters well for families, with play areas and a stock of children's games in the dining room, plus a children's menu. Dogs are also made welcome.
25 en suite (bth/shr) No smoking in 3 bedrooms CTV in all bedrooms Tea and coffee making facilities Direct dial from bedrooms 90P Last d 11pm
PRICE GUIDE
ROOMS: s £35-£45; d £40-£60✱
MEALS: Lunch £3.95-£10 Dinner £12-£20alc✱
CARDS: 🔲 🔲 🔲 🔲

ASHBURTON Devon Map **03** SX76

See also Bickington & Poundsgate

GH ⒬⒬⒬⒬ **Gages Mill** Buckfastleigh Rd TQ13 7JW ☎01364 652391
Jan/Mar-Nov
Carefully converted to retain its original character, this 14th-century wool mill offers prettily decorated bedrooms, all with en suite or private facilities, though the furnishings are of a simple standard. There are two sitting areas, one with arches leading into the dining room. Annie and Chris Moore are the welcoming hosts, and Chris prepares the imaginative dinners.
8 en suite (bth/shr) (1 fmly) No smoking in dining room CTV in 4 bedrooms Tea and coffee making facilities No dogs (ex guide dogs) Licensed Cen ht CTV No children 5yrs 10P No coaches Croquet Last d 3pm
PRICE GUIDE
ROOMS: s £22-£23; d £44-£46; wkly b&b £126-£136; wkly hlf-bd £196-£206.50

ASHBY-DE-LA-ZOUCH Leicestershire

See advertisement page 45.

ASHFORD Kent Map **05** TR04

GH ⒬⒬⒬ **Croft Hotel** Canterbury Rd, Kennington TN25 4DU ☎01233 622140 FAX 01233 622140
Situated beside the main A28 Canterbury road at Kennington, just over a mile from the town centre, this large private hotel is popular during the week with short-stay business travellers. Its bigger bedrooms are situated in two annexes, but all the ➡

accommodation is well equipped and provided with en suite facilities; some redecoration is planned during the winter months. 15 en suite (bth/shr) 13 annexe en suite (bth/shr) (4 fmly) No smoking in dining room CTV in all bedrooms Tea and coffee making facilities Direct dial from bedrooms Licensed Cen ht CTV 30P Croquet Last d 8pm

PRICE GUIDE
ROOMS: s £35-£42; d £45-£55✱
CARDS: 🂠 ▤ ▦ ▥

GH Q Q Q **Warren Cottage** 136 The Street, Willsborough TN24 0NB (exit M20 at junct 10 onto A20, 0.5m on left) ☎01233 621905 & 632929 FAX 01233 623400
Although only a few minutes from junction 10 of the M20, this 300-year-old cottage enjoys a peaceful country setting. The gardens and interior are charming, and bedrooms are all en suite. 4 en suite (shr) CTV in all bedrooms Tea and coffee making facilities No dogs (ex guide dogs) Licensed Cen ht CTV 10P No coaches Last d 9.30pm

PRICE GUIDE
ROOMS: s £25-£29.90; d £50-£59.80; wkly b&b £175-£209.30; wkly hlf-bd £238-£272.30
CARDS: 🂠 ▥ 🄂

ASHOVER Derbyshire Map **08** SK36

❤ Q Q Q Mr J A Wootton **Old School** *(SK323654)* Uppertown S45 0JF (off B5057, signposted left for Uppertown) ☎01246 590813
Mar-Oct
Set against a picturesque backdrop high amongst the hills, in total seclusion, this modern chalet-style farmhouse provides well kept, spacious accommodation with good facilities. 4 rms (2 shr) (2 fmly) CTV in all bedrooms Tea and coffee making facilities No dogs Cen ht CTV 10P 45 acres poultry sheep beef Last d 9.30am

PRICE GUIDE
ROOMS: s £16-£18; d £32-£36; wkly b&b £112-£126; wkly hlf-bd £154-£168✱

ASTHALL Oxfordshire Map **04** SP21

◀ Q Q Q **Maytime** OX18 4HW (0.25m N off A40) ☎01993 822068 FAX 01993 822635
The Maytime Inn sits square at the centre of this tiny, picturesque village three miles from Burford, the way from its huge car park to the original building leading through a courtyard where the smart modern bedrooms are located. Public areas are full of both colour and character: tables are covered in check gingham, rafters are home to a motley collection of stuffed toys, plump cushions and newspapers are strewn around and seating is a mixture of pews and trestles. Cuisine is modern in style, both full meals and snacks being served.
6 annexe en suite (bth) No smoking in area of dining room CTV in all bedrooms Tea and coffee making facilities Direct dial from bedrooms Cen ht 100P Last d 10pm

PRICE GUIDE
ROOMS: s fr £45; d fr £52.50✱
MEALS: Lunch £5-£14.50 Dinner £6.50-£14.50✱
CARDS: 🂠 ▤ ▦ ▥ 🄂

ASTON CLINTON Buckinghamshire Map **04** SP81

Selected

GH Q Q Q Q **West Lodge Hotel** London Rd HP22 5HL (on A41) ☎01296 630362 & 630331 FAX 01296 630151
This immaculately kept Victorian house is located on the A41,

---

a short distance from the town centre. All the bedrooms are en suite, furnished with modern pine. There are a bright lounge overlooking the well tended garden, and a breakfast room with two tables, one large and one small. A set dinner is served by prior arrangement.. The main feature of this friendly house is the indoor pool complex, which also contains a spa pool and sauna. The owner is a keen hot air balloonist and can arrange flights.
6 en suite (bth/shr) No smoking in dining room CTV in all bedrooms Tea and coffee making facilities Direct dial from bedrooms No dogs (ex guide dogs) Licensed Cen ht CTV 11P No coaches Indoor swimming pool (heated) Sauna Jacuzzi Last d 6pm
CARDS: 🂠 ▤ ▦ ▥ 🖭 ⬛

ASTON MUNSLOW Shropshire Map **07** SO58

Selected

GH Q Q Q Q *Chadstone* SY7 9ER (8m N of Ludlow off the B4368) ☎01584 841675
There are superb views across the Clee Hills from many of the bedrooms and the comfortable residents' lounge at this very modern bungalow. Bedrooms are freshly decorated and attractive fabrics are used to good effect. The house is licensed and evening meals are provided if required. Welcoming owners Muriel and Robert White create a peaceful, relaxing atmosphere.
5 rms (2 bth/shr) No smoking in bedrooms No smoking in dining room CTV in 1 bedroom Tea and coffee making facilities No dogs Licensed Cen ht CTV No children 12yrs 6P No coaches Last d 7pm

---

ASWARBY Lincolnshire Map **08** TF03

◀ Q Q Q **Tally Ho** NG34 8SA (3m S of Sleaford, on A15) ☎01529 455205
Located on the A15 in open countryside, with pleasant gardens to the rear, this delightful old inn provides plenty of charm in a refurbished bar complete with exposed beams and a real fire. The good range of food available in the bar supplements a range of interesting, well produced dishes served in the rear restaurant. Bedrooms are housed in a converted dairy to the rear and have been furnished along modern lines; all are en suite and have also been thoughtfully equipped.
6 annexe en suite (bth/shr) CTV in all bedrooms Tea and coffee making facilities Cen ht 40P Last d 10pm

PRICE GUIDE
ROOMS: s £30-£33; d £45-£48
MEALS: Lunch £8.25-£11&alc Dinner £11-£18.50alc
CARDS: 🂠 ▤ ⬤

AUDLEM Cheshire Map **07** SJ64

❤ Q Q Mrs H M Bennion **Little Heath** *(SJ663455)* CW3 0HE (take A529 from Nantwich for 5m, at 30mph sign turn right) ☎01270 811324
Apr-Nov
Set on a 50-acre dairy farm north of the village centre, this 200-year-old brick-built house retains something of its original character in the low beamed ceilings of a homely lounge and a traditionally furnished dining room where guests share a single large table. Spacious, well maintained bedrooms also have predominantly traditional furniture, the two without en suite facilities sharing a large modern bathroom and toilet.
3 rms (1 shr) No smoking Tea and coffee making facilities No dogs (ex guide dogs) Cen ht CTV 6P 50 acres dairy Last d 10am

AUDLEY Staffordshire Map 07 SJ75

Premier Selected

♥ QQQQQ Mrs E E
Oulton **Domvilles** *(SJ776516)*
Barthomley Rd ST7 8HT
(leave M6, junct 16, follow
signs to Barthomley)
☎01782 720378
Closed 25 Dec

Set in two hundred and forty
acres of beautiful Cheshire
countryside, within three
miles of Junction 15 of the
M6, this beautifully maintained 18th-century farmhouse is
still a part of the working dairy farm where the Oulton family
have lived for generations. The six en suite bedrooms are
attractively decorated, well equipped and have many personal
touches; family rooms and rooms with four-poster and half-
tester beds are available. The comfortably furnished lounge
features a period fireplace and the elegant breakfast room can
serve dinner by prior arrangement. An interesting range of
local crafts is kept on display in a converted outbuilding.
6 en suite (bth/shr) (2 fmly) CTV in all bedrooms Tea and
coffee making facilities No dogs (ex guide dogs) CTV 8P
Table tennis 225 acres dairy mixed Last d 6pm
PRICE GUIDE
ROOMS: s £20-£22; d £30-£36

AUSTWICK North Yorkshire Map 07 SD76

♥ QQQ Mrs M Hird *Rawlinshaw (SD781673)* LA2 8DD (on
A65,3.5m NW of Settle) ☎01729 823214
Etr-Sep
Mr & Mrs Hird have run this charming farmhouse for many years
now and the house dates back some 200 years. There is a very
comfortable lounge for guests and the dining room is full of charm
and character. The two bedrooms are quite delightfully furnished
and have very good comforts provided. It also provides pony
trekking on the farm and it is surrounded by delightful scenery.
2 rms (1 bth) No smoking in dining room CTV in all bedrooms
Tea and coffee making facilities No dogs (ex guide dogs) Cen ht
CTV 10P Riding 206 acres beef dairy horses sheep

AVETON GIFFORD Devon Map 03 SX64

♥ QQQ Mrs J Balkwill **Court Barton** *(SX695478)* TQ7 4LE
(follow signs for St Andrews Church)
☎01548 550312 FAX 01548 550312
Closed Xmas
Located next to the parish church and surrounded by well kept
gardens, this 16th-century farmhouse enjoys a picturesque setting.
Welcoming hosts John and Jill Balkwill have renovated the house
to provide large bedrooms with thoughtful extras. A comfortable
sitting room is available for guests, and breakfast is served in the
dining room.
7 rms (6 bth/shr) (2 fmly) No smoking in dining room Tea and
coffee making facilities No dogs (ex guide dogs) Cen ht CTV
10P Outdoor swimming pool Table tennis Pool table Croquet 40
acres mixed

AVONMOUTH Avon Map 03 ST57

GH Q **Bradford Hotel** 149/151 Avonmouth Rd BS11 9LW (off
junct 18 M5) ☎0117 982 3211

Situated about six miles from the city centre, this family-run hotel
is suited to both business people working in the area and
travellers, being very close to junction 18 of the M5 motorway.
The accommodation is well presented and comfortable, and a
hearty English breakfast is offered.
12 rms (2 bth 3 shr) CTV in all bedrooms Tea and coffee making
facilities No dogs (ex guide dogs) Licensed Cen ht CTV Last d
5pm
PRICE GUIDE
ROOMS: d £40; wkly hlf-bd fr £301✳

AXMINSTER Devon Map 03 SY29

Selected

♥ QQQQ Mrs S Gay **Millbrook Farmhouse**
(SY304987) Chard Rd EX13 5EG (on A358)
☎01297 35351
Closed Xmas, 2wks autumn & 3wks spring
A delightful thatched longhouse, dating back to the 10th
century and set in an acre of well tended gardens, is
conveniently located for both the town and coast. The
bedrooms are furnished with antiques, set off by attractive
fabrics, and provided with thoughtful extras such as fresh fruit
and flowers. The sitting room features oak-panelled walls and
a huge inglenook fireplace. A charming conservatory is a
recent addition, and guests may eat either here or in the dining
room, where local home-grown produce is served around a
large communal table at dinner. An attractive collection of
antique china is displayed throughout the house, and guests
can enjoy a game of croquet or badminton in the garden
during the summer months. ➡

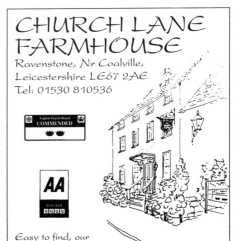

CHURCH LANE FARMHOUSE

Ravenstone, Nr Coalville,
Leicestershire LE67 2AE
Tel: 01530 810536

*Easy to find, our
Queen Anne Farmhouse
offers guests warm hospitality, comfort & style.
All rooms colour TV Radio/alarm, Kettle, en
suite bathrooms. Delicious dining in our
beamed parlour. Fully licensed bar. Guest
lounge with log burning stove. An artistic
household furnished with antiques and
paintings. A guest phone. Secure parking.
Your pleasure and comfort is our concern.*

3 rms (1 bth/shr) (2 fmly) No smoking CTV in all bedrooms
Tea and coffee making facilities No dogs (ex guide dogs)
Cen ht CTV 5P Putting Croquet Last d 5pm
PRICE GUIDE
ROOMS: d £31-£36; wkly b&b £217-£252; wkly hlf-bd
£294-£349✱

AYLSHAM Norfolk Map **09** TG12

GH ⓠⓠⓠ **Old Bank House** 3 Norwich Rd NR11 6BN (on
A140) ☎01263 733843
Closed 23 Dec-1 Jan
The Old Bank House is a Grade II listed red brick building which
dates back to around 1613; originally part of the Old Angel Inn, it
later became the private bank of Aylsham. Now the house offers
good accommodation with spacious character bedrooms and public
rooms that are traditionally appointed and retain such original
features of the house, as the Victorian bathrooms, pillared hall and
minstrels' gallery. Guest have the use of a comfortable small lounge
with many books and games, and meals are taken communally at a
highly polished table in the delightful dining room. Breakfast is
worthy of a mention, being a substantial meal in which home-made
bread rolls and jams feature prominently; evening meals are
available by prior arrangement. Private courtyard car parking is
provided and there is also a delightful walled garden. Please note
that smoking is not permitted within bedrooms.
3 rms (1 bth) (1 fmly) No smoking in bedrooms No smoking in
dining room CTV in all bedrooms Tea and coffee making
facilities Cen ht CTV 3P No coaches Half size snooker table
Table tennis Last d 10am
PRICE GUIDE
ROOMS: s £16-£18; d £32; wkly b&b £96-£108; wkly hlf-bd
£150-£162✱

BAKEWELL Derbyshire Map **08** SK26

See also Beeley

GH ⓠⓠ *Barleycorn Croft* Sheldon DE45 1QS (from A6,
1.5m from town, take right hand turn 500yds after turning to
Ashford. Into Sheldon and house is last one on left hand side
back from green) ☎01629 813636
A pleasant conversion of a small barn, set in the village of
Sheldon three miles west of Bakewell, Barleycorn Croft contains a
small TV lounge and diner together with two cosy bedrooms
which have co-ordinated decor and soft furnishings. Friendly
hostess Jenny Spafford provides a hearty breakfast (vegetarian by
prior arrangement). Please note that this a no-smoking
establishment.
2 rms No smoking Tea and coffee making facilities No dogs (ex
guide dogs) Cen ht CTV No children 7yrs 4P No coaches

GH ⓠⓠⓠ **Bene-Dorme** The Avenue DE45 1EQ (just off A6
near Rutland Recreation Ground) ☎01629 813292
Closed 21 Dec-1 Jan
Situated in a peaceful private road, the Bene Dorme offers two en
suite double bedrooms. A set breakfast is served in a no-smoking
dining room full of ornaments and family photographs.
2 en suite (bth/shr) (1 fmly) No smoking CTV in all bedrooms
Tea and coffee making facilities Cen ht 3P
PRICE GUIDE
ROOMS: s £35-£38

GH ⓠⓠⓠ **Castle Cliffe Private Hotel** Monsal Head
DE45 1NL (3m NW) ☎01629 640258
A very comfortable and cared for guest house perched high above
Monsal Dale, views of which are enjoyed by some of the fresh
looking bedrooms. The public rooms include a spacious dining
room where home produced British dishes are taken, a small well

stocked bar and a lounge furnished with deep cushioned sofas and
easy chairs around an open fire.
9 rms (4 shr) (2 fmly) No smoking in dining room CTV in 2
bedrooms Tea and coffee making facilities No dogs (ex guide
dogs) Licensed CTV 15P No coaches Last d 5pm
PRICE GUIDE
ROOMS: s £27.50-£37.50; d £40-£50; wkly b&b £140-£180;
wkly hlf-bd £220-£280
CARDS: 🖃 🚾   £

GH ⓠⓠⓠ **Cliffe House Hotel** Monsal Head DE45 1NL (3m
NW off B6465) ☎01629 640376
A very homely and traditionally furnished guest house which
enjoys a superb location at the head of Monsal Dale. The
bedrooms are all very well equipped and are generally spacious
and furnished with comfortable chairs. The public areas extend to
a large dining room and a comfortable television lounge.
9 en suite (bth/shr) (3 fmly) No smoking in dining room CTV in
all bedrooms Tea and coffee making facilities No dogs (ex guide
dogs) Licensed Cen ht CTV 14P No coaches
PRICE GUIDE
ROOMS: s £25-£30; d £40-£42; wkly b&b £130-£137
CARDS: 🖃 🚾   £

GH ⓠⓠ **Everton** Haddon Rd DE45 1AW ☎01629 813725
Etr-Oct
This semidetached Victorian house overlooks the park from a
setting close to Bakewell's centre. Three cheerfully decorated
bedrooms share a shower room on the first floor, and a full
English breakfast is served daily at 8.30am.
2 rms CTV in all bedrooms Tea and coffee making facilities No
dogs (ex guide dogs) Cen ht No children 10yrs 2P No coaches
PRICE GUIDE
ROOMS: d £32-£36✱   £

GH ⓠⓠ **Holly House** The Avenue DE45 1EQ (take A6
Matlock rd and after filling station turn right into The
Avenue) ☎01629 813207
Closed Xmas
Christine Wright cheerfully welcomes visitors to her pleasant
home which is situated in a quiet close near the centre of
Bakewell. Guests have their own small lounge, with a piano and
comfortable easy chairs, and breakfast is taken at one large table
in a delightful dining room with highly polished yew furniture.
The two attractively decorated bedrooms share one modern
bathroom across the landing and each has colour TV, books and
tea-making facilities. This is a no-smoking establishment.
2 rms No smoking CTV in all bedrooms Tea and coffee making
facilities No dogs (ex guide dogs) Cen ht CTV 4P No coaches
PRICE GUIDE
ROOMS: s £28; d £36-£40; wkly b&b fr £120✱   £

◀ ⓠⓠ *Red Lion* Rutland Square DE4 1BT
☎01629 812054 FAX 01629 814345
This 17th-century coaching inn at the centre of Bakewell, just off
the square, has recently been refurbished and now has attractive
bar areas which retain such original features as open fires and
beamed ceilings. A separate restaurant offers a good range of
meals. The three fresh, neat bedrooms share one general bathroom
along the corridor. Limited car parking is available at the rear of
the building.
6 rms (1 bth 2 shr) CTV in 5 bedrooms Tea and coffee making
facilities No dogs (ex guide dogs) Cen ht 4P Last d 8.45pm
CARDS: 🖃 🚾

BAMFORD Derbyshire Map 08 SK28

◀ Q Q **Ye Derwent Hotel** Main Rd S30 2AY (BW)
☎01433 651395
There is a very friendly, informal and relaxed atmosphere at this traditional village inn which is close to Ladybower Reservoir and popular with both walkers and families. Bedrooms, which vary in size and include some with en suite facilities, are soundly furnished and comfortable. A good range of home-cooked meals is available in the bar or the small restaurant. There is also a large garden, which is safe for children to play in, and ample car parking.
10 rms (1 bth 1 shr) (1 fmly) CTV in all bedrooms Tea and coffee making facilities Cen ht 40P Boat for hire Last d 9.15pm
PRICE GUIDE
ROOMS: s £25-£30; d £40-£45; wkly b&b £130-£145.50; wkly hlf-bd £185✱
MEALS: Lunch £6.35-£7.95&alc Dinner £6.35-£7.95&alc✱
CARDS: ⬛ 💳 £

BAMPTON Devon

See **Shillingford**

BANBURY Oxfordshire Map 04 SP44

GH Q Q **Belmont** 34 Crouch St OX16 9PR ☎01295 262308
Just around the corner from the famous Banbury Cross stands a tall Victorian town house offering bedrooms - some of them with attractively co-ordinated colour schemes - on all three floors. A cheerful dining room with red-checked table coverings leads off the small lounge.
8 rms (5 shr) (1 fmly) No smoking in dining room CTV in all bedrooms Tea and coffee making facilities No dogs (ex guide ➡

dogs) Cen ht No children 7-12yrs 7P No coaches
PRICE GUIDE
ROOMS: s £20-£25; d £35-£40
CARDS: 🃟 📧

GH Ⓠ Ⓠ Ⓠ *Calthorpe Lodge* 4 Calthorpe Rd OX16 8HS
☎01295 252325
Located in a quiet road close to the famous Banbury Cross, this
terraced Victorian guest house offers attractive recently
refurbished bedrooms which are well equipped and comfortable.
John and Eddie Blackwell provide a relaxed informal atmosphere
and value for money accommodation.
6 rms (4 bth/shr) (1 fmly) CTV in all bedrooms Tea and coffee
making facilities Cen ht CTV 6P No coaches
CARDS: 🃟 📧 ⓞ

Selected

GH Ⓠ Ⓠ Ⓠ Ⓠ **La Madonette Country** North Newington
OX15 6AA (3m W off B4035)
☎01295 730212 FAX 01295 730363
This former mill house is attractively located on the outskirts
of Banbury in its own spacious grounds with the millstream
running by. Bedrooms are comfortable with many fine pieces
of furniture and a super range of facilities including
telephones, television and tea making facilities. A pretty
lounge is available for guests and breakfast is served in the
smart dining room.
5 en suite (bth/shr) (2 fmly) CTV in all bedrooms Tea and
coffee making facilities Direct dial from bedrooms No dogs
(ex guide dogs) Licensed Cen ht CTV 20P No coaches
Outdoor swimming pool (heated)
PRICE GUIDE
ROOMS: s £28-£34; d £45-£58✳
CARDS: 🃟 📧 ⓞ 🈺

◖ Ⓠ Ⓠ Ⓠ *The Blinking Owl* Main St, North Newington
OX15 6AE ☎01295 730650
Once The Bakers Arms, this lovely ironstone inn is the oldest in
the village. Mr and Mrs Pursey have developed the owl theme
with custom-designed carpets and owl ornaments, and they have
scoured the countryside to find antique furniture for the two bars -
notably the big oak dresser and pews. There are three clean and
comfortable guest rooms. The ale is real - Abbot, Greene King,
IPA and Tetley's traditional - and food is served seven days a
week.
3 en suite (bth/shr) CTV in all bedrooms No dogs Cen ht No
children 8yrs 12P Last d 9pm

◖ Ⓠ Ⓠ **Roebuck** Stratford Rd, Drayton OX15 6EN (on A442)
☎01295 730542
Closed Dec
A friendly, traditional inn, the Roebuck is located on the fringes of
the quiet village of Drayton, a mile from Banbury. The bar and
restaurant extension offer a selection of snacks and meals
supplemented by daily specials, and accommodation with well
maintained facilities is provided on the two floors above.
2 rms No smoking in bedrooms No smoking in dining room
CTV in all bedrooms Tea and coffee making facilities No dogs
Cen ht 20P Last d 9.30pm
PRICE GUIDE
ROOMS: s fr £25; d fr £35✳
MEALS: Lunch £3.35-£6.95 Dinner £14-£18alc✳
CARDS: 🃟 📧 🈺

BANTHAM Devon Map **03** SX64

Premier Selected

GH Ⓠ Ⓠ Ⓠ Ⓠ Ⓠ **Widcombe
House** TQ7 3AA (off A379)
☎01548 561084
Mar-Oct
Although John Paine and Jill
Hutcheson have only recently
acquired this attractive
modern property, their high
standards are very much in
evidence. The house is set in
manicured gardens a short
drive from Bantham village

with both Salcombe and Kingsbridge within easy reach. The
three immaculate bedrooms are of a particularly high standard
with restful decor and quality furniture, each having a
spacious bathroom well equipped with extras. Jill is Cordon
Bleu trained and the delicious menus reflect this. The bread
and ice cream is all home made - stay a few days and you get
to choose the flavour! Our inspector particularly enjoyed the
Fresh Brill with Herb Crust accompanied by home grown
vegetables.
3 rms (2 bth/shr) No smoking CTV in all bedrooms Tea and
coffee making facilities No dogs Cen ht No children 14yrs
9P No coaches Last d 5pm
PRICE GUIDE
ROOMS: s £25-£30; d £40-£56; wkly b&b £120-£168;
wkly hlf-bd £239-£287✳
                                                                    £

◖ Ⓠ Ⓠ Ⓠ **Sloop** TQ7 3AJ ☎01548 560489 & 560215
FAX 01548 561940
Reputed to date back to the smuggling days of the 16th century,
the Sloop stands in the centre of this charming South Hams
village, close to Burgh Island and offering some fine estuary
views. The bedrooms have been updated to combine modern
facilities with original character; each is en suite and is attractively
appointed. Beamed, panelled bars display a good choice of food
on blackboards, the home-made puddings being particularly
appetising.
5 en suite (bth/shr) (2 fmly) CTV in all bedrooms Tea and coffee
making facilities Cen ht 35P No coaches Last d 10pm
PRICE GUIDE
ROOMS: d £52-£56✳
MEALS: Lunch £7.50-£11.50alc Dinner £7.50-£15alc✳
CARDS: 📧 🃟 🈺

BARDON MILL Northumberland Map **12** NY76

♥ Ⓠ Ⓠ Ⓠ Mrs J Davidson **Crindledykes** *(NY787672)* Nr
Housesteads NE47 7AF (on unclass rd, between A69 and
B6318) ☎01434 344316
Mar-Nov
This impeccably maintained traditional hill farm stands beside the
Newbrough road, northeast of Bardon Mill. A double bedroom
and a spacious twin share the bathroom, whilst downstairs there
are a guests' lounge and a dining room where meals are taken
around one table.
2 rms No smoking in bedrooms No smoking in dining room No
dogs Cen ht CTV 10P 475 acres stock Last d noon
PRICE GUIDE
ROOMS: s £20-£22; d £30-£34✳

BARHAM Kent Map 05 TR25

◾ 🔲🔲 **Old Coach House** Dover Rd (A2) CT4 6SA (on A2, 7m S of Canterbury) (Logis)
☎01227 831218 FAX 01227 831932
Located on the southbound side of the A2, this large, symmetrical red brick building can trace its history back for 250 years. There are five modestly furnished bedrooms with lofty ceilings, bright quilted bedspreads and old-fashioned writing desks. The French chef/owner is ably assisted by his wife in front-of-house duties. Full cooked/continental breakfast is available at extra charge.
5 en suite (bth/shr) (1 fmly) No smoking in bedrooms No smoking in area of dining room CTV in all bedrooms Tea and coffee making facilities No dogs Cen ht CTV 32P Last d 9pm
PRICE GUIDE
ROOMS: s fr £42; d fr £48✳
MEALS: Dinner fr £16.50alc✳
CARDS: (£)

BARNARD CASTLE Co Durham Map 12 NZ01

GH 🔲🔲🔲 *The Homelands* 85 Galgate DL12 8ES
☎01833 38757
Homelands is an attractive and well furnished house which stands close to the centre of town. Two bedrooms are contained within the main building while the others are located in two nearby houses. Breakfast is served in the first house, where there is also a delightfully comfortable lounge. Resident owner Kath Chesman provides friendly and attentive service.
4 rms (2 annexe en suite (bth/shr) CTV in all bedrooms Tea and coffee making facilities No dogs (ex guide dogs) Licensed Cen ht 5P No coaches Last d 8.15pm

♥ 🔲 R & Mrs D M Lowson **West Roods** (NZ022141) West Roods Working Farm, Boldron DL12 9SW (off A66, 2.5m E of Bowes) ☎01833 690116
Apr-Oct
A simply furnished farmhouse set at a high altitude, on a small caravan site in a very rural location, offers modest but clean and tidy accommodation, its pleasant owners providing plenty of tourist information.
3 rms (2 shr) (1 fmly) No smoking CTV in all bedrooms Tea and coffee making facilities No dogs (ex guide dogs) Cen ht 6P Table tennis Badminton 54 acres dairy
PRICE GUIDE
ROOMS: s £16-£20; d £32-£40; wkly b&b £100-£120✳
CARDS: 🔲

♥ 🔲🔲🔲 Mrs H Lowes **Wilson House** (N2018124) Barningham DL11 7EB (off A66) ☎01833 621218
Mar-Nov
A warm and friendly welcome awaits at this attractive farmhouse which stands in 475 acres amongst superb Pennine scenery. The bedrooms are attractively decorated and have colour televisions, full central heating and en suite facilities provided. There is a comfortable lounge, together with two cosy dining rooms where good home cooking is served, dishes being based on the best local produce available. The house is located close to the village of Barningham, which is signposted from the A66 at Greta Bridge.
3 rms (2 shr) (1 fmly) CTV in all bedrooms Tea and coffee making facilities No dogs (ex guide dogs) Cen ht CTV P 475 acres mixed livestock Last d 2pm
PRICE GUIDE
ROOMS: s £16; d £32✳

◾ 🔲🔲🔲 **The Fox and Hounds Country Inn & Restaurant** Cotherstone DL12 9PF (4m W on B6277) ☎01833 650241
Situated in the village of Cotherstone, overlooking the green and not far from the River Tees, this pleasant inn offers character bars

and beautifully furnished bedrooms. A good range of well cooked dishes is featured on interesting menus, and service is warm and friendly.
3 en suite (bth/shr) (1 fmly) No smoking in bedrooms No smoking in area of dining room No smoking in 1 lounge CTV in all bedrooms Tea and coffee making facilities Direct dial from bedrooms No dogs (ex guide dogs) Cen ht CTV 15P Last d 9.30pm
PRICE GUIDE
ROOMS: s £25-£37.50; d £50; wkly b&b £150-£175; wkly hlf-bd £240-£280
MEALS: Lunch £10-£20&alc Dinner £12-£20&alc
CARDS: (£)

BARNEY Norfolk Map 09 TF93

GH 🔲🔲🔲 **The Old Brick Kilns** Little Barney Ln, Barney NR21 0NL (NE of Fakenham, off A148 towards Barney)
☎01328 878305 FAX 01328 878948
A well cared for house in a peaceful location within the grounds of a caravan site, Old Brick Kilns offers fresh modern bedrooms equipped with modern facilities which include radio alarms. Breakfast is served around a large oval table and dinner is available by prior arrangement. Leading off the dining room there is a lounge with TV and a video recorder.
3 en suite (bth/shr) (2 fmly) No smoking CTV in all bedrooms Tea and coffee making facilities Direct dial from bedrooms No dogs (ex guide dogs) Licensed Cen ht CTV 15P No coaches Fishing Table tennis Boules Croquet Giant chess Last d 10am
PRICE GUIDE
ROOMS: s £20-£24; d £40-£48; wkly b&b £140; wkly hlf-bd £245
CARDS: 🔲

BARNSTAPLE Devon Map 02 SS53

See also Bratton Fleming

GH 🔲🔲 **Cresta** 26 Sticklepath Hill EX31 2BU
☎01271 74022
The Cresta is a detached pre-war house located at the top of Sticklepath Hill, on the old road to Bideford. It offers simply appointed bedrooms, including some with en suite facilities on the ground floor, and a no-smoking dining room where breakfast is served. Margaret Curtis is only too happy to arrange bridge games for her guests.
5 rms (1 shr) 1 annexe en suite (bth) (1 fmly) No smoking in dining room CTV in all bedrooms Tea and coffee making facilities Cen ht CTV 6P
PRICE GUIDE
ROOMS: s £15-£20; d £28-£32; wkly b&b fr £84✳

GH 🔲🔲🔲 **Heanton House** Kings Heanton, Marwood EX31 4ED ☎01271 46342
Heanton House is the family home of Colin and Sheila Gosling, who welcome guests to their home, quietly located on the edge of the village, about 3 miles from Barnstaple and conveniently located for visiting Marwood Gardens. The bedrooms are comfortable and well equipped, such thoughtful extras as a selection of books are included in each room. A comfortable sitting room is available for guests. Guests take meals around a large pine refectory table in the open plan, split level kitchen/dining room. Mrs Gosling is flexible about the types of meals that can be served, from a full three course meal to a lighter more informal meal. Packed lunches and bar-b-ques are also available by arrangement. Guests are encouraged to enjoy the 1.5 acres of gardens, from which there are glorious views over the surrounding countryside. A guest's laundry is available.
4 rms No smoking in bedrooms No smoking in dining room CTV in 2 bedrooms Tea and coffee making facilities No dogs (ex

guide dogs) Cen ht CTV No children 14yrs 5P No coaches Last d 5pm
PRICE GUIDE
ROOMS: s £17-£19; d £34-£38; wkly b&b £100-£115; wkly hlf-bd £125-£170✱

GH Q Q **West View** Pilton Causeway EX32 7AA (opposite Pilton Park) ☎01271 42079
West View is an end-of-terrace red brick Edwardian house overlooking the park, a short walk from the centre of town. Brightly decorated bedrooms are simply furnished, and a choice of dishes is offered at dinner in the small dining room.
7 rms (1 shr) 2 annexe rms (2 fmly) No smoking in dining room CTV in all bedrooms Tea and coffee making facilities Direct dial from bedrooms Cen ht 7P No coaches Last d 5.30pm
PRICE GUIDE
ROOMS: s £15-£16; d £30-£32; wkly b&b £105-£112; wkly hlf-bd £147-£161✱
CARDS: 🟦 🟥

GH Q Q Q *Yeo Dale Hotel* Pilton Bridge EX31 1PG (from A361 Barnstaple take A39 Lynton, hotel approx 0.25m from A361/A39 roundabout,on left past small park)
☎01271 42954
A listed three-storey building with a 19th-century façade, the Yeo Dale has evidence of earlier architectural eras within. The features of each period have been carefully retained in the modernisation of the property, creating an individual hotel of some character. There are comfortably furnished bedrooms, a quiet sitting room, a separate bar-lounge and an attractive dining room offering a choice of home cooked dishes.
10 rms (6 bth/shr) (3 fmly) No smoking in dining room CTV in all bedrooms Tea and coffee making facilities Licensed Cen ht CTV No parking Last d 5pm
CARDS: 🟦 🟥 🟥 🔵

Selected

♥ Q Q Q Q Mrs M Lethaby **Home Park** *(SS553360)* Lower Blakewell, Muddiford EX31 4ET ☎01271 42955
Closed 25-26 Dec
This small, well modernised farmhouse is set in a quiet position with uninterrupted views of rolling countryside. Mrs Lethaby provides cheerful hospitality and an excellent home-cooked dinner using fresh local ingredients. Two modern bedrooms have en suite facilities and there is good provision for children.
3 en suite (bth/shr) (2 fmly) No smoking in 2 bedrooms No smoking in dining room No smoking in lounges CTV in all bedrooms Tea and coffee making facilities Cen ht CTV 3P 70 acres sheep Last d 4pm
PRICE GUIDE
ROOMS: s £17.50-£20; d £30-£35; wkly b&b £110-£120; wkly hlf-bd £150✱

♥ Q Q Mrs J Dallyn **Rowden Barton** *(SS538306)* Roundswell EX31 3NP (2m SW B3232) ☎01271 44365
Rowden Barton, a modern farmhouse set in an elevated position overlooking glorious countryside, stands just a few hundred yards from the North Devon link road and close to the centre of Barnstaple. There are two letting bedrooms and a comfortable lounge. Breakfast is served around one large family table in the dining room.

---

2 rms No smoking No dogs (ex guide dogs) Cen ht CTV 4P 90 acres beef sheep
PRICE GUIDE
ROOMS: s fr £14; d fr £28✱

BARTON-ON-SEA Hampshire Map **04** SZ29

Selected

GH Q Q Q Q **Bank Cottage** Grove Rd BH25 7DN
☎01425 613677 FAX 01425 613677
Closed Xmas
This attractive property, dating from 1926, and with a warm, friendly atmosphere about it, stands in a peaceful location. A haven for those who are looking for a friendly relaxed place to stay, with charming proprietors who look after their guests well. The accommodation is comfortable and each bedroom is well equipped and nicely decorated and furnished. Dinners can be offered by arrangement but for those wishing to eat out, Mr and Mrs Neath are able to recommend many local restaurants. Guests are made to feel very welcome and many return here frequently.
3 rms (2 shr) No smoking CTV in all bedrooms Tea and coffee making facilities No dogs Cen ht CTV No children 7yrs 4P No coaches Last d noon
PRICE GUIDE
ROOMS: s £25-£30; d £35-£40; wkly b&b £110-£125; wkly hlf-bd £170-£185✱

Selected

GH Q Q Q Q **Cleeve House** 58 Barton Court Av BH25 7HG (Off A337) ☎01425 615211
4 rms (2 bth/shr) (1 fmly) No smoking Tea and coffee making facilities No dogs Cen ht CTV 8P No coaches
PRICE GUIDE
ROOMS: s £17; d £38-£42

Selected

GH Q Q Q Q **Hotel Gainsborough** Marine Dr East BH25 7DX ☎01425 610541
This delightful family-run hotel on the seafront continues to improve. The bedrooms have been tastefully redecorated, they are well equipped, with modern en suite facilities, and some have balconies. There is a comfortable residents lounge which now leads into a full bar, or for those wishing to benefit from the spectacular sea views there is an attractive sun lounge. The restaurant offers good traditional home-cooked evening meals. There is ample forecourt parking.
5 rms (2 bth 2 shr) (1 fmly) No smoking in bedrooms No smoking in dining room No smoking in 1 lounge CTV in all bedrooms Tea and coffee making facilities Licensed Cen ht No children 12yrs 10P No coaches Last d noon
PRICE GUIDE
ROOMS: d £20-£25; wkly b&b £140-£175; wkly hlf-bd £200-£250

BASINGSTOKE Hampshire Map **04** SU65

See also Hook

BASLOW Derbyshire Map **08** SK27

🔴 QQ *Rutland Arms* Calver Rd DE4 1RP ☎01246 582276
A small, refurbished, brewery-owned village inn, the Rutland
Arms offers good accommodation, pleasantly furnished in pine
with co-ordinating fabrics; the four bedrooms are served by two
modern bathrooms across the landing. The friendly couple who
manage the establishment encourage a relaxed atmosphere in the
bar area, and home-made bar meals are available.
4 rms (3 fmly) CTV in all bedrooms Tea and coffee making
facilities Cen ht 30P

🔴 QQQ *Wheatsheaf Hotel* Netherend DE4 1SR
☎01246 582240
The Wheatsheaf is a refurbished, brewery-owned inn offering
smart public areas geared to the service of meals in a friendly and
relaxed environment. Bedrooms are attractively decorated and
some have modern en suite facilities.
5 rms (1 bth) (1 fmly) No smoking in dining room No smoking
in lounges CTV in all bedrooms Tea and coffee making facilities
No dogs (ex guide dogs) Cen ht 100P Last d 9.30pm
CARDS: 🟦 🟥 🟦

BASSENTHWAITE Cumbria Map **11** NY23

GH 🔲🔲🔲 **Link House Hotel** CA13 9YD
☎017687 76291 FAX 017687 76670
This traditional Victorian house lies within walking distance of the northern end of Bassenthwaite Lake. Mike and Marilyn Tuppen took over in May 1995 and will be adding their personal touches to the house during the winter. Bedrooms are solidly furnished and include some nice singles; several others are well proportioned. In addition to the lounge there is a conservatory, and Marilyn's four-course dinners and hearty breakfasts are proving an attraction.
8 en suite (bth/shr) (2 fmly) No smoking in bedrooms No smoking in dining room CTV in all bedrooms Tea and coffee making facilities No dogs (ex guide dogs) Licensed Cen ht No children 7yrs 10P No coaches Last d 5pm
PRICE GUIDE
ROOMS: s £21-£26; d £42-£52; wkly hlf-bd £236
CARDS: 🟥 🟨 🟦 🟥 🔲

BATH Avon Map **03** ST76

See also Box, Bradford on Avon, Hinton Charterhouse, Keynsham, Swineford and Timsbury

GH 🔲 **Arney** 99 Wells Rd BA2 3AN (on A367)
☎01225 310020
Accommodation in simply furnished bedrooms is provided by this Victorian terraced property on the Wells road; breakfast is served at separate tables in the dining room.
3 rms (1 fmly) No smoking in dining room No smoking in lounges CTV in 1 bedroom Tea and coffee making facilities No dogs (ex guide dogs) Cen ht No parking
PRICE GUIDE
ROOMS: s £20-£23; d £32-£36   £

GH 🔲🔲🔲 **Ashley Villa Hotel** 26 Newbridge Rd BA1 3TZ
(W on A4) ☎01225 421683 & 428887 FAX 01225 313604
Situated close to the city centre, this well run little hotel offers comfortable accommodation in well equipped bedrooms, all of which have en suite facilities. A traditional English breakfast is served in the attractively furnished dining room, and there are two cosy lounge areas where guests are invited to relax, perhaps with a drink from the bar. Ample parking is provided.
14 en suite (bth/shr) (3 fmly) No smoking in dining room CTV in all bedrooms Tea and coffee making facilities Direct dial from bedrooms No dogs (ex guide dogs) Licensed Cen ht CTV 10P Outdoor swimming pool
PRICE GUIDE
ROOMS: s £43-£49; d £49-£69; wkly b&b £169-£343
CARDS: 🟥 🟨 🟦 🟥   £

GH 🔲🔲 **Astor House** 14 Oldfield Rd BA2 3ND (on entering Bath follow signs for Exeter, turn up Exeter Road (A367) second on right is Oldfield Road)
☎01225 429134 FAX 01225 429134
Closed Jan-mid Mar
An attractive Edwardian house in a quiet residential location, Astor House offers comfortable accommodation in a friendly and relaxed atmosphere. The proprietors, Mr and Mrs Beech, are constantly making improvements. An extensive breakfast menu may include cheese-filled Staffordshire oatcakes as well as a traditional English option. A small lounge is also provided for guests' use.
6 rms (4 shr) (1 fmly) No smoking CTV in 8 bedrooms Tea and coffee making facilities No dogs (ex guide dogs) Cen ht CTV

No children 2yrs 6P No coaches Special rates at 9 hole golf course
PRICE GUIDE
ROOMS: d £32-£40
CARDS: 🟥 🟨

Selected

GH 🔲🔲🔲🔲 **Badminton Villa** 10 Upper Oldfield Park
BA2 3JZ ☎01225 426347 FAX 01225 420393
Closed 24 Dec-1 Jan
This quality bed and breakfast establishment enjoys magnificent views of Bath from its setting in a pretty terraced garden on the city's southern slopes, only ten minutes from the centre. A large Victorian house personally restored by its enthusiastic owners, it offers only three bedrooms - each of them individually styled and well decorated with rich co-ordinating colours and fabrics. Attractively furnished in pine, they also feature first-class en suite facilities and are equipped to satisfy today's discerning traveller.
4 en suite (bth/shr) (1 fmly) No smoking CTV in all bedrooms Tea and coffee making facilities No dogs (ex guide dogs) Cen ht No children 4yrs 5P No coaches
PRICE GUIDE
ROOMS: s £38; d £50-£55✱
CARDS: 🟥 🟨

Selected

GH 🔲🔲🔲🔲 **Bailbrook Lodge** 35/37 London Rd West
BA1 7HZ ☎01225 859090 FAX 01225 859090
Closed 25-28 Dec
Just a mile from the city centre and seven miles from the M4, this handsome Georgian hotel offers comfortable accommodation in a choice of well equipped bedrooms, some with glorious views across the Avon Valley. Traditional English breakfast is served in the gracious dining room and an excellent dinner is also available. The hotel stands in its own well kept gardens and provides ample car parking.
12 en suite (bth/shr) (4 fmly) No smoking in 4 bedrooms No smoking in area of dining room CTV in all bedrooms Tea and coffee making facilities No dogs (ex guide dogs) Licensed Cen ht CTV 12P Last d 9pm
PRICE GUIDE
ROOMS: s £32-£47; d £48-£55
CARDS: 🟥 🟥 🟨 🟦   £

Selected

GH 🔲🔲🔲🔲 **The Bath Tasburgh** Warminster Rd,
Bathampton BA2 6SH (on A36, 1 mile east of city centre, signposted to Warminster)
☎01225 425096 FAX 01225 463842
Set in two acres of well tended gardens and five acres of pasture, yet close to the city centre, this Victorian house enjoys canal frontage and panoramic views over the Avon valley. The bedrooms have been tastefully decorated and are well equipped. There is a comfortable lounge leading into a conservatory, and breakfast is served in the dining room at separate tables.
13 rms (12 bth/shr) (4 fmly) No smoking in dining room No smoking in lounges CTV in all bedrooms Tea and coffee making facilities Direct dial from bedrooms No dogs

Licensed Cen ht CTV 15P Croquet
PRICE GUIDE
ROOMS: s £38-£50; d £50-£72
CARDS:
See advertisement on p.55.

(£)

Selected

GH ⬛⬛⬛⬛ **Blairgowrie House** 55 Wellsway BA2 4RT
☎01225 332266
This fine late-Victorian residence stands within walking
distance of the city centre and the main attractions of Bath.
Three bedrooms have been tastefully decorated and are
equipped with modern comforts and such thoughtful extras as
biscuits, bottled waters and shower gels. Downstairs,
armchairs are a feature of the elegant dining room where a
range of interesting dishes is available for breakfast.
3 rms (1bth 1shr) No smoking in dining room CTV in all
bedrooms Tea and coffee making facilities No dogs (ex
guide dogs) Cen ht No parking
PRICE GUIDE
ROOMS: s £30-36; d £42-£50

(£)

Selected

GH ⬛⬛⬛⬛ **Bloomfield House** 146 Bloomfield Rd
BA2 2AS ☎01225 420105 FAX 01225 481958
This imposing Grade II listed property, built around 200 ➡

QQQQ

Bailbrook Lodge

35/37 London Road West, Bath BA1 7HZ
Telephone & Fax: 01225 859090

This splendid Georgian house designed by
the famous architect John Everleigh is
situated one mile east of Bath. The tastefully
furnished accommodation offers 12 en-suite
bedrooms with TV and hospitality tray
(some 4-posters). The lounge bar overlooks
the grounds and the dining room offers
traditional English cuisine. Ample car
parking. B&B from £24 pp.

Ashley Villa Hotel, Bath

AA
QQQ

ETB

26 Newbridge Road, Bath BA1 3JZ
Telephone: (01225) 421683/428887   Fax: (01225) 313604

Comfortably furnished licensed hotel with relaxing informal atmosphere, situated close to the city
centre. All 14 well appointed bedrooms have en suite facilities, colour television, direct dial telephone,
tea and coffee making. Most Credit Cards welcome. This small friendly hotel has recently been
refurbished throughout. It has an outdoor swimming pool with garden, patio and car park.

You can be sure of a warm welcome from the resident owners,
Rod and Alex Kitcher, M.H.C.I.M.A.

years ago, stands in an elevated position overlooking the city. More recently the house has been sympathetically restored, retaining most of the original features yet at the same time providing modern comforts. Bedrooms are individually styled with velvet or hand-woven silk curtains, canopied or four-poster beds, and graced with antique furniture. Downstairs there is a comfortable lounge where reading material is provided. Bloomfield House, the home of Bridget and Malcolm Cox, is for non smokers only.

8 en suite (bth/shr) No smoking in all bedrooms Tea and coffee making facilities Direct dial from bedrooms No dogs Cen ht No children 10yrs 9P No coaches

PRICE GUIDE

ROOMS: s £35-£45; d £45-£95

CARDS: ▨ ▨

Selected

GH ▢▢▢▢ **Brocks** 32 Brock St BA1 2LN (MIN)
☎01225 338374 FAX 01225 334245

Closed Xmas & 2 wks Jan

Ideally situated in the loveliest part of Bath, between the Circus and the famous Royal Crescent, this elegant Georgian house offers comfortable accommodation in pleasantly furnished bedrooms, each with a style of its own. Breakfast is served in a gracious dining room with a cosy lounge area, and there is a good variety of dishes to suit most tastes. Pay and display parking is available during the day and there are local parks close by.

6 rms (5 bth/shr) (3 fmly) No smoking in dining room CTV in all bedrooms Tea and coffee making facilities No dogs (ex guide dogs) Cen ht 1P No coaches

PRICE GUIDE

ROOMS: s £40-£48; d £50-£56✱

CARDS: ▨ ▨

Selected

GH ▢▢▢▢ **Brompton House Hotel** St John's Rd
BA2 6PT ☎01225 420972 FAX 01225 420505

Closed Xmas & New Year

This fine Georgian Rectory built in 1777 has been more recently extended and, situated in award winning gardens, is but a few minutes' walk from the centre of the city. The Selby family extend a warm welcome to their guests, and the availability of parking is no small bonus in this busy area. Whilst the house has been renovated, care has been taken to retain the original elegance and charm of the building. The pastel shades of the comfortable bedrooms are complemented by co-ordinating fabrics, and they offer a range of facilities normally associated with larger establishments. Breakfast is served in an attractive dining room with an adjacent lounge.

18 en suite (bth/shr) (1 fmly) No smoking in bedrooms No smoking in dining room CTV in all bedrooms Tea and coffee making facilities Direct dial from bedrooms No dogs (ex guide dogs) Licensed Cen ht No children 5yrs 20P

PRICE GUIDE

ROOMS: s £32-£45; d £62-£74✱

CARDS: ▨ ▨ ▨

See advertisement on p.56.

Premier Selected

GH ▢▢▢▢▢ **Burghope Manor** Winsley BA15 2LA
☎01225 723557 FAX 01225 723113
(For full entry see Bradford on Avon)

GH ▢▢▢ **Carfax Hotel** Great Pulteney St BA2 4BS
☎01225 462089 FAX 01225 443257

The Carfax is situated in one of Bath's most beautiful Georgian streets and enjoys views across the city and into nearby Henrietta Park. There are a large reception area, a comfortable lounge and a conference room, all of which are warm and attractively furnished. Bedrooms vary in size and outlook, though they are all comfortable and well equipped, and there is a lift for guests' use. A traditional evening meal is offered, though the hotel has no drinks licence.

39 rms (34 bth/shr) (3 fmly) No smoking in 27 bedrooms No smoking in dining room No smoking in lounges CTV in all bedrooms Tea and coffee making facilities Direct dial from bedrooms No dogs (ex guide dogs) Lift Cen ht CTV 17P Games room Last d 7.50pm

PRICE GUIDE

ROOMS: s £22-£46; d £40-£72; wkly b&b £140-£238; wkly hlf-bd £182-£252✱

CARDS: ▨ ▨ ▨

See advertisement on p.57.

Selected

GH ▢▢▢▢ **Cheriton House** 9 Upper Oldfield Park
BA2 3JX (south of Bath, 0.5m along the A367)
☎01225 429862 FAX 01225 428403

Closed Xmas & New Year

The conscientious owners of this characterful stone-built Victorian villa continue to upgrade it and their painstaking renovation has provided commendable standards of comfort. Set in an elevated position with views over the city and beyond, enclosed in well kept gardens, it offers accommodation in bright, appealing bedrooms with quality en suite facilities; intimate public areas are attractively furnished and styled to be equally pleasing.

9 en suite (bth/shr) No smoking in 4 bedrooms No smoking in dining room CTV in all bedrooms Tea and coffee making facilities No dogs (ex guide dogs) Cen ht No children 9P No coaches

CARDS: ▨ ▨

See advertisement on p.57.

Selected

GH ▢▢▢▢ **Chesterfield Hotel** 11 Great Pulteney St
BA2 4BR ☎01225 460953 FAX 01225 448770

This Grade I listed property built by Georgian architect Thomas Baldwin in 1793 stands in a terrace of small hotels and guesthouses in Great Pulteney Street, just a few minutes' level walk from the city centre. Bedrooms are all tastefully decorated and equipped with modern facilities. Breakfast is served in an attractive dining room and there is also a lounge available for guests' use.

18 en suite (bth/shr) (3 fmly) CTV in all bedrooms Tea and coffee making facilities Direct dial from bedrooms No dogs (ex guide dogs) Licensed Cen ht CTV 8P

CARDS: ▨ ▨ ▨

See advertisement on p.57.

Tea and coffee making facilities No dogs Cen ht 6P No coaches
Last d 4pm
PRICE GUIDE
ROOMS: s £33-£35; d £45-£48; wkly hlf-bd
£229.25-£238.70✻
CARDS: ▧ ▦ £

Premier Selected

GH ▢▢▢▢▢ *Dorian
House* 1 Upper Oldfield Park
BA2 3JX (off A367)
☎01225 426336
FAX 01225 444699
This fine stone-built house
with good views of the city
and surrounding countryside
is located a pleasant walk
from the centre and all its
famous attractions. The
attractive bedrooms are

spacious, individually styled and extremely comfortable, two
rooms featuring four-poster beds. Full English breakfast is
served in the charming dining room, and there is a pleasant
lounge with a small honesty bar for guests' use.
8 en suite (bth/shr) (2 fmly) No smoking in dining room
CTV in all bedrooms Tea and coffee making facilities Direct
dial from bedrooms No dogs (ex guide dogs) Licensed Cen
ht 10P
CARDS: ▧ ▦ ▥ ⓞ

GH ▢▢ **Dorset Villa** 14 Newbridge Rd BA1 3JZ (W on A4)
☎01225 425975
A conveniently situated, early-Victorian property offers simple
accommodation in well equipped bedrooms enhanced by attractive
soft furnishings. Dinner is served in a pleasantly furnished dining
room which also has a residents' licence. Some on-site parking is
available.
7 rms (5 shr) (1 fmly) No smoking in dining room CTV in all
bedrooms Tea and coffee making facilities Cen ht CTV 6P
PRICE GUIDE
ROOMS: s £28-£36; d £36-£46✻
CARDS: ▧ ▦ £
See advertisement on p.58.

GH ▢▢▢ **Eagle House** Church St, Bathford BA1 7RS (3m
NE A363) ☎01225 859946 FAX 01225 859946
Closed 21-3 Jan
A magnificent Georgian residence, Eagle House is situated in the
attractive village of Bathford, a short drive from the city of Bath.
Guests receive a warm welcome into this family home and are
offered accommodation in large, comfortable bedrooms which
overlook a leafy garden complete with grass tennis court. There is
a gracious drawing room, and full English breakfast is served. A
cottage set in the old walled garden is also available.
6 en suite (bth/shr) 2 annexe en suite (bth/shr) (2 fmly) No
smoking in 1 bedrooms CTV in all bedrooms Tea and coffee
making facilities Direct dial from bedrooms Licensed Cen ht
10P Tennis (grass) Croquet lawn Children's play area
PRICE GUIDE
ROOMS: s £32-£42; d £39-£68✻
CARDS: ▧ ▦ £

Brompton House
St Johns Road, Bath BA2 6PT Tel: (01225) 420972 Fax: (01225) 420505

An elegant Georgian Rectory (1777), Brompton House has undergone extensive renovations and
upgrading to provide modern standards of comfort but retain the charm and original features of a
fine country residence. A peaceful setting with lovely mature gardens and our own private car park.
We are only 6 minutes level walk to the City centre and all main attractions.
The Selby family aim to give an efficient and friendly service at a competitive price.
All rooms are en-suite with colour TV, telephone and tea and coffee making facilities.
Choice of traditional English or wholefood breakfast. Smoking permitted in lounge only.
Brochure upon request

GH QQQ **Edgar Hotel** 64 Gt Pulteney St BA2 4DN
☎01225 420619
Closed 25 Dec
An impressive Regency town house situated in the centre of Great Pulteney Street provides comfortable accommodation close to the city centre. A full English breakfast is served in an attractive dining room overlooking the street.
14 en suite (shr) (1 fmly) No smoking in dining room CTV in all bedrooms Tea and coffee making facilities No dogs Licensed Cen ht CTV No parking
PRICE GUIDE
ROOMS: s £25-£35; d £35-£55✱
CARDS: 🟦 💳 ⓐ

GH QQQ **Gainsborough Hotel** Weston Ln BA1 4AB
☎01225 311380 FAX 01225 447411
Closed Xmas/New Year
The Gainsborough is an imposing Victorian property in a select residential area less than 15 minutes' walk from the city centre (via Victoria Park). All the rooms are tastefully decorated and well equipped to meet travellers' needs. A spacious residents' lounge overlooks the lawns and there is a friendly small bar. Ample parking facilities are provided.
16 en suite (bth/shr) (2 fmly) No smoking in dining room CTV in all bedrooms Tea and coffee making facilities Direct dial from bedrooms No dogs Licensed Cen ht 18P No coaches
PRICE GUIDE
ROOMS: s £30-£40; d £50-£65; wkly b&b £180-£280
CARDS: 🟦 💳 💳 ⓐ

GH QQ **Grove Lodge** 11 Lambridge, London Rd BA1 6BJ (heading east from city centre on the A4, establishment 200yds before junction of A4 and A46)
☎01225 310860 FAX 01225 429630
A lovely Regency home situated a short walk from the centre of Bath offers a friendly welcome and accommodation in comfortable bedrooms, some of which overlook the walled garden. There are a cosy lounge and an attractive dining room where breakfast is served at separate tables. On-street parking is available nearby.
8 rms (2 fmly) No smoking CTV in all bedrooms Tea and coffee making facilities No dogs (ex guide dogs) No parking No coaches
PRICE GUIDE
ROOMS: s £20-£25; d £40-£45; wkly b&b £100-£125 ⓐ

GH QQQ **Haute Combe Hotel** 174/176 Newbridge Rd BA1 3LE ☎01225 420061 & 339064 FAX 01225 420061
rs 25-26 Dec
This Edwardian family home is situated on the A4 Bristol road, about five minutes from the city centre. It has limited car parking space at the rear, as well as a garden and sun patio. Most bedrooms are fully en suite and two have private bathrooms. There is a choice of lounges, one for non-smokers, and a small bar forms part of the dining room.
11 rms (10 bth/shr) (5 fmly) No smoking in bedrooms No smoking in dining room No smoking in 1 lounge CTV in all bedrooms Tea and coffee making facilities Direct dial from bedrooms Licensed Cen ht CTV 10P No coaches Last d 6pm
PRICE GUIDE
ROOMS: s £39-£45; d £46-£64
CARDS: 🟦 💳 💳 ⓐ

GH ◖Q◗◖Q◗ **Henrietta Hotel** Henrietta St BA2 6LR
☎01225 447779 FAX 01225 466916
Closed 25 Dec
A Grade II listed building, this privately owned Georgian town house offers comfortable bed and breakfast accommodation. All the rooms are en suite and have colour TV and tea trays. The centre of Bath is just at the end of the road, and the Roman Baths and Pump Room are only 500 yards away.
10 en suite (bth/shr) (3 fmly) CTV in all bedrooms Tea and coffee making facilities No dogs (ex guide dogs) Cen ht CTV No parking
PRICE GUIDE
ROOMS: s £25-£35; d £35-£55✳
CARDS: ◪ ▧ ▨ (£)

Selected

GH ◖Q◗◖Q◗◖Q◗◖Q◗ **Hermitage** Bath Rd SN13 8DT BATH
☎01225 744187 FAX 01225 744187
(For full entry see Box)

Selected

GH ◖Q◗◖Q◗◖Q◗◖Q◗ **Highways House** 143 Wells Rd BA2 3AL
(on the A367) ☎01225 421238 FAX 01225 481169
Closed Xmas
This attractive Victorian house stands, surrounded by its own pretty terraced gardens, in a residential area within easy reach of the city centre. Enthusiastically run by conscientious owners David and Davina James, it offers comfortable, well equipped accommodation which includes one bedroom on the ground floor. Ample car parking space is provided, and the guest house is situated on the mini bus route into the city.
7 rms (6 bth/shr) No smoking in 1 bedrooms No smoking in dining room CTV in all bedrooms Tea and coffee making facilities No dogs (ex guide dogs) Cen ht No children 5yrs 8P
PRICE GUIDE
ROOMS: s £33-£38; d £50-£60;
wkly b&b £168-£196✳
CARDS: ◪ ▧ (£)

Premier Selected

GH ◖Q◗◖Q◗◖Q◗◖Q◗◖Q◗ *Holly*
Lodge 8 Upper Oldfield Park
BA2 3JZ (0.5m SW off A367)
☎01225 424042
FAX 01225 481138
Built in 1877, this gracious Victorian town house enjoys a pleasant location with spectacular views across the city, taking in the delights of its exceptional architecture. The garden here is quite  beautiful, having been lovingly created by George Hall, and equally superb standards in decor, style, comfort and hospitality can be enjoyed throughout the house. Bath is a wonderful city to explore, and Holly Lodge provides the ideal base from which to start.

---

6 en suite (bth/shr) No smoking CTV in all bedrooms Tea and coffee making facilities Direct dial from bedrooms No dogs Cen ht 8P No coaches
CARDS: ◪ ▧ ▨ ◉

GH ◖Q◗◖Q◗◖Q◗ **Holly Villa** 14 Pulteney Gardens BA2 4HG
☎01225 310331
Closed Xmas & New Year
An attractive mid-Victorian property with a pretty garden, Holly Villa is situated in a residential area of the city within easy walking distance of the centre. It has been sympathetically restored and now has seven comfortable letting rooms. Breakfast is served at separate tables in the dining room, where special diets can be catered for on request. A lounge with a colour TV is provided for guests; tea is offered on arrival and the service is always available. Please note that this is a no-smoking establishment.
7 rms (3 shr) (2 fmly) No smoking No dogs Cen ht CTV No children 4yrs 2P No coaches
PRICE GUIDE
ROOMS: d £45-£48
(£)

Selected

GH ◖Q◗◖Q◗◖Q◗◖Q◗ **Kennard Hotel** 11 Henrietta St BA2 6LL
☎01225 310472 FAX 01225 460054
Part of an attractive terrace close to Great Pulteney Bridge, this three-storey Georgian building is just a short walk from the town centre. Continued upgrading has resulted in well equipped, tastefully co-ordinated bedrooms, most of which ➡

have en suite shower rooms. There is a bright breakfast room where the friendly proprietors provide attentive service.

13 rms (11 shr) (2 fmly) No smoking in 2 bedrooms No smoking in dining room CTV in 12 bedrooms Tea and coffee making facilities Direct dial from bedrooms No dogs (ex guide dogs) Cen ht No children No parking No coaches

PRICE GUIDE

ROOMS: s £30-£35; d £54-£64

CARDS: (£)

GH ◗◗◗ *Lamp Post Villa* 3 Crescent Gardens, Upper Bristol Rd BA1 2NA (on A4, Bristol side of city)
☎01225 331221 FAX 01225 426783
Closed 24-26 Dec

This small, well run guesthouse is conveniently situated close to the city centre and near Victoria Park. Comfortable, well equipped bedrooms suit the needs of business guests or visitors to Bath. There is a pleasant dining room where a good choice of cooked or continental breakfasts is offered.

7 rms (4 bth/shr) (1 fmly) No smoking in bedrooms No smoking in dining room CTV in all bedrooms Tea and coffee making facilities Direct dial from bedrooms Cen ht CTV 4P No coaches

CARDS: 🔲 🔲

Selected

GH ◗◗◗◗ **Laura Place Hotel** 3 Laura Place, Great Pulteney St BA2 4BH (turn left off A4 at 1st traffic lights over Cleveland Bridge, past fire station then turn right along Henrietta Rd into Laura Place)
☎01225 463815 FAX 01225 310222
Mar-21 Dec

An elegant, beautifully preserved Georgian town house is conveniently situated for easy access on foot to the many places of interest in and around the city. The hotel also benefits from a small number of private parking places in a nearby yard. The spacious bedrooms, located on four floors, have been decorated and furnished in keeping with the building and are equipped with a good range of facilities. Breakfast is served at separate tables in the attractive dining room and there is a small lounge area at reception.

8 rms (7 bth/shr) (1 fmly) No smoking in 4 bedrooms No smoking in dining room CTV in all bedrooms Tea and coffee making facilities Direct dial from bedrooms No dogs (ex guide dogs) Cen ht No children 11yrs 10P No coaches

PRICE GUIDE

ROOMS: s fr £50; d £65-£85

CARDS: (£)

Premier Selected

GH ◗◗◗◗◗ **Leighton House** 139 Wells Rd BA2 3AL (on A367 Exeter rd out of Bath) ☎01225 314769 FAX 01225 443079

David and Kathy Slape, owners of this elegant Victorian house close to the city centre, just off the Wells Road, always ensure their guests are welcomed, made comfortable and well looked

after. The immaculately maintained and individually decorated bedrooms are all en suite, spacious and very well equipped. Guests also have the use of a very comfortable lounge overlooking the well tended gardens and the hills beyond, where drinks are available on request. Breakfast is served in the bright, attractively decorated, split-level dining room.

8 en suite (bth/shr) (1 fmly) No smoking in dining room CTV in all bedrooms Tea and coffee making facilities Direct dial from bedrooms No dogs (ex guide dogs) Cen ht 8P No coaches

PRICE GUIDE

ROOMS: d £62-£68; wkly b&b £185-£215✳

CARDS: (£)

Premier Selected

GH ◗◗◗◗◗ **Lodge Hotel** Bathford Hill, Bathford BA1 7SL
☎01225 858467 858575
FAX 01225 858173

This comfortable Georgian-style house, built of warm Bath stone, is situated in three acres of gardens, featuring an area of planted wild meadow in the quiet village of Bathford, two and

a half miles from the city centre. The house, still very much a family home, has six comfortably furnished and well appointed rooms including a small suite on the ground floor with doors opening onto a small terrace. A sumptuous breakfast is served in the richly decorated dining room which is warmed by an open fire on cooler days. Guests also have the use of a small sitting room on the first floor and there is also a heated outdoor swimming pool. Keith and Mary Johnson are always available to make sure everyone is well looked after.

5 en suite (bth/shr) (1 fmly) CTV in all bedrooms Tea and coffee making facilities Direct dial from bedrooms Cen ht 14P No coaches Outdoor swimming pool (heated)

PRICE GUIDE

ROOMS: s £47-£64; d £63-£84✳

CARDS: (£)

Selected

GH ◗◗◗◗ **Marlborough House** 1 Marlborough Ln BA1 2NQ ☎01225 318175 & 466127 FAX 01225 466127

Built of mellow Bath stone, this elegant semi-detached Victorian property adjoins Victoria Park and is within easy level walking distance of the city centre. Spacious bedrooms are tastefully decorated, and three have en suite facilities. Breakfast is served at two large tables in part of the bright lounge, where a wealth of local menus and information is provided. Please note that this is a no-smoking establishment.

5 rms (3 shr) (1 fmly) No smoking CTV in all bedrooms Tea and coffee making facilities No dogs Cen ht No children 5yrs 3P No coaches

PRICE GUIDE

ROOMS: s £20-£35; d £40-£55✳

CARDS: (£)

GH ⓠⓠⓠⓠⓠ **Newbridge House Hotel** 35 Kelston Rd BA1 3QH ☎01225 446676 FAX 01225 447541

This beautifully restored Georgian house, built in 1770 of distinctive Bath stone, is also a listed building and was formerly the home of Lord and Lady Kirkwood. Situated to the west of the city, it enjoys the most wonderful views over the Avon Valley. The public rooms are beautifully proportioned and include a traditionally furnished entrance hall and an elegant restaurant with doors opening onto the balcony which overlooks the gardens. Attractive bedrooms vary in size and have plenty of magazines as well as fresh fruit and flowers; They are all well equipped and include a ground-floor suite with its own private balcony. The hotel has rooms suitable for small private meetings or dinners and ample car parking.

10 en suite (bth/shr) (4 fmly) No smoking in dining room CTV in 25 bedrooms Tea and coffee making facilities Direct dial from bedrooms Licensed Cen ht 20P Last d 9.30pm
PRICE GUIDE
ROOMS: s fr £60; d fr £70✱
CARDS: 🔲 🔲 🔲 🔲

Selected

GH ⓠⓠⓠⓠ **Oakleigh House** 19 Upper Oldfield Park BA2 3JX (off A367) ☎01225 315698 FAX 01225 448223
Oakleigh stands in a pleasant residential area and offers well equipped, spacious bedrooms with views across the city. The resident proprietor serves a traditional English breakfast in the airy dining room.

4 en suite (bth/shr) No smoking in dining room No smoking in lounges CTV in all bedrooms Tea and coffee making facilities No dogs (ex guide dogs) Cen ht No children 14yrs 4P No coaches
PRICE GUIDE
ROOMS: s £35-£45; d £45-£60
CARDS: 🔲 🔲

GH ⓠⓠⓠ **Oldfields** 102 Wells Rd BA2 3AL (off A367) ☎01225 317984 FAX 01225 444471
This hospitable guest house - a large Victorian family residence built from Bath stone and attractively set in its own gardens - looks out over the city from an elevated position just ten minutes from the centre, Roman Baths and Abbey. Bedrooms have been sympathetically restored, Laura Ashley furnishings and fabrics complementing the original style of the house. On-site parking is available.

14 rms (1 bth 9 shr) No smoking in dining room CTV in all bedrooms Tea and coffee making facilities No dogs (ex guide dogs) Cen ht 10P
PRICE GUIDE
ROOMS: s £30-£48; d £42-£68; wkly b&b £133-£190✱
CARDS: 🔲 🔲

GH ⓠⓠⓠ **Old Red House** 37 Newbridge Rd BA1 3HE ☎01225 330464
Alfred Tayor's famous "Gingerbread House" was built 100 years ago and was for many years a high class patisserie and baker's shop. Situated one mile from the heart of the city, it has been more recently converted to a small no smoking guest house and now enjoys the unmistakable atmosphere of a warm and comfortable family home. The bedrooms have been tastefully decorated and equipped with modern facilities; one is contained in a small private lodge. An interesting selection of breakfast dishes is served in a sunny conservatory.

3 rms (1 bth 1 shr) (1 fmly) No smoking CTV in all bedrooms Tea and coffee making facilities Cen ht No children 4yrs 4P No coaches
PRICE GUIDE
ROOMS: s £25-£35; d £40-£55✱
CARDS: 🔲 🔲 🔲

Premier Selected

GH ⓠⓠⓠⓠⓠ **Old School House** Church St, Bathford BA1 7RR (3m NE on A363, beyond St Swithuns Church) ☎01225 859593 FAX 01225 859590

Built early in the19th century but now carefully modernised, this former school house in the village of Bathford (a few miles east of the city) offers comfortable bedrooms, each equipped with its own bathroom, a pay phone and such thoughtful extras as fresh flowers and boxed toiletries. Lounge and dining area are contained in a spacious reception room lavishly furnished with antique pieces and warmed by a log fire on winter evenings. Dinner is available by prior arrangement, the set main dish supplemented by a pleasing selection of starters and puddings. Guests are asked not to smoke.

4 en suite (bth/shr) (1 fmly) No smoking CTV in all bedrooms Tea and coffee making facilities Direct dial from bedrooms No dogs Licensed Cen ht 6P No coaches Last d noon
PRICE GUIDE
ROOMS: s £48-£60; d £60-£75
CARDS: 🔲 🔲

GH ⓠⓠⓠ *Orchard Lodge* Warminster Rd (A36), Bathampton BA2 6XG (MIN) ☎01225 466115
Conveniently situated two miles from the city centre, this small purpose-built establishment with its own large car park enjoys good views of the Avon Valley from an elevated position. It is comfortably furnished throughout, and en suite bedrooms are well equipped with a wide range of facilities. A sunbed, sauna and multi-gym are provided in the health area for guests' use.

14 en suite (bth/shr) (3 fmly) CTV in all bedrooms Tea and coffee making facilities Licensed Cen ht 16P No coaches Sauna Solarium Last d 7.45pm
CARDS: 🔲 🔲 🔲 🔲

 Selected

GH Q Q Q Q **Paradise House Hotel** Holloway BA2 4PX
☎01225 317723 FAX 01225 482005
Closed 3 days Xmas

This beautifully restored, elegant Georgian house boasts one
of the finest views over the city and offers commendable bed
and breakfast accommodation. The cosy public rooms are
styled with rich colours, deep furnishings and complementary
fabrics, and the building features a fine staircase, moulded
ceilings and decorative cornices. The lounge overlooks the
city and the splendid walled garden, and a hearty breakfast is
served in the bright, attractive breakfast room. The bedrooms
are particularly comfortable and individually styled - again
with good use of bold colours and fabrics. All are equipped to
a high standard and the majority have bright en suite facilities.
9 rms (6 bth 1 shr) (1 fmly) No smoking in bedrooms No
smoking in dining room CTV in all bedrooms Tea and coffee
making facilities Direct dial from bedrooms No dogs Cen ht
No children 10yrs 5P No coaches Croquet lawn Boules
pitch
PRICE GUIDE
ROOMS: s £34-£52; d £48-£70; wkly b&b £150-£220
CARDS: 🔲 🔲 🔲 (£)

GH Q Q **Parkside** 11 Marlborough Ln BA1 2NQ (just past
Queen Square and Charlotte St. car park, establishment on
right before Park gates) ☎01225 429444
Closed Xmas wk

An Edwardian family home built in mellow Bath stone stands near
the famous Royal Crescent, within walking distance of the city
centre. Bedrooms are continually being upgraded, so that most
now have their own shower rooms, and dinner is served in a
comfortable dining room overlooking the well tended garden.
5 rms (4 shr) (2 fmly) No smoking CTV in all bedrooms Tea
and coffee making facilities Cen ht CTV No children 5yrs 3P
No coaches Last d 6pm
PRICE GUIDE
ROOMS: s £35-£40; d £45-£52; wkly b&b £154.35
CARDS: 🔲 🔲

GH Q Q Q **Hotel St Clair** 1 Crescent Gdns, Upper Bristol Rd
BA1 2NA ☎01225 425543 FAX 01225 425543

The Hotel St Clair, well positioned for those who wish to visit the
city centre and all its attractions, is ideal for both business
travellers and tourists. The bedrooms are well equipped and some
have en suite facilities. An additional advantage is the large public
car park to the rear.
9 rms (6 bth/shr) (2 fmly) No smoking in dining room CTV in
all bedrooms Tea and coffee making facilities No dogs (ex guide
dogs) Licensed Cen ht No children 3yrs No parking
PRICE GUIDE
ROOMS: s £22-£38; d £34-£50✳
CARDS: 🔲 🔲 (£)

GH Q Q Q **St Leonards** Warminster Rd BA2 6SQ (leave M4
at junct 18, turn right at junct with A4 towards Bath. Turn left
on A36 Warminster road, climb hill and 200yds on left past
Bathampton sign) ☎01225 465838 FAX 01225 442800

St Leonards is an elegant mid-Victorian property set in an elevated
position on the Warminster road, with stunning views over the
Avon valley and the Kennet and Avon Canal. Three of the
bedrooms are fully en suite, the rest have showers, and all are
equipped with colour TV and hospitality trays. There are a small
reception lounge and an attractive dining room where a good
selection of dishes is served at breakfast.

---

6 rms (3 shr) No smoking in bedrooms No smoking in dining
room CTV in all bedrooms Tea and coffee making facilities No
dogs (ex guide dogs) Cen ht 10P No coaches
PRICE GUIDE
ROOMS: s £25; d £36-£45
 (£)

 Selected

GH Q Q Q Q **Sarnia** 19 Combe Park, Weston BA1 3NR
(opposite Royal United Hospital) ☎01225 424159
Closed 24 Dec-2 Jan

Jill and Rob Fradley welcome guests to their charming
Victorian home, which is located in the same road as the
Royal United Hospital. Guests can either walk to the city
centre or take one of the buses that regularly cover the 10-
minute journey. Spacious bedrooms are individually furnished
and recently re-decorated, hearty breakfasts include a
vegetarian option and a light supper is available by prior
arrangement. Children are particularly welcome, there being
both a play room with toys and a secluded rear garden.
3 en suite (bth/shr) (1 fmly) No smoking CTV in all
bedrooms Tea and coffee making facilities No dogs (ex
guide dogs) Cen ht CTV 3P No coaches
PRICE GUIDE
ROOMS: s £20-£30; d £40-£50
(£)

GH Q Q **Seven Springs** 4 High St, Woolley BA1 8AR
☎01225 858001
Closed 24 Dec-2 Jan

The hamlet of Woolley is situated to the north of Bath, just three
miles from the centre, and Seven Springs stands at the end of a
terrace of stone-built cottages. Lovely rural views can be enjoyed
from the gardens and patios. Breakfast is served at one large table
in the farmhouse-style kitchen and the bedrooms have comfortable
seating, en suite showers and colour TV.
3 en suite (bth/shr) (2 fmly) No smoking CTV in all bedrooms
Tea and coffee making facilities No dogs Cen ht 14P
PRICE GUIDE
ROOMS: d £35-£40✳
 (£)

 Selected

GH Q Q Q Q **Somerset House Hotel & Restaurant** 35
Bathwick Hill BA2 6LD (400yds up Bathwick Hill from St
Mary-the-Virgin church, at junct with A36) (Logis)
☎01225 466451 FAX 01225 317188

Individually styled bedrooms occupy three floors of this
classical Regency house which commands superb views of
the city from an elevated setting. Guests have a choice of
comfortable lounges, and the restaurant - like the rest of the
house - operates a no-smoking policy. Ample parking space is
available, and there is a well tended walled garden.
10 en suite (bth/shr) (5 fmly) No smoking Tea and coffee
making facilities Direct dial from bedrooms Licensed Cen
ht CTV 12P No coaches Last d 6.30pm
CARDS: 🔲 🔲 🔲 (£)

for anyone visiting the city. En suite bedrooms are generally very spacious and all are well equipped with tea and coffee making facilities and televisions; some enjoy wonderful views of the park. There are also a very smart lounge and a spacious and attractively decorated dining room where breakfast is served. The hotel has its own car park.

17 en suite (bth/shr) (4 fmly) No smoking in 4 bedrooms No smoking in dining room No smoking in lounges CTV in all bedrooms Tea and coffee making facilities Direct dial from bedrooms No dogs (ex guide dogs) Cen ht 19P No coaches

PRICE GUIDE

ROOMS: s £40-£49; d £50-£75✳

CARDS: (£)

BATTLE East Sussex Map **05** TQ71

GH 🔲🔲🔲 **Netherfield Hall** Netherfield TN33 9PS (3m NW of B2096) ☎01424 774450

Closed Feb rs Tue

Owners Jean and Tony Hawes offer hospitality of the highest standard at their home, which is situated in peaceful countryside and has excellent views. There are a range of comfortable, individually furnished ground-floor bedrooms, a shared family lounge and an attractive dining room with an open fire and lovely views over the veranda and garden. A self-catering apartment is also available.

3 rms (2 shr) 1 annexe en suite (shr) CTV in 3 bedrooms Tea and coffee making facilities Cen ht CTV 9P No coaches

PRICE GUIDE

ROOMS: s £25-£35; d £35-£50; wkly b&b £150-£210 (£)

 Selected

♥ 🔲🔲🔲🔲 Mrs F Ramsden **Brakes Coppice** *(TQ766134)* Telham Ln TN33 0SJ (off A2100 towards Crowhurst, 1m on left) ☎01424 830347 FAX 01424 830347

Closed 20 Dec-2 Jan

Located off the A2100, signed for Crowhurst, this modernised farmhouse is part of a farm specialising in the breeding of pedigree Charolais cattle. It stands about a mile from the famous battle field and quietly situated, with distant sea views and abundant wild life. The accommodation is totally non-smoking and has been tastefully and individually furnished with and rooms equipped with every modern amenity, including remote control TV with International satellite, direct dial telephones, hair-dryers and tea trays. There is an elegantly spacious and very comfortable lounge, and a delightful breakfast room with quality table appointments looks out on to the patio where breakfast can also be taken on warm sunny days. Service is personally provided by resident proprietors Michael and Fay Ramsden, who create a homely and relaxing atmosphere by their commitment to customer care. Full English breakfast based on good local produce and free range eggs is included in the room tariff.

3 en suite (bth/shr) No smoking CTV in all bedrooms Tea and coffee making facilities Direct dial from bedrooms No dogs Cen ht CTV 5P 70 acres cattle

PRICE GUIDE

ROOMS: s £29.50-£39.50; d £39.50-£49.50

CARDS: 🔳 ▨

♥ 🔲🔲🔲 Mr Mrs P Slater **Little Hemingfold Farmhouse Hotel** *(TQ774149)* Telham TN33 0TT (2.5m SE on N side of A2100) ☎01424 774338 FAX 01424 775351

Delightfully situated in woodland, overlooking a lake, this licensed farmhouse hotel is reached by way of a long bumpy track.

The accommodation has been individually furnished to provide a range of bedrooms, all equipped to a high standard. There are two lounges with log fires, a small reception area and an attractive dining room. A daily four-course dinner is served as well as good farmhouse breakfasts.

3 en suite (bth) 9 annexe rms (7 bth) No smoking in dining room No smoking in 1 lounge CTV in all bedrooms Tea and coffee making facilities Direct dial from bedrooms Licensed Cen ht 30P Outdoor swimming pool Tennis (grass) Fishing Boules Swimming in lake Croquet 40 acres mixed Last d 7pm

PRICE GUIDE

ROOMS: s £35-£38; d £60-£68; wkly b&b £200-£270; wkly hlf-bd £294-£315✳

CARDS: (£)

BEDALE North Yorkshire Map **08** SE28

See **Hunton & Patrick Brompton**

BEDFORD Bedfordshire Map **04** TL04

GH 🔲🔲 **Bedford Oak House** 33 Shakespeare Rd MK40 2DX (NW on connecting road between A6/A428) ☎01234 266972 FAX 01234 266972

This efficiently run family home offers an attractive wood-panelled breakfast room and a spacious conference room; guests can help themselves to tea and coffee from the lounge at any time.

15 rms (11 shr) (1 fmly) CTV in all bedrooms Tea and coffee making facilities No dogs (ex guide dogs) Cen ht CTV 17P No coaches

PRICE GUIDE

ROOMS: s £21-£32; d £30-£40

CARDS: 🔳 ▨ 🔲 (£)

GH 🔲🔲 **Hertford House Hotel** 57 De Parys Av MK40 2TP ☎01234 350007 & 354470 FAX 01234 353468

Closed 24 Dec-2 Jan

Most of the well kept bedrooms are spacious in this centrally located and family-run hotel; breakfast is served in a first-floor dining room which overlooks playing fields, and there is a combined reception, lounge and television room (with satellite TV) on the ground floor.

16 rms (14 bth/shr) (3 fmly) No smoking in 4 bedrooms No smoking in dining room CTV in all bedrooms Tea and coffee making facilities Cen ht CTV 14P

PRICE GUIDE

ROOMS: s £20-£34.50; d £35-£45✳

CARDS: (£)

BEELEY Derbyshire Map **08** SK26

 Selected

GH 🔲🔲🔲🔲 *Beeley House* DE4 2NT (off B6012, 5.50m N of Matlock) ☎01629 732194 FAX 01629 733960

Closed Xmas

The present owners, a freelance architect and a landscape design gardener, have transformed this former vicarage, accentuating its period features and creatively mixing contemporary furnishings and fabrics. Comfort and quality are foremost, and each of the bedrooms is unique. There is a downstairs room with gorgeous quatrefoil and trefoil mullioned windows, as well as a second room in a coaching inn reached by a wrought iron spiral staircase. The house is in a pretty village setting, within the Chatsworth Estate and overlooked by Beeley Moor.

2 en suite (bth/shr) No smoking CTV in all bedrooms Tea and coffee making facilities Cen ht No children 10yrs P
See advertisement under BAKEWELL

BEER Devon Map **03** SY28

GH Q **Bay View** Fore St EX12 3EE (turn off A3092 & follow signs to Beer) ☎01297 20489
Mar-Nov rs Nov-Mar
Bay View is at the end of the village overlooking the beach and sea.
6 rms CTV in 4 bedrooms Tea and coffee making facilities Cen ht CTV No children 5yrs No parking
PRICE GUIDE
ROOMS: s £15-£18; d £30-£36; wkly b&b £98-£110✱

BEERCROCOMBE Somerset Map **03** ST32

Premier Selected

♥ QQQQQ Mrs V Cole
Frog Street Farm *(ST317197)*
Frog St TA3 6AF
☎01823 480430
Mar-Oct
Mr and Mrs Cole extend a warm welcome to guests at their 15th-century farmhouse, which offers comfort and quality in idyllic surroundings. Spacious bedrooms are individually decorated in a fresh country style, and the beamed lounge with its wood-burning stove is the perfect place to relax after a delicious home-cooked dinner - perhaps fresh salmon and asparagus with baby carrots followed by chocolate mousse with Somerset cream.
3 en suite (bth/shr) No smoking Tea and coffee making facilities No dogs Cen ht CTV No children 11yrs Outdoor swimming pool (heated) 160 acres Dairy Racehorse stud Last d 2pm
PRICE GUIDE
ROOMS: d £44-£54; wkly b&b £154-£175✱

Premier Selected

♥ QQQQQ Mr & Mrs
Mitchem **Whittles** *(ST324194)*
TA3 6AH ☎01823 480301
Feb-Nov
This solid stone house is set within a 200-acre beef and dairy farm, well signed from the village of Beercrocombe. Bedrooms are individually furnished and decorated, and a comfortable lounge with an honesty bar is available to guests. An imaginative three-course set dinner will be provided by arrangement, and breakfast is served around a large refectory table in the front-facing dining room. A cosy self-catering flat for two is also available.

---

3 en suite (bth) No smoking in bedrooms No smoking in dining room No smoking in 1 lounge CTV in all bedrooms Tea and coffee making facilities No dogs Licensed Cen ht No children 12yrs 4P 200 acres beef dairy Last d 6.30pm(previous day)
PRICE GUIDE
ROOMS: s £27-£28; d £44-£46; wkly b&b £154-£161

BEESTON Nottinghamshire Map **08** SK53

GH QQ **Fairhaven Private Hotel** 19 Meadow Rd NG9 1JP (200yds after railway station) ☎0115 922 7509
Closed Xmas/New Year
The Fairhaven is a small commercial hotel located on the edge of town a short walk from the railway station and approximately three miles from Nottingham. At the time of our inspection, new en suite shower units were being added to some of the bedrooms, all of which have recently been redecorated. Guests have a comfortable lounge with a small dispense bar and TV.
12 rms (4 shr) (1 fmly) No smoking in 5 bedrooms No smoking in dining room No smoking in 1 lounge CTV in 7 bedrooms Tea and coffee making facilities No dogs Licensed Cen ht CTV 12P Last d 2pm
PRICE GUIDE
ROOMS: s £19-£29; d £28-£40; wkly b&b fr £133; wkly hlf-bd fr £182

BELLINGHAM Northumberland Map **12** NY88

Selected

GH 🅠🅠🅠🅠 *Westfield House* NE48 2DP (on B6320, Hexham to Bellingham)
☎01434 220340 FAX 01434 220340

A fine Edwardian house stands in its own gardens on the edge of the village, at the end of a tree-lined drive. The bedrooms are individual; one has a superb brass bed, others contain stripped pine, and rooms without en suite facilities provide bathrobes. There is a TV lounge and a larger room where enjoyable meals are served around a large table. The atmosphere is friendly and relaxed.
5 rms (2 shr) (1 fmly) No smoking Tea and coffee making facilities Cen ht CTV ch fac 8P
CARDS: 🔳 🔳

BELPER Derbyshire Map **08** SK34

See **Shottle**

BENENDEN Kent Map **05** TQ83

Selected

GH 🅠🅠🅠🅠 **Crit Hall** Cranbrook Rd TN17 4EU (off A229 onto B2086, on right after approx 2m)
☎01580 240609 FAX 01580 241743
Closed 16 Dec-14 Jan

Peacefully located with superb open views over the Weald, this elegant non-smoking Georgian country house offers exclusive accommodation for discerning guests. Each bedroom has been individually furnished and thoughtfully equipped with remote control TV, alarm clock radio, hair dryer, and tea tray. Antiques, matching porcelain and silverware, fresh flowers and magazines together with home-made preserves, cakes and shortbreads, all add to the overall effect. Public areas include as sumptuous lounge with a small conservatory extension, a separate dining room and a spacious kitchen/breakfast room. Light refreshments are available throughout the day, and dinner can be provided with a day's notice; vegetarian dishes are included and a short selection of wines features English examples from a local vineyard. Service is personally provided by the resident proprietors Susan and John Bruder.
3 en suite (bth/shr) No smoking CTV in all bedrooms Tea and coffee making facilities No dogs Licensed Cen ht No children 10yrs 6P No coaches Last d 9am
PRICE GUIDE
ROOMS: s fr £30; d £48-£50; wkly b&b fr £168; wkly hlf-bd fr £245

We endeavour to be as accurate as possible but changes in personnel and data can occur in establishments after the Guide has gone to press.

BEPTON West Sussex Map **04** SU81

Premier Selected

GH 🅠🅠🅠🅠🅠 **Park House Hotel** GU29 0JB (from centre of Midhurst take B2226 to Bepton)
☎01730 812880
FAX 01730 815643
Closed Xmas

A small private country house hotel, parts of which date back to the 1600s, stands in a peaceful, rural setting close to Cowdray Park, Goodwood and the South Downs. The spacious bedrooms are equipped with good beds and easy chairs for comfort. The elegant drawing room features soft lighting, deep sofas and thick Chinese rugs on the polished floor, while Mrs O'Brien serves generous portions of her delicious soups and savoury pies at the antique tables of the dining room.
10 en suite (bth/shr) 1 annexe en suite (bth) (2 fmly) CTV in all bedrooms Tea and coffee making facilities Direct dial from bedrooms Licensed Cen ht CTV 25P No coaches Outdoor swimming pool (heated) Tennis (grass) Croquet Pitch & putt Last d noon
PRICE GUIDE
ROOMS: s fr £60; d fr £110
CARDS: 🔳 🔳 🔳
See advertisement under MIDHURST

BERKELEY Gloucestershire Map **03** ST69

Selected

❤ 🅠🅠🅠🅠 Mrs B Evans **Greenacres** *(ST713008)* Breadstone GL13 9HF (2m W off A38, turn off A38 to Breadstone, in 0.75m on sharp left hand bend turn right up no through road, farm 300yds on right)
☎01453 810348 FAX 01453 810348
Closed 24 Dec-2 Jan

Well situated for touring the Cotswolds and visiting Bristol and Gloucester, this modern farmhouse enjoys an elevated position. Rooms are attractively decorated with co-ordinated soft fabrics and pine furniture, and have modern en suite facilities. Generous breakfasts are served in the dining room overlooking the garden, and there is also a comfortable lounge with TV.
4 en suite (bth/shr) CTV in all bedrooms Tea and coffee making facilities No dogs (ex guide dogs) Cen ht CTV No children 10yrs 10P Sauna 17 acres horse breeding
PRICE GUIDE
ROOMS: s £20-£23.50; d £39.50-£42

BERROW Somerset Map **03** ST25

🛏🔻 GH 🅠🅠 **Holly-Ferns** 223 Berrow Rd TA8 2JQ (from M5 junct 22 follow B3140) ☎01278 792031

This semi-detached family home, situated between Burnham-on-Sea and Brean, dates back in parts to 1735. Jenny and Paul Winship have sympathetically restored the brick-built house and exposed many of the original features. Breakfast is served at one

large table in the farm-house style kitchen and two bedrooms offer comfortable accommodation. Guests are requested not to smoke.
2 rms (1 shr) (1 fmly) No smoking CTV in all bedrooms Tea and coffee making facilities No dogs Cen ht 4P No coaches
PRICE GUIDE
ROOMS: s £15; d fr £26; wkly b&b £91-£105

BERRYNARBOR Devon Map **02** SS54

GH Ⓠ Ⓠ Ⓠ **The Lodge Country House Hotel and Restaurant**
EX34 9SG (1.5m W of A399) ☎01271 883246
Closed Jan
Berrynarbor is renowned for being one of the best kept villages in the country. The house, an attractive family-run establishment, is on a slope, with an acre of well tended gardens. Most of the comfortable bedrooms have lovely country views. Traditionally furnished public areas and home-cooked evening meals are provided.
7 rms (6 bth/shr) (2 fmly) No smoking in dining room CTV in all bedrooms Tea and coffee making facilities Licensed Cen ht No children 2yrs 8P No coaches Last d 8.30pm
PRICE GUIDE
ROOMS: s £20-£25; d £40-£50; wkly b&b £120-£150; wkly hlf-bd £171-£210
CARDS: 🔲 (£)
See advertisement under COMBE MARTIN

BERWICK-UPON-TWEED Northumberland Map **12** NT95

Selected

GH Ⓠ Ⓠ Ⓠ Ⓠ **Dervaig** 1 North Rd TD15 1PW (turn off A1 at A1167 (North Road) to town, last house on right before railway bridge) ☎01289 307378
Well maintained and spotlessly clean throughout, this detached Victorian house lies off the main road, north of the town centre and convenient for the railway station. The well proportioned bedrooms are comfortable and relaxing and the two rooms without en-suite facilities both have the private use of their own bathroom. There is an attractive lounge and the dining room features a fine collection of china plates. The sculpture of Laurel and Hardy on the landing will bring a smile on passing. The house has good parking and a large peaceful garden both front and rear.
5 rms (3 bth/shr) (3 fmly) No smoking in dining room No smoking in lounges CTV in all bedrooms Tea and coffee making facilities Cen ht 8P No coaches
PRICE GUIDE
ROOMS: d £36-£50; wkly b&b £120-£165

Selected

GH Ⓠ Ⓠ Ⓠ Ⓠ **Harvone** 18 Main St, Spittal TD15 1QY (leave A1 at roundabout marked A1167, follow to next roundabout, turn right to crossroads. Turn right and guesthouse on right hand side) ☎01289 302580
Sue Mechan offers a friendly welcome at this guest house in the main street of Spittal, an old estuary and ship-building port just south of Berwick. The bedrooms, which include one on the ground floor, are particularly attractive, with stylishly co-ordinated decor and fabrics as well as modern en suite bathrooms. There are a lounge and an adjoining dining room with individual tables. The interesting dinner carte and wine list tempt guests to 'dine in'.
3 en suite (bth/shr) No smoking CTV in all bedrooms Tea

and coffee making facilities No dogs Licensed Cen ht No children No coaches Last d 7pm
PRICE GUIDE
ROOMS: d £40-£44; wkly b&b £126-£139; wkly hlf-bd £149-£196✳

(£)

Selected

📖 📺 GH ⓠⓠⓠⓠ **The Old Vicarage** Church Rd, Tweedmouth TD15 2AN ☎01289 306909
This imposing 19th-century detached house lies in a quiet street opposite the church on the south side of the River Tweed. It has been sympathetically furnished to reflect its original character, with antique and period pieces as well as stripped pine. Bedrooms are very comfortable and have little touches such as sweets and toiletries. There is a cosy lounge with reading material, tourist information and board games, as well as a fridge with soft drinks and snacks. The elegant dining room is spacious and Tina Richarson puts a lot of care into her breakfasts, with local Craster kippers a speciality.
7 rms (4 shr) (1 fmly) No smoking in dining room No smoking in lounges CTV in all bedrooms Tea and coffee making facilities Cen ht CTV 5P
PRICE GUIDE
ROOMS: s £14-£17; d £28-£46; wkly b&b £98-£145

(£)

BETTISCOMBE Dorset Map **03** SY39

GH ⓠⓠⓠ *Marshwood Manor* DT6 5NS ☎01308 868442
Closed Dec-Jan
This peaceful Victorian manor house nestles in ten acres of garden and woodland, and offers a friendly and relaxed atmosphere. The spacious bedrooms are bright and prettily decorated, and have modern en suite facilities. There is a large comfortable lounge overlooking the putting green and croquet lawn, there is also a pool in the walled garden. Good English home cooked meals are served in the evenings, with delicious homemade bread and preserves, traditional puddings and most of the fresh fruit and vegetables come from the garden.
6 rms (2 bth 3 shr) (3 fmly) No smoking in dining room CTV in all bedrooms Tea and coffee making facilities Licensed Cen ht 15P No coaches Outdoor swimming pool (heated) Croquet Putting
CARDS:
See advertisement under BRIDPORT

BEVERLEY Humberside Map **08** TA03

See also Leven

GH ⓠⓠ **The Eastgate** 7 Eastgate HU17 0DR
☎01482 868464 FAX 01482 871899
A friendly, family-run guest house in the centre of this old town offers cosy bedrooms that are individual in style, mostly with light, cheerful decoration. Breakfast is served in an attractive dining room and refreshments are available within the comfortable ground-floor lounge.
18 rms (7 shr) (5 fmly) No smoking in bedrooms No smoking in dining room Cen ht CTV No parking
PRICE GUIDE
ROOMS: s £17.50-£27.50; d £30-£42✳

(£)

BEXHILL East Sussex Map **05** TQ70

GH ⓠⓠ **The Arosa** 6 Albert Rd TN40 1DG
☎01424 212574 & 732004 FAX 01424 212574 & 732004
A family-run hotel in a quiet location between the town centre and seafront provides accommodation in bright bedrooms which are furnished in modern style. There is a comfortable front lounge, and the recently refurbished dining room offers a three-course evening menu; light refreshments are available throughout the day. Dedicated personal service is provided by Christine and Tony Bayliss, who have recently been nominated for a Customer Care, Service and Hospitality Award. Seasonal winter and summer breaks are well worth enquiring about.
9 rms (3 bth/shr) (1 fmly) No smoking in dining room CTV in all bedrooms Tea and coffee making facilities Direct dial from bedrooms No dogs (ex guide dogs) Cen ht CTV No parking No coaches Last d noon
CARDS: 🔲 🔲 🔲 🔲 🔲 🔲

(£)

GH ⓠⓠⓠ **Bedford Lodge Hotel** Cantelupe Rd TN40 1PR (from Hastings on A259 (coast road), turn left at lights, then next left after Coombs Garage, then second left. Hotel 100yds on right) ☎01424 730097
This quietly located guest house has a warm and friendly atmosphere thanks to the involvment of owners Beryl and Michael Gebbie. All bedrooms are modern in style and have TV, tea trays and en suite toilets. A home-cooked, fixed-price menu is served in the dining room and there is a lounge available for guests.
6 rms (3 shr) (1 fmly) No smoking CTV in all bedrooms Tea and coffee making facilities Licensed Cen ht No children 10yrs No parking No coaches Last d 6pm
PRICE GUIDE
ROOMS: s £18-£24; d £36-£48; wkly b&b £100-£140; wkly hlf-bd £145-£199
CARDS: 🔲 🔲 🔲 🔲

(£)

GH ⓠⓠⓠ **Park Lodge** 16 Egerton Rd TN39 3HH
☎01424 216547 & 215041
Conveniently situated next to Egerton Park, not far from the seafront, this friendly family-run hotel offers a variety of bedrooms ranging from the very spacious furnished with period pieces to smaller rooms with bright modern furnishings. Breakfasts and home-cooked evening meals are served in a pretty dining room featuring lace tablecloths and fresh flowers.
10 rms (6 bth/shr) (2 fmly) No smoking in bedrooms No smoking in dining room CTV in all bedrooms Tea and coffee making facilities Direct dial from bedrooms Licensed Cen ht No coaches Last d 3pm
PRICE GUIDE
ROOMS: s £22-£28; d £39-£46; wkly b&b £127-£150; wkly hlf-bd £175-£195✳
CARDS: 🔲 🔲 🔲

(£)

BEYTON Suffolk Map **05** TL96

Selected

GH ⓠⓠⓠⓠ **Manorhouse** The Green IP30 9AF (4m E of Bury St Edmunds off A14)
☎01359 270960 FAX 01284 761611
Located on the north side of the village green, this well preserved, late-15th-century house offers two large, attractively decorated bedrooms. Old beams and an inglenook fireplace have been preserved downstairs, and the placing of armchairs in the wide windows of the dining room where breakfast is served is a welcome feature.
2 en suite (bth/shr) No smoking CTV in all bedrooms Tea and coffee making facilities No dogs Cen ht 6P No coaches

PRICE GUIDE
ROOMS: s £25; d £36-£38; wkly b&b £126

BIBURY Gloucestershire Map **04** SP10

Selected

GH Ⓠ Ⓠ Ⓠ Ⓠ **Cotteswold House** Arlington GL7 5ND (on B4425 between Cirencester and Burford)
☎01285 740609
An attractive Cotswold stone house recently built on the outskirts of the riverside village of Bibury offers three immaculate bedrooms, all prettily decorated and furnished. Breakfast is served at separate tables and guests have the use of a comfortable lounge and a small walled garden.
3 en suite (bth/shr) (1 fmly) No smoking CTV in all bedrooms No dogs (ex guide dogs) Cen ht 5P No coaches
PRICE GUIDE
ROOMS: s £25; d £38; wkly b&b £115.50

BICKINGTON (NEAR ASHBURTON) Devon Map **03** SX77

Selected

♥ Ⓠ Ⓠ Ⓠ Ⓠ Mrs E A Ross **East Burne** *(SX799711)* TQ12 6PA (1m from A38, off A382)
☎01626 821496 FAX 01626 821105
Closed Xmas & New Year
A Grade II listed medieval hall, this farmhouse is surrounded by a cobbled yard and old farm buildings, some of which have been converted to provide attractive self-catering accommodation. Three bedrooms, each with private facilities, are simply decorated to set off the old timbers and thick stone walls. There are a comfortable guests' lounge and a heavily timbered dining room where traditional English breakfast is served. Outside there are delightful gardens, a picnic area and a sheltered outdoor heated pool.
3 rms (2 shr) No smoking CTV in 2 bedrooms Tea and coffee making facilities No dogs (ex guide dogs) CTV 8P Outdoor swimming pool (heated) 40 acres cattle horses sheep
PRICE GUIDE
ROOMS: s £17.50-£20; d £35-£40; wkly b&b £115✳

BIDEFORD Devon Map **02** SS42

See also Parkham & Westward Ho!

GH Ⓠ Ⓠ Ⓠ **Mount Hotel** Northdown Rd EX39 3LP (turn off A39 then right at Raleigh garage) ☎01237 473748
Closed Xmas
This small, interesting Georgian building in a partly walled garden close to the historic riverside town offers comfortable, attractively decorated bedrooms. There are an attractive TV lounge and a small bar lounge, the only room where smoking is permitted. Resident proprietors Janet and Mike Taylor pride themselves both on good home cooking and on providing an establishment of character.
8 rms (1 bth 6 shr) (2 fmly) No smoking in bedrooms No smoking in dining room No smoking in lounges Tea and coffee making facilities No dogs (ex guide dogs) Licensed Cen ht CTV 4P No coaches Last d 5pm

PRICE GUIDE
ROOMS: s £21-£22; d £38-£40; wkly b&b £125-£147; wkly hlf-bd £175-£210
CARDS: 🔳 🔳   ⓔ

GH Ⓠ Ⓠ Ⓠ **Pines at Eastleigh** Old Barnstaple Rd, Eastleigh EX39 4PA (turn off A39 Barnstaple/Bideford road onto A386 signposted Torrington. After 0.75m turn left signposted Eastleigh, 2m to village, house on right)
☎01271 860561 FAX 01271 860561
Dating back to the 18th century, this former farmhouse is the home of Barry and Jenny Jones, who over the last few months have been upgrading the property. Set in seven acres of gardens and paddocks, on the edge of the village of Eastleigh, there is an attractive lounge with an honesty bar and in the dining room a choice of either two or four courses meals is served. The majority of the bedrooms are across the courtyard, all are comfortable and well equipped. Two self catering cottages are also available.
2 rms (1 shr) 4 annexe en suite (bth/shr) (2 fmly) No smoking CTV in all bedrooms Tea and coffee making facilities Direct dial from bedrooms Licensed Cen ht ch fac 12P No coaches 7.5 acre garden Arrangements for golf Last d 4pm
PRICE GUIDE
ROOMS: s £20-£30; d £40-£60; wkly b&b £112-£160; wkly hlf-bd £168-£216
CARDS: 🔳 🔳   ⓔ

GH Ⓠ Ⓠ Ⓠ *Sunset Hotel* Landcross EX39 5JA
☎01237 472962
Mar-Oct
Overlooking picturesque Devon countryside, this small country hotel offers accommodation in individually furnished and decorated bedrooms. A comfortable lounge adjoins the dining room where good home cooking is offered - everything is home-made from fresh local produce, including locally caught fish. Smoking is not permitted anywhere in the hotel.
4 en suite (shr) (2 fmly) CTV in all bedrooms Tea and coffee making facilities Licensed Cen ht CTV 6P No coaches Last d 6pm
CARDS: 🔳 🔳

BILLINGSHURST West Sussex Map **04** TQ02

GH Ⓠ Ⓠ Ⓠ **Newstead Hall Hotel** Adversane RH14 9JH (on A24) ☎01403 783196 FAX 01403 784228
An English country-house hotel built in Tudor style stands in the hamlet of Adversane, two miles south of Billingshurst. Skilfully extended, the house now provides modern, well equipped bedrooms, each with private bathroom, direct-dial telephone, TV and tea tray. The bar lounge forms the principal part of the hotel, with comfortable furniture and bar snacks available, and there is a well appointed wood-panelled restaurant. Ample car parking, a 4-poster bed and a small meeting room are to be provided, as the accommodation continues to be improved under new management.
15 en suite (bth/shr) CTV in all bedrooms Tea and coffee making facilities Direct dial from bedrooms Licensed Cen ht 61P No coaches Last d 9.30pm
PRICE GUIDE
ROOMS: s fr £32; d £42-£92✳
CARDS: 🔳 🔳 🔳 Ⓞ

Our inspectors never book in the name of the AA. They disclose their identity only after the bill has been paid.

Premier Selected

♥ Q Q Q Q Q Mrs M Mitchell *Old Wharf* *(TQ070256)* Wharf Farm, Newbridge RH14 0JG
☎01403 784096
FAX 01403 784096
Closed 2 wks Xmas & New Year

Ideally situated for the ferry, being only five minutes from the terminal, this deceptively spacious Victorian property has been skilfully restored and refurbished in recent years by the pleasant owners, Graham and Sandra Tubbs. Standards throughout the hotel are high and housekeeping is excellent. Some bedrooms have en suite facilities, and all are well equipped and comfortable. Day rooms have a warm atmosphere. Breakfast is taken in an attractive dining room, and can be served early for guests needing to get away in good time for a morning ferry. For evening meals, there is a wide choice of restaurants in easy walking distance.
4 en suite (bth/shr) No smoking CTV in all bedrooms Tea and coffee making facilities Direct dial from bedrooms No dogs (ex guide dogs) Licensed Cen ht No children 12yrs 10P Fishing 40 acres non-working
CARDS: 🔲 🔲 🔲 🔲

BINGHAM Nottinghamshire Map **08** SK73

Selected

GH Q Q Q Q **Bingham Court Hotel** Market St NG13 8AB ☎01949 831831 FAX 01949 838833
Closed 25-26 Dec
This purpose-built Chinese restaurant and hotel stands in the centre of the quiet market town. Although an unusual type of establishment it is a very good find for the discerning traveller looking for something a little different. The bedrooms are furnished to western tastes, have good facilities and are carefully maintained. Proprietor Tommy Cheung puts the same energy and enthusiasm into the cuisine and personally welcomes diners to the restaurant.
15 en suite (bth/shr) (2 fmly) No smoking in area of dining room No smoking in 1 lounge CTV in all bedrooms Tea and coffee making facilities Direct dial from bedrooms Licensed Lift Cen ht 30P Last d 8pm
PRICE GUIDE
ROOMS: s £39; d £50; wkly b&b £175-£273✳
CARDS: 🔲 🔲 🔲 🔲 (£)

BINGLEY West Yorkshire Map **07** SE13

Selected

GH Q Q Q Q **Five Rise Locks** Beck Ln BD16 4DD (off A650) ☎01274 565296 FAX 01274 568828
Closed 21 Dec - 1 Jan
This imposing hotel stands in well tended gardens with far-reaching views over the Aire Valley and the locks from which it takes its name. It provides a comfortable lounge, a large games room and an attractive dining room where Patricia

Oxley provides a good standard of home-cooked food. En suite bedrooms are attractively furnished and well equipped with telephones, colour televisions, clock radios and beverage trays. The hotel is found by turning up Park Road from the A650 then turning left at the crossroads into Beck Lane.
9 en suite (bth/shr) (2 fmly) No smoking in bedrooms No smoking in dining room No smoking in lounges CTV in all bedrooms Tea and coffee making facilities Direct dial from bedrooms Licensed Cen ht CTV 15P No coaches Pool table Last d 8.30pm
PRICE GUIDE
ROOMS: s £45-£50; d £45-£55; wkly b&b fr £294; wkly hlf-bd fr £374
CARDS: 🔲 🔲 (£)

BIRKENHEAD Merseyside Map **07** SJ38

GH Q **Gronwen** 11 Willowbank Rd, Devonshire Park L42 7JU (from Birkenhead Tunnel follow signs Town Centre/Tranmere Rovers FC) ☎0151 652 8306
A friendly and unassuming guest house, the Gronwen is conveniently situated close to the Glenda Jackson Theatre and Tranmere Rovers football ground. Although the accommodation is slightly dated, the double rooms are spacious and comfortable. A guests' lounge and a small breakfast room are provided.
5 rms (1 fmly) No smoking in dining room CTV in all bedrooms Tea and coffee making facilities Cen ht CTV No parking No coaches Last d 7.30pm
PRICE GUIDE
ROOMS: s £16; d £30; wkly b&b £108; wkly hlf-bd £140✳

🔲🔲 GH Q Q Q **Treetops** 506 Old Chester Rd, Rock Ferry L42 4PE ☎0151 645 0740
This fine Victorian house lies in its own grounds at Rockferry on the old Chester road. Bedrooms are attractively pine furnished, decorated with pretty papers and all have televisions, tea trays and full central heating. The house is run by the very friendly Swain family and, as well as good value meals, afternoon teas and morning coffees are served. A comfortable lounge is provided and ample car parking is available.
8 rms (2 shr) (1 fmly) CTV in all bedrooms Tea and coffee making facilities No dogs (ex guide dogs) Lift Cen ht CTV ch fac 12P No coaches Last d 9.30pm
PRICE GUIDE
ROOMS: s £12.95-£20; d £26-£40; wkly b&b £91-£140; wkly hlf-bd £112-£189 (£)

BIRMINGHAM West Midlands Map **07** SP08

See also Blackheath

GH Q Q **Ashdale House Hotel** 39 Broad Rd, Acock's Green B27 7UX (off A41, first on left after Acocks Green Centre) ☎0121-706 3598 & 0121-707 2324 FAX 0121-706 3598
Richard and Evelyn are friendly hosts concerned about the environment; they use eco-friendly products and serve breakfasts made from organic produce. Their three-storey Victorian terraced house is furnished with stripped pine and Victoriana.
9 rms (4 shr) (2 fmly) No smoking in dining room No smoking in lounges CTV in all bedrooms Tea and coffee making facilities Cen ht CTV 3P No coaches
PRICE GUIDE
ROOMS: s £20-£25; d £32-£37; wkly b&b £140-£175✳
CARDS: 🔲 🔲 🔲 🔲 🔲 (£)

GH **Awentsbury Hotel** 21 Serpentine Rd, Selly Park B29 7HU (take A38 from city centre, after 2m at end of dual carriageway, take 1st left into Barnbrook Rd & 1st right into Serpentine Rd) ☎0121 472 1258 FAX 0121 472 1258

Catering for a predominantly business clientele, the Awentsbury is situated in a quiet residential area close to the university and Pebble Mill. Bedrooms have all the usual facilities and public areas include a dining room and a small lounge.

16 rms (6 shr) (1 fmly) No smoking in dining room CTV in all bedrooms Tea and coffee making facilities Direct dial from bedrooms Cen ht 13P Last d 7pm

PRICE GUIDE

ROOMS: s £26-£36; d £39-£47

CARDS: 🟦 🟥 🟩 🟠   (£)

GH 🅀🅀🅀 **Bridge House Hotel** 49 Sherbourne Rd, Acocks Green B27 6DX ☎0121 706 5900 FAX 0121 624 5900

Closed Xmas

This substantial private hotel features excellent facilities and professional standards. A lounge/dining room leads through into a conservatory and there are two bars furnished in deep red with button-back seating. This extremely warm, security-conscious and well cared for hotel is convenient for the city centre and NEC.

30 en suite (bth/shr) (1 fmly) No smoking in 20 bedrooms No smoking in area of dining room CTV in all bedrooms Tea and coffee making facilities Direct dial from bedrooms No dogs Licensed Cen ht CTV 48P Last d 8.30pm

PRICE GUIDE

ROOMS: s fr £35.25; d fr £47

CARDS: 🟦 🟥 🟩 🟠

GH 🅀🅀 **Cape Race Hotel** 929 Chester Rd, Erdington B24 OHJ (on A452, 2m from juncts 5 and 6 of M6) ☎0121 373 3085 FAX 0121 373 3085

A large detached house north of the city, with its own garden, the Cape Race is convenient for access to the M6 and the city centre. The cleanly decorated bedrooms vary in size, but all have modern furnishings and a good range of equipment. Drinks can be dispensed to the cottage-style dining room or the cosy lounge from a small bar.

9 rms (8 shr) CTV in all bedrooms Tea and coffee making facilities Direct dial from bedrooms No dogs (ex guide dogs) Licensed Cen ht CTV 9P No coaches Outdoor swimming pool (heated) Tennis (hard) Last d 8.30pm

PRICE GUIDE

ROOMS: s £24-£29; d £40✷

CARDS: 🟦 🟥 🟩

🛏🎇 **GH** 🅀🅀 **Elston** 751 Washwood Heath Rd, Ward End B8 2JY ☎0121 327 3338

rs Sat & Sun

Created by the amalgamation of two houses and catering for a mainly business clientele, this splendid guest house is run by friendly Geordie landlady Mrs Bennett to provide comfortable no-frills accommodation. Evening meals are cooked according to guests' fancies and cost under £5 for a main course, pudding and hot drink. There are rarely any vacancies, so book well in advance.

11 rms (1 shr) No smoking in dining room No smoking in lounges CTV in all bedrooms Tea and coffee making facilities Cen ht CTV 11P No coaches Last d 8pm

PRICE GUIDE

ROOMS: s £15-£17.50; d £30-£32; wkly b&b fr £100   (£)

GH 🅀🅀🅀 **Fountain Court Hotel** 339-343 Hagley Rd, Edgbaston B17 8NH (on A456) ☎0121 429 1754 FAX 0121 429 1209

Made up of three houses, this hotel has a lounge, bar and dining room which are all bright and warm despite the dark oak

panelling. Bedrooms are modestly furnished but well equipped. The fixed-price menu for dinner has four or five choices at each course.

25 en suite (bth/shr) CTV in all bedrooms Tea and coffee making facilities Direct dial from bedrooms Licensed Cen ht CTV 20P Last d 8.30pm

PRICE GUIDE

ROOMS: s £30-£39; d £45-£55; wkly b&b £210-£273; wkly hlf-bd £311.50-£374.50✷

CARDS: 🟦 🟥 🟩 🟠   (£)

GH 🅀🅀 **Heath Lodge Hotel** Coleshill Road,Marston Green B37 7HT (1.5m from airport and NEC on edge of Marston Green village) ☎0121 779 2218 FAX 0121 779 2218

This hotel stands in a quiet but convenient location. The bedrooms vary in size and standard, and public areas include a beamed gallery restaurant, a bar and a comfortable lounge.

18 rms (13 bth/shr) (1 fmly) No smoking in dining room CTV in all bedrooms Tea and coffee making facilities Direct dial from bedrooms Licensed Cen ht CTV 20P Last d 8.30pm

PRICE GUIDE

ROOMS: s £28.50-£39.50; d £39.50-£49.50✷

CARDS: 🟦 🟥 🟩 🟠 🔵 🟥   (£)

GH **Homelea** 2399 Coventry Rd, Sheldon B26 3PN (exit M42 junct 6 on to A45, 2.5m on left near Arden Oak public house) ☎0121 742 0017

Closed Xmas

3 rms (2 shr) No smoking in 1 bedrooms No smoking in dining room No smoking in lounges CTV in all bedrooms Tea and coffee making facilities Cen ht CTV 5P No coaches

929 Chester Road • Erdington
Birmingham B24 0HJ
Telephone + Fax 0121 373 3085
Proprietors Phillip & Jill Jones
Hotel run personally by resident proprietors. All bedrooms with colour TV, phones and tea/coffee making facilities. Most rooms with shower & toilet en suite. Central Heating. Licensed Bar. Ample free car parking. Tennis court and outdoor pool in large garden. NEC and City Centre ten minutes, M6 junc 5 & 6 2 miles. Special weekly and weekend rates.

GH 🅀🅀 **Lyndhurst Hotel** 135 Kingsbury Road, Erdington B24 8QT (from M6 junct 6 follow A5127 then take right fork, signed Minworth, into Kingsbury Rd for hotel on right) ☎0121 373 5695 FAX 0121 373 5695
A large, considerably extended Victorian house, the Lyndhurst is conveniently located in the northern suburbs half a mile from junction 6 of the M6. The bedrooms, including those on the ground floor, have modern furnishings and equipment. Downstairs there are a large dining room with an adjacent lounge bar and a TV lounge.
14 rms (1 bth 12 shr) (3 fmly) CTV in all bedrooms Tea and coffee making facilities No dogs (ex guide dogs) Licensed Cen ht CTV 15P No coaches Last d 8.15pm
PRICE GUIDE
ROOMS: s £25-£39.50; d £39.50-£52.50; wkly b&b £195-£215; wkly hlf-bd £265-£285
CARDS: 🔲 🔲 🔲 🔲 🔲 ⓔ

GH 🅀🅀 **Robin Hood Lodge Hotel** 142 Robin Hood Ln, Hall Green B28 0JX (on A4040, 5m from city centre) ☎0121 778 5307 & 0121 608 6622 FAX 0121 608 6622
A commercial guest house with easy access to the city, NEC and airport offers functional but well equipped accommodation in the main building and two adjacent properties. There are a comfortable lounge with a bar and a small dining room.
9 rms (1 bth 4 shr) (1 fmly) CTV in all bedrooms Tea and coffee making facilities Licensed Cen ht CTV 11P No coaches Last d 8pm
PRICE GUIDE
ROOMS: s fr £24; d fr £36
CARDS: 🔲 🔲 🔲 ⓔ

GH 🅀 **Rollason Wood Hotel** 130 Wood End Rd, Erdington B24 8BJ (NE Birmingham on A4040) ☎0121 373 1230 FAX 0121 382 2578
A large commercial guest house, this establishment offers very simple accommodation, a good evening meal and a bar to relax in after a hard day's work.
35 rms (1 bth 10 shr) (4 fmly) CTV in all bedrooms Tea and coffee making facilities Licensed Cen ht CTV 35P Games room Last d 8.30pm
CARDS: 🔲 🔲 🔲 🔲

GH 🅀🅀 **Tri-Star Hotel** Coventry Road,Elmdon B26 3QR (on A45) ☎0121 782 1010 & 021-782 6131
Convenient for the NEC and airport, this mainly commercial hotel offers simple, well maintained accommodation. Public areas include a games room, small bar and comfortable TV lounge with an archway to the dining area.
15 rms (11 shr) (3 fmly) CTV in all bedrooms Tea and coffee making facilities No dogs Licensed Cen ht CTV 25P No coaches Pool table Last d 8pm
CARDS: 🔲 🔲 🔲

BIRMINGHAM (NATIONAL EXHIBITION CENTRE)
West Midlands

See **Hampton-in-Arden**

Prices quoted in the Guide are based on information supplied by the establishments themselves.

BISHAMPTON Hereford & Worcester Map **03** SO95

Premier Selected

♥ 🅀🅀🅀🅀🅀 Mrs H Robertson **Nightingale Hotel** *(SO988512)* WR10 2NH ☎01386 462521 FAX 01386 462522
This mock-Tudor farmhouse offers comfortable accommodation in bright, fresh and well equipped bedrooms with pretty co-ordinating soft furnishings and modern en suite facilities. There are three lounge areas with excellent seating, fresh flowers, books and magazines. The dining room is in two parts and the small restaurant has gained a good local reputation, for its high standard of cooking and imaginative menus. Proprietors Mr and Mrs Robertson are welcoming hosts whose concern for their guests' comfort ensures that visitors return regularly. The farmhouse is suitable for tourists and business guests alike, and small meetings can be accommodated.
4 en suite (bth/shr) (1 fmly) No smoking in dining room CTV in all bedrooms Tea and coffee making facilities No dogs Licensed Cen ht 30P Golf 18 Riding 200 acres beef arable Last d 9pm
PRICE GUIDE
ROOMS: s £35; d £50
CARDS: 🔲 🔲 🔲 🔲

BISHOP'S CASTLE Shropshire Map **07** SO38

GH 🅀🅀🅀 **The Old Brick Guesthouse** 7 Church St SY9 5AA (from A488, turn by Community College into Bishops Castle, follow road past church into town, 100yds on left hand side) ☎01588 638471
Closed Xmas
Probably dating, from 1720, this old building features exposed timbers, beams and an impressive staircase. The sitting room has great character, and a roaring fire burns in the inglenook fireplace in colder weather. Bedrooms include one at ground-floor level as well as some suitable for family use.
4 en suite (bth/shr) (1 fmly) No smoking in dining room Tea and coffee making facilities Licensed Cen ht CTV 5P No coaches Last d 3pm
PRICE GUIDE
ROOMS: s £25; d £40; wkly b&b £120-£150; wkly hlf-bd £174-£204
CARDS: 🔲 🔲 ⓔ

◀ 🅀🅀🅀 **The Boar's Head** Church St SY9 5AE (from A488 follow signs to livestock market, continue past market Inn is on the left at crossroads) ☎01588 638521
Public areas of this small town centre inn are enhanced by a variety of bric-á-brac and a welcoming real fire. The bedrooms are located on the ground floor of a converted former stable block and they all have modern furnishings, facilities and equipment.
4 en suite (bth/shr) (1 fmly) No smoking in dining room CTV in all bedrooms Tea and coffee making facilities Direct dial from bedrooms No dogs (ex guide dogs) Cen ht CTV 20P Pool table Last d 9.30pm
➡

PRICE GUIDE
ROOMS: s £30-£35; d £45-£50; wkly b&b fr £135; wkly hlf-bd fr £200
MEALS: Lunch £7-£10alc Dinner £8-£12alc
CARDS:

BISHOP'S STORTFORD Hertfordshire Map **05** TL42

Selected

GH **Q Q Q Q** **Cottage** 71 Birchanger Ln, Birchanger CM23 5QA (from M11 junct 8 take A120 Hertford rd then in 1m first right B1383 and right again into Birchington Lane) ☎01279 812349 FAX 01279 812349
A charming 17th-century Grade II listed cottage has been carefully modernised to retain its character. Set in a quiet rural location yet close to Bishop's Stortford, it offers well equipped accommodation which is attractively decorated and furnished. The panelled lounge is comfortable, and the delightful conservatory/dining room overlooks the garden.
15 rms (13 bth/shr) (1 fmly) No smoking CTV in all bedrooms Tea and coffee making facilities Direct dial from bedrooms No dogs (ex guide dogs) Licensed Cen ht 15P No coaches Croquet Last d 9.30am
PRICE GUIDE
ROOMS: s £24-£36; d £45✱
CARDS:

BLACKHEATH West Midlands Map **07** SO98

GH **Q Q** **Highfield House Hotel** Holly Rd, Rowley Regis B65 0BH ☎0121 559 1066
This popular commercial hotel is located at Blackheath, which is also known as Rowley Regis, just 1.5 miles from junction 2 of the M5. The rooms - though modest with plain decor and functional furnishings - are well kept, and standards of maintenance are good. Evening meals are served in the dining room, and there is a comfortable lounge with satellite TV.
14 rms (2 bth/shr) CTV in all bedrooms Tea and coffee making facilities No dogs (ex guide dogs) Licensed Cen ht CTV 12P No coaches Last d 6pm
CARDS:

BLACKPOOL Lancashire Map **07** SD33

GH **Q Q** **Arosa Hotel** 18-20 Empress Dr FY2 9SD ☎01253 352555
Only a short walk from the seafront, this private hotel offers spacious bedrooms with en suite bathrooms, TV and tea making facilities. Two are on the ground floor and some are suitable for families. There are a cosy bar, a sun lounge and forecourt car parking.
20 rms (3 bth 16 shr) (7 fmly) CTV in all bedrooms Tea and coffee making facilities Licensed Cen ht CTV 5P Last d 5pm

GH **Q Q** **Ashcroft Private Hotel** 42 King Edward Av FY2 9TA (turn off Queen Prom 2nd right after Savoy hotel) ☎01253 351538
This small, friendly hotel is just a short walk from Queens Promenade in a quiet area of the resort. Bedrooms are small but well equipped, and there are plans to add to those that already have en suite bathrooms.
10 rms (7 shr) (3 fmly) No smoking in dining room CTV in all bedrooms Tea and coffee making facilities No dogs Licensed Cen ht CTV 3P Last d 2pm

PRICE GUIDE
ROOMS: s £15-£18; d £30-£36; wkly b&b £98-£124; wkly hlf-bd £126-£152✱
CARDS:

GH **Q Q** **Berwick Private Hotel** 23 King Edward Av FY2 9TA ☎01253 351496
20 Mar-7 Nov
This small, popular and well maintained hotel is privately owned and personally run by Joan and Michael Wood, who take great pride in their establishment. Bedrooms, all but one of which are en-suite, are simply appointed and spotlessly clean. Joan Wood produces a choice of home-cooked dishes at dinner which are served in the small dining room, which has separate tables and next door to which is a small comfortable sun lounge.
8 rms (7 shr) No smoking in dining room No smoking in lounges Tea and coffee making facilities No dogs Licensed Cen ht CTV No children 3yrs 4P No coaches Last d 3pm

GH **Q Q Q** **Brooklands Hotel** 28-30 King Edward Av FY2 9TA ☎01253 351479
Mar-Nov rs Dec
This well maintained hotel, owned by Val and Ray Bird, is situated in a quiet residential area, just a hundred yards from Queens Promenade, but within easy reach of the towns many attractions. The eighteen freshly decorated bedrooms, four of which are on the ground floor, all have modern en suite shower facilities and are well equipped. A daily changing menu offering home cooked dishes is served in the spacious dining room and there is a comfortable lounge bar.
18 en suite (bth/shr) (4 fmly) No smoking in bedrooms No smoking in dining room CTV in all bedrooms Tea and coffee making facilities No dogs (ex guide dogs) Licensed Cen ht 5P Last d 5.30pm
PRICE GUIDE
ROOMS: s £18-£21; d £36-£42; wkly b&b £126-£147; wkly hlf-bd £154-£182
CARDS:

Selected

GH **Q Q Q Q** **Burlees Hotel** 40 Knowle Av FY2 9TQ (from Queens Promanade right at Uncle Toms cabin into Knowle Av) ☎01253 354535
Feb-Nov
Mike and Linda Lawrence take great pride in their immaculately maintained double fronted house, which is situated in a very pleasant and quiet residential area on the North Shore. The attractively decorated bedrooms are all en-suite and thoughtfully equipped. The bright dining room, which has matching pine furniture, is more modern in style, but is where guests can enjoy the good home-made food, cooked by Mike Lawrence. There is a very attractively furnished lounge with deep cushioned sofas, a small neat bar and guests in the summer also have the use of the well tended gardens.
9 en suite (shr) (2 fmly) No smoking in 6 bedrooms No smoking in dining room CTV in all bedrooms Tea and coffee making facilities No dogs Licensed Cen ht CTV 5P No coaches Last d 4pm
PRICE GUIDE
ROOMS: s £21-£24; d £42-£48; wkly b&b £129-£147; wkly hlf-bd £175-£199✱
CARDS:

GH 🅀🅀 **Claytons** 28 Northumberland Av, off Queens Promenade FY2 9SA (off Queens Promanade, nr Uncle Toms Cabin) ☎01253 355397 FAX 01253 500142

Claytons, which has been owned and personally run by Margaret and Gerry Clayton for the last seven years, is conveniently situated in a quiet area just off Queens Promenade. The comfortable bedrooms have en suite shower rooms and satellite television. A lounge/dining room serves a good range of good-value dishes. Mr and Mrs Clayton, who are keen jazz enthusiasts, also organise trips to local jazz clubs during the week.

6 en suite (shr) (1 fmly) No smoking in 2 bedrooms No smoking in dining room CTV in all bedrooms Tea and coffee making facilities No dogs (ex guide dogs) Cen ht CTV No children 7yrs No coaches Last d 4pm

PRICE GUIDE

ROOMS: s £17-£19; d £34-£38; wkly b&b £106-£112✱

CARDS: 🅰 🔳 🔳 ⓪   £

GH 🅀🅀 **Cliff Head Hotel** 174 Queens Promenade, Bispham FY2 9JN ☎01253 591086 FAX 01253 591086

Situated on Queens Promenade, this friendly hotel offers a cosy sun lounge, a bar and a dining room, in addition to well equipped bedrooms with en suite bathrooms.

10 en suite (bth/shr) (3 fmly) No smoking in dining room No smoking in lounges CTV in all bedrooms Tea and coffee making facilities Licensed Cen ht CTV 4P Last d 6pm

PRICE GUIDE

ROOMS: s £15-£19; d £30-£38; wkly hlf-bd fr £135✱

£

GH 🅀🅀🅀 **Cliftonville Hotel** 14 Empress Dr FY2 9SE ☎01253 351052 FAX 01253 540052

May-7 Nov & Xmas/New Year rs Apr

This well appointed hotel is situated just off Queens Promenade, close to Gynn Square. The en suite bedrooms are attractive and comfortably furnished, while public areas include a sun lounge, a bar with a pool table and a spacious restaurant serving a good choice of home-cooked dishes. There is a lift to all floors.

18 en suite (shr) (9 fmly) No smoking in dining room CTV in all bedrooms Tea and coffee making facilities No dogs (ex guide dogs) Licensed Lift Cen ht CTV 6P Pool table Last d 5.30pm

PRICE GUIDE

ROOMS: s £16-£28; d £32-£48; wkly b&b £96-£140; wkly hlf-bd £114-£160✱

CARDS: 🅰 🔳 🔳 🔳

GH 🅀🅀 **The Colby Hotel** 297 The Promenade FY1 6AL (on promenade midway between Blackpool Tower and Pleasure Beach) ☎01253 345845 FAX 01253 345845

This privately owned and personally run hotel is conveniently situated on the promenade between the Golden Mile and the Pleasure Beach. The en suite bedrooms, which include family and four-poster rooms, are equipped with televisions and tea/coffee making facilities; some have magnificent sea views. There are a modern dining room and a comfortable lounge which has a bar at one end, a pool table and satellite television.

14 en suite (shr) (5 fmly) CTV in all bedrooms Tea and coffee making facilities Direct dial from bedrooms No dogs Licensed Cen ht CTV 3P No coaches Pool table Last d 5pm

PRICE GUIDE

ROOMS: s £21-£26; d £38-£50; wkly b&b £120-£147; wkly hlf-bd £155-£189

CARDS: 🅰 🔳

GH 🅀🅀🅀 **Commodore Hotel** 246 Queens Promenade, North Shore FY2 9HA ☎01253 351440

Closed Nov-Mar

This well maintained hotel, which has been owned and personally run by Peter and Jean Turner for the last seven years, is quietly situated on Queens Promenade on the North Shore of the resort but is within easy reach of all the main attractions. The fully en suite bedrooms include ground-floor and family rooms as well as some with magnificent sea views; all are freshly decorated, comfortably furnished and well equipped. The attractively furnished open-plan lounge, bar and dining room serves a small choice of home-made dishes, usually on a good-value five-course dinner menu. The hotel also benefits from its own private car park.

18 en suite (shr) (4 fmly) No smoking in dining room CTV in all bedrooms Tea and coffee making facilities No dogs (ex guide dogs) Licensed 8P

PRICE GUIDE

ROOMS: s £18-£24; d £32-£44; wkly b&b £126-£135; wkly hlf-bd £125-£142✱

CARDS: 🅰 🔳 🔳   £

 GH 🅀🅀 **Denely Private Hotel** 15 King Edward Av FY2 9TA ☎01253 352757

Closed Xmas & New Year

Magnificent colour is provided by the huge array of plants in the small garden at the rear of this long established private hotel, which is situated in a quiet residential area, but only a short tram ride away from all the major attractions. The simple non smoking dining room, where evening meals are available overlooks the garden and there is also comfortable lounge. The bedrooms, including family rooms and two of which have en-suite facilities, are soundly furnished and simply decorated but do include hairdryers. The hotel also has a small car park at the rear.

9 rms (2 shr) (2 fmly) No smoking in dining room Tea and coffee making facilities No dogs Cen ht CTV 6P Last d 3.30pm

PRICE GUIDE

ROOMS: s £15.75-£17; d £31.30-£34; wkly b&b £99.22-£107.10; wkly hlf-bd £118.80-£120.65

𝕭𝖚𝖗𝖑𝖊𝖊𝖘 𝕳𝖔𝖙𝖊𝖑

40, Knowle Avenue, Blackpool FY2 9TQ
Tel: (01253) 354535
Proprietors: Mike and Linda Lawrence

Friendly, family run hotel situated off Queen's Promenade
in peaceful residential area.

★ Ideal for holidays, business or conference delegates
★ Easy access to town centre and amenities
★ Unrestricted car parking, some on premises
★ Comfort and excellent cuisine assured
★ Central heating throughout
★ All rooms en-suite
★ All rooms with TV, clock radio, hair dryer and
   tea/coffee making facilities
★ Licensed to residents
★ Low seasons rates Feb to May.
   Short Break Reductions,

GH ⓠⓠⓠ *Derwent Private Hotel* 8 Gynn Av, North Shore
FY1 2LD ☎01253 355194 FAX 01253 596618
A small privately-owned hotel is quietly located just off the Gynn
roundabout, close to the promenade. Bedrooms, which include
two family rooms, are attractively decorated and comfortably
furnished. The ground floor houses a spacious lounge with TV and
small dining room with a bar serving breakfast and dinner at
individual tables.
12 rms (4 shr) (2 fmly) No smoking in dining room Tea and
coffee making facilities Licensed Cen ht CTV 4P Last d 2pm
CARDS: 🔲 🔤

GH ⓠⓠ **The Garville Hotel** 3 Beaufort Av, Bispham
FY2 9HQ (2m N) ☎01253 351004
Closed Jan & 2 wks mid-May
Recent improvements that have been made to this small hotel by
its friendly owners Tony and Cath Dawson include adding en suite
shower rooms to most of the attractively furnished bedrooms. The
rooms themselves, including two with four poster beds and one on
the ground floor, include facilities such as tea and coffee making
facilities and televisions. Breakfast is served in the small dining
room and guests' have the use of a cosy lounge which also has a
bar.
6 rms (2 bth 3 shr) (3 fmly) No smoking in bedrooms No
smoking in dining room CTV in all bedrooms Tea and coffee
making facilities No dogs (ex guide dogs) Licensed Cen ht
CTV 5P No coaches Last d 2pm
PRICE GUIDE
ROOMS: s £17-£20; d £30-£34; wkly b&b £85-£95✱

GH ⓠⓠⓠ **Hartshead Hotel** 17 King Edward Av FY2 9TA
(off Promanade at Cliffs Hotel) ☎01253 353133 & 357111
Closed 7 Nov-Feb rs Mar-Etr
All guests are given a very warm welcome by Mrs Chantlay and
her staff who run this well maintained small hotel with great
enthusiasm. It is situated on the peaceful North Shore, just two
hundred yards from Queens Promenade. A choice of home cooked
dishes are served in the small attractively furnished dining room
and guests have the use of a comfortable lounge and a sun lounge.
The en-suite bedrooms, one or two of which are quite compact,
are comfortably furnished and equipped with telephones, clock
radios and tea and coffee making facilities. There is a small car
park at the rear of the hotel.
10 en suite (bth/shr) (3 fmly) No smoking in bedrooms No
smoking in dining room CTV in all bedrooms Tea and coffee
making facilities Direct dial from bedrooms Licensed Cen ht
CTV 6P No coaches Last d 3pm
PRICE GUIDE
ROOMS: s £21.50-£23; d £33-£36; wkly b&b £95-£117; wkly
hlf-bd £115-£138✱
CARDS: 🔲 🔤

GH ⓠⓠⓠ *Inglewood Hotel* 18 Holmfield Rd FY2 9TB
☎01253 351668
This immaculately maintained, family-run hotel is situated in a
quiet area just back from Queens Promenade. The bedrooms are
prettily decorated, and all have modern en suite shower rooms.
Good wholesome meals are served in the attractive dining room,
and guests also have the use of a cosy bar and a small sun lounge.
10 en suite (shr) (2 fmly) CTV in all bedrooms Tea and coffee
making facilities No dogs (ex guide dogs) Licensed Cen ht
CTV No children 2yrs No coaches Last d 10am

GH ⓠⓠⓠ **Lynstead Private Hotel** 40 King Edward Av
FY2 9TA (adjacent to Queens Promanade) ☎01253 351050
Closed 1st 2 wks Jan rs mid Nov-Dec & mid Jan-Etr
This long-established, privately owned guest house is
conveniently situated just off Queens Promenade. The en suite
bedrooms vary in size, but all are comfortable and attractively

---

decorated. The immaculate public areas have been decorated with
character and include a restaurant featuring an enormous
collection of teapots, an interesting bar with a tramcar theme, and
a very pleasant, comfortably furnished lounge and adjoining sun
lounge. All the bedrooms and the dining room are non smoking
and there is a chair lift between the first and second floors.
10 en suite (shr) (4 fmly) No smoking in bedrooms No smoking
in dining room Tea and coffee making facilities No dogs (ex
guide dogs) Licensed Lift Cen ht CTV No children 3yrs No
parking No coaches Last d 3pm
PRICE GUIDE
ROOMS: s £17-£20; d £34-£40; wkly b&b £119-£126; wkly hlf-
bd £119-£140✱

GH ⓠⓠⓠ **Lynwood** 38 Osborne Rd FY4 1HQ (adjoining
promenade, opposite Sandcastle Centre) ☎01253 344628
Closed Xmas & New Year
This delightful small guest house stands in a quiet street close to
the South Pier. There is a comfortable lounge, and good home
cooking is served in the pretty dining room. Most of the bedrooms
are en suite and all have televisions and clock radios.
8 rms (1 bth 5 shr) (1 fmly) No smoking in dining room CTV in
all bedrooms Tea and coffee making facilities No dogs Cen ht
1P No coaches Last d breakfast
PRICE GUIDE
ROOMS: s £13-£18; d £26-£36; wkly b&b £80-£100; wkly hlf-
bd £110-£140✱

GH ⓠⓠ **North Mount Private Hotel** 22 King Edward Av
FY2 9TD (off Queens Promenade, 1m N of North Pier)
☎01253 355937
This cosy family guest house is situated in a quiet area of the
town. The bedrooms are freshly decorated, and there is satellite
television in the residents' lounge.
8 rms (1 fmly) No smoking in dining room Tea and coffee
making facilities Licensed Cen ht CTV 1P Last d 3pm
PRICE GUIDE
ROOMS: s fr £14; d fr £28; wkly b&b £80-£98; wkly hlf-bd
£90-£126✱

GH ⓠⓠⓠ **The Old Coach House** 50 Dean St FY4 1BP
☎01253 344330
Set in award-winning gardens, this former mill owner's residence
was built in 1851. Only a short walk from the South Pier and other
attractions, the hotel offers extremely well equipped bedrooms, a
conservatory lounge and a recently extended restaurant which
enjoys a good local reputation.
5 en suite (shr) (2 fmly) No smoking in dining room CTV in all
bedrooms Tea and coffee making facilities Direct dial from
bedrooms No dogs (ex guide dogs) Licensed Cen ht 10P No
coaches Last d 9pm
PRICE GUIDE
ROOMS: s £22.90-£26.45; d £45.80-£52.90; wkly b&b £160.30;
wkly hlf-bd £278.95✱
CARDS: 🔲 🔤 🔤 💲

GH ⓠⓠⓠ **Sunny Cliff** 98 Queens Promenade, Northshore
FY2 9NS (1.5m N of Tower on A584, just past Uncle Toms
Cabin) ☎01253 351155
Etr-9 Nov & 4 days Xmas
Situated overlooking the seafront at the northern end of Queens
Promenade, this long-established and friendly guest house is now
adding en suite facilities to its compact bedrooms. Attractive
public areas comprise a cosy bar, comfortable lounge and well
appointed dining room where home-cooked meals are served.

9 rms (8 shr) (3 fmly) No smoking in dining room CTV in 8 bedrooms Tea and coffee making facilities Licensed CTV 8P No coaches Last d 5pm
PRICE GUIDE
ROOMS: s £15-£20; d £35-£40; wkly b&b £112-£122; wkly hlf-bd £140-£148✱

Selected

GH QQQQ **Sunray** 42 Knowle Av, Queens Promenade FY2 9TQ (from Tower, head N along Prom turning right at Uncle Toms Cabin, hotel 300yds on left)
☎01253 351937 FAX 01253 593307
Closed mid Dec-mid Jan
Sunray, which has been enthusiastically run by Jean and John Dodgson for the last twenty-five years, is situated in immaculate gardens in a quiet residential area just off Queens Promenade. Mr and Mrs Dodgson make every effort to ensure that their guests, many of whom return year after year, are comfortable and well looked after. This is typified by the thoughtful extras provided in the attractively decorated en suite bedrooms. There are also a very comfortable lounge and spacious dining room where a home cooked meal is served from 5.30pm.
9 en suite (bth/shr) (2 fmly) CTV in all bedrooms Tea and coffee making facilities Direct dial from bedrooms Cen ht CTV 6P No coaches Last d 3pm
PRICE GUIDE
ROOMS: s £25-£28; d £50-£56; wkly b&b £150-£168; wkly hlf-bd £222-£240✱
CARDS:

GH QQ **Surrey House Hotel** 9 Northumberland Av FY2 9SB (continue along Prom to Gynn Sq roundabout leading to Queens Prom, hotel is on fifth rd after roundabout)
☎01253 351743
Surrey House is conveniently situated in a quiet side street close to the seafront, to the north of the town. The bedrooms vary in size, but most are en suite and provide comfortable, simply furnished accommodation. Public areas comprise a comfortably furnished lounge, a pleasant sun lounge and a spacious dining room serving breakfast and dinner at separate tables.
12 rms (2 bth 9 shr) (2 fmly) No smoking in dining room CTV in 2 bedrooms Tea and coffee making facilities Cen ht CTV 7P Table tennis Pool table Last d 4.30pm
PRICE GUIDE
ROOMS: s £17-£23; d £34-£46; wkly b&b £119-£161; wkly hlf-bd £161-£203

GH QQQ **Westdean Hotel** 59 Dean St FY4 1BP
☎01253 342904
This well maintained and personally run hotel is conveniently situated just off the Promenade, close to the South Pier, Pleasure Beach and Sandcastle. The hotel has a small lounge, an interesting cellar bar, a games room and a spacious restaurant serving home-made meals. Bedrooms, most of which are en suite, include family rooms; all are freshly decorated and well equipped with tea and coffee making facilities, televisions, radio alarm clocks and fully controllable central heating.
12 rms (8 shr) (4 fmly) CTV in all bedrooms Tea and coffee making facilities No dogs Licensed Cen ht CTV 2P Games room Last d 5pm
PRICE GUIDE
ROOMS: s £17-£22; d £28-£44; wkly b&b £77-£115; wkly hlf-bd £98-£139✱
CARDS:

GH QQQ **Windsor Hotel** 53 Dean St FY4 1BP
☎01253 400232 FAX 01253 346886
A recently refurbished and immaculately maintained hotel is conveniently situated adjacent to the Promenade and close to the South Pier, the pleasure beach and Sandcastle. En suite bedrooms, including four-poster and family rooms, are attractively decorated and well equipped with satellite TV, tea/coffee making facilities and adjustable central heating. The spacious dining room serves breakfast and dinner, and there are a bar and a comfortable sun lounge.
12 en suite (shr) (3 fmly) No smoking in 6 bedrooms CTV in all bedrooms Tea and coffee making facilities No dogs (ex guide dogs) Licensed Cen ht CTV 8P Last d 7pm
PRICE GUIDE
ROOMS: s £16-£23; d £28-£46; wkly b&b £96-£114; wkly hlf-bd £120-£136✱
CARDS:

GH QQ **The Windsor & Westmorland Hotel** 256 Queens Promenade FY2 9HB ☎01253 354974 & 0500 657807 (free)
Constant improvements are taking place at this hospitable hotel which is conveniently situated on the quiet North shore. Bedrooms vary in size, but all are attractively decorated and en suite. Attractive public areas include a comfortable lounge bar and a spacious restaurant serving a choice of home-cooked dishes. A lift serves all floors and parking facilities are available.
30 en suite (bth/shr) (12 fmly) No smoking in bedrooms No smoking in dining room CTV in all bedrooms Tea and coffee making facilities Licensed Lift Cen ht CTV 12P
PRICE GUIDE
ROOMS: s fr £25; d fr £50✱
CARDS:

GH Q Q Q **Woodleigh Private Hotel** 32 King Edward Av,
North Shore FY2 9TA ☎01253 593624
Mar-Oct
Ann and Rick Partridge have welcomed visitors to this very well
maintained private hotel for many years. Bedrooms are prettily
decorated and have en suite shower rooms and satellite television.
The residents' lounge is spacious and comfortable, and good food
is served in the attractive dining room.
10 en suite (shr) (2 fmly) No smoking in dining room CTV in all
bedrooms Tea and coffee making facilities No dogs Cen ht CTV
No parking No coaches Last d 2pm
PRICE GUIDE
ROOMS: s £17-£20; d £34-£40; wkly b&b £110-£120; wkly hlf-
bd £126-£140

BLAGDON Avon Map **03** ST55

◀ Q Q **Seymour Arms** Bath Rd BS18 6TH (on A368)
☎01761 462279
This small country pub stands in an elevated position overlooking
a lake and surrounding countryside. The old world bar, with its
comfortable seating and warm atmosphere, offers a good range of
meals, and simply styled but well equipped bedrooms are newly
decorated throughout.
4 rms (3 shr) (1 fmly) No smoking in area of dining room No
smoking in 1 lounge CTV in all bedrooms Tea and coffee making
facilities No dogs Cen ht 20P Last d 9.30pm
PRICE GUIDE
ROOMS: s £20-£26; d £30-£39; wkly b&b £90-£156✱
MEALS: Bar Lunch £8.10-£14.70alc Dinner £8.10-£14.70alc✱

BLAKENEY Gloucestershire

See **Lydney**

BLAKENEY Norfolk Map **09** TG04

GH Q Q **Flintstones** Wiveton NR25 7TL (off A148 at
Letheringsett onto B1156 then 3m on left) ☎01263 740337
Closed 24-26 Dec
Flintstones is a proudly maintained house located near the pub in
the quiet village of Wiveton. A breakfast room is provided, where
dinner is also served.
5 en suite (shr) (3 fmly) No smoking CTV in all bedrooms Tea
and coffee making facilities Licensed Cen ht 5P No coaches
Last d 5pm
PRICE GUIDE
ROOMS: s £22; d £33-£37; wkly b&b fr £115.50; wkly hlf-bd fr
£189✱

BLANDFORD FORUM Dorset Map **03** ST80

GH Q Q Q *Fairfield House* Church Rd DT11 8UB (in village
of Pimperne, near A354)
☎01258 456756 FAX 01258 480053
This attractive Georgian house is quietly located on a country
lane, surrounded by its own well kept gardens. Bedrooms are
freshly decorated, bright and well equipped with modern facilities.
Two further rooms have been added, both spacious, with a shared
bathroom just across the hall; one bedroom in the stable block is
well equipped for disabled guests. There is a cosy lounge
complete with piano, games and books. A select carte is served in
the restaurant, which is open to non-residents and is gaining a
good local reputation.

5 en suite (bth/shr) (1 fmly) No smoking in bedrooms No
smoking in dining room CTV in all bedrooms Tea and coffee
making facilities No dogs (ex guide dogs) Licensed Cen ht 20P
Riding Clay shooting instruction Last d 9pm
CARDS: ◼ ◼ ◼ ◼

Selected

♥ Q Q Q Q Mr & Mrs J Tory **Home Farm** *(ST868069)*
Bryanston DT11 0PR (1.5m NW, opposite village shop)
☎01258 452919
This attractive 200-year-old farmhouse, surrounded by lovely
gardens where guests can sit and take tea in fine weather,
enjoys an idyllic setting in the heart of the village, opposite
the village stores. Well furnished bedrooms have such nice
touches as fresh flowers, pretty fabrics and pictures, and a
cosy lounge with its original oak panelling houses TV, a piano
and a guitar. Proprietor Jackie Tory is famous for the hearty
farmhouse breakfasts which are served at her kitchen table.
3 rms (2 bth/shr) Tea and coffee making facilities Cen ht
CTV 10P 800 acres dairy arable
PRICE GUIDE
ROOMS: s fr £18; d fr £36✱

BLICKLING Norfolk Map **09** TG12

◀ Q Q Q **Buckinghamshire Arms Hotel** Blickling, Aylsham
NR11 6NF (adjacent to Blickling Hall) ☎01263 732133
Situated at the gates of Blickling Hall, this National Trust property
offers well equipped guest rooms, all with trouser presses and
hairdryers, four-poster or tester beds and comfortable leather
armchairs. Originally an inn dating from the 17th century, it has a
popular bar and restaurant.
3 rms (1 shr) (1 fmly) No smoking in dining room CTV in all
bedrooms Tea and coffee making facilities Direct dial from
bedrooms No dogs (ex guide dogs) 80P Fishing Last d 9.30pm
PRICE GUIDE
ROOMS: s £45; d £60; wkly b&b £190; wkly hlf-bd £215✱
MEALS: Lunch £7.50-£12 Dinner £7.50-£12&alc✱
CARDS: ◼ ◼

BLOCKLEY Gloucestershire Map **04** SP13

Selected

GH Q Q Q Q **Lower Brook House** GL56 9DS
☎01386 700286 FAX 01386 700286
Lower Brook House is a well restored 17th-century building
with a pretty garden running down to a brook. Bedrooms,
though small, are interesting, with impressive antique
furnishings. The attractive breakfast room offers fresh fruit as
well as the traditional bacon and eggs, kedgeree or smoked
salmon and scrambled eggs. Two small lounge areas are also
available.
3 en suite (bth/shr) No smoking in bedrooms No smoking in
dining room CTV in all bedrooms Tea and coffee making
facilities Cen ht 10P No coaches

BODENHAM Hereford & Worcester Map **03** SO55

♥ Q Q Q Mr & Mrs P J Edwards *Maund Court (SO561505)*
HR1 3JA (E of Leominster, just off A417) ☎01568 797282
Closed Dec-Jan
Parts of this charming old house date back to the 15th century. It is
situated off the A417, about 8 miles south of Leominster. The

bedrooms have mainly period furnishings, including some antique pieces. All have modern equipment and facilities. Separate tables are provided in the traditionally furnished breakfast room and there is a comfortable lounge. Other facilities include a large garden, a croquet lawn and an outdoor swimming pool.
4 en suite (bth/shr) No smoking in dining room CTV in all bedrooms Tea and coffee making facilities Cen ht CTV 6P Outdoor swimming pool (heated) Croquet 130 acres mixed

---

BODLE STREET GREEN East Sussex Map **05** TQ61

♥ **Q Q** Mr & Mrs P Gentry **Stud** *(TQ652144)* BN27 4RJ (from Hailsham A271 turn left at Windmill Hill signposted Bodle Street, to White Horse Pub, take right fork signed Woods Corner, farm is 1.5m on left)
☎01323 833201 FAX 01323 833201
Closed Xmas
A Victorian-style farmhouse with 70 acres of farmland is peacefully situated in this small village northeast of Hailsham. Accommodation is simple, with modestly furnished but adequately equipped bedrooms. There is a small, comfortable lounge and a traditional English breakfast is served in the cosy dining room.
3 rms (1 shr) No smoking in bedrooms CTV in all bedrooms Tea and coffee making facilities No dogs Cen ht CTV 3P 70 acres cattle sheep
PRICE GUIDE
ROOMS: s £22-£25; d £34-£38; wkly b&b £119-£154; wkly hlf-bd £178.50-£213.50

BODMIN Cornwall & Isles of Scilly Map **02** SX06

GH **Q Q Q** **Mount Pleasant Moorland Hotel** Mount PL30 4EX (follow A30 signed Launceston for 4m, then t rt signed Mount for 3m) ☎01208 821342 FAX 01208 821417
Apr-Sep
Five miles east of Bodmin, this 17th-century Cornish stone and slate farmhouse is situated on the edge of the moor. The majority of the light, airy bedrooms have en suite facilities. Full English breakfast, including home-produced, free-range eggs, is served in the dining room, and a traditional home-cooked set dinner is offered each evening.
7 rms (6 bth/shr) (1 fmly) No smoking in bedrooms No smoking in dining room No smoking in 1 lounge Tea and coffee making facilities No dogs Licensed Cen ht CTV No children 5yrs 10P No coaches Last d 5pm
PRICE GUIDE
ROOMS: d £36-£42; wkly hlf-bd £140-£180

£

Selected

♥ **Q Q Q Q** Mrs P A Smith **Treffry** Lanhydrock PL30 5AF (take B3268 from Bodmin towards Lostwithiel, after 2.5m at mini roundabout turn right and farm is 300yds on the right) ☎01208 74405 FAX 01208 74405
Closed Xmas & New Year
Treffry Farm was the home farm of the Lanhydrock Estate, but is not owned by the National Trust as are the stately home, gardens and miles of scenic walks. It offers three pretty bedrooms, a panelled drawing room and a sunny dining room where breakfast is served. The house stands in established gardens with a children's play area which is shared with eight self-catering cottages.
3 rms (2 shr) No smoking CTV in all bedrooms Tea and coffee making facilities No dogs (ex guide dogs) Cen ht CTV No children 6yrs 4P Golf 18 Fishing Nature trail Woodland play area 200 acres dairy

PRICE GUIDE
ROOMS: s £19-£20; d £38-£40; wkly b&b fr £125※

£

BOLLINGTON Cheshire Map **07** SJ97

◀ **Q Q** *Turners Arms Hotel* 1 Ingersley Rd SK10 5RE ☎01625 573864
This old stone-built inn, well run along informal lines by family owners who provide friendly service, offers accommodation in carefully maintained, well equipped bedrooms furnished in modern style. Other facilities include a choice of bars and a bright dining room with an adjacent coffee lounge area. The hostelry is located on the outskirts of Bollington, on the road to Port Shrigley.
8 rms (2 bth 3 shr) (2 fmly) CTV in all bedrooms Tea and coffee making facilities Cen ht 3P Pool table Darts Last d 9.30pm
CARDS: 🔲 🔤 🔤

BOLTON Greater Manchester Map **07** SD70

GH **Q Q Q** **Broomfield Hotel** 33-35 Wigan Rd, Deane BL3 5PX ☎01204 61570 FAX 01204 650932
Considerable improvements have been made to this hotel, enhancing its quality throughout. Bedrooms, including ground-floor rooms, are modern, and there are a small lounge, a lounge bar and an attractive cottage-style breakfast room.
15 en suite (bth/shr) (1 fmly) No smoking in 2 bedrooms No smoking in dining room No smoking in 1 lounge CTV in all bedrooms Tea and coffee making facilities Licensed Cen ht 15P No coaches Last d 9pm

➡

The **FAIRFIELD**
COUNTRY HOUSE HOTEL

AA   QQQ   Licensed   👑👑👑
Recommended   Restaurant   Highly Commended

🦽 Full disabled facilities All major credit cards accepted

Frances and Alan Bromley extend you a warm welcome to their distinctive, Grade II, Georgian Manor House set in 1.5 acres of gardens and a peaceful village. The bedrooms are tastefully furnished carefully retaining much antiquity whilst offering modern en-suite facilities. Accessible to all the fine Dorset coast/beaches/ countryside and the abundant Historical Heritage of Dorset. The 'Fairfield' restaurant serves cream teas, Sunday lunch and 'à la carte' evening dinner from 7pm (last order 9.00). Stables, Riding, Clay shooting and Golf arranged on request.

CHURCH ROAD, PIMPERNE,
(A354) BLANDFORD FORUM,
DORSET DT11 8UB
Telephone: 01258 456756 Fax: 01258 452123

PRICE GUIDE
ROOMS: s £26.50-£28.50; d £38-£40; wkly b&b fr £185; wkly hlf-bd fr £252✱
CARDS: 🔲 🔲 🔲

BOLTONGATE Cumbria Map **11** NY24

Premier Selected

GH 🆀🆀🆀🆀🆀 **The Old Rectory** CA5 1DA
☎016973 71647
FAX 016973 71798
Closed Dec

This delightful house, situated in a hamlet with rural views towards the Lakeland hills, is the home of Kathleen and Anthony Peacock. Parts of the it, including the study, date from the 15th century when it was built as a peel tower to protect the occupants from Scots raiders. Pre-dinner drinks are served in the comfortable drawing room, and the 17th-century dining room provides the perfect setting for Anthony's fine cooking, served house-party style at a large polished oak table. The bedrooms are decorated and furnished to the highest standard.

3 rms (2 shr) No smoking Tea and coffee making facilities No dogs (ex guide dogs) Licensed Cen ht CTV No children 14yrs 10P No coaches Last d 4pm
PRICE GUIDE
ROOMS: s £36; d £72
CARDS: 🔲 🔲

BONSALL Derbyshire Map **08** SK25

GH 🆀🆀🆀 **Sycamore** 76 High St, Town Head DE4 2AR (leave A6 at Cromford onto B5036 then A5012. At Pig of Lead pub turn right into Bonsall) ☎01629 823903
An 18th-century house located in an elevated position, overlooking the village and surrounding countryside, offers fresh, neat accommodation, its bedrooms varying in size but all offering a good range of facilities. The lounge contains a small bar, and home-cooked meals are provided in the new dining room. Separate car parking is available below the house.
5 rms (3 bth 1 shr) (1 fmly) No smoking in bedrooms No smoking in dining room CTV in all bedrooms Tea and coffee making facilities No dogs (ex guide dogs) Licensed Cen ht 7P No coaches Last d noon
PRICE GUIDE
ROOMS: s £23-£27; d £41-£44; wkly b&b £137-£182; wkly hlf-bd £210-£259✱
See advertisement under MATLOCK

GH 🆀🆀🆀 *Town Head Farmhouse* 70 High St DE4 2AR
☎01629 823762
Tastefully converted and modernised in keeping with its 18th-century character, this house and its outbuildings are built around a small cottage garden and sited at the top of the town.
6 en suite (shr) CTV in all bedrooms Tea and coffee making facilities Cen ht CTV No children 6yrs 14P No coaches

---

BOROUGHBRIDGE North Yorkshire Map **08** SE36

Selected

🔳 🆀🆀🆀🆀 *The Crown* Roecliffe YO5 9LY
☎01423 322578 FAX 01423 324060
Situated in the village of Roecliffe, about a mile from Boroughbridge, this delightful old inn offers attractively furnished bedrooms with telephones and colour TV; the bars are full of character, and an extensive range of food is available either there or in the inviting restaurant.
12 en suite (bth/shr) CTV in all bedrooms Tea and coffee making facilities Direct dial from bedrooms Cen ht ch fac 70P Fishing Last d 9.30pm
CARDS: 🔲 🔲

BORROWDALE Cumbria Map **11** NY21

Selected

GH 🆀🆀🆀🆀 **Greenbank** CA12 5UY (3m S of Keswick on B5289) ☎017687 77215
Closed Dec-1 Feb
Greenbanks is a lovely Victorian house in an elevated position overlooking the valley and Derwentwater. Bedrooms are attractively styled with co-ordinated colour schemes and pine furniture. All have en suite facilities and several have fine views of the lake. Two comfortable lounges, one with TV, are provided, and four-course evening meals are served in the charming dining room. This hospitable house is run under the personal supervision of the proprietors, Trevor and Jennifer Lorton.
10 en suite (bth/shr) (1 fmly) No smoking in bedrooms No smoking in dining room Tea and coffee making facilities No dogs Licensed Cen ht CTV 15P No coaches Last d 5pm
PRICE GUIDE
ROOMS: s £26; d £46-£52; wkly b&b £133-£154; wkly hlf-bd £217-£238

Premier Selected

GH 🆀🆀🆀🆀🆀 **Hazel Bank** Rosthwaite CA12 5XB (6m from Keswick on B5289 Seatoller road, turn left at sign just before Rosthwaite village) ☎017687 77248
Closed Dec-Feb rs Mar & Nov

A delightful Victorian house surrounded by four acres of lawns and woodland commands magnificent views of the Borrowdale Valley from its elevated position in the village of Rosthwaite. Charming, enthusiastic hosts Gwen and John Nuttall have furnished and decorated their house in excellent taste; well proportioned bedrooms - including one with a four-poster bed - are individually furnished, thoughtfully equipped and very comfortable, while an elegant sitting room looks out over the garden and the dining room serves a set four-course dinner featuring John's cooking. There is a well constructed wine list, and house wines can be recommended. Smoking is not permitted, and terms are dinner, bed and breakfast only.

6 en suite (bth/shr) No smoking CTV in all bedrooms Tea and coffee making facilities Licensed Cen ht No children 6yrs 12P No coaches Last d 7pm

PRICE GUIDE

ROOMS: (incl. dinner) s £43; d £86; wkly hlf-bd £265

CARDS: £

BOSCASTLE Cornwall & Isles of Scilly Map **02** SX09

GH QQQ **Old Coach House** Tintagel Rd PL35 0AS (at junct of B3266 and B3263) ☎01840 250398

Mar-Oct rs Feb

Situated high above Boscastle harbour, in the upper village area, this 300-year-old property enjoys some fine views from its setting in pleasant gardens. Simply decorated and furnished bedrooms all have en suite facilities and many other useful extras; one of the two ground-floor rooms is fully equipped to meet the needs of disabled guests. Breakfast is served in a sunny conservatory overlooking the garden, and there is a pleasant lounge where guests can relax in front of an open fire.

6 en suite (bth/shr) (1 fmly) No smoking in dining room No smoking in lounges CTV in all bedrooms Tea and coffee making facilities No dogs (ex guide dogs) Cen ht No children 6yrs 7P No coaches

PRICE GUIDE

ROOMS: s £17-£24; d £34-£48; wkly b&b £102-£146✴

CARDS: £

GH QQQ **St Christophers Country House Hotel** High St PL35 0BD (from A39 at Camelford take B3266, first left past 30mph signs, first right) ☎01840 250412

Mar-Oct

This popular hotel attracts many returning guests with its warm hospitality, good food and unobtrusive service. The bedrooms are neat and well presented, and all offer either en suite or private facilities, Local books, jigsaw puzzles and tourist information are available in the comfortable lounge, and a choice of dishes made from local produce is served each evening in the spacious dining room.

9 rms (7 shr) No smoking in dining room CTV in all bedrooms Tea and coffee making facilities Licensed Cen ht CTV No children 12yrs 8P No coaches Last d 8pm

PRICE GUIDE

ROOMS: s £18-£19.50; d £36-£39; wkly hlf-bd £175-£181✴

CARDS:

Selected

GH QQQQ **Tolcarne House Hotel & Restaurant** Tintagel Rd PL35 0AS (at junct of B3266/B3263) ☎01840 250654

Feb-Oct

This charming Victorian residence has been enthusiastically improved by its new owners over the past two years. Set in glorious gardens which include a croquet lawn, the house offers lovely views down the valley to the sea. Spacious bedrooms which have been decorated with flair offer a high level of comfort. An open fire burns in the lounge in cooler weather, and there is a separate bar with easy chairs and high stools. Dinner, which is offered from both a carte and set menu, includes a variety of local dishes and there is a well-chosen wine list.

9 rms (8 bth/shr) (2 fmly) No smoking in 4 bedrooms No smoking in dining room CTV in all bedrooms Tea and coffee

---

making facilities Licensed Cen ht 15P No coaches Croquet
Last d 9pm
PRICE GUIDE
ROOMS: s £18-£21; d £38-£52; wkly b&b £114-£165; wkly
hlf-bd £184-£235*
CARDS: (£)

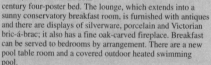
Selected

⌂▦ ♥ QQQQ Mr & Mrs Nicholls **Trerosewill**
(SX095905) Paradise PL35 0DL
☎01840 250545 FAX 01840 250545
Closed 15 Dec-15 Jan
There are spectacular views from this modern farmhouse, and
guests are assured of a genuinely warm welcome from owners
Cheryl and Steve Nicholls. Their natural enthusiasm for
looking after their guests makes this place a firm favourite;
there is evidence everywhere of attention to detail, and the
many little extras confirm this as a special place. The
bedrooms vary in size but not quality, and all come with co-
ordinating fabrics, tasteful decor and en suite facilities. The
comfortable lounge makes an ideal place in which to relax,
with its log-burning stove and children's board games. Typical
home-cooked farmhouse fare is served in the charming dining
room. This a no-smoking house.
7 rms (6 bth/shr) (2 fmly) No smoking CTV in all bedrooms
Tea and coffee making facilities No dogs (ex guide dogs)
Licensed Cen ht CTV 8P 92 acres dairy Last d 7pm
PRICE GUIDE
ROOMS: s £16-£25; d £34-£52; wkly b&b £115-£165; wkly
hlf-bd £220-£270
CARDS:

BOSHAM West Sussex Map **04** SU80

Premier Selected

GH QQQQQ **Kenwood**
Off A259 PO18 8PH (400m W
of Bosham roundabout on
A259)
☎01243 572727
FAX 01243 572738
Kenwood is a mid-Victorian
manor house set in three
acres of secluded grounds.
The comfortable bedrooms
provide many thoughtful
extras, and one has an 18th-
century four-poster bed. The lounge, which extends into a
sunny conservatory breakfast room, is furnished with antiques
and there are displays of silverware, porcelain and Victorian
bric-á-brac; it also has a fine oak-carved fireplace. Breakfast
can be served to bedrooms by arrangement. There are a new
pool table room and a covered outdoor heated swimming
pool.
3 en suite (bth/shr) (1 fmly) No smoking in dining room
CTV in all bedrooms Tea and coffee making facilities Direct
dial from bedrooms No dogs (ex guide dogs) Cen ht CTV
14P No coaches Outdoor swimming pool (heated) Fitness
equipment Pool table
PRICE GUIDE
ROOMS: d £40-£45; wkly b&b £140-£150*

BOURNEMOUTH Dorset Map **04** SZ09

See also Christchurch and Poole

GH QQQ **Alum Grange Hotel** 1 Burnaby Rd, Alum Chine
BH4 8JF ☎01202 761195
Located in Alum Chine, within easy walking distance of the beach
and promenade, this neat, well presented private hotel offers well
proportioned bedrooms; one room features a four-poster bed and
its own balcony with fine sea views, some rooms are on the
ground floor, and some rooms are reserved for non-smokers.
Public areas include a residents' bar and dining room, which
features a collection of nautical memorabilia. In addition to the set
dinner menu cooked by resident proprietor Mrs Hoath, there is a
short carte and an impressive vegetarian menu; bar snacks are also
served.
14 rms (5 bth 7 shr) (7 fmly) No smoking in 4 bedrooms No
smoking in dining room No smoking in 1 lounge CTV in all
bedrooms Tea and coffee making facilities Licensed Cen ht
CTV 10P Small snooker/pool table
PRICE GUIDE
ROOMS: s £15-£25; d £30-£50; wkly b&b £98-£147; wkly hlf-
bd £154-£203*
CARDS: (£)

⌂▦ GH QQQ **Amitie** 1247 Christchurch Rd BH7 6BP (on
A35 near junct with A3060 at Iford) ☎01202 427255
A warm welcome is assured at this personally run and very well
presented establishment. Bedrooms are attractive, with fresh decor
and modern facilities. Hearty breakfasts are served in a cosy room
adorned with treasures from far and wide.
8 rms (5 bth/shr) No smoking in dining room CTV in all
bedrooms Tea and coffee making facilities No dogs (ex guide
dogs) Cen ht 8P No coaches
PRICE GUIDE
ROOMS: s £14-£18; d £30-£40; wkly b&b £105-£112 (£)

Selected

GH QQQQ **The Boltons Hotel** 9 Durley Chine Rd
South, West Cliff BH2 5JT
☎01202 751517 FAX 01202 751629
Mar-Nov
In a convenient position, close to the West Cliff and only a
short distance from the town and the beaches, this personally
managed hotel offers a peaceful setting, a relaxed atmosphere
and very comfortable accommodation. Public areas include a
well appointed lounge area, a cosy bar with horse racing
memorabilia and a bright dining room.
12 en suite (bth/shr) (2 fmly) No smoking in dining room
CTV in all bedrooms Tea and coffee making facilities Direct
dial from bedrooms Licensed Cen ht CTV No children 3yrs
12P No coaches Outdoor swimming pool (heated) Last d
7pm
PRICE GUIDE
ROOMS: s £25-£29; d £50-£58; wkly b&b £125-£155;
wkly hlf-bd £165-£195
CARDS:

⌂▦ GH QQQ **Cairnsmore Hotel** 37 Beaulieu Rd, Alum
Chine BH4 8HY ☎01202 763705
Guest return to this comfortable hotel time and time again,
attracted by its relaxed and friendly atmosphere. Bedrooms have
modern facilities, though they are decorated in Victorian style,
with old paintings and ornaments covering the walls. The popular
lounge is both cosy and comfortably furnished, the bar has been

attractively decorated and the dining room - which serves a short, daily-changing menu of simple, home-cooked dishes - displays a large and fascinating collection of Victorian teapots.

10 en suite (bth/shr) (1 fmly) No smoking in dining room CTV in all bedrooms Tea and coffee making facilities Licensed Cen ht No children 5yrs 4P No coaches Last d 5pm

PRICE GUIDE

ROOMS: s £15-£21; d £30-£42; wkly b&b £102-£138; wkly hlf-bd £137-£173

CARDS: £

GH QQQ **Carisbrooke Hotel** 42 Tregonwell Rd BH2 5NT ☎01202 290432 FAX 01202 310499

This well presented, professionally managed private hotel enjoys a central location on the West Cliff, within walking distance of the BIC, Winter Gardens, seafront and shops. Modern in style, it offers bright well equipped bedrooms, a comfortable lounge, a small bar and an attractive dining room where individual, if closely spaced, tables are provided.

22 rms (19 bth/shr) (6 fmly) CTV in all bedrooms Tea and coffee making facilities Direct dial from bedrooms Licensed Cen ht CTV 18P Last d 7pm

PRICE GUIDE

ROOMS: s £18-£28; d £36-£56; wkly b&b £130-£190; wkly hlf-bd £155-£220

CARDS: £

GH QQQQ **Cherry View Hotel** 66 Alum Chine Rd BH4 8DZ ☎01202 760910

Comfortable and spotlessly maintained accommodation is offered at this family-owned hotel, which is fairly near Alum Chine and Westbourne. Each room has en suite facilities, mostly showers, and there is a tiny lounge, a smart bar, and a front-facing dining room where home-cooked evening meals are served.

11 en suite (bth/shr) (1 fmly) No smoking in 6 bedrooms No smoking in dining room CTV in all bedrooms Tea and coffee making facilities No dogs Licensed Cen ht No children 7yrs 11P Last d 4pm

PRICE GUIDE

ROOMS: s £27-£31; d £38-£44; wkly b&b £115-£140; wkly hlf-bd £160-£190

CARDS: £

Selected

GH QQQQ *Cliff House Hotel* 113 Alumhurst Rd BH4 8HS ☎01202 763003

Mar-Nov & Xmas

High up on the cliff top at Alum Chine, Letty and Alex Clark's popular house is easily distinguishable by the pretty, well kept garden. The spacious bedrooms are bright and spotlessly clean, several have magnificent views along the coast towards the pier, and two have balconies. There is a comfortable lounge, and Letty prepares good home cooked meals which are served in the attractive dining room.

12 en suite (bth/shr) (4 fmly) No smoking in dining room CTV in all bedrooms Tea and coffee making facilities No dogs Licensed Lift Cen ht No children 7yrs 12P No coaches Snooker Last d 6.30pm

GH QQQ *Cransley Private Hotel* 11 Knyveton Rd, East Cliff BH1 3QG (turn off A338 at St Paul's roundabout by ASDA Store, continue over first roundabout Knyveton Rd is the first on the left) ☎01202 290067

Etr-Oct

This small personally run hotel is situated in a quiet residential avenue on the East Cliff. Owners Judith and Mike Wilson offer a

warm welcome to this comfortable hotel. The bedrooms have ensuite facilities and are attractively decorated. There is a bright relaxing lounge overlooking the garden, and good traditional meals are served in the dining room.

12 rms (5 bth 6 shr) No smoking CTV in all bedrooms Tea and coffee making facilities No dogs (ex guide dogs) Licensed 10P No coaches Last d 5pm

GH QQ *Dean Park Hotel & Restaurant* 41 Wimborne Rd BH2 6NB (turn off A338 at Richmond Hill roundabout and take Wimbourne road. Hotel opposite St Augustines church, before traffic lights) ☎01202 552941 FAX 01202 556400

This small commercial and tourist hotel which is currently being upgraded, offers bedrooms that vary in size but are adequately furnished and equipped with modern facilities. The attractively appointed restaurant features a carte offering reasonably priced dishes, and dancing is provided on some evenings.

18 rms (16 bth/shr) (3 fmly) CTV in all bedrooms Tea and coffee making facilities Direct dial from bedrooms Licensed Cen ht CTV 40P Last d 8.30pm

CARDS:

GH QQQ *Dene Court* 19 Boscombe Spa Rd BH5 1AR ☎01202 394874

Well placed for both the centre of Boscombe and the pier, Dene Court offers comfortable accommodation in bright, attractively decorated bedrooms with modern en suite facilities. Downstairs, there are a comfortable lounge, a small games room with a snooker table, a well stocked bar and a dining room serving a short daily-changing menu of good home-cooked food.

16 rms (14 bth/shr) (7 fmly) CTV in all bedrooms Tea and coffee making facilities No dogs Cen ht CTV 15P Snooker

CARDS:

GH Q Q Q **Dorset House** 225 Holdenhurst Rd BH8 8DD
☎01202 397908
Closed 21 Dec-7 Jan
This neat and well presented guesthouse is located beside one of the main roads into town, convenient for the station and shops. Under the supervision of its friendly owners, it offers good-value accommodation in neat bedrooms; all are freshly decorated, and the two situated on the ground floor have modern en suite shower facilities. A hearty breakfast is served in the small dining room and dinner is available by prior arrangement. Smoking is not permitted anywhere in the house.
6 rms (2 bth/shr) No smoking CTV in all bedrooms Tea and coffee making facilities No dogs Cen ht No children 15yrs 6P No coaches Last d 6pm
PRICE GUIDE
ROOMS: s £16-£20; d £30-£34; wkly b&b £105-£112; wkly hlf-bd £150.50-£157.50*

GH Q Q Q **East Cliff Cottage Hotel** 57 Grove Rd BH1 3AT
☎01202 552788 FAX 01202 556400
Tucked away in a quiet road just three hundred yards from the seafront, this personally run hotel offers a warm welcome. The bedrooms are spacious and well equipped, many have been decorated to retain the original features of the building. There is an attractive dining room overlooking the pretty garden, and a comfortable guest lounge.
10 rms (5 bth) (2 fmly) CTV in all bedrooms Tea and coffee making facilities Direct dial from bedrooms Cen ht CTV 10P No coaches Last d 8.30pm
PRICE GUIDE
ROOMS: s £19.50-£25; d £39-£50; wkly b&b £165-£190; wkly hlf-bd £185-£215
CARDS:

GH Q Q **Hawaiian Hotel** 4 Glen Rd BH5 1HR
☎01202 393234
mid Apr-mid Oct
Especially popular with older guests, this comfortable and friendly hotel stands in a residential area of Boscombe, near the shops and the pier. Bedrooms are freshly decorated every year, food is home cooked, and the owners are proud of their awards from SAGA holidays.
12 rms (8 bth/shr) (3 fmly) No smoking in dining room CTV in all bedrooms Tea and coffee making facilities No dogs (ex guide dogs) Licensed Cen ht CTV 7P No coaches Last d 6pm
PRICE GUIDE
ROOMS: s £16.50-£18.50; d £31-£37; wkly b&b £90-£119; wkly hlf-bd £125-£169

GH Q Q Q **Highclere Hotel** 15 Burnaby Rd BH4 8JF (follow signs for Westbourne then Alum Chine,Earle Rd, Beaulieu Rd or Crosby Rd lead of main road into Burnaby Rd)
☎01202 761350
Apr-Sep
Situated in the quiet residential area of Alum Chine, this popular property has been run by the Baldwin family for eighteen years. The bedrooms are individually furnished and well equipped; some have lovely views over the bay. The Baldwins specialise in good home-cooked evening meals.
9 en suite (bth/shr) (5 fmly) No smoking in dining room CTV in all bedrooms Tea and coffee making facilities Licensed Cen ht CTV No children 3yrs 6P No coaches Last d 4pm
PRICE GUIDE
ROOMS: s £18-£22; d £36-£44; wkly b&b £126-£154; wkly hlf-bd £146-£165*
CARDS:

GH Q Q Q **Holmcroft Hotel** 5 Earle Rd BH4 8JQ
☎01202 761289 & 761395
This family-run hotel is located in the quiet residential area of Alum Chine, just a short walk from the sea. The bedrooms are bright and prettily decorated; all have en suite facilities. There is a cosy residents' bar with a piano, and the attractive dining room is decorated with paintings by local artists.
19 en suite (bth/shr) (2 fmly) No smoking in bedrooms No smoking in dining room CTV in all bedrooms Tea and coffee making facilities Direct dial from bedrooms Licensed Cen ht CTV No children 8yrs 13P No coaches Last d 5pm
PRICE GUIDE
ROOMS: s £18-£24; d £36-£48; wkly b&b £126-£168; wkly hlf-bd £154-£189
CARDS:

GH Q Q Q **Linwood House Hotel** 11 Wilfred Rd BH5 1ND
☎01202 397818
Mar-Oct
Built in the 1930s, this fine house with its lovely staircase and leaded windows stands on a quiet residential street in Boscombe, between the town centre and the promenade. The focal point is the attractive lounge, with French windows leading to a secluded garden - its comfort compensating for mainly compact bedrooms. A small bar is also provided in the dining room.
10 rms (1 bth 7 shr) (2 fmly) No smoking in dining room CTV in all bedrooms Tea and coffee making facilities Licensed Cen ht CTV No children 6yrs 7P No coaches Last d 9.30am
PRICE GUIDE
ROOMS: (incl. dinner) d £38-£46; wkly b&b £101-£133; wkly hlf-bd £136-£168*

GH Q Q *Mae-Mar Hotel* 91/95 West Hill Rd BH2 5PQ
☎01202 553167 FAX 01202 311919
This attractively presented hotel is family run and ideally placed for visiting the beach, town centre and attractions. There are two comfortably furnished lounge areas, in addition to a smart bar where there is regular live entertainment. The bedrooms offer simply furnished but comfortable accommodation, most with en suite facilities and many of them suitable for families.
39 rms (4 bth 25 shr) (11 fmly) No smoking in area of dining room No smoking in 1 lounge CTV in all bedrooms Tea and coffee making facilities Licensed Lift Cen ht CTV ch fac 8P Last d 5.30pm
CARDS:

GH Q Q Q **Mayfield Private Hotel** 46 Frances Rd BH1 3SA
☎01202 551839
Closed Dec
This small, cosy Guest house lies in a residential area to the eastern side of the town, overlooking Knyveton Gardens. Run by Mr and Mrs Barling for the past 14 years, it offers comfortable, neat accommodation with a welcoming atmosphere. Bedrooms are attractively decorated, and the cheerful dining room/bar, lounge and small no-smoking conservatory area are adorned with an interesting collection of historic items and bric-á-brac.
8 rms (4 shr) (1 fmly) No smoking in dining room CTV in all bedrooms Tea and coffee making facilities No dogs (ex guide dogs) Licensed Cen ht CTV No children 7yrs 5P No coaches Last d 9am
PRICE GUIDE
ROOMS: s £13-£15; d £26-£30; wkly b&b £84-£91; wkly hlf-bd £105-£128*

GH Q Q Q **Newfield Private Hotel** 29 Burnaby Rd BH4 8JF
☎01202 762724 & 760938
Quietly located in a residential area, this large family house dates from 1886. There are several family rooms, and those at the top of

the house have particular character, with their sloping ceilings; all, however, are bright and fresh with pretty floral fabrics. An evening meal of home-cooked dishes such as roasts and grills is served in the restaurant-cum-bar, and there is a comfortable lounge.

11 rms (1 bth 7 shr) (4 fmly) No smoking in dining room CTV in all bedrooms Tea and coffee making facilities Licensed Cen ht CTV 4P Last d 2pm

PRICE GUIDE
ROOMS: s £18.50-£23.50; d £37-£47; wkly b&b £115-£145; wkly hlf-bd £155-£190
CARDS: (£)

GH QQQ **Northover Private Hotel** 10 Earle Rd BH4 8JQ
☎01202 767349

This comfortable property is personally run by David and Anne Habgood; it is located in a quiet residential area of the town yet just 400 yards from the beach. There is a variety of rooms available, some suitable for families and some with en suite facilities. A full five-course dinner is served in the attractive dining room, and there is a bright television lounge for residents' use.

10 rms (7 bth/shr) (4 fmly) No smoking in 6 bedrooms No smoking in dining room No smoking in lounges Tea and coffee making facilities Licensed Cen ht CTV 11P No coaches Last d 5pm

PRICE GUIDE
ROOMS: s £17.50-£25; d £35-£50; wkly b&b £109-£130; wkly hlf-bd £149-£179
                                                              (£)

Selected

GH QQQQ **Silver Trees** 57 Wimborne Rd BH3 7AL (follow A338 into Bournemouth then A347 to Bournemouth University, Silvertrees is 1m from A338/A347 junct) ☎01202 556040 FAX 01202 556040

Both a warm welcome and a high standard of accommodation are offered at this lovely Victorian house, set back from the main road on the edge of town. Bedrooms are prettily decorated with co-ordinated fabrics, and all have en suite facilities. Beautiful stained-glass windows have been among the original features of the house which have been retained. Public rooms include a cosy lounge and a traditionally furnished dining room that overlooks the attractive garden.

5 en suite (shr) (1 fmly) No smoking in 3 bedrooms No smoking in area of dining room No smoking in 1 lounge CTV in all bedrooms Tea and coffee making facilities No dogs Cen ht 10P No coaches
CARDS:

GH QQ **Hotel Sorrento** 16 Owls Rd BH5 1AG (turn left off A35 at St Johns Church then turn left at crossroads)
☎01202 394019

Feb-Oct rs Xmas

The Sorrento, a family-run establishment with its own gardens, stands in a residential area of Boscombe between the shopping centre and the seafront. There are two lounges, one of which has a well stocked bar, and snacks are served in addition to dinner. A nominal payment is charged for the use of the bedroom TVs, which have satellite and video channels. The house is adorned with owner Richard Titcumb's paintings and prints.

19 rms (15 bth/shr) (5 fmly) No smoking in dining room CTV in all bedrooms Tea and coffee making facilities Licensed Cen ht CTV 19P No coaches Solarium Mini-gym Last d 4pm

PRICE GUIDE
ROOMS: s £15-£21; d £30-£42; wkly b&b £105-£147; wkly hlf-bd £120-£185✳
CARDS: (£)

GH QQQ **Thanet Private Hotel** 2 Drury Rd, Alum Chine BH4 8HA (follow signs for Alum Chine Beach hotel is on corner of Alumhurst Rd & Drury Rd)
☎01202 761135 FAX 01202 761135

Apr-Oct

A mill house dating from 1884, this property stands in a quiet residential area. The accommodation is neat, fresh and bright, and while TV is not available in every room there are sets available on request. Public areas have a traditional atmosphere and include a lounge, a tiny sun lounge and a dining room with a small but reasonably stocked dispense bar in one corner. A home-cooked evening meal is offered.

8 rms (5 shr) (1 fmly) No smoking in dining room CTV in all bedrooms Tea and coffee making facilities No dogs (ex guide dogs) Licensed Cen ht No children 7yrs 6P Last d 5pm

PRICE GUIDE
ROOMS: s £15.50-£18.50; d £30-£41; wkly b&b £103-£132; wkly hlf-bd £130-£162
CARDS: (£)

Selected

GH QQQQ **Tudor Grange Hotel** BH1 3EE (follow signs for East Cliff) ☎01202 291472 & 291463

Built originally in Berkshire, this handsome historic house was dismantled and moved to Bournemouth by a previous owner. It now stands in tree-studded gardens within walking distance of the promenade. As might be expected, wood panelling and leaded windows feature throughout, and both the lounge and dining room have ornate ceilings. A cosy bar is also provided. Bedrooms vary in size, and are furnished with modern fitted units which do not look out of place.

12 rms (11 bth/shr) (4 fmly) CTV in all bedrooms Tea and coffee making facilities Direct dial from bedrooms Licensed Cen ht CTV 11P No coaches Last d 7pm
CARDS:

GH QQQ **Valberg Hotel** 1a Wollstonecraft Rd BH5 1JQ
☎01202 394644

Built at the beginning of the century, this whitewashed villa is set in a quiet residential street midway between Boscombe centre and the promenade. There is an attractive lounge with contemporary seating, and French windows - both from here and the dining room - lead out to the well tended gardens. Bedrooms are small but bright and freshly maintained.

10 en suite (shr) (1 fmly) CTV in all bedrooms Tea and coffee making facilities No dogs Licensed Cen ht CTV No children 4yrs 9P No coaches Last d noon

---

GH QQQ **Weavers Hotel** 14 Wilfred Rd BH5 1ND
☎01202 397871

Apr-Oct

An attractive house is set in a quiet residential area, just a short walk from the shops and seafront. The en suite bedrooms are bright and fresh, while public rooms include a cosy lounge, a lounge with a bar and a pretty dining room serving traditional breakfasts and good home-cooked dinners.

7 rms (6 shr) (1 fmly) No smoking in dining room CTV in all bedrooms Tea and coffee making facilities No dogs Licensed Cen ht No children 7yrs 7P No coaches Last d 5pm

PRICE GUIDE
ROOMS: s £17.50-£20; d £37-£40; wkly b&b £124-£135; wkly hlf-bd £140-£160✳

GH QQQ *West Dene Private Hotel* 117 Alumhurst Rd BH4 8HS ☎01202 764843

14 Feb-5 Nov & 24-29 Dec rs 6 Nov-23 Dec & 30 Dec-13 Feb

Just a short walk from Alum Chine, this hotel commands wonderful sea views. Bedrooms are bright and neatly furnished, while public areas include both a cosy, well stocked bar and a comfortable lounge. Mr and Mrs Merson are personally involved in the daily running of the hotel and offer a traditional home-cooked meal in the evening.

17 rms (5 bth 7 shr) (4 fmly) No smoking in dining room CTV in 15 bedrooms Tea and coffee making facilities No dogs Licensed Cen ht CTV No children 4yrs 17P Last d 3.30pm
CARDS: 🔳 🔳 🔳 🔳

GH QQ *Woodford Court Hotel* 19-21 Studland Rd BH4 8HZ (1m from A35, turn-off at Frizzel roundabout in Westbourne. Follow signs for Alum Chine)
☎01202 764907 FAX 01202 761214

Conveniently situated for Alum Chine, this family-run hotel offers brightly decorated and well equipped bedrooms. Good home-cooked meals are served in the restaurant, and there are a cosy residents' bar and two spacious, comfortably furnished lounges.

35 rms (8 bth 18 shr) (11 fmly) No smoking in dining room No smoking in 1 lounge CTV in all bedrooms Tea and coffee making facilities Licensed Cen ht CTV No children 2yrs 18P No coaches Golf holidays arranged Last d 6.15pm
PRICE GUIDE
ROOMS: s £17-£22; d £34-£44; wkly b&b £119-£154; wkly hlf-bd £147-£195
CARDS: 🔳 🔳 🔳

Selected

GH QQQQ *Wood Lodge Hotel* 10 Manor Rd BH1 3EY ☎01202 290891

Mar-Jan

A putting green and bowls are provided for the energetic at this well run hotel, though guests can just sit in the pretty garden and enjoy the peaceful surroundings. Set a short walk from the East Cliff, it offers bright and spacious bedrooms with smart en suite facilities, together with two comfortable lounges, a cosy bar and a dining room looking out over the garden.

15 rms (14 bth/shr) (4 fmly) No smoking in dining room CTV in all bedrooms Tea and coffee making facilities Licensed Cen ht CTV 12P 9 hole putting green 2 bowls rinks Last d 7.30pm
PRICE GUIDE
ROOMS: s £21-£29; d £42-£58; wkly hlf-bd £170-£218✳
CARDS: 🔳 🔳

BOURTON-ON-THE-WATER Gloucestershire Map 04 SP12

Selected

GH QQQQ *Coombe House* Rissington Rd GL54 2DT ☎01451 821966 FAX 01451 810477

Closed 24, 25 & 31 Dec

An attractive Cotswold home stands in delightful well tended gardens within easy reach of many places of interest and

---

beauty. The attractive bedrooms are well equipped and include two ground-floor rooms. English or Continental breakfast is served in the dining room overlooking the garden. The friendly owners will help guests plan their route through the area.

7 en suite (bth/shr) (2 fmly) No smoking CTV in all bedrooms Tea and coffee making facilities No dogs Licensed Cen ht 10P No coaches
PRICE GUIDE
ROOMS: s £38-£45; d £51-£68; wkly b&b fr £161
CARDS: 🔳 🔳 🔳

Selected

GH QQQQ *The Ridge* Whiteshoots Hill GL54 2LE (0.5m S on A429) ☎01451 820660

This substantial detatched family home is set in two acres of grounds, in an elevated position overlooking beautiful Cotswold countryside only a short distance from Bourton-on-the-Water. Four of the spacious bedrooms are situated in an adjacent modern extension with access from the garden. All the rooms have private facillities and are equipped with colour television, central heating and tea trays. Breakfast is served at separate tables in the attractive dining room.

1 en suite (bth) 4 annexe en suite (bth/shr) (1 fmly) No smoking CTV in all bedrooms Tea and coffee making facilities No dogs Cen ht CTV No children 6yrs 12P No coaches
PRICE GUIDE
ROOMS: s £20-£25; d £40✳

BOVEY TRACEY Devon Map 03 SX87

GH QQ *Blenheim Hotel* Brimley Rd TQ13 9DH (A382 to Bovey Tracy, after 1m take first left on roundabout to Brimley. Follow road to end and turn left at T-junct. Hotel 100yds on right) ☎01626 832422

rs 25 & 26 Dec

A large Victorian house, the Blenheim has a large secluded garden leading onto open moorland. The owner, Mr Turpin, has a great interest in gardening, and he grows many unusual plants which are in evidence throughout the hotel. Accommodation is provided in large bedrooms with splendid views. Two guest lounges are provided, and meals cooked on the Aga are served in the bright dining room.

5 rms (1 shr) (1 fmly) No smoking in dining room No smoking in 1 lounge CTV in 4 bedrooms Tea and coffee making facilities Licensed Cen ht CTV 8P No coaches Last d 7.30pm
PRICE GUIDE
ROOMS: s £25-£26; d £50-£52; wkly b&b £160-£170; wkly hlf-bd £240-£260✳

Entries in this Guide are based on reports filed by our team of professionally trained, full-time inspectors.

Premier Selected

GH 🅀🅀🅀🅀🅀 **Front House Lodge** East St
TQ13 9EL ☎01626 832202
The welcome is warm and the atmosphere relaxed at this 16th-century property - one in a row of substantial houses on the main street, with a large car park and pretty garden to the rear. The house is full of character, the interior being predominantly Victorian in style. The lounge, dining room, bar and bedrooms are all lavishly decorated and full of curiosities and objets d'art. Bedrooms are en suite and equipped with colour TV and tea-making facilities. A set five-course dinner can be served in the beamed dining room by prior arrangement. No convenience foods are used, and all the soups, sauces and puddings are home-made.
6 rms (3 bth 2 shr) (2 fmly) No smoking CTV in all bedrooms Tea and coffee making facilities No dogs Licensed Cen ht CTV 6P Last d 10am
PRICE GUIDE
ROOMS: s £25-£30; d £36-£42
CARDS: 🔳 🔳 🔳

Selected

♥ 🅀🅀🅀🅀 Mrs H Roberts **Willmead** (*SX795812*)
TQ13 9NP ☎01647 277214
Closed Xmas & New Year
Guests at Willmead Farm are guaranteed a warm welcome from charming hostess Mrs Roberts. Visitors from all parts of the world have trodden a path to her door for the past 20 years and have been rewarded by the peace found at his picture-postcard cottage. The house dates from 1437 and many of the original features have been lovingly restored. The simply whitewashed rooms feature beams and inglenook fireplaces, and in the dining room guests eat at a communal table. The hall, complete with a minstrels' gallery from which the bedrooms lead, completes the interior picture. Outside there are charming gardens with a duck pond.
3 rms (1 shr) No smoking No dogs Cen ht CTV No children 10yrs 10P 32 acres beef & sheep
PRICE GUIDE
ROOMS: s £30; d fr £43.47

BOWES Co Durham Map **12** NY91

♥ 🅀🅀🅀 Mr & Mrs Milner **East Mellwaters** (*NY967127*)
DL12 9RH (off A66, south side, signposted) ☎01833 628269
Closed mid Dec-mid Jan
Well furnished accommodation with a traditional farmhouse atmosphere is offered at this busy working farm set beside the winding road which leads from the A66 to the west of Bowes. A cosy lounge is provided for guests, and carefully prepared home-cooked meals are served.
5 en suite (bth/shr) (1 fmly) No smoking CTV in all bedrooms Tea and coffee making facilities Cen ht CTV 10P 350 acres beef sheep Last d 5.30pm
CARDS: 🔳 🔳

BOWNESS-ON-SOLWAY Cumbria Map **11** NY26

GH 🅀🅀 **Wallsend** Church Ln CA5 5AF ☎01697 351055
Previously the rectory, this spacious house is situated on the edge of Bowness on Solway. The house contains thousands of books, many of which are for sale.
3 rms No smoking Tea and coffee making facilities Cen ht CTV No children 10yrs 3P No coaches Last d noon

BOWNESS-ON-WINDERMERE Cumbria

See **Windermere**

BOX Wiltshire Map **03** ST86

GH 🅀🅀🅀 *Cheney Cottage* Ditteridge SN13 8QF (take A4 Bath-Chippenham road and just before Box turn left signposted Ditteridge. Continue to T-junct and turn left, house 0.5m on left) ☎01225 742346
Closed 24 Dec-1 Jan
This delightful, thatched, no-smoking cottage stands in four acres of well kept grounds and gardens, in an elevated position with glorious views across the Box Valley. Three bedrooms have been tastefully decorated and thoughtful extras such as shoe cleaning kits and hairdryers provided. Breakfast is served around one table in the wood-panelled dining room where a TV is available to guests.
3 rms (1 shr) No smoking Tea and coffee making facilities No dogs (ex guide dogs) Cen ht CTV 5P No coaches Tennis (hard) Snooker
See advertisement under BATH

Selected

GH 🅀🅀🅀🅀 **Hermitage** Bath Rd SN13 8DT (5m from Bath on A4 towards Chippenham, Hermitage is first drive on left after 30mph signs)
☎01225 744187 FAX 01225 744187
This 16th-century country house was once a hermitage and has been renovated and refurbished to a high standard. The comfortable bedrooms are bright and well equipped, and a beautiful swimming pool is heated from May to September. The welcoming proprietors are happy to suggest local eating places and help plan sightseeing routes; Bath is just five miles away and Stonehenge, Avebury, Salisbury Lacock and Cheddar are all within driving distance.
3 en suite (shr) 2 annexe en suite (shr) (2 fmly) No smoking CTV in all bedrooms Tea and coffee making facilities No dogs (ex guide dogs) Cen ht 9P No coaches Outdoor swimming pool (heated)
PRICE GUIDE
ROOMS: d £42-£52

See advertisement under BATH

BOXFORD Suffolk Map **05** TL94

GH 🅀🅀🅀 **Cox Hill House** CO10 5JG (off A134 onto A1071, take second sign left to Boxford, next right to Kersey. House 0.5m at top of Cox Hill.) ☎01787 210449
Closed 24-26 Dec
Cox Hill House sits amid delightful grounds and gardens in a splendidly peaceful and rural location overlooking the old wool village of Boxford. Accommodation is attractively decorated and comfortably furnished: two bedrooms have en suite bathrooms whilst the other has a private bathroom adjacent; a ground floor ➡

bedroom has particular appeal to the more mature guests who find stairs difficult. Breakfast can be taken communally in either a well appointed dining room or the pleasant country kitchen. Please note that this is a non-smoking house which is not suitable for young children.

3 en suite (bth/shr) No smoking CTV in all bedrooms Tea and coffee making facilities No dogs (ex guide dogs) No children 12yrs 20P No coaches
PRICE GUIDE
ROOMS: s £20-£30; d £37-£44

BRADFORD ON AVON Wiltshire Map **03** ST86

See also Rode

Premier Selected

GH ◻◻◻◻◻ **Bradford Old Windmill** 4 Masons Ln
BA15 1QN ☎01225 866842
FAX 01225 866648
rs no dinner served Sun,Tues,Wed,Fri
Hidden among trees on the steep hillside above the town, this stump of a windmill, lovingly restored by Peter and Priscilla Roberts, is an enchanting place to stay. The intriguing building, with its circular lounge, is furnished with character. Distinctly different bedrooms might offer a round bed, a water bed or a minstrels' gallery. The Roberts are well travelled and a collection of artefacts acquired over the years adds further interest. Dinner may be ordered the previous day, and one might sample the delights of vegetarian recipes picked up in Mexico, Nepal, the Gambia and Jamaica, to name but a few.
4 rms (1 bth 2 shr) (1 fmly) No smoking CTV in all bedrooms Tea and coffee making facilities No dogs Cen ht No children 6yrs 4P No coaches Last d previous day
PRICE GUIDE
ROOMS: s £39-£55; d £39-£75; wkly b&b fr £280

Premier Selected

GH ◻◻◻◻◻ **Burghope Manor** Winsley BA15 2LA
☎01225 723557
FAX 01225 723113
Closed Xmas/New Year
Set in beautifully tended grounds and gardens, this 13th-century family home is steeped in history and intrigue. It has been lovingly restored to provide three comfortable bedrooms and fine pubic rooms, all with a relaxing ambience. Burghope Manor within easy driving distance of Bath, Bristol, Bradford-on-Avon, Cheltenham, Wells and Glastonbury.
3 en suite (bth/shr) (1 fmly) No smoking in bedrooms No smoking in dining room No smoking in lounges CTV in all bedrooms Tea and coffee making facilities No dogs Cen ht

CTV No children 10yrs 20P Shooting and fishing by arrangement
PRICE GUIDE
ROOMS: s £45-£55; d £60-£70✳
CARDS:
£

Premier Selected

GH ◻◻◻◻◻ **Fern Cottage** 74 Monkton Farleigh BA15 2QJ (Turn off A363 at sign for Monkton Farleigh. After 1m turn right at T-junct by Manor House gates, first cottage on left)
☎01225 859412
FAX 01225 859018
This 17th-century stone-built cottage nestles in the charming conservation village of Monkton Farleigh. Three beautifully presented bedrooms are available to guests, one in a coach house close to the cottage. Public areas feature oak beams, log fires and family possessions. A traditional breakfast may be taken at a large, attractively arranged table and there is a lovely conservatory where guests may relax looking out over the well tended cottage garden.
2 en suite (bth/shr) 1 annexe en suite (bth/shr) No smoking CTV in all bedrooms Tea and coffee making facilities No dogs (ex guide dogs) Cen ht 5P No coaches
PRICE GUIDE
ROOMS: s £28-£30; d £45-£50

Premier Selected

GH ◻◻◻◻◻ **Irondale** 67 High St BA3 6PB BATH
☎01373 830730 FAX 01373 830730
(For full entry see Rode)

Premier Selected

GH ◻◻◻◻◻ *Widbrook Grange* Trowbridge Rd BA15 1UH (1m from town centre beyond the canal bridge on A363)
☎01225 863173 & 864750
FAX 01225 862890
John and Pauline Price, together with their daughter Karen, welcome guests to this Grade II listed property which was formerly a working farm. The majority of the bedrooms are located in converted farm buildings set around the courtyard; each room is individually decorated and features lovely fabrics and antique furnishings. Fixed-price dinners offering a varied choice are served Monday-Thursday. An indoor pool and mini-gym are available to guests, and in the grounds the oldest remaining examples of red brick bee

boles can be seen.
4 rms (3 bth/shr) 15 annexe en suite (bth/shr) (2 fmly) No smoking in dining room CTV in all bedrooms Tea and coffee making facilities Direct dial from bedrooms No dogs Licensed Cen ht 60P Indoor swimming pool (heated) Gymnasium Last d 6.30pm
CARDS:

BRADING See **WIGHT, ISLE OF**

BRAFFERTON North Yorkshire Map **08** SE47

Selected

GH Q Q Q Q **Brafferton Hall** YO6 2NZ (take Hall Lane from village centre, house at top of road on left)
☎01423 360352 FAX 01423 360352
Best described as a private home accepting paying guests, this house was built in the 1740s and is set in a pleasant village by the River Swale. Delightfully furnished bedrooms offer good facilities, there are comfortable lounges, and dinner is served around one large communal table.
4 rms (2 bth 1 shr) No smoking CTV in all bedrooms Tea and coffee making facilities No dogs (ex guide dogs) Cen ht CTV 6P
PRICE GUIDE
ROOMS: s £30.50; d £60; wkly b&b £190; wkly hlf-bd £310
CARDS: (£)

BRAINTREE Essex Map **05** TL72

🖂 🖵 💙 Q Q Q Mrs J Reddington **Park** *(TL812223)* Church Rd, Bradwell CM7 8EP (turn off A120 beside The Swan PH signposted Bradwell Village continue for half a mile farmhouse stands back from the road on right)
☎01376 563584
Accommodation includes a four-poster bed.
2 rms No smoking Tea and coffee making facilities No dogs (ex guide dogs) Cen ht CTV No children 12yrs 3P 1 acres arable
PRICE GUIDE
ROOMS: s £16-£32

BRAITHWAITE Cumbria Map **11** NY22

GH Q Q Q **Maple Bank** CA12 5RY (just off A66 to N of Keswick) ☎01768 778229
Maple Bank is an attractive Edwardian residence set in an acre of garden two miles west of Keswick. Bedrooms are well equipped and tastefully decorated, and many have views of Skiddaw. There are a comfortable guests' lounge and an attractive dining room where well prepared evening meals are served.
7 en suite (shr) (1 fmly) No smoking in 1 bedrooms No smoking in dining room CTV in all bedrooms Tea and coffee making facilities No dogs Licensed Cen ht CTV No children 12yrs 10P No coaches Free access to lawn tennis/bowling club Last d 4pm
PRICE GUIDE
ROOMS: d £42-£45; wkly b&b £142-£150; wkly hlf-bd £200-£207
CARDS: (£)

BRAMPTON Cumbria Map **12** NY56

See also Castle Carrock

GH Q Q Q **Denton House** Low Row CA8 2LQ (4m E on A69) ☎016977 46278 FAX 016977 46278
This attractive Victorian house is situated in open countryside beside the A69, close to Hadrian's Wall. The main bedrooms are spacious and very well furnished, and there is a comfortable guest lounge with lovely views towards the Scottish border.
3 rms No smoking in bedrooms No smoking in dining room Tea and coffee making facilities Cen ht CTV 4P
PRICE GUIDE
ROOMS: s £13-£15; d £30✳
(£)

Selected

GH Q Q Q Q **Oakwood Park Hotel** Longtown Rd CA8 2AP (from M6 take the A69 at junct 43, to Brampton) ☎016977 2436
A large Victorian house standing in its own gardens and parkland off the A6071, just north, of the town offers generally spacious bedrooms, the master room being suitable for family use; all have en suite facilities and are comfortably furnished in traditional style. Downstairs there are an elegant lounge, an interesting library bar in which guests can enjoy pre-dinner drinks and a pleasant dining room - warmed by an open fire on chilly days - which is open to non-residents for afternoon tea and dinner.
5 en suite (bth/shr) (1 fmly) No smoking in bedrooms CTV in all bedrooms Tea and coffee making facilities No dogs (ex guide dogs) Licensed Cen ht CTV 12P No coaches Last d 8pm

---

Widbrook Grange

Trowbridge Road, Bradford-on-Avon
Wiltshire BA15 1UH
Tel: 01225 864750 & 863173 Fax: 01225 862890

John and Pauline Price extend a warm welcome to their elegant, peaceful Georgian home in eleven secluded acres. The house and courtyard rooms, and the Manvers Suite for conferences and seminars, have been lovingly restored and exquisitely decorated and furnished with antiques. New indoor swimming pool. Evening Dinner is offered in the Dining Room with an interesting selection of wines.

PRICE GUIDE
ROOMS: s fr £26; d fr £40✳
CARDS: ▨ ▨

Selected

❤ ℚℚℚℚ Mrs M Stobart *Cracrop* (NY521697)
Kirkcambeck CA8 2BW (off B6318, 7m N of town)
☎016977 48245 FAX 016977 48333
Jan-Nov
An early-Victorian farmhouse, situated on a 400-acre working
farm raising pedigree Ayrshire cattle, offers four carefully
modernised en suite bedrooms which still retain much of their
original character. Public areas include a very comfortable
guests' lounge, a games room and the pleasant dining room in
which traditional country breakfasts are served. Marked trails
make it easy for visitors to explore the farm.
3 en suite (shr) (2 fmly) No smoking CTV in all bedrooms
Tea and coffee making facilities No dogs (ex guide dogs)
Cen ht CTV No children 3P Fishing Sauna 425 acres
arable beef dairy mixed sheep Last d 1pm
CARDS: ▨

◀ ℚℚℚ **The Blacksmiths Arms** Talkin Village CA8 1LE
(A69 to Brampton, take B6413 to Castle Carrock, after
railway level crossing take second left sigposted Talkin)
☎016977 3452
This typical Cumbrian inn is situated in the village of Talkin,
winner of the best kept small village in the Carlisle area.
Bedrooms are of a very good standard, all with en suite facilities
and TV. A good range of bar food is provided, together with an
extensive choice of dishes in the cosy restaurant.
5 en suite (bth/shr) CTV in all bedrooms Tea and coffee making
facilities No dogs (ex guide dogs) 12P No coaches Games
room Last d 9pm
PRICE GUIDE
ROOMS: s £28; d £40✳
MEALS: Lunch £6-£17alc Dinner £6-£17alc✳
CARDS: ▨ ▨ ▨ £

BRANDON Suffolk Map **05** TL78

GH ℚℚℚ *Riverside Lodge* 78 High St IP27 0AU
☎01842 811236
Ideally situated by the river and on the fringe of the town centre,
this homely, family-run guest house offers comfortably appointed
bedrooms; all are en suite and have modern facilities. In addition,
guests have the use of a comfortable lounge. There are ample
parking facilities.
3 en suite (bth/shr) (1 fmly) CTV in all bedrooms Tea and coffee
making facilities No dogs (ex guide dogs) Cen ht CTV 10P No
coaches Tennis (grass) Fishing

BRANSFORD Hereford & Worcester Map **03** SO75

GH ℚ **Croft** WR6 5JD (on A4103, 4m from Worcester)
☎01886 832227
Dating back in part to the 16th century, this house stands in its
own mature gardens on the outskirts of Bransford village.
Bedrooms have a mixture of modern and older furniture, and all
have radios and tea trays; some rooms with en suite facilities are
available. There is a television in the cosy lounge, and separate
tables are provided in the pleasant, traditionally furnished dining
room.
5 rms (3 shr) (1 fmly) No smoking in bedrooms Tea and coffee
making facilities Licensed Cen ht CTV 5P No coaches Sauna

Jacuzzi Arrangement with golf course Last d 5.30pm
PRICE GUIDE
ROOMS: s £18-£25; d £35.50-£43; wkly b&b
£124.25-£161
CARDS: ▨ ▨ ▨ £

BRANSGORE Hampshire Map **04** SZ19

Selected

GH ℚℚℚℚ **Tothill House** Black Ln, off Forest Rd
BH23 8DZ (from A35, turn right into Forest Road, left into
Black Lane and house is third gate on the right)
☎01425 674414 FAX 01425 672235
In a remote New Forest location, this Edwardian gentleman's
residence is set in 12 acres of woodland. The spacious
bedrooms are individually furnished and provided with many
extras. There are a small library lounge and an impressive
breakfast room with a large communal table.
3 rms (2 shr) No smoking CTV in all bedrooms Tea and
coffee making facilities No dogs (ex guide dogs) Cen ht
CTV No children 16yrs 10P No coaches
PRICE GUIDE
ROOMS: d fr £50✳

Selected

GH ℚℚℚℚ **Wiltshire House** West Rd BH23 8BD
☎01425 672450
This attractive Victorian property, tucked away n the village
of Bransgore, in the west of the New Forest, is only a short
drive from the coast. The bedrooms are large and comfortably
furnished; all have colour television, hairdryers and en suite
facilities. Children are welcome and one of the rooms has a
small room with bunk beds adjoining it. There is a cosy
lounge with a log burning fire in the winter, and a pretty
garden.
3 rms (2 bth/shr) (2 fmly) No smoking CTV in 2 bedrooms
Tea and coffee making facilities No dogs (ex guide dogs)
Cen ht CTV 4P No coaches
PRICE GUIDE
ROOMS: s £16-£25; d £32-£40; wkly b&b £100-£120✳

BRATTON FLEMING Devon Map **03** SS63

Selected

GH ℚℚℚℚ **Bracken House** EX31 4TG (off A399,
signposted Bratton Fleming, left hand side, just after Post
Office) ☎01598 710320
late Mar-early Nov
Built as a rectory in 1840, the house stands in eight acres of
woodland and gardens, with a paddock and a small lake.
Bedrooms are well equipped and attractively decorated, and
two are on the ground floor. There is a comfortable lounge
with a well-stocked bar, and a wide range of books and
leaflets is available in the library. A fixed-price menu with a
vegetarian option is served in the dining room.
8 en suite (bth/shr) No smoking in dining room No smoking
in 1 lounge CTV in all bedrooms Tea and coffee making
facilities Licensed Cen ht No children 8yrs 12P No
coaches Croquet Library Last d 6pm

PRICE GUIDE
ROOMS: s £31-£47; d £52-£64; wkly b&b £147-£189;
wkly hlf-bd £245-£287
CARDS: £

BRAUNTON Devon Map **02** SS43

GH QQQ *Alexander Brookdale Hotel* 62 South St
EX33 2AN ☎01271 812075
Mike and Wendy Sargeant's friendly guest house provides neat,
light and airy bedrooms. A spacious bar-lounge is provided as
well as a separate first-floor lounge. Dinner is served by
arrangement in the simply furnished dining room.
8 rms (2 fmly) No smoking in bedrooms No smoking in dining
room CTV in all bedrooms Tea and coffee making facilities No
dogs (ex guide dogs) Licensed Cen ht CTV No children 8yrs
9P No coaches Last d 11am

BREDWARDINE Hereford & Worcester Map **03** SO34

Selected

GH QQQQ Bredwardine Hall HR3 6DB
☎01981 500596
Mar-Oct
A beautifully preserved stone-built manor house dating from
the middle of the 19th century, Bredwardine Hall is set in its
own spacious and mature gardens. There are four large
bedrooms (some of them suitable for family occupation) with
en suite facilities, and a fifth, smaller, room with a private
bathroom. All are attractively decorated and have modern
furnishings and equipment. The lounge is comfortable, and a
dining room with separate tables has its own small bar.
5 rms (3 bth 1 shr) No smoking in bedrooms No smoking in
dining room CTV in all bedrooms Tea and coffee making
facilities No dogs (ex guide dogs) Licensed Cen ht No
children 10yrs 7P No coaches Last d 4.30pm
PRICE GUIDE
ROOMS: s £33-£35; d £46-£50; wkly b&b £150.50-
£164.50; wkly hlf-bd £231-£245
£

See advertisement under HEREFORD

BRENDON Devon Map **03** SS74

GH Q Brendon House Hotel EX35 6PS ☎01598 741206
Closed 2 Nov-30 Dec rs 30 Dec-1 Mar
Brendon lies in one of the hidden valleys of Exmoor, on the banks
of the Lyn. Built in 1780, it now is the haunt of walkers, fishermen
and those who wish to explore north Devon. Bedrooms are cosy
and the lounge has antique furniture and paintings.
5 rms (1 bth 1 shr) (1 fmly) No smoking in dining room CTV in
2 bedrooms Tea and coffee making facilities Licensed Cen ht
CTV 5P Fishing permits sold for River Lyn Last d 5pm
PRICE GUIDE
ROOMS: s £18.50-£20.50; d £37-£41; wkly b&b £133-£140;
wkly hlf-bd £193-£200✶
£

BRENT ELEIGH Suffolk Map **05** TL94

♥ QQQ Mrs J P Gage Street *(TL945476)* CO10 9NU (access
from A1141 Lavenham/Hadleigh road) ☎01787 247271
Mar-Oct
A charming farmhouse with an attractive, well kept garden has
been thoughtfully furnished and tastefully decorated throughout. ➡

Breakfast is served round a communal table in the small dining room, and the relaxing sitting room - made homely by books, pictures and ornaments - features an inglenook fireplace. Spacious, comfortably appointed bedrooms retain their original high ceilings and wooden beams.

3 rms (2 bth/shr) No smoking in bedrooms No smoking in dining room Tea and coffee making facilities No dogs Cen ht CTV No children 12yrs 4P 143 acres arable

PRICE GUIDE

ROOMS: d fr £40✱

BRIDESTOWE Devon Map 02 SX58

♥ Q Q Mrs J E Down **Little Bidlake** *(SX494887)* EX20 4NS (turn off A30 at the Sourton Cross exit and take old A30 road to Bridestowe) ☎01837 861233

Etr-Nov

Little Bidlake is a lovely old farmhouse full of the bustle of family life and the everyday events of a large working farm. The two cheerful bedrooms, comfortable lounge and attractive dining room are complemented by the warm hospitality offered by the Downs family.

2 rms Tea and coffee making facilities No dogs (ex guide dogs) Cen ht CTV P Fishing 150 acres beef dairy mixed Last d 7.30pm

PRICE GUIDE

ROOMS: d £30-£35; wkly b&b £91-£100; wkly hlf-bd £140-£150

(£)

♥ Q Q Q Mrs M Hockridge **Week** *(SX519913)* EX20 4HZ ☎01837 861221

This 17th-century stone-built farmhouse on a working farm, is approached from the old A30, and has easy access to both the north and south coasts of Devon. Bedrooms include a family room on the ground floor. The comfortable lounge has an open fireplace, and guests can enjoy home-cooked dinners served at separate tables in the dining room. Mrs Hockridge offers a warm welcome and a relaxed atmosphere.

5 en suite (bth/shr) (2 fmly) No smoking in dining room No smoking in lounges CTV in all bedrooms Tea and coffee making facilities Cen ht CTV 10P Outdoor swimming pool (heated) 180 acres dairy mixed sheep Last d 5pm

PRICE GUIDE

ROOMS: s £20-£22; d £40-£44; wkly b&b £140-£154; wkly hlf-bd £210-£240✱

(£)

BRIDGNORTH Shropshire Map 07 SO79

GH Q Q Q **Severn Arms Hotel** Underhill St, Low Town WV16 4BB (turn off A442, onto B4363 and establishment facing river bridge crossing) ☎01746 764616

2 Jan-Nov

This tall, terraced property is situated at the foot of the cliff which separates Bridgnorth High and Low Towns, opposite the bridge which crosses the River Severn. The bedrooms have a mixture of modern and traditional furniture but all have modern equipment. One room is situated in an annexe cottage to the rear of the main house, and family rooms are available; front rooms have lovely views of the old bridge. There are a comfortable lounge with a small bar and a pleasant dining room with separate tables.

9 rms (2 bth 3 shr) (5 fmly) CTV in 8 bedrooms Tea and coffee making facilities Direct dial from bedrooms Licensed Cen ht CTV Fishing Last d 4pm

PRICE GUIDE

ROOMS: s £22.50-£34.50; d £37-£44; wkly b&b £123-£143; wkly hlf-bd £165-£185✱

CARDS: 🔳 🔳 🔳 🔳 🔳

(£)

◀ Q Q Q **Bulls Head** Chelmarsh WV16 6BA (S on B4555, 200 yds passed Chelmarsh church on right hand side) ☎01746 861469

rs 25 Dec

This friendly inn is situated south of Bridgenorth, alongside the B4555 in the village of Chelmarsh. Parts of it date back over 300 years, and it has been considerably extended at various times. Accommodation is smart and modern, all bedrooms having en suite bath or shower rooms. There is a quiet first floor lounge, and the bar, which is in three parts, features wood-burning stoves. There is a large car park available.

6 en suite (bth/shr) 1 annexe en suite (bth/shr) (2 fmly) No smoking in dining room No smoking in 1 lounge CTV in 6 bedrooms Tea and coffee making facilities Cen ht CTV 50P Solarium Jacuzzi Last d 9.30pm

CARDS: 🔳 🔳 🔳 🔳 🔳

◀ Q **Kings Head Hotel** Whitburn St WV16 4QN (off main street of High Town down narrow road) ☎01746 762141

Over 350 years old, this black and white timbered inn lies in the centre of the historic market town. Cosy bars featuring original oak beams, exposed timbers and inglenook fireplaces serve a good range of food, there is a separate breakfast room, and bedrooms include several suitable for family occupation.

5 rms (3 fmly) CTV in all bedrooms Tea and coffee making facilities No dogs (ex guide dogs) Cen ht 7P No coaches Snooker Last d 9pm

---

BRIDGWATER Somerset Map 03 ST33

🛏 💺 **GH** Q Q Q **Chinar** 17 Oakfield Rd TA6 7LX ☎01278 458639

The home of Guy and Rosemary Bret is located in a quiet residential area of the town, offering off street parking. Both bedrooms are neatly decorated and furnished, and the small double room whilst not fully ensuite has an ensuite WC. A comfortable lounge is available for guests use, and at the rear of the property is a charming, colourful garden. At breakfast time an imaginative selection of dishes are available, including muffins, waffles and scrambled eggs with smoked salmon, as alternatives to the full English breakfast.

2 rms (1 bth/shr) No smoking in bedrooms CTV in all bedrooms Tea and coffee making facilities Cen ht CTV No children 6yrs 2P No coaches

PRICE GUIDE

ROOMS: s £16-£20; d £34-£36; wkly b&b fr £96

Selected

GH Q Q Q Q **Woodlands** 35 Durleigh Rd TA6 7HX (from M5 junct24 head to Bridgwater, left at 1st major lights by Safeway, in approx 0.75m narrow drive on left to Woodlands) ☎01278 423442

This fine Victorian Grade II listed family home is quietly situated in two acres of well tended grounds and yet is only a short drive from the centre of town. Carefully restored by resident proprietors Mr and Mrs Palmer, it offers charming, individually styled bedrooms which enjoy pleasant views of the gardens. Breakfast is served in an elegant dining room which also has comfortable seating and a video for guests' use; dinner is offered by prior arrangement.

4 rms (3 bth/shr) No smoking in bedrooms No smoking in dining room CTV in all bedrooms Tea and coffee making facilities No dogs (ex guide dogs) Cen ht CTV No children 10yrs 4P No coaches Last d 3pm

PRICE GUIDE

ROOMS: s £18-£27; d £37-£42; wkly b&b £110-£175; wkly hlf-bd £180-£245

CARDS: 🔳 🔳

BRIDLINGTON Humberside Map 08 TA16

GH QQQ Bay Ridge Hotel Summerfield Rd YO15 3LF
☎01262 673425

A pleasantly run family hotel stands in a quiet side road close to the seafront and the town centre. Public rooms are inviting; the main lounge is comfortable and is backed up by a smaller non-smoking area, while the dining room serves interesting selections of well produced food. The owners are caring and provide friendly service.

14 rms (6 bth 6 shr) (5 fmly) No smoking in dining room CTV in all bedrooms Tea and coffee making facilities Licensed Cen ht CTV 7P Bar billiards Darts Library Last d 5.45pm

PRICE GUIDE
ROOMS: s £18.50-£19.50; d £37-£39; wkly b&b £115-£125; wkly hlf-bd £135-£155✱
CARDS: £

GH QQQ Langdon Hotel Pembroke Ter YO15 3BX
☎01262 400124 FAX 01262 400124

This family-owned hotel situated close to the seafront and the Spa Theatre offers comfortable accommodation. Ample public areas include a small patio and a cosy bar; bright bedrooms are well equipped, attractively decorated and mostly en suite.

20 rms (11 shr) (8 fmly) CTV in all bedrooms Tea and coffee making facilities No dogs (ex guide dogs) Licensed Lift Cen ht 3P Last d noon

PRICE GUIDE
ROOMS: s £20; d £40; wkly hlf-bd £162.50-£172.50✱ £

GH QQQ Marton Grange Flamborough Rd, Marton cum Sewerby YO15 1DU (on B1255, 600yds from Links golf club)
☎01262 602034 FAX 01262 602034

Located on the B1255 at Marton, this detached house in its own gardens provides very good facilities for the disabled guests for whom it caters in the main. Bedrooms are thoughtfully equipped and there are a cosy lounge and dining room, both of which overlook the pleasant gardens. It also has the benefit of a lift and special diets can be catered for.

10 en suite (bth/shr) (1 fmly) No smoking in 1 bedrooms No smoking in dining room No smoking in lounges CTV in all bedrooms Tea and coffee making facilities Lift Cen ht No children 2yrs 12P No coaches Last d 5pm

PRICE GUIDE
ROOMS: s £15-£17; d £28-£32✱ £

GH QQQ Southdowne Hotel 78 South Marine Dr YO15 3NS
☎01262 673270

This restful hotel is superbly positioned overlooking the sea, with uninterrupted views from Hornsea to Flamborough Head. The sunny dining room serves excellent-value home-cooked food. A comfortable lounge and a TV room are also available, and there is parking to the front of the house.

12 rms (8 shr) (2 fmly) CTV in 8 bedrooms Tea and coffee making facilities No dogs Licensed Cen ht CTV 10P No coaches Last d 5.30pm

PRICE GUIDE
ROOMS: s £18-£20; d £36-£40; wkly b&b £120-£130; wkly hlf-bd £160-£170✱

GH QQQ The Tennyson Hotel 19 Tennyson Av YO15 2EU (follow signs to North Beach, Tennyson Avenue is opposite sea front car park) ☎01262 604382 FAX 01262 604382

The Tennyson stands in a quiet side road close to the town centre and provides well equipped, individually styled bedrooms, one with a four-poster bed. The lounge is comfortable and the cosy dining room serves a high standard of food; Mrs Stalker has been

awarded a Heart Beat award for her healthy cooking, which is mainly British in style with occasional flambé dishes.

6 rms (3 bth 2 shr) No smoking in bedrooms No smoking in dining room CTV in all bedrooms Tea and coffee making facilities Licensed Cen ht No children 12yrs 3P Last d 8.30pm

PRICE GUIDE
ROOMS: s £20-£24.95; d £32-£44; wkly b&b £96-£132
CARDS: £

BRIDPORT Dorset Map 03 SY49

See also Bettiscombe

GH QQQQ Britmead House West Bay Rd DT6 4EG (approaching Bridport follow signs for West Bay,Britmead House is 800yds S of the A35)
☎01308 422941

This attractive private hotel is only a short walk from either the market town of Bridport or the quaint little harbour of West Bay. Bedrooms are equipped with every modern comfort and many thoughtful extras. There are a cosy lounge which overlooks the garden and an attractive dining room where fresh local produce is used wherever possible. A carefully chosen wine list complements the dishes served.

7 rms (6 bth/shr) (1 fmly) No smoking in dining room CTV in all bedrooms Tea and coffee making facilities Licensed Cen ht No children 5yrs 8P Last d 6pm

 AA ★

Bridge House is a pretty Georgian town house. Comfortable bedrooms with a bright and sunny breakfast room where you can enjoy a full breakfast menu. The hotel has gained an **AA rosette for food and service**. Family rooms available. All rooms are en suite and have tea and coffee facilities, colour TV and direct dial telephone. Major credit cards accepted. Own private car park.

**115 East Street, Bridport, Dorset DT6 3LB
Telephone: 01308 423371**

PRICE GUIDE
ROOMS: s £24-£34; d £38-£54; wkly b&b £105-£140; wkly hlf-bd £189-£224
CARDS: £

BRIGHTON & HOVE East Sussex Map **04** TQ30

See also Rottingdean

Selected

GH ◻◻◻◻ **Adelaide Hotel** 51 Regency Square BN1 2FF (on sea front opposite West Pier) (Logis) ☎01273 205286 FAX 01273 220904
Perfectly positioned close to the conference centre, exhibition halls, seafront and town centre, this quality hotel built about 170 years ago has been lovingly restored by proprietors Clive and Ruth Buxton in keeping with its Grade II listed status whilst providing every modern amenity. Bedrooms are once again being completely refurbished and upgraded, and the many thoughtful little extras, as well as room service of light refreshments and snacks, all add to the very high standards which regular guests have now come to expect at this good quality small hotel. There are a comfortable and well furnished lounge with writing desk and an attractive bright dining room where dinner is available by prior arrangement.
12 en suite (bth/shr) No smoking in dining room CTV in all bedrooms Tea and coffee making facilities Direct dial from bedrooms No dogs Licensed Cen ht No parking No coaches Last d 5pm
PRICE GUIDE
ROOMS: s £34-£60; d £55-£75; wkly b&b £154-£210; wkly hlf-bd £255.50-£311.50
CARDS: ◼◼◼◼ £

GH ◻◻◻ **Ainsley House Hotel** 28 New Steine BN2 1PD ☎01273 605310 FAX 01273 688604
Closed 24-27 Dec
This charming Regency terraced house near the front overlooks the sea and Palace Pier and offers comfortable accommodation in well maintained modern bedrooms. The smartly appointed breakfast room is combined with a small, comfortably furnished lounge, and proprietress Mrs King creates a welcoming and cheerful atmosphere throughout.
11 rms (8 shr) (3 fmly) No smoking in dining room CTV in all bedrooms Tea and coffee making facilities Direct dial from bedrooms No dogs (ex guide dogs) Cen ht CTV Last d 5pm
PRICE GUIDE
ROOMS: s £20-£30; d £42-£60
CARDS: ◼◼◼◼ £

GH ◻◻◻ *Allendale Hotel* 3 New Steine BN2 1PB ☎01273 675436 FAX 01273 602603
Closed 2 weeks over Christmas
Situated in one of Brighton's attractive seafront garden squares, this converted Regency town house is conveniently located close to the pier, conference centre, Royal Pavilion and shops. The bedrooms are immaculate, tastefully decorated and comfortably furnished; several are en suite, all are equipped with every possible convenience and front rooms enjoy fine sea views. A small lounge area adjoins the breakfast room, where full English or continental breakfast is served, and the hotel is licensed.
13 rms (6 shr) (5 fmly) No smoking in dining room CTV in all bedrooms Licensed Cen ht No parking Last d noon
CARDS:

GH ◻◻◻ **Alvia Hotel** 36 Upper Rock Gardens BN2 1QF ☎01273 682939
Ideally positioned for easy access to the seafront and town centre, this family-run bed and breakfast establishment has a friendly and informal atmosphere. Bedrooms vary in shape and size, but all are well furnished and modern. Guests have a choice of breakfast dishes, including vegan and vegetarian options. Continental breakfast, if preferred, can now be served to the room between 9 and 9.30am. There is a secure car park to the rear.
10 rms (7 bth/shr) (2 fmly) No smoking in 8 bedrooms No smoking in dining room No smoking in lounges CTV in 9 bedrooms Tea and coffee making facilities No dogs (ex guide dogs) Cen ht 5P
PRICE GUIDE
ROOMS: s £16-£18; d £38-£45; wkly b&b £96-£135
CARDS: £

GH ◻◻◻ **Ambassador Hotel** 22 New Steine, Marine Pde BN2 1PD ☎01273 676869 FAX 01273 689988
Thoughtfully decorated and furnished, this smart Regency terrace house near the Palace pier and seafront is also within walking distance of the town. Bedrooms vary in size, but all are well equipped and pleasantly furnished; a small, comfortably furnished sitting room and attractive dining room make up the public areas.
10 en suite (bth/shr) (3 fmly) No smoking in dining room CTV in all bedrooms Tea and coffee making facilities Direct dial from bedrooms No dogs Licensed Cen ht CTV No parking
PRICE GUIDE
ROOMS: s £23-£30; d £40-£60; wkly b&b £138-£180
CARDS: £

Selected

GH ◻◻◻◻ **Amblecliff Hotel** 35 Upper Rock Gardens BN2 1QF ☎01273 681161 & 676945 FAX 01273 676945
Bright and individually furnished in today's style, the predominantly non-smoking bedrooms of this friendly and personally run guest house have been carefully designed to combine good levels of comfort with every modern amenity. A continental breakfast can either be delivered to the bedroom or, like its English counterpart, served in a well appointed breakfast/sitting room. Restricted pay-and-display car parking is available, and private parking can usually be arranged.
8 en suite (bth/shr) (3 fmly) No smoking CTV in 11 bedrooms Tea and coffee making facilities Direct dial from bedrooms No dogs (ex guide dogs) Licensed Cen ht CTV No children 4yrs 3P
PRICE GUIDE
ROOMS: s £18.50-£20; d £37-£54; wkly b&b £117-£162✳
CARDS: £

Selected

GH ◻◻◻◻ **Arlanda Hotel** 20 New Steine BN2 1PD ☎01273 699300 FAX 01273 600930
This very comfortable, attractively furnished, residentially licensed guest house stands close to the sea front and within walking distance of the town centre and conference centre. Recent upgrading and refurbishment with good quality co-ordinated furnishings has improved the quality of the bedrooms to a high standard, and whilst some double rooms are smaller they are all well equipped with trouser presses, direct dial telephones, TV, luggage racks, controllable heating, and tea trays. The atmosphere is very friendly and informal

with service provided by the resident proprietors Karenza and Ken Matthews. Light refreshments can be provided throughout the daytime, breakfast is included in the room tariff and a fixed-price daily dinner menu and wine list are available, subject to last orders by 4pm.

12 en suite (bth/shr) (4 fmly) No smoking in dining room CTV in all bedrooms Tea and coffee making facilities Direct dial from bedrooms No dogs (ex guide dogs) Licensed Cen ht Last d 4pm

PRICE GUIDE
ROOMS: s £18-£36; d £44-£72; wkly b&b £112-£224✳

CARDS: 🄰 ▬ 🄫 🄿   £

GH 🄠🄠🄠 **Ascott House Hotel** 21 New Steine, Marine Pde BN2 1PD ☎01273 688085 FAX 01273 623733

This small, friendly hotel is situated in a smart garden square opposite the sea and personally run by proprietors Michael and Avril Strong. Most of the bedrooms have en suite facilities, and although they vary in size they are all attractively decorated, immaculately maintained and exceptionally well equipped. Snacks are available throughout the day, and there is a short but varied evening meal menu. The dining room is tastefully appointed in period style, and there is a cosy adjoining lounge as well as a foyer bar/reception area.

12 rms (10 shr) (8 fmly) No smoking in dining room CTV in all bedrooms Tea and coffee making facilities Direct dial from bedrooms No dogs Licensed Cen ht No children 3yrs No parking Last d 4pm

PRICE GUIDE
ROOMS: s £18-£36; d £42-£70✳

CARDS: 🄰 ▬ 🄫 🄿

GH ◻◻◻ **At The Twenty One** 21 Charlotte St, Marine Pde BN2 1AG (turn off A23 onto A259 towards Newhaven proceed for 0.5m) ☎01273 686450 FAX 01273 607711
This charming Victorian town house in the Kemp Town area has a good location close to the seafront and the Marina complex. Bedrooms are comfortably furnished with modern facilities; one room features a four-poster bed. Downstairs there is a pretty lounge with attractive soft furnishings and an attractively appointed, cosy dining room where breakfasts are served.
6 rms (5 shr) CTV in all bedrooms Tea and coffee making facilities Direct dial from bedrooms No dogs (ex guide dogs) Licensed Cen ht No children 9yrs No coaches Last d 9am
PRICE GUIDE
ROOMS: s £35-£50; d £46-£68
CARDS: ▨ ▧ ▨ £

GH ◻◻◻ **Brighton Marina House Hotel** 8 Charlotte St, Marine Pde BN2 1AG
☎01273 605349 & 679484 FAX 01273 605349
Conveniently located close to the seafront for easy access to the town centre, this family-run guest house offers a range of varied quality bedrooms, each of them equipped with TV, hairdryer, clock radio, and tea tray. Both continental and full English breakfasts are served in the small downstairs dining room which also contains the office and reception facilities. Dinner can be provided by prior arrangement, and authentic Indian curries are regularly featured. Friendly service is personally provided by the Jung family.
10 rms (7 shr) (3 fmly) CTV in all bedrooms Tea and coffee making facilities No dogs Licensed Cen ht No parking No coaches Last d 4pm
PRICE GUIDE
ROOMS: s £13.50-£25; d £33-£50; wkly b&b £81-£150; wkly hlf-bd £150-£220✳
CARDS: ▨ ▧ ▨ ⑩ £

GH ◻◻◻ **Cavalaire House** 34 Upper Rock Gardens BN2 1QF (follow A259 towards Newhaven, turn left at second set of traffic lights) ☎01273 696899 FAX 01273 600504
Closed Xmas & New Year
This well maintained guest house provides accommodation in compact but thoughtfully equipped bedrooms with attractive soft furnishings. Open-plan public areas are made up of a small, comfortable lounge and an attractively appointed dining room offering a choice of breakfasts.
9 rms (3 shr) (2 fmly) No smoking in dining room CTV in all bedrooms Tea and coffee making facilities Cen ht No children 5yrs No parking No coaches
PRICE GUIDE
ROOMS: s £16-£19; d £38-£44✳
CARDS: ▨ ▧ ▨ ⑩

GH ◻◻ **Cornerways Private Hotel** 18-20 Caburn Rd BN3 6EF (A270 Old Shoreham Road, adjacent to crossroads at junct with Dyke Road) ☎01273 731882
This large Victorian corner house offers basic but comfortable accommodation in modestly furnished bedrooms. The small lounge on the ground floor has recently been upgraded, a choice of breakfasts is provided and an evening meal is available at a reasonable price.
10 rms (1 shr) (2 fmly) CTV in 6 bedrooms Tea and coffee making facilities Licensed Cen ht CTV No parking Last d 2pm
PRICE GUIDE
ROOMS: s fr £17; d £34-£40; wkly b&b £106-£112; wkly hlf-bd £162-£168✳

GH ◻◻ **Dudley House** 10 Madeira Place BN2 1TN
☎01273 676794
Proprietors Mr and Mrs Lacey continue to provide well maintained accommodation in their smart terraced house which is located close to the seafront and all amenities. Simply furnished bedrooms vary in size but are all suitably equipped. The small sitting room and cosy dining room both feature attractive marble fireplaces, plants and flowers, and a good traditional English breakfast is served.
6 rms (3 shr) (3 fmly) CTV in all bedrooms Tea and coffee making facilities No dogs (ex guide dogs) Cen ht CTV No children 5yrs
PRICE GUIDE
ROOMS: d £30-£36; wkly b&b £100-£160✳

GH ◻◻◻ **Gullivers** 10 New Steine BN2 1PB
☎01273 695415 FAX 01252 372774
This mid-terrace Regency residence is close to the seafront and all amenities. The attractively decorated bedrooms feature floral duvets that co-ordinate with the curtains; all have direct-dial telephones and with the majority also benefit from en suite facilities. Breakfast is served in the bright dining room by the friendly owner, Sally Gannaway.
9 rms (5 shr) (3 fmly) No smoking in dining room No smoking in lounges CTV in all bedrooms Tea and coffee making facilities Direct dial from bedrooms Cen ht
PRICE GUIDE
ROOMS: s £18-£22; d £38-£48✳
CARDS: ▨ ▧ ▨ ⑩ £

GH ◻◻◻ **Kempton House Hotel** 33/34 Marine Pde BN2 1TR ☎01273 570248 FAX 01273 570248
This small hotel on the seafront, personally run in informal style by its proprietors, provides accommodation in attractive bedrooms which, though not large, are equipped with direct dial telephones, clock radios, TVs, hairdryers, trouser presses and tea trays. Public rooms comprise a combined dining room and bar reception area.
12 en suite (shr) (4 fmly) CTV in all bedrooms Tea and coffee making facilities Direct dial from bedrooms Licensed Cen ht Last d 9am
PRICE GUIDE
ROOMS: d £40-£50; wkly b&b £140-£165; wkly hlf-bd £225-£255
CARDS: ▨ ▧ ▨ ▨ £

GH ◻◻ **Kimberley Hotel** 17 Atlingworth St BN2 1PL
☎01273 603504 FAX 01273 603504
Quietly situated in a residential area, this family-run private hotel includes in its public areas a comfortable lounge and small bar as well as the large ground-floor dining room where a choice of breakfasts is offered. Bedrooms, though plainly decorated and furnished in a basic style, are of a good size and suitably equipped.
15 rms (4 bth/shr) (3 fmly) No smoking in dining room CTV in all bedrooms Tea and coffee making facilities No dogs (ex guide dogs) Licensed Cen ht CTV No children 2yrs
PRICE GUIDE
ROOMS: s £18-£22; d £34-£42; wkly b&b £120-£134✳
CARDS: ▨ ▧ ▨ ⑩ ▨

GH ◻◻ **Malvern Hotel** 33 Regency Square BN1 2GG
☎01273 324302 FAX 01273 324302
This well maintained guest house close to the sea and conference facilities provides bedrooms which, though not large, are thoughtfully equipped and suitably furnished. English and continental breakfasts are served in an attractive dining.
13 en suite (shr) No smoking in 3 bedrooms No smoking in dining room CTV in all bedrooms Tea and coffee making facilities Direct dial from bedrooms No dogs (ex guide dogs) Licensed Cen ht

PRICE GUIDE
ROOMS: s £30-£35; d £50-£60; wkly b&b £150-£210
CARDS: £

GH ⓠⓠⓠ **Melford Hall Hotel** 41 Marine Pde BN2 1PE
☎01273 681435 FAX 01273 624186
Closed 24-26 Dec
Further improvements have now been made to this small,
privately owned hotel which enjoys a prime position overlooking
the sea and close to the town centre. Bedrooms are freshly
decorated in a modern style with white furniture, floral duvets and
co-ordinating curtains, and the majority offer en suite facilities. A
choice of breakfasts is served in the dining room and there is a
guests' lounge to the front of the house. Car parking facilities,
though limited, are an added bonus.
25 rms (23 bth/shr) (4 fmly) No smoking in dining room CTV in
all bedrooms Tea and coffee making facilities Direct dial from
bedrooms No dogs (ex guide dogs) Cen ht CTV No children
2yrs 12P No coaches
PRICE GUIDE
ROOMS: s £30-£34; d £44-£54; wkly b&b £140-£175
CARDS: £

GH ⓠⓠⓠ **New Steine Hotel** 12a New Steine, Marine Pde
BN2 1PB ☎01273 681546
Mar-Dec
This delightful, long established hotel, personally run by its
resident proprietors, offers a good range of bedrooms furnished in
modern style. Public areas include a comfortable downstairs
lounge as well as the well appointed breakfast room - which will
serve a vegetarian meal by arrangement - and the atmosphere is
very friendly and informal throughout. Restricted pay-and-display
parking is usually available.
11 rms (9 bth/shr) No smoking in dining room CTV in all
bedrooms Tea and coffee making facilities Cen ht CTV No
children 8yrs No parking No coaches
PRICE GUIDE
ROOMS: s £18-£27; d £39-£45
£

GH ⓠⓠⓠ **Paskins Hotel** 19 Charlotte St BN2 1AG
☎01273 601203 FAX 01273 621973
Quietly located close to the seafront and within easy walking
distance of the town centre, this attractively decorated and well
designed guest house has a good range of well equipped modern
bedrooms, each with TV, direct dial telephone, and tea tray. The
downstairs breakfast room offers a choice of both vegetarian and
full English breakfasts, and there is a small bar lounge to the side.
Very friendly, helpful service is personally provided by the
proprietors Roger and Sue Marlowe.
19 rms (16 bth/shr) (2 fmly) No smoking in area of dining room
CTV in all bedrooms Tea and coffee making facilities Direct dial
from bedrooms No dogs (ex guide dogs) Licensed Cen ht No
children 5yrs No parking Last d 5.30pm
PRICE GUIDE
ROOMS: s £20-£33; d £30-£60; wkly b&b £120-£200; wkly hlf-
bd £230-£310
CARDS: £

GH ⓠⓠ **Prince Regent Hotel** 29 Regency Square BN1 2FH
☎01273 329962 FAX 01273 748162
This friendly guest house situated in a popular Regency square
offers comfortable, thoughtfully equipped accommodation - rooms
in a variety of sizes including a few which are spacious and well
appointed.
20 en suite (bth/shr) No smoking in dining room No smoking in
lounges CTV in all bedrooms Tea and coffee making facilities
Direct dial from bedrooms No dogs (ex guide dogs) Licensed
Cen ht CTV No children 12yrs No parking

PRICE GUIDE
ROOMS: s £35-£50; d £52-£85; wkly b&b fr £175
CARDS: ▧ ▨ ▨ ▨

GH Ⓠ Ⓠ *Queensbury Hotel* 58 Regency Square BN1 2GB
☎01273 325558 FAX 01273 324800
Closed 3 days Xmas
This large guest house, situated in the architectural set piece that is Regency Square, is convenient for the town centre and the sea front. Bedrooms are mixed in quality, though some have been recently updated. Breakfasts are served in the dining room and vegetarian diets can be catered for.
16 rms (6 bth/shr) (8 fmly) No smoking in dining room CTV in all bedrooms Tea and coffee making facilities Cen ht CTV
CARDS: ▧ ▨

GH Ⓠ Ⓠ Ⓠ **Regency Hotel** 28 Regency Square BN1 2FH (opposite West Pier) ☎01273 202690 FAX 01273 220438
A house of some character, comfortably appointed throughout, this hotel is conveniently situated for conference facilities and the seafront. An attractive dining room with Regency-style decor is open-plan with the small but comfortable lounge, and bedrooms - though they vary in size - are all well appointed and thoughtfully equipped.
13 rms (10 bth/shr) (1 fmly) No smoking in 2 bedrooms No smoking in dining room CTV in all bedrooms Tea and coffee making facilities Direct dial from bedrooms No dogs (ex guide dogs) Licensed Cen ht CTV ch fac No parking Golf riding & tennis can be arranged Last d 4pm
PRICE GUIDE
ROOMS: s £32-£38; d £55-£65✱
CARDS: ▧ ▨ ▨ ▨   (£)

GH Ⓠ Ⓠ Ⓠ **Trouville Hotel** 11 New Steine, Marine Pde
BN2 1PB ☎01273 697384
Closed Xmas & Jan
Part of an attractive seafront square, the Trouville is a tastefully restored Grade II listed building run by proud owners Mr and Mrs Hansell. In recent years much improvement has taken place, with co-ordinated decor and soft furnishings, and two more smart en suites have been added. The four-poster room has its own balcony. A choice of breakfasts is served in the ground-floor dining room which opens out to a small lounge, both having original marble fireplaces.
9 rms (4 shr) (1 fmly) No smoking in dining room CTV in all bedrooms Tea and coffee making facilities No dogs Licensed Cen ht CTV No coaches
PRICE GUIDE
ROOMS: s £20; d £34-£48; wkly b&b £133-£160
CARDS: ▧ ▨ ▨ ▨ ▨   (£)

GH Ⓠ Ⓠ **Westbourne Hotel** 46 Upper Rock Gardens BN2 1QF
☎01273 686920
A friendly, relaxing atmosphere pervades this small guest house which stands within easy reach of the seafront. A small sitting room and a ground-floor dining room serving a choice of English breakfasts make up the open-plan public areas, while modestly furnished bedrooms are attractively equipped and reasonably comfortable.
10 rms (6 shr) (4 fmly) No smoking in 1 bedrooms No smoking in dining room CTV in all bedrooms Tea and coffee making facilities No dogs Licensed Cen ht Last d 6pm
PRICE GUIDE
ROOMS: s £18-£28; d £32-£46; wkly b&b £120-£175; wkly hlf-bd £175-£225✱
CARDS: ▧ ▨ ▨ ▨

BRIGSTEER (NEAR KENDAL) Cumbria Map **07** SD48

♥ Ⓠ Ⓠ Ⓠ Mrs B Gardner **Barrowfield** *(SD484908)* LA8 8BJ
☎015395 68336
Apr-Oct
This delightful farmhouse dates back to the 16th century and is located on a sheep and dairy farm in a quiet, rural area. Bedrooms are traditionally and comfortably furnished, and all have central heating and washbasins. There are a spacious lounge and dining room in which hearty farmhouse breakfasts are served.
3 rms (1 fmly) No smoking No dogs Cen ht CTV 6P 180 acres dairy sheep
PRICE GUIDE
ROOMS: d £30-£34✱

BRISTOL Avon Map **03** ST57

GH Ⓠ Ⓠ Ⓠ *Alandale Hotel* 4 Tyndall's Park Rd, Clifton
BS8 1PG (adjacent to BBC studios) ☎0117 973 5407
Closed 2wks Xmas
This large, personally run, Victorian guest house stands next to the BBC studios and conveniently near the university, shops and business area. Bright, modern en suite bedrooms in a range of sizes are equipped with direct dial telephones and TV, while comfortable public areas include a bright breakfast room and spacious lounge with honesty bar. On-site car parking is limited.
17 en suite (bth/shr) CTV in all bedrooms Tea and coffee making facilities Direct dial from bedrooms Licensed Cen ht 10P No coaches
CARDS: ▧ ▨

GH Ⓠ Ⓠ **Alcove** 508-510 Fishponds Rd, Fishponds BS16 3DT (leave M32 junct2 follow signs into Fishponds & turn left into Fishponds Rd)
☎0117 965 3886 & 965 2436 FAX 0117 965 3886
Small and friendly, this personally run guest house catering mainly for business persons stands in a residential area just north of the city, with easy access to both the M4 and M32 motorways and the centre. Bedrooms offer adequate comfort and there is a cosy little breakfast room.
9 rms (3 shr) (2 fmly) No smoking in dining room CTV in all bedrooms Tea and coffee making facilities No dogs (ex guide dogs) Cen ht CTV 9P No coaches
PRICE GUIDE
ROOMS: s £24-£28; d £36-£40✱

GH Ⓠ Ⓠ *Birkdale Hotel* 11 Ashgrove Rd, Redland BS6 6LY (off Whiteladies road, 1m from city centre)
☎0117 973 3635 & 973 6332 FAX 0117 973 9964
Closed Xmas wk
This well appointed hotel is situated just off the main Whiteladies Road, only a mile from the city centre. Accommodation is provided in simply furnished bedrooms, each equipped with telephone, colour TV and tea/coffee tray. The large, comfortable lounge has a bar, and there are an attractively appointed and spacious dining room on the first floor.
42 en suite (bth/shr) CTV in all bedrooms Tea and coffee making facilities Licensed Cen ht 16P Last d 8pm
CARDS: ▧ ▨

GH Ⓠ Ⓠ Ⓠ **Downlands** 33 Henleaze Gardens, Henleaze
BS9 4HH ☎0117 962 1639
A charming, tall Victorian house set in a residential area near the Downs - yet within easy walking distance of the city centre - and personally run by conscientious owners offers accommodation in bright, individually styled bedrooms. There are a cosy breakfast room and a comfortable lounge, the secluded garden is popular in summer, and unrestricted street parking is available.

8 rms (2 shr) (1 fmly) CTV in 9 bedrooms Tea and coffee making facilities Cen ht No parking No coaches
PRICE GUIDE
ROOMS: s £25-£34; d £42-£46*
CARDS:

GH 🆀🆀🆀 **Mayfair Hotel** 5 Henleaze Rd, Westbury on Trym BS9 4EX ☎0117 962 2008
A semidetached Victorian property, the Mayfair is situated in a quiet residential area about 2.5 miles to the Clifton side of the city centre, off Dordham Downs and close to the zoo. It offers comfortable bedrooms, an attractive guests' lounge and a breakfast room. On-street parking is available outside the hotel.
9 rms (3 shr) (1 fmly) No smoking in dining room No smoking in lounges CTV in all bedrooms Tea and coffee making facilities 9P No coaches
PRICE GUIDE
ROOMS: s £22-£26; d £40-£44; wkly b&b fr £80
CARDS: 🔳

GH 🆀🆀 **Oakfield Hotel** 52-54 Oakfield Rd, Clifton BS8 2BG
☎0117 973 5556 FAX 0117 974 4141
Closed 24 Dec-1 Jan
Personally owned and run by Mrs Hurley since the 1940s, this well established hotel still deserves top marks for spotless housekeeping and refreshingly traditional standards, with classical silver and bone china in the breakfast room and service of early morning tea and hot drinks in the evening. Bedrooms have first-class beds and excellent linen. The Oakfield is in a convenient position close to Whiteladies Road, the BBC, Clifton and the university.
27 rms (4 fmly) No smoking in dining room No smoking in 1 lounge CTV in all bedrooms Tea and coffee making facilities Cen ht CTV 9P Last d 7pm
PRICE GUIDE
ROOMS: s £25-£27; d £35-£37; wkly b&b fr £175; wkly hlf-bd fr £220.50 ⓔ

GH 🆀🆀 *Rowan Lodge* 41 Gloucester Rd North, Filton Park BS7 0SN (on junct of A38 with Bronksea road)
☎0117 931 2170
Closed Xmas & New Year
This large detached house with its own car park is situated north of the city, close to the suburb of Filton and Bristol's business complex. Bedrooms are well equipped and there is a pleasant lounge/breakfast room.
6 rms (3 shr) (2 fmly) No smoking in dining room No smoking in lounges CTV in all bedrooms Tea and coffee making facilities Cen ht 8P No coaches
CARDS: 🔳 🔳

GH 🆀🆀 *Washington Hotel* 11-15 St Pauls Rd, Clifton BS8 1LX (follow A4018 into city, turn right at lights opposite BBC buildings, hotel is 200yds on left)
☎0117 973 3980 Telex no 449075 FAX 0117 974 1082
Closed 23 Dec-3 Jan
The Washington is a large, rambling, unlicensed hotel, conveniently situated for Clifton, the shops and the university. Bedrooms are well equipped and range from the more recently upgraded to those that are now in need of some decorative attention. There is a bright breakfast room, and guests can dine in Racks Restaurant, located in The Clifton, a sister hotel a few doors away.
46 rms (34 bth/shr) (5 fmly) CTV in all bedrooms Tea and coffee making facilities Direct dial from bedrooms Licensed Cen ht 20P Last d 11pm
CARDS: 🔳 🔳 🔳 🔳

GH ◨◨◨ **Westbury Park Hotel** 37 Westbury Rd, Westbury-on-Trym BS9 3AU (on A4018)
☎0117 962 0465 FAX 0117 962 8607
Situated on the famous Durdham Downs, between Bristol city centre and junction 17 of the M5, this detached Victorian family house is ideal for holiday-makers and business guests. There are an attractive lounge adorned with fresh flowers, a bar where snacks are available and an elegant dining room where breakfast is served. Bedrooms have all the creature comforts, and most are en suite.
8 en suite (bth/shr) (2 fmly) No smoking in dining room CTV in all bedrooms Tea and coffee making facilities Direct dial from bedrooms Licensed Cen ht CTV 4P No coaches Last d 8.30pm
PRICE GUIDE
ROOMS: s fr £27.50; d fr £43*
CARDS: ▨ ▨ ▨ ▨

BRIXHAM Devon Map **03** SX95

[⟲▼] GH ◨◨◨◨ **Harbour Side** 65 Berry Head Rd TQ5 9AA (follow signs for 'Marina') ☎01803 858899
This small, friendly guest house is ideally situated, overlooking the outer harbour with views over the marina and Torbay beyond, yet within a few minutes' walk of the town. Proprietors Jenny and Peter Tomlins provide dinner by prior arrangement, and a choice of dishes is offered at breakfast. Bedrooms are neatly furnished and adequately equipped.
5 rms (2 shr) (1 fmly) No smoking in dining room CTV in all bedrooms Tea and coffee making facilities No dogs (ex guide dogs) CTV No parking No coaches
PRICE GUIDE
ROOMS: s £16-£20; d £28-£34; wkly b&b £98-£112

GH ◨◨ **Harbour View Hotel** 65 King St TQ5 9TH
☎01803 853052
Guests arriving by sea would have no trouble spotting this house as it directly overlooks the entrance to the inner harbour and was once the home of a harbour master. Bedrooms are simple but attractive, with many facilities. Breakfast is served in the dining room/lounge.
9 rms (2 bth/shr) (1 fmly) CTV in all bedrooms Tea and coffee making facilities No dogs Cen ht 3P No coaches Last d breakfast
PRICE GUIDE
ROOMS: s £18-£23; d £30-£39; wkly b&b £94.50-£126*
CARDS: ▨ ▨ ▨

GH ◨◨◨ **Ranscombe House Hotel** Ranscombe Rd
TQ5 9UP ☎01803 882337 FAX 01803 882337
A little way from the town centre, with views over the rooftops to the harbour, this 18th-century property stands in its own garden. Bedrooms are comfortable, dinner and breakfast are served in a pleasant dining room and there is also a bar.
9 en suite (bth/shr) (2 fmly) No smoking in dining room No smoking in lounges CTV in all bedrooms Tea and coffee making facilities Direct dial from bedrooms No dogs (ex guide dogs) Licensed Cen ht CTV 16P No coaches Last d 4pm
PRICE GUIDE
ROOMS: s £24-£28; d £44-£52; wkly b&b £161-£189; wkly hlf-bd £215-£230*
CARDS: ▨ ▨ ▨ ▨

[⟲▼] GH ◨◨ **Sampford House** 59 King St TQ5 9TH
(follow signs for harbour Sampford House overlooks inner harbour on south side just above Southern Quay)
☎01803 857761
Closed Dec & Jan

Sampford House is a well maintained terraced property overlooking the inner harbour. Bedrooms are fairly compact, but there is a cosy lounge with tea-making facilities. The rear dining room overlooks a colourful courtyard and an evening meal can be provided by arrangement. Limited parking is available on the quay.
6 rms (5 bth/shr) No smoking in dining room CTV in all bedrooms Tea and coffee making facilities Cen ht CTV 2P No coaches Last d 10am
PRICE GUIDE
ROOMS: s £16-£18; d £32-£38

BRIZE NORTON Oxfordshire Map **04** SP20

♥ ◨◨ Mrs S Fryer **Rookery Farm** *(SP297080)* Burford Rd OX18 3NL (off A40 from Oxford, on reaching village turn right at mini-roundabout and right again. First house on left)
☎01993 842957
Parts of this stone farmhouse, which sits within its small-holding, date back to the 16th century. Breakfast is served around a large table where dinners can also be provided by prior arrangement. There are plans to add en suite facilities to the recently decorated bedrooms.
3 rms (1 fmly) CTV in all bedrooms Tea and coffee making facilities Cen ht 4P Outdoor swimming pool (heated) 6 acres horses/sheep
PRICE GUIDE
ROOMS: s £20; d £35

BROADSTAIRS Kent Map **05** TR36

GH ◨◨◨ **Bay Tree Hotel** 12 Eastern Esplanade CT10 1DR
☎01843 862502 FAX 01843 860589
A friendly, family-run guest house, the Bay Tree is located on the esplanade and has ample unrestricted parking. Most of the bedrooms are bright and spacious, but the one with a balcony overlooking the Channel is particularly attractive. A lounge is provided in addition to the cheerful dining room where a daily menu is offered.
11 en suite (bth/shr) No smoking in dining room CTV in all bedrooms Tea and coffee making facilities No dogs (ex guide dogs) Licensed Cen ht CTV No children 10yrs 12P No coaches Last d 4pm
PRICE GUIDE
ROOMS: s £20-£25; d £40-£50; wkly b&b £130-£150; wkly hlf-bd £170-£185*
CARDS: ▨ ▨

GH ◨◨ **Devonhurst Hotel** Eastern Esplanade CT10 1DR
☎01843 863010 FAX 01843 868940
Margaret and David Payne offer a warm welcome to guests at their small hotel, which overlooks the sea and sandy bay. The pretty bedrooms are continually being improved with added facilities, fabric canopies, silk flowers and fresh floral decor. Four rooms have splendid views and two have their own balcony. Downstairs, the dining room combines with a fully stocked bar, and there is a small lounge with satellite TV. Early breakfasts and special diets can be catered for.
9 en suite (shr) (1 fmly) No smoking in 4 bedrooms No smoking in dining room CTV in all bedrooms Tea and coffee making facilities No dogs (ex guide dogs) Licensed Cen ht CTV No children 5yrs No coaches Last d 5.30pm
PRICE GUIDE
ROOMS: s £23-£25; d £42-£50; wkly b&b £126-£142; wkly hlf-bd £167-£182*
CARDS: ▨ ▨ ▨ ▨

GH Q *East Horndon Private Hotel* 4 Eastern Esplanade
CT10 1DP ☎01843 868306
Mar-Nov

A large Victorian house in a quiet position on the East Cliff
seafront, this small private hotel, offers a range of bedrooms
varying from compact singles to spacious family rooms with en
suite facilities, all modestly furnished. There are a traditionally
styled lounge bar and a separate dining room where both breakfast
and dinner are served.

10 rms (4 bth/shr) (6 fmly) CTV in all bedrooms Tea and coffee
making facilities Licensed Cen ht No parking No coaches Last
d noon
CARDS:

GH QQQ *Gull Cottage* 5 Eastern Esplanade CT10 1DP
☎01843 861936
Closed Nov-Mar

A lovingly cared for home belonging to a friendly couple, Gull
Cottage is located on the peaceful eastern esplanade. The
bedrooms have been gradually improved with attractive decor and
pieces of highly varnished old furniture. The owners' private
lounge is available if required, and there is a south-facing
breakfast room. Guests should note that this is a no-smoking
establishment.

8 rms (6 shr) (3 fmly) No smoking CTV in 7 bedrooms Tea and
coffee making facilities No dogs (ex guide dogs) Licensed Cen
ht CTV No children 6yrs 6P
PRICE GUIDE
ROOMS: s £21; d £42; wkly b&b £140

GH QQQ *Oakfield Private Hotel* 11 The Vale CT10 1RB
☎01843 862506 FAX 01843 862506

Oakfield is a popular licensed establishment located close to the
centre, within easy reach of the bay, shops and railway station. It
can trace its history as a guest house from the turn of the century,
but nowadays the bedrooms are equipped with modern amenities
and extras such as toiletries. There are a games room with a pool
table, a well stocked bar and a bright dining room where dinner is
served.

11 rms (10 shr) No smoking in dining room CTV in all bedrooms
Tea and coffee making facilities No dogs (ex guide dogs)
Licensed Cen ht CTV 11P No coaches Games room Pool table
Last d 6pm
PRICE GUIDE
ROOMS: s £20-£24; d £40-£48; wkly b&b £125-£140; wkly hlf-
bd £165-£180
CARDS:

BROADWAY Hereford & Worcester Map **04** SP03

Selected

GH QQQQ *Bretforton Manor* Bretforton WR11 5JA
☎01386 833111 FAX 01386 833111
Closed 15 Dec-15 Jan

This beautifully preserved manor house, built of mellow
Cotswold stone, is situated near the church in the village of
Bretforton, which is equidistant from Broadway, Evesham and
Chipping Camden. Extensive grounds contain a duck pond, a
stream, a dovecote, a thatched timber framed barn and even
the village stocks, which date back to 1360. The house - once
owned by Elizabeth I - has a wealth of history and character
which is enhanced by original features such as the
magnificent carved oak panelling in the entrance hall and
stone flagged floors in this and other areas. Owners Janet and
Brian Crittenden have exercised great taste and care in
creating luxurious accommodation which combines modern

facilities with antique and period furnishings. Both twin and
double bedded rooms are available. All are spacious, as are
their high quality en suite bathrooms. Separate tables are
provided in the breakfast room. Dinners is only available for
party bookings.
3 en suite (bth/shr) No smoking CTV in all bedrooms Tea
and coffee making facilities No dogs Cen ht No children 6P
No coaches
PRICE GUIDE
ROOMS: s £45-£50; d £75-£85

Selected

GH QQQQ *Cowley House* Church St WR12 7AE (off
Village Green into Snowhill Rd) ☎01386 853262
This delightful old house is built of mellow Cotswold stone
and dates back to the 17th and 18th centuries. It is situated
close to the village centre, just off the A44. The house has a
wealth of charm and character which is enhanced by original
features such as exposed stone walls, stone-flagged floors and
ceiling beams. The bedrooms, which include a room with an
ornately carved, antique four-poster bed, have modern
equipment and facilities. The one room without an en suite
facilities has a private bathroom nearby. There are a very
attractive and comfortable lounge and a traditionally furnished
breakfast room. Other facilities include a small private car
park.
3 en suite (bth/shr) No smoking CTV in 2 bedrooms No
dogs Cen ht CTV No children 3P No coaches
PRICE GUIDE
ROOMS: d £45-£65; wkly b&b £157.50-£210*

Selected

GH QQQQ *Cusack's Glebe* Cusack's Glebe, Saintbury
WR12 7PX (2m NE off B4632 in Gloucestershire)
☎01386 852210 FAX 01386 853816
Closed 15 Dec-15 Jan

This charming 14th-century listed building enjoys
commanding views over an expanse of countryside and
retains a medieval atmosphere. Set in five acres of paddocks,
orchards and mature gardens, the house has been in Juliet
Carro's family since 1922. There are only two bedrooms but
both have antique four-poster beds, a profusion of period
furnishings and plenty of personal touches. Handsome
breakfasts are served in the cosy, flag-stoned breakfast room.
Smoking is not permitted.
2 en suite (bth/shr) (1 fmly) No smoking CTV in all
bedrooms Tea and coffee making facilities No dogs (ex
guide dogs) No children 8yrs 8P No coaches
PRICE GUIDE
ROOMS: d £50-£58*

Selected

GH QQQQ *Leasow House* WR12 7NA BROADWAY
☎01386 584526 FAX 01386 584596
(For full entry see Laverton)
See advertisement on p.107.

Selected

GH Q Q Q Q **Milestone House Hotel** 122 High St
WR12 7AJ ☎01386 853432
Closed Jan
Milestone House offers comfortable, individually furnished
rooms well equipped with the usual modern amenities. The
attractive conservatory restaurant, specialising in Italian
dishes, is popular with both residents and non-residents,
offering a good-value fixed-price menu in addition to the
carte. There are a rear car park and a delightful area with
hanging baskets, which is alive with colour in the summer.
4 en suite (bth/shr) (1 fmly) No smoking in bedrooms No
smoking in area of dining room CTV in all bedrooms Tea
and coffee making facilities No dogs (ex guide dogs)
Licensed Cen ht 8P No coaches Last d 9.30pm
PRICE GUIDE
ROOMS: d £55-£59.50✶
CARDS: 🔵 🟥

Premier Selected

GH Q Q Q Q Q **Old
Rectory** Church St WR12 7PN
(from Broadway take B4632
Stratford Rd for one and a
half miles turn right into
Church St at Bell Inn)
☎01386 853729
Closed 22-27 Dec
This 17th-century Cotswold-
stone village rectory provides
all the ingredients for a

perfect stay; the welcome is warm, the attractive rooms are
well equipped, and the setting, opposite the pretty church and
bordered by sheep-filled fields, is utterly tranquil. A delightful
walled garden offers guests complete privacy, and there are
many places of outstanding interest within a few miles of the
village; Broadway, one of the best known beauty spots in the
area, is only a mile and a half away. Among an excellent
choice of places to eat in the locality is a charming pub two
minutes' walk from the rectory.
6 en suite (bth/shr) 2 annexe en suite (bth/shr) (2 fmly) No
smoking CTV in all bedrooms Tea and coffee making
facilities Direct dial from bedrooms No dogs (ex guide dogs)
Cen ht No children 8yrs 10P No coaches
PRICE GUIDE
ROOMS: s £40-£80; d £60-£95; wkly b&b £175-£280✶
CARDS: 🔵 🟥 🟨 🟩

🏨 📺 **GH** Q Q **Olive Branch Guest House** 78 High St
WR12 7AJ (on A44) ☎01386 853440 FAX 01386 853440
Conveniently positioned in the High Street, this cosy, character
house is personally run and offers well equipped, if quite compact,
bedrooms. There are an attractive, stone flagged dining room and
a residents' lounge. The house is an ideal base for touring.
8 rms (6 bth/shr) (1 fmly) No smoking in dining room CTV in
all bedrooms Tea and coffee making facilities No dogs (ex guide
dogs) Cen ht 9P No coaches Last d 7.30pm
PRICE GUIDE
ROOMS: s £16-£19.50; d £40-£48
CARDS: 🟥

Selected

GH Q Q Q Q **Orchard Grove** Station Rd WR12 7DE
☎01386 853834
Closed Xmas & New Year
Set back off the Evesham road, a short walk from the village
centre, this immaculately kept house provides comfortable
modern accommodation in what is very much a family home.
It offers a cosy lounge, a breakfast room and well furnished
bedrooms, all nicely decorated, and there is a little terrace to
the rear overlooking the delightful garden.
3 rms (1 bth) (1 fmly) No smoking CTV in 1 bedroom Tea
and coffee making facilities No dogs (ex guide dogs) Cen ht
CTV No children 10yrs 3P No coaches
PRICE GUIDE
ROOMS: s £20-£25; d £42-£45

GH Q Q Q **Pennylands** Evesham Rd WR12 7DG
☎01386 858437
Closed Xmas
This large, semidetached house, built of Cotswold stone, dates
back to 1904. Set in a spacious and pleasant garden, it stands on
the A44, just west of Broadway. It provides soundly maintained
bedrooms equipped and furnished in modern style, including
family rooms and a room at ground-floor level which has its own
entrance from the car park and garden. All the bedrooms are no-
smoking. Separate tables can be provided in the traditionally
furnished dining room, which is also used as the lounge. Home-
cooked, wholesome evening meals are available by prior
arrangement.
3 en suite (bth/shr) No smoking in bedrooms CTV in all
bedrooms Tea and coffee making facilities No dogs (ex guide
dogs) Cen ht 6P No coaches
PRICE GUIDE
ROOMS: d £32-£37; wkly b&b fr £112✶

Selected

GH Q Q Q Q *Pond House* Lower Fields, Weston Rd,
Bretforton WR11 5QA (B4632 to Broadway, turn onto
B4035 at Weston-sub-Edge. House 0.5m on left after
crossing old railway bridge) ☎01386 831687
An impeccably maintained and modern detached house,
quietly set well back from the B4035 in its own extensive
gardens and paddock, offers panoramic views of the
surrounding countryside and hills. The comfortable lounge
opens on to a pleasant patio area. Bedrooms are tastefully
decorated and furnished, and all have modern equipment and
en suite facilities, while the comfortable lounge opens on to a
pleasant patio area and separate tables are provided in the
attractive breakfast room.
3 en suite (bth/shr) (1 fmly) No smoking CTV in all
bedrooms Tea and coffee making facilities No dogs Cen ht
10P No coaches
£

GH Q Q Q **Small Talk Lodge** Keil Close, 32 High St
WR12 7DP (on A44 in middle of High St next to Lygon Arms
Hotel) ☎01386 858953
Tucked away behind a High Street tea shop at the heart of this
popular Cotswold village, a hospitable, homely guest house offers
bright, comfortable, well equipped bedrooms, tastefully furnished
and decorated, which will appeal equally to holidaymaker or
business user. In the attractive little dining room which forms the
hub of the establishment, Lin Scrannage (formerly a chef in

Manchester) provides first-class breakfasts and imaginative candlelit dinners. A rear car park is an additional bonus.

8 rms (6 bth/shr) (1 fmly) No smoking in dining room No smoking in lounges CTV in all bedrooms Tea and coffee making facilities No dogs (ex guide dogs) Licensed CTV 8P No coaches

PRICE GUIDE
ROOMS: d £40-£50✻
CARDS: £

BROCKENHURST Hampshire Map **04** SU30

Premier Selected

GH ◰◰◰◰◰ **Thatched Cottage Hotel & Restaurant**
16 Brookley Rd SO42 7RR (off A337) ☎01590 623090
FAX 01590 623479
Closed 4-31 Jan

A charming establishment with a good deal of character, this hotel offers bedrooms individually decorated in romantic mood and equipped with many thoughtful touches. All are comfortable, attractive and provided with smart en suite facilities. Public areas include a cosy lounge and a very pretty, intimate restaurant - open to the public - which has gained a rosette for the quality of its food; imaginative menus feature an enjoyable range of elaborate dishes which are soundly based on good ingredients and very well presented. In summer, delicious cream teas are served in the carefully tended garden.

5 en suite (bth/shr) No smoking in dining room CTV in all bedrooms Tea and coffee making facilities Direct dial from bedrooms Licensed Cen ht No children 10yrs 10P No coaches Last d 9.30pm

PRICE GUIDE
ROOMS: d £80-£110; wkly b&b £265-£365
CARDS: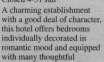

Selected

GH ◰◰◰◰ **The Cottage** Sway Rd SO42 7SH (from Lyndhurst on A337, turn right at Careys Manor into Grigg Lane. Continue 0.5m to crossroads, straight over and cottage next to war memorial)
☎01590 622296 FAX 01590 623014
Feb-Nov

Dating back 300 years and once a forester's cottage, this charming oak-beamed hotel is located in a picturesque village setting. The bedrooms are attractively decorated and all have modern en suite facilities, TVs, hairdryers, radio alarms and tea-making equipment. Traditional English breakfast is served in the dining room, and the cosy lounge has a fireplace and drinks cabinet. Proprietors Terry and Barbara Eisner provide a comprehensive list of personally recommended local restaurants and pubs.

7 en suite (bth/shr) (1 fmly) No smoking in bedrooms No smoking in dining room CTV in all bedrooms Tea and coffee making facilities Licensed Cen ht CTV No children 10yrs 12P No coaches Cream teas served in garden ➠

Leasow House
Laverton Meadows, Broadway,
Worcestershire WR12 7NA
Tel: Stanton (01386) 584 526 Fax: (01386) 584 596

Tranquilly situated approximately one mile off the B4632 (the Wormington-Dumbleton Road) and some three miles south of Broadway, making it ideally situated as a centre for touring the Cotswolds and the Vale of Evesham.
We offer spacious accommodation with all the refinements of the 20th century. All bedrooms have private shower/bathroom en suite, colour television, tea and coffee making facilities. Ground floor facilities for elderly and disabled people.
Leasow House is personally run by your hosts:
BARBARA & GORDON MEEKINGS
See gazetteer under Laverton

The Old Rectory
Church Street, Willersey
Nr. Broadway, Worcs. WR12 7PN

AA Premier Selected   English Tourist Board
Deluxe
Award winning Georgian Rectory with all amenities, situated at the end of a quiet country lane, opposite 11thC Church. Enjoy a delicious English Breakfast in our elegant dining room, warmed by a real log fire in winter. All rooms furnished to a very high standard. Beautiful and tranquil walled garden. Something for everyone from the romantic to the retired. Excellent walking from the house. Good base for touring. Many good restaurants nearby, ½ minutes walk to the 11thC Bell Inn. Special Breaks. 1½ miles Broadway – off the B4632
For Free colour brochure call Liz Beauvoisin
Tel: Broadway (01386) 853729 Fax: (01386) 858061

PRICE GUIDE
ROOMS: s £28.50-£47; d £57-£74; wkly b&b
£199.50-£259
CARDS:

BROMLEY Greater London Map **05** TQ46

GH Q Q **Glendevon House** 80 Southborough Rd, Bickley
BR1 2EN (turn off A222 at sign for railway station, hotel on
right) ☎0181 467 2183
This small family-run hotel has its own private car park and offers
easy access to central London from Bickley station. Bedrooms are
furnished in the modern style; most are fully en suite and all are
equipped with TV and tea tray. Guests may relax in the traditional
sitting room and take a full English breakfast or a light supper (the
latter by prior arrangement only) in the bright, comfortable dining
room. A top-floor flat with its own fully equipped kitchen is also
available.
11 rms (3 bth/shr) (2 fmly) CTV in 10 bedrooms Tea and coffee
making facilities Cen ht CTV 7P Last d 9pm
PRICE GUIDE
ROOMS: s £24-£32; d £37-£42✱
CARDS:

BROMPTON REGIS Somerset Map **03** SS93

♥ Q Mrs G Payne **Lower Holworthy** *(SS978308)* TA22 9NY
☎01398 371244
Closed Dec & Etr
Situated on the banks of Wimbleball Lake, popular for fishing and
water sports, this small farmhouse is in a secluded situation with
wonderful views across the lake and the rolling Exmoor
countryside. Part of a 200-acre livestock farm, it offers simple
bedroom accommodation and a cosy sitting room with a log fire.
Guests are given a hearty breakfast in the attractive dining room
which has a wood-burning stove.
2 en suite (bth/shr) Tea and coffee making facilities No dogs (ex
guide dogs) Cen ht CTV 6P 200 acres beef sheep

BROMSGROVE Hereford & Worcester Map **07** SO97

♥ Q Q Q Mr & Mrs A Gibbs **Lower Bentley** *(SO662979)*
Lower Bentley B60 4JB ☎01527 821286
Christine and Anthony Gibbs' family-run farmhouse provides
spacious, comfortable bedrooms with a good range of modern
creature comforts. This attractive red brick Victorian house
overlooks an expanse of countryside and is set in pretty gardens.
3 rms (2 bth) (1 fmly) CTV in all bedrooms Tea and coffee
making facilities Cen ht CTV 5P 346 acres dairy beef
PRICE GUIDE
ROOMS: s £20-£22.50; d £35; wkly b&b £105-£120✱

BROMYARD Hereford & Worcester Map **03** SO65

GH Q Q Q **Littlebridge House** Tedstone Wafre HR7 4PN (3m
N of B4203) ☎01885 482471
This impressive, large, stone built house is some 150 years old. It
is set in its own extensive gardens, and located in a picturesque
rural area, overlooking views of The Bromyard Downs. It is
reached by taking the B4203 (Stourport Road) from Bromyard.
The house is on the left after exactly 2.8 miles. The bedrooms are
traditionally furnished, including some antique pieces. All,
however, have modern equipment and en-suite facilities. A two
room family suite is available. Separate tables are provided in the
traditionally furnished dining room. Dinner is available by prior
arrangement. There is also an attractive and comfortably furnished
lounge, where a wood burning stove is lit during cold weather.

---

3 en suite (shr) (1 fmly) No smoking in bedrooms No smoking
in dining room CTV in all bedrooms Tea and coffee making
facilities No dogs (ex guide dogs) CTV ch fac 7P No coaches
Last d 7.30pm
PRICE GUIDE
ROOMS: s £20-£25; d £37-£40
CARDS:

♥ Q Q Q **Mrs P Morgan Nether Court** *(SO619494)* Stoke Lacy
HR7 4HJ (on A465) ☎01432 820247
This large Victorian house is set on a 300-acre mixed farm in the
village of Stoke Lacy. The three double bedrooms are furnished
with antique pieces and provided with either a modern en suite
bathroom or nearby private facilities. A welcoming log fire burns
in the cosy lounge, and there is also a fire in the original range of
the delightful dining room, where guests share one large table.
3 en suite (bth) (1 fmly) CTV in all bedrooms Tea and coffee
making facilities No dogs CTV 3P Fishing 300 acres mixed
Last d 24hr notice
PRICE GUIDE
ROOMS: s £20-£22; d £32-£35✱

BROUGH Cumbria Map **12** NY71

Selected

♥ Q Q Q Q Mrs J M Atkinson **Augill House** *(NY814148)*
CA17 4DX (400yds off A66) ☎017683 41305
This fine Georgian farmhouse lies in gardens on what used to
be the old road, on the east side of the town - turn off the by-
pass and then immediately right. Jeanette Atkinson keeps her
house in tip-top condition and welcomes her guests warmly.
Bedrooms are individually furnished and thoughtfully
equipped to include telephones, radios and hair dryers as well
as a selection of toiletries. The two rooms with en suite baths
also have a separate shower cubicle. Downstairs there is an
attractive and comfortable sitting room, and in summer
Jeanette's home-cooked meals are taken in the conservatory
looking out on to a large copper beech which dominates the
front garden.
3 en suite (bth/shr) No smoking CTV in all bedrooms Tea
and coffee making facilities Direct dial from bedrooms No
dogs (ex guide dogs) Cen ht CTV No children 12yrs 6P 40
acres mixed Last d 4pm
PRICE GUIDE
ROOMS: d £36-£40; wkly b&b £120-£125; wkly hlf-bd
£180-£185✱

BROUGHTON-IN-FURNESS Cumbria Map **07** SD28

◀ Q Q *Manor Arms* The Square LA20 6HY (take A5092
signposted to Millom and then follow signs to Broughton-in-
Furness) ☎01229 716286
The Manor Arms, a Grade II listed building situated overlooking
the village's Georgian square, is renowned for the quality of its
beer - particularly the six real ales - and the bar has a unique 18th-
century basket fireplace. It does not conform totally to our
definition of an inn because its food operation is limited to very
simple snacks, and breakfast is served in the rooms as there is no
dining room. However, bedrooms (all no-smoking) are of a good
standard, with en suite facilities and other modern features.
3 en suite (shr) (1 fmly) No smoking in bedrooms CTV in all
bedrooms Tea and coffee making facilities No dogs (ex guide
dogs) No parking No coaches Pool table
CARDS:

BRUNTINGTHORPE Leicestershire Map **04** SP68

♥ QQQQ Mrs A T Hutchinson **Knaptoft House Farm & The Greenway** *(SP619894)* Bruntingthorpe Rd, Bruntingthorpe LE17 6PR
☎0116 247 8388 FAX 0116 247 8388
Closed Xmas
Good accommodation is offered at this traditional mixed farm which stands in a secluded location with its own car park. The original farmhouse and adjoining modern bungalow are run by mother and daughter. Bedrooms at each (three of them ground-floor) are attractively decorated, thoughtfully furnished and maintained in pristine condition. Each house has its own comfortable lounge with log stove. The breakfast room is light and appealing and information is readily available as to where to obtain other meals. Guests are welcome to fish, by arrangement, in the restored medieval fishponds in the grounds.
3 rms (2 shr) 3 annexe rms (1 shr) No smoking in 1 bedrooms No smoking in dining room CTV in 4 bedrooms Tea and coffee making facilities No dogs Cen ht CTV No children 5yrs 10P Fishing Stabling 145 acres mixed
PRICE GUIDE
ROOMS: s fr £20; d fr £35✱

BUCKFAST Devon Map **03** SX76

GH QQQ *Furzeleigh Mill Country Hotel* Dart Bridge TQ11 0JP (beside A38 between Buckfast & Dartmoor)
☎01364 643476 FAX 01364 643476
Its location on the edge of the National Park makes this old mill house a convenient stopover on the way to the West Country or a good base for exploring Dartmoor. Bedrooms are small but comfortably furnished and well equipped. Ample public areas include two dining rooms offering a wide variety of food from a choice of menus. There are a comfortable residents' lounge and a large bar where hosts Bob and Ann Sandford endeavour to make all their guests feel at home.
15 rms (13 bth/shr) (2 fmly) No smoking in dining room CTV in all bedrooms Tea and coffee making facilities Licensed Cen ht CTV 32P Last d 8.30pm
CARDS: 🔲 🔲 🔲 🔲

BUCKFASTLEIGH Devon Map **03** SX76

GH QQ **Dartbridge Manor** 20 Dartbridge Rd TQ11 0DZ (beside A38 between Exeter & Plymouth) ☎01364 643575
A stone-built 400-year-old manor house full of character, with exposed beams and open fires, offers well furnished bedrooms and a comfortable lounge and breakfast room.
10 en suite (bth/shr) (2 fmly) No smoking in dining room No dogs Cen ht CTV 30P Fishing
PRICE GUIDE
ROOMS: s fr £20; d fr £35

◼ QQQQ *Dartbridge* Totnes Rd TQ11 0JR (turn off A38 onto A384) ☎01364 642214 FAX 01364 643977
Situated on the banks of the Dart, this inn is owned and managed by the Evans family. Bedrooms are attractive, a wide choice of menus is available in the large oak panelled bar, and a function room has recently been added.

11 en suite (bth/shr) (1 fmly) No smoking in dining room CTV in all bedrooms Tea and coffee making facilities Direct dial from bedrooms No dogs (ex guide dogs) Cen ht 100P Last d 9.30pm
CARDS: 🔲 🔲
See advertisement under Colour Section

BUDE Cornwall & Isles of Scilly Map **02** SS20

GH QQQQ *Cliff Hotel* Maer Down, Crooklets Beach EX23 8NG ☎01288 353110 FAX 01288 353110
Apr-Oct
This purpose-built hotel enjoys a wonderful position close to the cliff path, with views over Crooklets Beach. Comfortable en suite bedrooms are well designed and several have recently been refurbished; some have balconies and others overlook the terrace. The large, sunny bar/lounge has an adjoining games room, while a pool, jacuzzi, bowling green and tennis court are available in the extensive gardens. A choice of menus is featured in the dining room.
15 en suite (bth/shr) (12 fmly) No smoking in area of dining room No smoking in 1 lounge CTV in all bedrooms Tea and coffee making facilities Direct dial from bedrooms Licensed CTV 16P Indoor swimming pool (heated) Tennis (hard) Solarium Indoor spa pool Putting Last d 6pm

GH QQ **Links View** 13 Morwenna Ter EX23 8BU
☎01288 352561
Closed Dec
A popular traditional guest house, overlooking the golf course and within easy walking distance of the town centre, offers comfortable, neatly decorated bedrooms; several of them have lovely views, and three are equipped with private showers. Guests take breakfast in the sunny dining room/bar.
7 rms (2 fmly) No smoking in dining room CTV in all bedrooms Tea and coffee making facilities No dogs (ex guide dogs) Licensed Cen ht CTV 3P
PRICE GUIDE
ROOMS: s £14-£16; d £28-£32; wkly b&b £91-£99✱

 GH QQ **Pencarrol** 21 Downs View EX23 8RF (turn off A39 to town centre follow signs to Crooklets Beach, Downs View Road is ahead at Beach car park)
☎01288 352478
Closed Xmas rs Jan-Mar & Nov-Dec
Convenient for Crooklets Beach, Pencarrol overlooks the golf course from a corner position on a quiet street a short walk from the town centre. Appropriately furnished bedrooms, prettily decorated with co-ordinated fabrics, include two at ground level which are ideal for less mobile guests. A first-floor lounge takes advantage of enviable views, and Edna Payne prepares all the food herself, serving meals in the sunny, dual-aspect dining room.
8 rms (2 shr) (1 fmly) No smoking in dining room CTV in all bedrooms Tea and coffee making facilities No dogs (ex guide dogs) Cen ht CTV No parking No coaches Last d 5pm
PRICE GUIDE
ROOMS: s £14-£15; d £28-£30; wkly b&b £88-£94.50; wkly hlf-bd £140.50-£147 (£)

Selected

♥ QQQQ Mary Trewin **Court Farm** (SS224039) Marhamchurch EX23 0EN (opposite Post Office)
☎01288 361494 FAX 01288 361494
Closed 20 Dec-3 Jan
It is unusual to find a farmhouse located in the centre of the village, but Court Farm is the exception, as it is located opposite the church, village shop and 'local'. Chris and Mary Trewin welcome guests to their farmhouse home, and in addition a range of self catering cottages are also available, converted from former farm buildings. Bedrooms are neatly furnished and decorated, the majority having en suite facilities. Evening meals (mainly roasts) are provided for the many guests who return year after year. Recently the swimming pool has been fitted with a removable cover so that guests may use it whatever the weather.
5 rms (4 shr) (3 fmly) No smoking in dining room CTV in 4 bedrooms Tea and coffee making facilities No dogs (ex guide dogs) CTV 8P Indoor swimming pool (heated) Tennis (hard) Games room with pool table 180 acres beef/arable Last d noon
PRICE GUIDE
ROOMS: s fr £15; d £30-£34; wkly b&b £105-£112; wkly hlf-bd fr £144✱

♥ QQQ Mrs S Trewin **Lower Northcott** (SS215087) Poughill EX23 7EL ☎01288 352350 FAX 01288 352350
Set in a secluded valley about a mile from Bude, this charming Georgian farmhouse has its own large gardens with picnic benches. Free-range chickens, geese and ducks fulfil every child's dream of a farm holiday, and children are welcome to explore the 470-acre farm and watch the cows being milked. Predominantly en suite bedrooms - some with stunning coastline views - are

cheerfully decorated, while traditional breakfasts and evening meals are provided at separate tables in the dining room and there is a comfortable lounge where an open fire burns on chilly evenings. A children's games room is provided in the cellar.
5 rms (1 bth 3 shr) (3 fmly) Tea and coffee making facilities No dogs (ex guide dogs) Cen ht CTV 4P Indoor playroom 470 acres arable beef dairy sheep Last d 6.30pm
PRICE GUIDE
ROOMS: s fr £17; d fr £34; wkly hlf-bd fr £155✱

BUDLEIGH SALTERTON Devon Map **03** SY08

 Selected

GH QQQQ **Long Range Hotel** 5 Vales Rd EX9 6HS
☎01395 443321
Etr-Dec
The Long Range is a family-run hotel situated in its own gardens in a quiet residential area, 15 minutes' walk from the centre of town. Bedrooms are freshly decorated and equipped with modern comforts. There are a choice of lounges and a garden-facing conservatory where guests are encouraged to relax and enjoy the informal atmosphere. Dinner is available and the small selection of interesting dishes is prepared from the best fresh produce.
7 rms (2 bth 4 shr) (1 fmly) No smoking in bedrooms CTV in all bedrooms Tea and coffee making facilities No dogs Licensed Cen ht 6P Last d 8pm

GH QQQ **Willowmead** 12 Little Knowle EX9 6QS
☎01395 443115
A delightful family home with a colourful garden, Willowmead is set in a residential area within walking distance of the town centre and sea. Bedrooms are tastefully decorated and there is a most attractive first-floor lounge. A choice of dishes is offered in the cosy dining room, and the welcome is warm and friendly.
6 rms (4 shr) No smoking in bedrooms No smoking in dining room Tea and coffee making facilities Cen ht CTV No children 5yrs 6P No coaches

---

BUNGAY Suffolk Map **05** TM38

♥ QQQ Mrs B Watchorn **Park Farm** (TM304883) Harleston Rd, Earsham NR35 2AQ (3m SW of Bungay on A143)
☎01986 892180 FAX 01986 892180
A splendid Victorian farmhouse overlooking the Waveney Valley and was once part of the Duke of Norfolk's deer park. Bedrooms are airy and bright and the owner, Mrs Bobbie Watchorn, creates a friendly atmosphere.
3 en suite (bth/shr) No smoking CTV in all bedrooms Tea and coffee making facilities No dogs (ex guide dogs) Cen ht 11P 589 acres arable pigs poultry Last d 24hrs prior
PRICE GUIDE
ROOMS: s £22-£26; d £35-£40✱
CARDS: (£)

BUNTINGFORD Hertfordshire Map **05** TL32

♥ QQ Mrs P Hodge **Buckland Bury Farm** (TL357336) Buckland Bury SG9 0PY (On A10) ☎01763 272958
This delightful creeper-clad 300-year-old farmhouse sits on the brow of the hill at the edge of this small village, adjacent to the A10. The public rooms retain much of the original character of the house, the dining room in particular is impressive with its large communal dining table, exposed beams and large open fireplace; there is also a comfortable lounge for guests use. The traditionally furnished bedrooms are strictly non-smoking, each will be equipped with colour television, hairdryer, radio/alarm and tea making facilities.

3 rms (1 shr) No smoking in bedrooms CTV in all bedrooms Tea and coffee making facilities No dogs (ex guide dogs) Cen ht CTV P 550 acres arable Last d noon

PRICE GUIDE
ROOMS: s £15-£20; d fr £35

BURBAGE Wiltshire Map **04** SU26

Premier Selected

GH ⚲⚲⚲⚲⚲ **The Old Vicarage** SN8 3AG (in Burbage High Street turn into Taskers Lane take third right (Eastcourt) house on left beyond school sign) ☎01672 810495 FAX 01672 810663
Closed Xmas & New Year
This fine brick and flint-built former Victorian vicarage dates from 1853 and is set in its own pretty gardens beside the church. Each of the 3 bedrooms has been tastefully decorated and furnished in the period of the house, with many thoughtful extra touches. The resident proprietors are charming and extend a warm welcome into their home, where the high standard of tasteful décor and furnishings is evident throughout. The drawing room is elegant and comfortable, stocked with a wealth of reading material and beautiful fresh flower arrangements, together with a log fire; drinks are served here before dinner. Guests dine together around a large antique table in the candlelit dining room; home cooked dinners showing imagination and flair are served, using top quality fresh produce. Breakfast is informal, with a good choice of cooked and continental dishes. Smoking is not permitted.
3 en suite (bth) No smoking CTV in all bedrooms Tea and coffee making facilities No dogs (ex guide dogs) Cen ht CTV No children 18yrs 10P No coaches

PRICE GUIDE
ROOMS: s £35-£40; d £60-£80
CARDS: 🟦 ▦ 🟨

BURFORD Oxfordshire Map **04** SP21

Premier Selected

GH ⚲⚲⚲⚲⚲ **Andrews Hotel** High St OX18 4QA ☎01993 823151 FAX 01993 823240
Closed 23-27 Dec
This striking timbered Tudor building half way along the fashionable High Street contains a series of elegant lounges; these lead out to a terrace where the very efficient French staff serves  sumptuous teas - the cakes and pastries supplied by Maison Blanc. Bedrooms are superb in quality and generally similar in style. The latest to be refurbished, however is massive and features a Venetian marbled floor, a claw-footed bath and a four-poster bed. All offer such extras a mineral water,

---

magazines, books and an abundance of fresh flowers.
8 en suite (bth/shr) No smoking in bedrooms No smoking in dining room CTV in all bedrooms No dogs (ex guide dogs) Licensed Cen ht CTV No parking No coaches

PRICE GUIDE
ROOMS: d £65-£85
CARDS: 🟦 🟨

Premier Selected

GH ⚲⚲⚲⚲⚲ **Cottage-by-the-Church** Chapel Ln, Filkins GL7 3JG ☎01367 860613 FAX 01367 860613
(For full entry see Lechlade)

Selected

GH ⚲⚲⚲⚲ **Elm House** Meadow Ln, Fulbrook OX18 4BW (A361 towards Chipping Norton for 0.5m) ☎01993 823611 FAX 01993 823937
In a quiet and secluded part of this picturesque Cotswold village, this turn-of-the century house still retains such period features as generously proportioned rooms, stone mullioned windows and impressive open fireplaces. The new owner, David Brewster, is currently refurbishing the public areas to accentuate these features and reflect a country house style. Dinner is served in a pleasant bay-windowed room which looks out over the walled gardens and croquet lawn. The bedrooms have also received attention and are now all en suite.
7 rms (6 bth/shr) No smoking in bedrooms No smoking in dining room No smoking in 1 lounge CTV in all bedrooms Tea and coffee making facilities Direct dial from bedrooms Licensed Cen ht CTV No children 12yrs 10P No coaches Croquet lawn Last d 8.30pm

PRICE GUIDE
ROOMS: s £33-£55; d £45-£60; wkly b&b £231-£385; wkly hlf-bd £350-£504✱
CARDS: 🟦 🟨 ▦   (£)

BURLEY Hampshire Map **04** SU20

Selected

GH ⚲⚲⚲⚲ **Pikes Post** Chapel Ln BH24 4DJ (turn off A31 at Picket Post, follow sign posts to Burley village, pass Queens Head pub, turn into Chapel Lane in approx 0.5m Pikes Post on the left) ☎01425 402285
Closed Dec-Jan
3 en suite (bth/shr) No smoking CTV in all bedrooms Tea and coffee making facilities No dogs (ex guide dogs) Cen ht No children 4P

PRICE GUIDE
ROOMS: d £34-£38; wkly b&b fr £112

Selected

GH 🔵🔵🔵🔵 **Rosebay Cottage** Chapel Ln BH24 4DJ (turn off A31 at Picket Post, sign posted left to Burley. Turn left at Queen's Head public house into Chapel Lane, 0.5m on right) ☎01425 402471

With its five-bar gate, rose trellis, dovecote and pond, this lovely property is the epitome of a country cottage. En suite bedrooms are comfortably furnished; one has a four-poster bed. A cosy guest lounge and a dining room overlooking the garden are also available, and traditional breakfast includes home-produced eggs.

3 en suite (bth/shr) (1 fmly) No smoking CTV in all bedrooms Tea and coffee making facilities Cen ht 4P No coaches

PRICE GUIDE
ROOMS: s £15-£22; d £34-£38✻

BURNLEY Lancashire Map 07 SD83

GH 🔵🔵🔵 **Ormerod Hotel** 121/123 Ormerod Rd BB11 3QW ☎01282 423255

This privately owned and neatly maintained Victorian house faces Queen's Park, almost opposite the fire station. Bedrooms, all of which are en suite are comfortably furnished and freshly decorated with bright soft furnishings. Breakfast is served in the mahogany panelled dining room, opposite which is a comfortably furnished lounge which overlooks the park. Guests requiring dinner can visit the nearby Alexander Hotel which is under the same ownership.

9 en suite (bth/shr) (2 fmly) CTV in all bedrooms Tea and coffee making facilities Cen ht CTV 8P

PRICE GUIDE
ROOMS: s £20-£23; d £36✻ 							(£)

BURNSALL North Yorkshire Map 07 SE06

GH 🔵🔵 *Manor House* BD23 6BW (on B6160, approaching from Grassington) ☎01756 720231
Closed Jan

This family-run Victorian house offers good value accommodation. There is a cosy lounge and the bedrooms are homely and comfortable. There is also the benefit of a car park to the rear of the house. It is set on the edge of the village which is surrounded by beautiful Dales scenery and it is close to the River Wharfe.

7 rms (3 bth/shr) (2 fmly) No smoking in bedrooms No smoking in dining room Tea and coffee making facilities No dogs Licensed Cen ht CTV 7P No coaches Fishing Riding Solarium Last d 5pm

---

BURTON UPON TRENT Staffordshire Map 08 SK22

GH 🔵🔵🔵 **Delter Hotel** 5 Derby Rd DE14 1RU ☎01283 535115

A fully modernised house situated on the edge of town, on the busy Derby road. The bedrooms are bright and clean, and in the small basement bar snacks are served in the evening.

5 en suite (bth/shr) CTV in all bedrooms Tea and coffee making facilities No dogs (ex guide dogs) Licensed Cen ht CTV 8P No coaches Last d 6pm

PRICE GUIDE
ROOMS: s £27; d £38
CARDS: 							(£)

GH 🔵🔵🔵 **Edgecote Hotel** 179 Ashby Rd DE15 0LB (on A50, Leicester side of town) ☎01283 568966 FAX 01283 740118

This large, well maintained Victorian house, now a privately owned and personally run hotel, stands only half a mile from the town centre. Bright, modern bedrooms include some suitable for family occupation, drinks can be dispensed in the comfortable lounge, and a dining room furnished in cottage style retains its original panelled walls. The hotel has its own private car park.

12 rms (3 shr) (3 fmly) No smoking in bedrooms No smoking in dining room CTV in all bedrooms Tea and coffee making facilities No dogs (ex guide dogs) Licensed Cen ht CTV 8P

PRICE GUIDE
ROOMS: s £22-£33; d £36-£23; wkly b&b £133-£230✻
CARDS: 							(£)

BURWASH East Sussex Map 05 TQ62

❤ 🔵🔵 Mrs E Sirrell **Woodlands** *(TQ656242)* TN19 7LA (1m W of Burwash on A265, on right side of road, house set back 0.33m off road) ☎01435 882794
Etr-Oct

Located a mile west of Burwash village, this delightful 16th-century farmhouse is surrounded by 55 acres of rolling farmland. There is a good choice of ground-floor bedrooms, including one with a pine four-poster bed, and generous general bath and shower facilities. Mrs Liz Sirrell cooks a full English farmhouse breakfast using free-range eggs and good quality produce. The breakfast room incorporates some lounge seating and the atmosphere is friendly and relaxed.

3 rms (1 shr) No dogs Cen ht CTV 4P 55 acres mixed Last d am

PRICE GUIDE
ROOMS: s £16-£20; d £33-£37✻

BURY ST EDMUNDS Suffolk Map 05 TL86

GH 🔵🔵🔵 **Abbey Hotel** 35 Southgate St IP33 2AZ ☎01284 762020 FAX 01284 724770

At this hotel character accommodation is offered in four historic buildings dating from between 1150 and 1680, and the public areas are housed in a Tudor inn. Refurbishment work has been sympathetically undertaken to retain the original features of the buildings, and this is particularly evident in the pleasant lounge and informal eating area where breakfasts are served. Knowledgable advice can be given on sightseeing and eating out.

10 en suite (bth/shr) (2 fmly) No smoking in 5 bedrooms No smoking in dining room CTV in all bedrooms Tea and coffee making facilities Direct dial from bedrooms No dogs (ex guide dogs) Licensed Cen ht 14P No coaches

PRICE GUIDE
ROOMS: s £39.50-£42.50; d £49.50-£55✻
CARDS:

GH 🔵🔵🔵 **The Chantry Hotel** 8 Sparhawk St IP33 1RY ☎01284 767427 FAX 01284 760946
rs wknds

Conveniently located close to the town centre, this large Georgian house has the benefit of ample private car parking. Bedrooms are available in the main house and a Tudor annexe, and each comes with en suite facilities and a good range of facilities. There are a cosy lounge bar displaying a blackboard dinner menu and a spacious dining room.

14 en suite (bth/shr) 3 annexe en suite (bth/shr) (1 fmly) No smoking in dining room CTV in all bedrooms Tea and coffee making facilities Direct dial from bedrooms Licensed Cen ht 16P No coaches Last d 7pm

PRICE GUIDE
ROOMS: s £32.50-£44.50; d £49.50-£59.50
CARDS: £

GH ⚑⚑⚑ *Dunston Guest House/Hotel* 8 Springfield Rd
IP33 3AN ☎01284 767981
Dunston is a well established guest house providing
accommodation in both the main house and a cottage annexe, with
ample private car parking in the space between. Bedrooms are
generally light, with co-ordinated soft furnishings, and each is
equipped with colour TV, radio alarm and tea tray. Guests have the
use of a comfortable lounge and an adjacent conservatory sun
lounge which opens on to the guests' garden. Breakfast is taken in
the cheerful dining room.
11 rms (6 shr) 6 annexe rms (2 shr) (5 fmly) CTV in all
bedrooms Tea and coffee making facilities No dogs Licensed
Cen ht CTV 12P Last d 10pm previous day

Premier Selected

GH ⚑⚑⚑⚑⚑ **Twelve
Angel Hill** 12 Angel Hill
IP33 1UZ (in town centre by
Abbey ruins)
☎01284 704088
FAX 01284 725549
Closed Jan
A fine Georgian town house
stands in the centre of this
historic city and close to the
cathedral. The enthusiastic
owners are ideal hosts and
offer a warm welcome to their guests. There are four spcious
bedrooms and two smaller ones; all the rooms are en suite,
superbly furnished with fine period furniture and well
equipped with modern amenities and a few extra touches. An
elegant dining room offers a choice of breakfasts at individual
tables, the bar is cosy and guests can relax in the comfortable
sitting room. Limited parking is available.
6 en suite (bth/shr) No smoking CTV in all bedrooms Tea
and coffee making facilities Direct dial from bedrooms No
dogs Licensed Cen ht No children 16yrs 3P No coaches
PRICE GUIDE
ROOMS: s £45-£55; d £65-£75
CARDS: £

GH ⚑⚑ **York** 32 Springfield Rd IP33 3AR ☎01284 753091
Closed Feb
The York Guest House is a large red brick property located in a
quiet residential area close to the town centre; it is advisable to ask
for directions at the time of booking. Mrs Reeve is a cheerful
proprietor who provides sound accommodation, most of the
bedrooms being of good proportions and a few having en suite
facilities.
7 rms (1 bth 1 shr) No smoking in 2 bedrooms No smoking in
dining room No smoking in lounges CTV in all bedrooms Tea
and coffee making facilities Cen ht 3P No coaches
PRICE GUIDE
ROOMS: s £16-£18; d £32-£42✱ £

Selected

⚑ ⚑⚑⚑⚑ **The Six Bells Country Inn** The Green,
Bardwell IP31 1AW ☎01359 250820
Closed 25 & 26 Dec
A 16th-century inn in pleasant rural surroundings provides
accommodation in an annexe building; each of its good-sized
en suite bedrooms is furnished in modern pine and equipped
with colour television, direct-dial telephone and tea/coffee
making facilities. A cosy dining room in the main building
offers fixed-price and carte menus of uncomplicated dishes
based on good fresh produce.
8 en suite (shr) (2 fmly) No smoking in dining room CTV in
all bedrooms Tea and coffee making facilities Direct dial
from bedrooms Cen ht 40P No coaches Last d 9.30pm
PRICE GUIDE
ROOMS: s £35-£45; d £45-£65; wkly b&b £158-£200;
wkly hlf-bd £199-£250✱
MEALS: Lunch £10-£17.50alc Dinner £12-£22.50alc✱
CARDS: £

BUTTERMERE Cumbria Map **11** NY11

Premier Selected

GH ◻◻◻◻◻ *Pickett*
Howe Buttermere Valley
CA13 9UY ☎01900 85444
end Mar-mid Nov

Dating from 1650 and
renovated in 1991, this lovely
characterful farmhouse
features slate floors, oak
beams, mullioned windows
and spice cupboards; these
charms are enhanced by an
abundance of fresh flowers
and the many modern comforts provided by owners David
and Dani Edwards. The bedrooms, all of which are en suite,
are individually furnished and decorated, and Victorian brass
bedsteads, oak beams and chimney breasts give each room its
special charm. Mrs Edwards' cooking is a delight. The five-
course evening menu changes daily, reflecting the availability
of seasonal produce, and includes both British and
international dishes.

4 en suite (bth/shr) No smoking CTV in all bedrooms Tea
and coffee making facilities Direct dial from bedrooms No
dogs Licensed Cen ht No children 10yrs 4P No coaches
Fishing Last d noon
CARDS: 🔳 🔳

BUXTON Derbyshire Map **07** SK07

Premier Selected

GH ◻◻◻◻◻ *Brookfield*
On Longhill Brookfield Hall,
Long Hill SK17 6SU (1.5m W
of Buxton off A5004)
☎01298 24151
FAX 01298 24151

This luxurious Victorian
retreat is set in ten acres of
gardens and woodlands just a
mile and a half from Buxton.
Public rooms are furnished in
the country house genre with
authenticity as the keynote. There are a choice of dining
rooms (one of which leads through the conservatory and the
gardens) and two lounges (one of them is the library). The
grand hallway is licensed for wedding ceremonies and sweeps
majestically to the rooms above. Bedooms share the same
distinctive style and flair, with elaborately swagged drapes
and comfortable furniture.

7 en suite (bth/shr) No smoking in dining room CTV in all
bedrooms Tea and coffee making facilities Direct dial from
bedrooms Licensed Cen ht CTV 35P No coaches Riding
Last d 10.30pm
CARDS: 🔳 🔳 🔳 🔳

GH ◻◻◻ **Buxton View** 74 Corbar Rd SK17 6RJ
☎01298 79222 FAX 01298 79222
Closed Dec & Jan
This aptly named stone-built house stands north of the town amid
well maintained gardens and shrubberies which are colourful in

summer. The new owners, Mr & Mrs Howlett, have made
substantial improvements and the decoration and soft furnishings
have now been brought up to date. There is an attractive, well
appointed lounge and breakfasts are served in the conservatory.
5 en suite (bth/shr) (1 fmly) No smoking in bedrooms No
smoking in dining room CTV in all bedrooms Tea and coffee
making facilities Cen ht 7P No coaches Last d 9am
PRICE GUIDE
ROOMS: s £18-£20; d £36; wkly b&b £113;
wkly hlf-bd £183

Selected

GH ◻◻◻◻ **Buxton Wheel House Hotel** 19 College Rd
SK17 9DZ ☎01298 24869 FAX 01298 24869
Closed 24 Dec-2 Jan
Professionally run by a mother and daughter team, this
handsome Victorian house offers spacious accommodation,
including five no-smoking rooms, decorated in pale shades
with complementary soft furnishings. The lounge has good
sofas upholstered in deep greens, and the dining room can be
opened into a small bar area. At the entrance there is a good-
sized sun lounge used by walkers as a repository for outdoor
clothing.
9 en suite (bth/shr) (3 fmly) No smoking in 6 bedrooms No
smoking in dining room No smoking in 1 lounge CTV in all
bedrooms Tea and coffee making facilities No dogs
Licensed Cen ht CTV 10P Last d noon
PRICE GUIDE
ROOMS: s £24-£26; d £38-£44; wkly b&b £130-£140;
wkly hlf-bd £190-£199✳
CARDS: 🔳 🔳

Selected

GH ◻◻◻◻ **Coningsby** 6 Macclesfield Rd SK17 9AH
(between A515 and A53 on B5059)
☎01298 26735 FAX 01298 26735
Set back from the main road and surrounded by its own
carefully tended gardens, this impressive Victorian House has,
over the past twenty years, been faithfully restored and
refurbished in keeping with the period of its architecture.
Each of the large bedrooms is elaborately but tastefully
decorated, good use being made of Warners fabrics and
complementary wall coverings; two have living flame fires in
the original fireplaces, together with comfortable button-back
chairs in which to relax. There is a strictly observed no
smoking rule.
3 en suite (shr) No smoking CTV in all bedrooms Tea and
coffee making facilities No dogs Licensed Cen ht No
children 6P No coaches Last d 4pm
PRICE GUIDE
ROOMS: d £36-£50; wkly b&b £120-£137.75; wkly hlf-bd
£214.50-£232.50

GH ◻◻ **Griff** 2 Compton Rd SK17 9DN ☎01298 23628
Situated in a quiet, leafy and pleasantly established residential area,
The Griff has good, comfortable and well equipped rooms furnished
and finished predominantly in pine with modern en suite facilities.
In addition to a bright breakfast room there is also a cosy lounge.
5 en suite (shr) No smoking CTV in all bedrooms Tea and coffee
making facilities No dogs Cen ht CTV No children 5P No
coaches Last d noon

PRICE GUIDE
ROOMS: d fr £36; wkly b&b fr £120; wkly hlf-bd fr £158

Selected

GH Q Q Q Q **The Grosvenor House Hotel** 1 Broad Walk
SK17 6JE (nr Opera House)
☎01298 72439 FAX 01298 72439
Only a few minutes' walk from the Opera House and town
centre, this guest house enjoys an attractive location
overlooking the 55-acre Pavilion Gardens. Traditional and
more modern upholstery fabrics are delightfully blended in
the lounge's furnishings, while well equipped bedrooms have
good modern en suite facilities. To one side of the house
stands a cheerfully decorated coffee shop which opens at
weekends and in season.
8 en suite (bth/shr) (2 fmly) No smoking in bedrooms No
smoking in dining room CTV in all bedrooms Tea and coffee
making facilities No dogs (ex guide dogs) Licensed Cen ht
No children 8yrs 6P No coaches Last d breakfast
PRICE GUIDE
ROOMS: s £42.50-£47.50; d £50-£70; wkly b&b £157.50-
£210; wkly hlf-bd £230-£275
CARDS:

GH Q Q **Hawthorn Farm** Fairfield Rd SK17 7ED (on A6
Manchester/Stockport rd) ☎01298 23230
Apr-Oct
This lovely Tudor Farmhouse is set back from the road to
Manchester in beautiful gardens. Although thoroughly
modernised, the original architectural features have been carefully
maintained. Main house bedrooms are furnished in a mixture of
styles though all have very good beds while the 'shippen' houses
the annexe rooms, most of which have modern fully-tiled en
suites.
6 rms (1 shr) 6 annexe rms (4 shr) (1 fmly) No smoking in
dining room Tea and coffee making facilities Cen ht CTV 12P
No coaches
PRICE GUIDE
ROOMS: s £20-£21; d £40-£48✱

GH Q Q Q *Lakenham* 11 Burlington Rd SK17 9AL
☎01298 79209
This lovely guest house stands in its own gardens, set back from
the road and looking out over the Pavilion and its gardens.
Furnishings are in keeping with the house's period character with
some Art Deco ornaments. Comfortable, very spacious bedrooms
are equipped with good armchairs and refrigerators as well as the
more familiar modern facilities. All the furniture is highly
polished and well cared for.
6 en suite (bth/shr) (3 fmly) No smoking in dining room CTV in
all bedrooms Tea and coffee making facilities 9P No coaches
Last d 9am

GH Q Q **The Old Manse Private Hotel** 6 Clifton Rd,
Silverlands SK17 6QL ☎01298 25638
Closed Xmas & New Year
This Victorian dwelling faced in traditional local stone stands in a
leafy residential setting. Bedrooms are amply furnished while
reception rooms consist of a small bar counter which opens into
the dining room and a small sitting room with TV. Mrs Whitaker
offers plain English cooking.
8 rms (4 shr) (2 fmly) No smoking in dining room Tea and
coffee making facilities Licensed Cen ht CTV No children 5yrs
4P No coaches Last d 5pm

PRICE GUIDE
ROOMS: s fr £18; d £36-£40; wkly hlf-bd £175-£189

GH Q Q **Roseleigh Private Hotel** 19 Broad Walk SK17 6JR
☎01298 24904
Closed Jan rs Dec
Located opposite the Pavilion Gardens and lake, this hotel leads
out on to a pedestrian walkway to the opera house and town
centre; vehicular access is gained via Hartington road. The good-
sized bedrooms are furnished in traditional style, while the public
areas include a quiet lounge and a separate bar and dining room.
13 rms (8 bth/shr) (1 fmly) No smoking in bedrooms No
smoking in dining room CTV in all bedrooms Tea and coffee
making facilities Licensed 12P No coaches Last d 5pm
PRICE GUIDE
ROOMS: s £20; d £40-£42; wkly b&b £140-£147; wkly hlf-bd
£195-£200✱
CARDS: 🔲 💳

GH Q Q **Templeton** 13 Compton Rd SK17 9DN
☎01298 25275 FAX 01298 25275
This stone-faced Victorian house stands in a quiet residential area
of town. Accommodation is plainly furnished but the en suite
rooms are comfortable and a good size. Mrs Spider cooks a
traditional set dinner and is happy to take specific tastes into
consideration. There is also a good lounge to relax in.
6 rms (4 bth/shr) (2 fmly) No smoking in dining room CTV in
all bedrooms Tea and coffee making facilities No dogs Licensed
Cen ht CTV No children 3yrs 6P No coaches Last d noon
PRICE GUIDE
ROOMS: s £25.50-£27; d £35-£38; wkly b&b £115.50-£126;
wkly hlf-bd £168-£178.50✱

GH Q Q Q **Thorn Heyes Private Hotel** 137 London Rd
SK17 9NW (on A515) ☎01298 23539
Closed 2 wks Nov
A large imposing Victorian house stands in its own grounds and is
furnished in keeping with its character. The lounge is comfortable
and has a bar, and breakfast is served in the dining room
overlooking the garden.
8 en suite (shr) (2 fmly) No smoking in dining room CTV in all
bedrooms Tea and coffee making facilities Licensed Cen ht 12P
No coaches
PRICE GUIDE
ROOMS: s £18-£28; d fr £36; wkly b&b fr £123✱

Selected

GH Q Q Q Q **Westminster Hotel** 21 Broadwalk
SK17 6JT (approach via Hartington road)
☎01298 23929 FAX 01298 71121
Feb-Nov
The service at this friendly small hotel overlooking the
Pavillion and its grounds is very friendly. Well kept reception
rooms are spacious and comfortably furnished, bth lounge and
dining room having good views. The bedrooms are freshly
decorated and the more recently refurbished rooms are very
attractively co-ordinated.
12 en suite (bth/shr) No smoking in dining room CTV in all
bedrooms Tea and coffee making facilities No dogs (ex
guide dogs) Licensed Cen ht 14P Last d 3pm
PRICE GUIDE
ROOMS: s £26; d £42-£44; wkly b&b £147-£154; wkly hlf-
bd £200-£214✱
CARDS: 🔲 💳 💳

CADNAM Hampshire Map **04** SU31

GH QQ **The Old Well Restaurant** Romsey Rd, Copythorne
SO4 2PE (on A31) ☎01703 812321 & 812700
This popular family-owned restaurant with rooms is located in the
village of Copythorne, just off the motorway. Three of the rooms
have modern en suite facilities and attractive decor, while the
other three have the use of a bathroom and shower room and are
more simply decorated. There area small kitchen for guest use and
a television lounge.
6 rms (3 bth) (2 fmly) CTV in all bedrooms Tea and coffee
making facilities No dogs (ex guide dogs) Licensed Cen ht
CTV No children 3yrs 6P
PRICE GUIDE
ROOMS: s £22-£26; d £32-£42✱
CARDS: (£)

Selected

GH QQQQ **Walnut Cottage** Old Romsey Rd
SO40 2NP ☎01703 812275
Closed 24-26 Dec
This pretty Victorian cottage stands in a quiet New Forest
lane, its well tended back garden leading down to the river. En
suite bedrooms are neat and well presented, standards of both
housekeeping and maintenance being high. Comfortable
public areas with a relaxed atmosphere include the sunny
breakfast room where guests gather round a communal table
to enjoy a hearty traditional breakfast which will set them up
for the rest of the day. Helpful hosts will advise on where
other meals can be best obtained and also recommend places
worth visiting in and around the vicinity.
3 en suite (bth/shr) No smoking in dining room No smoking
in lounges CTV in all bedrooms Tea and coffee making
facilities No dogs (ex guide dogs) Cen ht CTV No children
14yrs 4P No coaches Free loan of bikes
PRICE GUIDE
ROOMS: s £28-£30; d £40-£43

❤ QQQ Mrs A M Dawe **Budds** *(SU310139)* Winsor Rd,
Winsor SO40 2HN ☎01703 812381
Apr-Oct
A property of great charm and character, this small farmhouse
offers two pretty bedrooms (one now provided with en suite
facilities) and cosy public areas. A hearty farmhouse breakfast is
the only meal served.
2 rms (1 bth) (1 fmly) No smoking Tea and coffee making facilities
No dogs (ex guide dogs) Cen ht CTV 3P 200 acres beef dairy
PRICE GUIDE
ROOMS: s fr £17; d fr £34; wkly b&b fr £110✱

Selected

❤ QQQQ Mrs A Dawe **Kents** *(SU315139)* Winsor Rd,
Winsor SO4 2HN ☎01703 813497
Apr-Oct
Dating from the 16th century, this delightful farmhouse is full
of character. Guests are warmly welcomed and well cared for,
the comfortable accommodation providing a home-from-
home environment. En suite facilities are modern and the
bedrooms well presented. Breakfast is the only meal served,
but Mrs Dawe is happy to recommend eating places, and there
is a cosy lounge in which guests can relax.
2 en suite (bth/shr) (1 fmly) No smoking No dogs Cen ht
CTV No children 2yrs 4P 200 acres beef dairy

CALLINGTON Cornwall & Isles of Scilly Map **02** SX36

◀ QQQ *Manor House* Rilla Mill PL17 7NT ☎01579 62354
A 300-year-old inn peacefully situated in the village of Rilla Mill
provides accommodation in six modern stone-built cottages in the
extensive grounds which front the River Lynher and benefit from
250 yards of fishing rights. Each cottage has two bedrooms, a well
equipped bathroom and an open-plan lounge/dining room and
modern kitchen area; the rooms are all named after Cornish rivers,
and two enjoy river frontage. Both self catering and bed and
breakfast accommodation are available, breakfast being served in
the restaurant which also offers home-cooked bar meals and an
extensive carte.
6 annexe en suite (bth/shr) (6 fmly) CTV in all bedrooms Tea
and coffee making facilities Cen ht CTV ch fac 50P Last d
9.30pm
CARDS: ▨ ▨

CALNE Wiltshire Map **03** ST97

Premier Selected

GH QQQQQ **Chilvester
Hill House** CALNE SN11 0LP
(A4 from Calne towards
Chippenham, after 0.5m take
right turn marked Bremhill.
Drive of house immediately
on right) ☎01249 813981 &
815785 FAX 01249 814217
This handsome Victorian
building stands in seven-and-
a-half acres of land, with an
outdoor heated swimming pool. The three bedrooms are all en
suite and well equipped with remote control TV and tea trays.
The house has a warm and friendly atmosphere, and dinner
may be served by arrangement.
3 en suite (bth) No smoking in dining room CTV in all
bedrooms Tea and coffee making facilities No dogs (ex
guide dogs) Licensed Cen ht CTV No children 12yrs 8P
No coaches Outdoor swimming pool (heated) Last d 11am
PRICE GUIDE
ROOMS: s £40-£50; d £60-£75
CARDS: ▨ ▨ ▨ ▨ (£)

CAMBRIDGE Cambridgeshire Map **05** TL45

See also Little Gransden

GH QQQ *Acorn* 154 Chesterton Rd CB4 1DA
☎01223 353888 FAX 01223 350527
A small, family run establishment offers light, fresh
accommodation and a friendly atmosphere. There are a couple of
ground-floor rooms, a family bedroom and a cosy dining room
where guests can have a hearty breakfast (vegetarian if desired).
Evening meals must be booked in advance and there is car parking
at the rear of the property.
5 rms (3 shr) (1 fmly) CTV in all bedrooms Tea and coffee
making facilities No dogs (ex guide dogs) Cen ht 5P Last d 6pm

GH QQQ *Assisi* 193 Cherry Hinton Rd CB1 4BX
☎01223 211466 & 246648 FAX 01223 412900
Closed 17 Dec-9 Jan
Popular with students, this large house provides soundly furnished
rooms with good en suite facilities. Its location is a 25-minute
walk south-east from the city centre.

17 en suite (bth/shr) (1 fmly) No smoking in 5 bedrooms No smoking in dining room No smoking in lounges CTV in all bedrooms Tea and coffee making facilities Direct dial from bedrooms No dogs (ex guide dogs) Cen ht CTV 15P
PRICE GUIDE
ROOMS: s £26-£29; d £36-£40✳
CARDS: £

GH **QQ** *Avimore* 310 Cherry Hinton Rd CB1 4AU (1.75m S of city centre just inside Cambridge Ring Rd)
☎01223 410956 FAX 01223 576957
This small, family-run guesthouse is on the southern edge of Cambridge and offers accommodation in simple but well equipped bedrooms. There is a small television lounge occupying part of the breakfast room.
4 rms (2 shr) (2 fmly) No smoking in dining room CTV in all bedrooms Tea and coffee making facilities Direct dial from bedrooms No dogs (ex guide dogs) Cen ht CTV 5P
PRICE GUIDE
ROOMS: s £18-£28; d £33-£40✳
CARDS: £

GH **QQ** *Benson House* 24 Huntingdon Rd CB3 0HH (on A604 near New Hall & Fitzwilliam House) ☎01223 311594
Located on one of the approach roads into the city, close to New Hall and Fitzwilliam Universities, Benson House offers sound accommodation in fresh looking, slightly compact bedrooms, including two on the ground floor. The small rear car park is of particular benefit in this area of Cambridge.
5 rms (2 shr) (3 fmly) No smoking in dining room CTV in all bedrooms Tea and coffee making facilities Cen ht 5P
See advertisement on p.119.

GH QQ *Bon Accord House* 20 St Margarets Square CB1 4AP (in cul-de-sac just off Cherry Hinton road)
☎01223 411188 & 246568
Closed Xmas & New Year
This well established, small, friendly guest house, situated in a quiet cul-de-sac to the south of the city centre. Bedrooms vary in size, there being some singles. There is a small lounge as well as the large separate dining room where a full choice of English breakfasts is served.
9 rms (1 shr) (1 fmly) No smoking CTV in all bedrooms Tea and coffee making facilities No dogs Cen ht 12P No coaches
CARDS: 🔼 ☴

GH QQQ *Brooklands* 95 Cherry Hinton Rd CB1 4BS
☎01223 242035 FAX 01223 242035
Friendly owners ensure good levels of comfort at this modernised, attractively decorated guest house. It is located about 20 minutes' walk south-east of the centre, and has many amenities including a sauna.
5 en suite (bth/shr) No smoking in bedrooms No smoking in dining room CTV in all bedrooms Tea and coffee making facilities No dogs (ex guide dogs) Cen ht CTV 5P No coaches Sauna Last d noon
PRICE GUIDE
ROOMS: s £28-£30; d £38-£45
CARDS: 🔼 ☴ 🔳 💿 💲   (£)

GH QQQ *Cristina's* 47 St. Andrews Rd CB4 1DL
☎01223 365855 & 327700
Closed 25-27 Dec
There is a friendly atmosphere at this small family-run guest house, located in a residential road north of the city centre. The high standards of maintenance are particularly impressive throughout the house. A no-smoking policy is applied to public rooms, which include a small lounge and a kitchen-themed dining room. Though they vary in size, all the bedrooms are neat and light in appearance, and the majority have en suite shower rooms.
6 rms (5 shr) (2 fmly) CTV in all bedrooms Tea and coffee making facilities No dogs Cen ht CTV 8P
PRICE GUIDE
ROOMS: s £25-£26✳

GH QQ *Dykelands* 157 Mowbray Rd CB1 4SP
☎01223 244300 FAX 01223 566746
This busy guest house is run by an energetic young couple who share lounge and garden with their guests. Bedrooms are spacious, simply furnished and well maintained.
8 rms (5 shr) (3 fmly) No smoking in dining room No smoking in lounges CTV in all bedrooms Tea and coffee making facilities Licensed Cen ht CTV 7P
PRICE GUIDE
ROOMS: s £19.75-£25.50; d £33-£39.50
CARDS: 🔼 ☴ 🔳 💿

GH QQQ *Fairways* 141-143 Cherry Hinton Rd CB1 4BX (from city centre towards Addenbrookes Hospital turn off A1307 (after bridge) then left into Cherry Hinton Rd)
☎01223 246063 FAX 01223 212093
Closed 24 Dec-1 Jan
This popular, family-run guest house catering predominantly for commercial guests continues to improve standards, and redecorated bedrooms now have direct dial telephones with integral radio alarms; most also have en suite showers. Public rooms include a pleasant, airy lounge which incorporates a well stocked bar and a pool table, and the comfortable dining room.
15 rms (8 shr) (3 fmly) No smoking in dining room CTV in all bedrooms Tea and coffee making facilities Direct dial from bedrooms No dogs (ex guide dogs) Licensed Cen ht CTV 20P

Pool table Last d 7pm
PRICE GUIDE
ROOMS: s £20-£28; d £35-£42
CARDS: 🔼 ☴

GH QQQ *De Freville House* 166 Chesterton Rd CB4 1DA (at junc of Ring Road and Elizabeth Way)
☎01223 354993 FAX 01223 321890
This attractively renovated and family-run Victorian house is located about a mile northeast of the city centre.
9 rms (5 bth/shr) (1 fmly) No smoking CTV in all bedrooms Tea and coffee making facilities No dogs Cen ht CTV No children 6yrs 2P No coaches
PRICE GUIDE
ROOMS: s £19-£35; d £34-£45

GH QQ *Hamden* 89 High St, Cherry Hinton CB1 4LU (2m E)
☎01223 413263
Friendly Italian proprietors maintain high standards of maintenance in this no-smoking guest house in Cherry Hinton. Whilst there is no lounge, bedrooms are generally of good proportions, each having remote control television, tea-making facilities and double glazing. Limited off-street car parking is provided.
5 en suite (shr) (1 fmly) No smoking CTV in all bedrooms Tea and coffee making facilities No dogs (ex guide dogs) Cen ht No children 10yrs 6P No coaches
PRICE GUIDE
ROOMS: s fr £25; d £35-£40

GH QQQ *Hamilton Hotel* 156 Chesterton Rd CB4 1DA (1m NE of city centre, off ring road A1134)
☎01223 365664 FAX 01223 314866
This charming guest house standing a mile to the northeast of the city centre offers well equipped, double-glazed bedrooms and smart public areas which include a restaurant (with dispense bar) serving snacks and evening meals. Car parking is available - a valuable asset in this area - and the hotel is very popular with commercial users.
18 rms (13 shr) (3 fmly) No smoking in area of dining room CTV in all bedrooms Tea and coffee making facilities Direct dial from bedrooms No dogs Licensed Cen ht No children 4yrs 10P No coaches Last d noon
CARDS: 🔼 ☴ 🔳 💿

GH QQQ *Helen Hotel* 167-169 Hills Rd CB2 2RJ (1m E, follow signs to A604 Colchester)
☎01223 246465 FAX 01223 214406
Closed 15 Dec-5 Jan
Hospitable owners work hard to maintain traditional values and good accommodation at this hotel about a mile east of the city. All bedrooms are equally well equipped, though sizes and styles do vary, while the comfortable lounge offers satellite TV and has a bar adjacent. Freshly home-cooked Italian and British dishes are served each evening, the day having begun with a hearty breakfast.
22 en suite (bth/shr) 5 annexe en suite (shr) (4 fmly) CTV in all bedrooms Tea and coffee making facilities Direct dial from bedrooms Licensed Cen ht CTV 20P Last d 7pm
CARDS: 🔼 ☴ 🔳 💿
See advertisement on p.121.

GH QQ *Kirkwood House* 172 Chesterton Rd CB4 1DA (Exit junc13 M11) ☎01223 313874
Closed Jan
This small Edwardian house offers reliable bed and breakfast accommodation, in freshly decorated, well maintained bedrooms, one of which is on the ground floor. Breakfast is generally taken in two sittings, in a small well appointed dining room which features ➡

a collection of antique plates.

5 rms (2 shr) No smoking CTV in all bedrooms Tea and coffee making facilities No dogs Cen ht No children 7yrs 2P No coaches

---

GH QQQ **Lensfield Hotel** 53 Lensfield Rd CB2 1EN (on SW side of city centre)
☎01223 355017 Telex no 818183 FAX 01223 312022
Closed 2wks Xmas
A well established, friendly, family-run hotel situated a few minutes' walk from the city centre offers bedrooms which vary considerably in both size and style. Those recently refurbished provide modern en suite accommodation and all rooms are well equipped and maintained. The smart restaurant features carte and fixed-price menus of international dishes at competitive prices, and the small bar which stands next to it is very well stocked.
36 rms (2 bth 18 shr) (4 fmly) No smoking in 4 bedrooms No smoking in area of dining room No smoking in lounges CTV in all bedrooms Tea and coffee making facilities Direct dial from bedrooms No dogs Licensed Cen ht CTV 7P Last d 8.45pm
PRICE GUIDE
ROOMS: s £42-£45; d £52-£58; wkly b&b £294-£315; wkly hlf-bd £343-£364✱
CARDS: 🅰 💳 🌐 ⑩

GH QQQ **Mowbray Lodge** 5 Mowbray Rd CB1 4SR
☎01223 240089 FAX 01223 240089
Good accommodation and smart public areas are provided at Mowbray Lodge, a small friendly guest house on the A1134. En suite bedrooms vary in size but are all attractively decorated and well equipped; smoking is not permitted in the bedrooms though guests may smoke in the comfortable lounge. Breakfast is served in a pleasant dining room and evening meals are available by prior arrangement.
6 en suite (shr) (1 fmly) No smoking in bedrooms No smoking in dining room CTV in all bedrooms Tea and coffee making facilities No dogs (ex guide dogs) Cen ht 6P Last d 5pm
PRICE GUIDE
ROOMS: s £28; d £36-£42; wkly b&b £126-£196✱
CARDS: 🅰 🌐 💳 🔷 ⑩ £

Selected

GH QQQQ **Old School Hotel & Guest House** 9 Greenside, Waterbeach CB5 9HW (0.50m from A10 in centre of Waterbeach village overlooking green)
☎01223 861609 FAX 01223 441683
An attractively converted old school overlooking Waterbeach's village green offers a friendly and informal environment, resident owners making every effort to meet guests' needs. Modern bedrooms and shower rooms - though in some cases small - are immaculately maintained, and refreshments and drinks are served during the day in a pleasant conservatory lounge. An annexe building just off the rear car parking area contains a sauna and indoor swimming pool.
8 en suite (shr) No smoking in dining room CTV in all bedrooms Tea and coffee making facilities Direct dial from bedrooms No dogs (ex guide dogs) Licensed Cen ht CTV 8P No coaches Indoor swimming pool (heated) Sauna Last d 7.45pm
PRICE GUIDE
ROOMS: s fr £30; d fr £45
CARDS: 🅰 💳 🌐 ⑩

GH QQQ **Sorrento Hotel** 196 Cherry Hinton Rd CB1 4AN
☎01223 243533 FAX 01223 213463
This family owned and managed hotel offers a good range of services and facilities including a TV lounge, a small bar and the recently extended restaurant, which features a good range of Italian and French dishes with daily and carte menus. Bedrooms are furnished to a good standard and very well equipped.
24 en suite (bth/shr) (5 fmly) No smoking in 4 bedrooms No smoking in area of dining room No smoking in 1 lounge CTV in all bedrooms Tea and coffee making facilities Direct dial from bedrooms Licensed Cen ht CTV 27P Petanque Last d 8.30pm
PRICE GUIDE
ROOMS: s £40-£47.50; d £55-£65; wkly b&b £280-£332.50; wkly hlf-bd £350-£575✱
CARDS: 🅰 💳 🌐 ⑩ 🔷 £

GH QQQ **Suffolk House Private Hotel** 69 Milton Rd CB4 1XA (1.5m on A1309)
☎01223 352016 FAX 01223 566816
This private hotel has fresh, attractive and tastefully furnished bedrooms, all with modern en suite facilities, TV, radios and tea tray. Hard working proprietors Mr and Mrs Cuthbert work hard to provide high standards of housekeeping and maintenance.
11 en suite (bth/shr) (5 fmly) No smoking in dining room No smoking in lounges CTV in all bedrooms Tea and coffee making facilities No dogs Cen ht No children 4yrs 11P No coaches
PRICE GUIDE
ROOMS: s £36-£45; d £50-£65✱
CARDS: 🅰 💳 🌐 🔷 ⑩ £

CANTERBURY Kent Map **05** TR15

See also Petham and Womenswold

GH Q **Castle Court** 8 Castle St CT1 2QF (at Norman castle turn left into Castle St guesthouse 200 metres on right)
☎01227 463441
A simple, well maintained guest house offers modest accommodation including a small dining room/lounge where a choice of English or Continental breakfast is served.
10 rms (2 shr) (2 fmly) No smoking in dining room CTV in all bedrooms Cen ht CTV 3P
PRICE GUIDE
ROOMS: s £18-£22; d £32-£45✱
CARDS: 🅰 💳 £

GH QQ **Cathedral Gate Hotel** 36 Burgate CT1 2HA (next to main gateway into cathedral precincts)
☎01227 464381 FAX 01227 462800
This small, family-run, private hotel is situated next to the cathedral. Low beam ceilings and sloping beams add to its character. Bedrooms are of various sizes, and a number have recently been redecorated. There are a comfortable lounge and a very small dining room, but guests can take breakfast in their rooms.
12 rms (2 bth) 12 annexe rms (10 bth/shr) (4 fmly) No smoking in dining room CTV in all bedrooms Tea and coffee making facilities Direct dial from bedrooms Licensed Cen ht 12P Last d 9pm
PRICE GUIDE
ROOMS: s £21-£46; d £40-£70
CARDS: 🅰 💳 🌐 ⑩ 💳 🔷 ⑩ £

GH QQQ **Chaucer Lodge** 62 New Dover Rd CT1 3DT (on A2 out of city centre to Dover, 0.25m S)
☎01227 459141 FAX 01227 459141
This well kept guest house is within a 10-minute walk of the city centre, The neat, bright bedrooms provide good amenities and the cheerful hosts make certain their guests get a warm welcome.

6 en suite (bth/shr) (2 fmly) No smoking in 2 bedrooms No smoking in dining room CTV in all bedrooms Tea and coffee making facilities No dogs (ex guide dogs) Cen ht 8P No coaches

PRICE GUIDE
ROOMS: d £35-£50*

Selected

GH QQQQ *Ebury Hotel* New Dover Rd CT1 3DX
☎01227 768433 FAX 01227 459187
Closed 15 Dec-14 Jan
An imposing, double-fronted Victorian building, the Ebury is set back from the main road in two acres of well kept grounds. The spacious bedrooms are furnished to a high standard and many have original fireplaces. Reception is staffed throughout the day and evening, and guests dining in the hotel can enjoy pre-dinner drinks in the elegant lounge. The short menu offers individually priced dishes in traditional English style.
15 en suite (bth/shr) (2 fmly) No smoking in dining room CTV in all bedrooms Tea and coffee making facilities Direct dial from bedrooms Licensed Cen ht CTV 21P No coaches Indoor swimming pool (heated) Spa Exercise equipment Last d 8.30pm
CARDS: ▨ ▆ ▆▆

Selected

GH QQQQ *Ersham Lodge* 12 New Dover Rd CT1 3AP
☎01227 463174 FAX 01227 455482
May-Oct
This large creeper-clad hotel has been run by the Pellay family for 16 years. A charming house close to the town centre, it has been tastefully decorated and furnished throughout to provide comfortable, well appointed accommodation. Guests have the use of a small lounge, and there is a spacious breakfast room leading on to the patio and garden.
14 rms (2 bth 11 shr) (1 fmly) No smoking in bedrooms No smoking in dining room CTV in all bedrooms Tea and coffee making facilities Direct dial from bedrooms No dogs (ex guide dogs) Licensed Cen ht 12P
CARDS: ▨ ▆ ▆▆

Selected

GH QQQQ *Magnolia House* 36 St Dunstan's Ter CT2 8AX (from A2 take turning for Canterbury. turn left at first roundabout approaching the city (signposted university). Third turning on right)
☎01227 765121 FAX 01227 765121
This well maintained Georgian house is set in a quiet residential area on the university side of town, within ten minutes' walk of the main shopping area. It has a great deal of charm and an air of quality. Nearly all the bedrooms are small and cosy, but they are well appointed; four have nicely tiled showers en suite and the other three have baths. A small but tastefully appointed TV lounge is the only area in which smoking is allowed.
7 en suite (bth/shr) No smoking CTV in all bedrooms Tea and coffee making facilities No dogs Cen ht CTV 4P No coaches

➡

PRICE GUIDE
ROOMS: s £36-£45; d £55-£80
CARDS:

13 rms (10 bth/shr) (2 fmly) CTV in all bedrooms Tea and coffee making facilities Direct dial from bedrooms Licensed Cen ht 10P Last d 8.15pm
PRICE GUIDE
ROOMS: s £32-£40; d £45-£55
CARDS:

Premier Selected

GH QQQQQ The Old Rectory Ashford Rd, Chartham CT4 7HS (take A28 towards Ashford, follow road for apprx 2.50 miles, Old Rectory on right just before x-roads signed Chartham)
☎01227 730075
FAX 01227 731929
Closed 17 Dec-10 Jan
A lovely Georgian house has been tastefully and thoughtfully decorated and furnished to reflect the character of the building. The bedrooms are spacious, comfortable and well equipped, with all those little extra touches that help to make guests feel at home. There is a comfortable sitting room which has recently been redecorated, and in the dining room Mrs Creasy provides three-course dinners and excellent English breakfasts.
3 en suite (bth/shr) No smoking CTV in 1 bedroom Tea and coffee making facilities No dogs (ex guide dogs) Cen ht CTV No children 14yrs 5P No coaches Last d noon
PRICE GUIDE
ROOMS: s £30-£40; d £45-£60
CARDS:

GH QQQ Oriel Lodge 3 Queens Av CT2 8AY (entering town on A2 from London, 400yds after first roundabout turn left into Queens Avenue) ☎01227 462845
This attractive detached Edwardian house, located in a residential area near the town centre, has been completely renovated by proprietors Keith and Anthea Rishworth. The bedrooms have been thoughtfully equipped and suitably furnished and they are all bright and modern; some have views of the cathedral. The open-plan dining room combines with a small comfortable lounge.
6 rms (2 shr) (1 fmly) No smoking in bedrooms No smoking in dining room CTV in all bedrooms Tea and coffee making facilities No dogs Cen ht No children 6yrs 6P No coaches
PRICE GUIDE
ROOMS: s £20-£26; d £35-£55; wkly b&b £110-£173
CARDS:

Selected

GH QQQQ Pointers Hotel 1 London Rd CT2 8LR (follow signs for university & Whitstable, Hotel opposite St Dunstan's Church) (Logis)
☎01227 456846 FAX 01227 831131
Closed 23 Dec-12 Jan
Perfectly situated within walking distance of the city centre, close to the university and cathedral, this delightful Georgian hotel is personally run by the resident proprietors Jack and Christine O'Brien. Bedrooms are particularly well decorated and equipped with direct dial telephone, TV, radio and tea trays. Public rooms comprise a well designed reception bar and lounge, and a pretty double-sided dining room. Both meals and light refreshments are served, service is friendly and the atmosphere informal. A private car park is available.

Selected

GH QQQQ Thanington Hotel 140 Wincheap CT1 3RY (on A28, just outside City Walls)
☎01227 453227 FAX 01227 453225
Black is the predominant colour of this unusual but visually appealing private hotel which stands some 15 minutes' walk from the town centre. Two modern wings - containing all the bedrooms and an indoor swimming pool - have been added to the original house, and facilities include a games room, snooker table and dispense bar as well as ample car parking space and an attractive garden.
10 en suite (bth) (2 fmly) No smoking in dining room CTV in all bedrooms Tea and coffee making facilities Direct dial from bedrooms Licensed Cen ht CTV 10P No coaches Indoor swimming pool (heated) Dart board pool table
PRICE GUIDE
ROOMS: s £42-£48; d £59-£65
CARDS:
See advertisement on p.125.

Premier Selected

GH QQQQQ Thruxted Oast Mystole, Chartham CT4 7BX (4m SW on A28)
☎01227 730080
Closed Xmas
This is a charming 18th-century oast house and barn is set in an area surrounded by hop gardens and orchards. Guests are made to feel relaxed and welcome by the friendly staff whose attention to detail makes comfort assured. Spacious bedrooms are tastefully furnished and the welcoming sitting room houses many books and magazines. Typically English food is carefully prepared using good, fresh produce and is served in the characterful dining room. Ample parking facilities are available.
3 en suite (shr) No smoking in bedrooms CTV in all bedrooms Tea and coffee making facilities Direct dial from bedrooms No dogs (ex guide dogs) Cen ht No children 8yrs 8P No coaches Croquet lawn
PRICE GUIDE
ROOMS: s £65; d £75
CARDS:

Selected

GH QQQQ Waltham Court Hotel Kake St, Petham CT4 5BS (1.5m through village towards Waltham)
☎01227 700413 FAX 01227 700127

MAGNOLIA HOUSE

36 St Dunstan's Terrace, Canterbury, Kent CT2 8AX
Tel and Fax: (01227) 765121 HIGHLY COMMENDED

This friendly, family run Georgian house, set in a quiet street, just a few minutes walk from the Westgate Towers and the City centre with its magnificent Cathedral, is ideally situated for the University and touring the Kentish coast and countryside. Enjoy our en suite facilities or luxurious 4 poster suite, varied and delicious breakfast, and relax in the beautiful walled garden. Car parking.

THE OLD RECTORY
Ashford Road, Chartham
Canterbury, Kent CT4 7HS
Telephone: 01227 730075
Fax: 01227 731929

AA QQQQQ Premier Selected

This elegant family home, formerly a rectory, set in 2 acres of well kept garden is furnished with antiques. The beautifully decorated rooms all have en-suite facilities, hairdryers and many extras. 2 bedroom suite with private lounge available. Within easy reach of Channel ports for continental travel or day trips to France. Canterbury is only 2½ miles away or 5 minutes by train. Safe parking within grounds.

FROM £22 pp including full English Breakfast

ORIEL LODGE
CANTERBURY

In a tree-lined residential road, five minutes' walk from the city centre, Oriel Lodge offers a clean, comfortable bed and breakfast in the warm and restful atmosphere of an Edwardian family house.

Tel: 01227 462845
Oriel Lodge, 3 Queens Avenue, Canterbury, Kent CT2 8AY

POINTERS HOTEL

1 London Road, Canterbury
Tel: 01227-456846 Fax: 01227 831131

Situated only a few minutes' walk from the City centre and Cathedral and close to the University.
Pointers is a family-run Georgian hotel offering home-produced English meals.
All bedrooms have either bath or shower and each is equipped with colour television, radio, direct-dial telephone and tea and coffee making facilities.

Private car park.   AA
QQQQ

This hotel is a spacious red-brick Georgian building quietly set in three acres of grounds midway between Petham and Waltham, which originally housed 30 of the parish poor. An informal reception area with comfortable sofas doubles as a bar and there are a large restaurant in country-house style and a cocktail bar. The four bedrooms are bright and cheerful, individually decorated in pale shades of pink and blue with solid pine furniture. Each has a smart modern bathroom en suite.

4 en suite (bth/shr) (1 fmly) No smoking in area of dining room CTV in all bedrooms Tea and coffee making facilities No dogs (ex guide dogs) Licensed Cen ht 45P Sauna Last d 9.45pm

PRICE GUIDE
ROOMS: s £35-£45; d £50-£65; wkly b&b £170-£200; wkly hlf-bd £230-£260
CARDS: £

Selected

GH Q Q Q Q **The White House** 6 St Peters Ln CT1 2BP (20yds off main shopping area) ☎01227 761836
There is a warm and friendly atmosphere within this attractive Regency house, which is personally run by the friendly owners, Mr and Mrs Blackman. Well maintained and attractive, The White House has good sized comfortable bedrooms, all very well-equipped. There is an elegant dining/sitting room, where guest take their breakfast at a large communal table.

9 en suite (bth/shr) (2 fmly) No smoking in dining room No smoking in lounges CTV in all bedrooms Tea and coffee making facilities No dogs Cen ht CTV 9P

PRICE GUIDE
ROOMS: s fr £30; d £35-£45
£

❤ Q Q Q Mr & Mrs R D Linch **Upper Ansdore** *(TR118498)* Duckpit Ln, Petham CT4 5QB (from Canterbury take B2068 and turn right through village. Take left hand fork and after 1.5m turn right to Upper Ansdore) ☎01227 700672
Closed Xmas & New Year
Parts of this peacefully located building date back to the 14th century. Immaculately kept, it offers well-laid out bedrooms, each of which has added character with exposed timbers. The location is ideal for outdoor pursuits.

3 en suite (shr) (1 fmly) No smoking Tea and coffee making facilities No dogs (ex guide dogs) Cen ht 5P 4 acres mixed smallholding

PRICE GUIDE
ROOMS: d £38
£

Selected

◀ Q Q Q Q **The Pilgrims Hotel** 18 The Friars CT1 2AS (from Canterbury follow signs for Marlowe Theatre,establishment situated opposite) ☎01227 464531 FAX 01227 762514
Opposite the Marlowe Theatre you will find a 350-year-old building which is now a friendly, relaxed hotel in which the proprietors are personally involved. Bedrooms are smartly furnished and fitted, and in the beamed bar a tempting range of meals and blackboard specials is available, as well as a number of real ales.

15 en suite (bth/shr) (1 fmly) CTV in all bedrooms Tea and

coffee making facilities Direct dial from bedrooms No dogs (ex guide dogs) Cen ht No parking Last d 10pm
PRICE GUIDE
ROOMS: s fr £45; d fr £55✱
CARDS: £

CANVEY ISLAND Essex Map **05** TQ78

Selected

GH Q Q Q Q **Maisonwyck** 194-196 Furtherwick Rd SS8 7BL ☎01268 510222 FAX 01268 694208
Maisonwyck is a friendly family-run hotel which is situated centrally between the town centre and the seafront. This smart house has been refurbished to a very good standard, offering a variety of public rooms which include a spacious and comfortably appointed lounge with a grand piano, a bar with a full size snooker table, a small fitness room and a delightful indoor swimming pool with jacuzzi. Bedrooms are all attractively decorated and have quality soft furnishings, the majority also having good comfortable armchairs; each room has smart modern en suite facilities; the occasional single room could be considered a little tight in comparison to the of bedrooms Please note that the lounge is designated a non-smoking room..

7 en suite (bth/shr) (2 fmly) No smoking in dining room No smoking in lounges CTV in all bedrooms Tea and coffee making facilities Direct dial from bedrooms No dogs (ex guide dogs) Licensed Cen ht CTV 14P Indoor swimming pool (heated) Snooker Gymnasium Jacuzzi Last d 8.30pm

PRICE GUIDE
ROOMS: s £35-£45; d £50-£65; wkly b&b £210-£259; wkly hlf-bd fr £280✱
CARDS:

CARLISLE Cumbria Map **11** NY45

See also Brampton, Castle Carrock, Longtown & Thursby

GH Q Q Q **Angus Hotel** 14 Scotland Rd CA3 9DG (N on A7) ☎01228 23546 FAX 01228 31895
This friendly, family-run, small hotel conveniently situated just north of the city, about two miles from junction 44 of the M6, provides secure overnight parking. The upgraded dining room offers a relaxed setting in which to enjoy the home-cooked meals served every evening except Sunday, while the majority of bedrooms have modern en suite facilities and are well equipped. Both business and leisure users will find this establishment very much to their liking.

12 rms (7 shr) (4 fmly) No smoking in 7 bedrooms No smoking in dining room CTV in all bedrooms Tea and coffee making facilities Licensed Cen ht 8P Last d 9pm

PRICE GUIDE
ROOMS: s £23.50-£35; d £34-£49
CARDS:

GH Q Q Q **Crossroads House** Brisco CA4 0QZ (0.75m from junct 42 of M6) ☎01228 28994
Closed 24-31 Dec
Formerly two cottages, this modern guest house three miles south of Carlisle - close to the village of Brisco - incorporates several interesting features including a Roman well in the hallway and a carved oak beam dating back to 1878 in the dining room. Bedrooms are very well maintained and comfortably furnished, while public areas include a spacious, relaxing lounge and a pleasant dining room. Smoking is not permitted in bedrooms.

5 rms (1 bth/shr) (1 fmly) No smoking No dogs (ex guide dogs) Licensed Cen ht CTV 12P No coaches Last d 10am
PRICE GUIDE
ROOMS: s fr £18; d £34-£40✳

GH 🄀🄀🄀 **East View** 110 Warwick Rd CA1 1JU (on main rd into city from junct 43 of M6) ☎01228 22112
A fine Victorian guest house located within ten minutes' walk of the city centre offers bedrooms which are brightly decorated though they vary considerably in size. A hearty breakfast is provided at individual tables in the attractive dining room.
8 en suite (shr) (3 fmly) No smoking in dining room CTV in all bedrooms Tea and coffee making facilities No dogs (ex guide dogs) Cen ht 4P
PRICE GUIDE
ROOMS: s fr £18; d fr £32✳

Selected

[♨🖥] GH 🄀🄀🄀🄀 **Howard House** 27 Howard Place CA1 1HR ☎01228 29159 & 512550
An elegant late-Victorian town house situated in a quiet conservation area close to the city centre offers four large, comfortable bedrooms equipped with radio alarm clocks and remote control TV; two of them have en suite facilities, one a four-poster bed. There is a fine Victorian fireplace in the homely lounge, and breakfast is served in an attractive rear dining room looking out over the small garden and patio.
5 rms (2 shr) (2 fmly) No smoking in dining room CTV in all bedrooms Tea and coffee making facilities No dogs (ex guide dogs) Cen ht CTV Last d 2.30pm
PRICE GUIDE
ROOMS: s £15-£17; d £30-£34; wkly b&b £100-£114; wkly hlf-bd £154-£168
CARDS: 🖪 🎴

GH 🄀🄀🄀 **Kenilworth** 34 Lazonby Ter CA1 2PZ (1.5m S, on A6) ☎01228 26179
This well maintained, family-owned Victorian house is situated on the A6 approaching the city from the south. Bedrooms are comfortably furnished and attractively decorated, and there is a spacious and comfortable lounge/dining room.
6 rms (2 fmly) CTV in all bedrooms Tea and coffee making facilities Cen ht CTV 5P No coaches
PRICE GUIDE
ROOMS: s £14-£20; d £26-£30✳

GH 🄀🄀🄀 **Kingstown Hotel** 246 Kingstown Rd CA3 0DE (exit M6 at junct 44, take A7 towards city centre. Hotel on left hand side) ☎01228 515292 FAX 01228 515292
Situated beside the A7 to the north of the city centre, convenient for the M6, this comfortable family-run hotel offers well furnished and pleasantly decorated bedrooms which include two on the ground floor. Also provided are a guests' lounge, a small bar and a separate dining room.
6 rms (4 bth/shr) (1 fmly) No smoking in dining room CTV in all bedrooms Tea and coffee making facilities Licensed Cen ht 12P No coaches Last d 9.30pm
PRICE GUIDE
ROOMS: s £23-£35; d £36-£42; wkly b&b £161-£245; wkly hlf-bd £202-£285
CARDS: 🖪 💳 🎴
See advertisement on p.127.

GH ⓆⓆⓆ *Parkland* 136 Petteril St CA1 2AW
☎01228 48331
This small guesthouse situated east of the town centre offers tastefully redecorated bedrooms furnished to a high standard. There are an attractive dining room, a neat lounge and a cosy little residents' bar.
5 rms (4 shr) (2 fmly) CTV in all bedrooms Tea and coffee making facilities Licensed Cen ht CTV 3P No coaches Last d 4pm

GH ⓆⓆⓆ **The Warren** 368 Warwick Rd CA1 2RU (exit M6 junct 43 and proceed 0.5m down main road. Opposite Esso petrol station) ☎01228 33663 & 512916
Built in 1839 and once known as the Star Inn, this guest house offers prettily decorated and well equipped accommodation, including two bedrooms at ground-floor level. Decorative antique chamber pots are a feature of the lounge, and in addition to the main lounge and dining room there are two conservatory lounges at the front of the hotel.
6 rms (5 shr) (1 fmly) No smoking in bedrooms No smoking in area of dining room CTV in all bedrooms Tea and coffee making facilities Direct dial from bedrooms No dogs (ex guide dogs) Cen ht CTV 6P No coaches Last d early am
PRICE GUIDE
ROOMS: s £20-£24; d £32-£34; wkly b&b £110-£115; wkly hlf-bd £154-£165✱

🛏🖤 ♥ⓆⓆ Mrs A Westmorland **Blackwell** *(NY387512)*
Blackwell, Durdar CA2 4SH (2m S, close to race course)
☎01228 24073
This comfortable farmhouse is set around a cobbled yard with cow sheds just outside the front door. It is situated on the edge of the city next to the racecourse and is to some extent a town farm. Bedrooms are attractively furnished, and though none of them have wash basins, the bathroom is close by. A cosy lounge and dining room are provided.
2 rms (1 fmly) No smoking in bedrooms Cen ht CTV ch fac 5P 120 acres dairy mixed
PRICE GUIDE
ROOMS: s £15-£16; d £30-£32
(£)

CARNFORTH Lancashire Map **07** SD47

Premier Selected

GH ⓆⓆⓆⓆⓆ **New Capernwray Farm**
Capernwray LA6 1AD (from B6254, left at village green in Over Kellet and continue for 2m) ☎01524 734284 FAX 01524 734284
Almost 300 years old, this white-painted farmhouse in the lovely Lunesdale area of north Lancashire has been completely modernised by Peter and Sally Townend. It is situated on the edge of the Lake District, easily reached from junction 35 of the M6. Bedrooms are attractively furnished and many display original ceiling timbers. There is an elegant lounge and a friendly, informal atmosphere prevails in the dining room where guests are seated at a communal table. Peter Townend has recently introduced discovery tours, conducting guests round Hadrian's Wall, the Yorkshire Dales and the Lake District.

3 rms (1 bth 1 shr) No smoking in bedrooms No smoking in dining room CTV in all bedrooms Tea and coffee making facilities Cen ht No children 10yrs 4P No coaches Last d 5pm
PRICE GUIDE
ROOMS: d £52-£62
CARDS:
(£)

CARSINGTON Derbyshire Map **08** SK25

Selected

GH ⓆⓆⓆⓆ **Henmore Grange** Hopton DE4 4DF (turn into Hopton from B5035 and take first left at Wirksworth end of bypass) ☎01629 540420
Set above Carsington Water in a quiet village street, Henmore Grange is converted from the cowsheds of a former farm estate. Many of the rooms on the ground floor overlook the carefully tended gardens while those above look out over the water; all have fine views and were carefully converted within the original framework. There are two lounges, one with a TV and the other warmed by a log burner. Guests can enjoy their breakfasts or evening meal in the attractive dining room.
11 rms (9 bth/shr) (2 fmly) No smoking in dining room Tea and coffee making facilities Licensed Cen ht CTV 14P Last d 6pm
PRICE GUIDE
ROOMS: s £20-£31; d £36-£55; wkly b&b £140-£217; wkly hlf-bd £210-£287✱
CARDS: ▬
(£)

CARY FITZPAINE Somerset Map **03** ST52

Selected

♥ⓆⓆⓆⓆ Mrs S Crang **Cary Fitzpaine** *(ST549270)*
BA22 8JB (from A303/A37 junct at Podimore take A37 signed Bristol/Shepton Mallet for 1m)
☎01458 223250 FAX 01458 223250
Closed 23-26 Dec
This attractive Georgian farmhouse, built of local stone, is set in 600 acres of farmland specialising in sheep, cattle, horses and arable crops. Andrew and Susie Crang welcome guests to their charming home, set in 1.5 acres of gardens, for a break in the heart of Somerset. The three large bedrooms are well furnished, having a refreshing country charm. Breakfast is taken in the delightful dining room with separate tables, or on summer mornings under the rose-clad verandah. The Crangs are only too happy to recommend a local inn or restaurant for dinner, there being many in the area.
3 en suite (bth/shr) (1 fmly) No smoking in dining room No smoking in lounges CTV in all bedrooms Tea and coffee making facilities Cen ht CTV 6P Fishing 600 acres arable beef horses sheep
PRICE GUIDE
ROOMS: s £19; d £36; wkly b&b £108

CASTLE ACRE Norfolk Map **09** TF81

♥ⓆⓆ Mrs E Coghill **Lodge Farm** *(TF824172)* Castle Acre PE32 2BS ☎01760 755506 FAX 01760 755103
This large old farmhouse sits in peaceful rural surroundings and is surrounded by its own 20 acres of mature paddocks and gardens; it

is also located approximately a mile and a half from the Peddars Way walking trail that passes through Castle Acre. The accommodation is spacious and traditionally furnished, providing colour television, tea-making facilities, mineral water and a range of books for guests use. Breakfast is taken in an airy dining room with a large communal dining table. Please note that this is a non-smoking house, and that it is not suitable for pets or very young children.

3 rms (1 bth) No smoking CTV in 1 bedroom Tea and coffee making facilities No dogs No children 2yrs 6P 20 acres
PRICE GUIDE
ROOMS: s £15-£18.50; d £36-£44; wkly b&b £100-£125✳

CASTLE CARROCK Cumbria Map **12** NY55

♥ Ⓠ B W Robinson *Gelt Hall* (NY542554) CA4 9LT (B6413 to Castle Carrock) ☎01228 70260
Characteristic of its period, with oak beams and low ceilings, this charming farmhouse dates back to 1818. It overlooks its own farmyard in the centre of the village and is part of a 200 acre dairy and sheep farm. Bedrooms are comfortably and traditionally furnished and there is a cosy lounge for guests.
3 rms (1 bth) (1 fmly) No dogs Cen ht CTV 7P 250 acres beef dairy sheep Last d 5pm

---

CASTLE CARY Somerset Map **03** ST63

Selected

▣ ◻◻◻◻ The George Hotel Market Place BA7 7AH
☎01963 350761 FAX 01963 350035
Located opposite the Market House, in the centre of this small town, The George dates back to the 15th century. Each of the

﬚essiestown ﬚arm

AA QQQQQ Premier Selected   OPEN ALL YEAR
Catlowdy, nr Longtown, Carlisle, Cumbria CA6 5QP
Telephone and Fax: 01228 577219

One of the nicest farm guesthouses. Warm and welcoming. Peaceful and quiet with pretty en suite bedrooms and delicious home cooking. Family accommodation – bed and breakfast or self-catering in comfortable courtyard cottages. The indoor heated swimming pool is open mid May – mid September.
Exit 44, M6 motorway – A7 to Longtown. Take road at Bush Hotel – 6½ miles to T-Junction – right 1½ miles to Catlowdy

bedrooms is individually furnished and particularly well equipped for both the business and leisure traveller. The George Bar, with its impressive inglenook fireplace, and an elm beam dating back to the 10th century, is supplemented by the non-smoking Snug. Both bars serve an extensive range of bar meals, with daily special dishes on a blackboard. In the panelled restaurant a relaxed atmosphere prevails, and guests are offered an interesting range of dishes from the carte menu.

12 en suite (bth/shr) 3 annexe en suite (bth/shr) (1 fmly) No smoking in area of dining room CTV in all bedrooms Tea and coffee making facilities Direct dial from bedrooms Cen ht 10P Last d 9pm

PRICE GUIDE
ROOMS: s £37-£45; d £65-£70*
MEALS: Lunch £5-£12 Dinner £5-£12&alc*
CARDS: 🔳 💳 💳 　　　　　　　　　　　£

CASTLE COMBE Wiltshire Map **03** ST87

GH 🆀🆀🆀 **Little Worth Cottage** Burton Rd, Acton Turville, GL9 1HN ☎01454 218308
Conrad and Adria Jones extend a warm welcome to their rurally situated stone-built cottage, parts of which date back to the 18th-century. Littleworth is surrounded by un-spoilt Cotswold countryside, close to the Badminton Estate and just four miles from historic Castle Combe. One large bedroom and one more cosy have been tastefully furnished and equipped with thoughtful extras like bottled water and fresh fruit and flowers. Guests are welcome to use the families comfortable drawing room where there is a colour television.

2 rms No smoking Tea and coffee making facilities No dogs (ex guide dogs) CTV No children 14yrs 4P No coaches Tennis (grass) Croquet lawn Last d 8pm

PRICE GUIDE
ROOMS: d £30-£36*

GH 🆀🆀🆀 **Paddock Barn** The Gib SN14 7LH
☎01249 782477
Situated only a mile from the famous village of Castle Combe, this beautiful 17th-century Cotswold barn has been expertly converted to create a home which displays a style and quality in keeping with the lovely building's age. Bedrooms are spacious and comfortable, with views across the countryside. In the gracious dining room a most beautiful table is set with delightful china, and the whole house is furnished with antiques and family possessions which are there for all to appreciate. There is a flower-filled patio where guests may relax after a day spent, perhaps, exploring Bath or the Cotswolds, which are within easy driving distance.

3 rms (1 bth) (3 fmly) No smoking in bedrooms No smoking in dining room Tea and coffee making facilities No dogs No children P No coaches Riding

---

CASTLE DONINGTON Leicestershire Map **08** SK42

For accommodation details see under **East Midlands Airport, Leicestershire**

CATLOWDY Cumbria Map **12** NY47

💟 🆀🆀🆀 Mr & Mrs Lawson **Craigburn** *(NY474761)* CA6 5QP (leave B6318 & follow signs to Catlowdy)
☎01228 577214 FAX 01228 577214
Poultry, pigs and goats, as well as various breeds of sheep and cattle - blackfaced ewes and suckler cows proving firm favourites with visitors - are kept on this 250-acre working farm situated in open country about 14 miles northeast of Carlisle; children are actively encouraged to touch the animals and to help with feeding. Accommodation is provided in modern en suite bedrooms and there are two lounges with books, games and TV as well as the

spacious dining room and a residents' bar.

6 en suite (bth/shr) (2 fmly) No smoking in bedrooms No smoking in dining room No smoking in lounges CTV in all bedrooms Tea and coffee making facilities No dogs (ex guide dogs) Licensed Cen ht CTV ch fac 20P 250 acres beef mixed sheep Last d 6pm

PRICE GUIDE
ROOMS: s £20-£21; d £40-£42; wkly b&b £112.40-£117.60; wkly hlf-bd £168-£179.20*
CARDS: 🔳 💳 　　　　　　　　　　　　　£
See advertisement under CARLISLE

CHADLINGTON Oxfordshire Map **04** SP32

GH 🆀🆀🆀 **Chadlington House Hotel** OX7 3LZ
☎01608 676437 FAX 01608 676503
Closed Jan
This large, peaceful hotel offers spacious, well equipped bedrooms, a ground floor bar and a restaurant serving a restricted menu.

10 en suite (bth/shr) (1 fmly) No smoking in bedrooms No smoking in dining room No smoking in lounges CTV in all bedrooms Tea and coffee making facilities Direct dial from bedrooms Licensed Cen ht CTV 20P No coaches Last d 7pm

PRICE GUIDE
ROOMS: s £30-£40; d £45-£65; wkly hlf-bd £140-£175
CARDS: 🔳 💳 　　　　　　　　　　　　　£

CHAGFORD Devon Map **03** SX78

Selected

GH 🆀🆀🆀🆀 **Glendarah House** TQ13 8BZ
☎01647 433270 FAX 01647 433483
Closed Xmas & 2 wks prior
This semidetached family home has recently been purchased by Allan and Pamela Simon, who have completely refurbished the accommodation. Each bedroom, now tastefully decorated and furnished, offers en suite facilities and modern equipment. Downstairs there are a cosy bar-lounge and an attractive dining room where breakfast is served.

5 en suite (bth) 1 annexe en suite (bth) No smoking in bedrooms No smoking in dining room No smoking in lounges CTV in all bedrooms Tea and coffee making facilities Licensed Cen ht No children 10yrs 7P No coaches

PRICE GUIDE
ROOMS: s £25-£30; d £45-£55
CARDS: 🔳 💳

Selected

GH 🆀🆀🆀🆀 **Thornworthy House** TQ13 8EY (from Chagford Square take the Fernworthy Road and follow signs to Thornworthy. House at end of road)
☎01647 433297 FAX 01647 433297
rs 3-31 Jan
This impressive stone-built property, 1,100 feet up on Dartmoor, offers superb views. The road stops at the house, which is about three miles from Chagford. Bedrooms are spacious, and two have en suite facilities. There is a large lounge where log fires blaze in cooler weather. Dinner and breakfast are served by arrangement at an additional charge.

3 rms (2 bth) No smoking in bedrooms No smoking in dining room CTV in 2 bedrooms Tea and coffee making facilities Licensed Cen ht CTV 8P No coaches Tennis (hard) Croquet Last d 10.30am
PRICE GUIDE
ROOMS: s £18-£23; d £42-£52.50; wkly b&b £147-£182

CHARD Somerset Map 03 ST30

GH 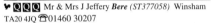 **Watermead** 83 High St TA20 1QT (on A30 through the High St continue up the hill from shopping centre) ☎01460 62834
An attractive Victorian house at the top of the High Street, set back from the busy road, Watermead offers comfortable accommodation and friendly hospitality from Doreen and Tony Botten. There are a cosy lounge and a sun room leading to the patio and garden. Delicious home-cooked dinners using traditional recipes are available by arrangement.
9 rms (6 shr) No smoking in dining room CTV in all bedrooms Tea and coffee making facilities Cen ht 9P No coaches Last d noon
PRICE GUIDE
ROOMS: s £16-£26; d £36; wkly b&b £112-£126; wkly hlf-bd £168-£182✱

♥ QQQ Mr & Mrs J Jeffery *Bere (ST377058)* Winsham TA20 4JQ ☎01460 30207
This stone Georgian house stands in beautiful surroundings on the Dorset/Somerset/Devon borders. Originally part of the Ford Abbey Estate, the house is set in eight acres of parkland with a stream, meadows, lawns and gardens. Bedrooms are spacious and well equipped with TVs and tea trays. Breakfast is served at a large refectory table.
2 en suite (bth/shr) (2 fmly) No smoking in area of dining room CTV in all bedrooms Tea and coffee making facilities CTV 6P 8 acres non working

---

CHARFIELD Gloucestershire Map 03 ST79

◼ QQ *Huntingford Mill Hotel* GL12 8EX ☎01453 843431
Enjoying a gloriously tranquil setting, yet only three miles from junction 14 of the M5, this was Gloucestershire's last working corn mill and is full of character. Guests have the use of over two miles of fishing on the Little Avon river, and there is space to wander as well as ample parking. The bedrooms provide comfortable standard accommodation, plus several cosy bar and lounge areas which have log fires. In the popular restaurant an extensive menu includes such specialities as Texas T-bone steaks.
5 rms (1 fmly) CTV in all bedrooms Tea and coffee making facilities No dogs (ex guide dogs) Cen ht CTV 25P Fishing Last d 10pm
CARDS: ◼ ▨

CHARING Kent Map 05 TQ94

♥ QQQ Mrs P Pym *Barnfield (TQ923484)* TN27 0BN (2.50 miles S off unclass road) ☎01233 712421
Some 500 acres of arable and sheep-grazing land surround this ancient farmhouse which has all the comfort and individuality of a well cared for home. It has low oak beams, open fires, an old tub in the communal bathroom, plus numerous family mementoes and books dotted around. Bedrooms are comfortable and interestingly furnished. Meals are served in two rooms, one of which doubles as a television lounge. Smoking is not permitted.
5 rms No smoking Tea and coffee making facilities No dogs Cen ht CTV 101P Tennis (hard) 30 acres sheep Last d 5pm

---

PRICE GUIDE
ROOMS: s £20; d fr £41; wkly hlf-bd £198.50-£210.50✱
CARDS: ▨

CHARMOUTH Dorset Map 03 SY39

GH QQQQ Newlands House Stonebarrow Ln DT6 6RA (take eastern slip road from Charmouth Bypass caravan park to bottom of hill at bend turn left into Stonebarrow Lane) ☎01297 560212
Mar-Oct
This delightful 16th century house is set in two acres of gardens and orchard on the edge of Charmouth. The bedrooms all have en suite facilities and are attractively decorated. There is a cosy bar and comfortable lounge; and the atmosphere is relaxed and friendly. Owner Clare Vear produces excellent home cooked meals using local produce, which are served in the charming dining room.
12 rms (11 bth/shr) (2 fmly) No smoking in bedrooms No smoking in dining room No smoking in lounges CTV in all bedrooms Tea and coffee making facilities No dogs (ex guide dogs) Licensed Cen ht CTV No children 6yrs 15P No coaches Last d noon
PRICE GUIDE
ROOMS: s £23-£25.75; d £46-£51.50; wkly b&b £146.50-£162.25; wkly hlf-bd £234.50-£250.50

CHATTERIS Cambridgeshire

See advertisement

THE CROSS KEYS
16 Market Hill, Chatteris,   **AA**
Cambridgeshire PE16 6BA   **★**
Tel: 01354 693036 Fax: 01354 693036

Built around 1540, Cross Keys is said to be the finest building of its time left in the area. Many of the original features still remain including two open fire places which during the winter months are lit welcoming guests. Situated in the centre in this pleasant Fenland town between the cities of Ely and Peterborough and surrounded by rich farmland. All seven bedrooms have been carefully decorated and furnished creating individual rooms, five of which are en suite. Restaurant meals are available 7 days a week using the finest meats, fresh fish and locally grown fresh vegetables. Ideal for enjoying or taking part in many sporting activities in the area.

CHEDDAR Somerset Map **03** ST45

GH Q Q **Market Cross Hotel** Church St BS27 3RA (in village centre) ☎01934 742264
Closed Nov
Personally run by Mr and Mrs Garland, this is an attractive Regency hotel in the middle of the village. Well equipped bedrooms are finished in soft colours, and there is a comfortable bar-cum-lounge overlooking the market cross. Children are welcome, and there is a toy area in the dining room where breakfast and dinner are served.
6 rms (3 shr) (2 fmly) No smoking in bedrooms No smoking in dining room CTV in all bedrooms Tea and coffee making facilities No dogs (ex guide dogs) Licensed Cen ht CTV ch fac 6P No coaches Last d 6pm
PRICE GUIDE
ROOMS: s £19-£20; d £37-£48; wkly b&b £130-£150∗
CARDS: 🅰 💳

Selected

❤ Q Q Q Q Mrs C Ladd **Tor Farm** *(ST455534)* Nyland BS27 3UD (take A371 from Cheddar towards Wells, after 2m turn right towards Nyland, Tor Farm 1.5m on right) ☎01934 743710
This modern stone-built farmhouse enjoys a peaceful location with splendid views of Glastonbury Tor, Wedmore and the Mendip hills, yet is within easy reach of the well known town of Cheddar. Mr and Mrs Ladd welcome guests to their attractive home, which is a good base for visiting the local attractions. Bedrooms are delightfully furnished and thoughtfully colour coordinated, some with pretty four-poster beds. The lounge has an open fire and the dining room is spacious and light, with wonderful views. A good choice is offered at dinner including many home-produced items, together with local wines.
8 rms (5 bth/shr) (1 fmly) No smoking in bedrooms No smoking in dining room Tea and coffee making facilities No dogs Licensed Cen ht CTV 12P 33 acres beef Last d 24hrs
PRICE GUIDE
ROOMS: s £19-£25; d £33-£46; wkly b&b £119.70-£157.55∗
CARDS: 🅰 💳

CHEDDLETON Staffordshire Map **07** SJ95

Selected

GH Q Q Q Q **Choir Cottage and Choir House** Ostlers Ln ST13 7HS (turn off A520 opposite Red Lion into Hollow Ln pass church & in 200yds Ostlers Ln on right) ☎01538 360561
Two comfortable bedrooms are offered at this 300-year-old cottage. The Pine Room has a splendid four-poster bed and two small children's beds so is ideal for family occupation, while the Rose Room has an attractively draped four-poster bed and its own small patio. Public rooms in the main house include a spacious lounge, a small conservatory and a room containing a pool table. Breakfast - and dinner by arrangement - are served at separate tables in the bright dining room.
2 en suite (bth/shr) 2 annexe en suite (bth/shr) (1 fmly) No smoking CTV in 2 bedrooms Tea and coffee making facilities Direct dial from bedrooms No dogs Cen ht No children 4yrs 5P No coaches Last d 24hrs notice

PRICE GUIDE
ROOMS: s £30-£35; d £45-£53

GH Q Q Q **Prospect House** 334 Cheadle Rd ST13 7BW (adjacent to A520, 2m from junct with A52 towards Leek) ☎01782 550639
Closed 25 Dec
An attractive 19th-century property, Prospect House is well situated for the many attractions of this part of the world - including Alton Towers and the Peak District. Pleasantly furnished bedrooms are divided between the main house and a rear coach house. A hearty breakfast is provided in the dining room, and all guests are offered a welcoming 'cuppa' on arrival.
1 rms 4 annexe en suite (shr) (1 fmly) No smoking in 1 bedrooms No smoking in dining room CTV in all bedrooms Tea and coffee making facilities Direct dial from bedrooms No dogs (ex guide dogs) Cen ht 6P No coaches Last d 3pm
PRICE GUIDE
ROOMS: s £19-£24; d £38-£40; wkly b&b £133-£140; wkly hlf-bd £189-£203∗

CHELMSFORD Essex Map **05** TL70

GH Q Q **Beechcroft Private Hotel** 211 New London Rd CM2 0AJ (turn off A12 onto B1007 follow through Galleywood for 3m) ☎01245 352462 FAX 01245 347833
Closed 24 Dec - 1 Jan
Beautifully maintained throughout, this friendly, family-run hotel offers comfortable bedrooms, a bright breakfast room and two lounges.
20 rms (9 shr) (2 fmly) No smoking in dining room CTV in 19 bedrooms Tea and coffee making facilities Cen ht CTV 15P No coaches
PRICE GUIDE
ROOMS: s £28-£36.50; d £40-£45
CARDS: 🅰 💳 💳   (£)

GH Q Q Q **Boswell House Hotel** 118-120 Springfield Rd CM2 6LF (Town centre at junct Victoria/Springfield Road's) ☎01245 287587 FAX 01245 287587
Closed 24 Dec-4 Jan
Conscientious, hard-working proprietors provide the backbone of this informal hotel, a solid-looking town house with plenty of off-street parking. Well equipped and predominantly non-smoking bedrooms include some designed with families in mind and there is a small bar which leads into the bright dining rooms where a three-course evening meal is served.
13 en suite (bth/shr) (2 fmly) No smoking in 9 bedrooms No smoking in dining room No smoking in 1 lounge CTV in all bedrooms Tea and coffee making facilities Direct dial from bedrooms No dogs (ex guide dogs) Licensed Cen ht CTV 15P Last d 8.30pm
PRICE GUIDE
ROOMS: s £42-£45; d £60; wkly b&b £294-£315; wkly hlf-bd £364-£385
CARDS: 🅰 💳 💳 💳 💳 💳   (£)

Selected

GH Q Q Q Q **Snows Oaklands Hotel** 240 Springfield Rd CM2 63P (near Essex Police HQ on A1113) ☎01245 352004 & 250357
A wealth of individual touches personalises this large house in a residential area: a variety of clocks keeps time in different public rooms, old family pictures abound and there are three pianos located in separate lounges (one of which is a conservatory overlooking a boisterous aviary). The

comfortable bar area leads into a television lounge with video recording facilities.
14 rms (13 bth/shr) (3 fmly) No smoking in 2 bedrooms No smoking in dining room No smoking in 1 lounge CTV in all bedrooms Tea and coffee making facilities No dogs (ex guide dogs) Licensed Cen ht CTV 14P
PRICE GUIDE
ROOMS: s £36-£41; d £43-£51✱

GH QQ **Tanunda Hotel** 219 New London Rd CM2 0AJ
☎01245 354295 FAX 01245 345503
Closed Xmas & New Year
Further improvements have now taken place at this small, family-run, private hotel. Bedrooms, though basic, are adequately furnished and equipped, and the attractively appointed dining room provides a choice of breakfasts.
20 rms (2 bth 9 shr) CTV in all bedrooms Tea and coffee making facilities Direct dial from bedrooms No dogs (ex guide dogs) Licensed Cen ht CTV 20P
PRICE GUIDE
ROOMS: s fr £28; d fr £42.50✱
CARDS:

CHELTENHAM Gloucestershire Map 03 SO92

GH QQQ **Battledown Hotel** 125 Hales Rd GL52 6ST (on B4075) ☎01242 233881 & 0374 899734
This impressive Grade II listed building well situated for the centre of the famous spa town offers comfortable accommodation; all the rooms have en suite facilities and are well equipped. Guests can enjoy a home-made set dinner in the dining room and relax in the cosy sitting room. Car parking is also available.
7 rms (5 shr) No smoking in 5 bedrooms No smoking in dining room No smoking in lounges CTV in all bedrooms Tea and coffee making facilities No dogs Cen ht 10P No coaches Last d 6pm
PRICE GUIDE
ROOMS: s £18-£29.50; d £38-£44; wkly b&b £126-£206.50; wkly hlf-bd £203-£283✱

Selected

GH QQQQ **Beaumont House Hotel** 56 Shurdington Rd GL53 0JE (SW side of town, on A46) ☎01242 245986 FAX 01242 520044
A distinctive Victorian hotel set back from the A46 in peaceful gardens, with ample private parking.
Accommodation styles vary: most of the 18 rooms are spacious, whilst those on the lower ground floor are small but more modern; most have private bathrooms and facilities include TV, direct-dial telephones and radio alarms. There is an elegant, comfortable lounge with a corner bar and a varied daily menu is served in the dining room on weekdays.
17 rms (16 bth/shr) (3 fmly) No smoking in dining room No smoking in lounges CTV in all bedrooms Tea and coffee making facilities Direct dial from bedrooms No dogs (ex guide dogs) Licensed Cen ht CTV 21P No coaches Last d 8pm
PRICE GUIDE
ROOMS: s £28-£36; d £40-£60; wkly b&b fr £156; wkly hlf-bd fr £239✱
CARDS:

GH Q Q Q Q **Beechworth Lawn Hotel** 133 Hales Rd
GL52 6ST (off the A40 London Rd) ☎01242 522583
A warm welcome awaits guests at this attractive Victorian
house. Bedrooms are spacious and well equipped with a good
range of facilities. Housekeeping is a real strength with
immaculately kept bedrooms and bathrooms. Beds are are of
excellent quality and very comfortable. The pretty dining
room has an attractive china display and serves good home
cooked fayre.
9 rms (5 shr) (2 fmly) CTV in all bedrooms Tea and coffee
making facilities Cen ht CTV 10P No coaches Last d 7pm
PRICE GUIDE
ROOMS: s £23-£30; d £40-£48; wkly b&b £145-£189;
wkly hlf-bd £215-£259✱

£

GH Q Q *Bideford* 220 London Rd GL52 6HW
☎01242 233311
This red brick Edwardian property enjoys a pleasant location in
leafy London Road, which is only a gentle twelve minutes' walk
from the delightful centre of this famous spa town. Mrs Verrion
offers five light, bright bedrooms, situated on two floors. The
pretty dining room has some comfortable chairs where guests are
welcome to relax. Specialist diets are well catered for, and the
produce used is all free-range and country grown. There is ample
car parking space.
5 rms P

GH Q Q Q Q *Charlton House* 18 Greenhills Rd, Charlton
Kings GL53 9EB ☎01242 238997 FAX 01242 238997
Closed 22 Dec-3 Jan
Mr and Mrs Stone welcome guests to their family-run
guesthouse located in a good residential area on the southern
outskirts of the town. Built in the 1930's, the house is set in
well tended gardens with ample off-road parking. Bedrooms
are situated on the first floor, and are all individually
furnished, decorated and very well equipped. A three-course
meal is available by prior arrangement, or guests may prefer
to choose a 'one plate meal': perhaps lasagne or omelette
served with salad and bread. Mrs Stone is a trained
nutritionist, so special dietary requirements can be catered for
by arrangement. Smoking is not permitted.
3 rms (1 shr) No smoking CTV in all bedrooms Tea and
coffee making facilities No dogs Cen ht CTV No children
10yrs 5P No coaches Last d early am
CARDS: 🔲 💳

Factual details of establishments in this Guide
are from questionnaires we send to all
establishments that feature in the book.

GH Q Q Q Q Q **Cleeve Hill
Hotel** Cleeve Hill GL52 3PR
(on B4632 2.5m from town
between Prestbury and
Winchcome)
☎01242 672052
Located in an area of
outstanding natural beauty
and having direct access to
the Cotswold Way, this
personally run hotel offers
thoughtfully equipped rooms
with superb views - all of them looking either to Cleeve
Common or across the valley to the Malvern Hills. The
comfortable, elegantly furnished lounge provides a quiet place
for guests to relax or enjoy a drink, and breakfast is served in
a light, airy conservatory-style room. Dinner can be taken at
one of the many good local restaurants which between them
cater for all tastes, but a light meal of soup, omelette or
sandwiches and salads can be taken at the hotel by
arrangement.
10 en suite (bth/shr) (1 fmly) No smoking CTV in all
bedrooms Tea and coffee making facilities Direct dial from
bedrooms No dogs (ex guide dogs) Licensed Cen ht No
children 8yrs 12P No coaches
PRICE GUIDE
ROOMS: s £45-£60; d £60-£75✱
CARDS: 🔲 💳 💳

GH Q Q **Crossways** Oriel Place, 57 Bath Rd GL53 7LH
☎01242 527683
An attractive end-of-terrace listed Regency building situated
conveniently close to the town centre. Pins on a world map in the
hallway indicate a truly international clientele, and some visitors
stay for months at a time. Bedrooms are well maintained and are
slowly benefiting from improvements to the decor; one room is on
the ground floor. Generous breakfasts are served in the dining
room.
6 rms (3 shr) (3 fmly) CTV in all bedrooms Tea and coffee
making facilities Cen ht No parking
PRICE GUIDE
ROOMS: s £18-£30; d £36-£42; wkly b&b £120-£200✱
CARDS: 🔲 💳

£

GH Q Q Q **Hallery House** 48 Shurdington Rd GL53 0JE
(directly adjacent to A46) (Logis)
☎01242 578450 FAX 01242 529730
This welcoming Victorian hotel with its own car park stands on
the A46 close to the town centre. Many of the bedrooms have en
suite facilities and all are well equipped. The delightful dining
room serves an impressive range of fresh local food.
16 rms (10 bth/shr) (2 fmly) No smoking in 3 bedrooms No
smoking in dining room CTV in all bedrooms Tea and coffee
making facilities Direct dial from bedrooms Licensed Cen ht ch
fac 20P Cycle hire Last d 8.30pm
PRICE GUIDE
ROOMS: s £20-£35; d £35-£65; wkly b&b £110-£280; wkly hlf-
bd £194-£360✱
CARDS: 🔲 💳 💳 💳

£

GH Q Q Q **Hannaford's** 20 Evesham Rd GL52 2AB (N on
A435 Evesham road)
☎01242 515181 & 524190 FAX 01242 515181
Closed 23-31 Dec

An attractive Regency terraced town house within walking distance of the town centre is run on personal, friendly lines by the Crowley family, who continue to make improvements. Bedrooms are modestly furnished but spacious and well equipped. Public rooms include a bright conservatory lounge bar and a comfortable sitting room. Home-cooked evening meals are available by prior arrangement, and parking is unrestricted in the roads surrounding the hotel.

8 en suite (bth/shr) (1 fmly) No smoking in dining room CTV in all bedrooms Tea and coffee making facilities Direct dial from bedrooms No dogs (ex guide dogs) Licensed Cen ht CTV No parking Last d breakfast

PRICE GUIDE

ROOMS: s £29-£33; d £48-£52*

CARDS:

GH QQQ **Hollington House Hotel** 115 Hales Rd GL52 6ST (0.5m from town on Prestbury road) (BW)
☎01242 256652 FAX 01242 570280

This large detached Victorian house is built from Cotswold stone. The nine bedrooms vary in size and style, the majority having modern en suite shower facilities. There is a comfortable lounge with a corner bar, and a choice of good food is offered at dinner and breakfast. Special interest tours can be arranged in the hotel's own mini-bus.

9 rms (8 shr) (2 fmly) No smoking in bedrooms No smoking in dining room CTV in all bedrooms Tea and coffee making facilities No dogs Licensed Cen ht No children 3yrs 16P Tours available Last d 5pm

PRICE GUIDE

ROOMS: s £26-£40; d £40-£60; wkly b&b £140-£210; wkly hlf-bd £231-£301*

CARDS:

GH QQ **Ivy Dene** 145 Hewlett Rd GL52 6TS
☎01242 521726 & 521776

This comfortable detached house with an attractive garden stands in a good residential area within walking distance of the town centre. Guests are made to feel welcome and are accommodated in well modernised bedrooms equipped with colour TV and tea-making facilities; breakfast is served in a small dining room overlooking the garden.

9 rms (5 shr) (2 fmly) No smoking in dining room CTV in all bedrooms Tea and coffee making facilities Cen ht CTV No parking

PRICE GUIDE

ROOMS: s £17.50-£25; d £35-£45*

GH QQ **Kielder** 222 London Rd, Charlton Kings GL52 6HW (1 mile from Cheltenham on A40 opposite Holy Apostles Church) ☎01242 237138

A late-Victorian suburban house just one mile from the town centre on the A40. Recently refurbished bedrooms are well equipped, and there is a stair lift with level access to one, and four steps up to the other two rooms. Evening meals are available by prior arrangement, and special diets are catered for. Smoking is not permitted.

3 rms (1 shr) (1 fmly) No smoking CTV in all bedrooms Tea and coffee making facilities No dogs (ex guide dogs) Cen ht 5P No coaches

PRICE GUIDE

ROOMS: s fr £18; d £32-£34; wkly b&b £105-£119*

GH QQ **Lonsdale House** Montpellier Dr GL50 1TX
☎01242 232379 FAX 01242 232379

rs Xmas

An attractive period house, centrally located, with limited parking.

Bedrooms are bright and airy and the blue and white breakfast room overlooks the garden. Guests may use the owners' lounge.
11 rms (3 shr) (3 fmly) No smoking in dining room CTV in all bedrooms Tea and coffee making facilities No dogs (ex guide dogs) Cen ht CTV 6P No coaches
CARDS:

 Premier Selected

GH QQQQQ **Lypiatt House** Lypiatt Rd GL50 2QW
☎01242 224994
FAX 01242 224996

A charming Victorian villa set in its own grounds a short walk from the Montpelier area of the town, Lypiatt House is conveniently situated for easy access to the A40. Stylishly decorated throughout, it offers accommodation in attractively furnished and very well equipped bedrooms. An honesty bar is provided in the conservatory and the set dinner (served by arrangement) might include an avocado and hot bacon salad followed by rack of lamb or fresh salmon, with a spicy pear and walnut sponge for pudding; house wines are available to accompany the meal.
10 en suite (bth/shr) No smoking in dining room CTV in all bedrooms Tea and coffee making facilities Direct dial from bedrooms No dogs (ex guide dogs) Licensed Cen ht 14P No coaches Last d 9am
PRICE GUIDE
ROOMS: s £48-£50; d £55-£70
CARDS: £

Selected

GH QQQQ **Malvern View** Cleeve Hill GL52 3PR (turn off A40 onto B4075, signposted to Broadway. Pass through Prestbury having joined B4632, follow signs to Broadway up Long Hill. House near top.)
☎01242 672017 FAX 01242 676207
Malvern View stands in an elevated position overlooking several counties, with wonderful views of the Malvern hills. The bedrooms are individually furnished and decorated, and all are equipped with colour TV and tea-making facilities; three of them benefit from the view. A hearty breakfast is served in the elegant dining room and a comfortable sitting room is available to guests. The rear garden has direct access on to Cleeve Common
3 en suite (bth/shr) No smoking in 1 bedrooms No smoking in dining room No smoking in lounges CTV in all bedrooms Tea and coffee making facilities No dogs (ex guide dogs) Cen ht No children 12P No coaches
PRICE GUIDE
ROOMS: s £25-£30; d £40-£45✱

GH QQQ **Manor Barn** Cowley GL53 9NN (6m S, off A435 Cheltenham/Cirencester road) ☎01242 870229
Linda and Andrew Roff's little guest house, a clever barn conversion set in rural surroundings five miles from Cheltenham, combines rustic charm with modern comfort. The spotless bedrooms feature stone walls and are nicely furnished in cane and pine, with excellent divans and attractive decor. This no-smoking establishment offers bed and breakfast only.
3 rms (1 shr) No smoking No dogs Cen ht CTV No children 7yrs 6P No coaches Last d by arrangement
PRICE GUIDE
ROOMS: s £15-£22.50; d £30-£38✱ £

Selected

GH QQQQ **Milton House** 12 Royal Pde, Bayshill Rd GL50 3AY ☎01242 582601 FAX 01242 222326
An imposing Regency house within the terrace of Royal Parade is benefiting from careful restoration by the owners Mr and Mrs Milton. Bright, comfortable bedrooms are individually styled and decorated, furnished in pine and provided with a good selection of modern creature comforts and facilities. Public rooms are equally attractive, with many of the original features retained. This elegant house is also very conveniently located, with direct rear access to Montpellier, the heart of Cheltenham's excellent shopping area. There is limited car parking available.
8 en suite (bth/shr) (3 fmly) No smoking in 2 bedrooms No smoking in dining room No smoking in 1 lounge CTV in all bedrooms Tea and coffee making facilities Direct dial from bedrooms No dogs Licensed Cen ht CTV 5P No coaches Last d 9am
PRICE GUIDE
ROOMS: s £35-£55; d £50-£68
CARDS: £

GH QQQ *Moorend Park Hotel* Moorend Park Rd GL53 0LA (first traffic lights after Bath road roundabout on right hand side) ☎01242 224441 FAX 01242 572413
This large Victorian house is located about twenty minutes' walk south of the centre. It is being carefully restored whilst maintaining original features such as the ceiling stucco work. It has a bar, a lounge and a restaurant where freshly made meals can be prepared by prior arrangement. Off-street parking is also available.
10 en suite (bth/shr) (3 fmly) No smoking in dining room No smoking in lounges CTV in all bedrooms Tea and coffee making facilities Direct dial from bedrooms Licensed Cen ht TV 25P No coaches Last d 8pm
CARDS:

GH QQ **North Hall Hotel** Pittville Circus Rd GL52 2PZ (1m E of town centre) ☎01242 520589 FAX 01242 216953
Closed 21 Dec-19 Jan
Quietly located in a tree-lined road only minutes from the town centre, this substantial period property has recently been modernised. The majority of the bedrooms are well furnished and equipped, although a few are more modest (this being reflected in the tariff). There are a spacious, comfortable lounge overlooking the rear garden, a cosy bar and a large dining room where a varied menu is served.
20 rms (16 bth/shr) No smoking in dining room CTV in all bedrooms Tea and coffee making facilities Direct dial from bedrooms Licensed Cen ht 20P Last d 7.15pm
PRICE GUIDE
ROOMS: s £18-£30; d £43.50-£48; wkly b&b £126-£168; wkly hlf-bd £171-£207✱
CARDS: £

Selected

GH ◨◨◨◨ *Stretton Lodge* Western Rd GL50 3RN
☎01242 528724 & 570771 FAX 01242 570771
This gracious Victorian residence has been well maintained
by owners of long standing. Bedrooms are comfortable,
comprehensively equipped and individually furnished, while a
lounge with an attractive old fireplace and ornate ceiling
mouldings proves a popular place in which to relax.
4 en suite (bth/shr) (1 fmly) No smoking CTV in all
bedrooms Tea and coffee making facilities Direct dial from
bedrooms No dogs (ex guide dogs) Licensed Cen ht 6P No
coaches Last d noon
CARDS: ▨ ▨ ▨

GH ◨◨◨ **Willoughby House Hotel** 1 Suffolk Square
GL50 2DR (150yds from A40 turn into Suffolk Rd, Suffolk Sq
off Suffolk Rd at 2nd traffic lights)
☎01242 522798 FAX 01242 256369
This beautiful Regency building enjoys a privileged location in the
Montpelier region of this famous spa town. Guests will appreciate
both the warm welcome they receive and the high standards of
accommodation provided in spacious, tastefully decorated and
furnished bedrooms. This is an ideal base from which to tour the
Cotswolds or go racing at Cheltenham.
9 en suite (bth/shr) (1 fmly) No smoking in 4 bedrooms No
smoking in dining room CTV in all bedrooms Tea and coffee
making facilities Direct dial from bedrooms Licensed Cen ht
CTV 12P No coaches Tennis (hard) Bowling Last d 9pm
PRICE GUIDE
ROOMS: s £25-£39.50; d £40-£50✷
CARDS: ▨ ▨

GH ◨◨ **Wishmoor** 147 Hales Rd GL52 6TD (just off B4075)
☎01242 238504 FAX 01242 226090
The atmosphere is relaxed and bedrooms are neatly furnished in
this semidetached Victorian guest house which stands in its own
gardens about a mile from the city centre. The ground floor
contains a traditional lounge with massive cheeseplant and a
separate dining room. Several rooms are designated non-smoking.
11 rms (5 shr) (1 fmly) No smoking in 3 bedrooms No smoking
in dining room CTV in all bedrooms Tea and coffee making
facilities No dogs (ex guide dogs) Cen ht 10P No coaches Last
d noon
PRICE GUIDE
ROOMS: s £18-£29; d £34-£45
CARDS: ▨ ▨

CHERITON FITZPAINE Devon Map 03 SS80

❤ ◨◨ Mrs D M Lock *Brindiwell* (SS896079) EX17 4HR
(approach from Bickleigh Bridge on A396, take road
signposted to Cadeleigh and after 3m a sign for farm on left)
☎01363 866357
Brindiwell Farm is a lovely, traditional, pink-painted farmhouse in
a picturesque setting surrounded by well-maintained gardens. The
four bedrooms have attractive floral decor and comfortable
furniture, and most also have stunning country views. The public
rooms feature ancient beams, oak screens and open fireplaces, and
breakfast is served at separate tables, with dinner by arrangement.
4 rms (1 fmly) No smoking in 1 bedrooms No smoking in 1
lounge CTV in 1 bedroom Tea and coffee making facilities No
dogs (ex guide dogs) CTV 5P 120 acres sheep Last d 5pm

CHESTER Cheshire Map 07 SJ46

GH ◨◨◨ **Bawnpark Hotel** 10 Hoole Rd, Hoole CH2 3NH
☎01244 324971 FAX 01244 310951
Bawn Park Hotel is conveniently situated on the A56 close to the
city centre. The five bedrooms are all equipped with small modern
en suite bathrooms and there is a bright breakfast room with
separate tables.
7 rms (5 bth/shr) (2 fmly) No smoking in dining room No
smoking in 1 lounge CTV in all bedrooms Tea and coffee making
facilities Cen ht CTV 12P
CARDS: ▨ ▨ ▨ £

GH ◨◨ **Egerton Lodge** 57 Hoole Rd, Hoole CH2 3NJ (on
A56) ☎01244 320712
Closed 19 Dec-3 Jan
This small guest house with a car park at the rear is part of a listed
early-Victorian terrace of houses which stands on the A56 just
north of the city centre. The soundly maintained bedrooms have
both modern and older furniture, and family rooms are available.
Separate tables are provided in the traditionally furnished
breakfast room.
7 rms (5 bth/shr) (4 fmly) No smoking in dining room CTV in
all bedrooms Tea and coffee making facilities No dogs Cen ht
No children 3yrs 5P No coaches
PRICE GUIDE
ROOMS: s £15-£19; d £25-£34✷
CARDS: ▨ ▨ ▨ £

GH ◨◨ *Eversley Hotel* 9 Eversley Park CH2 2AJ (off A5116
signed to Ellesmere Port) ☎01244 373744
Closed 24 Dec-2 Jan
North of the city centre, off the A5116, this large house provides ➡

Eversley Hotel

9 Eversley Park,
Chester, CH2 2AJ
Telephone: (01244) 373744

Attractive Victorian residence with all modern
facilities, relaxing atmosphere and good food.
¾ mile north of city centre just off the A5116.
Most rooms are en suite and have TV,
telephone, tea/coffee. Hotel has its own Bar &
Restaurant and car park.
Proprietors:
Bryn and Barbara Povey

modestly furnished but well equipped accommodation, including some ground-floor rooms. There are a cosy lounge, a lounge bar and a dining room with cottage-style furniture.
11 rms (4 bth 5 shr) (3 fmly) CTV in all bedrooms Tea and coffee making facilities No dogs Licensed Cen ht CTV 17P Last d 6pm
CARDS: ■ ▬

GH **Q** *Gables* 5 Vicarage Rd, Hoole CH2 3HZ (off A56)
☎01244 323969
Closed 23-27 Dec
This small, well cared for guest house is located just off the A56, convenient for the city centre and within easy reach of the M53. Facilities include six compact bedrooms (including two suitable for family use), a bright, cheerful lounge/breakfast room and a small car park.
6 rms (4 fmly) CTV in all bedrooms Tea and coffee making facilities No dogs CTV 6P

GH **QQQ** *Gloster Lodge Hotel* 44 Hoole Rd, Hoole
CH2 3NL (on A56) ☎01244 348410 & 320231
Closed 24-31 Dec
A large semidetatched house, fronted by a small car park, which provides modern, well equipped bedrooms, three of which are located in the single storey purpose-built annexe. There is a bright and pleasant breakfast room with separate tables.
5 en suite (bth/shr) 3 annexe en suite (bth/shr) (2 fmly) CTV in all bedrooms Tea and coffee making facilities Direct dial from bedrooms Licensed Cen ht 9P No coaches Last d 8pm
CARDS: ■ ▬ ▬

Selected

GH **QQQQ** *Golborne Manor* Platts Ln, Hatton Heath CH3 9AN (5m S off A41 Whitchurch road)
☎01829 770310 FAX 01829 318084
Golborne Manor is a mid-Victorian house set in three-and-a-half acres of grounds and gardens. It has been tastefully modernised to provide spacious guest bedrooms, one en suite and one served by a private bathroom. Breakfast is served at a large communal table in a pleasant room with period furniture. There is also a comfortable lounge.
3 rms (2 bth/shr) (1 fmly) No smoking CTV in all bedrooms Tea and coffee making facilities No dogs Cen ht 6P No coaches Table tennis Three-quarter snooker table
PRICE GUIDE
ROOMS: s £20-£28; d £38-£42✳

Selected

GH **QQQQ** *Green Gables* 11 Eversley Park CH2 2AJ (off A5116 signed 'Countess of Chester Hospital')
☎01244 372243 FAX 01244 376352
A large, impeccably maintained Victorian house, Green Gables provides good quality accommodation which includes a well equipped and tastefully furnished family room. There is a comfortable lounge, and the strikingly decorated dining room is supplemented by an elegant room which is available for private dinner parties or small conferences.
4 en suite (shr) (1 fmly) No smoking CTV in all bedrooms Tea and coffee making facilities Direct dial from bedrooms No dogs (ex guide dogs) Cen ht CTV 11P Last d 8pm

PRICE GUIDE
ROOMS: s £22-£23; d £34-£35; wkly b&b £154-£161; wkly hlf-bd £204-£245

Selected

GH **QQQQ** *Grove House* Holme St, Tarvin CH3 8EQ (5m E, between A51/A54 travel towards Tarvin house is on brow of hill set back off the A54 just before village)
☎01829 740893 FAX 01829 741769
Closed 20 Dec-5 Jan
Built in 1870, this house is beautifully set in the heart of the Cheshire countryside, no more than four miles from Chester itself. It is situated just outside Tarvin, on the A54 (after the roundabout where the A54 meets the A51). Bright, spacious and very comfortably furnished bedrooms offer such extra touches such as books and fresh flowers. The drawing room, which is also attractively decorated, has an open fire and French windows opening out on to a well maintained walled garden. Breakfast is served around one large table in the dining room.
3 rms (1 bth) No smoking in bedrooms No smoking in dining room CTV in 2 bedrooms Tea and coffee making facilities No dogs Cen ht CTV No children 12yrs 6P No coaches
PRICE GUIDE
ROOMS: s fr £18.50; d £40-£50; wkly b&b £130-£170✳

[symbols] **GH** **QQ** *Pear Tree* 69 Hoole Rd CH2 3NJ
☎01244 323260
This small, soundly maintained guest house which is conveniently situated for the city centre and the M53 Motorway is owned and run by the very friendly Alan and Jean Turnbull. Bedrooms, including family rooms and four rooms with en-suite shower facilities, are plainly but comfortably furnished. They are all equipped with tea and coffee making facilities and televisions. Breakfast is served in the bright dining room and the there is ample parking at the rear of the building.
9 rms (4 shr) (2 fmly) No smoking in dining room CTV in all bedrooms Tea and coffee making facilities No dogs Cen ht CTV 11P
PRICE GUIDE
ROOMS: s £16-£18; d £28

Premier Selected

GH **QQQQQ** Redland Private Hotel 64 Hough Green CH4 8JY (1m from town leaving on A483 Wrexham rd, then take A5104 Saltney rd for 200yds, opposite Westminster park)
☎01244 671024
FAX 01244 681309

Ideally situated a mile from Chester city centre, this carefully restored Victorian house retains many of its original features. The thirteen well equipped en suite bedrooms vary in size but all are tastefully decorated with antique or period

furniture; many contain four-poster or half-tester beds and one has a fascinating stained glass ceiling panel. Public areas include a grand dark-panelled entrance hall, a beautifully decorated drawing room with an ornate ceiling, a spacious breakfast room and an honesty bar. Sauna, solarium and ample car parking are also available.

13 en suite (bth/shr) (3 fmly) No smoking in 6 bedrooms No smoking in dining room CTV in all bedrooms Tea and coffee making facilities Licensed Cen ht 12P No coaches Sauna Solarium

PRICE GUIDE
ROOMS: s £40-£45; d £55-£70✱

GH QQQ **Vicarage Lodge** 11 Vicarage Rd, Hoole CH2 3HZ (just off A56) ☎01244 319533
This small, well maintained guest house, which has been personally run by Laura and Phillip Abbinante for the last nine years, is quietly situated just off Hoole Road, close to the M53 and only a mile from the city centre. The bedrooms, one or two of which are quite compact, are all attractively decorated, thoughtfully furnished and well equipped. Three rooms have modern en-suite shower rooms and the other two rooms have use of their own bathrooms. Breakfast is served in the bright dining room, which has separate tables and there is a small lounge area.

5 rms (3 shr) CTV in all bedrooms Tea and coffee making facilities No dogs Cen ht 7P No coaches

PRICE GUIDE
ROOMS: d £28-£34

CHESTER-LE-STREET Co Durham Map 12 NZ25

GH QQQ **Waldridge Fell** Waldridge DH2 3RY ☎0191 389 1908
This attractive stone-built guest house, formerly a chapel, enjoys panoramic views from its setting on the edge of a country park. Bedrooms are bright, fresh and well equipped while the combined lounge/dining room is a pleasant place in which to relax and enjoy the friendly service provided by owners Ken and Corris Sharratt.

5 rms (1 shr) (5 fmly) No smoking in dining room No smoking in lounges CTV in all bedrooms Tea and coffee making facilities Cen ht CTV 8P

PRICE GUIDE
ROOMS: s £22-£26; d £36-£40

CHILHAM Kent Map 05 TR05

GH QQQ **Jullieberrie House** Canterbury Rd CT4 8DX ☎01227 730488
A former family home is conveniently located close to Chilham Railway Station and easily accessed off the A28. Personally run by proprietors Pamela and Tony Hooker, it has a very friendly and relaxed atmosphere. Bedrooms are generous in size; all have remote control TV and tea trays, and overlook the well maintained rear garden. There is bright, comfortable breakfast room where a traditional cooked English breakfast includes home made jams and marmalades. Ample forecourt car parking is available.

3 rms (2 bth) CTV in all bedrooms Tea and coffee making facilities Cen ht 4P

PRICE GUIDE
ROOMS: s £20-£25; d £32-£38✱

◀ QQQ **Woolpack** High St CT4 8DL
☎01227 730208 & 730351 FAX 01227 731053
Situated near the village's main square and imposing castle, this

popular and welcoming inn dates back some 600 years. As well as a cosy, traditional bar there is an oak-beamed restaurant where home-produced meals are served. Well equipped bedrooms, including one with a four-poster bed and sizeable family rooms, are available in the main building and the nearby converted outbuildings.

3 en suite (bth) 10 annexe en suite (shr) (3 fmly) CTV in all bedrooms Tea and coffee making facilities Direct dial from bedrooms Cen ht CTV 30P Last d 9.30pm

PRICE GUIDE
ROOMS: s fr £37.50; d fr £47.50
CARDS: 🔲 🔲 🔲

CHIPPENHAM Wiltshire Map 03 ST97

See also Calne

GH QQ *Oxford Hotel* 32/36 Langley Rd SN15 1BX ☎01249 652542
The Oxford is a small family-run hotel convenient for the city centre. The bedrooms are well equipped and some of them offer en suite facilities. Full English breakfast and a traditional home-cooked dinner are served in the comfortable dining room.

13 rms (7 shr) (1 fmly) CTV in all bedrooms Tea and coffee making facilities Licensed Cen ht 9P Last d 5.30pm

CARDS: 🔲 🔲 🔲

Jullieberrie House
Canterbury Road, Chilham CT4 8DX
Telephone: 01227 730488

Just 5 minutes walk to the picturesque 15th century village and church from Jullieberrie House. Large, bright, modern rooms with every convenience and some en suite. Lovely garden and views. Enjoy home made bread and preserves with full English breakfast. An ideal base for exploring Kent, 30 minutes from Channel Ports and Tunnel. Situated on A28 Ashford to Canterbury road, near train and bus services, ample private parking.

CHIPPING CAMPDEN Gloucestershire Map **04** SP13

Premier Selected

GH ⓠⓠⓠⓠⓠ **The Malt House** Broad Campden
GL55 6UU (1m S, signposted from B4081)
☎01386 840295
FAX 01386 841334
The Brown family warmly welcomes guests to enjoy the quality and comfort of this 17th-century Malt House. The bedrooms offer a blend of comfortable furnishings with English antiques and beautiful floral displays. One wakes to enjoy views of the lovingly tended garden and orchard beyond. Dinner is available, served at a large table in the lovely beamed dining room.
7 rms (6 bth) No smoking in dining room No smoking in lounges CTV in 5 bedrooms Tea and coffee making facilities Licensed Cen ht 10P No coaches Croquet Last d noon
PRICE GUIDE
ROOMS: s £49.50-£65; d £65-£87.50
CARDS: 🔲 ▄▄

GH ⓠⓠⓠ **Orchard Hill House** Broad Campden GL55 6UU (follow Blockley rd to Broad Campden and in 1m pass The Bakers Arms for house 400yds on left)
☎01386 841473 FAX 01386 841030
Closed Xmas
This 17th-century farmhouse in the centre of Broad Camden has been beautifully restored. Bedrooms have oak doors and beams and there is a family room in a converted hayloft across a courtyard. A room is being constructed as a lounge for guests and substantial breakfasts are served round a large refectory table in the flagstoned dining room.
2 en suite (bth/shr) 2 annexe en suite (bth) No smoking CTV in all bedrooms Tea and coffee making facilities No dogs (ex guide dogs) Cen ht No children 4yrs 6P No coaches
PRICE GUIDE
ROOMS: s £38-£52; d £43-£55; wkly b&b £147-£182✱   (£)

CHIPPING NORTON Oxfordshire Map **04** SP32

Selected

GH ⓠⓠⓠⓠ **Forge House** Churchill OX7 6NJ
☎01608 658173
This large, well established guest house located next to the church in the centre of the village of Churchill, south of Chipping Norton. Bedrooms are spacious and well equipped, two of them featuring four-poster beds, one with a jacuzzi. There are two large lounges, and breakfast is served in an attractive cottage-style dining room.
4 en suite (bth/shr) (4 fmly) No smoking CTV in all bedrooms Tea and coffee making facilities No dogs (ex guide dogs) Licensed Cen ht CTV 6P
PRICE GUIDE
ROOMS: d £46-£56✱

CHISELDON Wiltshire Map **04** SU17

♥ ⓠⓠⓠ M Hughes *Parsonage* *(SU185799)* SN4 0NJ
☎01793 740204
This attractive stone-built farmhouse is in a quiet position beside the church in the village of Chiseldon, which is only a mile from junction 15 of the M4 and four miles from the centre of Swindon. The bedrooms are comfortable and very traditional in style. The public areas are full of character with some tasteful personal touches, and guests share one large antique table in the dining room.
4 rms (2 bth/shr) No smoking in dining room Tea and coffee making facilities Cen ht CTV 10P Riding 400 acres arable

---

CHISLEHAMPTON Oxfordshire Map **04** SU59

Selected

◀█ ⓠⓠⓠⓠ *Coach & Horses* Stadhampton Rd OX44 7UX (beside B480) ☎01865 890255 FAX 01865 890995
A listed, stone-built 16th-century inn set beside the B480 seven miles from Oxford features a series of cosy dining rooms with a wealth of exposed brick, oak timbers and horse brasses; these form the focal point of the inn, offering traditional pub dishes as well as more formal dinners, with specialities. The bar offers a choice of real ales, and drinks and snacks are served outside during the summer months. Chalet-style bedrooms are located in an annexe around the attractive rear courtyard; purpose-built and of a good size, they all have identical fittings and decor.
9 en suite (bth/shr) (1 fmly) CTV in all bedrooms Tea and coffee making facilities Direct dial from bedrooms Cen ht Last d 10pm
CARDS: 🔲 ▄▄ ▄▄ 🔘

CHOLMONDELEY Cheshire Map **07** SJ55

GH ⓠⓠⓠ **The Cholmondeley Arms** SY14 8BT (on A49)
☎01829 720300 FAX 01829 720123
This former school stands on the A49, close to Cholmondely Castle. The original building is now a spacious bar/bistro, where a wide range of dishes is served. Much of the original character has been preserved, and is enhanced by antique furniture and bric-á-brac. The former headmaster's house has four bedrooms, one of which is family-bedded and on the ground floor.
4 en suite (shr) (1 fmly) CTV in all bedrooms Tea and coffee making facilities Licensed Cen ht No parking No coaches Last d 10pm
PRICE GUIDE
ROOMS: s £34; d £46✱
CARDS: 🔲 ▄▄

CHORLEY Lancashire Map **07** SD51

GH ⓠⓠⓠ **Astley House Hotel** 3 Southport Rd PR7 1LB (on A581) ☎01257 272315
A Victorian house conveniently situated alongside the A581 near the town centre has been renovated and decorated in very attractive style by owner Carol Myerscough; many guests return regularly and, although bed and breakfast accommodation is the norm, she is happy to cook evening meals if given ample notice. Breakfast is served at individual tables in a bright dining room furnished with antiques, and there is a pleasant lounge. Outside there are a small private car park and a pretty rear garden.
6 rms (3 bth/shr) No smoking in dining room No smoking in lounges CTV in all bedrooms Tea and coffee making facilities No dogs (ex guide dogs) Cen ht 6P No coaches

---

PRICE GUIDE
ROOMS: s £20-£25; d £36✱
CARDS: £

CHRISTCHURCH Dorset Map **04** SZ19

See also Bournemouth & Highcliffe-on-Sea

GH Q Q *Belvedere Hotel* 59 Barrack Rd BH23 1PD
☎01202 485978
This spacious Victorian property on the main Christchurch-Bournemouth road - personally run by its proprietor for the last 40 years - provides a comfortable lounge, an attractive dining room and neat but simply furnished bedrooms with some modern facilities. Conveniently close to the county's rivers, it is particularly popular with fishermen, many of whom return year after year.
8 rms (3 fmly) CTV in all bedrooms Tea and coffee making facilities Licensed Cen ht CTV 12P Last d 4pm

---

CHULMLEIGH Devon Map **03** SS61

Selected

GH Q Q Q Q *Old Bakehouse* South Molton St EX18 7BW (off A377, opposite entrance to golf course on entering village) ☎01769 580074
This thatched 16th-century merchant's house forms part of a terrace of old properties in the centre of Chulmleigh, itself a charming and ancient town. The Burls family have converted the former bakehouse across the courtyard into three delightful bedrooms - each with its own shower, every modern facility and many thoughtful extras - and a cosy lounge. The dining room, with its exposed beams and stonework, is open to the public for lunches and afternoon teas, while in the evening dinner is served to residents only. Meals are home-cooked from the best of fresh local produce.
3 en suite (shr) (1 fmly) No smoking in all bedrooms Tea and coffee making facilities No dogs (ex guide dogs) Licensed Cen ht No children 5yrs ch fac No parking No coaches Last d 5pm
PRICE GUIDE
ROOMS: s £17-£22; d £30-£40; wkly b&b £105-£126; wkly hlf-bd £185-£234.50✱ £

CHURCHINFORD Somerset Map **03** ST21

◀ Q Q Q *The York Inn* Honiton Rd TA3 7RF
☎01823 601333
This inn of character is centrally situated in the village of Churchinford, which is surrounded by the Blagdon Hills. The bedrooms are attractively decorated and comfortably furnished. Open-plan bars have been carefully split into three sections, one with a pool table, another - more comfortable - with an inglenook fireplace, and the third a restaurant area where an extensive choice of dishes is offered from the carte or blackboard menus.
3 en suite (bth/shr) (1 fmly) CTV in all bedrooms Tea and coffee making facilities Cen ht 15P Last d 9.30pm
CARDS:

Our inspectors never book in the name of the AA. They disclose their identity only after the bill has been paid.

The Forge House

Churchill, nr. Chipping Norton, Oxfordshire OX7 6NJ
Tel: (01608) 658173

The Forge House is a 180-year-old traditional Cotswold stone cottage, with Inglenook log fires and exposed beams, combining the old world charm of tradition with the comfort of contemporary living. Four tastefully furnished en-suite rooms, two with four poster beds and one with a Jacuzzi en suite. All have colour TV, radio alarms and tea/coffee facilities. Lounge and garden available for guests' use. Personal service and advice on touring the area.
Convenient for Stratford-upon-Avon, Oxford, Warwick castle & the Cotswolds

THE OLD BAKEHOUSE

South Molton Street, Chulmleigh, Devon EX18 7BW
Telephone: (01769) 580074

Situated in a small hilltop town above the little Dart River, near the main Exeter to Barnstaple road. Ancient thatched cob cottages nestle around the beautiful 15th C. church. Very centrally situated for exploring the entire county of Devon. Our house was a 16th C. wool merchant's home, and up until 1963 the local bakery. We offer a licensed restaurant, en suite bedrooms, furnished to a very high standard, tranquillity in a beautiful conservation area, wood burning stoves, unique atmosphere, superb cuisine. Short breaks available.

OPEN ALL YEAR.

AA

CHURCH STRETTON Shropshire Map 07 SO49

See also Strefford

Selected

GH ◻◻◻◻ **Belvedere** Burway Rd SY6 6DP (turn W off A49 at Church Stretton and continue for 0.25m past war memorial) ☎01694 722232 FAX 01694 722232
This large late-Victorian detached house is situated a short walk from the town centre, on the lower slopes of the Long Mynd. All the soundly maintained bedrooms have modern furnishings and equipment, and many also have superb views of the surrounding hills; family rooms are available. There are a TV lounge and a large sitting room with a good selection of books. Separate tables are provided in the dining room, and the hotel is licensed. The attractive gardens feature fish ponds stocked with Coy carp, and there is a private car park.
12 rms (6 shr) (2 fmly) No smoking in dining room Tea and coffee making facilities Licensed Cen ht CTV ch fac 10P No coaches Last d 6pm
PRICE GUIDE
ROOMS: s £21-£23; d £42-£46; wkly b&b £132-£145; wkly hlf-bd £195-£208*
CARDS: £

GH ◻◻◻ *Brookfields* Watling St North SY6 7AR (NE edge of village, close to A49) ☎01694 722314
The extensive gardens of this large house reach as far as the eastern side of the A49, though access to the house is via the B4371 road to Much Wenlock. The attractive bedrooms, two of which overlook the Long Mynd hills, have modern furnishings and equipment as well as good quality en suite facilities. One room is located on the ground floor. There are a small lounge and an attractively decorated dining room with contemporary furniture.
4 en suite (bth/shr) (1 fmly) No smoking in bedrooms CTV in 3 bedrooms Tea and coffee making facilities Direct dial from bedrooms Licensed Cen ht 16P No coaches Last d 9pm

GH ◻◻◻ **Hope Bowdler Hall** Hope Bowdler SY6 7DD (from A49 take B4371) ☎01694 722041
Mar-Oct rs Nov
This fine country house is located in the village of Hope Bowdler, east of the town off the B4371. It is set in several acres of mature grounds with wildfowl pools, a tennis court and wooded slopes where guests may wander at leisure. The two spacious bedrooms are spacious and comfortably furnished and a large sitting room features an open fire.
2 rms No smoking No dogs Cen ht No children 12yrs 4P No coaches Tennis (hard)
PRICE GUIDE
ROOMS: s £18-£20; d £36

Selected

GH ◻◻◻◻ **Jinlye** Castle Hill, All Stretton SY6 6JP ☎01694 723243
Situated high above All Stretton, this delightful house has superb views over the local hills and countryside. It began as a crofter's cottage in the 16th century, and the lounge now occupies what used to be a barn. Beams and timbers abound, and both the lounge and entrance hall feature inglenook fireplaces with roaring log fires in colder weather. The modern bedrooms (which include one on the ground floor) are attractively decorated and have en suite facilities. Guests are

welcome to walk in the pretty gardens and the 15 acres of grounds.
8 rms (7 bth/shr) No smoking in bedrooms No smoking in dining room No smoking in 1 lounge CTV in 5 bedrooms Tea and coffee making facilities No dogs Licensed Cen ht CTV No children 12yrs 8P No coaches Mountain bikes for hire Last d 2pm
PRICE GUIDE
ROOMS: s £38; d £40-£64; wkly b&b £130-£210; wkly hlf-bd £214-£332*
 £

Premier Selected

❤ ◻◻◻◻◻ Mrs J Davies
Rectory (*SO452985*)
Woolstaston SY6 6NN (3.5m off B4370 at All Stretton) ☎01694 751306
Closed Mid Dec-25 Jan
A beautifully preserved timber-framed house dating back to 1620, surrounded by attractive spacious gardens, stands in the tiny village of Woolstaston, just over a mile

north of Church Stretton. It commands panoramic views of the surrounding countryside from its elevated position on the lower slopes of the Long Mynd, and is best reached by leaving the A49 at Leebotwood. The house has a wealth of charm and character, featuring exposed timbers, antique furnishings, a variety of bric-à-brac and an inglenook fireplace in the dining room. Bedrooms are spacious and comfortable, with modern equipment, sofas and armchairs. There are three comfortable lounge areas, and guests share one of two communal tables in the dining room at breakfast.
3 en suite (bth) No smoking in bedrooms No smoking in dining room No smoking in 1 lounge CTV in all bedrooms Tea and coffee making facilities No dogs Cen ht CTV No children 12yrs 10P 170 acres beef
PRICE GUIDE
ROOMS: s £25; d £40*

CIRENCESTER Gloucestershire Map 04 SP00

GH ◻◻◻ **The Bungalow** 95 Victoria Rd GL7 1ES ☎01285 654179
Conveniently located for the town centre, this well maintained detached house has recently benefitted from some major structural changes. The dining room now overlooks the back garden and there will be an additional ground floor room. The decor is contemporary and the bathrooms modern.
5 en suite (bth/shr) (2 fmly) No smoking in 1 bedrooms No smoking in dining room CTV in all bedrooms Tea and coffee making facilities Cen ht CTV 6P No coaches
PRICE GUIDE
ROOMS: s £17-£20; d £30; wkly b&b £120
£

GH ◻◻ *La Ronde Hotel* 52-54 Ashcroft Rd GL7 1QX ☎01285 654611 & 652216
This small family-run hotel with its own car park is conveniently situated in the historic Roman town of Cirencester. All the rooms offer en suite facilities and are centrally heated. The ring road, less than two hundred yards away, offers easy access to Swindon, Cheltenham, Gloucester, Bristol and the M4 motorway.

10 en suite (bth/shr) (2 fmly) No smoking in dining room CTV in all bedrooms Tea and coffee making facilities Licensed Cen ht 9P No coaches Last d 7pm
CARDS:

GH ⓆⓆⓆ **Smerrill Barns** Kemble GL7 6BW (off A429) ☎01285 770907 FAX 01285 770706
This guest house has recently been converted from 18th-century listed farm buildings to provide comfortable accommodation with modern facilities. The individually furnished bedrooms are tastefully decorated, and a ground-floor family suite with two adjoining bedrooms and a bathroom is available. Guests are requested to refrain from smoking.
7 en suite (bth/shr) (1 fmly) No smoking CTV in all bedrooms Tea and coffee making facilities No dogs (ex guide dogs) Cen ht No children 3yrs 8P No coaches
PRICE GUIDE
ROOMS: s £30-£35; d £45-£55; wkly b&b fr £122.50
CARDS: £

GH ⓆⓆⓆ **Wimborne House** 91 Victoria Rd GL7 1ES ☎01285 653890
A cheerful greeting, well kept accommodation and home-cooked food await visitors to this guest house conveniently located just a short distance from the centre of town and offering its own off-street parking. Two of the bedrooms have been refurbished and all are well designed, with immaculate private bathroom facilities.
5 en suite (bth/shr) No smoking CTV in all bedrooms Tea and coffee making facilities No dogs Cen ht No children 5yrs 8P No coaches Last d 4pm
PRICE GUIDE
ROOMS: s £20-£28; d £30-£35✱
£

Selected

◀ ⓆⓆⓆⓆ **Eliot Arms** Clark's Hay, South Cerney GL7 5UA (off A419) ☎01285 860215 FAX 01285 860215
An attractive 16th-century gabled inn in the village of South Cerney offers cosy, welcoming bar areas with exposed beams, brass and copper items and log fires. The ten bedrooms are immaculately furnished and there is a riverside garden.
12 en suite (bth/shr) (2 fmly) No smoking in 2 bedrooms No smoking in area of dining room No smoking in 1 lounge CTV in all bedrooms Tea and coffee making facilities Direct dial from bedrooms Cen ht 34P Last d 10pm
PRICE GUIDE
ROOMS: s fr £35; d fr £49.50✱
MEALS: Lunch £3.95-£10.95alc Dinner £3.95-£10.95alc✱
CARDS: £

◀ ⓆⓆⓆ **Masons Arms** Meysey Hampton GL7 5JT (off A417) ☎01285 850164 FAX 01285 850164
Ideally situated for touring local attractions, this delightful Cotswold inn stands beside the village green. Cosy en suite bedrooms are prettily furnished in cottage style are well equipped, the beamed bar displays a tempting variety of home-cooked dishes and a full English breakfast is available in the dining room.
8 en suite (shr) (1 fmly) No smoking in dining room CTV in all bedrooms Tea and coffee making facilities Cen ht No children 4yrs 8P No coaches Last d 9.30pm
PRICE GUIDE
ROOMS: s fr £28; d £44-£48✱
MEALS: Lunch £7-£14alc Dinner £8-£15alc✱
CARDS: £

CLACTON-ON-SEA Essex Map **05** TM11

GH ⓆⓆⓆ **Sandrock Hotel** 1 Penfold Rd, Marine Pde West CO15 1JN ☎01255 428215 FAX 01255 428215
Close to the pier and town centre, this Victorian house has large, well maintained bedrooms. Corridors are hung with watercolours painted by one of the family, the lounge is provided with games, books, and a music system, and there is a bar in the dining room.
8 en suite (bth/shr) (3 fmly) No smoking in 2 bedrooms No smoking in dining room CTV in all bedrooms Tea and coffee making facilities Licensed Cen ht 6P Last d 6pm
PRICE GUIDE
ROOMS: s £23.50-£29.50; d fr £47; wkly b&b fr £145; wkly hlf-bd fr £185✱
CARDS: £

CLAPHAM North Yorkshire Map **07** SD76

◀ ⓆⓆ **The Flying Horseshoe** LA2 8ES (1m W of A65 opposite railway station) ☎01524 251229
This popular inn stands opposite the railway station and has been considerably upgraded, especially in the public areas. The bedrooms are plain and fairly simple but are very neat and well maintained, whilst a good range of food is available either in the bar or the spacious dining room.
4 en suite (bth/shr) CTV in all bedrooms Tea and coffee making facilities Cen ht 50P Fishing Last d 9pm

CLAVERDON Warwickshire Map **04** SP16

GH ⓆⓆ **Woodside Country House** Langley Rd CV35 8PJ (0.75m S of B4095) ☎01926 842446
Closed 24 Dec-1 Jan
This small, pleasant guest house is situated on the Langley road, about a mile from the village, and is surrounded by 17 acres of woods and gardens. Bedrooms are traditionally furnished in cottage style and there is one on the ground floor. Excellent home-cooked dinners are available on request and Woodside has convenient access to Warwick, Stratford-upon-Avon, the NEC and the Midlands motorway network.
3 rms (1 fmly) No smoking CTV in 2 bedrooms Tea and coffee making facilities Cen ht CTV 13P No coaches Tennis Croquet Last d 2pm
PRICE GUIDE
ROOMS: s £18-£22; d £36-£44; wkly b&b £120-£148; wkly hlf-bd £176-£200✱
£

CLAWTON Devon Map **02** SX39

GH ⓆⓆⓆ **Clawford Vineyard** EX22 6PN (A388 Holsworth to Launceston road, turn left at Clawton cross roads, 1.5m to T-junct, turn left into village) ☎01409 254177
Situated in the peaceful Claw valley, Clawford is a working vineyard and cider orchard where guests are encouraged to sample the produce. Extensive coarse fishing in three well stocked lakes is also available - some monster carp awaiting keen anglers. There are two comfortable family bedrooms with colour televisions, and a cosy residents' lounge adjoins the conservatory style dining room where traditional breakfasts and dinners are served.
2 rms (2 fmly) No smoking CTV in all bedrooms Tea and coffee making facilities No dogs Licensed Cen ht CTV No children 5yrs 46P Tennis (grass) Fishing Last d 8pm
PRICE GUIDE
ROOMS: s £17; d £34; wkly b&b £107.10; wkly hlf-bd £155✱

CLAYTON-LE-WOODS Lancashire Map **07** SD52

Selected

GH Q Q Q Q **Brook House Hotel** 662 Preston Rd
PR6 7EH (on A6, 1m from junct 29 of M6)
☎01772 36403 FAX 01772 36403
rs Xmas
A 19th-century country residence, carefully modernised and
extended by the present owners to offer modern
accommodation, stands on the A6 just half a mile southeast of
junction 29 of the M6. Popular with business travellers, it has
spacious bedrooms equipped with such extras as satellite TV
and telephones; public areas include a bar and breakfast room,
and the conservatory which is currently being added will
provide a more formal dining area. A good range of bar meals
is available. There are pretty lawns and gardens, and ample
parking is provided.
21 rms (19 bth/shr) (3 fmly) No smoking in dining room No
smoking in 1 lounge CTV in all bedrooms Tea and coffee
making facilities Direct dial from bedrooms No dogs (ex
guide dogs) Licensed Cen ht 26P Last d 8.30pm
PRICE GUIDE
ROOMS: s £30-£38; d £38-£44✳
CARDS: 🔲 ▅ ▅ ▅ 💷

CLEARWELL Gloucestershire Map **03** SO50

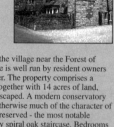

Premier Selected

GH Q Q Q Q Q **Tudor
Farmhouse Hotel &
Restaurant** GL16 8JS (turn
off A466 Monmouth/
Chepstow Road at Redbrook-
follow signs for Clearwell,
turn left at village cross,
hotel on left)
☎01594 833046
FAX 01594 837093
rs Sun evening
Tucked away on the edge of the village near the Forest of
Dean, this 13th-century house is well run by resident owners
Deborah and Richard Fletcher. The property comprises a
collection of stone cottages together with 14 acres of land,
some of which has been landscaped. A modern conservatory
forms an entrance hallway, otherwise much of the character of
the main building has been preserved - the most notable
feature being the 15th-century spiral oak staircase. Bedrooms
vary in size and style but they all offer modern facilities and
are full of charm; less mobile guests will appreciate the
ground-floor rooms contained in the converted stable
adjoining the house. A fine range of imaginative dishes -
including a full vegetarian selection - is offered by chef Bill
Denton in the intimate candlelit restaurant.
6 en suite (bth/shr) 4 annexe en suite (bth/shr) (3 fmly) No
smoking in 6 bedrooms CTV in all bedrooms Tea and coffee
making facilities Direct dial from bedrooms Licensed Cen
ht 20P No coaches Last d 9pm
PRICE GUIDE
ROOMS: s £45-£55; d £50-£75; wkly b&b £150-£210;
wkly hlf-bd £220-£270✳
CARDS: 🔲 ▅ ▅ ▅ ▅

CLEETHORPES Humberside Map **08** TA30

GH Q Q *Mallow View* 9-11 Albert Rd DN35 8LX
☎01472 691297
This long-established and predominantly commercial Victorian
terraced guest house stands between the town centre and the
seafront. Bedrooms are modestly appointed and generally
compact: the largest is situated on the ground floor and has its own
bathroom. There are also a small lounge bar with a piano, a pool
room and a neat dining room where dinner can be served by prior
arrangement.
16 rms (1 shr) (1 fmly) CTV in 15 bedrooms Tea and coffee
making facilities Licensed Cen ht CTV No parking Last d 7pm

CLIFTON UPON TEME Hereford & Worcester Map **03** SO76

◪ Q Q *Lion* 1 Village Rd WR6 6DH (on B4204)
☎01886 812617
A popular inn, full of character and situated on the B4204 at the
centre of this attractive village, the Lion dates back to 1207 when
it was a court house and hostelry. The en suite bedrooms are
comfortable. Open fires in the restaurant and lounge bar are
welcoming, and guests can choose between bar snacks and the
regularly-changing restaurant menu. The small public bar has
darts and pin ball.
2 en suite (bth/shr) (1 fmly) No smoking in area of dining room
Tea and coffee making facilities 20P Pool table Last d 9pm

CLIFTONVILLE Kent

See **Margate**

CLITHEROE Lancashire Map **07** SD74

GH Q Q Q **Brooklyn** 32 Pimlico Rd BB7 2AH
☎01200 28268
This immaculately maintained Victorian house, situated to the
north of the town but within easy walking distance of the town
centre itself, has been beautifully restored by Elizabeth and Colin
Underwood. The well tended patio garden at the back of the house
can be reached by way of the double doors at one end of the
comfortably furnished lounge where there is also a small bar. Both
dinner (between 6.30 and 7.30pm) and breakfast are served in the
bright dining room opposite. The four en suite bedrooms vary in
size but are all very attractively decorated and comfortably
furnished. Ample parking is available on the street.
4 en suite (bth/shr) No smoking in bedrooms No smoking in
dining room CTV in all bedrooms Tea and coffee making
facilities No dogs (ex guide dogs) Licensed Cen ht CTV 1P
No coaches Last d 5pm
PRICE GUIDE
ROOMS: s £23-£25; d £38-£40; wkly b&b £126-£154; wkly hlf-
bd £196-£224✳
CARDS: 🔲 ▅ ▅

Selected

GH Q Q Q Q **Peter Barn** Rabbit Ln, Cross Ln,
Waddington BB7 3JH ☎01200 28585
Closed 24 Dec-2 Jan
Peter Barn, just four miles from Clitheroe, enjoys the most
wonderful views from its magnificent position on the edge of
the Forest of Bowland. This lovingly restored tithe barn, set in
beautiful gardens, is reached from Clitheroe by driving
through the pretty village of Waddington and turning left into
Cross Lane (known locally as Rabbit Lane), just after the sign
for the Forest of Bowland. Guest accommodation, including
the comfortably furnished open-plan lounge/breakfast room,
is situated on the first floor. Two of the three pretty bedrooms

are en suite whilst the third has the private use of a nearby bathroom. Jean and Gordon Smith are not only renowned for their hospitality, but also for their home-made marmalade, jams and muesli provided at breakfast and their knowledge of gardening. Peter Barn is non-smoking throughout.
3 en suite (bth/shr) No smoking CTV in 1 bedroom Tea and coffee making facilities No dogs (ex guide dogs) Cen ht CTV 6P No coaches
PRICE GUIDE
ROOMS: d £35-£39; wkly b&b £98-£112

CLOUGHTON North Yorkshire Map **08** TA09

GH QQ *Cober Hill* Newlands Rd YO13 0AR (just off A171, 6m N of Scarborough) ☎01723 870310 FAX 01723 870271
Set within its own grounds on the edge of the Yorkshire Moors, to the north of Scarborough, Cober Hill serves mainly a conference centre and is open to the general public from early July to mid September only. Public areas are spacious, and several bedrooms have en suite facilities..
41 rms (8 bth/shr) 31 annexe en suite (bth/shr) (7 fmly) No smoking in bedrooms No smoking in dining room No smoking in 1 lounge Tea and coffee making Licensed Cen ht CTV 70P Tennis (hard) Bowling green Croquet Table tennis Clock golf Last d 6pm

▆ QQQ *Blacksmiths Arms* High St YO13 0AE
☎01723 870244
This charming village inn offers very well furnished and equipped bedrooms. A good range of home-cooked food is available in the pleasant bars, and breakfast is served in a cosy dining room.
6 en suite (bth/shr) (2 fmly) No smoking in bedrooms CTV in all bedrooms Tea and coffee making facilities No dogs (ex guide dogs) Cen ht 35P No coaches Last d 9.45pm
CARDS: ■ ■

CLOVELLY Devon Map **02** SS32

♥ QQQ Mrs E Symons *Burnstone* (SS325233) Higher Clovelly EX39 5RX ☎01237 431219
Burnstone Farm is a white-painted, 16th-century long house set back from the A39 between Bideford and Bude. The bedrooms have been equipped with many thoughtful extras such as wrapped toiletries, and sweets and biscuits with the tea facilities. Each room has a wash basin but they share one bathroom. Breakfast is served at a large table in an attractive lounge/diner.
2 rms (2 fmly) CTV in all bedrooms Tea and coffee making facilities Cen ht 3P Fishing 5 private lakes 500 acres arable mixed
PRICE GUIDE
ROOMS: d fr £32✳

CLUN Shropshire Map **07** SO38

♥ QQQ Mrs J Williams *Hurst Mill* (SO318811) SY7 0JA (1m E just off B4368) ☎01588 640224
Cosy bedrooms with modern furnishings, including one family room, are provided at this stone-built farmhouse which is located alongside the River Clun in a valley just east of Clun. There are a comfortable lounge, a conservatory and a dining room where guests eat at one communal table.
3 rms (1 shr) (1 fmly) No smoking in bedrooms No smoking in dining room No smoking in lounges CTV in 1 bedroom Tea and coffee making facilities CTV ch fac 6P Fishing Clay pigeon shooting 100 acres mixed Last d 6.30pm

PRICE GUIDE
ROOMS: s fr £17; d fr £24; wkly b&b fr £120; wkly hlf-bd fr £175✳

Selected

♥ QQQQ Mr & Mrs L Ellison *New House Farm* (SO275863) SY7 8NJ (take A488 Bishops castle rd then left at x-rds in Colebatch and follow rd through Cefn Einion and at next X-rds turn right) ☎01588 638314
Closed Dec & Jan
Some four miles north of Clun, this lovely stone-built house is quite remotely located on a large hill farm amid beautiful scenery. There are three spacious bedrooms, including a family room. One has modern furnishings while the others feature period pieces, but all are well equipped. There are also a comfortable lounge with a solid fuel stove and a cosy dining room with a shared table.
3 rms (2 bth/shr) (1 fmly) No smoking CTV in all bedrooms Tea and coffee making facilities CTV 6P 325 acres mixed Last d 2pm
PRICE GUIDE
ROOMS: d £36-£38; wkly b&b £120-£125; wkly hlf-bd £190-£195✳

COALVILLE Leicestershire Map **08** SK41

Selected

GH QQQQ *Church Lane Farm* Ravenstone LE67 2AE (at A50/A447 junct, take direction Ibstock and Church Lane first on right) ☎01530 810536
3 en suite (bth/shr) No smoking CTV in all bedrooms Tea and coffee making facilities Licensed Cen ht CTV No children 15yrs 6P No coaches Riding Water colour painting tuition Last d noon
PRICE GUIDE
ROOMS: s £17.50-£25; d £33-£40✳
CARDS: ■ ■
See advertisement under ASHBY-DE-LA-ZOUCH

COCKERMOUTH Cumbria Map **11** NY13

GH QQQ *Derwent Lodge Hotel* Embelton CA13 9YA
☎01768 776606
An attractive stone building standing back from the A66 in the small hamlet of Embleton. It has recently been completely refurbished and now offers modern well-equipped bedrooms whilst an extensive range of food is available in the spacious restaurant.
8 en suite (shr) CTV in all bedrooms Cen ht

Factual details of establishments in this Guide are from questionnaires we send to all establishments that feature in the book.

℘remier Selected

GH ◨◨◨◨◨ **Low Hall Country** Brandlingill CA13 0RE (3m S on unclass off A5086) ☎01900 826654 Mar-Oct

Hugh and Enid Davies have furnished their 17th-century farmhouse to a very high standard, retaining its distinctive character. All the bedrooms have modern en suite facilities and coordinated fabrics are very much a feature. There is a log fire in the beamed lounge on chilly days, and another equally comfortable lounge offers TV, books and magazines. There is a new menu each evening in the dining room, and breakfast is a memorable meal.

5 en suite (bth/shr) No smoking CTV in 1 bedroom Tea and coffee making facilities No dogs (ex guide dogs) Licensed Cen ht CTV No children 10yrs 10P No coaches Last d 7.15pm

PRICE GUIDE
ROOMS: s £20-£35; d £40-£70✳
CARDS: 🅰 💳

GH ◨◨◨ **Sundawn** Carlisle Rd, Bridekirk CA13 0PA (2m N on Carlisle road) ☎01900 822384

Closed 20 Dec-5 Jan

A friendly Victorian family home lies in its own gardens just off the A595, two miles east of Cockermouth. Public areas include a comfortable lounge/dining area and a sun lounge with panoramic views of the distant Lakeland fells. The front-facing bedrooms share the outlook and the relaxed atmosphere which fills the house.

4 rms (2 bth/shr) (1 fmly) No smoking Tea and coffee making facilities No dogs (ex guide dogs) Cen ht CTV 6P No coaches Last d before noon

PRICE GUIDE
ROOMS: s £15; d £30-£38; wkly b&b £105-£133; wkly hlf-bd £189-£217✳

CODSALL Staffordshire Map **07** SJ80

♥ ◨◨◨ Mrs D E Moreton **Moors Farm & Country Restaurant** (SJ859048) Chillington Ln WV8 1QF (between village of Codsall & Codsall Wood) ☎01902 842330 FAX 01902 847878

This busy working farm is beautifully situated in an isolated position five miles northwest of Wolverhampton. Many school parties have had their first introduction to a variety of farm animals here, with over 100 acres of mixed farming. The bright bedrooms are attractively decorated and traditionally furnished, while downstairs there are a small, cosy residents' lounge, an oak-beamed bar and an attractive non-smoking restaurant where a choice of home-cooked dishes is served at separate tables.

6 rms (3 shr) (3 fmly) No smoking in dining room CTV in all bedrooms Tea and coffee making facilities No dogs Licensed Cen ht No children 4yrs 20P 100 acres mixed Last d 2pm

PRICE GUIDE
ROOMS: s £25-£30; d £42-£50✳

COLCHESTER Essex Map **05** TL92

See also Frating

GH ◨◨ **Four Sevens** 28 Inglis Rd CO3 3HU (take B1022 Maldon rd the 2nd on rt) ☎01206 46093 FAX 01206 46093

To find Vas and Calypso Demetri's comfortable family home, take the Maldon road from the town centre, then second right and first left to reach this quiet residential area which is still close to the centre. Bedrooms are comfortable and dinner is available by arrangement. Traditional English cooking is a speciality.

6 rms (2 shr) (1 fmly) No smoking in dining room No smoking in lounges CTV in all bedrooms Tea and coffee making facilities No dogs Cen ht 2P No coaches Last d 8.30pm

PRICE GUIDE
ROOMS: s £25-£30; d £32-£40✳

GH ◨◨ **Old Manse** 15 Roman Rd CO1 1UR ☎01206 45154

Closed 23-31 Dec

A friendly welcome awaits at The Old Manse, a Victorian end-of-terrace house which was formerly a Methodist manse. There are three comfortably appointed bedrooms with quality soft furnishings and water colour paintings, each having a range of useful facilities and helpful extras; one of the bedrooms is located on the ground floor, and this proves to be particularly popular with mature guests. The bedrooms do not have wash basins, but they are served by three separate bathrooms that are conveniently close. A hearty breakfast is served at a communal dining table in the breakfast room. Please note that this is a non-smoking establishment, and that the house is not suitable for pets or very young children.

3 rms (2 bth/shr) No smoking CTV in all bedrooms Tea and coffee making facilities No dogs (ex guide dogs) Cen ht No children 6yrs 1P No coaches

---

GH ◨◨ **14 Roman Road** 14 Roman Rd CO1 1UR ☎01206 577905

Closed Xmas week

An attractive Victorian semidetached house stands in a peaceful residential road close to the castle and town centre. Bedrooms are immaculately kept and well furnished. Breakfast is cooked by charming proprietor Gill Nicholson at the large pine kitchen table and there is a small neat garden by part of Colchester's original Roman wall.

2 en suite (bth/shr) No smoking CTV in all bedrooms Tea and coffee making facilities No dogs Cen ht No children 12yrs 1P

PRICE GUIDE
ROOMS: s £26-£28; d £36-£38; wkly b&b £121-£196✳

GH ◨◨ **Tarquins** 26 Inglis Rd CO3 3HU ☎01206 579508 FAX 01206 579508

A Victorian house in a quiet position has been run for many years by Mrs Hudson. There is a comfortable lounge with ornaments and plants and bedrooms are on the first and second floors. At busy times, guests may have to share a table at breakfast.

6 rms (2 shr) (4 fmly) No smoking in dining room No smoking in 1 lounge CTV in all bedrooms Tea and coffee making facilities Cen ht CTV No children 5yrs 1P No coaches Last d 10am

PRICE GUIDE
ROOMS: s fr £20; d fr £30; wkly b&b fr £105; wkly hlf-bd fr £142

COLEFORD Gloucestershire Map **03** SO51

♥ ◨◨ Mrs S Davis **Lower Tump** (SO588160) Eastbach, English Bicknor GL16 7EU ☎01594 860253

This tranquil 16th-century farmhouse, delightfully situated amidst green fields, is the ideal base from which to explore the nearby Forest of Dean, and its two spaciously comfortable en suite bedrooms enjoy beautiful views across the working farm.

---

2 en suite (bth/shr) (1 fmly) CTV in all bedrooms Tea and coffee making facilities Cen ht CTV 10P 150 acres mixed
PRICE GUIDE
ROOMS: s £16.50-£17.50; d £28-£30; wkly b&b fr £84✱

COLESBOURNE Gloucestershire Map **04** SP01

◀ **Q Q Q** *Colesbourne* GL53 9NP (on A435 Cirencester to Cheltenham road) (Logis)
☎01242 870376 FAX 01242 870397
This inn is over 200 years old and retains a traditional bar and beamed restaurant. The former stable block, with its rare lunette windows, has been converted to provide excellent guest rooms.
10 annexe en suite (bth/shr) CTV in all bedrooms Tea and coffee making facilities Direct dial from bedrooms 70P Last d 10pm
CARDS: 🔳 ▀ ▀ ⑩

COLNE Lancashire Map **07** SD84

Selected

✔ **Q Q Q Q** Mrs C Mitson **Higher Wanless** *(SD873413)*
Red Ln BB8 7JP ☎01282 865301
Closed Dec
This 250-year-old whitewashed farmhouse is located in the most beautiful countryside, overlooking the Leeds/Liverpool canal and close to the Pendle Way. (Packed lunches and transport can be provided for walkers at a small charge). It is easily reached from junction 13 of the M65 Motorway by following signs for Barrowford. The farmhouse has two spacious and comfortably furnished bedrooms, one with an en suite shower room, the other with its own private bathroom located nearby. Both rooms are well equipped and have many personal touches. A fire is lit in the cosy beamed sitting room on cooler evenings and both breakfast and - by prior arrangement - a set dinner (with alternatives) are served in the dining room, where guests sit around a magnificent communal table.
2 rms (1 shr) (2 fmly) No smoking in bedrooms No smoking in area of dining room No smoking in 1 lounge CTV in 1 bedroom Tea and coffee making facilities No dogs Cen ht CTV No children 3yrs 4P 25 acres shire horses sheep Last d 9am
PRICE GUIDE
ROOMS: s £19-£22; d £38-£44✱

COLTISHALL Norfolk Map **09** TG21

Selected

GH **Q Q Q Q** **The Hedges** Tunstead Rd NR12 7AL (fron Norwich take B1150, turn right onto B1354, opposite river turn left into White Lion Rd at top take right fork)
☎01603 738361 FAX 01603 738361
Closed 24 Dec-1 Jan
The Hedges is a friendly guest house with two acres of lawns located a short distance from the village and the River Bure. The bedrooms are all en suite and equipped in a modern manner. There is a large lounge with a log burning fire and a corner bar with a supply of spirits and beers, and a south facing breakfast room with garden views. The house has its own deep-bore well ensuring a supply of fresh drinking water.
6 en suite (bth/shr) (2 fmly) No smoking in bedrooms No smoking in dining room No smoking in 1 lounge CTV in all bedrooms Tea and coffee making facilities No dogs (ex

guide dogs) Licensed Cen ht CTV 14P No coaches Last d 2pm
PRICE GUIDE
ROOMS: s £25; d £38-£40; wkly b&b £120✱

COMBE MARTIN Devon Map **02** SS54

See **Berrynabor**

CONGLETON Cheshire Map **07** SJ86

◀ **Q** **Egerton Arms Hotel** Astbury CW12 4RQ (off A34)
☎01260 273946
Set beside the A34 close to a church, this much-extended village inn offers well maintained simple accommodation. An attractive restaurant with a Cheshire brick fireplace serves breakfast and dinner, while lighter snacks can be enjoyed in the spacious lounge bar. Two of the bedrooms and areas in the lounge bar and restaurant are set aside for non-smokers.
8 rms No smoking in 2 bedrooms No smoking in area of dining room CTV in all bedrooms Tea and coffee making facilities Cen ht 100P No coaches Last d 9.30pm
CARDS: 🔳 ▀

CONISHOLME Lincolnshire Map **09** TF39

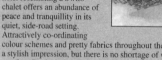

GH **QQQQ** Wickham House Church Ln LN11 7LX (turn into Church Lane from the A1031 at telephone kiosk in Conisholme, Wickham House next to church) ☎01507 358465
Closed Xmas & New Year

This lovely house, peacefully set next to the village church, is surrounded by delightful cottage gardens in the hamlet of Conisholme, just off the A1031. There are two comfortable lounges, one provided with a good selection of books. The guest bedrooms (one of them on the ground floor) are both very well furnished and thoughtfully equipped; warm, friendly service is provided by the resident owners and the house is fully no smoking.
4 en suite (bth/shr) No smoking CTV in all bedrooms Tea and coffee making facilities No dogs (ex guide dogs) Cen ht No children 8yrs 4P No coaches Last d noon
PRICE GUIDE
ROOMS: s fr £18.50

CONISTON Cumbria Map **07** SD39

GH **QQQ** Arrowfield Little Arrow, Torver LA21 8AU (on A593) ☎015394 41741
Feb-Nov

A delightful Victorian house set in well tended gardens, Arrowfield offers extensive views of the countryside and fells which surround it. The tastefully furnished and decorated bedrooms offer television and tea-making facilities, an open fire burns in the spacious lounge and home-cooked evening meals are served in a cosy dining room.
5 rms (2 shr) No smoking in bedrooms No smoking in dining room CTV in all bedrooms Tea and coffee making facilities No dogs (ex guide dogs) Licensed Cen ht CTV No children 3yrs 6P No coaches
PRICE GUIDE
ROOMS: s £18-£21; d £32-£46; wkly b&b £112-£137

Premier Selected

GH **QQQQQ** Coniston Lodge Hotel Sunny Brow LA21 8HH (at crossroads on A593 close to filling station) ☎015394 41201
rs Sun & Mon pm

This delightful family-run hotel resembling a Swiss chalet offers an abundance of peace and tranquillity in its quiet, side-road setting. Attractively co-ordinating colour schemes and pretty fabrics throughout the house create a stylish impression, but there is no shortage of warmth and comfort. Particularly spacious bedrooms are equipped with such extras such as telephones, radios, televisions, trouser presses and hair dryers; one room has a four-poster bed. Guests can enjoy Elizabeth Robinson's four-course evening meals in the inviting, relaxing setting of a dining room which, like the lounge, overlooks the garden. Of special interest are the Campbell Bluebird mementoes, presented to the family in 1951 and displayed in the lounge.

6 en suite (bth/shr) No smoking CTV in all bedrooms Tea and coffee making facilities Direct dial from bedrooms No dogs (ex guide dogs) Licensed Cen ht No children 10yrs 9P No coaches Last d 7.30pm
PRICE GUIDE
ROOMS: s £26-£39; d £52-£78✱
CARDS: £

Premier Selected

GH **QQQQQ** Wheelgate Country House Hotel Little Arrow LA21 8AU ☎015394 41418
15 Mar-3 Nov

Oak beams, low ceilings, wood panelling and antique furniture are features of this delightful country house hotel, converted from a 17th-century farmhouse. The bedrooms are attractively furnished and decorated, all have en suite facilities and one has a four-poster bed. Three rooms are located in a converted stable, one on the ground floor. Public areas include a beamed lounge with a log fire and fresh flowers, a cosy bar and a candlelit dining room where imaginative food is served.
5 en suite (bth/shr) 3 annexe en suite (bth/shr) (3 fmly) No smoking in bedrooms No smoking in dining room No smoking in lounges CTV in all bedrooms Tea and coffee making facilities No dogs (ex guide dogs) Licensed Cen ht 10P No coaches Free membership of Health Club Last d 7pm
PRICE GUIDE
ROOMS: s £25-£34; d £50-£68; wkly b&b £168-£205; wkly hlf-bd £245-£300
CARDS:

CONSETT Co Durham Map **12** NZ15

GH **QQQ** Greenhead Carterway Heads, (A68) DH8 9TP (just off A68, 2m from Shotley Bridge) ☎01207 255676
A delightful guest house set in a very rural location on the A68, three miles from Shotley Bridge, offers very pleasantly furnished and well equipped bedrooms with exposed beams and stone walls. The cosy lounge is warmed by a wood-burning fire, and friendly service is provided by the charming owners, Mr and Mrs Bates.
3 en suite (bth/shr) (1 fmly) CTV in all bedrooms Tea and coffee making facilities Licensed Cen ht CTV 10P No coaches Last d 5pm
PRICE GUIDE
ROOMS: s £20; d £30; wkly b&b £105-£140; wkly hlf-bd £140-£175✱

CONSTANTINE Cornwall & Isles of Scilly Map **02** SW72

◀ **QQQ** Trengilly Wartha Nancenoy TR11 5RP (from Constantine follow signs to Nancenoy) (Logis) ☎01326 340332 FAX 01326 340332
The public bar of this inn is very much a Cornish local with a good range of real ales and imaginative bar meals. The intimate restaurant serves a fixed price menu. Bedrooms are individually furnished and well equipped. Other features of the inn are its international size petanque pitch, and special events such as the sausage festival and pudding week.
6 rms (4 bth 1 shr) CTV in all bedrooms Tea and coffee making

facilities Direct dial from bedrooms Cen ht 55P Fishing
Petanque Last d 9.30pm
PRICE GUIDE
ROOMS: s £32-£40; d £44-£60; wkly b&b £150-£170; wkly hlf-
bd £250-£270✳
MEALS: Bar Lunch £8-£20alc✳
CARDS:  £

COPMANTHORPE North Yorkshire Map **08** SE54

GH ▣▣▣ *Duke of Connaught Hotel* Copmanthorpe Grange
YO2 3TN (off Appleton Roebuck/Bishopthorpe road)
☎01904 744318
Closed Xmas wk
In open countryside, this very skilfully converted group of farm
buildings has well furnished bedrooms, a cosy lounge and a
country-style dining room. The owners give friendly attention.
14 en suite (bth/shr) 4 annexe rms (2 fmly) CTV in 14 bedrooms
Tea and coffee making facilities No dogs (ex guide dogs)
Licensed Cen ht 40P Last d 6pm
CARDS:

COPPULL Lancashire Map **07** SD51

💟▣ Mrs Woodcock *Bridge Farm (SD569132)* Bridge Farm,
Coppull Moor Ln PR7 4LL ☎01257 792390
This modern farmhouse, which is still very much part of a
working mixed dairy farm and a family home, is conveniently
situated just off the A.49 at Coppull Moor, close to attractions
such as Camelot and Wigan Pier. The three bedrooms are
spacious, soundly furnished and share two bathrooms, one with a
shower cubicle. Breakfast is served in the large and attractively
furnished lounge/dining room.
3 rms Tea and coffee making facilities No dogs 6P 70 acres
dairy

CORBRIDGE Northumberland Map **12** NY96

Premier Selected

GH ▣▣▣▣▣ The
Courtyard Mount Pleasant,
Sandhoe NE46 4LX
☎01434 606850
In a beautiful pastoral setting
high above the valley of the
meandering Tyne, the
Courtyard is a quite
remarkable conversion of
once derelict farm buildings
restored in country-house
style. Though carefully

furnished and decorated with an eye for colour co-ordination
the atmosphere is relaxed and very welcoming. The bedrooms
- two with four-posters - are extremely comfortable, while
downstairs the huge lounge with its ancient oak timbers and
flagged floors leads into a split level dining room where
breakfasts and dinners (by arrangement) are served.
3 en suite (bth/shr) (1 fmly) No smoking in bedrooms No
smoking in dining room CTV in all bedrooms Tea and coffee
making facilities No dogs Cen ht No children 12yrs 3P No
coaches
PRICE GUIDE
ROOMS: s £25-£30; d £45-£55

GH ▣▣▣ **Morningside** Riding Mill NE44 6HL
☎01434 682350 FAX 01434 682350
Morningside, a stone-built former blacksmith's house, stands beside
the main road in the village of Riding Mill. It offers pleasant,
thoughtfully equipped bedrooms (two of them suitable for family
use), a relaxing guests' lounge, and a charming breakfast room.
5 rms (1 shr) (2 fmly) No smoking CTV in all bedrooms Tea
and coffee making facilities Cen ht CTV 5P No coaches Last d
breakfast
PRICE GUIDE
ROOMS: s £17-£25; d £30-£34✳

GH ▣▣▣ **Priorfield** Priorfield, Hippingstones Ln NE45 5JA
(from village centre through market place along Watling St
past Wheatsheaf pub and 2nd right into St Helens Lane then
1st rt) ☎01434 633179
Mar-Nov
This private house lies in a quiet residential cul-de-sac within
walking distance of the town centre. It offers one double and one
twin bedroom, both attractively decorated with stylish fabrics.
Breakfast is taken around a large refectory table in an area which
is also used as a lounge.
2 en suite (bth/shr) (1 fmly) No smoking in bedrooms CTV in all
bedrooms Tea and coffee making facilities No dogs Cen ht No
children 4yrs 2P No coaches
PRICE GUIDE
ROOMS: s £20-£28; d £32-£40✳

📧💟▣ Mrs C M Leech **Crookhill** *(NZ057656)* NE43 7UX
☎01661 843117
Apr-Oct rs Nov-Mar
This stone-built house stands in an elevated position off the A69
overlooking open countryside, and is reached via the B6309 to the
east of Newton. Bedrooms are simply appointed and there is a
pleasant combined lounge/breakfast room overlooking the garden.
3 rms (1 fmly) No smoking Tea and coffee making facilities No
dogs (ex guide dogs) Cen ht CTV 4P 23 acres beef mixed sheep
PRICE GUIDE
ROOMS: s fr £16; d £32-£34; wkly b&b fr £95

CORSHAM Wiltshire Map **03** ST87

Selected

💟▣▣▣ Mrs C Barton **Manor Farm** *(ST846679)*
Wadswick SN13 8JB (take B3109 from Corsham, past
mini-roundabout and turn left at Wadswick signpost.
Second farmhouse on left) ☎01225 810700
Feb-Nov
This handsome 17th-century farmhouse overlooking
beautifully tended gardens enjoys a quiet setting with rural
views extending to the Box Valley. Accommodation is offered
in three spacious, quality bedrooms, and the gracious drawing
room is an ideal place to relax after a day spent exploring the
Roman city of Bath or picturesque Bradford-on-Avon.
Breakfast - the only meal served in the large dining room -
may be enjoyed round a beautiful antique table.
3 en suite (shr) (1 fmly) No smoking CTV in all bedrooms
Tea and coffee making facilities No dogs (ex guide dogs)
Cen ht 3P Riding arranged 500 acres arable sheep
PRICE GUIDE
ROOMS: s £25-£30; d £38-£42✳
CARDS: £

COUNTISBURY (NEAR LYNTON) Devon Map **03** SS74

❤ **Q Q Q** Mrs R Pile **Coombe** *(SS766489)* EX35 6NF (0.5m off A39 on road to Brendon) ☎01598 741236
Apr-Oct rs Nov & Dec
Coombe Farm, with its 365 acres of hills and fields where Exmoor horned sheep and Devon cattle are reared, lies on the North Devon coastline within the boundary of Exmoor National Park. This early 17th-century house has a dining room with an inglenook fireplace, old beams and individual tables. A four-course dinner is served, and there is a cosy sitting room with TV where guests can relax. Bedrooms are warm and comfortable.
5 rms (2 shr) (2 fmly) No smoking Tea and coffee making facilities No dogs (ex guide dogs) Licensed Cen ht CTV 6P 365 acres sheep
PRICE GUIDE
ROOMS: d £34-£41; wkly b&b £100-£134

COVENTRY West Midlands Map **04** SP37

GH Q Q Ashleigh House 17 Park Rd CV1 2LH
☎01203 223804
Closed 23 Dec-1 Jan
The Ashleigh is a well established and popular house which is very handy for the station but quietly set in a pleasant residential street. The reception rooms have recently been refurbished and both the lounge and dining room are lovely. The bedrooms vary in size and are similarly styled with white desk and wardrobe units and clean fresh decoration. Their en suites are modern and fully tiled.
10 rms (8 shr) (5 fmly) CTV in all bedrooms Tea and coffee making facilities No dogs Licensed Cen ht CTV 12P No coaches Last d 8.45pm
PRICE GUIDE
ROOMS: s £18-£23.50; d £30-£34✳

GH Q Q Croft Hotel 23 Stoke Green, Off Binley Rd CV3 1FP (second turning on right after Humber Road traffic lights on A427/428) ☎01203 457846
The Croft is situated in an established residential area overlooking the green. Simple, bright bedrooms are offered, along with varied public areas. A bar complete with pool table serves draught beer and lager, and there are a set-price menu with grills and a range of bar snacks. Dogs and their owners are most welcome and are free to make use of the huge, enclosed rear garden.
12 rms (4 shr) (1 fmly) CTV in 6 bedrooms Tea and coffee making facilities Licensed Cen ht CTV 12P No coaches Pool table Last d 8.30pm
PRICE GUIDE
ROOMS: s £21-£28.50; d £34-£45✳
CARDS: 🅰 💳

GH Q Q Hearsall Lodge Hotel 1 Broad Ln CV5 7AA
☎01203 674543 & 678749
A pleasant semi detached dwelling near the city which is easy to find. It is well established, comfortable and the proprietor, Mrs Entwistle is friendly and concerned. The lounge is large and is connected to a cheerfully decorated dining room. The bedrooms are furnished with a mixture of styles and are both very clean and cared for.
12 rms (9 shr) (1 fmly) CTV in all bedrooms Tea and coffee making facilities Direct dial from bedrooms Licensed Cen ht CTV P No coaches
PRICE GUIDE
ROOMS: d £25✳
CARDS: 🅰 💳 💳

COWSHILL Co Durham Map **12** NY84

❤ **Q Q Q** Mrs J Ellis **Low Corn Riggs** *(NY845413)* DL13 1AQ
☎01388 537600
Situated in the heart of the North Pennines and at the head of Weardale, this well furnished farmhouse enjoys all of today's comforts. There are three pleasant bedrooms which are all en suite and have hospitality trays and there is also a very inviting lounge for guests'. Good home cooking is provided and there is also a riding stable on the farm. The house is located just to the west of Cowshill on the A689.
3 en suite (bth/shr) (1 fmly) No smoking in bedrooms No smoking in dining room Tea and coffee making facilities Licensed Cen ht CTV P Riding Last d 9pm
PRICE GUIDE
ROOMS: s £18; d £35✳

CRACKINGTON HAVEN Cornwall & Isles of Scilly
Map **02** SX19

Selected

📠 📺 GH **Q Q Q Q** Nancemellan EX23 0NN
☎01840 230283 FAX 01840 230283
Closed mid-Dec-mid Jan
Surrounded by National Trust land, Nancemellan is beautifully situated overlooking Crackington Haven and set in nine acres of peaceful gardens, being built in the style of Mackintosh. Lorraine and Eddie Ruff welcome guests to their family home, in its tranquil setting. The bedrooms are attractively presented and comfortable, during the winter 1995/6 one of the rooms is planned to be made ensuite, leaving the remaining rooms each having an exclusive use private bathroom. There is a drawing room available for the use of guests, which in cooler months has a log fire. Breakfast is taken in the kitchen, around a large family table, beside the Aga, the heart of the house. Light suppers are available by prior arrangement.
3 en suite (bth/shr) (1 fmly) No smoking CTV in all bedrooms Tea and coffee making facilities No dogs Cen ht No children 8yrs 3P No coaches Last d 6pm
PRICE GUIDE
ROOMS: s £16-£18; d £40-£50; wkly b&b £112-£175

Premier Selected

❤ **Q Q Q Q Q** Mrs M Knight **Manor** *(SX159962)* EX23 0JW ☎01840 230304
This delightful secluded manor house, listed in the Domesday Book, stands one mile from the sea at Crackington Have. Both the house and beautifully manicured gardens have been carefully restored by the owners to combine luxurious accommodation with discreet, traditional hospitality. Elegantly decorated and individually furnished bedrooms incorporate many fine pieces of antique furniture, and each room has either a private or an en suite bathroom. Downstairs, guests gather at the honesty bar for pre-dinner drinks before enjoying an evening meal which is taken in dinner party style

around the magnificent family dining table. Inventive menus make use of fresh local ingredients whenever possible. There are both summer and winter lounges, the latter with a cosy wood burner for chilly evenings. Breakfast is taken at individual tables in a sunny room overlooking the garden. Television is available in a separate, smaller lounge, while a full-sized snooker table is to be found in the barn - now converted for use as a games room - which is situated across the courtyard from the main building. Smoking is not permitted inside the house.

3 rms (2 bth) 2 annexe en suite (shr) No smoking No dogs Licensed Cen ht CTV No children 18yrs 6P Snooker Table tennis 30 acres beef Last d 5pm

PRICE GUIDE
ROOMS: s £42-£45; d £80-£84✳

Premier Selected

♥ QQQQQ Mrs J Crocker
Trevigue (SX136951)
EX23 0LQ ☎01840 230418
FAX 01840 230418
Mar-Sep
Built of local granite, Trevigue is a National Trust farmhouse dating back some 300 years and set in a simply stunning location on the North Cornish Coastal footpath. The hotel is surrounded by open countryside, the sea and Strangles Beach, and nestles within the protection of an enclosed cobbled courtyard. The Croker family treat their guests as family friends, offering them accommodation in attractively decorated and elegantly furnished bedrooms - whether in the historic main building or a modern Mediterranean-style villa a few hundred yards away - which are an ideal combination of traditional comfort and modern facilities. Most of the ground floor has lovely flagstone floors scattered with rugs, and there is a cosy lounge with wood-burning stove, relaxing chairs, attractive pictures and lots of reading material, which leads through to an additional, smaller, sitting room. The ancient dining room, complete with family dining table, now forms the entrance hall, and in what must have once been the breakfast room Mrs Croker serves fresh local food from imaginative menus. Outside, a barn has been converted to form an information area and restaurant in conjunction with the National Trust, so guests also have the choice of eating here or simply enjoying a cream tea on the lawn.

4 en suite (bth/shr) No smoking in bedrooms No smoking in dining room CTV in 2 bedrooms Tea and coffee making facilities No dogs Licensed CTV No children 12yrs 20P 500 acres dairy mixed Last d 5pm

PRICE GUIDE
ROOMS: s £30-£43; d £48-£55✳

Our inspectors never book in the name of the AA. They disclose their identity only after the bill has been paid.

Hearsall Lodge Hotel
1 BROAD LANE, COVENTRY CV5 7AA
Telephone: (01203) 674543

Family run hotel situated close to town centre in select residential area. Eighteen bedrooms with colour TV, tea and coffee making facilities and showers. Full central heating – Residents' TV lounge. Licensed bar. Ample parking space. Easy access to A45/M6 for National Exhibition Centre, Birmingham International Airport and Royal Showground at Stoneleigh.

TREVIGUE FARM
Crackington Haven

A superb 16th century farmhouse on a 500-acre dairy and beef farm with 2½ miles of spectacular coast-line. All bedrooms en-suite with tea-making facilities, two with colour TV. Beautifully appointed, tranquil sitting rooms with great emphasis placed on imaginative cuisine. An ideal location for touring Cornwall and Devon. Children over 12 years most welcome. Licensed. Trevigue is now licensed for civil marriages – a magical place to have your wedding.

Janet Crocker, Trevigue, Crackington Haven, Bude, Cornwall EX23 0LQ
Phone: St. Gennys (01840) 230418
Premier Selected

Premier Selected

❦ Q Q Q Q Q Mrs P Mount
Treworgie Barton *(SX178968)*
EX23 0NL ☎01840 230233
Apr-Sep rs Feb-Mar & Nov

Treworgie Barton is a 16th-century farmhouse peacefully situated at the head of the Millook valley, affording glorious views across open country and the rugged coastline to the sea. Five tastefully decorated
bedrooms are offered, two in a converted barn. There is a comfortable lounge, where a log fire burns on cooler evenings, and here guests are given tea and home-made biscuits on arrival. Dinner is served in the elegant dining room. It is a set meal but careful account is taken of guests' preferences. Food is freshly cooked and good use is made of local produce. The farmhouse is not licensed but wine can be brought in at no extra charge.
2 en suite (bth) 2 annexe en suite (bth/shr) (1 fmly) No smoking CTV in all bedrooms Tea and coffee making facilities No dogs No children 10yrs 5P 65 acres non working Last d 4pm
PRICE GUIDE
ROOMS: d £36-£46; wkly b&b £126-£161; wkly hlf-bd £214-£249

◆ Q Q Q **Coombe Barton** EX23 0JG
☎01840 230345 FAX 01840 230788
Mar-Oct rs Nov-Feb
Superbly positioned directly above the beach at Crackington Haven, this property originally built for the "captain" of the local slate quarry is now favoured by surfers and cliff walkers alike. Several of the comfortable bedrooms have en suite facilities, and most - like the bars - benefit from stunning views. The inn is popular with families, and has a large children's room in addition to three other bars. Blackboards display extensive menus (including daily specials) aimed at all age groups.
7 rms (3 bth) (1 fmly) CTV in 3 bedrooms Tea and coffee making facilities Cen ht CTV 40P Last d 9.30pm
PRICE GUIDE
ROOMS: s £17.50-£22.50; d £35-£58; wkly b&b £116-£195✳
CARDS: 🔳 🔳 🔳

CRANBROOK Kent Map 05 TQ73

Premier Selected

GH Q Q Q Q Q *Hancocks*
Tilsden Ln TN17 3PH
☎01580 714645

Further improvements have been made to this charming house and a small suite with its own sitting room is now available. Comfort and furnishings remain at a very high level, and the well appointed bedrooms have such special touches as
mineral water and bowls of fruit. An open fire in the spacious and comfortable lounge aids relaxation, particularly after a
good, well prepared evening meal. Breakfasts are hearty and enjoyable.
3 en suite (bth/shr) No smoking CTV in all bedrooms Tea and coffee making facilities Cen ht No children 9yrs 3P No coaches Last d 2pm

---

Selected

❦ Q Q Q Q Mrs S Wickham **The Oast** *(TQ755345)*
Hallwood Farm TN17 2SP (A229 1m S) ☎01580 712416
Mar-Oct rs Nov-Feb
This delightful farmhouse is set in peaceful rural surroundings. The furnishings are in keeping with the style of the house and the bedrooms are spacious. Guests have a choice of English or Continental breakfast.
2 en suite (bth/shr) No smoking CTV in all bedrooms Tea and coffee making facilities No dogs Cen ht No children 5yrs P 200 acres arable fruit sheep
PRICE GUIDE
ROOMS: s fr £25; d fr £35✳

CRANFORD Greater London

For accommodation details see **Heathrow Airport**

CRASTER Northumberland Map **12** NU22

◆ Q Q Q *Cottage* Dunstan Village NE66 3SZ (NW, off Howick to Embleton road) ☎01665 576658
Standing just a few minutes' drive from the coast in the village of Dunster, this family-run inn offers modern ground-floor bedrooms looking out on to secluded gardens to the rear. Food is available in the attractive restaurant, the cosy bar and a small conservatory. Meals are also served on the patio in good weather.
10 en suite (bth/shr) No smoking in area of dining room CTV in all bedrooms Tea and coffee making facilities Direct dial from bedrooms No dogs (ex guide dogs) Cen ht ch fac 35P Last d 9.30pm
CARDS: 🔳 🔳

CRAVEN ARMS Shropshire Map **07** SO48

GH Q Q **Hesterworth** Hesterworth, Hopesay SY7 8EX
☎01588 660487
Set in several acres of mature grounds and gardens, this Victorian mansion is now a centre for country holidays. Eleven units, each with its own lounge, small kitchen and two bedrooms, can be used either for self catering holidays or as serviced accommodation and evening meals are provided if required. There is a conservatory lounge which guests can use as an alternative to their bedrooms' private lounge and the large restaurant also has a small bar. This is an ideal centre for touring the area.
7 en suite (bth/shr) 11 annexe rms (2 bth 1 shr) (2 fmly) No smoking in area of dining room No smoking in 1 lounge Licensed Cen ht CTV 25P Tennis (grass) Last d 10am
PRICE GUIDE
ROOMS: s £17.25-£19.25; d £32.50-£36.25; wkly b&b fr £113.75; wkly hlf-bd fr £152.25

CRAWLEY West Sussex

For accommodation details see **Gatwick Airport**

CREWE Cheshire Map 07 SJ75

♥ Q Q Q Mrs Diana Edwards **Balterley Hall** *(SJ765499)*
Balterley CW2 5QG (4m SE) ☎01270 820206
Closed Xmas
An immaculately maintained Grade II listed building is beautifully
situated in the heart of the Cheshire countryside, yet is convenient
for Junction 16 of the M6, the Potteries, Crewe and Nantwich.
Two of the airy bedrooms are en suite and spacious, but all three
are well equipped and comfortably furnished. Breakfast is served
around a large table in the pleasant breakfast room which doubles
as a lounge and has a cupboard full of books and games. The
house is still part of a working farm and is reached by turning
down the lane opposite the village church.
3 rms (2 shr) (1 fmly) No smoking in 1 bedrooms No smoking
in dining room No smoking in lounges CTV in all bedrooms Tea
and coffee making facilities No dogs (ex guide dogs) CTV 6P
240 acres arable mixed pigs sheep Last d noon

Selected

♥ Q Q Q Q Ms M Hughes **Clayhanger Hall Farm**
(SJ728574) Maw Ln, Haslington CW1 1SH
☎01270 583952
Owned by the Hughes family for three generations, this very
successful dairy farm is set in the heart of the Cheshire
countryside. The four en suite bedrooms have pretty, colour
co-ordinated soft furnishings and are well equipped. Breakfast
and dinner (the latter available by prior arrangement before
4.00pm) can be enjoyed in the large bright breakfast room,
which also has a comfortable lounge area. A purpose-built
and fully equipped conference room has just been added, and
this can seat up to 40 delegates, theatre-style, in comfort.
4 en suite (shr) CTV in all bedrooms Tea and coffee making
facilities No dogs Cen ht CTV 6P Fishing 250 acres
dairy/sheep Last d 4pm

CREWKERNE Somerset Map 03 ST40

Premier Selected

GH Q Q Q Q Q **Broadview**
43 East St TA18 7AG (on the
Yeovil road) ☎01460 73424
Broadview is a unique
colonial-style bungalow, built
in 1926 and set in an elevated
position high above
Crewkerne. An immaculate
and well run establishment, it
offers guests every comfort
and the opportunity to
unwind in secluded
surroundings. A delightful lounge overlooking the terraced
garden is the ideal place to relax after a delicious dinner
cooked from fresh garden produce - perhaps home-made soup
with crusty bread, followed by roast Barbary duck with
vegetables and a tempting sweet to finish.
3 en suite (bth/shr) No smoking CTV in all bedrooms Tea
and coffee making facilities Cen ht 5P No coaches Last d
9am
PRICE GUIDE
ROOMS: s £35; d £46-£50; wkly b&b £161-£175; wkly hlf-
bd £245-£259✳

CRICKLADE Wiltshire Map 04 SU09

GH Q Q Q **Chelworth Hotel** Upper Chelworth SN6 6HD
☎01793 750440
Closed mid Dec-mid Jan
This attractive Cotswold-stone farmhouse is situated about a mile
from the Saxon town of Cricklade and only a short drive from
Swindon. Warm hospitality is offered here, and the bedrooms are
both modern and well equipped; a cosy, relaxing lounge is
warmed by a wood-burning stove, gardens are beautifully tended,
and there is a nursery selling plants across the road. Guests may
have dinner by arrangement.
7 rms (6 shr) (1 fmly) CTV in 6 bedrooms Tea and coffee
making facilities No dogs (ex guide dogs) Licensed Cen ht
CTV 10P No coaches Last d 7pm

Premier Selected

GH Q Q Q Q Q **Latton
House** Latton SN6 6DP
☎01793 751982
Latton House is a gracious
Georgian manor house
nestling in two acres of well-
tended gardens in the
peaceful village of Latton.
Everyone who visits this
lovely family home is
aassured of warm hospitality
in beautiful rooms furnished

PREMIER
SELECTED
BED &
BREAKFAST

with antiques and paintings. There is a wealth of interesting
pieces which have been acquired over the years. Guests are
welcome to share the heart of the family and are invited to relax in
the drawing room with its log fire and outlook to the gardens.
Dinner is served in the dining room and good traditional home
cooking is offered, while breakfast may be taken en famille in
the large kitchen complete with poppy red Aga. The small
town of Cricklade is only a mile away and the motorway 11
miles.
2 en suite (bth) No smoking in bedrooms CTV in all
bedrooms Tea and coffee making facilities No dogs (ex
guide dogs) Cen ht CTV 6P No coaches
PRICE GUIDE
ROOMS: s fr £30; d fr £60✳

CROMER Norfolk Map 09 TG24

GH Q Q Q **Beachcomber** 17 Macdonald Rd NR27 9AP
(leaving Cromer via Runton Road, first left after the
Cliftonville Hotel) ☎01263 513398
Closed 24-26 Dec
This well-maintained and comfortable guest offers individually
decorated bedrooms, most with en suite shower rooms. The owner
is enthusiastic and friendly and will readily cook a full dinner.
7 rms (5 shr) (1 fmly) No smoking in bedrooms No smoking in
dining room CTV in all bedrooms Tea and coffee making facilities
No dogs Cen ht CTV No parking No coaches Last d 4pm
PRICE GUIDE
ROOMS: s £15-£16; d £30-£34; wkly b&b £98-£115; wkly hlf-
bd £115-£138✳

GH Q Q **Birch House** 34 Cabbell Rd NR27 9HX
☎01263 512521
Great pride is taken in the maintenance of this no-smoking guest
house, which is located a short distance west of the town centre.

All the bedrooms have colour and satellite TV, and dinner is readily provided on request.
8 rms (1 bth 2 shr) (1 fmly) No smoking CTV in all bedrooms Tea and coffee making facilities Licensed No parking Last d 4pm
CARDS: 🔳 🔤

GH QQQ Brightside 19 Macdonald Rd NR27 9AP
☎01263 513408

Hazel Bright offers a friendly welcome at this smartly maintained guest house which provides a comfortable lounge, a small bar and a pleasant pine-panelled dining room; in which a set menu evening meal can be taken by prior arrangement. Bedrooms are fresh and light; each is double glazed and equipped with colour television and tea-making facilities; the majority have en suite shower rooms. There are two family bedrooms, one of which is slightly tight for space.
6 rms (5 shr) (3 fmly) No smoking in bedrooms CTV in all bedrooms Tea and coffee making facilities No dogs Licensed Cen ht CTV No children 4yrs No parking No coaches Last d 4pm
PRICE GUIDE
ROOMS: (incl. dinner) d fr £49; wkly b&b fr £116; wkly hlf-bd fr £138✱

GH QQQ Chellow Dene 23 MacDonald Rd NR27 9AP
☎01263 513251
Mar-Nov

A friendly welcome is assured from Mrs Leach at this bright, cheerful and well maintained guest house. Bedrooms vary in size, some have modern en suite shower rooms, all have a good level of facilities as standard. Breakfast and a set dinner are served in a pleasantly light dining room and guests also have the use of a small lounge and private car parking to the rear of the property.
7 rms (4 shr) (1 fmly) CTV in all bedrooms Tea and coffee making facilities Licensed Cen ht CTV 6P No coaches Last d 5pm

GH QQQ Morden House 20 Cliff Av NR27 0AN (off A140)
☎01263 513396

This charming, well kept Victorian house, a short distance from the town centre, has elegantly furnished public rooms, and an open stairwell which creates a feeling of spaciousness. Bedrooms are well equipped and maintained and there is an air of old-fashioned hospitality.
6 rms (4 bth/shr) (1 fmly) No smoking in dining room No smoking in lounges Tea and coffee making facilities Licensed Cen ht CTV 3P No coaches Last d 6pm
PRICE GUIDE
ROOMS: s fr £21; d fr £42; wkly b&b fr £140; wkly hlf-bd fr £189
CARDS: 💿   £

GH QQ Sandcliff Private Hotel Runton Rd NR27 9AS
☎01263 512888
Closed 21 Dec-4 Jan

The focal point of this large guest house is the bar and lounge area, which extend into the restaurant where evening meals are served. Bedrooms are modestly furnished and well cared for, some have unrestricted sea views. There is limited off street parking in front and plenty of spaces to the sides.
24 rms (9 bth 10 shr) (10 fmly) CTV in all bedrooms Tea and coffee making facilities Licensed 10P Last d 6pm

GH QQQ Westgate Lodge Private Hotel 10 MacDonald Rd
NR27 9AP ☎01263 512840
Mr Mrs Robson offer a friendly welcome and provide a good range of services within this attractively decorated and immaculately maintained small hotel. Accommodation is smart and decorative, with good use of co-ordinated soft furnishings and

appealing decor, all rooms have en-suite shower rooms and are particularly well equipped. Guests have the use of a comfortable lounge and small bar, the nicely appointed dining room is available for breakfast and evening meals, a good choice of dishes are provided. There is also easily accessible private car parking adjacent to the hotel.
11 en suite (shr) (4 fmly) No smoking in dining room CTV in all bedrooms Tea and coffee making facilities No dogs (ex guide dogs) Licensed Cen ht No children 3yrs 13P Last d 6.30pm
PRICE GUIDE
ROOMS: d £42.30-£49.36; wkly b&b £148.05-£172.76; wkly hlf-bd £193.88-£199.75

CROSTHWAITE Cumbria Map 07 SD49

Selected

GH QQQQ Crosthwaite House LA8 8BP
☎01539 568264
mid Mar-mid Nov

A delightful mid-18th century house situated at the northern end of the Lyth Valley and only five miles from Kendal and Windermere. Bedrooms are spacious and comfortable, and those at the front of the house have fine views over the valley. The dining rom, in which good home-cooked dinners are served, has a natural wood floor and other period features. There is also a comfortable lounge which looks out over the unspoilt countryside.
6 en suite (shr) CTV in all bedrooms Tea and coffee making facilities Licensed Cen ht CTV 12P No coaches Last d 5pm
PRICE GUIDE
ROOMS: s £20-£22; d £40-£44; wkly b&b fr £140; wkly hlf-bd fr £210
CARDS: 🔤

CROYDE Devon Map 02 SS43

GH QQQ West Winds Moor Ln EX33 1PA (at village centre
turn left and first left again following signs to Croyde Bay)
☎01271 890489 FAX 01271 890489
Apr-Nov

Chris and Roslyn Gedling enjoy welcoming guests to their small guest house with its panoramic views across Croyde Bay. Bedrooms are neatly furnished, there is a choice of light snack meals, and direct access to the beach from the garden.
4 rms (3 bth/shr) CTV in all bedrooms Tea and coffee making facilities Licensed Cen ht 6P No coaches Last d 7.30pm
CARDS: 🔳 🔤

Entries in this Guide are based on reports filed by our team of professionally trained, full-time inspectors.

Premier Selected

GH QQQQQ **Whiteleaf**
At Croyde EX33 1PN (turn
off A361 at Braunton for
Croyde, Whiteleaf is on left
at 'Road Narrows' sign)
☎01271 890266

Closed Jan-Feb rs Dec
Set back from Croyde Bay's
golden sands and away from
the centre of the village, a
1930s detached house
surrounded by colourful
gardens offers accommodation in well equipped, individually
furnished and decorated bedrooms. Dinner is served at
8.15pm, and guests are asked to make their choice two hours
earlier from the varied and imaginative range of dishes
available - salmon quenelles with a vermouth and pink
peppercorn sauce, for example, might be followed by soup
and a honeyed leg of Lunesdale duck served with fresh
vegetables. Breakfast is equally interesting, the house
speciality being baked eggs with smoked salmon, and a
choice of freshly made breads is also provided.
3 en suite (bth/shr) (1 fmly) No smoking in dining room No
smoking in 1 lounge CTV in all bedrooms Tea and coffee
making facilities Direct dial from bedrooms Licensed Cen
ht 10P No coaches Last d 6.30pm
PRICE GUIDE
ROOMS: s £35-£37; d £50-£54; wkly b&b £170-£184;
wkly hlf-bd £290-£300
CARDS: 🔲 🔲 🔲 🔲 🔲

♥ QQQ Mr & Mrs Barnes **Denham Farm & Country House**
(SS480404) North Buckland EX33 1HY
☎01271 890297 FAX 01271 890297
Closed 18-28 Dec
Jean and Tony Barnes' delightful farmhouse is in a village setting
some two miles from the breathtaking coastline at Croyde. The
bedrooms are bright, well furnished, and equipped with modern en
suite facilities. Jean offers good home cooked meals in the
informal restaurant, and a comfortable bar-lounge is provided with
a separate quiet lounge.
10 en suite (bth/shr) (2 fmly) No smoking in dining room No
smoking in 1 lounge CTV in all bedrooms Tea and coffee making
facilities No dogs Licensed Cen ht CTV ch fac 11P Games
room Table tennis Skittle alley 160 acres beef sheep Last d 6pm
PRICE GUIDE
ROOMS: d £50; wkly b&b £150-£160; wkly hlf-bd £205-£225✱
CARDS: 🔲 🔲

CROYDON Greater London Map 04 TQ36

Selected

GH QQQQ **Hayesthorpe Hotel** 48/52 St Augustines Av
CR2 6JJ ☎0181 688 8120 FAX 0181 688 8120
Quietly located in a residential part of South Croydon, this
delightful and improving hotel is personally run by resident
proprietors Michael Culley and Bruno Inzani, formerly of the
USA. Accommodation is still being upgraded but there is a
good choice of well equipped bedrooms, including one on the
ground floor with a conservatory lounge. Dinner is available
Monday-Friday from a three-course fixed-price menu. There
are a bar area, reception facilities, and an attractive summer

garden and terrace.
25 en suite (bth/shr) (5 fmly) No smoking in 5 bedrooms No
smoking in area of dining room CTV in all bedrooms Tea
and coffee making facilities Direct dial from bedrooms No
dogs (ex guide dogs) Licensed Cen ht 8P
PRICE GUIDE
ROOMS: s £35-£45; d £45-£60✱
CARDS: 🔲 🔲 🔲 🔲 🔲 🔲

GH QQQ **Kirkdale Hotel** 22 St Peter's Rd CR0 1HD (from
M25 junct 7 take A23 to Purley then A235 signed Croydon
and at Blue Anchor pub turn rt into Aberdeen Rd)
☎0181 688 5898 FAX 0181 680 6001
Closed 2 days Xmas
A popular and well maintained guest house standing close to
South Croydon railway station provides accommodation in
bedrooms which vary in size; all are freshly decorated, however,
and equipped with a range of facilities that includes direct dial
telephones. Breakfast is served in a modern rear-facing modern
dining room.
19 en suite (bth/shr) No smoking in bedrooms No smoking in
dining room CTV in all bedrooms Tea and coffee making
facilities Direct dial from bedrooms No dogs (ex guide dogs)
Licensed Cen ht CTV 12P
PRICE GUIDE
ROOMS: s £25-£39; d £40-£49; wkly b&b £138.50-£214
CARDS: 🔲 🔲 🔲

CULLOMPTON Devon Map 03 ST00

See also Uffculme

Selected

GH QQQQ **Rullands** Rull Ln EX15 1NQ
☎01884 33356 FAX 01884 35890
Rullands is a small country house restaurant with
accommodation, set in glorious rolling countryside only a few
minutes' drive from the M5. Though it dates from the 15th
century, the house offers every 20th-century comfort;
bedrooms are attractively decorated and all have en suite or
private facilities. Public areas include a restaurant (open to
non-residents) offering a short carte based on fresh
ingredients and specialising in local country fare. A choice
of lounges is provided, and there is a large garden with a terrace
overlooking open fields.
5 rms (4 bth/shr) (1 fmly) No smoking in bedrooms No
smoking in dining room CTV in all bedrooms Tea and coffee
making facilities Licensed Cen ht 20P No coaches Tennis
(hard) Last d 9.45pm
PRICE GUIDE
ROOMS: s £30-£35; d £55-£60; wkly b&b £210-£250;
wkly hlf-bd £300-£350✱
CARDS: 🔲 🔲

DALTON North Yorkshire Map 08 SE47

♥ QQQ Mrs P Richardson **Eldmire Hill** *(SE428752)* Eldmire
Hill YO7 3JH (6m N of Dalton) ☎01845 577252
Mar-Oct
Eldmire Hill Farm is situated on a very slight incline surrounded
by arable lands and a mature garden with lawns, shrubbery and
sheltered by tall trees. Inside the farmhouse is typical of its period,
the bedrooms spacious and furnished with co-ordinated fabrics
and wall coverings. To relax in there is a homely and very
comfortable looking lounge and a dining room where breakfasts
are served 'en famille'. ➡

2 rms (1 fmly) No smoking in bedrooms No smoking in dining room Tea and coffee making facilities No dogs (ex guide dogs) Cen ht CTV 3P Tennis (grass) 360 acres mixed
PRICE GUIDE
ROOMS: s £15-£16; d £28-£30; wkly b&b £98-£105✱

DARLINGTON Co Durham Map **08** NZ21

GH **Woodland** 63 Woodland Rd DL3 7BQ (on A68, opposite the Memorial Hospital) ☎01325 461908
Family owned and run, this guest house is part of a Victorian terrace beside the A68 just south of the centre of the town. Attractively furnished throughout, it offers well equipped bedrooms and a comfortable lounge.
8 rms (1 bth/shr) (2 fmly) No smoking in dining room CTV in all bedrooms Tea and coffee making facilities Cen ht CTV No parking
PRICE GUIDE
ROOMS: s £20-£28; d £34-£40✱

£

Selected

✦ Mr & Mrs D & A Armstrong **Clow Beck House** (NZ281100) Monk End Farm, Croft on Tees DL2 2SW ☎01325 721075 FAX 01325 721075
A modern-style farmhouse standing in open countryside on the edge of the village of Croft-on-Tees, Clow Beck has been extended to include three bedrooms in a nearby annexe. The house is handsomely furnished and bedrooms are well equipped and prettily decorated. There is a delightful lounge decorated in blue, with a superb Chinese carpet. Breakfast is served at one large table.
2 rms (1 shr) 7 annexe en suite (bth/shr) No smoking in dining room CTV in all bedrooms Tea and coffee making facilities No dogs Cen ht CTV 15P Fishing 90 acres mixed
PRICE GUIDE
ROOMS: s £25-£34; d £38-£47
CARDS: 🔲 🔲

£

DARTMOUTH Devon Map **03** SX85

Premier Selected

GH  **Boringdon House** 1 Church Rd TQ6 9HQ (turn rt into Townstal Rd opposite top gate of Royal Naval College then rt again at crossroad)
☎01803 832235
Mar-Dec
This charming Georgian house, set a little above the main shopping area and waterfront, enjoys stunning views from the front bedrooms and dining room. There are a large garden and a private courtyard where guests may park. The Greens have completely refurbished the accommodation since taking over, and the three bedrooms are simply decorated, emphasising their proportions with antique stripped-pine furniture, thick carpets, and an air of quiet luxury. Bathrooms are well equipped and have many little extras. Breakfast is taken in the dark green dining room, which has French windows leading

out into the garden. Guests eat together at one table, and there is a small, comfortable lounge. Smoking is not permitted.
3 en suite (bth) No smoking in all bedrooms Tea and coffee making facilities No dogs Cen ht No children 12yrs 6P No coaches
PRICE GUIDE
ROOMS: d £45-£55; wkly b&b £157.50-£175✱

£

Selected

GH **Broome Court** Broomhill TQ6 0LD
☎01803 834275
Converted from old farm buildings, Broome Court is tucked away into a south-facing hill overlooking three copses amidst rich South Devon countryside. The buildings are set around a paved courtyard filled with flowers and shrubs, with a goldfish pond and fountain in the middle. Breakfast is taken at separate tables in the farmhouse kitchen; the owners can advise guests on local restaurants and inns for dinner. The spacious bedrooms are individually furnished and well equipped with modern facilities. The establishment is a five minute drive from the historic port of Dartmouth, and its newly opened Golf and Country Club has an 18-hole championship course.
3 en suite (bth/shr) No smoking in bedrooms No smoking in dining room CTV in all bedrooms Tea and coffee making facilities Cen ht CTV 6P No coaches
PRICE GUIDE
ROOMS: s £28-£35; d £45-£50✱

Selected

GH **Captains House** 18 Clarence St TQ6 9NW
☎01803 832133
This charming little Georgian Grade II listed house, dating back to 1730, is conveniently situated a short distance from the main shopping area and the river Dart. The bedrooms are individually decorated, most featuring their original fireplaces, and there is a no-smoking bedroom. Tempting English breakfasts including home-made bread and preserves are served either in bedrooms or in the delightful dining room. There are local car parks nearby, and the house is within walking distance of the ferry and quayside.
5 en suite (bth/shr) No smoking in 1 bedrooms No smoking in dining room CTV in all bedrooms Tea and coffee making facilities Cen ht No children 5yrs No coaches
PRICE GUIDE
ROOMS: s £24-£28; d £36-£48; wkly b&b £112-£140
CARDS:

£

Factual details of establishments in this Guide are from questionnaires we send to all establishments that feature in the book.

GH ◨◨◨◨◨ **Ford House** 44 Victoria Rd
TQ6 9DX ☎01803 834047
FAX 01803 834047
Mar-Nov

This small, detached, Regency town house with a tiny walled garden stands 500 yards from the quayside and even closer to the main shopping area. The four individually furnished bedrooms are decorated with flair, featuring several antique pieces and objets d'art collected over the years by the owners. The rooms are well equipped, with fresh fruit and mineral water provided as welcome extra touches. Dinner is taken around a large mahogany table, the daily changing set Cordon Bleu menu uses fresh local produce, particularly the excellent supply of fresh fish. The adjoining drawing room offers a cosy log fire, interesting art work and a wide selection of reading material. The hotel is not licensed but will arrange local delivery, or guests may bring their own wine, and it is possible to book the whole house for private dinner party weekends.
3 en suite (bth/shr) No smoking in dining room CTV in all bedrooms Tea and coffee making facilities Direct dial from bedrooms Cen ht 4P No coaches Last d noon
PRICE GUIDE
ROOMS: s £50; d £50-£65; wkly b&b £175; wkly hlf-bd £350
CARDS: 🅰 💳 💳

Selected

GH ◨◨◨◨ *Hedley House* Newcomen Rd TQ6 9BN
☎01803 835849
Only a few moments from the town centre, overlooking the Lower Ferry and the steam railway on the other side of the estuary, this property has been lovingly refurbished in the last few years. The bedrooms all benefit from the lovely position, and each is individually furnished and decorated. There is a cosy sitting room, and dinner can be served by arrangement with Mrs Bird. Breakfast may be served in the courtyard in fine weather.
3 en suite (bth/shr) No smoking in bedrooms No smoking in dining room Tea and coffee making facilities No dogs (ex guide dogs) Cen ht CTV No children 12yrs No coaches Last d noon

GH ◨◨◨ **Sunny Banks** 1 Vicarage Hill TQ6 9EN (centre of town, 200yds from post office, behind bowling green)
☎01803 832766
Friendly owners Rosemary and Shaun Pound welcome guests to their guest house situated in a residential area two minutes' walk from the town centre and quay. The bedrooms are bright, attractively decorated and well equipped, and there is a small comfortable lounge. A set dinner using the best of local produce is available in the dining room if ordered in advance.
10 rms (6 bth/shr) (1 fmly) No smoking in 3 bedrooms No smoking in dining room CTV in all bedrooms Tea and coffee

making facilities Licensed Cen ht CTV 7P
PRICE GUIDE
ROOMS: s £18-£18.50; d £36-£50

Selected

◨ ◨◨◨◨ **Seale Arms** Victoria Rd TQ6 9SA
☎01803 832719
4 en suite (shr) (2 fmly) No smoking in 2 bedrooms No smoking in dining room CTV in all bedrooms Tea and coffee making facilities Cen ht No parking No coaches Last d 9pm
PRICE GUIDE
ROOMS: d £40-£50; wkly b&b £112-£140✱
MEALS: Lunch £5.60-£12.60 Dinner £5.60-£12.60✱

DAWLISH Devon Map 03 SX97

GH ◨ *Mimosa* 11 Barton Ter EX7 9QH (on entering Dawlish follow signs to Museum, Mimosa is directly opposite)
☎01626 863283
Close to the town centre and beaches, this holiday guest house is family run.
9 rms (1 shr) (4 fmly) No dogs (ex guide dogs) Licensed Cen ht CTV No children 3yrs 4P Last d 3pm

Broome Court

(Jan Bird & Tom Boughton)
Broomhill, Dartmouth, Devon TQ6 0LD
Tel: (01803) 834275

Standing in an area of outstanding natural beauty, affording peace and tranquillity of the rolling Devon countryside. No dinner, but area is renowned for excellent restaurants, pubs etc. Ideal for walking, riding, swimming and windsurfing. Championship 27-hole golf course 2m. (Our residents enjoy reduced green fees). Near to Dartmouth, Slapton Ley Field Centre/Nature Reserve, Torbay and Paignton. Dartmoor is 30 mins away. Plymouth 30m and Exeter 40m.

GH **Q|Q|Q** **Postern House** Priory Rd EX7 9JF
☎01626 888362
Closed Xmas
From its elevated hillside position Postern House enjoys attractive
views over the town and down to the seafront. The three bedrooms
are prettily furnished and are well equipped, each with hairdryer
and tea and coffee making facilities. The spacious wooden floored
hall leads on to a stylish breakfast room where guests dine at
separate tables.
4 en suite (bth/shr) (1 fmly) No smoking CTV in all bedrooms
Tea and coffee making facilities Cen ht 4P
PRICE GUIDE
ROOMS: d £32✳

───────────────────

Selected

GH **Q|Q|Q|Q** **Walton House** Plantation Ter EX7 9DR (off
A379) ☎01626 862760 FAX 01626 862760
Quietly located but within walking distance of the town centre,
Walton House is a grade II listed Georgian property, now run
by the welcoming owners, John and Doreen Newton. It has
comfortable, well equipped bedrooms and is immaculately
maintained. Hearty breakfasts are served by Mr Newton.
6 en suite (bth/shr) (1 fmly) No smoking in dining room
CTV in all bedrooms Tea and coffee making facilities No
dogs (ex guide dogs) Cen ht 6P
PRICE GUIDE
ROOMS: d £34-£38; wkly b&b £98-£126✳

───────────────────

DEAL Kent Map **05** TR35

Selected

GH **Q|Q|Q|Q** **Dunkerleys Restaurant** 19 Beach St
CT14 7AH ☎01304 375016 FAX 01304 380187
Primarily a restaurant, Dunkerley's also offers six comfortable
and well equipped bedrooms, furnished in a modern style with
good writing tables and some additional sofa-bed seating.
Some rooms are larger than others and the best have double
doors and attractive views. The establishment's raison d'être,
however, is clearly the provision of food, and chef Stephen
Harvey offers freshly prepared dishes using the best local
ingredients. There is a small dispense bar-lounge, and the
Ship Hold downstairs can be reserved for private functions.
Parking is available in a nearby pay-and-display car park.
6 en suite (bth/shr) (2 fmly) No smoking in area of dining
room CTV in all bedrooms Tea and coffee making facilities
Direct dial from bedrooms No dogs (ex guide dogs)
Licensed Cen ht No parking No coaches Last d 10pm
PRICE GUIDE
ROOMS: s £30-£40; d £40-£60
CARDS: ▨ ▤ ▤ ⊙ ▦ ▨ ▨

───────────────────

GH **Q|Q|Q** **Sondes Lodge** 14 Sondes Rd CT14 7BW
☎01304 368741
Lovingly restored by its resident proprietors Jayne and Tony Hulme
this charming Victorian terraced house has been carefully furnished
in the modern style to provide good value accommodation with a
friendly and relaxed informal atmosphere. The attractive bedrooms
come well equipped with remote control TV and tea trays, and all
rooms have private shower facilities. There is a small breakfast room
and an evening meal can also be provided with 24 hours notice.
3 en suite (shr) (1 fmly) No smoking in dining room CTV in all
bedrooms Tea and coffee making facilities No dogs (ex guide

dogs) Cen ht No coaches Last d 24hr notice
PRICE GUIDE
ROOMS: s £15-£20; d £30-£40; wkly b&b fr £105; wkly hlf-bd
fr £147✳
CARDS: ▨ ▤

───────────────────

DEBDEN GREEN Essex Map **05** TL53

♥ **Q** Mrs K M Low **Wychbars** *(TL579320)* Wychbars
CB11 3NA (at end of long unclassified lane off B1051)
☎01279 850362
Remotely situated, this 200-year-old moated, whitewashed
farmhouse stands in 3.5 acres and offers two simply furnished
bedrooms with a shared shower room.
2 rms CTV in all bedrooms Tea and coffee making facilities Lift
Cen ht CTV 10P 600 acres arable non-working
PRICE GUIDE
ROOMS: d £20-£22

───────────────────

DELPH Greater Manchester Map **07** SD90

GH **Q|Q** **Globe Farm** Huddersfield Rd, Standedge, Delph
OL3 5LU (on A62 between Oldham and Huddersfield, .75m
after junct with A670 from Uppermill) ☎01457 873040
Closed Xmas & New Year
Built in 1840, Globe Farm is situated in the Saddleworth Hills,
beside the A62, two miles from Delph and from its position 1100
feet above sea level enjoys the most magnificent views. The
freshly decorated, well equipped bedrooms all have fully en suite
shower rooms. There is a comfortable lounge, where a fire is lit on
cooler days and a dining room with its original stone flagged floor,
where a Mrs Mayall provides hearty breakfasts and a traditional
evening meal.
7 en suite (shr) No smoking in 2 bedrooms No smoking in dining
room CTV in all bedrooms Tea and coffee making facilities No
dogs (ex guide dogs) Cen ht CTV 25P No coaches
PRICE GUIDE
ROOMS: s £18; d £35; wkly b&b £120; wkly hlf-bd £160✳
CARDS: ▨

───────────────────

DERBY Derbyshire Map **08** SK33

See also Shottle

GH **Q|Q** **Dalby House Hotel** 100 Radbourne St, off Windmill
Hill Ln DE22 3BU (turn off A52 into Windmill Hill Lane near
A52/A38 junct) ☎01332 342353
Dalby House is set in a quiet residential area and has its own
ample car park and a pleasant walled garden. Public rooms include
a comfortable ground floor lounge and a light, appealing dining
room. Bedrooms vary in size and offer sound, modestly appointed
accommodation.
9 rms (2 fmly) No smoking in dining room CTV in all bedrooms
Tea and coffee making facilities Cen ht CTV 10P No coaches
Last d 4pm
PRICE GUIDE
ROOMS: s £17-£19; d £29-£34

───────────────────

GH **Q|Q|Q** **Georgian House Hotel** 32/36 Ashbourne Rd
DE22 3AD (0.5m W of city centre on A52 towards Ashbourne,
hotel on right) ☎01332 349806
Georgian House is a smart little hotel in a conservation area of the
city's west end. Public rooms, dominated by the restaurant, retain
much of their original character, and a further lounge area is being
created. A new style of food operation was being launched at the
time of our visit, with a good choice offered from market and carte
menus, now also served to non-residents. Bedrooms are pleasantly
furnished with dark wood fittings and floral fabrics. Four-poster
and ground-floor rooms are available.

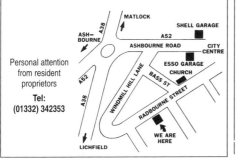

21 rms (14 bth/shr) (5 fmly) No smoking in 2 bedrooms No smoking in area of dining room No smoking in 1 lounge CTV in all bedrooms Tea and coffee making facilities Direct dial from bedrooms Licensed Cen ht CTV ch fac 24P Last d 9.30pm
PRICE GUIDE
ROOMS: s £27-£47; d £37-£60*
CARDS: ▤ ▦

GH Q Q Q **Heage House** 118 Duffield Rd DE22 1BG (on A6)
☎01332 349166
In an elevated position screened from the main road by a high stone wall this detached fairly modern dwelling has been furnished entirely with period furniture and antiques which look completely at home. The main entrance is via a lovely cottage style garden to the rear which the lounge cum dining room looks out over. The bedrooms are similarly furnished and though sharing a bathroom are very comfortable and immaculate.
3 rms No smoking CTV in all bedrooms Tea and coffee making facilities No dogs (ex guide dogs) Cen ht
PRICE GUIDE
ROOMS: s £15-£18; d £28-£34*

GH Q Q Q *Rangemoor Park Hotel* 67 Macklin St DE1 1LF
☎01332 347252 FAX 01332 369319
Recently refurbished, this city-centre guest house now boasts a stylish new entrance and impressive deluxe en suite bedrooms. Standard bedrooms have also been redecorated and the public areas are pleasantly decorated and furnished with colour co-ordinated soft fabrics. Ample car parking is a bonus in this city-centre location.
24 rms (13 bth/shr) (3 fmly) No smoking in dining room CTV in all bedrooms Tea and coffee making facilities Direct dial from bedrooms Cen ht CTV 37P
CARDS: ▤ ▦ ▦ ◐)

GH Q Q **Tree House** 69 Shardlow Rd DE24 0JP
☎01332 571421
A semi detached dwelling set back from the main road which offers very clean and nicely kept and thoughtfully furnished bedrooms and a spacious modern bathroom to share. Breakfasts are served in the dining room which doubles as a television lounge and is furnished with comfortable armchairs.
No smoking in bedrooms No smoking in lounges Tea and coffee making facilities No dogs Cen ht CTV No children 10yrs 3P No coaches
PRICE GUIDE
ROOMS: s £16.50-£18; d £32-£34*

GH Q **Victoria Park Hotel** 312 Burton Rd DE23 6AD (on A5250) ☎01332 341551
Just outside the city a splendid Victorian manse set back from the main road. Immaculately maintained throughout, it has a very comfortable lounge and a cheerful atmosphere.
11 rms (3 fmly) No smoking in dining room No smoking in lounges CTV in all bedrooms Tea and coffee making facilities Direct dial from bedrooms No dogs (ex guide dogs) Cen ht 15P No coaches
PRICE GUIDE
ROOMS: s £15-£17; d £25-£27*

DEVIZES Wiltshire Map **04** SU06

GH Q Q Q **Pinecroft** Potterne Rd SN10 5DA (0.25m S of town square on A360 to Salisbury opposite 'Southgate' public house) ☎01380 721433 FAX 01380 728368
A part-Georgian, part-Edwardian family home within easy walking distance of the town centre offers comfortable bedrooms. Breakfast is served at one large table.

5 en suite (bth/shr) (1 fmly) No smoking in 4 bedrooms No smoking in dining room No smoking in lounges CTV in all bedrooms Tea and coffee making facilities No dogs Cen ht ch fac 7P Mountain bikes for hire Badminton
PRICE GUIDE
ROOMS: s £20-£25; d £32-£40
CARDS: ▤ ▦ ▦

◀ Q Q Q **Wheatsheaf Inn** 9 High St, West Lavington SN10 4HQ (on A360, opposite Dauntseys School)
☎01380 813392 FAX 01380 818038
This roadside inn dates back to the 16th century but offers modern comforts, all rooms having en suite showers, TVs and tea trays. There is a choice of attractive bars and a restaurant serving freshly prepared dishes.
9 rms (7 shr) (1 fmly) No smoking in area of dining room CTV in all bedrooms Tea and coffee making facilities Cen ht 50P Pool table Skittle Alley Darts Last d 9.30pm
PRICE GUIDE
ROOMS: s fr £25; d fr £45; wkly b&b fr £140
MEALS: Lunch fr £5.95&alc Dinner fr £5.95&alc
CARDS: ▤ ▦ ▦

DIBDEN Hampshire Map **04** SU40

GH Q Q **Dale Farm** Manor Rd, Applemore Hill SO45 5TJ (A326 towards Fawley 1st rdbt sign to Applemore then 1st right after rdbt into Manor Rd after 200yds turn right)
☎01703 849632
Closed Xmas
This attractive 18th-century former farmhouse lies half hidden behind a riding stables down an unmade road. Modern bedrooms are bright and cosy, some overlooking the forest, and breakfast is served in a pine-furnished lounge/dining room.
6 rms (2 fmly) Tea and coffee making facilities No dogs (ex guide dogs) Cen ht CTV 20P No coaches Fishing Riding Last d 11am
PRICE GUIDE
ROOMS: s fr £17; d fr £32; wkly b&b fr £100; wkly hlf-bd fr £160*

DINTON Buckinghamshire Map **04** SP71

♥ Q Q Q Mrs J M W Cook **Wallace** *(SP770110)* HP17 8UF (from A418 take the turning marked Dinton/Ford, then 1st left signed Upton, where farm can be found on the right)
☎01296 748660 FAX 01296 748851
This delightful 16th-century farmhouse is situated in the heart of the countryside. The comfortable bedrooms are spacious and equipped with en suites or private bathrooms. There is a beamed sitting room with an open fire and TV, leading onto the patio. Breakfast is served at a communal table in the kitchen, beside an inglenook fireplace and bread ovens. A further highlight of a stay here is the range of animals at the farm: rare breeds of sheep, an aviary and heavy horses. The lovely grounds include a pond and pleasant walks.
3 rms (2 bth/shr) (1 fmly) No smoking in bedrooms No smoking in dining room Tea and coffee making facilities No dogs (ex guide dogs) Cen ht CTV 6P Fishing 24 acres beef cattle sheep
PRICE GUIDE
ROOMS: s fr £28; d £40-£42
CARDS: ▤ ▦ ▨

DISS Norfolk

See **Fressingfield and p.161.**

DODDISCOMBSLEIGH Devon Map **03** SX88

♥ **Q Q** Mrs B Lacey **Whitemoor** *(SX861866)*
Doddiscombsleigh EX6 7PU ☎01647 252423
A 16th century thatched farmhouse offering comfortable
accommodation. Bedrooms are simply furnished and decorated
and an attractive sitting room with an open fire is available to
guests. A two course dinner can be served by prior arrangement.
This is a no-smoking establishment.
4 rms No smoking Tea and coffee making facilities Cen ht CTV
4P Outdoor swimming pool 284 acres working
PRICE GUIDE
ROOMS: s £16.50-£17.50; d £33-£34; wkly hlf-bd £108.50-
£115.50* ⓔ

DONCASTER South Yorkshire Map **08** SE50

GH **Q Q** **Almel Hotel** 20 Christchurch Rd DN1 2QL (at rear of
Odeon cinema over rbt then next rt and left into Christchurch
Rd) ☎01302 365230 FAX 01302 341434
Set in a quiet residential road just off the town centre, this very large,
well kept period house provides accommodation in thoughtfully
equipped and freshly decorated bedrooms with some en suite
facilities. On the ground floor there are a good-sized bar and a
separate dining room where late suppers and breakfasts are served.
30 rms (24 bth/shr) (1 fmly) CTV in all bedrooms Tea and
coffee making facilities Licensed Cen ht CTV 8P Last d 8pm
PRICE GUIDE
ROOMS: s £21.50-£27.50; d £37-£41
CARDS: 💳 💳 💳 💳

◀ **Q Q** **Nelsons Hotel** Cleveland St DN1 1TR
☎01302 344550 FAX 01302 341596
Nelsons is a small inn located close to the main shopping area of

the town and within easy walking distance of the railway station.
There is no private parking but there are plenty of public car parks
in the area. Public areas are dominated by a lively modern bar
which offers a range of hot and cold bar meals, while bedrooms,
though simply decorated, have good modern furnishings and share
sound general bathrooms.
9 rms (2 fmly) No smoking in area of dining room CTV in all
bedrooms Tea and coffee making facilities Cen ht P Last d 8pm
PRICE GUIDE
ROOMS: s £12.50-£17.50; d £25-£30; wkly b&b £45-£70; wkly
hlf-bd £60-£82*
MEALS: Lunch £3.50-£7 Dinner £2.50-£7*
CARDS: 💳 💳 💳 ⓔ

DORCHESTER Dorset Map **03** SY69

See also Evershot, Ringstead, Sydling St Nicholas and
Winterbourne Abbas

Selected

GH **Q Q Q Q** **Westwood House Hotel** 29 High West St
DT1 1UP (Logis) ☎01305 268018 FAX 01305 250282
Originally built as a coaching house for Lord Ilchester in
1815, this handsome Georgian town house stands at the top
end of town. Personally managed by the proprietors, it offers
individually styled bedrooms with good facilities and
thoughtful extras such as bathrobes. Two of the en suite
bathrooms have spa baths. A good breakfast is served in the
bright and airy conservatory breakfast room and there is an
attractive lounge. Parking can be difficult during the day
although there is a public car park near by. ➡

7 rms (5 bth/shr) (1 fmly) CTV in all bedrooms Tea and coffee making facilities Direct dial from bedrooms Licensed Cen ht CTV

PRICE GUIDE
ROOMS: s £27.50-£39.50; d £42.50-£59.50; wkly b&b fr £149✳
CARDS:

Premier Selected

GH QQQQQ **Yalbury Cottage** Lower Bockhampton DT2 8PZ (2.5m E off A35) (Logis) ☎01305 262382 FAX 01305 266412
Closed 15-30 Jan

Located about two miles from Dorchester in a charming English village, Yalbury Cottage dates back over 400 years. Heather and Derek Furminger took over the delightful cottage late in 1994 and continue to provide friendly accommodation and good food. The majority of the well appointed bedrooms are on the ground floor, each overlooking either the garden or the adjacent fields. Guests can also relax in the comfortable beamed lounge with its inglenook fireplace. An imaginative three course dinner is served with choices at each course; a recent inspection meal started with a chilled yoghurt and cucumber soup, followed by noisette of lamb with a chicken and tarragon mousse on a tarragon sauce, served with carefully cooked fresh vegetables. Lemon tart, served warm, completed an enjoyable meal.

8 en suite (bth/shr) No smoking in 6 bedrooms No smoking in dining room CTV in all bedrooms Tea and coffee making facilities Direct dial from bedrooms Licensed Cen ht 20P Last d 8.30pm

PRICE GUIDE
ROOMS: s £41-£44; d £62-£68; wkly b&b £217-£308; wkly hlf-bd £301-£392
CARDS: £

🖼️📺 ❤ QQ Mrs M Tomblin **Lower Lewell** *(SY744897)* West Stafford DT2 8AP (1m east of Wise Man Inn) ☎01305 267169
Set in the heart of Hardy country, this attractive farmhouse was once the Talbothays Dairy, which was featured in Tess of the D'Urbervilles - home of Dairyman Crick. The house offers a warm and friendly atmosphere and the comfortable rooms overlook the neighbouring farmland. There is a cosy lounge and a good farmhouse breakfast is served.

3 rms (2 fmly) No smoking in dining room Tea and coffee making facilities No dogs Cen ht CTV 8P
PRICE GUIDE
ROOMS: s £16-£20; d £32-£36 £

DORKING Surrey

See advertisement opposite

DORRINGTON Shropshire Map **07** SJ40

GH QQQ **Ashton Lees** Ashton Lees SY5 7JW (6m S on A49) ☎01743 718378
This small, friendly guest house lies back off the A49 in an acre of mature lawns and gardens. Bedrooms look out to the rear over the

lovely Shropshire countryside and are equipped with TV and video. There are both a small bar and a comfortable lounge - the latter warmed by an open fire and provided with plenty of books and local guides. In fine weather afternoon teas are served in the rear gardens by Doreen Woodall, who also provides evening meals, with advance notice.

3 rms (1 bth/shr) No smoking in bedrooms No smoking in 1 lounge CTV in all bedrooms Tea and coffee making facilities No dogs Licensed CTV 6P No coaches Last d 9am
PRICE GUIDE
ROOMS: s £17-£20; d £34-£40; wkly b&b £100-£120✳ £

DOVER Kent Map **05** TR34

GH QQQ **Ardmore Private Hotel** 18 Castle Hill Rd CT16 1QW (on A258 next to Dover Castle) ☎01304 205895 FAX 01304 208229
Closed Xmas
The bedrooms in this cheerfully run guest house are bright and well kept; all but one have en suite facilities.

4 en suite (shr) (1 fmly) No smoking CTV in all bedrooms Tea and coffee making facilities No dogs Cen ht No parking
PRICE GUIDE
ROOMS: d £32-£45
CARDS:

GH QQQ **Beulah House** 94 Crabble Hill, London Rd CT17 0SA (on A256) ☎01304 824615
Conveniently located close to the town centre and western docks, this elegant late-Victorian house is slowly being upgraded yet retains much of its original character. The non-smoking accommodation is comfortably furnished and equipped with tea trays; one ground floor room has a four-poster bed and sole use of adjacent bathroom facilities. There is a bright breakfast room, a traditional TV lounge and a small conservatory lounge overlooking the lovely rear gardens. Cream teas ad light refreshments are also available and the house has its own forecourt parking.

7 rms (3 fmly) No smoking CTV in 3 bedrooms Tea and coffee making facilities No dogs Cen ht CTV 11P
PRICE GUIDE
ROOMS: s £19-£22; d £32-£38✳
CARDS:

GH QQQ **Castle House** 10 Castle Hill Rd CT16 1QW ☎01304 201656 FAX 01304 210197
Castle House is conveniently situated near to the castle, docks and town centre. Attractively decorated bedrooms are thaughtfully furnished and well-equipped, but public areas are limited to a very small lounge and a bright, fresh dining room serving a set price dinner menu and a choice of breakfast.

6 en suite (shr) (1 fmly) No smoking CTV in all bedrooms Tea and coffee making facilities No dogs (ex guide dogs) Licensed Cen ht CTV No parking No coaches Last d 6pm
PRICE GUIDE
ROOMS: s £20-£28; d £30-£40; wkly b&b £98-£133; wkly hlf-bd £140-£175✳
CARDS:

GH QQ **Dell** 233 Folkestone Rd CT17 9SL ☎01304 202422
The situation of this terraced house is not particularly inviting, so its well maintained interior is a pleasant surprise. Bedrooms may be cramped but beds and soft furnishings are of good quality and one room now has en suite facilities. A comfortable television lounge is provided for guests' use and on-street parking is available.

5 rms (1 shr) (3 fmly) Tea and coffee making facilities No dogs (ex guide dogs) Cen ht CTV 6P No coaches £

CHIPPENHALL HALL

Listed Tudor Manor, a period film location and of Saxon origin, with recordings in Domesday Book. Set in 7 acres of gardens and ponds giving total rural tranquillity. Unique atmosphere with beams and inglenook log fires. Fine food and wines. Heated outdoor pool set in rose covered courtyard. All rooms en-suite. ETB Highly Commended and holding Johansen Award for Excellence. One mile south of Fressingfield on B1116.

Fressingfield, Eye, Suffolk IP21 5TD
Tel: (01379) 588180 and 586733
Fax: (01379) 586272

CHURCHVIEW GUEST HOUSE

WINTERBOURNE ABBAS, DORCHESTER, DORSET DT2 9LS

QQQ

This 300-year-old Guesthouse, noted for its warm, friendly hospitality and delicious home cooking is located in a small village 5 miles west of Dorchester. Set in a designated area of outstanding natural beauty, Churchview makes an ideal touring base. All our comfortable rooms have tea making facilities and central heating, most en-suite. There are two lounges, one set aside for non-smokers, an attractive period dining room and well-stocked bar. Evening meal, bed and breakfast from £28.00 per person.

For further details please contact
Michael and Jane Deller. ☎ (01305) 889296

Rectory House

Fore Street, Evershot, Dorset DT2 0JW
Telephone: (0193583) 273

HIGHLY COMMENDED

An 18th century listed building of great charm, situated in this quiet and unspoilt Dorset village in an area of outstanding natural beauty made famous by Thomas Hardy's 'Tess of the D'Urbevilles'. Utmost comfort, with lovely centrally heated bedrooms each with en suite bathroom, colour TV, tea & coffee making facilities. The home cooking is superb with some exotic dishes to enjoy together with more traditional fare, including freshly baked bread from the Village Bakery and locally made sausages for your breakfast. Relax in the separate lounges with log fire during the winter months. Nearby many beautiful walks and places of interest to visit. Open all year except Christmas and New Year. Sorry no pets.

The Royal Oak

Holmbury St Mary, nr Dorking,
Surrey RH5 6PF
Telephone: 01306 730120

A 17th century Inn overlooking the village green previously frequented by smugglers and highwaymen. The Inn still offers travellers comfortable en suite bedrooms for overnight stops or longer stays to explore the surrounding countryside with superb walks and wildlife. Freshly prepared hot and cold meals, traditional beers, fine wines and a cheery atmosphere. The blazing log fire is a welcoming feature during the winter months. Central for main London station, Gatwick, Heathrow and Guildford

GH Q Q *Gateway Hovertel* Snargate St CT17 9BZ (between East & West Ferry Terminals)
☎01304 205479 FAX 01304 211504
Closed 23 Dec-6 Jan
Conveniently located beside the new A20 and open 24 hours a day, this hotel is part old house and part modern block. Accommodation is adequate, all rooms having en suite facilities and colour TV; good car parking arrangements include a secure area fitted with alarms.
27 en suite (bth/shr) (7 fmly) CTV in all bedrooms No dogs (ex guide dogs) Licensed Cen ht CTV 26P Last d 7pm
CARDS:

GH Q Q Q **Hubert House** 9 Castle Hill Rd CT16 1QW
☎01304 202253
Closed Oct
Conveniently situated for easy access to the town centre and within a few minutes' walk of the ferry ports this charming Georgian guest house has been home to the Hoynes family for nearly thirty years. The accommodation had been individually furnished in the modern style and all bedrooms come with remote control TV, clock radio alarm and tea tray. There are a small lounge and a well appointed breakfast room. Families are especially welcome, full English and healthy breakfasts can be provided and the atmosphere is very friendly, informal and welcoming. Whilst most rooms have en suite shower a general bathroom has been retained and there is ample free car parking.
8 en suite (bth/shr) (4 fmly) CTV in all bedrooms Tea and coffee making facilities No dogs (ex guide dogs) Cen ht 7P
PRICE GUIDE
ROOMS: s £26-£28; d £36-£42
CARDS:

★☞ **GH** Q Q Q **Linden** 231 Folkestone Rd CT17 9SL
☎01304 205449
Closed 24-26 Dec
Ideally situated on the B2011 Folkestone road this delightful double glazed Victorian terraced house has been tastefully furnished and modernised to provide quiet and comfortable beautifully maintained bedrooms all equipped to a high standard with remote control TV-Satellite, alarm clock radio, hair dryer, and tea trays. Other facilities include a combined traditionally well furnished lounge and well appointed breakfast room and a secure rear car park. Service is friendly and very helpful and personally provided by the resident proprietors Jean and Roger Walkden.
5 rms (3 bth/shr) (3 fmly) No smoking in dining room CTV in all bedrooms Tea and coffee making facilities Cen ht CTV 4P No coaches
PRICE GUIDE
ROOMS: s £14-£18; d £28-£40; wkly b&b £90-£120
CARDS:

GH Q Q Q **Number One** 1 Castle St CT16 1QH
☎01304 202007
Closed 25-27 Dec
A rather quaint house, owned by the same family for 20 years and made homely by their bric-á-brac and personal possessions, offers accommodation in bedrooms with mixed furnishings; these, though attractively decorated, tend to be cramped - partly because each contains a dining table at which breakfast is served. The small lounge opens out on to a pretty garden and some lock-up garage space is available.
5 en suite (shr) (3 fmly) No smoking in dining room No smoking in lounges CTV in all bedrooms Tea and coffee making facilities No dogs Cen ht 6P No coaches
PRICE GUIDE
ROOMS: d £36-£42

GH Q Q Q *Peverall House Hotel* 28 Park Av CT16 1HD
☎01304 202573 & 205088
This fine Victorian corner house is quietly situated in a residential area. Bedrooms are modestly furnished, well decorated and comfortable, and a relaxing sitting room leads to a dining room that serves a set menu of basic English dishes. Snacks are also available, as is a choice of breakfast.
6 rms (2 bth) (2 fmly) CTV in all bedrooms Tea and coffee making facilities No dogs Licensed Cen ht CTV 8P No coaches Last d noon

GH Q Q **St Brelades** 80/82 Buckland Av CT16 2NW
☎01304 206126 FAX 01304 211486
Set in a residential area on the fringe of the town centre, St Brelades offers clean simple accomodation, all en suite. The dinner menu offers a choice of Indian and English dishes. There is also a small sitting room.
6 rms (5 shr) (4 fmly) No smoking in dining room No smoking in lounges CTV in all bedrooms Tea and coffee making facilities No dogs Licensed Cen ht CTV 6P
PRICE GUIDE
ROOMS: s £20-£28; d £28-£42
CARDS:

GH Q Q Q **St Martins** 17 Castle Hill Rd CT16 1QW
☎01304 205938 FAX 01304 208229
Closed Xmas
Further improvements have taken place at this friendly guest house. There are now a number of spacious, comfortable and attractively decorated family rooms. There are also a relaxing lounge and a small dining room serving a choice of breakfasts.
6 en suite (shr) (3 fmly) No smoking CTV in all bedrooms Tea and coffee making facilities No dogs Licensed Cen ht No parking
PRICE GUIDE
ROOMS: s £25; d £32-£40

◆ Q Q **Cliffe Tavern** The High St, St Margarets at Cliffe CT15 6AT (follow A2 London rd then A258 towards Deal and 1st right) ☎01304 852400 FAX 01304 852400
Personally run by the proprietors Lucie, Lady Houstoun-Boswall, and Malcolm J M Walker, this part 16th-century Free House is situated in the High Street directly opposite the village church. Bistro-style home cooking and meals selected from the blackboard can be accompanied by a choice of four real ales from the cask and a range of fine wines. There is a front bar with a dart board as well as an elegant lounge and dining room overlooking the walled garden. Most of the bedrooms are located in two separate adjoining houses. Special events, gourmet weekends and long weekend breaks are featured, and the atmosphere is very friendly.
2 en suite (bth) 10 annexe en suite (bth/shr) (5 fmly) No smoking in dining room CTV in all bedrooms Tea and coffee making facilities Direct dial from bedrooms Cen ht CTV 40P No coaches Riding Last d 9.30pm
PRICE GUIDE
ROOMS: s fr £34.50; d fr £40✷
MEALS: Bar Lunch £5-£15alc Dinner £8.50-£22alc✷
CARDS:

We endeavour to be as accurate as possible but changes in personnel and data can occur in establishments after the Guide has gone to press.

DOVERIDGE Derbyshire Map **07** SK13

Premier Selected

♥ ⓠⓠⓠⓠⓠ Mrs B
Tunnicliffe **Beeches**
(SK125337) Waldley DE6 5LR
(A50 in westerly direction,
turn right at Doveridge and
down Marston Lane
signposted to Waldley. At
Waldley take first right then
first left) ☎01889 590288
FAX 01889 590288
Closed 24 Dec-3o Dec
Set in the fold of rolling hills with green fields, as far as the
eye can see, this Georgian farmhouse is very rural but also
very accessible. It is owner and chef Barbara Tunnicliffe who
greets guests, offering welcome refreshments and a friendly
smile. An elegant and intimate restaurant features the original
brickwork and oak beams, a rustic bar is furnished with
rough-hewn tables and settles around an open fire, and
thoughtfully furnished well equipped bedrooms are
thoroughly modern. In the restaurant there is a choice of two
menus, and although both are similar the supper menu is
marginally cheaper. The dishes are fresh and some
combinations show a keen passion for cooking. Cod fillets
and parsley sauce is served as a starter and a sliced duck
breast comes with a delicious well made rhubarb and caramel
gravy. Desserts are also home-made. Some of the farms brick
outbuildings have been converted and are utilised as
accommodation, but the majority remain essential to the
workings of a very active and substantial dairy farm. Guests
awaken to the sounds of the horses being turned out and
children are welcomed in the dairy sheds to watch the
milking.
10 rms (4 bth/shr) (7 fmly) No smoking in dining room No
smoking in lounges CTV in all bedrooms Tea and coffee
making facilities Direct dial from bedrooms No dogs (ex
guide dogs) Licensed Cen ht 30P 150 acres dairy Last d
9pm
PRICE GUIDE
ROOMS: s £38.50; d £46; wkly b&b £161; wkly hlf-bd
£227.50*
CARDS: 🔲 🔲 🔲 🔲
See advertisement on p.157.

DOWNHAM MARKET Norfolk Map **05** TF60

GH ⓠⓠⓠ *The Dial House* 12 Railway Rd PE38 9EB
☎01366 388358 FAX 01366 382198
rs 24-31 Dec
A delightful 17th-century house located on the fringe of the town
centre offers attractive bedrooms. There are two nicely appointed
lounges in which guests can relax. An evening meal is served with
the accent on healthy eating, and there is also a choice of
breakfasts. A warm welcome by proprietors Ann and David
Murray is assured.
3 rms (2 bth/shr) No smoking Tea and coffee making facilities
No dogs (ex guide dogs) Cen ht CTV 5P No coaches Last d
noon

DOWNTON Wiltshire Map **04** SU12

GH ⓠⓠⓠ **Warren** 15 High St SP5 3PG (take A338
signposted to Ringwood and after 5m turn left at traffic lights.
Guest house on left opposite Post Office) ☎01725 510263
Closed 20 Dec-6 Jan
A delightful 15th-century house in the village of Downton, The
Warren retains all the character and charm of its period. The
beamed rooms are furnished with antiques; one lounge has an
open fire and there is a beautiful oak panelled room overlooking a
walled garden with a profusion of flowers. Fresh flowers adorn
each of the bedrooms, and the dining room has French windows
opening on to the patio and garden.
6 rms (2 bth/shr) (1 fmly) No smoking in dining room Tea and
coffee making facilities Cen ht CTV No children 5yrs 8P No
coaches
PRICE GUIDE
ROOMS: s £25-£30; d £38-£42; wkly b&b fr £120*

See advertisement under SALISBURY

DREWSTEIGNTON Devon Map **03** SX79

GH ⓠⓠ *The Old Rectory* EX6 6QT
☎01647 281269 FAX 01647 21269
Closed 21-31 Dec
This large and rather Bohemian house was originally the vicarage
and stands close to the village centre in delightful grounds. The
wing bedrooms are individually decorated and artistically
furnished with interesting artefacts; breakfast is taken in the
delightful dining room overlooking the garden. A busy family
atmosphere pervades the house.
3 rms (1 bth/shr) No smoking Tea and coffee making facilities
No dogs Cen ht 3P

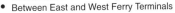

DROITWICH Hereford & Worcester Map **03** SO86

GH 🅠🅠 *The Larches* 46 Worcester Rd WR9 8AJ (on A38 by Highfields Hospital) ☎01905 773441
A fine old house dating back to 1729, set in wooded grounds on the Worcester road just a short distance from the town centre, offers accommodation in four modern bedrooms equipped with television sets and thoughtful extras like hot water bottles. Smoking is not permitted anywhere in the house. Car parking facilities are available.
4 rms No smoking CTV in all bedrooms Tea and coffee making facilities No dogs (ex guide dogs) Cen ht 7P No coaches Last d 10am

---

DUDDINGTON Northamptonshire Map **04** SK90

◀ 🅠🅠🅠 *Royal Oak Hotel* High St PE9 3QE ☎01780 83267
This delightful 17th-century stone-built inn, owned and run by the Morgado family, successfully retains the ambience and character of its period despite being smart and thoroughly modern. The charming bedrooms are well equipped and prettily furnished, and public areas have a lively atmosphere. A good selection of meals is available in either the dining area or the cosy bar.
6 en suite (bth/shr) (2 fmly) CTV in all bedrooms Tea and coffee making facilities Cen ht 75P Last d 9.30pm
CARDS: 🔵 🔴

DULVERTON Somerset Map **03** SS92

See also Oakford

Selected

GH 🅠🅠🅠 **Dassels Country House** TA22 9RZ
☎01398 341203 FAX 01398 341561
Situated three miles from Dulverton on the outskirts of East Anstey, this Georgian-style house stands in nine acres of grounds with panoramic views stretching from Wellington Monument to the Tors of Dartmoor. Bedrooms, including three garden rooms and one on the ground floor, are neatly decorated and furnished; all are equipped with remote control TVs and tea-making facilities. The comfortable, spacious lounge has a log fire, and a set dinner is served each evening featuring home-grown vegetables, local meats and, with advance notice, a vegetarian choice.
7 en suite (bth/shr) 3 annexe en suite (shr) (3 fmly) CTV in all bedrooms Tea and coffee making facilities Licensed Cen ht CTV 14P No coaches Last d 7pm
PRICE GUIDE
ROOMS: (incl. dinner) s £36; d £58-£68; wkly hlf-bd £185-£210*
CARDS: 🔵 🔴 🟰 🔴 🔵 £

Selected

GH 🅠🅠🅠🅠 **Highercombe** TA22 9PT ☎01398 323451
An imposing Grade II listed property with fine southerly views stands in mature gardens and grounds just two and a half miles from Dulverton, within easy reach of open moorland. Comfortable bedrooms are tastefully decorated and include furniture hand-made by the resident proprietor. The spacious lounge has a log fire and a TV. Breakfast is the normally the only meal served, but guests can eat well in several pubs in the village.
3 rms (2 shr) (1 fmly) No smoking CTV in all bedrooms

Tea and coffee making facilities Cen ht CTV 6P No coaches
PRICE GUIDE
ROOMS: s £17-£24; d £34-£38; wkly b&b £112-£122
 £

DUNSTER Somerset Map **03** SS94

See also Roadwater

Premier Selected

GH 🅠🅠🅠🅠🅠 **Dollons House** Church St TA24 6SH
☎01643 821880
Situated in the heart of the historic medieval village, this Grade II listed property has a Georgian façade, though it is believed to date back some four hundred years. Two of the comfortable, well equipped bedrooms have views of the Castle and each  is individually named; 'Kate's' has a half-tester bed and overlooks the lovely walled garden, while 'T-Bear Esq' is filled with teddy bears including a large mural in the shower room. There is also a delightful sitting room which opens onto a large veranda and the garden. The two front rooms of the house are run as a craft/flower shop.
3 rms

DURHAM Co Durham Map **12** NZ24

Selected

GH 🅠🅠🅠🅠 **Hillrise** 13 Durham Rd West, Bowburn DH6 5AU (junct 61 A1, Hillrise approx 200yds down on left from motorway)
☎0191 377 0302 FAX 0191 3770302
Conveniently located only 200 yards from the A1(M) in the village of Bowburn, this house has been lovingly furnished throughout and provides warm, friendly service. The pretty bedrooms are well equipped and guests can relax in a comfortable lounge. Well produced home-cooked meals are served in the conservatory dining room.
5 rms (4 shr) (3 fmly) CTV in all bedrooms Tea and coffee making facilities Cen ht CTV 4P Last d 4pm
PRICE GUIDE
ROOMS: s £17-£19; d £38; wkly b&b £119-£140; wkly hlf-bd £175-£189

GH 🅠🅠🅠 **Lothlorien** 48/49 Front St, Witton Gilbert DH7 6SY (3m on A691 Consett rd, opposite Glenridding Arms) ☎0191 371 0067
Situated in the village of Witton Gilbert, some three miles from Durham city, this well kept house offers value-for-money accommodation. Mrs Milne is a delightful hostess and cares greatly for the comfort of her guests, providing a cosy lounge and bright, well maintained bedrooms.
3 rms No smoking in dining room Tea and coffee making

---

facilities No dogs Cen ht CTV 3P No coaches
PRICE GUIDE
ROOMS: s £17-£18; d £34-£36; wkly b&b £119-£126✱

━━━━━━━━━━━━━━━━━━━━━━━━

◼ Ⓠ Ⓠ Ⓠ **Bay Horse** Brandon DH7 8ST (take A690 2.5m W)
☎0191 378 0498
This charming family owned and run stone inn in the village of
Brandon has recently been extended to provide well furnished
bedrooms and a delightful restaurant offering a wide range of food
which is also available in the bar.
10 annexe en suite (bth/shr) (1 fmly) CTV in all bedrooms Tea
and coffee making facilities Direct dial from bedrooms Cen ht
15P No coaches Last d 9.30pm
PRICE GUIDE
ROOMS: s £30; d £39✱
CARDS: 🆇 🆇

━━━━━━━━━━━━━━━━━━━━━━━━

DYMCHURCH Kent Map **05** TR12

GH Ⓠ Ⓠ **Chantry Hotel** Sycamore Gardens TN29 0LA
(200yds E of Dymchurch village on coast side of A259)
☎01303 873137
This part-timbered house stands in a private road with direct
access to the sea. Most of the bedrooms are of a good size, some
with adjoing bunk bedded rooms perfect for children; there are
plans to upgrade the rooms over the winter. A wide range of home
cooking is available and a separate TV lounge leads to a nice
lawn. There is car parking at the front of the house.
6 rms (5 bth/shr) (5 fmly) No smoking in dining room CTV in
all bedrooms Tea and coffee making facilities Licensed Cen ht
CTV 9P No coaches Table tennis Boules Last d 8.30pm
PRICE GUIDE
ROOMS: s £19.95-£30.50; d £39.90-£45; wkly b&b £125-£150;
wkly hlf-bd £175-£185✱
CARDS: 🆇 🆇 🆇 £

━━━━━━━━━━━━━━━━━━━━━━━━

⇄ ▦ **GH** Ⓠ Ⓠ **Waterside** 15 Hythe Rd TN29 0LN (on A259
5m W of Hythe) ☎01303 872253
Improvements continue at an extended house which stands by the
side of the A259 bordering a dyke and with views of the marsh to
the rear. Most bedrooms are small and quite simple in style though
three now have private facilities. A useful car park is available.
7 rms (3 shr) (1 fmly) No smoking in dining room CTV in all
bedrooms Tea and coffee making facilities No dogs Licensed
Cen ht CTV 7P No coaches Last d 8pm
PRICE GUIDE
ROOMS: s £15-£20; d £28-£37; wkly b&b £94-£126; wkly hlf-
bd £132-£164 £

━━━━━━━━━━━━━━━━━━━━━━━━

EARDISLAND Hereford & Worcester Map **03** SO45

♥ Ⓠ Ⓠ Ⓠ **Mary Johnson The Elms** *(SO418584)* HR6 9BN
☎01544 388405
Parts of this large farmhouse date back to the 17th century, but
most of it was built in late Victorian times; it stands five miles
west of Leominster, in pretty lawns and gardens at the centre of
the village. The house is also popular for afternoon teas, and Mary
Johnson extends a warm welcome to guests with an offer of tea on
arrival. There are four bedrooms, all comfortable and prettily
decorated, and a lounge is available for residents' use. This is a
no-smoking establishment.
4 rms No smoking No dogs No children 12yrs 6P 9 acres
grazing
PRICE GUIDE
ROOMS: s £17-£29; d £32.50-£33 £

EARLS COLNE Essex Map 05 TL82

◀ Q Q **Riverside Inn Motel** 40/42 Lower Holt St CO6 2PH (on A604) ☎01787 223487 FAX 01787 223487

On the banks of the River Colne, this part-timbered, purpose-built motel occupies the site of old farm buildings. The modern chalet-style rooms are plainly furnished but comfortable. Breakfast, charged separately, is cooked and served by the chatty owner, Mr Collyer, and guests may have to share tables. The adjacent freehold pub serves drinks and meals, and there is a garden with a children's play area.

11 en suite (shr) (3 fmly) No smoking in dining room No smoking in lounges CTV in all bedrooms Tea and coffee making facilities Cen ht 30P Last d 9.45pm

PRICE GUIDE
ROOMS: s fr £25; d fr £35✶
MEALS: Lunch £5-£10 Dinner £5-£10✶
CARDS: 🔲 💳

EASINGWOLD North Yorkshire Map 08 SE56

GH Q Q Q **Roseberry View** Easingwold Rd, Stillington YO6 1LR (from York, take B1363 to Stillington. Turn left for 0.5m, house on right) ☎01347 810795

This bungalow is situated half a mile from Stillington village and is set in open countryside, with an attractive large garden. There are comfortable, good-sized bedrooms, and a guests' lounge which doubles as a breakfast room.

2 rms (1 shr) No smoking CTV in all bedrooms Tea and coffee making facilities No dogs (ex guide dogs) Cen ht 5P No coaches

EASTBOURNE East Sussex Map 05 TV69

See also Wilmington

GH Q Q Q **Bay Lodge Hotel** 61 & 62 Royal Pde BN22 7AQ ☎01323 732515 FAX 01323 735009
Mar-Oct

Overlooking the Redoubt Gardens and the sea, this double-fronted Victorian house has bedrooms furnished in modern style; two of them have balconies. One side of the lounge is reserved for non-smokers and there is also a lounge bar. A four-course fixed-price menu is available in the non-smoking dining room and involved owners are attentive to their guests' needs.

12 rms (9 bth/shr) No smoking in dining room No smoking in 1 lounge CTV in all bedrooms Tea and coffee making facilities No dogs (ex guide dogs) Licensed Cen ht CTV No children 7yrs No parking No coaches Last d 6pm

PRICE GUIDE
ROOMS: s £17-£22; d £36-£46; wkly b&b £105-£148; wkly hlf-bd £165-£208✶
CARDS: 🔲 💳

Selected

GH Q Q Q Q **Beachy Rise** 20 Beachy Head Rd BN20 7QN ☎01323 639171

Built towards the end of the 19th century, this attractive semidetached house is quietly located in the conservation area of Meads Village, between the town centre and Beachy Head. Ample street parking is usually available. Bedrooms vary in shape and size, and are all individually furnished in an elegant style with period and co-ordinating furnishings. The lounge is comfortable and professional standards of cooking are provided in a dining room where the three-course dinner menu offers interesting home-made dishes; light refreshments

---

are available throughout the day, and service is personally provided by resident housekeeper Mrs Margaret Page. Smoking is not permitted in the dining room.

7 en suite (bth/shr) (1 fmly) No smoking in dining room CTV in all bedrooms Tea and coffee making facilities No dogs Licensed Cen ht No parking Last d noon

PRICE GUIDE
ROOMS: wkly b&b £135-£155; wkly hlf-bd £190-£210
CARDS: 🔲 💳

GH Q Q Q **Camelot Lodge** 35 Lewes Rd BN21 2BU (on A2021) ☎01323 725207

A 1920s mock Tudor house, beautifully maintained, offers well furnished bedrooms - one of them on the ground floor and some with spa baths; there are a lounge and a cosy bar through the dining room. A daily fixed-price menu with home grown vegetables and tasty desserts is available at dinner.

9 en suite (bth/shr) (1 fmly) No smoking in dining room CTV in all bedrooms Tea and coffee making facilities No dogs (ex guide dogs) Licensed Cen ht No children 5yrs 10P No coaches Last d 4pm

PRICE GUIDE
ROOMS: s £21.50-£24.50; d £43-£45; wkly b&b £136.50-£157.50
CARDS: 🔲 💳 🔲

GH Q Q Q **Chalk Farm Hotel & Restaurant** Coopers Hill, Willingdon BN20 9JD (1m S of Polegate crossroads t rt off A22, immediately after traffic lights) ☎01323 503800 FAX 01323 520331

In a quiet location off the A22, at the foot of the South Downs, this well run former farmhouse has a good range of comfortable and well equipped bedrooms, all furnished in the traditional style. There are a bar lounge, a cosy reading lounge, and a well appointed modern beamed restaurant. A new craft and garden centre, and a new bistro café are planned. There are also good function and conference facilities.

9 rms (2 bth 4 shr) (2 fmly) No smoking in dining room No smoking in 1 lounge CTV in all bedrooms Tea and coffee making facilities Direct dial from bedrooms Licensed Cen ht 15P No coaches Cycle hire Last d 9pm

PRICE GUIDE
ROOMS: s £30; d £43; wkly b&b £189; wkly hlf-bd £304.50✶
CARDS: 🔲 💳 🔲 ⓞ

GH Q Q Q **Far End Hotel** 139 Royal Pde BN22 7LH ☎01323 725666
Mar-Nov

Bedrooms furnished in modern style are provided by this seafront guest house next to Princes Park. Among the public rooms are a first-floor lounge and bar, and a daily four-course fixed-price menu is available in the bright, no-smoking, dining room.

10 rms (4 shr) No smoking in dining room No smoking in lounges CTV in all bedrooms Tea and coffee making facilities Licensed Cen ht CTV No children 4yrs 8P No coaches Last d 1pm

PRICE GUIDE
ROOMS: s £17-£21; d £34-£42; wkly b&b £110-£130; wkly hlf-bd £130-£180

GH Q Q Q **Flamingo Private Hotel** 20 Enys Rd BN21 2DN ☎01323 721654

This Victorian house in a residential area has kept many of its Victorian features, including a graceful staircase and a stained glass window. Bright spacious bedrooms include some on the ground floor, the dining room has a chandelier and a bar lounge with sun lounge extension overlooks the garden. A three-course evening meal is served.

12 en suite (bth/shr) (1 fmly) No smoking in dining room No smoking in 1 lounge CTV in all bedrooms Tea and coffee making facilities No dogs (ex guide dogs) Licensed Cen ht CTV No children 5yrs No parking No coaches Last d 4.30pm

PRICE GUIDE
ROOMS: s £21-£22.50; d £42-£45; wkly b&b £133-£140; wkly hlf-bd £175-£185.50*
CARDS: £

GH **QQ** *Mowbray Hotel* Lascelles Tce BN21 4BJ
☎01323 720012
Apr-Dec
Well placed for theatres, the seafront and Wish Tower, this long established hotel with traditionally furnished bedrooms is beautifully maintained and has lift access to all its upper levels. Guests have the use of a downstairs lounge, both breakfast and an evening meal are served and snacks are usually available all day. Owners provide attentive service and create a very friendly atmosphere.

15 rms (6 shr) CTV in all bedrooms Tea and coffee making facilities Lift CTV No children 6yrs No coaches Last d 5.30pm
CARDS: ⛝

Selected

GH **QQQQ** **Queens Cliff Hotel** 24 Carew Rd BN21 2JG
☎01323 726723
This quietly situated, family-run hotel, dating from the turn-of-the-century, offers refurbished accommodation, very comfortable and equipped with TVs and tea trays. There is a bar and a no-smoking dining room which serves a fixed-price four-course dinner.

8 en suite (bth/shr) (1 fmly) No smoking in dining room CTV in all bedrooms Tea and coffee making facilities Licensed Cen ht CTV 8P Last d 6pm
PRICE GUIDE
ROOMS: s £25-£30; d £42-£46; wkly b&b £147-£155; wkly hlf-bd £189-£205*
 £

GH **QQQ** *St Omer Hotel* 13 Royal Pde BN22 7AR
☎01323 722152
Apr-Sep rs Oct-Nov & Mar
Comfortable and well presented accommodation is offered by this seafront hotel personally run by friendly proprietors Andrew and Glynis Garman. Six of the bedrooms have sea views and there is one room especially equipped for disabled guests. Public rooms include a foyer lounge with dispense bar and a front sun lounge. The daily four-course menu available in the attractive panelled dining room features fresh produce, home-made pies and traditional hot puddings.

13 rms (4 bth 6 shr) (1 fmly) CTV in all bedrooms Tea and coffee making facilities No dogs (ex guide dogs) Licensed Cen ht CTV Last d 5pm
CARDS: ⛝

GH **QQ** **Sheldon Hotel** 9-11 Burlington Place BN21 4AS
☎01323 724120 FAX 01323 730406
Feb-Dec
A well run hotel with attentive service. There is a bar/lounge and dining room. Dinner by arrangement.

27 rms (14 bth/shr) (4 fmly) CTV in all bedrooms Tea and coffee making facilities Direct dial from bedrooms Lift Cen ht

CTV 16P Last d 6pm
PRICE GUIDE
ROOMS: s £23-£28; d £38-£48; wkly b&b £120-£140; wkly hlf-bd £140-£170
CARDS: £

GH **QQ** **Stirling House Hotel** 5-7 Cavendish Place BN21 3EJ
☎01323 732263
Mar-Oct
Ideally located for easy access to the seafront and town centre, this friendly terraced guesthouse is personally run by the proprietors, Eric and Elsa Norris. A good range of comfortably furnished bedrooms includes some on the ground floor while public areas are made up of a residents' bar/lounge, a TV lounge and a spacious dining room where home-cooked four-course dinners and generous English breakfasts are served.

20 rms (11 shr) No smoking in dining room CTV in all bedrooms Tea and coffee making facilities No dogs (ex guide dogs) Licensed CTV No children 10yrs Last d 9am
PRICE GUIDE
ROOMS: s £17-£19; d £34-£38; wkly b&b £112-£119; wkly hlf-bd £125-£150*
£

EAST DEREHAM Norfolk Map **09** TF91

GH **QQQ** **Clinton House** Well Hill, Clint Green, Yaxham NR19 1RX (leave A47 & join B1135 towards Wymondham, at Yaxham take rd towards Mattishall after 1m is Clint Green, turn right at school) ☎01362 692079
Clinton House offers spacious bedrooms. Guests are encouraged to use the lounge, too, with its comfortable seating, colour TV and video recorder. Breakfast is served in a large, bright conservatory overlooking the attractive lawns and tennis court. Smoking is not permitted in the house.

3 rms 1 annexe en suite (bth/shr) (2 fmly) No smoking CTV in 1 bedroom Tea and coffee making facilities No dogs (ex guide dogs) Cen ht CTV 10P No coaches Tennis (grass) Croquet
PRICE GUIDE
ROOMS: s £17-£20; d £28-£32; wkly b&b £182-£210*
 £

EAST MIDLANDS AIRPORT Leicestershire Map **08** SK42

GH **QQ** *The Four Poster* 73 Clapgun St DE7 2LF
☎01332 810335 & 812418
Mr Barker makes four-poster beds and oak dressers, and these are displayed in the front shop window of this colourful guesthouse; the main entrance is around the back, through an attractive courtyard filled with hanging baskets, tubs and borders. Simple but immaculate rooms are furnished mainly in traditional oak.

7 rms (3 bth/shr) 4 annexe rms CTV in all bedrooms Tea and coffee making facilities Cen ht CTV 18P No coaches

GH **QQQ** **Park Farmhouse Hotel** Melbourne Rd, Isley Walton DE74 2RN (Logis)
☎01332 862409 FAX 01332 862364
Closed Xmas & New Year
This attractive, elegantly proportioned farmhouse stands on the fringe of Donnington Park motor racing circuit yet overlooks rolling fields to Breedon church. Built around 1750 and featuring a slate roof and gables, it offers comfortable, well equipped accommodation: bedrooms are decorative, spacious and cosy, their furnishings and decor featuring a harmonious blend of country mansion and rustic farmhouse; there is a ground floor room adapted for disabled guests. The dining room has a quarry tiled floor and big pine tables arranged in front of a huge open range, and a blackboard menu offers traditional farmhouse meals. The

➡

pleasant lounge and bar retain the character and charm of the original building.

9 en suite (bth/shr) (2 fmly) No smoking in 2 bedrooms No smoking in dining room CTV in all bedrooms Tea and coffee making facilities Direct dial from bedrooms Licensed Cen ht 20P Last d 8.30pm

PRICE GUIDE
ROOMS: s £42-£46; d £56-£66; wkly b&b £165-£250
CARDS:

■ **QQQ** **Le Chevalier Bistro Restaurant** 2 Borough St
DE74 2LA ☎01332 812005 & 812106 FAX 01322 811372
A small, popular, cottage bistro set in a narrow side street in the town centre offers a room with a pool table as well as four cheerful and well appointed bedrooms which are accessed through a pretty courtyard. Competently cooked meals are served in an attractive bar and restaurant area featuring some fifty original charcoal sketches of movie stars on the raspberry-coloured walls.
4 en suite (bth/shr) (1 fmly) CTV in all bedrooms Tea and coffee making facilities No dogs (ex guide dogs) Cen ht CTV 2P Pool table Last d 10.30pm

PRICE GUIDE
ROOMS: s £25-£32; d £32-£38✽
MEALS: Dinner fr £14.95&alc✽
CARDS:

EDENBRIDGE Kent Map **05** TQ44

GH QQQ **Knowlands** Five Fields Ln TN8 6NA
☎01732 700314 FAX 01732 700314
Closed 20-30 Dec
This attractive guest house stands in a peaceful rural setting. The spacious bedrooms provide comfortable accommodation and are adequately equipped. The owners, Mr and Mrs Haviland, personally supervise and provide a high standard of hospitality.
2 rms No smoking CTV in all bedrooms Tea and coffee making facilities Cen ht 3P No coaches Tennis (hard)

PRICE GUIDE
ROOMS: d £50

ELTERWATER Cumbria Map **07** NY30

■ **QQQ** **Britannia** LA22 9HP
☎015394 37210 FAX 015394 37311
Closed 25 & 26 Dec
The Britannia is a traditional British inn, painted black and white, in a delightful village setting. The bedrooms are attractively furnished and have many modern features, whilst still retaining much of their original charm. The bars are small but atmospheric with open fires and oak beams. An extensive range of bar food is served at lunch time and in the evening, and on sunny days one can eat on the patio. The afternoon menu offers light snacks and cream teas. An attractive dining room and lounge are provided for residents.
9 rms (8 shr) 4 annexe rms (1 shr) No smoking in dining room CTV in all bedrooms Tea and coffee making facilities Direct dial from bedrooms Cen ht 10P No coaches Last d 9.30pm

PRICE GUIDE
ROOMS: s £17-£21.50; d £34-£59; wkly b&b £108.50-£196
MEALS: Bar Lunch £2.20-£10.70alc Dinner £2.20-£17.40alc
CARDS:

ELY Cambridgeshire Map **05** TL58

GH Q **Castle Lodge Hotel** 50 New Barns Rd CB7 4PW
☎01353 662276
Closed 23-27 Dec
A family owned small hotel situated in a quiet residential area within walking distance of the cathedral and town centre. The public rooms are quite comfortable and well maintained, providing a lounge bar and dining room, in which a good value daily changing menu of traditional British cooking is offered. Accommodation styles and sizes are varied, the first floor bedrooms are modestly furnished, whilst the second floor rooms are more basic.
12 rms (1 bth 2 shr) (2 fmly) No smoking in lounges CTV in 11 bedrooms Tea and coffee making facilities No dogs (ex guide dogs) Licensed Cen ht CTV 6P No coaches Last d 9pm

PRICE GUIDE
ROOMS: s £22.50-£30; d £40-£50✽
CARDS: 🔵 ▭

GH QQQ **Quarterway House** Ely Rd, Little Thetford
CB6 3HP (on A10 between Stretham and Little Thetford)
☎01353 648964
Quarterway House sits beside the A10 approximately 2 miles south of Ely, within 4 acres of gardens and paddocks. This newly built red brick house has been purposely furnished to retain a traditional character, this is evident with the restored period furnishings in the bedrooms and public rooms. Bedrooms are light and appealing but are a little tight for space, each is well equipped with thoughtful extras. Guests have the use of a comfortable lounge and an adjacent small conservatory, with breakfasts taken either communally in the kitchen or within the conservatory; evening meals are available by prior arrangement.
2 en suite (bth/shr) (1 fmly) No smoking CTV in all bedrooms Tea and coffee making facilities Direct dial from bedrooms Cen ht CTV No children 7yrs 9P No coaches Riding Last d 9pm

PRICE GUIDE
ROOMS: s £19-£20; d £35-£40; wkly b&b fr £100; wkly hlf-bd fr £145✽
CARDS: ▭

Selected

♥ **QQQQ** Mrs H Nix **Hill House** *(TL819487)* 9 Main St, Coveney CB6 2DJ (off A142) ☎01353 778369
This Victorian farm sits in the unspoilt village of Coveney, approximately 3 miles west of Ely. Mrs Nix is a charming and caring host who provides immaculately maintained accommodation. Bedrooms are fresh and appealing with colour co-ordinated decor and quality soft furnishings, each has a range of thoughtful extras and a modern en suite shower room; whilst being adjoined to the main house each bedroom has its own entrance. A carefully cooked breakfast is served at a highly polished communal table in the separate dining room and guests have the use of a quiet attractive sitting room. Please note that this is a non-smoking house which is not suitable for very young children or pets.
3 en suite (shr) No smoking CTV in all bedrooms Tea and coffee making facilities No dogs Cen ht No children 12yrs 6P 240 acres arable

PRICE GUIDE
ROOMS: d £36-£40✽

EMBLETON Northumberland Map **12** NU22

♥ 🔾🔾 A D Turnbull **Doxford** *(NU183233)* Doxford Farm NE6 75DY (signposted 'Doxford Country Store' from A1) ☎01665 579235 FAX 01665 579215
Closed Xmas & New Year
This appealing this farmhouse is set in secluded countryside yet only five minutes drive from the A1. The gardens have a grass tennis court and in addition to woodland walks the family own a farm shop nearby. Bedrooms are comfortable and there is a guests' lounge. Meals are served round two tables in the cosy dining room. The annexe room is in a rear outhouse and whilst more modest in standard it offers a touch of old fashioned character and includes a small sitting area with TV.
4 rms (1 fmly) No smoking CTV in 1 bedroom Tea and coffee making facilities CTV 6P Tennis (grass) Fishing Squash 400 acres arable/beef/sheep Last d 24hrs notice
PRICE GUIDE
ROOMS: s £16-£25; d £32-£38✱
CARDS: 🔳   £

EMSWORTH Hampshire Map **04** SU70

GH 🔾🔾🔾 **Jingles Hotel** 77 Horndean Rd PO10 7PU (turn off A259 towards Rowlands Castle and continue for approx 1m) ☎01243 373755 FAX 01243 373755
This family-run hotel is situated in a quiet location just north of the village. The bedrooms are neatly furnished and well equipped, all have colour television. There is a comfortable residents lounge, and a dining room with licensed bar, the Chapmans provide good home cooked meals in the evening and at lunchtime if required. The pretty patio and garden are available for guest use, as is the swimming pool.
13 rms (8 bth/shr) No smoking in 3 bedrooms No smoking in dining room CTV in all bedrooms Tea and coffee making facilities Licensed Cen ht CTV ch fac 14P Outdoor swimming pool (heated) Last d 7pm
PRICE GUIDE
ROOMS: s £23-£32.50; d £40-£52; wkly b&b £140-£189; wkly hlf-bd £196-£245✱
CARDS: 🔳   £

Selected

🏅 🔾🔾🔾🔾 *The Crown Hotel* 8 High St PO10 7TW ☎01243 372806 FAX 01243 370082
This popular inn is situated in the pretty little town of Emsworth, just a short walk from the quay, convenient for the coast and only five miles from Chichester. The bedrooms offer comfortable and well equipped accommodation, whilst retaining a lot of their original character. All rooms have trouser presses, hairdryers and satellite television; most also have en suite facilities. There is a cosy restaurant where all meals are served from an interesting and carefully prepared menu.
9 rms (7 bth/shr) (1 fmly) CTV in all bedrooms Tea and coffee making facilities Direct dial from bedrooms Cen ht 30P Last d 9.30pm
CARDS: 🔳

EPSOM Surrey Map **04** TQ26

GH 🔾🔾 *Epsom Downs Hotel* 9 Longdown Rd KT17 3PT ☎01372 740643 FAX 01372 723259
This hotel is quietly located in a residential area off the Alexandra Road, close to its junction with College Road. It offers a range of modern bedrooms, each well equipped with direct dial phone, TV and beverage-making facilities. The smart open-plan public areas

include a comfortable bar and an attractive dining room where dinner is available to both residents and non-residents from Monday to Saturday. Service is informal, there is ample car parking space, and conferences or functions can be catered for.
14 rms (3 bth 9 shr) CTV in all bedrooms Tea and coffee making facilities Direct dial from bedrooms No dogs Licensed Cen ht CTV 11P Last d 9pm
CARDS: 🔳   🔳

GH 🔾🔾🔾 **The White House** Downs Hill Rd KT18 5HW ☎01372 722472 FAX 01372 744447
Comfortable, well equipped accommodation is offered at this well maintained Victorian house, which is set back off the road in an attractive garden. A number of bedrooms have been upgraded with modern furniture and many have en suite facilities. A short, reasonably priced carte of plain English cooking is offered in the spacious dining room, and a choice is also available at breakfast.
15 rms (4 bth 3 shr) (1 fmly) No smoking in area of dining room CTV in all bedrooms Tea and coffee making facilities No dogs (ex guide dogs) Licensed Cen ht CTV 15P Last d 8.30pm
PRICE GUIDE
ROOMS: s £36-£49.50; d £49.50-£69.50
CARDS: 🔳   £
See advertisement on p.171.

ERLESTOKE Wiltshire Map **03** ST95

♥ 🔾🔾🔾 Mrs P Hampton **Longwater Park** *(ST966541)* Lower Rd SN10 5UE (turn off A360 at West Lavington onto B3908 for 3m, in Erlestoke village turn right by post office signed Marston/Worton,Longwater is 400yds on right) ☎01380 830095 FAX 01380 830095
Closed Xmas & New Year

Detached from the organically managed farm, this modern brick farmhouse overlooks parkland and lakes. The larger lake can be fished, while the smaller is set aside for waterfowl. Rooms are split between the main house and a separate building; all are comfortably furnished. There are an attractive lounge and conservatory. Organically produced ingredients are used wherever possible in the preparation of meals. Mr and Mrs Hampton encourage guests to be part of the family, which includes four cats.
3 en suite (bth/shr) 2 annexe en suite (bth/shr) (1 fmly) No smoking in bedrooms No smoking in dining room No smoking in 1 lounge CTV in all bedrooms Tea and coffee making facilities Licensed Cen ht CTV No children 12yrs 6P Fishing 166 acres beef waterfowl organic Last d 5pm
PRICE GUIDE
ROOMS: s £25.50; d £41; wkly b&b £133-£163; wkly hlf-bd £206-£236

£

ESCRICK North Yorkshire Map **08** SE64

GH 🔲🔲🔲 *Church Cottage* YO4 6EX
☎01904 728462 FAX 01904 728462
Church Cottage is situated in the village of Escrick to the south of York. It is an attractive house which has been carefully extended and furnished. All the bedrooms now have en suite facilities and a new residents' lounge was under construction at the time of our last visit.
7 rms (6 shr) (3 fmly) CTV in all bedrooms Tea and coffee making facilities No dogs (ex guide dogs) Licensed Cen ht 20P 9 hole garden putting Last d 8pm
CARDS: 🔳 🔳
See advertisement under YORK

🔳 🔲🔲🔲 *Black Bull Inn* Main St YO4 6JP
☎01904 728245 & 728154
This well furnished inn is close to the village centre, just of the A19 to the south of York. There is a wide choice of value-for-money food, and bedrooms are bright and modern with good facilities. The atmosphere in the bar is friendly and real ale is available.
8 en suite (bth/shr) (1 fmly) CTV in all bedrooms Tea and coffee making facilities Cen ht 15P No coaches Riding Last d 10pm
CARDS: 🔳 🔳
See advertisement under YORK

ETTINGTON Warwickshire Map **04** SP24

🔳🔳 ♥ 🔲🔲 Mrs B J Wakeham **Whitfield** *(SP265506)*
CV37 7PN (on A429, 1m from Ettington) ☎01789 740260
Closed Dec
A long driveway off the A429 north of the village leads to this spacious family farmhouse offering quiet, well maintained accommodation with friendly hosts; one bedroom is located on the ground floor. The house is set amongst 220 acres of mainly arable land, seven miles from Stratford-upon-Avon.
3 rms (2 shr) (1 fmly) No smoking in dining room Tea and coffee making facilities No dogs (ex guide dogs) Cen ht CTV 3P 220 acres mixed
PRICE GUIDE
ROOMS: s £14.50-£18; d £28-£33

£

Our inspectors never book in the name of the AA. They disclose their identity only after the bill has been paid.

EVERSHOT Dorset Map **03** ST50

Selected

GH 🔲🔲🔲🔲 **Rectory House** Fore St DT2 0JW (1.5m off A37 Yeovil to Dorchester rd)
☎01935 83273 FAX 01935 83273
Closed Dec
Situated in the centre of the picturesque village, this handsome stone-built house dates back to the 18th century and offers elegant accommodation. There are two spacious bedrooms in the main house and four other rooms, equally pretty, in a converted stable block. Thoughtful extras such as toiletries, fresh flowers and magazines are provided. Breakfast and dinner are served at a magnificent dining table, and the emphasis is on excellent home cooking and local ingredients. Two comfortable lounges are also provided.
6 en suite (bth/shr) No smoking in bedrooms No smoking in dining room No smoking in 1 lounge CTV in all bedrooms Tea and coffee making facilities No dogs (ex guide dogs) Licensed Cen ht TV No children 10yrs 6P No coaches Last d 7pm
PRICE GUIDE
ROOMS: s £30-£60; d £56-£75; wkly b&b £175-£210; wkly hlf-bd £245-£270
CARDS: 🔳 🔳
See advertisement under DORCHESTER

£

EVESHAM Hereford & Worcester Map **04** SP04

GH 🔲🔲🔲 **Church House** Greenhill Park Rd WR11 4NL
☎01386 40498
This large, attractive, Victorian house is set back off the A435 in a residential area close to the town centre. Owners Veronica and Michael Shaw create a very hospitable country house atmosphere, with an abundance of antiques and family mementoes. Cosy, bright and prettily decorated bedrooms are well equipped and furnished with good quality fabrics and period dressing tables and wardrobes. A substantial breakfast is served at the large, ornate table in the dining room, and the proprietors have a good knowledge of local restaurants and pubs for dinner.
3 en suite (bth/shr) (1 fmly) No smoking in dining room CTV in all bedrooms Tea and coffee making facilities Cen ht 3P No coaches
PRICE GUIDE
ROOMS: s £30-£35; d £38-£45

GH 🔲🔲🔲 **The Croft** 54 Greenhill WR11 4NF (0.5m on A435) ☎01386 446035
Set back within very attractive gardens, this substantial detached Georgian house offers spacious, comfortable bedrooms with a country house atmosphere. Boldly decorated public rooms are well stocked with books, magazines and games. Guests share a communal table in the elegant breakfast room, and the guest house is conveniently positioned close to the town centre.
3 rms (2 bth/shr) (1 fmly) No smoking in dining room CTV in all bedrooms Tea and coffee making facilities Cen ht CTV 6P No coaches
PRICE GUIDE
ROOMS: s £30-£35; d £38-£46✱

£

GH 🔲🔲 **Park View** Waterside WR11 6BS (0.25m SE on B4035) ☎01386 442639
Closed 22 Dec-6 Jan
Positioned overlooking the river and park, this busy guesthouse has spacious public rooms. Bedrooms are more modestly

furnished and offer budget accommodation.
26 rms (2 fmly) No smoking in dining room Licensed CTV
40P Last d 7pm
PRICE GUIDE
ROOMS: s £18.50-£22; d £34-£39
CARDS: £

EWELL Surrey Map **04** TQ26

GH Q Q **Nonsuch Park Hotel** 355/357 London Rd KT17 2DE
(on A24) ☎0181 393 0771 FAX 0181 393 1415
Situated on the A24, two miles from Epsom, this small, family-run
hotel has been completely refurbished. Bedrooms, some of which
are en suite, are equipped with direct dial telephones, TVs and
tea/coffee making facilities. The small lounge is comfortable, and
a carte dinner is served in the spacious dining room. There is a
patio for warmer weather and plenty of car parking space.
11 rms (2 bth 4 shr) (1 fmly) No smoking in dining room No
smoking in lounges CTV in all bedrooms Tea and coffee making
facilities Direct dial from bedrooms No dogs (ex guide dogs)
Licensed Cen ht CTV 11P Last d 9pm
PRICE GUIDE
ROOMS: s £36.50-£47; d £53-£57
CARDS: 🔳 🔳 £
See advertisement under EPSOM

EXETER Devon Map **03** SX99

See also Kenton, Starcross & Tedburn St Mary

GH Q **Braeside** 21 New North Rd EX4 4HF ☎01392 56875
Braeside is close to both the university and the city centre. The
seven bedrooms are spread over three floors and several have
shower cubicles. Breakfast is served in the attractive pine-
furnished dining room. Parking is limited to public car parks or
the road outside.
7 rms (3 shr) (1 fmly) No smoking in dining room CTV in all
bedrooms Tea and coffee making facilities Cen ht No parking
No coaches Last d 4pm
PRICE GUIDE
ROOMS: s £17-£20; d £29-£31; wkly b&b fr £119; wkly hlf-bd
fr £161
CARDS: 🔳 🔳 🔳

Selected

GH Q Q Q Q **The Edwardian** 30/32 Heavitree Rd
EX1 2LQ ☎01392 76102 & 54699
FAX 01392 76102 & 54699
Closed Xmas
Two Edwardian terraced houses have been converted to create
this guest house run by resident proprietors Michael and Kay
Rattenbury. The bedrooms are tastefully decorated and
furnished in period style, featuring the original fireplaces,
dried flowers and old local prints; several rooms have antique
furniture. Books and games are provided in the cosy lounge,
and breakfast is served in two adjoining dining rooms . Menus
from local restaurants are available, together with advice on
where to eat in the evenings. Private parking is limited but
there is a large public car park nearby.
14 rms (12 bth/shr) (1 fmly) No smoking in dining room
CTV in all bedrooms Tea and coffee making facilities Direct
dial from bedrooms Cen ht CTV 5P
PRICE GUIDE
ROOMS: s £22-£32; d £42-£46
CARDS: 🔳 🔳 🔳 £

GH Q Q Q **Hotel Gledhills** 32 Alphington Rd EX2 8HN
☎01392 430469 & 71439 FAX 01392 430469
Closed 2 wks Xmas/New Year
The Gledhills is an attractive red brick Victorian licensed hotel,
situated conveniently close to the shops, leisure centre and
Exeter's famous quay. The comfortable bedrooms have been
furnished with modern pieces and equipped with a range of
facilities. Charming hosts David and Suzanne Greening maintain
high standards and are rewarded by a large number of returning
guests. There is a sunny breakfast room, a cosy bar where a wide
variety of home cooked snacks is served, and a large rear car park.
12 rms (11 shr) (4 fmly) No smoking in dining room CTV in all
bedrooms Tea and coffee making facilities No dogs Licensed
Cen ht CTV 13P No coaches Last d 8pm
PRICE GUIDE
ROOMS: s £20-£28.50; d £40-£43; wkly b&b £132-£165✳
CARDS: 🔳 🔳 🔳 🔳

GH Q Q **Park View Hotel** 8 Howell Rd EX4 4LG (from M5
follow signs B3183 City Centre until you reach the clock
tower roundabout, 3rd exit Elm Grove at end of road T junct,
turn left Howell Road) ☎01392 71772 FAX 01392 53047
The Park View Hotel is located in a particularly quiet and
attractive residential area of town, yet close to the city centre,
station and university. It is a Grade II listed house with bright
accommodation on three floors. There are a comfortable lounge
with floor-to-ceiling windows and an attractive breakfast room
leading out to the rear garden and patio area.
15 rms (2 bth 7 shr) (2 fmly) No smoking in 1 bedrooms No
smoking in dining room CTV in all bedrooms Tea and coffee

The
White House Hotel

Downs Hill Road, Epsom,
Surrey KT18 5HW
Tel: (01372) 722472 Fax: (01372) 744447

ETB 🛏 🛏 🛏

✳ Situated ½ mile from Epsom Downs,
3 miles from M25

✳ Single & double rooms — most en suite
✳ Full English breakfast

✳ Weekend rates

making facilities Direct dial from bedrooms Cen ht CTV 6P
Swings Slide
PRICE GUIDE
ROOMS: s £20-£28; d £35-£43; wkly b&b £126-£182
CARDS: £

GH Ⓠ Ⓠ **Sunnymede** 24 New North Rd EX4 4HF
☎01392 73844
Closed 1 wk at Xmas
A city-centre guest house, Sunnymead is close to the university
and the main shopping area. The bedroooms are on three floors
and all have either en suite shower rooms or shower cubicles in
the rooms. Breakfast is served at separate tables in the dining
room, which is part conservatory. Parking is limited to public car
parks or to the road outside.
9 rms (5 shr) (1 fmly) No smoking in dining room CTV in all
bedrooms Tea and coffee making facilities No dogs Cen ht CTV
No parking No coaches Last d 9pm
PRICE GUIDE
ROOMS: s £16-£22; d £30-£32✳

[➡️ ⬛] **GH** Ⓠ **Telstar Hotel** 77 St Davids Hill EX4 4DW
☎01392 72466
A small, family-run guest house stands in a terrace of small hotels,
close to the university, station and city centre. Bedrooms are
comfortable, and the friendly proprietors serve breakfast in an
attractive dining room.
9 rms (1 fmly) No smoking in dining room Tea and coffee
making facilities Cen ht CTV 8P
PRICE GUIDE
ROOMS: s £14-£16; d £26-£40 £

GH Ⓠ Ⓠ *Trees Mini Hotel* 2 Queen's Crescent, York Rd
EX4 6AY ☎01392 59531
A family-run guest house, close to all the amenities and just a
short walk from the city centre, offers simple, comfortable
bedrooms. There is a quiet lounge, and a set evening meal is now
available in the dining room. Devonshire hospitality comes
naturally to the resident proprietors.
10 rms (1 bth) 2 annexe rms (1 fmly) CTV in all bedrooms Tea
and coffee making facilities No dogs Cen ht CTV 1P No
coaches Last d 10am
CARDS:

Selected

♥ Ⓠ Ⓠ Ⓠ Ⓠ Mrs S Glanvill **Rydon** *(SX999871)* Woodbury
EX5 1LB (B3179 to village and on entering village turn
right 10 yds before 30mph sign. Signposted)
☎01395 232341
The land round this charming Devon longhouse, down a 13th-
century country lane, has been farmed by the Glanvill family
for generations. Three large bedrooms are available for
guests' use, two with delightfully decorated bathrooms and
one with a beautifully draped four-poster bed. The
comfortable lounge has a colour television as well as various
board games, and there is a sunny dining room with separate
tables. Free-range eggs from the farm are part of the
traditional breakfast.
3 rms (2 bth) (1 fmly) No smoking in dining room Tea and
coffee making facilities Cen ht CTV 3P 280 acres dairy
PRICE GUIDE
ROOMS: s £17-£25; d £32-£44; wkly b&b
£112-£140✳ £

EYE Suffolk Map **05** TM17

◀ Ⓠ Ⓠ Ⓠ **Four Horseshoes** Wickham Rd, Thornham Magna
IP23 7HD ☎01379 678777 FAX 01379 678134
This is a charming thatched inn, located at a road junction in the
countryside. The low ceiling adds atmosphere to the various eating
areas, and there is an exposed deep-water well in one area.
Accommodation is modern in style but also retains the character
of the establishment.
8 rms (2 bth 5 shr) (1 fmly) No smoking in area of dining room
CTV in all bedrooms Tea and coffee making facilities Direct dial
from bedrooms Cen ht 120P Last d 10pm
PRICE GUIDE
ROOMS: s £35; d £50; wkly b&b £200-£300✳
CARDS: £

◀ Ⓠ Ⓠ Ⓠ **The White Horse** Stoke Ash IP23 7ET (on the
A140 between Ipswich/Norwich)
☎01379 678222 FAX 01379 678557
Spacious, comfortable bedrooms, furnished in up-to-date style and
suitably equipped, are provided in the modern annexe of this hotel.
A restaurant occupying two floors of the main building serves
everything from a light snack to a full three-course meal - all
dishes being freshly prepared; advance booking is recommended
for dinner.
7 annexe en suite (bth) CTV in all bedrooms Tea and coffee
making facilities Direct dial from bedrooms No dogs (ex guide
dogs) Cen ht 60P Last d 9.30pm
PRICE GUIDE
ROOMS: s fr £30; d fr £45✳
CARDS: £

EYNSFORD Kent Map **05** TQ56

Premier Selected

♥ Ⓠ Ⓠ Ⓠ Ⓠ Ⓠ Mrs Sarah
Alexander **Home Farm**
(TQ537656) Riverside
DA4 0AE ☎01322 866193
FAX 01322 868600
Mar-Nov
This delightful 18th-century
farmhouse in Queen Anne
style is located off the A225
to Sevenoaks, close to the
centre of the village and
overlooking the Darent
Valley. Personally run, it offers a very relaxed atmosphere,
with tea on arrival. The spacious lounge on the first floor has
TV and a grand piano, and there is a delightful beamed
breakfast room on the ground floor where guests enjoy a
freshly cooked and very tasty English breakfast. Bedrooms
are tastefully furnished and equipped, and there are three
gardens and 1000 acres of working grain farm.
3 en suite (bth/shr) No smoking Tea and coffee making
facilities No dogs (ex guide dogs) Cen ht CTV No children
12yrs 4P 850 acres arable

EYNSHAM Oxfordshire Map **04** SP40

GH Ⓠ Ⓠ Ⓠ *All Views* Main A40 OX8 1PU ☎01865 880891
Situated on the A40, this guest house is a modern chalet-style
bungalow which forms an integral part of the thriving nursery and
farm shop business operated by the Thomas family. The bedrooms
have excellent en suite bathrooms. There are also a breakfast room
and a comfortable lounge with a wood burning stove.

4 en suite (bth/shr) No smoking in dining room No smoking in lounges CTV in all bedrooms Tea and coffee making facilities Direct dial from bedrooms No dogs (ex guide dogs) Cen ht CTV No children 10yrs 10P No coaches

---

FAKENHAM Norfolk Map **09** TF92

See also Barney

◀ QQQ **Sculthorpe Mill** Lynn Rd, Sculthorpe NR21 9QG (2m SW, off A148, signposted)
☎01328 856161 & 862675 FAX 01328 856651
The completely refurbished bedrooms contain free standing cherry wood furniture and modern amenities. The ex water mill, commanding a scenic stream-side location, is licensed and offers a range of eating options in a choice of dining rooms.
6 en suite (bth/shr) (1 fmly) No smoking in 2 bedrooms CTV in all bedrooms Tea and coffee making facilities Direct dial from bedrooms Cen ht 60P Fishing Last d 9.30pm
PRICE GUIDE
ROOMS: s £35; d £55-£65; wkly b&b £140-£175; wkly hlf-bd £220-£275✳
MEALS: Lunch £11.95-£14.95&alc Dinner £11.95-£14.95&alc✳
CARDS: 🟦 💳 💳

FALFIELD Avon Map **03** ST69

GH QQ **Green Farm** GL12 8DL (1m N of village centre)
☎01454 260319
A 16th-century stone-built farmhouse with a pretty garden and ample parking space, this establishment offers basic country accommodation in comfortable bedrooms - some of them with lovely rural views. Cosy wood-burning stoves warm the large TV lounge and the flagstoned dining room where dinner is served ➡

THE WHITE HORSE INN
Stoke Ash, Eye, Suffolk IP23 7ET

A 17th Century Coaching Inn & Motel. A heavily timbered building inglenook fireplaces and friendly atmosphere.
In the grounds is a newly built Chalet Style Motel. Consisting of 3 Twin 4 Double spacious bedrooms all are en suite and have remote control colour television, direct dial telephone, tea/coffee making facilities.

Telephone: 01379 678 222

The Four Horseshoes Country Inn and Hotel
Thornham Magna, nr. Eye, Suffolk IP23 7HD
Telephone: 01379-678777 Fax: 01379-678134

A delightful 12th century thatched inn in a beautiful yet accessible part of Suffolk. The heavily beamed bar and restaurant areas serve real ales and a wide range of meals from bar snacks to à la carte. The wishing well adds to the enchanting atmosphere, with 8 en suite bedrooms and an attractive garden area there is something for everyone.

AA QQQ

Sculthorpe, nr. Fakenham, Norfolk NR21 9QG
Telephone: 01328 856161
Fax: 01328 856651

A privately owned 18th century listed watermill, situated just two miles from the market town of Fakenham and a ¼ mile off the A148. The building has recently undergone an extensive yet sympathetic renovation programme. Six well appointed, individual en suite bedrooms all with superb views, including one four poster suite. The oak beamed restaurant overlooks the river and provides a comprehensive menu complemented by a well balanced selection of fine wines also an excellent choice of bar food. Relax and unwind in the most idyllic surroundings. Ideally positioned as a base from which to explore the area.
Open all year and all day.

from an extensive menu of home-cooked fare. Well sited for the M4, the M5 and the cities of Bristol and Bath, the house also provides an ideal base from which to explore the Cotswolds.

7 rms No smoking in bedrooms Tea and coffee making facilities Cen ht CTV 10P No coaches Outdoor swimming pool Tennis (hard) Last d 8.30pm

PRICE GUIDE
ROOMS: s fr £20; d fr £32✳

FALMOUTH Cornwall & Isles of Scilly Map **02** SW83

GH 🇶🇶🇶 **Cotswold House Hotel** Melvill Rd TR11 4DF
☎01326 312077

Pamela and Graham Cain's small hotel is conveniently located just a few minutes' walk from the town centre, harbour and beach. It has limited on-site parking and a small sunny garden. Bedrooms are attractively co-ordinated and well equipped. A cosy bar and a comfortable lounge are provided for guests, and at dinner a choice of traditional dishes and salads is offered.

10 rms (9 bth/shr) (2 fmly) No smoking in dining room CTV in all bedrooms Tea and coffee making facilities No dogs Licensed No children 4yrs 10P Last d 7pm

PRICE GUIDE
ROOMS: s £18; d £36; wkly b&b £125; wkly hlf-bd £170

🚪🖥 **GH** 🇶🇶🇶 **Dolvean Hotel** 50 Melvill Rd TR11 4DQ
☎01326 313658

Paul and Carol Crocker have worked hard over the last twelve months to improve this comfortable Victorian hotel. A new family suite has been created on the ground floor as well as additional en suite facilities to other rooms. Several of the rooms have been totally redecorated and further work is planned. The spacious dining room is cheerfully decorated and evening meals are available by arrangement.

12 rms (6 bth 3 shr) (1 fmly) No smoking in dining room CTV in all bedrooms Tea and coffee making facilities No dogs (ex guide dogs) Licensed Cen ht CTV No children 2yrs 8P No coaches Last d 5.30pm

PRICE GUIDE
ROOMS: s £16-£20; d £32-£40
CARDS: 🔲 🔲 🔲

GH 🇶🇶🇶 **Harbour House** 1 Harbour Ter TR11 2AN
☎01326 311344

Mar-Dec

From its elevated position, overlooking the whole of the Carricks Roads estuary, Harbour House is conveniently located for the town, the beaches, yacht club and the ferries to St Mawes. The house has under gone extensive refurbishment, since young owners Celia and Ian Carruthers took over late in 1993. The bedrooms are comfortable and well equipped. In the simply furnished breakfast room, a varied menu is offered, packed lunches can be provided by arrangement. Facilities for storage and drying of sailing and diving equipment are available. It is planned to create private parking at the rear of the property during the winter of 1995/6.

6 rms (3 shr) (1 fmly) No smoking in bedrooms No smoking in dining room CTV in all bedrooms Tea and coffee making facilities No dogs Cen ht No parking

PRICE GUIDE
ROOMS: s £14-£16.50; d £28-£37✳

🚪🖥 **GH** 🇶🇶🇶 **Ivanhoe** 7 Melvill Rd TR11 4AS (follow signs Docks & Beach) ☎01326 319083

This family run guest house stands in an Edwardian terrace between the town centre and beaches. There is a comfortable lounge downstairs, and well kept bedrooms on the two floors above vary in size and headroom, but all are brightly decorated and have colourful duvets.

---

7 rms (4 shr) (2 fmly) No smoking in dining room CTV in all bedrooms Tea and coffee making facilities No dogs Cen ht CTV 4P No coaches

PRICE GUIDE
ROOMS: s £14-£18; d £28-£36
CARDS: 🔲 🔲 🔲 🔲

GH 🇶🇶🇶 **Melvill House Hotel** 52 Melvill Rd TR11 4DQ
☎01326 316645 FAX 01326 211608

Closed 23 -31 Dec

In a good position above the main town centre and yet still within easy walking distance of the harbour and beaches, this pink semi-detached guest house provides seven attractive bedrooms, each with private facilities. A choice is available at breakfast and a set four-course evening meal is served in the prettily decorated dining room. Stripped pine shutters in all the ground floor rooms, including the comfortable lounge, are a particular feature.

7 en suite (bth/shr) (3 fmly) CTV in all bedrooms Tea and coffee making facilities No dogs Licensed Cen ht CTV No children 7yrs 9P Last d 5.30pm

PRICE GUIDE
ROOMS: s £18.50-£24; d £33-£38; wkly b&b £105-£125; wkly hlf-bd £145-£165   £

Selected

GH 🇶🇶🇶🇶 **Penmere** "Rosehill", Mylor Bridge
TR11 5LZ ☎01326 374470

A large, detached, stone-built property built in 1862 stands on the edge of the village of Mylor Bridge, looking over its own neat gardens to the creek beyond. Lovingly restored by owners Ron and Ann Thomas, it is popular with the sailing fraternity, not least because they are both keen sailors - Ron being a qualified RYA instructor. The rooms are charmingly decorated with co-ordinating Laura Ashley soft furnishings, pine furniture and dried flowers, the style in keeping with their original period features. A sunny breakfast room and adjoining lounge - both with open fires and comfortable sofas - contain plenty of local information; smoking is not permitted in the open-plan dining room/lounge.

6 rms (4 bth/shr) (2 fmly) No smoking in dining room No smoking in lounges CTV in all bedrooms Tea and coffee making facilities No dogs (ex guide dogs) Cen ht 7P No coaches

---

Premier Selected

GH 🇶🇶🇶🇶🇶 **Prospect House** 1 Church Rd, Penryn TR10 8DA (on B3292 opposite Kessell's Volvo showroom do not follow town centre signs)
☎01326 373198
FAX 01326 373198

Barry Sheppard and Cliff Paul offer a house-party atmosphere at their Victorian property, which is situated some two miles from the centre of Falmouth. Many original features have been retained, including mahogany doors, coloured glass and elaborately painted plaster cornices. The comfortable, antique-furnished bedrooms offer extras such as chocolates and teddies, and on the first floor guests can help themselves to tea, coffee,

chocolate, orange juice and mineral water from a small pantry. Dinner is available by arrangement, chosen from a set menu served at one large table.
3 en suite (bth/shr) No smoking in dining room TV available Tea and coffee making facilities Cen ht CTV No children 12yrs 5P No coaches Last d 10am
PRICE GUIDE
ROOMS: s £28-£33; d £47-£53; wkly b&b £150-£168; wkly hlf-bd £275-£295

Selected

GH QQQQ **Rosemary Hotel** 22 Gyllyngvase Ter TR11 4DL ☎01326 314669
Apr-Nov
This cosy, family-run guest house stands close to both the town centre and beaches.
10 en suite (bth/shr) (2 fmly) No smoking in 5 bedrooms No smoking in dining room CTV in all bedrooms Tea and coffee making facilities No dogs Licensed Cen ht CTV 4P No coaches Last d 6.30pm
PRICE GUIDE
ROOMS: s £16.50-£19.50; d £33-£39; wkly b&b £109-£129; wkly hlf-bd £142-£169

GH QQQ **San Remo Hotel** Gyllyngvase Hill TR11 4DN (from Melville Rd turn rt down Gyllyngvase Hill) ☎01326 312076
Etr-Oct
The San Remo is situated close to Gyllyngvase beach, within walking distance of the town centre, harbour and port. The well maintained bedrooms are pleasantly decorated and furnished; several have views of the sea and three rooms are on the ground floor. The lounge is comfortable and a three-course evening meal is served in the cheerful dining room. Private car parking is available.
10 rms (8 bth/shr) (1 fmly) No smoking in dining room CTV in all bedrooms Tea and coffee making facilities No dogs (ex guide dogs) No children 5yrs 10P No coaches Last d 6pm
PRICE GUIDE
ROOMS: s £19-£22; d £38-£44; wkly b&b £125-£145; wkly hlf-bd £150-£175

GH QQQ **Treggenna** 28 Melvill Rd TR11 4AR (A39 for Falmouth docks) ☎01326 313881
With easy access to the beaches and the town centre, this property is neatly decorated and furnished throughout. The bedrooms vary in size, and there are a dining room, lounge and cosy bar.
5 rms (4 shr) (2 fmly) No smoking in 2 bedrooms No smoking in dining room No smoking in 1 lounge CTV in 6 bedrooms Tea and coffee making facilities Licensed Cen ht CTV 8P No coaches Last d 10am
PRICE GUIDE
ROOMS: s £16-£17.50; d £32-£34; wkly b&b £110-£120; wkly hlf-bd £150-£160✳

GH QQQ **Trelawney** 6 Melvill Rd TR11 4AS ☎01326 311858
Conveniently situated midway between the town centre and the beaches, this guest house is personally run by Ann and Colin Mackenzie. Bedrooms are well equipped and maintained to a high standard. Breakfast is served in the attractively decorated dining room.

6 rms (4 shr) (2 fmly) No smoking in dining room No smoking in lounges CTV in all bedrooms Tea and coffee making facilities Cen ht CTV 3P No coaches
PRICE GUIDE
ROOMS: s £14-£15; d £32-£34; wkly b&b £100-£110✳
CARDS: 🔳 💳

Selected

GH QQQQ *Westcott Hotel* Gyllyngvase Hill TR11 4DN (follow signs to beach) ☎01326 311309
3 Jan-Oct rs Jan-Mar
Bill and Sandra Ridden enjoy welcoming guests to their well maintained hotel, which is close to the beach and within walking distance of the town. Several of the bedrooms have sea views, and all are comfortable and well equipped. A lounge and an elegant dining room are provided. Dinner is available, with a choice of dishes, and a varied selection is also offered at breakfast.
10 en suite (bth/shr) 1 annexe en suite (bth) (2 fmly) No smoking in bedrooms No smoking in dining room CTV in all bedrooms Tea and coffee making facilities No dogs Licensed Cen ht CTV No children 5yrs 11P No coaches Last d 6pm

FALSTONE Northumberland Map **12** NY78

◀ QQQ **Pheasant** Stannersburn NE48 1DD ☎01434 240382 FAX 01434 240024
Closed 25-26 Dec rs Jan-Feb
Set in the Northumberland National Park just one mile from Kielder Water reservoir, this delightful country inn retains the character of a village pub whilst providing modern accommodation. Originally a farm house, it features stone walls and low beamed ceilings in bars which are adorned with brasses and bric-á-brac, and home-cooked meals are served either here or in a cosy pine-furnished dining room. The courtyard bedrooms - five of them on the ground floor and three upstairs - all have first-class shower rooms and external access.
8 annexe en suite (shr) (1 fmly) No smoking in bedrooms No smoking in dining room No smoking in lounges CTV in all bedrooms Tea and coffee making facilities Cen ht 40P No coaches Pool room Darts Last d 8.50pm
PRICE GUIDE
ROOMS: s £20-£30; d £40-£52; wkly b&b £140-£210
MEALS: Lunch £5.75-£6.50alc Dinner £10-£15.95alc
CARDS: 🔳 💳

FAREHAM Hampshire Map **04** SU50

Selected

GH QQQQ **Avenue House Hotel** 22 The Avenue PO14 1NS (Logis) ☎01329 232175 FAX 01329 232196
This smart family-run hotel is conveniently located on the A27 west of the town centre. The rooms are furnished and equipped to a high standard and provide bathrobes as well as direct-dial telephones, colour televisions and full en suite facilities. There are also a four-poster room, and some ground floor rooms. The lounge overlooks the garden and is equipped with local information, books and a 'tuck shop'. Ample parking space is provided.
17 en suite (bth/shr) (3 fmly) No smoking in 4 bedrooms CTV in all bedrooms Tea and coffee making facilities Direct ➡

dial from bedrooms Cen ht 19P
PRICE GUIDE
ROOMS: s £29.50-£45; d £39.50-£55✳
CARDS:

FARINGDON Oxfordshire Map **04** SU29

GH **Q Q Q** **Faringdon Hotel** Market Place SN7 7HL
☎01367 240536 FAX 01367 243250
A large building in the centre of town near the church, the
Faringdon's rooms, some in an annexe overlooking a small
courtyard, have excellent facilities, including satellite TV. There is
a fully licensed bar and the restaurant offers a short menu of
appetising dishes.
15 en suite (bth/shr) 5 annexe en suite (bth/shr) (3 fmly) CTV in
all bedrooms Tea and coffee making facilities Direct dial from
bedrooms Licensed Cen ht 5P No coaches Last d 9pm
PRICE GUIDE
ROOMS: s £46.50; d £56.50✳
CARDS:

FARMBOROUGH Avon Map **03** ST66

GH **Q Q Q** **Streets Hotel** The Street BA3 1AR
☎01761 471452 FAX 01761 471452
Closed 20 Dec-1 Jan
This small, private hotel is ideally situated between Wells and
Bath in the pretty village of Farmborough. The comfortable
bedrooms, some of which are situated in the coach house
immediately adjacent to the main house, are all en suite, well
equipped and include rooms with four-poster beds. There are a
choice of lounges, including a conservatory and a spacious
beamed lounge which is comfortably furnished and warmed by an
open fire in the winter. Breakfast (and dinner by prior
arrangement) are served in the attractive dining room and guests
also have the use of the gardens and heated outdoor swimming
pool.
3 en suite (bth/shr) 5 annexe en suite (bth/shr) CTV in all
bedrooms Tea and coffee making facilities Direct dial from
bedrooms No dogs Licensed Cen ht CTV No children 6yrs
10P No coaches Outdoor swimming pool (heated) Solarium
Last d 8.50pm
PRICE GUIDE
ROOMS: s fr £46; d fr £56✳
CARDS:

FAR SAWREY Cumbria Map **07** SD39

Selected

GH **Q Q Q Q** **West Vale Country** LA22 0LQ (2.75m
from Hawkshead on B5285) ☎015394 42817
Mar-Oct
A family-run guest house situated on the edge of the village
with superb open views of surrounding meadowland and hills.
It is built of lakeland stone and stands in its own neat gardens
in an area well known for its association with Beatrix Potter.
Bedrooms are comfortably furnished and most have private
showers. A spacious lounge extends from the front to the back
of the hotel and has an open log fire, and the dining room also
enjoys fine views. Enjoyable home-cooked evening meals are
provided, and service is friendly.
8 en suite (bth/shr) (3 fmly) No smoking in dining room Tea
and coffee making facilities No dogs (ex guide dogs)

Licensed Cen ht CTV No children 7yrs 8P No coaches
Coarse & trout fishing Last d 4pm
PRICE GUIDE
ROOMS: s £22; d £44; wkly hlf-bd fr £210

FAVERSHAM Kent Map **05** TR06

Selected

❤ **Q Q Q Q** Mrs S Chesterfield **Frith** *(TQ944555)*
Otterden ME13 0DD ☎01795 890701 FAX 01795 890009
A delightful late-Georgian farmhouse set in two acres of
attractive gardens and four acres of orchard has been carefully
furnished and decorated to retain its original charm. The three
spacious en suite bedrooms are well-equipped and furnished
with period furniture. Fine pictures and ornaments adorn the
comfortable sitting room which is filled with books and
magazines. A traditional English evening meal prepared using
fresh produce is served on a large wooden communal table, as
is a choice of breakfast.
3 en suite (shr) No smoking CTV in all bedrooms Tea and
coffee making facilities No dogs Cen ht No children 10yrs
12P Riding Carriage rides 6 acres non-working
PRICE GUIDE
ROOMS: s £25-£30; d £47-£54
CARDS:

◄ **Q Q Q** **White Horse** The Street, Boughton ME13 9AX
☎01227 751343 FAX 01227 751090
Dating back to the 15th-century, this inn provides a good standard
of accommodation in reasonably sized rooms which are furnished
in keeping with the style of the building. There are two bars and a
restaurant, where a menu of home made pies and grills is served.
A reasonable choice of popular, inexpensive wines is also
available.
13 en suite (bth/shr) (2 fmly) CTV in all bedrooms Tea and
coffee making facilities Direct dial from bedrooms Cen ht CTV
35P Last d 9.30pm
CARDS:

FAZELEY Staffordshire Map **04** SK20

GH **Q Q** **Buxton Hotel** 65 Coleshill St B78 3RG (on A4091 S
of Tamworth, near Drayton Manor Park)
☎01827 285805 & 284842 FAX 01827 285805
Closed 25-26 Dec & New Year
Originally a doctor's residence on the Peel Estate, the house is
situated alongside the A4091 just south of its junction with the
A5. Bedrooms are modestly appointed but all have TV and
telephones. There is an oak panelled bar, the dining room features
an ornately carved wooden fireplace, and the spacious lounge
includes a full size snooker table.
15 rms (4 bth 9 shr) (4 fmly) CTV in all bedrooms Tea and
coffee making facilities Direct dial from bedrooms Licensed
Cen ht CTV 16P No coaches Last d 8.15pm
PRICE GUIDE
ROOMS: s £26-£35; d £33-£39.95✳
CARDS:

FELIXSTOWE Suffolk Map **05** TM33

◄ **Q Q Q** **Fludyer Arms Hotel** Undercliff Rd East IP11 7LU
☎01394 283279 FAX 01394 670754
The needs of families are particularly well met by this seafront
hotel with a separate children's dining room and play area.

Spacious, comfortable bedrooms are furnished to an above-average standard, and a recently extended lounge bar offers a good selection of bar meals.

8 rms (6 bth/shr) (1 fmly) No smoking in area of dining room No smoking in 1 lounge CTV in all bedrooms Tea and coffee making facilities 8P Childrens playroom Last d 9pm

PRICE GUIDE
ROOMS: s £18-£32; d £38-£46✳
MEALS: Bar Lunch £3-£8 Dinner £3-£8✳
CARDS: 🖃 📇 📖

FELTHAM Greater London

For accommodation details see **Heathrow Airport**

FILEY North Yorkshire Map **08** TA18

GH 🇶🇶🇶 **Abbots Leigh** 7 Rutland St YO14 9JA (from A170 follow signs for town centre, then turn right at church clock tower, then second left) ☎01723 513334

Abbots Leigh stands in a quiet side road convenient for the town centre and the seafront. The pretty bedrooms are well equipped and offer many thoughtful little extras. There is a small lounge on the first floor and the dining room serves well cooked breakfasts and dinners.

6 en suite (bth/shr) (3 fmly) No smoking in bedrooms No smoking in dining room CTV in all bedrooms Tea and coffee making facilities No dogs (ex guide dogs) Licensed Cen ht No children 3yrs 4P No coaches Last d 4pm

PRICE GUIDE
ROOMS: s £20-£38; d £36-£52; wkly b&b £98-£113; wkly hlf-bd £154-£169
CARDS: 🖃 📖

Selected

GH 🇶🇶🇶🇶 *Downcliffe House* The Beach YO14 9LA
☎01723 513310 FAX 01723 516141
Mar-Nov

This refurbished Victorian house stands on the seafront overlooking Filey Bay. Bedrooms are comfortable, attractively appointed and well equipped with satellite TV and direct-dial telephones. The lounge bar is comfortable and service is friendly and attentive.

15 rms (4 bth 6 shr) (9 fmly) No smoking in dining room CTV in all bedrooms Tea and coffee making facilities Licensed Cen ht CTV 10P Pool table Last d 6.30pm
CARDS: 🖃 📖

GH 🇶🇶🇶 **Seafield Hotel** 9/11 Rutland St YO14 9JA
☎01723 513715

A family-run guest house stands in a quiet side road convenient for the town centre and the Crescent gardens. The pretty bedrooms are well equipped, the lounge is comfortable and the attractive dining room serves a well produced four-course dinner each evening.

13 rms (3 bth 7 shr) (7 fmly) No smoking in bedrooms No smoking in dining room No smoking in 1 lounge CTV in all bedrooms Tea and coffee making facilities No dogs Licensed Cen ht CTV 8P No coaches Last d 4pm

PRICE GUIDE
ROOMS: s £16.50-£20.50; d £33-£41; wkly b&b £110-£138; wkly hlf-bd £146-£174
CARDS: 🖃 📇 📖

FIR TREE Co Durham Map **12** NZ13

Premier Selected

GH 🇶🇶🇶🇶🇶 **Greenhead Country House Hotel**
DL15 8BL (on A68, turn right at Fir Tree Inn)
☎01388 763143

Conveniently located, this delightful small hotel is set just off the A68. It is superbly furnished and includes a comfortable lounge where exposed stonework adds to the appeal. The bedrooms are well furnished and thoughtfully equipped; one room features a four-poster bed and some rooms are reached by a spiral staircase. Suppers are available and attentive service is provided by the resident owners, Mr and Mrs Birbeck.

8 en suite (bth/shr) (1 fmly) No smoking in 2 bedrooms No smoking in dining room No smoking in 1 lounge CTV in 7 bedrooms Tea and coffee making facilities No dogs (ex guide dogs) Licensed Cen ht CTV No children 13yrs 20P No coaches Last d 5pm

PRICE GUIDE
ROOMS: s £35; d £45-£55; wkly b&b fr £245✳
CARDS: 🖃 📖

FLAX BOURTON Avon Map **03** ST56

◖ 🇶🇶🇶 **Jubilee** Main Rd BS19 3QX ☎01275 462741
Closed 25 Dec evening

A most attractive and very popular roadside inn on the outskirts of Bristol, with ample car parking space on site. The bedrooms offer neat accommodation with some nice extra touches, and there is a spacious guests' lounge on the first floor. Public areas are full of character, with pleasant bars, a log fire and a good range of home-cooked meals.

3 rms Tea and coffee making facilities Cen ht CTV No children 14yrs 51P No coaches Last d 10pm

PRICE GUIDE
ROOMS: s fr £28; d fr £56✳
CARDS: 🖃 📖

FORDINGBRIDGE Hampshire Map **04** SU11

GH 🇶🇶🇶 **Colt Green** Damerham SP6 3HA
☎01725 518240
Closed Jan & Dec

Set in an acre of walled riverside garden, Colt Green offers a tranquil country house environment. The ground-floor rooms are furnished with antiques but provide modern standards of comfort, and the no-smoking bedrooms are all well equipped. A cosy fire warms the lounge, and breakfast and high tea are served in the dining room. A four-course dinner prepared from fresh local ingredients is served at 8pm.

3 rms (1 shr) No smoking Tea and coffee making facilities No dogs (ex guide dogs) Cen ht CTV No children 8yrs 3P No coaches Last d 10am

PRICE GUIDE
ROOMS: s fr £22; d £38-£40✳

FOWEY Cornwall & Isles of Scilly Map **02** SX15

Selected

GH ◘◘◘◘ **Carnethic House** Lambs Barn PL23 1HQ
(off A3082, directly opposite "Welcome to Fowey" sign)
☎01726 833336 FAX 01726 833336
Closed Dec-Jan

This charming Regency manor house, located on the outskirts
of the picturesque harbour village of Fowey, is home to the
Hogg family. Elegantly set in its own beautifully kept
gardens, complete with outdoor heated swimming pool, it is
run as a small and friendly hotel offering comfortable
accommodation. Bedrooms have been equipped with modern
facilities and there is an attractive lounge where guests can
enjoy a drink from the bar. A choice is offered at dinner,
which is an informal affair. Quality ingredients are used to
produce imaginative dishes and locally caught fish is a
speciality.
8 rms (5 shr) (2 fmly) No smoking in 2 bedrooms No
smoking in dining room CTV in all bedrooms Tea and coffee
making facilities Licensed Cen ht ch fac 20P No coaches
Outdoor swimming pool (heated) Tennis (grass) Badminton
Putting Bowls Golf practice net Last d 8pm
PRICE GUIDE
ROOMS: s £30-£40; d £50-£62; wkly b&b £170-£210;
wkly hlf-bd £260-£300
CARDS: 🂠 ■ ➡ ⓪   (£)

GH ◘◘◘ **Trevanion** 70 Lostwithiel St PL23 1BQ
☎01726 832602
Mar-Dec
5 rms (1 fmly) No smoking CTV in all bedrooms Tea and
coffee making facilities No dogs (ex guide dogs) Cen ht No
children 4yrs 3P No coaches
PRICE GUIDE
ROOMS: s £16-£20; d £30-£34; wkly b&b £105-£126✳

GH ◘◘◘ **Wheelhouse** 60 Esplanade PL23 1JA
☎01726 832452
Mar-Oct
There are wonderful views across the estuary to Polruan from the
terrace, dining room and front bedrooms of this Victorian house. A
pleasant sitting room with a collection of houseplants has a small
honesty bar, and the dining room is decorated with an attractive
collection of china. Parking is difficult in Fowey and it is best to
make use of the car parks above the village.
6 rms (2 shr) (1 fmly) No smoking in dining room No smoking
in lounges CTV in 4 bedrooms Tea and coffee making facilities
No dogs Licensed Cen ht No parking No coaches
PRICE GUIDE
ROOMS: s £16-£18.50; d £32-£45; wkly b&b £112-£140✳   (£)

🅵 ◘◘◘ **King of Prussia** Town Quay PL23 1AT (St Austell
Brewery) ☎01726 832450
This pink, quayside inn is named after a local clergyman-cum-
smuggler who operated around Prussia Cove. All six bedrooms
enjoy delightful views across the estuary and have been tastefully
furnished and decorated with co-ordinating colour schemes. The
public bar, on the first floor, shares the beautiful outlook and here
a selection of interesting home-cooked meals and snacks is
offered. A more formal dining operation is available in the
character restaurant downstairs, where breakfast is also served.
6 en suite (bth/shr) (4 fmly) CTV in all bedrooms Tea and coffee

making facilities No dogs (ex guide dogs) Cen ht Last d 9.30pm
PRICE GUIDE
ROOMS: d fr £46; wkly b&b fr £140
MEALS: Bar Lunch £10-£15alc
CARDS: 🂠 ■ ➡

FOWNHOPE Hereford & Worcester Map **03** SO53

GH ◘◘◘ *Bowens Country House* HR1 4PS (6m SE of
Hereford on B4224) ☎01432 860430 FAX 01432 860430
This large stone-built farmhouse dating from the 17th century
retains much of its original character, with features such as the
inglenook fireplace in the lounge. It stands in one-and-a-half acres
of grounds, complete with putting green, opposite the village
church. Bedrooms vary in size and style, some having modern
furniture while others are more traditional; there are four ground-
floor rooms in two separate buildings to the rear. Individual tables
are provided in a cottage-style dining room.
8 rms (3 bth/shr) 4 annexe en suite (bth/shr) (2 fmly) No
smoking in dining room CTV in all bedrooms Tea and coffee
making facilities Licensed Cen ht No children 10yrs 15P No
coaches Tennis (grass) 9 hole putting Last d 8pm
CARDS: 🂠 ➡

FRAMLINGHAM Suffolk Map **05** TM26

💚 ◘◘◘ Mrs A Bater **Church Farm** *(TM605267)* Church Rd,
Kettleburgh IP13 7LF (behind church in Kettleburgh)
☎01728 723532
A 70 acre farm situated in a delightful rural setting. The friendly
owner, Mrs Bater, has a caring approach to her guests. The
spacious bedrooms are comfortably functional and there is a lounge
with a wood burning stove. Dinner is readily provided on request.
3 rms (1 shr) No smoking in bedrooms No smoking in dining
room Tea and coffee making facilities No dogs CTV P Clay
pigeon shooting 70 acres arable mixed Last d 6.30pm
PRICE GUIDE
ROOMS: d £34-£36; wkly b&b £119-£126; wkly hlf-bd £175-
£182   (£)

FRAMPTON ON SEVERN Gloucestershire Map **03** SO70

Premier Selected

GH ◘◘◘◘◘ **Old School
House** Whittles Ln GL2 7EB
(in village, take left turning
through middleof green.
300yds from end of green
turn right into Whittles Lane)
☎01452 740457
Closed 21-31 Dec
This lovely 18th-century
house is tucked away in
Frampton-on-Severn, a
charming Gloucestershire village with interesting houses and
cottages. The Old School House has two spacious bedrooms
beautifully furnished in in keeping with its character. Guests
are assured of warm hospitality and a relaxed atmosphere. A
traditional English breakfast may be enjoyed in the lovely
beamed dining room.
2 en suite (bth/shr) No smoking in bedrooms Tea and coffee
making facilities Cen ht CTV No children 10yrs 10P
PRICE GUIDE
ROOMS: d £40
 (£)

FRATING Essex Map 05 TM02

GH ▣▣▣▣ **Hockley Place** Frating CO7 7HF
☎01206 251703 FAX 01206 251578
Closed 15 Dec-14 Jan
3 en suite (bth/shr) No smoking CTV in all bedrooms Tea and coffee making facilities No dogs Licensed Cen ht CTV No children 12yrs 12P Outdoor swimming pool (heated) Gymnasium
PRICE GUIDE
ROOMS: s fr £30; d £60
CARDS: 🜏 💳

FRESHWATER See WIGHT, ISLE OF

FRESSINGFIELD Suffolk Map 05 TM27

GH ▣▣▣▣ *Chippenhall Hall* IP21 5TD (8m E of Diss on B1116) ☎01379 586733 & 588180
FAX 01379 586272
This listed Tudor manor (a mile south of Fressingfield on the B1116 Framlingham road) traces its history back to Saxon times, and is totally secluded in its seven acres of gardens and ponds. Inside, the rooms have preserved their ancient character with old beams and inglenook fireplaces. Bedrooms are decorated in a restrained but elegant style, and there are two lounges, one with television. By prior arrangement, especially for parties of friends, evening meals can be served in the candle-lit dining room. There is a heated outdoor swimming pool in the rose-covered courtyard.
3 en suite (bth/shr) No smoking in bedrooms Tea and coffee making facilities No dogs (ex guide dogs) Licensed Cen ht CTV No children 13yrs 20P No coaches Outdoor swimming pool (heated) Croquet lawn Clay pigeon shooting Last d 6pm
CARDS: 🜏 💳
See advertisement under DISS

FRINTON-ON-SEA Essex Map 05 TM21

GH ▣ **Forde** 18 Queens Rd CO13 9BL ☎01255 674758
Closed mid Dec-mid Jan
Decades of careful attention have resulted in the highest of standards being offered at this long-established, family-run guest house. Bedrooms are modest but neat, and there are a cosy television lounge and a breakfast room. Parking outside the building is unrestricted, and the road leads directly to the esplanade and seafront.
6 rms (1 fmly) No smoking in dining room Cen ht CTV No children 5yrs 1P No coaches
PRICE GUIDE
ROOMS: s £19.50; d £30; wkly b&b £105

Prices quoted in the Guide are based on information supplied by the establishments themselves.

FRITHAM Hampshire Map 04 SU21

♥ ▣▣▣▣ Mrs P Hankinson **Fritham Farm** *(SU243144)*
SO43 7HH (leave M27 at junct 1 and follow signs to Fritham) ☎01703 812333 FAX 01703 812333
Closed 24 Dec-28 Dec
This charming farmhouse, set in a leafy lane at the heart of the forest, provides a peace and tranquillity that brings visitors back time after time. Hospitality is cheerful and informal - you will feel at home from the moment that you are warmly welcomed and offered a cup of tea - and neat, attractive en suite bedrooms have such comfortable beds that you are assured of a good night's sleep. Cosy public areas include a dining room where hearty cooked breakfasts (and dinner by arrangement) are served round one well polished table. Guests should note that smoking is not permitted anywhere in the house and that credit cards are not accepted.
3 en suite (bth/shr) No smoking Tea and coffee making facilities No dogs (ex guide dogs) Cen ht CTV No children 10yrs 28P Forest walks 51 acres mixed grass
PRICE GUIDE
ROOMS: d £33-£36; wkly b&b £109.70-£126

FROGMORE Devon Map 03 SX74

◀ ▣▣ **Globe** TQ7 2NR (3.75m E of Kingsbridge on A379)
☎01548 531351
Situated between Dartmouth and Kingsbridge, the Globe is an ideal base from which to explore the beautiful South Devon ➡

CAR-N-ETHIC H·O·U·S·E

Lambs Barn • Fowey • Cornwall
Tel: (01726) 833336
David & Trisha Hogg

This delightful Regency house, situated in tranquil countryside close to the sea at Fowey, provides gracious accommodation and excellent food. Fresh local fish a speciality. Licensed bar & heated outdoor swimming pool. 1½ acres mature gardens AA selected in 1992 For FREE brochure write or telephone

QQQQ

AA SELECTED

countryside. It offers comfortable bedrooms, a cosy lounge bar, and the lively Sportsman Bar with pool, darts and satellite TV. The informal Barn Restaurant offers a good choice of meals including a children's menu, and hosts Duncan and Sheila Johnston provide a warm welcome.

6 rms (3 shr) (1 fmly) CTV in all bedrooms Tea and coffee making facilities Cen ht CTV 20P Pool Darts Cycle hire Canoe hire Last d 10pm

PRICE GUIDE
ROOMS: s £15-£25; d £30-£40; wkly b&b £110-£125✶
MEALS: Lunch £9-£20alc Dinner £9-£25alc✶
CARDS: 🃏 💳 (£)

FROME Somerset Map **03** ST74

GH 🇶🇶🇶 **Fourwinds** Bath Rd BA11 2HJ
☎01373 462618 FAX 01373 453029

Conveniently located on the outskirts of the town, this personally run guest house set in attractive gardens offers comfortable bedrooms and a welcoming atmosphere.

6 rms (1 bth 3 shr) (1 fmly) No smoking in dining room No smoking in lounges CTV in 13 bedrooms Tea and coffee making facilities Direct dial from bedrooms No dogs Licensed Cen ht 10P Last d 7pm

PRICE GUIDE
ROOMS: s £25-£30; d £40-£45; wkly b&b £150-£190; wkly hlf-bd £200-£240
CARDS: 🃏 💳 💳 (£)

FYLINGDALES North Yorkshire Map **08** NZ90

◀ 🇶🇶🇶 **Flask** Robin Hoods Bay YO22 4QH (on A171)
☎01947 880305 FAX 01947 880592

Originally a 16th-century monks' hostel, the Flask Inn is now a comfortable and well decorated inn. Suitably furnished bedrooms are equipped with good facilities, whilst the spacious bar provides a good range of home-cooked food.

6 en suite (bth/shr) (2 fmly) No smoking in dining room CTV in all bedrooms Tea and coffee making facilities No dogs Cen ht CTV 20P No coaches Last d 9.30pm

PRICE GUIDE
ROOMS: s £25; d £40; wkly b&b fr £130✶
MEALS: Bar Lunch £3.95-£7.95✶
 (£)

GAINSBOROUGH Lincolnshire

See **Marton**

GARBOLDISHAM Norfolk Map **05** TM08

GH 🇶🇶🇶 **Ingleneuk Lodge** Hopton Rd IP22 2RQ (turn S off A1066 on to B1111. 1m on right) ☎01953 681541
rs Xmas, New Year and Sun

Ingleneuk Lodge is located in a peaceful rural setting just south of the village. The neat bedrooms are furnished in a modern style and adequately equipped; some non-smoking rooms are available. An evening meal is served on request in the relaxing dining room, and there is also a comfortable lounge and bar.

9 rms (8 bth/shr) (2 fmly) No smoking in 4 bedrooms No smoking in dining room CTV in all bedrooms Tea and coffee making facilities Direct dial from bedrooms Licensed Cen ht 20P No coaches Last d 1pm

PRICE GUIDE
ROOMS: s £23-£33; d £37.50-£51; wkly b&b £124.25-£171.50; wkly hlf-bd £215-£262.50
CARDS: 🃏 💳 💳 (£)

GARGRAVE North Yorkshire Map **07** SD95

GH 🇶🇶 **Kirk Syke Hotel** 19 High St BD23 3RA (on A65 4m W of Skipton) ☎01756 749356
Closed 21-27 Dec

An impressive Victorian stone house stands on the A65 in the centre of the village. Modern bedrooms are available in a house in the grounds while more traditional rooms are found in the main house. The lounge is comfortable and good home cooking is served in the attractive dining room.

4 rms (3 bth) 6 annexe en suite (bth/shr) No smoking in dining room CTV in all bedrooms Tea and coffee making facilities No dogs Licensed Cen ht CTV No children 5yrs 12P No coaches Last d 10am

PRICE GUIDE
ROOMS: s £28-£29; d £40-£42; wkly b&b £140-£196; wkly hlf-bd £224-£280✶
CARDS: 🃏 💳

GARSTANG Lancashire Map **07** SD44

♥ 🇶🇶🇶 Mrs J Higginson **Clay Lane Head** *(SD490474)*
Cabus, Preston PR3 1WL (1m N on A6) ☎01995 603132
Mar-23 Dec

This 17th-century farmhouse standing alongside the A6 at Cabus, though considerably extended over the years, retains much of its original character in exposed beams and timbers. Bedrooms are suitable for families and include two with en suite facilities. There are a comfortable lounge and an impressive breakfast room with a wood-burning stove.

3 rms (2 bth/shr) (1 fmly) No smoking in bedrooms CTV in 2 bedrooms Tea and coffee making facilities No dogs (ex guide dogs) Cen ht CTV 5P 30 acres beef

PRICE GUIDE
ROOMS: s £17-£22; d £28-£36; wkly b&b £88-£113✶

GATWICK AIRPORT (LONDON) West Sussex Map **04** TQ24

GH 🇶🇶🇶 *Barnwood Hotel* Balcombe Rd, Pound Hill RH10 7RU ☎01293 882709 FAX 01293 886041
Closed Xmas-1 Jan

This fully licensed hotel situated in a residential area offers a range of bedrooms, all well equipped and some upgraded to a very high standard. Bar and lounge open out on to the rear gardens, and the restaurant adjoining them features both fixed-price and carte menus; snacks are also served in the bar. Two conference/function rooms are available and there is plenty of parking space. Breakfast is provided at a supplementary charge.

35 en suite (bth/shr) (3 fmly) CTV in all bedrooms Tea and coffee making facilities Direct dial from bedrooms No dogs (ex guide dogs) Licensed Cen ht 50P Last d 9pm
CARDS: 🃏 💳 💳 💳

GH 🇶🇶🇶 *Belmont House* 46 Massetts Rd RH6 7DS
☎01293 820500 FAX 01293 783812

This friendly bed and breakfast establishment, an Edwardian house set in a half-acre of gardens, has been lovingly restored and upgraded by its new owners. The comfortable lounge is well furnished and a front-facing breakfast room serves English and continental breakfasts. The grounds include a children's play area, and long-term parking is available by arrangement. A courtesy bus service to the airport is available and French and Italian are spoken if required.

6 rms (3 shr) 1 annexe en suite (shr) (3 fmly) No smoking CTV in all bedrooms Tea and coffee making facilities No dogs (ex guide dogs) Cen ht 22P No coaches
CARDS: 🃏 💳 💳

GH [Q][Q][Q] **Chalet** 77 Massetts Rd RH6 7EB (from M23 junct 9 follow A23 signed Redhill/London. At large rbt turn rt past Texaco Garage then 2nd rt, signed Horley Town Centre into Massetts rd) ☎01293 821666 FAX 01293 821619
Closed Xmas

This small, newly established and comfortable guest house provides ideal accommodation for travellers using the airport. Standards of housekeeping are high, and bedrooms are beautifully maintained and in excellent condition throughout. Very friendly service is provided by proprietors Daphne and Eric Shortland, and guests have use of the kitchen to make hot drinks as required. Good parking facilities are also provided.

6 rms (4 shr) (1 fmly) No smoking CTV in all bedrooms Tea and coffee making facilities No dogs (ex guide dogs) Cen ht CTV 12P No coaches

PRICE GUIDE
ROOMS: s fr £24; d fr £42
CARDS: ▦ ▦   (£)

GH [Q][Q][Q] **Copperwood** Massetts Rd RH6 7DJ (from M23 junc 9 pass airport onto A23 towards Redhill after 2nd roundabout, Massetts Rd is on right)
☎01293 783388 FAX 01293 420156

This tastefully restored corner house dates from 1904 takes its name from the copper beech trees that surround it. The prettily decorated modern bedrooms are well equipped and ideally furnished for the overnight guest. A full English breakfast is served in the bright non-smoking dining room where light refreshments are available until 9pm, and courtesy transport to and from the airport Terminal can be arranged.

5 rms (1 shr) (1 fmly) No smoking in dining room CTV in all bedrooms Tea and coffee making facilities Cen ht 5P

PRICE GUIDE
ROOMS: s £24-£32; d £35-£42✳
CARDS: ▦ ▦ ⓪

GH [Q][Q][Q] *Gainsborough Lodge* 39 Massetts Rd RH6 7DT (2m NE of airport adjacent A23)
☎01293 783982 FAX 01293 785365
rs 22 Dec-4 Jan

This delightful Edwardian house has a good range of bedrooms, some of which are on the ground floor. All are equipped with tv, clock radio, and tea trays. The no smoking breakfast room has been skilfully extended, with a new garden conservatory, and long term car parking can be arranged.

16 en suite (bth/shr) (5 fmly) No smoking in dining room No smoking in 1 lounge CTV in all bedrooms Tea and coffee making facilities No dogs (ex guide dogs) Cen ht CTV 20P No coaches

PRICE GUIDE
ROOMS: s £29.50-£33; d £39.50-£43✳
CARDS: ▦ ▦ ▦ ⓪   (£)

GH [Q][Q][Q] *Gatwick Skylodge* London Rd, County Oak RH11 0PF (2m S of airport on A23)
☎01293 544511 Telex no 878307 FAX 01293 611762
Closed 25-29 Dec

Long-term car parking is available by arrangement at this good-value modern hotel, and courtesy transport is provided to and from the airport terminals. Bedrooms - some of them conveniently located on the ground floor - are double-glazed and well equipped, while the very popular bar/dining area offers bar food at lunch time and a daily fixed-price menu in the evening; breakfast is not included in the room tariff.

51 en suite (bth) (7 fmly) CTV in all bedrooms Tea and coffee making facilities No dogs (ex guide dogs) Licensed Cen ht 60P No coaches Last d 9.15pm
CARDS: ▦ ▦ ▦

Selected

GH Q Q Q Q **High Trees Gatwick** Oldfield Rd RH6 7EP (follow signs for A23 London passing airport on left, turn right at next roundabout to Horley/Redhill. First right into Woodroyd Av and Oldfield Rd)
☎01293 776397 FAX 01293 785693
Closed 24-26 & 31 Dec
A new and conveniently situated non-smoking guest house located in an established residential area, within walking distance of the town centre, shops and restaurants. Bedrooms are modern, bright and furnished in pine, with thoughtful little extras. There is a very comfortable TV lounge, and a sitting/writing room on the first floor. The breakfast room overlooks the lawned rear garden, and reception and the kitchen are open plan. Continental breakfast is included in the room tariff, full English breakfast is subject to an additional charge. Light refreshments are usually available throughout the day.
8 en suite (bth/shr) (2 fmly) No smoking CTV in all bedrooms Tea and coffee making facilities No dogs Cen ht CTV 10P
PRICE GUIDE
ROOMS: s £33; d £44; wkly b&b fr £208✱
CARDS: 🔳 💳 £

Selected

GH Q Q Q Q *The Lawn* 30 Massetts Rd RH6 7DE
☎01293 775751 FAX 01293 821803
Closed Xmas
A most attractive Victorian house has been carefully preserved and tastefully furnished by friendly owners Ken and Janet Stocks. Bedrooms all have pretty co-ordinating fabrics and decor, good comfortable seating, TV and tea trays. The breakfast room is decorated in the style of the house, and old photographs throughout remind guests of the hotel's origins as a girls' school. There is a small lounge/reception area, and private car parking can be arranged.
7 rms (4 shr) No smoking CTV in all bedrooms Tea and coffee making facilities Cen ht No children 12yrs 10P No coaches
CARDS: 🔳 💳 💳 🔳

GH Q Q *Massetts Lodge* 28 Massets Rd RH6 7DE
☎01293 782738 FAX 01293 782738
This Victorian house offers adequately furnished and well equipped accommodation. Bedrooms in a variety of sizes include family, en suite and ground-floor rooms and downstairs there is an attractive breakfast room; the cost of breakfast is included in the room tariff, and an evening meal can be provided by arrangement.
8 rms (5 bth/shr) (2 fmly) No smoking in dining room CTV in all bedrooms Tea and coffee making facilities No dogs (ex guide dogs) Cen ht 10P No coaches Last d 7.45pm
CARDS: 🔳 💳 💳 🔳

GH Q Q **Rosemead** 19 Church Rd RH6 7EY
☎01293 784965 FAX 01293 820438
Comfortable and well presented accommodation - bedrooms are attractively furnished in the modern style, and all come with TV and tea trays. The best have new en suite shower rooms, and there are family rooms available. The dining room is no smoking and car parking can be arranged.

6 rms (2 shr) (2 fmly) No smoking CTV in all bedrooms Tea and coffee making facilities Cen ht 8P No coaches
PRICE GUIDE
ROOMS: s £23-£29; d £35-£42✱
CARDS: 🔳 💳 🔳 £

Selected

GH Q Q Q Q **Vulcan Lodge** 27 Massetts Rd RH6 7DQ
☎01293 771522
Dating from the late 17th century and originally a farm house, this attractive property is set back from the main road in a secluded position whilst still being convenient for both town centre and airport. Four individually decorated bedrooms show a wealth of feminine touches, the pretty breakfast room is furnished in pine, and guests have their own lounge with chintzy armchairs. Smoking is not permitted downstairs.
4 rms (3 shr) No smoking in dining room CTV in all bedrooms Tea and coffee making facilities No dogs Cen ht 10P No coaches
PRICE GUIDE
ROOMS: s £24-£31; d £42-£44✱
CARDS: 🔳 💳

GH Q Q **Woodlands** 42 Massetts Rd RH6 7DS (off A23 1m N of Gatwick Airport) ☎01293 782994 & 776358 FAX 01293 776358
This comfortable, non-smoking bed and breakfast establishment offers en suite bedrooms with TVs and beverage-making facilities. A bright front breakfast room serves a full English breakfast and other facilities include long term car parking and courtesy transport to and from the Airport terminal.
5 en suite (shr) (2 fmly) No smoking CTV in all bedrooms Tea and coffee making facilities No dogs Cen ht 22P No coaches
PRICE GUIDE
ROOMS: s £23-£30; d £32-£42✱ £

GAYHURST Buckinghamshire Map **04** SP84

🔳 ♥ Q Q Mrs K Adams **Mill** *(SP852454)* MK16 8LT (1m S off B526 unclass rd to Haversham)
☎01908 611489 FAX 01908 611489
Fresh-air pursuits such as tennis, fishing and riding are encouraged by the rural setting of this popular 17th-century farm house; it offers simple bedrooms in keeping with the original character of the building and an inviting open lounge/breakfast room overlooking fields.
3 rms (1 bth/shr) (1 fmly) No smoking in 2 bedrooms No smoking in dining room No smoking in 1 lounge CTV in all bedrooms Tea and coffee making facilities Cen ht CTV 13P Tennis (hard) Fishing Riding Rough shooting Trout fishing 550 acres mixed Last d 4pm
PRICE GUIDE
ROOMS: s £15-£20; d £30-£40; wkly b&b £105-£140 £

GIGGLESWICK North Yorkshire Map **07** SD86

◀ Q Q Q *Black Horse Hotel* Church St BD24 0BE
☎01729 822506
A small village inn dating back to 1663 enjoys a peaceful location next to the church. Pine-furnished bedrooms all have modern facilities, there is a small TV lounge on the first floor, and a wide range of food is served in the bar at lunchtime and in the cosy dining room in the evening. Traditional hand-pulled ales are

available in the convivial bars and service is down-to-earth and friendly.

3 en suite (bth/shr) No smoking in lounges Tea and coffee making facilities Cen ht CTV 20P No coaches Last d 8.45pm CARDS: ▦ ▭ ▣

GISLINGHAM Suffolk Map **05** TM07

Selected

GH ◻◻◻◻ **The Old Guildhall** Mill St IP23 8JT
☎01379 783361
Closed Jan
This immaculately maintained, thatched 15th-century Guildhall lies in the centre of the village. Original features include beams, timbers and fireplaces. Bedrooms are full of character, three having very low ceilings and the fourth room is reached by a spiral staircase; they all have modern en suite bathrooms. The comfortable lounge has a small but well equipped bar, and a snooker room is also available for meetings. Ray and Ethel Tranter ensure that their guests have a warm welcome, with a family atmosphere prevailing.
4 en suite (bth) No smoking CTV in all bedrooms Tea and coffee making facilities Licensed Cen ht 5P No coaches Last d 6pm
PRICE GUIDE
ROOMS: s £25-£35; d £45-£50; wkly b&b £150; wkly hlf-bd £200

GLASTONBURY Somerset Map **03** ST53

❤ ◻◻◻ Mrs J Tinney **Cradlebridge** *(ST477385)* BA16 9SD (take A39 from Glastonbury heading south, after Morlands factory take 2nd right signposted Meare/Wedmore farm is signposted on left after 1m) ☎01458 831827
Closed Xmas
This 200-acre dairy farm is situated one mile west of Glastonbury on the fringe of the Somerset Levels. The spacious ground floor bedrooms are located in a delightful barn conversion, with a patio area outside each offering extensive views to the Mendip Hills. A traditionally cooked farmhouse breakfast is served in the compact dining room where guests eat at a large communal table.
2 annexe en suite (shr) (2 fmly) No smoking in dining room CTV in all bedrooms Tea and coffee making facilities No dogs Cen ht 6P 200 acres dairy
PRICE GUIDE
ROOMS: s £25-£27.50; d £40; wkly b&b £120-£165✳

GLOUCESTER Gloucestershire Map **03** SO81

See also Lydney

▦▦ GH ◻ **Claremont** 135 Stroud Rd GL1 5JL (off A4173)
☎01452 529540 & 529270
Conveniently situated on the Stroud road, this well looked after guest house has been run by Mrs Powell for many years and is a welcoming, hospitable place to stay. Accommodation is offered in six immaculate bedrooms, and the cosy lounge/dining room is pleasantly furnished. Off road parking is provided at the rear of the house.
6 rms (1 bth/shr) (2 fmly) No smoking in dining room CTV in
➡

VULCAN LODGE
GUEST HOUSE
27 Massetts Road, Horley, Surrey RH6 7DQ
Tel: (01293) 771522

A charming picturesque house two miles from Gatwick offering very comfortable cottage style accommodation. 2 single, 1 double, 1 twin (3 en suite). All rooms have colour TV, tea coffee facilities and radio alarms.
Full English or continental breakfast provided. Quietly set back from main road we are two minutes walk from local restaurants, pubs and shops. Main line railway to London and coast five minutes.

WOODLANDS GUEST HOUSE
42 Massetts Road, Horley, Surrey RH6 7DS
Prop: Mr S. Moore
Tel: (01293) 782994 Fax: (01293) 776358
Est. 1983   W. S. Moore

A large detached Edwardian house close to town centre and railway station. **NON SMOKING** throughout. All rooms en suite, centrally heated, double glazed, C.T.V. and tea/coffee. A fast transfer service to and from **GATWICK AIRPORT** (1¼ miles) is provided by our courtesy car on request. Secure car parking on the premises.
Fire certificate awarded.

all bedrooms Tea and coffee making facilities No dogs Cen ht CTV 6P No coaches
PRICE GUIDE
ROOMS: s £16-£17; d £32-£35; wkly b&b £87.50-£91

GOATHLAND North Yorkshire Map **08** NZ80

GH **Fairhaven Country Hotel** The Common YO22 5AN (from A169 follw signs for Goathland, at parish church bear right hotel half a mile on right) ☎01947 896361
The Fairhaven Country Hotel is a family owned and run guest house which enjoys delightful all-round views from its setting in the moorland village of Goathland. Immaculately maintained bedrooms are steadily being upgraded, and guests have the use of a very spacious and relaxing lounge.
9 rms (4 bth/shr) (3 fmly) No smoking in dining room CTV in 5 bedrooms Tea and coffee making facilities Cen ht CTV 9P Putting green Games room Last d 5pm
PRICE GUIDE
ROOMS: s £18.50-£27.50; d £37-£45; wkly b&b £129.50-£157.50; wkly hlf-bd £190-£215
CARDS:

GH **Heatherdene Hotel** YO22 5AN ☎01947 896334
Once the vicarage, this appealing house stands in one of the most picturesque villages of Yorkshire, close to the North Yorkshire Moors. Some of the well furnished bedrooms are large, a lounge with a small bar offers fine views, and good meals are provided.
7 rms (2 bth 4 shr) (3 fmly) No smoking in 1 bedrooms CTV in all bedrooms Tea and coffee making facilities Licensed Cen ht 8P Last d 8pm
PRICE GUIDE
ROOMS: s £30-£35; d £45-£58; wkly b&b £180-£200; wkly hlf-bd £260-£300∗

See advertisement under WHITBY

GODALMING Surrey Map **04** SU94

GH **Fairfields** The Green, Elstead GU8 6DF (off A3 5m south of Guildford to Elstead, bear lt at Woolpack Inn then 200yds on lt) ☎01252 702345
Closed 21-29 Dec
This non-smoking establishment - a detached house built in 1947 - is conveniently situated at the centre of the village with both a garden and ample car parking space to the rear. Friendly and welcoming, it offers accommodation in well equipped, individually furnished bedrooms (including a suite of two rooms with private facilities); full English breakfast is included in the tariff, and the breakfast room has been extended to provide a conservatory lounge for guests.
3 rms (2 bth/shr) (1 fmly) No smoking CTV in all bedrooms Tea and coffee making facilities No dogs Cen ht No children 3yrs 3P No coaches
PRICE GUIDE
ROOMS: d £32-£39.50∗

GORRAN HAVEN Cornwall & Isles of Scilly Map **02** SX04

◗ **Llawnroc** PL26 6NU ☎01726 843461
The accommodation at this village inn is basic but comfortable. Bedrooms vary in size but are well equipped and there is a small first floor sitting room. The dining room is of typical inn style and offers simple English cooking on a choice of menus.
6 rms (2 bth 3 shr) (2 fmly) No smoking in dining room CTV in

all bedrooms Tea and coffee making facilities No dogs (ex guide dogs) Cen ht CTV 40P No coaches Last d 9.30pm
CARDS:
See advertisement under MEVAGISSEY

GOUDHURST Kent Map **05** TQ73

GH **Mill House** Church Rd TN17 1BN (on A262 from Sissinghurst Castle, opposite St Marys church) ☎01580 211703
This private home maintains the same 17th-century character as much of the village: only the siting of a mill stone in the large private lawns of the house indicate its purpose in earlier years. The informal young couple and their children live in a property full of character with a lived-in homely atmosphere. The two guest bedrooms are located at the top of a stairwell in a section separate from the owners. Both are spacious, one particularly so, and tastefully furnished. Neither has en suite facilities but within a short distance of each there is a private bathroom.
2 en suite (bth/shr) (1 fmly) No smoking CTV in all bedrooms Tea and coffee making facilities No dogs Cen ht CTV 4P No coaches
PRICE GUIDE
ROOMS: s £35; d £35-£40∗

GRAMPOUND Cornwall & Isles of Scilly Map **02** SW94

GH **Perran House** Fore St TR2 4RS (on the A390 between St Austell and Truro) ☎01726 882066
Well furnished bedrooms are available at this attractive, listed cottage in the centre of Cornwall, and the pine-furnished dining room serves light snacks and cream teas during the summer. The owner is an avid model collector. Smoking is discouraged.
5 rms (3 bth/shr) (1 fmly) No smoking in dining room No smoking in lounges CTV in all bedrooms Tea and coffee making facilities No dogs (ex guide dogs) Cen ht 8P No coaches
PRICE GUIDE
ROOMS: s £14-£18; d £28-£35; wkly b&b £90-£105
CARDS:

GRANGE-OVER-SANDS Cumbria Map **07** SD47

GH *Birchleigh* Kents Bank Rd LA11 7EY ☎01539 532592
Closed Jan
This small, friendly guest house is situated close to the town centre and within easy walking distance of the bay. It provides well maintained accommodation, including one bedroom located on the ground floor, and there is also an attractive breakfast room with individual tables.
5 en suite (bth/shr) (2 fmly) No smoking CTV in 4 bedrooms Tea and coffee making facilities Cen ht No parking No coaches
CARDS:

Entries in this Guide are based on reports filed by our team of professionally trained, full-time inspectors.

Premier Selected

GH ◻◻◻◻◻
Greenacres Lindale LA11 6LP (2m N, take B5277 & follow signs for Grange-Over-Sands & Lindale) ☎01539 534578 FAX 01539 534578
Closed 5 Nov-9 Jan

Anne and Joe Danson's lovely 19th-century cottage lies in the centre of Lindale village, two miles east of Grange-over-Sands. Lounges are a feature here and well worth enjoying, be it the cosy sun lounge or the delightful main one with its open fire in season. Anne's home-cooked dinners and hearty breakfasts gain praise. Bedrooms are not large, but are attractively decorated, furnished with mainly contemporary pieces and well equipped with radio clocks, hair dryers and magazines.
5 en suite (bth/shr) (1 fmly) No smoking CTV in all bedrooms Tea and coffee making facilities No dogs Licensed Cen ht 6P No coaches Last d noon
PRICE GUIDE
ROOMS: s £30-£33; d £49-£54; wkly b&b £171.50-£230; wkly hlf-bd £225-£250
CARDS: £

GRASMERE Cumbria Map 11 NY30

GH ◻◻◻ Bridge House Hotel Stock Ln LA22 9SN (turn off A591, onto B5287 establishment 1/4 mile on left immediately before St Oswalds Church and bridge)
☎015394 35425 FAX 015394 35523
14 Feb-8 Nov rs 9 Nov-4 Dec
Formerly a private residence, this hotel is set in secluded gardens in the centre of the village, close to the River Rothay. The bedrooms have been thoughtfully furnished and equipped with modern facilities. Public rooms include a comfortable lounge with an adjoining bar, and an attractive dining room in which five-course evening meals are served.
12 en suite (bth/shr) No smoking in bedrooms No smoking in dining room CTV in all bedrooms Tea and coffee making facilities Direct dial from bedrooms No dogs Licensed Cen ht No children 8yrs 20P No coaches Last d 7pm
PRICE GUIDE
ROOMS: s £25-£35; d £50-£70; wkly b&b £175-£204; wkly hlf-bd £207-£274✱
CARDS: £

GH ◻◻◻ Lake View Country House Lake View Dr LA22 9TD (turn off A591 after Prince of Wales then left at Wild Daffodil Tea Shop) ☎015394 35384
Mar-Nov rs Dec-Feb
An attractive stone house stands in its own well kept gardens in a quiet side road in the village centre, with a view of the lake. The house is comfortably furnished throughout and there are two cosy lounges. Service is very friendly.
6 rms (3 shr) No smoking in dining room CTV in all bedrooms Tea and coffee making facilities Cen ht No children 12yrs 11P No coaches Fishing permit for guests use Last d noon
PRICE GUIDE
ROOMS: s fr £23.50; d £47-£74; wkly b&b £154-£182; wkly hlf-bd £221-£249✱ £

GH ◻◻◻ Raise View White Bridge LA22 9RQ (turn off A591 opposite Swan Hotel and go to the corner of Swan Hotel and go to the corner of Swan Lane and Pye Lane)
☎015394 35215 FAX 015394 35126
Feb-Dec
A Lakeland stone cottage situated just a short walk from the village centre offers pleasant accommodation. The bedrooms are prettily decorated, there is a cosy lounge and friendly service is provided by the resident owners.
6 rms (4 shr) (1 fmly) No smoking CTV in all bedrooms Tea and coffee making facilities No dogs Cen ht No children 5yrs 6P No coaches
PRICE GUIDE
ROOMS: d £36-£46; wkly b&b £120-£153

GRASSINGTON North Yorkshire Map 07 SE06

Selected

GH ◻◻◻ Ashfield House Hotel BD23 5AE (take B6265 to village centre then turn off Main St into Ashfield) ☎01756 752584
Closed Jan rs Nov-Dec
Keith and Linda Harrison, the owners of this charming little guest house, are very friendly and caring hosts. Nestled in a quiet corner of the village, it has the benefit of its own car park and a secluded rear garden. The two homely lounges both offer log fires and plenty of books, whilst comfortable bedrooms have delightful pine furniture. The set four-course dinner served in the cottage-style dining room has been ➡

A spacious period house just west of Gloucester in an area of outstanding natural beauty. Ideally situated for touring the Cotswolds, Severn Vale, Royal Forest of Dean, Wye Valley and the Welsh Marches.
All guest rooms are en-suite and are comfortably furnished. All have hot and cold water, shaver points, tea/coffee making facilities with full central heating. Evening meals are available in the licensed dining room. The Guesthouse is open all year. Special interest and bargain breaks are available.

carefully prepared by Linda from the best produce available. Smoking is not permitted in the house.

7 rms (6 shr) No smoking CTV in all bedrooms Tea and coffee making facilities No dogs (ex guide dogs) Licensed Cen ht No children 5yrs 7P No coaches Last d 7pm

PRICE GUIDE
ROOMS: s £24-£37; d £54; wkly b&b £168-£189; wkly hlf-bd £231-£262.50
CARDS: ⬛ ▦

GH Q Q Q **The Lodge** 8 Wood Ln BD23 5LU
☎01756 752518
Mar-Oct rs Dec
This attractive, detached, grey-stone Victorian house stands on the edge of the village and provides good all-round standards of both accommodation and service. There is a cosy lounge for guests and the bedrooms are pleasantly furnished and decorated, most having views of the surrounding countryside.

8 rms (1 bth 2 shr) No smoking in dining room Tea and coffee making facilities Cen ht CTV 7P No coaches Last d 2pm
PRICE GUIDE
ROOMS: d £32-£44; wkly b&b £112-£132; wkly hlf-bd £175-£195✱
(£)

GRAVESEND Kent Map 05 TQ67

Selected

GH Q Q Q Q **Overcliffe Hotel** 15-16 The Overcliffe DA11 0EF (W side of town on A226)
☎01474 322131 FAX 01474 536737
This family-run hotel dates from 1860 and has been skilfully converted. The accommodation in both the main house and the nearby Victorian Lodge is well equipped and comfortable. the atmosphere is very friendly and welcoming, with attentive service being provided by polite uniformed staff. The attractive restaurant features an interesting selection of dishes which can be served on the terrace on warm sunny days. There is ample car parking, and access to the town centre is a only a few minutes walk away.

19 en suite (shr) 10 annexe en suite (bth/shr) CTV in all bedrooms Tea and coffee making facilities Direct dial from bedrooms Licensed Cen ht ch fac 45P Last d 9.30pm
PRICE GUIDE
ROOMS: s £50-£55; d £60-£75✱
CARDS: ⬛ ▦ ▦ ⓞ

GREAT AYTON North Yorkshire Map 08 NZ51

◄ Q Q Q **Royal Oak Hotel** 123 High St TS9 6BW
☎01642 722361 & 723270 FAX 01642 724047
rs Sun (closed 3pm-7pm)
Modern, attractively decorated bedrooms are a feature of this 18th-century former coaching inn. Bar meals are popular and a very good three-course luncheon has been added to the varied menus.

5 rms (4 bth/shr) CTV in all bedrooms Tea and coffee making facilities Direct dial from bedrooms Cen ht No parking Last d 9.30pm
PRICE GUIDE
ROOMS: s fr £25; d fr £45✱
MEALS: Lunch fr £5 Dinner £12.75&alc✱
CARDS: ⬛ ▦ ⓞ
(£)

GREAT DUNMOW Essex Map 05 TL62

GH Q Q **Cowels Cottage** Cowels Farm Ln, Lindsell CM6 3QG (take unclass road heading west, off B1057, 4m N of town)
☎01371 870454
This is a friendly, quiet farmhouse in which each bedroom has its own private facilities. There is a TV lounge which also serves as a breakfast room.

3 rms (1 bth/shr) (1 fmly) No smoking in bedrooms No smoking in dining room Tea and coffee making facilities No dogs Cen ht CTV P No coaches
PRICE GUIDE
ROOMS: s £16-£20; d £36; wkly b&b fr £156✱

Selected

GH Q Q Q Q **The Starr Restaurant with Rooms** Market Place CM6 1AX (directly off High St)
☎01371 874321 FAX 01371 876337
Closed 2-8 Jan
A restaurant operation in an old English setting and quality accommodation in a converted stable block, are offered at this establishment. Bedroom styles vary between antique and modern, but all are equally well equipped and have extras such as mineral water, cona coffee, books and tissues. The restaurant, which serves English dishes cooked in a French style, is smartly appointed and the service is professional. There is also a beamed bar. Please note that smoking is not permitted in either the bedrooms or the restaurant.

8 rms No smoking in bedrooms No smoking in dining room CTV in all bedrooms Tea and coffee making facilities Direct dial from bedrooms Licensed Cen ht 16P No coaches Last d 9.30pm
PRICE GUIDE
ROOMS: s fr £55; d £85-£100✱
CARDS: ⬛ ▦ ▦ ▦ ▦ ▨

GREAT YARMOUTH Norfolk Map 05 TG50

GH Q Q **Avalon Private Hotel** 54 Clarence Rd, Gorleston-on-Sea NR31 6DR (from A12 follow seafront signs, Clarence Rd is at right angle to Marine Parade)
☎01493 662114 FAX 01493 661521
The Avalon is situated in a residential road just a few minutes walk from the cliff tops and Gorleston's sandy beach. Paula and Ernie Winsor provide a personal service and clean accommodation, bedroom sizes are variable, a few have en-suite shower rooms and all have pay-and -view colour televisions with satellite channels. Guests also have the use of a small bar and a separate television lounge which is stocked with a range of books.

9 rms (4 shr) (3 fmly) No smoking in dining room CTV in all bedrooms Tea and coffee making facilities No dogs Licensed Cen ht CTV Last d 10.30am
PRICE GUIDE
ROOMS: s £12.50-£19; d £25-£36; wkly b&b £82-£89; wkly hlf-bd £126-£134.50✱

GH Q Q **Frandor** 120 Lowertoft Rd NR31 6ND (2m S off A12) ☎01493 662112
Warm and friendly, this family-run private hotel offers accommodation in adequately furnished bedrooms - some of them with en suite facilities. On the ground floor there are a comfortable lounge and a small dining room where both a traditional English breakfast and an evening meal are available.

6 rms (3 shr) (2 fmly) CTV in all bedrooms Tea and coffee making facilities Licensed Cen ht CTV 12P Last d 6.30pm
CARDS: ■■ £

GH QQ Georgian House 16-17 North Dr NR30 4EW (on seafront, N of Britannia Pier opposite entrance to Venetian Waterways) ☎01493 842623
Closed Xmas-Feb rs Nov-Etr
A popular, family-run guesthouse located in the quieter northern end of town, on the seafront. Gradual improvements to the decor will further enhance this immaculately kept establishment.
19 rms (11 bth 6 shr) (1 fmly) No smoking in dining room CTV in all bedrooms Tea and coffee making facilities No dogs Licensed Cen ht No children 5yrs 18P No coaches
PRICE GUIDE
ROOMS: d £32-£46; wkly b&b £100-£130✶ £

GH QQ Jennis Lodge 63 Avondale Rd NR31 6DJ (2m S off A12) ☎01493 662840
A personally run guesthouse lies within easy access of a sandy beach and the centre of Gorleston town. There is some emphasis on hospitality and ready service at the bar and restaurant.
11 rms (4 fmly) CTV in all bedrooms Tea and coffee making facilities Licensed Cen ht CTV No parking Last d 4pm

GH QQ Spindrift Private Hotel 36 Wellesley Rd NR30 1EU (follow signs for seafront continue along St Nicholas Rd & Euston Rd then first left into Wellesley Rd) ☎01493 858674
Closed Xmas
A well maintained guest house is set in tree-lined avenue running parallel to the seafront, to the north of the town centre. Resident owner Mrs Wells maintains a high standards of care and bedrooms are very satisfactory, if a little compact. There is a pleasant lounge with comfortable seating and TV.
8 rms (5 bth/shr) (3 fmly) CTV in all bedrooms Tea and coffee making facilities No dogs (ex guide dogs) Licensed Cen ht CTV No children 3yrs No coaches
PRICE GUIDE
ROOMS: s £15-£25; d £25-£40; wkly b&b £84-£125
CARDS: ■■ ■■ £

GH QQQ Squirrels Nest 71 Avondale Rd NR31 6DJ ☎01493 662746 FAX 01493 662746
Located near the seafront, this guest house provides well kept accommodation. Bedrooms are neatly furnished and well equipped. Public areas include a comfortable lounge, a small bar and a dining room where a good range of meals and snacks is available.
9 en suite (bth/shr) (1 fmly) No smoking in dining room CTV in all bedrooms Tea and coffee making facilities Licensed Cen ht CTV 5P Last d 8.30pm
CARDS: ■■ ■■

GREEN HAMMERTON North Yorkshire Map **08** SE45

◀ QQQ *Bay Horse* York Rd YO5 8BN ☎01423 330338 & 331113 FAX 01423 331279
An attractive former coaching inn stands just off the A59 between York and Harrogate, three miles east of its junction with the A1. Modern bedrooms are in a sympathetically designed building at the rear; all are equipped with every modern facility including showers, and most are on the ground floor. The bars are full of character, featuring beams, stone walls, horse brasses, prints and other bric-á-brac. A varied menu is provided in the attractive restaurant adjoining the bar areas, where an extensive choice of bar meals is offered at lunchtime.

10 annexe en suite (bth/shr) (1 fmly) CTV in all bedrooms Tea and coffee making facilities Direct dial from bedrooms Cen ht 40P Last d 9.30pm
CARDS: ■■ ■■
See advertisement under YORK

GREENHEAD Northumberland Map **12** NY66

♥ QQQ Mr B & Mrs P Staff **Holmhead** *(NY659661)* Hadrians Wall CA6 7HY (from B6318 turn between Waugh Coaches & youth hostel beside telephone box drive over bridge then quarter of a mile to Farm Road)
☎016977 47402 FAX 016977 47402
Closed 19 Dec-9 Jan
Whilst no longer a working farm, the approach to this interesting farmhouse, over a small bridge and through gated fields which run right up to the house, means that the farming atmosphere remains. The house itself is built of stone from Hadrian's Wall and Pauline Staff will lend her considerable knowledge to anyone seeking information on both local and Roman history. This is a real friendly family home and guests are made very welcome. There are two lounges, the one upstairs having an honesty bar, TV, books and games. Bedrooms are not large but are bright, cheery and thoughtfully equipped to include hair dryers, radios and all manner of toiletries. Meals are a feature of Holmhead and a talking point will be what is reputedly the longest breakfast menus in the world.
4 en suite (shr) 1 annexe rms (1 fmly) No smoking Tea and coffee making facilities No dogs Licensed Cen ht CTV 6P Fishing Table tennis 300 acres breeding sheep cattle Last d 3pm
PRICE GUIDE
ROOMS: d £45-£46; wkly b&b £132-£135; wkly hlf-bd £244-£247
CARDS: ■■ ■■ ■■

GRINDON Staffordshire Map **07** SK05

♥ QQQ Mrs P Simpson **Summerhill Farm** *(SJ083532)* ST13 7TT ☎01538 304264
This 200-year-old stone farmhouse set on a remote dairy farm offers traditionally furnished accommodation with modern facilities; this includes one small bedroom for children. Guests can relax in a very pleasant beamed lounge, and they share one large table in the attractive dining room. Smoking is not permitted indoors. The farmhouse is reached from Grindon village by taking the lane adjacent to the Cavalier Inn, marked as a no through road, for three-quarters of a mile.
3 rms (2 shr) No smoking CTV in 2 bedrooms Tea and coffee making facilities Cen ht CTV 6P 52 acres dairy
PRICE GUIDE
ROOMS: s £17.50-£20; d £32-£37; wkly b&b £112-£129; wkly hlf-bd £189-£206✶
See advertisement under LEEK

GUISBOROUGH Cleveland Map **08** NZ61

◀ QQQQ **Fox & Hounds** Slapewath TS14 6PX (2m on A171) ☎01287 632964 & 635280 FAX 01287 610778
Modern bedrooms are a feature of this popular hotel on the road to Whitby. The original building was once a railway station on the Saltburn to Guisborough line, but has now been extended and refurbished to include two restaurants, a traditional bar and a conservatory as well as the well appointed bedrooms. Meals are good value and a wide range of dishes is available. There is also a well equipped children's play area.
15 en suite (bth/shr) (2 fmly) CTV in all bedrooms Tea and ➡

coffee making facilities Direct dial from bedrooms Cen ht 150P
Last d 9.45pm
PRICE GUIDE
ROOMS: s fr £34; d fr £45
MEALS: Lunch £3.80-£12 Dinner £7-£12&alc
CARDS: ▣ ▬ ▬ ⊙

GUISELEY West Yorkshire Map **07** SE14

GH ◵◵◵ **Moor Valley Park Motel** Moor Valley Park, Mill
Ln, Hawksworth LS20 8PG (from A65 nera Harry Ramsdens
take 2nd left exit into Thorpe Ln right at golf club through
Hawksworth then left into Mill Ln)
☎01943 876083 FAX 01943 870335
Located between the villages of Hawksworth and Baildon, this
motel set amid fine grounds in a wooded valley provides very well
furnished chalet-style rooms with good facilities; continental
breakfast is included in the tariff. The main building houses
reception and a bar which is also used for the service of full
breakfasts.
    7 annexe en suite (shr) (2 fmly) CTV in all bedrooms Tea and
coffee making facilities No dogs (ex guide dogs) Licensed Cen
ht P Last d 10.30pm
PRICE GUIDE
ROOMS: s fr £32.50; d fr £39.50✱
CARDS: ▣ ▬ ▣   (£)

GUNNISLAKE Cornwall & Isles of Scilly Map **02** SX47

GH ◵◵ **Hingston Inn** St Anns Chapel PL18 9HB (on A390
half a mile from Gunnislake Railway Station heading towards
Callington) ☎01822 832468
This delightful late-Georgian property with a lovely old walled
garden enjoys superb views across the Tamar Valley from an
elevated position on the edge of St Ann's Chapel, some two miles
from the town; much of its varied history is described within the
house. The bedrooms are plainly decorated and furnished, but
most have en suite shower rooms and TVs. Downstairs, both the
large formal lounge and cosy bar have open fires while the
adjoining snug has a wood-burning stove. A traditional four-
course home-cooked meal is served in a dining room comprised of
two areas, one of them featuring attractive French windows
overlooking the patio.
    10 rms (8 shr) (1 fmly) CTV in all bedrooms Tea and coffee
making facilities Licensed Cen ht CTV 20P No coaches
Croquet Putting green Last d 9pm
PRICE GUIDE
ROOMS: s £30; d £50; wkly b&b £200-£330; wkly hlf-bd £330-
£380✱
CARDS: ▣ ▬   (£)

HADLEIGH Suffolk Map **05** TM04

GH ◵◵◵ *Odds & Ends* 131 High St IP7 5EJ (turn off A12
onto B1070 house at end of High St) ☎01473 822032
Half of this rambling house is an informal licensed restaurant
serving freshly prepared meals at lunchtime and by prior
arrangement in the evening. The courtyard bedrooms are generally
less well decorated than the main house rooms; one has been
adapted to accommodate disabled guests.
    6 rms (2 bth) 3 annexe en suite (shr) No smoking in dining room
No smoking in lounges CTV in all bedrooms Tea and coffee
making facilities Licensed Cen ht No children 8yrs 3P No
coaches Last d 5.30pm

◀ ◵◵ **The Marquis of Cornwallis** Upper Layham IP7 5JZ
(on B1070 between Hadleigh & A12)
☎01473 822051 FAX 01473 822051
There is an 'other world' atmosphere about this old inn which is
located a mile from the village of upper Layham, with a sloping

beer garden extending to the banks of the River Brett. The
alarming slope of some of the bedroom floors and the ticking of a
solitary grandfather clock in the corridor add to the simple, dated
character. Freshly made food is served at lunch and dinner time.
    3 en suite (bth/shr) No smoking in 1 bedrooms CTV in all
bedrooms Tea and coffee making facilities No dogs (ex guide
dogs) 22P Fishing Riding & coarse fishing can be arranged
Last d 9.30pm
PRICE GUIDE
ROOMS: s £29; d £40✱
MEALS: Lunch £1.95-£15alc Dinner £1.95-£15alc✱
CARDS: ▣ ▬ ▬ ⊙   (£)

HAINTON Lincolnshire Map **08** TF18

◴ ▼ **GH** ◵◵◵ **The Old Vicarage** School Ln LN3 6LW
(off A157) ☎01507 313660
Standing its own delightful cottage-style gardens, this spacious
house set beside the A157 near the church was once the vicarage.
There is a comfortable lounge for guests, pleasant bedrooms are
attractively furnished and friendly service is provided by resident
owners Mr & Mrs Ashton.
    3 rms No smoking CTV in all bedrooms Tea and coffee making
facilities No dogs Cen ht No children 12yrs 6P No coaches
Last d 3pm
PRICE GUIDE
ROOMS: s £15; d £30; wkly b&b fr £96; wkly hlf-bd
fr £140
                                                               (£)

HALFORD Warwickshire Map **04** SP24

◀ ◵◵ *Halford Bridge* Fosseway CV36 5BN ☎01789 740382
A listed Cotswold stone coaching inn on the A429 offering
modest, simply furnished bedrooms and a relaxed, informal
atmosphere with a welcoming open log fire. A wide range of food
is served in both the congenial lounge bar or in the cottage-style
dining room.
    6 rms (1 fmly) No smoking in area of dining room No smoking
in 1 lounge CTV in all bedrooms Tea and coffee making facilities
No dogs (ex guide dogs) CTV 40P Last d 9.30pm
CARDS: ▣ ▬

HALSTOCK Dorset Map **03** ST50

GH ◵◵◵ **Halstock Mill** BA22 9SJ (signposted from the
Cheddington road) ☎01935 891278
Closed Xmas
This cosy guest house, in a peaceful setting, is full of character.
The bedrooms are well equipped and comfortable and there is a
sitting room and a small dining room.
    4 en suite (bth) CTV in all bedrooms Tea and coffee making
facilities No dogs (ex guide dogs) Licensed Cen ht No children
5yrs 20P No coaches Stabling available Last d am
PRICE GUIDE
ROOMS: s £27-£30; d £44-£50; wkly b&b £139-£170; wkly hlf-
bd £237-£268✱
CARDS: ▣ ▬ ▬   (£)

HALTWHISTLE Northumberland Map **12** NY76

GH ◵◵◵ *Vallum Lodge* Military Rd, Twice Brewed, Bardon
Mill NE47 7AN (3.5m NE) ☎01434 344248
Closed Dec-Feb
A detached house stands three-and-a-half miles north of
Haltwhistle on the B6318; an old military road running close to
Hadrian's Wall. Mr and Mrs Wright offer a friendly atmosphere
and good-value home-cooked food. The ground-floor bedrooms
include two en suite rooms with new bathrooms. There are a
relaxing guest lounge and a cosy bar for residents and diners.

7 rms (2 bth/shr) (2 fmly) No smoking in bedrooms No smoking in dining room Tea and coffee making facilities Licensed Cen ht CTV 25P
CARDS:

Selected

♥ ⓠⓠⓠⓠ Mrs J Laidlow **Ald White Craig** *(NY713649)*
Shield Hill NE49 9NW (from B6318 turn off at Milecastle Inn, 0.75m on right) ☎01434 320565 & 321175
FAX 01434 320565
Lying high above the town to the north and with fine views across the valley, this original 17th-century croft has been modernised and extended to offer attractive bed and breakfast accommodation. Two doubles look out over the gardens, but it is the twin room to the side which has most style. Each room leads off from the open plan lounge and dining room, the latter with fine views from its picture window. Breakfasts are taken round the one circular table. From the A89 follow signs for Hadrian's Wall.
3 en suite (bth/shr) No smoking CTV in all bedrooms Tea and coffee making facilities No dogs (ex guide dogs) Cen ht No children 12yrs 3P 80 acres stock rearing rare breeds
PRICE GUIDE
ROOMS: s fr £25; d £38-£42; wkly b&b fr £133✳ (£)

Selected

♥ ⓠⓠⓠⓠ Mrs J Brown **Broomshaw Hill** *(NY706654)*
Willia Rd NE49 9NP ☎01434 320866 FAX 01434 320866
Mar-Nov
This farmhouse lies north of the town, in a picturesque setting overlooking the Halt Burn; a bridleway and footpath leads from the house to Hadrian's Wall, less than two miles away. Now carefully extended and converted into a stylish modern home, the house nevertheless retains much of its earlier character: exposed stone has been used to good effect, particularly in public areas which include a lounge with a wood-burning stove and a delightful dining room where breakfasts are taken round one big table. One of the bedrooms now has en suite facilities, whilst the other has a bathroom right next door.
3 rms (1 bth/shr) (1 fmly) No smoking in bedrooms No smoking in dining room CTV in all bedrooms Tea and coffee making facilities No dogs Cen ht CTV 6P 7 acres livestock horses
PRICE GUIDE
ROOMS: d £32-£40; wkly b&b £100-£130 (£)

HAMPSTHWAITE North Yorkshire Map **08** SE25

GH ⓠⓠⓠ *Lonsdale House* Village Green HG3 2EU
☎01423 771311
A late Victorian house which overlooks the green of this attractive village, situated in the beautiful Nidderdale countryside is only five miles from Harrogate. Most of the bedrooms have private bathrooms and are individually furnished and decorated, some having fine views. The restaurant specialises in wholesome English food using local produce, and there is a comfortable, spacious lounge.
5 rms (3 bth/shr) Tea and coffee making facilities Licensed Cen ht CTV 14P No coaches Last d noon

---

HAMPTON-IN-ARDEN West Midlands Map **04** SP28

GH ⓠⓠⓠ **Cottage** Kenilworth Rd B92 0LW (on A452)
☎01675 442323 FAX 01675 443323
Beside the A452, and handy for the NEC, this white cottage has gabled leaded windows. Space is at a premium, but the rooms are beautifully decorated and furnished. Owner Roger Howler is a popular, outgoing character who makes a stay here memorable.
9 rms (6 shr) (2 fmly) No smoking in dining room CTV in all bedrooms Tea and coffee making facilities Cen ht CTV 14P
PRICE GUIDE
ROOMS: s £20-£25; d £36-£39✳ (£)

GH ⓠⓠⓠ *Hollies* Kenilworth Rd B92 0LW (on A452, next to Jardenerie Garden Centre) ☎01675 442941 & 442681
FAX 01675 442941
rs 24-26 Dec
A modern detached house with a garden full of tubs and hanging baskets. The owners go out of their way to make guests feel comfortable. Breakfast is served in the lounge/diner and there are plenty of places to eat locally.
6 rms (4 shr) 2 annexe en suite (shr) (2 fmly) No smoking in 4 bedrooms No smoking in lounges CTV in all bedrooms Tea and coffee making facilities Cen ht CTV 12P
See advertisement under BIRMINGHAM (NATIONAL EXHIBITION CENTRE)

HANLEY CASTLE Hereford & Worcester Map **03** SO84

Selected

GH ⓠⓠⓠⓠ **Old Parsonage Farm** WR8 0BU (turn off B4211 onto B4209, 150yds on right) ☎01684 310124
Closed 2nd wk Dec-2nd wk Jan
This well-preserved and impeccably maintained 18th-century house is set in spacious gardens on the outskirts of the village. Two of the three comfortable bedrooms have en suite facilities whilst the third has a nearby private bathroom. An attractive dining room with separate tables features period-style furniture and an inglenook fireplace, and there are two comfortable lounges - one with a television.
3 en suite (bth) (1 fmly) No smoking No dogs Licensed Cen ht CTV No children 10yrs 6P No coaches Last d day before
PRICE GUIDE
ROOMS: s £29.50; d £41-£47; wkly hlf-bd £236-£256 (£)

HANWOOD Shropshire Map **07** SJ40

Selected

GH ⓠⓠⓠⓠ **White House** SY5 8LP (on A488)
☎01743 860414
Dating back some 400 years, this magnificent black and white farmhouse, surrounded by pleasant lawns and gardens, has been lovingly restored and converted in recent times by the friendly Mitchell family. The bedrooms are not particularly spacious as the original lines and walls have been retained, but beams and exposed timbers still feature. One room has a recently exposed wall section containing the original mud and straw used in its construction, which has been preserved for guests' interest. There are a cosy TV lounge, a bar with an inglenook fireplace, and an elegantly furnished sitting room.
6 rms (1 bth 1 shr) No smoking CTV in 1 bedroom Tea and coffee making facilities No dogs (ex guide dogs) Licensed ➡

Cen ht CTV No children 14yrs 15P No coaches Last d
8pm
PRICE GUIDE
ROOMS: s £20-£30; d £40-£50; wkly b&b £140-£210;
wkly hlf-bd £224-£294

HARLESTON Norfolk Map **05** TM28

◀ QQ *Swan Hotel* 19 The Thoroughfare IP20 9DQ
☎01379 852221 FAX 01379 854817
Friendly, helpful staff, personally supervised by the proprietors,
maintain a warm, relaxing atmosphere throughout this interesting
16th-century inn. A menu of popular, uncomplicated dishes is
provided in the recently upgraded beamed dining room, while
simply furnished and quite basic bedrooms are equipped with
colour TV, direct dial telephones and tea/coffee making facilities.
13 rms (10 bth) (1 fmly) CTV in all bedrooms Tea and coffee
making facilities Direct dial from bedrooms Cen ht CTV 75P
Last d 9pm
CARDS:

HARPFORD Devon Map **03** SY09

GH QQ Otter House EX10 0NH (turn off A3052 into
village, 0.25m on right after church) ☎01395 568330
A Grade II listed building dating back to the sixteenth century and
situated on the edge of the hamlet, this house offers stunning
views of Otter Valley - an area of outstanding natural beauty
which is particularly attractive to walkers and bird watchers.
Comfortable bedrooms are simply furnished, and a choice of
cooked breakfasts is served round one large table in the dining
room.
2 rms No smoking Tea and coffee making facilities No dogs (ex
guide dogs) Cen ht CTV 2P No coaches Last d 24hrs
PRICE GUIDE
ROOMS: s fr £17.50; d fr £35; wkly b&b fr £122.50✻
(£)

GH QQQ Peeks House EX10 0NH (off A3052, towards
Sidmouth turn first left after crossing River Otter)
☎01395 567664
An elegant Grade II listed building dating back to the 16th century
stands in this small village on the East Devon Way, with the
coastal resort of Sidmouth just over three miles away. Carefully
restored by owners Derek and Brenda Somerfield, the house now
provides modern accommodation with attractive fabrics used to
good effect in the bedrooms. The main public rooms feature
comfortable sofas and window seats in the drawing room and well
polished individual tables in the dining room. Meals can also be
served outside on the terrace when the weather permits.
5 en suite (bth/shr) No smoking in bedrooms No smoking in
dining room CTV in all bedrooms Tea and coffee making
facilities Licensed Cen ht CTV No children 5yrs 6P No
coaches Last d 1pm
PRICE GUIDE
ROOMS: d £42-£52; wkly b&b £140-£175; wkly hlf-bd £210-
£240
(£)

HARROGATE North Yorkshire Map **08** SE35

Selected

GH QQQQ Acacia Lodge 21 Ripon Rd HG1 2JL (on
A61 600yds N town centre) ☎01423 560752
Just a short walk from the town centre, this mellow, stone-
built semidetached Victorian house is set back from the A61.
Bedrooms, with a happy blend of modern and antique

---

furniture, are well equipped and attractively decorated. The
charming lounge is particularly inviting and has lots of
reading matter, and there is a pretty dining room.
5 en suite (bth/shr) (2 fmly) No smoking CTV in all
bedrooms Tea and coffee making facilities No dogs (ex
guide dogs) Cen ht CTV No children 5yrs 6P No coaches
PRICE GUIDE
ROOMS: s £32-£48; d £48-£58
(£)

Selected

GH QQQQ Alexa House & Stable Cottages 26 Ripon
Rd HG1 2JJ (on A61)
☎01423 501988 FAX 01423 504086
This attractive stone house, dating from 1830, is situated just
a short walk from the town centre on the Ripon road. The well
furnished accommodation includes a comfortable lounge and
dining room, where Yorkshire home cooking is served each
evening, as well as the prettily decorated and thoughtfully
equipped bedrooms. Some rooms are located in a converted
stable block to the rear.
9 en suite (bth/shr) 4 annexe en suite (shr) (1 fmly) No
smoking in 6 bedrooms No smoking in dining room CTV in
all bedrooms Tea and coffee making facilities Direct dial
from bedrooms Licensed Cen ht CTV 14P Last d 6.30pm
PRICE GUIDE
ROOMS: s £35-£40; d £52-£60
CARDS:
(£)

GH QQQ Anro 90 Kings Rd HG1 5JX (follow signs to
Conference Centre. House a short distance past on opposite
side of road) ☎01423 503087
Closed 22-28 Dec
This friendly guest house, situated almost opposite the Conference
Centre and close to the town centre, offers a good standard of
accommodation. Traditionally furnished bedrooms are bright and
fresh, and there are a cosy guests' lounge and a spacious dining
room where four-course dinners are served.
7 rms (4 shr) (1 fmly) No smoking in dining room CTV in all
bedrooms Tea and coffee making facilities No dogs Cen ht CTV
No children 7yrs Last d 4.15pm
PRICE GUIDE
ROOMS: s fr £19.50; d fr £39✻
(£)

Selected

GH QQQQ Ashley House Hotel 36-40 Franklin Rd
HG1 5EE ☎01423 507474 FAX 01423 560858
rs Dec
Three converted town houses make up this hotel, which is set
in a tree-lined road close to the International Conference
Centre. Bedrooms are attractively decorated and most have en
suite facilities and other modern features. There are two
lounges, a bar and a pretty dining room where breakfast and
evening meals are served.
17 en suite (bth/shr) (2 fmly) No smoking in 2 bedrooms No
smoking in dining room No smoking in 1 lounge CTV in all

bedrooms Tea and coffee making facilities Direct dial from bedrooms Licensed Cen ht CTV 6P Last d noon
PRICE GUIDE
ROOMS: s £27.55-£35; d £45-£65; wkly b&b £165-£210; wkly hlf-bd £225-£280
CARDS:

GH QQQ **Ashwood House** 7 Spring Grove HG1 2HS (off A61) ☎01423 560081 FAX 01423 527928
Closed 24-31 Dec
This handsome Edwardian house has been carefully furnished to a high standard. Attractive bedrooms have good facilities, the lounge is very comfortable and excellent breakfasts are served in an elegant dining room pleasantly decorated in Wedgwood blue.
8 en suite (bth/shr) (1 fmly) No smoking in 6 bedrooms No smoking in dining room CTV in all bedrooms Tea and coffee making facilities No dogs Licensed Cen ht CTV 5P No coaches
PRICE GUIDE
ROOMS: s £25-£30; d £40-£45✱
£

GH QQQ **Cavendish Hotel** 3 Valley Dr HG2 0JJ
☎01423 509637
Overlooking the Valley Gardens and convenient for the town centre, this large, family owned and run sandstone house offers a friendly welcome and caring service; attractively furnished bedrooms are well equipped, and there is a pleasant, very comfortable lounge.
9 en suite (bth/shr) No smoking in 1 bedrooms No smoking in dining room CTV in all bedrooms Tea and coffee making facilities Direct dial from bedrooms Licensed Cen ht Last d 8.30pm
PRICE GUIDE
ROOMS: s £25-£35; d £50-£65✱
CARDS:
£

Selected

GH QQQQ **The Dales Hotel** 101 Valley Dr HG2 0JP
☎01423 507248 FAX 01423 507248
rs Xmas
Overlooking the delightful Valley Gardens, this well furnished house has attractively co-ordinated bedrooms with a good range of facilities. An elegant lounge with an honesty bar is also provided, and there is a neat dining room to the rear. The house is enthusiastically run by resident owners.
8 rms (6 bth/shr) (2 fmly) No smoking in dining room CTV in all bedrooms Tea and coffee making facilities Licensed Cen ht CTV 1P Last d 9am
PRICE GUIDE
ROOMS: s £26-£28; d £48-£54
CARDS:
£

Selected

GH QQQQ *Delaine Hotel* 17 Ripon Rd HG1 2JL
☎01423 567974 FAX 01423 561723
Rupert and Marian Viner are the friendly hosts at the Delaine, an attractive house in lovely gardens, well worthy of its 'selected' award. It offers pretty bedrooms, a comfortable lounge, and good home cooking.
8 en suite (bth/shr) 2 annexe en suite (bth/shr) (2 fmly) No ➠

smoking in bedrooms No smoking in dining room CTV in all bedrooms Tea and coffee making facilities Direct dial from bedrooms No dogs Licensed Cen ht CTV 12P No coaches Last d 3pm
CARDS:

GH Q Q **Gillmore Hotel** 98 Kings Rd HG1 5HH (from town centre turn into Kings Rd pass conference centre hotel approx 200yds on right) ☎01423 503699 FAX 01423 503699
Within walking distance of the Conference Centre, this privately owned guest house provides modern bedrooms, including family rooms, and there is a comfortable lounge with a large-screen TV.
22 rms (2 bth 4 shr) (8 fmly) CTV in 9 bedrooms Tea and coffee making facilities Licensed Cen ht CTV 20P Snooker Last d 4pm
PRICE GUIDE
ROOMS: s £21-£22.50; d £35-£38

£

GH Q Q Q **Glenayr** 19 Franklin Mount HG1 5EJ ☎01423 504259
Situated in a quiet side road not far from the Conference Centre, this well maintained house offers high quality accommodation which represents good value for money. The comprehensively equipped bedrooms are bright and fresh, and guests also have the use of a cosy lounge.
6 rms (5 shr) No smoking in dining room CTV in all bedrooms Tea and coffee making facilities No dogs (ex guide dogs) Licensed Cen ht 3P No coaches Last d 4.30pm
PRICE GUIDE
ROOMS: s £18-£19; d £40-£45; wkly b&b £119-£133; wkly hlf-bd £199.50-£213.50
CARDS:

£

Selected

GH Q Q Q Q *Kimberley Hotel* 11-19 Kings Rd HG1 5JY ☎01423 505613 FAX 01423 530270
A large, completely refurbished hotel, the Kimberley is conveniently located for the conference centre and has well furnished bedrooms with a good range of equipment, including trouser presses, hairdryers and cable and satellite TV. There are extensive conference facilities as well as a lounge bar and a breakfast room.
49 en suite (bth/shr) (5 fmly) No smoking in dining room CTV in all bedrooms Tea and coffee making facilities Direct dial from bedrooms Licensed Lift Cen ht 45P
CARDS:

GH Q Q Q **Knox Mill House** Knox Mill Ln, Killinghall HG3 2AE (off A61, between Harrogate and Killinghall) ☎01423 560650
Built around 1785, this former mill owner's house is in a lovely location on the banks of a mill stream by the original waterwheel. All the attractively decorated bedrooms face south with views over the meadows and stream beyond. There is a comfortable lounge with colour TV and a single dining table in a vaulted alcove (once a dairy), with a small library adjoining.
3 rms (2 shr) No smoking Tea and coffee making facilities No dogs Cen ht CTV No children 10yrs 4P No coaches
PRICE GUIDE
ROOMS: d £38✱

£

GH Q Q Q **Lamont House** 12 St Mary's Walk HG2 0LW ☎01423 567143
Closed Xmas
Situated in a quiet side road, this Victorian house offers a good standard of accommodation, several bedrooms having been fully refurbished; there is also a comfortable lounge where guests can relax.
8 rms (5 shr) No smoking in bedrooms No smoking in dining room CTV in all bedrooms Tea and coffee making facilities Licensed Cen ht
PRICE GUIDE
ROOMS: s £20-£27.50; d £40-£50
CARDS:

£

GH Q Q **Prince's Hotel** 7 Granby Rd HG1 4ST (off A59) ☎01423 883469
This late-Victorian house stands just off the A59 as it enters The Stray. The bedrooms are well furnished in character with the rest of the house; one has a four-poster bed. The lounge is comfortable and the cosy rear dining room serves good home-cooked food.
6 rms (2 bth 2 shr) (1 fmly) No smoking in 1 bedrooms No smoking in dining room CTV in all bedrooms Tea and coffee making facilities No dogs Cen ht CTV No children 3yrs No parking No coaches Last d 9am

---

GH Q Q **The Richmond** 56 Dragon View, Skipton Rd HG1 4DG (off A59) ☎01423 530612 FAX 01423 530612
This family owned and run guest house stands close to the famous Stray, set back from the A59 on the east side of the town; comfortably appointed throughout, it offers value-for-money accommodation and good service. Public rooms include a lounge and a good-sized dining room.
6 rms (5 shr) No smoking in dining room CTV in all bedrooms Tea and coffee making facilities No dogs (ex guide dogs) Cen ht CTV 2P No coaches
PRICE GUIDE
ROOMS: s £20; d £40
CARDS:

£

GH Q Q **Roxanne** 12 Franklin Mount HG1 5EJ ☎01423 569930
Closed Xmas week
This small, Victorian house in a quiet side road is conveniently placed for the Conference Centre. Bright, pleasant bedrooms are provided, together with a combined lounge and dining room where there is a TV set.
5 rms (1 fmly) CTV in 3 bedrooms Tea and coffee making facilities No dogs (ex guide dogs) Cen ht CTV 2P Last d 4pm
PRICE GUIDE
ROOMS: s £16-£18; d £32-£36; wkly b&b £112-£126; wkly hlf-bd £150.50-£164.50✱

£

Factual details of establishments in this Guide are from questionnaires we send to all establishments that feature in the book.

GH Ⓠ *Shelbourne* 78 Kings Rd HG1 5JX ☎01423 504390
Situated close to the conference centre, this small guest house
offers an adequate standard of accommodation together with
friendly service. Public rooms comprise a cosy lounge and
breakfast room/bar.
8 rms (3 fmly) No smoking in dining room CTV in all bedrooms
Tea and coffee making facilities Licensed Cen ht CTV 1P No
coaches Last d noon
CARDS: 🅰 🖅

GH ⓆⓆⓆ **Stoney Lea** 13 Spring Grove HG1 2HS
☎01423 501524
Closed Xmas-after new Year
Set in a quiet side road, this well maintained house stands within
easy walking distance of both the town and the Conference
Centre. En suite bedrooms are well equipped, public areas include
a comfortable lounge and pleasant dining room.
7 en suite (bth/shr) No smoking in dining room CTV in all
bedrooms Tea and coffee making facilities No dogs (ex guide
dogs) Cen ht CTV No children 4yrs 3P No coaches
PRICE GUIDE
ROOMS: s fr £26; d fr £40

GH ⓆⓆⓆ **Wharfedale House** 28 Harlow Moor Dr HG2 0JY
(alongside the Valley Gardens in central Harrogate)
☎01423 522233
Pleasantly located overlooking Valley Gardens, this immaculately
kept hotel is also convenient for the town and Conference Centre.
Bedrooms are well appointed, and there are a comfortable lounge
where drinks are served and an attractive dining room. The owners
are both trained chefs and the meals are often prepared to an
individual's requirement.
8 en suite (bth/shr) (2 fmly) No smoking in dining room CTV in
all bedrooms Tea and coffee making facilities Direct dial from
bedrooms Licensed Cen ht 3P Last d 4pm
(£)

GH ⓆⓆⓆ **Wynnstay House** 60 Franklin Rd HG1 5EE (in
town centre turn into Strawberry Dale opposite the
conference centre left at the end of the road, last house on
left) ☎01423 560476
Situated in a side road convenient for the town and Conference
Centre, this well maintained guest house offers good all-round
standards of accommodation. Friendly service is provided by
resident owners Linda and Vince Spooner, and hearty breakfasts
are a feature.
5 en suite (shr) (2 fmly) No smoking in dining room CTV in 6
bedrooms Tea and coffee making facilities Cen ht No coaches
Last d 2pm
PRICE GUIDE
ROOMS: s £19-£21; d £38-£42; wkly b&b £126; wkly hlf-bd
£175✳
CARDS: 🅰 🖅
(£)

We endeavour to be as accurate as possible
but changes in personnel and data can occur
in establishments after the Guide has gone to
press.

HARROP FOLD Lancashire Map **07** SD74

Premier Selected

♥ ⓆⓆⓆⓆⓆ Mr & Mrs P
Wood *Harrop Fold Country
Farmhouse Hotel* (SD746492)
BBY 4PJ ☎01200 447600
Closed Jan
This delightful 16th-century
farmhouse, surrounded by
land which has been farmed
by the very hospitable Wood
family for the last thirty three
years, is ideally situated just
fifteen minutes from
Clitheroe and twenty minutes from the A59, providing a
wonderful base from which to explore both Lancashire and
Yorkshire. Pretty en suite bedrooms, including a small suite,
are all very comfortably furnished and filled with such
thoughtful touches as fruit and a small welcoming bottle of
wine. The first-floor sitting room enjoys the most wonderful
views and the cosy restaurant popular with many for the range
of carefully prepared, home-cooked dishes that are offered,
overlooks the gardens.
5 en suite (bth) 2 annexe en suite (bth/shr) No smoking in
bedrooms No smoking in dining room No smoking in 1
lounge CTV in all bedrooms Tea and coffee making facilities
Direct dial from bedrooms No dogs (ex guide dogs)
Licensed Cen ht 16P 280 acres sheep beef Last d 8pm
CARDS: 🅰 🖅

HARROW Greater London Map **04** TQ18

GH Ⓠ **Central Hotel** 6 Hindes Rd HA1 1SJ (off A409,
opposite Tesco supermarket)
☎0181 427 0893 FAX 0181 427 0893
There are plenty of car parking spaces at this modest but neatly
kept guest house located to the eastern end of the road. Guests are
looked after by a chatty resident owner who has been in charge for
ten years.
10 rms (3 shr) (3 fmly) CTV in all bedrooms Tea and coffee
making facilities No dogs Cen ht CTV 12P
PRICE GUIDE
ROOMS: s £25-£36; d £32-£48✳
CARDS: 🅰 🖅

GH ⓆⓆⓆ *Crescent Hotel* 58/62 Welldon Crescent HA1 1QR
☎0181 863 5491 FAX 0181 427 5965
Three houses have been linked together to create this friendly
hotel which is located in a quiet residential district. The bedrooms
vary in shape but are well equipped, offering direct dial telephones
and mini fridges. Dinner is served in a dining room which faces
the long lawns to the rear of the building.
21 rms (13 shr) (3 fmly) No smoking in dining room CTV in all
bedrooms Tea and coffee making facilities Direct dial from
bedrooms No dogs (ex guide dogs) Licensed Cen ht CTV 8P
Last d 8.15pm
CARDS: 🅰 🖃 🖅 ⓪

GH ⓆⓆ **Hindes Hotel** 8 Hindes Rd HA1 1SJ
☎0181 427 7468 FAX 0181 424 0673
Bedrooms are gradually being improved to match the comfortable
public areas at this friendly guest house. There are a bright open
kitchen and breakfast room as well as a large lounge with a colour
TV.
14 rms (7 shr) (2 fmly) No smoking in dining room CTV in all

bedrooms Tea and coffee making facilities No dogs (ex guide dogs) Cen ht CTV 30P Last d 4.30pm
PRICE GUIDE
ROOMS: s £25-£35; d £35-£49✳
CARDS: (£)

HARTFIELD East Sussex Map **05** TQ43

Selected

♥ QQQQ Mrs C Cooper **Bolebroke Watermill**
(TQ481373) Perry Hill, Edenbridge Rd TN7 4JP (off B2026 1m N of Hartfield) ☎01892 770425 FAX 01892 770425
Mar-Nov
A delightful old mill and barn has been converted into this unique and charming guest house. The barn has three bedrooms, two of which have four poster beds, and all are tastefully furnished and well-equipped. These rooms share a spacious comfortable lounge with lots of books and magazines. A narrow, steep staircase leads to the two compact bedrooms in the Mill, which also has its own lounge. Thoughtful touches such as a decanter of sherry and a bowl of fruit are welcome extras. Breakfast is served in the main house and Mrs Cooper has established a well deserved reputation for her breakfasts. Dinner is no longer served, but a light, cold snack can be served to guests in their bedrooms.
2 en suite (bth/shr) 3 annexe en suite (bth/shr) No smoking CTV in all bedrooms Tea and coffee making facilities No dogs (ex guide dogs) Cen ht No children 7yrs 8P 5 acres smallholding
PRICE GUIDE
ROOMS: s £48-£65; d £53-£70
CARDS:

HARTINGTON Derbyshire Map **07** SK16

GH QQ *Bank House* Market Place SK17 0AL
☎01298 84465
Closed Xmas & 2 wks annual holiday
Bank House, a listed Georgian building, stands in the main square of this delightful village. Mrs Blackburn maintains good standards of housekeeping, and the bedrooms are neat and fresh in appearance. Guests have sole use of a comfortable TV lounge on the top floor of the house, and breakfast is taken in the ground-floor dining room and evening meals are served by prior arrangement.
5 rms (1 bth/shr) No smoking in dining room Tea and coffee making facilities CTV 3P No coaches Last d previous day

---

HARTLAND Devon Map **02** SS22

GH QQ **Fosfelle** EX39 6EF (off A39 onto B3248 for 2m entrance on right) ☎01237 441273
A 17th-century manor house stands in well kept gardens and lovely countryside a short drive from the sea. Two lakes provide trout and coarse fishing, which are both popular. The bedrooms have comfortable beds and are furnished in country style with some antiques; modern facilities including telephones and tea-making equipment are also provided. The spacious dining room offers both carte and fixed-price menus.
7 rms (1 bth 3 shr) (2 fmly) No smoking in bedrooms CTV in 4 bedrooms Tea and coffee making facilities No dogs (ex guide dogs) Licensed Cen ht CTV ch fac 20P Fishing Snooker Last d 9pm
PRICE GUIDE
ROOMS: s £19-£24; d £36-£42; wkly b&b £120-£140; wkly hlf-bd £165-£185
CARDS: (£)

HARWICH Essex

See also Manningtree

♥ QQQQ Mrs H P Mitchell **New Farm House** *(TM165289)*
Spinnel's Ln CO11 2UJ ☎01255 870365 FAX 01255 870837
(For full entry see Wix)

HASELEY KNOB Warwickshire Map **04** SP27

Selected

GH QQQQ **Croft** CV35 7NL (from Warwick By-Pass take A4177 towards Solihull and in 4.5m turn right signed M6 Lichfield then in .5m turn right)
☎01926 484447 FAX 01926 484447
Closed Xmas wk
A family-run guest house and smallholding, The Croft is located in the small village of Haseley Knob, five miles from the centre of Warwick and only ten miles from the NEC in Birmingham. A warm welcome is provided by David and Pat Clapp, who have built up the house from a near derelict cottage. The lounge and bedrooms are full of personal touches, and the accommodation is immaculately kept; the two ground-floor rooms interconnect via a locked door in the bathrooms.
5 en suite (shr) (2 fmly) No smoking CTV in all bedrooms Tea and coffee making facilities Cen ht CTV 8P No coaches
PRICE GUIDE
ROOMS: s fr £20; d fr £40✳ (£)

See advertisement under WARWICK

HASTINGS & ST LEONARDS East Sussex Map **05** TQ80

GH Q Q **Argyle** 32 Cambridge Gardens TN34 1EN
☎01424 421294
Conveniently located within walking distance of the railway
station and town centre, this bed and breakfast guest house has
been run by the resident proprietor, Mr Emmanuel Jacob, for over
17 years. All the bedrooms have TV, tea trays, controllable heating
and double glazing. Downstairs there are a TV lounge and a cosy
breakfast room.
8 rms (3 shr) (3 fmly) No smoking in dining room CTV in all
bedrooms Tea and coffee making facilities No dogs Cen ht CTV
No children 4yrs No parking
PRICE GUIDE
ROOMS: s fr £16; d fr £30; wkly b&b fr £91✳

Premier Selected

GH Q Q Q Q Q **Bryn-y-
Mor** 12 Godwin Rd TN35 5JR
(A259 coast road keeping sea
on right bear left at Old
Town & follow road up hill,
at the Convent turn right into
Ashburton Rd then 2nd right)
☎01424 722744 FAX 01424
445933

This unique privately run
hotel recreates Victorian
standards of comfort and luxury. Together with modern
facilities, the bedrooms have been filled with Victoriana and
antiques, and are ornately furnished with four-poster or half-
tester beds, sofas and chaises longues. All rooms are en suite
except for one, which has sole use of a sumptuous bathroom
opposite. Bathrobes are provided, along with other thoughtful
extras. Dinner is no longer available, and breakfast is served
in the main lounge, which has stunning views over the town.
Two self catering cottages are also available, and
otherfeatures are a terraced garden and an outdoor swimming
pool.
4 rms (3 shr) (2 fmly) No smoking in bedrooms No smoking
in dining room No smoking in 1 lounge CTV in all
bedrooms Tea and coffee making facilities No dogs (ex
guide dogs) Licensed Cen ht CTV 4P No coaches Outdoor
swimming pool (heated)
PRICE GUIDE
ROOMS: s £28-£40; d £50-£70✳
CARDS: £

GH Q Q **Caspers** 8 Tackleway TN34 3DE (off A259)
☎01424 712880
Caspers, an 18th-century Grade II listed terraced house, provides a
friendly home from home with two letting rooms on the top floor,
and excellent views overlooking the harbour and town. The house
is personally run by proprietors Derek and Elaine Caspar, and
families are made particularly welcome. Meals are served by
arrangement in the attractive breakfast room, and special
vegetarian breakfasts are a feature. Street parking is usually
available.
2 rms (1 fmly) No smoking in dining room No smoking in
lounges CTV in all bedrooms Tea and coffee making facilities
No dogs
PRICE GUIDE
ROOMS: s fr £18; d £28; wkly b&b £87.50✳

GH Q Q Q **Eagle House** Pevensey Rd TN38 0JZ
☎01424 430535 & 441273 FAX 01424 437771
This peacefully located private hotel, was formerly occupied by an
army officer who fought in the Napoleonic wars and adopted the
consul's emblem, the eagle, as a crest for his residence. Bedrooms
are comfortable (with double glazing and traditional furnishings)
and well equipped; most have a writing table and chair, and all
have direct dial telephone, tv, clock radio, hair dryers and tea
trays. Room service is available between 7am and 11pm, and a
supper tray can be provided. A daily four-course dinner is also
served, prepared with fresh ingredients, and taken in the
sumptuous dining room with its silver table appointments and
crystal chandeliers.
20 en suite (bth/shr) (2 fmly) No smoking in dining room CTV
in 23 bedrooms Tea and coffee making facilities Direct dial from
bedrooms No dogs (ex guide dogs) Licensed Cen ht 13P No
coaches Last d 8.30pm
CARDS: ■ ■ ■ ■

Premier Selected

GH Q Q Q Q Q **Parkside
House** 59 Lower Park Rd
TN34 2LD (follow town centre
signs turn right at first traffic
lights then first right into
Lower Park Rd)
☎01424 433096
FAX 01424 421431

Quietly located in an elevated
position facing Alexandra
Park, this elegant Victorian
house has been lovingly restored and modernised whilst
retaining all the original architectural features. Non smoking
and individually furnished with every modern amenity and
lots of little extras, bedrooms have been furnished and
equipped to a very high standard and complemented by a first
class combined lounge and breakfast room. Friendly and
helpful service is personally provided by the resident
proprietor Mr Brian Kent the atmosphere is relaxed and
informal and there are no car parking restrictions.
5 rms (4 shr) (1 fmly) CTV in all bedrooms Tea and coffee
making facilities Direct dial from bedrooms No dogs (ex
guide dogs) Licensed Cen ht CTV No parking Last d 3pm

▭ ▭ **GH** Q Q **The Ridge Guest House & Restaurant** 361
The Ridge TN34 2RD ☎01424 754240
A popular, family run bed and breakfast establishment, The Ridge
offers functional modern bedrooms, some located on the ground
floor. Evening meals are available by prior arrangement, and
served in the spacious restaurant. A bar and TV lounge are
provided for guests.
11 en suite (shr) (2 fmly) CTV in all bedrooms Tea and coffee
making facilities No dogs Licensed Cen ht CTV 40P Last d
9.15pm
PRICE GUIDE
ROOMS: s £16-£18; d £26-£30; wkly b&b £90-£105
CARDS: ■

Selected

GH Q Q Q Q **Tower House Hotel** 26-28 Tower Rd West
TN38 0RG ☎01424 427217 & 423771
Quietly located above St Leonards-on-Sea, this Victorian
house has been skilfully extended to provide a choice of

bedrooms, some of which are on the ground floor. The rooms are individually decorated, some with private bathrooms, and all have TV and tea trays. A freshly prepared set menu is provided in the attractive, well furnished dining room, and other public rooms include a conservatory breakfast room, small well stocked bar, and a spacious comfortable lounge. Service is particularly helpful, available throughout the day from resident proprietors Roy and Joan Richards. There is no car park, but unrestricted street parking is readily available.

11 en suite (bth/shr) (2 fmly) No smoking in bedrooms No smoking in dining room CTV in 12 bedrooms Tea and coffee making facilities No dogs Licensed Cen ht CTV No parking No coaches Last d 4pm

PRICE GUIDE

ROOMS: s £25-£31.50; d £45-£50; wkly b&b £150-£189.50; wkly hlf-bd £230.50-£269.50

CARDS: £

GH QQ *Waldorf Hotel* 4 Carlisle Pde TN34 1JG (located on the main coastal road A259 from Folkestone to Brighton, between Hastings Old Town and the pier) ☎01424 422185

This long-established seafront hotel, offers a range of modern bedrooms, some with good sea views. There is an attractive restaurant and a traditionally furnished, cosy lounge, and a freshly prepared three-course evening meal is provided by prior arrangement. Service, by the Harding family, is friendly and helpful. There is a pay and display car park opposite.

12 rms (3 bth 2 shr) (3 fmly) CTV in all bedrooms Tea and coffee making facilities No dogs (ex guide dogs) Licensed CTV No parking Last d 11.30am

---

Selected

♥ QQQQ Mrs B Yorke **Filsham Farmhouse** *(TQ784096)* 111 Harley Shute Rd TN38 8BY ☎01424 433109 FAX 01424 461061

Closed Xmas & New Year

Although in what is now a residential area, Filsham is a Grade II listed 17th-century farmhouse, retaining much of its historic charm. Each of the three bedrooms has its own charm and all are furnished with quality antiques and pretty soft furnishings. The four-poster room is en suite whilst the other two share a large bathroom with separate showers and another has a WC with washbasin. The large hall doubles as an dining room and lounge with assorted antiques and objets d'art, original beams and an impressive inglenook fireplace with a real log fire. Mrs York is a natural hostess and plays her part in ensuring a memorable stay.

3 rms (1 shr) No smoking in bedrooms CTV in all bedrooms Tea and coffee making facilities Cen ht CTV 4P 1 acres non-working Last d am

PRICE GUIDE

ROOMS: s £20-£25; d £35-£45* £

◣ QQQ *Highlands* 1 Boscobel Rd TN38 0LU ☎01424 420299 FAX 01424 465065

rs 25 & 26 Dec

This former gentleman's residence is situated within easy reach of the sea front, on the western fringe of St Leonards. It has been skilfully converted to provide comfortable, well furnished accommodation, including a family room. The cosy bar is very popular locally, and serves freshly prepared bar meals and real ale. Breakfast is served in a small adjacent dining room, and the downstairs restaurant is now used as a function room. There is a front terrace summer patio, and some forecourt parking.

9 en suite (shr) (1 fmly) CTV in all bedrooms Tea and coffee

---

making facilities No dogs (ex guide dogs) Cen ht CTV 8P No coaches Last d 9.30pm

CARDS:

HATHERSAGE Derbyshire Map **08** SK28

♥ QQQ Mr & Mrs P S Wain **Highlow Hall** *(SK219802)* S30 1AX (off B6001 between Hathersage & Grindleford, turn towards Abney & Gliding Club for 1.5m) ☎01433 650393

This characterful 16th century stone house enjoys the most wonderful views from its position one-and-a-half miles from Hathersage, in the heart of the Peak District National Park. Its enthusiastic young owners will ensure that guests are given a very warm welcome and are well looked after. The spacious bedrooms, three of which are en suite, are very attractively decorated and comfortably furnished. Guests have the use of a comfortable lounge, and dinner is available in the spacious dining room. The house also has a magnificent Great Hall, largely unchanged since it was built, which is occasionally used for private parties.

6 rms (3 shr) (2 fmly) No smoking in bedrooms No smoking in dining room Tea and coffee making facilities No dogs Licensed CTV 12P 900 acres mixed sheep Last d 12hrs

PRICE GUIDE

ROOMS: s £18; d £40-£60; wkly b&b £120-£180; wkly hlf-bd £207.50-£267.50*

♥ QQQ Mrs Jill Salisbury **Land End** Abney S30 1AA (Take B6001 from Hathersage for 0.5m. Turn right opposite Plough Inn and travel 2.5m. House first on right after village sign) ☎01433 650371 FAX 01433 650371

This attractive stone-built farmhouse, which enjoys the most wonderful views of the Derbyshire Peak District, is situated in the beautiful hamlet of Abney, between Hathersage and Tideswell. Jill and Richard Salisbury take great care in looking after their guests ➡

and an equal amount of care has been given to the decoration of the very attractively and comfortably furnished bedrooms. One room has a smart en suite shower room and the other two share a large bathroom. There is a small comfortable sitting room and a dining room with a communal table, where breakfast is served. Stabling is available for guests who wish to bring their own horses.

3 rms (1 shr) No smoking in dining room No smoking in lounges Tea and coffee making facilities No dogs Cen ht CTV 74 acres beef sheep
PRICE GUIDE
ROOMS: d fr £33

◀ Q Q Q **Scotsman's Pack** School Ln S30 1BZ (off A625 turning onto School Ln, inn 50 yds from the turning, follow signs to the church) ☎01433 650253
Closed 24-26 Dec
This cosy inn is situated on the edge of a picturesque village in the heart of the Peak District National Park. The atmosphere is informal and hospitable proprietors Brian and Sally Williams ensure that their guests are comfortable and well looked after. Home-cooked dishes prepared by Sally are served in the open-plan bar which has a beamed ceiling, plenty of gleaming polished brass and an open fire. There are three non smoking tables in addition to a separate breakfast room. The four bedrooms, all of which are en suite, are comfortable, well equipped and very attractively furnished with pretty colour co-ordinated soft furnishings.

4 en suite (bth/shr) No smoking in area of dining room CTV in all bedrooms Tea and coffee making facilities No dogs (ex guide dogs) Cen ht No children 14yrs 13P Last d 9.30pm
PRICE GUIDE
ROOMS: s £27.50-£35; d £50-£55; wkly b&b £192.50✳
MEALS: Bar Lunch £4-£11 Dinner £10-£15✳

HATTON Warwickshire Map 04 SP26

Selected

GH Q Q Q Q *Northleigh House* Five Ways Rd CV35 7HZ (off A4177) ☎01926 484203
Closed 15 Dec-30 Jan
A large detached house, its attractive gardens surrounded by agricultural land, offers impeccably maintained accommodation, the majority of the individually styled bedrooms being quite spacious and including fridges among their good array of modern equipment. The attractive dining room is furnished in period style, as is the spacious lounge with its comfortable seating and wealth of reading material; evening meals can be provided (by prior arrangement) for parties of four or more. There is a total ban on smoking throughout the house.

7 en suite (bth/shr) No smoking CTV in all bedrooms Tea and coffee making facilities Cen ht CTV 10P No coaches Last d previous day
CARDS: 💳 💳
See advertisement under WARWICK

HAVANT Hampshire Map 04 SU70

See **Emsworth**

HAVERIGG Cumbria Map 07 SD17

GH Q Q Q **Dunelm Cottage** Main St LA18 4EX ☎01229 770097
Closed Jan
Situated in the centre of the village, close to the Harbour Inn, this delightful guest house has been converted from two white-painted cottages with leaded windows. Bedrooms are charmingly decorated and furnished, and although none have en suite facilities there are bath and shower rooms adjacent. There is a cosy lounge, and good home cooking is served at a long table in the dining room by resident owner Mrs Fairless, who also produces delicious home-made cakes and preserves. Just across the road is a very convenient car park.

3 rms Tea and coffee making facilities Cen ht CTV No children 10yrs No parking No coaches Last d 6.30pm
PRICE GUIDE
ROOMS: s fr £24; d fr £43; wkly b&b fr £155; wkly hlf-bd fr £220✳

HAWES North Yorkshire Map 07 SD88

GH Q Q Q **Steppe Haugh** Town Head DL8 3RH (on A684) ☎01969 667645
This charming cottage-style house dates back to 1643 and is said to be the oldest in Hawes. There are an attractive dining room with lace-covered tables and an inviting lounge. Bedrooms are mainly compact but are prettily decorated and furnished.

6 rms (2 shr) No smoking in bedrooms No smoking in dining room CTV in 2 bedrooms Tea and coffee making facilities Licensed Cen ht CTV No children 7yrs 6P No coaches Last d 6.30pm
PRICE GUIDE
ROOMS: s £18-£20; d £33-£46

HAWKHURST Kent Map 05 TQ73

GH Q Q Q **Southgate-Little Fowlers** Rye Rd TN18 5DA (on A268) ☎01580 752526
Closed Nov-Feb
Conveniently located on the outskirts of the village in an attractive garden, this former farm and dowagers house dates in part from the late 17th century. Accommodation has been individually furnished to retain the original character and is still being improved. A comfortable lounge and a separate conservatory breakfast room (featuring a Muscat grape vine) are available for guests' use and there is a children's play area in the rear garden. Freshly prepared full English breakfast is included in the room tariff, and service is friendly and helpful.

2 en suite (bth/shr) (1 fmly) No smoking CTV in all bedrooms Tea and coffee making facilities No dogs (ex guide dogs) Cen ht CTV 4P No coaches
PRICE GUIDE
ROOMS: d £38-£42✳

Our inspectors never book in the name of the AA. They disclose their identity only after the bill has been paid.

HAWKSHEAD Cumbria Map **07** SD39

See advertisement on p. 201

GH ⬜⬜⬜ **Ivy House** LA22 0NS ☎015394 36204
16 Mar-4 Nov

An attractive Grade II listed Georgian building situated close to
the centre of the village. Bedrooms are comfortably furnished and
all have en suite facilities. Some are in Mere Lodge, just across the
drive, and these rooms have TV, unlike those in the main house.
There is a comfortable guests' lounge and also a spacious and well
appointed dining room in which good English cooking is a feature.
6 en suite (bth/shr) 5 annexe en suite (bth/shr) (2 fmly) No
smoking in dining room CTV in 5 bedrooms Tea and coffee
making facilities Licensed Cen ht CTV 14P No coaches
Fishing Last d 6pm

PRICE GUIDE

ROOMS: s £26-£28; d £52-£56; wkly hlf-bd
£227-£241.50*

Selected

GH ⬜⬜⬜⬜ **Rough Close Country House** LA22 0QF
(1.25m S on Newby Bridge rd) ☎015394 36370
Apr-Oct rs Mar

This charming country house is peacefully situated in its own
grounds and gardens, overlooking beautiful Esthwaite Water, ➡

to the south of the village. The accommodation is immaculate andfurnishings and decoration are of a high standard. There are a very spacious and comfortable lounge and a cosy bar featuring a collection of horse brasses. A daily-changing dinner menu is provided in the delightful dining room, local produce being put to good use whenever possible.

5 en suite (bth/shr) No smoking in bedrooms No smoking in dining room Tea and coffee making facilities No dogs (ex guide dogs) Licensed Cen ht CTV No children 12yrs 10P No coaches Last d 7pm

PRICE GUIDE

ROOMS: (incl. dinner) s £41-£43.50; d £72-£77; wkly b&b £175-£192.50; wkly hlf-bd £241.50-£259

CARDS: £

◀ QQ **Kings Arms Hotel** LA22 0NZ (on Main Sq) ☎015394 36372

This old Lakeland inn with oak beams and an open fire, is situated in the centre of the village, and provides a good standard of accommodation and also a wide range of food, either in the bar or the attractive dining room. The Kings Arms prides itself on its selection of malt whiskies and choice of real ale. Parking is free with a hotel permit in the pay and display car park.

9 rms (6 shr) (2 fmly) No smoking in dining room CTV in all bedrooms Tea and coffee making facilities Direct dial from bedrooms Cen ht P Fishing Last d 9pm

PRICE GUIDE

ROOMS: s £24-£33; d £38-£56✳

MEALS: Lunch £7.70-£15 Dinner £7.70-£15&alc✳

CARDS: £

◀ QQQ **Sun** Main St LA22 0NT ☎015394 36236

The Sun is an 18th-century inn situated in the popular village of Hawkshead. Bedrooms, which have recently been upgraded, are particularly good and have lots of character with oak beams, wood panelling and stone walls as well as modern co-ordinated fabrics. All have en suite facilities and colour TV and some have brass bedsteads. Meals are served in the beamed bars and the two dining areas.

6 en suite (bth/shr) (1 fmly) No smoking in bedrooms No smoking in area of dining room CTV in all bedrooms Tea and coffee making facilities No dogs Cen ht No parking Last d 9.30pm

CARDS:

HAWNBY North Yorkshire Map 08 SE58

✿ QQQ Mrs S Smith **Laskill** (SE564905) Hawnby YO6 5NB (6m N of Helmsley on the B1257) ☎01439 798268

This charming farmhouse is situated in a beautiful valley just off the B1257, six miles north of Helmsley and is part of a 70-acre working sheep and cattle farm. All the bedrooms have thoughtful extra touches; some of them are located on the ground floor of a tastefully converted outbuilding, and most of the attractively decorated ones in the main house have their own showers. There is a very comfortable guests' lounge with an open fire and plenty of books in addition to the attractive little dining room, where Susan Smith's delicious home-cooked meals are served.

8 rms (6 bth/shr) CTV in all bedrooms Tea and coffee making facilities Licensed Cen ht CTV 20P Fishing Riding 600 acres beef sheep Last d 7pm

PRICE GUIDE

ROOMS: s fr £18.50; wkly b&b £129.50-£154; wkly hlf-bd £206-£231✳

£

HAWORTH West Yorkshire Map 07 SE03

GH QQQ **Ferncliffe Hotel** Hebden Rd BD22 8RS (on A6033 near junct with B6144) ☎01535 643405

This modern house stands in an elevated position on the Hebden road and has fine views over the valley where the steam railway is a popular attraction. The bedrooms are modern and a good range of food is available. It is family owned and run and offers warm hospitality.

6 en suite (shr) (1 fmly) No smoking in area of dining room No smoking in lounges CTV in all bedrooms Tea and coffee making facilities Licensed Cen ht CTV 12P Last d 8.30pm

PRICE GUIDE

ROOMS: s £22-£25; d £39-£50; wkly b&b £136.50-£175; wkly hlf-bd £195-£233.50✳

CARDS:

HAYES Greater London Map 04 TQ08

GH Q **Shepiston Lodge** 31 Shepiston Ln UB3 1LJ (leave M4 junct follow signpost for Hayes from slip road lodge 50 yds from fire station almost opposite Great Western pub) ☎0181 573 0266 & 0181 569 2536 FAX 0181 569 2536

A small guesthouse located conveniently close to the airport offering well maintained, adequately equipped bedrooms which are mostly spacious. There is a comfortable TV lounge and an evening meal is available in the small dining room. The house has a garden, and a large car park where guests may leave their car while abroad.

13 rms (3 fmly) CTV in all bedrooms Tea and coffee making facilities No dogs (ex guide dogs) Licensed Cen ht CTV 15P Last d 9pm

PRICE GUIDE

ROOMS: s £27.50-£31.50; d £40.50-£44.50

CARDS: £

HAYLING ISLAND Hampshire Map 04 SZ79

Premier Selected

GH QQQQQ **Cockle Warren Cottage Hotel** 36 Seafront PO11 9HL (take A3023 continue S to seafront then turn left & continue for 1m hotel on left) (Logis) ☎01705 464961 FAX 01705 464838

A small tile-hung farmhouse located at the eastern end of the seafront, with a large colourful garden. Personally run by the charming, very welcoming Skelton family, the accommodation is extremely well presented, with many extra touches. The standards of both maintenance and housekeeping are excellent, and each of the appealing bedrooms has its own individual style. The comfortable lounge area leads into the very pretty conservatory dining room, where Diane Skelton serves a set four-course dinner using fresh fish, seafood, poultry and game in dishes based on English and French provincial cuisine. Organically grown vegetables, home-baked bread and freshly made soups also feature, together with delicious rock cakes offered with tea on arrival. A buffet-style Continental breakfast is served, a cooked breakfast is available at extra charge.

4 en suite (bth/shr) 1 annexe en suite (shr) No smoking in bedrooms No smoking in dining room No smoking in l

lounge CTV in all bedrooms Direct dial from bedrooms
Licensed Cen ht No children 12yrs 9P No coaches Outdoor
swimming pool (heated) Last d 6pm
PRICE GUIDE
ROOMS: s £45-£65; d £64-£84✱
CARDS: 🃏 ▆ 🔲   (£)

HEASLEY MILL Devon Map **03** SS73

GH 🇶🇶🇶 *Heasley House* EX36 3LE (4m from A361,
through N Molton signposted Simons Bath & Heasley Mill)
☎01598 740213
Closed Feb
This small family-run hotel is set in a peaceful village with easy
access to Exmoor and the coast. Accommodation is comfortable
and the atmosphere relaxed; and home-cooked dishes make up the
predominantly set menus which are served round a large table in
the dining room.
8 rms (2 bth 3 shr) Tea and coffee making facilities Licensed
Cen ht CTV 11P No coaches Last d 5pm
CARDS: 🃏 🔲

HEATHROW AIRPORT Greater London Map **04** TQ07

See also Slough

GH 🇶🇶 **The Cottage** 150 High St, Cranford TW5 9PD (leave
M4 junct3 onto A312 continue to traffic lights & turn left The
Cottage on left) ☎0181 897 1815 FAX 0181 897 3117
Set in a quiet cul-de-sac off Cranford High Street, this guesthouse
offers comfortable and well maintained accommodation on the
ground and first floors. There is an informal and relaxed

Ees Wyke
· COUNTRY HOUSE ·

Blessed with a beautiful, tranquil setting
amidst rolling hills and overlooking the
peaceful, Esthwaite Water, this impressive
Georgian house has uninterrupted views
from all bedrooms of the lake, mountains,
forest and fells.

Once the holiday home of Beatrix Potter,
and only 5 mins walk from "Hill Top", her
Lakeland farmhouse, Ees Wyke now offers
accommodation of a high standard, a
growing reputation for first class cuisine, and
welcoming hospitality.

An ideal base for touring, walking or just
relaxing surrounded by the beauty of
Cumbria.

Near Sawrey, Hawkshead,
Cumbria LA22 0JZ
Telephone: Hawkshead (015394) 36393

Sun Inn

Main Street, Hawkshead,
Cumbria LA22 0NT
Telephone: (015394) 36236

The Sun Inn is situated in the unspoilt village
of Hawkshead which is rich in history and
magnificent surroundings. The 17th century
building contains original beamed ceilings and
open fires. The Sun is proud of its excellent
home made food with all dishes prepared using
the finest quality local produce. A wide range
of beers including real ales and an extensive
range of wines and spirits are also available all
served by friendly, welcoming staff.

CIVIC GUEST HOUSE

★ Ideally situated 10 mins from Heathrow
  Airport
★ 20 mins from Central London
★ 10 mins from M4 (Junction 3)
★ 200 yards from Hounslow Central Tube
  Station (Piccadilly Line)
★ 5 mins walk from town centre
★ Large private car park
★ Close to Twickenham Rugby ground
★ Hampden Court and Kew Gardens
★ All rooms with colour TV/Sky
★ Tea and coffee
★ Most rooms are en-suite
★ Full English breakfast

87/89 LAMPTON ROAD, HOUNSLOW,
MIDDLESEX TW3 4DP
TEL: 0181 572 5107/570 1851
FAX: 0181 814 0203

atmosphere under the proprietor Mrs Parry's personal supervision. 8 rms (1 bth/shr) (1 fmly) CTV in all bedrooms Cen ht CTV 12P
PRICE GUIDE
ROOMS: s £35-£42; d £42-£46
CARDS: 🖰 🚾

GH [Q][Q] **The Hounslow Hotel** 41 Hounslow Rd, Feltham TW14 0AU (off A244 hotel 200yds on left)
☎0181 890 2358 FAX 0181 751 6103
A cheerfully run hotel located close to Heathrow airport with a large car park, making it a useful stopover for onward air travel. The public areas comprise a bar with a prominently placed TV, and a restaurant where evening meal are served.
23 en suite (bth/shr) (2 fmly) No smoking in dining room CTV in all bedrooms Tea and coffee making facilities Direct dial from bedrooms Licensed Cen ht CTV 21P Last d 8.45pm
PRICE GUIDE
ROOMS: s £32-£40; d £40-£48; wkly b&b £224-£280; wkly hlf-bd £294-£350
CARDS: 🖰 🔳 🚾 ⓪ 🕦 🖎

GH [Q][Q][Q] **Longford** 550 Bath Rd, Longford UB7 0EE (approx 1.5m from junct 14 of M25)
☎01753 682969 FAX 01753 794189
Closed Xmas week
Situated in Longford village, within easy reach of the M25, M4 and Heathrow Airport, this 17th-century house retains its period character. Bedrooms are of a good size and are reserved for non-smokers - smoking being permitted only in the downstairs lounge. There is a private car park and the owners willingly arrange transport to the airport.
5 rms No smoking in bedrooms No smoking in dining room CTV in all bedrooms Tea and coffee making facilities No dogs Cen ht CTV No children 10yrs 5P No coaches
PRICE GUIDE
ROOMS: s fr £26; d fr £38*
CARDS: 🖰 🚾   (£)

HEBDEN BRIDGE West Yorkshire Map **07** SD92

Selected

GH [Q][Q][Q][Q] *Redacre Mill* Redacre, Mytholmroyd HX7 5DQ (on A646 towards Hebden Bridge) ☎01422 885563
Mar-Oct rs Nov-17 Dec & 10 Jan-Feb
This converted Victorian warehouse is delightfully located on the banks of the Rochdale Canal at Mytholmroyd. The bedrooms are attractively furnished, beautifully kept and thoughtfully equipped. There is a comfortable L-shaped dining room and lounge, where home-cooked meals can be enjoyed while watching the ducks and barges on the canal.
5 en suite (bth/shr) (1 fmly) No smoking CTV in all bedrooms Tea and coffee making facilities No dogs (ex guide dogs) Licensed Cen ht 8P No coaches Last d 8pm
CARDS: 🖰 🚾

HELMSLEY North Yorkshire Map **08** SE68

See also Hawnby

💌 [Q][Q] Mrs M E Skilbeck *Middle Heads (SE584869)* Rievaulx YO6 5LU (From Helmsley take B1257 Stokesley road, and in approx 2.75m turn right sign posted Middle Heads Farm follow road for 1m) ☎01439 798251
Mar-Nov
A very secluded farmhouse at the end of a long farm lane to the

north of Helmsley providing friendly service and comfortable accommodation. There is a cosy lounge and a beamed dining room. Bedrooms, while not ensuite, nevertheless, have private bathrooms and shower rooms.
3 rms No smoking in bedrooms No smoking in dining room Tea and coffee making facilities No dogs Cen ht CTV No children 5yrs 6P 170 acres arable beef mixed sheep

---

HELSTON Cornwall & Isles of Scilly Map **02** SW62

🖾 💌 💜 [Q][Q][Q] Mrs I White **Little Pengwedna** *(SW638318)*
Little Pengwedna Farm TR13 0AY (on B3302)
☎01736 850649
Cattle breeding has made this friendly farmhouse well known nationally. Its rooms retain the charm and character of the building, and are enhanced by many pretty ornaments, pictures and flowers from the well tended front lawn. Mrs White is a most welcoming hostess. Little Pengwedna is four miles north-west of Helston, on the Hayle road (B3302).
3 rms (2 shr) No smoking in bedrooms Tea and coffee making facilities No dogs (ex guide dogs) Cen ht CTV No children 5yrs 6P 60 acres beef/sheep Last d 6pm
PRICE GUIDE
ROOMS: s fr £15; d fr £26

🖾 💌 💜 [Q][Q] Mrs G Lawrance **Longstone** *(SW662319)*
Trenear TR13 0HG (take B3297 from Helston towards Redruth for 2m, turn left to Coverack Bridges, then first right and continue left to farm) ☎01326 572483
Mar-Nov
A simple but comfortable farmhouse is part of a working farm in a peaceful, remote setting amidst beautiful countryside. There is ample space both inside and out for families, and facilities include a playroom and sun lounge.
5 en suite (bth/shr) (2 fmly) No smoking in bedrooms No smoking in dining room Cen ht CTV 6P 62 acres beef Last d 9am
PRICE GUIDE
ROOMS: s £16-£18; d £30-£36; wkly b&b £105-£115; wkly hlf-bd £135-£150
   (£)

Selected

💜 [Q][Q][Q][Q] Mrs J Makin **Nanplough Farm Country House** *(SW682214)* Cury Whitecross TR12 7BQ
☎01326 241088 FAX 01326 241088
Guests can expect a friendly welcome from Jan and John Makin at their Victorian farmhouse located about five miles from Helston. The bedrooms have the usual modern comforts plus hair dryers and magazines. Dinner is provided by arrangement and guests can enjoy traditional English cooking with seasonal home-grown vegetables and fruit. There is a spacious lounge and outdoor amenities include a heated outdoor pool and, if weather permits, a weekly barbecue. Three self-catering cottages are available and there is a riding stable on the adjacent farm.
3 en suite (shr) No smoking in dining room CTV in all bedrooms Tea and coffee making facilities No dogs (ex guide dogs) Cen ht CTV 8P Outdoor swimming pool (heated) Games room 26 acres Last d 24hrs
PRICE GUIDE
ROOMS: £44-£50; wkly b&b £154-£175; wkly hlf-bd £241.50-£262.50*
CARDS: 🖰 🚾   (£)

Selected

☜ QQQQ **Halzephron Inn** Gunwalloe TR12 7QB (3m S of Helston on A3083 turn right signposted Gunwalloe,proceed through village Inn is on the left)
☎01326 240406
Closed 25 Dec
2 en suite (bth/shr) No smoking in dining room CTV in all bedrooms Tea and coffee making facilities No dogs (ex guide dogs) No children 14yrs 30P No coaches Last d 9.30pm
PRICE GUIDE
ROOMS: s £30-£35; d £40-£50; wkly b&b £140-£245✳
MEALS: Lunch £8-£15.90alc Dinner £9.55-£19alc✳
CARDS: 🗠 🏧 £

HENLEY-ON-THAMES Oxfordshire Map **04** SU78

GH Q *Flohr's Hotel & Restaurant* Northfield End RG9 2JG
☎01491 573412 FAX 01491 579721
This fine, listed Georgian town house is situated just east - and within easy walking distance - of the town centre. Plainly furnished but spacious bedrooms are located on the upper floors, and intending guests should note that one of the staircases is quite steep. There are also a smart bar and a cosy beamed restaurant where the set-price menu offers a choice of imaginative dishes.
9 rms (1 bth 2 shr) (4 fmly) CTV in all bedrooms Tea and coffee making facilities Direct dial from bedrooms Licensed Cen ht CTV 6P No coaches Last d 10pm
CARDS: 🗠 🏧 🏧

GH Q|Q|Q **Kenwade** 3 Western Rd RG9 1JL
☎01491 573468 FAX 0149 573468
An attractively mellow semidetached house built at the turn of the
century is located slightly west of the town in a residential area off
the Reading road. Bedrooms are all smartly co-ordinated, and the
decor features stripped pine and period furniture. Guests breakfast
family-style in the dining room and are welcome to use a lounge
which has satellite TV and an open fire.
3 rms (1 shr) No smoking CTV in all bedrooms Tea and coffee
making facilities Cen ht 2P
PRICE GUIDE
ROOMS: s £25-£30; d £33-£35✳

GH Q|Q|Q **Slater's Farm** Peppard Common RG9 5JL (leave
Henley up Gravel Hill at junct with B481 turn left. After
0.25miles after The Dog pub fork left farm on right after
200yds) ☎01491 628675
A lovely period house dating back in parts to 1726 stands beside
the village green and school four miles west of Henley: you are
advised to book by telephone and ask for detailed directions.
Furnished in character, the house features an abundance of oak
beams; cosy bedrooms have smart bathrooms, the breakfast room
and lounge are elegant and a sun room looks out on to a pretty
garden with facilities for tennis and croquet. Mrs Howden is a
hospitable proprietor, and the area has several pubs which are
popular for dinner.
3 rms No smoking in bedrooms CTV in 1 bedroom No dogs (ex
guide dogs) Cen ht CTV 3P No coaches Tennis (hard)
PRICE GUIDE
ROOMS: s fr £22; d fr £40

HENSTRIDGE Somerset Map 03 ST71

✸ Q|Q|Q Mrs P Doggrell *Toomer* (*ST708192*) Templecombe
BA8 0PH (entrance to farm on A30 between Milborne Port and
Henstridge traffic lights) ☎01963 250237
Amidst 400 acres of mixed farmland, this 300-year-old farmhouse
is surrounded by neat gardens. The good sized bedrooms are on
the first floor and provide pleasant accommodation. Breakfast is
taken around a communal table in a lovely dining room, and there
is a separate lounge with a TV and deep comfortable sofas.
3 rms (1 shr) (2 fmly) CTV in all bedrooms Tea and coffee
making facilities No dogs (ex guide dogs) Cen ht CTV 6P
Fishing 400 acres arable dairy

HEREFORD Hereford & Worcester Map 03 SO54

See also Bodenham & Little Dewchurch

Selected

GH Q|Q|Q|Q **Dormington Court Country House Hotel**
Dormington HR1 4DA (5m E, off A438)
☎01432 850370 FAX 01432 850370
Parts of this delightful house date back to Elizabethan times.
The rest is Georgian. Set in spacious gardens, it stands next to
the 13th-century church, in the village of Dormington, some 5
miles east of Hereford, via the A438. Its charm and character
is enhanced by original features, such as exposed beams, wall
timbers and a magnificent inglenook fireplace in the tastefully
appointed breakfast room. The well maintained bedrooms all
have modern equipment and facilities. Family bedded
accommodation and a room with a four-poster bed are
available.
6 en suite (bth/shr) (1 fmly) No smoking in dining room
CTV in all bedrooms Tea and coffee making facilities Cen ht

No children 5yrs 20P No coaches
PRICE GUIDE
ROOMS: s £29-£32; d £45-£60✳
CARDS: 🔲 🔲 🔲 🔲 🔲

Selected

GH Q|Q|Q|Q **Hermitage Manor** Canon Pyon HR4 8NR
(3.5m NW off A4110 towards Canon Pyon)
☎01432 760317
Mar-mid Dec
With eleven acres of grounds, sheltered by extensive deer
woodlands, this impressive manor house is set in an elevated
position overlooking rural Herefordshire. It has a magnificent
oak panelled lounge, a hall with polished floorboards and a
cheerful wood burning stove, plus a second no smoking
lounge, featuring an interesting carved wooden fireplace, and
a small TV lounge, all furnished with modern comfortable
seating. Most bedrooms are exceptionally large, well
furnished in mixed styles, and equipped with en suite
bathrooms and TV.
3 en suite (bth/shr) No smoking CTV in all bedrooms Tea
and coffee making facilities No dogs Cen ht No children
10yrs 12P No coaches Bowling Croquet
PRICE GUIDE
ROOMS: s £30; d £40-£50✳

GH Q|Q *Hopbine Hotel* Roman Rd HR1 1LE (on A4103,
beyond the race course) ☎01432 268722
A small, friendly hotel situated on the outskirts of the town with
modest but well equipped bedrooms. There are two lounge areas
and a small bar, and the hotel is particularly popular with business
guests. A set evening meal is served in the cosy dining room,
which is run on informal lines by owners Mr and Mrs Horne.
20 rms (14 bth) (4 fmly) No smoking in dining room No
smoking in lounges CTV in all bedrooms Tea and coffee making
facilities Licensed Cen ht CTV 20P Last d before noon

Selected

✸ Q|Q|Q|Q Mrs J Layton **Grafton Villa Farm**
(*SO500361*) Grafton HR2 8ED (2m S off A49)
☎01432 268689
Closed 23-28 Dec
A tastefully modernised 18th-century farmhouse, Grafton
Villa is set back from the A49 some two miles south of
Hereford. The bedrooms, including one suitable for family
occupation, have either antique or period style furniture and
modern equipment; two have en suite facilities and the third a
private bathroom nearby. Downstairs there are a cosy lounge
and a lovely dining room with a solid fuel stove.
3 rms (2 bth/shr) (1 fmly) No smoking in bedrooms No
smoking in dining room CTV in all bedrooms Tea and coffee
making facilities Cen ht CTV 6P 200 acres mixed
PRICE GUIDE
ROOMS: s £20-£22; d £35-£38; wkly b&b £110-£120

✸ Q|Q|Q Mr D E Jones **Sink Green** (*SO542377*) Rotherwas
HR2 6LE (on B4399 2m from junct of A49) ☎01432 870223
Closed Xmas
First impressions of this farmhouse give no hint of the charm and
quality of the accommodation within. The house dates from the
1500s and many original features, such as the low beamed

ceilings, are still in evidence. There is a small breakfast room with a stone-flagged floor and lovely period furniture, and the spacious lounge has several antique pieces and a solid fuel stove. Bedrooms, including one four-poster room, are attractively decorated and well equipped.
3 en suite (bth/shr) No smoking CTV in all bedrooms Tea and coffee making facilities No dogs (ex guide dogs) Cen ht CTV 10P 180 acres beef sheep
PRICE GUIDE
ROOMS: s £20-£25; d £36-£46

(£)

HEVERSHAM Cumbria Map **07** SD48

GH QQQ **Springlea** LA7 7EE (on A6 1m N of Milnthorpe traffic lights) ☎015395 64026
Springlea is a pleasant private house set in its own gardens a mile north of Milnthorpe. It offers two guest rooms, both with en suite facilities, furnished and decorated to a pleasing standard. There is a large lounge which guests may use and a well tended garden to the rear.
2 en suite (bth/shr) (1 fmly) No smoking in dining room No smoking in lounges CTV in all bedrooms Tea and coffee making facilities Cen ht 3P No coaches Sun lounge Last d 4pm
PRICE GUIDE
ROOMS: s £16.50-£18.50; d £31-£37; wkly b&b £100-£120

HEXHAM Northumberland Map **12** NY96

Selected

GH QQQQ **Dene House** Juniper NE46 1SJ (from town take B6306 and first right fork, then first left turn, both signposted Dye House. Follow road for 3.5m and Dene House past Juniper sign) ☎01434 673413
This delightful stone-built converted farmhouse is situated in its own gardens and nine acres of meadowland four miles south of Hexham. The three spacious bedrooms are furnished in pine, and one is en suite. Beamed ceilings and open fires are features of the elegant dining room and very comfortable lounge. Four-course evening meals can be served by prior arrangement, and breakfast is taken round the large pine kitchen table. To reach Dene House from Hexham, take the B6306, then turn right at the first fork, signed Dye House, then take the first left similarly signed and follow the road for three-and-a-half miles. Dene House is 100 yards past the Juniper sign,on the right-hand side. .
3 rms (1 shr) No smoking Tea and coffee making facilities Cen ht CTV ch fac 4P No coaches
PRICE GUIDE
ROOMS: s fr £18; d fr £36; wkly b&b fr £115✱

(£)

GH QQQ **Dukeslea** 32 Shaws Park NE46 3BJ ☎01434 602947
Immaculately maintained, this modern detached private house is set in a quiet estate on the western side of the town. Guests have use of the ground floor, where there are two compact but attractive bedrooms, as well as a lounge with TV and lots of tourist information. Breakfast is also taken here around the one table.
2 en suite (shr) No smoking Tea and coffee making facilities No dogs Cen ht CTV 5P No coaches
PRICE GUIDE
ROOMS: d £34-£36; wkly b&b £113-£115✱

Selected

GH QQQQ **Middlemarch** Hencotes NE46 2EB (on main street, next to St Mary's Church and overlooking Abbey and park) ☎01434 605003
This quietly elegant town house lies within walking distance of the town centre and has the benefit of its own car park. Bedrooms, including a four-poster, are traditionally furnished, well proportioned, and contain hairdryers and radios as well as the usual facilities. The cosy lounge provides board games, books and magazines, whilst tasty Aga-cooked breakfasts are taken round a big oak table in the kitchen.
3 rms (1 shr) (1 fmly) No smoking CTV in all bedrooms Tea and coffee making facilities Cen ht No children 10yrs 3P No coaches
PRICE GUIDE
ROOMS: s fr £26; d fr £40

(£)

Selected

♥ QQQQ Mrs S Carr *East Peterel Field* *(NY926615)* NE46 2JT ☎01434 607209 FAX 01434 601753
Hidden away outside the town of Hexham, this country home is full of elegance and charm, although the most impressive feature is the panoramic views which it enjoys over the surrounding countryside. The fields and adjoining stables are full of beautiful thoroughbred horses as the farm operates as a Stud. Mrs Carr offers a warm welcome and it is worth ➡

BREDWARDINE HALL

Mr & Mrs Jancey,
Bredwardine Hall, Bredwardine,
Nr Hereford HR3 6DB Moccas (01981) 500596
The Hall is a charming 19th-century Manor House with immense character and literary interest standing in secluded wooded gardens, providing elegant well appointed accommodation; five delightful bedrooms, spacious en-suite bathrooms; full central heating; tea/coffee facilities; colour TV's; ample parking. Excellent food and wine; relaxed friendly atmosphere; personal service. Situated in the tranquil unspoiled Wye Valley; 7 miles Hay-on-Wye; 12 miles Hereford. Sorry no pets or children under 10.

requesting at least one evening meal to enjoy her Cordon Bleu cookery which reflects the seasons by using fresh produce. Breakfast is taken in the kitchen round one table which is set close to the full length windows so that the views can be soaked up. Bedrooms are attractively appointed and furnished with thoughtful style.

3 rms (2 bth/shr) No smoking CTV in all bedrooms Tea and coffee making facilities No dogs (ex guide dogs) Cen ht CTV 5P Riding 120 acres equestrian Last d noon

---

♥ QQQ E A Courage **Rye Hill** *(NY958580)* Slaley NE47 0AH (5m S, off B6306) ☎01434 673259

Set in thirty acres of open farmland high above Hexham and enjoying fine panoramic views northwards, Rye Hill offers residents the opportunity to observe the day-to-day running of a small working farm. The bright cheery bedrooms, small lounge area with tourist information and games room with pool, TV and board games are all contained in two converted barns within the farm's courtyard, close to working outhouses and barns. Meals are taken at two pine tables in the house's dining room.

6 en suite (bth/shr) (2 fmly) No smoking in bedrooms No smoking in dining room CTV in all bedrooms Tea and coffee making facilities Licensed Cen ht CTV 6P Snooker Games room 30 acres sheep Last d 6pm
PRICE GUIDE
ROOMS: s £20; d £36; wkly b&b £113.40-£126; wkly hlf-bd £183.40-£196✱

◀ QQQ **Rose & Crown** Main St, Slaley NE47 0AA ☎01434 673263 FAX 01434 673263

This family-run inn lies in the village of Slaley, amidst open countryside five miles above Hexham to the south. There are two bar areas, the main one having a cosy fire and a low beamed ceiling hung with a fine collection of mugs. Real ale is on tap, and both bar meals and a carte menu are available. All the bedrooms - two twins and a single - are furnished in pine.

3 en suite (bth/shr) No smoking in bedrooms No smoking in area of dining room No smoking in 1 lounge CTV in all bedrooms Tea and coffee making facilities No dogs (ex guide dogs) Cen ht 35P Last d 10pm
PRICE GUIDE
ROOMS: s £18-£25; d £36-£45; wkly b&b £110-£155; wkly hlf-bd £180-£225
MEALS: Lunch £4.75-£9.25 Dinner £11-£19.75alc

HEYSHAM Lancashire Map **07** SD46

🛏🍽 GH QQ **Carr-Garth** Bailey Ln LA3 2PS (on A589 near Strawberry Gardens Hotel in 300yds keep right Carr-Garth in 100yds) ☎01524 851175
Etr-mid Oct

A solid, 17th-century house with pretty garden near the village and adjoining beach. Decor and housekeeping standards are high. There are two lounges and good-value home cooking is available.

8 rms (2 fmly) No smoking in dining room No smoking in 1 lounge Tea and coffee making facilities No dogs (ex guide dogs) CTV 8P No coaches Last d 5pm
PRICE GUIDE
ROOMS: s fr £15; d fr £27; wkly b&b fr £85.50; wkly hlf-bd fr £111

HIGHAM Suffolk Map **05** TM03

GH QQQQ **The Bauble** Higham CO7 6LA (on B1068, near the bridge at the foot of the hill approx 2 miles from A12) ☎01206 337254 FAX 01206 337263

This delightful 16th-century property is set in two acres of grounds and gardens on the edge of a sleepy Suffolk village in the heart of Constable country. The interior is tastefully decorated with period furniture, porcelain figurines and dried flower arrangements. The individually furnished bedrooms, two of them non-smoking, feature Laura Ashley or Sanderson soft furnishings and a range of thoughtful extras and amenities; one room has an en suite shower while the remaining two have private bathrooms nearby. Hearty breakfasts are served around a single mahogany table in the dining room. Other facilities include a relaxing guest lounge full of books, games and local information, and an outdoor pool and tennis court.

3 en suite (bth/shr) No smoking in 2 bedrooms No smoking in dining room CTV in all bedrooms Tea and coffee making facilities No dogs Cen ht No children 12yrs 5P No coaches Outdoor swimming pool (heated) Tennis (hard)
PRICE GUIDE
ROOMS: s £22-£25; d £40-£45

GH QQQQ **The Old Vicarage** CO7 6JY ☎01206 337248

An impressive timbered house sits on a quiet road on the outskirts of this small village with lovely views out over the surrounding meadowland. Bedrooms have assorted fixtures and furniture, but all have a homely feel. A comfortable guest lounge contains a large collection of reading material and French windows opening out onto a well tended gardens and an outdoor swimming pool. Service is friendly and the two resident Dalmatians are very affectionate.

3 rms (2 bth) (1 fmly) No smoking in dining room No smoking in lounges CTV in all bedrooms Tea and coffee making facilities Cen ht CTV 10P No coaches Outdoor swimming pool Tennis (hard) Fishing Boats
PRICE GUIDE
ROOMS: s £25-£35; d £48-£54✱

HIGH CATTON Humberside Map **08** SE75

♥ QQQ Mr & Mrs Foster **High Catton Grange** *(SE128541)* YO4 1EP (leave A166 in Stamford Bridge opposite 'Corn Mill' left at church for approx 1.5m take first turning right to High & Low Catton,first farm on left) ☎01759 371374
Closed early Dec-mid Jan

Standing in open countryside a mile from the village crossroads, this 18th-century farmhouse provides prettily decorated bedrooms with several thoughtful touches. There is a cosy guests' lounge and a pleasant dining room overlooking the garden.

3 rms (1 bth) (1 fmly) No smoking in dining room No smoking in lounges CTV in 1 bedroom Tea and coffee making facilities Cen ht CTV 6P 300 acres arable beef dairy
PRICE GUIDE
ROOMS: s £20-£25; d £30-£40

HIGHCLIFFE-ON-SEA Dorset Map 04 SZ29

GH Q Q Q *The Beech Tree* 2 Stuart Rd BH23 5JS (from Christchurch take A337 to New Milton, after 2m take 1st turning right past traffic lights into village) ☎01425 272038
This small, friendly guest house, personally run by its proprietors, continues to improve and has a loyal following of regulars. Its non-smoking bedrooms are modern, well equipped and attractively decorated with co-ordinated soft furnishings; all have en suite shower rooms. Downstairs there are a comfortable guests' lounge and a traditional dining room where the mainstays of a good home-cooked dinner are roasts and grills served with fresh vegetables and followed by desserts ranging from steamed syrup sponge to ice cream gateaux. There is a private car park.
7 rms (5 shr) CTV in all bedrooms Tea and coffee making facilities No dogs (ex guide dogs) Cen ht CTV No children 8P No coaches Last d 6pm

HIGH WYCOMBE Buckinghamshire Map 04 SU89

GH Q Q *Amersham Hill* 52 Amersham Hill HP13 6PQ (300yds from High Wycombe Railway Station on the A404) ☎01494 520635
Closed 15 Dec-6 Jan
A simple guest house on three floors, with comfortable bedrooms, lies close to the town centre and the railway station.
8 rms (1 shr) No smoking in dining room CTV in all bedrooms Tea and coffee making facilities No dogs (ex guide dogs) Cen ht No children 10yrs 9P No coaches
PRICE GUIDE
ROOMS: s £28-£30; d £45-£55✱

GH Q Q Q *Clifton Lodge Hotel* 210 West Wycombe Rd HP12 3AR ☎01494 440095 & 529062 FAX 01494 536322
West of the town centre this well cared for hotel has its bedrooms distributed among a maze of corridors. They are of various shapes but are all well equipped and include a four-poster room with a large whirlpool bath. The ground floor has a restaurant with conservatory, a bar and a lounge with satellite TV.
32 rms (12 bth 8 shr) (2 fmly) No smoking in dining room CTV in all bedrooms Tea and coffee making facilities Direct dial from bedrooms No dogs (ex guide dogs) Licensed Cen ht CTV 28P Sauna Jacuzzi Last d 8.45pm
CARDS: 🔲 🔲 🔲 🔲

HILTON Cambridgeshire Map 04 TL26

🔲 Q Q Q *Prince of Wales* Potton Rd PE18 9NG (follow B1040 to Biggleswade from A14 or B1040 to St Ives from A428) ☎01480 830257 FAX 01480 830257
rs 24-25 Dec
This small village public house offers public areas which, though limited, are cosy and welcoming, together with compact but well appointed accommodation and a good range of facilities. There is a comfortable lounge bar stocked with real ales, and breakfast and bar meals are served in the open-plan dining area. A blackboard specials list supplements a good range of bar meals that includes healthy eating and vegetarian dishes.
4 en suite (shr) CTV in all bedrooms Tea and coffee making facilities Direct dial from bedrooms Cen ht CTV No children 5yrs 8P Pool table Darts Last d 9.15pm
PRICE GUIDE
ROOMS: s £22.50-£33; d £45-£48
MEALS: Bar Lunch £1.50-£6.50alc Dinner £6.65-£16.50alc
CARDS: 🔲 🔲 🔲

HIMBLETON Hereford & Worcester Map 03 SO95

Selected

❦ Q Q Q Q Mrs P Havard **Phepson** *(SO941599)* WR9 7JZ (from Droitwich take B4090 for 2m then turn right & proceed for 2m) ☎01905 391205
Closed Xmas & New Year
Popular with business travellers and tourists alike, this rambling, traditional 17th-century farmhouse is set in the heart of the country, yet is only five miles from the M5. There is a very comfortable lounge with a good selection of games. Bedrooms are cosy and simple, and both rooms in the Granary annexe have good en suite facilities.
2 en suite (shr) 2 annexe en suite (bth) (1 fmly) No smoking in bedrooms No smoking in dining room CTV in all bedrooms Tea and coffee making facilities Cen ht CTV 6P 170 acres beef sheep
PRICE GUIDE
ROOMS: s £20-£25; d £36-£38✱

Clifton Lodge Hotel
210 West Wycombe Road, High Wycombe, Bucks HP12 3AR Tel: 01494 440095 & 529062 Fax: 01494 536322

Situated on the A40 West Wycombe approximately one mile from the M40 London to Oxford motorway and close to the centre of historic High Wycombe, the principal town of the Chilterns. Ideal for touring the Thames Valley, Oxford, Cotswold etc. There are ample car parking facilities and pleasant gardens. Good English breakfast, lunches and dinner available. All rooms have central heating, colour TV and direct dial telephone. Small functions catered for. Licensed.
Under the personal supervision of the proprietors

HINCKLEY Leicestershire Map **04** SP49

Selected

GH ◻◻◻◻ **Ambion Court Hotel** The Green,
Dadlington CV13 6JB (from Hinckley Police Station take
Stoke Golding Rd pass Safeway Superstore. At Stoke
Golding turn right into Dadlington) ☎01455 212292
FAX 01455 213141

A pleasant conversion of a red brick farm building, this hotel
overlooks the village green in Dadlington. It offers good
public rooms, including a comfortable lounge bar and a
lounge featuring exposed brickwork, and containing a piano,
books and board games. At dinner English cooking with
international influences is served. The bedrooms, all equally
well equipped, are split between the modern annexe and the
main house.

2 en suite (shr) 5 annexe en suite (bth/shr) (1 fmly) No
smoking in bedrooms No smoking in dining room CTV in
all bedrooms Tea and coffee making facilities Direct dial
from bedrooms Licensed Cen ht CTV 8P No coaches Last
d 8.30pm

PRICE GUIDE
ROOMS: s £35-£45; d £50-£60
CARDS: ▨ ▨ (£)

HINTON CHARTERHOUSE Avon Map **03** ST75

GH ◻◻◻ **Green Lane House** Green Ln BA3 6BL (turn off
B3110 in village by the Rose & Crown Inn) ☎01225 723631
This delightful guest house, converted from three 18th century
cottages, is situated in the conservation village of Hinton
Charterhouse, five miles from Bath and is in an ideal location for
exploring Wiltshire and Somerset. The four immaculately
maintained and brightly decorated bedrooms two of which are en
suite, are comfortably furnished. Guests also have the use of a
small lounge, with an open fire and the pretty gardens.

4 rms (2 shr) No smoking in dining room Tea and coffee making
facilities No dogs (ex guide dogs) Cen ht CTV 4P No coaches
PRICE GUIDE
ROOMS: s £24-£37; d £36-£49✷
CARDS: ▨ ▨ ▨ (£)

HITCHAM Suffolk Map **05** TL95

❤ ◻ Mrs B Elsden *Wetherden Hall (TL971509)* IP7 7PZ (take
B1115 from Stowmarket, at Hitcham White Horse turn onto
Bury St Edmunds road. After 100yds turn left to Lavenham.
Wetherden Hall is on right) ☎01449 740412
Mar-Sep

Warm hospitality is provided by the owner of this tidy farmhouse -
with chickens wandering across its lawn - which enjoys pleasant
views from its setting down a private drive on the outskirts of the
village. Two good-sized bedrooms and a combined lounge/dining
room are provided for guests' use.

2 rms (1 fmly) No smoking in bedrooms No dogs Cen ht CTV
No children 10yrs 4P Fishing 300 acres mixed

HITCHIN Hertfordshire Map **04** TL12

GH ◻◻◻ **Firs Hotel** 83 Bedford Rd SG5 2TY
☎01462 422322 FAX 01462 432051
rs 25 Dec-2 Jan & Sun

Originally a manor house, this roadside hotel close to the town
centre has varied accommodation, including some in modern
extensions. There is a fully licensed bar and the Classico
Restaurant offers a carte specialising in Italian cooking.

30 rms (24 bth/shr) (2 fmly) CTV in all bedrooms Tea and
coffee making facilities Direct dial from bedrooms Licensed
Cen ht CTV 30P Last d 9.30pm
PRICE GUIDE
ROOMS: s £27-£42; d £42-£52✷
CARDS: ▨ ▨ ▨ ▨ ▨ ▨ ▨ (£)

HOARWITHY Hereford & Worcester Map **03** SO52

❤ ◻◻◻ Mrs C Probert *The Old Mill (SO546294)* HR2 6QH
☎01432 840602

Dating from the 18th century and now converted into a small
country guest house, the Old Mill stands at the centre of the village;
the owners farm land elsewhere, but horses and sometimes sheep
are kept here. Guest rooms in cottage style are attractively decorated
and furnished, the comfortable television lounge is warmed by a log
fire in winter, and meals are taken in a beamed dining room.

6 rms (2 shr) No smoking Cen ht CTV 6P Last d 7pm

HOLBEACH Lincolnshire Map **08** TF32

GH ◻◻◻ **Pipwell Manor** Washway Rd, Saracens Head
PE12 8AL (off A17) ☎01406 423119

This period farmhouse is set amid arable farmland. Lesley Honnor
greets her guests warmly, inviting them on arrival to tea and cake
in a sunny lounge with highly polished tables and book-lined
walls. The dining room is dominated by a central oak table, and
original Georgian panelling is accentuated by candy-stripe
wallpaper, while greenery and dried flower arrangements in huge
baskets add further appeal. The bedrooms, two of which are really
roomy, all have an armchair or sofa; the soft furnishings and decor
are totally co-ordinated and quite lavish, in either Laura Ashley or
Sanderson fabrics. The house is immaculate and lovely to look at
but, more importantly, very comfortable and welcoming.

4 en suite (bth/shr) No smoking Tea and coffee making facilities
No dogs Cen ht CTV 4P No coaches Free use of cycles
PRICE GUIDE
ROOMS: s £20-£30; d £34-£38✷

HOLFORD Somerset Map **03** ST14

 GH ◻◻ **Haymans** TA5 1RY (leave A39 at Holford
turning into lane between the Texaco garage & the Plough
Inn Haymans on left) ☎01278 741627
Mar-Oct

A detached house set in well tended gardens, offering comfortable
accommodation. Rooms are equipped with TVs, tea trays and
magazines. Breakfast is served in the front facing dining room.
Haymans is an excellent base for walks in the Quantock Hills, and
a drying room is available by request. This is a no-smoking
establishment.

3 rms No smoking CTV in all bedrooms Tea and coffee making
facilities No dogs Cen ht No children 12yrs 3P No coaches
PRICE GUIDE
ROOMS: s £16; d £28; wkly b&b £96-£168 (£)

HOLMBURY ST MARY Surrey Map **04** TQ14

◼ ◻◻◻ *Royal Oak* The Glade RH5 6PF (turn off A25 onto
B2126 at Abinger Hammer, inn is 2.50m on right overlooking
village green) ☎01306 730120

This attractive village pub offers a good range of real ale and
blackboard bar meals. The bedrooms are individually furnished
and are particularly well equipped with modern amenities.

2 en suite (shr) No smoking in bedrooms CTV in all bedrooms
Tea and coffee making facilities No dogs (ex guide dogs) Cen ht
24P Last d 9.30pm
CARDS: ▨
See advertisement under DORKING

HOLMFIRTH West Yorkshire Map **07** SE10

GH ◙◙◙◙ **Holme Castle Country Hotel** Holme
Village HD7 1QG (2m S on A6024)
☎01484 686764 FAX 01484 687775
Located at the head of the Holme Valley and enjoying lovely
views over woods, moorland and a reservoir, this delightful
Victorian house is well cared for by the resident owners. The
drawing room features oak panelling and parquet flooring,
with an open fire during the colder months. Generally
spacious bedrooms bright and freshly decorated. Evening
meals are available by arrangement, with an emphasis on
fresh produce. Smoking is not permitted. The house stands in
the village of Holme, which is on the A6024 to the south west
of Holmfirth.
8 rms (5 bth/shr) (3 fmly) No smoking CTV in all bedrooms
No dogs (ex guide dogs) Licensed Cen ht CTV ch fac 12P
No coaches childrens playground Last d noon
PRICE GUIDE
ROOMS: s £20-£50; d £40-£65; wkly b&b £133-£259;
wkly hlf-bd £183-£354
CARDS: 🔲 🔲 🔲 🔲

◀ ◙◙◙ **White Horse** Scholes Road, Jackson Bridge
HD7 7HF (off A616 towards Sheffield, 1m from New Mill)
☎01484 683940
Closed 24-25 Dec & 31 Jan
Warm hospitality is provided at this typical Yorkshire pub -
famous for its appearances in 'Last of the Summer Wine'.
Attractive bedrooms offer good facilities, and a choice of freshly
cooked meals is served in the bar.
5 en suite (bth/shr) (3 fmly) CTV in all bedrooms Tea and coffee
making facilities No dogs (ex guide dogs) Cen ht 14P Last d
9.30pm
PRICE GUIDE
ROOMS: s £24; d £38✳
MEALS: Lunch £4.15-£10.60alc Dinner £4.15-£10.60alc✳

HOLNE Devon Map **03** SX76

♥ ◙◙◙◙ Mrs S Gifford **Wellpritton** *(SX716704)*
TQ13 7RX (from A38 follow signs for Ashburton, then
take Princeown & Two Bridges road for approx 3m at
AA telephone turn left then 1st right) ☎01364 631273
Wellpritten Farm is on the fringe of Dartmoor National Park
some 1.5 miles from the village, in an area ideal for walkers.
There are four attractive bedrooms, two of them family suites,
with many useful extras. Guests are invited to enjoy Sue
Townsend's home cooked fare in the dining room and relax in
the comfortable sitting room.
4 rms (1 bth 2 shr) (2 fmly) No smoking in bedrooms No
smoking in dining room Tea and coffee making facilities No
dogs (ex guide dogs) Cen ht CTV 6P Outdoor swimming
pool games room snooker table-tennis skittles 15 acres
mixed Last d 4pm
PRICE GUIDE
ROOMS: s £17.50; d £35; wkly b&b £122.50; wkly hlf-bd
£161✳

HOLSWORTHY Devon Map **02** SS30

See also Clawton

🏠 🔽 GH ◙◙◙◙ **Woodlands** Dunsland Cross
EX22 7YQ (4.5m E, junct A3072/A3079) ☎01409 221627
Closed Jan
A delightful bungalow set in two acres of level gardens some
50 yards down a private lane four miles from the market town
of Holsworthy. The National Trust owns the lane which leads
to the grounds of Old Dunsford House, burnt down in 1967,
and now providing a haven for wildlife. Suitable for the
partially able the two well-equipped rooms are found in a
separate guest wing and are each attractively decorated and
furnished. The sunny lounge/conservatory overlooks the
gardens and pond whilst freshly cooked breakfasts are served
in the dining room. Dinner is not available although light
snacks and cream teas are available.
2 en suite (shr) No smoking in dining room CTV in all
bedrooms Tea and coffee making facilities No dogs Cen ht
2P No coaches
PRICE GUIDE
ROOMS: s £16; d £29-£31; wkly b&b £90-£98

ambion court hotel
The Green, Dadlington, Nuneaton CV13 6JB
Telephone: (01455) 212292
Fax: (01455) 213141

Charming, modernised Victorian farmhouse overlooking
Dadlington's tranquil village green, 2 miles north of
Hinckley, convenient for Birmingham, Coventry,
Leicester, NEC, M1 and M6. All rooms are en-suite and
extremely comfortably appointed, particularly the
imposing Pine Room honeymoon suite. There is a
delightful lounge, cocktail bar and a restaurant offering
creative International fare and extensive function menus.
Conference facilities are also available. Ambion Court
offers comfort, hospitality and exceptional tranquillity
for tourists and business people alike.

Resident proprietors John & Wendy Walliker
See gazetteer under Hinckley

♥ Q Q Mr & Mrs E Cornish **Leworthy** *(SS323012)* EX22 6SJ (leave Holsworthy via Bodmin St, past the Chapel in the direction of North Tamerton, Leworthy is signposted left after 3m) ☎01409 253488 FAX 01409 254671

Guests return year after year to enjoy the home cooking and peaceful surroundings of Leworthy Farm. The ten bedrooms in the main house vary in both size and level of equipment and all are simply furnished; several self-catering properties are also available. Leisure facilities include a nine-hole pitch-and-putt course, a well stocked fishing lake, farm tours and a hay ride.

10 rms (3 shr) (5 fmly) No smoking in dining room No smoking in 1 lounge Tea and coffee making facilities No dogs (ex guide dogs) Licensed CTV ch fac 20P Tennis (hard) Fishing Covered barn for skittles & badminton 235 acres mixed Last d 6pm

PRICE GUIDE
ROOMS: s £17.50-£20; d £35-£40; wkly b&b £114-£120; wkly hlf-bd £171-£186∗

HOLT Norfolk Map **09** TG03

GH Q Q Q **Lawns Private Hotel** 26 Station Rd NR25 6BS (hotel located opposite Greshams cricket ground) ☎01263 713390

The Lawns is a Victorian red brick property offering well proportioned bedrooms with many modern amenities. Fresh home-cooked food is served for all meals and real ale is available in the bar.

11 en suite (bth/shr) No smoking in dining room CTV in all bedrooms Tea and coffee making facilities No dogs Licensed Cen ht No children 16yrs 12P No coaches Last d 8pm

PRICE GUIDE
ROOMS: s £37; d £70-£75
CARDS: ▨ ▨ ▨

HONITON Devon Map **03** ST10

Selected

GH Q Q Q Q **Colestocks House** Payhembury Rd, Feniton EX14 0JR (turn off A30 at Pattersons Cross, to Feniton/Payhembury. Hotel 2m on left) ☎01404 850633 FAX 01404 850901

Apr-Oct

The thatched roof, pale pink walls and well-tended gardens of Colestocks House are just visible over the garden walls which surround this charming listed 16th-century property. The large bedrooms are comfortable and attractively decorated in Laura Ashley style, and one ground-floor room boasts a four-poster bed. There are French doors leading out to the secluded gardens from the drawing room, and the dining room has a huge inglenook fireplace. A carte with a wide range of English and Continental dishes is available each evening, and there is a separate bar.

10 en suite (bth/shr) No smoking in bedrooms No smoking in dining room No smoking in 1 lounge CTV in all bedrooms Tea and coffee making facilities No dogs (ex guide dogs) Licensed Cen ht CTV No children 10yrs 10P No coaches Last d 7pm

PRICE GUIDE
ROOMS: s £24.95-£27.50; d £55-£60; wkly b&b fr £180; wkly hlf-bd £253-£264∗
CARDS: ▨ ▨

GH Q Q Q **The Crest** Moorcox Ln, Wilmington, Honiton EX14 9JU (3m E of Honiton on A35 at eastern end of village, after the river bridge turn left, the Crest is 100 metres on right) ☎01404 831419

This modern chalet-style bungalow is situated in its own sheltered gardens on the edge of the village of Wilmington, an area of outstanding natural beauty, three miles from the market town of Honiton. Three immaculate bedrooms have been freshly decorated and are well equipped. There is a small sun lounge, and guests are welcome to enjoy the well kept gardens where a pitch and putt course and a badminton court have been provided.

3 en suite (bth/shr) (1 fmly) No smoking in 2 bedrooms No smoking in dining room CTV in all bedrooms Tea and coffee making facilities Cen ht CTV 6P No coaches Pitch & putt course Badminton court Last d 9.30pm

PRICE GUIDE
ROOMS: s £16-£20; d £32; wkly b&b fr £100; wkly hlf-bd fr £135∗

♥ Q Q Mrs I Underdown **Roebuck** *(ST147001)* EX14 0PB (western end of Honiton-by-pass) ☎01404 42225

This farmhouse offers comfortable accommodation and is situated in a prominent position on the A30 just outside the town centre, which is famous for its lace and numerous antique shops. Breakfast is served at individual tables in the dining room, and there is a comfortable lounge. Smoking is not permitted in the bedrooms or dining room.

4 rms (1 fmly) No smoking in bedrooms No smoking in dining room CTV in 1 bedroom Tea and coffee making facilities Cen ht CTV P 180 acres dairy mixed

£

Selected

■ Q Q Q Q **The Heathfield** Walnut Rd EX14 8UG (from A30 onto A375 Sidmouth rd and in .5m at mini-rbt turn right the right again. Walnut Av 1st on right) ☎01404 45321 & 45322 FAX 01404 45321

Closed 25-26 Dec & 1 Jan

The approach to this beautiful and sympatheticaly restored 16th century longhouse is well signed through a modern housing estate. Bedrooms are spacious, tastefully furnished with pine and equipped with every modern comfort. The bars and restaurant are open-plan, exposed stone walls and wooden beams adding to the character of the establishment. There is a carte as well as a blackboard of bar snacks.

5 en suite (bth/shr) CTV in all bedrooms Tea and coffee making facilities Direct dial from bedrooms No dogs (ex guide dogs) Cen ht 50P Skittle alley Last d 10pm

PRICE GUIDE
ROOMS: s fr £32.50; d fr £45; wkly b&b fr £204.75
CARDS: ▨ ▨ ▨

HOOK Hampshire Map **04** SU75

GH Q Q **Cedar Court Country** Reading Rd RG27 9DB (1m N of Hook on B3349) ☎01256 762178

Surrounded by lovely woodland, this attractive single-storey house is tucked well away from the road at the end of a shared private drive. Bedrooms overlook the pretty garden and are neat and well equipped, while public areas include a comfortable lounge and small breakfast room.

6 rms (3 shr) (1 fmly) No smoking in dining room CTV in all bedrooms Tea and coffee making facilities No dogs (ex guide

dogs) Cen ht CTV 6P No coaches
PRICE GUIDE
ROOMS: s £22-£28; d £32-£38
CARDS: ▨ ▧

GH 🇶🇶 *Cherry Lodge* Reading Rd RG27 9DB (on B3349)
☎01256 762532 FAX 01256 762532
Closed Xmas
Cherry Lodge is a small, extended bungalow on the northern edge
of the village. Being completely family run and lacking any
pretentions, it has become a home from home for travelling
business people. The modern bedrooms all have en suite facilities
and direct dial telephones. There is a comfortable TV lounge with
deep armchairs and a simple conservatory-type dining room where
the set two-course dinner is of the hearty British 'meat and two
veg' variety.
6 en suite (bth/shr) (1 fmly) No smoking in dining room Tea and
coffee making facilities Direct dial from bedrooms Cen ht CTV
20P Last d midnight
CARDS: ▨ ▧ ▧

GH 🇶🇶 *Oaklea* London Rd RG27 9LA (on A30, 200yds
from centre of Hook) ☎01256 762673 FAX 01256 762150
A detached Victorian family-run guest house offers good value for
money, in a convenient location on the A30, with a delightful
large walled garden. Personally managed for many years by Mr
and Mrs Swinhoe, it offers a warm welcome and caters well for
both leisure and business guests, many of whom return frequently.
Bedrooms vary in size but are neat and nicely presented in an old
fashioned style. There is a licensed bar area and a pleasant lounge,
and a four-course evening meal is offered.
10 rms (4 shr) (1 fmly) No smoking in 4 bedrooms No smoking
in dining room CTV in 5 bedrooms Tea and coffee making
facilities Licensed CTV ch fac 11P No coaches Last d noon
CARDS: ▧
See advertisement under BASINGSTOKE

HOPE Derbyshire Map **07** SK18

Selected

GH 🇶🇶🇶🇶 **Underleigh House** Off Edale Rd S30 2RF
(from village church on A625 take Edale rd for 1m then
left into lane) ☎01433 621372 FAX 01433 621372
This immaculately maintained house, converted from a
former barn, is situated one and a half miles from the village
of Hope and set in very well tended and colourful gardens and
from the small terrace, guests' can enjoy the most wonderful
views of the unspoilt countryside beyond. Barbara and Tony
Singleton are enthusiastic and welcoming hosts with Tony
taking charge in the kitchen, where he produces a very good
range of home-cooked dishes. Dinner and breakfast are served
in the attractive stone flagged dining room, which has a
communal table, and next door to which is a spacious and
comfortably furnished sitting room, which also enjoys the
most wonderful views and where a fire is lit on cooler
evenings. The six bedrooms are en suite and each has its own
resident teddy bear, all are comfortably furnished, freshly
decorated and include many little extras.
6 en suite (bth/shr) No smoking in dining room No smoking
in lounges CTV in all bedrooms Tea and coffee making
facilities No dogs (ex guide dogs) Licensed Cen ht No
children 12yrs 6P No coaches Last d noon
PRICE GUIDE
ROOMS: d £50-£56; wkly hlf-bd £266-£280✱
CARDS: ▨ ▧ £

HORLEY Surrey

For accommodation details see under **Gatwick Airport, London**

HORNCASTLE Lincolnshire Map **08** TF26

Selected

♥ 🇶🇶🇶🇶 Mrs J Bankes Price **Greenfield Farm**
(TF175745) Minting LN9 5RX (take A158 eastward,
through Wragby and after 3m turn right at Midge pub,
farm 1m on right) ☎01507 578457
Closed Xmas & New Year
A modern and very substantial farmhouse in the heart of the
tranquil Lincolnshire Wolds. It is an ideal touring base for
either the nearby Spa resort, the antiques trail, Lincoln or the
coast. The bedrooms are delightful, traditionally furnished
though their purpose built en suite are thoroughly modern.
Apart from a comfortable lounge with its inviting and
warming wood burning stove there are acres of countryside to
enjoy and gardens with a huge well stocked pond to enjoy.
3 rms (2 shr) No smoking Tea and coffee making facilities
No dogs (ex guide dogs) Cen ht CTV 6P 387 acres arable
PRICE GUIDE
ROOMS: s £20; d £36-£38; wkly b&b fr £126

HORNCHURCH Greater London Map **05** TQ58

◀ 🇶🇶🇶 **The Railway Hotel** Station Ln RM12 6SB (adjacent
to railway station) ☎01708 476415 FAX 01708 437315
A well managed purpose-built inn dating from the 1930s and
located on the fringe of the town centre offers good standards of
accommodation. Modern bedrooms are well equipped, and there is
a large open-plan public area featuring pleasant seating areas and
polished woodwork. A good selection of bar meals is available in
the comfortable lounge bar.
11 en suite (bth/shr) (3 fmly) CTV in all bedrooms Tea and
coffee making facilities Direct dial from bedrooms No dogs (ex
guide dogs) Cen ht 60P Last d 9pm
PRICE GUIDE
ROOMS: s fr £39; d £39-£49✱
MEALS: Lunch £3.35-£7.95 Dinner £3.35-£7.95✱
CARDS: ▨ ▧ ▧ ◉

HORN'S CROSS Devon Map **02** SS32

Premier Selected

GH 🇶🇶🇶🇶🇶 **Lower
Waytown** EX39 5DN (from
Bude through Horns Cross
then .5m past Hoops Inn on
left) ☎01237 451787
Etr-Oct
A beautiful conversion of a
barn and roundhouse has
created this delightfully
spacious and comfortable
home, where Caroline and
Chris May are the welcoming
hosts. The unique round sitting room with beams and an
inglenook adjoins the spacious dining room where the
excellent breakfasts are served. The bedrooms, one of which ➡

is on the ground floor, are tastefully decorated and furnished (smoking in the bedrooms is not permitted). There are five acres of gardens and grounds with stream-fed ponds and ornamental waterfowl.

3 en suite (bth/shr) No smoking CTV in all bedrooms Tea and coffee making facilities No dogs Cen ht CTV No children 12yrs 8P No coaches

PRICE GUIDE
ROOMS: s £30-£35; d £40-£47; wkly b&b £126-£207

HORSFORD Norfolk Map **09** TG11

GH QQQ **Church Farm** Church St NR10 3DB
☎01603 898020 & 898582 FAX 01603 891649
A well-kept property in a rural setting south of the village, this guest house offers a dining room, lounge and five spacious bedrooms, each with its own shower.

6 en suite (shr) (2 fmly) No smoking in dining room CTV in all bedrooms Tea and coffee making facilities No dogs (ex guide dogs) Cen ht CTV 20P No coaches

PRICE GUIDE
ROOMS: s £17-£20; d £32-£36; wkly b&b £112∗
CARDS: (£)

HORSHAM West Sussex Map **04** TQ13

See advertisement opposite

HORSHAM ST FAITH Norfolk Map **09** TG21

GH QQQ **Elm Farm Chalet Hotel** Norwich Rd NR10 3HH (on A140 Cromer road from Norwich, pass airport, take right hand turning into village)
☎01603 898366 FAX 01603 897129
rs 25-26 Dec
Once a working farm, this hotel is in the centre of a village set amongst open fields. Lunch and dinner are served daily, with garden teas in the summer, and the bedrooms are housed in modern brick annexes, in the style of a motel. All are well equipped with modern amenities, including direct dial telephone.

18 annexe rms (16 bth/shr) (2 fmly) No smoking in 10 bedrooms No smoking in dining room No smoking in 1 lounge CTV in all bedrooms Tea and coffee making facilities Direct dial from bedrooms No dogs (ex guide dogs) Licensed Cen ht CTV 20P No coaches Last d 6.30pm

PRICE GUIDE
ROOMS: s £31-£36; d £49.50-£56; wkly b&b £217-£252; wkly hlf-bd £294-£329
CARDS: (£)

Entries in this Guide are based on reports filed by our team of professionally trained, full-time inspectors.

HORTON Dorset Map **04** SU00

Premier Selected

GH QQQQQ **Northill House** BH21 7HL (7m N of Wimborne, off B3078)
☎01258 840407
Closed 21 Dec-15 Feb
Just off the edge of a small village, this delightful country house offers a warm welcome and a cosy, relaxing atmosphere. The spacious public rooms are light, airy and comfortable, and the dining room has a conservatory extension which is very popular with guests during the summer months. The bedrooms are well equipped and maintained. The Garnsworth family continue to offer hospitality of the highest standard. A selection of books and magazines are provided for guests in the lounge, where winter guests can warm themselves by the log fire.

9 en suite (bth/shr) (1 fmly) No smoking in dining room CTV in all bedrooms Tea and coffee making facilities Direct dial from bedrooms No dogs (ex guide dogs) Licensed Cen ht No children 8yrs 9P No coaches Last d 7pm

PRICE GUIDE
ROOMS: s £38; d £67
CARDS: ▤ ▤ ▤ (£)
See advertisement under WIMBORNE MINSTER

◀ QQQ **Horton** Cranborne Rd BH21 5AD (on B3078 between Wimborne and Cranbourne)
☎01258 840252 FAX 01258 841400
Further improvements have taken place at this popular country inn. The comfortable bedrooms are well-equipped, and the redecorated, refurnished dining room offers simple English dishes. Service is friendly and attentive.

8 rms (3 bth/shr) CTV in all bedrooms Tea and coffee making facilities Cen ht 100P Last d 9.30pm

PRICE GUIDE
ROOMS: s £17.50-£30; d £40-£50; wkly b&b £122.50-£140; wkly hlf-bd £199-£220
MEALS: Lunch £9-£12.50
CARDS: ▤ ▤

HORTON IN RIBBLESDALE North Yorkshire Map **07** SD87

◀ QQ **Crown Hotel** BD24 0HF (take B6479 from Settle)
☎01729 860209 FAX 01729 860444
This family-run village inn is said to date back to the 17th century and stands right on the Pennine Way as it passes through the Ribble Valley. Bedrooms are sizeable but simply decorated. Tasty home-made meals are a feature of the two bars, where beams and open fires create a traditional atmosphere. There are also a dining room, two guests' lounges with television, and a spacious beer garden behind the inn.

9 rms (7 bth/shr) (4 fmly) Tea and coffee making facilities Cen ht CTV 15P Last d 8.30pm

PRICE GUIDE
ROOMS: s £18-£23; d £36-£46; wkly b&b £120-£150
MEALS: Bar Lunch £4-£5.75alc Dinner £4.50-£6.50alc

HOUNSLOW Greater London Map **04** TQ17

GH 🔲🔲 *Civic* 87/89 Lampton Rd TW3 4DP
☎0181 572 5107
Close to the centre of Hounslow, this guest house has the benefit
of a spacious private car park. Bedrooms are being gradually
improved and all have satellite TV.
15 rms (7 shr) (3 fmly) No smoking in 3 bedrooms CTV in all
bedrooms Tea and coffee making facilities No dogs Cen ht CTV
8P Last d 7.30pm
PRICE GUIDE
ROOMS: s £29-£35; d £40-£45; wkly b&b £175-£210✱
CARDS: 🔳 🔳
See advertisement under HEATHROW AIRPORT

GH 🔲🔲 *Omar* 97 Hanworth Rd TW3 1TT (on A314)
☎0181 577 9969
Conveniently located within walking distance of the High Street
and London underground station, and having its own car park, this
guest house offers bed and breakfast with a range of good value
standard bedrooms, some of which are located on the ground floor.
There are a no-smoking TV lounge and a breakfast room. The
atmosphere is very relaxed and informal, with service provided by
the Saeed family.
16 rms (1 bth/shr) (1 fmly) No smoking in dining room No
smoking in lounges CTV in 6 bedrooms No dogs (ex guide dogs)
Cen ht CTV 10P

GH 🔲🔲 *Shalimar Hotel* 215-221 Staines Rd TW3 3JJ
☎0181 577 7070 & 0181 572 2816 FAX 0181 569 6789
Recently extended to provide more en suite bedrooms and larger
public areas, this popular family-run hotel is conveniently situated
within walking distance of the town centre. Attractive bedrooms
are all well equipped with every modern amenity. The open-plan
TV lounge has a residents' bar adjacent, and three-course evening
meals are available Monday-Thursday in the well furnished dining
room. A function room which accommodates up to 100 guests is
ideal for wedding receptions, with an attractive rear garden and
terrace. Formal reception facilities and forecourt parking are
provided.
31 rms (22 shr) (7 fmly) No smoking in 2 bedrooms No smoking
in area of dining room CTV in all bedrooms Tea and coffee
making facilities Direct dial from bedrooms No dogs Licensed
Cen ht CTV 8P Last d noon
PRICE GUIDE
ROOMS: s £34-£38; d £44-£48; wkly b&b £200✱
CARDS: 🔳 🔳 🔳 🔳   ⓔ

HOVE East Sussex

See **Brighton & Hove**

HUBY North Yorkshire Map **08** SE56

GH 🔲🔲 *The New Inn Motel* Main St YO6 1HQ (between
A19 & B1363) ☎01347 810219
This modern brick-built motel stands behind the inn of the same
name, though unconnected with it. Bedrooms in the chalet-style
building are functional, and there is a small breakfast room. Car
parking space outside the chalets is more than adequate.
8 en suite (shr) (2 fmly) No smoking in dining room No
smoking in lounges CTV in all bedrooms Tea and coffee making
facilities Licensed Cen ht CTV 15P No coaches Fishing
PRICE GUIDE
ROOMS: d £40; wkly b&b £140-£160; wkly hlf-bd £155-£175✱   ⓔ

HUCKNALL Nottinghamshire Map **08** SK54

◀ 🔲🔲 *Station Hotel* Station Rd NG15 7TQ ☎0115 963 2588
A friendly atmosphere prevails at this large Victorian public
house, located about a quarter of a mile from the town's High
Street and easily found by following signs to the railway station.
Refurbishment in recent years has added to the appeal both of the
bars and of generally spacious bedrooms which are equipped with
colour TVs and tea-making facilities.
6 rms (2 fmly) CTV in all bedrooms Tea and coffee making
facilities No dogs (ex guide dogs) Cen ht 20P Last d 9.30pm
CARDS: 🔳 🔳

HUDDERSFIELD West Yorkshire Map **07** SE11

GH 🔲🔲🔲 *Elm Crest* 2 Queens Rd, Edgerton HD2 2AG
(A629 signed Halifax, 100yds on right after traffic lights)
(Logis) ☎01484 530990 FAX 01484 516227
An attractive Victorian property set in well tended gardens about a
mile from the city centre, Elm Crest is very well equipped and
furnished, providing guests with comfortable accommodation.
There are a cosy lounge with a log fire and a bright dining room.
Derek and Margaret Gee enjoy meeting and caring for their
guests, and they run a totally no-smoking house.
8 rms (5 shr) (2 fmly) No smoking CTV in all bedrooms Tea
and coffee making facilities Direct dial from bedrooms No dogs
Licensed Cen ht CTV No children 5yrs ch fac 12P No coaches
Last d 9pm
PRICE GUIDE
ROOMS: s fr £32; d fr £57; wkly b&b fr £220; wkly hlf-bd fr
£320
CARDS: 🔳 🔳 🔳 🔳 🔳 🔳   ⓔ

HULL Humberside Map **08** TA02

GH QQQ *Earlesmere Hotel* 76/78 Sunny Bank, Spring Bank West HU3 1LQ ☎01482 341977 FAX 01482 473714
Closed Xmas rs wknds
This mostly commercial hotel is located in a residential area, about a mile from the city centre. It offers a good number of en-suite rooms, as well as more modestly appointed accommodation. There is a good range of dishes available at dinner, there is a small bar and a pleasant, comfortable lounge.
15 rms (7 shr) (4 fmly) No smoking in dining room CTV in all bedrooms Tea and coffee making facilities Licensed Cen ht CTV No parking Last d 6pm
CARDS: 🂠 🔤

HUNGERFORD Berkshire Map **04** SU36

GH QQQ *Marshgate Cottage Hotel* Marsh Ln RG17 0QX (from A338 turn right beside railway bridge into Church St, 0.5m cross stream & turn sharp right)
☎01488 682307 FAX 01488 685475
Closed 24 Dec-15 Jan
This aptly named hotel is a low, red brick cottage complex arranged round a pretty courtyard. All bedrooms overlook the Kennet and Avon Canal, and many are on the ground floor. Whilst the exterior of the building is 17th century, inside the decoration is wholly Scandinavian, with natural pine floors, lots of rugs, and simple, comfortable furniture. There is a large dining room where evening meals (ordered when booking) are served. Cooking is mostly traditional English, but there is also the odd Scandanavian dish, too.
9 rms (1 bth 6 shr) (1 fmly) No smoking in 3 bedrooms No smoking in area of dining room No smoking in 1 lounge CTV in all bedrooms Tea and coffee making facilities Direct dial from bedrooms No dogs (ex guide dogs) Licensed Cen ht No children 5yrs 10P Last d 7.30pm
PRICE GUIDE
ROOMS: s £25.50-£35.50; d £39.50-£48.50✳
CARDS: 🂠 🔤 🔤 (£)

HUNSTANTON Norfolk Map **09** TF64

GH QQQQ *Claremont* 35 Greevegate PE36 6AF (off A149, turn left at Greevegate, opposite recreation ground. House is 300mtrs on right before St Edmunds church)
☎01485 533171
A warm and friendly atmosphere pervades this comfortable, well appointed guest house which stands close to the seafront and town centre. A number of thoughtful touches have been added to well appointed bedrooms with quality furnishings, while the cosy lounge is provided with books and magazines for guests' use and the attractive dining room serves a hearty English breakfast (with some alternatives). Limited car parking facilities are available.
7 en suite (bth/shr) (1 fmly) No smoking CTV in all bedrooms Tea and coffee making facilities Licensed Cen ht CTV No children 5yrs 4P No coaches
CARDS: 🂠 🔤

GH QQQ **Pinewood House** 26 Northgate PE36 6AP (turn off A149 into Greevegate, 2nd right by bank, 200yds on right)
☎01485 533068
Smart and well appointed, this guest house offers a small, comfortable sitting room and an attractive dining room; bedrooms vary in size, but all are furnished in modern style, comfortable and well equipped.

8 rms (4 shr) (4 fmly) No smoking in bedrooms No smoking in dining room CTV in all bedrooms Tea and coffee making facilities Licensed Cen ht 6P No coaches
PRICE GUIDE
ROOMS: s £17.50-£39; d £35-£50✳
CARDS: 🂠 🔤 🔤 (£)

GH QQQ **Sutton House Hotel** 24 Northgate PE36 6AP
☎01485 532552
Further improvements have been made to this friendly family-run guest house; all bedrooms are now en suite, brightly decorated and well equipped. Additional facilties include a comfortable first-floor lounge and a well appointed dining room. An evening meal is served with a choice of home-cooked English dishes in a relaxing atmosphere.
7 en suite (bth/shr) (2 fmly) No smoking in bedrooms No smoking in dining room CTV in all bedrooms Tea and coffee making facilities Licensed Cen ht CTV 5P No coaches Last d 4pm
PRICE GUIDE
ROOMS: s £25-£30; d £40-£50; wkly b&b £140-£210; wkly hlf-bd £210-£245
CARDS: 🂠 🔤 (£)

HUNTON North Yorkshire Map **07** SE19

Selected

◀ QQQQ **The Countryman's** DL8 1PY (just off A684 Bedale/Leyburn Road between Patrick Brompton and Constable Burton) ☎01677 450554
An attractive village inn offers well equipped bedrooms and a friendly atmosphere. The inviting bar serves a good range of real ales, and well produced food is also available. A rear car park is provided for guests' use.
7 en suite (bth/shr) No smoking in bedrooms No smoking in dining room CTV in all bedrooms Tea and coffee making facilities No dogs Cen ht No children 14yrs 20P No coaches Pool table Last d 9.30pm
PRICE GUIDE
ROOMS: s £30-£35; d £45-£60
MEALS: Bar Lunch £4-£6.95alc Dinner £5-£11.50alc
CARDS: 🂠 🔤 (£)

HUTTON-LE-HOLE North Yorkshire Map **08** SE79

GH QQ *The Barn Hotel & Tearooms* YO6 6UA
☎01751 417311
Closed Xmas
An attractive stone-built guest house and tea room, this establishment enjoys a pretty village setting where sheep are allowed to roam freely. Bedrooms are modern in style and there is a comfortable residents' lounge with an open fire. A good range of food is available in a dining room full of Yorkshire character.
8 rms (3 bth/shr) (1 fmly) No smoking Tea and coffee making facilities No dogs (ex guide dogs) Licensed Cen ht CTV 15P
CARDS: 🂠 🔤

Factual details of establishments in this Guide are from questionnaires we send to all establishments that feature in the book.

HYDE Greater Manchester Map **07** SJ99

Selected

❤ QQQQ Mr & Mrs I Walsh **Needhams** *(SJ968925)*
Uplands Rd, Werneth Low, Gee Cross SK14 3AQ
☎0161 368 4610 FAX 0161 367 9106
This delightful stone built farm house, with its adjoining barn,
is owned and run by the very hospitable Mrs Walsh and has
been extensively restored and modernised. It enjoys the most
spectacular views over three counties from its elevated
position close to Werneth Low Park and the golf course and it
is located at the very end of Uplands Road, which is in some
places is just an unmade track. The bedrooms, most of which
have en-suite shower facilities, are modern, cosy and very
well equipped with televisions, direct dial telephones, radio
alarm clocks and many personal touches, in addition to a good
range of information on what to do in the area. Many of the
house's original features remain, including the exposed beams
and low ceilings of the lounge/dining room where a real fire is
lit in the winter. Dinner is available with orders taken in
advance from the speciality menu and a courtesy service is
offered to and from the airport or railway station for a small
charge.
7 rms (6 shr) (1 fmly) CTV in all bedrooms Tea and coffee
making facilities Direct dial from bedrooms Licensed Cen
ht CTV 14P Golf 12 Riding 30 acres beef Last d 9pm
PRICE GUIDE
ROOMS: s £18-£20; d £30-£34
CARDS: 🔳 ▬ ▬

HYTHE Kent Map **05** TR13

GH QQ *Sunny Bank House* 3 Station Rd CT21 5PN
☎01303 267087
Delightfully situated on the fringe of the town, only 5 minutes
from the Channel Tunnel terminus, this guesthouse has been
tastefully furnished and decorated with some fine furniture. The
bedrooms are not large but comfortably appointed. There is a
small sitting room and breakfast room where a choice of breakfast
is offered.
3 rms (1 fmly) No smoking in bedrooms CTV in 1 bedroom
Cen ht CTV 4P No coaches

GH QQQ **The White House** 27 Napier Gardens CT21 6DD
☎01303 266252
This large house is situated at the end of a cul-de-sac overlooking
the cricket ground and about half a mile from the sea. Bedrooms
are large and all have en suite facilities. An attractive garden with
tables and chairs provides a quiet place to relax, and the upstairs
breakfast room and balcony is an agreeable venue for the
Kennett's excellent breakfast. There is no lounge, but a
conservatory housing a three piece suite is about to be built.
3 en suite (shr) (1 fmly) CTV in all bedrooms Tea and coffee
making facilities No dogs (ex guide dogs) Cen ht CTV 4P No
coaches
PRICE GUIDE
ROOMS: s £22-£25; d £36-£38✳

ILFORD Greater London Map **05** TQ48

GH QQQ *Cranbrook Hotel* 24 Coventry Rd IG1 4QR
☎0181 554 6544 & 4765 FAX 0181 518 1463
A privately owned hotel conveniently situated in a residential area
close to the town centre offers modern accommodation. The small
bar lounge is comfortably appointed and well stocked, and both a
choice of breakfasts and an evening meal are offered in the

pleasant dining room. Friendly service is provided by the Perry
family, who have made significant improvements to the hotel
during their 19 years of ownership.
30 rms (26 bth/shr) (5 fmly) No smoking in 10 bedrooms No
smoking in dining room CTV in all bedrooms Tea and coffee
making facilities Direct dial from bedrooms Licensed Cen ht
CTV 30P Last d 7.30pm
CARDS: 🔳 ▬ ▬ 🔟
See advertisement under LONDON

GH QQ **Park Hotel** 327 Cranbrook Rd IG1 4UE (on A123
just south of junct with A12, Gantshill Rbt)
☎0181 554 9616 & 0181 554 7187 FAX 0181 518 2700
Privately owned and busy, this commercial hotel is modestly
furnished and decorated throughout. Well equipped bedrooms
offer trouser presses, hair dryers, telephones and tea-making
facilities, however, and a small but comfortable TV lounge is
provided for guests' use. Dinner is served Monday-Thursday.
20 rms (7 bth 10 shr) (3 fmly) CTV in all bedrooms Tea and
coffee making facilities Licensed Cen ht CTV 23P Last d
7.45pm
PRICE GUIDE
ROOMS: s £28.50-£36.50; d £40-£46.50✳
CARDS: 🔳 ▬ ▬ 🔳 🔟
See advertisement under LONDON

GH QQQ **Woodville** 10-12 Argyle Rd IG1 3BQ
☎0181 478 3779
Individually furnished comfortable modern well maintained
bedrooms and very good quality shower facilities combine with
double glazing and TV to provide good standards of
accommodation. Families with children are particularly welcome,
with service of light refreshment available throughout the day
personally supervised by the resident proprietor Joan Murray.
There is a comfortable sitting area combining with a beamed
dining room and a furnished rear garden and terrace. The
atmosphere is very friendly and relaxed and forecourt car parking
is provided.
15 rms (2 bth 1 shr) (3 fmly) No smoking in dining room CTV
in all bedrooms No dogs (ex guide dogs) Cen ht 11P
PRICE GUIDE
ROOMS: s fr £21; d £35-£40; wkly b&b £105-£150

ILFRACOMBE Devon Map **02** SS54

See also West Down

GH QQQ *Collingdale Hotel* Larkstone Ter EX34 9NU
☎01271 863770
Mar-27 Dec
Enjoying a good location, this hotel offers bedrooms on three
floors. Those at the back enjoy fine views across the golf course to
the sea. Golfers and cricketers are among the regular guests here
and advance booking is advisable. The hotel has been upgraded
and the en suite bedrooms have been redecorated and furnished
with coordinating soft fabrics. Further improvements have also
taken place in the bar and dining room.
9 rms (8 bth/shr) No smoking in bedrooms No smoking
in dining room Tea and coffee making facilities Licensed CTV
No parking No coaches Last d 5.30pm
CARDS: 🔳 ▬

GH QQQ *Cresta Hotel* Torrs Park EX34 8AY
☎01271 863742
May-Oct
A well established hotel, the Cresta has been in the Seddon family
for many years. The current generation continue to make
improvements and, overall, the bedrooms are bright, well
furnished and comfortable. Some ground-floor rooms are

➡

available, and a lift serves all floors. There is a cosy lounge area, a bar with a dance floor, and a bright dining room.

29 en suite (shr) (15 fmly) No smoking in area of dining room No smoking in 1 lounge CTV in all bedrooms Tea and coffee making facilities Licensed Lift Cen ht CTV 35P Putting green Last d 7pm

CARDS: ■ ■ ■

GH ⓆⓆ *Dedes Hotel* 1-3 The Promenade EX34 9BD
☎01271 862545 FAX 01271 862234
Closed 23-26 Dec

Dedes is in a central location directly opposite the beach and the Pavilion Theatre, the front facing rooms enjoying good views. Bedrooms, all but a few en suite, tend to be small but are nicely furnished and have good quality beds. There is a residents' lounge and lounge bar, in addition to the public bar, and for meals there is a choice between a cafÈ and more formal restaurant. The hotel specialises in clay shooting holidays.

17 rms (10 bth 2 shr) (6 fmly) No smoking in area of dining room CTV in all bedrooms Tea and coffee making facilities Licensed CTV 6P Clay pigeon shooting Last d 9.45pm

CARDS: ■ ■ ■ ⊙

GH ⓆⓆⓆ *Merlin Court Hotel* Torrs Park EX34 8AY
☎01271 862697

A fine example of late Victorian architecture, the Merlin Court looks out across the rooftops to the town beyond. It is a friendly place with many regular guests. Bedrooms are bright and fresh and there is a cosy lounge area, dining room and bar. The bar and skittle alley is a great attraction.

13 rms (3 bth 9 shr) (5 fmly) No smoking in bedrooms No smoking in dining room CTV in all bedrooms Tea and coffee making facilities Licensed Cen ht CTV 14P No coaches Skittle alley Last d 6.30pm

PRICE GUIDE
ROOMS: s £19-£21; d £38-£42; wkly b&b £126-£140; wkly hlf-bd £168-£180

CARDS: ■ ■ ■ £

GH ⓆⓆ *Southcliffe Hotel* Torrs Park EX34 8AZ
☎01271 862958
Spring BH-17 Sep rs Mar-Apr

A substantial brick-built Victorian property set in its own lawned garden just a short hilly walk from the town centre and beaches caters very well for families, most rooms having bunks or adjacent children's rooms. The lower ground floor contains extensive games and play rooms, there is a "Mums' kitchen", and a separate sitting room provides a quiet alternative to the bar lounge.

13 en suite (shr) (8 fmly) No smoking in dining room No smoking in lounges Tea and coffee making facilities No dogs Licensed CTV ch fac 12P No coaches Games room Last d 6pm

CARDS: ■ ■

GH ⓆⓆ *Strathmore Hotel* 57 St Brannocks Rd EX34 8EQ (on A361 approach into Ilfracombe, 0.25 from Mullacot Cross roundabout) ☎01271 862248 FAX 01271 864044

Rosemary and Nigel Pilch took over this handsome Victorian semi-detached property towards the end of 1994. They have continued a programme of upgrading to the bedrooms, installing smartly tiled shower rooms. A recently refurbished bar is provided, and in the dining room a short fixed-price menu is served. There is also a cosy no-smoking TV room.

9 rms (8 bth/shr) (3 fmly) No smoking in dining room No smoking in 1 lounge CTV in all bedrooms Tea and coffee making facilities Licensed Cen ht CTV 8P No coaches Last d 8.30pm

PRICE GUIDE
ROOMS: s £14; d £30-£36; wkly b&b £98-£116.80; wkly hlf-bd £140-£172✳

CARDS: ■ ■ ■ ▧

Selected

GH ⓆⓆⓆⓆ **Varley House** 13 Chambercombe Park Ter, Chambercombe Park EX34 9QW (follow A399 Combe Martin rd and at swimming pool turn right)
☎01271 863927 FAX 01271 863927
mid Mar-Oct

At Varley House Roy and Barbara Gable offer a warm welcome and well equipped accommodation in tastefully decorated bedrooms, including one on the ground floor. The bar is the social centre, but there is a beautifully proportioned lounge with a good selection of books and magazines. Barbara prepares imaginative dinners with a choice of dishes, including home-made soups, pâtés and traditional steak and kidney pie. Guests are asked to smoke only in the lounge and bar.

9 rms (8 bth/shr) (3 fmly) No smoking in bedrooms No smoking in dining room CTV in all bedrooms Tea and coffee making facilities Licensed Cen ht CTV No children 5yrs 8P No coaches Last d 5.30pm

PRICE GUIDE
ROOMS: s £21-£22; d £44-£47; wkly hlf-bd £190-£210

CARDS: ■ ■ ■ ■ ▧

GH ⓆⓆⓆ **Westwell Hall Hotel** Torrs Park EX34 8AZ
☎01271 862792

Standing in its own grounds in an elevated position, Westwell Hall has good views of the harbour and out across the town. The well proportioned bedrooms have fresh decor and en suite facilities, and there is a warm, cosy feel to the public areas, which include a games room where children may play. Home cooked fare is served in the dining room, and gourmet weekends in March and October are very popular.

9 en suite (bth/shr) (1 fmly) No smoking in dining room CTV in all bedrooms Tea and coffee making facilities Licensed Cen ht 14P No coaches Snooker Croquet Table tennis Last d 7pm

CARDS: ■ ■ £

INGLEBY GREENHOW North Yorkshire Map **08** NZ50

Selected

❤ ⓆⓆⓆⓆ Mrs M Bloom **Manor House Farm** *(NZ586056)* TS9 6RB (entrance to farm drive opposite church) ☎01642 722384
Closed 21-29 Dec

Set in woods and parkland beside the ancient Ingleby manor house, this lovely old farmhouse offers spacious and comfortable accommodation. All areas are very well furnished, the three bedrooms having every possible comfort while the inviting lounge is made cosy by a wood-burning stove. A good home-cooked dinner is served every evening in the pretty dining room, and delightful owners provide warm, friendly service. The farm is signed from the church in the village.

3 en suite (bth) No smoking Tea and coffee making facilities No dogs Licensed Cen ht CTV No children 12yrs 50P Fishing Riding Rough shooting 168 acres mixed Last d 3pm

PRICE GUIDE
ROOMS: (incl. dinner) d £71-£84; wkly hlf-bd £248.50

INGLETON North Yorkshire Map **07** SD67

Selected

GH ◻◻◻◻ **Ferncliffe** Main St LA6 3HJ (turn off A65 onto B6255, 75yds on right) ☎015242 42405
Closed Nov rs Dec-Jan

An attractive stone house set close to the village centre, Ferncliffe has been tastefully appointed throughout with quality furnishings to provide both pretty bedrooms and a comfortable lounge. The tick of the grandfather clock adds to the charm of a dining room where good English fare is served.

5 en suite (shr) No smoking in dining room CTV in all bedrooms Tea and coffee making facilities Cen ht CTV 6P No coaches
PRICE GUIDE
ROOMS: s fr £26; d fr £40; wkly b&b £133-£172; wkly hlf-bd £212-£250✱

(£)

GH ◻◻ **Langber Country** Tatterthorne Rd LA6 3DT (off A65 between Mason's Arms and Tatterthorne Road car park) ☎015242 41587
Closed 23 Dec-3 Jan

Standing in an elevated position in open countryside, this modern house offers sound accommodation together with spacious public rooms, all enjoying fine views.

7 rms (2 bth 1 shr) (3 fmly) No smoking in bedrooms No smoking in dining room Tea and coffee making facilities Cen ht CTV 6P Last d 5pm
PRICE GUIDE
ROOMS: s £15.25-£21; d £29.90-£40; wkly b&b £99-£120; wkly hlf-bd £134-£162✱

(£)

Selected

GH ◻◻◻◻ *Oakroyd Old Rectory* Main St LA6 3HJ ☎01524 241258

A former rectory is now a family hotel conveniently situated just off the A65, on the edge of the village. Bedrooms are furnished in contemporary style; many have fine views of the surrounding countryside. There is a comfortable guests' lounge with TV, books, magazines and board games. The dining room is very attractively furnished and decorated, enhanced by a collection of paintings and prints; excellent home-cooked food is served, with a set evening menu offering an extensive choice. The cosy bar is the only area where smoking is allowed. Resident owners Peter and Ann Hudson are genial hosts, and Peter's cooking has been highly praised.

6 en suite (shr) (2 fmly) No smoking in bedrooms No smoking in dining room No smoking in lounges CTV in all bedrooms Tea and coffee making facilities No dogs (ex guide dogs) Licensed Cen ht CTV No children 11yrs 6P No coaches Last d 5.30pm

---

GH ◻◻◻ **Pines Country House Hotel** LA6 3HN (on A65) ☎01524 241252 FAX 01524 241252

Located in an elevated position on the A65 and only a short walk from the village, this charming country house hotel offers warm and friendly service in a peaceful house. There is a lovely comfortable lounge and the sunny conservatory is the setting for the well produced home cooking which is backed by a select list of wines. Bedrooms are pleasantly furnished and are thoughtfully equipped.

Look out for the 80 year old grape vine in the conservatory.
5 rms (4 bth/shr) (2 fmly) No smoking in bedrooms No smoking in dining room No smoking in 1 lounge CTV in all bedrooms Tea and coffee making facilities Licensed Cen ht CTV 16P No coaches Last d 6pm
PRICE GUIDE
ROOMS: s £27-£35; d £40-£44; wkly hlf-bd £134-£154✱
CARDS: 🔳 💳

GH ◻◻◻ **Springfield Private Hotel** Main St LA6 3HJ (off A65) ☎01524 241280
Closed Xmas

Situated close to the village and having the benefit of a delightful rear garden which leads down to the river, this late Victorian house offers very good value for money. The house is comfortable and cosy and the bedrooms are well equipped and are spotlessly clean. Very friendly service is provided by the resident owners who have been running the guest house for many years now. There is private fishing on the river Greta

5 en suite (shr) (1 fmly) No smoking in dining room No smoking in 1 lounge CTV in all bedrooms Tea and coffee making facilities Licensed Cen ht CTV 12P No coaches Fishing Last d 5pm
PRICE GUIDE
ROOMS: s £20; d £36-£40; wkly hlf-bd £182

(£)

GH ◻◻ **Stacksteads** Tatterthornm Rd LA6 3HS (from A65 towards Settle, turn right at Masons Arms public house into Tamerthorn Road, farm 300 yds on right) ☎01524 241386

Situated about one mile from the village centre and set in beautiful open countryside, this old farmhouse is well furnished and offers very good value for money. There is a cosy lounge for guests and a good hearty breakfast is served in the pleasant dining room. ➡

Evening meals are available on request.
3 rms (2 shr) No dogs Cen ht CTV 4P No coaches Last d 8.30am
PRICE GUIDE
ROOMS: s £15; d £30✳

INSTOW Devon Map **02** SS43

GH ◗◗◗ **Anchorage Hotel** The Quay EX39 4HX
☎01271 860655 & 860475 FAX 01271 860767
Closed 16 Jan - Feb
Standing on the quay, only a few minutes' walk from a sandy beach, this well presented Victorian guesthouse offers easy access to the North Devon Link and M5. Bedrooms with en suite showers are centrally heated and equipped with telephones, colour televisions and tea-making facilities. There is a choice of comfortable, well furnished lounges on the first floor, with an attractive restaurant and bar lounge at ground level.
17 en suite (bth/shr) (6 fmly) No smoking in area of dining room CTV in 2 bedrooms Tea and coffee making facilities Direct dial from bedrooms Licensed Cen ht CTV 18P Last d 9.30pm
CARDS: 🔳 🔤

IPSWICH Suffolk Map **05** TM14

GH ◗◗◗ *Bentley Tower Hotel* 172 Norwich Rd IP1 2PY
(turn right off A12 at Chevalier roundabout)
☎01473 212142 FAX 01473 212142
Closed 24 Dec-4 Jan
The atmosphere is welcoming at this well-established guest house, and public areas include a relaxing sitting room with satellite television, a spacious bar and a pleasant dining room where evening meals are served. Bedrooms are spacious and well appointed, all having en suite facilities. Private parking is available.
11 en suite (shr) (2 fmly) No smoking in 2 bedrooms CTV in 13 bedrooms Tea and coffee making facilities No dogs (ex guide dogs) Licensed Cen ht 16P No coaches Last d 8.45pm
CARDS: 🔳 🔤

GH ◗ **Cliffden** 21 London Rd IP1 2EZ
☎01473 252689 FAX 01473 252689
Only five minutes walk from the city centre, this large building has its bedrooms divided between three floors, including the ground floor. They vary greatly in size and appointments. Breakfast is served in a room divided from an informal lounge by a partion.
15 rms (7 shr) (3 fmly) No smoking in 1 bedrooms No smoking in dining room CTV in all bedrooms Tea and coffee making facilities No dogs (ex guide dogs) Cen ht 7P
PRICE GUIDE
ROOMS: s £18-£20; d £25-£30; wkly b&b £84-£105✳

GH ◗◗◗ **Highview House Hotel** 56 Belstead Rd IP2 8BE
(nr Railway Station) ☎01473 601620 & 688659
An hotel conveniently located near the town centre and railway station provides sound accommodation in adequately furnished and equipped bedrooms. A set dinner menu is offered in the lower-ground-floor dining room (which also houses a full-size snooker table at one end).
11 rms (9 bth/shr) (1 fmly) CTV in all bedrooms Tea and coffee making facilities Direct dial from bedrooms Licensed Cen ht CTV 15P No coaches Snooker Last d 7.30pm
PRICE GUIDE
ROOMS: s £33-£38.50; d £48.50✳
CARDS: 🔳 🔤

IRONBRIDGE Shropshire Map **07** SJ60

GH ◗◗◗ **Broseley** The Square, Broseley TF12 5EW (from Ironbridge-Bridgenorth rd B4373 into Broseley and at petrol station turn right into Church St) ☎01952 882043
Closed 22-27 Dec
A comfortable guesthouse stands in the centre of the town with an adjacent public car park. The rooms are well equipped and have all the facilities required by the business or tourist visitor.
6 en suite (bth/shr) (3 fmly) No smoking in dining room No smoking in lounges CTV in all bedrooms Tea and coffee making facilities Direct dial from bedrooms Licensed Cen ht No parking No coaches Last d by arrangement
PRICE GUIDE
ROOMS: s £25-£29; d £40-£45✳
CARDS: 🔳 🔤

Selected

GH ◗◗◗◗ **The Library House** 11 Severn Bank TF8 7AN (50yds from the Iron Bridge)
☎01952 432299 FAX 01952 433967
Situated just 100yds from the famous landmark, this small family-run guesthouse was until 1960 the local library. The lounge now occupies this spot and is furnished with deep modern easy chairs and settees, with a drinks table for diners. The quarry tiled dining room is pine furnished and dates from 1750, and was once a doctor's surgery. Bedrooms are individually decorated with coordinated fabrics and have comfortable armchairs. There are terraced gardens to the rear with fine views of the local church, and free car parking is available nearby. George and Chris Maddocks are a very friendly couple and offer warm hospitality at their totally no smoking establishment.
3 en suite (bth/shr) (1 fmly) No smoking CTV in all bedrooms Tea and coffee making facilities Licensed Cen ht CTV No parking No coaches
PRICE GUIDE
ROOMS: s fr £35; d fr £48

ISLE OF

Placenames incorporating the words 'Isle of' or 'Isle' will be found under the actual name, eg Isle of Wight is under Wight, Isle of.

ITCHEN ABBAS Hampshire Map **04** SU53

Selected

◀ ◗◗◗◗ **Trout Inn** Main Rd ☎01962 779537
Closed 25-26 Dec
Situated 3.5m from Winchester in the Ichen Valley on the B3047 Kingsworthy to Alresford road, this popular, delightful, tile-hung village pub has six comfortable, individually furnished bedrooms all equipped with TV and tea trays. Families are particularly welcome; there is a children's play area and special meals can be provided. Personally run by the proprietor, David Lee Smith, the atmosphere is very cordial, relaxed and friendly; there is a good range of real ale (including Pedigree and Burton hand pulled cask bitter) and a ready supply of fresh trout from the nearby River Itchen. The cooking style is British, specialising in fresh fish, and as well as a separate no-smoking dining room featuring a carte there is a very good selection of bar meals. The bar is cosy and well

appointed and local pursuits include Darts, Bar Billiards, and shove ha'ppenny, local fishing can readily be arranged, as can bicycle hire. There is a good sized garden, summer barbecue and ample car parking.
6 en suite (shr) (2 fmly) No smoking CTV in 5 bedrooms Tea and coffee making facilities No dogs (ex guide dogs) Cen ht 29P Last d 8.30pm
PRICE GUIDE
ROOMS: s fr £27.50; d £46
MEALS: Lunch £3.95-£9.95&alc Dinner £3.95-£9.95&alc
CARDS: 💳 💳 💳

IVER HEATH Buckinghamshire Map 04 TQ08

GH ◙◙◙ **Bridgettine Convent** Fulmer Common Rd SL0 0NR (from Iver Heath roundabout take Pinewood Road pass Film Studios to cross roads and turn left into Fulmer Common Road) ☎01753 662073 & 662645 FAX 01753 662172
There is unstinting hospitality in this Tudor building which is run by the order of St. Bridget in Rome. Although the bedrooms are simple they are all well looked after and are slowly being provided with full en suite bathroom facilities. There are a large peaceful library and a further room which can be used for small meetings.
13 rms (3 shr) (3 fmly) No smoking No dogs Cen ht CTV P No coaches Last d 2pm
PRICE GUIDE
ROOMS: s £17-£19; d £34-£38

JACOBSTOWE Devon Map 02 SS50

❤ ◙◙◙ Mr & Mrs J King **Higher Cadham** *(SS585026)* EX20 3RB (from Jacobstowe village take A3072 towards Hatherleigh/Bude, a few yards after church turn sharp right in front of Cottage Farm continue for 0.5m) ☎01837 851647 FAX 10837 851410
Closed Dec
A Devon longhouse with a farm which is part of the Tarka Trail scheme, allowing the public to walk part or all of the 180 miles of river and countryside path. The charming bedrooms are named after four of the rivers mentioned in Tarka The Otter; one room has a four-poster bed. The lounge and dining room have beamed ceilings and log burners, and traditional farmhouse fare is provided at the large dining room table. A restaurant and five additional en suite bedrooms are being created by barn conversions.
9 rms (3 fmly) No smoking in dining room No smoking in 1 lounge CTV in 1 bedroom Tea and coffee making facilities Licensed Cen ht CTV 10P Play room Nature Trail 139 acres Beef Sheep Last d 7pm
PRICE GUIDE
ROOMS: s £16.50-£22.50; d £33-£45; wkly b&b £110-£145; wkly hlf-bd £155-£195
CARDS: 💳 💳 💳 💳
See advertisement under OKEHAMPTON

KEIGHLEY West Yorkshire Map 07 SE04

GH ◙◙◙ **Bankfield** 1 Station Rd, Cross Hills BD20 7EH (turn off A650/A629 Aire Valley trunk road at Kildwick roundabout and take weight limit restriction road towards Cross Hills. 0.5m on right) ☎01535 632971
Family owned and run, this stone-built house situated in the village of Crosshills, between Keighley and Skipton, offers a good standard of well maintained accommodation. Spacious rooms are pleasantly decorated, and the comfortable lounge provides both TV and plenty of reading matter.

---

3 rms (1 shr) (1 fmly) No smoking in bedrooms CTV in 1 bedroom Tea and coffee making facilities Cen ht CTV 5P No coaches
PRICE GUIDE
ROOMS: s £17-£19; d £34-£38; wkly b&b £119-£133✳

KENDAL Cumbria Map 07 SD59

See also Brigsteer

Selected

GH ◙◙◙◙ **Burrow Hall Country Guest House** Plantation Bridge LA8 9JR (on A591) ☎01539 821711
Dating back to 1648, this delightful country house is situated on the A591, west of Kendal and only 10 minutes' drive from junction 36 of the M6. The main lounge features original oak beams and open log fires, and there is another comfortable TV lounge. A well produced four-course evening meal is served at individual tables in the cosy dining room and is very much a feature at Burrow Hall.
3 en suite (shr) No smoking in bedrooms No smoking in dining room Tea and coffee making facilities No dogs Licensed Cen ht CTV No children 16yrs 12P No coaches Last d 6.30pm
PRICE GUIDE
ROOMS: d £45; wkly b&b £157.50; wkly hlf-bd £220
CARDS: 💳 💳

GH QQQQ **Higher House Farm** Oxenholme Ln, Natland LA9 7QH ☎015395 61177 FAX 015395 61177
No longer part of a farm, but secluded in gardens which include an orchard, this attractive house dates from the 17th century and has been carefully modernised to retain such original featuresas old beams. A tasteful and inviting lounge has a log fire in cold weather, whilst on fine days one can sit out on the patio and admire the sweeping views. Val Sunter's meals cater for a variety of tastes and preferences. Bedrooms are sensibly furnished and have thoughtful touches like hair dryers, fresh fruit and flowers and radios.
3 en suite (bth/shr) No smoking CTV in 2 bedrooms Tea and coffee making facilities Cen ht CTV 9P No coaches Golf 9 Last d 1pm
PRICE GUIDE
ROOMS: s £18-£23; d £36-£40; wkly b&b £126; wkly hlf-bd £217✳

GH QQQQQ **Lane Head Country House Hotel** Helsington LA9 5RJ (0.5m S off A6) ☎01539 731283 & 721023 FAX 01539 721023
Closed Nov
Signposted off the A6, this 17th-century country residence is situated to the south of the town with views over Kendal and the surrounding countryside.

Bedrooms are modern and comfortable and have TVs and telephones as standard; one also has a private lounge. The spacious sitting room is elegantly furnished and has a wood-burning stove for colder weather. It is here that pre-dinner drinks are served to tables, and there follows a choice of five carefully cooked and well presented dishes. The hotel also has a pretty rear garden and ample car parking.
7 en suite (bth/shr) No smoking in 2 bedrooms No smoking in dining room CTV in all bedrooms Tea and coffee making facilities Direct dial from bedrooms Licensed Cen ht 10P No coaches Last d 5pm
PRICE GUIDE
ROOMS: s £35-£40; d £50-£65
CARDS: 🔲 ▬ ▬

We endeavour to be as accurate as possible but changes in personnel and data can occur in establishments after the Guide has gone to press.

GH QQQQQ **Low Jock Scar** Selside LA8 9LE (6m N on A6) ☎01539 823259 FAX 01539 823645
Mar-Oct

This small country guest house enjoys an idyllic setting , secluded in six acres of attractively laid-out gardens and woodland, with a stream running by. Philip and Alison Midwinter are charming and enthusiastic hosts and Alison's five-course dinners and hearty breakfasts draw praise. The house has a relaxed and inviting atmosphere, with a lovely lounge full of books and tourist maps, a conservatory dining room overlooking the gardens and pleasant individually furnished and airy bedrooms, one of which has its own outside entrance. Low Jock Scar is totally non-smoking and lies off the A6 six miles north of Kendal.
5 rms (3 bth/shr) No smoking Tea and coffee making facilities Licensed Cen ht CTV No children 12yrs 7P Last d 10am
PRICE GUIDE
ROOMS: s £27-£32; d £40-£50

GH QQQ **Martindales** 9-11 Sandes Av LA9 4LL (N on A6, before Victoria Bridge) ☎01539 724028
This comfortable terraced guest house is located within walking distance of the town centre. The attractively decorated modern bedrooms are sensibly furnished and include a spacious family room on the top floor. The welcoming bar/lounge has a cheery coal fire.
8 en suite (shr) (1 fmly) No smoking in dining room CTV in all bedrooms Tea and coffee making facilities No dogs (ex guide dogs) Licensed Cen ht No children 8yrs 7P No coaches Last d 1pm
PRICE GUIDE
ROOMS: s fr £25; d £40-£42; wkly b&b £140-£175; wkly hlf-bd £210-£245✳
CARDS: 🔲 ▬

♥ QQQ Mrs S Beaty **Garnett House** *(SD500959)* Burneside LA9 5SF (0.5m from the A591 Kendal/Windermere road, 2m from Kendal) ☎01539 724542
Closed Xmas & New Year
Amongst the rolling hills with views over Howgill Fell in the distance this ancient fifteenth century stone farmhouse sits squarely amid its barns and yard, fronted by a pretty cottage garden. Inside the house is furnished in character with modern facilities. Mrs Beatty offers a substantial dinner of traditional farm house cooking.
5 rms (3 shr) (2 fmly) No smoking in dining room CTV in all bedrooms Tea and coffee making facilities No dogs CTV 6P 750 acres Dairy Sheep Last d 5pm
PRICE GUIDE
ROOMS: d £30-£33; wkly b&b £102-£110

♥ QQQ Mrs J Ellis **Gateside** *(NY494955)* Windermere Rd LA9 5SE (2m from Kendal travelling towards Windermere on A591) ☎01539 722036
Closed Xmas & New Year
An attractive white painted farmhouse situated on a working farm

on the A591 Windermere road, with easy access to junction 36 of the M6. Bedrooms are prettily decorated and full of character, some featuring beams. There is a cosy guests' lounge and a spacious dining room, with friendly service provided by owner Mrs June Ellis.

5 rms (2 shr) (1 fmly) No smoking in dining room CTV in all bedrooms Tea and coffee making facilities Cen ht 6P 280 acres dairy sheep Last d 4.30pm

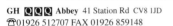

¥ Q Q Q Mrs E M Gardner **Natland Mill Beck** *(SD520907)* LA9 7LH (1m from Kendal on A65, close to Westmoreland General Hospital) ☎01539 721122

Mar-Oct

This 17th century farmhouse is quietly secluded in attractive gardens only 200 metres from the A65. An interesting building, it has low beamed ceilings and many original architectural features. There are two lounges, one with a dining area serving enjoyable meals around a large table. Bedrooms reflect the character of the house and are brightly decorated; the largest has an en suite shower room. The smaller twin has a shower cubicle and shares a bathroom with the small double.

3 rms (1 shr) Tea and coffee making facilities No dogs Cen ht CTV 3P 100 acres dairy

PRICE GUIDE

ROOMS: s fr £16; d fr £32✱

(£)

KENILWORTH Warwickshire Map **04** SP27

GH Q Q Q **Abbey** 41 Station Rd CV8 1JD ☎01926 512707 FAX 01926 859148

A proudly run establishment, this guest house is located within a short distance of the main shopping area and has a large pay-and-display car park to the rear. Two of the rooms have en suite facilities and all are considerably equipped. There are a cosy TV lounge and a breakfast room where a collection of miniature houses is displayed.

7 rms (3 shr) (1 fmly) No smoking CTV in all bedrooms Tea and coffee making facilities No dogs (ex guide dogs) Licensed Cen ht CTV 2P No coaches Last d 5pm

PRICE GUIDE

ROOMS: s £19-£24; d £34-£40

(£)

GH Q Q Q **Castle Laurels Hotel** 22 Castle Rd CV8 1NG (on A452, opposite Castle) ☎01926 56179 FAX 01926 54954

Closed 22 Dec-2 Jan

Castle Laurels is an impeccably maintained Victorian house close to the castle. The bedrooms are traditionally furnished and vary in size, though all have modern equipment. One is furnished for family occupancy. There is a comfortable lounge and a dining room with separate tables.

12 en suite (shr) (1 fmly) No smoking CTV in all bedrooms Tea and coffee making facilities Direct dial from bedrooms No dogs (ex guide dogs) Licensed Cen ht No children 5yrs 14P No coaches Last d 7pm

PRICE GUIDE

ROOMS: s £30-£33; d £48-£54✱

CARDS:

(£)

GH Q Q Q **Ferndale** 45 Priory Rd CV8 1LL ☎01926 53214 FAX 01926 58336

The friendly and easy-going manner of the owner, Mrs Wilson, makes this a popular guest house. She is helped by her mother who takes care of the many bright flowering pots during the warmer months. Bedrooms are individually furnished and variously sized.

7 en suite (bth/shr) (2 fmly) No smoking in bedrooms No smoking in dining room CTV in all bedrooms Tea and coffee

➡

making facilities Licensed Cen ht CTV 8P
PRICE GUIDE
ROOMS: s £20-£25; d £35-£42✷

GH ◖Q◗◖Q◗◖Q◗ **Hollyhurst** 47 Priory Rd CV8 1LL (on A452)
☎01926 53882
This bright semidetached house is now under the ownership of
Mary Millar, a friendly and conscientious hostess. Bedrooms are
simply furnished but reasonably spacious, and some family rooms
are available. There is a small dispense bar as well as a guests'
lounge - the only room in the house where smoking is permitted.
7 rms (3 shr) (1 fmly) No smoking CTV in all bedrooms Tea
and coffee making facilities No dogs Licensed Cen ht CTV No
children 5yrs 9P No coaches Last d 10am
PRICE GUIDE
ROOMS: s £19-£25; d £38-£46; wkly b&b £120-£180; wkly hlf-
bd £150-£220

Selected

GH ◖Q◗◖Q◗◖Q◗◖Q◗ **Victoria Lodge Hotel** 180 Warwick Rd
CV8 1HU (0.25m S on A452, opposite St Johns Church)
☎01926 512020 FAX 01926 58703
Smartly furnished and individually styled accommodation is
offered at this modern guest house which has been cleverly
converted from a series of old flats. The character is
contemporary, but there are a few reminders of the past in the
form of personal memorabilia. Recent changes to the public
areas have allowed for an extra bedroom on the ground floor.
The hallway provides a small lounge area and a reception
counter, their contemporary decor shared by a breakfast room
where dinner is also served.
7 en suite (bth/shr) No smoking CTV in all bedrooms Tea
and coffee making facilities Direct dial from bedrooms No
dogs (ex guide dogs) Licensed Cen ht No children 14yrs
11P No coaches
PRICE GUIDE
ROOMS: s £34-£36; d £47-£51✷
CARDS:

KENTON Devon Map 03 SX98

◖✉◗◖🛏◗ ♥ ◖Q◗◖Q◗◖Q◗ Mrs D Lambert **Mill Farm** (SX959839)
EX6 8JR (take A379 to Dawlish and bypassing Exminster go
across mini roundabout by Swans Nest. Farm 1.5m on right)
☎01392 832471
Closed Xmas
This imposing farmhouse is set back from the Exeter to Dawlish
road, and surrounded by its own pasture. Bedrooms are
comfortable and nicely decorated and furnished, two have en-suite
showers, and the other three share two bathrooms. There is a
homely lounge and breakfast is served in a bright and attractive
dining room.
6 rms (2 shr) (2 fmly) No smoking in dining room No smoking
in lounges CTV in 2 bedrooms Tea and coffee making facilities
No dogs Cen ht CTV 12P 60 acres beef
PRICE GUIDE
ROOMS: s £15-£20; d £28-£35; wkly b&b £91-£140

KESWICK Cumbria Map 11 NY22

Selected

GH ◖Q◗◖Q◗◖Q◗◖Q◗ **Abacourt House** 26 Stanger St CA12 5JU
☎017687 72967
A charming Victorian house standing in a quiet side road,
only a short way from the town centre has been tastefully
refurbished to a very high standard. Bill and Sheila Newman
are good hosts, and there is a very pleasant atmosphere, with
convenient car parking to the rear.
5 en suite (shr) No smoking CTV in all bedrooms Tea and
coffee making facilities No dogs Cen ht No children 5P No
coaches
PRICE GUIDE
ROOMS: d £40

Selected

GH ◖Q◗◖Q◗◖Q◗◖Q◗ **Acorn House Hotel** Ambleside Rd CA12
4DL (500yds from town centre opposite St John Church)
☎017687 72553 FAX 017687 75332
Feb-Nov
This traditional Georgian hotel features antique furniture in
some bedrooms, three also having four-poster beds. All rooms
have private facilities and such extras as colour television,
radio alarms, and tea-making equipment; four situated on the
top floor are attractively decorated but slightly smaller than
the others. An elegant drawing room offers comfortable sofas
and winged armchairs, while the spacious, lofty dining room
looks out over a well tended garden. Smoking is not permitted
in the bedrooms.
10 rms (9 bth/shr) (3 fmly) No smoking in bedrooms No
smoking in dining room CTV in all bedrooms Tea and coffee
making facilities No dogs (ex guide dogs) Licensed Cen ht
No children 5yrs 10P No coaches
PRICE GUIDE
ROOMS: s £25-£35; d £45-£60; wkly b&b £155-£170✷
CARDS: ◼ ▦

GH ◖Q◗◖Q◗◖Q◗ **Allerdale House** 1 Eskin St CA12 4DH
☎017687 73891
A substantial end of row terraced house just five minutes from the
town centre and its high street which runs parallel. The Allerdale
is a very well cared for establishment which in addition to the
thoughtfully co-ordinated rooms has a lovely sitting room and a
brightly decorated dining room. dinners are home made and use
local produce such as the local trout. Although there is no choice,
menus are displayed in the morning and changes are easily made
to suit.
6 en suite (bth/shr) (2 fmly) No smoking CTV in all bedrooms
Tea and coffee making facilities Direct dial from bedrooms
Licensed Cen ht No children 5yrs 6P No coaches Last d 5pm
PRICE GUIDE
ROOMS: s £18-£22; d £36-£44; wkly b&b £126-£154; wkly hlf-
bd £199.50-£231✷

GH Ⓠ Ⓠ Ⓠ Ⓠ **Applethwaite Country House Hotel**
Applethwaite, Underskiddaw CA12 4PL (off A591)
☎017687 72413 FAX 017687 75706

Situated high above the Borrowdale Valley en route to
Lattrigg and Skiddaw beyond the Applethwaite was built as a
gentleman's residence around the turn of the century and has
gracefully proportioned reception rooms and bedrooms above.
The latter are gradually being furnished in the Edwardian
style and are both spacious and very comfortable. The views
are splendid and especially from the second floor and from
the oriole window. The drawing room is also furnished in
character and in the dining room a short menu includes four
courses.

12 en suite (bth/shr) (4 fmly) No smoking in 7 bedrooms No
smoking in dining room No smoking in lounges CTV in all
bedrooms Tea and coffee making facilities No dogs (ex
guide dogs) Licensed Cen ht CTV 10P No coaches
Bowling green Putting Croquet lawn Last d 6.45pm
PRICE GUIDE
ROOMS: s £27.50-£31.50; d £55-£63; wkly b&b £190;
wkly hlf-bd £275-£290
CARDS: £

GH Ⓠ Ⓠ Ⓠ **Avondale** 20 Southey St CA12 4EF (take first left
at Cenotaph into Southey St Avondale 100yds on right)
☎017687 72735

Situated in a quiet side road close to the town centre, this
attractive terraced guest house is family run and offers well
furnished accommodation. Smoking is not permitted.

6 rms (4 shr) No smoking CTV in all bedrooms Tea and coffee
making facilities No dogs (ex guide dogs) Licensed Cen ht No
children 12yrs No coaches Last d breakfast
PRICE GUIDE
ROOMS: s £14.50-£18.50; d £29-£37; wkly b&b £101.50-
£122.50; wkly hlf-bd £168-£188✳
CARDS: £

GH Ⓠ Ⓠ Ⓠ **Beckside** 5 Wordsworth St CA12 4HU (turn off
A66 onto A5271, Wordsworth St just beyond Shell Petrol
Station next to Fitz Park) ☎017687 73093

A very attractive terraced cottage built in 1878 of Lakeland stone
stands just a stone's throw from the River Greta and Fitz Park.
Bedrooms are bright and fresh and public areas comfortable and
inviting, with plenty of fresh flowers in evidence. Fruit cake is
offered to guests on arrival by hospitable owner Carol Wraight.
Smoking is not permitted inside the house.

4 en suite (bth/shr) No smoking CTV in all bedrooms Tea and
coffee making facilities No dogs (ex guide dogs) Cen ht No
children 8yrs No parking No coaches Last d 1pm
PRICE GUIDE
ROOMS: d £34-£37; wkly b&b £120; wkly hlf-bd £200 £

GH Ⓠ Ⓠ Ⓠ **Brierholme** 21 Bank St CA12 5JZ (on A591,
100yds from post office) ☎017687 72938

Brierholme is set in a small terraced row in the centre of town and
from its elevated position affords fine views from the upper floors.
Bedrooms are bright and modern with good en suite bathrooms,
and the attic room is full of character. A comfortable lounge is
provided on the first floor and a dining room downstairs.

6 en suite (bth/shr) (2 fmly) No smoking in bedrooms No
smoking in dining room CTV in all bedrooms Tea and coffee

making facilities Licensed Cen ht 6P No coaches Last d 3pm
PRICE GUIDE
ROOMS: d £34-£42✳

GH Ⓠ Ⓠ Ⓠ **Charnwood** 6 Eskin St CA12 4DH (0.5m S of
A591 near town centre) ☎017687 74111

This attractive Victorian house is a Grade I listed building, which
is situated in a quiet but convenient area of the town. All but one
bedroom have modern en-suite facilities, and there is a
comfortable guests room and a pleasant dining room.

5 en suite (shr) (2 fmly) No smoking CTV in all bedrooms Tea
and coffee making facilities No dogs (ex guide dogs) Licensed
Cen ht CTV No children 5yrs No coaches Last d 4pm
PRICE GUIDE
ROOMS: d £36-£42; wkly b&b £119-£133; wkly hlf-bd £192-
£206
CARDS: £

GH Ⓠ Ⓠ Ⓠ **Claremont House** Chestnut Hill CA12 4LT (SE
on A591) ☎017687 72089

This comfortable house, built more than 150 years ago as a lodge
for a manor house, is now the home of Geoff and Hilda
Mackerness. Individually decorated bedrooms are attractively
furnished, and there are also a guests' lounge and a smart dining
room. The garden is pleasant and private parking facilities are
available. Vegetarians are welcome.

5 en suite (bth/shr) No smoking in bedrooms No smoking in
dining room Tea and coffee making facilities No dogs Licensed
Cen ht CTV 8P No coaches Last d 4pm
PRICE GUIDE
ROOMS: s £30-£35; d £44-£50✳

 £

See advertisement on p.225.

GH Q Q Q **Clarence House** 14 Eskin St CA12 4DQ (second turning on left after Shell garage Greta St leads to Eskin St)
☎017687 73186

Closed 23-26 Dec

Clarence House is a Victorian property situated within easy walking distance of the town centre. The bedrooms are freshly decorated, comfortable and equipped with modern facilities. There is a spacious dining room with individual tables and a small cosy lounge on the first floor. Please note that this is a no-smoking establishment.

9 rms (8 bth/shr) (3 fmly) No smoking CTV in all bedrooms Tea and coffee making facilities No dogs (ex guide dogs) Cen ht No children 5yrs No parking
PRICE GUIDE
ROOMS: s £18-£21; d £36-£44

Selected

GH Q Q Q Q **Craglands** Penrith Rd CA12 4LJ (guesthouse at the foot of Chestnut Hill on right entering Keswick) ☎017687 74406

rs Nov-Mar

This semi-detached Victorian house lies by the main road in an elevated position leading into Keswick from the south and east. Attractively decorated throughout, it offers bedrooms which are not large, but are thoughtfully equipped and with most providing small seating areas. There is a comfortable lounge where a complementary sherry is served before enjoying Wendy Dolton's delicious home-cooked dinners. The house is not licensed but one is welcome to bring one's own beverage.

5 en suite (bth/shr) No smoking CTV in all bedrooms Tea and coffee making facilities No dogs (ex guide dogs) Cen ht No children 8yrs 6P No coaches Last d 4pm
PRICE GUIDE
ROOMS: s £24-£27; d £40-£44; wkly b&b £130-£150; wkly hlf-bd £220-£240✱

Selected

GH Q Q Q Q **Dalegarth House Country Hotel**
Portinscale CA12 5RQ (approach Portinscale from A66 pass Farmers Arms approx 100yds on left to hotel)
☎017687 72817

A delightful house standing above landscaped gardens and a prominently placed Monkey Puzzle tree in a small lakeside village. Inside the house the furnishings, decor and facilities are thoroughly modern bright and light. The bedrooms are very generously proportioned and their lay out practical. Dinners are home made and served in a relaxing and friendly atmosphere.

10 en suite (bth/shr) (1 fmly) No smoking CTV in all bedrooms Tea and coffee making facilities No dogs (ex guide dogs) Licensed Cen ht CTV No children 5yrs 12P No coaches Last d 5.30pm
PRICE GUIDE
ROOMS: s £25-£27; d £50-£54; wkly b&b £165-£175; wkly hlf-bd £245-£255
CARDS: 💳 💳

Premier Selected

GH Q Q Q Q Q **Derwent Cottage** Portinscale
CA12 5RF ☎017687 74838
Mar-Oct

Tucked away in the centre of the village secluded by extensive gardens Derwent Cottage is something of a misnomer as inside it is a substantial period house furnished in a contemporary style though quiet and elegant. The reception rooms extend to a well appointed dining room overlooking the glorious gardens and a lounge and small well stacked bar. The bedrooms are furnished to hotel standard both for their size and facilities and are furnished very comfortably with many thoughtful extras. Mr and Mrs Newman are a delightful couple who run the business personally with an enthusiasm and efficiency which is especially noteworthy. Dinner is home cooked and a set, four-course affair in the Lakeland tradition.

5 en suite (bth/shr) No smoking CTV in all bedrooms Tea and coffee making facilities No dogs (ex guide dogs) Licensed Cen ht No children 12yrs 10P No coaches Last d noon
PRICE GUIDE
ROOMS: d £48-£64; wkly b&b £161-£189; wkly hlf-bd £245-£273✱
CARDS: 💳 💳

GH Q Q Q **Edwardene** 26 Southey St CA12 4EF
☎017687 73586 FAX 017687 73824

This large Victorian end-of-terrace house stands in a quiet area, close to the town centre. Bedrooms are pleasantly decorated, and it is planned to make most of them en suite in the near future. There is a well appointed dining room and two comfortable lounges, one on the ground floor.

11 en suite (bth/shr) (1 fmly) No smoking in bedrooms No smoking in dining room CTV in all bedrooms Tea and coffee making facilities Direct dial from bedrooms No dogs (ex guide dogs) Licensed Cen ht CTV No coaches Last d 6pm
PRICE GUIDE
ROOMS: s £19-£20; d £38-£40; wkly b&b £125-£135; wkly hlf-bd £185-£195✱
CARDS: 💳 💳 💳 💳 💳

GH Q Q Q **Fell House** 28 Stanger St CA12 5JU
☎017687 72669

Closed 24-26 Dec

A small Victorian property in a quiet side road a few minutes' walk from the town centre, Fell House offers well furnished accommodation with colour TV and some en suite facilities. There are a comfortable lounge and a dining room with individual tables. Private parking is available at the rear.

6 rms (2 shr) (1 fmly) No smoking in dining room No smoking in lounges CTV in all bedrooms Tea and coffee making facilities No dogs Cen ht 5P No coaches
PRICE GUIDE
ROOMS: s £15.50-£16.50; d £31-£38; wkly b&b £108.50-£126✱

GH Q Q *Foye House* 23 Eskin St CA12 4DQ
☎017687 73288
An attractive Victorian terraced house situated in a quiet area not far from the town centre offers well appointed bedrooms, several of them en suite. There is a pretty dining room in which breakfast and home cooked evening meals are served and there is also a comfortable lounge. This is a non-smoking house.
8 rms (4 shr) (2 fmly) No smoking CTV in all bedrooms Tea and coffee making facilities Cen ht No parking

GH Q Q Q *Goodwin House* 29 Southey St CA12 4EE
☎017687 74634
Closed 25-26 Dec
Goodwin House is a late Victorian property set on the corner of a quiet side road close to the town centre. Bedrooms are comfortably furnished and some have en suite facilities. There is a residential licence, and a range of beers, wines and spirits is available to guests.
5 rms (2 shr) (2 fmly) No smoking in dining room CTV in all bedrooms Tea and coffee making facilities No dogs (ex guide dogs) Licensed Cen ht No coaches Last d midday
PRICE GUIDE
ROOMS: s £12-£15; d £24-£38; wkly b&b £75-£133; wkly hlf-bd £131-£189

Selected

GH Q Q Q Q *Greystones* Ambleside Rd CA12 4DP
(opposite St John's Church) ☎017687 73108
Feb-Nov
Built of Lakeland stone and fronted by a flower-filled patio, this attractive end-of-terrace house stands in a quiet area close to the town centre. The en suite bedrooms are particularly well equipped and are prettily decorated in modern co-ordinated fabrics. There are a comfortable lounge and a spacious dining room serving well presented meals based on fresh produce. The atmosphere is friendly and private parking is available.
8 en suite (bth/shr) No smoking CTV in all bedrooms Tea and coffee making facilities No dogs (ex guide dogs) Licensed Cen ht No children 8yrs 9P No coaches Last d 2pm
PRICE GUIDE
ROOMS: s £21.50-£22.50; d £43-£46✳
CARDS: 💳 💳

GH Q Q Q *Heatherlea* 26 Blencathra St CA12 4HP
☎017687 72430
Closed Xmas
This attractive Lakeland stone house is in a quiet street close to the town centre. All bedrooms are nicely decorated and have en suite facilities, and there is a small and beautifully furnished dining room. Smoking is not permitted.
4 en suite (shr) (2 fmly) No smoking CTV in all bedrooms Tea and coffee making facilities No dogs (ex guide dogs) Licensed Cen ht No parking No coaches Last d 10am

GH Q Q Q *Lynwood Hotel* 12 Ambleside Rd CA12 4DL
☎017687 72081 FAX 017687 75021
Closed 24-26 Dec
Lynwood is a commodious and comfortable Victorian house set in a quiet side road convenient for the town centre. The bedrooms are prettily decorated and well equipped, and the proprietors are friendly and caring. This is a no-smoking establishment.
7 rms (6 shr) (1 fmly) No smoking CTV in all bedrooms Tea and coffee making facilities No dogs Licensed Cen ht CTV No

coaches Last d 4pm
PRICE GUIDE
ROOMS: s £18.50-£25; d £40-£52; wkly b&b £129.50-£175; wkly hlf-bd £208.25-£253.75
CARDS: 💳 💳 💳

GH Q Q *Melbreak House* 29 Church St CA12 4DX (A66 to Keswick, then take Penrith road and turn off at Greta Street leading to Erskin Street and Church Street) ☎017687 73398
An attractively decorated lounge and dining room, the latter adorned with memorabilia, are features of this compact guest house. Bedrooms vary in size and style, but are being upgraded, and good use is made of tasteful fabrics.
10 rms (8 shr) (2 fmly) No smoking CTV in all bedrooms Tea and coffee making facilities Licensed Cen ht CTV No parking No coaches Last d 9.15am

Selected

GH Q Q Q Q *Ravensworth Hotel* 29 Station St CA12 5HH (turn off A591 into Station Street at War Memorial, hotel is on right) ☎017687 72476
Closed Dec-Jan
Prominently placed close to the park and town centre, this substantial Victorian house can be recognised in season by its colourful display of flowers and window boxes. Bedrooms are enhanced by stylish decor and are well equipped to include hair dryers. There is a delightful upstairs lounge complete with magazines and books as well as a marble fire place and ticking clock that adds to the relaxing atmosphere. On the ground floor you will find the attractive dining room and residents bar.

➡

8 en suite (bth/shr) (1 fmly) No smoking in bedrooms No smoking in dining room CTV in all bedrooms Tea and coffee making facilities No dogs Licensed Cen ht CTV No children 6yrs 5P
PRICE GUIDE
ROOMS: s £15-£45; d £30-£48; wkly b&b £105-£147
CARDS: £

GH Q Q **Richmond House** 37-39 Eskin St CA12 4DG (enter Keswick on main road take second left after Shell petrol station into Greta St continue into Eskin St) ☎017687 73965
A double fronted Victorian terraced house situated in a quiet street not far from the town centre. Most bedrooms have en suite facilities, there is a comfortable guest lounge, a bar and a pleasant dining room. This is a no smoking establishment.
9 rms (7 shr) (1 fmly) No smoking CTV in all bedrooms Tea and coffee making facilities No dogs (ex guide dogs) Licensed Cen ht CTV No children 4yrs No parking Last d 5pm
PRICE GUIDE
ROOMS: s £15-£22; d £31-£38; wkly b&b £95-£120; wkly hlf-bd £155-£170✱
CARDS: £

GH Q Q Q **Rickerby Grange Country House Hotel**
Portinscale CA12 5RH (by-pass Keswick on A66 Cockermouth road turn left at Portinscale sign, pass Farmer Arms Inn on left & turn down second lane to the right) ☎017687 72344
Closed 5 Nov-mid Feb
Situated down a private lane in the peaceful village of Portinscale, close to the northwesterly tip of Lake Derwentwater, this attractive hotel offers predominantly en suite bedrooms furnished and decorated in modern style; one has a four-poster bed and some are located on the ground floor. The dining room is spacious, and there is a lounge bar as well as a comfortable lounge. Private parking is available at the rear of the building.
12 rms (11 bth/shr) (3 fmly) No smoking in dining room No smoking in 1 lounge CTV in 13 bedrooms Tea and coffee making facilities Direct dial from bedrooms Licensed Cen ht No children 5yrs 20P No coaches Last d 5pm
PRICE GUIDE
ROOMS: s £25; d £50; wkly b&b £165; wkly hlf-bd £240 £

GH Q Q Q **Skiddaw Grove Hotel** Vicarage Hill CA12 5QB (turn off at Keswick rbt, junc A591, into Keswick, turn right into Vicarage Hill hotel 20 yds on left) ☎017687 73324
Closed Xmas
An early Victorian house stands in its own grounds in a quiet part of the town between Bassenthwaite and Derwentwater, with extensive views of Skiddaw. Bedrooms are modern and well equipped, all with private bathrooms, clock radios and tea trays; TVs are also available. Public areas include a bar lounge, residents' lounge and dining room, with magnificent views over Bassenthwaite Lake and Skiddaw. Home-cooked food is prepared from fresh local produce, and special diets can be catered for by prior arrangement. An outdoor heated pool is available in summer months, and the hotel has a private garden with a sun terrace and a car park. Smoking is only permitted in the bar lounge.
10 en suite (bth/shr) (1 fmly) No smoking in bedrooms No smoking in dining room No smoking in lounges CTV in all bedrooms Tea and coffee making facilities No dogs (ex guide dogs) Licensed Cen ht 12P No coaches Outdoor swimming pool (heated) Table tennis Last d 5pm
PRICE GUIDE
ROOMS: s £22-£24; d £44-£48; wkly b&b £154; wkly hlf-bd £245

GH Q Q Q **Stonegarth** 2 Eskin St CA12 4DH ☎017687 72436
This Grade II listed Victorian house is situated in a quiet area of the town, with the advantage of a large private car park. Bedrooms are tastefully furnished and decorated in a modern style, and there is a particularly impressive dining room, with recently restored plasterwork.
9 en suite (bth/shr) (2 fmly) No smoking in 5 bedrooms No smoking in dining room No smoking in lounges CTV in all bedrooms Tea and coffee making facilities Direct dial from bedrooms Licensed Cen ht No children 5yrs 9P No coaches Last d 6pm
PRICE GUIDE
ROOMS: s £17-£24; d £34-£48; wkly hlf-bd £185-£230
CARDS: £

GH Q Q **Sunnyside** 25 Southey St CA12 4EF ☎017687 72446
Closed 15 Dec-15 Feb rs 15 Nov-15 Dec
This sizeable house features comfortable bedrooms, a relaxing first floor lounge, a downstairs dining room and its own car park.
8 rms (2 fmly) No smoking in dining room CTV in all bedrooms Tea and coffee making facilities No dogs (ex guide dogs) Cen ht 8P No coaches
CARDS: ⬛ ▨

GH Q Q **Swiss Court** 25 Bank St CA12 5JZ ☎017687 72637
Attractive leaded windows and a first-floor lounge with views over the town are features of this comfortable guest house just a minute's walk from the main shops. All the bedrooms have en suite facilities and, as well as the lounge, there is a breakfast room with individual tables.
7 rms No dogs Cen ht CTV No children 6yrs 3P No coaches

GH Q Q Q **Thornleigh** 23 Bank St CA12 5JZ (on A591 opposite Bell Close Car Park) ☎017687 72863
Feb-Nov
A friendly town-centre guest house, Thornleigh has recently been upgraded to a high standard with much thought to guests' comfort. Bedrooms have been tastefully re-decorated and re-carpeted and new lighting has been installed, together with more modern and efficient shower units. All rooms are en suite and extremely well appointed. There is a comfortable guests' lounge and an attractive dining room.
6 en suite (shr) No smoking in 4 bedrooms No smoking in dining room CTV in all bedrooms Tea and coffee making facilities No dogs Cen ht No children 16yrs 3P No coaches
PRICE GUIDE
ROOMS: d £38-£42
CARDS: ⬛ ▨

GH Q Q **Yew Tree House** 28 Eskin St CA12 4DG (turn left off A591 opposite Fitz Park straight across two junctions into Eskin St, Yew Tree third GH on left) ☎017687 74323
Yew Tree House is a small, pleasantly furnished house in a quiet side road near the town centre. Bedrooms are prettily decorated and there is a cosy residents' lounge.
5 rms (2 shr) (1 fmly) No smoking in dining room No smoking in lounges CTV in all bedrooms Tea and coffee making facilities Cen ht CTV No parking Last d 1pm
PRICE GUIDE
ROOMS: s £14-£15; d £28-£34; wkly b&b £98-£112; wkly hlf-bd £150-£165✱ £

KETTERING Northamptonshire Map **04** SP87

GH QQ *Headlands Private Hotel* 49-51 Headlands NN15 7ET
☎01536 524624 FAX 01536 83367
A large Victorian house located in an attractive suburb off
Queensberry Road, close to the town centre, is run by involved
proprietors who place comfort high on their list of priorities. Some
of the bedrooms on the top floor are very generously proportioned,
and they are all neatly presented and furnished in pastel tones and
floral prints.
13 rms (7 bth/shr) (3 fmly) No smoking in dining room CTV in
all bedrooms Tea and coffee making facilities Cen ht CTV 10P
Last d 5pm
CARDS: 🔲 🔲

KETTLEWELL North Yorkshire Map **07** SD97

See also Starbotton

GH QQQQ *Langcliffe Country* BD23 5RJ (off B6160,
at 'Kings Head' take road marked 'Access Only')
☎01756 760243 & 760896
A charming double-fronted detached house quietly situated in
this attractive Dales village with a southern aspect down
Wharfedale and splendid views of the surrounding fells. The
house stands in well tended gardens, and all rooms have fine
views. Bedrooms are spacious and comfortable, tastefully
furnished and particularly well equipped, most with private
bathrooms. There is also a self-contained cottage annexe
adjacent which has been equipped for elderly and disabled
guests; one room on the ground floor has also been adapted
for similar use, with wheelchair access from the car park.
Home-cooked four-course dinners are served in the
conservatory dining room overlooking the gardens, or in an
adjacent room with a large oak table, ideal for families or
parties. There is a log fire in the cosy sitting room, and a
private car park adjacent to the house.
6 rms (4 bth/shr) CTV in all bedrooms Tea and coffee
making facilities Direct dial from bedrooms Licensed Cen
ht CTV 6P No coaches Last d 9am
CARDS: 🔲 🔲

KEXBY North Yorkshire Map **08** SE75

➽ QQQ Mrs K R Daniel **Ivy House** (*SE691511*) YO4 5LQ
☎01904 489368
This late-Victorian farmhouse stands on the A1079, only five
miles from York. Part of a dairy and mixed arable farm of 130
acres, it provides very well cared for accommodation with
comfortable, spacious bedrooms, a lounge overlooking the
gardens and a dining room with individual tables. Guests are
assured of a warm welcome in this friendly, cheerful and
conveniently located guest house.
3 rms (1 fmly) CTV in all bedrooms Tea and coffee making
facilities No dogs Cen ht CTV 5P 132 acres mixed £

Our inspectors never book in the name of the
AA. They disclose their identity only after the
bill has been paid.

KEYNSHAM Avon Map **03** ST66

GH QQQQ **Grasmere Court Hotel** 22/24 Bath Rd
BS18 1SN (on A4 between Boliston and Bath)
☎0117 986 2662 FAX 0117 986 2762
Equidistant from Bristol and Bath, this small family-run hotel
offers immaculate accommodation and high standards
throughout. Bedrooms are tastefully furnished in warm colour
coordinating fabrics, and there is a congenial bar/lounge.
Dinner and breakfast are served in the pleasant dining room,
with home-grown vegetables used whenever possible. An
outdoor swimming pool is available for guests during warmer
months.
16 en suite (bth/shr) (3 fmly) No smoking in bedrooms No
smoking in dining room CTV in all bedrooms Tea and coffee
making facilities Direct dial from bedrooms No dogs
Licensed Cen ht CTV 19P No coaches Last d 7.30pm
PRICE GUIDE
ROOMS: s £34-£43; d £40-£49✳
CARDS: 🔲 🔲 🔲 🔲 🔲 £

➽ Q Mrs L Sparkes **Uplands** (*ST663664*) Wellsway BS18 2SY
(off B3116) ☎0117 986 5764 & 986 5159
This large, rambling, creeper-clad farmhouse dating back over 200
years occupies a convenient position near Keynsham and close to
both Bath and Bristol. Bedrooms are spacious enough to be used
for families. Breakfast is served at separate tables in the dining
room.
7 rms (3 shr) (4 fmly) No smoking in 2 bedrooms No smoking

THE MILL INN
MUNGRISDALE
Nr. Penrith, Cumbria CA11 0XR
Telephone: 017687 79 632

A fine 16th century Inn in a peaceful
village setting by the River
Glendermackin nestling under the
Skiddaw range of fells and close to
Blencathra. 2 miles off the A66, 10 miles
from Keswick and 8 miles from
Ullswater. Old fashioned hospitality,
modern facilities, real ale and
imaginative home cooked food.

in dining room No smoking in lounges CTV in all bedrooms Tea and coffee making facilities No dogs (ex guide dogs) Cen ht CTV 20P 200 acres dairy
PRICE GUIDE
ROOMS: s £17.50-£20; d £40-£45; wkly b&b £120-£140✷

£

KIDDERMINSTER Hereford & Worcester Map **07** SO87

Selected

GH QQQQ **Cedars Hotel** Mason Rd DY11 6AL (turn off ring rd onto A442 to Bridgenorth then 1st left, hotel opposite police station) (MIN)
☎01562 515595 FAX 01562 751103
Closed 6 Dec-2 Jan
Just north of the town centre, this well maintained private hotel provides good quality, well equipped accommodation. Small conferences can be accommodated. Breakfast is available at a supplementary charge.
20 en suite (bth/shr) (6 fmly) No smoking in 7 bedrooms CTV in 22 bedrooms Tea and coffee making facilities Direct dial from bedrooms Licensed Cen ht 23P Last d 8.30pm
PRICE GUIDE
ROOMS: s £29.90-£51; d £42-£62✷
CARDS:

£

GH QQQ **Collingdale Hotel** 197 Comberton Rd DY10 1UE
☎01562 515460 & 862839
A friendly small hotel just half a mile from the town centre. Bedrooms are pretty, with floral wallpaper and fabrics, and many are pine furnished. Evening meals are available.
9 rms (1 bth 3 shr) (2 fmly) No smoking in dining room CTV in all bedrooms Tea and coffee making facilities Licensed Cen ht 7P Last d 2pm
PRICE GUIDE
ROOMS: s £20-£25; d £32-£38; wkly b&b £112.50-£175; wkly hlf-bd £150-£213✷

£

GH QQ **Gordonhouse Hotel** 194 Comberton Rd DY10 1UE (100yds from jct A449/A448)
☎01562 822900 FAX 01562 865626
A large early-Victorian property, this hotel is situated about half a mile from the town centre, close to both the railway station and the Severn Valley Steam Railway. It offers sound, fairly modern accommodation which includes ground-floor and family-bedded rooms. Other facilities include a comfortable lounge, a cosy bar, a large garden and a private car park.
15 rms (1 shr) 3 annexe rms (2 fmly) No smoking in dining room CTV in all bedrooms Tea and coffee making facilities Licensed Cen ht CTV 25P No coaches Last d 7pm
PRICE GUIDE
ROOMS: s £19-£26; d £32-£40; wkly b&b fr £125✷
CARDS:

£

KIDLINGTON Oxfordshire Map **04** SP41

Selected

GH QQQQ **Bowood House** 238 Oxford Rd OX5 1EB (on the A4260, 4m N of Oxford, opposite Thames Valley Police H.Q.) ☎01865 842288 FAX 01865 841858
Closed 24 Dec-1 Jan
This attractive red brick property is situated only four miles

---

from the centre of Oxford on the old Banbury road. Bedrooms are well decorated and equipped with TV, telephone, radio alarm trouser press and hair dryers. The majority of rooms are in the main house but an attractive garden wing houses the remainder, one of which is equipped for disabled guests. There is a cosy lounge and well stocked bar. The attractive dining room is useful for guests wishing to choose from the well priced carte.
10 rms (8 bth/shr) 12 annexe en suite (bth/shr) (4 fmly) No smoking in lounges CTV in all bedrooms Tea and coffee making facilities Direct dial from bedrooms No dogs (ex guide dogs) Licensed Cen ht 25P Last d 8.30pm
PRICE GUIDE
ROOMS: s £32-£45; d £55-£62
CARDS:
See advertisement also under OXFORD

KILBURN North Yorkshire Map **08** SE57

◖ QQQ *Forresters Arms Hotel* YO6 4AH
☎01347 868386 & 868550 FAX 01347 868386
This attractive village inn is situated beneath the famous Kilburn White Horse, next to the parish church, which, together with the inn was built by the Normans in the 12th century. Bedrooms are modern in style, and although rather compact, are all individually furnished and decorated, with a mixture of pine and mahogany furniture; two rooms have four-poster beds. There are two bars serving a wide range of bar meals at lunchtime and in the evenings. There is also an attractive dining room for evening meals.
10 en suite (bth/shr) (2 fmly) No smoking in dining room CTV in all bedrooms Tea and coffee making facilities Direct dial from bedrooms Cen ht 40P Last d 9.30pm
CARDS: ⬛ ▒

KILVE Somerset Map **03** ST14

Premier Selected

◖ QQQQQ **Hood Arms**
TA5 1EA (12m W of Bridgwater on the A39)
☎01278 741210
Closed 25 Dec
The Hood Arms, dating back to the 17th-century and situated at the centre of this busy village, is the ideal venue from which to explore the Quantocks and the Somerset coast. Comfortable, well equipped bedrooms have such thoughtful touches as fresh flowers and iced water, while the bar's extensive blackboard menu of interesting dishes includes chicken and broccoli mornay, spinach and garlic lasagne and Mrs B's faggots. The restaurant is open from Wednesday to Saturday, offering the usual range of grills. At the rear of the property are some delightful walled gardens and a patio area. The inn has a good reputation locally for its warm friendly atmosphere and value-for-money meals.
5 en suite (bth) No smoking in dining room CTV in all bedrooms Tea and coffee making facilities Direct dial from bedrooms Cen ht No children 7yrs 12P No coaches Last d 10pm
PRICE GUIDE
ROOMS: s fr £38; d fr £62; wkly hlf-bd fr £297
MEALS: Lunch £9-£15alc Dinner £12-£18alc
CARDS:

£

KINETON Warwickshire Map **04** SP35

 ♥ QQQ Ms C Howard **Willowbrook** *(SP334518)* Lighthorne Rd CV35 0JL (exit M40 junct12 and take B4451 to Kineton. In village take first right into Lighthorne Road)
☎01926 640475 FAX 01926 641747
Closed Xmas
This peacefully located farmhouse with its speciality smallholding of sheep and old breeds of poultry is located half a mile from the village. It is suitably placed for most of the main tourist attractions in the area. The well travelled owners (who speak French and Spanish) are relaxed hosts and happy to welcome non-smoking guests. The three bedrooms are spacious and individually decorated with many helpful extras.
3 rms (1 shr) No smoking CTV in all bedrooms Tea and coffee making facilities Cen ht CTV No children 6P 5 acres smallholding
PRICE GUIDE
ROOMS: d £31-£38*

£

KINGHAM Oxfordshire Map **04** SP22

 Selected

GH QQQQ **Conygree Gate** Church St OX7 6YA (centre of village off A429 & A361) ☎01608 658389
Closed 3-4 Jan
Standing in the centre of the village, this attractive stone-built farmhouse dates back to the 17th century. It offers comfortable, stylish accommodation in keeping with the period with leaded windows and stone fireplaces. Bedrooms are imaginatively decorated and feature lovely antique furniture; two garden suites at ground-level are also available. The delightful restaurant offers excellent country cooking and a choice of wines.
10 rms (1 bth 7 shr) (3 fmly) No smoking in dining room CTV in all bedrooms Tea and coffee making facilities Licensed Cen ht 12P No coaches Last d 5pm
PRICE GUIDE
ROOMS: s fr £28; d fr £54; wkly b&b fr £189; wkly hlf-bd fr £276.50*
CARDS: 🔳 💳

£

KINGSBRIDGE Devon Map **03** SX74

See also Bantham

GH QQQ *Ashleigh House* Ashleigh Rd, Westville TQ7 1HB
☎01548 852893 FAX 01548 852893
rs Nov-Mar
Situated on the edge of the town off the Salcombe road, this friendly guest house is an ideal base for touring the South Hams. Bedrooms are well equipped, and the first-floor en suite rooms feature attractive patchwork quilts. Colour TV is available by prior arrangement. Cooked dishes are offered in the spacious, no-smoking dining room.
8 rms (3 shr) (1 fmly) No smoking in bedrooms No smoking in dining room CTV in 4 bedrooms Tea and coffee making facilities Licensed CTV 5P No coaches Last d 4pm
CARDS: 🔳 💳

GH QQQ *South Allington House* Chivelstone TQ7 2NB
☎01548 511272 FAX 01548 511272
The Baker family farm locally and Barbara Baker welcomes guests to their charming listed period house, where a no-smoking policy is in force and morning coffees and afternoon teas are

served. Bedrooms are attractively decorated and comfortable, and electric blankets are supplied for the colder months.
11 rms (5 bth/shr) (2 fmly) No smoking CTV in 1 bedroom Tea and coffee making facilities No dogs (ex guide dogs) Cen ht CTV 15P No coaches Fishing Croquet Bowls

KINGSDOWN Kent Map **05** TR34

GH QQQ **Blencathra Country** Kingsdown Hill CT14 8EA
☎01304 373725
An attractive modern detached country guest house, surrounded by a pleasant garden and close to the sea, is quietly situated in a peaceful side road of this sleepy village. Rooms are attractively decorated and of a good size. There is a well appointed, comfortable lounge, a small honesty bar and a smart dining room which overlooks the garden.
7 rms (4 shr) (3 fmly) No smoking in bedrooms No smoking in dining room CTV in all bedrooms Tea and coffee making facilities No dogs (ex guide dogs) Licensed CTV 7P No coaches Croquet Last d 6.30pm
PRICE GUIDE
ROOMS: s £17-£20; d £34-£38; wkly b&b £102-£120*

£

GH QQQ **Kingsdown Country Hotel & Captains Table** Cliffe Rd CT14 8AJ ☎01304 373755 FAX 01304 373755
A large family home with private access to the sea, this hotel is located in a quiet hamlet close to Deal. The façade betrays its previous existence as a restaurant, and the friendly owner willingly provides home-cooked meals for residents and, by arrangement, for non-residents. A lounge and a large bar counter adjoin the restaurant and above them are four guest bedrooms, each with an en suite shower and hairdryer.
4 en suite (shr) No smoking in bedrooms No smoking in dining

BOWOOD HOUSE

238 Oxford Road,
Kidlington, Oxford
OX5 1EB

Situated on the A4260, 4 miles from Oxford, Bowood House offers accommodation of a high standard and a warm friendly atmosphere.

★ Private bathrooms
★ Satellite TVs
★ Direct Dial telephones
★ Tea/Coffee making facilities
★ Radio alarms
★ Residential Licence

AA SELECTED

 OXFORD
(01865) 842288

room CTV in all bedrooms Tea and coffee making facilities No dogs (ex guide dogs) Licensed Cen ht 8P Last d 9pm
PRICE GUIDE
ROOMS: s £18-£25; d £36-£50; wkly b&b £120-£175; wkly hlf-bd £150-£200

KINGSEY Buckinghamshire Map **04** SP70

❤ Q Q Q Mr & Mrs N M D Hooper **Foxhill** *(SP748066)*
HP17 8LZ (from Thame take A4129 to Kingsey, farm is last house on right) ☎01844 291650
Closed Dec & Jan
The Hoopers offer a friendly welcome at their white-painted, listed farmhouse, which is set back in lovely grounds complete with duck pond. An added bonus is the swimming pool, which is available for use during warmer weather. The first floor bedrooms are spacious with oak-beamed ceilings, and pleasantly furnished. Downstairs there is an entrance hall with polished quarry tiles and a cheerful lounge/breakfast room.
3 rms No smoking CTV in all bedrooms Tea and coffee making facilities No dogs (ex guide dogs) Cen ht CTV No children 5yrs 40P Outdoor swimming pool (heated) 4 acres non-working
PRICE GUIDE
ROOMS: s £20-£23; d £38-£42; wkly b&b £133-£161

KINGSLEY Cheshire Map **07** SJ57

GH Q Q Q **Charnwood** Hollow Ln WA6 8EF
☎01928 787097 FAX 01928 788566
Situated close to the Delamere Forest, at the bottom of the village (just past the post office and garage), Charnwood is a large modern house with lovely gardens. The attractively decorated and well equipped bedrooms, one twin and the other double, share a large bathroom and have their own entrance leading into a comfortably furnished sitting room. Breakfast is served in a pleasant room with French windows opening on to a patio and magnificent pergola.
2 rms (1 bth/shr) (1 fmly) No smoking CTV in all bedrooms Tea and coffee making facilities Direct dial from bedrooms No dogs Cen ht CTV 5P
PRICE GUIDE
ROOMS: s £20-£25; d £36-£40; wkly b&b £126-£140✳

KING'S LYNN Norfolk Map **09** TF62

See also Tottenhill

Selected

GH Q Q Q Q **Andel House** 211 Station Rd, Watlington PE33 0JG (5m S at A134/Watlington Junction)
☎01553 811515 FAX 01553 811429
This modern house, set between the Great Ouse river and a man-made relief channel, stands in a peaceful rural location some six miles south of King's Lynn and is the home of the Hurrell family. Much attention has been given to detail, features ranging from a miniature fish pond and fountain at the front entrance to the array of figurines in one of the two guest lounges. Two richly decorated bedrooms are equipped with modern amenities; the third, slightly smaller and less extravagantly furnished, is located in a separate extension overlooking the immaculate lawn. Secure parking is available, and the owners will happily provide dinner.
2 en suite (bth) 1 annexe en suite (bth) No smoking in bedrooms No smoking in 1 lounge CTV in all bedrooms Tea and coffee making facilities No dogs (ex guide dogs) Cen ht

CTV 6P No coaches Last d 6.30pm
PRICE GUIDE
ROOMS: s £25-£29.50; d £35.50-£42.50; wkly b&b £122.50-£150; wkly hlf-bd £185.50-£213

GH Q Q **Beeches** 2 Guannock Ter PE30 5QT
☎01553 766577 FAX 01553 776664
A family-run Victorian house, the Beeches is located in a quiet residential area to the south-east of the town. Freshly cooked meals are served in the dining room which overlooks a well tended garden. Most of the bedrooms are spacious and each one has a direct-dial telephone.
7 rms (4 bth/shr) (2 fmly) No smoking in dining room CTV in all bedrooms Tea and coffee making facilities Direct dial from bedrooms Licensed Cen ht CTV 3P No coaches Last d 4.30pm
PRICE GUIDE
ROOMS: s £22-£28; d £36-£42; wkly b&b £150-£195; wkly hlf-bd £180-£252✳
CARDS: 🔴 🟰 🔳

GH Q **Buckingham Lodge** 29 Tennyson Av PE30 2QG
☎01553 764469 FAX 01553 764469
The new owners of this family run guest house are set to improve standards of the modestly appointed accommodation. Bedroom styles and sizes are variable, 5 rooms have shower cubicles within the rooms. Breakfasts are taken in a small dining room, snacks are also available during the evening. Off road parking is also available in the private road adjacent to the house.
6 rms No smoking in dining room CTV in all bedrooms Tea and coffee making facilities No dogs (ex guide dogs) Cen ht 10P Last d 4pm
PRICE GUIDE
ROOMS: s £18; d £34✳

Selected

GH Q Q Q Q **Fairlight Lodge** 79 Goodwins Rd PE30 5PE ☎01553 762234 FAX 01553 770280
Closed 24-26 Dec
To find Fairlight Lodge take the A17 to the town, take last exit on the roundabout to Gaywood, and follow the road until you find this Victorian house which sits in attractive gardens, with ample private car parking. Inside this tastefully furnished house there is a comfortable lounge with open fire, books and music system, also a smaller dining room where Tim Rowe serves a good choice hearty breakfast. Accommodation is divided between the main house and three garden bedrooms, all are light and inviting with attractive quality soft furnishings and complimenting decor; housekeeping and attention to detail are strengths here.
7 rms (4 shr) (1 fmly) No smoking in 2 bedrooms No smoking in dining room No smoking in lounges CTV in all bedrooms Tea and coffee making facilities Cen ht 8P No coaches
PRICE GUIDE
ROOMS: s £20-£30; d £32-£38

GH Q Q **Guanock Hotel** South Gate PE30 5JG (follow signs to town centre. Establishment immediately on right of South Gates) ☎01553 772959 FAX 01553 772959
A predominantly business establishment, the Guanock is located south of the centre just inside the town gate. The bedrooms tend to be small but are neat in appearance. An evening meal is served in the cheerful dining room, and bar meals and light refreshments are

available in either the pool lounge or small bar.

17 rms (5 fmly) No smoking in 8 bedrooms No smoking in dining room CTV in all bedrooms Tea and coffee making facilities No dogs (ex guide dogs) Licensed Cen ht 12P Pool room Last d 5pm

PRICE GUIDE
ROOMS: s £20-£23; d £34-£36✱
CARDS: 💳 💳 💳 💳 (£)

GH Q Q Q **Havana** 117 Gaywood Rd PE30 2PU (opposite King Edward VII High School) ☎01553 772331
Closed 23 Dec-1 Jan

To find the Havana from the A17 to the town centre, take the last exit at the mini roundabout to Gaywood and continue to the very end; turn right at the T-junction and the guesthouse is a few yards along on the left. A turn-of-the-century semi-detached building which is continually being improved by proprietors Mr and Mrs Breed. Most of the attractively decorated bedrooms are en-suite and the two ground floor bedrooms are larger than the others. There is a shared lounge and breakfast room and there are parking spaces to the front and rear of the building.

5 rms (3 shr) 2 annexe en suite (shr) (1 fmly) No smoking in 1 bedrooms No smoking in dining room No smoking in lounges CTV in all bedrooms Tea and coffee making facilities No dogs Cen ht CTV 8P No coaches Sport & leisure complex close by

PRICE GUIDE
ROOMS: s £16-£25; d £28-£36; wkly b&b £91-£119✱ (£)

GH Q Q **Maranatha** 115 Gaywood Rd PE30 2PU
☎01553 774596

Competitively priced accommodation is offered at this guest house catering mainly for the business traveller. Bedrooms, although on the small side, are generally fresh looking. The strikingly decorated lounge has a good gas fire, colour TV and an organ for guests' use. Evening meals and snacks are readily available.

6 rms (1 shr) 1 annexe en suite (bth) (2 fmly) No smoking in dining room CTV in all bedrooms Tea and coffee making facilities Cen ht CTV 12P No coaches Last d 6pm

PRICE GUIDE
ROOMS: s £15-£17; d £28-£30✱

Selected

GH Q Q Q Q *Russet House Hotel* 53 Goodwins Rd
PE30 5PE ☎01553 773098 FAX 01553 773098
Closed Xmas & New Year

A warm welcome is provided by owners Rae and Barry Muddle at this extended Victorian house. There are twelve well-kept bedrooms of varying size, all with private facilities and many additional personal touches. Cosy public rooms include a bar, lounge and dining room where home-cooked food is served. In addition there is a garden and plenty of parking.

12 en suite (bth/shr) (1 fmly) No smoking in 1 bedrooms No smoking in dining room CTV in all bedrooms Tea and coffee making facilities Direct dial from bedrooms No dogs (ex guide dogs) Licensed Cen ht 14P No coaches Last d 7.45pm
CARDS: 💳 💳 💳 💳

KINGSTON Devon Map **03** SX64

Selected

GH Q Q Q Q **Trebles Cottage Hotel** TQ7 4PT
☎01548 810268 FAX 01548 810268

Hidden among a maze of country lanes - but good directions are given when a booking is confirmed! - this pretty cottage stands at the top of a peaceful village, just a mile from a sandy beach and 12 miles from Plymouth. Bedrooms vary in size and furnishings, but all are well equipped. A small cocktail bar leads through an archway into the dining room, where breakfast and an optional four-course evening meal are served. A choice of starters is offered - perhaps hot Salcombe smokie with gooseberry sauce or minestrone soup - followed by a set main course such as whole roast spring chicken with dill stuffing accompanied by fresh local vegetables. Home-made puddings include real sherry trifle and spotted dick, all served with clotted cream.

5 en suite (bth/shr) No smoking in 3 bedrooms No smoking in dining room CTV in all bedrooms Tea and coffee making facilities Licensed Cen ht No children 12yrs 10P No coaches Last d 4pm

PRICE GUIDE
ROOMS: s £32-£40; d £45-£60; wkly hlf-bd £240-£300
CARDS: 💳 💳 💳 (£)

KINGSTON UPON THAMES Greater London

See advertisement on p.233.

Commended

Russet House Hotel

Tel: King's Lynn (01553) 773098

One of the nicest old houses in one of the most historic Towns in England. Set in beautiful secluded gardens a short walk from Town Centre and River Ouse. Four poster suite. Pretty en suite rooms with TV and courtesy Tea/Coffee.

Cosy little bar – roaring fire in winter! Open to garden in Summer!

Elegant Dining Room – good food. Ample room to park your car.

Rae & Barry Muddle (we try not to live up to our name!)

Vancouver Ave/Goodwins Road, King's Lynn Norfolk PE30 5PE

KINVER Staffordshire Map **07** SO88

◀ QQQ **Kinfayre Restaurant** 41 High St DY7 6HF
☎01384 872565 FAX 01384 877724
Dating from 1650, this fully modernised inn in the attractive
village's main street has been owned and personally run by Henry
and Ann Williams for the last 20 years. En suite bedrooms are
located in a modern annexe adjacent to the main building, behind
which there are attractive gardens containing a large heated
swimming pool (for residents' use only). Public areas include a
lounge bar which retains many original features, an attractive non-
smoking restaurant and two skittle alleys which are very popular
with the locals.
11 en suite (shr) (1 fmly) No smoking in dining room No
smoking in lounges CTV in all bedrooms Tea and coffee making
facilities No dogs (ex guide dogs) Cen ht CTV 22P Outdoor
swimming pool (heated) Skittle alley Last d 10pm
PRICE GUIDE
ROOMS: s fr £30; d fr £50; wkly b&b fr £175; wkly hlf-bd fr
£250
MEALS: Lunch £4.95-£7.95&alc Dinner fr £7.95&alc
CARDS: 🔳 🔳

KIRKBY LONSDALE Cumbria Map **07** SD67

Premier Selected

GH QQQQQ **Cobwebs
Country House** Leck, Cowan
Bridge LA6 2HZ
☎015242 72141 FAX
015242 72141
mid Mar-Dec rs Sun & Mon
This charming small country

house and restaurant lies
surrounded by farmland in
the village of Cowan Bridge,
two miles south of Kirkby
Lonsdale (turn off the A65 at
the signpost for Leck). The enthusiastic owners Paul Kelly and
Yvonne Thompson have maximised the house's period
character; the two lounges retain the style of a Victorian
parlour, whilst the well equipped en suite bedrooms feature
antique and old stripped pine furniture, pretty decor and
original fireplaces in most of the rooms. The attractive
conservatory restaurant offers a daily-changing four-course
menu including a good regional selection of cheeses; both the
cooking and the wine list have won awards.
5 en suite (bth/shr) No smoking in dining room CTV in all
bedrooms Tea and coffee making facilities Direct dial from
bedrooms No dogs Licensed Cen ht No children 12yrs 20P
No coaches Fishing Last d 7.30pm
PRICE GUIDE
ROOMS: s fr £45; d fr £60
CARDS: 🔳 🔳 (£)

Entries in this Guide are based on reports
filed by our team of professionally trained,
full-time inspectors.

Premier Selected

GH QQQQQ **Hipping
Hall Hotel** Cowan Bridge
LA6 2JJ (on A65)
☎015242 71187
FAX 015242 72452
Mar-Nov

This handsome country
house in beautiful, secluded
gardens stands back from the
A65 two miles southeast of
Kirkby Lonsdale, on the
Cumbrian/Yorkshire border;
the remains of a hamlet dating back to the fifteenth century, it
gains great character and charm from retained features
reminiscent of a bygone age. Attractively decorated and very
comfortable bedrooms furnished with antiques offer en suite
facilities, telephones and television sets, the two in an
adjacent converted coach house also being equipped for self
catering. A five-course evening meal is served, dinner party
style, in the Great Hall (complete with minstrels' gallery), the
price including a different wine to complement each dish.
This delightful hotel will please not only the holiday-maker
but also any business person looking for peace and seclusion.
7 en suite (bth/shr) No smoking in dining room CTV in all
bedrooms Tea and coffee making facilities Direct dial from
bedrooms Licensed Cen ht CTV No children 12yrs 12P
No coaches Croquet Last d 6.30pm
PRICE GUIDE
ROOMS: s £63; d £79-£89⁕
CARDS: 🔳 🔳 🔳 (£)

KIRKBYMOORSIDE North Yorkshire Map **08** SE68

Selected

GH QQQQ **Appletree Court** Town Farm, 9 High
Market Place YO6 6AT ☎01751 431536
Appletree Court, a charming cottage-style guest house, was
once part of a working farm, and many of the original timbers
from the old hay loft are still visible. The four bedrooms are
named after apple varieties and decorated with Laura Ashley
fabrics. Downstairs, there is an attractive lounge/breakfast
room with individual tables. Smoking is not permitted.
4 en suite (bth/shr) No smoking CTV in all bedrooms No
dogs Cen ht No children 12yrs 2P No coaches Last d noon
PRICE GUIDE
ROOMS: s £25-£27; d £40-£44

KIRKBY THORE Cumbria Map **12** NY62

Selected

♥ QQQQ Mrs Y Dent **Bridge End** CA10 1UZ
☎017683 61362
This spacious 18th-century farmhouse lies by the A66 in a
small village midway between Appleby and Temple Sowerby.
Yvonne Dent has worked enthusiastically to upgrade the
house since moving in last year. She has created three
delightful, well proportioned bedrooms adorned with antique
furniture and her own hand-made cushions and patchwork
quilts as well as remote control TVs, radio sets and hair

dryers. Two have en suite bathrooms whilst the third room has sole use of its own private bathroom close by. There are a comfortable lounge and a dining room where meals are taken around the one table. This is a lovely house in which to relax despite its proximity to the main road and there are some fine views across open farmland.

3 rms (2 bth/shr) No smoking CTV in all bedrooms Tea and coffee making facilities No dogs Cen ht CTV 3P Fishing 550 acres Last d noon

PRICE GUIDE

ROOMS: s fr £17; d £20

KIRK IRETON Derbyshire Map **08** SK25

◀ Q Q *Barley Mow* Main St, Kirk Ireton DE6 3JP
☎01335 370306

Closed Xmas wk

Set in the middle of a quaint little hilltop village the Barley Mow is an amazing inn. Built in 1683, it stands untouched by time - a series of small quarry-tiled rooms, their ancient rough-hewn walls worn with age, appropriately furnished with old pine and oak settles and stools. Hook Norton and Old Hooky ales are served, their casks stacked at eye level behind the counter. Bedrooms with smooth stone walls are modern but furnished with scrubbed pine bedroom units; bathrooms are fully tiled. The courtyard planted with old English roses leads to a sitting room warmed by a log burner.

5 en suite (bth/shr) (1 fmly) CTV in all bedrooms Tea and coffee making facilities Cen ht P No coaches Last d noon

---

KIRKOSWALD Cumbria Map **12** NY54

Selected

GH Q Q Q Q **Prospect Hill Hotel** CA10 1ER
☎01768 898500 FAX 01768 898088

Closed 24-26 Dec

Sympathetically developed from an interesting collection of 18th-century farm buildings several years ago, this delightful hotel set in open countryside a mile north of the village provides an excellent base from which to explore the area. Bedrooms - many of them retaining their stone walls - are individually decorated and furnished; some feature brass bedsteads while others have patchwork quilts, homespun curtains and thick carpets. Guests can relax over a drink in the former byre, now a charming and characterful bar with beamed ceiling, flagged floor and an abundance of old farm implements.

9 rms (4 bth/shr) 2 annexe en suite (bth/shr) (2 fmly) No smoking in area of dining room CTV in 2 bedrooms Tea and coffee making facilities No dogs Licensed Cen ht CTV ch fac 31P Croquet Last d 8.45pm

PRICE GUIDE

ROOMS: s £20-£45; d £46-£66✳

CARDS: 🟦 💳 💳   ⓔ

KIRKWHELPINGTON Northumberland Map **12** NY98

Selected

GH Q Q Q Q **Shieldhall** Wallington, Cambo NE61 4AQ (towards Wallington Hall & Rothbury 0.25m E of crossroads A696/B6342)
☎01830 540387 FAX 01830 540387

An 18th-century house and adjoining farm buildings have

been converted to form a charming country guest house. Self-contained bedroom suites open onto a courtyard; they are not large but contain furniture hand-crafted in the on-site workshops. Public areas filled with curios and objets d'art and include a cosy TV lounge and an elegant main lounge looking out on to the gardens. Meals are served in a delightful little dining room which has an inglenook fireplace.

5 en suite (bth/shr) (1 fmly) No smoking in bedrooms No smoking in dining room No smoking in lounges CTV in 4 bedrooms Tea and coffee making facilities No dogs (ex guide dogs) Licensed Cen ht CTV No children 13yrs 10P No coaches Croquet lawn Last d noon

PRICE GUIDE
ROOMS: s £25-£30; d £38-£46

KIRTLING Cambridgeshire Map **05** TL65

❤ QQ Mrs C A Bailey **Hill** *(TL685585)* CB8 9HQ
☎01638 730253
Situated midway between Saxon Street and the village of Kirtling, this traditional 16th-century farmhouse with a modern exterior, surrounded by arable and pasture farmland. Accommodation is comfortable and the public rooms include a lounge and dining room with open log fires and a games room.

3 rms (2 shr) CTV in 1 bedroom Tea and coffee making facilities Licensed Cen ht CTV 15P Games room 500 acres arable Last d 8.30pm

PRICE GUIDE
ROOMS: s £22; d £40✳

See advertisement under NEWMARKET

KIRTON Nottinghamshire Map **08** SK66

GH QQQ *Old Rectory* Main St NG22 9LP
☎01623 860083 Telex no 378505 FAX 01623 860751
Closed Xmas & New Year
A former Georgian rectory, set back from the village High Street in neatly tended grounds, offers fresh, inviting bedrooms and a choice of eating styles - informal meals in the lounge bar or a more substantial choice in the dining room.

10 rms (5 shr) (1 fmly) Tea and coffee making facilities No dogs (ex guide dogs) Licensed CTV 18P No coaches Last d 7pm
CARDS: 🅰 🔲

KNARESBOROUGH North Yorkshire Map **08** SE35

GH QQQ *Newton House Hotel* 5/7 York Place HG5 0AD (on A59, 2.5m from A1 turnoff)
☎01423 863539 FAX 01423 869748
This charming and well furnished Georgian house is close to the town centre and provides a good standard of comfort and service. There is a large lounge and an elegant dining room, and the bedrooms are equipped with phones, televisions, and tea trays.

9 rms (8 bth/shr) 3 annexe en suite (bth/shr) (4 fmly) No smoking in dining room CTV in all bedrooms Tea and coffee making facilities Direct dial from bedrooms Licensed Cen ht CTV 8P No coaches Last d 11am

PRICE GUIDE
ROOMS: s £32.50-£37.50; d £50-£60; wkly b&b £150-£210; wkly hlf-bd £240-£285✳
CARDS: 🅰 🔲 🔲 🔲 🔲
See advertisement under HARROGATE

GH QQQ *The Villa* The Villa Hotel, 47 Kirkgate HG5 8BZ
☎01423 865370 FAX 01423 867740
This charming character house standing next to the railway station, near the town centre, offers accommodation in attractively furnished bars equipped with telephones and mini-bars. A

---

delightful breakfast lounge overlooks the River Nidd, and there is also a comfortable lounge; service is attentive and the atmosphere warm and friendly throughout.

6 rms (4 shr) (1 fmly) No smoking in dining room CTV in all bedrooms Tea and coffee making facilities Direct dial from bedrooms Licensed Cen ht CTV No parking No coaches

---

KNOWLE West Midlands Map **07** SP17

GH QQQ *Ivy House* Warwick Rd, Heronfield B93 0EB (3m from junct 5 of M42, on A4141)
☎01564 770247 FAX 01564 770247
A 250-year-old property, rendered white and attractively covered in virginia creeper, Ivy House is situated a mile and a half out of Knowle on the Warwick side. Guest accommodation is separate from that of the owners and bedrooms are improving all the time; en suite facilities are modern and of a good size. There is a lounge and dining room combination where light evening snacks can be provided.

8 en suite (shr) (1 fmly) No smoking CTV in all bedrooms Tea and coffee making facilities Cen ht CTV 20P Fishing

---

KNUTSFORD Cheshire Map **07** SJ77

Selected

GH QQQQ *The Hinton* Town Ln, Mobberley WA16 7HH ☎01565 873484 FAX 01565 873484
At the time of our last inspection, this large house was being further extended to provide more bedrooms and a conservatory. The house provides well maintained and equipped modern bedrooms, two of which can be let as a family suite.

4 rms (2 bth/shr) (1 fmly) No smoking CTV in all bedrooms Tea and coffee making facilities No dogs (ex guide dogs) Licensed Cen ht 10P No coaches Last d 4.30pm
CARDS: 🅰 🔲 🔲 🔲

Selected

GH QQQQ *Laburnum Cottage* Knutsford Rd, Mobberley WA16 7PU
☎01565 872464 FAX 01565 872464
Situated on the B5085 between Knutsford and Mobberley and very convenient for Manchester Airport, this delightfully furnished house is surrounded by prize winning gardens and has good parking for guests. Bedrooms are all well equipped and have many thoughtful extras, and the comfortable lounge is the perfect place to unwind. Hearty breakfasts are served around a large table and the house is no-smoking throughout.

5 rms (3 bth/shr) (1 fmly) No smoking CTV in all bedrooms Tea and coffee making facilities No dogs (ex guide dogs) Cen ht CTV 12P No coaches

PRICE GUIDE
ROOMS: s £30-£39; d £42-£50✳

GH QQQ *Pickmere House* Park Ln, Pickmere WA16 0JX ☎01565 733433
Closed Xmas
Dating from 1772, this imposing house stands in the village of Pickmere. Its mainly spacious bedrooms are traditionally furnished but equipped with modern facilities. There is a comfortable lounge extending into two rooms, and dinner is served by prior arrangement in the beamed dining room. The

house is no-smoking throughout.
9 rms (5 shr) (3 fmly) CTV in all bedrooms Tea and coffee making facilities Cen ht CTV 9P No coaches

Selected

◀ QQQQ **The Dog Inn** Well Bank Ln, Over Peover WA16 8UP (from A50 turn left at Whipping Stocks continue straight on for approx 2m)
☎01625 861421 FAX 01625 861421
This popular and very well maintained inn stands in the village of Over Peover. Traditionally furnished bedrooms have modern facilities plus thoughtful extras such as fresh fruit, biscuits etc. A good selection of home-cooked dishes is displayed on a blackboard menu and can be served either in the pleasant lounge bar or adjacent dining room.
3 en suite (bth/shr) No smoking in area of dining room CTV in all bedrooms Tea and coffee making facilities No dogs (ex guide dogs) Cen ht 30P No coaches Pool table Last d 9.30pm
PRICE GUIDE
ROOMS: s fr £39.50; d fr £59.50✳
MEALS: Lunch £3.85-£14.60 Dinner £3.85-£15.10✳

LACOCK Wiltshire Map 03 ST96

Premier Selected

GH QQQQQ *At the Sign of the Angel* 6 Church St SN15 2LA ☎01249 730230 FAX 01249 730527
Closed 23 Dec-30 Dec

This charming 15th century wool merchants house nestles in the famous National Trust village of Lacock, which is only a short drive away from the M4 and the city of Bath. There are oak beams, log fires and a collection of antiques to enjoy, the atmosphere here is relaxed and hospitable with the family always on hand to help.The eight bedrooms on offer to guests are beautifully furnished and thoughtfully equipped. There are two bedrooms in the annexe which are reached by footbridge across the delightful garden stream. The Angel has gained a reputation for fine cooking, and certainly the menu is extensive and appealing, and meals are served in a beamed dining room with an enormous log fire and candles by night.
6 en suite (bth) 3 annexe en suite (bth) (1 fmly) CTV in all bedrooms Tea and coffee making facilities Direct dial from bedrooms Licensed Cen ht No children 10yrs 1P No coaches Last d 9pm
CARDS: 🔲 ▦ ▦

LAMBERHURST Kent Map 05 TQ63

◀ QQ *George & Dragon* School Hill TN3 8DQ
☎01892 890277
Set in the centre of this small village on the main A21, the George and Dragon offers basic accomodation in good-sized bedrooms, attractively decorated and well equipped. The main bar has some comfortable seating and a good selection of bar snacks, while a carte is seved in the well-appointed dining room.
6 rms (4 bth/shr) (1 fmly) CTV in all bedrooms Tea and coffee

making facilities No dogs (ex guide dogs) Cen ht 30P Pool table Last d 9.30pm
CARDS: 🔲

LAMBOURN Berkshire Map 04 SU37

Selected

GH QQQQ **Lodge Down** The Woodlands RG16 7BJ (take B3400 from Lambourn, then follow signs for Baydon, farm 1m E of Baydon)
☎01672 540304 FAX 01672 540304
Set in tranquil countryside with splendid views across the gallops of Lambourn Downs, this attractive and welcoming hotel contains a training course for horses and a summer swimming pool within its grounds. Breakfast is served round a large communal table, and in winter an open fire warms the spacious sitting room where guests watch television. There are three bedrooms on the first floor, each of a good size, furnished with period pieces and provided with a modern en suite bathroom.
3 en suite (bth/shr) (1 fmly) No smoking in bedrooms No smoking in dining room Tea and coffee making facilities No dogs (ex guide dogs) Cen ht CTV 10P No coaches Indoor swimming pool Tennis (hard)
PRICE GUIDE
ROOMS: s £20-£25; d fr £40; wkly b&b fr £140✳ ⓕ

LANCASTER Lancashire Map 07 SD46

GH QQQ **Lancaster Town House** 11/12 Newton Ter, Caton Rd LA1 3PB (1m from exit 34 of M6) ☎01524 65527
Neat bedrooms and comfortable public areas are offered at this well furnished guesthouse, which caters for business guests and tourists alike. Service is friendly and helpful.
5 en suite (bth/shr) (1 fmly) No smoking in dining room No smoking in lounges CTV in all bedrooms Tea and coffee making facilities No dogs (ex guide dogs) Cen ht No children 4yrs No parking No coaches
PRICE GUIDE
ROOMS: s £22-£25; d £34.50-£40✳

LANGPORT Somerset Map 03 ST42

Premier Selected

GH QQQQQ *Hillards* High St, Curry Rivel TA10 0EY ☎01458 251737 FAX 01458 253233

A listed former farmhouse dating from the 17th century, this charming old building offers the intimate atmosphere created by a wealth of oak and elm panelling, beamed ceilings and large open fireplaces. Each bedroom has its own style but the emphasis throughout is on guests' comfort. A hearty breakfast is served in the dining room, at one large oak table in winter and separate tables in summer. Converted outbuildings provide self-catering accommodation of a high standard.

4 rms (1 bth/shr) 2 annexe en suite (bth/shr) No smoking No dogs (ex guide dogs) Cen ht CTV No children 25P No coaches

---

LAUNCESTON Cornwall & Isles of Scilly Map **02** SX38

Selected

🏠 🍴 ♥ Q Q Q Q Mrs Margaret Smith **Hurdon** *(SX333828)* PL15 9LS (leave A30 at first Launceston exit (A388) and continue towards Industrial Estate. Then follow signs for 'Trebullet') ☎01566 772955
May-Oct
This handsome 18th-century stone-built farmhouse is situated at the end of a tree-lined drive, south of the town of Launceston, on a 400-acre working farm. Much of the original character of the house has been retained and is now combined with modern facilities to provide six spacious bedrooms. There is an attractive lounge, and dinner is served at separate tables in the elegant dining room. The Smith family welcome guests, but respectfully request them not to smoke in the house.
6 rms (4 bth) (1 fmly) No smoking Tea and coffee making facilities No dogs (ex guide dogs) Cen ht CTV 10P 400 acres mixed Last d 4.30pm
PRICE GUIDE
ROOMS: s £15.50-£18.50; d £31-£37; wkly b&b £95-£116; wkly hlf-bd £155-£176

♥ Q Q Q Mrs K Broad **Lower Dutson** *(SX340859)* PL15 9SP (on A388) ☎01566 776456
Neatly furnished and decorated bedrooms are offered in a farmhouse which has been the home of the Broad family since 1897; the original building on the same site dated back to the seventeenth century. Guests have the use of a spacious lounge/dining room, and a three-bedroomed self-catering cottage attached to the house is also available. The mixed farm of 180 acres includes a coarse fishing lake as well as fishing on a stretch of the River Tamar where, in September 1993, a salmon weighing 20.5lbs. was caught.
3 rms (1 bth) (1 fmly) No smoking Tea and coffee making facilities No dogs (ex guide dogs) Cen ht CTV 4P Fishing 180 acres beef sheep
PRICE GUIDE
ROOMS: s £15-£17; d £26-£32; wkly b&b £91-£112✳

LAVERTON Gloucestershire Map **04** SP03

Selected

GH Q Q Q Q **Leasow House** WR12 7NA (take B4632 from town to Cheltenham for 2m & turn right to Wormington then 1st on right)
☎01386 584526 FAX 01386 584596
This early 17th-century Cotswold stone farmhouse is situated southwest of Broadway off the A4632 (signposted Wormington and Dumbleton, it is the first farm on the right). Bedrooms are very modern and well equipped, all with en suite facilities, yet the character of the farmhouse has been retained. The comfortable library has a wide range of books and guides. Two new bedrooms have recently been added, and these share a mini kitchen and comfortable lounge.
5 en suite (bth/shr) 2 annexe en suite (bth) (2 fmly) No smoking in bedrooms No smoking in dining room CTV in

all bedrooms Tea and coffee making facilities Direct dial from bedrooms Cen ht 10P No coaches
PRICE GUIDE
ROOMS: s £30-£40; d £48-£62
CARDS: 🔲 💳
See advertisement under BROADWAY

LEAMINGTON SPA (ROYAL) Warwickshire Map **04** SP36

GH Q Q **Charnwood** 47 Avenue Rd CV31 3PF (approaching from A452, under railway bridge, guesthouse on right in .5m)
☎01926 831074
Conveniently located for the town centre, this friendly, personally run guest house with bright, value for money acommodation and homely public rooms.
6 rms (1 bth 1 shr) (1 fmly) No smoking in dining room No smoking in lounges CTV in all bedrooms Tea and coffee making facilities Cen ht 6P Last d noon
PRICE GUIDE
ROOMS: s £17-£27; d £32-£37; wkly b&b £119-£189; wkly hlf-bd £189-£259✳
CARDS: 🔲 💳

GH Q Q Q **Coverdale Private Hotel** 8 Portland St CV32 5HE
☎01926 330400 FAX 01926 833388
This attractive, detached Regency house is centrally located and conveniently placed for most of the town's amenities. The bedrooms have high ceilings in keeping with the character of the building which allows for spacious and well lit rooms. Two of the bedrooms are located on the ground floor and they all have private bathroom facilities.
8 rms (2 bth 4 shr) (2 fmly) No smoking in 2 bedrooms CTV in all bedrooms Tea and coffee making facilities Direct dial from bedrooms Cen ht 3P
CARDS: 🔲 💳 🔲 🔲

GH Q Q Q **Flowerdale House** 58 Warwick New Rd CV32 6AA (on the junct B4099/B4453)
☎01926 426002 FAX 01926 883699
This delightful, lovingly restored Victorian house is situated on the Warwick road on the fringes of Leamington. The bedrooms all vary in size, style of decor and layout which contributes to an original atmosphere. There is a small dispense bar next to the lounge and the breakfast room can spill over into a bright back facing conservatory.
6 en suite (bth/shr) No smoking in dining room No smoking in lounges CTV in all bedrooms Tea and coffee making facilities Licensed Cen ht 8P No coaches
PRICE GUIDE
ROOMS: s £22-£26; d £36-£46
CARDS: 🔲 💳

GH Q Q *Glendower* 8 Warwick Place CV32 5BJ (300yds W of Fire Station) ☎01926 422784
This semidetached Victorian house is situated on the B4099 west of the town centre. It provides simple but soundly maintained modern accommodation suitable for commercial visitors and tourists alike; family rooms are also available. The spacious public rooms retain many original features, and the guesthouse has a bar license. Street parking nearby is usually available.
9 rms (2 bth) (3 fmly) No smoking in dining room CTV in all bedrooms Tea and coffee making facilities Licensed Cen ht CTV 2P Last d 7pm

---

GH Q Q **Guys Cliffe** 157 Rugby Rd, Milverton CV32 6DJ
☎01926 336217 FAX 01926 336217
A character Edwardian house, personally run, and offering bright, comfortable and well equipped bedrooms, together with homely

public rooms. Well suited to both business guest and tourist.
7 en suite (bth/shr) (1 fmly) No smoking in dining room No smoking in lounges CTV in all bedrooms Tea and coffee making facilities Cen ht CTV 4P No coaches

PRICE GUIDE
ROOMS: s £24-£44; d £48-£88; wkly b&b £140-£280*

♥ Q Q Q Mrs R Gibbs **Hill** (*SP343637*) Lewis Rd, Radford Semele CV31 1UX (2m from Leamington Spa on the A425) ☎01926 337571
Closed Xmas & New Year
Located on a mixed farm, and popular with both business people and tourists, this well maintained mid-Victorian house lies east of Leamington Spa. Bedrooms vary in size and their furnishings range from modern to period style. Public areas include a comfortable TV lounge and conservatory/breakfast room with solid pine furniture. Smoking is not permitted.
5 rms (3 shr) (1 fmly) No smoking CTV in all bedrooms Tea and coffee making facilities No dogs Cen ht CTV 6P 350 acres arable beef mixed sheep

PRICE GUIDE
ROOMS: s £18-£22; d £32-£40

LECHLADE Gloucestershire Map **04** SU29

Premier Selected

GH Q Q Q Q Q **Cottage-by-the-Church** Chapel Ln, Filkins GL7 3JG (off A361 between Burford and Lechlade, alongside Filkins church) ☎01367 860613 FAX 01367 860613
This charming 17th-century cottage does indeed stand opposite the church in the beautiful village of Filkins, just two miles from Lechlade. Guests receive warm hospitality and can choose between two delightful bedrooms furnished in character with the building. The garden is lovingly cared for, and Stratford, Warwick, Oxford and Cheltenham are all within easy reach.
2 en suite (bth/shr) No smoking in bedrooms Tea and coffee making facilities Cen ht CTV No children 10yrs 4P

PRICE GUIDE
ROOMS: d £39-£50; wkly b&b £120-£140*

LEDBURY Hereford & Worcester Map **03** SO73

GH Q Q Q **Barn House** New St HR8 2DX ☎01531 632825
The front part of this delightful town house dates from the early 18th century, but the rear is much older. The "Barn Room", a fascinating timber framed room now used for functions, was once a barn and dates from about 1612. Other period features include the graceful staircase, with Chinese Chippendale screens. The bedrooms are tastefully furnished in a style befitting the character of the house. There is a comfortable lounge and a traditionally furnished breakfast room, with a beamed ceiling, where separate tables are provided. Other facilities include a bar, extensive and attractive gardens and a secure car park.
3 rms (1 shr) No smoking in bedrooms No smoking in dining room CTV in 2 bedrooms Tea and coffee making facilities No

dogs Licensed Cen ht CTV No children 14yrs 6P

PRICE GUIDE
ROOMS: d £54*
CARDS:

GH Q Q Q **Wall Hills Country Guesthouse** Hereford Rd HR8 2PR (off A438) ☎01531 632833
Closed Xmas/New Year
The long private drive leading to this 250-year-old former farmhouse is reached from the A438 on the western outskirts of town. Privately owned and personally run, the guest house offers spacious, traditionally furnished accommodation which includes a family room; all the bedrooms are no-smoking. Separate tables are provided in the dining room, and there is a spacious lounge where welcoming log fires burn in cold weather.
3 rms (1 bth 1 shr) (1 fmly) No smoking in bedrooms No smoking in dining room Tea and coffee making facilities No dogs Licensed Cen ht CTV 8P No coaches Arrangement with local golf course Last d 8.30pm

PRICE GUIDE
ROOMS: s £35-£39; d £47-£58
CARDS:

LEEDS West Yorkshire Map **08** SE33

GH Q Q Q **Ash Mount Hotel** 22 Wetherby Road, Oakwood LS8 2QD ☎0113 265 8164 FAX 0113 265 8164
A large, well furnished Victorian house fronted by a attractive garden stands off the main road in the pleasant residential area of Oakwood, close to Roundhay Park; modern bedrooms are all well equipped, though they vary in size and downstairs there are a comfortable lounge and a neat dining room. Private car parking facilities are available.
11 rms (7 bth/shr) (1 fmly) No smoking in dining room No smoking in lounges CTV in all bedrooms Tea and coffee making facilities Direct dial from bedrooms Licensed Cen ht CTV 10P Last d breakfast

PRICE GUIDE
ROOMS: s £21-£30; d £38-£44*
CARDS:

GH Q Q Q **Merevale Hotel** 16 Wetherby Rd, Oakwood LS8 2QD ☎0113 265 8933 & 273 7985 FAX 0113 265 8933
This elegant house is set back from the main road and also has the benefit of a car park to the rear. It is close to Roundhay Park in a pleasant residential area of Leeds. It provides well equipped bedrooms which are bright, fresh and modern and there is also a comfortable lounge together with an inviting dining room.
14 rms (6 bth/shr) (1 fmly) No smoking in dining room No smoking in lounges CTV in all bedrooms Tea and coffee making facilities Direct dial from bedrooms No dogs Licensed Cen ht CTV 11P Last d 8pm

PRICE GUIDE
ROOMS: s £20-£30; d £36-£44*
CARDS:

GH Q Q Q *Pinewood Private Hotel* 78 Potter Newton Ln LS7 3LW (leave town centre on A61 Harrogate Road. Turn right at roundabout at top of hill, hotel 600yds on left) ☎0113 262 2561 FAX 0113 262 2561
This family owned and run guest house is only two miles from the city centre and is located in a pleasant residential area. Well furnished bedrooms have many thoughtful extras and public rooms include two lounges and a very pleasant dining room.
10 en suite (bth/shr) (2 fmly) No smoking in dining room No smoking in 1 lounge CTV in all bedrooms Tea and coffee making facilities Licensed Cen ht CTV P No coaches Last d 10am
CARDS:

GH **Q Q Q Trafford House & Budapest Hotel** 18 Cardigan Road, Headingley LS6 3AG ☎0113 275 2034 & 275 6637 FAX 0113 274 2422

Closed 24 & 25 Dec

Only two miles from the city, and with some bedrooms overlooking the cricket ground, this pleasantly furnished throughout, the hotel provides very good value for money.

18 rms (4 shr) (4 fmly) No smoking in dining room CTV in all bedrooms Tea and coffee making facilities Direct dial from bedrooms No dogs (ex guide dogs) Licensed Cen ht CTV 30P Last d noon

PRICE GUIDE

ROOMS: s £22-£39; d £34-£55; wkly b&b £140-£210

CARDS:

LEEK Staffordshire Map **07** SJ95

GH **Q Peak Weavers Hotel** King St ST13 5NW (in town centre behind St Mary's Church, off A53) ☎01538 383729

An extended 1930s property (converted from a convent) this hotel lies close to the centre of Leek - an ideal location for exploring the Peak District. The bedrooms are compact and simply furnished, but some have en suite facilities. Public rooms comprise a recently refurbished licensed bar and dining room.

10 rms (3 bth 1 shr) (2 fmly) No smoking in dining room CTV in 6 bedrooms Tea and coffee making facilities Licensed Cen ht 16P Last d 8.30pm

PRICE GUIDE

ROOMS: s £18-£27; d £32-£38

CARDS: 🔳 ▬ ▬

◀ **Q Q Q Abbey** Abbey Green Rd ST13 8SA (off A523, 0.5m outside Leek on the Macclesfield road) ☎01538 382865

Located just outside the moorland town of Leek, this inn offers good-value bar food and is popular with locals. All the comfortable modern bedrooms are housed in a converted sandstone barn and have en suite shower rooms as well as many additional facilities. Breakfast is served in the main building.

7 annexe en suite (shr) CTV in all bedrooms Tea and coffee making facilities Direct dial from bedrooms No dogs (ex guide dogs) Cen ht No children 14yrs 60P Last d 8pm

CARDS: 🔳 ▬ ▬ ▣

LEICESTER Leicestershire Map **04** SK50

GH **Q Q** *Alexandra House* 342 London Road, Stoneygate LE2 2PJ (1m S, near University) ☎0116 270 3056 FAX 0116 270 5464

Located just over a mile south of the city centre on the A6 London road, this guest house is sheltered from the noise of traffic by mature trees. Bedrooms - all of which are situated on on the first floor - are colour co-ordinated in striking, rich Laura Ashley fabrics and wall coverings. Public areas are particularly spacious and comfortable, but breakfast is the only meal served.

4 en suite (shr) No smoking in bedrooms No smoking in dining room Tea and coffee making facilities Direct dial from bedrooms No dogs Cen ht 10P No coaches

CARDS: 🔳 ▬

GH **Q Q Q Burlington Hotel** Elmfield Av LE2 1RB (just off A6, 0.75m from railway station) ☎0116 270 5112 FAX 0116 270 4207

Closed 23 Dec-2 Jan

Just off the A6 and very handy for the city or university, this family-owned hotel is a fine Victorian residence with splendid period features. A carved and panelled oak inglenook with integral settles either side dominates the lounge. There is a cosy bar combined with the reception area, while modern bedrooms are equipped with writing desks and co-ordinated soft furnishings.

Careful and enthusiastic management is evident throughout.

16 rms (11 bth/shr) (1 fmly) CTV in all bedrooms Tea and coffee making facilities No dogs (ex guide dogs) Licensed Cen ht CTV 23P Last d 8.30pm

PRICE GUIDE

ROOMS: s £27-£38; d £40-£46

CARDS: 🔳 ▬ ▬

GH **Q Q Croft Hotel** 3 Stanley Rd LE2 1RF (close to main line railway station) ☎0116 270 3220 FAX 0116 270 3220

Just off the A6 and close to the city centre, the Croft is a fine looking turn-of-the-century house which has a good and varied selection of similarly furnished rooms. There are a small lounge and a cheerful dining room where breakfasts and home-made evening meals are served.

26 rms (8 bth/shr) (2 fmly) No smoking in dining room CTV in all bedrooms Tea and coffee making facilities Licensed Cen ht CTV 16P Last d 6.30pm

PRICE GUIDE

ROOMS: s £22-£34; d £32-£38; wkly b&b £140-£150; wkly hlf-bd £175-£190

CARDS: 🔳 ▬

GH **Q Q** *Scotia Hotel* 10 Westcotes Dr LE3 0QR (take 3rd turning on the right after A46 leaves the A47 west end of Leicester) ☎0116 254 9200

The Scotia is just off the Narborough Road and was built at the turn of the century as a private residence. The period features are still clear to see, and homely, comfortably furnished public rooms are highlighted with cheerful decoration. Each of the bedrooms (some of which are across the road) is fitted with a small desk, and the evening meal offers a choice of three dishes prepared from fresh ingredients.

11 rms (4 bth/shr) (1 fmly) CTV in all bedrooms Tea and coffee making facilities Licensed Cen ht 5P No coaches Last d 8pm

---

GH **Q Q The Stanfre House Hotel** 265 London Rd LE2 3BE (turn left at roundabout on A6) ☎0116 270 4294

Closed 25 Dec-2 Jan

Stanfre House was built at the turn of the century. Whilst it is painted white on the outside, the interior is a myriad of colour - due in part to the healthy leaf plants filling each room. The lounge looks very welcoming, its ornaments and surfaces polished until they gleam, while bright yellow table mats give the dining room a cheerful air. Adequately equipped bedrooms reflect the character of the rest of the hotel.

12 rms (1 fmly) No smoking in dining room CTV in all bedrooms Licensed Cen ht CTV 6P

PRICE GUIDE

ROOMS: s £19; d £30✳

GH **Q Q Q Stoneycroft Hotel** 5/7 Elmfield Av LE2 1RB ☎0116 270 7605 FAX 0116 270 6067

This is a very substantial guest house quietly located just off the A6. The bedrooms are uniformally furnished with good modern fittings which include a comfortable desk, writing area and suitable chairs. Public areas provide a conference room and a separate bar combined with a large, attractively decorated restaurant.

44 rms (25 bth/shr) (4 fmly) No smoking in dining room CTV in all bedrooms Tea and coffee making facilities No dogs (ex guide dogs) Licensed Cen ht CTV 20P Pool table Last d 9pm

PRICE GUIDE

ROOMS: s £26-£34; d £37-£39; wkly b&b £182-£273; wkly hlf-bd £250-£341✳

CARDS: 🔳 ▬ ▬ ▣ ▦ ▦ ▣

LELANT Cornwall & Isles of Scilly Map 02 SW53

Selected

◄ QQQQ Badger TR26 3JT ☎01736 752181
This village inn is situated just off the A30, convenient for St Ives and close to the Hayle Estuary. Bedrooms are comfortable, attractive, and well equipped. The spacious bars retain their character and there is a no-smoking conservatory restaurant where a hot carvery is offered on Saturday nights and at lunch on Sunday. The good daily selection of bar meals includes popular home-made puddings.
6 en suite (bth/shr) No smoking in dining room No smoking in lounges CTV in all bedrooms Tea and coffee making facilities Direct dial from bedrooms No dogs (ex guide dogs) Cen ht No children 6yrs 100P No coaches Last d 10.15pm
PRICE GUIDE
ROOMS: s £28-£30; d £45-£48✳
MEALS: Lunch £2.50-£7.50&alc Dinner £2.50-£7&alc✳
CARDS: ![cards] (£)

LEOMINSTER Hereford & Worcester Map 03 SO45

See also Bodenham

GH QQ Knapp House Luston HR6 0DB (2.5m N on B4361) ☎01568 615705
Dating back to the 16th century, this black and white timbered house has a pleasant garden. Bedrooms are smart and brightly decorated, and the impressive panelled lounge has a cheerful log fire burning in the colder weather.
2 rms (1 fmly) Tea and coffee making facilities Cen ht CTV 4P Last d 5pm
PRICE GUIDE
ROOMS: s £16; d £30; wkly b&b £100✳ (£)

Selected

♥ QQQQ Mrs J Conolly **The Hills** *(SO564638)* Leysters HR6 0HP ☎01568 750205
Feb-Oct
Jane and Peter Conolly offer a warm welcome to guests at their creeper-clad 15th-century farmhouse located at Leysters, between Leominster and Tenbury Wells. There are two bedrooms in the main house, one of which was a chapel in the 1920s, and a third room is contained in a cleverly converted stone-built barn; at the time of our visit a second barn was being converted into another two spacious bedrooms. A wood-burning stove warms the timbered lounge, and in the slab-floored dining room Jane provides good home cooked meals at individual tables.
3 en suite (bth/shr) 3 annexe en suite (bth) No smoking CTV in all bedrooms Tea and coffee making facilities Cen ht No children 12yrs 8P 120 acres arable Last d noon
PRICE GUIDE
ROOMS: d £40-£46; wkly b&b £140-£161; wkly hlf-bd £245-£266
CARDS: (£)

♥ Q Mrs E Thomas **Woonton Court** *(SO548624)* Leysters HR6 0HL (take A39, 2.5m from town onto A4112 and pass through Kimbolton, turning right for Woonton before Leysters village. Farm 0.5m down lane.) ☎01568 750232
Closed 22-27 Dec
Neatly tucked away in a secluded spot yet convenient to the A49 Ludlow-Leominster road this Tudor farmhouse offers homely accommodation and a warm welcome. Ideally positioned for visiting National Trust properties, the Welsh marshes and Hereford. Hearty breakfasts, using the farm produce, including free-range eggs and milk from the Guernsey herd.
2 rms (1 bth) No smoking in 1 bedrooms No smoking in area of dining room CTV in all bedrooms Tea and coffee making facilities Cen ht CTV 4P 250 acres mixed Last d previous day
PRICE GUIDE
ROOMS: s £18; d £32; wkly b&b fr £110 (£)

LEVEN Humberside Map 08 TA14

◄ QQ *The New Inn* 44 South St HU17 5NZ (off A1035) ☎01964 542223
This red brick coaching inn is almost 200 years old and has been recently refurbished. Meals are taken in the lounge bar. Bedrooms have all had en suite shower rooms added, although the rooms themselves do tend to be compact.
4 rms (3 shr) (1 fmly) No smoking in area of dining room CTV in 3 bedrooms Tea and coffee making facilities No dogs (ex guide dogs) Cen ht CTV 55P Last d 9pm
CARDS: ![cards]

SUMMERHILL FARM

Grindon, Leek, Staffordshire ST13 7TT
Telephone: 01538 304264

A traditional family farmhouse set in a secluded position within the Peak District National Park amid rolling countryside and spectacular scenery. Overlooking the valleys of the Dove and Manifold, wonderful for walkers. Cars can be safely parked all day at Summerhills. The farmhouse is tastefully furnished with period furniture. Breakfast and evening meals are taken in the conservatory with panoramic views across green pastures where the cattle peacefully graze. Ideally situated for the spa towns of Ashbourne and Buxton, Chatsworth House, the Potteries, Alton Towers and mnay other places of interest.

LEVENS Cumbria Map **07** SD48

GH ꞯꞯꞯ **Birslack Grange** Cotes LA8 8PA (take A590 into Village, past Hare & Hounds and village crossroads, turn left into Hutton Lane. House 300yds on left) ☎015395 60989

A private residence tastefully converted from a barn and set in neat gardens on the edge of the village enjoys views over meadowland towards the south lakeland hills. There are three bedrooms, a spacious dining room with quarry-tiled floor and large pine dresser, and a comfortable guests' lounge with TV. Ample parking is provided in the grounds.

4 rms (3 shr) No smoking Tea and coffee making facilities No dogs (ex guide dogs) Cen ht CTV 4P No coaches Last d 8pm

PRICE GUIDE
ROOMS: s £20-£22; d £28-£33; wkly b&b £90-£100; wkly hlf-bd £160-£170✱

(£)

◀ ꞯꞯꞯ *Gilpin Bridge Hotel & Restaurant* Bridge End LA8 8EP (on A5074, 100mtrs from junct with A590) ☎015395 52206

An attractive inn with a beamed bar and restaurant, the Gilpin Bridge serves real ale and a wide choice of bar meals. The restaurant is open for dinner and table reservations are advisable, especially at weekends. Bedrooms are modern in style and very well equipped. One room has a four-poster bed and another an impressive brass bedstead.

10 en suite (bth/shr) No smoking in 2 bedrooms CTV in all bedrooms Tea and coffee making facilities No dogs (ex guide dogs) Cen ht 100P Last d 9pm

CARDS: ▬ ▬

LEW Oxfordshire Map **04** SP30

Selected

♥ ꞯꞯꞯꞯ Mrs M Rouse **The Farmhouse Hotel** *(SP322059)* University Farm OX18 2AU (on the A4095, 3m SW of Witney on the Bampton Road) ☎01993 850297 & 851480 FAX 01993 850965

Closed Xmas & New Year rs Sun

This lovely 17th-century Cotswold stone longhouse stands, surrounded by pretty landscaped gardens and terraces, on a working farm. Each of the bedrooms is furnished to accentuate its own unique features, with distinctive colour schemes, cottage prints, patchwork quilts, plants and an abundance of fresh flowers. A sitting room offering deep cushioned sofas and armchairs around its beamed inglenook fireplace leads into another sitting room, a small bar offering draught ales, an attractive conservatory which is used mainly as a breakfast room and a restaurant. The latter is open to non-residents, and a daily-changing menu offers a variety of seasonal choices; smoking is not permitted here or in the bedrooms.

6 en suite (bth/shr) (2 fmly) No smoking in bedrooms No smoking in dining room No smoking in 1 lounge CTV in all bedrooms Tea and coffee making facilities Direct dial from bedrooms No dogs (ex guide dogs) Licensed Cen ht No children 5yrs 25P 216 acres dairy Last d 6pm

PRICE GUIDE
ROOMS: d fr £50; wkly b&b fr £168

CARDS: ▬ ▬

LEWES East Sussex Map **05** TQ41

Premier Selected

PREMIER SELECTED BED & BREAKFAST

GH ꞯꞯꞯꞯꞯ **Fairseat House** Newick BN8 4PJ (on A272 between Haywards Heath and Uckfield) ☎01825 722263 FAX 01825 722263

Carole and Roy Pontifex extend a warm welcome to guests in their home. Carole likes to get to know her guests and by the time you arrive you are greeted as an old friend. Each of three bedrooms has its own distinctive character. The Elizabethan room offers an elegantly draped four poster bed where romantic breakfasts can be served. Two drawing rooms feature open fireplaces and some fine works of art, be sure to see the dramatic, textured portrait at the top of the stairs. Dinners are first rate with produce coming from the garden which also features a covered heated swimming pool. Breakfasts are delicious with eggs coming from the resident hens and fine home made preserves.

3 en suite (bth/shr) No smoking No dogs Cen ht CTV No children 6P No coaches Outdoor swimming pool (heated)

PRICE GUIDE
ROOMS: s £25-£27; d £38-£60✱

CARDS: ▬

(£)

GH ꞯꞯꞯ **Hyde Cottage** The Street, Kingston BN7 3PB ☎01273 472709

Home to Jennifer Maddock and her family this delightful 200 years old non-smoking cottage bed and breakfast guest house is hidden away behind a thick hedge row in the quiet and relaxing residential surroundings with views of the South Downs. The house is very spacious and the accommodation has been individually furnished with period pine and antique furniture, and whilst two bedrooms are without wash hand basins all come with tea tray. There is a small study lounge, kitchen breakfast room (a private dining room can also be made available), and Jennifer Maddock makes all her own marmalades and jams with generous English breakfasts being cooked on the Aga. Car parking is limited.

Selected

GH ꞯꞯꞯꞯ **Nightingales** The Avenue, Kingston BN7 3LL ☎01273 475673

This attractive house in the pretty village of Kingston-near-Lewes has a magnificent garden which has won many awards. The two stylish bedrooms are comfortable and feature many extras such as complimentary fruit, sherry and biscuits. The airy lounge overlooks the garden and breakfasts are served at an attractive polished wooden table.

2 rms (1 bth/shr) No smoking CTV in all bedrooms Tea and coffee making facilities Cen ht CTV 2P No coaches

PRICE GUIDE
ROOMS: d £40-£45

CARDS: ▬ ▬ ▬

(£)

LEYBURN North Yorkshire Map **07** SE19

GH 🔲🔲🔲 *Eastfield Lodge Private Hotel* 1 St Matthews Ter DL8 5EL (on A684, near St Matthews Church) ☎01969 23196

Situated on the edge of the delightful town of Leyburn, this spacious and well furnished house provides a good standard of accommodation. The bedrooms are well equipped, having colour televisions and, in most cases, en suite showers. There is a cosy lounge bar and service is friendly and attentive.

9 rms (4 shr) (2 fmly) CTV in all bedrooms Tea and coffee making facilities Licensed Cen ht 10P

CARDS: 🔲 🔲

Selected

GH 🔲🔲🔲🔲 **Park Gate House** Constable Burton DL8 5RG (on A684 opposite Constable Burton Hall Park) ☎01677 450466

An eighteenth century roadside gatehouse which used to form part of the Constable Burton Estate. Under new ownership the spacious house has been refurbished and modernised within the original framework. The lounge has retained the inglenook log fire and the dining room is furnished in dark polished oaks. The bedrooms are furnished in the country manner with pretty cottage style fabrics and old pine furniture and each has its own lovely bathroom a few strides away. Mr and Mrs Thornber are a friendly couple and the house is immaculate throughout.

3 rms 1 annexe en suite (shr) No smoking CTV in all bedrooms Tea and coffee making facilities No dogs (ex guide dogs) Licensed Cen ht CTV No children 12yrs 6P No coaches

PRICE GUIDE

ROOMS: s £25-£35; d £36-£50

◀ 🔲🔲🔲 *Foresters Arms* Carlton-in-Coverdale DL8 2BB (5m SW) ☎01969 40272

This delightful old inn is located in the peaceful village of Carlton in Coverdale, five miles from Leyburn. The bar area features low beams, log fires and real ales, the restaurant offers a wide choice of well prepared food, and three very well furnished bedrooms provide restful accomodation.

3 rms (2 shr) (1 fmly) No smoking in area of dining room CTV in all bedrooms Tea and coffee making facilities Direct dial from bedrooms Cen ht 10P No coaches Last d 9.30pm

CARDS: 🔲 🔲

LICHFIELD Staffordshire Map **07** SK10

GH 🔲🔲 *Coppers End* Walsall Rd, Muckley Corner WS14 0BG (on A461, 100yds from Muckley Corner rbt off the A5) ☎01543 372910

This detached property built in 1935 as a police station and cell (hence the name) is now a personally run guesthouse, located three miles southwest of Lichfield. It provides bedrooms with modern furnishings and equipment, two of which are located on the ground floor; smoking is not permitted in bedrooms. There is a pleasant comfortable lounge, and a small cosy dining room where tables are shared.

6 rms (1 shr) No smoking in bedrooms No smoking in area of dining room CTV in all bedrooms Tea and coffee making facilities Licensed Cen ht CTV 12P No coaches Last d noon

PRICE GUIDE

ROOMS: s £22-£29; d £35-£41

CARDS: 🔲 🔲 🔲 🔲 🔲

GH 🔲🔲🔲 *The Oakleigh House Hotel* 25 St Chads Rd WS13 7LZ ☎01543 262688 & 255573

Closed 27 Dec-1 Jan rs Sun evening & Mon

This well preserved and charming house set in attractive gardens next to Stowe Pool, less than half a mile from the cathedral, dates back to 1909. Bedrooms in the main house have mainly period-style furniture, while those in the single-storey annexe have modern furniture. They are all well equipped. There is a cosy lounge, a small pleasant bar and an attractive conservatory restaurant.

5 rms (3 bth/shr) 5 annexe en suite (bth/shr) CTV in all bedrooms Tea and coffee making facilities Direct dial from bedrooms Licensed Cen ht No children 20P No coaches Last d 9.30pm

CARDS: 🔲 🔲

LIFTON Devon Map **02** SX38

GH 🔲🔲 *Mayfield House* PL16 0AN ☎01566 784401

This detached house, set in a village close to both the Dartmoor National Park and the Cornish border, offers accommodation in three bedrooms; the lounge bar has a homely atmosphere, and breakfast is served in a simply appointed dining room.

3 rms (1 fmly) No smoking in bedrooms CTV in all bedrooms Tea and coffee making facilities No dogs (ex guide dogs) Licensed 10P No coaches

CARDS: 🔲

LIGHTHORNE Warwickshire Map **04** SP35

♥ 🔲🔲🔲 Mrs J Stanton **Redlands** *(SP334570)* Banbury Rd CV35 0AH (off B4100, 5m S of Warwick) ☎01926 651241

Closed Xmas

Redlands Farm, the cheerful home of Mr and Mrs Stanton, is surrounded by 100 acres of arable land, ideal for short rambles. All the bedrooms are spacious and one features a raised brass bedstead. Parts of the building date back to the 16th century, but the overall impression is one of modern-day comfort.

3 rms (1 bth) (1 fmly) No smoking in bedrooms No smoking in dining room Tea and coffee making facilities No dogs (ex guide dogs) Cen ht CTV 7P Outdoor swimming pool 100 acres arable

PRICE GUIDE

ROOMS: s £15-£17.50; d £34-£38✱

LINCOLN Lincolnshire Map **08** SK97

See also Horncastle & Swinderby

GH 🔲🔲 *Brierley House Hotel* 54 South Park LN5 8ER ☎01522 526945 & 522945

Located on a quiet avenue overlooking South Common Golf Course, Brierley House is about half a mile from the city centre. Modest but sound accommodation is offered and guests have the use of a comfortable lounge. There is a dining room with a small bar, and evening meals are available by prior arrangement.

7 rms (2 bth 4 shr) CTV in all bedrooms Tea and coffee making facilities No dogs Licensed Cen ht CTV No parking Adjacent 18 hole golf course Last d breakfast

---

Selected

GH 🔲🔲🔲🔲 **Carline** 1-3 Carline Rd LN1 1HL ☎01522 530422

Closed Xmas & New Year

Enthusiastic owners offer a warm welcome at this popular guest house in a quiet residential area below the castle. The bedrooms vary in size and are individually furnished and

➡

attractively decorated in cheerfully coordinated colour schemes. Annexe rooms have their own comfortable lounge, and there is an additional lounge in the main house. This is a no-smoking establishment.

9 en suite (bth/shr) 3 annexe rms (1 shr) (2 fmly) No smoking CTV in all bedrooms Tea and coffee making facilities No dogs (ex guide dogs) Cen ht No children 2yrs 13P No coaches

PRICE GUIDE
ROOMS: s £20-£30; d £32-£40✱

Selected

GH Ⓠ Ⓠ Ⓠ Ⓠ **D'Isney Place Hotel** Eastgate LN2 4AA
☎01522 538881 FAX 01522 511321

D'Isney Place is an unusual establishment, close to the cathedral, offering quality accommodation in bedrooms of varying size. Each room is individually furnished, with en suite facilities and personal touches such as fresh milk and good towelling bathrobes. Deluxe rooms have even more comforts, perhaps a four-poster bed and a jacuzzi bathroom. There is no lounge or dining room, and breakfast is served to the bedroom in fine Minton china.

18 en suite (bth/shr) (2 fmly) No smoking in 7 bedrooms CTV in all bedrooms Tea and coffee making facilities Direct dial from bedrooms Cen ht 10P

PRICE GUIDE
ROOMS: s £51-£61; d £55-£84✱
CARDS: 🅰 ▬ ▬ 🅾 💷

Selected

GH Ⓠ Ⓠ Ⓠ Ⓠ **Minster Lodge Hotel** 3 Church Ln
LN2 1QJ ☎01522 513220 FAX 01522 513220

Minster Lodge is a pleasant red brick house with a colourful garden frontage situated within 500yds of the historic Newport Arch and a short walk from the cathedral. The house is beautifully kept and provides light, fresh accommodation in well equipped rooms with double glazing and modern bathrooms. Guests have sole use of a comfortable lounge, with a chesterfield suite, writing desk and small corner bar. A good choice is offered at breakfast, which is served in the bright dining room.

6 en suite (bth/shr) (2 fmly) No smoking in dining room CTV in all bedrooms Tea and coffee making facilities Direct dial from bedrooms Licensed Cen ht CTV 6P No coaches

PRICE GUIDE
ROOMS: s £39-£45; d £50-£55✱
CARDS: 🅰 ▬

GH Ⓠ Ⓠ Ⓠ **Tennyson Hotel** 7 South Park LN5 8EN (S of city centre on A15, nr South Park Common)
☎01522 521624 FAX 01522 521624

An immaculately maintained house with friendly owners, the Tennyson is situated on the southern inner ring road. The bedrooms, which vary in size, are fresh and light in appearance, and comfortable armchairs are provided where space permits. A good choice of dishes is available at dinner; light refreshments are served in the small lounge area during the day.

8 en suite (bth/shr) (1 fmly) No smoking in dining room CTV in all bedrooms Tea and coffee making facilities Direct dial from

bedrooms No dogs Licensed Cen ht 8P No coaches Last d 7.45pm

PRICE GUIDE
ROOMS: s £24-£26; d £36-£38
CARDS: 🅰 ▬ ▬ 🅾

LISKEARD Cornwall & Isles of Scilly Map **02** SX26

GH Ⓠ Ⓠ Ⓠ **Elnor** 1 Russell St PL14 4BP (between town centre & railway station)
☎01579 342472 FAX 01579 345673
Closed Xmas

This neat guesthouse has recently been extended to provide an additional three en suite bedrooms. Public areas are cosy and simply styled and a good home-cooked breakfast is served, but now there are more restaurants in the town an evening meal is only available on request. The small rear car park is an added bonus here.

9 rms (7 shr) (1 fmly) No smoking in dining room CTV in 7 bedrooms Tea and coffee making facilities Direct dial from bedrooms No dogs Licensed Cen ht CTV 6P No coaches Last d 5pm

PRICE GUIDE
ROOMS: s £16.50-£19.50; d £33-£39; wkly b&b £105-£126; wkly hlf-bd £175-£196

Selected

❤ Ⓠ Ⓠ Ⓠ Ⓠ Mrs S Rowe **Tregondale** (SX294643)
Menheniot PL14 3RG (E of Liskeard 1.5m N of A38)
☎01579 342407 FAX 01579 342407

This attractive farmhouse forms part of a 200-acre farm whose interests include pedigree South Devon cattle and long wool sheep. The house has been sympathetically modernised to retain its original character and friendly atmosphere. Bedrooms are tastefully decorated and furnished with co-ordinating colour schemes, a comfortable lounge is available and traditional farmhouse fare is served around a communal table in the dining room.

3 en suite (bth/shr) (1 fmly) CTV in all bedrooms Tea and coffee making facilities No dogs CTV 3P Tennis (hard) 180 acres arable beef mixed sheep Last d 6pm

PRICE GUIDE
ROOMS: s £20; d £35-£38; wkly b&b £122.50-£125; wkly hlf-bd £182-£189✱

LITTLEBOURNE Kent Map **05** TR25

◀ Ⓠ Ⓠ Ⓠ *King William IV* 4 High St CT3 1ST (turn off M2 at the Howletts Zoo junct, proceed to Littlebourne, when you join A257 establishment is directly opposite)
☎01227 721244 FAX 01227 721244

Lying in the centre of the village, this is a country inn of some character. A good local clientele enjoys simple wholesome cooking, lunch and dinner being served seven days a week and the blackboard menu changing daily. A sample meal consisted of flavoursome home-smoked salmon with scrambled egg, a braised rabbit with leeks and ale, and a well-prepared caramel and almond pudding with sauce anglaise. A short wine list features inexpensive wines and service is friendly.

4 en suite (bth/shr) (1 fmly) CTV in all bedrooms Tea and coffee making facilities No dogs (ex guide dogs) Cen ht No children 10yrs 20P No coaches Traditional pub games Last d 9.20pm
CARDS: 🅰 ▬

LITTLE CHEVERELL Wiltshire Map 03 ST95

Premier Selected

GH Q Q Q Q Q **Little Cheverell House** Little Cheverell SN10 4JJ
☎01380 813322
FAX 01380 813322

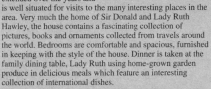

A splendid stone-built Georgian rectory enjoys a beautiful tranquil setting in this pretty village. Standing in well tended gardens, it has been sympathetically extended over the years and is well situated for visits to the many interesting places in the area. Very much the home of Sir Donald and Lady Ruth Hawley, the house contains a fascinating collection of pictures, books and ornaments collected from travels around the world. Bedrooms are comfortable and spacious, furnished in keeping with the style of the house. Dinner is taken at the family dining table, Lady Ruth using home-grown garden produce in delicious meals which feature an interesting collection of international dishes.

2 en suite (bth/shr) No smoking Tea and coffee making facilities No dogs (ex guide dogs) Cen ht CTV No children 12yrs P No coaches Tennis (hard) Last d 9am

LITTLE DEWCHURCH Hereford & Worcester Map 03 SO53

♥ Q Q Mrs G Lee **Cwm Craig** *(SO535322)* HR2 6PS
☎01432 840250

This attractive Georgian farmhouse is run with pride by Mrs Lee. Although it is close to the village centre, it is advisable to ask for directions. The spacious bedrooms are furnished with some interesting antique pieces, and there are several very comfortable sitting areas, as well as a snooker room. Any children who are staying here between December and Easter will enjoy seeing the young calves hand-fed.

3 rms (1 shr) (1 fmly) No smoking in dining room CTV in 1 bedroom Tea and coffee making facilities No dogs (ex guide dogs) Cen ht CTV 5P Snooker/pool table Darts 190 acres arable beef

PRICE GUIDE

ROOMS: s £16; d £30-£34; wkly b&b £98-£105✳

LITTLE GRANSDEN Cambridgeshire Map 04 TL25

♥ Q Q Q Mrs M Cox **Gransden Lodge** *(TL288537)*
Longstowe Rd SG19 3EB (2m off A1198)
☎01767 677365 FAX 01767 677647

Gransden Lodge is a proudly kept farmhouse on the B1046 between Little Gransden and Longstowe. Animal lovers will be interested to know that the owners have two bulldog mastiffs and there are some pedigree Gelbwieh cattle on the predominantly arable holding. Smoking is not permitted in the house.

3 en suite (bth/shr) No smoking CTV in all bedrooms Tea and coffee making facilities No dogs Cen ht CTV 6P 860 acres arable beef mixed

PRICE GUIDE

ROOMS: s £18-£20; wkly b&b fr £110✳

LITTLE PETHERICK Cornwall & Isles of Scilly
Map **02** SW97

GH 🇶🇶🇶 **The Old Mill Country House** PL27 7QT (off A30
onto A389) ☎01841 540388
Mar-Oct rs Nov-Etr
A listed 16th-century converted corn mill, this hotel in its own
carefully tended gardens enjoys a village setting, by a stream.
There is a choice of lounges where drinks are available, and dinner
is served at separate tables in the Mill Room.
6 rms (1 bth 4 shr) No smoking in 1 bedrooms No smoking in
dining room No smoking in 1 lounge Tea and coffee making
facilities No dogs (ex guide dogs) Licensed Cen ht CTV No
children 14yrs 10P No coaches Sun terrace Last d 6pm
PRICE GUIDE
ROOMS: d £42-£56
CARDS: (£)

LIVERPOOL Merseyside Map **07** SJ39

GH 🇶🇶🇶 **Aachen Hotel** 91 Mount Pleasant L3 5TB
☎0151 709 3477 & 1126 FAX 0151 709 1126 & 3633
Closed 22 Dec-2 Jan
A friendly, popular, family-run establishment, this attractive little
hotel near the city centre provides small but prettily decorated and
very well equipped bedrooms, many of which have en suite
facilities. It also offers a cosy lounge bar and a neat breakfast
room. Lime Street Station, the Roman Catholic cathedral and the
main shopping areas are within easy walking distance.
17 rms (11 bth/shr) (6 fmly) No smoking in 10 bedrooms No
smoking in dining room CTV in all bedrooms Tea and coffee
making facilities Direct dial from bedrooms No dogs (ex guide
dogs) Licensed Cen ht CTV 2P Snooker Last d 8.30pm
PRICE GUIDE
ROOMS: s £22-£30; d £34-£44; wkly b&b £154-£210; wkly hlf-
bd £194.25-£250.25✱
CARDS: (£)

GH 🇶🇶🇶 **The Blenheim** 37 Aigburth Dr, Sefton Park
L17 4JE ☎0151 727 7380
A restored Victorian villa, this guest house overlooks the lake at
Sefton Park and is only ten minutes' drive from the airport and
city centre. The accommodation is modern and bright, a variety of
rooms ranging from singles to family suites. Public rooms
comprise a comfortable lounge bar and a breakfast room. Ample
parking is provided in the grounds.
17 rms (3 shr) (4 fmly) No smoking in dining room CTV in all
bedrooms Tea and coffee making facilities No dogs Cen ht CTV
22P Last d 7pm
CARDS:

Prices quoted in the Guide are based on
information supplied by the establishments
themselves.

LIZARD Cornwall & Isles of Scilly Map **02** SW71

GH 🇶🇶🇶🇶🇶
**Landewednack
House**
Church Cove TR12 7PQ (left
off A3083 at Lizard Village
signed Church Cove then in
.25m fork left)
☎01326 290909
FAX 01326 290192
Peter and Marion Stanley
welcome non-smoking guests
to their beautiful 17th-
century rectory, which stands in a walled garden overlooking
the sea between Black Head and the Lizard Point. The
bedrooms are individually furnished with great style; one
features an antique four-poster bed and the other overlooks
the garden, the church tower and the sea beyond. There is a
cosy sitting room with a log fire, and a house party
atmosphere is encouraged, with guests dining together at one
large table (though any who prefer can eat alone). Dinner is
provided by prior arrangement only, and Marion is an
imaginative cook; breakfast is a feast not to be missed.
3 en suite (bth/shr) No smoking CTV in all bedrooms Tea
and coffee making facilities Direct dial from bedrooms No
dogs Licensed Cen ht No children 12yrs 4P No coaches
Boules Croquet lawn Last d 8pm
PRICE GUIDE
ROOMS: d £56-£72; wkly hlf-bd £176.40-£226.80✱

GH 🇶🇶🇶 **Penmenner House Hotel** Penmenner Rd
TR12 7NR ☎01326 290370
Located in its own grounds, with spectacular views of the
lighthouse and magnificent coastal scenery, this small hotel is run
by Muriel and Ray Timporley in friendly relaxed style. Bedrooms
on the first floor are all well equipped, and there is a comfortable
lounge with a small bar. Evening meals are available by prior
arrangement, served in the elegant dining room.
8 rms (5 shr) No smoking CTV in all bedrooms Tea and coffee
making facilities No dogs (ex guide dogs) Licensed Cen ht
CTV No children 3yrs 10P No coaches Table tennis Pool table
Last d 5pm
PRICE GUIDE
ROOMS: s £23-£25; d £40-£44; wkly b&b £127-£163✱
CARDS: (£)

LONDON Greater London

Places within the London postal area are listed below in postal
district order commencing East then North, South and West, with
a brief indication of the area covered. Other places within the
county of London are listed under their respective placenames.

E7 FOREST GATE

GH 🇶🇶🇶 **Forest View Hotel** 227 Romford Rd, Forest Gate
E7 9HL (from A406 turn left onto A118 for approx 2m hotel is
on right) ☎0181 534 4844 FAX 0181 534 8959
Conveniently located on the A118 between Ilford and Forest Gate
this popular family run residentially licensed and well equipped
hotel has a range of modern bedrooms including some furnished
for families and several annexe rooms to the rear. There is a
spacious bar and small non-smoking dining room serving a la
carte dinner including vegetarian dishes daily from 6.30pm to

8.45pm. Light refreshment service is also available along with business services, reception office and night porter service. Good car parking is provided.

20 rms (7 shr) (3 fmly) No smoking in dining room CTV in all bedrooms Tea and coffee making facilities Direct dial from bedrooms No dogs (ex guide dogs) Licensed Cen ht CTV No children 2yrs 15P Last d 8.45pm

PRICE GUIDE

ROOMS: s £32.90; d £47-£56.40; wkly b&b £230.30; wkly hlf-bd £275.10-£289.80✱

CARDS: 🔲 🔲

E11 LEYTONSTONE

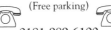

across the main road. Many original 1930s features have been retained, including a white-panelled hall, continental stained glass and high ceilings. Bedrooms are of a good size and attractively furnished in modern style; a freshly cooked breakfast is available, and resident proprietors personally provide service which is both enthusiastic and convivial. Other facilities include free car parking and garage. Smoking is not permitted anywhere within the house.

3 en suite (bth/shr) No smoking CTV in all bedrooms Tea and coffee making facilities No dogs Cen ht No children 12yrs 4P No coaches
PRICE GUIDE
ROOMS: d £39.50✶

E18 SOUTH WOODFORD

GH QQQ **Grove Hill Hotel** 38 Grove Hill, South Woodford E18 2JG (off A11 London Rd, close to South Woodford tube station) ☎0181 989 3344 & 530 5286 FAX 0181 530 5286
A small private, hotel in a residential area. The accommodation is modest in style with clean and nicely maintained bedrooms. A choice of English or Continental breakfast is available.
21 rms (10 bth 2 shr) (2 fmly) No smoking in dining room CTV in all bedrooms Tea and coffee making facilities Direct dial from bedrooms Licensed Cen ht CTV 12P Last d 9pm
PRICE GUIDE
ROOMS: s £23.50-£35.25; d £41.71-£49.35; wkly b&b £164.50-£246.75
CARDS: 🔲 🔲 🔲

N4 FINSBURY PARK

Selected

GH QQQQ **Mount View** 31 Mount View Rd N4 4SS ☎0181 340 9222 FAX 0181 342 8494
An attractive and tastefully appointed Victorian house, Mount View is situated in a quiet residential area, close to Finsbury Park underground station. The bedrooms are spacious and thoughtfully furnished, with extra welcoming touches. Breakfast is served in the open-plan dining room at a communal table, and the choice of dishes including a healthy option. A patio garden is also available to guests.
3 rms (2 bth/shr) No smoking CTV in all bedrooms Tea and coffee making facilities No dogs Cen ht No parking No coaches
PRICE GUIDE
ROOMS: s fr £23; d £42-£50✶

N8 HORNSEY

GH QQ **Aber Hotel** 89 Crouch Hill N8 9EG ☎0181 340 2847 FAX 0181 340 2847
The accommodation at this small guest house is basic but well maintained and comfortable. The bedrooms vary in size and are suitably equipped. There are a small lounge and dining room, and a choice is offered at breakfast.
9 rms (4 fmly) No smoking in 2 bedrooms No smoking in dining room No dogs Cen ht CTV No parking No coaches
PRICE GUIDE
ROOMS: s £20-£26; d £34-£38; wkly b&b £120-£140
CARDS: 🔲 🔲 🔲

GH QQQ *White Lodge Hotel* 1 Church Ln, Hornsey N8 7BU ☎0181 348 9765 FAX 0181 340 7851
There is a warm, friendly atmosphere at this comfortable bed and

breakfast establishment. Bedrooms come in a variety of sizes and some have en suite facilities. Breakfast is served in a small ground-floor dining room.
16 rms (8 shr) (5 fmly) CTV in all bedrooms Tea and coffee making facilities No dogs (ex guide dogs) Cen ht CTV No parking No coaches Last d at breakfast
CARDS: 🔲 🔲

N19 UPPER HOLLOWAY

GH QQQ **Parkland Walk** 12 Hornsey Rise Gardens N19 3PR ☎0171 263 3228 & 0973 382982 FAX 0171 831 9489
A fine Victorian house offers homely accommodation in a quiet residential area. Bedrooms vary in size, but all have fine period furniture. There are two equally comfortable rooms in an annexe house across the road.
4 rms (2 bth/shr) 2 annexe en suite (bth/shr) (1 fmly) No smoking CTV in all bedrooms Tea and coffee making facilities No dogs (ex guide dogs) Cen ht CTV No parking
PRICE GUIDE
ROOMS: s £23-£32; d £42-£55✶
CARDS: 🔲

NW1 REGENT'S PARK

GH QQQ *Four Seasons Hotel* 173 Gloucester Place, Regents Park NW1 6DX ☎0171 724 3461 & 0171 723 9471 FAX 0171 402 5594
Situated within easy reach of Madam Tussaud's and the Sherlock Holmes Museum, this small, family-run bed and breakfast establishment offers comfortable accommodation with a warm atmosphere. The bedrooms are bright and pleasantly furnished, and a continental-style breakfast is served in the conservatory. English breakfast is available on request.
16 rms (14 bth/shr) (2 fmly) CTV in all bedrooms No dogs Cen ht
CARDS: 🔲 🔲 🔲 🔲

NW2 CRICKLEWOOD

GH Q **Clearview House** 161 Fordwych Rd NW2 3NG ☎0181 452 9773
In a quiet residential area, this small guest house provides well maintained accommodation. The bedrooms are neatly furnished and equipped, and there is a good size dining/lounge on the ground floor.
6 rms (1 fmly) No smoking CTV in 2 bedrooms No dogs (ex guide dogs) Cen ht CTV No children 5yrs No parking No coaches
PRICE GUIDE
ROOMS: s £20; d £35; wkly b&b £86✶

GH QQQ *The Garth Hotel* 64-76 Hendon Way NW2 2NL ☎0181 455 4742
Comfortable and well appointed, this privately owned hotel is situated on the southbound carriageway of the A41 Hendon Way. Extensively redeveloped, it offers a wide range of accommodation. Bedrooms are spacious, well equipped and furnished in bright modern style. The impressive marble foyer leads to the attractive Tivoli Restaurant and bar, which specialises in Italian cuisine. Extensive conference and banqueting facilities are available and the hotel is located 5 minutes' drive from the M1.
53 rms (30 bth 10 shr) (9 fmly) CTV in all bedrooms Tea and coffee making facilities Licensed Cen ht CTV 58P Last d 11pm
CARDS: 🔲 🔲 🔲 🔲

NW3 HAMPSTEAD

GH 🅀🅀 **La Gaffe** 107-111 Heath St NW3 6SS (located at the top end of Heath St 200yds from Hampstead Underground) ☎0171 435 4941 & 435 8965 FAX 0171 794 7592
Originally built around 1734 as a shepherd's cottage, this Italian wine bar and restaurant is very popular with the locals. A range of non-smoking bedrooms is available, some of them located above the wine bar and others in two separate annexes upstairs and to the rear. Continental breakfast is included in the room tariff. Arrival by taxi is recommended, as parking is limited.
18 annexe en suite (shr) No smoking in bedrooms CTV in all bedrooms No dogs (ex guide dogs) Licensed Cen ht No parking Last d 11.30pm
PRICE GUIDE
ROOMS: s £45; d £70-£72✱
CARDS: 🅰 ▬ ▬ ⓞ
See advertisement on p.249.

Selected

GH 🅀🅀🅀🅀 **The Langorf Hotel** 20 Frognal, Hampstead NW3 6AG ☎0171 794 4483 FAX 0171 435 9055
An attractive terraced house in a quiet residential area offering accommodation of a high standard. The well equipped bedrooms are thoughtfully furnished and feature attractive soft furnishings. The breakfast room also has a small bar, and light meals and snacks are available 24 hours a day. Lounge facilities are limited to a small but comfortable foyer/lounge. Guests can choose from either English or continental breakfast.
31 en suite (bth/shr) (2 fmly) CTV in all bedrooms Tea and ➡

ABER HOTEL

A quiet family run hotel with a warm and friendly atmosphere. Situated in a pleasant residential area of North London and within easy access of the city centre by public transport. Also, we are on a direct route via the Piccadilly line Underground from Heathrow Airport to Finsbury Park. All rooms are centrally heated. There is a lounge for guests with CTV. Included in our realistic prices is a full English breakfast. Unrestricted parking outside hotel. Many excellent restaurants within walking distance.

89, Crouch Hill, Hornsey, London N8 9EG.
Telephone/Fax. No: 0181-340-2847

coffee making facilities Direct dial from bedrooms No dogs
Licensed Lift Cen ht CTV No parking
PRICE GUIDE
ROOMS: s £55-£66; d £80-£90; wkly b&b £360✷
CARDS: ▨ ▤ ▨ ◑ ▨

Premier Selected

GH ⓆⓆⓆⓆⓆ
Sandringham Hotel 3
Holford Rd, Hampstead
NW3 1AD ☎0171 435 1569
FAX 0171 431 5932

A delightful period house in
a very elegant village
neighbourhood, within
walking distance of the
underground station and all
the local attractions. The
accommodation which is still
being upgraded is furnished with antiques, enhancing the
English country house atmosphere. Personally run by the
resident proprietors Michael and Jill von Grey, the hotel's
reputation lies in the personal attention to customer care.
Bedrooms are non smoking and individually furnished with
thoughtful little extras. There is a formal sitting room and an
attractive, well appointed breakfast room, where traditional
cooked breakfast usually includes fresh baked muffins, choice
of teas and coffees, and fresh fruit. Service of light
refreshments is available throughout the day, and local
restaurants can be recommended.
17 rms (15 bth/shr) (2 fmly) No smoking in bedrooms No
smoking in area of dining room CTV in all bedrooms Direct
dial from bedrooms No dogs Licensed Cen ht No children
6yrs 5P No coaches
PRICE GUIDE
ROOMS: s £60-£75; d £82-£95
CARDS: ▨ ▨

NW4 HENDON

GH ⓆⓆⓆ **Peacehaven Hotel** 94 Audley Rd, Hendon Central
NW4 3HB (turn off A41 at Hendon Central, turn right into
Vivian Avenue then 5th left into Audley Road)
☎0181 202 9758 & 0181 202 1225 FAX 0181 202 9758
Improvements have been made at this friendly little guest house,
including new carpets and beds. The bedrooms are comfortable
and well furnished, and a choice of breakfasts is served in the
bright breakfast room.
13 rms (7 bth/shr) CTV in all bedrooms Tea and coffee making
facilities No dogs (ex guide dogs) Cen ht 2P
PRICE GUIDE
ROOMS: s £38-£48; d £50-£66✷
CARDS: ▨ ▨ ◑

NW11 GOLDERS GREEN

GH ⓆⓆⓆ **Anchor Hotel** 10 West Heath Dr, Golders Green
NW11 7QH ☎0181 458 8764 FAX 0181 455 3204
A charming guesthouse offering a friendly atmosphere and
comfortable, well appointed accommodation. Bedrooms do vary
in size, but they are tastefully decorated with modern furniture and
attractive soft furnishings. There is a choice of a Danish-style
buffet or cooked English breakfast in the small dining room.
12 rms (9 shr) (2 fmly) No smoking in area of dining room CTV
in all bedrooms Tea and coffee making facilities Direct dial from

bedrooms No dogs (ex guide dogs) Cen ht CTV 9P No coaches
PRICE GUIDE
ROOMS: s £29-£33; d £40-£49✷
CARDS: ▨ ▨

GH ⓆⓆ **Central Hotel** 35 Hoop Ln, Golders Green
NW11 8BS ☎0181 458 5636 FAX 0181 455 4792
Accommodation at this privately run hotel is split between two
adjacent houses and continues to improve. Main house bedrooms
have more modern furnishings, but all rooms are adequately
furnished and well equipped. A choice of breakfasts is available
each morning.
13 en suite (bth/shr) 13 annexe en suite (bth/shr) CTV in all
bedrooms Direct dial from bedrooms No dogs Cen ht 8P
PRICE GUIDE
ROOMS: s £30-£40; d £50-£60✷
CARDS: ▨ ▨ ▨ ◑

SE9 ELTHAM

GH ⓆⓆⓆ *Yardley Court Private Hotel* 18 Court Rd SE9 5PZ
☎0181 850 1850
Situated in the centre of Eltham, this privately owned bed and
breakfast hotel offers comfortable accommodation at a reasonable
price. The bedrooms are adequately equipped and furnished, and a
choice of breakfast is served in the attractive conservatory area
which overlooks the garden.
9 rms (8 shr) (1 fmly) CTV in all bedrooms Tea and coffee
making facilities No dogs (ex guide dogs) Cen ht 8P No
coaches
CARDS: ▨ ▨

SE10 GREENWICH

◀ ⓆⓆ **The Pilot Inn** 68 Riverway, Greenwich SE10 0BE
(follow signs for Greenwich Yacht Club)
☎0181 858 5910 FAX 0181 293 0371
This popular inn stands close to the river. It offers modern annexe
bedrooms which are well equipped with colour TV and tea/coffee
making facilities. Wholesome British fare is served in a separate
dining area.
7 rms (1 fmly) CTV in all bedrooms No dogs Cen ht Last d
8.45pm
PRICE GUIDE
ROOMS: s £30; d £45✷
MEALS: Lunch £2.50-£5.50 Dinner £5-£10.95✷
CARDS: ▨ ▨ ▨

SE19 NORWOOD

GH ⓆⓆ **Crystal Palace Tower Hotel** 114 Church Rd, Crystal
Palace SE19 2UB ☎0181 653 0176
A small privately owned and run guesthouse offering suitably
furnished and equipped bedrooms of a good size which are well
maintained. There is a small lounge and a choice of breakfast is
offered at separate tables in the dining room.
10 rms (4 bth 4 shr) (4 fmly) No smoking in dining room CTV
in 7 bedrooms Tea and coffee making facilities Cen ht CTV 10P
No coaches
PRICE GUIDE
ROOMS: s £25-£27; d £36-£39✷
CARDS: ▨ ▨

SE22 EAST DULWICH

GH ⓆⓆⓆ **Bedknobs** 58 Glengarry Rd, East Dulwich
SE22 8QD (opposite Dulwich Hospital) ☎0181 299 2004
This small, terraced, Victorian house offers well appointed
bedrooms, tastefully furnished in keeping with its period.

Generous English or continental breakfast is offered at a large wooden table in the cosy dining room.

3 rms (1 fmly) No smoking CTV in all bedrooms Tea and coffee making facilities No dogs Cen ht No parking No coaches
PRICE GUIDE
ROOMS: s £19.50-£27.50; d £34.50-£45; wkly b&b £135✳

SW1 WESTMINSTER

GH QQ Annanadale House Hotel 39 Sloane Square, Sloane Square SW1W 8EB ☎0171 730 5051 FAX 0171 730 4778
A fine terraced house close to Sloane Square, with a warm and friendly atmosphere. Bedrooms vary in size, and all are pleasantly furnished and well equipped. A vegetarian breakfast is available in the dining room.
13 rms (9 bth/shr) (2 fmly) No smoking in lounges CTV in all bedrooms Tea and coffee making facilities Direct dial from bedrooms Cen ht No parking
PRICE GUIDE
ROOMS: s £38-£70; d £70-£85
CARDS: 🟥 ⚌ 🟦 💳

GH QQQ The Executive Hotel 57 Pont St, Knightsbridge SW1X 0BD ☎0171 581 2424 FAX 0171 589 9456
This fine Victorian house near Harrods is being refurbished to provide modern accommodation. Bedrooms are thoughtfully furnished and well equipped, and a good choice of buffet breakfast is served in the dining room.
27 en suite (bth/shr) (3 fmly) No smoking in dining room CTV in all bedrooms Tea and coffee making facilities Direct dial from bedrooms No dogs (ex guide dogs) Licensed Lift Cen ht No parking No coaches
PRICE GUIDE
ROOMS: s £55-£70; d £75-£99✳
CARDS: 🟥 ⚌ ⚌ 💿 💳

GH QQQ *Melbourne House Hotel* 79 Belgrave Rd, Victoria SW1V 2BG ☎0171 828 3516 FAX 0171 828 7120
Melbourne House, a family-run bed and breakfast establishment, is conveniently situated for Victoria coach and rail stations and has recently been refurbished throughout in a modern style. Comfortably furnished, well equipped bedrooms vary in size and include a few family rooms, and breakfast is served in a bright dining room.
15 rms (13 bth/shr) (2 fmly) No smoking in 8 bedrooms No smoking in dining room No smoking in lounges CTV in all bedrooms Tea and coffee making facilities Direct dial from bedrooms No dogs Cen ht CTV P
CARDS: 🟥 ⚌ 💳

GH QQ *Willett Hotel* 32 Sloane Gardens, Sloane Square SW1W 8DJ ☎0171 824 8415 Telex no 926678 FAX 0171 730 4830
This elegant London town house is situated in a quiet, tree-lined street leading off Sloane Square and offers a range of comfortable, attractively furnished bedrooms, mostly with en suite facilities. Guests have a wide choice of dishes from the buffet-style breakfast served in the brightly decorated dining room.
18 rms (15 bth/shr) (6 fmly) CTV in all bedrooms Tea and coffee making facilities Direct dial from bedrooms No dogs Cen ht
CARDS: 🟥 ⚌ ⚌ 💿

GH QQQ Winchester Hotel 17 Belgrave Rd SW1V 1RB ☎0171 828 2972 Telex no 269674 FAX 0171 828 5191
The standard of accommodation remains high at this friendly hotel, and the owner, Mr McGoldrick takes great pride in the quality of his English breakfasts. The good-sized bedrooms are well appointed and suitably equipped with modern facilities. ➡

18 en suite (bth/shr) (2 fmly) No smoking in lounges CTV in all bedrooms No dogs Cen ht No children 10yrs No parking No coaches
PRICE GUIDE
ROOMS: d £60✱

Selected

GH ⓆⓆⓆⓆ **Windermere Hotel** 142/144 Warwick Way, Victoria SW1V 4JE ☎0171 834 5163 & 834 5480
FAX 0171 630 8831
With continued improvements, this small private hotel offers accommodation of the highest standard. The comfortable bedrooms are brightly decorated, well equipped and furnished in modern style. A small, tastefully furnished lounge is provided, and there is an attractive dining room, where a short dinner carte and a choice of English or continental breakfasts are available.
23 rms (19 bth/shr) (7 fmly) No smoking in dining room No smoking in lounges CTV in all bedrooms Tea and coffee making facilities Direct dial from bedrooms No dogs (ex guide dogs) Licensed Cen ht CTV No parking Last d 9.30pm
PRICE GUIDE
ROOMS: s £34-£55; d £48-£82✱
CARDS: 🄰 💳 🄽 💳 💷

SW3 CHELSEA

Selected

GH ⓆⓆⓆⓆ **Claverley House** 13-14 Beaufort Gardens, Knightsbridge SW3 1PS
☎0171 589 8541 FAX 0171 584 3410
This attractive Edwardian house is quietly situated within easy reach of Hyde Park, the West End and the main shops in Knightsbridge. Comfortably and elegantly appointed throughout, it offers bedrooms which are all stylishly furnished and decorated though they vary in size. A lounge/reading room furnished with chesterfields is well stocked with books and magazines, and a choice of good English breakfast dishes is provided in the spacious, gaily decorated dining room.
32 rms (29 bth/shr) (5 fmly) No smoking in 20 bedrooms No smoking in dining room CTV in all bedrooms Direct dial from bedrooms No dogs (ex guide dogs) Lift Cen ht No parking No coaches
PRICE GUIDE
ROOMS: s £65-£110; d £95-£195✱
CARDS: 🄰 💳 💳 🔘

SW5 EARLS COURT

Selected

GH ⓆⓆⓆⓆ **Henley House Hotel** 30 Barkston Gardens, Earls Court SW5 0EN
☎0171 370 4111 FAX 0171 370 0026
The programme of upgrading at this hotel is now complete. The decor is very colourful throughout, particularly in the bedrooms - these being of a reasonable size, comfortably furnished and well equipped with modern facilities; framed prints, together with dried and artificial flowers, add to the colour. There are a small reception lounge with a number of

books and magazines and a well appointed breakfast room where a buffet breakfast is served.
20 en suite (shr) (2 fmly) No smoking in dining room CTV in all bedrooms Tea and coffee making facilities Direct dial from bedrooms No dogs (ex guide dogs) Cen ht No parking Last d 6.45pm
PRICE GUIDE
ROOMS: s £49-£58; d £73-£84✱
CARDS: 🄰 💳 🄽 🔘 💳 💳 £

GH ⓆⓆ **Swiss House Hotel** 171 Old Brompton Rd, South Kensington SW5 0AN ☎0171 373 2769 & 373 9383
FAX 0171 373 4983
The comfortable, well equipped bedrooms offered by this small bed and breakfast hotel now all have en suite facilities. A choice is offered at breakfast and snacks can be obtained from midday.
16 rms (14 bth/shr) (7 fmly) No smoking in 4 bedrooms No smoking in dining room CTV in all bedrooms Direct dial from bedrooms Cen ht CTV No parking No coaches Last d 9.30pm
PRICE GUIDE
ROOMS: s £36-£52.50; d £67.50✱
CARDS: 🄰 💳 🄽 🔘 💷 £

SW7 SOUTH KENSINGTON

Selected

GH ⓆⓆⓆⓆ **Five Sumner Place Hotel** 5 Sumner Place, South Kensington SW7 3EE (300yds from South Kensington underground station)
☎0171 584 7586 FAX 0171 823 9962
Mr and Mrs Palgan's Victorian terraced house offers attractively decorated bedrooms with quality furniture and a good range of equipment (including hairdryers and a combined unit with a trouser press, iron and board); complimentary mineral water is a nice touch. A choice of English or continental breakfast is served in the colourful conservatory.
13 en suite (bth/shr) (4 fmly) No smoking in 6 bedrooms No smoking in dining room No smoking in lounges CTV in all bedrooms Direct dial from bedrooms No dogs Lift Cen ht CTV No parking No coaches
PRICE GUIDE
ROOMS: s £69-£82; d £99-£116
CARDS: 🄰 💳 💳 £

Selected

GH ⓆⓆⓆⓆ *Kensington Manor Hotel* 8 Emperors Gate SW7 4HH ☎0171 370 7516 FAX 0171 373 3163
This small family-run hotel stands on the west side of the city. Bedrooms vary in size, but all are well furnished and adequately equipped. A choice of English and continental breakfast is served in the attractive dining room.
14 rms (13 bth/shr) (4 fmly) CTV in all bedrooms Tea and coffee making facilities No dogs (ex guide dogs) Licensed Cen ht No parking No coaches
CARDS: 🄰 💳 💳 🔘

SW19 WIMBLEDON

GH Q Q Q **Kings Lodge Hotel** 5 Kings Rd SW19 8PL
☎0181 545 0191 FAX 0181 545 0381
Kings Lodge is a well appointed small hotel situated in a quiet
residential area. The bedrooms vary in size and are furnished in a
modern style. A comfortable lounge is available for guests' use
and breakfast is served in the bright dining room. Dinner can be
provided on request.
7 en suite (bth/shr) (4 fmly) CTV in all bedrooms Tea and coffee
making facilities Direct dial from bedrooms No dogs (ex guide
dogs) Cen ht CTV 6P No coaches Last d 8pm
PRICE GUIDE
ROOMS: s £45-£65; d £59-£79
CARDS: £

GH Q Q **Trochee Hotel** 21 Malcolm Rd SW19 4AS
☎0181 946 1579 & 3924 FAX 0181 785 4058
Comfortable accommodation is offered by this well maintained
hotel, which is situated in a quiet residential area. A lounge/dining
room is also provided on the ground floor.
17 rms (2 fmly) CTV in all bedrooms Tea and coffee making
facilities No dogs (ex guide dogs) Cen ht CTV 3P
PRICE GUIDE
ROOMS: s £34-£37; d £48-£51
CARDS: £

GH Q Q **Wimbledon Hotel** 78 Worple Rd SW19 4HZ
☎0181 946 9265 & 946 1581 FAX 0181 946 9265
The Wimbledon Hotel is a friendly bed and breakfast
establishment close to the town centre. The bedrooms are
modestly but suitably furnished and equipped with modern
facilities. There are a comfortable small lounge and a no-smoking
breakfast room where full English breakfast is served.
14 rms (11 bth/shr) (6 fmly) No smoking in bedrooms No
smoking in dining room CTV in all bedrooms Tea and coffee
making facilities Direct dial from bedrooms No dogs Cen ht
CTV 10P
CARDS: £

GH Q Q Q **Worcester House** 38 Alwyne Rd SW19 7AE
☎0181 946 1300 FAX 0181 785 4058
Standing in a quiet residential area close to the town centre,
Worcester House offers a comfortable standard of accommodation
in well equipped and adequately furnished bedrooms. A choice of
breakfasts is available.
9 en suite (shr) (1 fmly) CTV in all bedrooms Tea and coffee
making facilities Direct dial from bedrooms No dogs (ex guide
dogs) Cen ht CTV P
PRICE GUIDE
ROOMS: s £45.50-£49.50; d £59.50-£62.50
CARDS: £

W1 WEST END

GH Q Q Q **Blandford Hotel** 80 Chiltern St W1M 1PS
☎0171 486 3103 FAX 0171 487 2786
Conveniently located for Baker Street tube station, this large bed
and breakfast hotel offers basic but adequate accommodation.
Bedroom vary in size but are suitably equipped and attractively
appointed. There is a small bar/lounge, and a choice of English or
continental breakfast is served in the pleasant dining room.
33 en suite (bth/shr) (3 fmly) No smoking in dining room No
smoking in 1 lounge CTV in all bedrooms Tea and coffee making
facilities Direct dial from bedrooms No dogs (ex guide dogs)
Licensed Lift Cen ht CTV No parking
CARDS:

GH Q Q Q Q **Bryanston Court** 60 Great Cumberland
Place W1 (BW) ☎0171 262 3141 Telex no 262076
FAX 0171 262 7248
This remarkably quiet, three-storey hotel is conveniently
located for Oxford Street and just a few minutes' walk from
Marble Arch. The smartly decorated public areas include a
'clubby' bar and a breakfast room where a full continental
spread is served with the additional option of cooked items.
No other meals are available. Bedroom decor is similar
throughout, but rooms vary in shape, having been built within
the existing walls; all have en suite facilities but some are a
little tight for space.
54 en suite (bth/shr) (3 fmly) CTV in all bedrooms Tea and
coffee making facilities Direct dial from bedrooms No dogs
Licensed Lift Cen ht No parking No coaches Last d 10pm
PRICE GUIDE
ROOMS: s £73-£85; d £85-£95✶
CARDS:

GH Q Q Q **Hotel Concorde** 50 Great Cumberland Place
W1H 7FD ☎0171 402 6169 Telex no 262076
FAX 0181 724 1184
Closed 24 Dec-4 Jan
Adjoining the Bryanston Court hotel which the Theodore family
also own this well managed hotel has been recently renovated.
Bedrooms are all furnished to the same standard, with good
quality modern showers, direct-dial telephones, radios, TV, hair
dryers and tea making facilities. There is a lift to all levels, a club-
style foyer sitting area and a small basement breakfast room; a
supplementary charge is made for full English breakfast. The
Theodore family have managed the hotel for over two family
generations, and it enjoys a loyal international clientele. There is
no car park but parking meters can usually be found nearby and
there is a local NCP car park.
28 en suite (bth/shr) (1 fmly) CTV in all bedrooms Tea and
coffee making facilities Direct dial from bedrooms No dogs (ex
guide dogs) Licensed Lift Cen ht CTV 2P No coaches
PRICE GUIDE
ROOMS: s £65-£75; d £75-£85✶
CARDS:

GH Q **Edward Lear Hotel** 28-30 Seymour St W1
☎0171 402 5401 FAX 0171 706 3766
Close to Oxford Street, this former home of artist and writer
Edward Lear offers bed and breakfast accommodation at prices
that represent good value for the West End. The bedrooms, though
simply furnished, are well equipped and maintained. The dining
room is pleasantly appointed and serves a choice of breakfasts.
Parking is difficult in this area so nearby multi-storeys are the best
solution.
31 rms (3 bth 1 shr) (2 fmly) No smoking in dining room No
smoking in 1 lounge CTV in all bedrooms Tea and coffee making
facilities Direct dial from bedrooms No dogs Cen ht CTV No
parking No coaches
PRICE GUIDE
ROOMS: s £39.50-£47.50; d £55-£67.50✶
CARDS: £

GH Q Q Q **Georgian House Hotel** 87 Gloucester Place,
Baker St W1H 3PG ☎0171 935 2211 & 486 3151
FAX 0171 486 7535
The standard of accommodation remains high at this privately
owned and run hotel, which is situated conveniently close to
Baker Street. The bedrooms are furnished in modern style and are
suitably equipped. Lounge facilities are restricted, but the dining

room is well appointed, and a continental breakfast is served here, or an English breakfast is available on request. There is a lift serving all floors.

19 rms (8 bth 3 shr) (3 fmly) No smoking in dining room CTV in all bedrooms Tea and coffee making facilities Direct dial from bedrooms No dogs Licensed Lift Cen ht No children 5yrs No parking No coaches

PRICE GUIDE
ROOMS: s £55-£60; d £70-£75
CARDS: 💳 ▬ ▬

GH QQQ Hart House Hotel 51 Gloucester Place, Portman Sq W1H 3PE ☎0171 935 2288 FAX 0171 935 8516
This Georgian town house offers well equipped, attractively styled bedrooms and there is a small, pleasant dining room which, with its oak furniture and lace cloths, is reminiscent of an English tearoom. It is situated close to Oxford Street and the West End and has been steadily upgraded by the resident owner, Andrew Bowden.

16 rms (11 bth/shr) (4 fmly) No smoking in dining room No smoking in lounges CTV in all bedrooms Tea and coffee making facilities Direct dial from bedrooms No dogs Cen ht CTV No parking No coaches

PRICE GUIDE
ROOMS: s £43-£55; d £60-£80
CARDS: 💳 ▬ ▬   (£)

GH QQQ London Continental Hotel 88 Gloucester Place W1H 3HN (near Baker Street underground)
☎0171 486 8670 FAX 0171 486 8671
A full programme of refurbishment has been completed at this fine Victorian terraced house which is located within easy reach of Marble Arch and Madam Tussaud's. The bedrooms are small but adequately furnished and well equipped. There is a bright ➡

conservatory breakfast room where a continental buffet breakfast is served (English breakfast being available on request).

25 en suite (shr) (4 fmly) No smoking in dining room CTV in all bedrooms Tea and coffee making facilities Direct dial from bedrooms No dogs (ex guide dogs) Lift Cen ht CTV 2P

PRICE GUIDE
ROOMS: s £45-£55; d £55-£65*
CARDS:

choose English or Continental breakfasts. Standards of housekeeping are commendably high.

42 en suite (bth/shr) (3 fmly) CTV in all bedrooms Tea and coffee making facilities Direct dial from bedrooms No dogs (ex guide dogs) Licensed Lift Cen ht CTV No parking Last d 8pm

PRICE GUIDE
ROOMS: s fr £75.50; d fr £89*
CARDS:

Selected

GH 🇶🇶🇶🇶 **The Regency Hotel** 19 Nottingham Place W1M 3FF ☎0171 486 5347 FAX 0171 224 6057

A redecoration programme is in progress to maintain the high standard now expected of this small friendly hotel located close to Oxford Circus. Bedrooms vary in size but are well furnished and equipped with several extras, including mini bars; a few family rooms are available. A choice of English and continental breakfast is served in the breakfast room, and room service is available between 7.00am and 11.00am, including hot meals and light refreshments. Lounge facilities are limited to some seating in the reception lobby.

20 en suite (bth/shr) (2 fmly) No smoking in 2 bedrooms No smoking in area of dining room No smoking in 1 lounge CTV in all bedrooms Tea and coffee making facilities Direct dial from bedrooms No dogs (ex guide dogs) Licensed Lift Cen ht No parking Last d 9pm

PRICE GUIDE
ROOMS: s £50-£60; d £70-£79; wkly b&b £290-£420; wkly hlf-bd £370-£490
CARDS:

GH 🇶🇶 **Wigmore Court Hotel** 23 Gloucester Place W1H 3PB (MIN) ☎0171 935 0928 FAX 0171 487 4254

Conveniently situated for the West End, this family-run bed and breakfast hotel is being upgraded and improved. Bedrooms are well equipped, with direct dial telephones, radios, TVs and teatrays. There is a small breakfast room and a cosy lounge. Car parking can be very difficult but there is an NCP almost next door.

18 rms (11 bth 5 shr) (4 fmly) CTV in all bedrooms Tea and coffee making facilities Direct dial from bedrooms No dogs (ex guide dogs) Cen ht CTV No parking

PRICE GUIDE
ROOMS: s £30-£50; d £40-£65*
CARDS:

W2 BAYSWATER, PADDINGTON, NOTTING HILL GATE

GH 🇶🇶🇶 **Blakemore Hotel** 30 Leinster Gardens W2 3AN ☎0171 262 4591 Telex no 291634 FAX 0171 724 1472

A popular hotel with a concierge, a bar and a dining room for breakfast and dinner. Bedrooms modestly furnished.

163 en suite (bth/shr) CTV in all bedrooms Tea and coffee making facilities Direct dial from bedrooms Lift Cen ht CTV No parking
CARDS:

Selected

GH 🇶🇶🇶🇶 **Byron Hotel** 36-38 Queensborough Ter W2 3SH (just off the Bayswater Rd close to Queensway) ☎0171 243 0987 FAX 0171 792 1957

Only a few yards from Hyde Park, this elegant Victorian house with five floors and a lift has beautifully designed public areas. Bedrooms, too, are richly furnished and well equipped. In the attractively appointed dining room guests can

---

GH 🇶🇶🇶 **Camelot Hotel** 45-47 Norfolk Square W2 1RX ☎0171 723 9118 & 262 1980 FAX 0171 402 3412

This well appointed and comfortable private hotel stands close to Paddington Station, well situated in a quiet square. Bedrooms are particularly well equipped and a modern automatic lift serves all floors except the sixth. Car parking can be difficult.

44 rms (36 bth/shr) (8 fmly) No smoking in dining room CTV in all bedrooms Tea and coffee making facilities Direct dial from bedrooms No dogs (ex guide dogs) Lift Cen ht CTV No parking

PRICE GUIDE
ROOMS: s £37-£51; d fr £71*
CARDS:

GH 🇶🇶🇶 *Kingsway Hotel* 27 Norfolk Square, Hyde Park W2 1RX ☎0171 723 7784 & 0171 723 5569 Telex no 885299 FAX 0171 723 7317

Under the personal supervision of the owners, Mr and Mrs Shaw, this small hotel overlooks the gardens of an attractive square close to Paddington Station. The comfortable accommodation is well equipped and reasonably priced, with carefully maintained bedrooms and modern facilities. There is a small foyer lounge, and breakfast is served in the attractive dining room.

33 rms (30 bth/shr) (4 fmly) CTV in all bedrooms Tea and coffee making facilities No dogs (ex guide dogs) Lift Cen ht CTV
CARDS: ▓ ▓ ▓

GH 🇶🇶🇶 **Mitre House Hotel** 178-184 Sussex Gardens, Hyde Park W2 1TU ☎0171 723 8040 Telex no 914113 FAX 0171 402 0990

A popular, family run hotel has been modernised over the last few years to provide comfortable and well-equipped bedrooms. There is a small bar and a comfortable lounge, as well as a spacious dining room where a choice of breakfasts is offered.

70 rms (64 bth/shr) (3 fmly) No smoking in 10 bedrooms No smoking in area of dining room CTV in all bedrooms Direct dial from bedrooms No dogs (ex guide dogs) Licensed Lift Cen ht CTV 25P

PRICE GUIDE
ROOMS: s £50-£60; d £70*
CARDS: ▓ ▓ ▓
See advertisement on p.257.

Selected

GH 🇶🇶🇶🇶 **Mornington Hotel** 12 Lancaster Gate W2 3LG (BW) ☎0171 262 7361 FAX 0171 706 1028

This busy tourist hotel is located close to Hyde Park and within easy striking distance of Oxford Street. It provides modern standards of comfort in carefully maintained spacious bedrooms. Breakfast, which is entirely self service, is a broad continental spread including cold cuts of meat. An added feature is the cosy library bar which is open through the evening.

68 en suite (bth/shr) (6 fmly) No smoking in 12 bedrooms No smoking in area of dining room CTV in all bedrooms Tea

➡

and coffee making facilities Direct dial from bedrooms
Licensed Lift Cen ht No parking No coaches
PRICE GUIDE
ROOMS: s fr £89; d £99-£119
CARDS: £

Selected

GH QQQQ *Norfolk Plaza Hotel* 29/33 Norfolk Square,
Paddington W2 1RX ☎0171 723 0792 Telex no 266977
FAX 0171 224 8770
A large privately owned and run terraced hotel situated in an
attractive square close to Paddington Station offers above
average accommodation. Bedrooms vary in size but are
attractively decorated, with modern furnishings and facilities;
there are also several small suites with separate sitting rooms.
Public rooms include an open-plan reception/lounge/bar, and
an attractive dining room where a buffet breakfast is served.
87 en suite (bth/shr) (25 fmly) No smoking in 5 bedrooms
No smoking in dining room CTV in all bedrooms Tea and
coffee making facilities Direct dial from bedrooms No dogs
(ex guide dogs) Licensed Lift Cen ht No parking No
coaches
CARDS:

Selected

GH QQQQ **Norfolk Towers Hotel** 34 Norfolk Place
W2 1QW (close to Paddington Station & St Mary's
Hospital) ☎0171 262 3123 Telex no 268583
FAX 0171 224 8687
Further improvements have been made to this well appointed
hotel. Bedrooms, some quite spacious, are furnished in a
modern style and have recently been redecorated with
colourful wallpaper. A comfortable reception lobby, bar and
dining room are provided, and a choice is offered at breakfast.
Although it is primarily a bed and breakfast establishment,
there is a wine bar where light meals and snacks are available
at lunch and dinner.
85 en suite (bth/shr) (3 fmly) CTV in all bedrooms Direct
dial from bedrooms No dogs (ex guide dogs) Licensed Lift
Cen ht No parking Last d 10pm
CARDS:

GH QQ **Park Lodge Hotel** 73 Queensborough Ter, Bayswater
W2 3SU ☎0171 229 6424 FAX 0171 221 4772
A tall terraced house in Bayswater situated close to Queensway
and Bayswater tube stations, giving easy access to the West End.
Bedrooms vary in size but are adequately furnished and equipped,
and a complete redecoration programme is in progress to improve
the general standard. Public areas are limited but there is a
pleasantly appointed dining room.
29 en suite (bth/shr) (2 fmly) No smoking in 5 bedrooms No
smoking in dining room No smoking in lounges CTV in all
bedrooms Tea and coffee making facilities Direct dial from
bedrooms No dogs (ex guide dogs) Lift Cen ht No parking Last
d noon
PRICE GUIDE
ROOMS: s fr £47.50; d fr £57.50✳
CARDS: £

GH QQ **Parkwood Hotel** 4 Stanhope Place, Marble Arch
W2 2HB ☎0171 402 2241 FAX 0171 402 1574
The Parkwood is a small, privately owned bed and breakfast

establishment situated close to Marble Arch. Compact bedrooms
are well equipped and suitably furnished, and there is a little
reception lounge as well as a pleasantly appointed breakfast room
where a choice of breakfasts is offered.
18 rms (13 bth/shr) (4 fmly) No smoking in 2 bedrooms No
smoking in dining room CTV in all bedrooms Tea and coffee
making facilities Direct dial from bedrooms No dogs Cen ht
CTV No parking No coaches
PRICE GUIDE
ROOMS: s £44-£59.50; d £54.50-£74.50
CARDS: £

GH QQQ *Rhodes Hotel* 195 Sussex Gardens W2 2RJ
☎0171 262 5617 & 0171 262 0537 FAX 0171 723 4054
This attractive terraced house offers compact bedrooms which
have been refurbished in a modern style and are now very well
equipped. While English breakfast incurs a small additional
charge, continental is included in the tariff; both are served in the
stencilled dining room.
18 rms (15 bth/shr) (5 fmly) CTV in all bedrooms Tea and
coffee making facilities Direct dial from bedrooms No dogs Cen
ht CTV P
CARDS:

GH QQQ **Slavia Hotel** 2 Pembridge Square W2 4EW (next
to Public Library) ☎0171 727 1316 FAX 0171 229 0803
Situated close to Notting Hill Station, in a quiet residential area,
this well maintained hotel offers comfortable accommodation.
There are a small lounge and a spacious dining room; English and
continental breakfasts are served.
31 en suite (shr) (8 fmly) CTV in 12 bedrooms Direct dial from
bedrooms Licensed Lift Cen ht CTV 1P
PRICE GUIDE
ROOMS: s £35-£51; d £45-£70✳
CARDS: £

W4 CHISWICK

Selected

GH QQQQ **Chiswick Hotel** 73 Chiswick High Rd
W4 2LS ☎0181 994 1712 FAX 0181 742 2585
The Chiswick is a popular privately owned hotel with
spacious, tastefully appointed bedrooms. The lounge is small
but attractively decorated and there is a good sized dining
room with individual tables. A carte is offered at dinner and
there is a choice of dishes at breakfast.
33 en suite (bth/shr) (5 fmly) CTV in all bedrooms Tea and
coffee making facilities Direct dial from bedrooms Licensed
Cen ht CTV 15P Last d 8.30pm
PRICE GUIDE
ROOMS: s fr £69; d fr £94; wkly b&b £310-£485; wkly hlf-
bd £418-£595
CARDS: £

W5 EALING

GH QQ **Creffield Lodge** 2-4 Creffield Rd, Ealing W5 3HN
☎0181 993 2284 Telex no 935114 FAX 0181 992 7082
Refurbishment has begun at Creffield Lodge introducing a more
modern feel with bright decor and soft furnishings. Older style
bedrooms remain, but these are all clean and well equipped.
Guests breakfast and have use of facilities at the adjoining
Carnarvon Hotel.
24 rms (11 bth/shr) (1 fmly) No smoking in area of dining room
No smoking in 1 lounge CTV in all bedrooms Tea and coffee
making facilities Direct dial from bedrooms No dogs (ex guide ➡

dogs) Licensed Cen ht 20P Last d 9.15pm
PRICE GUIDE
ROOMS: s £30-£55; d £45-£70✳
CARDS: ⓔ

W6 HAMMERSMITH

GH Ⓠ Ⓠ Ⓠ *Premier West Hotel* 28-34 Glenthorne Rd,
Hammersmith W6 OLS ☎0181 748 6181
Further improvements are in progress at this busy commercial
hotel - namely the refurbishment of the public areas. Bedrooms
vary in size, some being more spacious than others, but all are
equipped to a high standard and include trouser presses and
hairdryers; some have small tub showers while the remainder have
more conventional baths. A set-price dinner is served in the large
dining room.
26 en suite (bth/shr) 15 annexe en suite (bth/shr) (5 fmly) CTV
in all bedrooms Tea and coffee making facilities No dogs (ex
guide dogs) Licensed Cen ht CTV 5P
CARDS:

W7 HANWELL

Selected

GH Ⓠ Ⓠ Ⓠ Ⓠ **Wellmeadow Lodge** 24 Wellmeadow Rd
W7 2AL ☎0181 567 7294 FAX 0181 566 3468
This is a justly popular guest house which is conveniently
located close to the M4 motorway, Heathrow airport and
Boston Manor underground station. It has the added
advantage of being surprisingly quiet owing to its location on
a residential street with unrestricted parking. The eight fully
en suite bedrooms are all spacious and have well laid out
bathrooms which have excellent water pressure. Guests are
welcome to use a lounge with soft armchairs and a small bar
run on an honesty basis. A carefully cooked breakfast is
served in the kitchen around a large pine table.
8 en suite (bth/shr) No smoking CTV in all bedrooms Tea
and coffee making facilities Direct dial from bedrooms No
dogs (ex guide dogs) Cen ht No parking No coaches Last d
noon
PRICE GUIDE
ROOMS: s £47-£60; d £70-£107
CARDS: ⓔ

W8 KENSINGTON

GH Ⓠ Ⓠ **Apollo Hotel** 18-22 Lexham Gardens W8 5JE (first
turning on left after Cromwell Hospital continue for 100yds
hotel on right) ☎0171 835 1133 Telex no 264189
FAX 0171 370 4853
This family-run bed and breakfast hotel continues to improve
steadily. Bedrooms, which have been modernised to a comfortable
standard and are well equipped, include a few more spacious
family rooms, and the dining room was in process of
refurbishment at the time of our visit. A choice of English and
continental breakfast is offered.
52 rms (35 bth 11 shr) (4 fmly) CTV in all bedrooms Direct dial
from bedrooms No dogs (ex guide dogs) Licensed Lift Cen ht
No parking No coaches
PRICE GUIDE
ROOMS: s £55-£60; d £65-£70
CARDS:

GH Ⓠ Ⓠ **Atlas Hotel** 24-30 Lexham Gardens W8 5JE
☎0171 835 1155 Telex no 264189 FAX 0171 370 4853
Like its sister establishment the Apollo, this popular hotel

continues to improve. A number of bedrooms have been upgraded
to a more modern style and are spacious and attractively equipped.
At the time of our visit, the dining room was being fitted with
brighter modern lighting and new carpeting. The hotel also has a
small bar and a reception lounge.
57 rms (14 bth 31 shr) (6 fmly) CTV in all bedrooms Direct dial
from bedrooms No dogs (ex guide dogs) Licensed Lift Cen ht
No parking
PRICE GUIDE
ROOMS: s £55-£60; d £65-£70
CARDS:

W14 WEST KENSINGTON

Selected

GH Ⓠ Ⓠ Ⓠ Ⓠ **Aston Court Hotel** 25/27 Matheson Rd
W14 8SN ☎0171 602 9954 Telex no 919208
FAX 0171 371 1338
Situated in a quiet residential area close to Olympia, this
private, family-run hotel offers a high standard of
accommodation. The comfortable bedrooms are attractively
appointed and suitably equipped with modern facilities.
Guests also have the use of a comfortable lounge and bar, and
there is a bright little conservatory dining room; breakfast can
also be served to the bedrooms. Newspapers and magazines
are provided.
29 en suite (bth/shr) (3 fmly) CTV in all bedrooms Tea and
coffee making facilities Direct dial from bedrooms No dogs
(ex guide dogs) Licensed Lift Cen ht CTV No parking
PRICE GUIDE
ROOMS: s £55-£59; d £65-£79.50✳
CARDS: ⓔ

GH Ⓠ Ⓠ Ⓠ **Avonmore Hotel** 66 Avonmore Rd W14 8RS (off
Hammersmith Road opposite Olympia Exhibition Centre)
☎0171 603 4296 & 3121 FAX 0171 603 4035
Close to Olympia and within easy reach of Kensington High
Street, this delightful little hotel is personally run by Mrs
McKenzie. Bedrooms are attractive and very well equipped. There
is a small bar, a light and airy dining room and a friendly
atmosphere. Car parking in this area is limited but public transport
is good.
9 rms (7 bth/shr) (3 fmly) CTV in all bedrooms Tea and coffee
making facilities Direct dial from bedrooms No dogs Licensed
Cen ht CTV No parking
PRICE GUIDE
ROOMS: s £43-£58; d £56-£68✳
CARDS: ⓔ

GH Ⓠ Ⓠ **Centaur Hotel** 21 Avonmore Rd W14 8RP
☎0171 602 3857 & 603 5973 FAX 0171 603 9193
Its friendly atmosphere is the most important feature of this well
kept, family-run guest house which stands in a quiet, residential
area, convenient for Olympia and Earls Court. Bedrooms are
attractively decorated and there are a small lounge and a dining
room with shared tables. Car parking is metered in the immediate
vicinity.
10 rms (4 shr) (2 fmly) CTV in all bedrooms Direct dial from
bedrooms No dogs Cen ht CTV No parking
PRICE GUIDE
ROOMS: s £35-£45; d £60-£70✳

WC1 BLOOMSBURY, HOLBORN

GH Q Q **Mentone Hotel** 54-55 Cartwright Gardens
WC1H 9EL ☎0171 387 3927 & 388 4671
FAX 0171 388 4671

A striking feature of this small, private hotel is the attractive floral display outside the building. The bedrooms are well-equipped and there is an attractive dining room where both English and Continental breakfast is offered.

27 rms (17 shr) (10 fmly) No smoking in dining room CTV in all bedrooms Tea and coffee making facilities No dogs Cen ht No parking Tennis (hard)

PRICE GUIDE
ROOMS: s £30-£48; d £45-£60*
CARDS: £

LONGLEAT Wiltshire Map 03 ST84

✦ Q Q Q Mrs J Crossman **Stalls** *(ST806439)* BA12 7NE (turn off A362 at Corsley beside the White Hart, follow road for 2m towards Longleat House farmhouse is on right hand side)
☎01985 844323

Surrounded by delightful countryside and once part of the Longleat estate, this 120-year-old farmhouse stands on what is still a working farm. Bedrooms are comfortable and well equipped, and there is a cosy sitting room. Should guests want some entertainment, there is a good country pub only a short drive away.

3 rms No smoking in bedrooms No smoking in dining room No smoking in 1 lounge CTV in all bedrooms Tea and coffee making facilities No dogs Cen ht CTV 6P Table tennis Childrens play area 350 acres dairy

PRICE GUIDE
ROOMS: s fr £15.50; d fr £31* £

Selected

✦ Q Q Q Q Mrs L N Corp **Sturford Mead** *(ST834456)* BA12 7QU (on A362 half way between Warminster & Frome) ☎01373 832213

This welcoming farmhouse enjoys views across National Trust land close to Longleat House. Spacious, well equipped bedrooms are decorated in co-ordinating colour schemes and each has a pleasant outlook. A traditional English breakfast is served at separate tables in the attractive dining room, and there is a comfortable guests' lounge.

3 en suite (bth/shr) No smoking CTV in all bedrooms Tea and coffee making facilities No dogs (ex guide dogs) Cen ht CTV ch fac 10P 5 acres pig

LONGRIDGE Lancashire Map 07 SD63

Selected

✦ Q Q Q Q Mrs E J Ibison **Jenkinsons** *(SD611348)* Alston Ln PR3 3BD (off B6243 Preston to Longridge road - follow signs to Alston Hall College) ☎01772 782624 rs Xmas

This immaculately renovated farmhouse, which is over two hundred years old, is owned by the very hospitable Ibison family and is still very much part of a working farm. It is only a few miles from Preston and is an ideal base for exploring Lancashire and the surrounding counties. There is a spacious and very comfortably furnished lounge which is dominated by a huge inglenook fireplace and large sofas covered in rich

fabrics; off this is a characterful dining room where breakfast (and dinner by arrangement) are served. The six immaculate bedrooms, whilst not en suite, are traditionally and very attractively furnished, one with a magnificent half-tester bed. The house is non-smoking throughout.

6 rms No smoking Tea and coffee making facilities No dogs (ex guide dogs) Cen ht CTV No children 12yrs 10P 100 acres dairy sheep Last d 4pm

LONGTOWN Cumbria Map 11 NY36

Premier Selected

✦ Q Q Q Q Q Mr & Mrs J Sisson **Bessiestown** *(NY457768)* Catlowdy CA6 5QP (from Bush Hotel, 6.5m to Bridge Inn, turn right onto B6318 one and a half miles to Catlowdy, farm first on left) ☎01228 577219 FAX 01228 577219

This delightful farmhouse stands on a small sheep and beef farm in a tiny village close to the Scottish border. Six spacious and very attractively decorated bedrooms with modern en suite facilities offer TV, radio alarms and beverage-making equipment, while downstairs there are two lounges (one with an honesty bar) and a very pleasant dining room where hearty breakfasts and home-cooked dinners are ➡

served at individual lace-covered tables. An indoor heated swimming pool is open from mid-May to mid-September, and one of the old farm buildings has been converted into a games room.

4 en suite (bth/shr) (1 fmly) No smoking in bedrooms No smoking in dining room No smoking in 1 lounge CTV in all bedrooms Tea and coffee making facilities No dogs (ex guide dogs) Licensed Cen ht CTV 10P Indoor swimming pool (heated) Games room 80 acres beef sheep Last d 4pm

PRICE GUIDE
ROOMS: s £24.50-£29.50; d £39-£45; wkly b&b £130-£140*
CARDS: 🏧 💳 💳 (£)
See advertisement under CARLISLE

LOOE Cornwall & Isles of Scilly Map **02** SX25

Selected

GH 🅀🅀🅀🅀 **Coombe Farm** Widegates PL13 1QN (on B3253 just S of Widegates village, 3.5m east of Looe) ☎01503 240223
Mar-Oct
Coombe Farm is home to Sally and Alex Low, their family and pets. The 1920s house is set in 10 acres of lawns, meadows, streams and ponds with views down the valley to the sea. Bedrooms are equipped with modern comforts, and three occupy a converted barn close to the house. There are a comfortable lounge and an elegant dining room furnished with antique pieces. Log fires blaze on cooler evenings and fresh flowers adorn the tables and sideboards. A four-course dinner is available, as are drinks, but guests are asked not to smoke. A swimming pool and games room are also provided.
7 en suite (shr) 3 annexe en suite (shr) (6 fmly) No smoking CTV in all bedrooms Tea and coffee making facilities Direct dial from bedrooms Licensed Cen ht CTV No children 5yrs 20P No coaches Outdoor swimming pool (heated) Table tennis Snooker Croquet Last d 7pm

PRICE GUIDE
ROOMS: s £20-£26; d £40-£52; wkly b&b £140-£182; wkly hlf-bd £214-£260* (£)

 GH 🅀🅀 **Gulls Hotel** Hannafore Rd PL13 2DE ☎01503 262531
Etr-Oct & Xmas
This hotel features a sun lounge and a patio which look down on the beach, the village and out to sea. Many bedrooms have the same view and there is also a bar and dining room where supper is served.
11 rms (2 shr) No smoking CTV in 7 bedrooms Tea and coffee making facilities Licensed Cen ht CTV 3P Last d at breakfast

PRICE GUIDE
ROOMS: s £13-£16; d £26-£38; wkly b&b £78-£114; wkly hlf-bd £141-£177 (£)

Selected

GH 🅀🅀🅀🅀 **Harescombe Lodge** Watergate PL13 2NE ☎01503 263158
Originally the shooting lodge to the Trelawny Estate, Harescombe Lodge dates back to 1760. It is quietly positioned in a delightful hamlet on the creek side of the West Looe

River, surrounded by attractive gardens with streams, waterfalls and small stone bridges, yet is within half an hour's walk (along the river path) of Looe. The bedrooms are cosy and individually furnished with some fine antiques, and offer country views and modern, well presented bathrooms. A generous breakfast is served in the tastefully restored dining room, freshly prepared by the friendly Mrs Wynn.
3 en suite (bth/shr) Tea and coffee making facilities No dogs (ex guide dogs) Cen ht No children 12yrs 10P No coaches Last d 9am

PRICE GUIDE
ROOMS: d £36-£40; wkly b&b £119-£133; wkly hlf-bd £189-£203* (£)

 GH 🅀🅀 **'Kantara'** 7 Trelawney Ter PL13 2AG (on main Looe/Polperro road, 120yds above Looe Bridge opposite car park) ☎01503 262093
At this hillside house overlooking the river, John and Hazel Storer make everyone feel at home, especially families. The bar/lounge is an obvious meeting point and breakfast is served in the sunny dining room.
5 rms (3 fmly) No smoking in dining room CTV in all bedrooms Tea and coffee making facilities Licensed CTV 1P Registered boat available fo fishing/cruising Last d 4pm

PRICE GUIDE
ROOMS: s £13-£15.50; d £26-£31; wkly b&b £87-£104; wkly hlf-bd £150-£167
CARDS: 🏧 💳 💳 💳 (£)

Selected

GH 🅀🅀🅀🅀 **Panorama Hotel** Hannafore Rd PL13 2DE (in West Looe overlooking pier & beach) ☎01503 262123 FAX 01503 265654
As its name suggests, this friendly hotel is superbly situated in an elevated position with outstanding views over Looe, the harbour and the surrounding coastline. Some of the brightly decorated bedrooms have balconies and all are equipped with modern facilities. Guests gather to enjoy a drink in the lounge bar before going into an attractive dining room for dinner.
10 en suite (bth/shr) (4 fmly) No smoking in dining room No smoking in lounges CTV in all bedrooms Tea and coffee making facilities No dogs Licensed Cen ht CTV 13P Last d 6.30pm

PRICE GUIDE
ROOMS: s £22-£32; d £44-£64; wkly b&b £132-£192; wkly hlf-bd £195-£255*
CARDS: 🏧 💳 💳 💳 💳 💳 (£)

GH 🅀🅀🅀 **Polraen Country House Hotel** Sandplace PL13 1PJ (2m N, at jct of A387/B3254) ☎01503 263956
This attractive 18th-century granite house stands in two acres of well kept gardens in the Looe Valley. En suite bedrooms are comfortable and equipped to modern standards, while public areas include a cosy lounge, a separate bar lounge and a character dining room with an old fashioned range.
5 en suite (bth/shr) (2 fmly) No smoking in dining room CTV in all bedrooms Tea and coffee making facilities Licensed Cen ht 21P No coaches Last d 8pm
CARDS: 🏧 💳

GH **St Aubyns** Marine Dr, Hannafore,West Looe PL13 2DH (from Looe Bridge take West Quay rd signed Hannafore. House in .75m) ☎01503 264351

Etr-end Oct

A fine Victorian house dating back to 1894 situated on Marine Parade in West Looe, close to the beach, surrounded by attractive gardens and with uninterrupted views of the coast. Bedrooms are comfortably furnished and attractively decorated; some larger rooms at the front of the house have sunny balconies overlooking the beach. Many original features have been retained, and the large public rooms contain many fine pieces of furniture as well as paintings and tapestries.

8 rms (4 bth/shr) (6 fmly) No smoking in dining room No smoking in lounges CTV in 4 bedrooms Tea and coffee making facilities No dogs CTV 4P No coaches

PRICE GUIDE

ROOMS: s fr £20; d £40-£55✶

CARDS: 🂱 🂱 🂱 🂱 🂱   (£)

Selected

GH **Woodlands** St Martins Rd PL13 1LP (on B3253, 1m from St Martins Church) ☎01503 264405

You will find this pleasant Victorian house on the edge of woodlands overlooking the river and only a short walk from the village. All bedrooms are agreeably furnished and both the sitting room with its open fire and the dining room have a warm, country house feel, with stripped pine doors. Home cooking is an attraction, using local, home-grown and organic produce.

5 rms (4 shr) (2 fmly) No smoking in 3 bedrooms No smoking in dining room CTV in all bedrooms Tea and coffee ➡

making facilities No dogs (ex guide dogs) Licensed Cen ht 6P No coaches Last d 6.30pm
PRICE GUIDE
ROOMS: s £17-£19; d £36-£42; wkly b&b £126-£140; wkly hlf-bd £190-£210

LORTON Cumbria Map **11** NY12

Premier Selected

GH ⬛⬛⬛⬛⬛ **New House Farm** CA13 9UU (6m S, on B5289 between Lorton and Loweswater)
☎01900 85404
FAX 01900 85404

New House Farm enjoys a beautiful location, nestling in Lorton Vale between the villages of Lorton and Loweswater. It is no longer a working farm, but the house has been skilfully renovated to reveal many of its fine seventeenth-century features - for example, the exposed beams, stone fireplaces and flagged floors in the restful lounges and cosy dining room. The bedrooms, which have spectacular views, are furnished with large beds and antique pine furniture, while such thoughtful touches as fresh fruit and flowers add a homely feel. Hazel Hatch is responsible for some fine home-cooking which sometimes includes game or fish freshly caught by husband John.
3 en suite (bth/shr) No smoking Tea and coffee making facilities Licensed Cen ht No children 12yrs 30P No coaches Last d 7pm
PRICE GUIDE
ROOMS: s £30-£40; d £60-£70; wkly b&b £210-£245; wkly hlf-bd £315-£385✻

LOUGHBOROUGH Leicestershire Map **08** SK51

GH ⬛⬛⬛ *De Montfort Hotel* 88 Leicester Rd LE11 2AQ (on A6 Leicester rd) ☎01509 216061 FAX 01509 233667
Now fully refurbished the decoration and furnishings throughout are pretty and contrast well with the furniture and character of the house. There is a really comfortable lounge which leads off from the dining room. Here the dark polished woods are off set by deep purple chintz pelmets. A freshly cooked set evening dish of the day is offered as well as popular grill type dishes. The bedrooms are fresh and light and well equipped with good desk surfaces and seating.
9 rms (7 bth/shr) (3 fmly) No smoking in 3 bedrooms No smoking in dining room CTV in all bedrooms Tea and coffee making facilities Licensed Cen ht CTV No coaches Last d 6pm
CARDS: 🟦 🟥 🟫

GH ⬛⬛⬛ **Garendon Park Hotel** 92 Leicester Rd LE11 2AQ
☎01509 236557 FAX 01509 265559
A very friendly and cared for hotel which continually strives for improvement. The bedrooms, some of which are brightly decorated are very clean and well equipped. There is a cosy dining room which opens into an equally comfortable lounge furnished with Chesterfield armchairs and sofa. Evening meals are freshly cooked and vary from a set dish of the day to a list of popular grill dishes.
9 rms (5 bth/shr) (2 fmly) No smoking in 1 bedrooms No

---

smoking in dining room CTV in all bedrooms Tea and coffee making facilities Licensed Cen ht CTV ch fac Last d 8pm
PRICE GUIDE
ROOMS: s £21.50-£30; d £35-£45✻
CARDS: 🟦 ▬ 🟫 🟦 🟥 🔲

LOUTH Lincolnshire Map **08** TF38

Selected

GH ⬛⬛⬛⬛ **Wickham House** Church Ln LN11 7LX
☎01507 358465
(For full entry see Conisholme)

Selected

◀⬛⬛⬛⬛ **Masons Arms** Cornmarket LN11 9PY
☎01507 609525
A very friendly and popular coaching inn tucked away in the corner of the market place. It has a great atmosphere, welcoming as a meeting, drinking or eating place for locals and visitors especially on market days. The bedrooms are comfortably furnished with thoroughly modern facilities.
10 rms (5 bth/shr) No smoking in area of dining room CTV in all bedrooms Tea and coffee making facilities No dogs (ex guide dogs) Cen ht No parking Last d 9.30pm
PRICE GUIDE
ROOMS: s £20-£35; d £35-£50; wkly b&b £175-£200; wkly hlf-bd £200-£250✻
MEALS: Lunch fr £6.50 Dinner £10-£17.50alc✻
CARDS: 🟦 🟫

LOW CATTON Humberside Map **08** SE75

Selected

GH ⬛⬛⬛⬛ **Derwent Lodge** YO4 1EA (from York take the A1079 Hull rd through Kexby then take the 1st turn left after the Kexby Bridge Hotel and at next junction fork left) ☎01759 371468
Feb-Nov
An attractive white-washed house, Derwent Lodge is set within its own well tended gardens in a sleepy village eight miles east of York. Dating from the 1850s, it retains some of the building's original character in oak beams and York stone fireplaces. The spacious lounge provides games and jigsaw puzzles, and a five-course dinner menu is available if ordered in advance. Bedrooms (including one on the ground floor) are light and inviting, each having an en suite bathroom or shower room. This is a no-smoking establishment.
5 en suite (bth/shr) No smoking CTV in all bedrooms Tea and coffee making facilities Licensed Cen ht No children 8yrs 8P No coaches Last d 4pm
PRICE GUIDE
ROOMS: s £31.50; d £47; wkly b&b £164.50; wkly hlf-bd £224

LOWER BEEDING West Sussex Map **04** TQ22

❤ QQQ Mr J Christian *Brookfield Farm Hotel (TQ214285)* Winterpit Ln, Plummers Plain RH13 6LU
☎01403 891568 FAX 01403 891499
Quietly located in rural surroundings, this friendly hotel offers a choice of bedrooms all furnished in the modern style. There is a cosy beamed lounge, bar and a restaurant, which overlooks the lake and golf course. Other facilities include a golf driving range, boating lake, putting green, six-hole practice golf course with PGA pro-tuition, sauna, and children's play area.
20 en suite (bth/shr) (2 fmly) No smoking in area of dining room No smoking in lounges CTV in all bedrooms Tea and coffee making facilities Direct dial from bedrooms Licensed Cen ht CTV 100P Outdoor swimming pool Golf 7 Fishing Snooker Sauna Games room Putting 300 acres mixed Last d 9.30pm
CARDS: 🔳 🔳 🔤
See advertisement under HORSHAM

LOWER BRAILES Warwickshire Map **04** SP33

❤ QQQ Mrs H Taylor *New House Farm (SP305382)* Lower Brailes OX15 5BD ☎01608 686239
Closed Xmas
This well proprtioned 400-year-old house, made of local red brick, has been owned by the same family for sixty years. Bedrooms have a welcoming atmosphere and there is a comfortable lounge. Breakfast is served in a north facing conservatory which overlooks the well maintained lawns.
3 rms (2 shr) (1 fmly) No smoking in 2 bedrooms No smoking in dining room No smoking in 1 lounge CTV in all bedrooms Tea and coffee making facilities Cen ht CTV P Golf 18 Snooker 500 acres arable/sheep
PRICE GUIDE
ROOMS: s £18-£20; d £30-£35; wkly b&b £98-£115✳ ⓔ

LOWESTOFT Suffolk Map **05** TM59

Selected

GH QQQQ *Abbe* 322 London Rd South NR33 0BG (on main A12 London road) ☎01502 581083
Enthusiastic owners Nick and Diane Murphy offer a warm welcome at this small family run guest house, where friendly personal service features highly. The public rooms offer a comfortably appointed lounge with a small corner bar and pleasant dining room decorated in pastel shades; it's here that guests are offered a good choice at both breakfast and dinner, the latter available by prior arrangement. The accommodation might not be particularly spacious, but all the bedrooms are thoughtfully laid out and individually decorated, with co-ordinated colour schemes through the decor and quality soft furnishings; each room is very well equipped and have many thoughtful extras.
3 rms (2 shr) (1 fmly) No smoking in bedrooms No smoking in dining room CTV in all bedrooms Tea and coffee making facilities No dogs (ex guide dogs) Licensed Cen ht CTV 1P No coaches Last d 7pm
PRICE GUIDE
ROOMS: s £22-£25; d £32-£38; wkly b&b £102-£112; wkly hlf-bd £157.50-£172✳

GH QQ *Fairways* 398 London Rd South NR33 0BQ (S of town centre on A12) ☎01502 572659
Set back from the seafront at the southern end of the town, this well run guest house offers bright bedrooms, a comfortable lounge with colour TV and a video recorder, and a dining room with a

dispense bar.
7 rms (4 bth/shr) (2 fmly) No smoking in dining room CTV in all bedrooms Tea and coffee making facilities Licensed Cen ht CTV 2P Last d 7pm
CARDS: 🔳 🔤

GH QQ *Kingsleigh* 44 Marine Pde NR33 0QN (on the A12 overlooking the seafront) ☎01502 572513
Closed Xmas
Central to the town and on the seafront, this well kept guest house offers good sea views from the front rooms. The car park is on London Road South near to the building.
4 rms No smoking in 2 bedrooms No smoking in dining room CTV in all bedrooms Tea and coffee making facilities Cen ht No children 3yrs 4P No coaches
PRICE GUIDE
ROOMS: s £17-£20; d £30-£32✳ ⓔ

GH QQQ *Rockville House* 6 Pakefield Rd NR33 0HS (enter town from south on A12, 1m past water tower take sharp turning right immediately after 'no entry' sign on right) ☎01502 581011 & 574891 FAX 01502 581011
rs Oct-Apr
In a quiet road near the seafront, this tidy guesthouse has a welcoming lounge with games and books and a dining room where dinner or supper trays are served by arrangement. Bedrooms are thoughtfully arranged.
7 rms (2 bth 1 shr) No smoking in dining room CTV in all bedrooms Tea and coffee making facilities No dogs (ex guide dogs) Licensed Cen ht No children 12yrs No parking No ➡

coaches Beach hut Last d 10am
PRICE GUIDE
ROOMS: s £21-£33; d £37-£43; wkly b&b £110-£130; wkly hlf-bd £175-£195∗
CARDS: ◪ ▭ £

GH ◪◪◪ **Somerton House** 7 Kirkley Cliff NR33 0BY (on seafront 100yds from Claremont Pier)
☎01502 565665 FAX 01502 501176
This is a distinctive blue and white house on the seafront. The bedrooms, one with a four-poster, one with a half tester, all have individual character and thoughtful extras.
8 rms (4 shr) (4 fmly) No smoking in 2 bedrooms No smoking in dining room CTV in all bedrooms Tea and coffee making facilities Licensed Cen ht CTV P Last d 5pm
PRICE GUIDE
ROOMS: s £20-£25; d £34-£39; wkly b&b £120-£140; wkly hlf-bd £183-£203∗
CARDS: ◪ ▬ ▭ ◉ £

LOW ROW North Yorkshire Map **07** SD99

Selected

GH ◪◪◪◪ **Peat Gate Head** DL11 6PP
☎01748 886388
Set in the midst of one of Yorkshire's most beautiful dales, this 400-year-old house is full of charm and character, with low ceilings, beams and exposed stone walls. The hospitable owner, Alan Earl, is a very capable cook producing excellent Yorkshire dinners. The accommodation includes warm, cosy bedrooms and two lounges.
6 rms (3 shr) No smoking in bedrooms No smoking in dining room No smoking in 1 lounge Tea and coffee making facilities No dogs Licensed Cen ht CTV No children 5yrs No parking No coaches Last d 5.30pm
PRICE GUIDE
ROOMS: (incl. dinner) s fr £35.50; d £75.90-£79.90

LUDGVAN Cornwall & Isles of Scilly Map **02** SW53

▣▣ ♥◪ Mrs C E Blewett **Menwidden** (*SW502337*) TR20 8BN (at Crowlas x-rds on A30 turn onto Ludgvan road then turn right signed Vellanoweth for farm in 1m on left)
☎01736 740415
Closed Dec-Jan
First-time visitors would be well advised to ask for directions to this small market garden and dairy farm within easy reach of Land's End, Penzance, St Ives and the Lizard Peninsula. The pebble-dashed family house has extensive views, and accommodation is sound (though most of the bedrooms lack wash basins). Well cooked, wholesome meals are served in the dining room, and guests can take their ease in a cosy lounge with TV.
5 rms (1 fmly) Tea and coffee making facilities CTV 6P 40 acres market gardening Last d 1pm
PRICE GUIDE
ROOMS: s fr £14.50; d fr £29; wkly b&b fr £97; wkly hlf-bd fr £130
£

LUDLOW Shropshire Map **07** SO57

GH ◪◪◪ **The Brakes** Downton SY8 2LF (5.5m NW, on edge of Downton village)
☎01584 856485 FAX 01584 856485
Mar-Oct
This tastefully modernised former farmhouse dates back to the

1750's. Set in extensive and attractive gardens, it is situated in a picturesque and peaceful area, on the edge of Downton Village, some five and a half miles north-west of Ludlow. Two of the bedrooms have traditional style furnishings, whilst the third has modern type. All are similarly equipped. There is a comfortable lounge, where welcoming real fires burn when the weather is chilly. Drinks can be served in here. Separate tables are provided in the traditionally furnished dining room, where home cooked meals are served. Guests are more than welcome to indulge in a game of croquet or badminton in the grounds, or simply relax.
3 en suite (bth/shr) (1 fmly) No smoking in dining room No smoking in lounges CTV in all bedrooms Tea and coffee making facilities Licensed Cen ht No children 12yrs 6P No coaches Croquet Badminton Last d 6pm
PRICE GUIDE
ROOMS: s fr £25; d fr £45
CARDS: ◪ ▭

GH ◪◪◪ **Cecil** Sheet Rd SY8 1LR (off A49. Ludlow By-pass) ☎01584 872442 FAX 01584 872442
Closed Xmas
This friendly little guest house with its own forecourt car park stands on the town side of the A49 bypass, in pretty lawns and gardens. Run by Gillian and Maurice Phillips, the accommodation - which includes two ground-floor bedrooms - is immaculately maintained. There are a cosy bar with TV and a comfortable modern lounge, and Gillian provides good home cooking, catering for vegetarians and special diets if given advance notice.
10 rms (3 shr) (1 fmly) No smoking in bedrooms No smoking in dining room No smoking in 1 lounge CTV in all bedrooms Tea and coffee making facilities Licensed Cen ht CTV 11P Last d 9am
PRICE GUIDE
ROOMS: s fr £18; d £42; wkly b&b £115-£135; wkly hlf-bd £181-£201
CARDS: ◪ ▭ £

Selected

GH ◪◪◪◪ **Moor Hall** SY8 3EG
☎01584 823209 & 823333 FAX 01584 823387
This Georgian Palladian style house, built in 1789 is situated in attractive gardens four miles from Ludlow on the B4364 Bridgenorth Road. The Chivers family have lived here for the last fourteen years and very much enjoy welcoming guests in to their home. Dinner (by prior arrangement) when the Chivers normally sit and join their guests and breakfast, are served around a communal table in the dining room. The atmosphere is very informal and guests are free to enjoy many rooms in the house including the blue sitting room and the drawing room, which has windows which open out on to the gardens and in the winter is warmed by an open fire. The three bedrooms, all of which are en-suite, are attractively furnished and well equipped.
3 en suite (shr) No smoking in bedrooms No smoking in dining room No smoking in lounges CTV in all bedrooms Tea and coffee making facilities No dogs Licensed Cen ht CTV 12P No coaches Fishing Archery Clay shooting Boules Croquet
PRICE GUIDE
ROOMS: d £37-£45; wkly b&b £110-£130; wkly hlf-bd £170-£200∗
£

Selected

GH [Q][Q][Q][Q] **Number Twenty Eight** 28 Lower Broad St SY8 1PQ ☎01584 876996 FAX 01584 876996
This attractive half-timbered cottage stands on the south side of the town centre, close to Ludford Bridge and the River Teme. There is also a charming mews cottage with two bedrooms, a lounge and a large garden just across the street beside the Broad Gate. The main house is where the genial hosts meet guests and serve meals (including a fixed price dinner accompanied by a good range of wines) a cosy dining room with patio doors looking out on to the neat garden. There is also a pleasant lounge with a wealth of reading material. Street parking is available.
2 en suite (bth/shr) 2 annexe en suite (bth/shr) No smoking in bedrooms No smoking in dining room CTV in all bedrooms Tea and coffee making facilities Direct dial from bedrooms Licensed Cen ht No parking No coaches Last d 8.30pm
PRICE GUIDE
ROOMS: s £40-£60; d £50-£70; wkly b&b £160-£190; wkly hlf-bd £260-£290✱
CARDS: 🅰 ━ 🔤

◖ [Q][Q][Q] **The Church** The Buttercross SY8 1AW (in town centre) (BW) ☎01584 872174 FAX 01584 877146
Closed Xmas Day
Occupying a site that dates back seven centuries, this pleasant inn provides modern bedrooms and a character bar. It lies in the centre of town, directly behind the Buttercross, and there is ample public parking nearby. A wide range of bar food is always available.
8 en suite (bth/shr) (1 fmly) No smoking in dining room No smoking in lounges CTV in all bedrooms Tea and coffee making facilities No dogs (ex guide dogs) Cen ht P No coaches Last d 9pm
PRICE GUIDE
ROOMS: s £28-£40; d £40✱
MEALS: Lunch £6.50-£12 Dinner £8.50-£12.50&alc✱
CARDS: 🅰 🔤

LUSTLEIGH Devon Map 03 SX78

Selected

GH [Q][Q][Q][Q] **Eastwrey Barton Hotel** TQ13 9SN (turn off A38 onto A382 towards Mortonhampstead, hotel situated 0.5m on right) ☎01647 277338
Closed Nov-Feb
Originally a farmhouse, this 17th century building is quietly set in its own grounds with splendid views along the Wray Valley across to Lustleigh Cleave. A small, welcoming hotel, it offers comfortable accommodation in spacious bedrooms containing fresh flowers. The public areas benefit from the views and include a cosy bar and an airy sun lounge. A short set-price menu is served in the dining room; the food is interesting, the wine list includes some local bins and the water is provided from the hotel's own spring.
6 en suite (bth) No smoking CTV in all bedrooms Tea and coffee making facilities Licensed Cen ht CTV No children 12yrs 10P No coaches Last d 6pm
PRICE GUIDE
ROOMS: d £58; wkly b&b £182; wkly hlf-bd £264
CARDS: 🅰 🔤 🔲

LUTON Bedfordshire Map 04 TL02

GH [Q][Q] *Arlington Hotel* 137 New Bedford Rd LU3 1LF (on A6) ☎01582 419614 FAX 01582 459047
Set back from the A6, towards Bedford, this detached commercial hotel is convenient for Luton airport and the M1. The bedrooms are well equipped, with en suite facilities and direct dial telephones being standard. There is a small traditionally styled bar and large dining room where simple evening meals are served.
19 en suite (bth/shr) (3 fmly) CTV in all bedrooms Tea and coffee making facilities Direct dial from bedrooms No dogs (ex guide dogs) Licensed Cen ht 25P Last d 8.30pm
CARDS: 🅰 ━ 🔤 ◉

GH [Q][Q] **Leaside Hotel** 72 New Bedford St LU3 1BT ☎01582 417643 FAX 01582 34961
A large Victorian hotel, the Leaside is popular for its comfortable bar and elegant restaurant. Bedrooms are well equipped but do not match the style of the public areas. The hotel can be difficult to find so it is worth asking for directions.
11 en suite (bth/shr) 1 annexe en suite (shr) (1 fmly) CTV in all bedrooms Tea and coffee making facilities Direct dial from bedrooms No dogs (ex guide dogs) Licensed Cen ht CTV 30P No coaches Threequarter size snooker table Last d 9.30pm
PRICE GUIDE
ROOMS: s £35-£45; d £45-£55
CARDS: 🅰 ━ 🔤 ◉

LUTTERWORTH Leicestershire

See **Shearsby**

EASTWREY BARTON HOTEL
Lustleigh, Devon TQ13 9SN
Telephone: 01647 277338
A Country House Hotel within the Dartmoor National Park.

A 17th Century farmhouse set in its own grounds with views along the Wray Valley. Six en suite bedrooms all individually designed. Traditional English cooking and a good selection of excellent wines. Enjoy an aperitif or a leisurely after dinner drink in the cosy bar. With the emphasis on peace and quiet, the hotel provides a relaxing and stress free holiday. Ideally situated for touring South Devon.

LYDFORD Devon Map 02 SX58

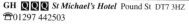

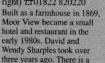
Premier Selected

GH ◗◗◗◗◗ **Moor View Hotel** Vale Down EX20 4BB (turn off A30 at Sourton Cross onto A386 Tavistock road, hotel is approx 4m on right) ☎01822 820220

Built as a farmhouse in 1869, Moor View became a small hotel and restaurant in the early 1980s. David and Wendy Sharples took over three years ago. There is a stylishly decorated drawing room, a separate bar (the only room in which smoking is allowed) and a dining room named Crockers, after the previous owners, where a fixed-price dinner menu is offered. Sunday lunches and cream teas are also served. In cool weather, open fires are lit in the public rooms.

6 rms (4 bth/shr) (1 fmly) No smoking in bedrooms No smoking in dining room CTV in all bedrooms Tea and coffee making facilities Licensed Cen ht CTV No children 12yrs 15P No coaches Croquet Last d 10am

---

LYDNEY Gloucestershire Map 03 SO60

GH ◗◗◗ **Viney Hill Country** Viney Hill GL15 4LT (2.5m from Lydney off A48 on unclassed road) ☎01594 516000 FAX 01594 516018

This charming, cottage-style guest house is well maintained and professionally run by a friendly and helpful couple. Located just outside the village of Blakeney, off the A48, it has been sympathetically extended and the rooms are quite spacious, comfortable and full of personal touches; many have lovely views of the surrounding countryside. There are two lounges and dinner can be provided. Smoking is not permitted.

6 en suite (bth/shr) No smoking CTV in all bedrooms Tea and coffee making facilities No dogs (ex guide dogs) Licensed Cen ht CTV 10P No coaches Last d 1pm

PRICE GUIDE
ROOMS: s fr £32; d fr £42
CARDS: 🔲 🔳
See advertisement under GLOUCESTER

LYME REGIS Dorset Map 03 SY39

GH ◗◗◗ **Coverdale** Woodmead Rd DT7 3AB (off A35 onto B1365 through Uplyme, over mini rbt tthe 2nd left before Mariners Hotel) ☎01297 442882
Feb-Nov rs Dec-Jan

Situated high above the town, yet within five minutes' walk of the centre, this neat guest house makes the ideal base from which to explore this beautiful coastal area. The no-smoking bedrooms are simply furnished and well maintained, some enjoying superb views to West Bay and Portland, with Lyme Regis Bay in the foreground. There is a comfortable lounge and a dining room where Mrs Harding offers a home cooked dinner.

8 rms (6 shr) (2 fmly) No smoking Tea and coffee making facilities Cen ht CTV No children 18mths 9P No coaches Last d 4pm

PRICE GUIDE
ROOMS: s £15-£17; d £26-£38; wkly b&b £86-£126✱ £

GH ◗◗◗ **St Michael's Hotel** Pound St DT7 3HZ ☎01297 442503

This friendly family-run hotel is conveniently situated a short walk from the town and the seafront. The spacious bedrooms are well appointed; some have fine sea views. Other facilities include an attractive breakfast room, a comfortable lounge, a hairdressing salon, a sun bed and the services of a reflexologist.

12 rms (4 bth 6 shr) (1 fmly) No smoking in dining room No smoking in 1 lounge CTV in all bedrooms Tea and coffee making facilities Licensed Cen ht No children 3yrs 13P No coaches Solarium
CARDS: 🔲 🔳

GH ◗◗◗ **The White House** 47 Silver St DT7 3HR (on A3070 Axminster-Lyme Regis rd approx 50mtrs from jct with A3052) ☎01297 443420
Apr-Oct

This charming house offers bright, attractively furnished rooms with modern en suite facilities. There is a comfortable lounge, a pretty breakfast room and a private car park at the rear of the building and the owners can give details of all the local walks.

7 en suite (shr) No smoking in dining room CTV in all bedrooms Tea and coffee making facilities Cen ht No children 10yrs 7P No coaches

PRICE GUIDE
ROOMS: d £36-£40; wkly b&b £112-£126 £

LYMINGTON Hampshire Map 04 SZ39

Selected

GH ◗◗◗◗ **Albany House** Highfield SO41 9GB ☎01590 671900
Closed 2wks in winter

A lovely early Victorian house built around 1840, Albany House enjoys an elevated position close to the town centre. The front facing bedrooms have excellent views, and several are very spacious and comfortable, with quality bathrooms. All are furnished with antiques and come with TV and tea trays. Inventive home cooking is served, using fresh local produce in a choice of daily menus. Dinner is available by arrangement. There is a sumptuous dining room with a log fire, a well furnished dining room, and an attractive walled garden.

3 en suite (bth/shr) (1 fmly) No smoking in dining room CTV in all bedrooms Tea and coffee making facilities Cen ht CTV 4P No coaches Last d noon

PRICE GUIDE
ROOMS: s £26-£39; d £48-£56; wkly b&b £158-£186; wkly hlf-bd £210-£230✱ £

GH ◗◗◗ **Cedars** 2 Linden Way, Highfield SO41 9JU (from A337 take 3rd turning in right part Toll House pub into Alexandra Rd then left into Fullerton Rd and right into Beresford Rd for Linden Av) ☎01590 676468

A neat bungalow which offers three bedrooms, all freshly decorated and with smart en-suite or private facilities. A sunny breakfast room looks out on the pretty garden, and Mr and Mrs Puzey are friendly and capable hosts.

3 rms (2 shr) No smoking CTV in all bedrooms Tea and coffee making facilities No dogs Cen ht No children 4P No coaches

PRICE GUIDE
ROOMS: d £34-£38; wkly b&b fr £119 £

GH ◻◻◻◻ *Durlston House* Gosport St SO41 9EG
☎01590 676908
Situated within walking distance of the town centre, this
attractive family-run hotel continues to improve, and offers a
warm welcome. The bedrooms are very pleasantly decorated
and have modern en suite facilities and colour televisions.
There is now a well equipped bar, and, after enjoying a good,
home-cooked evening meal guests may relax in the
comfortable lounge.
4 en suite (shr) (1 fmly) No smoking CTV in all bedrooms
Tea and coffee making facilities No dogs Cen ht CTV 4P

GH ◻◻◻◻ *Efford Cottage* Milford Rd, Everton
SO41 0JD (2m west on A337)
☎01590 642315 & 0374 703075 FAX 01590 642315
Efford Cottage is a part-Georgian house, surrounded by trees
and a well tended garden and set back from the Milford road
between Milford and Lymington - ideally located for both the
New Forest and the sea. Bedrooms are prettily decorated and
well equipped with colour TV, mini-fridges, trouser presses
and en suite shower rooms. Guests are offered a variety of
teas in the bright lounge on arrival, and there is an optional
evening meal, traditionally cooked and using home-grown
and local produce wherever possible. Breakfast is a
sumptuous affair, the large menu offering an English grill, a
vegetarian option, cold meats and cheese, fresh fruit, home-
made bread and preserves.
3 en suite (shr) (1 fmly) No smoking in bedrooms No
smoking in dining room CTV in all bedrooms Tea and coffee
making facilities Cen ht No children 12yrs 4P No coaches
Last d 1.5 hrs prior
PRICE GUIDE
ROOMS: d £30-£40; wkly b&b £113-£133; wkly hlf-bd
£157.50-£233.10

GH ◻◻◻◻◻ *The Nurse's Cottage* Station Rd
SO41 6BA ☎01590 683402 FAX 01590 683402
(For full entry see SWAY)

GH ◻◻◻◻ *Our Bench* Lodge Rd, Pennington
SO41 8HH (from A337 turn right signposted Pennington
Village, pass the church, then 2nd right guesthouse on
left) ☎01590 673141 FAX 01590 673141
Closed 24-26 & 31 Dec
Situated in a residential street in the village of Pennington, this
modern, chalet-style bungalow offers comfortable and very
well maintained accommodation. In addition to the dining
room, where breakfast and evening meals are served, there is a
cosy, conservatory-style lounge which overlooks the well
tended gardens. A separate building houses a heated swimming
pool, a jacuzzi and a sauna. Smoking is not permitted.

3 en suite (shr) No smoking Tea and coffee making facilities
No dogs Cen ht CTV No children 14yrs 5P No coaches
Indoor swimming pool (heated) Sauna Jacuzzi Mountain
bikes Last d 6pm
PRICE GUIDE
ROOMS: s £18-£25; d £38-£42; wkly b&b £126-£175;
wkly hlf-bd £173-£215

LYNDHURST Hampshire Map **04** SU30

See also Fritham

GH ◻◻◻◻ *Ormonde House* Southampton Rd
SO43 7BT ☎01703 282806 FAX 01703 282004
Closed 10 days Xmas
Set just off the main Southampton-Lyndhurst road in its own
flower-filled gardens, this friendly family-run establishment
has much to commend it. Following refurbishment work in
recent months, the accommodation is comfortable, attractively
decorated and well equipped. Public areas are smart and well
furnished, and the dining room's daily changing blackboard
menu offers an abundance of home-made fare - dinner being
served every evening except Sunday.
15 en suite (bth/shr) (1 fmly) No smoking in 2 bedrooms No
smoking in dining room CTV in all bedrooms Tea and coffee
making facilities Direct dial from bedrooms Licensed Cen
ht 15P No coaches Last d 6.30pm
PRICE GUIDE
ROOMS: s £24-£35; d £40-£70; wkly b&b £155-£210;
wkly hlf-bd £220-£270
CARDS: ◼◼◼◼◼

GH ◻◻◻ *Penny Farthing Hotel* Romsey Rd SO43 7AA
(from M27 junct 1 follow A337, hotel on left at entrance to
village) ☎01703 284422 FAX 01703 284488
An attractive, personally run hotel conveniently situated near the
town centre provides accommodation in well equipped and
attractively decorated bedrooms which vary in size; they are all
named after types of bicycle. There are a bright, spacious
breakfast room and a small lounge bar, and ample parking space is
provided at the rear of the building.
11 rms (10 bth/shr) (2 fmly) No smoking in bedrooms No
smoking in dining room No smoking in 1 lounge CTV in all
bedrooms Tea and coffee making facilities Licensed Cen ht
CTV 15P No coaches
PRICE GUIDE
ROOMS: s £25-£35; d £45-£70✱
CARDS: ◼◼
See advertisement on p.269.

GH ◻◻◻ *Whitemoor House Hotel* Southampton Rd
SO43 7BU ☎01703 282186
Closed 23 Dec-4 Jan
Whitemoor House, a family-owned establishment located on one
of the main roads into Lyndhurst, offers freshly decorated
accommodation with a traditional feel; Some bedrooms offer en
suite facilities, and those at the front of the house enjoy good
views across to the forest. Breakfast, the only meal provided, is
served in an attractive dining room and forecourt parking is
available.
8 rms (1 bth 6 shr) (2 fmly) No smoking CTV in all bedrooms
Tea and coffee making facilities No dogs (ex guide dogs)

Licensed Cen ht CTV 10P No coaches Golf 18 Last d 6pm
PRICE GUIDE
ROOMS: s £25-£30; d £50-£60; wkly b&b £157.50-£165; wkly hlf-bd £210-£245
CARDS: ◼️ ▦ (£)

LYNMOUTH Devon Map 03 SS74

See also Lynton

Selected

GH Ⓠ Ⓠ Ⓠ Ⓠ **Bonnicott House** Watersmeet Rd EX35 6EP (opposite Anglican church) ☎01598 753346
Mar-Nov
Built as a rectory in 1820, this eight-bedroomed hotel boasting splendid views over Lynmouth Bay has now been upgraded to an attractive standard. All the bedrooms have pretty, co-ordinated soft furnishings; the smaller among them have built-in furniture, but others feature fine period pieces. Next to the well stocked bar is a spacious lounge with a very pleasant outlook. A set dinner based on the freshest of produce is available by prior arrangement and breakfast offers a good choice of cooked dishes. Smoking is allowed in the bar.
8 en suite (shr) (2 fmly) No smoking CTV in all bedrooms Tea and coffee making facilities Licensed Cen ht No children 5yrs No coaches
PRICE GUIDE
ROOMS: s £20-£25; d £38-£50; wkly b&b £130-£158

GH Ⓠ Ⓠ Ⓠ *Corner House* Riverside Rd EX35 6EH ☎01598 753300
Mar-Oct
The spacious bedrooms of this guest house have been completely refurbished to a high standard. They are all attractively decorated, thoughtfully furnished and well equipped with comfortable sofas, colour TVs and tea-making facilities. There is no sitting room but the large restaurant is open all day serving coffee.
3 en suite (shr) No smoking in bedrooms CTV in all bedrooms Tea and coffee making facilities No dogs Licensed Cen ht No children 3P Last d 8pm
CARDS: ◼️ ▦ ▨ (£)

Selected

GH Ⓠ Ⓠ Ⓠ Ⓠ **Countisbury Lodge Hotel** Tors Park EX35 6NB (enter town from A39 and down Countisbury Hill) ☎01598 752388
Mar-Dec
This stone built former Victorian vicarage, in a peaceful secluded setting with a steep terraced garden, retains all the original charm of the period and from its position high above the town and harbour enjoys stunning views across a deep wooded valley. Now, run as a friendly hotel by Margaret & John Hollinshead, Countisbury Lodge offers comfortable accommodation and good home cooking. Bedrooms have been tastefully decorated with co-ordinating floral soft fabrics and equipped with modern comforts. There is an attractive lounge with a colour television and a small bar area built into the exposed rock face. A choice of interesting dishes is offered from the menu and prepared from the best of fresh ingredients.
6 en suite (bth/shr) (1 fmly) No smoking in bedrooms No smoking in dining room No smoking in lounges Tea and coffee making facilities Licensed Cen ht CTV 8P No

coaches Last d 5pm
PRICE GUIDE
ROOMS: d £80; wkly b&b £171; wkly hlf-bd £262
CARDS: ◼️ ▦

Selected

GH Ⓠ Ⓠ Ⓠ Ⓠ **The Heatherville** Tors Park EX35 6NB (1st left hand fork in Tors Rd) ☎01598 752327
Mar-Oct
Dating back over 100 years, this guesthouse run by Roy and Pauline Davis enjoys a superb location overlooking the river Lyn and Summerhouse Hill despite being within easy walking distance of the town of Lynmouth. Bedrooms are comfortably furnished, and delicious home-cooked meals are varied enough to suit all tastes. Guests can relax in a pleasant sitting room with bar.
9 rms (1 bth 4 shr) (2 fmly) No smoking in dining room CTV in 5 bedrooms Tea and coffee making facilities Licensed Cen ht CTV No children 7yrs 9P No coaches Last d 5.30pm
PRICE GUIDE
ROOMS: s fr £22.50; d £45-£50; wkly b&b £157.50-£175; wkly hlf-bd £215.50-£231.50✳

LYNTON Devon Map 03 SS74

See also Lynmouth

Selected

GH Ⓠ Ⓠ Ⓠ Ⓠ **Alford House Hotel** Alford Ter EX35 6AT (enter via Lynbridge and up hill past the Old Station then 2nd right) (Logis) ☎01598 752359
Set high on a hillside overlooking the bay, this charming Georgian house offers accomodation of the highest standard. The lounge is comfortable and thoughtfully appointed and some of the attractively decorated, well furnished bedrooms have four-poster beds. The elegant dining room offers a choice of breakfast and a set dinner menu and displays the same warm, friendly atmosphere as the rest of the hotel.
8 rms (1 bth 6 shr) No smoking in bedrooms No smoking in dining room CTV in all bedrooms Tea and coffee making facilities No dogs (ex guide dogs) Licensed Cen ht CTV No children 12yrs No parking No coaches Last d 5pm
PRICE GUIDE
ROOMS: s fr £20; d £40-£52; wkly b&b £126-£140; wkly hlf-bd £224-£238✳
CARDS: ◼️ ▦

GH Ⓠ Ⓠ Ⓠ **Castle Hill House** Castle Hill EX35 6JA ☎01598 752291 FAX 01598 752291
Bedrooms in this small hotel are all named after local villages, and well equipped with, television, clock radio and tea making facilities. As well as the bar lounge, there is a cosy sitting room, and a dining room for both residents and non-residents.
9 en suite (bth/shr) (3 fmly) No smoking in 2 bedrooms No smoking in dining room No smoking in 1 lounge CTV in all bedrooms Tea and coffee making facilities Licensed Cen ht CTV ch fac No parking Last d 9.45pm
PRICE GUIDE
ROOMS: s £20-£25; d £36-£50; wkly b&b £120-£165
CARDS: ◼️ ▦ ▥ ▨ (£)

269

GH Q Q Q Q *Hazeldene* 27 Lee Rd EX35 6BP
☎01598 752364
Closed mid Nov-28 Dec

A high standard of accommodation is offered at this well-established guest house. Bedrooms vary in size but all are attractively decorated and thoughtfully furnished. There are two small, comfortable lounges, one for non-smokers, and a pleasant dining room where an evening meal is available.

9 en suite (bth/shr) (2 fmly) No smoking in 2 bedrooms No smoking in dining room No smoking in 1 lounge CTV in all bedrooms Tea and coffee making facilities Licensed Cen ht CTV No children 5yrs 8P No coaches Last d 5pm
CARDS: 🔳 🔳 🔳 🔳

GH Q Q Q Q **Highcliffe House** Sinai Hill EX35 6AR (turn off A39 at Lynton, left fork at main car park 300yds up Sinai Hill) ☎01598 752235 FAX 01598 752235

John Bishop with partner Steven Phillips have restored this Victorian 'Gentleman's Summer Residence' to its former glory, with the discreet addition of modern comforts. The views from the property are stunningly beautiful, over Lynton, the coastline and the surrounding countryside. Each bedroom is individually furnished and decorated, all are well equipped. In the well furnished, candlelit dining room, imaginative dinners are served, guests having a varied choice of dishes, prepared from fresh local ingredients, complimented with a fine selection of wines from around the world. Adjoining the dining room is a conservatory, where guests can enjoy a pre-dinner drink, or just watch the setting sun. A separate sitting room is also available to guests.

6 en suite (bth/shr) No smoking CTV in all bedrooms Tea and coffee making facilities No dogs (ex guide dogs) Licensed Cen ht No children 10P No coaches Last d 7pm
PRICE GUIDE
ROOMS: s £25-£30; d £50-£60; wkly b&b £159-£185; wkly hlf-bd £257-£283
CARDS: 🔳 🔳 🔳

GH Q Q Q Q *Ingleside Hotel* Lee Rd EX35 6HW (on private rd between Town Hall & Methodist church) ☎01598 752223
Mar-Oct

This attractive Victorian house is set above the village with views across the Watersmeet Valley to Lynton Bay and the hills of Exmoor. Built in 1895 as a gentleman's residence, it now makes a very comfortable hotel. Bedrooms are warm and pleasantly furnished and the dining room is light and bright. Guests are asked not to smoke in the large sitting room where a fire burns on cold evenings.

7 en suite (bth/shr) (2 fmly) No smoking in dining room No smoking in lounges CTV in all bedrooms Tea and coffee making facilities No dogs Licensed Cen ht No children 12yrs 10P No coaches Last d 5.30pm
CARDS: 🔳 🔳

GH Q Q Q Q *Lynhurst Hotel* Lyn Way EX35 6AX
☎01598 752241 FAX 01598 752241
Mar-Oct

The Lyndhurst, an attractive Victorian house overlooking a charming wood and the bay, is personally managed by Mr and Mrs Townsend, who always offer guests a genuine welcome. Pretty fabrics, ornaments and dried flowers are features of the interior, along with a resident troupe of teddy bears, and Mrs Townsend prepares a tasty selection of home-cooked meals. Parking can be a little difficult but Lynton's main car park is only a short walk away.

7 rms (2 bth 2 shr) (1 fmly) No smoking CTV in all bedrooms Tea and coffee making facilities Licensed CTV No parking No coaches Last d noon

GH Q Q Q Q *Mayfair Hotel* Lynway EX35 6AY
☎01598 753227 & 753327

A recent change of ownership has seen improvements to this character house, now with a comfortable lounge and brightly styled dining room, both with Victorian marble fireplaces and assorted antiques and period pieces. The house itself is set high above the town and enjoys splendid views of an expanse of National Trust headland and out to sea.

9 en suite (bth/shr) No smoking in dining room CTV in all bedrooms Tea and coffee making facilities No dogs (ex guide dogs) Licensed Cen ht CTV No children 10P No coaches Last d 11am
CARDS: 🔳 🔳

🚪 🍽 **GH** Q Q **Retreat** 1 Park Gardens, Lydiate Ln EX35 6DF (top end of Lydiate Rd which runs parallel to main town road (Lee Rd)) ☎01598 753526
Mar-Oct

This well-maintained guest house has basic but adequate accomodation. Reasonably sized bedrooms are thoughtfully decorated and comfortable as is the small lounge. Breakfast and an evening meal are served in the bright dining room.

5 rms No smoking in dining room Tea and coffee making facilities Cen ht CTV No children 7yrs 3P No coaches
PRICE GUIDE
ROOMS: s £15-£16; d £30-£32; wkly b&b £100-£107
(£)

GH Q Q Q **Rockvale Hotel** Lee Rd EX35 6HW (short private road to left of Lynton Town Hall and Tourist Information Office) ☎01598 752279 & 753343
Mar-Oct

The Woodlands offer a high standard of hospitality at this small, bright, cosy hotel. The individually furnished bedrooms vary in size. Judith Woodland also offers a good evening menu with vegetarian dishes.

8 rms (5 bth 1 shr) (2 fmly) No smoking CTV in all bedrooms Tea and coffee making facilities Direct dial from bedrooms No dogs Licensed Cen ht No children 4yrs 8P No coaches Last d 5pm
PRICE GUIDE
ROOMS: s £18; d £44-£48; wkly b&b £120-£146; wkly hlf-bd £204-£244
CARDS: 🔳 🔳

GH ◻◻◻ **St Vincent** Castle Hill EX35 6JA
(adjacent to Exmoor Museum) ☎01598 752244
Closed Dec-Jan
A charming period building set in a colourful cottage garden near
the centre of Lynton (adjacent to the Exmoor Museum), this guest
house includes a splendid Regency staircase among its many
period features. One of the neatly furnished and decorated
bedrooms is on the ground floor, and an evening meal is available
- guests making their choice after breakfast from a menu offering
three starters and main courses. Limited parking space is available
behind the house.
6 rms (1 bth 2 shr) No smoking CTV in all bedrooms Tea and
coffee making facilities No dogs (ex guide dogs) Licensed Cen
ht CTV No children 8yrs 3P No coaches Last d 11.30am
PRICE GUIDE
ROOMS: s £16-£17; d £32-£39; wkly b&b £102-£125; wkly hlf-
bd £170-£195
(£)

Premier Selected

GH ◻◻◻◻◻ **Victoria
Lodge** Lee Rd EX35 6BS (off
A39 opposite Post Office)
☎01598 753203
FAX 01598 753203
Dec-Jan
A Victorian theme recurs
throughout Victoria Lodge,
from the double-fronted
exterior to its interior
furnishings, fireplaces and
mantlepieces. Mr and Mrs
Bennett, the resident proprietors, prepare a four-course
evening meal which is served in the charming dining room.
Smoking is not permitted within the hotel.
10 en suite (bth/shr) (1 fmly) No smoking CTV in all
bedrooms Tea and coffee making facilities No dogs
Licensed Cen ht 8P No coaches Last d 3pm
PRICE GUIDE
ROOMS: s £21-£32; d £36-£60; wkly b&b £113-£185; wkly
hlf-bd £197-£283
CARDS: ◼◼

Selected

GH ◻◻◻◻ *Waterloo House Hotel* Lydiate Ln
EX35 6AJ ☎01598 753391
Waterloo House is an attractive Georgian hotel run in a
friendly and relaxed style by its owners Sheila and Roger
Mountis. The individually furnished bedrooms are
comfortable and well equipped, and the choice of lounges
includes a no-smoking room with a log fire and a TV lounge
with a dispense bar. The elegant dining room features
imaginative menus of home-cooked dishes, and (with notice)
vegetarian and other special diets can be catered for.
9 rms (8 bth/shr) (2 fmly) No smoking in 4 bedrooms No
smoking in dining room No smoking in 1 lounge CTV in all
bedrooms Tea and coffee making facilities Licensed Cen ht
CTV 4P No coaches Last d 7pm

LYTHAM ST ANNES Lancashire Map **07** SD32

GH ◻◻ **Cullerne Hotel** 55 Lightburne Av, St Annes
on Sea FY8 1JE ☎01253 721753
This well maintained Victorian house is quietly and conveniently
situated very close to the Promenade. The five bright and airy
bedrooms are freshly decorated and share a good bathroom.
Guests have the use of a very comfortable lounge, a pleasant bar
and a spacious dining room with separate tables. Forecourt
parking is available.
5 rms (2 fmly) No smoking in dining room CTV in all bedrooms
Tea and coffee making facilities No dogs Licensed Cen ht CTV
4P No coaches Last d noon
PRICE GUIDE
ROOMS: s £14.50; d £29; wkly b&b £101.50;
wkly hlf-bd £116
(£)

GH ◻◻◻ **Endsleigh Private Hotel** 315 Clifton Dr South
FY8 1HN ☎01253 725622
This well maintained small hotel is conveniently situated close to
the seafront and St Annes Square. Well equipped en suite bedrooms
include family rooms and two ground-floor rooms with a patio and
private access. Traditional home-cooked meals are served in the
two-part restaurant with separate tables and there is a comfortable
lounge. Car parking is available at the front of the hotel.
15 en suite (bth/shr) (3 fmly) No smoking in 6 bedrooms No
smoking in dining room No smoking in lounges CTV in all
bedrooms Tea and coffee making facilities No dogs Licensed
Cen ht 8P No coaches Last d 4pm
PRICE GUIDE
ROOMS: s £18-£2; d £36-£42; wkly b&b £125-£130;
wkly hlf-bd £168-£178✳
(£)

INGLESIDE HOTEL
Lee Road, Lynton. Tel: (01598) 752223

Since 1972 Clive and Lesley Horn have been offering
a warm welcome to their guests at Ingleside – a small
family run AA hotel in premier position overlooking
the village. High standards of accommodation, food
and wine assured. All rooms ensuite, colour TV,
tea/coffee makers. Safe car park in hotel grounds.
LYNTON is the perfect centre to enjoy the
magnificent beauty of **EXMOOR'S** coast, cliffs, rivers
& countryside, whether walking, strolling or motoring.
Brochure with sample menus & information sheet of
local & surrounding area gladly sent.

GH 🅀 *Lyndhurst Private Hotel* 338 Clifton Dr North FY8 2PB
☎01253 724343

Conveniently situated close to the centre of town opposite Ashton Gardens, Lyndhurst has been run as a private hotel by Mr and Mrs Clegg for the last twenty seven years. The bedrooms are simply furnished and vary in size; two are en suite, some are family rooms and those at the front of the house benefit from lovely views of the park. There is also a spacious lounge with a television, and a dining room serving breakfast and an evening meal.

12 rms (1 bth 3 shr) (4 fmly) CTV in 4 bedrooms Tea and coffee making facilities CTV 11P No coaches Last d noon

GH 🅀🅀🅀 **Strathmore Hotel** 305 Clifton Dr South FY8 1HN
☎01253 725478

This well maintained small hotel, which is owned and personally run by the very hospitable Mr and Mrs Brocklesby, is well situated on Clifton drive, close to both the beach and town centre. The bedrooms are bright, well equipped and attractively decorated and there is also a very comfortable lounge and small dining room where both breakfast and home-made dishes for dinner are served.

10 rms (2 bth 3 shr) No smoking in dining room CTV in all bedrooms Tea and coffee making facilities No dogs Licensed Cen ht No children 9yrs 10P No coaches Last d 5pm

PRICE GUIDE

ROOMS: s £17-£21; d £34-£42; wkly b&b £119-£140; wkly hlf-bd £147-£168✱

MACCLESFIELD Cheshire Map **07** SJ97

GH 🅀🅀🅀 **Moorhayes House Hotel** 27 Manchester Rd, Tytherington SK10 2JJ (on A538 0.5m N of town centre)
☎01625 433228

This large detached house stands in spacious gardens on the A523 Stockport road, just north of the town centre. The accommodation, whilst not luxurious, is modern and soundly maintained: bedrooms vary in size from compact to quite spacious. Proprietors Ann and Owen Thomas aim to provide a 'home from home' atmosphere for their guests, who comprise both commercial visitors and tourists.

9 rms (5 shr) No smoking in dining room No smoking in lounges CTV in all bedrooms Tea and coffee making facilities Cen ht 15P No coaches

PRICE GUIDE

ROOMS: s £25-£35; d £39-£44✱

Selected

♥ 🅀🅀🅀🅀 Mrs Anne Read **Hardingland Farm Country House** *(SJ958725)* Macclesfield Forest SK11 0ND
☎01625 425759

Mar-Nov

This well maintained 18th-century farmhouse enjoys an elevated position beside Macclesfield Forest, and is convenient for Macclesfield , Buxton, Chatsworth and Haddon House. Two of the bedrooms are en suite and all are bright, airy and attractively decorated. A spacious lounge and a dining room with a communal table are both comfortably furnished and traditional in style. To find the house, turn off the A537 into a lane immediately opposite the millstone which acts as a boundary marker for the Peak National Park.

3 rms (2 bth/shr) No smoking Tea and coffee making facilities No dogs Cen ht CTV No children 16yrs 3P 17 acres smallholding beef sheep Last d 9am

PRICE GUIDE

ROOMS: d £36-£44; wkly b&b £126-£154; wkly hlf-bd fr £165✱

MAIDENHEAD Berkshire Map **04** SU88

Premier Selected

GH 🅀🅀🅀🅀🅀 **Beehive Manor** Cox Green Ln
SL6 3ET ☎01628 20980

Closed Xmas

This large, lovingly preserved house dates in part to the 16th century, and is located in a peaceful suburban setting, convenient for the M4 and A40. The style of the house and gardens, and the gentle nature of its owners all contribute to a special atmosphere. Wood panelling, mullion windows and stained glass reflect the character of the graceful house. The lounge is used as a greeting room where drinks are served to welcome guests; it also houses the communal TV (bedroom TV being available by request). Breakfast is served around a highly polished oak table in a west-facing room and features home-baked bread. Bedrooms are decorated in a restrained manner and each has its own private bathroom facilities.

3 en suite (bth/shr) No smoking No dogs Cen ht CTV No children 12yrs 6P No coaches

PRICE GUIDE

ROOMS: s £36; d £56

MAIDSTONE Kent Map **05** TQ75

Selected

GH 🅀🅀🅀🅀 **Conway House** 12 Conway Rd ME16 0HD
☎01622 88287

Conway House is quietly situated and well positioned for easy access from Junction 5 of the M20 to Maidstone West. Home to proprietors Tony and Sue Backhouse it offers an atmosphere which is very friendly, relaxed and welcoming. The accommodation comprises a combined lounge and breakfast room and a good range of comfortable double-glazed bedrooms all well furnished in the modern co-ordinated style. All rooms come well equipped with remote control TV, trouser press and tea tray, and some have controllable heating. The standard of maintenance and housekeeping is very high and service is personally provided by the proprietors. There is a large rear garden and ample forecourt car parking.

3 rms (1 shr) (1 fmly) CTV in all bedrooms Tea and coffee making facilities Cen ht CTV 5P No coaches Last d 24hrs

PRICE GUIDE

ROOMS: s £20-£25; d £34-£38

CARDS: 🔲 🔲

GH 🅀🅀 **Rock House Hotel** 102 Tonbridge Rd ME16 8SL (on A26, 0.5m from town centre)
☎01622 751616 FAX 01622 756119

Closed 24 Dec-1 Jan

A long established and well run bed and breakfast establishment, Rock House is well situated west of the town centre. The accommodation is particularly well maintained, and resident proprietors Madeleine and Roy Salter provide polite service in a

cheerful atmosphere. There is a small TV lounge, and cooked English breakfast is served in the sunny, no-smoking breakfast room.
11 rms (5 bth/shr) (3 fmly) No smoking in dining room CTV in all bedrooms Tea and coffee making facilities No dogs Cen ht CTV 7P No coaches
PRICE GUIDE
ROOMS: s £26-£38; d £36-£46; wkly b&b £175-£210*
CARDS: (£)

Selected

 GH ◙◙◙◙ Willington Court Willington St ME15 8JW (1.5m E, at junct of A20 Asford Rd & Willington St) ☎01622 738885
Conveniently located on the A20 Ashford Road, this late-Victorian Tudor-style house dates from c1896 and is personally run in a relaxed manner by Mrs Mandy Waterman. The non-smoking bedrooms have been individually furnished and equipped with every modern amenity; all have fresh flowers and one features a four-poster bed. Other facilities include two small, cosy lounges, (one for smokers), and a very attractive beamed breakfast room. Ample car parking is available.
3 en suite (bth/shr) No smoking in bedrooms No smoking in dining room No smoking in 1 lounge CTV in all bedrooms Tea and coffee making facilities No dogs (ex guide dogs) Cen ht CTV No children 16yrs 6P No coaches
PRICE GUIDE
ROOMS: s £25-£33; d £38-£4; wkly b&b £119-£217 (£)
CARDS:

MALDON Essex Map 05 TL80

◙◙◙ Swan Hotel Maldon High St CM9 7EP
☎01621 853170 FAX 01621 854490
This freshly kept inn close to the centre of the attractive town offers public areas neatly divided into a bar/eating area and a separate breakfast room occasionally used for conferences; bedrooms are located above these.
6 en suite (bth/shr) (2 fmly) No smoking in 2 bedrooms CTV in all bedrooms Tea and coffee making facilities No dogs Cen ht 31P Last d 9pm
PRICE GUIDE
ROOMS: s £35; d £48-£50*
CARDS:

MALHAM North Yorkshire Map 07 SD96

GH ◙◙◙ Sparth House Hotel BD23 4DA (in centre of village) ☎01729 830315
Sparth House is one of the oldest houses in Malham and dates back in part to 1664. The bedrooms, some of which are in a more modern extension to the rear, are all well furnished and pleasantly equipped. There is a cosy bar to the rear, a spacious dining room and a games room available. There is also a comfortable lounge and service is warm and friendly from the resident owners.
10 rms (7 bth/shr) No smoking in bedrooms No smoking in dining room No smoking in 1 lounge CTV in 7 bedrooms Tea and coffee making facilities No dogs (ex guide dogs) Licensed Cen ht CTV 7P Table-tennis Darts Last d 5pm
PRICE GUIDE
ROOMS: s £20.50-£27; d £37-£50; wkly b&b £129.50-£175; wkly hlf-bd £145-£210* (£)

MALMESBURY Wiltshire Map 03 ST98

See also Alderton

 ♥ ◙◙◙ Mrs R Eavis Manor *(ST922837)* Corston SN16 0HF (on A429, 3m from junct 17 of M4) ☎01666 822148 FAX 01666 822148
Closed 2wks Xmas
This attractive stone-built farmhouse dates back to the 18th century and is part of a working farm in the village of Corston, and ideally placed for exploring nearby Malmesbury and the Cotswolds. Bedrooms are comfortable and tastefully decorated; there is an elegant lounge with an open fireplace and an adjacent breakfast room. For evening meals, there is a good choice of places within walking distance.
6 rms (3 bth/shr) (2 fmly) No smoking CTV in all bedrooms Tea and coffee making facilities No dogs Cen ht CTV 8P 436 acres arable dairy
PRICE GUIDE
ROOMS: s £16-£25; d £32-£40
CARDS: (£)

♥ ◙◙ Mrs E G Edwards Stonehill *(SU986894)* Charlton SN16 9DY (3.5m from town on B4040) ☎01666 823310
This 15th-century Cotswold-stone farmhouse is situated just over three miles from the ancient borough of Malmesbury on the B4040. The bedrooms are comfortable and there is a cosy dining room where breakfast is served. John and Edna Edwards welcome guests and will happily accommodate pets.
3 rms (1 shr) (1 fmly) No smoking in bedrooms CTV in 2 bedrooms Tea and coffee making facilities Cen ht CTV ch fac ➡

5P 180 acres dairy
PRICE GUIDE
ROOMS: s £15-£20; d £30-£40; wkly b&b £98-£122.50✱

MALPAS Cheshire Map **07** SJ44

Selected

GH 🆀🆀🆀🆀 **Broughton House** Threapwood SK14 7AN
(A41 into Malpas then B5069 to Threapwood 3m turn
left into Broughton House drive)
☎01948 770610 FAX 01948 770610
This interesting conversion of a number of original Georgian
stables, built for a former 17th century house, stands in the
rolling countryside close to the Welsh border and offers well
appointed and very comfortable accommodation. The three
ground floor bedrooms which have either a king-size four-
poster or twin beds, are spacious, attractively furnished and
well equipped with many small extras. Breakfast in the
summer, is served in the conservatory which overlooks the
gardens, open fields and the Welsh hills and in the winter, in
the traditionally furnished dining room or a continental
breakfast tray can be delivered to your room. Guests also have
the use of the six acres of gardens should they wish to play
croquet or tennis. Broughton House is no smoking throughout
and all three bedrooms have wheelchair access.
3 en suite (bth/shr) No smoking CTV in all bedrooms Tea
and coffee making facilities No dogs (ex guide dogs) Cen ht
No children 10yrs 3P No coaches Tennis (hard) Croquet
PRICE GUIDE
ROOMS: s £35-£45; d £46-£54; wkly b&b £150-£189✱
CARDS: ▆▆▆

Selected

GH 🆀🆀🆀🆀 **Laurel Farm** Chorlton Ln SY14 7ES (from
Malpas take B5069 towards Bangor-on-Dee, in 1m turn
right to Chorlton further mile turn right opp tel kiosk,
0.25m to Laurel Farm)
☎01948 860291 FAX 01948 860291
Set in attractive gardens, parts of this former farmhouse date
back to the 17th century, though most of it is early 19th-
century. There are four individually styled bedrooms,
including one at ground level and a family suite. All have a
good array of modern equipment and such thoughtful touches
as flowers and pictures. Dinner is available by prior
arrangement, guests eating at one large table in the quarry-
tiled dining room. The cosy first-floor lounge contains a small
kitchen and is sometimes used by self-catering guests. The
house is surrounded by attractive gardens and has ample car
parking space.
3 en suite (bth/shr) (1 fmly) No smoking CTV in all
bedrooms Tea and coffee making facilities Cen ht CTV No
children 12yrs P No coaches Last d on arrival
PRICE GUIDE
ROOMS: d £48-£55; wkly b&b £165✱

Premier Selected

♥ 🆀🆀🆀🆀🆀 Mrs K M
Ritchie **Tilston Lodge**
(SJ463511) Tilston SY14 7DR
(3m N of Malpas)
☎01829 250223
FAX 01829 250223

Owned by the Ritchie family
for the last five years, this
beautifully preserved and
restored early-Victorian
house is situated in the heart
of the lovely Cheshire
countryside on the edge of the village of Tilston. It was once a
hunting lodge, and the original billiard room is now a
comfortable summer sitting room with a wood-burning stove
and French windows which open out on to the spacious and
attractive gardens. Beautifully furnished public rooms also
include the front hall with its original tiled floor, a dining
room with an open fire and separate tables where breakfast is
served (dinner being available by prior arrangement only) and
the main drawing room. The attractively decorated and
comfortably furnished en suite bedrooms have high ceilings,
and one has a four-poster bed; all are well equipped and have
such thoughtful extras such as fruit, home-made biscuits,
fresh flowers, games and books. Smoking is discouraged.
3 en suite (bth/shr) (1 fmly) No smoking CTV in all
bedrooms Tea and coffee making facilities No dogs (ex
guide dogs) Cen ht CTV 10P Croquet Table tennis 16 acres
rare breeds poultry sheep Last d 6pm
PRICE GUIDE
ROOMS: s £30-£40; d £50-£60

MALVERN Hereford & Worcester Map **03** SO74

GH 🆀🆀🆀 **Bredon House** 34 Worcester Rd WR14 4AA (on
A449) ☎01684 566990 FAX 01684 575323
Closed 21 Dec-1 Jan
Bredon House is a listed Regency building, in elevated position
with extensive views. There is a friendly, informal atmosphere.
The bedrooms are comfortable and there is a cosy lounge and
pleasant gardens.
9 en suite (bth/shr) (2 fmly) No smoking in dining room CTV in
all bedrooms Tea and coffee making facilities Direct dial from
bedrooms Licensed Cen ht 9P No coaches
PRICE GUIDE
ROOMS: s £30-£36; d £45-£55✱
CARDS: ▆▆ ▆▆ ▆▆

GH 🆀🆀🆀 **Pembridge Hotel** Graham Rd WR14 2HX
☎01684 574813 FAX 01684 574813
This character Victorian house has recently seen the benefit of
substantial refurbishment. Comfortable, brightly decorated
bedrooms boast quality modern en suites, and the spacious public
rooms offer a choice of lounges and a restaurant which is also
open to non-residents.
8 en suite (bth/shr) No smoking in dining room CTV in all
bedrooms Tea and coffee making facilities Direct dial from
bedrooms No dogs (ex guide dogs) Licensed Cen ht No
children 8P No coaches Last d 8pm
PRICE GUIDE
ROOMS: s £36-£39; d £55-£60
CARDS: ▆▆ ▆▆ ▆▆ ▆▆ ▆

GH QQQ **Sidney House Hotel** 40 Worcester Rd WR14 4AA (alongside the A449) ☎01684 574994

Enviably positioned in an elevated location, with extensive views over the Severn Valley towards the Vale of Evesham and the Cotswolds, this Grade II listed building dates from 1823. The bedrooms are attractively decorated and mostly furnished with stripped pine. An excellent range of modern facilities is provided and there are some thoughtful extras. There are a comfortable lounge and a pleasant dining room where a commendable breakfast is served.

8 rms (5 shr) (1 fmly) No smoking in dining room CTV in all bedrooms Tea and coffee making facilities Licensed Cen ht CTV 9P No coaches Last d 3pm

PRICE GUIDE

ROOMS: s £20-£40; d £39-£59

CARDS: ■ ■ ■ ■ (£)

Selected

GH QQQQ **Wyche Keep** 22 Wyche Rd WR14 4EG (off B4218, Great Malvern to Colwall) ☎01684 567018 FAX 01684 892304

An impeccably maintained, castellated country house, built at the turn of the century for the Baldwin family, is situated high on the slopes of the Malvern Hills with spectacular views, and there is direct access from the delightful gardens on to the hills. Judith and Jon Williams are warm and friendly hosts who go to great lengths to make their guests welcome. One of the three comfortable bedrooms boasts a four-poster bed, and all have modern en suite facilities. The charming dining room has antique furniture and log fires, and there is a spacious, comfortable lounge. Guests can enjoy a summer evening drink on the verandah. The organised historical tours offered by Jon Williams, a historian, are very popular.

3 en suite (bth/shr) No smoking Tea and coffee making facilities No dogs Licensed Cen ht CTV No children 13yrs 6P No coaches Last d 7pm

PRICE GUIDE

ROOMS: d £50-£60; wkly b&b £175-£210; wkly hlf-bd £287-£322✳

MANCHESTER Greater Manchester Map **07** SJ89

GH QQ **Kempton House Hotel** 400 Wilbraham Rd, Chorlton-Cum-Hardy M21 0UH (on A6010) ☎0161 881 8766

Closed 24Dec-1 Jan

Situated in the suburb of Chorlton-cum-Hardy, three miles south of the city centre, this large Victorian house is within easy reach of the airport and motorway network. The bedrooms, while not luxurious, have modern furnishings and equipment. Other facilities include a lounge, a small bar and a car park.

13 rms (5 shr) CTV in all bedrooms Tea and coffee making facilities No dogs (ex guide dogs) Licensed Cen ht CTV 9P No coaches Last d 5pm

PRICE GUIDE

ROOMS: s £22-£27; d £32-£36.50✳

CARDS: ■ ■ (£)

GH QQ **New Central Hotel** 144-146 Heywood St, Cheetham M8 0PD (1.5m from city centre, off Cheetham Hill Rd) ☎0161 205 2169 FAX 0161 205 2169

This large detached house situated in a quiet residential area, is conveniently located just off the A665 Cheetham Hill Road, approximately one and a half miles from Victoria station. (Heywood Street is reached coming out of the city on the A665, by turning left in to it opposite the Manchester Northern Hospital and an Esso service station). The bedrooms, some of which benefit

from their own shower cubicles are soundly furnished and the public areas include a bright and traditionally furnished breakfast room with an adjoining lounge. The hotel also provides secure car parking.

10 rms (5 shr) CTV in all bedrooms Tea and coffee making facilities Licensed Cen ht CTV 10P No coaches Last d 7.30pm

PRICE GUIDE

ROOMS: s fr £21.50; d £33-£35✳ (£)

MANCHESTER AIRPORT Greater Manchester Map **07** SJ88

GH QQQ **Rylands Farm** Altrincham Rd SK9 4LT (leave M56 junct 6 take A358 towards Wilmslow guesthouse in 1m on left just past Wilmslow Moat House) ☎01625 535646 FAX 01625 535646

Closed 25 Dec

Rylands is a tastefully modernised old farmhouse on the A538 north of Wilmslow, convenient for Manchester Airport and the M56. All six bedrooms are located in a purpose built annexe, half on ground floor level. Some are rather small but all have modern facilities. The cottage-style dining room is in the main house and guests eat at a communal table. Self-catering units are also available.

6 annexe en suite (shr) No smoking in 3 bedrooms No smoking in dining room No smoking in 1 lounge CTV in all bedrooms Tea and coffee making facilities Direct dial from bedrooms Licensed Cen ht CTV 14P No coaches Last d 7pm

PRICE GUIDE

ROOMS: s £33; d £38✳

CARDS: ■ ■

MANNINGTREE Essex Map 05 TM13

Selected

♥ QQQQ Mrs B Whitworth **Dairy House** *(TM148293)*
Bradfield Rd CO11 2SR
☎01255 870322 FAX 01255 870186
(For full entry see Wix)

MARGARET RODING (NEAR GREAT DUNMOW) Essex Map 05 TL51

♥ QQ Mr & Mrs J Matthews **Greys** *(TL604112)* Ongar Rd
CM6 1QR (in Margaret Roding village turn off A1060 by
telephone kiosk, second house on left approx 0.5m)
☎01245 231509
The guest bedrooms at Greys Farm are neat and tidy, and have
shared use of a bathroom. Guests are greeted with hot drinks,
which are provided at all reasonable hours. Full English breakfast
is served at separate pine tables in the small dining room, and
there is a comfortable beamed lounge for relaxing and reading up
on local information.
3 rms No smoking No dogs Cen ht CTV No children 10yrs 3P
340 acres arable sheep
PRICE GUIDE
ROOMS: d fr £37

MARGATE Kent Map 05 TR37

GH QQ **Beachcomber Hotel** 3-4 Royal Esplanade, Westbrook
CT9 5DL ☎01843 221616
Some of the bedrooms at this well kept guest house have views
over the sands of Westbrook Bay. There is a well stocked bar and
a cosy lounge area, as well as the TV lounge and dining room
where freshly prepared meals are served.
15 rms (3 fmly) No smoking in dining room Tea and coffee
making facilities No dogs Licensed Cen ht CTV 1P Last d
10am
PRICE GUIDE
ROOMS: s £15-£17; d £30-£34; wkly b&b £98-£105; wkly hlf-
bd £145-£160✳

Selected

GH QQQQ **The Greswolde Hotel** 20 Surrey Road,
Cliftonville CT9 2LA ☎01843 223956
This comfortable house has a warm, friendly atmosphere and
a high level of hospitality. Lounge and dining room are well-
furnished and decorated in period Victorian style as are the
spacious bedrooms which are equipped with most of the
essentials.
6 en suite (bth/shr) (2 fmly) No smoking in dining room
CTV in all bedrooms Tea and coffee making facilities
Licensed Cen ht No coaches
PRICE GUIDE
ROOMS: s £22-£25; d £36
CARDS: 🔳 🔳

GH QQ *Westbrook Bay House* 12 Royal Esplanade,
Westbrook CT9 5DW ☎01843 292700
This is an improving small guest house providing comfortable
accomodation. Bedrooms are simply but adequately furnished and
equipped. A welcoming lounge is available to guests and breakfast

is served in the well-appointed dining room.
11 rms (4 shr) (4 fmly) CTV in 10 bedrooms Tea and coffee
making facilities No dogs (ex guide dogs) Licensed Cen ht
CTV No coaches Last d 4.30pm

MARKET DRAYTON Shropshire Map 07 SJ63

Selected

♥ QQQQ Mrs P Williamson *Mickley House* *(SJ615325)*
Faulsgreen, Tern Hill TF9 3QW (A41 to Tern Hill
roundabout, then A53 towards Shrewsbury, first right for
Faulsgreen, 4th house on right) ☎01630 638505
Closed Xmas
A large Victorian property, Mickley House is surrounded by
lovely gardens and situated on a 125-acre beef farm some four
miles west of Market Drayton. The house has been
extensively altered to provide good quality accommodation,
and the ease of access to, and spaciousness of the rooms, plus
the availability of ground-floor accommodation makes it
especially suitable for disabled guests. Bedrooms have every
modern facility and many welcoming touches such as flowers,
plants and complimentary wine. The combined lounge/dining
room features exposed ceiling beams and a solid fuel stove in
a large fireplace.
3 en suite (bth/shr) (1 fmly) No smoking CTV in all
bedrooms Tea and coffee making facilities No dogs Cen ht
CTV 10P 125 acres beef

Selected

♥ QQQQ Mr J M Thomas **Stoke Manor** *(SJ646278)*
Stoke-on-Tern TF9 2DU (in village of Stoke-on-Tern
midway between A41 & A53)
☎01630 685222 FAX 01630 685666
Closed Dec
An 18th-century farmhouse set in 250 acres of arable land, is
situated in the village of Stoke-on-Tern, reached off the A53
at Hodnet. The three bedrooms all have en suite bathrooms,
and are furnished with stripped pine, TV and tea making
facilities. There are lovely views of the Shropshire Plain from
the comfortable, modern sitting room. No evening meal is
served, but there are ample local restaurants nearby. Artefacts
and pottery dating from the 12th century are displayed in the
house, and the unusual cellar bar features a collection of old
farm implements. The grounds include a lake stocked with
crayfish and tench, and there are fishing rights on a stretch of
the River Tern.
3 en suite (bth/shr) (1 fmly) No smoking in bedrooms No
smoking in dining room CTV in all bedrooms Tea and coffee
making facilities No dogs (ex guide dogs) Licensed Cen ht
No children 5yrs 20P Fishing Vintage tractor collection
Farm trail 250 acres arable
PRICE GUIDE
ROOMS: s £25-£27.50; d £40-£50✳

MARKET LAVINGTON Wiltshire Map 03 SU05

GH QQQ **Old Coach House** 21 Church St SN10 4DU (Off
B3098 in centre of village opposite church) ☎01380 812879
The Old Coach House is an attractive 200-year-old house situated
in the village of Market Lavington. Bright bedrooms have a
pleasing outlook across rooftops to fields and the dining room
(where an evening meal is served by prior arrangement) is
furnished in a style in keeping with the house. The old stables are

now converted to offer a pleasant ground-floor room with a self-contained flat above. Market Lavington is the ideal base from which to visit such places of interest as Salisbury, Avebury, Longleat, Lacock and Stourhead.

3 en suite (shr) 1 annexe en suite (shr) No smoking CTV in all bedrooms Tea and coffee making facilities No dogs (ex guide dogs) Cen ht 4P No coaches

PRICE GUIDE

ROOMS: s £21-£23; d £39; wkly b&b £122.50-£145✻

MARKSBURY Avon Map **03** ST66

GH 🇶🇶 **Wansdyke Cottage** Crosspost Ln BA2 9HE (junct A39/B3116 in direction of Compton Dando)
☎01225 873674 FAX 01225 873674

Wansdyke Cottage is a stone-built 18th-century property conveniently situated on the A39/B3116 crossroads south of Bath. The reception rooms, with coal fires in cooler weather, offer views to Stantonbury hill and the surrounding farmland. The guest bedrooms, including one ground-floor room, are individually furnished and there is access to bathrooms close by. An extensive dinner menu is offered.

4 rms (1 bth) Tea and coffee making facilities Cen ht CTV 4P No coaches Last d 6pm

PRICE GUIDE

ROOMS: s £15-£18; d £30-£35; wkly b&b £105-£126; wkly hlf-bd £154-£175✻ £

MARLBOROUGH Wiltshire Map **04** SU16

See also Burbage & West Grafton

Premier Selected

GH 🇶🇶🇶🇶🇶 **Laurel Cottage** Southend, Ogbourne St George SN8 1SG (on A346)
☎01672 841288
Apr-Oct rs Mar

This attractive 16th-century thatched farm cottage is set in well kept gardens between Junction 15 of the M4 and the delightful town of Marlborough. It has been sympathetically modernised to provide every modern comfort, yet still retains the features of the original building. There are three bedrooms in the main house and one in a converted coach house in the garden; all are equipped with colour TVs, central heating and hospitality trays. A comfortable lounge is available and breakfast is served around one large table in the beamed dining room. The resident proprietors welcome guests and provide friendly service in their non-smoking home.

2 en suite (bth/shr) 1 annexe en suite (bth) (1 fmly) No smoking CTV in 4 bedrooms Tea and coffee making facilities No dogs Cen ht CTV 5P No coaches

PRICE GUIDE

ROOMS: d £42-£50

Selected

GH 🇶🇶🇶🇶 **The Vines** High St SN8 1HJ
☎01672 516583 & 515333 FAX 01672 515338

Six comfortable bedrooms are situated in a character property on the main street of the delightful town of Marlborough. Guests have full use of the elegant public areas and choice of eating operations at the Ivy House Hotel across the road. The en suite rooms are tastefully decorated and furnished, and equipped with modern comforts including trouser press and mini bars. Parking is available at the rear of the house and the location is ideal for exploring Wiltshire's many areas of beauty.

6 en suite (bth/shr) (2 fmly) No smoking in area of dining room CTV in all bedrooms Tea and coffee making facilities Licensed Cen ht 36P Last d 9.15pm

PRICE GUIDE

ROOMS: s £20; d £50-£55

CARDS: £

MARLOW Buckinghamshire Map **04** SU88

Selected

GH 🇶🇶🇶🇶 **Holly Tree House** Burford Close, Marlow Bottom SL7 3NF (1.5m N of Marlow, off A4155)
☎01628 891110 FAX 01628 481278

This modern property is situated in a quiet residential area overlooking a wooded valley and convenient for the M4 and M40. The attractively furnished bedrooms vary in size and are equipped with the usual modern comforts including TV, direct-dial telephone and ironing boards; the carpeted bathrooms all have shower attachments. The informal breakfast room is adjacent to a small comfortable lounge with TV and video, which overlooks the sun patio. Guests have the use of an outdoor heated pool and are assured of a friendly welcome from Tina Wood.

5 en suite (bth/shr) CTV in all bedrooms Tea and coffee making facilities Direct dial from bedrooms No dogs (ex guide dogs) Cen ht CTV 8P No coaches Outdoor swimming pool (heated)

PRICE GUIDE

ROOMS: s £54.50-£62.50; d £62.50-£67.50

CARDS: £

MARTOCK Somerset Map **03** ST41

GH 🇶🇶🇶 **Wychwood** 7 Bearley Rd TA12 6PG
☎01935 825601
Closed Xmas & New Year

This modern detatced family home backs onto farmland, a short walk from the centre of the village. Bedrooms are thoughtfully equipped. There is a spacious and comfortable lounge, and breakfast is served in the attractive dining room. Dinner can be taken by arrangement.

No smoking CTV in 3 bedrooms Tea and coffee making facilities No dogs Cen ht CTV No children 3P No coaches

PRICE GUIDE

ROOMS: s £24-£28; d £34-£38; wkly b&b £115-£129; wkly hlf-bd £213-£227

CARDS: £

MARTON Lincolnshire Map **08** SK88

Selected

GH Q Q Q Q **Black Swan Coaching Inn** 21 High St
DN21 5AH (on A156)
☎01427 718878 FAX 01427 718878
Myra and Brian Cunliffe are enthusiastic and friendly hosts
who welcome guests to their newly refurbished guest house
complex in the village of Marton on the A156, 6 miles from
Gainsborough. The house was originally a coaching inn,
consequently bedroom sizes are variable but each one is light
and inviting and has pleasant floral soft furnishing. They have
a range of modern facilties and modern en-suite shower room.
Two nicely appointed lounges offer spacious surroundings
and real comfort. There is a dipenser bar for service of drinks
to the lounges and a cosy dining room where dinner and a
hearty breakfast is served. There are also two courtyard
apartments available for longer lets, these can be self-
contained. This is a totally non-smoking establishment. The
owners of this attractive inn are happy to make a special offer
for 1996 of three consecutive nights' bed & breakfast for the
price of two on presentation of a copy of the 1996 guidebook.
6 en suite (shr) 2 annexe en suite (shr) (3 fmly) No smoking
CTV in all bedrooms Tea and coffee making facilities No
dogs (ex guide dogs) Licensed Cen ht CTV 8P No coaches
Last d 8.30pm
PRICE GUIDE
ROOMS: s £24-£29; d £39-£49; wkly b&b £140-£180;
wkly hlf-bd £210-£250

MARTON Warwickshire Map **04** SP46

♥ Q Q Q Mrs P Dronfield *Marton Fields* (*SP402680*)
CV23 9RS (1m off A423 take left bend at church through
village then take left fork in road farm on right)
☎01926 632410
Closed Xmas
Marton Fields, an attractive red brick house, set in mixed
farmland, is located about one mile down a lane leading from the
village church. The spacious bedrooms are mainly furnished in
traditional style, and modern comforts include electric blankets
when necessary. There are two lounges, one of which has a wood-
burning stove. Breakfast is served in a traditionally furnished
room and there is seating for six people at one table. Mrs
Drunfield is a talented artist and examples of her work can be seen
throughout the house.
3 rms (1 shr) No smoking Tea and coffee making facilities No
dogs (ex guide dogs) Cen ht CTV 10P Fishing Croquet lawn
Painting holidays 240 acres arable mixed sheep Last d 6pm

MARY TAVY Devon Map **02** SX57

🖂 💺 ♥ Q Q Q Mrs B Anning *Wringworthy* (*SX500773*)
PL19 9LT (take A386 farm signed 2 miles after Mary Tavy)
☎01822 810434
Mar-Oct
Parts of Wringworthy Farm date back to the Domesday Book, and
there are many interesting architectural features to note. It is to be
found at the end of a private drive in a lovely setting about three
miles from the ancient stannery town of Tavistock. The bedrooms
are large and comfortable, and there is a huge fireplace with a
woodburner in the lounge. Breakfast is served at a 16-foot-long
antique table in a room with polished flagstones and linenfold wall
panelling.
3 rms No smoking in bedrooms CTV in all bedrooms Tea and
coffee making facilities No dogs (ex guide dogs) Cen ht CTV

3P 80 acres beef sheep
PRICE GUIDE
ROOMS: s £16; d £32

MASHAM North Yorkshire Map **08** SE28

Selected

GH Q Q Q Q **Bank Villa** HG4 4DB ☎01765 689605
Mar-Oct
A charming Georgian house stands in its own well tended
gardens only a short walk from the village centre; well
furnished throughout, it features dark beams and antique pine
furniture in the bedrooms. There is a spacious dining room
serving good home cooking and the lounge is comfortable and
inviting.
7 rms No smoking in bedrooms No smoking in dining room
No smoking in 1 lounge Licensed Cen ht CTV No children
5yrs 7P No coaches Last d noon
PRICE GUIDE
ROOMS: s £26-£30; d £36; wkly b&b fr £110; wkly hlf-bd
fr £200

MATLOCK Derbyshire Map **08** SK36

GH Q Q *Bradvilla* 26 Chesterfield Rd DE4 3DQ (on A632
towards Chesterfield, below convent school) ☎01629 57147
Closed 22-28 Dec
This privately owned Victorian house stands in an elevated
position above the A632 Chesterfield road, just beyond the town
centre. It offers a friendly atmosphere, light, fresh bedrooms and a
sun lounge overlooking the colourful garden. A hearty breakfast is
served in the cheerful breakfast room and a small multi-functional
room has been added on the first floor for guests' use.
2 rms (1 bth) (1 fmly) No smoking in bedrooms No smoking in
dining room No smoking in lounges CTV in 1 bedroom Tea and
coffee making facilities Cen ht 4P No coaches

GH Q **5 Clarence Terrace** Holme Rd DE4 3NY (turn
off A6 at County & Station Hotel) ☎01629 55555
Closed 21 Dec-2 Jan
This Victorian terraced house, which stands in a quiet residential
road on the hillside of Matlock Bath, provides sound but modest
standards of accommodation. The flexible range of bedrooms
includes one on the ground floor, a family room and some
reserved for non-smokers; two of the rooms do not have
washbasins. There is a reasonably comfortable lounge/dining
room where breakfast is served at individual tables. On-street car
parking permits are provided for residents.
3 rms (2 fmly) No smoking No dogs Cen ht CTV No parking
PRICE GUIDE
ROOMS: s £14-£15; d £20-£26; wkly b&b £70

Selected

GH Q Q Q Q **Hodgkinsons Hotel** 150 South Pde
DE4 3NR ☎01629 582170 FAX 01629 584891
Closed 24-27 Dec & 3-14 Jan
This delightful small Georgian hotel offers attentive service
and a warm welcome. It has been refurbished in Victorian and
Georgian styles using authentic William Morris designs and
comfortable period/antique furniture; all the modern essentials
have been also been sympathetically added. The hallway

opens into a bar and restaurant to one side and a comfortably furnished lounge with an open fire on the other. There is another equally charming lounge on the first floor.
7 en suite (shr) CTV in all bedrooms Tea and coffee making facilities Direct dial from bedrooms Licensed Cen ht 6P No coaches Hairdressing salon within hotel Last d 8pm
PRICE GUIDE
ROOMS: s £30-£35; d £50-£90*
CARDS:

GH QQ **Kensington Villa** 84 Dale Rd DE4 3LU
☎01629 57627
Set in a slightly elevated position in the town, this semi-detached Victorian building offers three delightfully decorated rooms, each adjacent to the modern bathroom. The dining room opens out to a yard and a terraced rock garden liberally decorated with hanging baskets and tubs. Mr and Mrs Gorman are a very friendly and hospitable couple who keep their rooms in a pristine condition.
3 rms No smoking CTV in all bedrooms Tea and coffee making facilities No dogs (ex guide dogs) Cen ht 3P No coaches
PRICE GUIDE
ROOMS: s £16; d £32; wkly b&b fr £105*

Selected

GH QQQQ **Lane End House** Green Ln, Tansley DE4 5FJ (off A615 at Tansley, opposite Gate Inn public house) ☎01629 583981
The house, aptly named, stands within its own carefully tended and colourful gardens and in parts dates from the 18th century. The bedrooms, each of which is en suite or has its own adjacent bathroom, are furnished with a plethora of personal touches which not only add to their comfort but also add a very homely and appealing feel to them. Home cooked dinners and breakfast are served around a large oval table in the dining hall where French windows lead out to the gardens. The drawing room or lounge is truly lovely furnished and decorated to a high standard. The honesty 'bar' rests on a polished dresser.
4 en suite (bth/shr) No smoking CTV in all bedrooms Tea and coffee making facilities Licensed Cen ht CTV 6P No coaches Croquet Last d 6pm
PRICE GUIDE
ROOMS: s £29-£35; d £38-£50
CARDS: £

GH QQ **Manor House** Wensley DE4 2LL (from A6, turn onto B5057 signed Wensley. Past Square & Compass pub and 500yds up hill, house signposted) ☎01629 734360
A relaxed and welcoming atmosphere pervades this non-smoking establishment - a charming old farm cottage situated on the B5057 between Darley Dale and Winster. Its two simply furnished but freshly decorated bedrooms share a modern bathroom and guests can relax in a splendid garden as well as the comfortable public areas. The hearty breakfast served at a communal dining table includes home-made preserves, cobs and fresh fruit.
2 rms (1 fmly) No smoking Tea and coffee making facilities No dogs (ex guide dogs) Cen ht CTV No children 10yrs 6P No coaches
PRICE GUIDE
ROOMS: s £20-£27.50; d £35-£40 £

GH QQ **Radley House Hotel** 14 Dale Rd DE4 3LT
☎01629 582677
This warm and comfortable home from home guest house is

situated right in the centre of the town on the two upper floors above the traffic and a row of shops. The accommodation is family oriented though business visitors are equally well catered for. Evening meals are home cooked from fresh produce and generously portioned.
7 rms (4 fmly) No smoking in dining room CTV in all bedrooms Tea and coffee making facilities Licensed Cen ht CTV 6P No coaches Last d noon
PRICE GUIDE
ROOMS: s £16-£18.50; d £32-£37; wkly b&b £105-£122.50; wkly hlf-bd £145-£165*

♥ QQ Mrs M Brailsford **Farley** *(SK294622)* Farley DE4 5LR (1.5m to the NW of Matlock) ☎01629 582533
Closed Xmas & New Year
This traditional stone built farmhouse stands just a mile and a half from the town centre amidst horses, dogs, sheep, pigs, dairy and beef herds and arable land. The accommodation comfortable with fine views to Riber and Crich. Mrs Brailsford is a very cheerful and welcoming character and offers a good value home cooked set dinner featuring meats reared on the farm and her own baking, jams and preserves. There is also an enclosed garden for children to play in.
3 rms (1 shr) (2 fmly) No smoking in bedrooms CTV in 1 bedroom Tea and coffee making facilities Cen ht CTV 8P Riding 275 acres arable beef dairy Last d 5pm
PRICE GUIDE
ROOMS: d £32-£36; wkly b&b £112-£126; wkly hlf-bd £130-£144* £

SYCAMORE HOUSE

An 18th Century Grade II listed building tastefully converted to a delightful and comfortable guest accommodation, overlooking the quiet and unspoilt village of Bonsall and the Derbyshire hills beyond. Situated 1½ miles off the A6 and an ideal base for the many and varied Peak District attractions including Chatsworth House, Haddon Hall, Dove Dale, Alton Towers and Carsington Water.
5 bedrooms all en-suite, and with colour TV, hairdryer and tea/coffee making facilities.
Central heating. Residential licence. Car park.
Full English breakfast. Open all year.
Ray & Pauline Sanders
Town Head, Bonsall, Nr Matlock, Derbyshire DE4 2AR
Telephone: (01629) 823903

BL & S Haynes **Packhorse** *(SK323617)*
Tansley DE4 5LF (2m NE of Matlock off A632 at Tansley)
☎01629 580950
Built of the local stone this farmhouse rests at the end of a long
lane in peaceful solitude amidst the Dales. Mr & Mrs Haynes have
handed over the running to their son and plans to refurbish the
bedrooms may be completed during 1996/7. The bedrooms are
each spacious and comfortable decorated in light pastel shades. As
well as a cosy lounge there is a separate dining room. Gloucester
Old Spots and Large Whites are reared on the farm producing all
the breakfast bacon.
4 rms (2 fmly) No smoking in bedrooms No smoking in dining
room CTV in all bedrooms Tea and coffee making facilities No
dogs (ex guide dogs) Cen ht CTV No children 3yrs 20P 40
acres mixed
PRICE GUIDE
ROOMS: s £15-£18; d £30-£36

Mrs Janet Hole **Wayside** *(SK324630)* Matlock Moor
DE4 5LF ☎01629 582967
Closed Xmas & New Year
This family farm sits high above Matlock, approximately 2 miles
from the town centre on the A632. There is a warm welcome and
neat accommodation waiting within this 17th century farmhouse.
Bedrooms vary in size and style, and there is a pleasant and
comfortable lounge. There are also two self-catering cottages
available.
6 rms (2 fmly) No dogs (ex guide dogs) Cen ht CTV 8P 60
acres dairy

MAWGAN PORTH Cornwall & Isles of Scilly Map **02** SW86

GH **White Lodge Hotel** TR8 4BN (on coast road
between Newquay & Padstow opposite Mawgan Porth pitch
& putt) ☎01637 860512
Mar-Nov & Xmas
Especially popular with golfers and dog owners, this family-run
hotel is generally busy with many regular guests. There are bright
bedrooms and comfortable public areas, including a lounge, an
attractive bar and a dining room where a good variety of meals is
served.
16 rms (11 bth/shr) 2 annexe en suite (bth/shr) (7 fmly) CTV in
17 bedrooms Tea and coffee making facilities Licensed CTV
17P Games room Last d 7.30pm
CARDS:

MAXEY Cambridgeshire Map **04** TF10

GH **Abbey House** West End Rd PE6 9EJ
☎01778 344642 FAX 01778 344642
In a peaceful village location, this delightful Georgian house
offers accommodation in both the main building and the converted
coach house. All bedrooms are simply furnished and decorated in
pastel colours. There is a comfortable lounge, an elegant breakfast
room and gardens which contain what is claimed to be the oldest
yew tree in the county.
3 rms (1 shr) 6 annexe en suite (bth/shr) (1 fmly) No smoking in
6 bedrooms No smoking in dining room CTV in all bedrooms
Tea and coffee making facilities No dogs (ex guide dogs) Cen ht
CTV 12P No coaches Fishing
PRICE GUIDE
ROOMS: s £19-£30; d £33-£47; wkly b&b £112-£154✳

See advertisement under STAMFORD

MAYFIELD East Sussex Map **05** TQ52

Selected

Rose & Crown Fletching St TN20 6TE (off
A267) ☎01435 872200 FAX 01435 872200
A delightful, family-run free house with oak beamed bars and
log burning fires, this village inn has been welcoming guests
since the early 16th century. It has recently been refurbished
to provide comfortable, individually furnished bedrooms with
access from the outside. Chef Kevin Shaw offers a wide
selection of bar meals and light snacks, including the
recommended Chef's Specials, and an á la carte menu is
offered in the informal restaurant. A range of enjoyable dishes
is served such as smoked salmon quenelles, home-made steak
and ale pie and a number of salads. The dessert menu is also
popular and the interesting wine list includes some quality
wines.
4 en suite (bth/shr) CTV in all bedrooms Tea and coffee
making facilities No dogs (ex guide dogs) Cen ht No
children 5yrs 15P Last d 9.30pm
CARDS:

MENDHAM Suffolk Map **05** TM28

Mrs J E Holden **Weston House** *(TM292828)*
IP20 0PB (from A143 or B1123 follow signs for Mendham
then follow signs from centre of village) ☎01986 782206
Mar-Nov
An ideal setting for peaceful relaxation, this charming farmhouse
offers thoughtfully furnished accommodation, two of its spacious,
well equipped bedrooms now also having en suite facilities. The
comfortable sitting room provides a selection of books as well as
colour TV, and both a traditional English breakfast and an evening
meal are served in the cosy dining room. Though well off the
beaten track, the farmhouse is signposted and you should find it
easily enough.
3 rms (2 shr) (1 fmly) No smoking in bedrooms No smoking in
dining room No smoking in lounges Tea and coffee making
facilities Cen ht CTV 6P 300 acres arable beef mixed Last d
2pm
PRICE GUIDE
ROOMS: s £21; d £36; wkly b&b £101.50; wkly hlf-bd
£171.50
CARDS:

MERE Wiltshire Map **03** ST83

Selected

GH **Chetcombe House Hotel** Chetcombe Rd
BA12 6AZ (off A303) ☎01747 860219
This elegant detached property is set in an acre of colourful
gardens on the edge of the village, within easy access of the
A303. Five immaculate en suite bedrooms have been
tastefully decorated and furnished, and all come with modern
facilities. There is a comfortable lounge with wood-burning
stove and access to the gardens and a small bar at reception.
The imaginative home-cooked dinners served in the dining
room make use of home-grown vegetables in season.
5 en suite (bth/shr) (1 fmly) No smoking CTV in all
bedrooms Tea and coffee making facilities Licensed Cen ht

10P No coaches Last d 5pm
PRICE GUIDE
ROOMS: s £29-£33; d fr £50; wkly b&b £150-£200; wkly hlf-bd £245-£295✳
CARDS: 🔲 🔲 🔲

MEREWORTH Kent Map **05** TQ65

◀ Q Q Q **Queen's Head** 133 Butchers Ln ME18 5QD (7m E of Maidstone) ☎01622 812534
A Grade II Listed early Victorian country pub located approximately six miles from Maidstone off the A26 with three spacious attractive and well furnished, well equipped bedrooms. There are two bars open all day featuring hand pulled cask ales, popular and good value home made bar food, lots of board games and dart board. The separate non smoking dining room can be reserved for private parties, and families with children are very welcome. There is large garden with children's play area, barbecue, wishing well with spring water, and Thursday night Bat and Trap. Service is personally provided by the resident tenants Jim and Judy Hogan.
3 en suite (shr) No smoking in dining room CTV in all bedrooms Tea and coffee making facilities No dogs (ex guide dogs) Cen ht 50P Last d 9.15pm
PRICE GUIDE
ROOMS: d £36-£39✳

MERIDEN West Midlands Map **04** SP28

GH Q Q Q **Meriden Hotel** Main Rd CV7 7NH (on B4104) ☎01676 522005 FAX 01676 523744
Well placed for the NEC, this licensed guest house offers some good rooms with added facilities for the business user. The bar and connecting dining room are in a chintz and stained wood style which creates a cheerful cottage effect. Under the new ownership, the dining room has been opened in the evening to offer a good range of freshly cooked and accurately flavoured dishes, prepared to order.
13 en suite (bth/shr) (1 fmly) No smoking in area of dining room CTV in all bedrooms Tea and coffee making facilities Licensed Cen ht CTV 15P No coaches Last d 9.30pm
PRICE GUIDE
ROOMS: s £32.50-£38.80; d £62.50-£64.50✳
CARDS: 🔲 🔲 🔲 🔲 🔲

MEVAGISSEY Cornwall & Isles of Scilly Map **02** SX04

GH Q Q Q **Headlands Hotel** Polkirt Hill PL26 6UX (follow one way system through village & ascend towards Port Mellon, hotel 0.25m on right) ☎01726 843453
Feb-Nov & Xmas/New Year
Perched above the village, the enviable position of this small, family-run hotel provides spectacular views from many of the bedrooms as well as the terrace, bar, sitting room and newly refurbished dining room. There are 14 attractive bedrooms, and a comfortable sitting room leads to the sunny bar lounge. Dinner is not to be missed, with friendly Maureen Grist offering good home cooking using local produce and some local recipes, including patisserie, ice cream and sorbets.
14 rms (9 shr) (3 fmly) No smoking in dining room No smoking in 1 lounge CTV in 9 bedrooms Licensed Cen ht CTV 11P No coaches Last d 7.30pm
PRICE GUIDE
ROOMS: s £19-£26; d £38-£52; wkly b&b £119-£168; wkly hlf-bd £203-£252

GH Q Q Q Q **Mevagissey House** Vicarage Hill PL26 6SZ ☎01726 842427 FAX 01726 842427
Mar-Oct
Originally the vicarage until the property was sold in 1948, this lovely Georgian house has been carefully restored by Diana and John Owens. Set in four acres of attractive mature gardens with views right across the valley, it stands only a short stroll from the village centre. The individually furnished bedrooms offer guests a high level of comfort, and all offer fine views. Spacious public rooms include a comfortable lounge (where smoking is discouraged), a sun lounge and small bar, all furnished with antique furniture collected over the years by the Owens. A daily set four-course evening meal is served in the elegant dining room, where a small carte and a well chosen wine list are also available.
6 rms (1 bth 3 shr) (2 fmly) No smoking in bedrooms No smoking in dining room No smoking in lounges CTV in all bedrooms Tea and coffee making facilities No dogs (ex guide dogs) Licensed Cen ht No children 7yrs 12P No coaches Last d 5pm
PRICE GUIDE
ROOMS: s £17-£22; d £38-£50; wkly b&b £112-£168; wkly hlf-bd £217-£259✳
CARDS: 🔲 🔲

GH Q Q Q **Spa Hotel** Polkirt Hill PL26 6UY ☎01726 842244 FAX 01726 842244
Peacefully situated in an acre of mature grounds, the hotel has been recently acquired by Eric and Lesley Bailey, who have ➡

worked hard to upgrade the accommodation offered. The newly decorated bedrooms almost all have sea or garden views, and offer a wide range of extra facilities. The cheerful public areas have also benefited from redecoration and refurbishment, and comprise a comfortable lounge, a separate bar in Tudor style and an attractive beamed dining room where Eric offers a very good-value four-course dinner.

12 rms (11 bth/shr) (3 fmly) No smoking in dining room No smoking in lounges CTV in all bedrooms Tea and coffee making facilities Licensed Cen ht CTV 14P Pool table Pitch & putt Darts Putting green Last d 7pm

PRICE GUIDE
ROOMS: s £20; d £40; wkly b&b £140; wkly hlf-bd £194
CARDS: 🟥 ▦ ⓪

GH Ⓠ Ⓠ Ⓠ *Tremarne Hotel* Polkirt PL26 6UY
☎01726 842213 FAX 01726 843420
Mar-Oct
The O'Connor family took over here early last year and have almost totally refurbished the accommodation. The quietly situated hotel now offers well appointed rooms which are attractively decorated with coordinating colour schemes. Several rooms overlook the outdoor swimming pool and terrace to the rear of the property, while those at the front benefit from sea views; the spacious family room has a large balcony. Public areas include a small bar, a large comfortable sitting room and a bright cheerful dining room leading to the attractive sun lounge which runs across the front of the property.

14 en suite (bth/shr) (2 fmly) No smoking in dining room No smoking in 1 lounge CTV in all bedrooms Tea and coffee making facilities Licensed Cen ht 13P No coaches Outdoor swimming pool (heated) Last d 7pm
CARDS: 🟥 ▦ ▦ ⓪

Selected

♥ Ⓠ Ⓠ Ⓠ Ⓠ Mrs L Hennah **Kerryanna** *(SX008453)*
Treleaven Farm PL26 6RZ (off B3273 on enterence to village, by tennis courts) ☎01726 843558
Mar-Oct
Percy and Linda Henneh's well furnished modern farmhouse, enjoys lovely views of the village and sea below, specially from the lounge. Bedrooms have recently been upgraded with pine and pretty fabrics. The daily four-course dinner is excellent value, orders for the main course usually taken in advance. Vegetarian and children's menus are provided.
6 en suite (bth/shr) (2 fmly) No smoking in bedrooms No smoking in dining room CTV in all bedrooms Tea and coffee making facilities No dogs Licensed Cen ht CTV No children 5yrs 7P Outdoor swimming pool (heated) Games room Putting 200 acres arable beef Last d 5pm
PRICE GUIDE
ROOMS: d £36-£48

♥ Ⓠ Ⓠ Ⓠ Mrs A Hennah *Treleaven* (*SX008454*) PL26 6RZ
(turn right at foot of hill when entering Mevagissey)
☎01726 842413
Closed 15 Dec-7 Jan
The farmhouse looks down over the rooftops of Mevagissey and is only a short stroll from the sea. Bedrooms are all attractive and the large dining room is also open to non-residents. There is a good choice of fixed-price and carte menus, including a 'carve your own joint', and the restaurant is open for lunch and cream teas as well. There is a heated swimming pool and an 18-hole putting course.
6 en suite (shr) (1 fmly) No smoking in dining room CTV in all bedrooms Tea and coffee making facilities No dogs Licensed

Cen ht 6P Outdoor swimming pool (heated) Games room Putting 200 acres mixed Last d 8pm
CARDS: 🟥 ▦

◀ Ⓠ Ⓠ *The Ship* Fore St PL26 6UQ (St Austell Brewery)
☎01726 843324
A historic inn dating back to the reign of Elizabeth I and situated in the centre of this famous fishing village has its nautical atmosphere enhanced by a pine-panelled public bar featuring a flagstone floor and portholes for windows. A variety of menus displayed on large blackboards include local shellfish as well as dishes for children. Bedrooms, situated on the first and second floors, though compact in size and basically decorated, are modern and furnished in pine. There is a separate breakfast room on the first floor. Parking is difficult in the village centre but there is a pay-and-display car park nearby.
6 rms (2 fmly) CTV in all bedrooms Tea and coffee making facilities Cen ht No parking Last d 8.30pm

---

MIDDLEHAM North Yorkshire Map **07** SE18

◀ Ⓠ Ⓠ Ⓠ **The Black Swan Hotel** Market Place DL8 4NP
(CON) ☎01969 622221
rs 24-27 Dec
An attractive, Grade II listed, 17th-century inn set in the centre of this fascinating Dales town is dominated by the castle which was once the home of Richard III. Bedrooms, though not large, are full of charm, prettily furnished (two rooms having four-poster beds) and equipped with good facilities. Bars are full of character, and a good choice of well produced food ranges from bar meals to the carte offered in a cosy dining room; in warmer weather you may choose to eat outside in a delightful rear garden backing on to the castle, which is floodlit on summer evenings.
7 en suite (bth/shr) (1 fmly) CTV in all bedrooms Tea and coffee making facilities Direct dial from bedrooms Cen ht 3P Last d 9pm
PRICE GUIDE
ROOMS: s £26-£29; d £44-£60
MEALS: Lunch £7.25-£10.50alc Dinner £11.50-£19.50alc
CARDS: 🟥 ▦

MIDDLETON-IN-TEESDALE Co Durham Map **12** NY92

GH Ⓠ Ⓠ Ⓠ **Brunswick House** 55 Market Place DL12 0QH
(opposite St Mary's church) ☎01833 640393
Brunswick House, an attractive property dating from 1760 and set in the market place, offers pretty bedrooms with a good range of facilities and mainly pine furniture. There is a cosy lounge and the dining room doubles up as a tea shop during the summer.
4 rms (3 shr) (1 fmly) No smoking in bedrooms No smoking in dining room CTV in all bedrooms Tea and coffee making facilities No dogs (ex guide dogs) Licensed Cen ht 4P No coaches Last d 7pm
PRICE GUIDE
ROOMS: s £20-£27.50; d £40; wkly b&b £125; wkly hlf-bd £195
CARDS: 🟥 ▦ ⓔ

MIDDLEWICH Cheshire Map **07** SJ76

♥ Ⓠ Ⓠ Mrs S Moss **Forge Mill** *(SJ704624)* Forge Mill Ln, Warmingham CW10 0HQ ☎01270 526204
The oldest part of this house dates back to the early 18th century but it was enlarged in mid-Victorian times. Original features, such as the tiled entrance hall, have been preserved and the house is furnished throughout in a style befitting its age and character. There are two spacious bedrooms, both no-smoking, a comfortable lounge and a boldly decorated breakfast room where separate tables are provided. Dinner is available by prior arrangement only.

2 rms No dogs (ex guide dogs) Cen ht CTV 10P 150 acres
mixed
PRICE GUIDE
ROOMS: s £17.50; d £32; wkly b&b £112✳

MIDHURST West Sussex

See **Bepton** & **Rogate**

MILLER'S DALE Derbyshire Map **07** SK17

GH QQ **Dale Cottage** SK17 8SN (turn off A6 between
Buxton and Bakewell onto B6049 at signposted stating
Millers Dale/Tideswell. Opposite "Craft Supplies"")
☎01298 872400
A 19-century Dales cottage set in the lee of the valley on the
Monsal Trail and next to the river. The accommodation is on the
ground floor with the two well furnished and attractive rooms
sharing a very good bathroom. Breakfast is served around a
communal table in an equally comfortable lounge. There is a craft
centre opposite the cottage which is a Mecca for wood turning
devotees an enthusiasm shared by the proprietor Mr McAuliffe.
2 rms No smoking CTV in all bedrooms Tea and coffee making
facilities No dogs (ex guide dogs) Cen ht 2P No coaches Last d
10am
PRICE GUIDE
ROOMS: s £20; d £35; wkly b&b £105-£120✳

MILTON COMMON Oxfordshire Map **04** SP60

◖ QQ **Three Pigeons** OX9 2JN
☎01844 279247 FAX 01844 279483
rs 24-25 Dec
This small country inn is conveniently located for the M40,
making it a popular refreshment spot for coach parties. A good
variety of bar meals is available at lunchtime and in the evening.
The comfortable bedrooms are individually furnished and
decorated, and are located above the public area facing the rear of
the building, reached by an external staircase.
3 en suite (bth/shr) (2 fmly) CTV in all bedrooms Tea and coffee
making facilities Direct dial from bedrooms Cen ht CTV 50P
Pool table Clay pigeon shooting by arrangement Last d 9pm
PRICE GUIDE
ROOMS: s £35; d £50; wkly b&b £196✳
MEALS: Lunch £9.50-£15alc Dinner £9.50-£15alc✳
CARDS:

MILTON KEYNES Buckinghamshire Map **04** SP83

See also **Gayhurst**

Selected

GH QQQQ **Old Bakery** Main St, Cosgrove Village
MK19 7JL (off A508 towards Northampton. Take first
right for Cosgrove, hotel on left after the bridge over
Grand Union Canal) ☎01908 263103 & 262255
FAX 01908 263620
Located in the peaceful village of Cosgrove. An L-shaped
building, much renovated, which is divided into two parts. the
main part comprises a cosy open area with a small bar and
reception which overlooks the restaurant. The owner's
intention is to offer popular, well-cooked food. Most of the
bedrooms are remarkably spacious, well maintained and
furnished to modern standards. A full cooked or Continental
breakfast is available at a supplementary charge.
8 en suite (bth/shr) (1 fmly) No smoking in 2 bedrooms No

smoking in dining room CTV in all bedrooms Tea and coffee making facilities Direct dial from bedrooms No dogs (ex guide dogs) Licensed Cen ht 10P No coaches Last d 9pm
PRICE GUIDE
ROOMS: s £36-£43.50; d £43.50
CARDS: £

GH [Q][Q][Q] **Thurstons Private Hotel** 90 High St, Newport Pagnell MK16 8EH ☎01908 611377
This establishment is part of a subtantial town house on the High Street of Newport Pagnell. Bedrooms are on three floors and are simply appointed with en suite facilities. There is a small lounge area adjoining the breakfast room, and a large car park.
8 en suite (bth/shr) No smoking in dining room CTV in all bedrooms Tea and coffee making facilities No dogs (ex guide dogs) Licensed Cen ht 14P No coaches
PRICE GUIDE
ROOMS: s £27-£35; d £39-£45✱
CARDS: £

MILTON-UNDER-WYCHWOOD Oxfordshire Map **04** SP21

Selected

GH [Q][Q][Q][Q] **Hillborough Hotel** The Green OX7 6JH (off A424 Burford-Stow village centre)
☎01993 830501 FAX 01993 832005
This three-storey, stone-built property stands at the heart of the Cotswolds, overlooking the village green from the setting of its own garden.. Bedrooms in both the house and annexe are attractive, spacious, comfortable and equipped to maximise guests' comfort. Public areas include a bistro and bar decorated in simple but delightful rustic style, with oak tables and polished floorboards; this leads into a conservatory featuring deep sofas and an abundance of plants.
6 en suite (bth/shr) 4 annexe en suite (bth) (3 fmly) No smoking in dining room CTV in all bedrooms Tea and coffee making facilities Direct dial from bedrooms Licensed Cen ht ch fac 15P No coaches Croquet Last d 5pm
PRICE GUIDE
ROOMS: s £30-£40; d £40-£58; wkly b&b £168; wkly hlf-bd £273✱
CARDS: £

MINEHEAD Somerset Map **03** SS94

See also Dunster

⊨☎ **GH** [Q][Q][Q] **Avill House** 12 Townsend Rd TA24 5RG
☎01643 704370 & 0500 121291
This Victorian semidetached three-storey house with a brightly painted façade and colourful flower beds, is conveniently located a short walk from the town and seafront. The accommodation is being steadily improved, and bedrooms have smart, functional furniture, pretty coordinating dÈcor and interesting paintings of local attractions; they are all comfortable. The bar has recently been extended and is cosy and comfortable, and a new sitting room is currently being built. The front-facing dining room is simple in décor, and a small choice for an evening meal is offered, along with a huge breakfast served by Mrs Wood. There is ample forecourt parking.
9 rms (3 shr) (4 fmly) No smoking in dining room No smoking in 1 lounge CTV in all bedrooms Tea and coffee making facilities

---

Licensed CTV 7P Games room Last d 5.30pm
PRICE GUIDE
ROOMS: s £16-£17.50; d £29-£36; wkly b&b £89-£110; wkly hlf-bd £139-£166
  £

GH [Q][Q][Q] **Bactonleigh** 20 Tregonwell Rd TA24 5DU
☎01643 702147
Mar-1 Nov
An informal atmosphere and attentive service is provided at this small family-run hotel, which is only a three-minute, level walk from the beach and the town centre. Additional en suite facilities have been installed in the bedrooms, where guests are requested to refrain from smoking. The fixed-price dinner menu offers good value for money.
8 rms (4 shr) (1 fmly) No smoking in bedrooms No smoking in dining room CTV in all bedrooms Tea and coffee making facilities Licensed Cen ht CTV 5P Last d 5pm
PRICE GUIDE
ROOMS: s £15-£16.50; d £30-£35; wkly b&b £101.50-£119; wkly hlf-bd £147-£164.50✱

Selected

GH [Q][Q][Q][Q] *Gascony Hotel* The Avenue TA24 5BB
☎01643 705939
Mar-Oct
In a good location in the centre of the town, and only 200 yards from the seafront, this Victorian property has been transformed over the years by its owners Kay and John Luckett into a most attractive and comfortable hotel. The accommodation is maintained to a high standard and it offers good sized bedrooms, bright and modern with smartly tiled en suite bathrooms. The open plan lounge and bar are welcoming and have recently been redecorated. There is a pretty pink and green dining room which has a Welsh dresser with a collection of pewter on display.
13 en suite (bth/shr) (2 fmly) No smoking in dining room CTV in all bedrooms Tea and coffee making facilities Licensed Cen ht No children 5yrs 15P No coaches Last d 5.30pm
CARDS:

Selected

GH [Q][Q][Q][Q] **Marston Lodge Hotel** St Michaels Rd TA24 5JP (situated just before St Michaels church on North Hill) ☎01643 702510
Mar-Oct
This substantial Edwardian house - now a small but attractive hotel - stands in an elevated position with superb views over Dunster, Minehead Bay, the Quantocks and the rolling hills of Exmoor. Valerie and Frank Allen welcome guests to their home, offering accommodation in particularly well appointed and equipped bedrooms. A varied choice is offered at dinner, dishes making good use of fresh local ingredients, some of them straight from the garden. The south-facing grounds are a fine feature of the hotel, and there are several seating areas for guests.
12 en suite (bth/shr) No smoking CTV in all bedrooms Tea and coffee making facilities No dogs Licensed Cen ht No children 10yrs 9P No coaches Last d 7pm
PRICE GUIDE
ROOMS: (incl. dinner) s £24-£28; d £48-£56; wkly b&b £148-£183; wkly hlf-bd £221-£249✱ £

GH ◨◨◨ **Mayfair Hotel** 25 The Avenue TA24 5AY
☎01643 702719
Mar-Nov
Located in the town centre but within easy walking distance of the seafront, this private hotel offers old-fashioned standards of hospitality and comfort. Jack and Anne Segenhout have welcomed guests for over eighteen years and provide good home-cooked meals in a traditional English style. The bedrooms are neatly decorated and stocked with thoughtful extras, while a comfortable lounge is available in addition to the separate bar lounge. There is an extremely useful car park at the rear.
16 en suite (bth/shr) 9 annexe en suite (bth/shr) (10 fmly) No smoking in dining room CTV in all bedrooms Tea and coffee making facilities No dogs (ex guide dogs) Licensed Cen ht 23P Last d 6pm
PRICE GUIDE
ROOMS: s £24-£28; d £46-£50; wkly b&b £142-£150; wkly hlf-bd £165-£178✱
CARDS: ▨ ▧

◨ ◨◨◨ **Kildare Lodge** Townsend Rd TA24 5RQ
☎01643 702009 FAX 01643 706516
Sympathetic conversion of this building - designed in the style of Sir Edwin Lutyens and dating back to 1907 - has retained its original character. Situated in a peaceful area of the town, the inn is only a short walk from the shops and the seafront. Marion and Martin Beckett welcome guests, either in the bar or to stay longer. Half the well equipped bedrooms are located in a converted stable block, while the baronial-style restaurant with its high ceiling and massive stone fireplace offers a wide choice of dishes from both a fixed-price menu and carte.
4 en suite (bth/shr) 5 annexe en suite (bth/shr) (3 fmly) No smoking in area of dining room No smoking in 1 lounge CTV in all bedrooms Tea and coffee making facilities Direct dial from bedrooms Cen ht CTV 25P Golf 18 Childrens play area Last d 9pm
PRICE GUIDE
ROOMS: s £19.50-£33; d £38-£66; wkly b&b £120-£180; wkly hlf-bd £180-£240
MEALS: Lunch £3.50-£16alc Dinner £12.50&alc
CARDS: ▨ ▧ ▨ ⓞ   (£)

MINSTER LOVELL Oxfordshire Map **04** SP31

♥ ◨◨◨ Mrs Katharine Brown **Hill Grove** *(SP314115)*
OX8 5NA (off B4047) ☎01993 703120 FAX 01993 700528
Closed Xmas
A modern farmhouse with views over the Windrush and its valley, Hill Grove is situated off the B4047 towards Crawley. Each of the comfortable, pleasantly furnished bedrooms has a colour TV, and guests are invited to use the owner's sitting room. This is a no-smoking establishment.
2 en suite (bth/shr) No smoking CTV in all bedrooms Tea and coffee making facilities No dogs (ex guide dogs) Cen ht CTV 3P 300 acres arable beef mixed
PRICE GUIDE
ROOMS: d £38-£44✱   (£)

MISTLEY Essex Map **05** TM13

◨ ◨◨◨ *Thorn Hotel* Mr T Newman, High St CO11 1HE
☎01206 392821 FAX 01206 392133
This town centre inn has been given a new lease of life by the current owner who used to renovate old buildings. The well proportioned bedrooms have new furniture and fittings, and a rather grisly mural in the dining room serves as a reminder of Mistley's 17th century Witchfinder General.

4 en suite (shr) CTV in all bedrooms Tea and coffee making facilities No dogs Cen ht CTV No children 5yrs 4P Last d 9.30pm
CARDS: ▨ ▧

MOLESWORTH Cambridgeshire Map **04** TL07

◨ ◨◨ **Cross Keys** PE18 0QF (turn off A14 follow signs to Molesworth) ☎01832 710283
A whitewashed village pub just off the A14 offers accommodation both in the main house and in an annexe block; rooms in the original building are more modest in appointment and less up-to-date, all have en suite facilities and are equipped with TV and tea trays. Home-made meals are served in an open-plan bar area where the comprehensive list is displayed on a large blackboard. A supplementary charge is made for breakfast, either full cooked or Continental.
4 en suite (bth/shr) 6 annexe en suite (bth/shr) (1 fmly) CTV in all bedrooms Tea and coffee making facilities Direct dial from bedrooms Cen ht 30P Last d 10.15pm
PRICE GUIDE
ROOMS: s £25.25-£26.25; d £36.50-£38.50
MEALS: Lunch £5-£7&alc Dinner £5-£7&alc
CARDS: ▨ ▧

MORCHARD BISHOP Devon Map **03** SS70

Premier Selected

♥ ◨◨◨◨◨ Mr & Mrs S Chilcott **Wigham** *(SS757087)* EX17 6RJ (1.5m NW of Morchard Bishop in the direction of Chulmleigh)
☎01363 877350
FAX 01363 877350
In a rural area with views over farmland this 16th-century thatched Devon longhouse is run by Stephen and Dawn Chilcott. They are organic farmers and Stephen cooks using home-grown produce including beef, pork, lamb and chicken. Guests dine together round one large table. Bedrooms are imaginatively furnished with locally hand-carved wooden pieces. Open log fires burn in the lounges and there is a snooker room.
5 en suite (bth/shr) (1 fmly) No smoking CTV in all bedrooms Tea and coffee making facilities No dogs Licensed Cen ht No children 10yrs 9P Outdoor swimming pool (heated) Riding 7ft snooker table 31 acres cattle sheep hay
PRICE GUIDE
ROOMS: (incl. dinner) d £80-£110✱
CARDS: ▨ ▧ ▨   (£)
See advertisement on p.285.

MORECAMBE Lancashire Map **07** SD46

GH ◨◨◨ **Ashley Private Hotel** 371 Marine Rd, Promenade East LA4 5AH ☎01524 412034
A privately-owned hotel is conveniently situated on the Eastern Promenade, close to the town centre and with wonderful views over Morecambe Bay. The comfortable bedrooms are bright and freshly decorated; all but one are en suite. Public areas consist of a first floor lounge and a combined dining room and bar where a good choice of home-cooked dishes are available. The resident ➡

owners are very hospitable and make every effort to ensure that their guests are well looked after.

13 rms (11 bth/shr) (3 fmly) CTV in all bedrooms Tea and coffee making facilities Licensed Cen ht 4P Last d 3pm

PRICE GUIDE

ROOMS: s £17-£19; d £32.40-£36; wkly b&b £99.90-£111; wkly hlf-bd £146-£162✳

CARDS: £

GH Q Q Q **Beach Mount** 395 Marine Rd East LA4 5AN
☎01524 420753

mid Mar-Oct

A very well cared for family owned hotel overlooking the bay which offers a full range of facilities in thoughtfully furnished rooms. The lay out of the public rooms is designed to take advantage of its prominent position.

23 en suite (bth/shr) (4 fmly) CTV in all bedrooms Tea and coffee making facilities Licensed Cen ht CTV 6P Last d 7pm

PRICE GUIDE

ROOMS: s £20.25-£21.25; d £37.50-£39.50; wkly b&b £118.50-£129; wkly hlf-bd £142-£159.50✳

CARDS: £

GH Q *Ellesmere Private Hotel* 44 Westminster Rd LA4 4JD
☎01524 411881

In a quiet location central to the town and resort's amenities which is just three blocks from the sea front. The rooms are comfortably furnished and well kept and the lounge is really cosy and homely.

6 rms (2 fmly) No smoking in bedrooms No smoking in dining room CTV in all bedrooms Tea and coffee making facilities No dogs (ex guide dogs) Cen ht CTV No parking No coaches Last d 3pm

GH Q Q **New Hazelmere Hotel** 391 Promenade East
LA4 5AN ☎01524 417876 FAX 01524 414488

Apr-3 Jan

This large hotel is well situated on the promenade and enjoys the most superb sea views. The variously sized bedrooms, most of which are en suite, are soundly furnished and well equipped. Some rooms are situated on the ground floor and a chair lift is available for guests' use. The impressive public areas, which have been decorated with real character and a nautical theme, include a spacious restaurant, comfortable lounge and bar. Unrestricted car parking is available at the front of the hotel on the promenade.

50 rms (17 bth 23 shr) (23 fmly) CTV in all bedrooms Tea and coffee making facilities Licensed Cen ht CTV 3P Last d 5.30pm

PRICE GUIDE

ROOMS: s fr £18; d fr £36; wkly b&b fr £99; wkly hlf-bd fr £160✳

CARDS: £

GH Q Q Q *Hotel Prospect* 363 Marine Rd East LA4 5AQ
☎01524 417819

Etr-Nov

A very well established and family run guest house which has maintained good standards of quality consistently. The bedrooms, half of which enjoy the fine bay views, are furnished comfortably and with modern facilities. The dining room extends at the front to a small lounge area with its own well stocked bar.

14 en suite (bth) (9 fmly) No smoking in 8 bedrooms No smoking in dining room CTV in all bedrooms Tea and coffee making facilities Licensed Cen ht CTV 6P Last d 3pm

CARDS:

GH Q Q Q **Wimslow Private Hotel** 374 Marine Rd East
LA4 5AW ☎01524 417804

Closed 1 week Nov & 1 week Jan

This very pleasant private hotel stands on a quiet corner of the

promenade, at the eastern end, with lovely views of the Cumbrian Hills. Freshly decorated bedrooms have en suite facilities, and the quiet lounge provides an alternative to a bar which - like the first-floor dining room -takes advantage of seafront views. New proprietors bring with them years of experience in the hospitality business.

14 en suite (bth/shr) (2 fmly) No smoking in dining room No smoking in lounges CTV in 13 bedrooms Tea and coffee making facilities No dogs (ex guide dogs) Licensed Cen ht CTV 11P Last d 4.30pm

PRICE GUIDE

ROOMS: s £17; d £34; wkly b&b £110; wkly hlf-bd £158✳

CARDS: £

MORETONHAMPSTEAD Devon Map **03** SX78

Premier Selected

GH Q Q Q Q Q **Blackaller Hotel & Restaurant** North Bovey TQ13 8QY
☎01647 440322
FAX 01647 4403222

Closed Jan & Feb

This former 17th-century wool mill situated on the banks of the River Bovey has been converted into a charming small hotel. Bedrooms are individually furnished and decorated; public areas are a delight, with comfortable easy chairs and plenty of reading material in the spacious sitting room, a well stocked bar, and a small restaurant. Hazel Phillips and Peter Hunt offer a choice of menu at dinner, and the hotel prides itself justifiably for its excellent home cooking using local fresh produce, including Devon lamb and beef, and fish fresh from Brixham or the rivers Dart and Teign.

5 en suite (bth/shr) No smoking in bedrooms No smoking in dining room CTV in all bedrooms Tea and coffee making facilities Licensed Cen ht 5P No coaches Fishing Riding Last d 8pm

PRICE GUIDE

ROOMS: s £27-£30; d £60-£66✳

GH Q Q Q **Cookshayes** 33 Court St TQ13 8LG
☎01647 440374

mid Mar-Oct

Topsy Harding's love of antiques is evident throughout this guest house, which is situated on the edge of the moorland town. It is filled with many small collectable items along with some fine pieces of furniture. The majority of the rooms have en suite facilities and one has a four-poster bed. There is a comfortable lounge with bay windows overlooking the garden, and set home cooked meals are available each evening in the dining room. A cosy bar is also provided.

8 rms (6 shr) (1 fmly) No smoking in dining room No smoking in lounges CTV in all bedrooms Tea and coffee making facilities Licensed Cen ht CTV No children 7yrs 15P No coaches Putting green Last d 5.30pm

CARDS: £

Premier Selected

GH ◖◗◖◗◖◗◖◗◖◗ **Gate House** North Bovey TQ13 8RB ☎01647 440479 FAX 01647 440479

Sheila and John Runham-Williams are relatively new to the hospitality industry, but they have obviously found their vocation. The Gate House is a magnificent medieval thatched cottage set in immaculate gardens which feature a swimming pool. Guests are welcomed with a pot of tea and cakes - hot cross buns at our Easter visit. Dinner is taken in a charming room, warmed by a blue Aga, where fine china and crystal provide a sparkling setting for Sheila's home cooking - the meal probably following soup by salmon or trout from the Teign or Dart rivers. Bedrooms are stylish and thoughtfully equipped, and a massive granite fireplace is a feature of the lounge. The house is unlicensed, but guests are welcome to bring their own wine without corkage charge.

3 en suite (bth/shr) No smoking CTV in all bedrooms Tea and coffee making facilities Cen ht CTV No children 15yrs 3P No coaches Outdoor swimming pool (heated) Last d 6pm

PRICE GUIDE
ROOMS: s £29; d £48

COOKSHAYES
Country Guest House

COURT STREET, MORETONHAMPSTEAD
DEVON. TEL: 01647 440374

LES ROUTIERS. Member of the West Country Tourist Board.

An exceptional licensed country guest house on the edge of Dartmoor. Renowned for comfort and cuisine. Traditionally furnished, including four poster, colour TV and tea/coffee all rooms. Ample secure parking in ornamental gardens. Excellent centre for touring, walking, fishing, golf, riding and shooting. Brochures and tariff by return. Credit cards taken.

Wigham

Stephen & Dawn Chilcott,
Morchard Bishop, Nr. Crediton, Devon, EX17 6RJ   Telephone/Fax: 01363 877350

A 16th century thatched Longhouse within a 30 acre smallholding in a delightful rural setting with views over peaceful farming valley. Situated 1½ miles out of the village of Morchard Bishop with Exeter, Tiverton, Barnstaple, Dartmoor, Exmoor and beaches both north and south all easy car rides. Delicious freshly cooked food using own produce, free range eggs, soft and pressed cheeses, cream, fruit and organically grown vegetables, also an excellent wine list and Devon farm cider. Five guest rooms including one family suite and one delightful 4-poster honeymoon suite, all with colour TV, **VHS Video** and luxury private bathrooms.

Stock includes poultry, pigs, calves, sheep and house cow.

Heated outdoor pool. 2 sitting rooms, snooker lounge, full central heating, guest kitchen.

Sorry NO SMOKERS, CASUAL CALLERS or SMALL CHILDREN. Open all year.

FULL COLOUR BROCHURE   AA Premier Selected ◖◗◖◗◖◗◖◗◖◗   Licensed

Selected

GH Ⓠ Ⓠ Ⓠ Ⓠ *Moorcote* TQ13 8LS ☎01647 440966
Apr-Oct
Mrs Gabrielle O'Brien welcomes guests to her home, a
Victorian house set well back from the road in a neat garden.
Bedrooms are individually furnished and decorated,
combining modern facilities with charm and character. A
hearty breakfast, proves popular with the many regular
Dartmoor National Park tourists and walkers.
6 rms (4 shr) No smoking in 2 bedrooms CTV in all
bedrooms Tea and coffee making facilities No dogs Cen ht
CTV No children 12yrs 6P No coaches

Selected

♥ Ⓠ Ⓠ Ⓠ Ⓠ Mrs T Merchant **Great Sloncombe**
(SX737864) TQ13 8QF (from Moretonhampstead take
A382 towards Chagford for 1.5m. At sharp double bend
take left turning and farm is 0.5m up lane)
☎01647 440595
Great Sloncombe is a listed granite and cob-built longhouse of
13th-century origins. None of its character has been lost in the
provision of modern facilities; a beautiful granite inglenook
fireplace, lots of exposed beams, low ceilings and flagstones
are all features of the rambling old house. Three en suite
bedrooms have been tastefully furnished and decorated in
keeping with the building, and there are many thoughtful
extras. Dinner is available by arrangement, served at separate
tables in the cosy dining room.
3 en suite (shr) No smoking CTV in all bedrooms Tea and
coffee making facilities Cen ht No children 8yrs 3P 170
acres dairy
PRICE GUIDE
ROOMS: d £38-£40✱

♥ Ⓠ Ⓠ Ⓠ Mrs M Cuming **Wooston** *(SX764890)* TQ13 8QA
☎01647 440367 FAX 01647 440367
Closed Xmas
Wooston is a 280-acre mixed farm high above the Teign Valley,
with glorious views across the moors. The tastefully decorated
bedrooms are comfortably furnished. Two are en suite and one has
sole use of the bathroom across the landing. Of the two attractive
lounges, one is for non smokers (guests are requested not to smoke
in the bedrooms). Home-cooked farmhouse fare is served around
one large table in the spacious dining room.
3 rms (2 shr) No smoking in bedrooms No smoking in dining
room No smoking in 1 lounge CTV in all bedrooms Tea and
coffee making facilities CTV ch fac 6P 280 acres mixed
Last d 5pm
PRICE GUIDE
ROOMS: d £35-£42✱

MORETON-IN-MARSH Gloucestershire Map **04** SP13

GH Ⓠ Ⓠ **Acacia** 2 New Rd GL56 0AS ☎01608 650130
A small terraced stone house only a few paces from the attractive
High Street. The accommodation is comfortable and immaculate;
though rooms are compact, they are all light and crisp. Guests also
have use of a welcoming lounge with an open fire.
4 rms (1 shr) (1 fmly) No smoking in bedrooms CTV in all
bedrooms Tea and coffee making facilities Cen ht
PRICE GUIDE
ROOMS: s £18-£21; d £34-£36

Premier Selected

GH Ⓠ Ⓠ Ⓠ Ⓠ Ⓠ **College
House** Chapel St, Broadwell
GL56 0TW ☎01451 832351
Closed 24-26 Dec
A lovely wisteria clad 16th-
century house in a tranquil
village. The bedrooms and
bathrooms are large and many
old features are still intact
although the furnishings are
modern. Sybil Gisby, an ex-
restaurateur, is an excellent

cook, helped by her hundreds of cookbooks.
3 en suite (bth) No smoking in bedrooms No smoking in
dining room CTV in all bedrooms Tea and coffee making
facilities No dogs Cen ht No children 16yrs 5P No coaches
Last d noon
PRICE GUIDE
ROOMS: d £42-£58; wkly b&b £147-£203; wkly hlf-bd
£262.50-£318.50

GH Ⓠ Ⓠ **Moreton House** High St GL56 0LQ (at junct of A44
& A429) ☎01608 650747 FAX 01608 652747
There is a delicious smell of baking bread at this friendly guest
house and tea shop which is open for coffees, lunches, teas and
dinner for residents. Bedrooms are simple with a small lounge
area and bar next to the tea shop.
12 rms (5 bth/shr) No smoking in area of dining room CTV in all
bedrooms Tea and coffee making facilities Licensed Cen ht 7P
Last d 8pm
PRICE GUIDE
ROOMS: s £21.50-£23; d £40-£60; wkly b&b £126-£196✱
CARDS: 🅰 💳

MORLEY Derbyshire Map **08** SK34

GH Ⓠ Ⓠ Ⓠ **Alambie** 189 Main Rd DE7 6DG (facing Rose &
Crown public house) ☎01332 780349
Tucked away behind a screen of mature conifers, Alambie -
Aborigine for "rest a while", is a very welcoming and comfortable
place to stay whether on business or pleasure. The proprietors Mr
& Mrs Green-Armytage invite guests into their home with
enthusiasm. The bedrooms are carefully furnished with some very
thoughtful extras. The reception rooms consist of a small
conservatory and a dining room where meals are taken around a
communal table.
3 en suite (shr) (1 fmly) No smoking CTV in all bedrooms Tea
and coffee making facilities Cen ht CTV 5P No coaches
PRICE GUIDE
ROOMS: d fr £32; wkly b&b fr £140; wkly hlf-bd fr £196✱

MORLEY West Yorkshire Map **08** SE22

GH Ⓠ Ⓠ Ⓠ *The Old Vicarage* Bruntcliffe Rd LS27 0JZ
☎01532 532174 FAX 01532 533549
Set next to a church on the A650, this attractive stone-built house
is furnished with antiques and interesting Victoriana. The en suite
bedrooms offer good facilities (including direct dial telephones);
guests also have access to two comfortable lounges and can take
evening meals in the delightful Victorian-style dining room.
17 en suite (bth/shr) No smoking in 5 bedrooms No smoking in
dining room No smoking in 1 lounge CTV in all bedrooms Tea and
coffee making facilities Direct dial from bedrooms No dogs (ex
guide dogs) Licensed Cen ht CTV 20P No coaches Last d 8pm
CARDS: 🅰 💳 💳

MORPETH Northumberland Map **12** NZ18

◀ Q Q Q *Granary Hotel* Links Rd, Amble NE65 0SD (off A1068) ☎01665 710872 FAX 01665 710681
Only 100 yards from the sea and not far from the town centre, The Granary has well equipped bedrooms, a small lounge, and a pub and conservatory restaurant serving a range of food including home-made pizzas.
13 en suite (shr) (1 fmly) No smoking in 1 bedrooms CTV in all bedrooms Tea and coffee making facilities Direct dial from bedrooms Cen ht 50P Last d 9.30pm
CARDS: ▨ ▩ ▨

MORTEHOE Devon Map **02** SS44

See also Woolacombe

Selected

GH Q Q Q Q Sunnycliffe Hotel EX34 7EB
☎01271 870597 FAX 01271 870597
Closed Dec & Jan
This small hotel is delightfully situated on a hillside overlooking the sea. Bedrooms are very comfortable with lots of thoughtful extras, including quite a range of books, and the lounge bar and restaurant are bright, inviting rooms. Mr Bassett personally prepares all the dishes fresh on the day, even the pudding, and Mrs Bassett ensures that guests are happy and comfortable.
8 en suite (bth/shr) No smoking in 4 bedrooms No smoking in dining room No smoking in 1 lounge CTV in all bedrooms Tea and coffee making facilities No dogs Licensed Cen ht No children 10P No coaches Last d 6pm
PRICE GUIDE
ROOMS: s £25; d £50; wkly b&b fr £175; wkly hlf-bd £245-£275✱

MOUSEHOLE Cornwall & Isles of Scilly Map **02** SW42

◀ Q Q Q Old Coastguard Hotel The Parade TR19 6PR
☎01736 731222
rs Jan & Feb
Known locally as the 'Coastie', this lively establishment has a spacious bistro with superb views of St Clements Isle and across St Mount's Bay to The Lizard. A good choice of dishes is offered, the 'specials' board - which changes daily - featuring a selection of seafood from nearby Newlyn as well as meat and vegetarian dishes. The individually decorated bedrooms vary in size and shape but most have sea views.
11 en suite (bth/shr) 7 annexe en suite (shr) (1 fmly) No smoking in area of dining room CTV in 11 bedrooms Tea and coffee making facilities Cen ht 12P No coaches Access to beach from garden Last d 9.30pm
PRICE GUIDE
ROOMS: s £18-£26; d £36-£56✱
MEALS: Lunch £10-£15alc Dinner £10-£20alc✱
CARDS: ▨ ▩

MUCH WENLOCK Shropshire Map **07** SO69

◀ Q Q Q The Plume of Feathers Inn Harley SY5 6LP (on A458, 1.5m towards Shrewsbury)
☎01952 727360 FAX 01952 727360
This hostelry standing beside the A458 just north of Much Wenlock -almost exactly halfway between Shrewsbury and Bridgnorth - has been much extended in recent times but parts of

the building date back to 1620. Bedrooms have modern equipment and facilities while the lounge bar retains an old world character enhanced by such features as exposed stone walls and ceiling beams. The bright, spacious restaurant is furnished in cottage style, and outside there are a beer garden, a children's play area and a heated swimming pool.
8 en suite (bth/shr) (4 fmly) No smoking in bedrooms No smoking in dining room CTV in all bedrooms Tea and coffee making facilities No dogs (ex guide dogs) Cen ht 70P Last d 9.30pm
PRICE GUIDE
ROOMS: s £20-£28; d £36-£42✱
MEALS: Lunch £7.45-£17.65alc Dinner £7.45-£17.65alc✱
CARDS: ▨ ▩

MUKER North Yorkshire Map **07** SD99

♥ Q Q Q Mrs A Porter **Oxnop Hall** *(SD931973)* Low Oxnop, Gunnerside DL11 6JJ (off B6270) ☎01748 886253
Closed Xmas
Situated amid the fine scenery of Swaledale between Muker and Gunnerside, this 17th century farmhouse has been sympathetically modernised retaining original features such as its mullion windows and oak beams. Attractively appointed bedrooms vary in size but all are thoughtfully equipped, well maintained and have modern en suite facilities. Annie Porter gives guests a warm welcome, provides them with fresh local produce and is a mine of information on local sites and attractions. Guests should note that smoking is not allowed anywhere inside the house.
5 en suite (bth/shr) 1 annexe en suite (shr) (1 fmly) No smoking CTV in 3 bedrooms Tea and coffee making facilities No dogs (ex guide dogs) Licensed Cen ht CTV No children 7yrs 10P 700 acres beef sheep Last d 6.30pm
PRICE GUIDE
ROOMS: s £20; d £40; wkly b&b £117.50; wkly hlf-bd £194✱

MUNDESLEY Norfolk Map **09** TG33

GH Q Q Q Manor Hotel NR11 8BG (at junct of B1145 & B1159) ☎01263 720309 FAX 01263 721731
Closed 2-12 Jan
The Manor Hotel is a large Victorian building perched on the cliff top with direct access to the sea. It is popular with a regular clientele who enjoy the wide range of public areas and simply appointed but comfortable bedrooms.
26 en suite (bth/shr) 4 annexe en suite (bth) (2 fmly) No smoking in dining room CTV in all bedrooms Tea and coffee making facilities Licensed Cen ht CTV 50P Outdoor swimming pool (heated) Last d 9pm
PRICE GUIDE
ROOMS: s £33-£35; d £50-£55; wkly hlf-bd £190-£210✱

MUNGRISDALE Cumbria Map **11** NY33

♥ Q Q Q Mr G Weightman **Near Howe** *(NY286373)* CA11 0SH (1.5m from the A66)
☎017687 79678 FAX 017687 79678
Mar-Nov
An ideal retreat, this traditional Cumbrian farmhouse is set in beautiful countryside just a mile from the A66. Bedrooms are modern in style, with pleasant decor and furnishings; good home cooking and a comfortable lounge and bar are also provided.
7 rms (5 shr) (3 fmly) No smoking in bedrooms No smoking in dining room Tea and coffee making facilities Licensed Cen ht CTV 10P Snooker 350 acres beef sheep Last d 5pm
PRICE GUIDE
ROOMS: d £34-£40; wkly b&b £119-£140; wkly hlf-bd £189-£203✱

◼ QQQ **The Mill Inn** CA11 0XR (2m N of A66 signposted 'Mungrisdale & Caldbeck' midway between Keswick & Penrith) ☎017687 79632
Closed 25 Dec
This 16th-century inn is set against an impressive backdrop of fellside, close to a running beck. Bars are full of character and the bedrooms well furnished and thoughtfully equipped; a good range of food is served in either the bar or the cosy restaurant.
6 rms (5 bth/shr) No smoking in dining room CTV in all bedrooms Tea and coffee making facilities Cen ht 30P Pool table Last d 9pm
PRICE GUIDE
ROOMS: s £27-£38.50; d £54-£60✱
MEALS: Lunch fr £5alc Dinner £6-£12alc✱
See advertisement under KESWICK

NAILSWORTH Gloucestershire Map 03 ST89

GH QQQ **Apple Orchard House** Springhill GL6 0LX ☎01453 832503 FAX 01453 836213
Apple Orchard House, set in a pleasant location with views across beautiful Gloucester countryside, offers three comfortable bedrooms (one of them on the ground floor). Guests have use of a lounge overlooking the garden, an adjacent dining room serving breakfast and dinner, and a private car park.
3 en suite (bth/shr) No smoking in bedrooms No smoking in dining room No smoking in lounges CTV in all bedrooms Tea and coffee making facilities Direct dial from bedrooms Cen ht CTV 3P Last d 5pm
PRICE GUIDE
ROOMS: s £20-£28; d £34-£40; wkly b&b £108-£126; wkly hlf-bd £195.50-£213.50
CARDS: ■■ ■■

NANTWICH Cheshire Map 07 SJ65

See also Wybunbury

Selected

GH QQQQ **Oakland House** 252 Newcastle Rd, Blakelow, Shavington CW5 7ET (on A500) ☎01270 67134 FAX 01270 651752
Mr and Mrs Wetton welcome guests warmly to their comfortable home situated two miles east of Nantwich on the A500, just five miles from the M6. The modern bedrooms, including two in an annexe, are furnished to a high standard, and there are also a spacious sitting room and a large conservatory overlooking the well kept garden. This is a no-smoking establishment.
3 en suite (shr) 2 annexe en suite (bth/shr) (1 fmly) No smoking in bedrooms No smoking in dining room No smoking in lounges CTV in all bedrooms Tea and coffee making facilities Cen ht CTV 10P No coaches
PRICE GUIDE
ROOMS: s £25; d £32-£36
CARDS: ■■ ■■ ■■

NAYLAND Suffolk Map 05 TL93

GH QQQ **Hill House** Gravel Hill CO6 4JB (enter town from A134 into Bear Street, continue past T junction into Birch Street, Gravel Hill is 100yds on left. Hill House is 50yds on right) ☎01206 262782
Hill House sits within a quiet secluded position within this attractive Constable Village, through which passes the Stour Valley walk and the Essex Way. Mrs Heigham offers a warm

welcome to her delightful 16th century home, a Grade II listed timber frame hall house that retains many of its original features. Guests are welcome to use the quiet and tastefully furnished sitting room, with its log fire and comfortable sofas. Breakfast is taken in a delightful dining area which has a highly polished communal dining table and good appointments. There are two bedrooms, one of good comfortable proportions and another which is more cosy by comparison; these share two general bathrooms. Please note that this is a non-smoking house, which is not suitable for very young children.
2 rms (1 fmly) No smoking CTV in all bedrooms Tea and coffee making facilities No dogs Cen ht 3P No coaches Croquet
PRICE GUIDE
ROOMS: s £18-£20; d £36-£38; wkly b&b £120

NEAR SAWREY Cumbria Map 07 SD39

GH QQQ **Buckle Yeat** LA22 0LF ☎015394 36446 & 36538 FAX 015394 36446
This charming 200-year-old cottage, mentioned in Beatrix Potter's 'Tale of Tom Kitten', still retains much of its original character despite the modern furnishings in the prettily decorated bedrooms; the delightful lounge offers deep armchairs and a log fire, while full English breakfast, morning coffee and afternoon teas are served in a beamed dining room featuring an old cooking range. There are a small gift shop in the entrance to the cottage and a private car park to one side of it.
7 en suite (bth/shr) No smoking in dining room CTV in all bedrooms Tea and coffee making facilities Cen ht CTV 10P No coaches
PRICE GUIDE
ROOMS: s £20-£22; d £40-£44; wkly b&b £133-£147✱
CARDS: ■■ ■■

Premier Selected

GH QQQQQ **Ees Wyke Country House** LA22 0JZ (1.5m outside Hawkshead on B5285) ☎015394 36393 FAX 015394 36393
Mar-Dec
A charming Georgian country house situated in its own grounds with stunning views over Esthwaite Water and the surrounding fells. Well proportioned, individually furnished and decorated bedrooms have tasteful colour schemes and a blend of modern and antique furniture, and many benefit from fine views. Delicious evening meals and hearty Cumbrian breakfasts are served in the spacious dining room, and the comfortable lounges offer open log fires and plenty of reading material.
8 en suite (bth/shr) No smoking in dining room CTV in all bedrooms Tea and coffee making facilities Licensed Cen ht No children 10yrs 12P No coaches Last d 7.15pm
PRICE GUIDE
ROOMS: d £76-£80; wkly hlf-bd £330-£350
See advertisement under HAWKSHEAD

Selected

GH 🔲🔲🔲🔲 *The Garth* LA22 0JZ ☎015394 36373
Closed Dec & Jan
A fine Victorian country house standing in its own grounds and gardens, with views of Esthwaite Water and the Langdale mountains. Much of the period character has been retained, but bedrooms now have every modern facility; two rooms have four-poster beds and there is also a family suite on the ground floor. The spacious lounge has an open fire, and freshly cooked English cuisine is offered in the dining room at individual tables.
7 rms (4 shr) (1 fmly) CTV in 4 bedrooms Tea and coffee making facilities Licensed Cen ht CTV No children 5yrs 12P No coaches Last d 4pm

---

GH 🔲🔲 **High Green Gate** LA22 0LF (on B5285 between Bowness & Hawkshead via ferry) ☎015394 36296
Apr-Oct
This 18th-century converted farmhouse, surrounded by a cottage garden, stands at the centre of this village made famous by Beatrix Potter - her house, Hill Top, being only a short walk away. Most of the traditionally furnished bedrooms have en suite facilities and some are suitable for family use. One of the two lounges contains a television set, and there is also a pleasant dining room where breakfast and an evening meal are served.
5 rms (1 bth 2 shr) (4 fmly) No smoking in dining room Cen ht CTV 7P Last d 6pm
PRICE GUIDE
ROOMS: s £22-£25; d £38-£44; wkly b&b £133-£154; wkly hlf-bd £178.50-£199.50✳ £

NEATISHEAD Norfolk Map **09** TG32

GH 🔲🔲🔲 **Regency** The Street NR12 8AD ☎01692 630233
A 17th century house is situated in a popular and picturesque village, ideal for touring the coast or the Broads. Bedrooms are prettily decorated, comfortable and well maintained; some en suite facilities are available.
5 rms (1 bth 1 shr) (1 fmly) No smoking in dining room No smoking in lounges CTV in all bedrooms Tea and coffee making facilities 6P No coaches
PRICE GUIDE
ROOMS: s fr £20; d fr £39✳
CARDS: 💳 £

NEEDHAM MARKET Suffolk Map **05** TM05

Selected

GH 🔲🔲🔲🔲 **Pipps Ford** Norwich Rd Rdbt IP6 8LJ (entrance off roundabout junct A14/A140)
☎01449 760208 FAX 01449 760561
Closed mid Dec-mid Jan
This large, white painted farmhouse offers a homely lounge and a conservatory dining room. Here Mrs Hackett-Jones provides dinner and breakfast, stressing the importance of fresh ingredients. Bedrooms are divided between the main house and the converted barn, those in the farmhouse itself are full of character, whilst those in the conversion have a more contempory feel. All bedrooms have en-suite facilities and individual decor.
3 en suite (bth/shr) 4 annexe en suite (bth/shr) No smoking in bedrooms No smoking in dining room Tea and coffee making facilities No dogs (ex guide dogs) Licensed Cen ht

---

CTV No children 5yrs 12P No coaches Outdoor swimming pool Tennis (hard) Fishing Last d 5pm
PRICE GUIDE
ROOMS: s £17-£37.50; d £45-£65; wkly b&b £150-£220; wkly hlf-bd £261-£331✳

NETHER BROUGHTON Leicestershire Map **08** SK62

GH 🔲🔲🔲 **Cherry Trees Farmhouse** 26 Middle Ln LE14 3HD ☎01664 822491
Built as a cottage farmhouse, this attractive guesthouse has been extended over the last 200 years to include a Georgian frontage. Chequered quarry tiles line the hallway and lead into the lounge and dining room, where elaborately swagged windows and polished antique furniture add the period elegance. Each room is quite distinctive, fireplaces framing open grates ranging from black marble to pine, and bedrooms also feature comfortable armchairs, fresh flowers and books - welcoming extra touches from enthusiastic proprietor Mrs Greaves.
3 en suite (bth) CTV in all bedrooms Tea and coffee making facilities Cen ht CTV 4P No coaches
PRICE GUIDE
ROOMS: s fr £25; d fr £40

NETLEY Hampshire Map **04** SU40

GH 🔲🔲🔲 **La Casa Blanca** SO31 5DQ
☎01703 453718 FAX 01703 453718
A small, family run private hotel situated close to the village centre, with views of Southampton Water. The accommodation has been extensively improved by proprietors Jane and Nigel Poole, and more en suite facilities are being provided. All rooms have direct-dial telephones, clock radios and TV; three have shower units, and the others are en suite. There is a well stocked bar and home-cooked food is served in the attractive dining room. Forecourt car parking is provided.
9 en suite (bth/shr) (3 fmly) CTV in all bedrooms Tea and coffee making facilities Direct dial from bedrooms No dogs (ex guide dogs) Licensed Cen ht CTV 9P No coaches Last d 9.30pm
PRICE GUIDE
ROOMS: s £25; d £44-£46; wkly b&b £133-£175; wkly hlf-bd £175-£245✳
CARDS: 💳 💳 💳 £

NETTLECOMBE Dorset Map **03** SY59

Selected

🔲 🔲🔲🔲🔲 **Marquis of Lorne** DT6 3SY
☎01308 485236 FAX 01308 485666
This 16th-century inn is surrounded by beautiful Dorset countryside. Now completely refurbished, The Marquis of Lorne provides modern accommodation yet retains all the character of the old building. Bedrooms are all en suite and downstairs is a choice of bars, some with exposed walls, open fireplaces and beams. An extensive selection of dishes is offered on the display blackboard and includes a range of home-cooked fare. Resident proprietors Ian and Anne Barrett afford a friendly welcome to guests seeking a peaceful rural location.
6 en suite (shr) (1 fmly) No smoking in area of dining room CTV in all bedrooms Tea and coffee making facilities Direct dial from bedrooms No dogs (ex guide dogs) Cen ht No ➡

children 10yrs 50P Boules Last d 9.30pm
PRICE GUIDE
ROOMS: s £30-£35; d £55✳
MEALS: Lunch £6.50-£16.50alc Dinner
£7.50-£17.50alc✳
CARDS: 🔳 ▩ (£)

NETTLETON Wiltshire Map **03** ST87

Selected

GH 🔲🔲🔲🔲 **Fosse Farmhouse Country Hotel** Nettleton
Shrub SN14 7NJ (off B4039, 1.5m past Castle Combe race
circuit take 1st left at Gib Village for farm 1m on right)
☎01249 782286 FAX 01249 783066
This 18th-century farmhouse constructed of Cotswold stone
stands beside the Roman Fosse Way, close to the village and
deep in the heart of Beaufort hunting country. Considerable
renovation has recently taken place, the original period
fittings complementing the French decorative antique
furniture and pretty English chintzes now creating a unique
style and ambience. Dinner is served in an intimate dining
room featuring first-class home cooking, and there is a
comfortable guests' lounge. Afternoon teas are available in
the attractive garden or in the old barn tea rooms, where
breakfast is also served.
2 en suite (bth/shr) 3 annexe en suite (shr) No smoking in 1
bedrooms No smoking in dining room CTV in all bedrooms
Tea and coffee making facilities Licensed Cen ht ch fac 10P
Golf 18 Last d 8.30pm
PRICE GUIDE
ROOMS: s £35-£55; d £70-£110; wkly b&b fr £225; wkly
hlf-bd fr £350
CARDS: 🔳 ▬ ▩ (£)

NEWARK-ON-TRENT Nottinghamshire Map **08** SK75

See also Kirton

◀ 🔲🔲 *Willow Tree* Front St, Barnby in the Willows NG24 2SA
(take A17 to Sleaford and turn by Newark Golf Club
signposted Barnby) ☎01636 626613 FAX 01636 626613
rs 25 Dec
Parts of this small village inn date back to 1680 and it is set in the
conservation village of Barnby-in-the-Willows, about two miles
east of Newark. Bedrooms are available within the main house
and in a small adjacent annexe to the rear. Guests have the choice
of informal food and real ale in the public bar or carte and daily
menus in the pleasant beamed restaurant.
5 rms (2 fmly) CTV in all bedrooms Tea and coffee making
facilities No dogs (ex guide dogs) 20P Last d 10.30pm
CARDS: 🔳 ▬ ▩

NEWBIGGIN Cumbria Map **12** NY42

GH 🔲🔲🔲 **Tymparon Hall** Newbiggin, Stainton CA11 0HS
(exit M6 at junct 40 and take A66 towards Keswick for
approx 3m, then take right turn for village) ☎017684 83236
Closed 5 Nov-5 Mar
This 18th century manor house lies at the end of the village in it
own gardens and grounds adjacent to farm buildings, yet is within
easy reach of the A66 and the M6. Do not be inhibited by its grand
title, this lovely traditional house has a friendly and relaxing
atmosphere and you will be made to feel at home by owner
Margaret Taylor. Bedrooms are lofty and well proportioned, there
is a comfortable sitting room and spacious dining room with
beamed ceiling.

4 rms (2 bth/shr) (2 fmly) No smoking Tea and coffee making
facilities No dogs Cen ht CTV P Last d 4pm
PRICE GUIDE
ROOMS: s £17-£18.50; d £36-£40; wkly b&b £115-£130; wkly
hlf-bd £185-£200✳ (£)

NEWBIGGIN-ON-LUNE Cumbria Map **12** NY70

🛏🔽 GH 🔲🔲🔲 **Low Lane House** CA17 4NB
☎015396 23269
Closed Xmas/New Year
Originally a farmhouse, this traditional 17th-century house is
steeped in history and full of charm and character. Sympathetically
developed by Janet and Graham Paxman, interesting features
abound, such as old woodwork and original fireplaces, a spice
cupboard in the dining room, fine panelling and a parquet floor in
the sitting room, and a bread oven in the lobby. Bedrooms reflect
the period style and are well proportioned. Whilst they do not have
wash basins, the bathroom is nearby. Meals are taken round the
one table and guests are also invited to use the conservatory which
gives fine views of the gardens and the valley.
3 rms No smoking Tea and coffee making facilities No dogs (ex
guide dogs) Licensed Cen ht CTV No children 8yrs 3P No
coaches Last d noon
PRICE GUIDE
ROOMS: s £16; d £32

NEWBOLD ON STOUR Warwickshire Map **04** SP24

💙🔲🔲 Mrs J M Everett **Newbold Nurseries** *(SP253455)*
CV37 8DP ☎01789 450285 FAX 01789 450285
Mar-29 Oct
A modern farmhouse on a holding which produces hydroponically
grown tomatoes and cucumbers. There is one very large bedroom
for families, a twin-bedded room, a large, comfortable lounge and
a breakfast room where guests share a table.
2 rms (1 bth/shr) (1 fmly) CTV in all bedrooms Tea and coffee
making facilities Cen ht CTV 2P 25 acres arable tomato nursery
PRICE GUIDE
ROOMS: d fr £30 (£)

NEWBURY Berkshire

See **Lambourn**

NEWBY BRIDGE Cumbria Map **07** SD38

🛏🔽 GH 🔲 **Browside Cottage** Ayside LA11 6JE (on A590
S through High Newton on the right after Aireys butcher
shop. Right at phone box)
☎015395 31500 FAX 015395 31857
A country cottage situated just off the A590 about three miles
south of Newby Bridge offers comfortable, cosy accommodation.
The two bedrooms are situated in a wing of the cottage and do not
have wash basins, but there are two bathrooms for guests' use (one
of them in the main part of the house).
2 rms No smoking in bedrooms CTV in all bedrooms Tea and
coffee making facilities Cen ht 2P No coaches Last d 9am
PRICE GUIDE
ROOMS: s £14-£18; d £28-£36; wkly b&b £90-£115; wkly hlf-
bd £153-£178 (£)

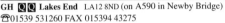
Selected

GH QQQQ **Hill Crest** Brow Edge LA12 8QP
☎015395 31766
Mar-Oct
A split-level bungalow built of blue Lakeland stone with leaded windows, Hill Crest stands in an elevated position about a mile west of Newby Bridge. There are two luxurious bedrooms with en suite facilities, beautiful pine furniture and attractive decor; the delightful small lounge, which opens onto the patio, doubles as a breakfast room.
2 en suite (shr) (1 fmly) No smoking CTV in all bedrooms Tea and coffee making facilities No dogs Cen ht CTV 4P No coaches
PRICE GUIDE
ROOMS: s £23-£25; d £34-£40; wkly b&b £105-£120; wkly hlf-bd £114-£129
£

GH QQ **Lakes End** LA12 8ND (on A590 in Newby Bridge)
☎01539 531260 FAX 015394 43275
Aptly named this very friendly, well situated and accessible Guest House lies at the outfall of Lake Windermere. It is a detached gentlemen's residence within substantial terraced gardens and woods which guests are encouraged to enjoy. The bedrooms are generously proportioned and furnished comfortably. There is also some lounge seating in the dining area.
4 rms (1 fmly) No smoking in dining room CTV in all bedrooms Tea and coffee making facilities Licensed Cen ht CTV 7P No coaches Free use of local Leisure Club
PRICE GUIDE
ROOMS: d £33-£36; wkly b&b £94-£103✳
£

NEWCASTLE-UNDER-LYME Staffordshire Map 07 SJ84

GH QQ **Durlston** Kimberley Rd, Cross Heath ST5 9EG (on north side of town on A34 opposite the Hanging Gate pub)
☎01782 611708
Simple but well maintained accommodation, including some family rooms, is offered by this guest house on the A34, just north of the town centre. Drinks from the licensed bar can be served in either the bright dining room or comfortable lounge. There is no car park but street parking is generally available.
7 rms (2 fmly) No smoking in bedrooms No smoking in dining room CTV in all bedrooms Tea and coffee making facilities Licensed Cen ht CTV No parking No coaches
PRICE GUIDE
ROOMS: s £19; d £34; wkly b&b £126✳
CARDS:
£

NEWCASTLE UPON TYNE Tyne & Wear Map 12 NZ26

GH QQQ **Chirton House Hotel** 46 Clifton Rd NE4 6XH (turn right at General Hospital) ☎0191 273 0407
Chirton House is a large semi-detached property set in its own grounds in a quiet residential area of the city, close to the General Hospital. Bedrooms are comfortably furnished and well decorated, and some are suitable for family use. There are also a lounge and cosy cocktail bar.
11 rms (2 bth 3 shr) (3 fmly) No smoking in 1 lounge CTV in all bedrooms Tea and coffee making facilities Licensed Cen ht CTV 12P No coaches Last d 5.30pm
PRICE GUIDE
ROOMS: s £23-£33; d £34-£44; wkly b&b £140-£180; wkly hlf-bd £180-£230
CARDS:
£

GH QQ **The George Hotel** 88 Osborne Rd, Jesmond NE2 2AP (on B1600 off A1058) ☎0191 281 4442 FAX 0191 281 8300
The George is a privately run family hotel in the popular Jesmond area, within easy reach of the city centre. Many of the well equipped bedrooms have en suite facilities, and a lounge bar and an attractive dining room are provided.
14 rms (10 bth/shr) (4 fmly) CTV in all bedrooms Tea and coffee making facilities Direct dial from bedrooms Cen ht CTV 9P Last d 4pm
CARDS:

NEWHAVEN East Sussex Map 05 TQ40

GH QQ **Harbour View** 22 Mount Rd BN9 0LS
☎01273 512096
Harbour View is a small bungalow in a quiet residential area close to the port. There are three guest bedrooms, all modern and nicely kept, and a shared bathroom. Len and Margaret Bailey are friendly hosts who happily provide early breakfasts for guests catching the morning ferry.
3 rms (1 shr) (2 fmly) No smoking in bedrooms No smoking in dining room CTV in all bedrooms Tea and coffee making facilities Direct dial from bedrooms No dogs (ex guide dogs) Cen ht CTV 4P No coaches
PRICE GUIDE
ROOMS: s £15-£20; d £30-£32; wkly b&b £105✳
£

GH QQQ **Newhaven Marina Yacht Club Hotel** Fort Gate, Fort Rd BN9 9DR ☎01273 513976
Situated on the banks of the River Ouse, this popular yacht club has a range of modern bedrooms on the first floor. Many are compact but have pleasant coordinated fabrics and furniture.

Guests have full use of the club bar and restaurant which offer fine views of the marina.

7 rms (1 shr) 1 annexe en suite (bth) CTV in all bedrooms Tea and coffee making facilities No dogs (ex guide dogs) Cen ht 50P No coaches Marina facilities Last d 9.30pm/10.30pm
CARDS: 🔼 🎫

NEWLAND Gloucestershire Map **03** SO50

Selected

GH ◻◻◻◻ **Millend House and Gardens** GL16 8NF
☎01594 832128
Closed 23-27 Dec
Dating back some 250 years, Millend House is situated in an elevated position looking down the valley to Newland. Set in well-tended, hillside gardens which are open to the public during the summer, it is the home of the Tremlett family. Bedrooms are comfortably furnished and well equipped, thoughtful touches such as magazines and books are placed in the bedrooms. Guests take breakfast around one table in the spacious dining room, which doubles as a guests' sitting romm with comfortable easy chairs and sofa. The majority of guest have dinner at one of the local inns and restaurants of which there are several. This is a no smoking establishment.
3 rms (2 bth/shr) No smoking CTV in all bedrooms Tea and coffee making facilities No dogs (ex guide dogs) Cen ht 4P No coaches
PRICE GUIDE
ROOMS: d £36-£40

(£)

NEWMARKET Suffolk Map **05** TL66

See **Kirtling**

NEW MILTON Hampshire Map **04** SZ29

GH ◻◻ **Copthorne** St Johns Rd, Bashley BH25 5SA (off A35 onto B3058, turn right at Rising Sun public house, after 0.5m turn left at petrol station. House on left) ☎01425 618716
Closed 22 Dec-1 Jan
This personally run property is in the pretty village of Bashley, close to New Milton and the New Forest. The bedrooms are bright and neatly decorated, offering comfortable accommodation. The attractive dining room over looks the garden and Mrs Cheney's lovely collection of Bonsai.
1 rms (1 fmly) No smoking in bedrooms No smoking in dining room No smoking in lounges CTV in all bedrooms Tea and coffee making facilities No dogs Cen ht CTV No children 12yrs 1P
CARDS: 🔳 🎫

 GH ◻◻◻ **St Ursula** 30 Hobart Rd BH25 6EG
☎01425 613515
Located in a residential area, this 1930s house has good accommodation including a ground floor garden room suitable for a disabled person. The sitting room is full of ornaments and family mementoes creating a friendly atmosphere. Full English breakfast is served and in sunny weather you may be able to enjoy a barbecue.
4 rms (2 shr) No smoking in bedrooms No smoking in dining room CTV in 2 bedrooms Tea and coffee making facilities Cen ht CTV 5P No coaches
PRICE GUIDE
ROOMS: s £16-£18; d £32-£38

(£)

NEWPORT Shropshire Map **07** SJ71

◧ ◻◻ **Fox & Duck** Pave Ln TF10 9LQ (1.5m S)
☎01952 825580
This small family-run inn lies just off the bypass near the National Sports Centre. It is set in pleasant lawns and gardens which include a children's play area. Bedrooms are in an extension and in the older part of the inn are two traditional bars with panelled walls and open fires. Guests can choose between a bar meal and something more substantial in the separate panelled restaurant.
9 rms (7 bth/shr) (2 fmly) No smoking CTV in all bedrooms Tea and coffee making facilities No dogs (ex guide dogs) Cen ht 75P Last d 10pm
PRICE GUIDE
ROOMS: s £17.50-£35; d £40-£45; wkly b&b £140-£175✳
MEALS: Lunch £5.50-£9.50 Dinner £5.50-£9.50&alc✳
CARDS: 🔼 🎫

NEWQUAY Cornwall & Isles of Scilly Map **02** SW86

See also Watergate Bay

🏼 ▾ GH ◻◻ **Aloha** 124 Henver Rd TR7 3EQ (located on the A3058, on the northern side of Newquay)
☎01637 878366
One mile from the centre of Newquay, this guest house has a comfortable lounge with a separate bar leading to a conservatory which overlooks the garden. A choice of meals is available in the evening. Bedrooms are attractive but not over large.
13 rms (6 shr) (6 fmly) No smoking in dining room No smoking in lounges CTV in all bedrooms Tea and coffee making facilities No dogs Licensed Cen ht CTV 14P Games room Pool table Darts Last d 6pm
PRICE GUIDE
ROOMS: s £12-£20; d £24-£36; wkly b&b £70-£120; wkly hlf-bd £100-£150
CARDS: 🔼 🎫 🎫 ⓪ 🎫 🔳 (£)

GH ◻◻◻ **Arundell Hotel** Mount Wise TR7 2BS
☎01637 872481 & 874105 FAX 01637 850001
This family-run hotel is situated close to the town and offers a wide variety of leisure facilities. Accommodation is bright and nicely equipped. Most rooms are quite spacious, with en suite facilities; there is a lift to all floors. The varied public areas include a large bar/lounge where evening entertainment takes place six nights a week during the season. There is an excellent leisure complex which includes a large indoor heated pool, together with sauna, solarium and whirlpool. There is also a popular sun terrace and ample car parking.
35 en suite (bth/shr) (8 fmly) No smoking in dining room CTV in all bedrooms Tea and coffee making facilities Direct dial from bedrooms No dogs Licensed Lift Cen ht CTV 34P Indoor swimming pool (heated) Snooker Sauna Solarium Min-gym Pool room Last d 7pm
CARDS: 🔼 🎫 🎫 ⓪

🏼 ▾ GH ◻◻◻ **Bon-Ami Hotel** 3 Trenance Ln TR7 2HX (take A3058 Newquay road, then 3rd left to Newlyn East and take 2nd farm lane on left) ☎01637 874009
Apr-Sep
Enjoying a fine location overlooking the park and boating lake, this very friendly small hotel provides modern, bright and well maintained bedrooms, all with private shower, WC and heated towel rails. The spacious dining room offers a varied menu (special diets can be catered for on request), whilst light refreshments and cream teas are served throughout the day on the sun terrace. There is a separate bar and service is friendly and helpful.
9 en suite (shr) No smoking in dining room CTV in all bedrooms Tea and coffee making facilities No dogs Licensed Cen ht CTV

No children 9P No coaches Last d 5pm
PRICE GUIDE
ROOMS: s £16-£18; d £32-£36; wkly b&b £98-£121; wkly hlf-bd £126.50-£149.50
CARDS: (£)

GH Q Q Q **Copper Beech Hotel** 70 Edgcumbe Av TR7 2NN
☎01637 873376
Etr-mid Oct & Xmas & New Year
This family-run hotel is situated in its own grounds in a quiet area of town opposite Trenance Gardens, and has been owned by the Lentern family for the past 20 years. Continued improvements now provide comfortable accommodation with bright, pretty coordinating decor; there are 14 bedrooms, some on the ground floor, most with private bathrooms. Public areas are well furnished and smartly decorated and include a TV lounge, spacious lounge bar opening on to a patio area and an attractive dining room.
14 en suite (bth/shr) (3 fmly) No smoking in dining room CTV in all bedrooms Tea and coffee making facilities No dogs (ex guide dogs) Licensed Cen ht CTV 14P Last d 6pm
PRICE GUIDE
ROOMS: wkly hlf-bd £155.10-£186.78

GH Q Q Q **Hotel Trevalsa** Whipsiderry Beach, Porth
TR7 3LX ☎01637 873336 FAX 01637 878843
Apr-mid Oct
In a stunning position overlooking Porth Beach and within a minute's walk of Whipsiderry Beach, this guest house offers a variety of bedrooms, some with magnificent views, some with four-poster beds and one on the ground floor. There is a spacious bar and separate lounge as well as a games room for children. A four-course meal with a choice of dishes is served each evening. Ample private parking is provided to the rear of the property.
24 rms (20 bth/shr) (7 fmly) No smoking in dining room CTV in all bedrooms Tea and coffee making facilities Licensed Cen ht CTV 19P Last d 7pm
PRICE GUIDE
ROOMS: (incl. dinner) s £20-£29; d £40-£58; wkly b&b £109-£169; wkly hlf-bd £139-£199*
CARDS: (£)

GH Q Q Q *Kellsboro Hotel* 12 Henver Rd TR7 3BJ
☎01637 874620
Etr-Oct
There is an indoor heated swimming pool with a sun terrace at this hotel. Above is a large bar with dance floor and pool table with live entertainment twice a week. Bedrooms are simply decorated. In the newly decorated dining room a choice is offered at both breakfast and dinner.
14 rms (10 bth 3 shr) (8 fmly) CTV in all bedrooms Tea and coffee making facilities Licensed Cen ht 20P Indoor swimming pool (heated) Pool table Last d 7pm
CARDS:

GH Q Q Q *Links Hotel* Headland Rd TR7 1HN
☎01637 873211
Apr-Oct
A well established family run hotel in a convenient position between Fistral Beach and the town centre, very close to the golf course. The bedrooms all have satellite TV, and most enjoy views of either the sea or golf course. Hearty breakfasts and optional evening meals are available in the dining room, and there is a large bar and games room which features original beer barrels for seats. Mr and Mrs Newton are welcoming, friendly hosts and many of their guests return year after year.
15 rms (10 bth 3 shr) (3 fmly) CTV in all bedrooms Tea and coffee making facilities Licensed Cen ht CTV No parking Last d 4pm

 Selected

GH Q Q Q Q **Pendeen Hotel** Alexandra Road, Porth TR7 3ND ☎01637 873521 FAX 01637 873521
Closed Nov-2 Jan
Many of the bedrooms have fine views over Porth Beach at a hotel which has a reputation for high standards of comfort and friendliness. A choice of menus is available at breakfast and dinner, and snacks and light lunches can be had throughout the day in the bar or on the sun terrace.
15 en suite (bth/shr) (5 fmly) No smoking in 3 bedrooms No smoking in dining room CTV in all bedrooms Tea and coffee making facilities No dogs (ex guide dogs) Licensed Cen ht 15P No coaches Last d 6.30pm
PRICE GUIDE
ROOMS: s £16.50-£22.50; d £35-£49; wkly b&b £105-£150; wkly hlf-bd £135-£189
CARDS: (£)
See advertisement on p.297.

Selected

GH Q Q Q Q **Porth Enodoc** 4 Esplanade Rd, Pentire TR7 1PY ☎01637 872372
Mar-Oct
Splendidly situated overlooking Fistral Beach, this family-run hotel maintains exceptionally high standards throughout. The comfortable bedrooms are simply and tastefully furnished; all have en suite shower rooms and many other useful extras. Public areas include a cosy bar, a lounge in soft shades of ➡

Hill Farm
Kirtling, Nr Newmarket, Suffolk CB8 9HQ
Telephone: (01638) 730253

A 400 year old farmhouse which commands superb views, offers spacious well appointed accommodation. All rooms have tea/coffee facilities and some en suite. Full central heating. Access at all times – own key. Choice of menu with home cooking and special diets catered for by prior arrangement.
Fully licensed. Open all year.

pink and green and a sunny dining room. Dinner is served each evening, offering a choice of traditional menus which make good use of fresh local produce.

15 en suite (shr) (3 fmly) No smoking in dining room CTV in all bedrooms Tea and coffee making facilities No dogs Licensed Cen ht No children 2yrs 15P No coaches Last d 6.45pm

PRICE GUIDE
ROOMS: s £17.50-£23.50; d £30-£47; wkly b&b £99-£150; wkly hlf-bd £139-£185

GH QQQQ *Priory Lodge Hotel* Mount Wise TR7 2BH (turn left at traffic lights in town centre on to the one way system & Berry Rd, right on to Mount Wise B3282 hotel is approx 0.5m on right) ☎01637 874111
Mar-Nov & Xmas rs Mar & Nov

With lovely sea views over the bay from many bedrooms and public areas, Priory Lodge stands in well maintained gardens close to the town centre, beaches and harbour. The Pocklington family maintain high standards of decor throughout the establishment, continually improving and updating the accommodation. Spacious, attractively decorated and well equipped bedrooms, some of them with balconies, include four family rooms grouped around the heated outdoor swimming pool; a sauna and solarium are provided, as well as a games room with pool table and fruit machines. A wide variety of freshly cooked food is offered in the large wood-panelled dining room, a small but relaxing lounge has family trophies on show, and, during the season, live entertainment is staged in the lively lounge bar with its adjoining dance floor.

22 rms (7 bth 13 shr) 4 annexe en suite (shr) (17 fmly) No smoking in dining room CTV in all bedrooms Tea and coffee making facilities Direct dial from bedrooms No dogs (ex guide dogs) Licensed Cen ht 30P Outdoor swimming pool (heated) Sauna Solarium Pool table Video machines Last d 7.30pm

CARDS: ☒ ▬ ▥

GH QQQ **Rolling Waves** Alexandra Rd, Porth TR7 3NB (off A30 & join A3059 then onto B3276 into Porth) ☎01637 873236
Attractively positioned, with views over Porth beach and Newquay Bay, this establishment offers accommodation in bedrooms which are comfortable but not over large, five of them situated on the ground floor. The pleasant lounge has good views and a home-cooked evening meal is served in the dining room.

9 rms (8 shr) (2 fmly) No smoking in bedrooms No smoking in dining room No smoking in lounges CTV in all bedrooms Tea and coffee making facilities Licensed Cen ht CTV 10P Last d 6.30pm

PRICE GUIDE
ROOMS: s £16-£24; d £32-£48; wkly b&b £115-£145; wkly hlf-bd £155-£185
CARDS: ☒ ▥

GH QQQ **Tir Chonaill Lodge** 106 Mount Wise TR7 1QP ☎01637 876492 FAX 01637 876492
Guests are well looked after at this friendly guesthouse, which is personally run by Mr and Mrs Watts and family. Bedrooms are brightly decorated and simply furnished, and there is a small lounge, well stocked bar and front-facing dining room.

22 rms (21 bth/shr) (10 fmly) No smoking in 2 bedrooms No smoking in area of dining room CTV in all bedrooms Tea and

coffee making facilities Licensed Cen ht CTV 21P Darts Pool table Last d 5pm

PRICE GUIDE
ROOMS: s £18-£26; d £35-£44; wkly b&b £115-£155; wkly hlf-bd £145-£175
CARDS: ☒

GH QQQQ **Towan Beach Hotel** 7 Trebarwith Crescent TR7 1DX ☎01637 872093
A delightful small terraced Guest house situated close to the town centre and beach. The property has been totally refurbished by the present owners and now provides a high standard of accommodation in single, double and family rooms. Downstairs a small cocktail bar leads out on to a terraced area, and there is an attractive lounge with an open fire and a separate dining room. The resident chef/proprietor Andrew Medhurst creates a wide choice of menus, and barbecues are held on the terrace on summer evenings. There is limited private parking available by arrangement.

6 rms (3 shr) (1 fmly) No smoking in dining room CTV in all bedrooms Tea and coffee making facilities No dogs (ex guide dogs) Licensed Cen ht CTV No children 8yrs 2P No coaches Last d 4.30pm

PRICE GUIDE
ROOMS: (incl. dinner) s £18-£23; d £36-£46; wkly b&b £108-£140; wkly hlf-bd £150-£182
CARDS: ☒ ▥

GH QQQ **Wheal Treasure Hotel** 72 Edgcumbe Av TR7 2NN ☎01637 874136
Apr-mid Oct
An attractive detached house standing in its own grounds, set slightly outside the town centre, close to Trenance Gardens and boating lake. The standard of decor and furnishing throughout the house is high, and bedrooms are well equipped, with several family rooms available. The dining room and bar have been extended into a large conservatory which leads out on to a terrace and the mature garden. A varied choice of menus is offered and dishes are freshly cooked by the resident proprietor Mr Franks. The dining room is a no-smoking area.

12 rms (3 bth 8 shr) (3 fmly) Tea and coffee making facilities No dogs Licensed Cen ht CTV No children 3yrs 10P No coaches Last d 5pm

GH QQQQ **Windward Hotel** Alexandra Road, Porth TR7 3NB (approaching Newquay on the A3508, turn right onto B3276 Padstow road, hotel in 1m on right) ☎01637 873185
This hotel, 200 yards from Porth beach, was built only a few years ago and so benefits from many modern luxuries. There are panoramic views from the lounge, bar and many of the bedrooms and the latter are decorated using pretty borders with matching curtains and bedspreads while the modern free-standing furniture provides plenty of space for holiday luggage. Besides the lounge there is a smaller TV lounge and in the attractive dining room there is a choice of menu for breakfast and dinner. Mr and Mrs Sparrow are very good hosts and guests return year after year.

14 en suite (bth/shr) (3 fmly) No smoking in bedrooms No smoking in dining room CTV in all bedrooms Tea and coffee

making facilities No dogs (ex guide dogs) Licensed Cen ht
CTV 14P Last d 6.30pm
PRICE GUIDE
ROOMS: d £40-£50; wkly b&b £99-£149; wkly hlf-bd
£125-£198
CARDS: (£)

Selected

♥ ⓠⓠⓠⓠ Mrs K Woodley **Degembris** *(SW852568)*
Newlyn East TR8 5HY
☎01872 510555 FAX 01872 510230
Closed Xmas
This attractive 18th-century slate-hung farmhouse stands in
the depths of the countryside on an arable working farm, only
five miles from Newquay. Bedrooms are individually
decorated, each with a pretty coordinating theme; there is a
general bathroom and shower room and standards of
housekeeping are high. Public areas include a comfortable
lounge with TV and a cosy dining room where home-cooked
evening meals are served at separate tables. The attractive,
well kept grounds include a country trail, and there is parking
close to the house. To find the house, turn right at the traffic
lights in Summercourt to Newquay A3058. Take the third
turning on the left to Newlyn East, about two miles from
Summercourt, then take the second farm lane on the left.
5 rms (3 bth/shr) (2 fmly) No smoking CTV in all bedrooms
Tea and coffee making facilities No dogs Cen ht CTV 8P
165 acres arable Last d 10am
PRICE GUIDE
ROOMS: s fr £18; d fr £36

Selected

♥ ⓠⓠⓠⓠ J C Wilson **Manuels** *(SW839601)* Quintrell
Downs TR8 4NY (signposted on the A392, 3m from
Newquay) ☎01637 873577
Closed 23 Dec-1 Jan
This delightful 17th-century farmhouse is surrounded by
charming gardens and set in a sheltered valley just two miles
from Newquay's town centre and beaches. There is a country
atmosphere in the stylish bedrooms, enhanced by stripped
pine furniture, Laura Ashley fabrics and dried flowers; two
rooms interconnect to provide a large and adaptable family
suite. There are a traditional drawing room, and a fascinating
dining room with huge inglenook fireplace and an antique
dining table around which guests gather for substantial
farmhouse breakfasts; evening meals and nursery teas are also
available. The owners are happy for guests to explore their
farm, and there are both pet and farm animals to visit, as well
as a guided walk. Pony rides can be arranged.
4 rms (1 shr) (1 fmly) No smoking Tea and coffee making
facilities No dogs (ex guide dogs) Cen ht CTV ch fac 6P
Farm trail Pony riding 100 acres mixed Last d 4pm
PRICE GUIDE
ROOMS: s £19; d £38; wkly hlf-bd £198.50-£207.50
(£)

NEWTON ABBOT Devon Map **03** SX87

GH ⓠⓠ **Lamorna** Ideford Combe TQ13 0AR (3m N A380)
☎01626 65627
Situated slightly off the beaten track, some three miles from
Newton Abbot and about eight from Torquay, this guest house ➡

benefits from peaceful surroundings and delightful country views. The eight traditionally decorated bedrooms vary in size, one being a large family suite; three are located on the ground floor. Public rooms include a comfortable bar-lounge, dining room and sun room, and there is even an indoor heated swimming pool.

8 rms (1 bth/shr) (2 fmly) No smoking in dining room CTV in 2 bedrooms Tea and coffee making facilities No dogs (ex guide dogs) Licensed Cen ht CTV 14P No coaches Indoor swimming pool (heated)

PRICE GUIDE

ROOMS: s fr £20; d fr £36; wkly b&b £140✳

➥ Q Q Q Mrs A Dallyn **Bulleigh Park** (*SX860660*) Ipplepen TQ12 5UA (turn off A381 for Compton at BP garage follow for approx 1m. Signposted) ☎01803 872254

Set in a tranquil country lane, this delightful family farm specialises in pedigree Aberdeen Angus cattle. The house is relatively modern, built some 30 years ago, and is spacious and comfortable throughout. There are a lounge with an open fireplace and a dining room which benefits from charming country views. Two bedrooms are located in the main house and a family suite in an adjacent cottage which is also let on a self-catering basis.

2 rms (1 bth) No smoking in bedrooms No smoking in dining room CTV in all bedrooms Tea and coffee making facilities No dogs (ex guide dogs) Cen ht CTV 6P 40 acres beef ponies

PRICE GUIDE

ROOMS: s £15-£18; d £30-£36; wkly b&b fr £101.50✳

Selected

🔲 Q Q Q Q **The Barn Owl** Aller Mills, Kingskerswell TQ12 5AN (turn off A380 at signpost for Aller Mills) ☎01803 872130 & 872968 FAX 01803 875279

Closed 25-27 Dec

This 16th-century farmhouse has been lovingly restored by Derek and Margaret Warner and the characterful interior features old beams, flagstoned floors and rough exposed stone walls. The six recently created bedrooms are cottage style, with black beams, white plaster walls, locally made, dark-stained pine furniture, and individual floral decor. The rooms are well equipped with TV, hair dryers, direct-dial telephones and tea trays, together with extra touches such as fresh fruit and flowers. The three interconnecting bars have log fires, an inglenook fireplace, black leaded range and the largest bar has oak panelling and ornate plaster work. An extensive range of bar meals includes grills, salads, sandwiches and a blackboard with daily special dishes. A separate restaurant in a converted barn provides dinner six nights a week and Sunday lunch, with a carte menu and seasonal local specialities.

6 en suite (bth/shr) CTV in all bedrooms Tea and coffee making facilities Direct dial from bedrooms No dogs Cen ht No children 14yrs 45P No coaches Last d 9.30pm

PRICE GUIDE

ROOMS: s fr £40; d £60-£75✳

MEALS: Bar Lunch £10-£17alc Dinner £14.75-£20.50alc✳

CARDS: 🔲 🔲 🔲 🔲

NEWTON FERRERS Devon Map **02** SX54

GH Q Q Q **Maywood Cottage** Bridgend PL8 1AW (off A379 at Yealmpton onto B3186) ☎01752 872372

Maywood Cottage stands between Noss Mayo and Newton Ferriers, two delightful villages at the side of the estuary which are connected at low tide by a causeway. Two bedrooms are available; both are neatly appointed and one is en suite. Guests have access to a book-lined lounge and an atmospheric dining room with

exposed stone walls. Jill Cross has a good local reputation for her cooking and can adapt to suit most tastes.

2 rms (1 shr) (2 fmly) No smoking in bedrooms Tea and coffee making facilities Cen ht CTV 2P No coaches Last d 7pm

PRICE GUIDE

ROOMS: s £20-£25; d £35-£45; wkly b&b £120-£150; wkly hlf-bd £170-£200✳

NITON See **WIGHT, ISLE OF**

NORTHALLERTON North Yorkshire Map **08** SE39

GH Q Q Q **Alverton** 26 South Pde DL7 8SG (at south end of High Street) ☎01609 776207

This friendly Victorian terraced house, conveniently situated close to the town centre, offers accommodation which is both well furnished and homely. Bedrooms are bright, fresh and well equipped, and guests have access to a recently refurbished lounge.

5 rms (3 shr) (1 fmly) No smoking in bedrooms No smoking in dining room CTV in all bedrooms Tea and coffee making facilities No dogs (ex guide dogs) Cen ht CTV 4P No coaches Last d 1pm

PRICE GUIDE

ROOMS: s £16.25-£23; d £33.30-£37; wkly b&b £113.50-£161; wkly hlf-bd £183-£230

GH Q Q Q **Windsor** 56 South Pde DL7 8SL (on A684 at southern end of High Street) ☎01609 774100

Closed 24 Dec-2 Jan

Situated within easy reach of the town centre. this well maintained Victorian house offers bright, fresh and very clean bedrooms together with a cosy and well furnished lounge. Mrs Peacock the resident owners is friendly and caring whilst a neat and well tended garden is found to the rear of the house.

6 rms (2 shr) (1 fmly) No smoking in bedrooms CTV in all bedrooms Tea and coffee making facilities Cen ht CTV No coaches Last d 3pm

PRICE GUIDE

ROOMS: s £20-£25; d £31-£37; wkly b&b fr £108.50; wkly hlf-bd fr £171.50

CARDS: 🔲 🔲

NORTHAMPTON Northamptonshire Map **04** SP76

GH Q **Hollington** 22 Abington Grove NN1 4QW (take A5123 Kettering rd the 1st right turn after White Elephant junct then 1st right again) ☎01604 32584

Closed Xmas

Guests receive a warm welcome at this friendly guest house. The bedrooms are modestly furnished and attractively decorated; all are equipped with colour TV and tea/coffee making facilities. A choice of breakfasts is served in the nicely appointed dining room. Some car parking is available.

7 rms (2 fmly) No smoking in dining room CTV in all bedrooms Tea and coffee making facilities Cen ht 7P No coaches

PRICE GUIDE

ROOMS: s £16-£18; d £25-£30✳

CARDS: 🔲 🔲 🔲

GH Q Q Q **Poplars Hotel** Cross Street, Moulton NN3 1RZ (off A43 into Moulton Village and follow signs for Collage) ☎01604 643983 FAX 01604 790233

Closed Xmas wk

The Gillies family have owned this village farmhouse since the 1920s, although it has only relatively recently been converted into a successful guesthouse. Extremely comfortable throughout, it offers bedrooms equipped with all the modern amenities, a pleasant lounge with satellite TV and a cosy dining room where the daily-changing dinner menu offers a range of home-cooked dishes.. Smoking is only permitted in the TV lounge.

21 rms (16 bth/shr) (4 fmly) No smoking in 17 bedrooms No smoking in area of dining room No smoking in 1 lounge CTV in all bedrooms Tea and coffee making facilities Licensed Cen ht CTV 22P Last d 7.30pm

PRICE GUIDE
ROOMS: s £20-£37.50; d £40-£47.50∗
CARDS: 🔳 📷 🔳

Selected

❤ 🆀🆀🆀🆀 Mrs M A Turney **Quinton Green** *(SP783532)* Quinton NN7 2EG (turn off A508 S of town, continue past Quinton village and farm is 1m on right)
☎01604 863685 FAX 01604 862230
Closed Xmas

A mellowed stone longhouse dating from the 17th century, this delightful farmhouse is set in a totally secluded rural location surrounded by 1200 acres of arable land and the various outbuildings and milking sheds necessary for a herd of 400 Freesian/Holstein cattle. Inside, a country house atmosphere is fostered by the smart lounge with its deep sofas and armchairs, pastoral pictures, fresh flowers and an open fire. Each of the three spacious bedrooms is furnished with comfortable armchairs and has its own very modern tiled bathroom. Breakfast is served around a refectory table. Mrs Turney is an enthusiastic host, and the accommodation she provides is ideal for both business and leisure guests.

3 rms (2 shr) CTV in all bedrooms Tea and coffee making facilities 10P 1200 acres dairy arable

PRICE GUIDE
ROOMS: s £20; d £38-£40; wkly b&b fr £126

NORTH ELMHAM Norfolk Map **09** TF92

◀ 🆀🆀🆀 **Kings Head Hotel** Crossroads NR20 5JE
☎01362 668856 FAX 01362 668856
A charming country inn, thoughtfully modernised in keeping with the character of the original building, offers both lunch and dinner in its attractive restaurant; there is also a small dining room where bar meals can be served to guests not wishing to eat in the bar itself. Two spacious, comfortably appointed bedrooms both offer en suite facilities and converted stables provide a function room.

2 en suite (bth/shr) (1 fmly) No smoking in area of dining room CTV in all bedrooms Tea and coffee making facilities Direct dial from bedrooms No dogs (ex guide dogs) Cen ht 30P Last d 9.30pm

PRICE GUIDE
ROOMS: s £35; d £45∗
CARDS: 🔳 📷 🔳

NORTH MOLTON Devon Map **03** SS72

🛏🖥 GH 🆀🆀🆀 **Homedale** EX36 3HL (off A361)
☎01598 740206
This compact but warm and comfortable Victorian house, built 100 years ago, offers visitors a warm welcome and informal hospitality. Individually styled bedrooms are equipped with colour TV and tea trays, while an attractive dining room with views of the Devon countryside serves traditional homely fare - dinner being available, as well as a hearty breakfast.

4 rms (1 shr) No smoking in bedrooms No smoking in dining

---

room CTV in all bedrooms Tea and coffee making facilities Cen ht CTV 5P No coaches Last d 5.30pm

PRICE GUIDE
ROOMS: s £11.50-£15; d £23-£40; wkly b&b £80.50-£105; wkly hlf-bd £150.50-£175

NORTH NIBLEY Gloucestershire Map **03** ST79

GH 🆀🆀🆀 **Burrows Court Hotel** Nibley Green, Dursley GL11 6AZ (off A38, at North Nibley, Stinchcombe and Blanchworth sign) ☎01453 546230
Set in a quiet rural location, this stone built converted mill house offers well equipped, prettily decorated bedrooms with modern facilities and yet retains many original features. On reaching North Nibley, follow signs to Berkley and the house is just past the crossroads, set back from the road in its own grounds.

10 en suite (bth/shr) No smoking in dining room CTV in all bedrooms Tea and coffee making facilities No dogs Licensed Cen ht 12P No coaches Outdoor swimming pool Last d 8pm

PRICE GUIDE
ROOMS: s £27.50-£30; d £40-£45; wkly b&b £90-£105; wkly hlf-bd £160-£175
CARDS: 🔳 📷 🔳

NORTH PERROTT Somerset Map **03** ST40

◀ 🆀🆀🆀 **The Manor Arms** TA18 7SG (on A3066, signposted Bridport) ☎01460 72901
Visitors are sure of a warm welcome to this delightful sixteenth-century inn in picturesque North Perrott. Olde worlde bars display tempting menus to suit all tastes and pockets, their home-cooked dishes representing excellent value for money. Small but well equipped and pleasantly furnished non-smoking bedrooms are ➡

located in the Coach House, away from the hubbub of the main building, and there is both a garden and car park at the rear of the pub.

5 en suite (shr) No smoking in bedrooms No smoking in dining room No smoking in 1 lounge CTV in all bedrooms Tea and coffee making facilities No dogs (ex guide dogs) Cen ht 22P No coaches Last d 9.45pm
PRICE GUIDE
ROOMS: s £32; d £42-£48
MEALS: Lunch £10-£14alc Dinner £10-£14alc
CARDS: 🅰 💳

NORTH STAINLEY North Yorkshire Map 08 SE27

◀ Q Q Q *Staveley Arms* (turn off A61 onto A6108, 3.25m on right beyond Lightwater Valley Theme Park) ☎01765 635439 FAX 01765 635359
This extensive old inn offers a very good range of food, which may be served either in the bar or one of the bistro style dining rooms. There are exposed beams and stone work and lots of horse racing memorabilia throughout the public rooms. There are three delightful bedrooms, each with a private bathroom and a decidedly country feel.
4 en suite (bth) CTV in all bedrooms Tea and coffee making facilities No dogs (ex guide dogs) Cen ht 70P Last d 9.30pm
CARDS: 🅰 💳

NORTH TAWTON Devon Map 03 SS60

♥ Q Q Q Mrs J Pyle **Lower Nichols Nymet** *(SS705016)* EX20 2BW (on A3072 halfway between Okehampton and Crediton) ☎01363 82510
Closed Nov-mid Mar
A modern, no-smoking establishment, this farmhouse enjoys a rural setting between Crediton and Okehampton. It is a dairy farm and guests are free to watch at milking time and enjoy marked trails in glorious countryside. The two en suite bedrooms have been comfortably decorated and there is a spacious lounge with a wood-burning stove. Dinner can be served by arrangement.
2 en suite (bth/shr) (1 fmly) No smoking Tea and coffee making facilities No dogs Cen ht CTV 3P Farm trail 160 acres dairy Last d breakfast
PRICE GUIDE
ROOMS: d £34-£37; wkly b&b £100-£110; wkly hlf-bd £160-£170

NORTH WALSHAM Norfolk Map 09 TG23

GH Q Q Q **Beechwood Hotel** 20 Cromer Rd NR28 0HD (B1150 out of Norwich turn left at first set of traffic lights and right second) ☎01692 403231 FAX 01692 407284
A delightful Georgian building close to the town centre, Beechwood Hotel provides parking spaces on the gravel driveway, and the immaculately kept lawns at the front and the back reflect the high standards throughout. The accommodation is simply furnished and most bedrooms have en suite facilities. There are two lounges and a dining room where residents can sample Mrs Townsend's home cooked food.
9 en suite (bth/shr) (4 fmly) No smoking in 5 bedrooms No smoking in dining room CTV in all bedrooms Tea and coffee making facilities Direct dial from bedrooms Licensed Cen ht No children 10yrs 22P Games room Last d 9pm
PRICE GUIDE
ROOMS: s £29-£33; d £50-£52; wkly b&b £175-£182; wkly hlf-bd £210-£252
CARDS: 🅰 💳 💳 💳 🔵 💷

Selected

GH Q Q Q Q **Toll Barn** Norwich Rd NR28 0JB (1m S, off B1150, signposted)
☎01692 403063 FAX 01692 406582
Toll Barn is a uniquely charming house which lies one mile south of North Walsham off the B1150. The main house has been created within the shell of an 18th century barn and has been sympathetically furnished to retain the character and atmosphere of the old barn. Accommodation is in tastefully appointed lodges which surround a central fountain within delightful courtyard gardens. Bedrooms are spacious, comfortable and fresh, the quality soft furnishings and individual decor all create a welcoming and restful environment. All but one the rooms have modern en suite shower facilities, the remaining room has a full tester king size bed and a corner bath; each of the rooms are very well equipped and have a range of thoughtful extras. Breakfast can be taken communally within the delightful breakfast room or alternatively full English breakfast can be served to your lodge. Please note that this is a non-smoking establishment.
6 annexe en suite (bth/shr) (1 fmly) No smoking CTV in all bedrooms Tea and coffee making facilities No children 8yrs 12P No coaches Croquet
PRICE GUIDE
ROOMS: s £25-£30; d £38-£44✳

NORTH WARNBOROUGH Hampshire Map 04 SU75

◀ Q Q Q **The Jolly Miller** Hook Rd RG29 1ET (off M3 junct 5) ☎01256 702085 FAX 01256 704030
Situated in the village of North Warnborough, this attractive pub is ideally located for the M3, Basingstoke, Odiham and Farnham. The rooms are prettily decorated, and some have modern en suite facilities.
8 rms (4 bth/shr) (1 fmly) CTV in all bedrooms Tea and coffee making facilities Direct dial from bedrooms Cen ht CTV ch fac 60P Pool room Skittles Last d 10.30pm
PRICE GUIDE
ROOMS: s £32.50-£42.50; d £41.50-£51.50
CARDS: 🅰 💳 💳

NORTH WHEATLEY Nottinghamshire Map 08 SK78

Premier Selected

GH Q Q Q Q Q **The Old Plough Country Guest House** Top St, North Wheatley DN22 9DB ((off A620) ☎01427 880916
This delightful grade II listed building has been lovingly refurbished by its friendly owners and accommodation throughout combines comfort with quality. There is a no-smoking rule in the bedrooms and in the dining room where Mrs Pasley serves imaginative four-course dinners at a communal table. The house, in a quiet village midway between Retford and Gainsborough, is not considered suitable for young children.
3 en suite (bth/shr) No smoking in bedrooms No smoking in dining room CTV in all bedrooms Tea and coffee making

facilities No dogs (ex guide dogs) Licensed Cen ht CTV
No children 15yrs 4P No coaches Last d 8.30pm
PRICE GUIDE
ROOMS: s £27.50; d £55; wkly b&b £192.50; wkly hlf-bd
£287
See advertisement under RETFORD

NORTHWOOD Greater London Map **04** TQ09

GH Ⓠ **Frithwood House** 31 Frithwood Av HA6 3LY (off
Watford Rd) ☎01923 827864
Frithwood is a large, detached Edwardian house located in a
peaceful residential area about 10 minutes' walk from the
underground station. Mr Mistry is an amiable host, and he is
gradually making improvements to the bedrooms, which are
modest but well kept. Breakfast is served family-style in the
kitchen at two big pine tables.
11 rms (1 bth 1 shr) (4 fmly) No smoking in bedrooms No
smoking in dining room CTV in 3 bedrooms No dogs (ex guide
dogs) Cen ht CTV 10P
PRICE GUIDE
ROOMS: s £22-£30; d £38-£45; wkly b&b fr £175✱

NORTH WOOTTON Somerset Map **03** ST54

⇥▼ ✔ ⓆⓆⓆ Mrs M White **Barrow Farm** *(ST553416)*
BA4 4HL ☎01749 890245
Closed Dec-Jan
Peacefully located in beautiful countryside, this 15th-century
working dairy farm offers four immaculate, well furnished
bedrooms, each with a tea/coffee tray. Mrs White provides a
traditional evening meal, and one of the two pleasant lounges is
provided with TV.
3 rms (1 fmly) No smoking in dining room No smoking in 1
lounge CTV in all bedrooms Tea and coffee making facilities No
dogs CTV 4P 150 acres working dairy Last d 9am
PRICE GUIDE
ROOMS: s £15-£16; d £30; wkly b&b £98; wkly hlf-bd £150

NORTON FITZWARREN Somerset Map **03** ST12

GH ⓆⓆⓆ **Old Manor Farmhouse** TA2 6RZ (on B3227 3n
west of Taunton) (Logis)
☎01823 289801 FAX 01823 289801
Accommodation is offered in neat, comfortable rooms at this
Edwardian farmhouse which stands in its own grounds three miles
from Taunton. The dining room is warmed by a wood-burning
stove in cooler weather, and dinner is available on request. Ample
parking is provided and there is a pleasant garden for guests to
enjoy.
7 en suite (bth/shr) No smoking in dining room CTV in all
bedrooms Tea and coffee making facilities Direct dial from
bedrooms No dogs (ex guide dogs) Licensed Cen ht 12P No
coaches Last d 4pm
PRICE GUIDE
ROOMS: s £34-£36; d £44-£46; wkly b&b £147-£154; wkly hlf-
bd £203-£210✱
CARDS:

NORTON ST PHILIP Somerset Map **03** ST75

Premier Selected

GH ⓆⓆⓆⓆⓆ **Monmouth
Lodge** BA3 6LH (on B3110)
☎01373 834367
Closed 20 Dec-2 Jan
This is the charming home of
Mr and Mrs Graham who go
out of their way to make
guests feel welcome. The
three ground-floor bedrooms,
all prettily furnished with
good quality fabrics and
thoughtful touches, offer
space and comfort; two of the rooms open out onto a patio. In
the imaginatively furnished lounge and stylish dining room
there is the same attention to detail and quality. Well kept
gardens and views across to the hills of Somerset, with the
village church in the foreground, add to the considerable
appeal of Monmouth Lodge.
3 en suite (bth/shr) (1 fmly) No smoking CTV in all
bedrooms Tea and coffee making facilities No dogs Cen ht
No children 5yrs 5P No coaches
PRICE GUIDE
ROOMS: s £35-£40; d £46-£55✱
CARDS:

Selected

GH 🇶🇶🇶🇶 **The Plaine** BA3 6LE (off A366 signed Radstock, house at x-rds in village)
☎01373 834723 FAX 01373 834101
Closed 21 Dec-2 Jan

The Plaine Guest House is located in the centre of the village and the home of Gill and Terry Gazzard. Dating back to the 16th century, the house retains many original features, including natural stone walls, intriguing fireplaces and a flagstone entrance hall. Breakfast is served in the heavily beamed dining room with guests seated around one table. Each bedroom, containing a four-poster bed, is individually furnished and decorated.

3 en suite (bth/shr) No smoking CTV in all bedrooms Tea and coffee making facilities No dogs Cen ht CTV 6P No coaches
PRICE GUIDE
ROOMS: s £30-£35; d £45-£55
CARDS: £

NORWICH Norfolk Map 05 TG20

GH 🇶🇶🇶 **Earlham** 147 Earlham Rd NR2 3RG (from northern by-pass A47 take B1108 and follow signs City Centre. over 2 rbts for guesthouse on left after Earlham House Shopping Centre)
☎01603 454169 FAX 01603 454169
Closed 23-26 Dec

A friendly atmosphere and hospitality of the highest standard are provided by this charming Victorian house, thoughtfully decorated and furnished throughout. Bright, comfortable bedrooms are well equipped - though, in some cases, rather small - while public areas are made up of a relaxing sitting room and an attractive dining room which offers traditional English, continental and vegetarian breakfasts.

7 rms (2 shr) (1 fmly) No smoking in 4 bedrooms No smoking in dining room No smoking in lounges CTV in all bedrooms Tea and coffee making facilities No dogs Cen ht CTV No parking No coaches
PRICE GUIDE
ROOMS: s £19-£24; d £34-£40; wkly b&b fr £125
CARDS: ▆▆▆ £

GH 🇶🇶 **Grange Hotel** 230 Thorpe Rd NR1 1TJ (from the by-pass A47 take A1042 for 2.5m through 3 sets traffic lights for hotel on right) ☎01603 34734 FAX 01603 34734
Closed 26-30 Dec

A large hotel on the Great Yarmouth road, the Grange has attractive public areas, including a bar, pretty restaurant and formal reception area. Accommodation is serviceable and offers a good range of facilities.

35 en suite (bth/shr) (1 fmly) No smoking in dining room CTV in all bedrooms Tea and coffee making facilities Direct dial from bedrooms Licensed Cen ht 40P Sauna Solarium Pool room Last d 9.30pm
PRICE GUIDE
ROOMS: s £35-£40; d £55-£60✳
CARDS: £

GH 🇶🇶🇶 *Hotel Belmonte* 60-62 Prince of Wales Rd NR1 1LT ☎01603 622533 FAX 01603 760805

There is a continental atmosphere about this restaurant with rooms. The ground floor is made up of a popular, cosy bar area with a large restaurant to the rear; entertainment is provided here at the weekends, and there is also a basement night club which opens on Fridays and Saturdays. Continental breakfast is served to

the well planned, thoughtfully furnished bedrooms, and full breakfast is available if required.

9 en suite (bth/shr) CTV in all bedrooms Tea and coffee making facilities No dogs (ex guide dogs) Licensed Cen ht No parking Last d 11pm
CARDS: ▆ ▆▆ ▆▆ ▣

GH 🇶🇶 **Marlborough House Hotel** 22 Stracey Road, Thorpe Rd NR1 1EZ ☎01603 628005 FAX 01603 628005

A proudly kept private hotel with some compact bedrooms, Marlborough House is conveniently located for the railway station and football ground. A cosy lounge and a breakfast room are provided.

12 rms (7 bth/shr) (2 fmly) No smoking in 3 bedrooms No smoking in area of dining room No smoking in 1 lounge CTV in all bedrooms Tea and coffee making facilities Licensed Cen ht CTV 10P Last d 4.30pm
PRICE GUIDE
ROOMS: s £18-£28; d £38-£42; wkly b&b £126-£196; wkly hlf-bd £168-£238 £

NOTTINGHAM Nottinghamshire Map 08 SK54

GH 🇶🇶 *Crantock Hotel* 480 Mansfield Rd NG5 2EL
☎0115 962 3294

Set back from the A60 and extremely accessible to the city and the local neighbourhood of Sherwood. The Crantock is a large house set in its own grounds which are a good setting for the various functions held at the hotel. The bedrooms and the reception rooms are generally of a good size. The bar is especially attractive, furnished with plump cushioned rattan chairs.

10 rms (1 bth/shr) 10 annexe rms (7 bth/shr) (5 fmly) CTV in all bedrooms Tea and coffee making facilities Licensed Cen ht CTV 70P Pool table Last d 9pm
CARDS: ▆ ▆▆

GH 🇶🇶 **Gallery Hotel** 8-10 Radcliffe Rd, West Bridgford NG2 5FW (on A52) ☎0115 981 3651 & 981 1346 FAX 0115 981 3732

A very well placed predominantly commercial guest house which is only yards away from Trent Bridge and the County Cricket and Football Grounds. The public areas are really good consisting of a very comfortable and cheerful lounge, a separate breakfast room and a well furnished convivial cellar bar which is decorated with the owners' collection of football photographs and memorabilia from his days as a professional footballer. The bedrooms, are very well presented with crisp laundered bed linens and good beds. Eleven have shower cubicles and public toilets are near to all the rooms.

15 rms (11 bth/shr) (3 fmly) No smoking in dining room CTV in all bedrooms Tea and coffee making facilities No dogs (ex guide dogs) Licensed Cen ht CTV 35P Pool table Last d 7.30pm
PRICE GUIDE
ROOMS: s £21-£25; d £34-£38; wkly b&b £147; wkly hlf-bd £203✳
CARDS: ▆ ▆▆

GH 🇶🇶🇶 **Grantham Hotel** 24-26 Radcliffe Rd, West Bridgford NG2 5FW (follow signs for Nottingham South/Trent Bridge/National Water Sports Centre, hotel is 0.75m from E end of ring road A52) ☎0115 981 1373 FAX 0115 981 8567

Major refurbishment of the ground floor public areas has recently been completed at this commercial guest house, which is close to Trent Bridge cricket ground. A comfortable small lounge has been created, together with an open-plan bar next to the appealing dining room. Neat, well equipped (though in some cases quite small) bedrooms remain unchanged.

22 rms (14 bth/shr) (2 fmly) No smoking in dining room CTV in all bedrooms Tea and coffee making facilities Licensed Cen ht

CTV No children 3yrs 10P Last d 7.15pm
PRICE GUIDE
ROOMS: s £19.95-£27; d £34-£39; wkly b&b £99.75-£135;
wkly hlf-bd £135.45-£170.70∗
CARDS: 💷

GH 🇶🇶 *P & J Hotel* 277-279 Derby Rd, Lenton NG7 2DP (on
main Derby Rd A52, 0.75m from city centre)
☎0115 978 3998 FAX 0115 978 3998
rs 24-29 Dec
A well established guest house conveniently sited within five
minutes' drive of the city centre (and close to the Queens Medical
Centre) has the advantage of its own rear car park. Some of the
thoughtfully equipped bedrooms have en suite facilities, and there
is a high ratio of public bathrooms for those without. Breakfast
and an evening meal are served in a cheerful dining room
decorated with plate, tea pot and brass collections.
19 rms (9 shr) (8 fmly) No smoking in area of dining room No
smoking in lounges CTV in all bedrooms Tea and coffee making
facilities Licensed Cen ht CTV 12P No coaches Last d 9.30pm
CARDS: 🔲 💷 💷

GH 🇶🇶🇶 *Royston Hotel* 326 Mansfield Rd, Sherwood
NG5 2EF ☎0115 962 2947
One of a row of commercially oriented hotels just a mile from the
city and one with a special homely appeal. The bedrooms are a
good size, immaculate, individually and comfortably furnished.
Their beds are inviting - made up with crisp starched co-ordinated
fabrics and plump pillows. As well as a breakfast room there is a
separate lounge and some off street parking.
8 rms (6 shr) 4 annexe en suite (shr) (2 fmly) CTV in all
bedrooms Tea and coffee making facilities No dogs (ex guide
dogs) Cen ht CTV 16P
CARDS: 🔲 💷 💷

GH 🇶🇶🇶 *St Andrews Private Hotel* 310 Queens Rd,
Beeston NG9 1JA (leave M1 at junct 25 onto A52 and through
2 sets traffic lights then right signed Beeston onto B6006)
☎0115 925 4902 FAX 0115 925 4902
Located on the south-west edge of Beeston, about three miles
from Nottingham city centre, this small hotel offers appealing
accommodation. Guests are welcome to use the comfortable
lounge, which has TV, books, games and a giant jigsaw puzzle.
Dinners are available Monday to Thursday, and special diets can
be catered for with advance notice. There is a more restricted
service some weekends.
10 rms (3 shr) (1 fmly) No smoking in 5 bedrooms No smoking
in dining room CTV in all bedrooms Tea and coffee making
facilities Cen ht CTV 6P No coaches Last d 1pm
PRICE GUIDE
ROOMS: s £19-£28; d £32-£36; wkly b&b £133-£196; wkly hlf-
bd £161-£224∗

Selected

GH 🇶🇶🇶🇶 **Windsor Lodge Hotel** 116 Radcliffe Rd,
West Bridgford NG2 5HG (0.5m from Trent Bridge cricket
ground on A6011 to Grantham)
☎0115 952 8528 & 981 3773 FAX 0115 952 0020
Windsor Lodge is a large, family-run hotel with spacious
public areas which are decorated in a Victorian style
sympathetic to the building. These include quiet lounges, a
lounge bar, a room containing a full-sized snooker table and a
large dining room where dinner is served Monday-Thursday.
Immaculately maintained bedrooms offer modern
accommodation with a good range of facilities, and the secure
parking provided at the rear of the hotel is an added bonus.

48 en suite (bth/shr) (8 fmly) CTV in all bedrooms Tea and
coffee making facilities Direct dial from bedrooms No dogs
Licensed Cen ht CTV 50P No coaches Snooker Solarium
Last d 8.30pm
PRICE GUIDE
ROOMS: s £25-£42; d £40-£52∗
CARDS: 🔲 💷 💷

Selected

♥ 🇶🇶🇶🇶 Mr & Mrs R C Smith **Hall Farm House**
(SK679475) Gonalston NG14 7JA (A612 towards
Southwell then left into Gonalston. In 1.5m take 1st right
into village) ☎0115 966 3112 FAX 0115 966 4844
Closed 17 Dec-6 Jan
This rambling old farmhouse stands in the centre of this
unspoilt village, surrounded by a beautiful cottage garden
complete with tennis court and swimming pool. The Smiths
have brought up their family here and the reception rooms and
bedrooms have a lived in feel to them. Family photographs
hang alongside fine original paintings including those of
Rosie Smith. Flagged and oak floors are covered with rugs,
and the polished carved oak furniture looks thoroughly at
home with open fires and beamed ceilings. Although there is a
formal dining room, guests generally find their way to the
kitchen and eat next to the Aga.
3 rms (1 bth/shr) (1 fmly) Tea and coffee making facilities
No dogs Cen ht CTV ch fac 5P Outdoor swimming pool
(heated) Tennis (hard) Playroom with piano Table tennis 22 ➡

AA **Marlborough**
QQ **House Hotel** •••
Guesthouse
22 Stracey Road, Norwich NR1 1EZ
Tel & Fax: (01603) 628005

A cheerful and clean family owned
hotel situated just off the Great Yarmouth
road, within easy distance of the
station and city centre.
All double/twin and family rooms have
private showers and toilets.
Licensed bar, lounge and car park.
Full central heating.
All bedrooms have colour TV and tea
& coffee making facilities.

acres sheep/poultry Last d 5pm
PRICE GUIDE
ROOMS: s £20-£25; d £40-£45; wkly b&b £140-£175✱

NUNEATON Warwickshire Map 04 SP39

GH 🅀🅀🅀 **Drachenfels Hotel** 25 Attleborough Rd CV11 4HZ
(off M6 junct 3 signed Town Centre and turn right at last rbt
on dual-carriageway then right again for hotel on right)
☎01203 383030
A large Edwardian property on the B4114 about a quarter of a
mile from the town centre overlooks playing fields and parkland.
Comfortable bedrooms are well looked after and there are a
congenial little bar and an attractive dining room.
8 rms (2 shr) (2 fmly) CTV in all bedrooms Tea and coffee
making facilities Licensed Cen ht 8P Last d 8pm
PRICE GUIDE
ROOMS: s £21-£29; d £31-£39✱
CARDS: 🔳 🔳

Selected

GH 🅀🅀🅀🅀 **Leathermill Grange** Leathermill Ln,
Caldecote CV10 0RX (from A5, take turning for Hartshill,
at give way sign go under railway bridge follow road
towards Nuneaton. Leathermill Ln 400yds on left)
☎01827 716094 & 716422 FAX 01827 716422
Closed 24-27 Dec & 2 wks annual holiday
Looking for all the world like a revamped farmhouse, this
delightful building prefers to be considered a country house;
despite some "grand" touches, the overall atmosphere is one
of informality and cheerfulness. There are a gravel
courtyard and a landscaped lawn, complete with ornamental
lake, which leads down to the banks of the River Anker; the
garden also provides much of the produce for the kitchen.
Meals are served at two oval tables, and there is a large
lounge-cum-function room with a well stocked bar. Bedrooms
are gradually benefiting from the introduction of attractively
crafted pinewood furniture.
4 en suite (bth/shr) No smoking in dining room No smoking
in 1 lounge CTV in all bedrooms Tea and coffee making
facilities No dogs Licensed Cen ht CTV 30P No coaches
Fishing Croquet Pool table Last d 6pm
PRICE GUIDE
ROOMS: s £25; d £45✱

GH 🅀🅀 **La Tavola Calda** 68 & 70 Midland Rd CV11 5DY
(through town centre take B4111 Atherstone/Coleshill rd for
.5m) ☎01203 383195 & 381303 FAX 01203 381816
This terraced property is family owned and run and consists of a
Trattoria style restaurant with rooms above. These are compact but
modern and well furnished.
8 en suite (bth/shr) (2 fmly) CTV in all bedrooms Tea and coffee
making facilities No dogs (ex guide dogs) Licensed Cen ht
CTV 25P No coaches Last d 9.45pm
PRICE GUIDE
ROOMS: s £18-£20; d £32✱
CARDS: 🔳 🔳 🔳 🔳

OAKAMOOR Staffordshire Map 07 SK04

Premier Selected

GH 🅀🅀🅀🅀🅀 **Bank
House** Farley Ln
ST10 3BD ☎01538 702810
FAX 01538 702810
A sympathetically restored
farmhouse just outside the
village, Bank House can only
be fully appreciated on
entering the wrought iron
gates and progressing down
the drive past well kept
lawns. Bedrooms are very

comfortable, with four-poster beds in both the singles and
doubles. Dinner is available; the menu is discussed in
advance, and the meal is elegantly served in the dining room
where the owners, Mr and Mrs Orme, enjoy dining with their
guests and imparting their local knowledge. There is also a
spacious guests' lounge with a veritable library of books. The
Orme family extends to two dogs and three cats who are also
very friendly.
3 en suite (bth/shr) (2 fmly) No smoking in bedrooms No
smoking in dining room No smoking in 1 lounge CTV in all
bedrooms Tea and coffee making facilities No dogs (ex
guide dogs) Licensed Cen ht CTV 6P No coaches Last d
11am
PRICE GUIDE
ROOMS: s fr £38; d £50-£70✱
CARDS: 🔳 🔳

❤ 🅀🅀🅀 Mrs I Craigie *Cotton Lane* (SK058471) Cotton
ST10 3DS ☎01538 702033 FAX 01538 702033
Mar-Nov
This delightful brick built house is situated in an elevated position
overlooking the Churnett Valley on the edge of the Peak District,
just two miles from Alton Towers. Three bedrooms offer
comfortable accommodation and the spacious lounge is
attractively furnished and warmed by a log fire on cooler days.
Breakfast is served at separate tables in the conservatory dining
room, home made bread being a speciality. Elaine and Ian Craigie
and their family enjoy welcoming guests and showing people the
family's Tamworth pig, Peggy or Pollyanna the Jersey calf.
3 rms (1 shr) (1 fmly) No smoking in bedrooms No smoking in
dining room CTV in all bedrooms Tea and coffee making
facilities No dogs (ex guide dogs) Cen ht CTV 12P Riding 10
acres non-working

Selected

❤ 🅀🅀🅀🅀 Mrs Christine Shaw **Ribden Farm**
(*SK075471*) Three Lows, Oakamoor ST10 3BW (on B5417
Cheadle/Ashbourne road, on right 0.5m before junction
with A52) ☎01538 702830 & 702153
FAX 01538 702830
Mar-Nov
Well maintained bedrooms with comfortable modern
furnishings are offered at this stone-built farmhouse, one
room being suitable for family occupation. Smoking is not
permitted in the bedrooms but is allowed in the lounge.
Separate tables are provided in a breakfast room which looks
out over the garden and the 100-acre sheep farm. Located on
the edge of the Peak District, this establishment offers

convenient access to both the Staffordshire moorland and Alton Towers.
3 rms (2 shr) (1 fmly) No smoking in bedrooms No smoking in dining room CTV in all bedrooms Tea and coffee making facilities No dogs Cen ht CTV 4P 100 acres sheep
PRICE GUIDE
ROOMS: d £36-£42✶
CARDS:

OAKFORD Devon Map **03** SS92

Selected

♥ QQQQ Anne Boldry **Newhouse** *(SS892228)* EX16 9JE (on B3227, 5m west of Bampton) ☎01398 351347
Closed Xmas
Set back off the old South Molton road in 40 acres within a peaceful valley and bordered by a trout stream, this 17th-century farmhouse retains much of its charm and character whilst providing modern comfort. Two en suites have recently been installed. Home-made soups, patés, bread and preserves, as well as home-produced vegetables can be enjoyed here. The farmhouse is well sited for touring Devon, together with access to Somerset and the coast.
3 en suite (bth) (1 fmly) CTV in all bedrooms Tea and coffee making facilities No dogs Cen ht CTV No children 10yrs 3P Fishing 42 acres beef sheep Last d 4pm
PRICE GUIDE
ROOMS: s £17-£20; d £32-£38; wkly b&b £105-£112; wkly hlf-bd £170-£175
(£)

ODDINGTON Gloucestershire Map **04** SP22

◗ QQQ **Horse & Groom** Upper Oddington GL56 0XH
☎01451 830584
Beams, creaking floorboards and blazing log fires add character to this privately owned village centre inn, parts of which date back to the 16th century. Bedrooms are all similar in style and furnished in a modern fashion. There is a large rear garden with a children's play area.
8 en suite (bth/shr) (2 fmly) CTV in all bedrooms Tea and coffee making facilities No dogs (ex guide dogs) Cen ht 40P Last d 9.30pm
CARDS:

ODIHAM Hampshire Map **04** SU75

Premier Selected

GH QQQQQ **Poland Mill** Poland Ln RG21 1JL (from M3 junct 5 take A287 signed Farnham/Guildford. In 2m turn left B3016 signed Winchfield/Hartley Witney past cattle grid and left into Poland Ln) ☎01256 702251
This lovely old mill house can be traced back to the 15th century and is one of eight

mills mentioned in Greater Domesday. The house, mill stream and pond are located at the end of a single track in the middle ➥

Leathermill Lane, Caldecote, Nuneaton, Warwickshire CV10 0RX
Tel: 01827 716094   Fax: 01827 716422
A recently refurbished Victorian House located in a quiet country setting, bordering the river Anker. Tastefully decorated and with licensed bar. All the bedrooms have full en suite facilities and colour TV etc. There is ample parking and easy access to M6, M42, M69 and NEC plus airports at Birmingham and East Midlands. All within 25 miles. Nearby is Arbury Hall and Twycross Zoo.

The Horse and Groom Inn

Upper Oddington, Moreton-in-Marsh, Gloucestershire GL56 0XH
Telephone: (01451) 830584
Ideally situated for exploring all the picturesque Cotswold villages and within easy reach of the many places of interest in the area. This XVIth century Cotswold stone Inn of great character is family run and offers seven en suite bedrooms. There are two delightful olde worlde bars and cheery Inglenook fireplace where reals ales can be enjoyed. The small, cosy dining room is renowned for its high standard of cuisine using mostly local produce with daily home made specialities. A large beer garden with stream and fishponds are interesting features.

of beautiful countryside, yet the M3 is within easy reach. Owner Janice Cole collects antique lace and linen, the latter adding a final touch of luxury to the bedrooms. The rooms provide every homely touch, including robes, biscuits and fresh fruit. Breakfast is an indulgent affair, served at one table in the dining room and consisting of freshly squeezed juice, fresh eggs from the garden, and warm brioche served with home-made lemon curd and jams.

4 rms (2 shr) CTV in 2 bedrooms Tea and coffee making facilities Cen ht CTV 6P No coaches

PRICE GUIDE

ROOMS: s £20-£22; d £40-£47

OFFTON Suffolk Map **05** TM04

♥ ◲◲◲ Mrs P M Redman **Mount Pleasant** *(SS066495)* IP8 4RP (on A1100) ☎01473 658896 FAX 01473 658896

Located in peaceful rural surroundings with views of the countryside, this 16th-century farmhouse offers a warm welcome and comfortable accommodation. The bedrooms are attractively decorated, suitably furnished and well equipped. An evening meal is served by arrangement in the well appointed dining room; there is also a cosy lounge in which to relax.

3 en suite (bth/shr) No smoking in lounges CTV in all bedrooms Tea and coffee making facilities No dogs (ex guide dogs) Licensed Cen ht CTV No children 14yrs 6P 8 acres mixed Last d 9am

PRICE GUIDE

ROOMS: s £18-£20; d £28-£30; wkly b&b £98-£140; wkly hlf-bd £154-£196

OKEHAMPTON Devon Map **02** SX59

See also Holsworthy

GH ◲◲◲ **Fairways Lodge** Thorndon Cross EX20 4NE (4m W, on A3079. On right hand side, before hump back bridge) ☎01837 52827

This recently constructed stone property with outstanding views over Yes Tor and Will Hayes. There are three bedrooms, one on the ground floor with ramped access to the rear. An evening meal can be provided by arrangement, using fresh local produce and home-grown organic vegetables.

3 rms (1 bth 1 shr) (1 fmly) No smoking in 1 bedrooms No smoking in dining room Tea and coffee making facilities Cen ht CTV 8P No coaches Last d 8pm

PRICE GUIDE

ROOMS: s £15-£18; d £30-£36; wkly b&b £105-£126; wkly hlf-bd £157.50-£178.50✱

♥ ◲◲◲ Mrs K C Heard **Luxridge** *(SX561932)* Hughslade Farm EX20 4LR (from town centre follow B3260 for 2m , past Petrol Station, bungalow on right) ☎01837 52883

Closed Xmas

The Heard family extends a warm welcome to Luxridge bungalow, which is part of Hughslade Farm, two miles west of Okehampton. The bedrooms are freshly decorated and have modern en suite facilities, colour TV and tea-making equipment. There is a spacious lounge, and breakfast is served in a bright conservatory with glorious views of the surrounding countryside.

2 en suite (bth/shr) No smoking in dining room CTV in all bedrooms Tea and coffee making facilities CTV 10P Riding

Snooker Games room Horse riding 600 acres beef sheep Last d 6pm

PRICE GUIDE

ROOMS: d £36-£44✱

OLD DALBY Leicestershire Map **08** SK62

GH ◲◲◲ **Home Farm** Church Ln LE14 3LB (6m NW of Melton Mowbray) ☎01664 822622

Closed Xmas

An 18th century farm with a delightful cottage garden in the middle of a typically rural English village. The inside of the house is furnished with antiques, oak floors and rich coloured rugs and upholstery. All the bedrooms have modern tiled bathrooms and breakfast is served around a refectory table.

3 rms (2 shr) 2 annexe en suite (shr) CTV in 2 bedrooms Tea and coffee making facilities No dogs (ex guide dogs) Cen ht CTV 5P

PRICE GUIDE

ROOMS: s £25-£27; d £40-£45; wkly b&b £126-£170

CARDS: ◲ ◲

OLDHAM Greater Manchester Map **07** SD90

♥ ◲◲◲ Mrs A Heathcote **Higher Quick Farm** *(SD973043)* Lydgate, Saddleworth OL4 4JJ ☎01457 872424

Closed 25-26 Dec

A farmhouse dating back to 1750, which offers three bright, spacious and comfortable bedrooms, one of which is en suite. There is also a large lounge/breakfast room which has an open fire and superb views across the garden to the moors. The house is no-smoking throughout.

3 rms (1 shr) (1 fmly) No smoking CTV in all bedrooms Tea and coffee making facilities No dogs (ex guide dogs) Cen ht CTV 8P 45 acres beef

PRICE GUIDE

ROOMS: s £20; d £36; wkly b&b £100-£120✱

OLD SODBURY Avon Map **03** ST78

Selected

GH ◲◲◲◲ **The Sodbury House Hotel** Badminton Rd BS17 6LU ☎01454 312847 FAX 01454 273105

Closed 24 Dec-3 Jan

An efficiently run little country hotel, Sodbury House offers comfortable accommodation within easy reach of the M4, M5 and the Cotswolds. The spacious bedrooms in the main house have views over the garden and farmland, there are further well equipped rooms in the garden annexe, and a delightful honeymoon/executive suite is available. The coach house makes an ideal conference room, and buffet lunches are served here. A traditional evening meal is provided during the week.

6 en suite (bth/shr) 7 annexe en suite (shr) (3 fmly) No smoking in dining room CTV in all bedrooms Tea and coffee making facilities Direct dial from bedrooms Licensed Cen ht 28P No coaches Croquet Boules

PRICE GUIDE

ROOMS: s £40-£47.50; d £58-£75✱

CARDS: ◲ ◲ ◲ ◲ ◲

OLNEY Buckinghamshire Map 04 SP85

GH Q Q Q **Queen Hotel** 40 Dartmouth Rd MK46 4BH (on A509) ☎01234 711924 FAX 01234 711924
This large building with a separate block of rooms has been extensively renovated under the management of the new owners. Continuing improvements will enhance the overall decor, and the bar and lounge have a welcoming ambience. Although some of the bedrooms are on the small side, they have modern amenities.
4 rms (3 shr) 5 annexe en suite (shr) CTV in all bedrooms Tea and coffee making facilities No dogs (ex guide dogs) Licensed Cen ht 9P No coaches
PRICE GUIDE
ROOMS: s £22.50-£27.50; d £35-£37.50✶
CARDS: 🅰 ▦ 🆅🆂🅰 ▦ ▦

Prices quoted in the Guide are based on information supplied by the establishments themselves.

FAIRWAY LODGE GUEST HOUSE
Thorndon Cross • Okehampton •
Devon EX20 4NE
Telephone: 01837 52827

Fairway Lodge. Stone built farmhouse, set in beautiful ¾ acre gardens. Organic small-holding, breeding miniature Shetland ponies, surrounded by North Dartmoor countryside, for horse riding (stables nearby), walking, ornithology, and golf, or just enjoy the scenery and clean air. Large comfortable well appointed rooms with beverage facilities.
Enjoy the care of resident owners and the relaxed atmosphere.

Higher Cadham Farm
Jacobstowe, Okehampton,
Devon EX20 3RB
Tel: Okehampton (01837) 851647
Fax: Okehampton (01837) 851410

Close to Dartmoor and on the Tarka Trail.
Higher Cadham offers the best in farm holidays and short breaks
• Scrumptious food • Licensed
• Some en-suite • Children welcome
• Pets corner
A real family atmosphere with value for money assured

Telephone
for brochure
Credit cards accepted

Commended

LUXRIDGE
Hughslade, Okehampton, Devon EX20 4LR
Telephone: 01837 52883

A traditional bungalow next to Hughslade Farm where guests are made very welcome to see the farming activities on this large working farm. The bungalow has two en suite bedrooms, one twin and one double, both have colour TV and tea making facilities. The large lounge has colour television and comfortable furnishings. All rooms command glorious views of farmland and the surrounding countryside. Breakfast is served in the conservatory overlooking Dartmoor. Games room with full sized snooker table. An ideal base for touring Devon and Cornwall with beautiful walks arranged daily from beauty spots on Dartmoor. Okehampton is only 2 miles away and well worth a visit especially the Castle and museum. There is also a swimming pool and an unspoilt park. Moderate terms on request from **Mrs K. C. Heard.**

OTLEY Suffolk Map **05** TM25

Premier Selected

GH ⓠⓠⓠⓠⓠ **Otley House** Helmingham Rd IP6 9NR (turn off A12 at Woodbridge onto B1079 signposted Grundisburgh. Approx 5m to village, house 300yds on right after Post Office) ☎01473 890253 FAX 01473 890009 rs Nov- Feb

Situated at the edge of the quiet village of Otley, north of Ipswich, this 17th-century manor house stands in two acres of peaceful mature grounds with a small duck pond. The spacious entrance hall boasts a fine Georgian staircase leading to four spacious, luxurious bedrooms; all are en suite and thoughtfully equipped with a few extra touches. Tea, coffee and after-dinner drinks are served in the elegantly furnished drawing room, and the billiard room is the only area in which guests can smoke. Evening meals are served Thursday to Saturday and reflect the Swiss/French background of the chef. The atmosphere is relaxing and guests will receive a warm welcome.
4 rms (3 bth) No smoking in bedrooms No smoking in dining room No smoking in 1 lounge CTV in 3 bedrooms Tea and coffee making facilities No dogs Licensed Cen ht CTV No children 12yrs 8P No coaches Threequarter size snooker table Last d 1pm

PRICE GUIDE
ROOMS: s £42-£52; d £58-£72✳

 £

OTTERY ST MARY Devon Map **03** SY19

GH ⓠ **Fluxton Farm Hotel** Fluxton EX11 1RJ
☎01404 812818
Apr-Oct & Xmas rs Nov-Apr
This listed 16th-century longhouse is surrounded by attractive gardens and is a haven for both cat lovers and small gauge railway enthusiasts. Bedrooms are well equipped and comfortably furnished. The traditional home-cooked dinners served each evening are popular with guests, and the breakfast porridge has quite a reputation.
12 rms (6 bth 4 shr) (2 fmly) No smoking in dining room No smoking in 1 lounge CTV in 11 bedrooms Tea and coffee making facilities Licensed Cen ht CTV 15P No coaches Fishing Putting Garden railway Last d 5.30pm

PRICE GUIDE
ROOMS: s £23-£25; d £46-£50; wkly b&b £150-£170; wkly hlf-bd £195-£220✳

£

Selected

❤ ⓠⓠⓠⓠ Mrs Jayne Burrow **Claypits Farm** *(SY112927)*
East Hill, Ottery St Mary EX11 1QD ☎01404 814599
Etr-Nov
This attractive farmhouse, converted from old barns, stands in an elevated position four miles from Sidmouth and enjoys picturesque views of the surrounding countryside of East Devon. Claypitts is a 60 acre working farm and guests are

welcome to make the acquaintance of the pony, pigs, sheep, geese, ducks and chicken. Three bedrooms offer comfortable accommodation and breakfast is served at separate tables in the dining room which leads to the spacious lounge where a wood burning stove is lit on chilly evenings and books and games are provided.
3 rms (1 shr) No smoking Tea and coffee making facilities No dogs Cen ht CTV No children 3yrs 3P 65 acres arable sheep

PRICE GUIDE
ROOMS: d £30-£32; wkly b&b £105-£112✳

OUNDLE Northamptonshire Map **04** TL08

◀ ⓠⓠ **The Ship Inn** 18-20 West St PE8 4EF (BW)
☎01832 273918
A rustic coaching inn full of character, located in the main street of this picturesque market town, offers a range of real ales and bar meals in its cosy bar with inglenook fireplace. The coach and boat houses have been tastefully converted into well equipped bedrooms, mostly furnished in antique pine and striking co-ordinated fabrics, and a breakfast/sitting room.
11 en suite (bth/shr) (1 fmly) No smoking in area of dining room CTV in all bedrooms Tea and coffee making facilities Cen ht CTV 70P Last d 10pm

PRICE GUIDE
ROOMS: s fr £27.50; d £48-£55; wkly b&b fr £190; wkly hlf-bd £225-£280✳
MEALS: Lunch £6-£8.80 Dinner £6.80-£12✳
CARDS: £

OXFORD Oxfordshire Map **04** SP50

See also Yarnton

GH ⓠ *Acorn* 260 Iffley Rd OX4 1SE (From ring-road take A4158 north for 1m. On left opposite Toyota garage)
☎01865 247998
Closed Xmas-New Year
A friendly guest house located exactly a mile south of the centre is run along traditional lines and maintains good standards. Bedrooms are mostly spacious and provide the necessary facilities.
6 rms (3 fmly) No smoking in 1 bedrooms No smoking in dining room CTV in all bedrooms Tea and coffee making facilities No dogs Cen ht 5P
CARDS: 🔲 🔲

GH ⓠⓠⓠ **All Seasons** 63 Windmill Rd, Headington OX3 7BP (off North Eastern By-pass onto A420 then left at central traffic lights into Windmill Rd) ☎01865 742215
Closed 8 Dec-2 Jan
A small friendly guesthouse within easy walking distance of the shops in Headington and the regular bus service to the city centre. Three of the bedrooms are furnished to a high standard with private bathrooms, and rooms on the first floor share a shower room. The small breakfast room is freshly decorated, and there is ample car parking at the rear of the property. This establishment is totally no smoking.
6 rms (3 shr) No smoking CTV in all bedrooms Tea and coffee making facilities No dogs Cen ht No children 12yrs 6P No coaches

PRICE GUIDE
ROOMS: s £25-£35; d £45-£48✳

GH ⓠⓠ **Balka Lodge** 315 Iffley Rd OX4 4AG
☎01865 244524 FAX 01865 244524
There is a large car park at the back of this guest house which is located to the east of the centre. It has recently changed hands and

the new owners have ambitious plans to fully upgrade the interior and add an extension. The standards of the bedrooms currently vary but they are all neatly kept.

8 rms (5 bth/shr) (1 fmly) No smoking in bedrooms No smoking in dining room CTV in all bedrooms Tea and coffee making facilities Cen ht CTV 8P

PRICE GUIDE
ROOMS: s £35-£45; d £48-£55✳
CARDS:

GH **QQ** **Bravalla** 242 Iffley Rd OX4 1SE (south east of city centre on A4158 Reading/Henley rd)
☎01865 241326 & 250511
This semidetached guest house stands on the Iffley road, which has a regular bus service to the city centre. Small and informal, it provides neat, well equipped bedrooms, with breakfast served in a modest conservatory at the rear of the property.

6 rms (4 shr) (2 fmly) No smoking in dining room CTV in all bedrooms Tea and coffee making facilities Cen ht CTV 6P No coaches

PRICE GUIDE
ROOMS: s £18-£24; d £38-£44✳
CARDS: (£)

GH **QQ** *Bronte* 282 Iffley Rd OX4 4AA ☎01865 244594
A red brick Victorian semidetached house situated within walking distance of the city centre. Bedrooms on two upper floors are neatly furnished and cheerfully decorated, with good modern beds. There is a pleasant TV lounge, and the dining room opens out through French windows into a pretty, well tended garden.

5 rms (1 shr) (1 fmly) CTV in all bedrooms Tea and coffee making facilities No dogs (ex guide dogs) Cen ht CTV 5P
CARDS:

GH 🅠🅠 **Brown's** 281 Iffley Rd OX4 4AQ (from city centre take High St over Magdalen Bridge, Iffley Rd 3rd exit on roundabout) ☎01865 246822 FAX 01865 246822

A warm welcome awaits visitors to this red brick Victorian property. Some of the bedrooms are small, but all offer good facilities. Smoking is not permitted in the breakfast room.

9 rms (2 shr) (3 fmly) No smoking in dining room CTV in all bedrooms Tea and coffee making facilities No dogs Cen ht 4P No coaches

PRICE GUIDE
ROOMS: s £20-£28; d £32-£48✳
CARDS: 🅫 🏧

GH 🅠🅠 *Casa Villa* 388 Banbury Rd OX2 7PW (1.25m north of city centre 200yds from A40 link to M40)
☎01865 512642 FAX 01865 512642

7 rms (5 shr) (1 fmly) No smoking CTV in all bedrooms No dogs Cen ht CTV 5P

PRICE GUIDE
ROOMS: s £30-£50; d £50-£59✳
CARDS: 🅫 🏧 🏧

Selected

GH 🅠🅠🅠🅠 **Chestnuts** 45 Davenant Rd, off Woodstock Rd OX2 8BU (off A40/A34 at Peterlee rbt to Woodstock Rd rbt then on A4144 and second left) ☎01865 53375 due to change to 553375 FAX 01865 53375

Closed 23 Dec-5 Jan

Chestnuts is an immaculately maintained modern home located off the Woodstock road to the north of the city. Regular buses run into the centre and there is private parking for four cars. Recent changes include an extension to the lounge, an opening up of the rear patio and the addition of a large bedroom. Breakfast is served in a bright conservatory extension, and the overall atmosphere is one of care and a willingness to please. A friendly resident labrador contributes to the warm hospitality. Smoking is permitted in the sitting room only.

4 en suite (shr) (1 fmly) No smoking CTV in all bedrooms Tea and coffee making facilities No dogs (ex guide dogs) Cen ht No children 12yrs 5P No coaches

PRICE GUIDE
ROOMS: s £31-£33; d £49-£56

GH 🅠🅠 *Combermere* 11 Polstead Rd OX2 6TW (from jct with A40 proceed S down A4144 for 1.5m then turn right into Polstead road) ☎01865 56971 due to change to 556971

A three-storey red brick house, this establishment is located on a quiet residential street off the Woodstock road. Bedrooms vary in size and all have modern en suite showers. Limited off street parking is available.

9 en suite (shr) (2 fmly) No smoking in dining room CTV in all bedrooms Tea and coffee making facilities Cen ht 3P No coaches

CARDS: 🅫 🏧 🏧 🏧

GH 🅠🅠🅠 **Conifer** 116 The Slade, Headington OX3 7DX
☎01865 63055 FAX 01865 63055

This family run guesthouse is situated west of the city centre in Headington and offers well maintained simple bed and breakfast accommodation. Bedrooms are reasonable in size with neat decor, and there is a small lounge/breakfast room. Guests can make use of the outdoor heated swimming pool in the summer months.

8 rms (1 bth 2 shr) (1 fmly) No smoking in dining room No smoking in lounges CTV in all bedrooms Tea and coffee making facilities No dogs Cen ht 8P No coaches Outdoor swimming pool (heated)

PRICE GUIDE
ROOMS: s £21-£35; d £35-£50✳
CARDS: 🅫 🏧

Premier Selected

GH 🅠🅠🅠🅠🅠 **Cotswold House** 363 Banbury Rd OX2 7PL (off A40)
☎01865 310558
FAX 01865 310558

Situated two miles north of the city centre, Jim and Anne O'Kane's stone-built house was constructed relatively recently to high standards. Bedrooms vary in size but each features good quality, comfortable furnishings and good equipment; one ground-floor room is available. A choice is offered at breakfast which includes the traditional cooked meal, vegetarian with fresh fruit or home-made muesli. This is a no-smoking establishment.

7 en suite (shr) (2 fmly) No smoking CTV in all bedrooms Tea and coffee making facilities No dogs Cen ht No children 6yrs 6P No coaches

PRICE GUIDE
ROOMS: s £35-£37; d £52-£55

GH 🅠🅠🅠 **Courtfield Private Hotel** 367 Iffley Rd OX4 4DP (on A4158, south east of city centre)
☎01865 242991 FAX 01865 242991

The Courtfield is a meticulously maintained house located just over a mile south of the centre, with plenty of off street parking. Bright bedrooms are spacious and the lounge (where tea and coffee are served) also acts as a breakfast room; there is a distinguished art deco marble bathroom, together with other touches of the same period.

6 rms (4 bth/shr) (1 fmly) No smoking in dining room No smoking in lounges No dogs Cen ht CTV No children 3yrs 8P No coaches

PRICE GUIDE
ROOMS: s £28-£32; d £36-£45; wkly b&b £140-£150
CARDS: 🅫 🏧 🏧 🏧

Selected

GH 🅠🅠🅠🅠 **Dial House** 25 London Rd, Headington OX3 7RE ☎01865 69944 FAX 01865 742208

An elegant detached half-timbered building set in well tended gardens within a mile and a half of the town, this friendly guest house offers accommodation in spacious centrally heated non-smoking bedrooms. There is a quiet lounge where guests can read or plan their next day's activities from the literature on display, and the area provides a good choice of restaurants and eating places. Off-street parking is available - and buses stop only a few steps from the front door.

8 en suite (bth/shr) (2 fmly) No smoking in bedrooms No smoking in dining room CTV in all bedrooms Tea and coffee making facilities Cen ht No children 6yrs 8P No coaches

PRICE GUIDE
ROOMS: d £46-£50✳

GH QQQ *Earlmont* 322-324 Cowley Rd OX4 2AF
☎01865 240236
Closed 24 Dec-1 Jan
A double-fronted terraced property situated on the busy Cowley road on the eastern side of the city. There are eight bedrooms in the main building, the majority furnished in pine, with private bathrooms; the remaining rooms are situated across the road in a small annexe. Public rooms are nicely furnished and decorated, although fairly small. Smoking is not permited in the main building.
8 rms (1 bth 6 shr) 7 annexe rms (2 fmly) CTV in all bedrooms Tea and coffee making facilities No dogs Cen ht No children 5yrs 11P

GH QQQ **Falcon Private Hotel** 88-90 Abingdon Rd OX1 4PX (from A34 take 3rd exit on rbt then left again)
☎01865 722995
Situated along the Abingdon road just east of the city, this guesthouse has been created by the conversion of two Victorian houses and carefully refurbished by the new proprietors. Bedrooms are particularly well equipped and comfortable, with excellent en suite facilities. Public areas are comfortable, if a little limited in space. The owners are friendly, helpful and eager to provide for their guests' comfort.
11 en suite (shr) (4 fmly) No smoking in bedrooms No smoking in dining room CTV in all bedrooms Tea and coffee making facilities Direct dial from bedrooms No dogs (ex guide dogs) Cen ht CTV 10P Jacuzzi Last d 5pm
PRICE GUIDE
ROOMS: s £26-£28; d £42-£45; wkly b&b £182; wkly hlf-bd £238
CARDS: ◼◼◼ (£)

COMBERMERE HOUSE
11 Polstead Road, Oxford OX2 6TW
Telephone/Fax: Oxford (01865) 56971

Family run guest-house in quiet tree-lined road off Woodstock Road, North Oxford, 15 minutes walk from City Centre and Colleges. Frequent bus services. Parking. All rooms have television, tea and coffee-making facilities and are en suite. Full English breakfast. Open all year. Central heating. All major credit cards accepted.

COURTFIELD PRIVATE HOTEL

367 Iffley Road, Oxford OX4 4DP
Tel: Oxford (01865) 242991

An individually designed house situated in tree-lined road; with modern spacious bedrooms, majority are **en suite.** Close to picturesque Iffley Village and River Thames yet easily accessible to Oxford's historic city centre and Colleges.

PRIVATE CAR PARK

THE DIAL HOUSE

25 LONDON ROAD, OXFORD
Tel: (01865) 69944   Fax: (01865) 742208
THE DIAL is just 1.5 miles from the city centre. There is off-street parking, and for the pedestrian, bus stops only a few steps from the door.
All bedrooms have private facilities, colour TV and beverages. Smoking in guest lounge only. The proprietors, in providing the atmosphere of an elegant half-timbered house, offer a high standard of comfort to guests who prefer friendly personal service and attention.

AA Kindly note we do not
QQQQ have facilities for
Selected children under 6 years.

Premier Selected

GH ◉◉◉◉◉
Fallowfields Kingston
Bagpuize, with Southmoor
OX13 5BH (10 miles SW off
A420, signed Kingston
Bagpuize and at mini-rbt turn
right through the village to
Southmoor and at last
lampost turn left)
☎01865 820416
FAX 01865 821275

Fallowfields is a large grey-stone family house, located on the western fringes of the village of Southmoor. The guest house is building a local reputation both for its small meeting facilities and its cooking. With the 'fetish for freshness' in the kitchen, much work has been undertaken in a garden which also extends to include an outdoor heated pool and a flat lawn ideal for croquet. Inside, the house is bright and airy, with a lived-in feel, large bedrooms being furnished with simple home comforts.

3 en suite (bth/shr) No smoking CTV in all bedrooms Tea and coffee making facilities Direct dial from bedrooms Licensed Cen ht No children 8yrs 17P No coaches Outdoor swimming pool (heated) Tennis (hard) Croquet lawn Last d 7.30pm
PRICE GUIDE
ROOMS: s £55-£75; d £64-£89✽
CARDS: 🔳 🔳 🔳

GH ◉◉◉ **Gables** 6 Cumnor Hill OX2 9HA (off A420)
☎01865 862153 FAX 01865 864054
Closed 24 Dec-1 Jan
A very attractive white Victorian gabled house is set in a small garden, just off the A34. Completely gutted and refurbished some years ago, it offers modern well furnished accommodation with good facilities, crisp linens and coordinating colour schemes. All the en suite bathrooms are smart, modern and fully tiled.
6 rms (1 bth 4 shr) (1 fmly) No smoking in 2 bedrooms No smoking in dining room No smoking in lounges CTV in all bedrooms Tea and coffee making facilities Direct dial from bedrooms No dogs (ex guide dogs) Cen ht CTV 6P
PRICE GUIDE
ROOMS: s £24-£26; d £42-£46; wkly b&b £130-£150✽
CARDS: 🔳 🔳   (£)

Selected

GH ◉◉◉◉ *Galaxie Private Hotel* 180 Banbury Rd
OX2 7BT ☎01865 515688 FAX 01865 56824
A popular, privately run commercial hotel is to be found in the Summertown area just north of the city, surrounded by shops and restaurants. Recent refurbishment has added an attractive reception area and lounge/dining room housed in a modern conservatory. The bedrooms have also received attention and have furnishings of an equivalent standard, with excellent facilities.
31 rms (27 bth/shr) (3 fmly) No smoking in bedrooms No smoking in dining room CTV in all bedrooms Tea and coffee making facilities Direct dial from bedrooms Lift Cen ht CTV 30P

GH ◉◉◉ **Green Gables** 326 Abingdon Rd OX1 4TE (off Oxford Ring Rd, south side, signed Headington Rbt then .5m on left) ☎01865 725870 FAX 01865 725870
Closed 23-31 Dec
Green Gables is a large Edwardian house located about a mile from the city centre. The friendly owners personally oversee service and are gradually making improvements to the interior. Bedrooms, most of which are spacious and equipped with en suite facilities, include two on the ground floor - one of them suitable for disabled guests. There is a bright breakfast room, and ample off street parking is provided.
9 rms (6 bth/shr) (3 fmly) No smoking in dining room No smoking in lounges CTV in all bedrooms Tea and coffee making facilities No dogs (ex guide dogs) Cen ht 8P No coaches
PRICE GUIDE
ROOMS: s £20-£33; d £34-£47
CARDS: 🔳 🔳

GH ◉◉◉ *Highfield* 91 Rose Hill OX4 4HT (on A4158)
☎01865 774083 & 718524
Doreen and Bertram Edwards provide a warm welcome at their smart and very well run guesthouse, which is just off the ring road to the east of the city. The bright and freshly decorated dining room is appealing, and there is a pleasant lounge with thick rugs and comfortable sofas. The modern bedrooms are of a high standard, making this a popular choice with the local business community.
7 rms (5 shr) (2 fmly) No smoking in 3 bedrooms No smoking in dining room No smoking in lounges CTV in all bedrooms Tea and coffee making facilities No dogs Cen ht CTV 5P
CARDS: 🔳 🔳

GH ◉◉◉ *Homelea* 356 Abingdon Rd OX1 4TQ
☎01865 245150
Peggy and John Hogan have created a warm and welcoming home here where generally spacious bedrooms are especially comfortable because of the excellent quality of the beds. Homelea is obviously placed on Abingdon Road and has its own parking and small garden.
6 en suite (shr) (3 fmly) No smoking in 2 bedrooms CTV in all bedrooms Tea and coffee making facilities No dogs (ex guide dogs) Cen ht CTV 6P

Selected

GH ◉◉◉◉ **Marlborough House** 321 Woodstock Rd OX2 7NY (from A34/A44 junct north of city Centre signs inti Woodstock Rd for horel on right adjacent to traffic lights)
☎01865 311321 FAX 01865 515329
Closed 23 Dec-2 Jan
A modern, purpose-built, three-storey hotel has immaculate and smartly furnished bedrooms, each fully equipped with TV, direct dial telephone with radio and alarm, and a mini bar. Meals are not served, but each room has its kitchen with a fridge, microwave, kettle and sink. Pre-packed continental-style breakfasts are delivered to the rooms in the evenings so that guests may prepare their own, and there are restaurants in the neighbourhood for evening meals. Drinks are available from reception, and free tea and coffee is offered in the coffee lounge. Smoking in bedrooms is discouraged.
12 en suite (bth/shr) (2 fmly) No smoking in bedrooms CTV in all bedrooms Tea and coffee making facilities Direct dial

from bedrooms No dogs Licensed Cen ht No children 8yrs
6P No coaches
PRICE GUIDE
ROOMS: s £55; d £65✳
CARDS:

(£)

GH Q Q Q **Pickwicks** 17 London Rd, Headington OX3 7SP
☎01865 750487 & 68413 FAX 01865 742208
Two Victorian properties have been joined by a lounge/bar area to
create this family-run hotel conveniently situated about one and a
half miles from the city centre. Bedrooms vary in size, but all are
well equipped and the majority have en suite facilities; ground-
floor rooms are available. A set evening meal is served by
arrangement and, again by arrangement, cars may be left in the car
park. Frequent buses pass the hotel.
15 rms (3 bth 6 shr) (5 fmly) No smoking in bedrooms No
smoking in dining room CTV in all bedrooms Tea and coffee
making facilities Direct dial from bedrooms Licensed Cen ht
CTV 12P Last d noon
PRICE GUIDE
ROOMS: s £25-£35; d £36-£50✳
CARDS: ▨ ▨ ▨ ◎ ▨

GH Q Q Q **Pine Castle Hotel** 290/292 Iffley Rd OX4 4AE
(off Ring Rd onto A4158) ☎01865 241497 & 728887
FAX 01865 727230
Closed Xmas
A small Edwardian semidetached house on the Iffley road, just
east of the city, stands in a popular central location. The four
attractive cottage-style bedrooms feature carefully chosen
coordinating decor and furnishings, with pretty patchwork quilts
complementing the pine furniture. Public rooms are well

GABLES

6 Cumnor Hill, Oxford
Tel: (01865) 862153
Fax: (01865) 864054

Gables is situated in a perfect location just 5
minutes drive into the City Centre. The
Railway and Bus Stations are within a short
distance and we are on a regular bus route.
All rooms have private facilities, direct dial
telephones, satellite TV, radio, hair dryer and
tea/coffee facilities. A warm and friendly
welcome awaits you on arrival and we hope to
ensure your stay with us is pleasant and
comfortable.
Major credit cards accepted.

𝕲𝖆𝖑𝖆𝖝𝖎𝖊 𝕻𝖗𝖎𝖛𝖆𝖙𝖊 𝕳𝖔𝖙𝖊𝖑

180 BANBURY ROAD, OXFORD
Telephone: (01865) 515688
Fax: (01865) 56824

This is a small, select, family hotel, recently
refurbished to a very high standard. It is situated 1
mile from the City Centre. All 30 bedrooms are fully
equipped with colour TV, telephone and the majority
have private facilities. There is ample car parking.
Terms include full English breakfast.

The hotel is open all year round and enjoys
international patronage.

AA QQQQ

𝕲𝖗𝖊𝖊𝖓 𝕲𝖆𝖇𝖑𝖊𝖘

326 Abingdon Road, Oxford
Tel: (01865) 725870   Fax: (01865) 723115

- Characterful, secluded and detached Edwardian
  house, set in mature gardens.
- Bright, spacious rooms with TV and tea/coffee
  making facilities. The majority have en suite
  shower and W.C. One room is on the ground floor,
  with facilities for the disabled.
- Off street, secluded parking is guaranteed.
- Full English breakfast with real coffee.
- One mile to the first of the colleges. Bus stop 20
  yds away with buses every 10 minutes.
- On the A4144, ½ mile from the ring road. Easy
  access, therefore, to sights and countryside,
  including Blenheim, the Cotswolds, Stratford
  upon Avon.

---

decorated and comfortably furnished, and include a small licensed bar and reception desk.

8 rms (4 bth/shr) (2 fmly) No smoking in 4 bedrooms No smoking in dining room CTV in all bedrooms Tea and coffee making facilities Direct dial from bedrooms No dogs (ex guide dogs) Licensed Cen ht CTV 4P No coaches Last d 8.30am
PRICE GUIDE
ROOMS: d £42-£65*
CARDS: (£)

GH ◨◨◨◨ **Tilbury Lodge Private Hotel** 5 Tilbury Ln, Eynsham Rd, Botley OX2 9NB (off the B4044)
☎01865 862138 FAX 01865 863700
Two miles west of the city centre in a quiet suburban lane, Tilbury Lodge is a pretty guest house run by friendly proprietors, Mr and Mrs Trafford. Bedrooms are bright, modern and well equipped with telephones, hair dryers and, in one room, a romantic four poster bed. A ground floor bedroom is available for guests unable to use the stairs and a spa bath can be used between 11am and 6pm. Children are also very welcome and a play area in the back garden helps keep them amused.

9 en suite (bth/shr) (1 fmly) No smoking in bedrooms No smoking in dining room CTV in all bedrooms Tea and coffee making facilities Direct dial from bedrooms No dogs Cen ht CTV 10P No coaches Jacuzzi
PRICE GUIDE
ROOMS: s £38-£42; d £57-£62
CARDS: (£)

GH ◨◨◨ **Westwood Country Hotel** Hinksey Hill Top OX1 5BG (South West off Ring Rd) (MIN)
☎01865 735408 FAX 01865 736536

Closed 22 Dec-9 Jan
Situated on top of Hinksey Hill, this large, well-established hotel stands in four acres of lovely woodland, now designated a nature reserve. The size allows for small conferences and week-end functions. Bedrooms are individually furnished and variously sized and there is a room with a sauna, spa bath and fitness machine. Award winning facilities for disabled people are also available.

21 en suite (bth/shr) (2 fmly) No smoking in dining room CTV in all bedrooms Tea and coffee making facilities Direct dial from bedrooms No dogs (ex guide dogs) Licensed Cen ht CTV ch fac 30P Sauna Jacuzzi Wildlife nature garden & trail Last d 8.15pm
PRICE GUIDE
ROOMS: s £55; d £80; wkly hlf-bd £266-£392
CARDS: (£)

GH ◨◨◨ **Willow Reaches Hotel** 1 Wytham St OX1 4SU (from town centre take A4144 for 0.75m past Hinksey Park. Turn right into Norreys Avenue and at end of road turn right again. Hotel next to church)
☎01865 721545 FAX 01865 251139

A small hotel tucked away in a quiet cul-de-sac off the Abingdon road, within easy walking distance of the city centre. The modern comfortable bedrooms are well equipped, with clock radios and satellite TV, and some have private bathrooms. A comfortable lounge with TV and a bar adjoins the dining room. A good choice is offered at breakfast, and both English and Indian meals are available at dinner, which is served by arrangement. There is adequate parking, some covered.

9 en suite (bth/shr) (1 fmly) No smoking in dining room No smoking in lounges CTV in all bedrooms Tea and coffee making

facilities Direct dial from bedrooms No dogs Licensed Cen ht CTV P No coaches Last d 6pm
PRICE GUIDE
ROOMS: s £36-£45; d £49-£55; wkly b&b £210-£252; wkly hlf-bd £280-£357*
CARDS: ▪▪▪

OXHILL Warwickshire Map **04** SP34

♥ ◨◨◨◨ Mrs S Hutsby **Nolands Farm** *(SP312470)* CV35 0RJ (1m E of Pillarton Priors on A422)
☎01926 640309 FAX 01926 641662
Closed 1 Dec-15 Jan
This farm is situated in a tranquil valley. Guest rooms are located in carefully restored stables, totally separate from the owner's accommodation. The comfortable bedrooms are generally spacious: two have four-poster beds and they offer a good range of facilities including private bathrooms. Public areas include a cosy dining room and a small comfortable bar area. There is a well stocked trout lake and clay pigeon shooting and riding can be arranged nearby.

9 annexe en suite (bth/shr) (2 fmly) No smoking in dining room No smoking in 1 lounge CTV in all bedrooms Tea and coffee making facilities No dogs (ex guide dogs) Licensed Cen ht No children 7yrs 12P Fishing Clay pigeon shooting Bicycle hire 200 acres arable Last d 12hrs notice
PRICE GUIDE
ROOMS: d £32-£44
CARDS: ▪▪▪

PADSTOW Cornwall & Isles of Scilly Map **02** SW97

See also Little Petherick and St Merryn

GH ◨◨ **Alexandra** 30 Dennis Rd PL28 8DE (from A39 Wadebridge take A389 to Padstow. At outskirts of Padstow take first turning right down Sarah's Lane leading into Dennis Road) ☎01841 532503
Mar-Oct
The Alexandra overlooks the beautiful Camel Estuary from an elevated, quiet residential position. Built in 1906, this fine Victorian house is the family home of proprietor Maureen Williams and offers a relaxing, informal atmosphere. The bedrooms are furnished in a traditional style with a TV and tea/coffee making facilities provided. A comfortable sitting room augments a small dining room, and unrestricted parking is available.

5 rms (5 fmly) No smoking in dining room CTV in all bedrooms Tea and coffee making facilities No dogs No children 5yrs 5P No coaches
PRICE GUIDE
ROOMS: s £16-£17; d £32-£34; wkly b&b £105-£110*

GH ◨◨◨ **Newlands Hotel** PL28 8QX (1.5m from Padstow on B3276) ☎01841 520469
The sheltered coves and rocky pools of Trevone's sandy beach are situated about 150 yards from this family hotel, run by owners John and Beverley Philpott. In the spacious dining room a table d'hote menu is offered and guests are asked to make their choice at breakfast, to ensure availability and high quality. The bedrooms are comfortable, facilities are modern and each room is equipped with remote controlled television and beverage making facilities. Trevone is about one and a half miles from Padstow.

10 rms (3 bth 6 shr) (1 fmly) No smoking in dining room No smoking in 1 lounge CTV in all bedrooms Tea and coffee making ➡

TILBURY LODGE

PRIVATE HOTEL

TEL: (01865) 862138
FAX: (01865) 863700

Tilbury Lodge is situated in a quiet country lane just two miles west of the city centre and one mile from the railway station. Good bus service available. Botley shopping centre is a few minutes walk away with restaurants, shops, banks, pubs etc.

All rooms en suite with direct dial telephone, colour TV, radio, hair dryer and tea/coffee facilities. Jacuzzi. Four poster. Ground floor bedrooms. Central heating, double glazing. Ample parking.

TILBURY LODGE PRIVATE HOTEL
5 TILBURY LANE, EYNSHAM ROAD,
BOTLEY, OXFORD OX2 9NB

Oxford Oxfordshire
Westwood Country Hotel
E.T.B. ♛♛♛

Hinksey Hill Top, OX1 5BG
Tel: **Oxford (01865) 735408**
Fax: **(01865) 736536**
Proprietor: **Mr and Mrs A.J. and M. Parker**

WINNER OF DAILY MAIL HOTEL AWARD 1991
A family run hotel with 21 bedrooms, all with private facilities, radio, intercom, colour TV, hairdryer, video and tea/coffee making facilities. Three acres of gardens and woodlands. Excellent food. Intimate bar. For Hotel guests, jacuzzi, sauna and mini gym available. Catering for up to 130 for weddings and 60 for conferences.

Willow Reaches Hotel
1 Wytham St., Oxford
Tel: Oxford (01865) 721545 Fax: (01865) 251139

English Tourist Board Commended

A private hotel with a high standard of comfort, in a quiet location just a mile south of Oxford city centre.

The hotel is near a fishing lake and a public park with swimming pools and children's boating lake.

Every bedroom has a direct dial telephone, colour television, radio and tea/coffee-making facility; all bathrooms en suite. Bridal suite.

Central Heating throughout. Residents' lounge with teletext TV. Bar, restaurant serving English and Indian meals. A large garden. Children welcome.

Parking facilities.

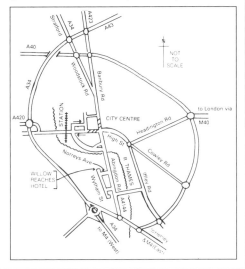

facilities Licensed Cen ht CTV 12P No coaches Last d 4.30pm

PRICE GUIDE
ROOMS: s £18.50-£25; d £37-£50; wkly b&b £125-£160; wkly hlf-bd £150-£190✳

Premier Selected

GH 🅀🅀🅀🅀🅀 **St Petroc's House** 4 New St, Padstow PL28 8EA ☎01841 532700 FAX 01841 533344
Xmas

The fifth oldest property in Padstow, St Petroc's is a delightful terraced property set in a narrow street leading to the harbour front and village centre. The beamed bedrooms retain the character of the old building and have been tastefully decorated and equipped with modern facilities. There are an elegant first-floor lounge and, downstairs, an attractive bar-lounge and adjacent bistro where lunch and dinner are served in informal surroundings. Fresh fish is a speciality and the cooking skills of head chef Paul Hearn have earned St Petroc's restaurant a two-rosette award.

8 en suite (bth/shr) (2 fmly) No smoking in dining room CTV in all bedrooms Tea and coffee making facilities Direct dial from bedrooms Licensed Cen ht 8P Last d 9.30pm

PRICE GUIDE
ROOMS: s £25-£34.30; d £52-£77✳
CARDS: 🅰 ▭ ▭ ▭ 🅂

PAIGNTON Devon Map **03** SX86

GH 🅀🅀🅀 **Beresford** 5 Adelphi Rd TQ4 6AW
☎01803 551560
Closed 7 Dec-7 Jan

Occupying a position close to the seafront, pier, festival hall and main shopping centre, this traditionally run family establishment attracts many regular visitors. All the rooms have either en suite or private shower rooms and two are reserved for non-smokers. Home-cooked fare is served in the dining room, and a large lounge is provided for guests' use. On-street parking is available to the front of the hotel.

8 rms (6 shr) (1 fmly) No smoking in 2 bedrooms No smoking in dining room CTV in all bedrooms Tea and coffee making facilities No dogs Licensed Cen ht CTV 3P No coaches Last d 10am

PRICE GUIDE
ROOMS: d £40-£44; wkly b&b fr £120; wkly hlf-bd fr £150✳

GH 🅀🅀🅀 **Channel View Hotel** 8 Marine Pde TQ3 2NU (from A380 Prestondown Rbt follow signs Preston down hill to traffic lights then forward under railway bridge and turn left) ☎01803 522432 FAX 01803 528376
rs Dec & Jan

This guest house is located in a quiet cul-de-sac on the esplanade, not far from the centre of town. Owned by Margaret and David Teague for over 14 years, the friendly, cheerful atmosphere draws guests back time after time. Bedrooms are light and airy, some rooms having a sea view, and all are well equipped; there is a ground-floor lounge available. The front-facing dining room with a bar has superb sea views, and there is a patio for guests.

12 en suite (bth/shr) (3 fmly) No smoking in dining room CTV in all bedrooms Tea and coffee making facilities No dogs (ex

guide dogs) Licensed Cen ht CTV 10P Last d noon

PRICE GUIDE
ROOMS: s £20-£25; d £36-£40; wkly hlf-bd £110-£210
CARDS: 🅰 ▭

GH 🅀🅀 **Cherra Hotel** 15 Roundham Rd TQ4 6DN
☎01803 550723
Mar-Nov

A small private hotel in a quiet residential area a short distance from the town centre, beaches and harbour. The bedrooms are comfortable though some are compact; all have TV. A colourful garden surrounds the property.

14 rms (9 shr) (7 fmly) No smoking in dining room CTV in all bedrooms Tea and coffee making facilities Licensed Cen ht CTV 15P Last d 5.30pm

PRICE GUIDE
ROOMS: s £12-£20; d £24-£40; wkly b&b £80-£130; wkly hlf-bd £110-£160✳

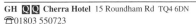

Selected

GH 🅀🅀🅀🅀 **Clennon Valley Hotel** 1 Clennon Rise, Goodrington TQ4 5HG
☎01803 550304 FAX 01803 550304

Situated close to the town centre and safe sandy beaches, this stylish establishment has a friendly atmosphere and offers attractive bedrooms, most of which are en suite. A bistro style restaurant and adjoining bar offer interesting home cooked dishes, and the lounge is comfortable and elegant. Smoking is not permitted in the bedrooms, and there is ample private parking.

10 rms (1 bth 7 shr) (2 fmly) No smoking in bedrooms CTV in all bedrooms Tea and coffee making facilities Direct dial from bedrooms No dogs (ex guide dogs) Licensed Cen ht CTV 6P Last d 10am

PRICE GUIDE
ROOMS: s £19-£25; d £38-£42; wkly b&b £125-£135; wkly hlf-bd £160-£175
CARDS: 🅰 ▭

GH 🅀🅀🅀 **Danethorpe Hotel** 23 St Andrews Rd TQ4 6HA
☎01803 551251

This friendly establishment - which is constantly being improved - stands in a quiet side street just a short walk from the seafront and harbour. Ten comfortably furnished bedrooms are well decorated with co-ordinated fabrics, a large bar overlooks the garden and the redecorated dining room serves both fixed-price and carte menus. Ample private parking is available.

10 rms (6 shr) (2 fmly) CTV in all bedrooms Tea and coffee making facilities No dogs Licensed Cen ht 10P
CARDS: 🅰 ▭ ▭

GH 🅀🅀🅀 **Oldway Links Hotel** 21 Southfield Rd TQ3 2LZ
☎01803 559332 FAX 01803 526071

A particularly attractive Georgian mansion, this hotel enjoys a quiet location in the heart of Paignton. Most of the simply decorated bedrooms have en suite facilities as well as numerous extras. Spacious public areas include a comfortable lounge leading to a sun terrace overlooking the landscaped gardens. There are a cosy bar with a flagstone floor and an attractive navy and peach dining room which is also available for seminars and meetings during the day. The set-price menu offered each evening specialises in local produce.

15 rms (13 bth/shr) (3 fmly) No smoking in area of dining room No smoking in lounges CTV in all bedrooms Tea and coffee making facilities No dogs (ex guide dogs) Licensed Cen ht

CTV ch fac 30P Last d 7.30pm
PRICE GUIDE
ROOMS: s £19.50-£25.50; d £39-£51; wkly b&b £78-£164.50;
wkly hlf-bd £206.50-£234.50✴
CARDS: ■ ■ £

GH ◙◙◙ *Redcliffe Lodge Hotel* 1 Marine Dr TQ3 2NL
☎01803 551394
Apr-mid Nov
Redcliffe Lodge stands a short walk from the town centre and the
beach with stunning views of Paignton Green and the sea. Well
equipped bedrooms include three ground-floor rooms; a large sun
lounge adjoins a quieter sitting room and a sunny bar/dining room.
Pride is taken in the variety of dishes available on the dinner menu
with at least five home-made sweets on the dessert trolley.
17 en suite (bth/shr) (2 fmly) No smoking in dining room CTV
in all bedrooms Tea and coffee making facilities No dogs
Licensed Cen ht CTV 20P No coaches Last d 6.30pm
CARDS: ■ ■

GH ◙◙◙ *St Weonard's Private Hotel* 12 Kernou Rd
TQ4 6BA ☎01803 558842
A small, well maintained terraced house is close to the seafront,
the shops and the Festival Hall. Bedrooms are comfortable and
there is a television lounge and a dining room where snacks are
available between breakfast and supper.
8 rms (5 shr) (2 fmly) No smoking in dining room Tea and
coffee making facilities No dogs Licensed CTV 2P No coaches
Last d 3.30pm
PRICE GUIDE
ROOMS: s £14-£16; d £28-£32; wkly b&b £90-£105; wkly hlf-
bd £139-£154✴
CARDS: ■ ■

GH ◙◙◙ *Sattva Hotel* 29 Esplanade TQ4 6BL
☎01803 557820
Mar-Oct
Terry and Margaret Nadin welcome guests to their seafront hotel
just a level two-minute walk to the beach. Virtually all the
bedrooms are en suite, some have private balconies and a lift is
provided to all floors. Entertainment is provided in the bar-lounge
during the season, and the atmosphere is lively.
20 en suite (bth/shr) (2 fmly) No smoking in dining room CTV
in all bedrooms Tea and coffee making facilities No dogs
Licensed Lift Cen ht CTV 10P Last d 5pm
PRICE GUIDE
ROOMS: s fr £20; d fr £40; wkly hlf-bd £180-£205✴
CARDS: ■ ■

GH ◙◙◙ *The Sealawn Hotel* Sea Front, 20 Esplanade Rd
TQ4 6BE ☎01803 559031
Situated on the esplanade overlooking the beaches, the pier and
most of Torbay, this hotel is still within a stone's throw of the
town centre. The bedrooms are attractively decorated and well
equipped and some have stunning views. There are a cosy bar
where snacks are available, a large lounge, and a dining room
where traditional breakfasts and evening meals are served. Ample
private parking is provided.
12 en suite (bth/shr) (3 fmly) No smoking in dining room CTV
in all bedrooms Tea and coffee making facilities Direct dial from
bedrooms No dogs Licensed Cen ht CTV ch fac 13P Solarium
Last d 5.30pm
PRICE GUIDE
ROOMS: s £18-£27; d £36-£44; wkly b&b £119-£182; wkly hlf-
bd £161-£224✴
£

Clennon Valley Hotel
Clennon Rise, Paignton, Devon TQ4 5HG.
Telephone & Fax: 01803 550304

AA
Selected
◙◙◙◙

A beautifully presented Victorian Hotel
situated at Goodrington, between Torquay
and Brixham. This quiet Hotel offers a good
selection of non-smoking bedrooms with a
high profile on security and personal service.
The Clennon Valley Hotel is managed by the
owners who enjoy the company of selected
guests from Europe, America and many
areas of the United Kingdom.

Redcliffe Lodge

**1 Marine Drive,
Paignton TQ3 2NJ**
 VISA
Reception (01803) 551394
Visitors (01803) 525643

RIGHT BY THE BEACH . . . The Hotel is situated
in one of Paignton's finest sea front positions in its
own grounds with an easy level walk to most
facilities including two safe sandy beaches,
harbour, theatre, shops and town centre.

DINE IN STYLE . . . Sea air sharpens appetites
remarkably. Meals in our sunny dining room
overlooking the sea front are to be lingered over
and savoured. We are proud of our cuisine, the
result of careful thought to give pleasure, variety
and interest.

All principal rooms and most of the bedrooms have
extensive seaviews. All bedrooms en-suite with
colour TV, radio and intercom to reception, tea
making facilities.

Ground floor bedrooms available. Hotel is heated
throughout making it ideal for late holidays, mid-
week bookings accepted. Large car park – perfect
touring centre. Colour brochure on request from
resident proprietors Allan & Hilary Carr.

GH [Q][Q][Q] **Sea Verge Hotel** Marine Dr, Preston TQ3 2NJ
☎01803 557795
Etr-Oct
The enthusiastic Birchall family create a friendly atmosphere at
this hotel, which occupies an advantaged position on Preston
Green, close to the town centre and promenade. There are eleven
attractive bedrooms, each with en suite or private facilities and
many useful extras, and three of the first-floor rooms have
balconies. Public areas are decorated to a high standard and
include a large lounge, a sun lounge, and a cosy bar and dining
room where traditional home-cooked fare is offered.
11 rms (9 shr) (2 fmly) No smoking in bedrooms Tea and coffee making facilities No dogs Licensed
Cen ht CTV No children 9yrs 14P No coaches Last d 6pm
PRICE GUIDE
ROOMS: s £18-£38; d fr £36; wkly b&b fr £126; wkly hlf-bd fr
£182✱

£

GH [Q][Q] *Toad Hall* 49 Dartmouth Rd TQ4 5AE
☎01803 558638
A personally run establishment, Toad Hall is situated close to the
town centre and a little walk from the esplanade and beaches. The
bedrooms are named after Kenneth Grahame's familiar characters,
and the theme is taken up with posters, sepia photographs and old
theatre memorabilia. There is a comfortable lounge leading out to
an attractive covered verandah and a separate dining room where
home-cooked food is served.
5 rms (2 shr) (2 fmly) No smoking in dining room No dogs
Licensed Cen ht CTV No children 10yrs 6P No coaches Last d
10am

GH [Q][Q][Q] **Torbay Sands Hotel** 16 Marine Pde, Preston Sea
Front TQ3 2NU ☎01803 525568
Vera and Eddie Hennequin have created a hospitable atmosphere
at their modern hotel which has panoramic views of the bay. The
bright, cosy bedrooms are complemented by comfortable and
tasteful public rooms.
13 rms (11 shr) (4 fmly) No smoking in dining room CTV in all
bedrooms Tea and coffee making facilities Licensed Cen ht
CTV 5P
PRICE GUIDE
ROOMS: s £13.50-£18; d £27-£36; wkly b&b £90-£117; wkly
hlf-bd £120-£142✱
CARDS: 🟥 🟰 🟥 💷

£

GH [Q][Q][Q] *Waterleat House* 22 Waterleat Rd TQ3 3UQ
☎01803 550001 FAX 01803 550001
This large detached residence stands in a quiet area of Paignton
overlooking the zoo. The bedrooms - most of which offer en suite
or private facilities - are cheerfully decorated and all have TVs
and tea trays. Snacks available in the cosy bar provide an
alternative to the meals served in a large dining room.
6 en suite (bth/shr) (1 fmly) No smoking in dining room CTV in
5 bedrooms Tea and coffee making facilities No dogs (ex guide
dogs) Licensed Cen ht 4P No coaches Tennis (hard) Riding
Last d 9.30pm

Prices quoted in the Guide are based on
information supplied by the establishments
themselves.

PARKHAM Devon Map **02** SS32

Premier Selected

GH [Q][Q][Q][Q][Q] **The Old
Rectory** EX39 5PL
☎01237 451443
Closed 11 Dec-14 Jan
Situated in the quiet village
of Parkham near Horns
Cross, this extended
Georgian house has been
restored by Jean and Jack
Langton who treat their
guests as family friends.
Bedrooms are spacious and

beautifully decorated, with many personal touches. Each has
either an en suite or private bathroom. Deep, comfortable
sofas furnish the drawing room, which is brightened by
displays of ornaments, pictures and fresh flowers. Jean
Langton is a talented cook and our inspector praised highly a
meal which began with a creamed mushroom tartlet with
brandy sauce, continued with local venison accompanied by
excellent vegetables, and finished with a selection of delicious
'melt in the mouth' desserts.
3 en suite (bth/shr) No smoking No dogs (ex guide dogs)
Licensed Cen ht CTV No children 12yrs 12P No coaches
Last d 6pm
PRICE GUIDE
ROOMS: s £50-£55; d £70-£78; wkly b&b £220.50-£245;
wkly hlf-bd £395.50-£420
CARDS: 🟥

£

PATELEY BRIDGE North Yorkshire Map **07** SE16

♥ [Q][Q] Mrs C E Nelson *Nidderdale Lodge (SE183654)* Felbeck
HG3 5DR ☎01423 711677
Etr-Oct
Surrounded by a working farm and standing beside the B6265 two
miles east of Pately Bridge, this large bungalow overlooks the
Nidderdale valley from an elevated setting. Bedrooms are both
bright and modern, and a cosy lounge is also provided.
3 rms (1 bth/shr) (1 fmly) Tea and coffee making facilities No
dogs (ex guide dogs) Cen ht CTV 3P 30 acres mixed

PATRICK BROMPTON North Yorkshire Map **08** SE29

Selected

GH [Q][Q][Q][Q] **Elmfield House** Arrathorne DL8 1NE (2m
N unclass towards Catterick Camp)
☎01677 450558 FAX 01677 450557
This large and attractive house enjoys delightful all-round
views of open countryside from a setting in carefully tended
gardens complete with a well stocked pond. Furnished along
modern lines, it offers thoughtfully equipped bedrooms
(including two on the ground floor which are suitable for
disabled persons) and a comfortable, spacious dining room in
which to enjoy quality home-cooked meals. Guests also have
the use of a games room and solarium.
9 en suite (bth/shr) (2 fmly) No smoking in dining room
CTV in all bedrooms Tea and coffee making facilities Direct
dial from bedrooms No dogs (ex guide dogs) Licensed Cen

ht 12P Fishing Solarium Last d before noon
PRICE GUIDE
ROOMS: s fr £29.50; d £39-£44; wkly b&b £129.50-£170;
wkly hlf-bd £210-£227✳
CARDS:

♥ ◨◨◨ Mrs P Knox **Mill Close** *(SE232922)* DL8 1JY (leave
A684 at Crakehall turning right to Catterick and Hackforth.
After 1m turn first left, first farm on right)
☎01677 450257 FAX 01677 450585
Mar-Nov
Dating in part from the 16th century, this attractive farmhouse is in
a delightful rural setting. The two guest bedrooms are spacious
and well furnished, and each has its own bath or shower room
across the landing. A cosy lounge is provided and breakfast is
served in the pleasant dining room.
2 en suite (bth/shr) (1 fmly) No smoking in bedrooms Tea and
coffee making facilities No dogs Cen ht CTV 3P 230 acres
arable/beef Last d 9am
PRICE GUIDE
ROOMS: s £20; d £32-£36; wkly b&b fr £112; wkly hlf-bd fr
£182

PAWLETT Somerset Map 03 ST24

♥ ◨◨◨ Mrs Worgan **Brickyard** *(ST298421)* River Rd
TA6 4SE ☎01278 683381
This attractive farmhouse is over 450 years old and is situated
down a long unmade road within a mile of the village, close to
junctions 22 and 23 of the M5. The comfortable bedrooms are
prettily decorated and furnished, and downstairs there are a cosy
lounge with TV and a small bar where guests can relax over a
drink whilst choosing supper from an extensive menu of enjoyable
home-cooked dishes. There are views across the garden to a lake
beyond, and boats pass frequently on the nearby River Parrett.
3 rms (1 fmly) No smoking in bedrooms Tea and coffee making
facilities No dogs Licensed Cen ht CTV 14P Fishing 2 acres
non working Last d 6pm
PRICE GUIDE
ROOMS: s £15-£17; d £30-£35; wkly b&b £105-£119; wkly hlf-
bd £140-£154✳

PENRITH Cumbria Map 12 NY53

See also Newbiggin

GH ◨◨◨ **Brandelhow** 1 Portland Place CA11 7QN (in town
centre) ☎01768 864470
Closed 24-25 Dec & 31 Dec
This terraced guest house lies within walking distance of the town
centre. Bedrooms are attractively decorated and include one very
large family room; guests also have use of the establishment's
stylish lounge.
6 rms (3 fmly) No smoking in 2 bedrooms No smoking in dining
room CTV in all bedrooms Tea and coffee making facilities Cen
ht CTV 1P No coaches
PRICE GUIDE
ROOMS: s £18-£20; d £28-£32; wkly b&b £105-£119✳

GH ◨◨◨ **Limes Country Hotel** Redhills, Stainton
CA11 0DT (2m W A66 turn left immediately before Little
Chef and follow road for 0.25 miles "The Limes" is on the
right) ☎01768 863343
Situated just a short distance from Penrith, this red sandstone
Victorian house enjoys glorious views from the setting of its own

gardens. There are a comfortable lounge and dining room, and
predominantly en suite bedrooms are all of a good standard.
6 en suite (bth/shr) (2 fmly) No smoking in dining room CTV in
all bedrooms Tea and coffee making facilities No dogs (ex guide
dogs) Licensed Cen ht 7P No coaches Last d 3pm
PRICE GUIDE
ROOMS: s £23-£25; d £38-£40; wkly b&b £119-£165; wkly hlf-
bd £157.50-£240
CARDS:

GH ◨◨◨ **Woodland House Hotel** Wordsworth St
CA11 7QY (at foot of Beacon Hill, close to Town Hall)
☎01768 864177 FAX 01768 890152
An elegant Victorian end-of-terrace house, five minutes' walk
from the centre, offers attractive bedrooms, a pleasant dining room
and a choice of lounges - one of them having a bar. Dinner is
served by arrangement. Smoking is not permitted on the premises.
8 en suite (bth/shr) (2 fmly) No smoking CTV in all bedrooms
Tea and coffee making facilities No dogs Licensed Cen ht CTV
10P No coaches Last d 4.30pm
PRICE GUIDE
ROOMS: s £25; d £40; wkly b&b £129-£166

PENSHURST Kent Map 05 TQ54

Premier Selected

GH ◨◨◨◨◨ **Swale**
Cottage Old Swaylands Ln,
Off Poundsbridge Ln
TN11 8AH (off A26 onto
B2176 after 2.75m turn left
onto Poundsbridge Lane)
☎01892 870738
In a superb and peaceful rural
setting, this delightful guest
house offers accommodation
of a very high standard. The
spacious, well equipped

bedrooms are not only very comfortable, but are full of
charm. The attractive lounge is relaxing, too, and all round the
house are paintings by the owner, an accomplished artist. A
traditional English breakfast is served in the elegant dining
room.
3 en suite (bth/shr) No smoking CTV in all bedrooms Tea
and coffee making facilities No dogs Cen ht No children
10yrs 5P No coaches
PRICE GUIDE
ROOMS: s £36-£42; d £54-£60✳

PENZANCE Cornwall & Isles of Scilly Map 02 SW43

See also Porthcurno & St Hilary

Selected

GH ◨◨◨◨ **Blue Seas Hotel** 13 Regent Ter TR18 4DW
☎01736 64744 FAX 01736 330701
Set in a quiet, south-facing terrace, this early Victorian
property overlooks the promenade. Pat and Derek Davenport
are welcoming hosts and many guests return time after time.
The majority of the well presented bedrooms are fitted with ➡

modern en suite facilities and a spacious lounge is available for guests' use; the cheerful dining room serves traditional meals featuring home-cooked bread, soups and puddings as well as main courses based on fresh local produce - including locally caught fish.

10 en suite (bth/shr) (3 fmly) No smoking in bedrooms No smoking in dining room CTV in all bedrooms Tea and coffee making facilities No dogs Licensed Cen ht CTV No children 5yrs 12P No coaches Last d 6.30pm

PRICE GUIDE
ROOMS: s £18.50; d £37; wkly b&b fr £129; wkly hlf-bd fr £217✳

CARDS: ▬ ▬   (£)

GH QQQ **Camilla Hotel** 12 Regent Ter TR18 4DW (take seafront road to Promenade, Regent Terrace is at eastern end)
☎01736 63771
Closed Xmas

Forming part of a Regency terrace, the Camilla Hotel is in a quiet position overlooking the seafront, and convenient for the town centre and parks. The comfortable bedrooms are attractively decorated and well equipped. Dinner is a set meal and special diets can be catered for by prior arrangement.

8 rms (1 bth 3 shr) (3 fmly) No smoking in bedrooms No smoking in dining room CTV in all bedrooms Tea and coffee making facilities Licensed Cen ht CTV No children 10yrs 5P

PRICE GUIDE
ROOMS: s fr £19; d £38-£42; wkly b&b £125-£140✳
CARDS: ▬ ▬

GH QQQ **Carlton Private Hotel** Promenade TR18 4NW
☎01736 62081
mid Mar-mid Oct

There are uninterrupted views from all the rooms at the front out across the beach to the sea and St Michael's Mount in the distance. The lounge has some interesting pieces of furniture brought back from Java and many original paintings. The dining room looks over the small garden which is a blaze of colour in the summer and has won several awards in Penzance. Bedrooms are simply decorated and provide all modern comforts.

10 rms (8 shr) No smoking in dining room No smoking in lounges CTV in all bedrooms Tea and coffee making facilities No dogs (ex guide dogs) CTV No children 12yrs No coaches

PRICE GUIDE
ROOMS: s £16.50-£25; d £40-£45✳

                                                           (£)

Selected

GH QQQQ **Chy-an-Mor** 15 Regent Ter TR18 4DW
☎01736 63441
Closed Dec-Jan

Mr and Mrs Russell took over this charming Georgian hotel overlooking the sea in the spring of 1993 and they have done much to modernise the facilities but have also taken care to respect the original character of the building. Bedrooms are of a good size and attractively decorated. Lounge and dining room are inviting, with comfortable seating and furnished in keeping with the style of the house.

8 en suite (shr) (1 fmly) No smoking CTV in all bedrooms Tea and coffee making facilities No dogs Licensed Cen ht CTV No children 10yrs 10P No coaches Last d breakfast

PRICE GUIDE
ROOMS: s £17.50-£21.50; d £35-£43; wkly b&b £122.50-£150.50✳
CARDS: ▬ ▬ ▬ ▬ ▬

 GH QQQ **Dunedin** Alexandra Rd TR18 4LZ (follow sea front along to mini roundabout, turn right into Alexandra road 500yds up on right) ☎01736 62652
Closed 10 Dec-10 Jan

Situated on the tree-lined road not far from the town centre and the Promenade, this Victorian terrace house is larger than it appears. The bar/dining room is at garden level with polished tables and cheerful decor and bedrooms have all the usual facilities.

9 en suite (bth/shr) (4 fmly) No smoking in dining room CTV in all bedrooms Tea and coffee making facilities Licensed Cen ht CTV No children 3yrs No parking

PRICE GUIDE
ROOMS: s £13-£16; d £26-£32; wkly b&b £85-£105

GH QQQ **Georgian House** 20 Chapel St TR18 4AW
☎01736 65664
Closed Xmas

This centrally located hotel is situated mid-way between the town centre and the sea front, within easy walking distance of the Isles of Scilly ferry docks. There are plans to upgrade the well equipped bedrooms during the winter of 1995/6. A small rear car park is available.

12 rms (4 bth 2 shr) (4 fmly) No smoking in 2 bedrooms No smoking in area of dining room CTV in all bedrooms Tea and coffee making facilities No dogs (ex guide dogs) Licensed Cen ht CTV 11P Last d 8pm

PRICE GUIDE
ROOMS: s £18.50-£25; d £34-£42; wkly b&b £110.50-£162.50✳
CARDS: ▬ ▬ ▬   (£)

GH QQ *Kimberley House* 10 Morrab Rd TR18 4EZ (take Promenade road, pass Harbour and turn right into Morrab Road) ☎01736 62727
Closed Dec

A large Victorian property built of Cornish granite, this hotel is set midway between the town centre and the promenade, within a 10-minute walk of the bus and rail terminals. The bedrooms are simply appointed, and it should be noted that the rather narrow stairs to the second floor could present difficulties for some guests. There is a comfortable lounge with colour TV as well as a cosy bar.

9 rms (2 fmly) No smoking in dining room CTV in all bedrooms Tea and coffee making facilities No dogs (ex guide dogs) Licensed Cen ht CTV No children 5yrs 4P Last d 5pm
CARDS: ▬ ▬

GH QQQ **Hotel Minalto** Alexandra Rd TR18 4LZ
☎01736 62923

Standing close to the quieter end of the promenade, this spacious Victorian house forms the end of a terrace and offers very comfortable, well modernised accommodation. Public rooms include two lounges, one with a bar, and the house has a light and friendly atmosphere.

12 rms (10 shr) (3 fmly) CTV in all bedrooms Tea and coffee making facilities Licensed Cen ht CTV 8P No coaches Last d 6pm

PRICE GUIDE
ROOMS: s £13.50-£17.50; d £26-£35; wkly b&b £85-£110; wkly hlf-bd £135-£155✳
CARDS: ▬ ▬

GH QQ *Mount Royal Hotel* Chyandour Cliff TR18 3LQ (on the old A30 entering Penzance) ☎01736 62233
Mar-Oct

Situated on the edge of the town overlooking Mounts Bay, this solid Victorian house offers modestly furnished bedrooms, a spacious dining room with period features and a simple lounge.

9 rms (5 bth) (3 fmly) No smoking in dining room CTV in 3 bedrooms Tea and coffee making facilities Cen ht CTV 10P No coaches

GH ◎◎◎ **Penalva** Alexandra Rd TR18 4LZ ☎01736 69060
A haven for non-smokers, this well modernised Victorian house situated within easy walking distance of seafront and town centre offers accommodation in attractively decorated and furnished bedrooms. Guests have the use of a spacious lounge, and traditionally cooked evening meals are available by arrangement.
5 rms (4 shr) (3 fmly) No smoking CTV in all bedrooms Tea and coffee making facilities No dogs Cen ht CTV No children 3yrs No parking No coaches Last d 6.30pm
PRICE GUIDE
ROOMS: s £11-£16; d £22-£32; wkly b&b £70-£105; wkly hlf-bd £140-£175✱   ⓔ

✉ ☎ **GH** ◎◎◎ **Penmorvah Hotel** Alexandra Rd TR18 4LZ ☎01736 63711
Owned and personally run by Colin and Mary Williams, this hotel stands in a tree-lined avenue, conveniently positioned for easy access to both the promenade and shopping centre. Bedrooms, including one on the ground floor, are simply furnished and well equipped, and a choice of menu is offered at both breakfast and dinner.
8 en suite (bth/shr) (4 fmly) No smoking in dining room CTV in all bedrooms Tea and coffee making facilities Licensed Cen ht Last d 6pm
PRICE GUIDE
ROOMS: s £13-£20; d £26-£40; wkly b&b £85-£135; wkly hlf-bd £135-£180
CARDS: ▦ ▬ ▭   ⓔ

✉ ☎ **GH** ◎◎ **Trenant Private Hotel** Alexandra Rd TR18 4LX (from A30 at Penzance Station follow road by harbour for about 1m, turn right into Alexandra Road) ☎01736 62005
A spacious double fronted Victorian mid-terrace house with comfortable public rooms stands in a tree-lined area within easy walking distance of both town centre and seafront. Dinner features plain, traditional Cornish home cooking, and bedrooms - some of them with stylish bed drapes - vary in size.
9 rms (5 shr) (3 fmly) No smoking in dining room No smoking in lounges CTV in all bedrooms Tea and coffee making facilities Licensed Cen ht CTV No parking No coaches Last d noon
PRICE GUIDE
ROOMS: s £13-£16; d £30-£40; wkly b&b £80-£135; wkly hlf-bd £150-£190   ⓔ

GH ◎◎ **Trevelyan Hotel** 16 Chapel St TR18 4AW (turn left at the top of the town centre into Chapel St hotel halfway along on left) ☎01736 62494
This restored terraced house dates back to the 18th century and stands in the older part of the town close to the main shopping areas. Bedrooms are furnished in keeping, but have modern standards of comfort. Lounge and dining room (with its small bar) are attractively furnished.
6 rms (5 shr) 2 annexe en suite (bth/shr) (4 fmly) No smoking in 4 bedrooms No smoking in dining room CTV in all bedrooms Tea and coffee making facilities No dogs (ex guide dogs) Licensed Cen ht CTV 8P No coaches Last d am
PRICE GUIDE
ROOMS: s £15-£25; d £30-£50; wkly b&b £105-£110✱   ⓔ

GH ◎◎◎ **Treventon** Alexandra Place TR18 4NE ☎01736 63521
7 rms (4 shr) (2 fmly) No smoking in dining room CTV in all bedrooms Tea and coffee making facilities Cen ht CTV No children 5yrs No parking No coaches Last d 3pm
PRICE GUIDE
ROOMS: s £13-£16; d £26-£32; wkly b&b £93-£106; wkly hlf-bd £140-£155✱   ⓔ

See advertisement on p.323.

✉ ☎ **GH** ◎◎◎ **Trewella** 18 Mennaye Rd TR18 4NG ☎01736 63818
Mar-Oct
Television sets have recently been installed in the neat bedrooms of this bright, cheerful guesthouse near the seafront and football ground. Proprietors proud of their reputation for traditional home-cooked food are happy to cater for special diets by prior arrangement. Smoking is not allowed in any public area, including the comfortable residents' lounge with bar.
8 rms (4 shr) (2 fmly) No smoking in 1 bedrooms No smoking in dining room No smoking in lounges CTV in all bedrooms Tea and coffee making facilities Licensed Cen ht CTV No children 5yrs No parking No coaches Last d noon
PRICE GUIDE
ROOMS: s £12.50-£15.50; d £25-£31; wkly b&b £80-£101; wkly hlf-bd £129-£150
See advertisement on p.323.

Selected

♥ Q Q Q Q Mrs P Lally **Rose Farm** *(SW446290)*
Chyanhal, Buryas Bridge TR19 6AN (take A30 to Land's
End, at Drift turn left (behind phone box), 0.75m down
lane on left) ☎01736 731808
Closed 24-27 Dec
2 en suite (shr) 1 annexe en suite (shr) (1 fmly) No smoking
in bedrooms No smoking in dining room CTV in all
bedrooms Tea and coffee making facilities No dogs (ex
guide dogs) Cen ht 8P 23 acres beef
PRICE GUIDE
ROOMS: d £35-£38; wkly b&b £122.50-£133✳

Selected

◾ Q Q Q Q **The Yacht** The Promenade TR18 4AU
(opposite Jubilee swimming pool)
☎01736 62787 FAX 01736 331604
Situated on the seafront, this popular pub was built in the
1930s to an eye-catching design. Recent refurbishment has
created a spacious lounge bar, where an extensive range of bar
meals is served. The well equipped bedrooms are on the first
floor, most having splendid sea views.
8 en suite (bth/shr) (2 fmly) No smoking in bedrooms No
smoking in dining room CTV in all bedrooms Tea and coffee
making facilities Direct dial from bedrooms Cen ht P Last d
9pm
PRICE GUIDE
ROOMS: s £20-£25; d £40-£50; wkly b&b £120-£150;
wkly hlf-bd £170-£200✳
MEALS: Lunch £3.50-£6&alc Dinner £3.50-£6&alc✳
CARDS: £

PERRANUTHNOE Cornwall & Isles of Scilly Map **02** SW52

GH Q Q Q **Ednovean House** TR20 9LZ (turn off A394 at
Perran x-rds, then take first lane on the left and continue to
very end of the lane) ☎01736 711071
Arthur and Val Compton are welcoming hosts at this small,
relaxing hotel, quietly situated in an acre of lawns and gardens
with magnificent views across Mounts Bay. A safe sandy beach is
just a short walk away. Bedrooms are neat and tidy, the majority
sharing the superb view. A varied set-price menu and a vegetarian
selection are offered each evening.
9 rms (6 shr) (1 fmly) No smoking in dining room Tea and
coffee making facilities Licensed Cen ht CTV No children 7yrs
12P No coaches 9 hole putting green Last d 6pm
PRICE GUIDE
ROOMS: s £21-£23; d £38-£46; wkly b&b £120-£145; wkly hlf-
bd £208-£234
CARDS: £

Selected

♥ Q Q Q Q Mr & Mrs C Taylor **Ednovean** *(SW912299)*
TR20 9LZ ☎01736 711883
Dating back to the 17th century, this granite barn has been
lovingly converted to a comfortable home. It now comprises a
small working farm of 22 acres and is situated above the
village, with views to Mount's Bay and St Michael's Mount.
Bedrooms are located on the ground floor, furnished and
decorated in country style with pretty chintz fabrics and fresh

fruit and flowers. Guests take breakfast around a communal
table, and dinner is available by arrangement, but there are
many small restaurants in the area.
3 rms (2 bth) No smoking CTV in 2 bedrooms Tea and
coffee making facilities Cen ht CTV No children 9yrs 6P
22 acres arable grassland horticultural
PRICE GUIDE
ROOMS: s £20-£40; d £30-£50; wkly b&b £140-£280 £

PETERBOROUGH Cambridgeshire Map **04** TL19

GH Q Q **Aaron Park Hotel** 109 Park Rd PE1 2TR
☎01733 64849 FAX 01733 64849
Accommodation at the Aaron Park Hotel is divided between the
main Victorian house and an annexe house in the same avenue.
Bedroom styles vary considerably from modern rooms with en
suite facilities to older, smaller and more modestly furnished
rooms.
9 rms (5 bth/shr) 5 annexe en suite (bth/shr) (3 fmly) CTV in all
bedrooms Tea and coffee making facilities Licensed Cen ht
CTV 10P No coaches Last d 6.30pm
PRICE GUIDE
ROOMS: s £29-£39; d £38-£44✳
CARDS: £

GH Q Q Q **Hawthorn House Hotel** 89 Thorpe Rd PE3 6JQ
☎01733 340608 & 313470
This well preserved Victorian house is located near the hospital on
the A1179, south of the centre. The bedrooms are generally well
equipped and individually furnished. There is a conservatory
lounge and a dining room with a corner bar.
8 en suite (bth/shr) (2 fmly) No smoking in 5 bedrooms No
smoking in dining room CTV in all bedrooms Tea and coffee
making facilities Direct dial from bedrooms No dogs (ex guide
dogs) Licensed Cen ht CTV 5P No coaches Last d 8.30pm
PRICE GUIDE
ROOMS: s £25-£36; d £40-£48
CARDS: £

GH Q Q Q **Lodge Hotel** 130 Lincoln Rd PE1 2NR (N of city
at junct with Lincoln Road and Limetree Avenue)
☎01733 341489 FAX 01733 52072
The Lodge is a welcoming small hotel situated about 10 minutes'
walk from the cathedral. The friendly proprietors maintain good
standards of housekeeping, and each of the bedrooms has a
modern en suite shower room. There are a comfortable small bar
and an attractive, no-smoking restaurant where a range of home-
cooked dishes is available from a set-priced three-course menu.
9 en suite (shr) No smoking in dining room CTV in all bedrooms
Tea and coffee making facilities Licensed Cen ht No children
10yrs 6P No coaches Last d 8.30pm
PRICE GUIDE
ROOMS: s £35-£45; d £45-£55; wkly b&b £200-£220; wkly hlf-
bd £278
CARDS: £

PETERSFIELD Hampshire Map **04** SU72

See also **Rogate**

◾ Q Q Q **The Master Robert** Buriton GU31 5SW (S on A3,
signposted for Buriton) ☎01730 267275 FAX 01730 231817
This busy, popular inn stands in the village of Buriton, two miles
from Petersfield on the A3. Parts of the main building date back to
the 15th century, but the bedrooms are a more recent addition, and
are well furnished and very well equipped with every modern
convenience for both business and leisure guests. An extensive
range of blackboard meals and snacks is offered, together with a

selection of real ales. Staff are friendly and helpful.
6 en suite (bth/shr) CTV in all bedrooms Tea and coffee making facilities Direct dial from bedrooms Cen ht 35P Last d 10pm
CARDS:

PEVENSEY East Sussex Map **05** TQ60

GH Q Q **Napier** The Promenade BN24 6HD ☎01323 768875
This modern guest house enjoys an enviable location on the beach yet is within a short drive of Eastbourne. Well maintained throughout, it provides modestly furnished but suitably equipped bedrooms, two of them with balconies. There is a small, comfortable sun lounge, and a choice of breakfasts is served in the pleasantly appointed dining room.
10 rms (5 shr) (3 fmly) No smoking in dining room CTV in all bedrooms Tea and coffee making facilities No dogs Licensed Cen ht CTV 7P No coaches Fishing Last d 4pm
PRICE GUIDE
ROOMS: s £15-£18; d £30-£36; wkly b&b £102-£118✱

PEWSEY Wiltshire Map **04** SU16

◾ Q Q **Woodbridge** North Newnton SN9 6JZ (2.5m SW on A345) (Logis) ☎01980 630266 FAX 01980 630266
Closed 25 Dec
This inn of character is situated beside the A345 in a rural location. Lou and Terry Vertessy have renovated the bars, and extensive blackboard menus offer a range of dishes including many Mexican specialities. The bedrooms are very comfortable and thoughtful extras such as bottled waters and reading materials are provided.
3 rms (1 shr) No smoking in dining room CTV in all bedrooms Tea and coffee making facilities No dogs (ex guide dogs) Cen ht
➡

CTV 60P No coaches Fishing Pentanque Bar billiards Darts
Last d 10.30pm

PRICE GUIDE
ROOMS: s £25-£30; d £30-£35; wkly b&b £175-£210; wkly hlf-
bd £245-£280
MEALS: Lunch £7.90-£20&alc Dinner £7.90-£20&alc
CARDS: £

PICKERING North Yorkshire Map **08** SE88

⚫■ GH Q Q Q **Bramwood** 19 Hallgarth YO18 7AW (off
A169) ☎01751 474066

This 18th-century Grade II listed building near the town centre has
the advantage of its own car park. The bedrooms are well
maintained, public areas are comfortable and service is warm and
friendly.

6 rms No smoking Tea and coffee making facilities No dogs (ex
guide dogs) CTV 6P No coaches Last d 2.30pm

PRICE GUIDE
ROOMS: s £15-£16; d £30-£36; wkly b&b £90-£102; wkly hlf-
bd £153-£165
CARDS: £

Selected

❤ Q Q Q Q Mr & Mrs S Ducat **Rawcliffe House Farm**
(SE797917) Stape YO18 8JA ☎01751 473292

Feb-Oct rs Feb

This luxurious accommodation is situated at Snape, about six
miles from Pickering, in a beautiful location amidst 40 acres
of pasture and meadows. The bedrooms are housed in
converted barns and are set round a south-facing courtyard. Meals
are served at a large communal table in the farmhouse, where
there is also a spacious, comfortable guests' lounge. Owners
Eddy and Sheila Ducat are congenial hosts providing
excellent accommodation in a delightful setting.

3 annexe en suite (bth/shr) No smoking in bedrooms No
smoking in dining room CTV in all bedrooms Tea and coffee
making facilities No dogs (ex guide dogs) Cen ht No
children 8yrs 20P 40 acres non-working Last d 24hrs prior

PRICE GUIDE
ROOMS: s £22.50-£25; d £35-£41; wkly b&b £122.50-
£140; wkly hlf-bd £185.50-£203
 £

PIDDLETRENTHIDE Dorset Map **03** SY79

GH Q Q Q **Old Bakehouse Hotel** DT2 7QR
☎01300 348305

Closed 24-26 Dec & Jan

The Old Bakehouse supplied bread to the Piddle Valley for over
20 years, but it is now a popular family-run guest house. It retains
many original features, such as low beamed ceilings and open
fireplaces. The bedrooms are divided between the main house and
a small extension which overlooks the garden and pool, and they
offer simple, well equipped accommodation with en suite
facilities. The cosy lounge leads into the dining room where a
traditional breakfast is served.

2 en suite (bth) 7 annexe en suite (bth/shr) No smoking in dining
room No smoking in lounges CTV in all bedrooms Tea and
coffee making facilities Cen ht CTV 16P No coaches Outdoor
swimming pool (heated)

PRICE GUIDE
ROOMS: s £22-£27.50; d £44
CARDS: ▨ ▨

◀ Q Q Q **The Poachers** DT2 7QX (on B3143 from
Dorchester) ☎01300 348358

Nestling in the heart of the Piddle Valley, this family run inn offers
a friendly base from which to discover the beautiful countryside.
The fully en suite bedrooms are comfortably furnished, well
equipped, and can cater for families. There is a heated outdoor
pool with attractive patio area and garden. The restaurant offers a
good range of home cooked meals to suit all tastes and appetites.

2 en suite (bth/shr) 9 annexe en suite (bth/shr) (2 fmly) CTV in
all bedrooms Tea and coffee making facilities Direct dial from
bedrooms Cen ht CTV 40P Outdoor swimming pool (heated)
Last d 9pm

PRICE GUIDE
ROOMS: s £30; d £46
CARDS: ▨ ▨ £

PLUCKLEY Kent Map **05** TQ94

Selected

❤ Q Q Q Q Mr & Mrs V Harris **Elvey Farm Country
Hotel** *(TQ916457)* TN27 0SU
☎01233 840442 FAX 01233 840726

Standing in the peaceful Kent countryside on the outskirts of
the village, Elvey farm offers accomodation in three
buildings. The en suite bedrooms are furnished and decorated
in keeping with the style of the farm and are well-equipped.
Guests can also use a small, comfortable bar lounge and a
large dining room with wooden tables which serves an
evening meal on request.

10 en suite (bth/shr) (6 fmly) CTV in all bedrooms Tea and
coffee making facilities Licensed Cen ht ch fac 20P 75
acres mixed

PRICE GUIDE
ROOMS: s £35.50-£43.50; d £45.50-£59.50
CARDS: ▨ ▨ £

PLYMOUTH Devon Map **02** SX45

Selected

GH Q Q Q Q **Bowling Green Hotel** 9-10 Osborne Place,
Lockyer St, The Hoe PL1 2PU
☎01752 667485 FAX 01752 255150

Closed 24-26 Dec

Overlooking Drake's Bowling Green and close to Plymouth
Hoe, this Georgian terrace house has well equipped and
comfortable bedrooms. Breakfast is in an attractive open-plan
dining room, at one end of which is the lounge.

12 rms (8 bth/shr) (3 fmly) CTV in all bedrooms Tea and
coffee making facilities Direct dial from bedrooms Cen ht
CTV 4P

PRICE GUIDE
ROOMS: s £28-£34; d £36-£46✴
CARDS: £

GH Q Q Q **Caraneal** 12/14 Pier St, West Hoe PL1 3BS
☎01752 663589 & 261931

A two-minute walk from the seafront, and conveniently positioned
for the ferry terminal, city centre and Hoe, this neat mid-terrace
house provides a friendly and relaxed atmosphere. Limited private
parking is available and there is ample pay and display parking
nearby. A range of bar meals is served during the evening.

9 en suite (bth/shr) (1 fmly) No smoking in dining room CTV in

all bedrooms Tea and coffee making facilities No dogs (ex guide dogs) Licensed Cen ht CTV 2P Last d 8pm
PRICE GUIDE
ROOMS: s fr £20; d £30-£35*
CARDS: (£)

GH QQ **Cranbourne Hotel** 282 Citadel Road,The Hoe
PL1 2PZ ☎01752 263858 & 661400 FAX 01752 263858
An end-of-terrace Georgian hotel near to the Hoe, the Barbican and city centre. Bedrooms are simply furnished and breakfast is served in a bright dining room.
14 rms (6 shr) (3 fmly) No smoking in dining room CTV in all bedrooms Tea and coffee making facilities Licensed Cen ht CTV 3P Hairdressing salon
PRICE GUIDE
ROOMS: s £15-£25; d £26-£40*
CARDS: (£)

GH QQ **Devonshire** 22 Lockyer Rd, Mannamead PL3 4RL
☎01752 220726 FAX 01752 220766
A period, double-fronted, stone-built, terraced property situated in a quiet residential road very close to the Mutley Plain shopping area. The comfortable bedrooms are bright and airy and all have TV and tea-making facilities; there are three bedrooms available on the ground floor. A set dinner is served at 6pm in the dining room. The lounge bar has a cosy atmosphere, and the guesthouse is personally run by the owners Mary and Phil Collins in a friendly and relaxed style.
10 rms (3 shr) (4 fmly) No smoking in dining room CTV in all bedrooms Tea and coffee making facilities No dogs Licensed ➡

Cen ht CTV 6P Last d 2pm
PRICE GUIDE
ROOMS: s fr £17; d fr £32; wkly b&b fr £112; wkly hlf-bd fr £168
CARDS: ▨ ▧

GH 🅀🅀🅀 **Dudley** 42 Sutherland Road, Mutley PL4 6BN
☎01752 668322 FAX 01752 673763
The Dudley is a family-run guest house close to the railway station in a quiet residential area. The seven bedrooms are cheerfully decorated and most have en suite facilities as well as colour TVs and tea-making equipment. There is a comfortable lounge with ample seating and a newly decorated dining room.
7 rms (5 shr) (2 fmly) No smoking in dining room CTV in all bedrooms Tea and coffee making facilities Cen ht CTV 3P Last d 9am
PRICE GUIDE
ROOMS: s £16-£22; d £34-£36; wkly b&b £95-£120; wkly hlf-bd £144-£176✱
CARDS: ▨ ▧ (£)

GH 🅀🅀🅀 **Four Seasons** 207 Citadel Rd East, The Hoe PL1 2JF ☎01752 223591
Closed 23 Dec-1 Jan
7 rms (5 shr) (2 fmly) No smoking in dining room CTV in all bedrooms Tea and coffee making facilities No dogs (ex guide dogs) Cen ht No parking
PRICE GUIDE
ROOMS: s £18-£25; d £26-£32; wkly b&b fr £112✱
CARDS: ▨ ▧ ▧

GH 🅀🅀 **Georgian House Hotel** 51 Citadel Rd, The Hoe PL1 3AU ☎01752 663237 FAX 01752 253953
Ideally situated for both the Hoe and the city centre, this family-run establishment is also close to the cross channel ferry terminal. The bedrooms are fairly small, although they all have the benefit of en suite facilities, and there are an attractive bar and a separate dining room which offers a variety of dishes on its carte; parking space is limited, and the majority of guests park in the street.
10 en suite (bth/shr) (1 fmly) CTV in all bedrooms Tea and coffee making facilities Direct dial from bedrooms No dogs (ex guide dogs) Licensed Cen ht CTV 2P Last d 9pm
PRICE GUIDE
ROOMS: s £29; d £39✱
CARDS: ▨ ▧ ▧ ▧

GH 🅀🅀🅀 **Grosvenor Park Hotel** 114-116 North Rd East PL4 6AH ☎01752 229312 FAX 01752 252777
Well maintained modern accommodation is offered at this smart hotel which is located close to the railway station, a short distance from the city centre; several of the rooms have en suite showers. Public areas include a lounge, a separate bar and a spacious dining room which provides a choice of menus. Limited private parking is available.
18 rms (9 shr) No smoking in 3 bedrooms No smoking in area of dining room CTV in all bedrooms Tea and coffee making facilities No dogs (ex guide dogs) Licensed Cen ht CTV 6P Last d 8pm
PRICE GUIDE
ROOMS: s £17.50; d £30-£35; wkly b&b £105-£122.50; wkly hlf-bd £157.50-£175✱
CARDS: ▨ ▧ (£)

GH 🅀🅀🅀 **The Lamplighter Hotel** 103 Citadel Rd, The Hoe PL1 2RN ☎01752 663855
Closed 24-26 Dec
Janie and Tony Achilles and their young family have managed to create a relaxed and welcoming atmosphere at this establishment conveniently situated on Plymouth's historic Hoe, close to both

---

the city centre and ferry terminal. There are nine cheerfully decorated bedrooms, all with either en suite or private facilities, and breakfast is served in a big sunny dining room which combines with the comfortable lounge area.
9 en suite (shr) (2 fmly) CTV in all bedrooms Tea and coffee making facilities Cen ht CTV 4P
PRICE GUIDE
ROOMS: s £18-£25; d £28-£35
CARDS: ▨ ▧ ▧ (£)

GH 🅀🅀 **Oliver's Hotel & Restaurant** 33 Sutherland Rd, Mutley PL4 6BN ☎01752 663923
An end-of-terrace house in a quiet residential street, Oliver's is situated close to the railway station, city centre and university. The hotel - which is renowned for its food - is open to both residents and non-residents, offering a wide selection of interesting dishes. Bedrooms vary in size and style, four of them having en suite facilities.
6 rms (4 shr) (1 fmly) No smoking in dining room CTV in all bedrooms Tea and coffee making facilities Direct dial from bedrooms No dogs (ex guide dogs) Licensed Cen ht No children 11yrs 2P No coaches Last d 7.30pm
PRICE GUIDE
ROOMS: s £20-£30; d £45; wkly b&b £126-£189✱
CARDS: ▨ ▧ ▧ ▧ (£)

GH 🅀🅀🅀 **Rosaland Hotel** 32 Houndiscombe Rd, Mutley PL4 6HQ ☎01752 664749 FAX 01752 256984
The neat exterior of the Rosalind Hotel reflects its immaculate interior, which is characterised by stripped pine and dried flowers. A small family-run establishment, convenient for the station, university and city centre, it is one of our inspector's favourites in Plymouth. The bedrooms have a charming country feel as well as all the modern amenities. Breakfast is served in the cheerful dining room, which has a bar in one corner. There is also a comfortable lounge.
8 rms (4 shr) (2 fmly) No smoking in dining room No smoking in lounges CTV in all bedrooms Tea and coffee making facilities Direct dial from bedrooms No dogs (ex guide dogs) Licensed Cen ht CTV 3P Last d noon
PRICE GUIDE
ROOMS: s £17-£22; d £30-£34✱
CARDS: ▨ ▧ ▧ ▧ (£)

Selected

♥ 🅀🅀🅀🅀 Mrs L Brunning **Netton** (*SX552464*) Noss Mayo PL8 1HB ☎01752 873080 FAX 01752 873080
Built from traditional materials about 100 years ago, and subsequently sympathetically restored, Netton Farmhouse is located about a mile from the village of Noss Mayo and two minutes by car from the South Devon Coastal Path. Bedrooms are comfortable and provided with thoughtful extras such as toiletries and mineral water. The friendly owner, Lesley Ann Brunning, is delighted to prepare dinner for guests, which may take the form of a barbecue on balmy summer evenings. An indoor pool, hard tennis court and a games room with pool, table tennis and darts are available.
3 en suite (bth/shr) (2 fmly) No smoking Tea and coffee making facilities No dogs (ex guide dogs) Cen ht CTV ch fac P Indoor swimming pool (heated) Tennis (hard) Last d 4pm
PRICE GUIDE
ROOMS: s £17-£25; d £34-£40

POCKLINGTON Humberside Map **08** SE74

♥ Ⓠ Mr & Mrs Pearson *Meltonby Hall (SE800524)* Meltonby YO4 2PW (2m N unclass) ☎01759 303214
Etr-Oct
Located in the tiny hamlet of Meltonby at the foot of the Wolds, this friendly farm offers simple accommodation in a peaceful location. Guests have their own comfortable lounge and evening meals can be served with advance notice.
2 rms (1 fmly) Tea and coffee making facilities No dogs Cen ht CTV 4P 118 acres mixed

POLMASSICK Cornwall & Isles of Scilly Map **02** SW94

GH ⓆⓆⓆ *Kilbol House Country Hotel* PL26 6HA
☎01726 842481
This attractive 18th-century white-washed house surrounded by acres of grounds and charming gardens enjoys a peaceful location near a vineyard. Most of the simply decorated and furnished bedrooms overlook the gardens and open farmland beyond; three of them are on the ground floor and two others are located in the cottage annexe. As well as the comfortable lounge with TV there is a large separate bar lounge with an inglenook fireplace featuring a wood-burning stove. The varied choice of freshly prepared food served in the dining room includes local vegetables and home-made puddings, and the wine list is well chosen.
8 rms (4 bth) 2 annexe en suite (shr) (2 fmly) No smoking in bedrooms No smoking in dining room CTV in 1 bedroom Tea and coffee making facilities Direct dial from bedrooms Licensed Cen ht CTV 13P No coaches Outdoor swimming pool (heated) Last d noon
CARDS: 🔳 🔳 🔳

POLPERRO Cornwall & Isles of Scilly Map **02** SX25

Selected

GH ⓆⓆⓆⓆ *Landaviddy Manor* Landaviddy Ln PL13 2RT (follow road through Polperro until Landaviddy is reached on west side of village) ☎01503 272210
Closed Nov-Jan
Dating back over 200 years, this lovely manor house sits within two acres of well tended gardens on a quiet lane just above the centre of the fishing village, enjoying lovely rural and sea views. Bedrooms are decorated in a feminine style, with co-ordinated soft fabrics and a mixture of modern and antique furniture. All are nicely equipped, some have en suite facilities and some have four-poster beds. Public areas are attractive and comfortable, and a relaxed atmosphere prevails throughout, cultivated by the warm and friendly proprietors.
7 rms (4 shr) No smoking in bedrooms No smoking in dining room CTV in all bedrooms Tea and coffee making facilities No dogs Licensed Cen ht CTV No children 10yrs 9P No coaches Last d breakfast
CARDS: 🔳 🔳
See advertisement on p.329.

Selected

GH ⓆⓆⓆⓆ *Lanhael House* PL13 2PW (on entering Polperro turn right at small roundabout guesthouse 75yds on right) ☎01503 272428 FAX 01503 273077
Apr-Oct
Mrs Taylor is very welcoming and guests return on a regular basis to stay in this attractive and appealing guest house, parts

of which date back to the 17th century. Some of the bedrooms open directly onto the terrace garden, and all have such extras as good toiletries, antique furniture and a selection of books. A full English breakfast, or a variation of it, is still popular with guests, but a large number now choose the vegetarian alternative of fresh fruit salad, waffles and maple syrup.

4 rms (1 bth 1 shr) 1 annexe en suite (shr) CTV in all bedrooms Tea and coffee making facilities No dogs (ex guide dogs) Cen ht CTV No children 14yrs 5P No coaches Outdoor swimming pool (heated)

PRICE GUIDE
ROOMS: s £25; d £36-£39

Premier Selected

♥ Q Q Q Q Q Mrs L Tuckett **Trenderway** *(SX214533)* Pelynt PL13 2LY (from Looe take A387 to Polperro, farm is signposted on main road) ☎01503 272214

Luxury accommodation amidst beautiful surroundings is on offer at this 16th-century farmhouse set in 400 acres at the head of the Polperro Valley. Two substantial granite barns have been converted to provide some of the five stylishly decorated and individually furnished bedrooms, each one with a large bath and shower room equipped to a very high standard. The farm's own chickens produce the free range eggs which go into substantial breakfasts, and these are served in a sunny conservatory. There is a relaxing sitting room with a log fire. A further barn has been decorated in a Mediterranean style, and is available as quality self-catering accommodation.

2 en suite (bth/shr) 2 annexe en suite (bth/shr) No smoking CTV in all bedrooms Tea and coffee making facilities No dogs Cen ht No children 5P 400 acres arable mixed sheep cattle

PRICE GUIDE
ROOMS: s £30-£35; d £56-£60

(£)

POOLE Dorset Map **04** SZ09

See also Bournemouth

Selected

GH Q Q Q Q **Acorns** 264 Wimborne Rd, Oakdale BH15 3EF (on A35 1m from town centre) ☎01202 672901 FAX 01202 672901

Set back from the main road, this guest house offers attractive, co-ordinated and well furnished bedrooms, most of which are en suite. The remaining two have sole use of adjacent bath or shower rooms. There is a cosy lounge and bar area and a comfortable dining room where dinner is served on request. The house has a friendly and informal atmosphere and is popular with business travellers.

5 rms (4 shr) No smoking in dining room No smoking in lounges CTV in all bedrooms Tea and coffee making facilities No dogs Licensed Cen ht CTV No children 14yrs

---

6P No coaches Last d noon
PRICE GUIDE
ROOMS: s £18-£20; d £36-£40✳
CARDS: ⬛ ▥ ▥ ▥ ⑤   (£)

⟦⟧ **GH** Q Q **Avoncourt Private Hotel** 245 Bournemouth Rd, Parkstone BH14 9HX (on A35 between Poole & Bournemouth) ☎01202 732025 FAX 01202 732025

This small private hotel has a small car park at the rear. The style of accommodation is cosy, neat and well presented. Some bedrooms have private shower cubicles in the rooms, and another now has en suite facilities. There is a bright, comfortable and well decorated combined bar/breakfast room, and resident proprietors Mr and Mrs Jones take great pride in their home and work hard to maintain high housekeeping standards.

6 rms (1 bth/shr) (3 fmly) No smoking in area of dining room CTV in all bedrooms Tea and coffee making facilities No dogs Licensed Cen ht CTV 6P Last d 10am

PRICE GUIDE
ROOMS: s £16-£20; d £30-£46; wkly b&b fr £95; wkly hlf-bd fr £140

CARDS: ⬛ ▥ ▥ ⑩ (£)

GH Q Q Q **Seacourt** 249 Blandford Rd, Hamworthy BH15 4AZ (on A350 between Upton and Poole Bridge) ☎01202 674995

Located close to the cross channel ferry terminal, this guesthouse has recently been taken over by the Hewitt family, who have implemented a programme of redecoration and improvements since their arrival. All bedrooms now have en suite facilities, and overall the standard of accommodation is high. Bedrooms are neat and bright, with pretty coordinating decor, and three are conveniently located on the ground floor. There is a cosy lounge and bright, front-facing breakfast room. Car parking is available, and the atmosphere is relaxed and friendly.

5 en suite (bth/shr) (1 fmly) No smoking in 1 bedrooms CTV in all bedrooms Tea and coffee making facilities Cen ht CTV 6P No coaches

---

GH Q Q **Sheldon Lodge** 22 Forest Rd, Branksome Park BH13 6DH (turn off A35 at Frizzel rdbt & take B3065 to traffic lights turn right & first left) ☎01202 761186

This attractive property stands in a quiet residential area on the outskirts of Poole. The en suite bedrooms are neatly furnished and have colour TVs. Other attractions include a residents' bar with a full size snooker table, a sun lounge area and convenient street parking.

12 en suite (bth/shr) (1 fmly) No smoking in dining room CTV in 14 bedrooms Tea and coffee making facilities Licensed Cen ht 3P Solarium Last d 7pm
CARDS: ⬛

PORLOCK Somerset Map **03** SS84

GH Q Q Q **Lorna Doone Hotel** High St TA24 8PS (on A39) ☎01643 862404
Closed 24-26 Dec

Owners Toni and Dick Thornton continue to upgrade and improve this property conveniently located in the centre of the village. New bedrooms, three of which are on the ground floor, have been created from the former stables in the courtyard at the rear of the property. The attractive and well appointed no-smoking restaurant is open to non-residents and is complemented by a well stocked bar and a short, select wine list. A comfortable lounge is available for guests, with a log fire on cooler evenings adding to the warm, friendly, informal atmosphere.

10 en suite (bth/shr) 5 annexe en suite (shr) (2 fmly) No smoking in dining room CTV in all bedrooms Tea and coffee

making facilities Licensed Cen ht CTV 9P Last d 8.45pm
PRICE GUIDE
ROOMS: s £22.50; d £38-£47; wkly b&b £126-£157.50
CARDS: ▨ ▨   (£)

GH Q Q Q *Seapoint* Upway TA24 8QE (behind Ship Inn)
☎01643 862289
Seapoint is the comfortable, Edwardian home of Christine and
Steven Fitzgerald, overlooking Porlock Bay and surrounded by the
beautiful hills of Exmoor. The cosy, well equipped bedrooms are
tastefully furnished and decorated. Evening meals are home made,
using wholefood ingredients. Many guests with dietary needs
return annually, vegetarian, vegan and traditional meals are always
available, guests with other diets should give prior notice to the
Fitzgeralds. Guided or unguided walks on Exmoor are another
speciality of Seapoint, each bedroom is supplied with a special
folder outlining the walks available.
3 en suite (bth/shr) No smoking CTV in all bedrooms Tea and
coffee making facilities Licensed Cen ht CTV 4P No coaches
Last d 3pm

PORTHCURNO Cornwall & Isles of Scilly Map **02** SW32

🚪 🖵 **GH** Q Q *Corniche* Trebehor TR19 6LX (at Sennen
turn left off the A30 at the Wreckers Inn on to B3315,
establishment 1m on left) ☎01736 871685
Closed Nov-Jan
Near the hamlet of Porthcurno with its popular open air Minack
Theatre, this spacious detached house offers well equipped
modern bedrooms and bright attractive public rooms. There are
magnificent views over the surrounding countryside.
6 rms (1 fmly) No smoking Tea and coffee making facilities No
dogs Licensed Cen ht CTV No children 5yrs 7P No coaches
Last d 3.30pm
PRICE GUIDE
ROOMS: s £12-£14; d £24-£28; wkly b&b £80-£94; wkly hlf-bd
£115-£129   (£)

GH Q Q Q *Grey Gables* TR19 6JT (turn off A30 onto
B3283 then follow road signs for Minack Theatre, continue
for another 400 metres. Grey Gables opposite St Levan
church) ☎01736 810421
Mar-Oct
A solid house of Cornish stone, Grey Gables is set in an acre and a
quarter of gardens and lawns on a magnificent stretch of cliff.
From the garden, a cliff path leads to Porthchapel Beach, and the
world-renowned Minack open air theatre is within walking
distance. In the no-smoking dining room Mrs Thomas provides a
good-value dinner of traditional home-cooked dishes, and a
separate lounge with TV is available for guests' use.
7 rms (4 bth/shr) No smoking in dining room No smoking in
lounges CTV in 1 bedroom Tea and coffee making facilities No
dogs (ex guide dogs) Cen ht No children 5yrs 9P No coaches
Last d 4pm
PRICE GUIDE
ROOMS: s £15.50-£17.50; d £31-£38; wkly b&b £108.50-£133;
wkly hlf-bd £171.50-£196✳   (£)

Factual details of establishments in this Guide
are from questionnaires we send to all
establishments that feature in the book.

PORT ISAAC Cornwall & Isles of Scilly Map **02** SW98

Selected

GH ⓆⓆⓆⓆ **Archer Farm Hotel** Trewetha PL29 3RU
(on B3267) ☎01208 880522
Etr-Oct
An old Cornish farmhouse has been converted to provide this
small family hotel. The five bedrooms all have en suite
facilities and some also have balconies and/or rural views. A
family suite with two interconnecting rooms is available.
Bedrooms have soft, co-ordinated colour schemes, and the
standard of decor is equally high in cheerful public areas. The
latter include a small bar, comfortable lounge and separate TV
lounge as well as the sunny dining room where Vickie
Welton's cordon bleu menus are served. Outside there are
extensive gardens and a patio.
5 en suite (bth/shr) (1 fmly) No smoking in dining room No
smoking in 1 lounge CTV in all bedrooms Tea and coffee
making facilities Direct dial from bedrooms Licensed Cen
ht CTV 8P No coaches Last d 8pm
PRICE GUIDE
ROOMS: s £20-£22.50; d £40-£45; wkly b&b £142-£192;
wkly hlf-bd £232-£282✶

GH ⓆⓆ **Bay Hotel** 1 The Terrace PL29 3SG (turn off A39
onto B3314 then onto B3267) ☎01208 880380
Etr-Oct
Enjoying a good position overlooking the sea, this long-
established hotel has been run by Mary and Jim Andrews for over
13 years. The bedrooms are furnished to a satisfactory standard in
a conventional style and several are suitable for families. There is
a comfortable lounge facing the sea, with a separate bar and a
plain but practical dining room where an à la carte menu is usually
available. Parking can be a little difficult at times but there is a pay
and display car park opposite.
10 rms (4 bth/shr) (4 fmly) No smoking in dining room CTV in
all bedrooms Tea and coffee making facilities Licensed Cen ht
10P Last d 7pm
PRICE GUIDE
ROOMS: s £18-£21.50; d £36-£43; wkly b&b £108-£132; wkly
hlf-bd £168-£189.50

PORTLAND Dorset Map **03** SY67

GH ⓆⓆⓆ **Alessandria Hotel & Italian Restaurant** 71
Wakeham Easton DT5 1HW ☎01305 822270 & 820108
FAX 01305 820561
This bright Portland stone house stands towards the southern tip of
Portland Bill. It is well-maintained throughout with comfortable
accomodation, including a small lounge with welcoming seating
and a nicely appointed restaurant serving the well-prepared Italian
menu of propietor Giovanni Bisogno.
15 rms (1 bth 10 shr) 1 annexe en suite (bth/shr) (3 fmly) No
smoking in dining room CTV in all bedrooms Tea and coffee
making facilities No dogs (ex guide dogs) Licensed Cen ht
CTV 16P No coaches Last d 9pm
PRICE GUIDE
ROOMS: s £25-£35; d £45-£50; wkly b&b £145-£195; wkly hlf-
bd £230-£245
CARDS: 🔳 🔳 🔳 ⓪

PORTREATH Cornwall & Isles of Scilly Map **02** SW64

Selected

GH ⓆⓆⓆⓆ **Benson's** 1 Hillside TR16 4LL (off B3300)
☎01209 842534
A recently built modern guest house is situated in an elevated
position with beautiful views over the village, harbour and
coastline. Bedrooms are all located on the ground floor and
are very well equipped. Self-service breakfast is taken in the
conservatory, which offers spectacular views. Much of the
coastline and surrounding countryside are owned by the
National Trust, and there are marvellous clifftop walks and
secluded coves to explore.
4 en suite (shr) No smoking CTV in all bedrooms Tea and
coffee making facilities No dogs (ex guide dogs) Cen ht No
children 6P No coaches
PRICE GUIDE
ROOMS: s £25-£36; d £36; wkly b&b £119✶

GH ⓆⓆ **Cliff House** The Square TR16 4LB ☎01209 842008
This white painted stone cottage dates back some 200 years.
Bedrooms are simply furnished and well equipped, with tvs, tea
trays and radio alarms. A hearty breakfast is served in the rear
dining room. There are several pubs and small restaurants in the
village for evening meals.
4 en suite (shr) No smoking in dining room CTV in 1 bedroom
Tea and coffee making facilities No dogs Cen ht No children
7yrs 6P No coaches
PRICE GUIDE
ROOMS: s £15; d £30✶

PORTSMOUTH & SOUTHSEA Hampshire Map **04** SZ69

GH ⓆⓆ **Abbey Lodge** 30 Waverley Rd PO5 2PW (follow sea
front signs towards pier turn left into Granada, Clarendon or
Burgoyne Road to roundabout for Waverley Road)
☎01705 828285 FAX 01705 872943
Cheerful proprietor Mrs Forbes takes great care of her guests at
this small establishment set in a residential area between the shops
and the seafront. Bedrooms vary in shape and size but all are
brightly decorated; some have en suite facilities, and more are
planned. The comfortable public areas have a traditional feel, and
dinner is available by arrangement.
9 rms (1 bth 2 shr) (2 fmly) CTV in all bedrooms Tea and coffee
making facilities No dogs (ex guide dogs) Cen ht CTV No
parking Last d 9am
PRICE GUIDE
ROOMS: s £16-£25; d £30-£37✶
CARDS: 🔳 🔳 🔳 ⓪ 🔳 🔳

GH ⓆⓆⓆ **Bembell Court Hotel** 69 Festing Rd PO4 0NQ
(road opposite Natural History Museum)
☎01705 735915 & 750497 FAX 01705 756497
Guests are assured of both a friendly welcome and a relaxed
atmosphere at this small hotel. Bedrooms - half of which offer en
suite facilities - vary in size and comfortable public areas include a
dining room where home-cooked dishes are served with home-
grown vegetables. The hotel has won a number of awards for its
flower displays, which are particularly lovely in the summer
months.
13 rms (8 bth/shr) (3 fmly) No smoking in 4 bedrooms No
smoking in dining room No smoking in 1 lounge CTV in all
bedrooms Tea and coffee making facilities Direct dial from

---

bedrooms No dogs (ex guide dogs) Licensed Cen ht CTV 10P
Last d 4pm
PRICE GUIDE
ROOMS: s £20-£35; d £40-£48; wkly b&b £145-£160; wkly hlf-
bd £199-£225
CARDS: (£)

[icons] **GH** [Q][Q] **Birchwood** 44 Waverley Rd PO5 2PP
(keeping South Parade Pier on left take 1st right onto rdbt
leave at 3rd exit into Waverley Rd) ☎01705 811337
This Victorian terraced house is situated five minutes' walk from
the seafront and has a welcoming, informal atmosphere. Bedrooms
offer modern facilities and there is a comfortable lounge and an
attractive breakfast room.
6 rms (3 shr) (2 fmly) No smoking in 2 bedrooms No smoking
in dining room CTV in all bedrooms Tea and coffee making
facilities No dogs (ex guide dogs) Licensed Cen ht CTV No
parking Last d 3pm
PRICE GUIDE
ROOMS: s £15-£25; d £30-£36; wkly b&b £94.50-£113.40;
wkly hlf-bd £132.30-£151.20
CARDS: [icons] (£)

GH [Q][Q] *Collingham* 89 St Ronans Rd PO4 0PR
☎01705 821549
Closed 24-26 Dec
In a residential part of town, not far from either the shops or
seafront, this small hotel offers neat, freshly decorated bedrooms
and a breakfast room/lounge, all with a warm and friendly
atmosphere. Breakfast is the only meal served, but there are a
number of dining options in the town.
6 rms (3 fmly) No smoking in 4 bedrooms No smoking in dining
room No smoking in lounges CTV in all bedrooms Tea and
coffee making facilities Cen ht CTV No parking

GH [Q][Q] **The Elms** 48 Victoria Rd South PO5 2BT (left at
roundabout at end of M275, straight ahead at next 3
roundabouts & traffic lights guesthouse 300yds on right)
☎01705 823924 FAX 01705 823924
Conveniently located close to the shops and seafront, this
Victorian property offers simply furnished, clean, reasonably
equipped bedrooms particularly aimed at families, with several
bunk beds. The front-facing lounge is shared with the Erskine
family, and the atmosphere is informal. There is a small bar, and
breakfast is served downstairs, with early breakfasts available for
those catching ferries.
6 rms (2 shr) (3 fmly) No smoking in dining room CTV in all
bedrooms Tea and coffee making facilities No dogs (ex guide
dogs) Licensed Cen ht CTV 2P No coaches
PRICE GUIDE
ROOMS: s £17; d £34-£40; wkly b&b £110
 (£)

GH [Q][Q][Q] **Fortitude Cottage** 51 Broad St, Old Portsmouth
PO1 2JD ☎01705 823748 FAX 01705 823748
Closed 25 & 26 Dec
This attractive house is easily located by the year-round flower
baskets and tubs outside. Personally run for many years by Mrs
Harbeck, it is ideally situated just five minutes from the ferry
ports, making it a perfect overnight stop. The bedrooms are bright
and pretty, and now all have private facilities. Breakfast is served
in the sunny dining room, and there is parking in the street as well
as in a car park opposite the building.
3 en suite (bth/shr) No smoking CTV in all bedrooms Tea and
coffee making facilities No dogs Cen ht No children No parking
No coaches
PRICE GUIDE
ROOMS: d £42-£44*
CARDS: (£)

GH [Q][Q] **Gainsborough House** 9 Malvern Rd PO5 2LZ
☎01705 822604
Closed Xmas
Many guests return time and time again to this friendly guesthouse
which is quietly situated in a residential area fairly close to the
shops and seafront. Neat, tidy bedrooms are well kept, while the
lounge and dining room are both attractive and comfortable.
7 rms (2 fmly) No smoking in dining room No smoking in
lounges CTV in all bedrooms Tea and coffee making facilities
No dogs Cen ht CTV No children 3yrs No parking No coaches
PRICE GUIDE
ROOMS: s £14.50-£15; d £29-£30*

GH [Q][Q] **Glencoe** 64 Whitwell Rd PO4 0QS ☎01705 737413
Conveniently situated for the sea and the town, this personally run
hotel is in a quiet residential area. The bedrooms are bright, pretty
and comfortable , several have modern showers en suite. There is
a well appointed breakfast room overlooking an attractive patio,
and a cosy guest lounge.
7 rms (5 shr) (1 fmly) No smoking CTV in all bedrooms Tea
and coffee making facilities No dogs Cen ht CTV No children
5yrs No parking
PRICE GUIDE
ROOMS: s fr £16.50; d £35-£38*
CARDS: (£)

[icons] **GH** [Q][Q][Q] **Hamilton House** 95 Victoria Rd North
PO5 1PS ☎01705 823502 FAX 01705 823502
This spacious Victorian property has been carefully renovated by
Graham and Sandra Tubb to provide bright, comfortable
accommodation. The bedrooms all have colour television and
three of them offer modern en suite facilities. There is a
comfortable guest lounge where guests can relax, and easy parking ➡

---

is available in the adjoining street. This is an ideal stopover point for the ferry, which is just five minutes away.

8 rms (3 shr) (3 fmly) No smoking in 1 bedrooms No smoking in dining room No smoking in lounges CTV in all bedrooms Tea and coffee making facilities No dogs Cen ht CTV No parking Last d noon

PRICE GUIDE

ROOMS: s £16-£21.50; d £32-£43; wkly b&b £109-£147; wkly hlf-bd £144-£182

£

GH Ⓠ Ⓠ Ⓠ *Mallow* 82 Whitwell Rd PO5 0QS
☎01705 293829 & 293892

7 rms (3 shr) (1 fmly) No smoking in 1 bedrooms No smoking in dining room CTV in all bedrooms Tea and coffee making facilities No dogs Licensed Cen ht CTV No parking No coaches Last d 1pm

CARDS: ▰ ▰

GH Ⓠ Ⓠ Ⓠ **St Margarets Hotel** 3 Craneswater Gate PO4 0NZ
☎01705 820097 FAX 01705 820097

Closed 2 wks Xmas

14 rms (11 bth/shr) (2 fmly) No smoking in dining room CTV in all bedrooms Tea and coffee making facilities No dogs Licensed Cen ht CTV 4P Last d noon

PRICE GUIDE

ROOMS: s £20-£26; d £34-£42

CARDS: ▰ ▰

Selected

GH Ⓠ Ⓠ Ⓠ Ⓠ **Upper Mount House Hotel** The Vale, Clarendon Rd PO5 2EQ ☎01705 820456

Located in a residential area between the shopping centre and seafront, this colonial-style house built over 150 years ago continues to be renovated with great care by Mr and Mrs Moth. Much of the property's original character has been retained and the house is attractively decorated, with co-ordinated fabrics in the bedrooms and a traditional feel to the public rooms. Home-cooked fare is offered in the dining room and car parking is provided on site.

12 en suite (bth/shr) (3 fmly) No smoking in dining room CTV in all bedrooms Tea and coffee making facilities No dogs (ex guide dogs) Licensed Cen ht CTV 12P Last d 6pm

PRICE GUIDE

ROOMS: s £20-£28; d £36-£48; wkly hlf-bd £169-£200✳

CARDS: ▰ ▰

£

GH Ⓠ Ⓠ Ⓠ *Victoria Court* 29 Victoria Rd North PO5 1PL
☎01705 820305

Located in a residential area, this semidetached Victorian property continues to be upgraded and improved by resident proprietors Mr and Mrs Johnson. The comfortable bedrooms are well furnished and equipped, with bright decor and modern en suite shower rooms. There is a small first floor lounge, and a set home-cooked evening meal is offered in the dining room, where there is also a tiny bar.

7 en suite (shr) (3 fmly) No smoking in dining room CTV in all bedrooms Tea and coffee making facilities Direct dial from bedrooms No dogs (ex guide dogs) Licensed Cen ht No coaches Last d am

CARDS: ▰ ▰ Ⓓ

POUNDSGATE Devon Map **03** SX77

Premier Selected

GH Ⓠ Ⓠ Ⓠ Ⓠ Ⓠ **Leusdon Lodge** Leusdon TQ13 7PE
☎01364 631304

A granite-built family-run guesthouse in an elevated position affording glorious views across Dartmoor. The bedrooms are conventionally furnished and equipped with many modern conveniences. There is a wood panelled dining room where a choice of dishes is served from a small daily changing menu. A popular resting place for walkers, and an ideal setting from which to explore Dartmoor.

7 en suite (bth/shr) CTV in all bedrooms Tea and coffee making facilities Licensed Cen ht 14P No coaches Croquet Bowls lawn Last d 6.30pm

PRICE GUIDE

ROOMS: d £50-£100✳

CARDS: ▰ ▰

❤ Ⓠ Ⓠ Ⓠ Mrs Margaret Phipps **New Cott Farm** *(SX703727)* TQ13 7PD (take Two Bridges/Princetown turning off A38 at 2nd Ashburton junct (Pear Tree). Through Poundsgate village then 1st left and follow farm signs)
☎01364 631421 FAX 01364 631338

A delightful single-storey farmhouse with a large garden - set on the southern slopes of Dartmoor in almost total seclusion, yet close to the A38 and only three miles from Ashburton - offers very attractively decorated bedrooms with co-ordinating fabrics; each has a fully tiled shower room, and they are suitable for partially disabled guests. Traditional puddings with clotted cream, as well as local meat and vegetables, feature in the enjoyable home-cooked meals which Mrs Phipps serves in the comfortable dining room which leads into a stunning conservatory with extensive views of moorland. There are two private trout ponds for guests' use.

4 en suite (bth/shr) No smoking Tea and coffee making facilities No dogs (ex guide dogs) Cen ht CTV No children 3yrs 4P Fishing 130 acres cattle, sheep Last d 5pm

PRICE GUIDE

ROOMS: d £34-£36; wkly hlf-bd fr £170✳

PRAA SANDS Cornwall & Isles of Scilly Map **02** SW52

Selected

❤ Ⓠ Ⓠ Ⓠ Ⓠ Mr & Mrs W Jenkin **Higher Trevurvas** Higher Trevurvas, Ashton TR13 9TZ (signposted from A394) ☎01736 763613

Jan-Oct

This small farm stands in peaceful surroundings off the A394 Helston to Penzance Road, about five miles from Helston. Two of the four bedrooms are en suite, one has a shower with a private WC across the corridor and one room has an adjoining bathroom. The cosy dining room is well appointed and the ideal setting for one of Mrs Jenkin's traditionally cooked, five course set dinners. There is also a spacious guest lounge where a fire is lit on cooler nights.

4 en suite (bth/shr) No smoking CTV in all bedrooms Tea

and coffee making facilities No dogs (ex guide dogs) Cen ht
CTV No children 10yrs 6P 25 acres beef sheep Last d 10am
PRICE GUIDE
ROOMS: d £34-£40; wkly b&b £115-£130; wkly hlf-bd
£192-£207

PRESTON Lancashire Map **07** SD52

See also Longridge

GH ⓠⓠⓠ **Tulketh Hotel** 209 Tulketh Road, Ashton PR2 1ES
(leave M6 junct 31 or M55 junct 1 towards Blackpool on
A5085, turn left onto A5072 at St Andrews Church)
☎01772 726250 & 728096 FAX 01772 723743
Closed 24 Dec-1 Dec
This very well maintained Edwardian House, which retains many
of its original features such as the magnificent tiled floor in the
front hall, is situated in the residential area of Ashton, northwest
of the town centre has been owned by the Hardwick family for the
last eight years. Bedrooms, all but one of which are en-suite are
attractively decorated and well equipped. Breakfast and dinner,
where a good range of dishes are available from an a la carte
menu, are served in the spacious dining room opposite which is a
comfortably furnished lounge bar with access to the well tended
gardens.
12 rms (11 bth/shr) (1 fmly) No smoking in dining room CTV in
all bedrooms Tea and coffee making facilities Direct dial from
bedrooms No dogs (ex guide dogs) Licensed Cen ht CTV 12P
No coaches Last d 7.30pm
PRICE GUIDE
ROOMS: s £32-£40; d £42-£50
CARDS: 🟥 ▆ 🟨 ⓞ

GH ⓠⓠ **Withy Trees** 175 Garstang Road, Fulwood PR2 4LL
(2m N on A6) ☎01772 717693 FAX 01772 717693
This friendly, enthusiastically run and well appointed guest house
is conveniently situated beside the A6, in Fulwood, to the north of
the town. Eight out of the ten comfortably furnished bedrooms,
some of which are non smoking, are en-suite and all are equipped
with televisions and tea and coffee making facilities. There is a
comfortably furnished lounge and a bright, spacious dining room,
with separate tables, where breakfast and dinner, by prior
arrangement, are very willingly served.
10 en suite (bth/shr) (4 fmly) No smoking in 7 bedrooms No
smoking in dining room CTV in all bedrooms Tea and coffee
making facilities Cen ht CTV 20P Last d 2pm
PRICE GUIDE
ROOMS: s £20-£27; d £30-£37; wkly b&b £100-£120; wkly hlf-
bd £130-£150

◀ⓠⓠⓠ *Birley Arms Motel* Bryning Ln, Warton PR4 1TN
(leave M55 at junct 3 then A585 to Kirkham, follow signs to
Wrea Green & Warton, Birley Arms between the two)
☎01722 679988 FAX 01772 679435
This popular country inn is situated a short distance off the A584
and guests should take the turning for Wrea Green from the village
of Warton. The original inn has been considerably extended and
now offers a good standard of modern accommodation, pleasantly
appointed bedrooms being furnished in old pine and well equipped
with extra facilities (including trouser presses). An extensive
range of bar meals is offered at both lunch and dinner, and there is
an enclosed play area outside for children.
16 en suite (shr) CTV in all bedrooms Tea and coffee making
facilities No dogs (ex guide dogs) Cen ht 80P Last d 9.15pm
CARDS: 🟥 ▆ 🟨 ⓞ

"Hamilton House"
95 VICTORIA ROAD NORTH, SOUTHSEA
PORTSMOUTH, HANTS PO5 1PS
TELEPHONE & FAX: (01705) 823502

Delightful family-run guest house, centrally located
just 5 mins by car, to continental ferry terminal,
Guildhall/City Centre and main Tourist attractions of
Portsmouth/Southsea. Ideal touring base.
The bright, modern bedrooms have heating, colour
TVs and tea/coffee making facilities.
Some en suite rooms available.
Traditional English, Vegetarian or Continental
breakfast is served from 6.00 a.m.
Holidaymakers, business people & travellers are
assured a warm welcome & pleasant stay
at any time of the year.
For brochure please send SAE to
Graham & Sandra Tubb & quote ref AA.

VICTORIA COURT
29 Victoria Road North, Southsea,
Hampshire PO5 1PL
Telephone: (01705) 820305

Victoria Court offers the warmth of a comfortable
licensed Victorian house representing value and
the kind of facilities demanded by todays business
traveller combined with a friendly service for the
holiday maker.

All rooms have: en suite facilities, colour TV. clock,
radio, tea/coffee making facilities, direct dial
telephone, hair dryer and individual temperature
control. Breakfasts available for ferry travellers
from 6am.

RAMSGATE Kent Map **05** TR36

GH [Q][Q] **Eastwood** 28 Augusta Rd CT11 8JS (east side of harbour near Granville Theatre)
☎01843 591505 FAX 01843 591505
This well-maintained establishment provides accomodation in two houses. Each has its own brightly decorated dining room serving a set evening meal. A small sitting room is also available for guests' use. Some bedrooms are small but all have colourful soft furnishings.
7 rms (2 bth/shr) 6 annexe en suite (bth/shr) (4 fmly) No smoking in 4 bedrooms No smoking in dining room No smoking in 1 lounge CTV in all bedrooms Tea and coffee making facilities Cen ht CTV 18P Last d 6pm
PRICE GUIDE
ROOMS: s £18-£26; d £30-£40; wkly b&b £130-£170; wkly hlf-bd £150-£200*

(£)

[📺💷] **GH** [Q] **St Hilary Private Hotel** 21 Crescent Rd CT11 9QU (follow A253 to B2054 at small roundabout turn into Westcliff road, take second left into Crescent Road)
☎01843 591427
rs 25-26 Dec
A modest, traditional and professionally run guest house, St Hilary is located in a Victorian residential district. It provides a lounge with a TV and video recorder, and a bar-cum-breakfast room. Some of the bedrooms have shower cubicles.
7 rms (4 fmly) No smoking in 2 bedrooms No smoking in dining room No smoking in lounges Tea and coffee making facilities No dogs Licensed CTV No children 4yrs No parking No coaches Last d 3.30pm
PRICE GUIDE
ROOMS: s £16-£18; d £28-£32; wkly b&b £70-£84; wkly hlf-bd £90-£110
CARDS: ■

(£)

RASKELF North Yorkshire Map **08** SE47

Selected

GH [Q][Q][Q][Q] **Old Farmhouse Country Hotel** YO6 3LF (Logis) ☎01347 821971 FAX 01347 822392
Closed 22 Dec-Jan
Originally the farmhouse for the village farm, this lovely old building is now a well furnished and comfortable hotel with a reputation for hospitality and good food. It is ideal for exploring the North York Moors and the Hambleton Hills. The beamed bedrooms, which include two family rooms and one room with a four-poster bed, are decorated in a mixture of styles and are well equipped. Two very comfortable lounges are available, one smaller with a TV, and the very popular restaurant offers a wide choice of home-cooked dishes.
10 en suite (bth/shr) (2 fmly) No smoking in dining room CTV in all bedrooms Tea and coffee making facilities Direct dial from bedrooms Licensed Cen ht 12P No coaches Last d 7pm
PRICE GUIDE
ROOMS: s £40-£45; d £74-£82; wkly hlf-bd £259-£294

RAVENSCAR North Yorkshire Map **08** NZ90

GH [Q][Q][Q] **The Smugglers Rock Country** YO13 0ER (leave A171 towards Ravenscar guesthouse half mile before Ravenscar opposite an old stone windmill) ☎01723 870044
A delightful stone-built property standing in open countryside, this house has links with smuggling activities along the coast. A light

from a window in the east wall would signal when it was safe to bring contraband through tunnels from the beach. Today it is a comfortable guest house with a well furnished lounge and bedrooms.
8 en suite (bth/shr) (1 fmly) No smoking in dining room No smoking in lounges CTV in all bedrooms Tea and coffee making facilities Licensed Cen ht CTV No children 3yrs 12P Last d 4.30pm
PRICE GUIDE
ROOMS: s £21-£24; d £40-£44

RAVENSTONEDALE Cumbria Map **07** NY70

◀ [Q][Q] *Kings Head* Coldbeck CA17 4NH
☎015396 23284 FAX 015396 23604
A delightful old inn standing on the approach to the village offers pleasantly furnished accommodation which includes family rooms. The bars are particularly attractive, and a good range of home-cooked meals is served in the dining room.
4 rms (2 bth) (1 fmly) No smoking in area of dining room CTV in all bedrooms Tea and coffee making facilities Direct dial from bedrooms Cen ht CTV 10P Fishing Last d 9.30pm

READING Berkshire Map **04** SU77

GH [Q][Q][Q] **Abbey House Hotel** 118 Connaught Rd RG3 2UF (take A329 towards Tilehurst after Reading West Railway bridge take 3rd left) (MIN)
☎01734 590549 FAX 01734 569299
Closed Xmas-New Year
Situated in a quiet residential road off the A329 and convenient for Reading West Station and the town centre, this friendly family-run hotel provides a sound standard of accommodation. Bedrooms vary in size and style from the relatively modest to some with three-star comfort and extras such as trouser presses and telephone computer terminals. There is a comfortable lounge and a small bar adjoins the dining room serving an extensive range of meals each evening.
20 rms (14 bth/shr) (1 fmly) No smoking in dining room CTV in all bedrooms Tea and coffee making facilities Direct dial from bedrooms No dogs (ex guide dogs) Licensed Cen ht CTV 14P Last d 8.30pm
PRICE GUIDE
ROOMS: s £24.50-£45.50; d £50.50-£59.50
CARDS: ■ ■ ■ ■

GH [Q][Q][Q] **Aeron Private Hotel** 191-193 Kentwood Hill, Tilehurst RG31 6JE (3m W off A329)
☎01734 424119 FAX 01734 451953
This family run hotel is in Tilehurst on the North West edge of Reading. It has been extensively upgraded to offer bedrooms in two adjacent houses in a variety of styles to suit all pockets. All the rooms are well maintained and equipped with direct dial telephone and TV but en suite rooms have been more recently refurbished and provide such extras as writing desks and hairdryers. There is a smartly decorated lounge and dinner is served Monday to Thursday in the licensed dining room and includes dishes such as lasagne or chicken kiev and home made spotted dick or treacle sponge. A large car park is available for guests' use.
13 rms (7 shr) (1 fmly) No smoking in area of dining room CTV in all bedrooms Tea and coffee making facilities Direct dial from bedrooms Licensed Cen ht CTV 20P
PRICE GUIDE
ROOMS: s £25-£41; d £33-£54*
CARDS: ■ ■ ■

REDCAR Cleveland Map **08** NZ62

GH Ⓠ Ⓠ Ⓠ **Claxton Hotel** 196 High St TS10 3AW (leave A174 at double rdbt signed Redcar continue across railway crossing turn left at traffic lights by St Peter's Church hotel on left) ☎01642 486745 FAX 01642 486522
Situated at the end of the High Street, this well established hotel provides well appointed accommodation, with both the business and leisure guest in mind. The spacious, attractive open-plan bar and restaurant are popular, and there is a cosy TV lounge; some rooms enjoy sea views.
27 rms (21 shr) (3 fmly) No smoking in dining room CTV in all bedrooms Tea and coffee making facilities Licensed Cen ht CTV 10P Last d 9pm
PRICE GUIDE
ROOMS: s £18-£21; d £33-£36.50✳

REDHILL Surrey Map **04** TQ25

Selected

GH Ⓠ Ⓠ Ⓠ Ⓠ **Ashleigh House Hotel** 39 Redstone Hill RH1 4BG ☎01737 764763 FAX 01737 780308
Closed Xmas
Further improvements have been made to this small hotel situated to the east of the town. Bedrooms, all of which have en suite facilities, are bright and colourful with modern furnishings. The dining room on the ground floor is equally cheerful, and a choice is offered at breakfast. Guests have use of the outdoor pool, weather permitting.
8 rms (2 bth 4 shr) (2 fmly) CTV in all bedrooms Tea and coffee making facilities No dogs (ex guide dogs) Cen ht 9P ➡

No coaches Outdoor swimming pool (heated)
PRICE GUIDE
ROOMS: s £26-£40; d £40-£52✱
CARDS: 🆑 💳

GH 🆀🆀🆀 **Lynwood House** 50 London Rd RH1 1LN (on
A23 approx 500yds from railway station)
☎01737 766894 & 778253
There has been further upgrading to this conveniently situated
guest house. The bedrooms are attractively decorated, and guests
have use of small lounge. The dining room has individual tables,
and a choice is offered at breakfast.
9 rms (3 shr) (4 fmly) No smoking in dining room CTV in all
bedrooms Tea and coffee making facilities No dogs (ex guide
dogs) Cen ht 8P
PRICE GUIDE
ROOMS: s £23-£26; d £38-£45✱

REDMILE Leicestershire Map **08** SK73

GH 🆀🆀🆀 **Peacock Farm Guest House & Restaurant**
NG13 0GQ (follow signs for Belvoir Castle Peacock Farm half
a mile from village) ☎01949 842475 FAX 01949 43127
There are clear signs to this roadside building, located to the north
of Redmile. The restaurant provides generous meals to overnight
guests as well as encouraging local and passing trade. Five of the
individually furnished bedrooms are in the main building, while
the remainder are in an extension with separate entrances.
4 rms 4 annexe en suite (bth/shr) No smoking in dining room
CTV in 4 bedrooms Tea and coffee making facilities No dogs (ex
guide dogs) Licensed Cen ht CTV 30P Indoor swimming pool
Snooker Solarium Table tennis Croquet Last d 8.30pm
PRICE GUIDE
ROOMS: s fr £32; d fr £45✱
CARDS: 🆑 💳

REEDHAM Norfolk Map **05** TG40

GH 🆀🆀🆀 **Briars** 10 Riverside NR13 3TF (approach on
B1140, turn right at Reedham railway station, 0.5m to war
memorial and fork right)
☎01493 700054 FAX 01493 700054
This small, welcoming home has a wonderful location
overlooking the River Yare and Broads, in a quiet village. The
ground floor is taken up by a tea shop and hair salon by day, and
on certain nights a dinner menu is offered. The three comfortable
bedrooms are furnished in pine; there is also a lounge and
conservatory with sweeping views over the Broads.
3 en suite (bth/shr) No smoking in dining room CTV in all
bedrooms Tea and coffee making facilities No dogs (ex guide
dogs) Cen ht CTV 6P Fishing Last d 9pm
PRICE GUIDE
ROOMS: s £30; d £42.50
CARDS: 🆑 💳 🆑

We endeavour to be as accurate as possible
but changes in personnel and data can occur
in establishments after the Guide has gone to
press.

REETH North Yorkshire Map **07** SE09

Premier Selected

GH 🆀🆀🆀🆀🆀 **Arkleside
Hotel** DL11 6SG (follow
B6160 then B6270 from
Richmond to Reeth. Hotel on
top right corner of village
green) ☎01748 884200
Closed Jan
There are fine views along
the dale from the rear of this
delightful, friendly and
enthusiastically run little
hotel - originally a row of cottages dating back to the 1600s.
Attractively decorated bedrooms offer many thoughtful
extras, while both the comfortable sitting room and a separate
bar lounge provide an abundance of books and magazines.
The well produced four-course dinner is served in a dining
room featuring natural stonework and enjoying a delightful
outlook.
8 en suite (shr) 1 annexe en suite (bth) (1 fmly) No smoking
in bedrooms No smoking in dining room No smoking in
lounges CTV in all bedrooms Tea and coffee making
facilities Licensed Cen ht CTV No children 10yrs 6P No
coaches Walking trips arranged Last d 7.30pm
PRICE GUIDE
ROOMS: s £28.50-£41; d fr £57; wkly b&b fr £190; wkly
hlf-bd fr £273
CARDS: 🆑 💳

◀ 🆀🆀🆀 *Buck Hotel* DL11 6SW
☎01748 884210 FAX 01748 884802
Standing at the top corner of the village, overlooking the green,
this well furnished hotel and inn offers modern, well equipped
bedrooms. The public areas are spacious, with a games room to
the rear; service is friendly, and a good range of food is available
in either the bar or the cosy restaurant.
10 en suite (bth/shr) (2 fmly) CTV in all bedrooms Tea and
coffee making facilities Cen ht CTV Last d 9pm
CARDS: 🆑 💳

REIGATE Surrey Map **04** TQ25

Selected

GH 🆀🆀🆀🆀 **Cranleigh Hotel** 41 West St RH2 9BL (on
A25 at end of High St heading towards Dorking) (MIN)
☎01737 223417 FAX 01737 223734
Closed 24 Dec-1 Jan
Situated just beyond the end of the High Street, on the
Dorking road, this personally run private hotel offers
bedrooms furnished in modern style and equipped with every
facility, some of them also having sole use of an adjacent
bathroom. Public areas include a traditional lounge which
retains some original features, a well stocked bar and a very
attractive conservatory restaurant where carte dinners are
served Monday-Thursday; the menu represents excellent
value for money, there is a good selection of house wines, and
particularly friendly service helps to create a relaxed, informal
atmosphere. Two-acre grounds offer a swimming pool, a very
attractive rear garden and good forecourt car parking. The
restaurant can be reserved for private meetings and dining.
9 rms (7 bth) (1 fmly) CTV in all bedrooms Tea and coffee

making facilities Direct dial from bedrooms No dogs (ex guide dogs) Licensed Cen ht CTV 6P No coaches Outdoor swimming pool (heated) Tennis (hard & grass) Last d 9pm

PRICE GUIDE

ROOMS: s £49-£55; d £65-£75

CARDS: £

RENDCOMB Gloucestershire Map **04** SP00

GH QQQQQ *Shawswell Country House* GL7 7HD (from Cirencester take A435 towards Cheltenham for 5m and then then right into village. Follow direction sign 'Shanswell No Through Road' for 1.5m) ☎01285 831779
Closed Dec-Jan

Shawswell Country House dates back in part to the 17th century and has been lovingly and tastefully restored by its resident owners. Most of the bedrooms are spacious, comfortable and well equipped; one has an impressive four-poster bed. Dinner, which is served by arrangement on several days during the week, consists of interesting dishes based on home-produced vegetables and fruit wherever possible. Smoking is only permitted in the lounge.

5 en suite (bth/shr) No smoking in bedrooms No smoking in dining room CTV in all bedrooms Tea and coffee making facilities No dogs (ex guide dogs) Licensed Cen ht No children 10yrs 8P No coaches

---

RETFORD Nottinghamshire

See **North Wheatley**

RICHMOND North Yorkshire Map **07** NZ10

See also Low Row, Reeth and Thwaite

GH QQQ *Pottergate* 4 Pottergate DL10 4AB (leave A1 Richmond/Catterick slip road across rdbt in direction of Richmond continue 100yds to traffic lights guesthouse just beyond light) ☎01748 823826
Friendly service and a good standard of accommodation are guaranteed at this Georgian terraced house near the town centre. Bedrooms are fairly compact but are well equipped, and there are a small lounge and a cosy breakfast room on the ground floor. There is also a bar.
6 rms (2 fmly) CTV in all bedrooms Tea and coffee making facilities Licensed Cen ht CTV No children 2yrs 5P No coaches

PRICE GUIDE

ROOMS: s £20-£22; d £34; wkly b&b £110-£130✱

♥ QQQ Mr & Mrs P Chilton *Mount Pleasant* (NZ149058) Whashton DL11 7JP ☎01748 822784
Closed 20-28 Dec
There are lovely all-round views to be enjoyed from this 19th-century farmhouse which has been owned by the Chilton family for over a hundred years. The house is set in open countryside, and most of the bedrooms are in converted outbuildings with quaint ➡

Shawswell

Country House

AA QQQQQ Tel: 01285 831779
De-Luxe
Rendcomb, Cirencester, Gloucestershire GL7 7HD

"Far from the Madding Crowd"

Glorious hillside location offering peace and tranquillity. A lovely 17C house set in 25 acres overlooking The Churn Valley. It boasts a wealth of beams and cosy inglenooks, 5 superb en-suite bedrooms including a four-poster. Emphasis on personal service and very high standards to ensure an enjoyable and restful break. Centrally situated, perfect for walking and touring. Bath, Stratford, Oxford all under 1 hour.

Awarded AA QQQQQ
Premier Selected

The Old Plough

Country Guest House
Top Street, North Wheatley, Retford,
Nottinghamshire DN22 9DB
Tel: (01427) 880916

Situated in a quiet unspoiled rural village, The Old Plough has, been acclaimed by the AA, and graded ⚐⚐ De Luxe by the ETB. Its elegant and comfortable accommodation leaves nothing to be desired and is complemented by superb cuisine. Fully licensed for a relaxing and peaceful stay.

Colour brochure on request.

names like The Piggery and The Bull Pen. Mrs Chilton is proud of her Yorkshire cooking, which she ably demonstrates both in the evening meal and some very substantial breakfasts.

6 rms (4 bth/shr) (2 fmly) CTV in all bedrooms Tea and coffee making facilities Licensed Cen ht CTV 8P 280 acres sheep/beef Last d 6pm

---

Premier Selected

♥ QQQQQ Mrs M F Turnbull *Whashton Springs* *(NZ149046)* DL11 7JS (in Richmond turn left at traffic lights towards Ravensworth, 3m down steep hill farm at bottom on left)
☎01748 822884
Closed late Dec-Jan

Very warm and friendly service is provided by the family who own this charming Georgian farmhouse set in delightful countryside to the north of Richmond. Wholesome Yorkshire breakfasts and well prepared dinners are served in the cosy dining room, and guests can relax in a comfortable lounge (warmed by a log fire during the colder months) which has lovely views over the garden. Bedrooms in the garden annexe are modern in style whilst those in the main house are more traditional, but all are thoughtfully equipped as well as attractively furnished and decorated. Guests are encouraged to explore the farm or to wander down to the stream through well tended grounds.

3 en suite (bth/shr) 5 annexe en suite (bth/shr) (2 fmly) No smoking in 3 bedrooms No smoking in dining room CTV in all bedrooms Tea and coffee making facilities Direct dial from bedrooms No dogs (ex guide dogs) Licensed Cen ht No children 5yrs 10P 600 acres arable beef mixed sheep Last d am

---

RICHMOND UPON THAMES Surrey Map **04** TQ17

GH QQ *Hobart Hall Hotel* 43-47 Petersham Rd TW10 6UL (on A307, 200yds from Richmond Bridge) ☎0181 940 0435
This pleasant hotel by the river, on the fringe of the town, is made up of two Victorian houses. Some of the spacious, comfortable and well equipped bedrooms have views of the river, while public areas include a well appointed lounge and a bright dining room - its walls painted with murals - where a choice of breakfasts is served. Some car parking is available.

19 en suite (bth/shr) (3 fmly) No smoking CTV in all bedrooms Tea and coffee making facilities Direct dial from bedrooms No dogs (ex guide dogs) Cen ht CTV 15P
CARDS: 🔲 ■ 🔲

RINGSTEAD Dorset Map **03** SY78

Selected

GH QQQQ *The Creek* DT2 8NG (take A352 Wareham rd,turn right after approx 4m onto A353 towards Weymouth. After 1m turn left to Ringsted Beach) ☎01305 852251
Home to Michael and Freda Fisher this delightful family house is situated on a protected Heritage Coastal Path close to the shingle beach which forms part of Ringstead Bay. With superb views from the lounge and dining room, two comfortable bedrooms (both with a private shower facility)

and friendly, attentive service this establishment has a lot to commend it. Home made biscuits, preserves and marmalades, freshly cooked traditional English breakfast, and offers of refreshment on arrival and during the evening all add to the homely and very relaxing atmosphere. Dinner can usually be arranged by giving 24 hours' notice, and the Smugglers Inn at Osmington Mills (1.75m walk) is also recommended for the more energetic. Other facilities include the garden, use of the family swimming pool and ample car parking.

2 en suite (shr) No smoking in bedrooms Tea and coffee making facilities No dogs (ex guide dogs) Cen ht CTV No children 10yrs 4P No coaches Outdoor swimming pool (heated) Last d 10am
PRICE GUIDE
ROOMS: s £17.50; d £35✳

RINGWOOD Hampshire Map **04** SU10

Premier Selected

GH QQQQQ *Little Forest Lodge Hotel* Poulner Hill BH24 3HS (1.5m E on A31) ☎01425 478848
This Edwardian family house is personally run by Eric Martin and his wife Jane. The bedrooms are pleasantly furnished and the house is decorated with interesting artefacts from a bygone era. There is a comfortable residents' lounge with a bar and an open fire. The neatly kept garden has mature trees and a children's play area. the dining room with Edwardian panelling is the setting for a three-course dinner based on fresh produce - this being available only to guests who pre-book dinner bed and breakfast.

5 en suite (bth/shr) (2 fmly) No smoking in 3 bedrooms CTV in all bedrooms Tea and coffee making facilities Licensed Cen ht 12P No coaches Last d 4pm
CARDS: 🔲 🔳

Selected

GH QQQQ *The Nest* 10 Middle Ln, off School Ln BH24 1LE (off A31 into B3347 at 2nd pedestrian lights turn sharp left into School Lane then left again) ☎01425 476724 & 0589 854505 FAX 01425 476724
Follow directions from the B&B sign on the main road to reach this delightful former school house tucked away in a quiet road on the edge of the town. Much care has been taken in the decoration of the rooms, with their pretty co-ordinating fabrics and interesting pictures, and a traditional English breakfast is served in the conservatory overlooking the garden; there is parking space in front of the building. Guests are asked to refrain from smoking.

3 rms No smoking CTV in all bedrooms Tea and coffee making facilities Cen ht 6P No coaches
PRICE GUIDE
ROOMS: s £18-£25; d £32-£36; wkly b&b £112-£140✳

RIPON North Yorkshire Map **08** SE37

♥ **QQQ** Mrs V Leeming **Bay Tree** *(SE263685)* Aldfield
HG4 3BE (approx 4m W, take unclass road S off B6265)
☎01765 620394
This converted 17th-century barn stands in open countryside in the
village of Aldfield, close to Fountains Abbey. Bedrooms are bright
and fresh; some have exposed beams and one has a four-poster
bed. The lounge is comfortable, and home-cooked breakfasts and
dinners are served in the pleasant dining room.
6 rms (2 bth 3 shr) (1 fmly) No smoking in bedrooms CTV in all
bedrooms Tea and coffee making facilities Licensed Cen ht ch
fac 10P 400 acres dairy beef arable Last d 10am
PRICE GUIDE
ROOMS: s fr £25; d £37-£40; wkly b&b fr £129.50; wkly hlf-bd
fr £203∗
CARDS: 🔲 🔲   £

ROADWATER Somerset Map **03** ST03

Selected

♥ **QQQQ** Mr & Mrs Brewer **Wood Advent** *(ST037374)*
TA23 0RR ☎01984 640920 FAX 01984 640920
Part of a working 360-acre mixed farm, this secluded 19th-
century farmhouse nestles at the foot of the Brendon hills in
the beautiful Exmoor National Park. The no-smoking
bedrooms are spacious, comfortable, and beautifully
furnished, with delightful views over the large garden, woods
and fields. A set five-course dinner cooked by Mrs Brewer is
served at separate tables in the dining room. Possible leisure
pursuits include walking, riding, clay-pigeon shooting and
golf.
5 rms (1 bth 3 shr) (3 fmly) No smoking in bedrooms No
smoking in dining room No smoking in lounges Tea and
coffee making facilities No dogs Licensed Cen ht CTV ch
fac 12P Outdoor swimming pool (heated) Tennis (grass)
Clay pigeon shooting 350 acres arable beef sheep Last d
9.30am

ROCHDALE Greater Manchester Map **07** SD81

♥ **QQ** Mrs J Neave **Leaches** *(SD837139)* Ashworth Valley
OL11 5UN ☎01706 41116 & 228520
Closed 22 Dec-2 Jan
Surrounded by a pleasant garden and remotely situated on a beef
and sheep rearing farm, this 17th-century stone-built farmhouse is
reached by taking the A680 to Ashworth Reservoir and then
turning into Ashworth Road and following it for about a mile. The
no-smoking bedrooms are simply but comfortably furnished, and
there are a lounge and breakfast room, both with low beamed
ceilings. Proprietors Mr and Mrs Neave are a hospitable couple
with a wealth of local knowledge.
3 rms (2 fmly) No smoking in bedrooms No smoking in dining
room CTV in all bedrooms Tea and coffee making facilities Cen
ht CTV 6P Fishing 140 acres beef sheep
PRICE GUIDE
ROOMS: s fr £18; d fr £34∗   £

ROCHESTER Northumberland Map **12** NY89

♥ **Q** Mrs J M Chapman **Woolaw** *(NY821984)* NE19 1TB
☎01830 520686
This traditional farmhouse offers charmingly unpretentious bed
and breakfast accommodation in lovely rural surroundings. The
ground-floor en suite bedrooms are compact and modestly
furnished; the first-floor room offers greater comfort, but shares a

bathroom with the owners.
3 rms (2 shr) (1 fmly) TV available No dogs (ex guide dogs)
Cen ht CTV 10P Fishing 740 acres beef horses sheep Last d
5.30pm
PRICE GUIDE
ROOMS: s £14-£16; d £28-£32∗

ROCK Cornwall & Isles of Scilly Map **02** SW97

GH QQ Roskarnon House Hotel PL27 6LD
☎01208 862329 FAX 01208 862785
Mar-Nov
Set in an acre of mature grounds, this detached Edwardian house
has been owned by the same family for over 35 years. Standing in
an elevated position, it has spectacular panoramic views over the
Camel Estuary, and offers peaceful relaxation at an affordable
price. Two of the bedrooms have a private shower, some have TV
and two are conveniently located on the ground floor; most have
sea views. The lounge and dining room overlook the lawns and
beach. A fixed-price menu is served, using home-grown produce,
and the friendly service is personally supervised by the proprietor
Ian Veall. Table tennis is available in the games room, and local
sports including sailing, golf, tennis, riding, water skiing, surfing
and fishing can be arranged.
12 rms (9 bth/shr) (5 fmly) No smoking in dining room CTV in
all bedrooms Tea and coffee making facilities No dogs (ex guide
dogs) Licensed CTV 16P No coaches Last d 8pm
PRICE GUIDE
ROOMS: s fr £20; d fr £40; wkly hlf-bd fr £200
CARDS: 🔲

RODBOURNE Wiltshire Map **03** ST98

🔲 🔲 ♥ **QQQ** Mrs C Parfitt **Angrove** *(ST949842)* SN16 0ET
(take A429 from Malmesbury and 0.5m after police station,
turn left into Grange Lane and continue to top of hill. Turn
left into Angrove Lane) ☎01666 822982
Feb-Nov
A long private drive through pretty countryside leads to this
peacefully situated stone-built farmhouse. Bedrooms are spacious;
each has its own private shower room and has been equipped with
modern comforts. There is a cosy lounge and breakfast is served in
an airy dining room with access to the well kept gardens. The
Parfitt family extend a warm welcome to their guests but request
that they refrain from smoking in the house.
3 en suite (shr) No smoking Tea and coffee making facilities No
dogs Cen ht CTV P Fishing 204 acres beef
PRICE GUIDE
ROOMS: s £14-£18; d £28-£36; wkly b&b £98-£112

RODE Somerset Map **03** ST85

Premier Selected

GH QQQQQ Irondale
67 High St BA3 6PB
☎01373 830730
FAX 01373 830730
Closed 24-27 Dec
An elegant three-storey
stone-built house in the
village centre, conveniently
located for the city of Bath
and many places of interest.
Guests are assured of a warm
welcome, and treated as part
of the Holder family, sharing the two delightful sitting rooms ➡

and taking breakfast at one large table in the pleasant dining room. The bedrooms are tastefully furnished and decorated, with attractive coordinating soft furnishings, and each room has its own bathroom across the landing. There is a variety of inns and restaurants within easy driving distance for dinner.

3 en suite (bth/shr) No smoking in bedrooms CTV in all bedrooms Tea and coffee making facilities No dogs Cen ht CTV No children 14yrs 3P No coaches

PRICE GUIDE
ROOMS: s £35-£40; d £45-£50; *
CARDS:

See advertisement under BATH

GH ◻◻◻◻ *Wheelbrook Mill* Laverton BA3 6QY
☎01373 830263

This 200-year-old stone-built mill is the home of Andrew and Shelley Weeks and their two young sons. It is situated in the picturesque hamlet of Laverton, just off the A36 and within easy reach of Bath. The mill is well set back from a quiet lane overlooking Wheel Brook and open fields and woods. The oak-beamed bedrooms are furnished with antique stripped pine, brass beds and attractively co-ordinating soft furnishings. There is a comfortable sitting room with an open fire, and dinner can be arranged with 24 hours' notice. Breakfast is taken around the long communal table in the kitchen, often with the family.

4 rms (2 bth) CTV in 2 bedrooms Tea and coffee making facilities No dogs Cen ht CTV ch fac 6P No coaches Last d 24hr notice

---

ROGATE West Sussex Map **04** SU82

Premier Selected

♥ ◻◻◻◻◻ Mrs J C Francis **Mizzards** *(SU803228)* GU31 5HS (from x-rds in Rogate go S for 0.50miles cross river continue for 300yds then turn right (signed Mizzards Farm) ☎01730 821656 FAX 01730 821655 Closed Xmas

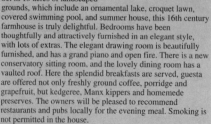

Set in 13 acres of landscaped grounds, which include an ornamental lake, croquet lawn, covered swimming pool, and summer house, this 16th century farmhouse is truly delightful. Bedrooms have been thoughtfully and attractively furnished in an elegant style, with lots of extras. The elegant drawing room is beautifully furnished, and has a grand piano and open fire. There is a new conservatory sitting room, and the lovely dining room has a vaulted roof. Here the splendid breakfasts are served, guesta are offered not only freshly ground coffee, porridge and grapefruit, but kedgeree, Manx kippers and homemede preserves. The owners will be pleased to recommend restaurants and pubs locally for the evening meal. Smoking is not permitted in the house.

3 en suite (bth/shr) No smoking CTV in all bedrooms Tea and coffee making facilities No dogs Cen ht No children 9yrs 12P Outdoor swimming pool (heated) Croquet 13

acres sheep non-working
PRICE GUIDE
ROOMS: s £30-£36; d £48-£56

♥ ◻◻◻ Mrs J Baigent **Trotton** *(SU835225)* GU31 5EN (on A272 between Midhurst and Petersfield)
☎01730 813618 FAX 01730 816093

A busy working farm well located off the A272 between Petersfield and Midhurst, offers well presented, modern accommodation in a converted barn. A third bedroom has been added recently, conveniently sited on the ground floor, and all bedrooms have smart, modern en suite shower rooms. The sitting room offers a good supply of games and books, including table tennis and darts, and children are welcome. The farm is situated in an area of outstanding natural beauty with good fishing.

3 en suite (shr) No smoking Tea and coffee making facilities No dogs (ex guide dogs) Cen ht CTV P Fishing Table tennis Darts 230 acres arable beef mixed
PRICE GUIDE
ROOMS: s £25-£30; d £35-£40*

ROMFORD Greater London Map **05** TQ58

GH ◻ *The Orchard Guest House* 81 Eastern Rd RM1 3PB
☎01708 744099
Closed Xmas

This red brick Edwardian guest house is set in a quiet residential road near the town centre. Many of its original features have been retained, and adequately furnished bedrooms are equipped with reasonable comfort. There is a small, comfortable, open-plan lounge/dining room where both a traditional English breakfast and an evening meal are available.

5 rms (1 shr) (2 fmly) CTV in all bedrooms No dogs (ex guide dogs) Cen ht CTV 6P Last d am

---

ROMSEY Hampshire Map **04** SU32

Selected

GH ◻◻◻◻ *Country Accommodation* The Old Post Office, New Rd, Michelmersh SO51 0NL (leave A3057 at Timsbury New Rd, Michelmersh, guesthouse at top of hill) ☎01794 368739

This old Post Office has seen many changes over the years, having started life as a forge in the 1820's. A bakery and village shop were gradually added, which have now been carefully converted. Bedrooms are attractively decorated and have modern en suite shower rooms, TVs, books, fresh flowers and unlimited supplies of tea and coffee. Beakfast is served in the attractive dining room.

4 annexe en suite (shr) (1 fmly) No smoking in dining room Tea and coffee making facilities No dogs Cen ht 5P No coaches
PRICE GUIDE
ROOMS: s £25; d £40; wkly b&b £175-£280
CARDS:

Entries in this Guide are based on reports filed by our team of professionally trained, full-time inspectors.

GH Q Q Q Q Q **Highfield House** Newtown Rd, Awbridge SO51 0GG (take A27 signed Salisbury/Whiteparish for 3 miles then 1st right into Danes Rd for 1 mile the 1st left signed Newtown, Highfield 1st house on right) ☎01794 340727 FAX 01794 341450

Although it is only five years old, this house set in 1.5 acres of mature grounds feels as though it has been here for ever. The en suite bedrooms are attractively decorated and furnished, and thoughtful extras such as bathrobes, courtesy trays and remote control TVs are provided. A traditional breakfast and a good home-cooked evening meal are served at a communal table, and guests can enjoy tea and home-made cake in a comfortable lounge overlooking the beautiful garden.

3 en suite (bth/shr) CTV in all bedrooms Tea and coffee making facilities No dogs (ex guide dogs) Cen ht CTV No children 14yrs 10P No coaches Last d 4pm

PRICE GUIDE
ROOMS: d £45※

ROSLEY Cumbria Map 11 NY34

GH Q Q Q Q **Causa Grange** CA7 8DD ☎016973 45358

This elegant Victorian house stands amid an acre of well-tended gardens in open countryside on the fringe of the Lake District National Park. The beautiful home of Mrs Ann Falck and her family, it offers luxurious accommodation with many additional comforts and personal touches. There are two very relaxing lounges where log fires burn on cooler evenings, and the dining room features a lovely hand-carved fireplace and, like the rest of the house, the ornate original plasterwork. Meals are served by arrangement.

2 en suite (bth/shr) No smoking Tea and coffee making facilities No dogs Cen ht CTV No children 12yrs 8P No coaches Last d noon

PRICE GUIDE
ROOMS: s £21-£25; d £40-£48; wkly b&b £133-£168; wkly hlf-bd £190-£245※

ROSS-ON-WYE Hereford & Worcester Map 03 SO52

See also St Owen's Cross

GH Q Q **The Arches Country House** Walford Rd HR9 5PT (take B4234 from town centre continue for approx half a mile The Arches is on the left just below Chasedale Hotel) ☎01989 563348

Just off the B4243 on the outskirts of the town, this guest house has small bedrooms made attractive by co-ordinated decor. A comfortable conservatory overlooks the neat garden and guests are well looked after by the owners.

➡

8 rms (2 bth 2 shr) (2 fmly) No smoking CTV in all bedrooms Tea and coffee making facilities No dogs (ex guide dogs) Licensed Cen ht CTV 9P No coaches Last d 5pm
PRICE GUIDE
ROOMS: s £18-£25; d £34-£42; wkly hlf-bd £179-£213

GH **Brookfield House** Ledbury Rd HR9 7AT (approaching town from M50 Brookfield House is on the left at the bottom of the hill before town cwntre) ☎01989 562188
Closed 3 days Xmas rs Dec-Jan

This popular guesthouse within walking distance of the town centre has modestly furnished bedrooms of varying size, a traditional lounge and small dining room where breakfasts are served.

8 rms (1 bth 2 shr) No smoking in dining room CTV in all bedrooms Tea and coffee making facilities Licensed Cen ht No children 5yrs 10P No coaches
PRICE GUIDE
ROOMS: s £17.50-£18.50; d £34-£40; wkly b&b £115.50-£126.50*
CARDS: 🔳 🔳 🔳

Selected

GH ◻◻◻◻ **Edde Cross House** Edde Cross St HR9 7BZ (approach from rdbt where A49 joins A40 onto B4260 into Ross. Turn left at top of hill into Edde Cross St, house 300yds on left) ☎01989 565088
Feb-Nov

This attractively refurbished Grade II listed Georgian town house is just a short walk from the town centre, with the added advantage of off-street parking. Well cared for, it offers light bedrooms pleasantly decorated and well equipped with some thoughtful extras; some rooms have lovely views over the River Wye and most are furnished in old pine. There is a small comfortable lounge bar and a cosy dining room where a good choice is offered for breakfast, including a vegetarian menu. Guests also have the use of the delightful rear walled garden which offers fine views. Smoking is not permitted.

3 en suite (bth/shr) No smoking CTV in all bedrooms Tea and coffee making facilities No dogs Cen ht No children 10yrs 3P No coaches
PRICE GUIDE
ROOMS: s £30; d £42-£46; wkly b&b £140-£147

GH ◻◻◻ *Ryefield House Hotel* Gloucester Rd HR9 5NA ☎01989 563030

A charming family-run hotel which has received awards for its decorative gardens, situated on the Gloucester road a short distance from the town centre. Mr and Mrs Edwards are enthusiastic owners, creating a welcoming atmosphere in comfortable public rooms which have been attractively furnished. Bedrooms vary in size and are well equipped, together with many thoughtful touches such as fresh flowers, fudge and books. Carefully produced home-cooked evening meals are available on advance request.

8 rms (5 bth/shr) (4 fmly) CTV in all bedrooms Tea and coffee making facilities Direct dial from bedrooms Licensed Cen ht CTV 11P No coaches Last d 5pm

---

GH ◻◻◻ **Sunnymount Hotel** Ryefield Rd HR9 5LU ☎01989 563880
rs 21-31 Dec

This licensed hotel is located in a quiet residential area close to the town centre, with its own parking. Bedrooms vary in size and style and there are two lounges offering TV, books and games: one is

no-smoking. Mr and Mrs Williams are welcoming hosts and provide enjoyable home-cooked meals.

9 rms (7 bth/shr) No smoking in dining room No smoking in 1 lounge Tea and coffee making facilities No dogs (ex guide dogs) Licensed Cen ht CTV 7P No coaches Last d 6.30pm
PRICE GUIDE
ROOMS: s £28-£30; d £47-£51; wkly b&b £154-£160; wkly hlf-bd £230*
CARDS: 🔳 🔳 🔳

ROTHBURY Northumberland Map **12** NU00

Selected

GH ◻◻◻◻ **Orchard** High St NE65 7TL (turn off A697 onto B6334 to Rothbury Orchard Guesthouse on right side of village) ☎01669 620684
Mar-Nov

Hospitality and Sheila Jefferson's excellent home-cooked meals - dinner being an occasion to which one can look forward - are the lynch pins of this spotlessly clean main street guesthouse. There are lots of books and magazines in the lounge as well as a small honesty bar. Bedrooms are comfortable and thoughtfully equipped and one will find an "essentials kit", including hair dryer, scissors, plasters and sewing materials, on each floor.

6 rms (4 shr) (1 fmly) No smoking in dining room CTV in all bedrooms Tea and coffee making facilities No dogs Licensed Cen ht No parking No coaches Last d 7pm
PRICE GUIDE
ROOMS: s £20-£22.50; d £40-£45; wkly b&b £140-£157; wkly hlf-bd £220-£238

ROTHERHAM South Yorkshire Map **08** SK49

Selected

GH ◻◻◻◻ *Stonecroft* Main St, Bramley S66 0SF (4m E of Rotherham) ☎01709 540922

An amazing gem among guest houses, this small cottage and mews in the village centre offers bedrooms which are attractively and very comfortably furnished and have an excellent range of facilities (including video players). Between the house and the mews lies a lovely courtyard with lawns, a fountain and colourful shrubberies. The lounge is furnished with deep cushioned sofas, a library selection of videos which guests can borrow and a television with Sky channels. Though only breakfast is provided, billing arrangements have been made with the local inn and hotel. Mr and Mrs Shepherd go out of their way to make their guests really welcome and comfortable, providing what is very much a home from home.

3 en suite (bth/shr) 5 annexe en suite (shr) (1 fmly) No smoking in bedrooms No smoking in dining room No smoking in 1 lounge CTV in all bedrooms Tea and coffee making facilities Licensed Cen ht CTV 10P No coaches
CARDS: 🔳 🔳

ROTTINGDEAN East Sussex Map **05** TQ30

GH ◻◻ **Braemar House** Steyning Rd BN2 7GA ☎01273 304263
A well appointed family house near the centre of the village offers accommodation well furnished in traditional style. The

comfortable TV lounge has board games and magazines.
15 rms (2 fmly) No smoking in dining room Cen ht CTV No parking No coaches
PRICE GUIDE
ROOMS: s £15; d £30*

ROWSLEY Derbyshire Map **08** SK26

◀ QQQ **Grouse and Claret** Station Rd DE4 2EL (on A6 between Matlock and Bakewell) ☎01629 733233
A popular and appealing roadside inn which has very good quality spacious bedrooms decorated and furnished in a co-ordinated and contemporary style. Though they are not en suite each room is only a few steps away from either of the modern bathrooms. The public areas are open plan, their furnishings and decoration accentuate both the Grouse and the Claret themes. Meals either light or full are extensive and cater for popular tastes.
5 rms No smoking in area of dining room No smoking in 1 lounge CTV in all bedrooms Tea and coffee making facilities No dogs (ex guide dogs) Cen ht 77P Last d 9.30pm
PRICE GUIDE
ROOMS: s £20; d £35*
MEALS: Lunch £8.50-£15 Dinner £8.50-£15*
CARDS: 🅰 ■ 🔳

ROXTON Bedfordshire Map **04** TL15

♥ QQQ Mrs J Must *Church (TL153545)* 41 High St MK44 3EB (from A428 turn into Roxton village, at crossroads go south down High St, Church Farm is second house on left after Parish Hall) ☎01234 870234 FAX 01234 871576
Set in the middle of a quiet village, this welcoming farm house is bounded by arable fields. The two bedrooms it offers are fresh and spacious, and there is a lounge with colour television; breakfast is served round a large wooden table.
2 rms (1 fmly) No smoking Tea and coffee making facilities Cen ht CTV 6P 66 acres arable

---

RUCKHALL Hereford & Worcester Map **03** SO43

Selected

◀ QQQQ *The Ancient Camp* HR2 9QX
☎01981 250449 FAX 01981 251581
rs Sun evening & Mon
Named after a nearby Iron Age settlement, this charming stone-built inn is quietly located four miles southwest of Hereford. The modern bedrooms include two with fine views of the Golden Valley and the River Wye. The bars and dining areas are full of character with exposed beams, stone walls, stone-flagged floors and a variety of old world bric-á-brac.
5 en suite (bth/shr) CTV in all bedrooms Tea and coffee making facilities Direct dial from bedrooms No dogs (ex guide dogs) Cen ht No children 10yrs 30P No coaches Fishing Last d 9.30pm
CARDS: 🅰 🔳

RUFFORTH North Yorkshire Map **08** SE55

GH QQQ **Wellgarth House** Wetherby Rd YO2 3QB (from A1237, at 2nd roundabout turn left onto B1224 signposted Wetherby, after 1 mile 1st house on left entering village) ☎01904 738592 & 738595 FAX 01904 738595
Closed 25-26 Dec
Situated on the edge of the village, only four miles west of York, this large modern house offers well furnished, mainly en suite

---

bedrooms. A cosy lounge and a separate breakfast room are also provided.
8 rms (6 shr) (1 fmly) No smoking in 5 bedrooms No smoking in dining room CTV in all bedrooms Tea and coffee making facilities Cen ht CTV 8P No coaches
PRICE GUIDE
ROOMS: s £17-£25; d £30-£45
CARDS: 🅰 🔳

RUGBY Warwickshire Map **04** SP57

GH QQ **Avondale** 16 Elsee Rd CV21 3BA ☎01788 578639
This semidetached house is located close to the famous public school in a quiet residential area; it is advisable to ask for directions. The bedrooms are mostly spacious and modestly furnished. Breakfast is served at separate tables in the large lounge/breakfast room.
4 rms (1 shr) (1 fmly) CTV in all bedrooms Tea and coffee making facilities No dogs Cen ht CTV 8P No coaches
PRICE GUIDE
ROOMS: s £20-£25; d £34-£38*

RUSHLAKE GREEN East Sussex Map **05** TQ61

Selected

GH QQQQ **Great Crouch's** TN21 9QD (off B2096, 200yds past village green on right) ☎01435 830145
Closed 16-31 Dec
Grade 11 listed house built around C1720 and set in 15 acres of gardens and pasture land. Home to Ruth and Richard ➠

Ryefield House Hotel
Gloucester Road, Ross-on-Wye,
AA LISTED
Herefordshire HR9 5NA
Telephone: 01989 563030

Our lovely hotel is efficiently run with warmth and humour – a most relaxing base from which to tour the Wye Valley, Forest of Dean, Malvern Hills and Welsh Mountains. Alternatively, forget all that and simply wander around our little town and stroll along the river bank.
All bedrooms have television, direct dial telephone, fresh flowers and fudge and you may breakfast as early or late as you wish.
We will happily guide you on your choice of restaurant, cafe or 'pub at which to dine each evening. You may just about be hungry again by then having sampled one of our renowned gargantuan breakfasts earlier in the day. *Proprietors: The Edwards family*

Thomas the non-smoking accommodation comprises the spacious and beautifully furnished self contained converted beamed Sussex out house suite, and one bedroom in the main house with sole use of adjoining first class facilities. Whilst there is no lounge the bedrooms are very comfortable and come equipped with every modern facility. Mrs Ruth Thomas makes all her own jams, marmalades and cakes, and breakfast cooked on the Aga using home grown and local produce is served in the elegant breakfast room. Service is very friendly and refreshments are offered on arrival, there is a local pub close by which also serves good home cooked pub food, and there are several local prestigious restaurants. Other facilities include a furnished garden, heated indoor swimming pool and plenty of car parking space.

1 en suite (bth/shr) 1 annexe en suite (bth/shr) No smoking CTV in all bedrooms Tea and coffee making facilities No dogs (ex guide dogs) Cen ht 6P Indoor swimming pool (heated)

PRICE GUIDE
ROOMS: d £45-£50; wkly b&b £140-£157.50

RUSHTON SPENCER Staffordshire Map **07** SJ96

♥ QQ Mrs J Brown *Barnswood* (*SJ945606*) SK11 0RA (on A523, 5m from Leek) ☎01260 226261
Closed 24 Dec-5 Jan
This 300-year-old stone-built farmhouse is ideally situated on the A523 Macclesfield/Leek road, enjoying the most spectacular views over Rudyard Lake and the valley beyond. The combined lounge/breakfast room is cosy and traditionally furnished, and soundly maintained bedrooms include a family room.

4 rms (2 fmly) No smoking in bedrooms Tea and coffee making facilities No dogs Cen ht CTV 4P 100 acres dairy

---

RUSTINGTON West Sussex Map **04** TQ00

Selected

GH QQQQ Kenmore Claigmar Rd BN16 2NL (from A259 follow signs for Rustington turn off for Claigmar Rd is between War Memorial & Alldays Shop. Kenmore on right as Claigmar Rd bends)
☎01903 784634 FAX 01903 784634
Quietly situated in a residential area just off the main shopping street, this well run and attractively furnished guesthouse continues to be improved. The bedrooms offer good levels of comfort and several are ideal for families. There is a small lounge, and a freshly prepared set three-course meal is served in the sunny dining room every day if arranged in advance.

7 rms (1 bth 5 shr) (2 fmly) No smoking in dining room No smoking in lounges CTV in all bedrooms Tea and coffee making facilities Cen ht CTV 7P No coaches Last d noon

PRICE GUIDE
ROOMS: s £22.50-£25; d £45-£50; wkly b&b £145-£160✱
CARDS: 🔳 💳 💳

RYDAL Cumbria

See **Ambleside**

RYDE See **WIGHT, ISLE OF**

RYE East Sussex Map **05** TQ92

Premier Selected

GH QQQQQ Green Hedges Hilly Fields, Rye Hill TN31 7NH (on A268, look for 'Private Road' signs on left)
☎01797 222185
Closed Xmas & New Year
This fine Victorian country house stands in 1.5 acres of delightful, mature and well kept gardens with a heated swimming pool. Bedrooms have been individually

furnished to the highest standard and are all equipped with TV, clock radio alarms, hair dryers and tea trays; the comfortable lounge is provided with board games and books, and an elegant, antique-furnished breakfast room overlooks the garden. The atmosphere is very relaxed and homely, with service personally supervised by the owner.

3 en suite (shr) No smoking CTV in all bedrooms Tea and coffee making facilities No dogs Cen ht No children 12yrs 8P No coaches Outdoor swimming pool (heated)

PRICE GUIDE
ROOMS: d £51-£58; wkly b&b fr £175✱
CARDS: 🔳 💳

Selected

GH QQQQ Holloway House High St TN31 7JF
☎01797 224748
Its rooms individually furnished with antiques, this historic creeper-clad hotel is ideally situated at the heart of the town centre. Generally spacious bedrooms have been furnished to retain their original character, most of them boasting brass or four-poster beds, and the fine wood-panelled bar and feature dining rooms are open throughout the day for meals and light refreshments - the blackboard menu including home-made soups, pies and traditional desserts; dinner, however, is only available by arrangement. Particularly helpful service is provided by the owner and members of her family. Guests are advised to leave their cars in the town pay-and-display car park.

6 en suite (bth/shr) (2 fmly) No smoking in area of dining room CTV in all bedrooms Tea and coffee making facilities No dogs (ex guide dogs) Licensed Cen ht No parking No coaches Last d 8pm

PRICE GUIDE
ROOMS: s £39-£90; d £50-£90✱
CARDS: 🔳 💳

Factual details of establishments in this Guide are from questionnaires we send to all establishments that feature in the book.

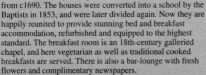

GH ◯◯◯◯◯ **Jeakes House** Mermaid St TN31 7ET (within the cobbled medieval town centre, approached either from High St or from The Strand Quay) ☎01797 222828 FAX 01797 222623

Jeake's House, and Quaker's House next door, have a well documented history dating from c1690. The houses were converted into a school by the Baptists in 1853, and were later divided again. Now they are happily reunited to provide stunning bed and breakfast accommodation, refurbished and equipped to the highest standard. The breakfast room is an 18th-century galleried chapel, and here vegetarian as well as traditional cooked breakfasts are served. There is also a bar-lounge with fresh flowers and complimentary newspapers.

12 rms (8 bth 2 shr) (2 fmly) No smoking in dining room CTV in all bedrooms Tea and coffee making facilities Direct dial from bedrooms Licensed Cen ht No parking No coaches

PRICE GUIDE
ROOMS: s fr £22.50; d £41-£59; wkly b&b fr £199.50✱
CARDS: 🅰 💳 💳 (£)

GH ◯◯◯ *Little Saltcote* 22 Military Rd TN31 7NY
☎01797 223210

Built in 1901, this delightful house nestles under a cliff overlooking the River Rother and the Romney Marshes. It has an attractive terraced garden with forecourt parking, and all the bedrooms - including one conveniently located on the ground floor - have been individually furnished in cottage style. Guests are offered a good-choice breakfast menu which includes vegetarian options, free-range eggs, locally produced herb sausages and home-made marmalade.

6 rms (2 shr) (2 fmly) CTV in all bedrooms Tea and coffee making facilities No dogs Cen ht P No coaches

GH ◯◯◯◯ **Mint Lodge** 38 The Mint TN31 7EN
☎01797 223268 FAX 01797 223268

A tiny but elegantly refurbished guest house dating from around 1500, Mint Lodge is personally run by proprietor Yvonne Cronshaw and her daughter Tracy. One of the individually furnished bedrooms is located on the ground floor, and all are well equipped with a wealth of little extras. The front door opens directly on to the dining room, where fresh flowers, complimentary daily newspapers and generous traditional breakfasts (vegetarian by arrangement) can be enjoyed; the breakfast menu also includes fish and speciality teas and coffees. Car parking is not possible, so the town car park or taxi arrivals are recommended.

3 en suite (bth/shr) (1 fmly) CTV in all bedrooms Tea and coffee making facilities No dogs (ex guide dogs) Cen ht No children 3yrs No parking

PRICE GUIDE
ROOMS: s £25-£30; d £36-£40✱
CARDS: 🅰 💳 (£)

GH ◯◯◯◯ **Old Borough Arms** The Strand TN31 7DB (off A259) ☎01797 222128 FAX 01797 222128

A 300-year-old sailors' inn incorporating part of Rye's town wall, this family-run hotel is conveniently located for easy access to all the local attractions. Accommodation has been extensively upgraded in recent years, bedrooms being furnished in a modern style which is nevertheless in keeping with the original building. Public rooms include a historic restaurant and bar lounge warmed by a log fire in the winter months, but dinner is now served by arrangement only; a choice of full English, continental or vegetarian breakfasts is available. Friendly proprietors provide helpful service, and adjacent restricted car parking is usually supplemented by two under-cover spaces.

9 en suite (shr) (2 fmly) CTV in all bedrooms Tea and coffee making facilities Licensed Cen ht CTV 2P Last d 8pm

PRICE GUIDE
ROOMS: s £25-£35; d £40-£60; wkly b&b £140-£205
CARDS: 🅰 💳 (£)

Mermaid Street, Rye, East Sussex TN31 7ET
Tel: Rye (01797) 222828 Fax: (01797) 222623
Beautiful listed building built in 1689. Set in medieval cobblestoned street, renowned for its smuggling associations. Breakfast – served in eighteenth century galleried former chapel – is traditional or vegetarian. Oak-beamed and panelled bedrooms overlook the marsh and roof-tops to the sea. Brass, mahogany or four-poster beds, linen sheets and lace. En-suite bathrooms, hot drink trays, direct dial telephones and televisions.
Honeymoon suite and family rooms available. Residential licence.
Write or telephone for further details to the proprietors: Mr & Mrs F Hadfield

GH ◎◎◎◎ **The Old Vicarage Guesthouse** 66 Church Square TN31 7HF (follow Town Centre signs from A259, enter town via Landgate Arch, 3rd left in High St into West St, by St Mary's Church footpath leads to Vicarage) ☎01797 222119 FAX 01797 227466

Closed 22-26 Dec

This 400-year-old listed building, its Georgian façade painted pink, has many interesting features. It stands directly opposite St Mary's church and graveyard in a picturesque square, and should not be confused with the private hotel of the same name! The bedrooms have been very prettily decorated and furnished with Laura Ashley fabrics and reproduction pine furniture; two rooms have four-poster beds and all have private bathrooms due to recent modernisation. There is an attractive lounge where guests can help themselves to a glass of sherry, and a smart dining room with a log fire overlooks the pretty walled garden. A choice of breakfast is offered, including free range eggs, home-made marmalade and freshly baked scones, and Julia and Paul Masters are charming, unobtrusive hosts. Smoking is not permitted in bedrooms.
6 rms (5 bth/shr) (1 fmly) No smoking in bedrooms No smoking in dining room CTV in all bedrooms Tea and coffee making facilities No dogs (ex guide dogs) Cen ht No children 10yrs
PRICE GUIDE
ROOMS: s £30-£50; d £40-£59; wkly b&b £119-£182

GH ◎◎◎◎◎ **The Old Vicarage Hotel & Restaurant** 15 East St TN31 7JY (Logis) ☎01797 225131 FAX 01797 225131

Closed Jan

Housed in a building dating from about 1706, quietly located and overlooking the River Rother and Romney Marsh to its rear, this hotel offers individually furnished bedrooms (including two with four-poster beds) which are equipped with many thoughtful extras as well as every modern amenity. The comfortable cocktail bar/reception and foyer lounge area leads on to a very well appointed restaurant with summer terrace - an attractive setting in which to choose from a dinner menu of interesting dishes freshly prepared in predominantly classical style. Service is personally supervised by the proprietors, limited room service is also available, and there is a good selection of English and European wines.
4 en suite (bth/shr) (2 fmly) CTV in all bedrooms Tea and coffee making facilities Direct dial from bedrooms Licensed Cen ht No parking No coaches Last d 9pm
PRICE GUIDE
ROOMS: s £45-£48; d £76-£84; wkly b&b £228-£252; wkly hlf-bd £288-£330
CARDS: 🔲 🔲 🔲

GH ◎◎◎◎ **Playden Cottage** Military Rd TN31 7NY (leave Rye in direction of Appledore, Playden Cottage is last house on left, at the de-limit sign) ☎01797 222234

Peacefully situated just a short distance from the town centre and fronted by a lovely terraced garden, this pretty cottage dating from the 1700's has views of Romney Marsh. Two of its individually furnished bedrooms overlook the garden and the other faces on to woodland, while the lounge offers a well tuned piano, TV, books and guides to local attractions. Dinner can sometimes be arranged, and breakfast - taken round a large communal table - provides a wide choice which includes large field mushrooms cooked in butter and fresh fruit as well as more traditional items. Service is relaxed and ample car parking space is available.
3 en suite (shr) (1 fmly) No smoking in dining room Tea and coffee making facilities No dogs (ex guide dogs) Cen ht CTV No children 12yrs 5P No coaches Last d by arrangement
PRICE GUIDE
ROOMS: s £37.50-£60; d £50-£60; wkly b&b £157.50-£189; wkly hlf-bd £259-£385
CARDS: 🔲 🔲

♥ ◎◎ Mrs P Sullivin **Cliff Farm** *(TQ933237)* Iden Lock TN31 7QE (2m along the Military Road to Appledore turn left at hanging milk churn) ☎01797 280331

Mar-Oct

This attractive Sussex peg tile hung farmhouse looks out over Romney Marsh. The rooms are simple in style with a floral decor and traditional furniture. A full English breakfast is served at separate tables in the small dining room and there is an adjoining cosy sitting room with TV and a wood burning stove. The patio in the front garden has lovely views over the Marsh and the River Rother which flows in front of the house.
3 rms (1 fmly) No smoking in bedrooms Tea and coffee making facilities Cen ht CTV 6P 6 acres smallholding
PRICE GUIDE
ROOMS: d £29-£30✳

SAFFRON WALDEN Essex Map **05** TL53

GH ◎◎◎ **Rowley Hill Lodge** Little Walden CB10 1UZ (1.25m north of town centre on B1052. On left of road with three tall chimneys) ☎01799 525975 FAX 01799 516622

Situated on the Linton road, this Lodge comprises a pair of extended farm-workers' cottages. The bedrooms have attractive period furnishings and there is a modern bathroom. Breakfast is served family-style around a large table and guests are welcome to use Mr and Mrs Haslam's comfortable sitting room.
2 en suite (bth/shr) No smoking in bedrooms CTV in all bedrooms Tea and coffee making facilities No dogs (ex guide dogs) Cen ht CTV 4P No coaches
PRICE GUIDE
ROOMS: s £19.50; d £35✳

◼ ◎◎◎ **Cricketer's Arms** CB11 3YG ☎01799 543210 FAX 01799 543512

This mellow, red-brick pub sits beside the village green, and its friendly owners and staff create a welcoming and informal atmosphere. The bedrooms are housed in a modern extension, and all are nicely appointed and well equipped, each with an en suite shower. Major refurbishments to the public rooms in 1995 will provide greater flexibility and comfort for guests and locals alike.
7 en suite (shr) (2 fmly) CTV in all bedrooms Tea and coffee

making facilities Cen ht P Last d 10pm
PRICE GUIDE
ROOMS: s £40-£50; d £50-£60✱
MEALS: Lunch £1.99-£17alc✱
CARDS:

ST AGNES Cornwall & Isles of Scilly Map **02** SW75

GH 🆀🆀 **Penkerris** Penwinnick Rd TR5 0PA (1st house on right after village sign) ☎01872 552262
Designed by the Cornish architect Sylvanus Trevail, this Edwardian residence is on the outskirts of the village with views over glorious countryside. The owner is able to recommend many walks and places to visit. Bedrooms are simply decorated and the dining room and sitting room are large and look out over the garden.
6 rms (2 shr) (2 fmly) CTV in all bedrooms Tea and coffee making facilities Licensed CTV 8P No coaches Last d 10am
PRICE GUIDE
ROOMS: d £27-£35; wkly b&b £90-£100; wkly hlf-bd £125-£160✱
CARDS: ⬛ 💳   (£)

GH 🆀🆀🆀 **Porthvean Hotel** Churchtown TR5 0QP (off A30 at Chiverton Rbt onto B3277, hotel opposite parish church) ☎01872 552581 FAX 01872 553773
Closed 18 Dec-22 Jan
Right at the centre of the village this is a good spot to watch the Flora Dances Carnival and Victorian Street Fayre. Parts of the building date back some 400 years and many original features still exist. Bedrooms have attractive antique pine furniture with modern comforts.
7 en suite (shr) (2 fmly) No smoking in dining room CTV in all bedrooms Tea and coffee making facilities Direct dial from bedrooms No dogs (ex guide dogs) Licensed Cen ht 8P No coaches Last d 9pm
CARDS: ⬛ 💳 🟦   (£)

ST ALBANS Hertfordshire Map **04** TL10

Selected

GH 🆀🆀🆀🆀 *Ardmore House* 54 Lemsford Rd AL1 3PR (Logis) ☎01727 859313 & 861411 FAX 01727 859313
Close to the town centre, in a peaceful residential area, this small, welcoming, family-run hotel has been considerably improved over recent years. All the rooms now offer the expected modern comforts, with those in the new wing being the most spacious. The lounge bar is elegant with attractive soft furnishings and decorative fireplaces, and evening meals and snacks can be served here, or in the dining room which overlooks the garden.
26 en suite (bth/shr) (3 fmly) No smoking in dining room CTV in all bedrooms Tea and coffee making facilities Direct dial from bedrooms Licensed Cen ht CTV 30P Last d 8.30pm
CARDS: ⬛ 💳 🟦

GH 🆀🆀 **Melford** 24 Woodstock Rd North AL1 4QQ ☎01727 853642 & 830486 FAX 01727 853642
Friendly owners are justifiably proud of their simply furnished but well maintained home, a large detached house with both garden and car parking space. The television lounge has an honesty bar, and guests share several large tables at breakfast.
12 rms (4 shr) (3 fmly) No smoking in dining room Tea and

coffee making facilities Licensed Cen ht CTV 12P No coaches
PRICE GUIDE
ROOMS: s £25-£40; d £40-£47✱

ST AUSTELL Cornwall & Isles of Scilly Map **02** SX05

GH 🆀🆀 **Alexandra Hotel** 52-54 Alexandra Rd PL25 4QN ☎01726 74242
A neat, well presented private hotel situated just outside the town centre, close to he railway station. The bedrooms vary in size and are bright and well maintained. Guests have the use of a comfortable lounge, and a set evening menu is served in the nicely appointed dining room if required, or light snacks are available in the cosy, well stocked bar.
14 rms (4 shr) (1 fmly) No smoking in dining room CTV in all bedrooms Tea and coffee making facilities Licensed Cen ht CTV 20P Last d 5.30pm
PRICE GUIDE
ROOMS: s £24-£29; d £42-£52; wkly b&b £138-£170; wkly hlf-bd £180-£212
CARDS: ⬛ 💳 🟦 ⬛ 🟦 🟦   (£)

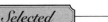

Selected

GH 🆀🆀🆀🆀 **T'Gallants** 6 Charlestown Rd, Charlestown PL25 3NJ ☎01726 70203
This elegant Georgian property is situated close to the pier in the picturesque port of Charlestown, just one mile from the town of St Austell. There are seven smart bedrooms, five of which have en suite showers, the other two have showers and share a toilet and bathroom. Breakfast is served in the attractive dining room, and there is also a cosy bar lounge.
➡

8 rms (6 bth/shr) No smoking in area of dining room No smoking in 1 lounge CTV in all bedrooms Tea and coffee making facilities No dogs Licensed Cen ht CTV 20P No coaches

PRICE GUIDE

ROOMS: s £25-£30; d £34-£38*

CARDS: 🔲 ▨   (£)

Selected

❧ ⓠⓠⓠⓠ Mrs J Nancarrow **Poltarrow** *(SW998518)*
PL26 7DR (off A390 turn right at St Mewan School entrance to farmhouse within 0.25m on left)
☎01726 67111
Closed 16 Dec-5 Jan

Situated in the scattered hamlet of St Mewen, with views over rolling farmland, this wisteria-clad farmhouse is a wonderful base for touring. The high quality bedrooms are individually furnished and decorated with lots of flair. Judith Nancarrow's set three-course dinners, made using local produce, are very popular, with farmhouse cookery being the order of the day. A cosy lounge is provided for guests, with a log fire burning on chilly evenings. There are three large, attractive self-catering cottages also available to let.

3 en suite (bth/shr) 2 annexe en suite (bth/shr) (1 fmly) No smoking in bedrooms No smoking in dining room CTV in all bedrooms Tea and coffee making facilities No dogs (ex guide dogs) Licensed Cen ht CTV 10P Pool table 45 acres mixed Last d noon

PRICE GUIDE

ROOMS: s £19-£22; d £36-£40; wkly b&b £126-£140; wkly hlf-bd £196-£210*

CARDS: 🔲 ▨

◀ ⓠⓠⓠ **Rashleigh Arms** Quay Rd, Charlestown PL25 3NJ
(A390, signposted on St Austell roundabout)
☎01726 73635 FAX 01726 69246

This large, friendly inn is found on the harbour approach in the unusual fishing port of Charlestown, which is frequently used for the filming of historical films. Spacious public areas include two bars and a restaurant (where breakfast is served) as well as a children's room. The bedrooms are bright and cheerful, pleasantly decorated and furnished with pine. There is a large private car park.

5 en suite (shr) CTV in all bedrooms Tea and coffee making facilities No dogs (ex guide dogs) Cen ht 120P Last d 10pm

PRICE GUIDE

ROOMS: s £24; d £48; wkly b&b £168*

MEALS: Lunch £8.15-£18.95 Dinner £8.20-£25.50*

CARDS: 🔲 ▨

Our inspectors never book in the name of the AA. They disclose their identity only after the bill has been paid.

ST BLAZEY Cornwall & Isles of Scilly Map **02** SX05

Premier Selected

GH ⓠⓠⓠⓠⓠ
Nanscawen House Prideaux Rd PL24 2SR
☎01726 814488
FAX 01726 814488
Closed 22-27 Dec

This very fine granite-built Georgian house beautifully set in the Luxulyan Valley is owned and run by the Martin family who strive to provide guests with the utmost in quality and comfort. The three bedrooms are decorated and furnished to a luxurious standard, each with their own spa bath and teddy bear. A spacious drawing room, comfortably furnished with matching chairs and sofas, leads into the conservatory where breakfast and dinner is served. All the food is home-cooked, using as much home-grown produce as possible and reviving many long-forgotten recipes. Five acres of mature south-facing gardens surround the house and an outdoor swimming pool is heated between April and September. There is also an outdoor whirlpool bath. Smoking is not permitted in the house.

3 en suite (bth/shr) No smoking CTV in all bedrooms Tea and coffee making facilities Direct dial from bedrooms No dogs Licensed Cen ht No children 12yrs 6P No coaches Outdoor swimming pool (heated) Putting green Jacuzzi/Whirlpool

PRICE GUIDE

ROOMS: s £35-£68; d £68-£78*

CARDS: 🔲 ▨   (£)

ST HILARY Cornwall & Isles of Scilly Map **02** SW53

Premier Selected

❧ ⓠⓠⓠⓠⓠ S L White
Ennys *(SW559328)*
Goldsithney TR20 9BZ
☎01736 740262
FAX 01736 740262
Closed 25-26 Dec

This beautiful 17th-century Cornish granite farmhouse stands on a small working farm, at the end of a long tree-lined drive and surrounded by sheltered gardens where guests are welcome to wander. A grass tennis court is available for guests' use, as is a heated swimming pool at stated hours. Two bedrooms (one of them a family suite) are located in a converted barn, and two of the three rooms in the main house have four-poster beds. There is a comfortable sitting room with a log fire in winter, and good dinners are served - the summertime set menu perhaps preceded by sherry in the garden on pleasant evenings. Local produce is used with care and imagination to create interesting meals which are served by candlelight at separate tables. The premises are not licensed, but guests are welcome to bring their own wine.

3 en suite (bth/shr) 2 annexe en suite (bth/shr) (1 fmly) No smoking in bedrooms No smoking in dining room CTV in all bedrooms Tea and coffee making facilities No dogs Cen ht CTV 2P Outdoor swimming pool (heated) Tennis (grass) 50 acres arable Last d 7.30pm

PRICE GUIDE
ROOMS: s £30-£35; d £45-£52*
CARDS:
See advertisement under PENZANCE

ST IVES Cornwall & Isles of Scilly Map **02** SW54

GH 🇶🇶🇶 *Bay View* Headland Road, Carbis Bay TR26 2NX
☎01736 796469
Mar-Oct
This family-run hotel is located in a residential area close to the beach at Carbis Bay, within easy access of St Ives. It offers modern, bright, comfortable bedrooms which are well appointed. Public areas are cosy and inviting, with ornaments, books and plants, and there is a TV lounge and bar. An evening meal is offered, cooked by Mrs Beaver.
9 rms (8 shr) (3 fmly) No smoking in bedrooms CTV in all bedrooms Tea and coffee making facilities No dogs (ex guide dogs) Licensed Cen ht CTV No children 5yrs 11P Last d 6pm

GH 🇶🇶🇶 **Blue Mist** The Warren TR26 2EA
☎01736 795209
Etr-Oct
This is a homely, friendly guesthouse, close to the seafront and the town centre. Well-equipped bedrooms are attractively decorated and have modern furnishings. The bar is small but comfortable and a choice of breakfasts is offered in the open-plan dining room.
8 en suite (shr) CTV in all bedrooms Tea and coffee making facilities Direct dial from bedrooms No dogs (ex guide dogs) Cen ht No children 4yrs 4P

PRICE GUIDE
ROOMS: s £20.75-£23.75; d £37.50-£49.50; wkly b&b £151.75-£172.75*
CARDS:

GH 🇶🇶🇶 **Channings Hotel** 3 Talland Rd TR26 2DF (on entering St Ives on the A3074 fork left at Porthminster Hotel then turn 1st left & 1st left again into Talland Rd. Hotel 2nd on right) ☎01736 795681 FAX 01736 797863
The focal point of this friendly, family-run private hotel is its bar/lounge, though there is also a small, cosy TV lounge. The hotel continues to improve and the bedrooms are well equipped. A set price dinner is served in the attractive dining room.
10 en suite (bth/shr) (5 fmly) No smoking in 6 bedrooms No smoking in dining room CTV in all bedrooms Tea and coffee making facilities Licensed Cen ht CTV 10P Last d 4pm

PRICE GUIDE
ROOMS: s £17-£25; d £34-£50; wkly b&b £119-£175; wkly hlf-bd £160-£212
CARDS:

GH 🇶🇶🇶 **Chy-an-Creet Private Hotel** Higher Stennack TR26 2HA (on B3311 into harbour, opposite Leach Pottery) ☎01736 796559 FAX 01736 796559
On the edge of town and just a short walk from the beaches is this family run small hotel. The bedrooms are all en suite, and public areas are cosy and attractive. Dinner is served in the pretty dining room and guests have a choice of dishes. Guests will enjoy their holiday at this welcoming guesthouse.
10 en suite (bth/shr) (4 fmly) No smoking in bedrooms No smoking in dining room Tea and coffee making facilities

---

Licensed CTV 16P Last d 4pm
PRICE GUIDE
ROOMS: s £15-£23; d £30-£46; wkly b&b £105-£161; wkly hlf-bd £148-£200
CARDS:

GH 🇶🇶🇶 **Countryman at Trink** Old Coach Rd TR26 3JQ
☎01736 797571
The atmosphere is welcoming at this small hotel set in two acres of landscaped gardens. A log fire burns in the cosy lounge and guests dine by candlelight.
6 en suite (shr) (2 fmly) No smoking CTV in all bedrooms Tea and coffee making facilities No dogs Licensed Cen ht No children 8yrs 20P No coaches Last d 8.30pm

PRICE GUIDE
ROOMS: s £35; d £50; wkly b&b £161-£172; wkly hlf-bd £238-£245
CARDS:

Selected

GH 🇶🇶🇶🇶 **Dean Court Hotel** Trelyon Av TR26 2AD
☎01736 796023 FAX 01736 796233
Mar-Oct
Joy and Ian Alford provide accommodation of the highest standard. There are two comfortable lounges with sea views, and picture windows in the attractive restaurant take full advantage of the vista. The bedrooms are comfortable and well-equipped, and those that do not have sea views overlook woodland.
12 en suite (bth/shr) (2 fmly) No smoking in dining room No smoking in 1 lounge CTV in all bedrooms Tea and coffee making facilities No dogs Licensed Cen ht No children 14yrs 12P No coaches Last d 6pm

PRICE GUIDE
ROOMS: s £28-£35; d £52-£68; wkly b&b £180-£215; wkly hlf-bd £215-£250*
CARDS:

GH 🇶🇶🇶 *The Hollies Hotel* 4 Talland Rd TR26 2DF
☎01736 796605
A friendly family run guesthouse is situated in a quiet residential area. The bedrooms are comfortable and well-equipped. There is a welcoming lounge and a good size dining room.
10 en suite (bth/shr) (4 fmly) No smoking in dining room CTV in all bedrooms Tea and coffee making facilities No dogs Licensed Cen ht CTV 12P Last d 5.30pm

GH 🇶🇶 *Island View* 2 Park Av TR26 2DN ☎01736 795111
Mar-Oct
With easy access to the shops by way of the carefully concealed narrow steps for which St Ives is well known, Island View overlooks the harbour and bay from its elevated setting. Regular guests are welcomed back year after year, and, whilst some of the rooms are a little compact, all are well equipped with televisions and tea trays. There are a cosy lounge and an adjoining dining room where an evening meal is available from Whitsun onwards.
10 rms (2 shr) (4 fmly) CTV in all bedrooms Tea and coffee making facilities Cen ht No parking No coaches Last d 6.30pm

GH 🇶🇶🇶 **Kandahar** 11 The Warren TR26 2EA
☎01736 796183
Closed Xmas, New Year & owners hols rs Part Nov & part Feb
Standing on a quaint, narrow street close to the sea, Kandahar offers clean, comfortable accomodation in spacious, well-maintained bedrooms, some with sea views. A small dining room ➡

also looks out over the sea where guests can relax and enjoy a sound English breakfast.

5 rms (3 bth/shr) (1 fmly) No smoking in dining room CTV in all bedrooms Tea and coffee making facilities No dogs Cen ht CTV 6P No coaches

PRICE GUIDE
ROOMS: s £18-£20; d £34-£48

GH Q Q Q Q **Kynance** The Warren TR26 2EA (take A3074 into town centre taking sharp right hand turn before bus/coach terminus, into railway station approach road. Kynance 20yds on left) ☎01736 796636
Closed mid Nov-mid Feb

In a convenient location, within sight and sound of the ocean, and close to the town centre, this charming former tin miner's cottage is full of character. The owners, Mr and Mrs Norris have tastefully decorated and furnished the house throughout, and bedrooms are attractive, comfortable and well-equipped. Public areas are small and cosy. There is an attractive dining room and a choice of English and Continental breakfast is offered.

7 rms (5 bth/shr) (2 fmly) No smoking in dining room No smoking in lounges CTV in all bedrooms Tea and coffee making facilities No dogs Cen ht CTV No children 7yrs 5P No coaches

PRICE GUIDE
ROOMS: s £19-£24; d £33-£40; wkly b&b £115.50-£140✳

GH Q Q Q **Longships Hotel** Talland Rd TR26 2DF
☎01736 798180 FAX 01736 798180

The Longships Hotel enjoys an enviable position above St Ives, offering stunning views over the harbour and bay; the town centre, however, is only a few minutes' walk away. This is a popular hotel, providing well appointed bedrooms, all of which have en suite facilities. An imaginative four-course evening meal can be enjoyed in the well decorated dining room, while nightly entertainment takes place in the large bar.

25 en suite (bth/shr) (7 fmly) No smoking in dining room No smoking in 1 lounge CTV in all bedrooms Tea and coffee making facilities Licensed Cen ht CTV 18P Last d 7pm

PRICE GUIDE
ROOMS: s £18-£26; d £36-£52; wkly b&b £125-£180; wkly hlf-bd £155-£210
CARDS: 🔲 🔲 🔲

GH Q Q Q Q **Lyonesse Hotel** 5 Talland Rd TR26 2DF (A3074 to St Ives fork left at Porthminster, left again at Albert Rd. Lyonesse 50yds on right) ☎01736 796315 FAX 01736 796315
Closed Dec-Jan

A few minutes' walk from the town centre and beaches, the Herbert family's hotel is run to ensure that guests have all they could wish for. This is evident not only in the provision of a wide variety of Aga-cooked dishes - including many vegetarian choices - but also in the high standards of housekeeping maintained throughout the spacious, well equipped bedrooms and pleasant relaxation areas. Private parking is available behind the hotel.

15 en suite (shr) (4 fmly) No smoking in bedrooms No smoking in dining room No smoking in lounges CTV in all

---

bedrooms Tea and coffee making facilities No dogs Licensed Cen ht CTV 10P Last d 6.30pm

PRICE GUIDE
ROOMS: s £17-£24; d £34-£48
CARDS: 🔲 🔲

GH Q Q Q Q **Monowai Private Hotel** Headland Road, Carbis Bay TR26 2NR (on entering Carbis Bay turn right off A3074 into Porthrepta Rd, Headland Rd is on the right after 300yds) ☎01736 795733
Mar-Sep

A family-run, character establishment stands in an elevated position commanding glorious views across the bay. The brightly decorated bedrooms have been furnished in a cottage style, and a cosy atmosphere is a feature of the bar and lounge. A choice of home-cooked dishes is offered on the fixed-price menu, with vegetarian specialities. A friendly welcome awaits guests.

8 en suite (shr) (3 fmly) No smoking Tea and coffee making facilities Licensed Cen ht CTV No children 5yrs 7P No coaches Outdoor swimming pool (heated) Pool table Darts Last d 6.30pm

PRICE GUIDE
ROOMS: s £16-£28; d £36-£60; wkly b&b £126-£210; wkly hlf-bd £210-£294

GH Q Q Q **The Old Vicarage Hotel** Parc-An-Creet TR26 2ET
☎01736 796124 FAX 01736 796124
Etr-Oct

A lovely mellowed stone 1850s vicarage which positively gleams with polish. Public areas are furnished in keeping with the period and one WC is reputedly the oldest in town - a Delft style metropolitan ceramic. Bedrooms are decorated with matching soft furnishings and there is a well stocked bar.

8 rms (4 bth/shr) (3 fmly) No smoking in bedrooms No smoking in dining room CTV in 7 bedrooms Tea and coffee making facilities Licensed Cen ht CTV 12P No coaches Putting green

PRICE GUIDE
ROOMS: s £20-£23; d £36-£40; wkly b&b £112-£126✳
CARDS: 🔲 🔲 🔲

GH Q Q Q *Pondarosa Hotel* 10 Porthminster Ter TR26 2DQ (approach town by A3074, fork left at Porthminster Hotel and follow road to left hand bend) ☎01736 795875

This terraced guest house is set above the town, close to the train and bus stations and within easy walking distance of the harbour and beaches. The housekeeping is of a particularly high standard throughout. Almost all the neatly co-ordinated bedrooms now have en suite facilities, and public areas include a cosy lounge and an attractive dining room and conservatory where guests tend to take their coffee after enjoying the four-course evening meal. There is also private parking available behind the hotel.

10 rms (1 bth 7 shr) (4 fmly) No smoking in 2 bedrooms No smoking in dining room No smoking in 1 lounge CTV in all bedrooms Tea and coffee making facilities No dogs (ex guide dogs) Licensed Cen ht CTV 12P Last d 4pm
CARDS: 🔲 🔲 🔲 🔲

GH QQQQ **Regent Hotel** Fernlea Ter TR26 2BH (in centre of town, close to bus & railway station)
☎01736 796195 FAX 01736 794641
One of the many attributes of the Regent Hotel is its proximity to the town centre, railway and bus stations as well as the beaches and harbour. Bedrooms are stylishly decorated and well equipped, the stunning views across the beaches and harbour which many of them have being particularly pleasant at night when the area is attractively lit up. Information on many of the local attractions and galleries is provided in the elegant lounge, while the restaurant (open to the public by day as a coffee shop) offers both a carte breakfast and an imaginative fixed-price evening menu.
9 rms (7 shr) No smoking in 4 bedrooms No smoking in area of dining room CTV in all bedrooms Tea and coffee making facilities No dogs Licensed Cen ht CTV No children 7yrs 12P No coaches Last d 7pm
PRICE GUIDE
ROOMS: s £23-£26; d £52-£60; wkly b&b £180-£200; wkly hlf-bd £239-£260✱
CARDS: 🌑 🌑 🌑 🌑 🌑 🌑 🌑   (£)

GH QQQ *St Merryn Hotel* Trelyon TR26 2PN
☎01736 795767 FAX 01736 797248
Mar-Nov
Standing in its own carefully tended gardens some fifteen minutes' walk from the town centre, the St Merryn combines traditional hospitality with all the modern comforts of well equipped en suite bedrooms. There are two lounges here, as well as a large bar where evening entertainment is often provided during the season . The Holder family serve well prepared home-cooked English meals in a sunny dining room which has had a new conservatory extension since last year.
19 en suite (bth) (8 fmly) No smoking in dining room CTV in all bedrooms Tea and coffee making facilities Direct dial from bedrooms No dogs Licensed Cen ht CTV No children 4yrs 20P Last d 6pm
CARDS: 🌑 🌑

GH QQQ **Sunrise** 22 The Warren TR26 2AT
☎01736 795407
Jan-Oct
This terraced cottage in the town centre has glorious views of the harbour from the top-floor bedrooms. The attractive bedrooms are comfortably furnished, with spotless en suite facilities. Traditional English breakfasts are a speciality, and complement the warm welcome offered by the proprietors.
7 rms (5 bth/shr) (2 fmly) No smoking in dining room CTV in all bedrooms Tea and coffee making facilities Cen ht CTV 5P
PRICE GUIDE
ROOMS: s £16-£20; d £30-£40✱   (£)

See advertisement on p.353.

GH QQQ **Tregorran Hotel** Headland Bay, Carbis Bay TR26 2NU (at Carbis Bay turn right down to beach along Porthrepta Rd. Take last turning on the right into Headland Rd, Tregorran Hotel halfway along) ☎01736 795889
Etr-1 Oct
The wide range of facilities makes this Spanish-looking hotel ideal for families. There are a games room and small gymnasium as well as the newly redesigned and improved swimming pool, and these - like the large bar - all benefit from stunning views of St Ives Bay; paths from the garden lead down to the beaches, and the ➡

coastal railway to St Ives is only a few minutes' walk away. For less clement days there is a lounge for those wishing to read or play games, and carte breakfasts and evening meals are attractively presented in a redecorated dining room.

15 rms (13 shr) (5 fmly) No smoking in dining room CTV in all bedrooms Tea and coffee making facilities Licensed Cen ht CTV 25P No coaches Outdoor swimming pool (heated) Solarium Gymnasium Pool table Games room Last d 3pm

PRICE GUIDE
ROOMS: s £15-£30; d £30-£60; wkly b&b £105-£210; wkly hlf-bd £154-£259*
CARDS: 🔳 ▆▆ 📇   (£)

GH 🆀🆀🆀 *Trevail Hotel* 7 Talland Rd TR26 2DF
☎01736 797030

Upgraded over the past few years, this guest house provides comfortable, spacious bedrooms. The airy lounge is comfortably furnished, and there is also a cosy bar. A home-cooked three-course meal is served each evening, and breakfasts are hearty and traditional.

8 en suite (shr) (5 fmly) No smoking in dining room CTV in all bedrooms Tea and coffee making facilities No dogs (ex guide dogs) Licensed Cen ht CTV 10P Last d 3pm
CARDS: 🔳 📇

Selected

🔁📺 **GH** 🆀🆀🆀🆀 Trewinnard 4 Parc Av TR26 2DN (A3074 to St Ives, on entering town turn left at Nat West bank and then turn left at mini roundabout. Go past car park and house 150yds on right) ☎01736 794168
Apr-Oct

This house in an elevated setting offers superb views over the town, harbour and St Ives Bay. Bedrooms, although a little compact, are well equipped and most comfortable, while downstairs there are an attractively decorated lounge and an engaging dining room leading into a small bar (the only room where smoking is allowed).

7 rms (5 shr) (1 fmly) No smoking CTV in all bedrooms Tea and coffee making facilities No dogs Licensed Cen ht No children 7yrs 4P No coaches Last d noon

PRICE GUIDE
ROOMS: s £15-£18; d £27-£36; wkly b&b £91-£126; wkly hlf-bd £136.50-£171.50
CARDS: 🔳 📇 📇 🔳   (£)

🍺 🆀🆀🆀 **Queens Tavern** High St TR26 1RR (St Austell Brewery) ☎01736 796468

This popular inn situated in the town centre offers well-equipped bedrooms. There is a small dining room on the first floor where a selection of meals and snacks are available and a choice of breakfasts is served.

5 en suite (shr) (3 fmly) CTV in all bedrooms Tea and coffee making facilities No dogs (ex guide dogs) Cen ht CTV Last d 8.15pm

PRICE GUIDE
ROOMS: d fr £42; wkly b&b fr £125
MEALS: Bar Lunch £10-£15alc
CARDS: 🔳 📇 🔳

ST JUST (NEAR LAND'S END) Cornwall & Isles of Scilly
Map **02** SW33

🍺 🆀🆀🆀 **Wellington Hotel** Market Square TR19 7HL
☎01736 787319 FAX 01736 787906

This historic old inn in the town's Market Square traces its history back to the mid 14th century. Its cosy bars are warm and

hospitable, inviting guests to try the good range of local beers and the home-cooked bar food. Modern bedrooms are housed in the converted former stables.

6 annexe en suite (bth/shr) (4 fmly) CTV in all bedrooms Tea and coffee making facilities Direct dial from bedrooms Cen ht CTV No parking Last d 9pm

PRICE GUIDE
ROOMS: s £25-£30; d £35-£40; wkly b&b £160-£180*
MEALS: Lunch £7-£10&alc Dinner £7-£10&alc*
CARDS: 🔳 ▆▆ 📇 ⓞ 📇 🔳

ST JUST-IN-ROSELAND Cornwall & Isles of Scilly
Map **02** SW83

Selected

GH 🆀🆀🆀🆀 *Rose-Da-Mar Hotel* TR2 5JB (turn off A390 onto B3287 to Tregony and then A3078 to St Just-in-Roseland, turn right at Crossroads along B3289,hotel 500yds on left) ☎01326 270450
mid Mar-mid Oct

Situated along a quiet country lane on the Roseland peninsula, this delightful property with its well tended gardens has splendid views over the River Fal. Bedrooms are delightfully decorated and all benefit from the view. Imaginative five course meals are served in the sunny dining room, and the Rose-Da-Mar has a loyal clientele, many of whom return several times a year.

8 rms (4 bth 1 shr) (1 fmly) No smoking in dining room Tea and coffee making facilities Licensed Cen ht CTV No children 11yrs 9P No coaches Last d 6.30pm

---

ST KEYNE Cornwall & Isles of Scilly Map **02** SX26

💗 🆀🆀🆀 Mrs B N Light **Penbugle Farm** *(SX228602)* PL14 4RS (establishment is approximately 3 miles along B3243 past Dobwalls) ☎01579 320288
Mar-Oct

This Duchy of Cornwall farm raises attractive South Devon beef cattle on 300 acres of land. Accommodation is comfortable and particularly spacious, and guests can relax in the inviting lounge with its wood-burning stove and television. Breakfast is a communal meal, served around an antique dining table.

2 en suite (shr) (2 fmly) No smoking in bedrooms Tea and coffee making facilities No dogs (ex guide dogs) Cen ht CTV 4P 287 acres arable beef sheep

PRICE GUIDE
ROOMS: d fr £30; wkly b&b fr £95*

See advertisement under LOOE

ST MARY'S See **SCILLY, ISLES OF**

ST MAWGAN Cornwall & Isles of Scilly Map **02** SW86

🍺 🆀🆀 **The Falcon** TR8 4EP (from A30 follow signs RAF St Mawgan, then St Mawgan village. Pub at bottom of hill in village centre) ☎01637 860225

Award winning gardens make an inviting setting for this magnolia-and wisteria-clad inn. The bar is no less inviting with pine furniture and a log fire during the winter months. There is also a pleasing lack of juke boxes and games machines. St Austell Brewery provide the house beer and there is a small, separate, no-smoking dining/breakfast room. The bedrooms are well-equipped. During the summer months a barbecue is held in the garden every evening.

3 rms (2 shr) No smoking in dining room CTV in all bedrooms
Tea and coffee making facilities Direct dial from bedrooms Cen
ht 20P Last d 10pm
PRICE GUIDE
ROOMS: s £17-£20; d £34-£50
MEALS: Lunch £6-£18alc Dinner £6-£18alc
CARDS:

ST MERRYN Cornwall & Isles of Scilly Map **02** SW87

◖ QQQ *Farmers Arms* PL28 8NP (St Austell Brewery)
☎01841 520303
A lively and informal atmosphere prevails at this old village inn,
which has kept much of its original character. The bars are heavily
beamed, with slate floors and open fireplaces. A wide
selection of dishes is offered along with a range of real ales.
Bedrooms are well equipped with modern creature comforts.
4 en suite (shr) (2 fmly) CTV in all bedrooms Tea and coffee
making facilities Cen ht 100P Last d 9.30pm
CARDS: ███

ST OWEN'S CROSS Hereford & Worcester Map **03** SO52

♥ QQ Mrs F Davies **Aberhall** (*SO529242*) HR2 8LL
☎01989 730256
Closed Dec
This 16th-century farmhouse is off the B4521. Accommodation is
comfortable, the views are panoramic and the owner Freda Davis
is full of energy and hospitality. Guests have the use of a modern
and comfortable lounge and there is a games room and an outdoor
tennis court. It is a mixed working farm, with livestock, trees and
turkeys. No evening meals are served.
3 rms (1 shr) No smoking Tea and coffee making facilities No
dogs (ex guide dogs) Cen ht CTV No children 10yrs 3P Tennis
(hard) Pool table Table tennis 132 acres arable beef mixed
PRICE GUIDE
ROOMS: d £32-£35   (£)

ST WENN Cornwall & Isles of Scilly Map **02** SW96

Selected

GH QQQQ **Wenn Manor** PL30 5PS (take B3274
through Tregonethen turn right for St Wenn, hotel next to
church) ☎01726 890240 FAX 01726 890680
This attractive old manor house stands in its own grounds.
The three bedrooms are individually decorated and furnished
with fine old furniture, and they all have excellent modern en
suite bathrooms. Wood panelling, flag-stone floors and
antique furniture lend character and charm to the public areas,
and a recently discovered well in the cosy bar has been made
into an attractive feature, together with a wood-burning fire.
An array of tempting fresh dishes is offered in the restaurant,
and a relaxed and friendly atmosphere prevails throughout.
3 en suite (bth) No smoking in bedrooms No smoking in area
of dining room CTV in all bedrooms Tea and coffee making
facilities Direct dial from bedrooms No dogs (ex guide dogs)
Licensed Cen ht CTV No children 12yrs 32P No coaches
Croquet lawn Last d 9.30pm
PRICE GUIDE
ROOMS: (incl. dinner) s £45; d £90✳
CARDS: ███   (£)

SALCOMBE Devon Map **03** SX73

Selected

GH QQQQ **Devon Tor Hotel** Devon Rd TQ8 8HJ
☎01548 843106
Closed Dec
A small private hotel in a fine position commands magnificent
views of the estuary from many of the bedrooms. Rooms are
cosily decorated, each with its own colour scheme, and there
is a sunny dining room and a small but comfortable guests'
lounge.
6 en suite (bth/shr) (2 fmly) No smoking CTV in all
bedrooms Tea and coffee making facilities No dogs
Licensed Cen ht CTV 5P No coaches Last d 4.30pm
PRICE GUIDE
ROOMS: s £20-£35; d £40-£55; wkly b&b £140-£169;
wkly hlf-bd £198-£248
                                              (£)

GH QQQ **Lyndhurst Hotel** Bonaventure Rd TQ8 8BG
☎01548 842481 FAX 01548 842481
Jan-Oct
Standing high above the town, this personally managed private
hotel enjoys glorious views across the rolling countryside and
estuary. Bedrooms are attractive and freshly decorated, with smart
en suite shower facilities; many have fine views and testify to
good standards of housekeeping. There is a comfortable lounge
and a well stocked bar in addition to the attractive, bright dining
room where Geoff and Sheila Sharp offer their renowned four-
course dinners.
                                              ➡

GUEST · HOUSE

Your Friendly Award Winning Guest House

Accommodation consists of seven bedrooms, most
with private facilities. All bedrooms have colour TV,
central heating and tea/coffee making facilities.
Large inviting dining room to enjoy our extensive
choice of Breakfast Menu including vegetarian
specialities. Beautiful views of harbour and bay, 200
yards from the beach and a few minutes walk to
the harbour, town centre and Tate Gallery. Two sun
terraces give access to car park, St.Ives Railway
Station and Bus/Coach terminus.

SUNRISE ENSURES A WARM WELCOME!
Recommended QQQ
'Sunrise' The Warren, St.Ives, Cornwall.
Telephone (01736) 795407

8 en suite (shr) (1 fmly) No smoking CTV in all bedrooms Tea and coffee making facilities No dogs Licensed Cen ht No children 7yrs 4P No coaches Last d 4.30pm

PRICE GUIDE

ROOMS: s £18.50-£25; d £37-£50; wkly b&b £126-£168; wkly hlf-bd £210-£238

GH 🇶🇶🇶 *Torre View Hotel* Devon Rd TQ8 8HJ
☎01548 842633

6 Feb-4 Nov

A neat, friendly hotel in a fine position overlooking the sea, with glorious views across the estuary to the hills beyond. Bedrooms are nicely decorated and comfortable and those without en suite facilities have use of their own private bath and shower room nearby. Home-cooked evening meals are offered in the front-facing dining room, with a daily choice written on the blackboard. In addition to the comfortable lounge there is also a bar/lounge with a well stocked bar, darts and skittles.

8 en suite (bth/shr) (2 fmly) No smoking in dining room CTV in all bedrooms Tea and coffee making facilities No dogs Licensed Cen ht CTV No children 4yrs 4P No coaches Last d 6pm

CARDS: 🔲 🔲

GH 🇶🇶🇶 **Trennels Hotel** Herbert Rd TQ8 8HR (take A381 to Salcombe, from main road turn left into Devon Road then left again into Herbert road, hotel is 50yds on right)
☎01548 842500

Mar-Oct

A private, licensed hotel conveniently situated for the town centre and harbour in a residential area has superb views over the town, estuary and National Trust land. Bedrooms are all comfortable and simply furnished, the majority having estuary views. Home-cooked meals are served in the dining room, with a set four-course table fixed-price menu. Smoking is not permitted here.

7 rms (5 shr) (1 fmly) No smoking CTV in 5 bedrooms Tea and coffee making facilities No dogs Licensed Cen ht CTV No children 4yrs 8P No coaches

PRICE GUIDE

ROOMS: s £17-£19; d £36-£44; wkly b&b £119-£140

SALFORD Greater Manchester Map **07** SJ89

GH 🇶🇶🇶 **Hazeldean Hotel** 467 Bury New Rd M7 3NE (on A56 2m from M62 junct 17)
☎0161 792 6667 & 0161 792 2079 FAX 0161 792 6668

Closed 24 Dec-2 Jan

A large Victorian property some 2.5 miles north of Manchester city centre and within a few minutes' drive of the M61 and M62, the Hazeldean provides soundly maintained accommodation which includes some ground floor bedrooms and a few rooms in an adjacent house. Bedrooms vary in style - some being traditionally furnished and some modern - but all have a good array of equipment including telephones and private bars. Public areas offer a restaurant, bar and quiet lounge and there is also a function room for up to 36 people.

21 rms (17 bth/shr) 3 annexe rms (2 bth/shr) (2 fmly) No smoking in dining room CTV in 21 bedrooms Tea and coffee making facilities Direct dial from bedrooms No dogs (ex guide dogs) Licensed Cen ht CTV 23P Last d 8.30pm

PRICE GUIDE

ROOMS: s £35-£40; d £44-£50✱

CARDS: 🔲 🔲 🔲 🔲 🔲 🔲

SALISBURY Wiltshire Map **04** SU12

See also Downton, Whiteparish & Winterbourne Stoke

GH 🇶🇶🇶 **Byways House** 31 Fowlers Rd SP1 2QP
☎01722 328364 FAX 01722 322146

Closed Xmas & New Year

Byways is a Victorian property in a quiet residential area of Salisbury, just a short hilly stroll from the city centre. Accommodation is offered in well furnished, light and airy rooms, including one on the ground floor which caters especially for disabled guests. (One can drive right up to the patio doors of the latter.) A full English or vegetarian breakfast is served in an attractively organised breakfast room overlooking the pretty garden.

23 rms (19 bth/shr) (5 fmly) No smoking in dining room No smoking in lounges CTV in all bedrooms Tea and coffee making facilities Licensed Cen ht 15P

PRICE GUIDE

ROOMS: s £23-£30.50; d £39-£49; wkly b&b £154-£213.50✱

CARDS: 🔲 🔲

GH 🇶🇶🇶 **Cricket Field Cottage** Skew Bridge, Wilton Rd SP2 7NS (off A36 Warminster rd) ☎01722 322595

This modernised old gamekeeper's cottage is set back from the Wilton Road and enjoys views of the village church and the South Wiltshire cricket ground. Bedrooms have been equipped with modern comforts and breakfast is served in a bright and airy dining room.

13 rms (3 shr) No smoking CTV in all bedrooms Tea and coffee making facilities No dogs (ex guide dogs) Cen ht No children 2yrs 13P No coaches

PRICE GUIDE

ROOMS: s £25-£32; d £38-£42✱

£

GH 🇶🇶🇶 **The Edwardian Lodge** 59 Castle Rd SP1 3RH (.5n north off A345) ☎01722 413329

This fine Edwardian house has spacious rooms which have been recently refurbished and tastefully decorated. Situated within easy walking distance of the city centre and cathedral.

7 en suite (shr) (2 fmly) No smoking in 3 bedrooms No smoking in dining room CTV in all bedrooms Tea and coffee making facilities Cen ht CTV 8P Last d 8pm

PRICE GUIDE

ROOMS: s £25-£27.50; d £35-£40✱

GH 🇶🇶🇶 **Glen Lyn** 6 Bellamy Ln, Milford Hill SP1 2SP (from A36 at traffic lights into Tollgate Rd then at traffic lights right up Milford Hill) ☎01722 327880

This substantial Victorian family home stands in beautifully kept gardens in a quiet tree-lined lane, just a five minute walk from the city centre. There is a comfortable lounge and the bedrooms have been equipped with modern facilities. The house is no smoking throughout, and offers bed and breakfast only.

9 rms (2 bth 2 shr) (1 fmly) No smoking CTV in all bedrooms Tea and coffee making facilities No dogs (ex guide dogs) Licensed Cen ht CTV No children 12yrs 7P No coaches Last d 7pm

PRICE GUIDE

ROOMS: s £20-£22; d £36-£40; wkly b&b £126-£137; wkly hlf-bd £190-£200

£

Selected

GH 🇶🇶🇶🇶 **Grasmere House** 70 Harnham Rd SP2 8JN
☎01722 338388 FAX 01722 333710

An elegant example of late Victorian architecture, Grasmere House is set back off the Harnham Road, in well kept grounds that lead down to the River Adder and enjoys glorious views across fields to the cathedral. The hotel has recently been extended and the new bedrooms equipped and furnished to a high standard. Dinner is served in a conservatory dining room where a choice of interesting home-cooked dishes is available. There is a comfortable lounge and Dale Naug and his staff assure guests of attentive and friendly service.

21 en suite (bth/shr) (1 fmly) No smoking in bedrooms No smoking in dining room CTV in all bedrooms Tea and coffee making facilities Direct dial from bedrooms Licensed Cen ht 30P Fishing Croquet Badminton Last d 9.30pm

PRICE GUIDE

ROOMS: s £42.50-£48.50; d £65-£95✳

CARDS: 💳 💳 💳 💳

GH 🇶🇶 Hayburn Wyke 72 Castle Rd SP1 3RL (.5m N on A345) ☎01722 412627

This Victorian brick-built guesthouse on the Amesbury road is in walking distance of the city centre and has the advantage of some parking spaces. The bedrooms are well equipped, and breakfast is served in an attractive dining room.

6 rms (2 shr) (2 fmly) No smoking in dining room No smoking in lounges CTV in all bedrooms Tea and coffee making facilities No dogs (ex guide dogs) Cen ht CTV ch fac 6P

PRICE GUIDE

ROOMS: s £23-£35; d £34-£40   (£)

GH 🇶 Holmhurst Downton Rd SP2 8AR (follow ring rd around city taking south coast route) ☎01722 410407

Karen and Trevor Hayward's family home is on the Ringwood road, close to the city centre and cathedral. Bedrooms are well

➡

NEWTON FARMHOUSE

Southampton Road (A36), Whiteparish, Salisbury, Wiltshire SP5 2QL

Telephone: (01794) 884416

Proprietors: John & Suzi Lanham

Grade II, Part 16c farmhouse, formerly part of the Trafalgar Estate, 8 miles south of Salisbury on A36 Southampton Road. Convenient for Stonehenge, Winchester, Romsey and New Forest. 8 en-suite rooms (2 with 4 poster) with colour TV, tea/coffee facilities. Beamed dining room with flagstone floor. Large grounds, outdoor swimming pool. Evening meals by arrangement.

ETB 🏵🏵 Commended   *AA QQQ* Recommended

Grasmere House

70 Harnham Road, Salisbury, Wiltshire SP2 8JN
Telephone: 01722 338388   Fax: 01722 333710

A large, late Victorian house situated in 1½ acres of colourful and mature grounds. Built as a family residence for prosperous Salisbury merchants it has been delightfully converted whilst retaining all the features and atmosphere of a comfortable family home. The luxurious twenty bedrooms, all of distinctive character have en suite facilities and beautiful views. The Conservatory Restaurant serves freshly cooked English food with a French flavour. Centrally situated for the town with a regular bus service or either, an 8 minute walk via the Cathedral Close or a 20 minute walk via the Old Mill and town path. Enjoy a unique experience staying with us at Grasmere where comfort and attentive service go hand in hand

---

10 minutes drive from Salisbury.
Come to the quiet, unspoilt village
of Downton for a comfortable bed
and delicious breakfast at

THE WARREN

HIGH STREET, DOWNTON, SALISBURY, WILTS.

A modernised Georgian house of great antiquity and character offering pleasant English fare and homely high-class accommodation.

Tel: Downton (01725) 510263

2 MILES FROM THE NEW FOREST.

equipped and comfortable, and breakfast is served at separate tables in a pleasant dining room.

6 rms (4 shr) (2 fmly) No smoking in dining room No smoking in lounges CTV in all bedrooms Tea and coffee making facilities No dogs (ex guide dogs) Cen ht 9P

PRICE GUIDE
ROOMS: s £20-£25; d £32-£38✳

GH **Q Q** **Leena's** 50 Castle Rd SP1 3RL (off A303 onto A345 to Castle Road) ☎01722 335419

This family-run establishment in walking distance of the centre has parking space and a garden. There is an attractive breakfast room and a comfortable lounge.

6 rms (5 shr) (1 fmly) No smoking in bedrooms CTV in all bedrooms Tea and coffee making facilities No dogs (ex guide dogs) Cen ht CTV 6P No coaches

PRICE GUIDE
ROOMS: s £17-£22; d £32-£39✳

Selected

GH **Q Q Q Q** **The Old House** 161 Wilton Rd SP2 7JQ (on the A30 between Wilton and Salisbury, close to the police station) ☎01722 333433

Full of character, this attractive brick house is set in its own large gardens, within easy reach of the city and railway station. The en suite bedrooms are brightly decorated, each furnished in its own individual style and all are equipped with remote-control TV and tea-making facilities. A comfortable lounge, featuring exposed beams and brick walls, is available to guests, and home-cooked English breakfasts are served in the tasteful dining room, furnished and decorated in a country-cottage style with china plates on the walls and a Welsh dresser in one corner. Smoking is only permitted in the lounge.

7 en suite (bth/shr) (2 fmly) No smoking in bedrooms No smoking in dining room No smoking in 1 lounge CTV in all bedrooms Tea and coffee making facilities No dogs (ex guide dogs) Licensed Cen ht CTV 10P No coaches Games room Table tennis Darts Last d 3.30pm

PRICE GUIDE
ROOMS: s £20-£30; d £32-£40; wkly b&b £140-£210; wkly hlf-bd £210-£280✳

GH **Q** **Richburn** 23/25 Estcourt Rd SP1 3AP (from A30 take 5th exit off Weeping Cross rdbt) ☎01722 325189

Closed Xmas

This detached Victorian family home is situated close to the ring road and just a few minutes walk from the city centre. The bedrooms are no smoking and whilst quite simply furnished are clean and comfortable. There is a guests lounge with a colour television, and a car park at the rear.

10 rms (2 bth/shr) (2 fmly) No smoking in bedrooms No smoking in dining room Cen ht CTV 10P

PRICE GUIDE
ROOMS: s £17-£17.50; d £29-£38

Selected

GH **Q Q Q Q** *Stratford Lodge* 4 Park Ln, Off Castle Rd SP1 3NP ☎01722 325177 FAX 01722 412699

Closed 23 Dec-31 Jan

Guests are assured of a warm welcome to this delightful house, built in 1890 and retaining much of the character of the period. Though tucked away down a leafy lane, it is only minutes from the centre of historic Salisbury. Individually styled bedrooms are furnished with antiques and special little treasures collected by the family. Breakfast is served in a delightful terracotta-tiled conservatory with pretty tables and chairs, while the elegant dining room has French windows out to the secluded garden.

8 en suite (bth/shr) (2 fmly) No smoking CTV in all bedrooms Tea and coffee making facilities Direct dial from bedrooms No dogs Licensed Cen ht No children 8yrs 12P Indoor swimming pool (heated) Small gymnasium Last d 8.30pm

CARDS:

GH **Q Q** **Victoria Lodge** 61 Castle Rd SP1 3RH (take A345 off Salisbury ring road. Castle Road 400yds on right) ☎01722 320586 FAX 01722 414507

Closed 25-26 Dec

This red brick, detatched property, which benefits from its own car park. Neat bedrooms are well equipped and simply furnished, and a choice of evening meal is available if required. There is a cosy lounge with satellite TV.

13 rms (11 bth/shr) (1 fmly) No smoking in bedrooms No smoking in dining room CTV in all bedrooms Tea and coffee making facilities Licensed Cen ht CTV 13P Last d 9pm

PRICE GUIDE
ROOMS: s fr £28.50; d fr £42

♥ **Q Q** A Shering **Swaynes Firs** *(SU068221)* Grimsdyke, Coombe Bissett SP5 5RF (7m SW Salisbury & 3m SW of Coombe Bissett on left side of A354 Blandford road) ☎01725 519240

Set well away from the main Dorchester to Blandford road, this attractive farmhouse enjoys country views, with the home paddocks containing household pets in the foreground. Accommodation is offered in a choice of three light rooms, each equipped with tea trays and TV. The lounge is large and cosy and on cold evenings a wood burning stove is lit. A full country breakfast is served in the spacious dining room, and vegetarians are catered for.

3 en suite (shr) (1 fmly) No smoking in bedrooms No smoking in dining room CTV in all bedrooms Tea and coffee making facilities Cen ht CTV 6P 11 acres beef horses poultry

PRICE GUIDE
ROOMS: d fr £36

SALTASH Cornwall & Isles of Scilly Map **02** SX45

Selected

⬛ **Q Q Q Q** *The Crooked Inn* Stoketon Cross, Trematon PL12 4RZ ☎01752 848177 FAX 01752 843203

Conveniently situated just off the A38 six miles from Plymouth, this friendly inn provides accommodation in well equipped bedrooms which are sited in a modern building across the courtyard from the bar and dining room. Menus offer an extensive selection of dishes, and a good choice of real ales is available from the well stocked cellar; children's meals are served in a separate room upstairs.

12 annexe rms (9 bth/shr) (2 fmly) CTV in 8 bedrooms Tea and coffee making facilities Cen ht CTV 45P Outdoor swimming pool (heated) Childrens play area Last d 9.30pm
CARDS: 🔲 🔲

SANDBACH Cheshire Map **07** SJ76

GH 🔲🔲 **Poplar Mount** 2 Station Rd, Elworth CW11 9JG (off A533 into Station Rd) ☎01270 761268 FAX 01270 761268
Situated just off the A533, opposite the railway station, this small guest house offers a good range of facilities. Some bedrooms are en suite and all have TVs, tea/coffee trays and radio alarm clocks. The dining room has separate tables, and in the sitting room there is a display of the owner's handicrafts for sale.
7 rms (2 bth 2 shr) (1 fmly) No smoking in dining room CTV in all bedrooms Tea and coffee making facilities No dogs (ex guide dogs) Cen ht CTV 7P No coaches Last d 7.45pm
PRICE GUIDE
ROOMS: s £19-£28; d £38*
CARDS: 🔲 🔲 (£)

SANDHURST Kent Map **05** TQ82

♥ 🔲🔲🔲 Mrs A Nicholas **Hoads Farm** Crouch Ln TN18 5PA ☎01580 850296 FAX 01580 850296
An original farm house dating from the 16th century beautifully restored and personally run by Mrs Anne Nicholas. Furnished with period and antique furniture and comprising three comfortable bedrooms, one of which can have sole use of private facilities, are all furnished to a good standard and equipped with tea trays. There is a spacious, elegant, beamed lounge with log burning fire, and a separate candle lit dining room overlooking the garden; dinner can be arranged with 24 hours notice. Families are especially welcome and the Nicholas family also own the adjoining Sandhurst Vineyard (and a wine shop) which has produced some award-winning English table wines. There are plenty of signposted local walks.
3 rms Tea and coffee making facilities No dogs Licensed Cen ht CTV P 350 acres apple hops vines sheep
PRICE GUIDE
ROOMS: d £34; wkly b&b fr £102; wkly hlf-bd fr £179*
CARDS: 🔲 🔲 🔲

SANDOWN See **WIGHT, ISLE OF**

SANDWICH Kent Map **05** TR35

◀ 🔲🔲🔲 **St Crispin** The Street, Worth CT14 0DF ☎01304 612081 FAX 01304 614838
Set in the peaceful small village of Worth, this friendly inn is particularly popular in summer with a busy bar meal trade and a well-maintained garden. Bedrooms in the main building are well-appointed with old pine and attractive soft furnishings; there is also accommodation in an outhouse. Full meals and breakfasts are served in the pleasant dining room.
4 en suite (bth/shr) 3 annexe en suite (bth) (2 fmly) CTV in all bedrooms Tea and coffee making facilities Cen ht 30P Last d 9.30pm
CARDS: 🔲 🔲

SANDY Bedfordshire Map **04** TL14

Selected

♥ 🔲🔲🔲🔲 Mrs M Codd **Highfield** *(TL515166)* Great North Rd SG19 2AQ (1.5m N on A1) ☎01767 682332
Closed 24 Dec-1 Jan
Mrs Codd is an enthusiastic and friendly hostess who takes great pride in this immaculately maintained farmhouse which

---

is surrounded by comparatively peaceful arable farmland. This pretty whitewashed house offers tastefully appointed accommodation, the bedrooms being divided between the main house and a nicely converted stable block; which provides ground floor rooms. Breakfast is taken communally at a large table in a nicely appointed dining room and guests also have the use of an inviting and comfortable lounge, decorative with pictures and dried flower arrangements and providing a range of books and games for guests use.
3 rms (1 bth 1 shr) 3 annexe en suite (shr) (2 fmly) No smoking CTV in 3 bedrooms Tea and coffee making facilities Cen ht CTV 14P 300 acres arable
PRICE GUIDE
ROOMS: s £20-£27.50; d £35-£40; wkly b&b £116-£135*

SARISBURY GREEN Hampshire Map **04** SU50

Selected

GH 🔲🔲🔲🔲 **Dormy House Hotel** 21 Barnes Ln SO31 7DA (Take A27 towards Fareham, turn right at Warsash) ☎01489 572626
Situated between Southampton and Portsmouth, this large Victorian house has been tastefully extended to provide modern accommodation. The bedrooms all have en suite facilities and are bright and attractively decorated. There is a comfortable lounge, and the dining room has a cosy atmosphere. Evening meals provide a good, interesting variety to suit all tastes. Ground-floor rooms are available and there is ample parking.
12 en suite (bth/shr) (1 fmly) No smoking in 3 bedrooms CTV in all bedrooms Tea and coffee making facilities Direct ➡

dial from bedrooms Licensed Cen ht CTV 18P No coaches
Last d 5pm
PRICE GUIDE
ROOMS: s £29.50-£37.60; d £46-£46*
CARDS:

SAXELBY Leicestershire Map **08** SK62

♥ Ⓠ Ⓠ Ⓠ Mrs M A Morris **Manor House** *(SK701208)*
LE14 3PA (1.5m off A6006, the Manor is at the bottom of
Church Lane) ☎01664 812269
Etr-Oct
Part Elizabethan, this lovely old building is in a cul-de-sac past the
church in the hamlet of Saxelby. There is a snug breakfast room
where dinner is also provided by the friendly hostess.
3 rms (1 shr) (1 fmly) No smoking in dining room CTV in all
bedrooms Tea and coffee making facilities No dogs (ex guide
dogs) Cen ht CTV 6P 125 acres dairy sheep Last d noon
PRICE GUIDE
ROOMS: s fr £25; d fr £36; wkly b&b fr £120; wkly hlf-bd fr
£180

SCARBOROUGH North Yorkshire Map **08** TA08

GH Ⓠ Ⓠ **Alga Court** 5 Alga Ter, off St Martins Square
YO11 2DF ☎01723 366078
A small terraced house situated in a quiet side street on the South
Cliff offers well equipped bedrooms ranging from smallish singles
to family rooms. There is a comfortable lounge and a dining area
downstairs.
6 rms (3 bth/shr) (3 fmly) No smoking in dining room No
smoking in lounges CTV in all bedrooms Tea and coffee making
facilities Cen ht CTV No coaches Last d 3pm
PRICE GUIDE
ROOMS: s fr £14; d fr £28; wkly b&b fr £98; wkly hlf-bd fr
£119*

GH Ⓠ Ⓠ Ⓠ **Anatolia Hotel** 21 West St YO11 2QR
☎01723 503205 & 360864
Closed Nov-Etr
Situated in a quiet side road close to the south beach, this well
furnished, family-run hotel provides warm and friendly service.
Bedrooms have many thoughtful extras, and public rooms include
a spacious and comfortable lounge as well as a cosy dining room
where a five-course dinner is served.
8 en suite (shr) (3 fmly) No smoking in dining room CTV in all
bedrooms Tea and coffee making facilities No dogs (ex guide
dogs) Licensed Cen ht CTV No parking No coaches Last d
3.30pm
PRICE GUIDE
ROOMS: s £16-£20; d £32-£40; wkly b&b £112-£140; wkly hlf-
bd £145-£155*

GH Ⓠ Ⓠ **Avoncroft Hotel** 5-7 Crown Ter YO11 2BL (fron
Station take Filey rd A165 over Valley Bridge and left
opposite St Andrews Church then left again for Crown
Crescent) ☎01723 372737 FAX 01723 372737
This small hotel in the centre of a Georgian terrace is convenient
for both the seafront and the town centre. Bedrooms are simply
furnished and decorated. There is a comfortable lounge for
residents, a spacious dining room and an adjoining lounge bar.
34 rms (1 bth 20 shr) (13 fmly) CTV in all bedrooms Tea and
coffee making facilities Licensed Cen ht CTV Games room

Pool table Last d 6.15pm
PRICE GUIDE
ROOMS: s £19.50-£25.50; d £39-£51; wkly b&b £136.50-
£178.50; wkly hlf-bd £169-£210

GH Ⓠ Ⓠ Ⓠ **Dolphin Hotel** 151 Columbus Ravine YO12 7QZ
(from A64 left at Station and over two sets of lights and rbs,
hotel on right) ☎01723 374217
A small terraced house close to North Bay, the cricket ground and
Peasholm Park. Bedrooms are particularly well equipped, with
private bathrooms, and home-cooked dinners and breakfasts with
a good choice of menu are served by the friendly resident owners.
5 en suite (shr) (2 fmly) No smoking in dining room No
smoking in lounges CTV in all bedrooms Tea and coffee making
facilities Direct dial from bedrooms No dogs Licensed Cen ht
No children 5yrs No coaches Last d 8.30pm
PRICE GUIDE
ROOMS: d £32-£36; wkly b&b £112-£126; wkly hlf-bd £154-
£168
CARDS:

GH Ⓠ Ⓠ Ⓠ *Geldenhuis Hotel* 145-147 Queens Pde YO12 7HU
☎01723 361677
Mar-Oct rs Xmas
Standing high above the North Bay, this large guest house enjoys
excellent sea views and has its own car parking area to the front.
Public rooms are spacious and the bedrooms, including some with
en suite facilities, are bright and modern.
30 rms (3 bth 10 shr) (4 fmly) No smoking in dining room No
smoking in 1 lounge CTV in 20 bedrooms Tea and coffee making
facilities Licensed Cen ht CTV 22P Last d 6pm

GH Ⓠ Ⓠ **Manor Heath Hotel** 67 Northstead Manor Dr
YO12 6AF (follow signs for North Bay and Peasholme Park)
☎01723 365720
Closed Dec-1 Jan
This family run holiday guesthouse is situated on the North Bay
beside Peasholme Park, within easy reach of central amenities.
Public areas are cosy, with a small lounge, a bar and a bright
modern dining room. Bedrooms are in various sizes with practical
appointments.
15 rms (2 bth 10 shr) (6 fmly) No smoking in dining room CTV
in all bedrooms Tea and coffee making facilities No dogs
Licensed Cen ht CTV 16P No coaches Last d 4.30pm
PRICE GUIDE
ROOMS: s £17.50-£20; d £35-£40; wkly b&b £122.50-£140;
wkly hlf-bd £150-£165

GH Ⓠ *Meadow Court* Queens Ter YO12 7HJ ☎01723 360839
A friendly guest house situated close to the North Bay and
Peasholme Park offers fairly simple accommodation at a
reasonable price. There are a cosy lounge and a small bar together
with a pleasant dining room.
10 rms (2 fmly) Tea and coffee making facilities Licensed Cen
ht CTV Last d 2pm

GH Ⓠ Ⓠ Ⓠ *Mount House Hotel* 33 Trinity Rd, South Cliff
YO11 2TD ☎01723 362967
Mar-Oct
A delightful semidetached Victorian house is situated in a quiet
residential area on the south side of the town. Bedrooms are very
well maintained and there are two very comfortable lounges, one
designated a quiet lounge. Both are furnished and decorated to a
very high standard. There is also a cosy bar which features
humorous golfing prints and a conservatory. In the attractive
dining room four-course dinners are served. The hotel is owned
and managed by Audrey and Alf Dawson, who pride themselves

on good service and value for money. Their attention to detail is evident throughout the hotel.

7 en suite (bth/shr) (3 fmly) CTV in all bedrooms Tea and coffee making facilities No dogs (ex guide dogs) Licensed Cen ht CTV 6P No coaches Last d 4pm

CARDS: ▣ ▩

Selected

GH ▢▢▢▢ **Paragon Hotel** 123 Queens Pde YO12 7HU (on A64) ☎01723 372676 FAX 01723 372676
2 Jan-Oct

This delightful hotel overlooks the North Bay and Scarborough Castle and is also close to the cricket ground. The modern bedrooms are individually decorated, with many enjoying fine sea views. The very comfortable bar lounge features a large picture window, and a telescope for viewing passing ships. A choice of menu is offered at dinner which is served in the attractively appointed dining room. The hotel's car park takes up most of the front garden, but there is a patio.
15 en suite (bth/shr) (2 fmly) No smoking in 6 bedrooms No smoking in dining room CTV in all bedrooms Tea and coffee making facilities Licensed Cen ht No children 2yrs 6P No coaches Last d 7pm

PRICE GUIDE

ROOMS: s £20-£22; d £40-£44; wkly b&b £140-£154; wkly hlf-bd £178-£198

CARDS: ▣ ▩

GH ▢▢▢ *Parmelia Hotel* 17 West St YO11 2QN
☎01723 361914
Apr-Oct

This very comfortable private hotel is situated on the South Cliff only a short distance from the Esplanade and Cliff tramway. Bedrooms are modern and tastefully furnished with attractive coordinated fabrics. There is an elegant and relaxing guests lounge and also a spacious lounge bar. Five-course evening meals are served in the bright and attractive dining room. The standards of hospitality and maintenance are very high.
15 rms (1 bth 12 shr) (3 fmly) No smoking in dining room CTV in all bedrooms Tea and coffee making facilities No dogs (ex guide dogs) Licensed Cen ht CTV No parking Last d 5.45pm

GH ▢▢▢ **Phoenix** 157 Columbus Ravine YO12 7QZ
☎01723 368319
mid Feb-mid Dec

A cosy, well furnished guest house, the Phoenix is conveniently placed for all the attractions of the North Bay. The bedrooms have remote control TVs with video link up, and there is a lounge with plenty of books and games for children. It is a family-run establishment, providing warm and friendly service.
6 rms (4 shr) (3 fmly) CTV in all bedrooms Tea and coffee making facilities No dogs (ex guide dogs) Licensed Cen ht CTV No parking Last d 11am

PRICE GUIDE

ROOMS: d £26-£30; wkly b&b £90-£105; wkly hlf-bd £127-£142✱

CARDS: ▣ ▩ ⓔ

GH ▢▢▢ **Premier Hotel** 66 Esplanade, South Cliff YO11 2UZ ☎01723 501062 FAX 01723 501062
Mar-Nov

Large Victorian property with fine views of the sea and coastline. The hotel has a very comfortable lounge and spacious dining room and several of the well equipped and nicely decorated bedrooms also have sea views. Many of the original features of the building have been retained, and their Victorian elegance is enhanced by

the friendly and relaxed atmosphere.
19 en suite (bth/shr) (2 fmly) No smoking in dining room CTV in all bedrooms Tea and coffee making facilities Licensed Lift Cen ht 6P Last d 6pm

PRICE GUIDE

ROOMS: s £30-£34; d £54-£58; wkly b&b £175-£189; wkly hlf-bd £250-£264

CARDS: ▣ ▩ ⓔ

GH ▢▢▢ **The Ramleh** 135 Queens Pde YO12 7HY (from A64 left at Station and at traffic lights left then 2nd right and 1st left) ☎01723 365745
Mar-Oct

This friendly family run establishment forms part of a terraced row overlooking the North Bay close to Peasholm Park. The comfortable residents' lounge has recently been refurbished, and further improvements are planned for the front facing dining room and bar. Bedrooms are also gradually being upgraded to offer comfortable modern standards.
9 rms (1 bth 6 shr) (4 fmly) No smoking in dining room CTV in all bedrooms Tea and coffee making facilities No dogs (ex guide dogs) Licensed Cen ht CTV 5P Last d 2pm

PRICE GUIDE

ROOMS: s £15-£21; d £30-£38; wkly b&b £98-£105; wkly hlf-bd £133-£161✱

CARDS: ▣ ▩ ⓔ

GH ▢▢ **Rayvil Hotel** 133 Queens Pde YO12 7HU
☎01723 364901
Closed Xmas & New Year rs Jan-Mar & Oct-Dec

A fresh, bright and very clean establishment situated in a prominent location overlooking the North Bay. Bedrooms are compact, but all have colour television and two have modern en-suite shower rooms. The comfortable guests' lounge has splendid sea views, there is an attractively appointed dining room, a small bar and a private car park at the front of the hotel.
9 rms (2 shr) (2 fmly) No smoking in dining room CTV in all bedrooms Tea and coffee making facilities No dogs (ex guide dogs) Licensed Cen ht CTV No children 4yrs 8P No coaches Last d 1pm

PRICE GUIDE

ROOMS: (incl. dinner) s £21-£23; d £42-£46; wkly b&b £112-£122.50; wkly hlf-bd £147-£161

CARDS: ▣ ▩ ⓔ

GH ▢▢▢ *Riviera Hotel* St Nicholas Cliff YO11 2ES
☎01723 372277

This charmingly elegant hotel occupies a prime position close to the south beach and the town centre. The lounges reflect not only contemporary styles, but also the elegance of the Victorian era to which the building belongs. Public rooms and half of the bedrooms have recently been extensively modernised and re-furbished. Five course evening meals are served in the attractive dining room with its tented ceiling.
20 en suite (bth/shr) (3 fmly) CTV in all bedrooms Tea and coffee making facilities Direct dial from bedrooms No dogs (ex guide dogs) Licensed Lift Cen ht No parking No coaches Last d 7pm

CARDS: ▣ ▩

GH ▢▢ **Sefton Hotel** 18 Prince of Wales Ter YO11 2AL
☎01723 372310
Mar-Oct

A traditional guest house overlooking attractive gardens on the North Cliff offers comfortable bedrooms and spacious public rooms. There is a lift between floors and service is friendly and attentive.
14 rms (8 bth) No smoking in 8 bedrooms No smoking in dining room No smoking in 1 lounge No dogs (ex guide dogs) Licensed ➡

Lift Cen ht CTV No children 12yrs No coaches Last d 6pm
PRICE GUIDE
ROOMS: (incl. dinner) s £23-£24; d £46-£48; wkly b&b £140-£147; wkly hlf-bd £161-£168✳

 GH 🅀🅀 West Lodge Private Hotel 38 West St, South Cliff YO11 2QP (close to Italian Gardens) ☎01723 500754
Situated close to the South Cliff, this Victorian house offers adequate accommodation in bedrooms which are, for the most part, fairly spacious. There is a good lounge, and home-cooked dinners are available in the attractively appointed dining room, which also incorporates a small bar.
7 rms (3 shr) (4 fmly) No smoking in dining room CTV in all bedrooms Tea and coffee making facilities Licensed Cen ht CTV Garden swing Last d 10am
PRICE GUIDE
ROOMS: s £14-£17; d £28-£34; wkly b&b £98-£119; wkly hlf-bd £133-£154
CARDS: 🆇 🆇 🆇 🆇

GH 🅀🅀🅀 The Whiteley Hotel 99/101 Queens Pde YO12 7HY (follow signs North Bay) ☎01723 373514
Feb-Oct
Superb views are enjoyed from this family-run establishment overlooking North Bay. The bedrooms are prettily decorated and furnished along modern lines, and the lounges are comfortable and inviting.
12 rms (10 shr) (3 fmly) No smoking in dining room No smoking in 1 lounge CTV in all bedrooms Tea and coffee making facilities Licensed Cen ht CTV 10P No coaches Last d 2pm
PRICE GUIDE
ROOMS: s £16-£17; d £38-£40; wkly b&b £130-£135; wkly hlf-bd £170-£175✳
CARDS: 🆇 🆇

 ❤ 🅀🅀 Mrs M A Edmondson Plane Tree Cottage Farm (SE999984) Staintondale YO13 0EY (7m N) ☎01723 870796
May-Oct
Plane Tree Farm is off the beaten track, near the scattered hamlet of Staintondale about eight miles north of Scarborough. Near the coast and on the edge of the moors, it offers the friendly atmosphere of a typical Yorkshire farmhouse. There are two guest rooms and a cosy lounge, and guests are welcomed by the friendly sheep dog, the cat and, of course, Mrs Edmondson the owner.
2 rms Tea and coffee making facilities No dogs Cen ht CTV No children 2P 60 acres rare breed sheep pigs hens Last d am
PRICE GUIDE
ROOMS: s £16; d £32; wkly b&b £105; wkly hlf-bd £155

◀ 🅀🅀🅀 Pickwick Huntriss Row YO11 2ED
☎01723 375787 FAX 01723 374284
Closed 25 Dec
The Pickwick Inn is a listed building situated in the centre of town close to all amenities. The bedrooms are modern and well appointed, and some have four-poster beds. The inn has no restaurant (though there are plenty in the vicinity) but there is an attractive first-floor breakfast room, and snacks are served in the bars at lunch time. A lift is available to all floors.
10 en suite (bth/shr) CTV in all bedrooms Tea and coffee making facilities Direct dial from bedrooms No dogs (ex guide dogs) Lift Cen ht No children 10yrs No coaches
PRICE GUIDE
ROOMS: s £22.50-£32; d £35-£55; wkly b&b £105-£135
MEALS: Bar Lunch £1.75-£3.50
CARDS: 🆇 🆇 🆇 🆇

SCILLY, ISLES OF Map 02

ST MARY'S Map 02

 Selected

GH 🅀🅀🅀🅀 Carnwethers Country House Carnwethers, Pelistry Bay TR21 0NX ☎01720 422415
30 Apr-2 Oct
This fine guest house is located on the far side of Saint Mary's from the quay in a secluded location; it is advisable to ask for directions. Roy and Joyce Graham take pains to make sure their guests are well looked after; their beautiful gardens have won the Scilly in Bloom competition and a croquet lawn and swimming pool help ensure guests spend a lot of time outdoors. Indoors are well presented bedrooms, a comfortable lounge and a smart dining room.
9 rms (8 bth/shr) 1 annexe en suite (bth/shr) (2 fmly) No smoking CTV in all bedrooms Tea and coffee making facilities Licensed Cen ht CTV No children 7yrs 4P No coaches Outdoor swimming pool (heated) Sauna Pool table Table tennis Last d 6.30pm
PRICE GUIDE
ROOMS: (incl. dinner) s £40-£55; d £76-£94; wkly hlf-bd £210-£315

Selected

GH 🅀🅀🅀🅀 Crebinick House Church St TR21 0JT ☎01720 422968
30 Mar-26 Oct Closed 1-26 Oct rs B&B only
This 18th century house is located in Hugh Town, the "capital" of these lovely islands, and retains many period features. The bright modern bedrooms feature stylish en suite shower rooms with fluffy towels and toiletries, and the work of local artists. The fresh dining room is pretty with lace tablecloths and Portmerion crockery; Mrs Jones cooks traditional dishes and is happy to cater to any dietary needs given notice. The house is no smoking throughout.
6 en suite (shr) No smoking Tea and coffee making facilities No dogs Licensed Cen ht CTV No children 7yrs No parking No coaches Last d 9.30am
PRICE GUIDE
ROOMS: (incl. dinner) d £33.50-£38.50; wkly b&b £168-£210; wkly hlf-bd £234.50-£269.50

SCOTCH CORNER North Yorkshire Map 08 NZ20

Selected

◀ 🅀🅀🅀🅀 Vintage Hotel DL10 6NP (leave A1 at Scotch Corner and take A66 towards Penrith, hotel is 200yds on left) ☎01748 824424 & 822961
Closed 25 Dec & 1 Jan rs Nov-Mar
This friendly roadside hotel is situated on the A66 near the junction with the A1 at Scotch Corner. Bedrooms are modern and well equipped, while the bar and restaurant offer an extensive range of food.
8 rms (5 bth/shr) No smoking in dining room CTV in all bedrooms Tea and coffee making facilities Direct dial from

bedrooms No dogs (ex guide dogs) Cen ht CTV 50P Last
d 9.15pm
PRICE GUIDE
ROOMS: s £23.50-£32.50; d £36.50-£39.50✳
MEALS: Lunch £10.45-£11.75 Dinner £12.50-£20.65alc✳
CARDS: (£)

SEAFORD East Sussex Map **05** TV49

Selected

GH Ⓠ Ⓠ Ⓠ Ⓠ **Avondale Hotel** Avondale Rd BN25 1RJ
(on A259 edge of town)
☎01323 890008 FAX 01323 490598
Very comfortable and well run, this welcoming family hotel
fronted by a terrace and flower garden stands on flat ground
within easy walking distance of the town centre.
Accommodation - which is now entirely non-smoking - has
been extensively upgraded over the years to provide
bedrooms equipped with every modern amenity. Service of all
meals is provided seven days a week in the pleasant
lounge/dining room, and light refreshments can be obtained
throughout the day; room service is also available. Street
parking is unrestricted.
16 rms (9 shr) (6 fmly) No smoking CTV in all bedrooms
Tea and coffee making facilities Direct dial from bedrooms
No dogs (ex guide dogs) Lift Cen ht CTV No coaches Last
d 12.30pm
PRICE GUIDE
ROOMS: s £18-£20; d £37-£39.50; wkly b&b £126-£135;
wkly hlf-bd £168-£180✳
CARDS:

🛏️ ☎ GH Ⓠ Ⓠ **Silverdale** 21 Sutton Park Rd BN25 1RH (on
A259 in the centre of Seaford, close to War Memorial)
☎01323 491849 FAX 01323 891131
Ideally located close to the town centre and only ten minutes'
drive from the ferry port at Newhaven, this personally run and
very friendly licensed guest house offers a good range of
bedrooms, a cosy lounge and a combined bar and breakfast room.
Meals (which are available by request) include vegetarian and
home-made dishes and are accompanied by a good selection of
wines.
4 rms (2 bth/shr) (3 fmly) No smoking in 2 bedrooms No
smoking in area of dining room No smoking in lounges CTV in
all bedrooms Tea and coffee making facilities Direct dial from
bedrooms No dogs (ex guide dogs) Licensed Cen ht CTV 4P
No coaches Last d 9pm
PRICE GUIDE
ROOMS: s £13-£25; d £25-£40; wkly b&b £90-£140; wkly hlf-
bd £130-£180
CARDS: (£)

SEATON Devon Map **03** SY29

Selected

GH Ⓠ Ⓠ Ⓠ Ⓠ **Boshill House** Boshill Cross, Axmouth
EX12 4BL (left off A358 onto A3052 (Lyme Regis and
Sidmouth) for house on right) ☎01297 553201
An attractive stone built house in grounds of five acres, with
stunning views across the Axe valley. Ideally situated for
Lyme Regis, Sidmouth, the coast and country villages.
Bedrooms are spacious, well equipped with modern facilities
and each has its own sitting area. Mrs Silvester has provided

some thoughtful touches.
3 en suite (bth/shr) (2 fmly) No smoking CTV in all
bedrooms Tea and coffee making facilities Direct dial from
bedrooms Cen ht CTV 10P No coaches Outdoor
swimming pool
PRICE GUIDE
ROOMS: d £32-£40; wkly b&b £112-£142✳ (£)

GH Ⓠ Ⓠ Ⓠ **Mariners Hotel** Esplanade EX12 2NP
☎01297 20560
This small, private hotel, personally run by the proprietors, has a
superb seafront position overlooking Lyme Bay. Bedrooms are all
en suite and a ground-floor room is available. There is a residents'
lounge and an additional spacious sun lounge, and a varied choice
of menu is offered at dinner.
10 en suite (bth/shr) (1 fmly) No smoking in dining room CTV
in all bedrooms Tea and coffee making facilities Licensed Cen ht
CTV 10P No coaches Last d 6pm
PRICE GUIDE
ROOMS: s £24-£28; d £42; wkly b&b £118-£131.75; wkly hlf-
bd £188-£210.75
CARDS:

SEAVIEW See **WIGHT, ISLE OF**

SEDBERGH Cumbria Map **07** SD69

GH Ⓠ Ⓠ **Cross Keys Hotel** LA10 5NE (4m from Sedbergh on
A683) ☎015396 20284
Closed 7 Jan-20 Mar
Situated on the A638 four miles north of Sedbergh, this National
Trust property dates in part from the 16th century and features
low beamed ceilings, flagstone floors, mullioned windows and
a spiral stone staircase. Open fires burn in both the dining room
and lounge in cooler weather and there is also a small sun
lounge which offers fine views of the valley, nearby fells and
the Cautley Spout waterfall. Bedrooms are modest but full of
character.
5 rms (1 bth/shr) No smoking Tea and coffee making facilities
No dogs (ex guide dogs) Cen ht 9P No coaches Riding Last d
24hr notice
PRICE GUIDE
ROOMS: s £25; d £50-£60; wkly b&b £175-£2100; wkly hlf-bd
£301-£336✳ (£)

SEDGEFIELD Co Durham Map **08** NZ32

🍴 Ⓠ Ⓠ Ⓠ *Dun Cow* High St TS21 3AT ☎01740 20894
This is a popular town-centre pub with a long history. The bars are
attractive and the food has a good reputation. Bedrooms are
comfortable and well furnished, many with exposed beams.
6 rms CTV in all bedrooms Tea and coffee making facilities
Direct dial from bedrooms Cen ht 25P Last d 10pm
CARDS:

SELBY North Yorkshire Map **08** SE63

GH Ⓠ **Hazeldene** 32-34 Brook St, Doncaster Rd YO8 0AR (off
A19 south of town centre)
☎01757 704809 FAX 01757 709300
Closed Xmas wk
Accommodation in traditional style is offered at this Victorian
villa which stands on the A19 just south of the town. Friendly
service is provided by Mr and Mrs Leake, the resident owners.
7 rms (1 shr) (2 fmly) No smoking CTV in all bedrooms Tea ➡

and coffee making facilities No dogs No children 2yrs 5P No coaches
PRICE GUIDE
ROOMS: s £16-£18; d £29-£36✶

SELSEY West Sussex Map **04** SZ89

Selected

GH Q Q Q Q St Andrews Lodge Chichester Rd PO20 0LX (on right past Police Station)
☎01243 606899 FAX 01243 606899
Closed Xmas
This comfortable and well run private hotel has recently been completely renovated and refurbished. Bedrooms are non-smoking and well equipped with remote control satellite TV and tea trays, and furnished in a comfortable modern style. There are a pleasant breakfast room, a bar lounge and small conservatory, and dinner can be provided with prior arrangement. Smoking is only permitted in the bar area, and there is ample forecourt parking.
5 en suite (bth/shr) 1 annexe en suite (shr) (2 fmly) No smoking in bedrooms No smoking in dining room No smoking in lounges CTV in all bedrooms Tea and coffee making facilities Licensed Cen ht CTV 15P Last d 1pm
PRICE GUIDE
ROOMS: s £20-£40; d £36-£50; wkly b&b £126-£175; wkly hlf-bd £185-£234.50✶
CARDS: ▆▆ ▆▆

SEMLEY Wiltshire Map **03** ST82

◀ Q Q **Benett Arms** SP7 9AS (on village green, opposite church) ☎01747 830221 FAX 01747 830152
Closed 25 & 26 Dec
This country inn, situated in a picturesque village between Tisbury and East Knoyle, is personally run by resident proprietor Joseph Duthie. The well equipped bedrooms are simply furnished and comfortable; three rooms are located in a rear annexe on ground-floor level. The friendly informal bar is split-level, with an open fire in the bar area. An extensive range of bar meals and a more formal restaurant is available.
2 en suite (bth/shr) 3 annexe en suite (shr) CTV in all bedrooms Tea and coffee making facilities Direct dial from bedrooms Cen ht ch fac 30P Last d 9.45pm
PRICE GUIDE
ROOMS: s £30; d £46✶
MEALS: Lunch £12.50-£19.50alc Dinner £12.50-£19.50alc✶
CARDS: ▆ ▆▆ ▆▆ ▆

SENNEN Cornwall & Isles of Scilly Map **02** SW32

GH Q Q *The Old Manor Hotel* TR19 7AD (on A30, opposite St Sennens Church) ☎01736 871280 FAX 01736 871280
Closed 23-28 Dec
A friendly guesthouse offering comfortable bedrooms, some with private shower, and all with open views. There is a separate TV lounge/library with a video, and outside guests have the use of the walled garden and putting green. A wide choice of meals is available all day, ranging from snacks and quick orders to set-price menus featuring locally caught fish; Cornish cream teas are served in the garden. Holiday cottages are also available to rent.
8 rms (5 shr) (3 fmly) No smoking in 1 bedrooms CTV in 7 bedrooms Tea and coffee making facilities Direct dial from bedrooms No dogs Licensed Cen ht CTV 50P No coaches putting green Last d 5.30pm
CARDS: ▆ ▆▆ ▆▆

GH Q Q Sunny Bank Hotel Sea View Hill TR19 7AR (on A30, 8m W of Penzance just after sign for Sennen)
☎01736 871278
Closed Dec
This large, detached house stands in acres of gardens on the outskirts of the town. Part of the gardens are maintained in a natural state and are home to many kinds of birds as well as squirrels and badgers. There are two lounges and bedrooms vary in size and decor. Hospitality and good food are provided by the owners, Ralph and Valerie Comber.
11 rms (2 fmly) Tea and coffee making facilities No dogs (ex guide dogs) Licensed Cen ht CTV 12P No coaches Last d 7pm
PRICE GUIDE
ROOMS: s £14-£15; d £28-£34; wkly b&b £98-£119; wkly hlf-bd £125-£144✶

SETTLE North Yorkshire Map **07** SD86

GH Q Q Liverpool House Chapel Square BD24 9HR (turn off B6480 by side of police station (Chapel Street) and take 2nd turning on right) ☎01729 822247
Closed 1-21 Jan
A mid 18th-century property, this was once the gatehouse for the Leeds-Liverpool Canal. The house is well maintained, pleasantly furnished and filled with interesting Victoriana, and there is a tea shop on the ground floor. Guests should note that this is a no-smoking establishment.
7 rms No smoking Tea and coffee making facilities No dogs Licensed CTV No children 12yrs 8P No coaches Last d 10am
PRICE GUIDE
ROOMS: s £17.50; d £35; wkly b&b £122.50; wkly hlf-bd £210
CARDS: ▆ ▆▆ ▆▆

GH Q Q The Oast Guest House 5 Pen-y-Ghent View, Church St BD24 9JJ ☎01729 822989
Situated on the edge of the town with views of the surrounding peaks, this family-run guest house offers pleasantly furnished accommodation. There are a delightful lounge and a cosy dining room providing good home cooking.
6 rms (3 bth/shr) No smoking in bedrooms CTV in 5 bedrooms Tea and coffee making facilities No dogs (ex guide dogs) Licensed Cen ht CTV No children 5yrs 4P No coaches Last d noon
PRICE GUIDE
ROOMS: s £14.50-£15.50; d £35-£40; wkly b&b £122.50-£140; wkly hlf-bd £157.50-£185.85✶

GH Q Q *Whitefriars Country Guesthouse* Church St BD24 9JD ☎01729 823753
Closed Xmas Day
Standing its own gardens and yet close to the town centre, this charming house dating back to the 17th century offers bedrooms in traditional style together with a comfortable lounge. There are many original features, including beams and a marble fireplace. The house is fully non-smoking and there is adequate car parking available.
9 rms (3 shr) (3 fmly) CTV in 3 bedrooms Tea and coffee making facilities No dogs (ex guide dogs) Licensed Cen ht CTV 9P No coaches Last d 5pm

◀ Q Q **Golden Lion** 5 Duke St BD24 9DU (in town centre opposite Barclays Bank) ☎01729 822203
rs 25 Dec
The Golden Lion is a town-centre establishment offering an extensive range of well produced food in both the restaurant or the bar, along with some good real ales. The hotel is family run and

constantly being improved. There are plans to install more en suite facilities soon.
11 rms (1 shr) CTV in 1 bedroom Tea and coffee making facilities No dogs (ex guide dogs) Cen ht CTV 11P Last d 10pm
PRICE GUIDE
ROOMS: s £20-£25.75; d £40-£50.50
MEALS: Lunch £8.95 Dinner £12-£16
CARDS: 🔲 🔲

SEVENOAKS Kent

See **Wrotham**

SHAFTESBURY Dorset

See **Tollard Royal**

SHALDON Devon

See **Teignmouth**

SHANKLIN See **WIGHT, ISLE OF**

SHAP Cumbria Map **12** NY51

GH ㉯㉯㉯ *Brookfield* CA10 3PZ (junct 39 of M6)
☎01931 716397
Closed 21 Dec-Jan
Set in pleasant gardens on the A6 to the south of the village, this friendly guest house offers comfortably furnished bedrooms which are spacious and freshly decorated. Downstairs there are an inviting lounge and a very attractive dining room where home-cooked evening meals are served. A small bar adjoins the dining room, and there is ample private car parking.
6 rms (3 fmly) CTV in all bedrooms Tea and coffee making facilities No dogs Licensed Cen ht CTV 36P No coaches Last d 8.15pm

🔲🔲 💗🔲 E & S Hodgson **Green Farm** *(NY565143)*
CA10 3PW (on A6 in Shap village) ☎01931 716619
Etr-Sep
This traditional 18th-century Cumbrian farmhouse is situated on a working farm to the south of the town, set back from the A6. The three bedrooms are simply furnished, two with washbasins in the rooms and one with an adjacent bathroom. There is a cosy lounge and tables are set up for breakfast in another room. This friendly establishment has meadowland extending to the distant hills above.
3 rms (2 fmly) No smoking in bedrooms No smoking in dining room Tea and coffee making facilities No dogs CTV 4P 200 acres mixed
PRICE GUIDE
ROOMS: s £15; d £30-£30

SHEFFIELD South Yorkshire Map **08** SK38

GH ㉯㉯㉯ **Hunter House Hotel** 685 Ecclesall Rd, Hunters Bar S11 8TG (on A625 overlooking Endcliffe Park, 1m from City Centre) ☎0114 266 2709 FAX 0114 268 6370
This large hotel consists of three houses, one of which is the original Toll House, some 250 years old. Bedrooms are very well equipped, although some are a little compact. There is a bar, dining room and a comfortable lounge, making this a welcome addition to our guide.
23 rms (10 bth/shr) (9 fmly) No smoking in dining room CTV in all bedrooms Tea and coffee making facilities Direct dial from

bedrooms Licensed Cen ht 8P Last d 8.45pm
PRICE GUIDE
ROOMS: s £22.50-£37.95; d £34.95-£43.95; wkly b&b £155-£210; wkly hlf-bd £215-£270✱
CARDS: 🔲 🔲 🔲 🔲

GH ㉯㉯㉯ *Lindrick Hotel* 226 Chippinghouse Rd S7 1DR (1.5m from city centre)
☎0114 258 5041 FAX 0114 255 4758
Closed 24 Dec-first Sat in Jan
A small hotel in a quiet, tree-lined, residential area of Nether Edge, a short distance from the city centre. Friendly proprietors provide a warm welcome and high standards throughout. Bedrooms are pleasantly decorated, with the more compact, cheaper rooms being mostly on the second floor. Public rooms are inviting and include a small cosy bar and separate lounge. Breakfast, with its good selection of dishes, is the only meal served at weekends; a supper menu of home-made bar snacks is available Monday - Thursday. Smoking is not permitted in the breakfast room and lounge. There is both on-site and unlimited on-street parking.
23 rms (15 shr) (1 fmly) No smoking in dining room No smoking in 1 lounge CTV in all bedrooms Tea and coffee making facilities Direct dial from bedrooms Licensed Cen ht CTV 20P Last d 8.45pm
CARDS: 🔲 🔲 🔲 🔲   £

GH ㉯㉯㉯ **Millingtons** 70 Broomgrove Rd S10 2NA (off A625, signposted Castleton, Eccleshall Rd) ☎0114 266 9549
Millingtons is a small guest house set in a relatively quiet tree-lined road to the southwest of the city centre, convenient for the universities and the Hallamshire Hospital. Friendly proprietors offer a warm welcome and maintain good levels of housekeeping. Guests take breakfast at a communal table.

SNAKE PASS INN

Snake Pass, Bamford, Sheffield S30 2BJ
Telephone: (01433) 651480 ㉯㉯㉯

Built by the Duke of Devonshire as a coaching house in the 18th century, and set in the beautiful Ashopton Woodlands of the Peak District on the A57 Snake Pass Road. All seven bedrooms are en suite and have satellite TV, tea and coffee making facilities, and radio alarm clock. Ample car parking and ideal as a centre for the Peak District.

6 rms (3 bth/shr) No smoking in dining room CTV in all bedrooms Tea and coffee making facilities No dogs (ex guide dogs) Cen ht CTV No children 12yrs 4P No coaches
PRICE GUIDE
ROOMS: s £20-£27; d £33-£42✱

SHERBORNE Dorset Map **03** ST61

See also **Halstock.**

Selected

GH ◻◻◻◻ **The Alders** Sandford Orcas DT9 4SB (from town take B3148 towards Marston Magna, after 2.5m take signposted turning to Sandford Orcas. 1m after entering village turn left at T-junct) ☎01963 220666
This non-smoking property is set in the picturesque village of Sandford Orcas, three miles from Sherborne. It has been designed and built by the owners to create an old fashioned atmosphere, and is decorated with the owner's painting of local scenes. The en suite bedrooms are attractively appointed and overlook the garden, while the cosy lounge features a log fire. Traditional breakfasts are available.
2 en suite (bth/shr) No smoking CTV in all bedrooms Tea and coffee making facilities No dogs (ex guide dogs) Cen ht CTV 5P No coaches Arrangement with Sherborne Golf Club
PRICE GUIDE
ROOMS: s £18.50-£26; d £37-£42

Selected

GH ◻◻◻◻ **Pheasants Restaurant with Rooms** 24 Greenhill DT9 4EW (centre of town on A30) (Logis) ☎01935 815252 FAX 01935 815252
Closed 2 wks mid-Jan rs Sun & Mon
Six letting bedrooms are now available at this restaurant-with-rooms, an establishment already enjoying a good reputation for its food. The en suite rooms are well appointed with antique furnishings and co-ordinated fabrics. There is a comfortable lounge and private parking to the rear of the property.
6 rms (4 bth/shr) (2 fmly) No smoking in 3 bedrooms CTV in all bedrooms No dogs (ex guide dogs) Licensed Cen ht P No coaches Last d 10pm
PRICE GUIDE
ROOMS: s fr £37.50; d fr £55; wkly b&b fr £250; wkly hlf-bd fr £375✱
CARDS: ◼ ▆

Selected

GH ◻◻◻◻ **Wheatsheaf House** Corton Denham DT9 4LQ (from town take B3145 and follow sign for corton Denham. Fork right at sign for Blackford, house 200 yds beyond) ☎01963 220207 & 0378 017808
Closed Dec-20 Feb
This delightful property is situated on the edge of Corton Denham, just four miles from Sherborne. Set in eight acres of beautiful gardens, the house enjoys breathtaking views over the Dorset countryside. Bedrooms are spacious and comfortable, one being en suite whilst the other has private use of a bathroom.

2 rms (1 bth) No smoking in bedrooms CTV in 1 bedroom Tea and coffee making facilities Cen ht CTV 1P No coaches
PRICE GUIDE
ROOMS: s £16-£20; d £34-£45; wkly b&b £119-£130✱

Selected

♥ ◻◻◻◻ Mrs J Mayo **Almshouse Farm** *(ST651082)* Hermitage, Holnest DT9 6HA (take A352 Dorchester rd for 5m and at Holnest x-rds turn right signed Hermitage for farm 1.2m on left) ☎01963 210296
Closed Xmas & New Year
A former monastery, this farmhouse dates from the 16th century and is part of a 160-acre working dairy farm. The spacious bedrooms now offer modern en suite and private facilities and extras such as hairdryers, colour TVs, toiletries and sewing kits. Full English breakfast is served in the oldest part of the house, which has a magnificent inglenook fireplace with wood-burning stove, and there is also a comfortable residents' lounge. Guests are welcome to watch the milking and other farming activities.
3 en suite (bth/shr) (1 fmly) No smoking in dining room CTV in all bedrooms Tea and coffee making facilities No dogs (ex guide dogs) CTV 6P 160 acres dairy
PRICE GUIDE
ROOMS: d £37-£21✱

♥ ◻◻ Mrs P T Tizzard **Venn** *(ST684183)* Milborne Port DT9 5RA (on the A30 3m E of Sherborne, on edge of village of Milborne Port) ☎01963 250598
Neat, bright and well presented, this dairy farm stands beside the A30 only three miles from the famous abbey town. Pretty bedrooms now offer TV sets as well as tea-making facilities, and there are excellent views across the fields from the comfortable lounge where a log fire burns on cooler days; breakfast menus offer a lighter option as well as the traditional hearty meal. Cheerful hosts, a warm welcome and a relaxed atmosphere attract many guests back time and time again.
3 rms (1 fmly) No smoking in bedrooms No smoking in dining room No smoking in lounges CTV in all bedrooms Tea and coffee making facilities No dogs (ex guide dogs) Cen ht CTV P 375 acres dairy/beef
PRICE GUIDE
ROOMS: s fr £15; d fr £28✱

SHERIFF HUTTON North Yorkshire Map **08** SE66

GH ◻◻◻ **Rangers House** Sheriff Hutton Park YO6 1RH (off A64 between York and Malton signed Sherrif Flaxton/Sherrif Hutton and through Flaxton and West Lilling to T-junct where turn sharp right) ☎01347 878397 FAX 01347 878666
Standing next to the hall in Sheriff Hutton Park, this attractive and well furnished guest house was built in 1639 as a brewhouse and stable for the royal hunting lodge. Ample lounges are full of interesting items and service is friendly and helpful.
6 rms (2 bth 2 shr) (1 fmly) No smoking in area of dining room Tea and coffee making facilities No dogs Licensed Cen ht CTV 30P No coaches Multigym Last d 9.30pm
PRICE GUIDE
ROOMS: s £32; d £60-£64; wkly b&b 60p-£202; wkly hlf-bd £315-£345✱

SHERINGHAM Norfolk Map **09** TG14

Selected

GH ◻◻◻◻ **Fairlawns** 26 Hooks Hill Rd NR26 8NL
(from A149 turn inti Holt Rd opposite Police Station then
2nd left and at T-junct turn right)
☎01263 824717 FAX 01263 824717
Etr-Oct
This large Victorian house has been sympathetically
converted to provide fresh and inviting accommodation. Set in
its own spacious grounds, it is located in a quiet and secluded
residential cul-de-sac just a few minutes from the town centre.
The bedrooms are all of a comfortable size, with modern en
suite bathrooms, TV and tea trays. Mrs McGill is a charming
and enthusiastic hostess who prides herself on providing good
quality food, including Sunday 'brunch'.
5 en suite (bth/shr) No smoking in dining room CTV in all
bedrooms Tea and coffee making facilities No dogs (ex
guide dogs) Licensed Cen ht No children 12yrs 6P No
coaches Croquet Last d noon
PRICE GUIDE
ROOMS: d fr £40; wkly b&b fr £128✶
(£)

SHIFNAL Shropshire Map **07** SJ70

GH ◻◻◻ **Village Farm Lodge** Sheriffhales TF11 8RD (from
A5 turn onto the B4379 into the village of Sheriffhales and
pass sub-post office on left for the house in 100yds on left))
☎01952 462763 FAX 01952 677912
Former farm buildings have been converted into fine modern
accommodation at this pleasant little guest house which is located
in the hamlet of Sheriffhales, north of the town. Bedrooms include
some suitable for family use and several at ground-floor level,
some with external access from the car park. There are a pretty,
pine furnished, cottage-style dining room with individual tables,
and a cosy conservatory lounge.
8 en suite (shr) (3 fmly) No smoking in 4 bedrooms CTV in all
bedrooms Tea and coffee making facilities No dogs (ex guide
dogs) Licensed Cen ht CTV 12P No coaches
PRICE GUIDE
ROOMS: s £25-£28.50; d £35-£39
CARDS: ◼ ◼
(£)

SHILLINGFORD Devon Map **03** SS92

Selected

GH ◻◻◻◻ **The Old Mill** EX16 9BW (on B3227)
☎01398 331064
A carefully restored stone-built mill is set in pretty gardens by
a stream on the edge of the village. The spacious well
equipped bedrooms are furnished in pine, and two are
arranged in suites with private lounges. The lounge in the
main house is reserved for guests taking dinner. Proprietor Di
Burnell offers a set menu of home-cooked food with fresh
local vegetables; special dietary needs are provided for by
arrangement. The wine list features about 25 wines all very
reasonably priced. Smoking is not permitted.
2 en suite (bth/shr) 2 annexe en suite (shr) (2 fmly) No
smoking CTV in all bedrooms Tea and coffee making
facilities No dogs Licensed Cen ht CTV No children 5yrs

20P No coaches Fishing Last d noon
PRICE GUIDE
ROOMS: d £44-£52; wkly b&b £140-£161; wkly hlf-bd
£266-£287
(£)

SHIPBOURNE Kent Map **05** TQ55

Selected

◼ ◻◻◻◻ **The Chaser** Stumble Hill TN11 9PE (next to
church) ☎01732 810360 FAX 01732 810941
The front part of this imposing Victorian building is a rustic
inn, but to the rear there is a popular restaurant with a high,
vaulted ceiling. Here, freshly made dishes drawn from local
produce are served. The well equipped accommodation is
divided between the main building and the converted stable
block.
15 en suite (bth/shr) (1 fmly) CTV in all bedrooms Tea and
coffee making facilities Direct dial from bedrooms Cen ht
30P Last d 9.30pm
PRICE GUIDE
ROOMS: s fr £45; d fr £55✶
MEALS: Lunch fr £12.50 Dinner fr £19.95✶
CARDS: ◼ ◼ ◼
(£)

SHIPSTON ON STOUR Warwickshire Map **04** SP24

See also Lower Brailes

GH ◻◻◻ **The Manor** Main St, Long Compton CV36 5JJ
(centre of Long Compton village on A3400 50yds S of St
Peter & St Pauls church)
☎01608 684218 FAX 01608 684218
Closed 23 Dec-8 Jan
There is no shortage of space in the bedrooms and three lounges of
this large, rambling manor house, located in the centre of the
village of Long Compton. Dinner is served in the dining room,
guests choosing their meals earlier in the morning. The house
(which dates from 1524) is occasionally used for social functions.
5 en suite (bth/shr) (1 fmly) No smoking in dining room Tea and
coffee making facilities No dogs (ex guide dogs) Licensed Cen
ht CTV 8P
PRICE GUIDE
ROOMS: s £35; d £60; wkly b&b £210-£245; wkly hlf-bd £216-
£251✶
(£)

See advertisement on p.367.

SHOTTLE Derbyshire Map **08** SK34

Selected

GH ◻◻◻◻ **Shottle Hall** Shottle DE56 2EB (leave
A517 at crossroads with B5023, 200yds towards
Wirksworth then turn right & proceed for 0.5m)
☎01773 550276 & 550203 FAX 01773 550276
Closed Nov & Xmas
Guests are assured of a warm welcome at this large family
home. Surrounded by three acres of grounds and a large farm,
this is the ideal spot for a relaxing holiday.
7 rms (5 bth) 2 annexe en suite (bth) (3 fmly) No smoking
in bedrooms CTV in 3 bedrooms Tea and coffee making
➡

facilities Licensed Cen ht CTV 30P No coaches Last d
6pm
PRICE GUIDE
ROOMS: s £25-£35; d £44-£60

See advertisement under DERBY

Premier Selected

❤ ▢▢▢▢▢ Mrs J L Slack
Dannah (SK314502)
Bowmans Ln DE56 2DR (from
Belper A517 Ashbourne road
for approx 1.50m Hanging
Gate pub on right take next
right to Shottle continue 1m
to village over x-rds turn rt)
☎01773 550273 & 550630
FAX 01773 550590
Closed Xmas

Dannah Farm is part of Chatsworth Estate and is set in open
countryside amongst the rolling hills of Ecclesbourne Valley.
The Georgian Farmhouse has over recent years been
sympathetically converted into a really good hotel. The
bedrooms are housed in the connected barns, and furnished in
character with a mix of period pieces and country pines; all
are comfortably furnished, one with a canopied four poster,
another with a small sitting room on a split level and one
approached via a spiral staircase. The reception rooms are
connected by the kitchen and comprise a cosy restaurant and a
separate bar. Two more lounges are reserved purely for
residents.
8 rms (7 bth/shr) (1 fmly) No smoking in bedrooms No
smoking in dining room No smoking in 1 lounge CTV in all
bedrooms Tea and coffee making facilities No dogs (ex
guide dogs) Licensed Cen ht 20P 128 acres mixed Last d
6.15pm
PRICE GUIDE
ROOMS: s £35-£55; d £54-£75; wkly b&b £175-£250
CARDS: 🔲 🔲
See advertisement under DERBY

SHREWSBURY Shropshire Map **07** SJ41

Selected

GH ▢▢▢▢ Fieldside 38 London Rd SY2 6NX
☎01743 353143
Closed 18 Dec-18 Jan

Fieldside is a beautifully preserved and impeccably
maintained Victorian house close to the Shire Hall. It provides
tastefully decorated bedrooms with a good array of modern
equipment. There is an attractive breakfast room with period-
style furniture, and other facilities include a large rear garden
and a private car park. The whole house is no-smoking.
9 rms (6 shr) No smoking CTV in 7 bedrooms Tea and
coffee making facilities Direct dial from bedrooms No dogs
Cen ht No children 9yrs 12P No coaches
CARDS: 🔲 🔲 🔲

Selected

GH ▢▢▢▢ Mytton Hall Montford Bridge SY4 1EU
☎01743 850264
A very large house dating from 1790, Mytton Hall has been
extended at various times over the centuries. It is quietly
situated in its own extensive grounds on the edge of the
village of Mytton. There are three double rooms, two of
which are very spacious, and all have antique furnishings and
modern en suite facilities. Welcoming fires burn in both the
cosy sitting room and the lovely breakfast room, where guests
eat at a communal table.
3 en suite (bth) No dogs Cen ht CTV No children 14yrs P
No coaches Fishing

GH ▢▢ Restawhile 36 Coton Crescent SY1 2NZ
☎01743 240969
A cosy little guest house, Restawhile is situated just off the A528
Ellesmere road north of the town centre. Its four en suite
bedrooms have modern equipment, a comfortable residents'
lounge is provided and, although there is no car park, five lock-up
garages are available to guests.
4 en suite (bth/shr) No smoking in dining room CTV in all
bedrooms Tea and coffee making facilities Direct dial from
bedrooms No dogs Cen ht CTV No children 11yrs 5P No
coaches Last d 6pm
CARDS: 🔲 🔲 🔲

GH ▢▢▢ Roseville 12 Berwick Rd SY1 2LN (.75m north
and 80yds from junct with A528) ☎01743 236470
Closed 17 Dec-31 Jan
A superbly maintained late Victorian house, Roseville always
looks as if it has been freshly decorated. The three bedrooms are
attractively furnished in pine; two have en suite facilities and the
other a private bathroom. A comfortable residents' lounge is also
provided. Please note that only non-smokers are accommodated.
3 rms (2 shr) No smoking No dogs Cen ht CTV No children
12yrs 3P No coaches Last d noon
PRICE GUIDE
ROOMS: s £20-£22; d £40-£44; wkly b&b £135-£154; wkly hlf-
bd £190-£230✱

Selected

GH ▢▢▢▢ Sandford House Hotel St Julians Friars
SY1 1XL (cross River Severn over 'English Bridge' and
take first sharp left) ☎01743 343829
Ornate ceilings and walls are a feature of this delightful
Georgian townhouse situated near the English bridge over the
river, within easy walking distance of the town centre. Many
good walks are also available nearby. The bedrooms - most of
them spacious - are modern and freshly decorated, the
majority having en suite facilities.
11 rms (9 bth/shr) (3 fmly) No smoking in dining room
CTV in all bedrooms Tea and coffee making facilities
Licensed Cen ht CTV 3P No coaches
PRICE GUIDE
ROOMS: s £25-£33; d £39-£44.50✱
CARDS: 🔲 🔲 🔲

GH ⓠⓠⓠ **Sydney House Hotel** Coton Crescent, Coton Hill
SY1 2LJ (jct of A528/B5067) (Logis) ☎01743 354681 &
Freecall 0500 130243 FAX 01743 354681
Closed 25 Dec- 1 Jan
Modern accommodation is provided at this Edwardian house
situated north of the town centre and is easily seen from the
Ellesmere road. Bedrooms are equipped with every modern
facility, including telephones, TVs and hairdryers. There are an
attractively panelled lounge bar for residents and a large car park.
7 rms (4 shr) (1 fmly) No smoking in dining room No smoking
in lounges CTV in all bedrooms Tea and coffee making facilities
Direct dial from bedrooms No dogs (ex guide dogs) Licensed
Cen ht 7P No coaches Last d 8.30pm
PRICE GUIDE
ROOMS: s £34-£48; d £44-£63; wkly b&b £142.50-£205; wkly
hlf-bd £217.50-£280
CARDS: 🅽 ▬ ▬ £
See advertisement on p.369.

GH ⓠⓠⓠ **Tudor House** 2 Fish St SY1 1UR (enter town by
crossing English Bridge, ascend Wyle Cop after 50yds first
right) ☎01743 351735
Closed 23-26 Dec
Dating from 1460, this beautifully preserved house stands in the
town centre opposite St Alkmund's Church. The bedrooms are
traditionally furnished but have modern facilities and equipment.
The cosy lounge contains a small bar, and separate tables are
provided in the pleasant dining room. A warm welcome from Mair
Harris awaits all her guests, many of whom are regular visitors.
3 rms (2 shr) No smoking in 2 bedrooms No smoking in dining
room CTV in all bedrooms No dogs Licensed Cen ht CTV No ➡

Fieldside
38 London Road, Shrewsbury SY2 6NX
Tel: (01743) 353143

A lovely Victorian house with attractive
gardens. Centrally heated bedrooms have
shower en-suite, colour television, direct line
telephone and tea/coffee making facilities. The
hotel is situated 1½ miles from town centre of
Shrewsbury, famous for its floral displays,
ancient buildings and interesting museums.
Adjacent to Fieldside is St Giles church visited
by 'Brother Cadfel' the medieval sleuth in Ellis
Peters novels.
NON SMOKING
Enclosed parking. S.A.E. for details.
Resident proprietors: Pat & Ian Fraser

parking No coaches
PRICE GUIDE
ROOMS: s £25-£34; d £38-£46✱

♥ ◙◙◙ Mrs P A Roberts **The Day House** *(SJ465104)*
Nobold SY5 8NL (2.5m SW between A488 & A49)
☎01743 860212
Closed Xmas & New Year
The original part of this large house dates back to 1720; it was
enlarged in 1860, and the Gothic-style architecture is quite
impressive. Located on an arable farm and surrounded by
extensive mature gardens, the house is reached by a private lane
from the Longden road near the village of Nobold. Bedrooms,
which include family accommodation, are spacious, and there are
a comfortable lounge and an attractive antique-furnished breakfast
room.
3 en suite (bth/shr) (3 fmly) CTV in all bedrooms Tea and coffee
making facilities No dogs (ex guide dogs) Cen ht CTV 11P
Fishing Rough & game shooting 400 acres arable dairy
PRICE GUIDE
ROOMS: s fr £30; d £40-£46; wkly b&b fr £133✱

♥ ◙◙◙ Mrs J M Jones **Grove** *(SJ537249)* Preston Brockhurst
SY4 5QA (6m N on A49) ☎01939 220223
Closed 16 Dec-14 Jan
Dating back to the late 18th century, this timber-framed house
stands on a large, mainly arable farm in the village of Preston
Brockhurst, north of Shrewsbury. Well maintained
accommodation includes a single, a twin and a spacious family
room, all furnished with both modern and antique items. There is a
combined breakfast room and lounge, plus a second, more
spacious, sitting room. Guests are welcome to use the large
pleasant gardens. This is a no-smoking house.
3 rms (1 shr) (1 fmly) No smoking CTV in 1 bedroom Tea and
coffee making facilities No dogs (ex guide dogs) Cen ht CTV
6P 322 acres Arable Pigs
PRICE GUIDE
ROOMS: s £16.50; d £37✱

♥ ◙◙◙ Mrs C Yates **Upper Brompton** *(SJ548078)* Cross
Houses SY5 6LE (from town take A452 to Cross Houses and
turn first left after Fox public house, past houses and down
lane for 0.5m) ☎01743 761629
This delightful Georgian farmhouse is set in pretty gardens and
surrounded by 300 acres of arable farmland. Three bedrooms, all
of which are en suite, are offered, one of them also having four-
poster beds. Christine Yates enjoys welcoming visitors to her
home and serves up hearty breakfasts and fresh home-cooking in
the evenings. There is a comfortable lounge with an open fire in
cooler weather, and the house is non-smoking throughout. The
farm is signed off the A458 at the village of Cross Houses, south
east of the town.
3 en suite (bth/shr) (1 fmly) No smoking CTV in all bedrooms
Tea and coffee making facilities ch fac 20P 315 acres arable
Last d 10am

SIDMOUTH Devon Map **03** SY18

See also Harpford

GH ◙◙◙◙◙ **Broad Oak**
Sid Rd EX10 8QP (from
A3052) ☎01395 513713
Closed Dec & Jan
Situated in a quiet residential
area close to the town centre
and seafront, this pleasant
hotel has its own car parking
to the rear. The well equipped
bedrooms are individually
appointed and are provided
with thoughtful extras; two
rooms have en suite facilities and the single has its own
bathroom. Public areas include a comfortable sitting room
(shared with the owners) and an attractive dining room which
serves a good choice of English and Continental breakfasts.
3 rms (2 shr) No smoking CTV in all bedrooms Tea and
coffee making facilities No dogs (ex guide dogs) Cen ht No
children 4P
PRICE GUIDE
ROOMS: s £20; d £46-£50; wkly b&b £144.90-£157.50✱

 GH ◙◙◙ **Canterbury** Salcombe Rd EX10 8PR
(200yds from central Sidmouth, next to River Sid hump back
bridge) ☎01395 513373
Mar-Nov
Small and homely, this is a well-maintained guest house.
Bedrooms vary in size but are reasonably equipped, all with en
suite facilities. Public rooms are small yet comfortable with a set
price menu available at dinner. Parking is limited.
8 rms (7 bth/shr) (4 fmly) CTV in all bedrooms Tea and coffee
making facilities Licensed CTV 6P No coaches Last d 4.30pm
PRICE GUIDE
ROOMS: s £15.50-£18.50; d £31-£37; wkly b&b £102-£122;
wkly hlf-bd £154-£174
CARDS: ▨ ▆ ▆ ◉ ▨

GH ◙◙◙ **Kinellan Lodge** 5 Fortfield Place, Station Rd
EX10 8NX ☎01395 514442
Janet and Michael Allen welcome guests to their gabled, semidetached No Smoking family home which is situated a short level
walk from the sea front and town centre. There is a comfortable
lounge and the bedrooms have been equipped with modern
facilities. Breakfast is served in an attractive dining room where
dinner is available by arrangement.
6 en suite (shr) No smoking CTV in all bedrooms Tea and coffee
making facilities No dogs Cen ht Last d noon
PRICE GUIDE
ROOMS: s £17.50-£20; d £30-£35; wkly b&b £94.50-£110.25;
wkly hlf-bd £150-£166.25✱

GH ◙◙◙ **Mariners** 69 Sidford High St EX10 9SH (exit M5
at junct 30 and take B3052) ☎01395 515876
A delightful Victorian residence stands in an acre of well kept
gardens in the village of Sidford, just a mile from Sidmouth. The
atmosphere is friendly and the bedrooms have been equipped with
modern comforts. The guest lounge is comfortable and the
attractive dining room serves tasty breakfasts and dinners.
7 en suite (shr) (1 fmly) No smoking in bedrooms No smoking
in dining room CTV in all bedrooms Tea and coffee making

facilities No dogs Cen ht CTV No children 7yrs 10P No coaches
PRICE GUIDE
ROOMS: s £17-£19; d £34-£38; wkly b&b £133.05-£125.35; wkly hlf-bd £166.25-£179.55

Selected

GH [Q][Q][Q][Q] **Number Four** 4 Fortfield Place, Station Rd
EX10 8NX (leave A3052 towards Sidmouth for approx
2 m house on right just before Fortfield Hotel)
☎01395 578733
Closed 24 Dec-1 Jan
Christine and Ernie Barnes extend a warm welcome to their
Victorian semi-detached family home with it's pretty enclosed
gardens. The sea-front and town centre are just a short level
walk away and the beautiful countryside of East Devon is
easily accessible. Three en-suite bedrooms have been
tastefully decorated and equipped with modern comforts.
Breakfast is served in an airy dining room and secure parking
is available at the rear.
3 en suite (bth/shr) No smoking CTV in all bedrooms Cen
ht 3P No coaches
PRICE GUIDE
ROOMS: d £28-£35; wkly b&b £90-£112

GH [Q][Q][Q] **The Old Farmhouse** Hillside Rd EX10 8JG
☎01395 512284
Closed Dec & Jan
This delightful thatched 16th-century farmhouse is in a residential
area, within easy walking distance of the sea and shops.
Bedrooms, some in a small cottage across the patio, are decorated
with pretty floral papers and soft furnishings. The lounge and
dining room are full of character with exposed beams and original
fireplaces. The dinner menu offers a choice at each course, and
features home-made soups and patés and lovely old-fashioned
puddings. Smoking is not permitted in the bedrooms or dining
room.
4 rms (1 bth) 4 annexe en suite (bth/shr) (2 fmly) No smoking in
bedrooms No smoking in dining room CTV in 3 bedrooms Tea
and coffee making facilities Licensed Cen ht CTV 4P No
coaches
PRICE GUIDE
ROOMS: s £17-£23; d £34-£46; wkly b&b £105-£138; wkly hlf-
bd £174-£208✳
CARDS: 🔲 🔲

GH [Q][Q] *Ryton House* 52-54 Winslade Rd EX10 9EX
☎01395 513981
Feb-Oct
Set in a quiet residential area about a mile from the seafront,
Ryton House offers bright bedrooms, some with en suite facilities.
There is a TV lounge and a licensed dining room where a
traditional set dinner is served.
9 rms (2 bth 4 shr) (4 fmly) No smoking in dining room No
smoking in lounges Tea and coffee making facilities Licensed
Cen ht CTV 9P Last d 4.30pm

SILECROFT Cumbria Map **06** SD18

◀ [Q][Q] **Miner's Arms** Main St LA18 5LP (from M6 follow
A590 singposted Barrow as far as Greenwood at which point
turn right and follow signs for A595 Whitehaven/Broughton.)
☎01229 772325 & 773397
This family run pub lies in the centre of the village and is popular
➡

for its food. There is a series of lounges including a cosy sug with log fire and one for non-smokers. Bedrooms vary in size but are cheerfully decorated and come with modern bathrooms. There is also a small residents sitting room upstairs.

4 en suite (bth/shr) No smoking in bedrooms No smoking in dining room Tea and coffee making facilities No dogs (ex guide dogs) Cen ht CTV 50P Last d 9.30pm

PRICE GUIDE

ROOMS: s £20-£25; d £32-£35

MEALS: Lunch £7-£15&alc Dinner £7-£15&alc

£

SILLOTH Cumbria Map **11** NY15

GH **Q Q Q** *Nith View* 1 Pine Ter CA5 4DT (on the sea front) ☎016973 31542

Nith View is a family-run licensed guesthouse, situated at the end of a terrace overlooking the Solway Firth. Bedrooms are comfortably furnished and most have en suite facilities. There is also a guests' lounge, a small bar and an attractive dining room. All groups are catered for and those playing golf on the nearby Championship Course will find it particularly convenient.

8 rms (5 shr) (4 fmly) No smoking in 2 bedrooms No smoking in area of dining room No smoking in 1 lounge CTV in 5 bedrooms Tea and coffee making facilities Licensed Cen ht CTV 9P

CARDS:

SILVERSTONE Northamptonshire Map **04** SP64

♥ **Q Q Q** Mr & Mrs Branch **Silverthorpe** *(SP661456)* Silverthorpe Farm, Abthorpe Rd NN12 8TW (off A43 for Silverstone Village) ☎01327 858020

This spacious modern bungalow, surrounded by a mushroom farm and five acres of pastureland on which sheep are grazed, is particularly handy for visitors to Silverstone motor racing circuit. Ample secure parking is available.

3 rms No smoking CTV in all bedrooms Tea and coffee making facilities 4P 5 acres mushroom

PRICE GUIDE

ROOMS: s fr £20; d fr £38✱

£

SITTINGBOURNE Kent Map **05** TQ96

Premier Selected

GH **Q Q Q Q Q**
Hempstead House London Rd, Bapchild ME9 9PP (on A2, 1.5m E opposite turning to Tonge) ☎01795 428020 FAX 01795 428020

Surrounded by beautiful countryside, this Victorian family house stands in three acres of gardens that include a kitchen garden. The Holdstock family treat guests as friends and invite them to dine with the family, or privately if they so wish. Large bedrooms include dressing areas. There is a large drawing room leading into a conservatory, a smaller sitting room and a dining room. Breakfast is served in the huge kitchen.

7 en suite (bth/shr) (1 fmly) No smoking in bedrooms No smoking in area of dining room No smoking in 1 lounge CTV in all bedrooms Tea and coffee making facilities Direct

dial from bedrooms Licensed Cen ht CTV ch fac 100P Outdoor swimming pool (heated) Play area Croquet Pitch & putt Last d 10m

PRICE GUIDE

ROOMS: s £55; d £62; wkly b&b £173.60-£195.30; wkly hlf-bd £271.60-£305.55

CARDS:

Selected

♥ **Q Q Q Q** Mrs Y P Carter **Saywell Farmhouse** *(TQ874575)* Bedmonton, Wormshill ME9 0EH (take B2163 S from Sittingbourne after approx 5m turn E onto unclassified road towards Wormshill) ☎01622 884444 Closed Xmas

Dating back in part to the 13th century, this property stands in a quiet, rural area, though convenient for major roads. The bedrooms are attractive and the house has a congenial feeling about it. Mrs Carter's home-cooked meals are much appreciated by her guests. This is a no-smoking house.

3 en suite (bth/shr) No smoking CTV in all bedrooms Tea and coffee making facilities No dogs Cen ht No children 12yrs 6P 5 acres

PRICE GUIDE

ROOMS: s £25-£35; wkly b&b £175-£245; wkly hlf-bd £290.50-£360.50✱

£

SKEGNESS Lincolnshire Map **09** TF56

GH **Q Q Q** *Crawford Hotel* South Pde PE25 3HR ☎01754 764215

A very respectable and reliable small hotel which has consistently offered comfortable accommodation and good facilities and amenities to their holidaying guests. High standards of cleanliness, maintenance and a lovely warm atmosphere are the keywords here.

20 rms (10 bth 7 shr) (8 fmly) CTV in all bedrooms Tea and coffee making facilities No dogs Licensed Lift Cen ht CTV No parking Indoor swimming pool (heated) Sauna jacuzzi games room Last d 5pm

CARDS:

GH **Q Q Q** *Northdale* 12 Firbeck Av PE25 3JY ☎01754 610554

This small and friendly hotel is set in a quiet side road near all the town's attractions. Bright modern bedrooms are provided, a separate bar lounge and comfortable no-smoking lounge are available, and a choice of menus is available in the pleasant dining room.

12 rms (2 bth 7 shr) (3 fmly) No smoking in dining room No smoking in lounges CTV in 8 bedrooms Tea and coffee making facilities Licensed Cen ht CTV 8P Last d 5.30pm

---

SKIPTON North Yorkshire Map **07** SD95

⊨ ▼ **GH** **Q Q** *Craven House* 56 Keighley Rd BD23 2NB ☎01756 794657 Closed 25 Dec-3 Jan

This double-fronted Victorian house stands beside the A629 Keighley road only a short walk from the town centre. Family owned and run, it provides good all-round standards of accommodation and service; individually furnished bedrooms offer good facilities, and there is an attractive breakfast room.

7 rms (2 bth 1 shr) No smoking in dining room CTV in all

bedrooms Tea and coffee making facilities Cen ht 3P
PRICE GUIDE
ROOMS: s £16-£24; d £30-£38
CARDS: £

GH Ⓠ Ⓠ Ⓠ **Highfield Hotel** 58 Keighley Rd BD23 2NB (on A629 heading towards Keighley, 0.25m from town centre)
☎01756 793182
Closed 23-27 Dec & 3-20 Jan rs New Years Eve
An attractive Victorian house on a corner site offers pleasantly furnished bedrooms with good facilities and a comfortable bar lounge and dining room; resident owners provide friendly service.
10 rms (3 bth 6 shr) (2 fmly) No smoking in dining room CTV in all bedrooms Tea and coffee making facilities Licensed Cen ht CTV No parking No coaches Last d 8pm
PRICE GUIDE
ROOMS: s £19.50-£28; d £37-£39✱
CARDS: £

◀ Ⓠ Ⓠ **Red Lion Hotel** High St BD23 1DT (WB)
☎01756 790718
Situated in the High Street, this pleasant old inn is said to be the oldest in Skipton and dates back to 1205. The bedrooms are comfortably furnished and well equipped. The bars have been refurbished and are spacious and full of charm and character; home-made bar meals are served at lunchtime.
3 en suite (bth/shr) (2 fmly) CTV in all bedrooms Tea and coffee making facilities No dogs Cen ht 4P Last d 7.30pm
PRICE GUIDE
ROOMS: s fr £25; d fr £35
MEALS: Lunch fr £3.95 Dinner £2.95-£5.95
CARDS: £

SLAIDBURN Lancashire Map **07** SD75

Premier Selected

GH Ⓠ Ⓠ Ⓠ Ⓠ Ⓠ **Parrock Head Farm House Hotel**
Woodhouse Ln BB7 3AH (1m NW, up Back Lane to Newton on left)
☎01200 446614
FAX 01200 446313
Picturesquely surrounded by sheep and rolling countryside, this very comfortable seventeenth-century farmhouse stands in

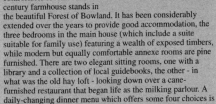

the beautiful Forest of Bowland. It has been considerably extended over the years to provide good accommodation, the three bedrooms in the main house (which include a suite suitable for family use) featuring a wealth of exposed timbers, while modern but equally comfortable annexe rooms are pine furnished. There are two elegant sitting rooms, one with a library and a collection of local guidebooks, the other - in what was the old hay loft - looking down over a cane-furnished restaurant that began life as the milking parlour. A daily-changing dinner menu which offers some four choices is made up of totally fresh and attractively presented dishes; a full lunch is served only on Sundays, though snacks are available on other days.
3 en suite (bth/shr) 4 annexe en suite (bth/shr) (1 fmly) No smoking in dining room No smoking in lounges CTV in all bedrooms Tea and coffee making facilities Direct dial from

bedrooms Licensed Cen ht ch fac 20P No coaches Last d 8.30pm
PRICE GUIDE
ROOMS: s £40-£44.50; d £60-£69
CARDS: £

SLEAFORD Lincolnshire Map **08** TF04

See also Aswarby

Selected

◀ Ⓠ Ⓠ Ⓠ Ⓠ *Carre Arms Hotel* Mareham Ln NG34 7JP
☎01529 303156 FAX 01529 303139
A large red brick building handy for the town's station which has been thoroughly modernised over recent years. The bedrooms are prettily furnished with antiqued pine furniture and modern tiled bathrooms. The reception room are spacious and though furnished in a contemporary style the effect is good. The bar is open plan and convivial extended out to a Brasserie and the gardens and patio beyond. For more formal dining the restaurant offers a carte menu which has freshly cooked dishes.
13 en suite (bth/shr) (2 fmly) No smoking in area of dining room CTV in all bedrooms Tea and coffee making facilities Direct dial from bedrooms No dogs (ex guide dogs) Cen ht 75P Last d 9.45pm
CARDS:

SLEDMERE Humberside Map **08** SE96

◀ Ⓠ Ⓠ **Triton** YO25 0XQ ☎01377 236644
This simple but well kept 18th-century inn, with its cream-washed walls, nestles in the picturesque wolds. The bar is oak panelled with a warm open fire and offers hand-pumped real ales and interesting bar meals, hence its popularity with the locals. There is a separate dining room with deep brown dralon banquettes and light pink flock wallpaper. The bedroom furniture is solid, with floral duvets, plain carpets and light wallpaper.
7 rms (3 bth 2 shr) (1 fmly) CTV in all bedrooms Tea and coffee making facilities Cen ht CTV 31P Last d 9pm
PRICE GUIDE
ROOMS: s £19.50-£21.50; d £39-£43; wkly b&b fr £160✱
MEALS: Lunch £7-£14 Dinner £7-£14✱
CARDS: £

SLOUGH Berkshire Map **04** SU97

GH Ⓠ Ⓠ **Colnbrook Lodge** Bath Rd, Colnbrook SL3 0NZ (3m E A4, between Punchbowl pub and level crossing)
☎01753 685958 FAX 01753 685164
Closed 23 Dec-2 Jan
This revamped Edwardian house is conveniently located for the M4 and M25 motorways as well as Heathrow airport. There is a range of bedroom styles which are being gradually updated.
8 rms (5 bth/shr) (2 fmly) No smoking in dining room CTV in all bedrooms Tea and coffee making facilities Direct dial from bedrooms No dogs (ex guide dogs) Licensed Cen ht CTV ch fac 12P Last d 7pm
PRICE GUIDE
ROOMS: s £25-£35; d £30-£42; wkly b&b £150-£200
CARDS: £

SNAKE PASS Derbyshire Map **07** SK19

◾ ⓆⓆⓆ Snake Pass Inn S30 2BJ (on A57)
☎01433 651480 FAX 01433 651480
5 en suite (bth/shr) (1 fmly) CTV in all bedrooms Tea and coffee making facilities No dogs (ex guide dogs) 40P Last d 9pm
PRICE GUIDE
ROOMS: s £19.50-£25; d £39-£45; wkly b&b £136.50-£175✱
MEALS: Lunch fr £15 Dinner fr £15✱
CARDS: 🖃 ▅ 🖭

SOLIHULL West Midlands Map **07** SP17

GH ⓆⓆⓆ The Gate House Barston Ln, Barston B92 0JN
☎01675 443274
A Victorian property on the edge of the pretty village, very handy for the NEC, the Gate House offers particularly spacious individually furnished bedrooms with modern bathrooms. It has retained much of its period charm and is tranquilly set in three acres of grounds where guests are welcome to wander.
3 rms (2 bth/shr) No smoking CTV in all bedrooms Tea and coffee making facilities No dogs (ex guide dogs) Cen ht CTV 20P No coaches
PRICE GUIDE
ROOMS: s £22-£27; d £38-£44✱

SOMERTON Somerset Map **03** ST42

GH ⓆⓆⓆ *Church Farm* Compton Dundon TA11 6PE
☎01458 272927
Closed 20 Dec-7 Jan
Quietly located opposite the church in the village, well off the B3151 Street to Somerton road, this cottage offers simply furnished but well equipped bedrooms; the majority of rooms are located in an adjacent converted stable block. There is a comfortable lounge, and dinner is served by arrangement in the attractive beamed, split-level dining room.
1 en suite (bth/shr) 5 annexe en suite (bth/shr) (2 fmly) No smoking in dining room No smoking in lounges CTV in all bedrooms Tea and coffee making facilities Licensed Cen ht No children 5yrs 6P No coaches Fishing Last d 10am

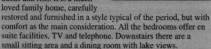

Premier Selected

GH ⓆⓆⓆⓆⓆ The Lynch Country House 4 Behind Berry TA11 7PD
☎01458 272316
FAX 01458 272590
Set in beautiful countryside on the edge of Somerton, this house is surrounded by well kept grounds boasting a lake with black swans, exotic ducks and fish. It is a much loved family home, carefully restored and furnished in a style typical of the period, but with comfort as the main consideration. All the bedrooms offer en suite facilities, TV and telephone. Downstairs there are a small sitting area and a dining room with lake views.
5 en suite (bth/shr) CTV in all bedrooms Tea and coffee making facilities Direct dial from bedrooms No dogs (ex guide dogs) Licensed Cen ht 15P No coaches
PRICE GUIDE
ROOMS: s £40-£50; d £45-£65✱
CARDS: 🖃 🖭

♥ ⓆⓆ Mr D Grindley Rookery *(ST534288)* Charlton Mackrell TA11 7AL ☎01458 224030 FAX 01458 224090
Philomena and David Grindley took over this farmhouse last year, after it had stood empty for six years. The house has been refurbished to a good standard, whilst still retaining original features such as the superb inglenook fireplace in the kitchen. Breakfast is served here, round a large table. There is a sitting room for guests, and also a sauna and mini gym. Set in nine acres, surrounded by worked farmland, the house enjoys pleasant rural views.
3 rms (1 fmly) No smoking CTV in all bedrooms Tea and coffee making facilities Cen ht CTV No children 5yrs 10P Sauna Gymnasium 9 acres sheep
PRICE GUIDE
ROOMS: s £16-£18; d £32-£35✱

SOUTHAMPTON Hampshire Map **04** SU41

GH ⓆⓆ Banister House Hotel Banister Rd SO15 2JJ (.5m north east of city centre off A33) ☎01703 221279 & 225753 FAX 01703 221279
Closed 25-27 Dec
Banister House stands in a residential area close to the city centre on a site where there has been a hotel for many years. The bedrooms offer simply decorated yet well equipped accommodation; all rooms have telephones and colour television and several have en suite showers. There is a well appointed restaurant with a bar, and evening meals are popular.
23 rms (13 bth/shr) (3 fmly) CTV in all bedrooms Tea and coffee making facilities Direct dial from bedrooms Licensed Cen ht CTV 14P No coaches Last d 7.45pm
PRICE GUIDE
ROOMS: s £21.50-£25.50; d £29.50-£36
CARDS: 🖃 ▅ 🖭

GH ⓆⓆⓆ Capri 52 Archers Rd SO1 2LU ((in city centre near Railway Station) ☎01703 632800 FAX 01703 630100
An Italian-inspired house close to the Dell and cricket ground provides comfortable, individually furnished bedrooms; the Ambassador Suite, which features a water bed, jacuzzi and steam room. The dining room offers home-cooked meals and the well furnished lounge has a marble fireplace.
15 rms (11 bth/shr) (2 fmly) No smoking in 1 bedrooms No smoking in 1 lounge CTV in all bedrooms Tea and coffee making facilities Direct dial from bedrooms No dogs (ex guide dogs) Licensed Cen ht 15P Last d 5pm
PRICE GUIDE
ROOMS: s £21; d £39✱
CARDS: 🖃 🖭

GH ⓆⓆⓆ Dodwell Cottage Dodwell Ln, Bursledon SO31 1AD ☎01703 406074 FAX 01489 578659
Closed 23 Dec-30 Jan
This attractive old house is ideally located for access to the M27 and the coast and offers good comfortable accommodation. The bedrooms retain much of their original character yet all have smart en suite facilities, and some overlook the garden. There is a comfortable guest lounge, and breakfast is taken around a lovely polished wood table in the dining room.
3 rms (1 bth/shr) (1 fmly) No smoking Tea and coffee making facilities No dogs (ex guide dogs) Cen ht CTV No children 5yrs ch fac 10P No coaches Last d 6pm

![Selected]

GH **Q Q Q Q** *Hunters Lodge Hotel* 25 Landguard Rd,
Shirley SO1 5DL ☎01703 227919 FAX 01703 230913
Closed 17 Dec-7 Jan
Veronica and Steve Dugdale will ensure you receive a warm
welcome in this personally run hotel, conveniently situated for
the city centre, ferry ports and motorways. The bedrooms are
bright and attractively decorated; all have telephones and
satellite television, and most have en suite facilities. There is a
cosy lounge with a well stocked bar, and evening meals are
available on request.
18 rms (8 bth 4 shr) (2 fmly) No smoking in 4 bedrooms No
smoking in area of dining room No smoking in 1 lounge
CTV in all bedrooms Tea and coffee making facilities Direct
dial from bedrooms Licensed Cen ht CTV 20P Last d 6pm
CARDS: 🔲 🔲 🔲

![Selected]

 GH **Q Q Q Q** Landguard Lodge 21 Landguard Rd
S015 5DL (between Shirley Rd and Hill Lane, just north of
Railway Station) ☎01703 636904 FAX 01703 636904
This smart personally run property is ideally located for the
city centre, theatres, hospitals and university. The attractive
bedrooms are comfortable and well appointed, most have en
suite facilities. There is a spacious comfortable lounge, and
evening meals can be provided in the bright dining room.
13 rms (9 shr) (1 fmly) No smoking in dining room No
smoking in lounges CTV in all bedrooms Tea and coffee
making facilities No dogs (ex guide dogs) Cen ht CTV No
children 5yrs 4P No coaches Last d 9am
PRICE GUIDE
ROOMS: s £16-£19; d £30-£32
CARDS: 🔲 🔲 🔲 🔲

GH **Q Q** Linden 51-53 The Polygon SO15 2BP
☎01703 225653
Closed 2wks Xmas
This personally run property is located in a quiet residential area
of the city, and within walking distance of the shops. The
bedrooms are comfortable and simply furnished, they all have
quality soft furnishings. There is an attractive breakfast room, and
a bright guests' lounge. Some off-street parking is available.
12 rms (4 fmly) No smoking in dining room No smoking in
lounges CTV in all bedrooms Tea and coffee making facilities
No dogs Cen ht CTV 7P
PRICE GUIDE
ROOMS: s £14-£15; d £27-£30✱ (£)

GH **Q Q Q** Lodge 1 Winn Rd, The Avenue SO2 1EH (take
A33 into city and at end of Common, and at Cowherds pub
turn left) ☎01703 557537
Closed 23 Dec-1 Jan
Situated close to the university, this very well maintained,
personally managed Victorian hotel is a busy and popular one.
Bedrooms are well equipped and a good choice of meals is offered
in the evening. There is a lounge area and a licensed bar.
14 rms (1 bth 7 shr) (2 fmly) No smoking in dining room CTV
in all bedrooms Tea and coffee making facilities Direct dial from

bedrooms Licensed Cen ht CTV 10P No coaches Last d 9pm
PRICE GUIDE
ROOMS: s £22.50-£30.50; d £39.50-£42.50✱
CARDS: 🔲 🔲 🔲 (£)

GH **Q Q** Madison House 137 Hill Ln SO1 5AF (A33 then
A35, at next roundabout turn left, straight over mini-
roun·labout into Hill Ln, 0.75m on left)
☎01703 333374 FAX 01703 322264
Closed 24 Dec-1 Jan
This family run property offers bright simply furnished rooms, and
a friendly environment. Breakfast is served in a well appointed
dining room, and there is a residents' lounge with a piano. There is
a off-street parking.
9 rms (3 bth/shr) (1 fmly) No smoking in dining room CTV in
all bedrooms Tea and coffee making facilities No dogs (ex guide
dogs) Cen ht CTV 6P
PRICE GUIDE
ROOMS: s £15-£21.50; d £30-£42✱
CARDS: 🔲 🔲

GH **Q** Wayside Lodge 2 Midanbury Ln, Bitterne SO18 4HP
☎01703 228780
Located on the east carriageway of the Bitterne road, not far from
Northam Bridge, this very friendly guesthouse is personally run
by resident proprietors Bob and Ingrid Tyley. Bedrooms are
reasonably well furnished, with plans for further upgrading. There
is a well appointed breakfast room and guests can also use the
family lounge. Evening meals can be provided by prior
arrangement.
8 rms (2 fmly) CTV in all bedrooms Tea and coffee making
facilities Cen ht CTV 6P No coaches Last d 8.30pm
PRICE GUIDE
ROOMS: s £15.50; d £30✱ (£)

SOUTHEND-ON-SEA Essex Map 05 TQ88

GH **Q Q** Argyle Hotel 12 Clifftown Pde SS1 1DP
☎01702 339483
Closed Xmas
Overlooking the sea and the bandstand, this terraced house offers
comfortable bedrooms with shared bathrooms. The hotel is
licensed and the breakfast room/restaurant serves good value
home cooking. The restaurant is open at lunchtime only.
11 rms (3 fmly) CTV in all bedrooms Tea and coffee making
facilities No dogs Licensed Cen ht CTV No children 5yrs No
parking No coaches
PRICE GUIDE
ROOMS: s £18-£19; d £35-£37✱ (£)

GH **Q Q** Marine View 4 Trinity Av, Westcliff on Sea SSO 7PU
☎01702 344104
As its name suggests, this semidetached guesthouse is close to the
seafront. It is situated in an attractive tree lined avenue. The
bedrooms are furnished in a traditional style and a small lounge
adjoins the ground floor dining room.
6 rms (1 fmly) No smoking in dining room CTV in all bedrooms
Tea and coffee making facilities No dogs (ex guide dogs) Cen ht
CTV No children 3yrs No parking No coaches
PRICE GUIDE
ROOMS: s £15-£17.50; d £28-£32; wkly b&b £80-£87.50✱

GH **Q Q** Mayflower Hotel 5-6 Royal Ter SS1 1DY
☎01702 340489
Closed 10 days Xmas & New Year
The Regency ironwork balcony of this Grade II listed building is ➡

ablaze with geraniums during the summer months. Bedrooms on four floors (including some at ground level) and are simply furnished but equipped with television and radio; some have en suite shower rooms. Communal tea and coffee making facilities are provided in a bright room on the first floor, where there is also a pool table.

23 rms (4 shr) (3 fmly) CTV in all bedrooms Tea and coffee making facilities Cen ht CTV 2P Pool table

PRICE GUIDE

ROOMS: s £19-£28; d £32-£40✱

GH Q Q *Terrace Hotel* 8 Royal Ter SS1 1DY (Royal Terrace can only be approached from Southend seafront, via Pier Hill, opposite the pier) ☎01702 348143

Part of an attractive listed terrace above the cliffs and overlooking the sea, this small hotel looks particularly appealing in the summer with its many colourful hanging baskets. Bedrooms are simply furnished and two have their own balcony. Downstairs there are three small public rooms: a TV lounge, bar and breakfast room.

9 rms (3 shr) (3 fmly) No smoking in lounges CTV in all bedrooms Tea and coffee making facilities Licensed Cen ht CTV No parking No coaches

---

GH Q Q Q *Tower Hotel* 146 Alexandra Rd SS1 1HE (off A13 at Cricketers Inn into Milton Rd then left into Cambridge Rd and take 3rd turn on right into Wilson Rd)

☎01702 348635 FAX 01702 433044

Attractively painted in 'Essex cream', this well-established local hotel has recently won recognition for conservation and restoration from the Southend Society. Bedrooms in the annexe are larger than those in the main building but all are well equipped and have direct-dial telephones. Public rooms include a large corner bar and an elegant restaurant where a short set-price menu is offered.

16 rms (14 bth/shr) 17 annexe en suite (bth/shr) (6 fmly) No smoking in area of dining room CTV in all bedrooms Tea and coffee making facilities Direct dial from bedrooms Licensed Cen ht CTV ch fac 2P Residents membership of nearby sports club Last d 9pm

PRICE GUIDE

ROOMS: s £25-£43; d £35-£55; wkly b&b £150-£270; wkly hlf-bd £190-£350

CARDS: 🔲 🔲 🔲 🔲

SOUTH MOLTON Devon Map 03 SS72

Premier Selected

♥ Q Q Q Q Q Mrs Theresa Sampson **Kerscott** *(SS793255)* Ash Mill EX36 4QG (6m east on B3227, 1.5m from A361) ☎01769 550262

Closed mid Dec-mid Jan

This delightful farmhouse, surrounded by 70 acres of pasture land, stands beside the B3227 between Bampton and South Molton - the views from its elevated position directly opposite the foot hills of Exmoor encompassing miles of rural Devon and stretching as far as the Tors of Dartmoor. Many places of interest and beauty in this unspoilt area of the southwest are within easy reach and the riverside towns of Barnstaple and Bideford just a short drive away. Mentioned in the Domesday Book, Kerscott Farm retains such original features as a host of exposed beams and four inglenook fireplaces with bread and cream ovens; all the bedrooms have

been ingeniously upgraded to provide such modern facilities as shower rooms and central heating, but great care has been taken not to detract from the character of the building. Honest home-cooked meals are based on local meat and vegetables, springs and wells provide the water and bread is baked on the premises. Smoking is not permitted anywhere in the house.

3 en suite (shr) No smoking Tea and coffee making facilities No dogs Cen ht CTV No children 10yrs 4P 72 acres beef sheep Last d 10am

PRICE GUIDE

ROOMS: s £20; d £34; wkly b&b £140; wkly hlf-bd £168-£196

SOUTHPORT Merseyside Map 07 SD31

GH Q Q Q **Ambassador Private Hotel** 13 Bath St PR9 0DP ☎01704 543998 & 530459 FAX 01704 536269

Closed Xmas & New Year

A centrally situated and privately run hotel, the Ambassador offers well equipped bedrooms, all of which have en suite facilities. A comfortable bar adjoins the attractive restaurant, and there is a small first-floor guests' lounge. The accommodation is impeccably maintained throughout.

8 en suite (shr) (4 fmly) No smoking in 4 bedrooms No smoking in dining room CTV in all bedrooms Tea and coffee making facilities Licensed Cen ht No children 5yrs 6P Last d 7pm

PRICE GUIDE

ROOMS: s £29; d £46; wkly b&b £140; wkly hlf-bd £180✱

CARDS: 🔲 🔲 🔲

GH Q Q **Lake Hotel** 55-56 The Promenade PR9 0DY ☎01704 530996 & 501900

Conveniently located overlooking Marine Walk and Gardens, only a short walk from well known Lord Street, this large end-of-terrace house offers simply decorated and furnished bedrooms which nevertheless provide en suite facilities, televisions, radios and telephones; a chair lift has recently been installed to make it easier for less mobile guests to reach the first floor. Downstairs there are a lounge, bar and pleasantly appointed dining room.

20 en suite (shr) (5 fmly) No smoking in dining room CTV in all bedrooms Tea and coffee making facilities Direct dial from bedrooms Licensed Cen ht CTV No children 8yrs 14P Last d 4.30pm

PRICE GUIDE

ROOMS: s £25-£26; d £40-£46✱

CARDS: 🔲 🔲

GH Q **Lyndhurst** 101 King St PR8 1LQ (off A570 at McDonalds on corner of King St) ☎01704 537520

The Lyndhurst, an attractive small terraced house close to the town centre, provides comfortable accommodation and a congenial atmosphere. The property is well maintained throughout and includes a lounge and well furnished dining room.

7 rms CTV in all bedrooms Tea and coffee making facilities No dogs (ex guide dogs) Licensed Cen ht CTV No children 5yrs 2P No coaches Last d noon

PRICE GUIDE

ROOMS: s £14; d £28; wkly b&b £91; wkly hlf-bd £133✱

GH Q Q Q *Oakwood Private Hotel* 7 Portland St PR8 1LJ ☎01704 531858

Etr-Nov

This comfortable private hotel is only a short walk from Lord Street, Southport's main shopping area. Its en suite bedrooms, one of which is at ground floor level, are spacious and comfortable, with a mixture of traditional and modern furniture. There are an attractive dining room and two lounges - a comfortably furnished

quiet lounge and a smaller lounge with a TV set. Ample car parking space is available at the front of the hotel.
7 rms (4 shr) No smoking CTV in all bedrooms Tea and coffee making facilities No dogs Licensed Cen ht CTV No children 5yrs 8P No coaches

GH QQ **Rosedale Hotel** 11 Talbot St PR8 1HP (enter by A570 and left into Talbot St)
☎01704 530604 FAX 01704 530604
Situated close to the town centre and the renowned Lord Street, this friendly, family-run hotel offers comfortable accommodation in predominantly en suite bedrooms; some family rooms are also available. Public areas are made up of a residents' bar, lounge and attractive dining room, and private parking facilities are available at the front of the building.
10 rms (7 shr) (2 fmly) No smoking in bedrooms No smoking in dining room CTV in all bedrooms Tea and coffee making facilities No dogs (ex guide dogs) Licensed Cen ht 8P Last d 4pm
PRICE GUIDE
ROOMS: s £20-£26; d £40-£52✱
CARDS: 🔲 🔲 🔲

GH QQQ **The White Lodge Private Hotel** 12 Talbot St PR8 1HP (in town centre) ☎01704 536320
This comfortable licensed hotel situated close to Southport's famous Lord Street is also within easy reach of the many championship golf courses in the area. Most bedrooms have en suite facilities and other modern amenities, while public areas include an interesting bar on the lower ground floor as well as the relaxing lounge and pleasantly appointed dining room at street level. There is private parking at the front of the hotel.
8 rms (1 bth 4 shr) (3 fmly) No smoking in dining room CTV in 7 bedrooms Tea and coffee making facilities No dogs (ex guide dogs) Licensed CTV ch fac 6P Last d 6pm
PRICE GUIDE
ROOMS: s £18-£24; d £36-£48; wkly b&b £105-£140; wkly hlf-bd £115-£175
£

SOUTHSEA Hampshire

See **Portsmouth & Southsea**

SOUTHWELL Nottinghamshire Map 08 SK65

◖ QQQ *Crown Hotel* 11 Market Place NG25 0HE
☎01636 812120
The Crown is an attractive Georgian inn located in the town centre. The refurbished public areas are effectively a pleasant open-plan pub, in which breakfast and bar snack lunches are taken. The bedrooms are nicely appointed, with light wood furniture and pretty fabrics.
7 rms (1 shr) CTV in all bedrooms Tea and coffee making facilities No dogs (ex guide dogs) Cen ht 10P Last d 9.30pm
CARDS: 🔲 🔲

SOUTHWOLD Suffolk Map 05 TM57

GH QQQ **Oldhurst** 24 High St IP18 6AD (opposit Kings Head) ☎01502 723829
A well maintained whitewashed Victorian house located at the western end of the High Street. There are three large bedrooms, mostly furnished with old pieces of wooden furniture, and the breakfast room on the ground floor also has a few armchairs for extra comfort.
3 en suite (bth/shr) No smoking in dining room CTV in all

bedrooms Tea and coffee making facilities Cen ht No parking No coaches
PRICE GUIDE
ROOMS: s £25-£40; d £40-£50✱
£

SOUTH ZEAL Devon Map 03 SX69

GH QQQ **Poltimore** EX20 2PD (leave A30 at Whidden Down towards South Zeal and turn left after Rising Sun public house) ☎01837 840209
A peacefully situated cottage offering character accommodation with easy access to the A30. Bedrooms are compact but comfortable, and there are two lounges with exposed timbers and feature fireplaces. A choice of food is served in the informal dining room.
7 rms (2 bth 2 shr) No smoking in dining room CTV in all bedrooms Tea and coffee making facilities Licensed Cen ht CTV No children 8yrs 25P No coaches Last d 9pm
PRICE GUIDE
ROOMS: s £23-£27; d £46-£50; wkly b&b £129-£157; wkly hlf-bd £216.50-£246.50
CARDS: 🔲 🔲 🔲
£

SPAXTON Somerset Map **03** ST23

Selected

GH Ⓠ Ⓠ Ⓠ Ⓠ **Gatesmoor** Hawkridge TA5 1AL (from
Bridgewater follow signs Spaxton and through village,
house on right adjacent to Hawkridge Reservoir)
☎01278 671353

Gatesmoor is a white painted 17th-century cottage set in a
beautiful garden bordering a scenic reservoir, close to the
Quantocks and within easy driving distance of Taunton. The
bedrooms are attractively furnished, and share a bathroom.
Many extras are provided for the comfort of guests who also
have their own sitting room with colour TV. A four-course
dinner is served in the beamed dining room.
2 rms No smoking Tea and coffee making facilities No dogs
(ex guide dogs) Cen ht CTV No children 10yrs 4P No
coaches
PRICE GUIDE
ROOMS: d £32-£35; wkly b&b £102-£122.50; wkly hlf-bd
£172-£192.50✳

(£)

SPENNYMOOR Co Durham Map **08** NZ23

GH Ⓠ Ⓠ Ⓠ *Idsley House* 4 Green Ln DL16 6HD (off junct
A167/A688, signposted Green Lane) ☎01388 814237
Closed Xmas
Well equipped accommodation is offered at this detached house
conveniently situated near the junction of the A167 and the A688.
Guests have the use of a comfortable lounge, and a hearty
breakfast is served in the rear conservatory.
5 rms (4 shr) (1 fmly) No smoking in dining room CTV in all
bedrooms Tea and coffee making facilities Cen ht CTV 7P

STAFFORD Staffordshire Map **07** SJ92

See also Adbaston

GH Ⓠ Ⓠ **Bailey Hotel** 63 Lichfield Rd ST17 4LL (on A34 1m
south of town centre) ☎01785 214133
Closed 20 Dec-2 Jan
This small, friendly, privately owned guesthouse is conveniently
situated beside the A34 and is within easy reach of either Junction
13 or 14 of the M6. The bedrooms, which vary in size, are all
freshly decorated, have modern furnishings and are well equipped.
Guests' also have the use of a comfortable lounge which has a
flame effect fire and there is a bright dining room and which is
furnished with cottage style furniture.
11 rms (3 shr) (1 fmly) No smoking in dining room CTV in all
bedrooms Tea and coffee making facilities Direct dial from
bedrooms Licensed Cen ht CTV 11P No coaches Last d
6.45pm
PRICE GUIDE
ROOMS: s £16.50-£26; d £30-£38
CARDS:

(£)

GH Ⓠ Ⓠ Ⓠ **Leonards Croft Hotel** 80 Lichfield Rd ST17 4LP
(A34, on right after railway bridge) ☎01785 223676
Closed Xmas
This large gabled house, set in delightful gardens beside the A34,
is conveniently situated for junction 13 of the M6. Owned and
personally run by Mr and Mrs Johnson for the last eight years, the
hotel is soundly maintained, and bedrooms (including two on the
ground floor) are traditionally and comfortably furnished. Dinner
and breakfast are served in attractive restaurant which has a small
bar, and there is a spacious lounge - all these areas overlooking the

gardens.
11 rms (4 shr) (3 fmly) No smoking in dining room CTV in 9
bedrooms Tea and coffee making facilities Licensed Cen ht
CTV 10P Last d 8.30pm
PRICE GUIDE
ROOMS: s £18-£25; d £36-£45✳

GH Ⓠ Ⓠ Ⓠ **Stone Cliff** Brook Ln, Brocton ST17 0TZ
☎01785 662217
This interesting individually designed house is situated right on
the edge of the Cannock Chase country park, just outside Stafford
and is within easy reach of the M6. Guests' have the use of a
spacious first floor lounge/dining room, which has huge windows
overlooking the park and which in the winter months is warmed
by a wood burning stove. The two bedrooms, one of which is en-
suite and the other which has the use of a private bathroom, are
spacious, comfortably furnished, and one even has a small
balcony.
2 rms (1 bth/shr) No smoking CTV in all bedrooms Tea and
coffee making facilities No dogs (ex guide dogs) Cen ht CTV
2P No coaches
PRICE GUIDE
ROOMS: d £36-£40; wkly b&b fr £126

STAMFORD Lincolnshire Map **04** TF00

Selected

GH Ⓠ Ⓠ Ⓠ Ⓠ **The Priory** Church Rd, Ketton PE9 3RD
(off A6121 Morcot rd 3m from A1, opposite village
church) ☎01780 720215 FAX 01780 721881
The Priory is an impressive stone-built house with gardens
running down to the River Chater. Enthusiastic hosts Moya
and John Acton work continually to upgrade the amenities,
and have recently put telephones into the bedrooms and had
showers fitted to the baths. The bedrooms (all no-smoking)
are quite spacious and imaginatively decorated using designer
fabrics. Public areas are enhanced by colourful flower
arrangements and numerous paintings. There is a lounge, a
conservatory where meals are served in summer, and a richly
decorated dining room used in the winter months. Evening
meals, including vegetarian dishes, are available by prior
arrangement.
3 rms (2 bth/shr) No smoking in bedrooms No smoking in
dining room CTV in all bedrooms Tea and coffee making
facilities Direct dial from bedrooms No dogs (ex guide dogs)
Licensed Cen ht ch fac 9P No coaches Fishing Croquet
Last d 7pm
PRICE GUIDE
ROOMS: s £29-£37.50; d £38-£55; wkly b&b £120-£173;
wkly hlf-bd £207.50-£260.50✳
CARDS: ▣ ▦

(£)

STAMFORD BRIDGE Humberside

See Low Catton & High Catton

STANLEY Co Durham Map **12** NZ15

♥ Ⓠ Ⓠ Mrs P Gibson **Bush Blades Farm** *(NZ168533)*
Harperley DH9 9UA (after Stanley follow sign for Harperley,
farm on right 0.5m after crossroads) ☎01207 232722
Closed 20 Dec-2 Jan
This large detached house stands in its own grounds and enjoys
some fine views to the rear. There are three pleasant bedrooms all
with colour televisions and with two of the rooms sharing a
shower room. A cosy lounge/breakfast room is available whilst
friendly service is provided by the resident owners. It is found by

following the signs for Harperley from the A693, is about one mile from Stanley and is only 10 minutes from the A1(M).
3 rms (1 bth) No smoking in dining room No smoking in lounges CTV in all bedrooms Tea and coffee making facilities No dogs Cen ht No children 12yrs 4P 50 acres sheep
PRICE GUIDE
ROOMS: s £20-£25; d £32-£37*

◖ Ⓠ Ⓠ Ⓠ **Oaktree** Tantobie DH9 9RF (1.75m NE)
☎01207 235445
A typical pub situated in the village of Tanobie, near Stanley, the Oaktree also has a Victorian dining room where good home-made French-style cooking is served. The bedrooms have many interesting features; some are in a separate building to the rear, and all now have en suite facilities.
2 en suite (bth/shr) 3 annexe en suite (bth/shr) (1 fmly) No smoking in area of dining room CTV in all bedrooms Tea and coffee making facilities Cen ht 12P Snooker Last d 10.30pm
PRICE GUIDE
ROOMS: s £20.50-£26; d fr £40*
MEALS: Bar Lunch fr £1 Dinner £9.50&alc*
CARDS: 🔳 🔳 🔳 💳   (£)

STANSTED Essex Map **05** TL52

GH Ⓠ Ⓠ Ⓠ **The Laurels** 84 St Johns Rd CM24 8JS (from A120 take B1383 and turn right before Q8 Petrol Station)
☎01279 813023 FAX 01279 813023
A welcoming guest house situated in a quiet lane in the centre of the village, The Laurels offers bright public areas which include an open-plan lounge bar and dining room where guests can enjoy a three-course meal or a snack from the bar menu. Bedrooms are fresh and inviting, with a good range of equipment. Transportation to and from Stansted Airport can be provided by prior ➡

Whitgreave Manor
AA QQQQ

Situated in own mature grounds in peaceful country surroundings.
1 mile junction 14, M6 motorway.
All rooms en-suite, tastefully furnished, colour TV, tea/coffee facilities and direct dial telephone.
Breakfast is served in our elegant dining room – excellent evening meals available at local Inns and Restaurants.
Ample private car-parking. Tennis court.
Fishing by arrangement.
Ideally located for: Alton Towers – Wedgewood – Staffs County Showground – Shugborough Hall.

For reservations call Barbara Challinor
Whitgreave Manor, Whitgreave,
STAFFORD, Staffordshire ST18 9SP
Tel: (01785) 51767   Fax: (01785) 57078

Abbey House

Though mainly Georgian in appearance, the house dates in part from 1190AD having been formerly owned by Thornley Abbey and Peterborough Minster before its later use as a Rectory. Set in pleasant gardens in a quiet village between Stamford and Market Deeping, and offering 7 rooms with private facilities. Abbey House provides an ideal base for touring the Eastern Shires with their abundance of stately homes, abbeys, cathedrals and delightful stone villages and market towns.

AA QQQ
Proprietors: Mr and Mrs A B Fitton
Abbey House, West End Road, Maxey, PE6 9EJ
Telephone: Market Deeping (01778) 344642

THE PRIORY
• CHURCH ROAD •
• KETTON • STAMFORD • LINCOLNSHIRE •

Historic 16th Century Country House near Stamford – "England's finest stone town". Quiet setting in picturesque village. Luxury ensuite bedrooms overlook delightful gardens. Colour TVs, phones, tea and coffee and teddy bears in all rooms. Private parking. Convenient for A1. Near Rutland Water, Burghley House and forest walks. Colour brochure available.

Tel: 01780 720 215 Fax: 01780 721 881

arrangement.
7 rms (5 bth/shr) (2 fmly) No smoking in bedrooms CTV in all bedrooms Tea and coffee making facilities Licensed Cen ht CTV 10P Last d 10pm
PRICE GUIDE
ROOMS: s £25-£32; d £40-£45✱

STANTON Derbyshire Map **08** SK21

GH QQ Homesclose House DE6 2DA (off A52)
☎01335 324475
Feb-Nov
This small, modern and well maintained house is situated in the centre of the village of Stanton, just outside Ashbourne and is ideally situated for guests wishing to visit Alton Towers. The two bedrooms, one of which is on the ground floor, are bright and attractively decorated and both share a first floor bathroom. Breakfast is served around a communal table in the dining room, which enjoys views over the well tended garden and the open countryside beyond.
2 rms (1 fmly) No smoking CTV in all bedrooms Tea and coffee making facilities Cen ht 6P
PRICE GUIDE
ROOMS: d £30-£33✱

STANTON IN PEAK Derbyshire Map **08** SK26

GH QQ Byres Off Main St DE4 2LX (off B5056, signposted Stanton in Peak, turn left 25yds before public house)
☎01629 636561
In a picturesque hill top village The Byres is a tasteful barn conversion. The two good sized rooms are in the eves with plenty of character exposed timbers, co-ordinated soft furnishings and deep armchairs. The bathroom which the rooms share is situated between. Breakfasts are served around a large pine table in a farmhouse style kitchen which is both warm and comfortable.
2 rms (2 fmly) No smoking in bedrooms No smoking in lounges CTV in all bedrooms Tea and coffee making facilities No dogs (ex guide dogs) Cen ht 2P No coaches
PRICE GUIDE
ROOMS: s £20-£22; d £30-£34

STARBOTTON North Yorkshire Map **07** SD97

Premier Selected

GH QQQQQ Hilltop Country BD23 5HY (on B6160) ☎01756 760321
mid Mar-mid Nov
Dating back to the 17th century, this charming farmhouse is situated in the pretty hamlet of Starbotton, on the road between Kettlewell and Buckden. Standing in an elevated position, the house has fine views of the surrounding hills, and the grounds slope down to Cam Gill Beck. Tasteful use of modern fabrics has ensured that the house has retained much of its character. Bedrooms are spacious and comfortable, although one in the converted barn is more compact. The drawing room is comfortable and relaxing, with a log fire for cooler evenings. Excellent meals

---

are taken in the former parlour where guests enjoy superb meals at antique tables - dinner is served only on Friday and Saturday. The owners, Mr and Mrs Rathmell, have written a book containing Hilltop recipes, on sale to guests. A typical meal might include smoked fillet of Kilnsey trout, breast of Nidderdale chicken stuffed with mushroom pâté, served with sherry sauce, and followed by lemon meringues and local cheeses.
4 en suite (bth/shr) 1 annexe en suite (shr) (1 fmly) No smoking in bedrooms No smoking in dining room No smoking in lounges CTV in all bedrooms Tea and coffee making facilities No dogs (ex guide dogs) Licensed Cen ht 6P No coaches Last d 6pm
PRICE GUIDE
ROOMS: s £35; d £50

STARCROSS Devon Map **03** SX98

◧ **QQ** *The Galleon* The Strand EX6 8PR ☎01626 890412
Situated at the centre of the village, opposite Brunels' Museum, this inn has views of the Exe estuary. Bedrooms - which have an entrance from the car park - are simply appointed, but several have full en suite facilities. Fresh, locally caught fish is usually featured in both an extensive range of home-made bar dishes and the oak-beamed restaurant's carte.
9 rms (1 bth) (3 fmly) CTV in all bedrooms Tea and coffee making facilities No dogs (ex guide dogs) Cen ht CTV 15P Pool table Darts Last d 9.30pm

---

STAVERTON Devon Map **03** SX76

Premier Selected

GH QQQQQ Kingston House Staverton TQ9 6AR (take A38 Exeter/Plymouth at Buckfastleigh take A384 Totnes road for 2.5m turn left to Staverton, at Sea Trout Inn take left fork signposted Kingston) ☎01803 762235
FAX 01803 762444
3 rms (2 bth/shr) No smoking in bedrooms No smoking in dining room Tea and coffee making facilities Direct dial from bedrooms No dogs (ex guide dogs) Licensed Cen ht CTV No children 16yrs 19P No coaches Last d 6.30pm
PRICE GUIDE
ROOMS: s £60-£67.50; d £90-£105; wkly b&b £409.50-£478; wkly hlf-bd £632.50-£701
CARDS: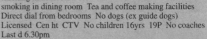

STEEPLE ASTON Oxfordshire Map **04** SP42

GH QQQ Westfield Farm Motel The Fenway OX6 3SS (off A4260, 0.5m from junction with B4030)
☎01869 340591 FAX 01869 347594
In a pretty village location, this single storey accommodation block converted from an old milking parlour and stables is set around a quad. Friendly owners offer a warm welcome, bedrooms are spacious and good breakfasts include Wiltshire bacon and free range eggs. There are two acres of lovely gardens leading down to a wood and stream.
7 en suite (shr) (2 fmly) No smoking in 2 bedrooms CTV in all

bedrooms Tea and coffee making facilities Direct dial from bedrooms Licensed Cen ht CTV 12P No coaches Riding Last d 8.30pm
PRICE GUIDE
ROOMS: s £34-£36; d £50-£60✳
CARDS:

STEYNING West Sussex Map **04** TQ11

GH QQQ **Nash Hotel** Horsham Rd BN4 3AA (off B2135)
☎01903 814988
An attractive Elizabethan manor house, with more recent additions, stands in peaceful countryside overlooking the South Downs. The formerly bumpy drive has recently been much improved. Bedrooms are spacious and furnished in traditional style. There is a large comfortable lounge with TV, books and a piano. The hotel owns the Steyning Vineyard and serves their wines at dinner; tastings are arranged occasionally in the special tasting room. Facilities include an all-weather tennis court and outdoor swimming pool. Smoking is not permitted. There are also three self-catering cottages to let.
4 rms (1 bth) (2 fmly) No smoking in 1 bedrooms No smoking in dining room No smoking in lounges CTV in all bedrooms Tea and coffee making facilities Licensed Cen ht CTV 20P No coaches Outdoor swimming pool Tennis (hard) Last d 8pm
PRICE GUIDE
ROOMS: s £30; d £48
£

Selected

GH QQQQ **Springwells Hotel** 9 High St BN44 3GG (from A283,by-pass, take main road through vilage for house on right opposite Methodist Church)
☎01903 812446 & 812043 FAX 01903 879823
Closed 24 Dec-1 Jan
Conveniently situated close to the village centre, this fine Georgian merchant's house has been sympathetically converted to provide a range of individually furnished bedrooms, including four-poster and family rooms. Among the attractive features are the walled garden with its 300-year-old yew trees, the outdoor heated pool, the new conservatory and the elegantly furnished TV lounge. A generous English breakfast including whisky porridge and fish alternatives is served.
10 rms (8 bth/shr) (1 fmly) No smoking in 1 lounge CTV in all bedrooms Tea and coffee making facilities Direct dial from bedrooms Licensed Cen ht CTV 6P No coaches Outdoor swimming pool (heated) Sauna Last d 8.45pm
PRICE GUIDE
ROOMS: s £26-£35; d £43-£70; wkly b&b £182-£245✳
CARDS:

STIPERSTONES Shropshire Map **07** SJ30

GH QQ **Tankerville Lodge** SY5 0NB
☎01743 791401
A well hidden house in a rural setting is reached by turning off the A488 Shrewsbury to Bishops Castle road, signed to Snailbeach, and passing through Stiperstones; in three quarters of a mile there is a bed and breakfast sign on a bend in the road. The rooms are neat, there is a lounge full of touring information, and a daily weather chart is posted in the country-style dining room. A self-catering cottage is also available.
4 rms No smoking in dining room Tea and coffee making

facilities Licensed Cen ht CTV No children 5yrs 4P No coaches
PRICE GUIDE
ROOMS: s £15.75-£18.25; d £31.50; wkly b&b £99.26-£116.76; wkly hlf-bd £160.51-£178.01
£

STOCKBRIDGE Hampshire Map **04** SU33

GH QQQ **Carbery** Salisbury Hill SO20 6EZ (on A30)
☎01264 810771 FAX 01264 811022
Closed 2 wks Xmas
Mr and Mrs Hooper are the charming hosts at this attractive Georgian property, which stands just two minutes from the centre of the small town. The bedrooms are neat, freshly decorated and nicely furnished, and the majority of them have en suite facilities. Public areas are comfortable and a home-cooked evening meal is offered in the dining room. There is an outdoor heated swimming pool, a terrace and an acre of gardens, so guests can take full advantage of fine weather.
11 rms (2 bth 6 shr) (2 fmly) No smoking in dining room CTV in all bedrooms Tea and coffee making facilities No dogs Licensed Cen ht 14P Outdoor swimming pool (heated) Pool table Last d 6pm
PRICE GUIDE
ROOMS: s £23-£30; d £46-£49

GH QQQ *Old Three Cups Private Hotel* High St SO20 6HB
☎01264 810527
24 Dec-early Jan rs Jan
A 15th-century inn, now run as a private hotel with a restaurant and residential licence, the Old Three Cups is situated on the main street of the charming village. Public areas include a bar and ➡

Springwells Hotel

STEYNING, WEST SUSSEX (Nr. Brighton)
Telephone: 01903-812446 Fax: 01903-879823
Once a Georgian merchant's town house now an elegant ten-bedroomed bed & breakfast hotel. All rooms have telephones & colour TV and most have private facilities.
Tea/coffee making facilities if required.
Some four-poster beds. Lovely walled gardens, outdoor swimming pool. Victorian style conservatory. Half hour from Gatwick/Newhaven.
£26-£70 per room

restaurant with exposed beams and low ceilings. The bedrooms are attractively decorated.

8 rms (4 bth/shr) (2 fmly) CTV in all bedrooms No dogs (ex guide dogs) Licensed Cen ht 12P No coaches Last d 9.30pm
CARDS: 🔳 🔤

STOCKTON-ON-TEES Cleveland Map **08** NZ41

Selected

GH 🆀🆀🆀🆀 **The Edwardian Hotel** 72 Yarm Rd TS18 3PQ ☎01642 615655

Conveniently located for the town centre and the A66, this pleasant house has been carefully furnished, with some particularly nice touches in the bedrooms. A comfortable lounge is provided and dinner is available by prior arrangement.

6 rms (5 bth/shr) (2 fmly) CTV in all bedrooms Tea and coffee making facilities No dogs (ex guide dogs) Licensed Cen ht CTV P
CARDS: 🔳 🔤

STOKE-BY-NAYLAND Suffolk Map **05** TL93

Selected

🚩 🆀🆀🆀🆀 **The Angel Inn** Polstead St CO6 4SA (off A12 on B1068) ☎01206 263245 FAX 01206 337324
Closed 25-26 Dec

A popular and at times very busy inn dating from the 16th-century, situated in one of Suffolk's most interesting villages and surrounded by lovely countryside, has been totally restored and refurbished whilst retaining such original features as exposed brickwork, beams, two large open fireplaces in the bars and a gallery overlooking the high-ceilinged dining room. Individually decorated and furnished bedrooms of a high standard are provided with good modern en suite facilities. The restaurant serves the same dishes as are listed on the daily blackboard bar-meals menu - both bars and restaurant being much frequented by local customers.

5 en suite (bth/shr) 1 annexe en suite (bth/shr) No smoking in area of dining room CTV in all bedrooms Tea and coffee making facilities Direct dial from bedrooms No dogs (ex guide dogs) Cen ht No children 8yrs 25P No coaches Last d 9pm
PRICE GUIDE
ROOMS: s £46; d £59
MEALS: Lunch £11.75-£24.20alc Dinner £13.55-£24.20alc
CARDS: 🔳 🔴 🔤 🔘 £

STOKE HOLY CROSS Norfolk Map **05** TG20

💚 🆀🆀 Mrs Harrold **Salamanca** *(TG235022)* NR14 8QJ (at A47/A140 intersection take minor road to Caistor St Edmunds, then first right, farm approx 1m on left) ☎01508 492322
Closed 15 Dec-15 Jan & Etr

Parts of this large red brick farmhouse date back to the 16th century, and it is still located on a working farm. The bedrooms are all spacious and well maintained, and all are either en suite or have private facilities. There is a guest lounge with TV and a separate breakfast room.

3 en suite (bth/shr) 1 annexe en suite (bth) No smoking CTV in 1 bedroom Tea and coffee making facilities No dogs Cen ht

---

CTV No children 6yrs 7P 165 acres beef mixed
PRICE GUIDE
ROOMS: s £19-£21; d £38-£42
CARDS: 🔘 £

STOKE-ON-TRENT Staffordshire Map **07** SJ84

Selected

GH 🆀🆀🆀🆀 **Old Dairy House** Trentham Park ST4 8AE (from M6 junct 15 turn right at 1st roundabout, left at lights and then 3rd turning right, following signs for Trentham Park Golf Club)
☎01782 641209 FAX 01782 712904

Dating back to early Victorian times when it was an estate house and dairy, this very attractive black and white timber-framed property has been tastefully restored and modernised without loss of character; it now offers two en suite bedrooms with separate lounges, one with direct access to the garden. Both rooms have quality period furnishings and a good range of modern equipment. The old circular dairy makes an unusual but comfortable lounge, with its high domed ceiling, and welcoming fire. A pleasant dining room has oak-panelled walls and period furniture, and dinner (by prior arrangement) is served at one large table. The house stands in two acres of pleasant gardens and grounds within Trentham Park, close to the famous Trentham Gardens complex.

2 en suite (bth/shr) No smoking CTV in all bedrooms Tea and coffee making facilities Direct dial from bedrooms No dogs (ex guide dogs) Cen ht No children 7yrs 10P Tennis (hard) Last d 3pm
PRICE GUIDE
ROOMS: s £30; d £40-£44; wkly b&b fr £140; wkly hlf-bd fr £175

GH 🆀🆀🆀 **White Gables Hotel** Trentham Rd, Blurton ST3 3DT (2 miles past Trentham Gardens, off A34) ☎01782 324882 FAX 01782 598302

This small privately owned hotel stands on the A5035, close to both Trentham Gardens and the Wedgwood factory. It is also within easy reach of Junction 15 of the M6, and is convenient for access to the city centre. Bedrooms vary in size and style, but all are very well equipped and one has a four-poster bed. Recreational facilities include a hard-surface tennis court and a games room with snooker, pool and darts.

9 rms (3 bth 3 shr) (2 fmly) No smoking in dining room No smoking in lounges CTV in all bedrooms Tea and coffee making facilities Direct dial from bedrooms No dogs (ex guide dogs) Licensed Cen ht CTV 14P No coaches Tennis (hard) Games room Last d 7.30pm
PRICE GUIDE
ROOMS: s £20-£40; d £38-£52
CARDS: 🔳 🔴 🔤 🔘 £

GH 🆀🆀🆀 **The White House Hotel** 94 Stone Rd, Trent Vale ST4 6SP (1.5m from junct 15 of M6 at crossroads of A500 and A34) ☎01782 642460 FAX 01782 657189

Conveniently situated on the A34 close to its junction with the A500, this small family-run hotel is well positioned for access to Trentham Gardens as well as the city centre and other local amenities. Junction 15 of the M6 is only a mile away. Recent improvements include the building of extra bedrooms. Ground-floor rooms are available, and two are situated in a separate annexe building. There is a small lounge, and a dining room where dinner and breakfast are available during the week, but only breakfast is served at weekends.

10 rms (3 shr) 2 annexe en suite (shr) (2 fmly) No smoking in bedrooms No smoking in dining room CTV in all bedrooms Tea

and coffee making facilities Direct dial from bedrooms No dogs (ex guide dogs) Licensed Cen ht CTV 12P No coaches
PRICE GUIDE
ROOMS: s £20-£35; d £30-£48*
CARDS: £

STONE Staffordshire Map **07** SJ93

GH ◻◻◻◻ **Whitgreave Manor** Whitgreave ST18 9SP (off M6 junct 14 towards Stone and in .5m left into Whitgreave Lane)
☎01785 51767 FAX 01785 57078
Built in 1850 and standing in mature gardens, this house is conveniently situated just off the A34 between Stafford and Stone, close to junction 14 of the M6. The four en suite bedrooms are tastefully decorated and well equipped, although one is smaller than the rest. French windows lead to the garden from a large, comfortable drawing room, and breakfast is served around a polished table in the dining room. There are also two smaller sitting rooms with open fires, one also having TV, and a fax machine is available for guests' use.
4 en suite (bth/shr) (1 fmly) No smoking in bedrooms No smoking in dining room No smoking in 1 lounge CTV in all bedrooms Tea and coffee making facilities Direct dial from bedrooms No dogs (ex guide dogs) Cen ht CTV ch fac 20P Outdoor swimming pool Tennis (grass) Fishing Table tennis
PRICE GUIDE
ROOMS: s £25-£30; d £43-£45 £

See advertisement under STAFFORD

STONEHOUSE Gloucestershire Map **03** SO80

◼ ◻◻◻ **Rose & Crown Inn** Nympsfield GL10 3TU (turn off B4066 at Coaley Peak, 0.75m to village)
☎01453 860240 FAX 01453 860240
This popular 300 year old Country Pub stands in the pretty village of Nympsfield. Extensive bar areas which feature attractive Cotswold stone walls, an inglenook fire place and a wood burning stove. The meals on offer look tempting, and there are dishes to suit all tastes and budgets. Accommodation is offered in four spacious well equipped bedrooms, each one bright, crisp and comfortable. Nympsfield is an easy drive from Stroud, Dursley, Nailsworth and Cirencester, and many other places of interest and beauty.
4 rms (3 bth/shr) (3 fmly) CTV in all bedrooms Tea and coffee making facilities No dogs (ex guide dogs) Cen ht CTV 20P Last d 9.30pm
PRICE GUIDE
ROOMS: s £24-£28; d £39-£38
MEALS: Lunch £4.25-£18alc Dinner £4.25-£18alc
CARDS: £

STOW-ON-THE-WOLD Gloucestershire Map **04** SP12

GH ◻◻◻◻ **Bretton House** Fosseway GL54 1JU (S on A429, on left 0.5m beyond Little Chef) ☎01451 830388
Closed Xmas
This elegant Edwardian residence was once the vicarage, and is set in an elevated position on the edge of the town. It enjoys glorious views of the Cotswold countryside. Three en-suite rooms have been tastefully decorated and furnished and each

is equipped with colour TV, central heating and tea trays. There is a guests lounge and an attractive dining room, and the atmosphere is that of a friendly family home.
3 en suite (bth/shr) No smoking in bedrooms No smoking in dining room CTV in all bedrooms Tea and coffee making facilities Cen ht CTV No children 10yrs 10P Last d 10am
PRICE GUIDE
ROOMS: d £42-£45; wkly b&b fr £140

GH ◻◻◻◻ **Cotswold Cottage** Chapel St, Bledington OX7 6XA (4m SE off B4450)
☎01608 658996 FAX 01608 658996
As its name suggests, this delightful cottage is set in the charming village of Bledington, which has a typical village green and a variety of quaint cottages. There are three lovely bedrooms to choose from, each thoughtfully furnished and decorated to a high standard; the newly created garden room, a few paces from the main building, boasts a fine four-poster bed. A most attractive dining room looking out on to the well tended cottage garden offers full English breakfasts, and dinner can be taken in the pub, a short stroll away.
3 rms (2 bth/shr) (2 fmly) No smoking CTV in all bedrooms Tea and coffee making facilities No dogs Cen ht No children 16yrs 4P No coaches
PRICE GUIDE
ROOMS: d £44-£50; wkly b&b £150-£165* £

PROSPECT HOUSE
334 Cheddleton Road, Cheddleton, Leek, Staffordshire ST13 7BW
 Tel: 01782 550639 AA QQQ Recommended

Situated in the heart of the Staffordshire moorlands, close to the Churnet Valley, this 19th Century Coach House boasts a homely atmosphere with friendly service in a beautiful part of the country.
All bedrooms have en-suite facilities with colour television, tea and coffe making facilities and are individually heated. Private car parking. Children welcome. Easy access for wheelchairs.

GH Ⓠ Ⓠ *Cotswold View* Nether Westcote OX7 6SD (4m E, signed from A424) ☎01993 830699

A Cotswold-stone house is situated in the sleepy village of Nether Westcote, just off the A424 between Stow-on-the-Wold and Burford. Accommodation is comfortable and bright; one or two rooms are a little compact, but the hayloft and granary rooms adjacent to the main building are spacious and well equipped. The dining room has a conservatory and serves dinner, breakfast and cream teas.

6 rms (3 shr) 2 annexe en suite (bth/shr) No smoking CTV in all bedrooms Tea and coffee making facilities CTV 11P No coaches Last d 4pm

---

Selected

GH Ⓠ Ⓠ Ⓠ Ⓠ **Crestow House** GL54 1JY
☎01451 830969 FAX 01451 832129

Closed Jan

This splendid Victorian manor house, accessed from the B4068 Lower Swell road, is perched on the crest of the hill overlooking the town of Stow-on-the-Wold on one side and the Dikler Valley on the other. Individually-styled bedrooms are spacious and comfortable, while public areas include a welcoming sitting room, a south-facing conservatory and a breakfast room where a choice of newspapers is offered each morning. Dinner is served - by arrangement - around a single table in the elegantly furnished dining room, the imaginative set menu making good use of fresh local produce. Guests have the use of a heated outdoor swimming pool during the summer months.

4 en suite (bth/shr) No smoking CTV in 2 bedrooms Tea and coffee making facilities No dogs Cen ht CTV No children 15yrs 4P No coaches Outdoor swimming pool (heated) Last d noon

PRICE GUIDE

ROOMS: s £34-£40; d £60-£68; wkly b&b fr £199; wkly hlf-bd fr £210✳

CARDS: 🆘 📧

See advertisement under CHELTENHAM

GH Ⓠ Ⓠ **Limes** Evesham Rd GL54 1EJ ☎01451 830034

Closed 24-30 Dec

Mr and Mrs Keyte offer a warm welcome to their guests, providing warm hospitality and comfortable, well equipped rooms. The bright dining room overlooks a pretty garden with a busy pond and an aviary buzzing with cockatiels and budgies, while a large lounge has views of rolling Gloucestershire farmland.

3 rms (1 shr) 1 annexe en suite (shr) (1 fmly) CTV in all bedrooms Tea and coffee making facilities Cen ht CTV 4P No coaches

PRICE GUIDE

ROOMS: d £32-£39

GH Ⓠ Ⓠ Ⓠ **Stowaway** 14 Park St GL54 1AQ (500yds from centre of village on A436) ☎01451 831839

This small terraced guest house in the centre of Stow is run with gusto by Julian Brown a young man who is deeply committed to hospitality. Mr Brown is a keen chef and dining at Stowaway should not be missed. There are many special features including some original works of art. The kitchen is a cooks paradise be sure to drop in.

3 en suite (shr) CTV in all bedrooms Tea and coffee making facilities Cen ht No parking

PRICE GUIDE

ROOMS: s £25-£35; d £30-£45; wkly b&b fr £122.50✳

CARDS: 🆘 📧

🏨 🖵 ♥ Ⓠ Ⓠ Mr R Smith **Corsham Field** *(SP217249)*
Bledington Rd GL54 1JH ☎01451 831750

There are superb views of rolling Gloucestershire farmland from this modern Cotswold stone farmhouse. The 100-acre working farm is owned by Mr Smith, who is also responsible for the well-being of guests in his home. Accommodation is offered in three comfortable rooms, one of which has en suite facilities. Breakfast is served in a lounge/dining room overlooking the garden. There is a good pub within five minutes' walk, and Stow-on-the Wold is only a short drive away.

3 rms (1 bth) (1 fmly) No smoking in dining room CTV in all bedrooms Tea and coffee making facilities Cen ht CTV 10P 100 acres arable beef sheep

PRICE GUIDE

ROOMS: s £15-£25; d £27-£37; wkly b&b £94.50-£129.50

Selected

🍴 Ⓠ Ⓠ Ⓠ Ⓠ **Kings Head Inn & Restaurant** The Green, Bledington OX7 6HD (4m SE off B4450)
☎01608 658365 FAX 01608 658902

Closed Xmas day

A delightful Cotswold inn, the Kings Head enjoys a peaceful location beside the village green, with its brook and resident ducks. There are 12 well equipped bedrooms to choose from, all beautifully furnished and provided with thoughtful extras. An award-winning restaurant offers the most delicious meals, and on chilly days a tasty lunch can be taken by the blazing log fire in the old world bar.

6 en suite (bth) 6 annexe en suite (bth/shr) (2 fmly) No smoking in bedrooms No smoking in area of dining room CTV in all bedrooms Tea and coffee making facilities Direct dial from bedrooms No dogs (ex guide dogs) Cen ht CTV 70P Last d 9.45pm

PRICE GUIDE

ROOMS: s £42-£45; d £60-£75✳

MEALS: Lunch £2-£9.95 Dinner £6.25-£9.95&alc✳

CARDS: 🆘 📧

Selected

🍴 Ⓠ Ⓠ Ⓠ Ⓠ **Royalist Hotel** Digbeth St GL54 1BN (turn off A429 onto A436)
☎01451 830670 FAX 01451 870048

The oldest building in Stow, this private hotel features in the Guinness Book of Records. Besides its wealth of history and character, it has a warmth and comfort which enhances its charm. The bedrooms, all of which have en suite facilities, are well equipped and attractively decorated. Morning coffees, lunches and teas are served in a gracious lounge warmed by a large log fire, and a good food choice is available in the evening.

12 en suite (bth/shr) CTV in all bedrooms Tea and coffee making facilities Direct dial from bedrooms Cen ht 12P

PRICE GUIDE

ROOMS: s £40-£60; d £50-£75

MEALS: Bar Lunch £2.25-£10

CARDS: 🆘 📧

STRATFORD-UPON-AVON Warwickshire Map **04** SP25

See also Newbold on Stour

GH Ⓠ Ⓠ Ⓠ **Aberfoyle** 3 Evesham Place CV37 6HT
☎01789 295703
Mrs McGregor, the friendly owner of this well kept guest house,
takes pleasure in changing and upgrading its bedroom furnishings.
Breakfast is served in a room which doubles as the guests' lounge.
2 en suite (shr) (1 fmly) No smoking CTV in all bedrooms Tea
and coffee making facilities Cen ht No children 5yrs 2P No
coaches
PRICE GUIDE
ROOMS: s £22-£25; d £38-£44; wkly b&b £110-£125

GH Ⓠ Ⓠ Ⓠ **Ambleside** 41 Grove Rd CV37 6PB (turn off
A3400 onto B439, through traffic lights, guesthouse on right)
☎01789 297239 & 295670 FAX 01789 295670
Closed Xmas
Positioned on the Evesham Road, just a few minutes to the west of
he town centre, this house offers nicely maintained and furnished
bedrooms, including family rooms. Public rooms are limited, the
lounge and dining room being combined.
7 rms (3 shr) (3 fmly) No smoking in 4 bedrooms No smoking
in dining room CTV in all bedrooms Tea and coffee making
facilities Cen ht CTV 8P
CARDS: 🌑 🔳 🔳 🌑 🔳 (£)

GH Ⓠ Ⓠ Ⓠ **Brook Lodge** 192 Alcester Rd CV37 9DR (W on
A422 opposite turning to Anne Hathaway's Cottage)
☎01789 295988 FAX 01789 295988
Closed 22 Dec-1 Jan
An added bonus to this large detached house is the availability of
off-street parking. The business is conscientiously run by a
cheerful and friendly couple who have gradually stamped their
mark on the character of the building. Nearly all the bedrooms are
spacious and well laid out. The owners have compiled useful

directories and maps of town centre and local sights of interest.
7 en suite (shr) (1 fmly) No smoking CTV in all bedrooms Tea
and coffee making facilities No dogs (ex guide dogs) Cen ht
CTV 10P No coaches
PRICE GUIDE
ROOMS: s £25-£40; d £38-£50
CARDS: 🌑 🔳 🔳 (£)

GH Ⓠ Ⓠ **Courtland Hotel** 12 Guild St CV37 6RE (on A3400)
☎01789 292401
This Georgian guest house is conveniently located for the town
centre and offers modest but sound accommodation. Bedrooms
feature some modern and some traditional furnishings and all are
well equipped. There is a small lounge and a charming breakfast
room.
7 rms (3 bth/shr) (1 fmly) No smoking in dining room No
smoking in 1 lounge CTV in all bedrooms Tea and coffee making
facilities No dogs (ex guide dogs) Cen ht CTV 3P
PRICE GUIDE
ROOMS: s £18-£22; d £35-£50✳
CARDS: 🌑 🔳 🔳 🌑 🔳 (£)
See advertisement on p.385.

GH Ⓠ Ⓠ Ⓠ **Craig Cleeve House** 67-69 Shipston Rd
CV37 7LW ☎01789 296573 FAX 01789 299452
Two adjoining houses, Craig and Cleeve, were knocked together
to form this spacious guest house which is run by an enthusiastic
couple who maintain very good standards. Several of the
bedrooms are located on the ground floor.

15 rms (9 shr) (5 fmly) No smoking in bedrooms No smoking in dining room No smoking in lounges CTV in all bedrooms Tea and coffee making facilities Licensed Cen ht 15P
CARDS: 🔲 🔲 🔲

GH 🔲🔲🔲 *The Croft* 49 Shipston Rd CV37 7LN (on A3400, 400 yds from Clopton Bridge)
☎01789 293419 FAX 01789 293419
Five minutes' walk south of the town centre, this large semidetached Victorian house offers well equipped bedrooms, most of which have been redecorated and upgraded. Family rooms and a ground-floor room are also available. There is a comfortable residents' lounge and a small dining room, where evening meals are available by prior arrangement. The large rear garden includes a heated swimming pool.
9 rms (4 shr) (5 fmly) No smoking in 2 bedrooms No smoking in dining room CTV in all bedrooms Tea and coffee making facilities Licensed Cen ht CTV 4P Outdoor swimming pool (heated) Last d noon
CARDS: 🔲 🔲 🔲

GH 🔲🔲 **Curtain Call** 142 Alcester Rd CV37 9DR (follow A46 then turn left onto A422 towards Stratford. Curtain Call 1m on left) ☎01789 267734
This friendly guest house appeals to all ages and owner Mrs Herdman enjoys making her guests feel at home. Bedrooms are modestly furnished but pleasant and there is a cosy breakfast room.
4 rms (3 shr) (2 fmly) No smoking in 2 bedrooms No smoking in dining room No smoking in lounges CTV in all bedrooms Tea and coffee making facilities Cen ht 5P Last d 8pm
PRICE GUIDE
ROOMS: s £16-£19; d £32-£38; wkly b&b £105-£126✳
CARDS: 🔲 🔲 🔲 🔲   (£)

GH 🔲🔲🔲 **The Dylan** 10 Evesham Place CV37 6HT
☎01789 204819
This friendly family guest house is centrally located with bright, comfortable bedrooms, some with impressive Victorian tiled fireplaces. The stylish breakfast room has as its centrepiece a working Wurlitzer juke box with many of the eponymous artists' tracks.
5 en suite (shr) (1 fmly) No smoking in 2 bedrooms No smoking in dining room No smoking in lounges CTV in all bedrooms Tea and coffee making facilities Cen ht 3P No coaches
PRICE GUIDE
ROOMS: s £20-£24; d £36-£44✳

GH 🔲🔲 *East Bank House* 19 Warwick Rd CV37 6YW (Take A439 into town and turn 1st right at St Gregory's church)
☎01798 292758 FAX 01798 292758
There is a friendly atmosphere at this elegant Victorian residence, where two types of room are offered, those with en-suite bathrooms are a little more luxurious than the more compact and functional rooms. There is a cosy lounge and a bright breakfast room.
11 rms (6 bth/shr) (2 fmly) No smoking in bedrooms No smoking in dining room CTV in all bedrooms Tea and coffee making facilities No dogs (ex guide dogs) Cen ht 5P
CARDS: 🔲 🔲

Selected

GH 🔲🔲🔲🔲 **Eastnor House Hotel** Shipston Rd CV37 7LN (follow A3400 Shipston Rd hotel 1st on right close to Clopton Bridge)
☎01789 268115 FAX 01789 266516
Spacious, wood-furnished bedrooms with higher than usual

ceilings are offered at this large Victorian house located close to the river bridge crossing. Breakfast is served in a bright front-facing room and there is a lounge with deep sofas and armchairs.
9 en suite (bth/shr) (3 fmly) No smoking in bedrooms No smoking in dining room CTV in all bedrooms Tea and coffee making facilities Licensed Cen ht 9P No coaches
PRICE GUIDE
ROOMS: d £42-£62; wkly b&b fr £180✳
CARDS: 🔲 🔲 🔲 🔲   (£)

GH 🔲🔲 *Eversley Bears* 37 Grove Rd CV37 6PB
☎01789 292334
This friendly guest house offers a warm welcome and an amazing collection of about 700 teddy bears.
6 rms (2 shr) (2 fmly) Tea and coffee making facilities No dogs (ex guide dogs) Cen ht CTV No children 14yrs 3P

Selected

GH 🔲🔲🔲🔲 *Graveside Barn* Binton CV37 9TU
☎01789 750502 & 297000 Telex no 311827
FAX 01789 298056
A gem of a B&B, this stone-built barn has been cleverly converted by proprietors Denise and Guy Belchambers to provide good quality modern accommodation in a delightful rural setting. Each of the attractive bedrooms has a spectacular view. One room is conveniently located on the ground floor and another has its own external entrance reached by a spiral staircase. There is a comfortable open plan lounge area and a dining room offering a good choice at breakfast. Smoking is not permitted in the bedrooms or dining room.
3 en suite (shr) No smoking CTV in all bedrooms Tea and coffee making facilities Direct dial from bedrooms No dogs (ex guide dogs) Cen ht No children 12yrs 6P No coaches Golf 18 Tennis (hard)
CARDS: 🔲 🔲
See advertisement on p.387.

GH 🔲🔲🔲 **Hardwick House** 1 Avenue Rd CV37 6UY (turn right off A439 at St Gregory's Church into St Gregory's Rd, Hardwick House 200yds on left)
☎01789 204307 FAX 01789 296760
Closed 3 days at Xmas
Cricket memorabilia adorns the walls of this large Victorian house - the owner once played county cricket. Accommodation is in spacious rooms and modern touches are making a gradual impact on the style of the establishment.
14 rms (9 bth/shr) (3 fmly) No smoking in bedrooms No smoking in dining room CTV in all bedrooms Tea and coffee making facilities No dogs (ex guide dogs) Cen ht 12P
PRICE GUIDE
ROOMS: s £19-£23; d £38-£60✳
CARDS: 🔲 🔲 🔲 🔲 🔲 🔲   (£)
See advertisement on p.387.

GH 🔲🔲🔲 **Highcroft** Banbury Rd CV37 7NF (on A422 out of town, 2m from river bridge on left)
☎01789 296293 FAX 01789 415236
A friendly family house with extensive gardens, Highcroft is situated next to the main Banbury road, two miles from the town centre, with an attractive rural backdrop. Period-style furniture is combined with modern equipment in the bedrooms, and one room in the ground floor extension has its own entrance. There is a

Courtland Hotel

12 Guild Street, Stratford-on-Avon CV37 6RE

Bed and Breakfast
From/to £17.50-£25

En suite facilities available.
Personal attention in well appointed Georgian House. Full English & Continental breakfast with home made preserves. All rooms with H&C, central heating, double glazing, colour television, tea & coffee making facilities. Antique furniture. Town centre situation. 3 minutes' level walk to theatre.

Tel: (01789) 292401

AA
LISTED

Mrs. Bridget Johnson
Recommended by
Arthur Frommer

ENGLISH TOURIST BOARD
APPROVED

CRAIG CLEEVE HOUSE
Licensed Private Hotel

67-69 Shipston Road, Stratford upon Avon, Warwickshire CV37 7LW
Telephone: 01789 296573   Fax: 01789 299452

From/To £19.50-£25.00

Good friendly service, family atmosphere and comfortable rooms of a high standard plus a breakfast where no one is left feeling hungry! Just five minutes walk to the town centre with all it's amenities. Ideal for visiting Shakespeare Country and the Cotswolds. All rooms have tea/coffee making facilities and colour TV. Most have en suite facilities and there are 4 rooms available on the ground floor.

"Our sole aim is to make our guests feel comfortable and welcome."

DOSTHILL COTTAGE

The Green, Wilmcote,
Stratford upon Avon CV37 9XJ
Telephone & Fax: 01789 266480

One of the original properties of this Shakespearean village, overlooking Mary Arden's House and Garden. Walk 3 miles down the canal past 14 locks into Stratford upon Avon or take an easy drive to NEC, Royal Show Ground or Cotswolds.
Car parking, garage if required.
All rooms have private facilities.

The Dylan

10 Evesham Place, Stratford upon Avon CV37 6HT
Telephone: (01789) 204819

A spacious Victorian house with original fireplaces. Centrally situated in the town only five minutes from the shops and the Royal Shakespeare Theatre. Comfortable, friendly accommodation, all rooms are tastefully furnished and decorated with en suite facilities, colour television, tea/coffee making facilities and central heating. Ground floor bedroom available. Car parking. An ideal base for touring the Heart of the Midlands.

lounge/breakfast room with lots of comfortable seating, and a tennis court is provided in the grounds.
1 en suite (bth/shr) 1 annexe en suite (bth/shr) (1 fmly) No smoking CTV in all bedrooms Tea and coffee making facilities Cen ht CTV 5P No coaches Tennis (hard)
PRICE GUIDE
ROOMS: s £25; d £35; wkly b&b fr £100

GH Q Q Q *Hollies* 'The Hollies', 16 Evesham Place CV37 6HQ ☎01789 266857
This friendly guest house and is personally run by proprietor Mrs Morgan. The fresh en suite bedrooms have modern furnishings and some family rooms are available. The attractive dining room features a display of crystal and although there is no lounge all rooms are equipped with TV.
6 rms (3 bth/shr) (3 fmly) No smoking CTV in all bedrooms Tea and coffee making facilities Cen ht CTV 6P

GH Q Q Q **Hunters Moon** 150 Alcester Rd CV37 9DR (on A422 5m from M40 junct 15) ☎01789 292888
Closed 25-26 Dec
Optimum use is made of space in this personally run guest house. It is well maintained and looked after by the resident couple. Original features include a smokers' lounge on the first floor and a self contained bedroom in the back garden which contains a pond with an ornamental fountain.
7 rms (6 shr) (3 fmly) No smoking in bedrooms No smoking in dining room No smoking in lounges CTV in all bedrooms Tea and coffee making facilities No dogs (ex guide dogs) Cen ht CTV 6P
PRICE GUIDE
ROOMS: s £18-£24; d £34-£46
CARDS: 💳 💳

GH Q Q Q **Marlyn** 3 Chestnut Walk CV37 6HG (from Evesham Road A439 towards town centre, second right after roundabout) ☎01789 293752
Modern improvements are being made on a gradual basis to this establishment (a hotel since 1890) without greatly affecting its character. Bedroom sizes vary but the furniture is carefully laid out. The energetic owner will happily cook dinner as well as sharing his expertise as an aromatherapist and reflexologist.
8 rms (3 shr) (1 fmly) No smoking in 2 bedrooms No smoking in dining room CTV in all bedrooms Tea and coffee making facilities Licensed Cen ht No parking No coaches Aromatherapy & reflexology treatment Last d breakfast
PRICE GUIDE
ROOMS: s £17-£19; d £34-£44; wkly b&b fr £112; wkly hlf-bd fr £168✳
CARDS: 💳 💳

GH Q Q Q **Melita Private Hotel** 37 Shipston Rd CV37 7LN (on A3400, 200yds from Clopton Bridge) ☎01789 292432 FAX 01789 204867
Closed 20-28 Dec
The well tended garden, particularly attractive in summer, is a feature of this large Victorian house. There are plans to set up a more formal bar in the lounge, which is the only place where smoking is allowed. Bedrooms are predominantly spacious and furnished in a contemporary style.
12 en suite (bth/shr) (3 fmly) No smoking in bedrooms No smoking in dining room CTV in all bedrooms Tea and coffee making facilities Direct dial from bedrooms Licensed Cen ht CTV 12P
PRICE GUIDE
ROOMS: s £29-£49; d £49-£69
CARDS: 💳 💳 💳 💳
See advertisement on p.389.

GH Q Q Q **Moonraker House** 40 Alcester Rd CV37 9DB (on A422, 900yds NW of town centre) (MIN) ☎01789 299346 & 267115 FAX 01789 295504
This popular, personally owned and run guesthouse is rather unusual, comprising four different properties within the same street. This makes for very varied accommodation, with some bedrooms being more luxurious than others, but all are well furnished and equipped with modern comforts and facilities; some rooms are on the ground floor. Continued improvements include a range of good quality bedrooms and an appealing new sun lounge.
10 en suite (bth/shr) 9 annexe en suite (bth/shr) (3 fmly) No smoking in 13 bedrooms No smoking in dining room No smoking in lounges CTV in all bedrooms Tea and coffee making facilities Cen ht 22P
PRICE GUIDE
ROOMS: s £25-£35; d £39-£60; wkly b&b £136-£210✳
CARDS: 💳 💳
See advertisement on p.389.

GH Q Q Q **Nando's** 18-19 Evesham Place CV37 6HT (on A439) ☎01789 204907 FAX 01789 204907
The style of this busy guest house is geared around groups of tourists. Tea and coffee is provided via vending machines in the lobby, next to the bright breakfast room. Bedrooms vary in size and are reached by one of three staircases.
21 rms (1 bth 6 shr) (10 fmly) No smoking in bedrooms No smoking in dining room CTV in all bedrooms Cen ht CTV 8P
PRICE GUIDE
ROOMS: s £20-£28; d £28-£44
CARDS: 💳 💳 💳 💳

GH Q Q **No 10 Bed & Breakfast** 10 Chestnut Walk CV37 6HQ ☎01789 266424
Closed Xmas/New Year
This small, personally run guest house is informally run by the chatty owner. Breakfast is served in a lounge/dining area adorned by personal items creating a homely atmosphere.
2 en suite (bth/shr) CTV in all bedrooms Tea and coffee making facilities No dogs Lift Cen ht CTV 1P
PRICE GUIDE
ROOMS: d £40✳

GH Q Q Q **Parkfield** 3 Broad Walk CV37 6HS (just off B439 to left on way out of Stratford, immediately before first rdbt) ☎01789 293313
This charming Victorian house dates back to 1875 and is within easy walking distance of the town centre. Mr and Mrs Pettitt are a friendly couple who are very keen on the theatre so this is an ideal place to stay for visitors to the Royal Shakespeare Theatre. Bedrooms are furnished in a mixture of modern and traditional styles and feature some nice touches such as sewing kits, tissues and clock radios. Some good works of art can be seen throughout the house, many by family members. Dinner is not served but the owners are delighted to recommend some local restaurants.
7 rms (5 shr) (1 fmly) No smoking CTV in all bedrooms Tea and coffee making facilities No dogs (ex guide dogs) Cen ht No children 7yrs 8P No coaches
PRICE GUIDE
ROOMS: s £18-£19; d £36-£42✳
CARDS: 💳 💳 💳
See advertisement on p.389.

GH Q Q Q *The Payton Hotel* 6 John St CV37 6UB (follow A439 from town centre towards Warwick and M40, then first left) ☎01789 266442 FAX 01789 266442
Closed 23-27 Dec
An attractive late-Georgian house centrally located within walking distance of the town centre is personally run by Mr and Mrs

➡

A warm welcome awaits you at Hardwick House

A delightful Victorian Building dating from 1887 situated in a quiet area of town, yet only a few minutes walk to the Shakespearian properties and Royal Shakespeare Theatre. Ideal position for Warwick Castle, Birmingham Arena and the National Exhibition Centre.

Large comfortable rooms. Ensuite and standard available. All with colour T.V., Tea/Coffee making facilities, hot & cold water, full central heating, **AMPLE CAR PARKING.**

RESIDENT PROPRIETORS

DRENAGH AND SIMON WOOTTON

Hardwick House, 1 Avenue Road,
Stratford-upon-Avon, Warwickshire. CV37 6UY

AA QQQ   **TELEPHONE RESERVATIONS**   English Tourist Board COMMENDED

01789 204307
Fax: 01789 296760

AA QQQ Recommended

All rooms are en-suite and are attractively furnished with colour television, tea and coffee making facilities, and fitted hairdryers. Single, twin, double and family rooms are available.

Hunters Moon is close to Anne Hathaway's cottage, and is an ideal base for visiting the Cotswold villages, Warwick Castle and all the other Shakespearian properties. Car parking. An excellent English breakfast is served by resident hosts – Stratfordians Rosemary and David Austin. Visa and Access accepted.

Recommended by Arthur Frommer.

Telephone for further details and reservations.

150 ALCESTER ROAD,
STRATFORD-UPON-AVON,
WARWICKSHIRE CV37 9DR
TELEPHONE: (01789) 292888

English Tourist Board

GRAVELSIDE BARN

Offers the discerning traveller all the modern conveniences and comforts of today in a stunning and tranquil setting.

Serenely situated on a hilltop in the middle of rolling Warwickshire farmland, with magnificent views of the countryside and Cotswold Hills.

A great base for exploring Shakespeare's Country and the Heart of England, or somewhere to relax and feel the cares and stresses slip away.

3½ miles from Stratford and 10 minutes from Junction 15 of the M40.

Please ring or fax for a brochure.

"Your place in the country"

GRAVELSIDE BARN

Denise & Guy Belchambers
Gravelside Barn, Binton, Stratford-upon-Avon,
Warwickshire CV37 9TU
Tel: 01789 750502/293122   Fax: 01789 298056

English Tourist Board HIGHLY COMMENDED

AA

Rickett. Bedrooms, although not overly spacious, are attractive and modern, with several extra welcoming touches. There are a pleasant little breakfast room and small lounge area on the ground floor.

5 rms (4 shr) No smoking CTV in all bedrooms Tea and coffee making facilities No dogs (ex guide dogs) Cen ht 3P No coaches

CARDS:

GH 🅀🅀🅀 **Penryn House** 126 Alcester Rd CV37 9DP (0.5m past railway station, right hand side of A422)
☎01789 293718

This is a well maintained guest house with good-sized and well looked after en-suite bathroom facilities. Breakfast is served in a large room with a view of the back garden. One of the bedrooms is located on the ground floor and another is located off the rear car park and is fully self contained. The owner finds time to pay extra attention to his colourful flower beds.

7 rms (5 shr) 1 annexe en suite (shr) (3 fmly) No smoking in dining room No smoking in lounges CTV in all bedrooms Tea and coffee making facilities Cen ht 9P

PRICE GUIDE
ROOMS: s £16-£23; d £35-£48; wkly b&b £100-£170
CARDS: 🅂 🔲 🔲 🔲   £

See advertisement on p.391.

GH 🅀🅀 **Ravenhurst** 2 Broad Walk CV37 6HS
☎01789 292515
Closed Xmas

This Victorian guest house is well positioned for the town centre and local amenities. Bedrooms are bright, modern and well equipped and there is a four-poster room. The ground floor features a combined lounge and breakfast room.

5 en suite (bth/shr) (1 fmly) No smoking CTV in all bedrooms Tea and coffee making facilities No dogs Cen ht 4P No coaches

PRICE GUIDE
ROOMS: d £38-£45
CARDS: 🅂 🔲 🔲 🔲

GH 🅀 **Salamander** 40 Grove Rd CV37 6PB (on A439 towards Evesham, just behind the police station)
☎01789 205728 FAX 01789 205728

Conveniently positioned close to the town centre, this semidetached house provides simple but sound accommodation. Bedrooms are furnished with a mixture of old and new and some have TV.

6 rms (4 shr) (3 fmly) No smoking in dining room CTV in all bedrooms Tea and coffee making facilities Cen ht CTV 6P Last d 6.30pm

PRICE GUIDE
ROOMS: s £16-£20; d £32-£42✳

Selected

GH 🅀🅀🅀🅀 **Sequoia House Private Hotel** 51-53 Shipston Rd CV37 7LN (on A3400 close to Clopton Bridge) ☎01789 268852 FAX 01789 414559
Closed 21-27 Dec

A very pleasing little hotel, this extended Victorian house stands close to the river and town centre (guests can walk into town via the rear garden). Bedrooms vary in size and some are more opulent than others but all are well equipped and brightly decorated. Five rooms are located in a converted cottage, and no-smoking rooms are available. There is also a lounge bar and a large air-conditioned conference/function room.

19 rms (15 bth/shr) 5 annexe en suite (shr) (4 fmly) CTV in all bedrooms Tea and coffee making facilities Direct dial

from bedrooms No dogs Licensed Cen ht CTV No children 5yrs 26P

PRICE GUIDE
ROOMS: s £29-£49; d £39-£72
CARDS: 🅂 🔲 🔲 🔲 🔲 🔲 🔲

See advertisement on p.391.

GH 🅀🅀🅀 **Stretton House Hotel** 38 Grove Rd CV37 6PB
☎01789 268647

A well kept semidetached house stands near the town centre. Bedrooms have modern furniture and include family rooms. There is a combined breakfast room and lounge.

7 rms (4 shr) (2 fmly) No smoking CTV in all bedrooms Tea and coffee making facilities No dogs (ex guide dogs) Cen ht No children 8yrs 4P Last d 4pm

PRICE GUIDE
ROOMS: s £20-£25; d £36-£48✳

Selected

GH 🅀🅀🅀🅀 **Twelfth Night** Evesham Place CV37 6HT (on A439) ☎01789 414595

This Victorian villa is situated west of the town centre with convenient access to the local amenities. Bedrooms are tastefully decorated and have been recently restored with colourful bold fabrics. They feature high quality facilities, brass beds and some extra personal touches. The comfortable lounge and attractive dining room have period furnishings and good quality fittings. The house is no smoking throughout.

6 en suite (shr) No smoking CTV in all bedrooms Tea and coffee making facilities No dogs Cen ht No children 12yrs 7P No coaches

PRICE GUIDE
ROOMS: d £44-£56
CARDS: 🅂 🔲

Selected

GH 🅀🅀🅀🅀 **Victoria Spa Lodge** Bishopton Ln CV37 9QY (1.50miles N on A3400 intersected by A46. 1st exit left Bishopton Lane, 1st house on right)
☎01789 267985 FAX 01789 204728

In recent times Paul and Doreen Tozer have transformed their early Victorian house with significant upgrading to the bedrooms. These are now prettily decorated and comfortable with quality furnishings, efficient en suite showers and a good range of modern equipment. The attractive lounge/dining room is similarly well furnished in period style, and handsome English or vegetarian breakfasts start the day.

7 en suite (shr) (3 fmly) No smoking CTV in all bedrooms Tea and coffee making facilities No dogs Cen ht CTV 12P No coaches

PRICE GUIDE
ROOMS: s £35-£38; d £40-£45✳
CARDS: 🅂 🔲

See advertisement on p.391.

GH 🅀🅀🅀 **Virginia Lodge** 12 Evesham Place CV37 6HT
☎01789 292157
Closed Xmas

Original Victorian features have been retained in the hallway of this well kept guest house. Individually styled bedrooms include one at the back with access to the garden.

➡

7 en suite (shr) (1 fmly) No smoking in bedrooms No smoking in dining room CTV in all bedrooms Tea and coffee making facilities Licensed Cen ht CTV 9P
PRICE GUIDE
ROOMS: s £18-£21; d £36-£46*

GH [Q][Q] **Winterbourne** 2 St Gregory's Rd CV37 6UH (from A439 Warwick to Stratford road turn right by church) ☎01789 292207 FAX 01789 292207
Closed 23-27 Dec
This large guest house, located to the east of the centre, retains some of its 1900s character. The bedrooms are mostly large and are gradually showing the results of ongoing improvements. Some have wide views over the rear garden with its variety of fruit trees. Parking is not usually difficult to find in this area.
5 rms (4 shr) (1 fmly) No smoking CTV in all bedrooms Tea and coffee making facilities No dogs Cen ht 4P No coaches
PRICE GUIDE
ROOMS: s £20-£45; d £40-£50*

 Y [Q][Q] Mrs R M Meadows **Monk's Barn** *(SP206516)* Shipston Rd CV37 8NA (on A3400 approx 1.25m S) ☎01789 293714
Closed 25-26 Dec
Monk's Barn Farm, two miles south of Stratford, has its origins in the 16th century, but the pretty farmhouse is more recent. Bedrooms are modern and well equipped and there are two newer rooms in the old milking parlour. The split-level dining room/lounge is warm and cosy.
4 rms (2 shr) 2 annexe en suite (shr) (1 fmly) No smoking in 2 bedrooms No smoking in dining room No smoking in lounges CTV in all bedrooms Tea and coffee making facilities No dogs (ex guide dogs) Cen ht CTV 5P Fishing 75 acres mixed
PRICE GUIDE
ROOMS: s £16-£18; d £29-£33; wkly b&b £87.50-£100

STREFFORD Shropshire Map **07** SO48

Y [Q][Q][Q] Mrs C Morgan **Strefford Hall** *(SO444856)* Strefford SY7 8DE ☎01588 672383
Closed Xmas & New Year
Stefford Hall is an impressive Victorian farmhouse, part of a large working farm, nestling at the foot of Wenlock Edge. There are three spacious bedrooms, two of which have modern en suite shower rooms, while the third has exclusive use of an adjoining bathroom; the amenities provided include TVs and hairdryers. There is a residents' lounge, complete with wood-burning stove, and the house is fronted by pleasant lawns and gardens. Please note that only non-smokers are accommodated.
3 en suite (bth/shr) No smoking CTV in all bedrooms Tea and coffee making facilities CTV 3P 350 acres arable beef sheep
PRICE GUIDE
ROOMS: s fr £18; d £36-£38; wkly b&b fr £126*

STRETFORD Greater Manchester Map **07** SJ89

GH [Q][Q] **Thistlewood Hotel** 203 Urmston Ln M32 9EF (leave M63 junct 3 towards Urmston, onto Stretford Rd, then Urmston Ln) ☎0161 865 3611
This large Edwardian house, though set in a pleasant residential area, stands not far from junction 7 of the M63. Public areas are spacious, while modern bedrooms all provide hair dryers and trouser presses. Family owned and run, the hotel offers friendly, attentive service.
9 en suite (shr) (1 fmly) No smoking in dining room CTV in all bedrooms Tea and coffee making facilities No dogs (ex guide

dogs) Licensed Cen ht CTV 8P No coaches Last d 5pm
PRICE GUIDE
ROOMS: s £29; d £43*
CARDS:

STROUD Gloucestershire Map **03** SO80

GH [Q][Q][Q] **Ashleigh House** Bussage GL6 8AZ (take A419 to Brinscombe and turn into Toadsmoor Road. After 1.5m turn right and right again 0.5m after phone box. Turn right into gates of house) ☎01453 883944 FAX 01453 886931
Feb-Nov
9 en suite (bth/shr) (3 fmly) No smoking in bedrooms CTV in all bedrooms Tea and coffee making facilities No dogs Licensed Cen ht 9P No coaches Last d 11am
PRICE GUIDE
ROOMS: s £21-£27; d £36-£48.50; wkly b&b fr £126; wkly hlf-bd fr £173.25*

GH [Q][Q][Q] **Downfield Hotel** 134 Cainscross Rd GL5 4HN (2m W on A419) ☎01453 764496 FAX 01453 753150
Closed 2 wks Xmas & New Year
This family-run hotel stands only a mile from the centre of the small town of Stroud. Some of the comfortable, well equipped bedrooms have en suite facilities, guests can enjoy a drink in the pleasant lounge before eating in a spacious dining room, and on-site parking is available.
21 rms (11 bth/shr) (4 fmly) CTV in 17 bedrooms Tea and coffee making facilities Direct dial from bedrooms Licensed Cen ht CTV 25P No coaches Last d 8pm
PRICE GUIDE
ROOMS: s £20-£29; d £29-£35
CARDS:

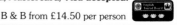

Selected

GH Q Q Q Q **Hunters Lodge** Dr Browns Rd,
Minchinhampton GL6 9BT
☎01453 883588 FAX 01453 731449
Closed Xmas
3 en suite (bth/shr) (1 fmly) No smoking CTV in all
bedrooms Tea and coffee making facilities No dogs 8P No
coaches
PRICE GUIDE
ROOMS: s £25-£28; d £36-£44✳

STUDLEY Warwickshire Map 04 SP06

♥ Q Q Q Miss S A Walters *Bug In The Blanket (SP089643)*
Castle Farm B80 7AH ☎01527 854275 & 852254
FAX 01527 854897
Do not be put off by the name; this reflects the quirky but pleasing
nature of this farmhouse. Set in the grounds of a 500-acre estate,
the majority of accommodation is offered in 'The Wing',
converted from old garden buildings. These modern en suite
rooms have a good range of facilities including a kitchenette. Two
rooms are situated in the 15th-century black and white cottage,
'The Bug'; these rooms have access to shower facilities only via
public areas. 'The Bug' also contains the dining room where
appetising meals are served around a communal table, helping to
maintain the convivial and fun atmosphere of the place.
Continental breakfast can be left in room refrigerators,
alternatively, a cooked breakfast is available in the cottage. There
is also a cosy lounge and the restaurant is licensed.
2 rms 6 annexe en suite (bth/shr) (1 fmly) CTV in 6 bedrooms
Tea and coffee making facilities No dogs (ex guide dogs)
Licensed Cen ht CTV 15P Outdoor swimming pool (heated)
Sauna 500 acres arable beef sheep Last d 2pm

STURMINSTER NEWTON Dorset Map 03 ST71

♥ Q Q Q Mrs S Wingate-Saul *Holebrook (ST743117)* Lydlinch
DT10 2JB ☎01258 817348
rs 25 Dec-1 Jan
This charming Georgian farmhouse is situated amid beautiful
peaceful countryside. Guests have the choice of staying in the
main house , or any of the attractively converted stables or cow-
byres, which are equipped for self catering or can be B&B. There
is a large games room with pool table, table tennis and a range of
exercise equipment; outside there is a swimming pool, croquet
lawn and of course the animals - guests are welcome to assist in
some of the day to day chores such as feeding and egg collecting.
2 rms 4 annexe rms (3 shr) No smoking in dining room No
smoking in 1 lounge CTV in 4 bedrooms Tea and coffee making
facilities No dogs (ex guide dogs) Licensed Cen ht CTV 12P
Outdoor swimming pool Games room Mini-gym 126 acres
mixed Last d 4pm

STURTON BY STOW Lincolnshire Map 08 SK88

Selected

♥ Q Q Q Q Mrs Brenda Williams **Gallows Dale Farm**
(SK874809) Stow Park Rd LN1 2AH (1m W on A1500)
☎01427 788387
This attractive 18th-century brick-built house has been
extended and carefully furnished to a very pleasant standard.
There is a cosy lounge to the rear, and a very substantial
breakfast is served in the inviting dining room. Bedrooms are
pleasantly furnished and have radios and tea-making facilities.

The house is fully non-smoking and service is naturally
friendly.
3 rms (1 shr) (1 fmly) No smoking Tea and coffee making
facilities No dogs Cen ht CTV 5P 33 acres cattle & horses
PRICE GUIDE
ROOMS: s £15-£18; d £30-£40; wkly b&b fr £90✳

SUDBURY Suffolk Map 05 TL84

GH Q Q *Hill Lodge Private Hotel* 8 Newton Rd CO10 6RL
☎01787 377568
Well maintained and comfortable, this small commercial hotel is
personally supervised by its owners. Simply decorated but
attractively furnished bedrooms are well equipped, the spacious
bar has a lounge area and an evening meal is served in the bright
dining room. Conference facilities are also available.
17 rms (7 shr) CTV in all bedrooms No dogs (ex guide dogs)
Licensed Cen ht CTV 2P
CARDS: 🔴

GH Q Q *Old Bull And Trivets* Church St CO10 6BL
☎01787 374120 FAX 01787 379044
Whether you enter by the main door of the hotel or go into the
restaurant from the car park, you will be warmly welcomed. On
the ground floor you will find a pizzeria and lounge, whilst
upstairs, among the beams, are seven large bedrooms - two of
them having raised mezzanines which hide an extra bed.
7 rms (4 bth/shr) 3 annexe en suite (bth/shr) (5 fmly) CTV in all
bedrooms Tea and coffee making facilities Direct dial from
bedrooms Licensed Cen ht 15P Last d 10pm
CARDS: 🔲 🔲 🔲 🔴

SUNDERLAND Tyne & Wear Map 12 NZ35

GH Q Q Q **Bed & Breakfast Stop** 183 Newcastle Rd, Fulwell
SR5 1NR (on A1018, 0.5m on right past windmill)
☎0191 548 2291
This semidetached dormer bungalow is situated on the A1018 at
Fulwell, just north of Sunderland, offering good standards of
accommodation in a convenient location. The three bedrooms do
not have washbasins, but all rooms are tastefully and comfortably
furnished and there are ample general facilities for guests' use.
There is a very comfortable lounge downstairs incorporates an
attractive dining area. Private parking is provided.
3 rms (1 fmly) No smoking CTV in all bedrooms Tea and
coffee making facilities No dogs Cen ht CTV No children 3yrs
3P No coaches Last d noon
PRICE GUIDE
ROOMS: s £15-£17; d £28-£30; wkly b&b £98-£110; wkly hlf-
bd £133-£140✳

SURBITON Greater London Map 04 TQ16

GH Q Q **Warwick** 321 Ewell Rd KT6 7BX (on A240 towards
Kingston Warwick Guesthouse is in half a mile on the right))
☎0181 296 0516 FAX 0181 296 0517
This small guesthouse, convenient for the A3, is run by a cheerful
proprietress. Bedrooms are simply furnished and best suited for
single guests. Public areas are limited.
9 rms (1 bth/shr) (1 fmly) CTV in all bedrooms Tea and coffee
making facilities Direct dial from bedrooms Cen ht CTV 8P
Last d 2pm
PRICE GUIDE
ROOMS: s £28-£34; d £38-£44; wkly b&b fr £175; wkly hlf-bd
fr £225
CARDS: 🔲 🔲

SUTTON Greater London Map **04** TQ26

GH 🔲🔲🔲 **Ashling Tara Hotel** 50 Rosehill SM1 3EU
☎0181 641 6142 FAX 0181 644 7872
Located opposite the Rose Hill tennis centre and sports complex
and only a mile from the nearest tube for quick access to central
London, this hotel is ideal for business and pleasure. The
accommodation is slowly being upgraded: Ashling House
comprising reception, bar, restaurant, lounge and function room,
while most of the bedrooms, which have every modern facility, are
in the Ashling Tara Annexe.
12 en suite (bth/shr) 4 annexe en suite (shr) (2 fmly) No
smoking in bedrooms No smoking in dining room No smoking in
lounges CTV in all bedrooms Tea and coffee making facilities
Direct dial from bedrooms No dogs Licensed Cen ht CTV 25P
Last d 9.30pm
PRICE GUIDE
ROOMS: s fr £50; d fr £60∗
CARDS: 🔲 🔲 🔲 £

GH 🔲 **Dene Hotel** 39 Cheam Rd SM1 2AT (W on A232 one
way system opposite Selcombe Centre)
☎0181 642 3170 FAX 0181 642 3170
The Dene has been personally run as a bed and breakfast hotel for
many years, in a very friendly manner. It is a pair of linked houses,
very close to the town centre, opposite the Holiday Inn, offering
bedrooms in a variety of sizes, some with garden views.
28 rms (12 bth/shr) (3 fmly) No smoking in dining room CTV in
all bedrooms Tea and coffee making facilities Direct dial from
bedrooms No dogs (ex guide dogs) Cen ht 18P No coaches
PRICE GUIDE
ROOMS: s £19.98-£37.63; d £39.95-£49.35∗ £

SUTTON West Sussex Map **04** SU91

🔲 🔲🔲🔲🔲🔲 **The White
Horse** RH20 1PS
☎01798 869221
FAX 01798 869291
Recently restored and
completely refurbished, this
privately owned inn has
offered comfort and
sustenance to travellers and
locals alike since 1746.
Bedrooms vary in shape and
size, but all have been
thoughtfully equipped and attractively refurnished in modern
style; should you wish to get away from it all, the Cottage
Annexe with its quiet garden setting and absence of telephone
provides the ideal opportunity. The bar is double-sided - the
'public' featuring a comprehensive range of real ales, the
other complementing a more sophisticated choice of drinks by
a blackboard menu of meals and snacks. There is also a
slightly more formal eating area, and the beer garden and
patio add a further dimension during the warmer months.
5 en suite (bth) CTV in all bedrooms Tea and coffee making
facilities Direct dial from bedrooms No dogs Cen ht 10P
No coaches Last d 9.30pm
PRICE GUIDE
ROOMS: s £48; d £58; wkly b&b £134-£218; wkly hlf-bd
£206-£290
MEALS: Lunch £12&alc Dinner £12&alc
CARDS: 🔲 🔲 🔲 🔲 £

SUTTON COLDFIELD West Midlands Map **07** SP19

GH 🔲🔲 **Standbridge Hotel** 138 Birmingham Rd B72 1LY
(1m S on A5127) ☎0121 354 3007
A handsome early Victorian property, the Standbridge offers well
maintained accommodation. There are a homely residents' lounge
and, beyond it, a lovely enclosed garden with terrace. Mrs Watts
serves alternative dishes for the health-conscious.
8 rms No smoking in 4 bedrooms No smoking in dining room
No smoking in lounges CTV in all bedrooms Tea and coffee
making facilities Licensed Cen ht CTV No children 5yrs 8P
No coaches Jacuzzi Spa bath Last d 6pm
PRICE GUIDE
ROOMS: s £20-£25; d £35∗
CARDS: 🔲 🔲

SUTTON UPON DERWENT Humberside Map **08** SE74

GH 🔲🔲🔲 **Manor Farmhouse** Main St YO4 5BN (7.5m S of
York off B1228. Follow B1228 through Elvington over stone
bridge to Sutton on Derwent, pass church) ☎01904 608009
An attractive detached former farmhouse standing in the delightful
village of Sutton on Derwent and opposite the church. There are
three well furnished bedrooms and a cosy lounge is provided for
guests. Breakfast is served around a large table and service is very
friendly and attentive.
3 en suite (shr) No smoking CTV in all bedrooms No dogs (ex
guide dogs) Cen ht CTV 6P No coaches
PRICE GUIDE
ROOMS: s £20; d £36-£40; wkly b&b £126-£140 £

See advertisement on p.395.

SWAFFHAM Norfolk Map **05** TF80

Selected

GH Q Q Q Q **Corfield House** Sporle PE32 2EA (3m E, on S edge of village, 0.5m from A47) ☎01760 723636 end Mar-mid Dec

Corfield is an immaculately kept house dating from 1820 with a 1950s extension. The bedrooms are neat and attractively furnished and there is a small lounge with plenty of useful leaflets (the owner works in a local tourist information centre). The set dinner is discussed at the start of the day, enthusiastically prepared, and served in the cosy dining room. Smoking is not permitted in the house.

5 en suite (bth/shr) No smoking CTV in all bedrooms Tea and coffee making facilities No dogs Licensed Cen ht 5P No coaches Last d 5.30pm
PRICE GUIDE
ROOMS: s £23; d £37-£43; wkly b&b £129.50-£161; wkly hlf-bd £205-£230
CARDS: ▨ ▨

◀ Q Q Q **Red Lion Hotel** 87 Market Place PE37 7AQ
☎01760 721022

A popular centrally-located town public house with a cheerful team of staff. Newly built accommodation is situated to the rear and provides bright, colourfully furnished bedrooms, each with shower room and colour TV. Some of the bedrooms are designed to contain family groups.

9 annexe en suite (shr) CTV in all bedrooms Tea and coffee making facilities Cen ht 8P Last d 9.30pm
PRICE GUIDE
ROOMS: s £25-£30; d £35-£37✱
CARDS: ▨ ▨ ▨   (£)

SWANAGE Dorset Map **04** SZ07

GH Q Q Q **Bella Vista Hotel** 14 Burlington Rd BH19 1LS (from A351 travel towards Studland, take 2nd right opposite Crows Nest PH. Bella Vista is next to Grand Hotel)
☎01929 422873
Mar-Oct rs Jan-Feb

This small, friendly guesthouse continues to provide a high standard of accommodation. The bedrooms are attractive and reasonably equipped. There is a comfortable lounge and a choice of breakfasts is served in the dining room.

7 rms (5 shr) (4 fmly) No smoking CTV in all bedrooms Tea and coffee making facilities No dogs Licensed Cen ht 6P No coaches Last d 10am
PRICE GUIDE
ROOMS: d £32-£45; wkly b&b £100-£142; wkly hlf-bd £163-£204

GH Q Q Q **Burlington House Hotel** 7 Highcliffe Rd BH19 1LW ☎01929 422422
8 Apr-28 Oct

This small private hotel provides comfortable and well-equipped accommodation. There is a relaxing lounge and separate bar. Dinner and breakfast are served in the dining room.

8 rms (7 bth/shr) (6 fmly) No smoking in dining room CTV in all bedrooms No dogs Licensed Cen ht CTV 9P Last d 5pm

⋈ ▦ GH Q Q Q **Chines Hotel** 9 Burlington Rd BH19 1LR
☎01929 422457
2 Mar-19 Oct

A friendly atmosphere prevails at this popular family-run hotel.

Airy bedrooms include a large number with en suite facilities; a cosy lounge bar is also provided, as is an attractive dining room where a good home-cooked evening meal can be enjoyed.

12 rms (8 shr) (3 fmly) No smoking in bedrooms No smoking in dining room CTV in all bedrooms Tea and coffee making facilities No dogs Licensed Cen ht CTV 9P Last d 4pm
PRICE GUIDE
ROOMS: s £16-£22; d £32-£44; wkly b&b £112-£154; wkly hlf-bd £112-£224   (£)

⋈ ▦ GH Q Q Q **Crowthorne Hotel** 24 Cluny Crescent BH19 2BT (from town centre follow uphill beside White Swan public house. Hotel just beyond the youth hostel)
☎01929 422108
Apr-Oct

In a quiet residential area, this Victorian villa-style house provides a high standard of accommodation and friendly service. There is a choice of dishes at dinner and the cooking is a good balance of English dishes.

8 rms (2 bth 3 shr) (2 fmly) No smoking Tea and coffee making facilities No dogs Licensed Cen ht CTV 8P No coaches Last d 5pm
PRICE GUIDE
ROOMS: (incl. dinner) s £16-£20; d £32-£48; wkly b&b £100-£144; wkly hlf-bd £150-£205
CARDS: ▨ ▨   (£)

GH Q Q *Eversden Private Hotel* Victoria Rd BH19 1LY
☎01929 423276
Mar-Nov

A small comfortable family-run hotel is pleasantly situated in New Swanage, with fine open views, convenient for the Isle of Purbeck golf club and the sandy beach. Public areas include a small TV lounge, a lounge bar for residents and a light, spacious dining room where a set-price dinner is served at separate tables. There is ample private parking.

12 rms (2 bth 3 shr) (3 fmly) No smoking in 5 bedrooms No smoking in dining room CTV in 10 bedrooms Tea and coffee making facilities No dogs Licensed Cen ht CTV 12P No coaches Last d 6pm

GH Q Q Q *Firswood Hotel* 29 Kings Rd BH19 1HF
☎01929 422306
Closed Xmas rs Jan-Mar & Nov-Dec

Enjoying a central location close to the shops and steam railway, this attractive and very well presented property is personally run by the cheerful Mr and Mrs Baker. Bedrooms are neat, well decorated and nicely furnished, with four of the six rooms having smart en suite facilities. The first floor lounge has comfortable sofas and TV, and the dining room is smartly decorated and nicely furnished. This is a very friendly place to stay, offering a good standard of accommodation at good value prices.

6 rms (2 bth 2 shr) (2 fmly) No smoking in dining room CTV in all bedrooms Tea and coffee making facilities No dogs Cen ht CTV No children 5yrs 7P No coaches Last d 4.30pm

GH Q Q Q **Havenhurst Hotel** 3 Cranbourne Rd BH19 1EA
☎01929 424224

In a quiet residential area, this family run private hotel continues to improve. A number of bedrooms have been upgraded and new modern showers installed. Public areas include a comfortable bar and a small television lounge. A choice of menus is available at lunch and dinner, which include a good selection of home made desserts.

17 en suite (bth/shr) (4 fmly) No smoking in dining room CTV in all bedrooms Tea and coffee making facilities No dogs (ex

guide dogs) Licensed Cen ht CTV 17P Last d 7pm
PRICE GUIDE
ROOMS: s £17.50-£30; d £35-£60; wkly b&b £120-£200; wkly hlf-bd £170-£235✱

GH ⓠⓠⓠ **Oxford Hotel** 3/5 Park Rd BH19 2AA
☎01929 422247
In a pleasant location on the edge of the town and close to the seafront, this comfortable guesthouse offers attractive and well equipped bedrooms. There is a good sized lounge and bar as well as a dining room.
14 rms (7 bth/shr) (4 fmly) CTV in all bedrooms Tea and coffee making facilities No dogs Licensed Cen ht CTV Last d 4.30pm
PRICE GUIDE
ROOMS: s £13-£17.50; d £30-£35✱

GH ⓠⓠⓠ **St Michael Hotel** 31 Kings Rd BH19 1HF
☎01929 422064
This neat and well managed private hotel has recently changed hands, and new owners are already introducing attractive soft fabrics and fresh decor into the comfortable, predominantly en suite bedrooms; relaxing public areas have a warm, friendly atmosphere. A small forecourt car park is available for guests' use.
5 en suite (shr) (3 fmly) No smoking in dining room CTV in all bedrooms Tea and coffee making facilities Licensed Cen ht CTV No children 5yrs 5P No coaches Last d 2pm
PRICE GUIDE
ROOMS: d £30-£35; wkly b&b £95-£115; wkly hlf-bd £144-£164✱

GH ⓠⓠⓠ **Sandringham Hotel** 20 Durlston Rd BH19 2HX
(Follow signs for 'Durlston Country Park') ☎01929 423076
Mr and Mrs Sill are the owners of this well maintained and comfortable guest house. Situated in a quiet residential area, it offers well appointed bedrooms and restful public areas.
11 rms (9 shr) (5 fmly) No smoking in dining room Tea and coffee making facilities No dogs (ex guide dogs) Licensed Cen ht CTV 8P No coaches Last d 6.30pm
PRICE GUIDE
ROOMS: s £22-£26; d £44-£52; wkly b&b £150-£175; wkly hlf-bd £192-£216
CARDS: 🔳 💳

GH ⓠⓠⓠ **White Lodge Hotel** Grosvenor Rd BH19 2DD
☎01929 422696 & 425510
rs Dec & Feb
Improvements have recently been made to this small but comfortable guesthouse. The bedrooms are nicely furnished and equipped with the usual facilities. Public areas are compact and a choice of breakfasts is available in the dining room.
14 rms (13 bth/shr) (4 fmly) No smoking in 10 bedrooms No smoking in dining room No smoking in 1 lounge CTV in all bedrooms Tea and coffee making facilities Licensed Cen ht CTV No children 2yrs 12P Last d 6pm
PRICE GUIDE
ROOMS: (incl. dinner) s £20-£25; d £36-£44; wkly b&b £140-£160; wkly hlf-bd £170-£190✱
CARDS: 🔳 💳

Our inspectors never book in the name of the AA. They disclose their identity only after the bill has been paid.

SWAY Hampshire Map **04** SZ29

Premier Selected

GH ⓠⓠⓠⓠⓠ **The Nurse's Cottage** Station Rd SO41 6BA (off B3055 in village next to post office)
☎01590 683402
FAX 01590 683402
Closed 15 Nov-15 Dec
This popular little cottage offers accommodation which has been completely refurbished, with admirable attention to detail, by the present owner Tony Barnfield. Well equipped bedrooms are decorated in attractive co-ordinating fabrics, there are a cosy lounge and dining room, and the evening meal is not to be missed, with a seasonally-changing, three-course menu at a very reasonable price. The wine list is also a real treat, containing over 70 wines, many of them as half bottles. Short break holidays and leisure pursuits are available, and car parking can be provided.
3 en suite (shr) No smoking CTV in all bedrooms Tea and coffee making facilities Licensed Cen ht No children 5yrs 6P No coaches Last d 7.30pm
PRICE GUIDE
ROOMS: (incl. dinner) s £45; d £80; wkly hlf-bd £230-£265
CARDS: 🔳 💳 💳 💳 💳
See advertisement on p.397.

MANOR FARMHOUSE

Sutton upon Derwent,
York YO4 5BN
Telephone: 01904 608009

An 18th century farmhouse situated in an attractive village location next to the church and 4 minutes walk to the village pub. All the bedrooms are decorated to a high standard with en suite facilities and tea/coffee making. Comfortable guest lounge with an inglenook fireplace. Lovely garden. Ample car parking. Non-smoking. An ideal base for visiting York (7 miles) and Castle Howard (15 miles). Contact Diana Arnold

SWINDERBY Lincolnshire Map 08 SK86

GH ◨◨◨ *Halfway Farm Motel & Guest House* A46
LN6 9HN (8m N of Newark on A46, 8m SW Lincoln)
☎01522 868749 FAX 01522 868082
Standing beside the A46 midway between Lincoln and Newark,
this 18th-century farmhouse and stable complex has been cleverly
converted into a modern motel, with some main house
accommodation. The motel rooms all have modern en suite
shower rooms, and all the bedrooms have a good range of
facilities. The farmhouse retains much of its original character,
offering a beamed lounge and an attractive dining room.
7 rms (5 shr) 10 annexe en suite (shr) (3 fmly) No smoking in
dining room CTV in all bedrooms Tea and coffee making
facilities Direct dial from bedrooms Cen ht CTV 20P No
coaches
CARDS:
See advertisement under LINCOLN

SWINDON Wiltshire Map 04 SU18

GH ◨◨◨ **Fir Tree Lodge** 17 Highworth Rd, Stratton St
Margaret SN3 4QL (opposite 'The Rat Trap' public house.
Follow A419 until Highworth/Burford turn right at rdbt Fir
Tree Lodge 100yds on right) ☎01793 822372
A large, modern family home with a spacious car park and rear
garden, situated on the A361, just over two miles from the town
centre. Bedrooms offer modern decor, furnishings and facilities,
and breakfast is served in the attractive dining room. Mr and Mrs
Duggan extend a friendly welcome to their guests.
11 en suite (shr) No smoking in bedrooms CTV in all bedrooms
Tea and coffee making facilities No dogs (ex guide dogs) Cen ht
CTV 14P No coaches
PRICE GUIDE
ROOMS: s £25-£29; d £35-£45

(£)

Selected

GH ◨◨◨◨ **Portquin** Highworth Rd, Blunsdon
SN2 4DH (turn off A419 at Blunsdon onto B4019
signposted Highworth, half a mile from A419)
☎01793 721261 FAX 01793 721261
The family home of Ann and Roger Scratchley, this
guesthouse enjoys a rural situation within an easy drive of
Swindon centre and the M4. Bedrooms have been tastefully
decorated and equipped with modern facilities. Breakfast is
served in an attractive dining room which is open plan and
combines with a spacious, comfortable lounge.
6 en suite (shr) 3 annexe en suite (shr) (2 fmly) No smoking
in 6 bedrooms No smoking in dining room No smoking in
lounges CTV in all bedrooms Tea and coffee making
facilities Direct dial from bedrooms Cen ht 12P No coaches
PRICE GUIDE
ROOMS: s £23-£26; d £35-£40∗

(£)

♥ ◨◨◨ Mrs J Hussey **Weir Farm** *(SU114772)* Broad Hinton
SN4 9NE (6m SW of Swindon, on A4361 adjacent to Broad
Hinton/Uffcott crossroads)
☎01793 731207 FAX 01793 731207
Closed 24 Dec-Feb
This elegant farmhouse, in its own well kept gardens with a tennis
court, is set back from the A361 on the Swindon side of Broad
Hinton. The three bedrooms are spacious and have been equipped
with many thoughtful extras such as sewing kits, tissues and
writing paper. There is a lounge for guests' use and breakfast is

served at one large table in the dining room. The Weir is a no-
smoking establishment.
3 rms No smoking Tea and coffee making facilities No dogs
Cen ht CTV No children 8yrs 6P Tennis (hard) Riding 2000
acres arable beef dairy
PRICE GUIDE
ROOMS: s £20-£24; d £30-£38∗

(£)

SWINEFORD Avon Map 03 ST66

Premier Selected

GH ◨◨◨◨◨ **Gaites
House** Swineford, Bitton
BS15 6LR (situated off A431
Bristol/Bath road, at village
of Swineford)
☎0117 932 9800
FAX 0117 932 8882
This newly refurbished country
house which stands in seven
acres of grounds with the most
marvellous views of the
surrounding Cotswold
escarpment is conveniently situated between Bath and Bristol,
just off the A431 at Swineford. Its enthusiastic owners Nick
and Liz Sandy make every effort to ensure that their guests
are comfortable and well looked after. Bedrooms are en suite
or with private bathroom and are beautifully decorated, well
appointed and have many extras. A sumptuous breakfast
which includes a generous buffet with fresh fruit, home-made
muesli and jams is served around a communal table in the
long dining room. Guests also have use of a very comfortable
and elegantly decorated drawing room with doors opening out
on to the terrace. Hot-air ballooning and clay-pigeon
shooting can also be arranged and the owners are very willing,
for a small charge, to drop you off and collect you from the
local village pub.
3 en suite (bth/shr) No smoking in bedrooms No smoking in
dining room CTV in all bedrooms Tea and coffee making
facilities Direct dial from bedrooms Cen ht 20P No coaches
PRICE GUIDE
ROOMS: s £45-£55; d £65-£75
CARDS:

(£)

SYDLING ST NICHOLAS Dorset Map 03 SY69

GH ◨◨◨ **Lamperts Cottage** Sydling St Nicholas DT2 9NU
(from A37 turn off right just beyond Grimstone, follow valley
road to Sydling St Nicholas, Lamperts Cottage 1st thatched
cottage on right) ☎01300 341659 FAX 01300 341699
Lamperts Cottage offers comfortable accommodation in an
attractive village setting. There is a little footbridge across the
stream to the front door, and Nicky Willis ensures that guests are
warmly welcomed on arrival. Well furnished bedrooms have
pretty co-ordinated fabrics and original features. There is a huge
fireplace in the breakfast room, and a traditional breakfast includes
home-made preserves and local eggs.
3 rms No smoking in 3 bedrooms No smoking in dining room
No smoking in lounges Tea and coffee making facilities No dogs
No children 8yrs
PRICE GUIDE
ROOMS: s £20-£30; d £36; wkly b&b £108

(£)

SYMONDS YAT (EAST) Hereford & Worcester Map **03** SO51

GH 🇶🇶🇶 **Garth Cottage Hotel** HR9 6JL (turn off A40 at Little Chef, Whitchurch & follow signs for Symonds Yat East) ☎01600 890364
Apr-Oct
The Eden family runs this impeccably maintained little guest house which stands beside the River Wye, offering river views from all the bedrooms. The cosy lounge has a conservatory extension and solid fuel stove, a pleasant dining room furnished in sturdy pine provides separate tables, and there is a small bar.
4 en suite (shr) No smoking in dining room Tea and coffee making facilities No dogs (ex guide dogs) Licensed Cen ht CTV No children 12yrs 9P No coaches Fishing Last d 3pm
PRICE GUIDE
ROOMS: d £46; wkly b&b £147; wkly hlf-bd £252

SYMONDS YAT (WEST) (NEAR ROSS-ON-WYE)
Hereford & Worcester Map **03** SO51

GH 🇶🇶🇶 **Woodlea Hotel** HR9 6BL (on B4164, 1.5m from junct with A40) ☎01600 890206 FAX 01600 890206
A family-run hotel dating back to the 16th century is idyllically situated on wooded slopes overlooking the River Wye with views of this famous beauty spot. Bedrooms are simply furnished and there are attractive public areas including two lounges and a cosy cottage-style bar. The gardens contain terraced lawns and a patio.
9 rms (6 bth/shr) (2 fmly) No smoking in dining room Tea and coffee making facilities Direct dial from bedrooms Licensed Cen ht CTV 9P No coaches Last d 6.30pm
PRICE GUIDE
ROOMS: s £22-£40; d £44-£60; wkly b&b £154-£195; wkly hlf-bd £210-£245
CARDS: 🖸 🖸 🖸 £

TADCASTER North Yorkshire Map **08** SE44

GH 🇶🇶 **Shann House** 47 Kirkgate LS24 9AQ (leave A64 at Tadcaster turn off, Shann House is opposite St Mary's Church) ☎01937 833931
There are plans to carry out a complete refurbishment of this imposing Georgian house in the centre of the town. Bedrooms are simply furnished, and there are a guests' lounge and a rear dining room where breakfast is served.
8 en suite (bth/shr) (1 fmly) No smoking in dining room CTV in all bedrooms Tea and coffee making facilities Licensed Cen ht No coaches
PRICE GUIDE
ROOMS: s £20.50-£23; d £36-£40; wkly b&b £143.50-£161✳
CARDS: 🖸 🖸 £

TARRANT MONKTON Dorset Map **03** ST90

◀ 🇶🇶🇶 *Langton Arms* DT11 8RX
☎01258 830225 FAX 01258 480053
This attractive 17th-century thatched inn stands in the centre of the peaceful Dorset village. The chalet-style bedrooms are located in a modern annexe building and are all of a good size, with modern furnishings and facilities. The inn is full of charm and character, and there are two small cosy bars, one with a large inglenook fireplace; the extensive range of bar snacks is also served in the separate, more formal dining room. Traditional English fare is offered, and the dishes are well prepared and full of flavour. Breakfast is served in a sunny conservatory, and the atmosphere throughout is relaxed and friendly.
6 annexe en suite (bth/shr) (2 fmly) No smoking in area of dining room CTV in all bedrooms Tea and coffee making facilities Direct dial from bedrooms 80P Skittles Last d 9.45pm
CARDS: 🖸 🖸 🖸

TAUNTON Somerset Map **03** ST22

See also Churchingford

GH 🇶🇶🇶 **Brookfield** 16 Wellington Rd TA1 4EQ (just out of town on A38) ☎01823 272786
Just five minutes from the centre of Taunton, Brookfield offers seven comfortable guest rooms, all of which should have en suite facilities in 1995. Full English breakfast is served in the spacious dining room and Mrs Boyce is happy to cook dinner by prior arrangement. Guests also have the use of a cosy lounge.
8 rms (6 bth/shr) in 2 bedrooms No smoking in dining room CTV in all bedrooms Tea and coffee making facilities Licensed Cen ht CTV 8P No coaches
PRICE GUIDE
ROOMS: s £17-£20; d £32-£40; wkly b&b £119-£140 £

GH 🇶🇶🇶 **Jays Nest** Meare Green, Stoke St Gregory TA3 6HZ ☎01823 490250 FAX 01823 490250
The Jay's Nest stands in an acre of grounds just a short walk from the Willows and Wetlands Centre, the home of basket-making crafts. New owners have just taken over and plan to make a number of changes including the upgrading of bedrooms. Public areas include a comfortable lounge, a bar and a dining room overlooking the patio and serving a choice of dishes at dinner.
5 rms (1 bth 2 shr) No smoking in bedrooms No smoking in dining room No smoking in 1 lounge Tea and coffee making facilities Licensed CTV No children 10yrs 20P Last d 8.30pm
PRICE GUIDE
ROOMS: s £27; d £44-£50; wkly b&b £154-£175; wkly hlf-bd £224-£245✳ £

See advertisement on p.399.

Selected

GH ◨◨◨◨ **Meryan House Hotel** Bishop's Hull
TA1 5EG (take A38 out of town)
☎01823 337445 FAX 01823 322355
Dating back over 300 years, this charming period property is
located in the centre of the village, only a mile from Taunton.
Owners Mr and Mrs Clark have modernised the house with
care, exposing beams and three inglenook fireplaces. There is
a comfortable lounge as well as a cosy bar, where guests
choose from the varied dinner menu. Dishes are prepared
from the best of fresh local produce, including vegetables
from the garden. The bedrooms are simply decorated but
enhanced by attractive fabrics and pieces of antique furniture.
12 en suite (bth/shr) (3 fmly) No smoking in 4 bedrooms No
smoking in dining room No smoking in 1 lounge CTV in all
bedrooms Tea and coffee making facilities Direct dial from
bedrooms Licensed Cen ht CTV 17P No coaches Last d
6.30pm
PRICE GUIDE
ROOMS: s £35-£40; d £40-£58✳
CARDS: 🟦 🟥 £

Selected

♥ ◨◨◨◨ Mrs M Fewings **Higher Dipford** *(ST216205)*
Trull TA3 7NU ☎01823 275770 & 257916
An attractive Somerset long house in a farmyard setting at the
foot of the Blagdon Hills, this hotel affords easy access to the
M5 and the centre of Taunton. The interior reflects good taste,
quality and charm. A choice of beamed lounges includes one
with an inglenook fireplace and a small bar. Farmhouse
cooking based on local ingredients is served at separate tables
in the dining room.
3 en suite (bth/shr) No smoking in 2 bedrooms No smoking
in dining room No smoking in 1 lounge CTV in all
bedrooms Tea and coffee making facilities No dogs (ex
guide dogs) Licensed Cen ht CTV 6P 120 acres beef dairy
Last d 8pm
PRICE GUIDE
ROOMS: s £28-£32; d £46-£54; wkly b&b £161-£175;
wkly hlf-bd £266-£294✳
CARDS: 🟥 £

TAVISTOCK Devon Map **02** SX47

See also Mary Tavy

Selected

GH ◨◨◨◨ **Old Coach House Hotel** Ottery PL19 8NS
(2m W) ☎01822 617515
Originally built for the Duke of Bedford in 1857, this former
farm coach house is situated in the hamlet of Ottery.
Sympathetically renovated in 1989, it has been converted into
a small hotel of character with well equipped bedrooms, of
which three are conveniently on the ground floor. Both the
cosy lounge and the intimate restaurant have access to the
patio and south-facing rear garden. Both set meal and carte
meals are offered.
6 en suite (bth/shr) (1 fmly) No smoking in dining room
CTV in all bedrooms Tea and coffee making facilities Direct

---

dial from bedrooms Licensed Cen ht CTV No children 5yrs
8P Last d 10pm
PRICE GUIDE
ROOMS: s £19.50-£30; d £39-£56; wkly b&b £119-£168;
wkly hlf-bd £140-£198
CARDS: 🟦 🟥 🟥 🟦 🟥 🟩 £

TEBAY Cumbria Map **07** NY60

GH ◨◨◨ **Carmel House** Mount Pleasant CA10 3TH (0.25m
from M6 junct 38) ☎015396 24651
Closed 24-25 Dec & 1 Jan
This attractive little guest house is located in the centre of the
village, just off junction 38 of the M6. Bedrooms are thoughtfully
equipped, and guests have use of a cosy lounge and an appealing
pine-furnished dining room.
5 en suite (shr) 2 annexe en suite (shr) No smoking in bedrooms
No smoking in dining room CTV in all bedrooms Tea and coffee
making facilities No dogs (ex guide dogs) Cen ht CTV 7P No
coaches Tennis (hard)
PRICE GUIDE
ROOMS: s £16.50-£17.50; d £33-£35
CARDS: 🟥

◧ ◨ **Cross Keys** CA10 3UY (on A685) ☎015396 24240
This family-run inn sits in the centre of the village which is only
half a mile from junction 38 of the M6. A good selection of food
can be taken in the cosy low beamed bar or in the adjoining dining
room. Bedrooms are modestly furnished but cheerily decorated
and offer good value.
6 rms (2 fmly) CTV in all bedrooms Tea and coffee making
facilities No dogs (ex guide dogs) CTV 30P Fishing Pool Last
d 9pm
PRICE GUIDE
ROOMS: s £15-£17.50; d £22-£30; wkly b&b fr £77✳
MEALS: Lunch fr £3.75&alc Dinner fr £3.75&alc✳

TEDBURN ST MARY Devon Map **03** SX89

◧ ◨◨◨ **Kings Arms** Tedburn St Mary EX6 6EG
☎01647 61224 FAX 01647 61931
This attractive inn is situated in the centre of the village, within
easy reach of Dartmoor National park and a few miles from the
city of Exeter. The bedrooms are simply furnished and have
recently been redecorated. The bars are full of character with log
fires, exposed beams and a small dining area.
7 rms (3 fmly) CTV in all bedrooms Tea and coffee making
facilities No dogs Cen ht P Last d 9.30pm
PRICE GUIDE
ROOMS: s £19.50-£22.50; d £39-£45✳
MEALS: Bar Lunch fr £2.95✳
CARDS: 🟦 🟥

TEIGNMOUTH Devon Map **03** SX97

Selected

GH ◨◨◨◨ **Fonthill** Torquay Rd, Shaldon TQ14 0AX
(on B3199) ☎01626 872344 FAX 01626 872344
This Georgian manor house has been owned by the Graeme
family for over 120 years, and is set in 25 acres of gardens
and grounds overlooking the River Teign. Two of the three
delightful bedrooms in the west wing have en suite bathrooms
and there is also a combined breakfast and sitting room.
Breakfast is attractively served, with a good choice of starters
and hot dishes available. Mrs Graeme is happy to advise
guests of local inns and restaurants for dinner.

Smoking is not permitted.
3 en suite (bth/shr) No smoking Tea and coffee making facilities No dogs Cen ht CTV 6P No coaches Tennis (hard)
PRICE GUIDE
ROOMS: d £46-£52

GH 🅠🅠🅠 **Hill Rise Hotel** Winterbourne Rd TQ14 8JT (A381 Teignmouth railway station turn left into Shute Hill, across crossroads hotel on left) ☎01626 773108
The Potter family are keen to make all their guests feel at home in this friendly guest house - a large, red-brick, Edwardian residence set in well tended gardens within easy walking distance of the town centre. The Potters continue to upgrade the property and now have three en suite bedrooms with another planned. There is a small bar, where snacks are available in the evening, as well as a comfortable lounge and newly decorated dining room. Guests are asked to refrain from smoking, except in the bar.
8 rms (3 shr) (2 fmly) No smoking in bedrooms No smoking in dining room No smoking in 1 lounge CTV in all bedrooms Tea and coffee making facilities No dogs (ex guide dogs) Licensed Cen ht CTV 5P No coaches
PRICE GUIDE
ROOMS: s £15-£20; d £26-£30; wkly b&b £91-£98

GH 🅠🅠 *Lyme Bay House Hotel* Den Promenade TQ14 8SZ ☎01626 772953
Apr-Oct
A large Victorian house overlooking the sea on Den Promenade, next to the church, is situated close to the town's amenities. Three of the bedrooms have private bathrooms, and TVs are available in rooms on request. A lift serves all floors. ➡

9 rms (3 shr) (1 fmly) Tea and coffee making facilities Licensed Lift Cen ht CTV No parking No coaches

GH QQ ***Rathlin House Hotel*** Upper Hermosa Rd TQ14 9JW ☎01626 774473

Closed Xmas rs Nov-Mar

This attractive Victorian villa is set in a quiet residential area a little way from the town centre and seafront. Several of the rooms are designed for families; some rooms have views over the large gardens. The sitting room and dining room both have attractive bay windows looking onto the south-facing gardens and sunny terrace.

7 en suite (bth/shr) (4 fmly) No smoking in dining room CTV in all bedrooms Tea and coffee making facilities Licensed CTV 12P Last d 6.15pm

Premier Selected

GH QQQQQ **Thomas Luny House** Teign St TQ14 8EG ☎01626 772976

Closed Jan

Thomas Luny, the marine artist, built this beautifully proportioned house in the late 18th century. It is situated in the old quarter of Teignmouth, approached through an archway into a courtyard. Inside there is an elegant drawing room with French windows leading into a walled garden. Guests gather round a large table in the dining room for dinner, a set meal skilfully prepared from fresh produce. John and Alison Allan spare no effort in attending to every detail. Bedrooms are well decorated and comfortably furnished with many antique pieces and you can also enjoy the flowers, bottled water and other extras that are provided.

4 en suite (bth/shr) No smoking in dining room CTV in all bedrooms Direct dial from bedrooms No dogs (ex guide dogs) Licensed Cen ht No children 12yrs 8P No coaches Last d 8pm

PRICE GUIDE

ROOMS: s £27.50-£30; d £55-£60; wkly b&b £192.50; wkly hlf-bd £280

TELFORD Shropshire Map **07** SJ60

Selected

GH QQQQ ***Church Farm*** Wrockwardine, Wellington TF6 5DG (in centre of village, opposite church) ☎01952 244917

A large brick-built farmhouse dating from 1750, Church Farm stands opposite the church in Wrockwardine village. Much of the original character has been preserved and there is an inglenook fireplace and exposed beams. The dining room is furnished with antiques and guests share one large table. Bedrooms have a mixture of furnishings from antique to modern. One ground-floor room is available in the house and there is another room in a single-storey converted outbuilding.

5 rms (2 bth/shr) 1 annexe en suite (shr) (1 fmly) No smoking in dining room CTV in all bedrooms Tea and coffee making facilities Cen ht CTV 10P No coaches Last d 9am

CARDS:

QQ ***Cock Hotel*** 148 Holyhead Rd, Wellington TF1 2ED (1m W off M54 junct 6, on B5061) ☎01952 244954

This traditional town inn is situated at the busy junction of the B5061 and the A5 close to junction 7 of the M54. Simply furnished bedrooms are available, together with ample parking facilities.

7 rms (1 fmly) CTV in all bedrooms Tea and coffee making facilities No dogs (ex guide dogs) Cen ht 30P No coaches Last d 9pm

QQQ **Swan Hotel** Watling St, Wellington TF1 2NH ☎01952 223781 FAX 01952 223782

Since purchasing the hotel from the brewery, the proprietors have made great improvements to the accommodation; the rooms are now smart and modern, and the meal choices vary from an á la carte menu to lighter bar snacks.

12 rms (7 bth/shr) (2 fmly) CTV in all bedrooms Tea and coffee making facilities Cen ht 150P Last d 10pm

PRICE GUIDE

ROOMS: s £20-£25; d £35-£45*

CARDS: (£)

TEMPLE CLOUD Avon Map **03** ST65

QQQ Mr & Mrs Wyatt **Temple Bridge** *(ST627575)* BS18 5AA (0.5m S of village, on A37 towards Wells) ☎01761 452377

Closed Xmas

A 17th-century white-washed farmhouse is situated at the end of a short drive set back from the A37. Accommodation is provided in neat bedrooms, and a cosy lounge is available to guests. Features include mullioned windows, oak beams, and a large garden. Breakfast is served in a pleasant dining room, and there is a good variety of places to eat nearby. Bath, Bristol and Wells are within an easy drive.

2 rms (2 fmly) No smoking in bedrooms No smoking in dining room CTV in all bedrooms Tea and coffee making facilities No dogs (ex guide dogs) Cen ht CTV No children 2yrs 3P 150 acres arable

PRICE GUIDE

ROOMS: s £17-£19; d £32-£34

(£)

TETBURY Gloucestershire Map **03** ST89

Premier Selected

GH QQQQQ **Tavern House** Willesley GL8 8QU (3m SW on A433) ☎01666 880444 FAX 01666 880254

This delightful stone-built property was once a 17th-century staging post, and is situated in the hamlet of Willesley, near the glorious Westonbirt Arboretum. Run by Tim and Janet Tremellen, the house has been delightfully restored, and the well equipped bedrooms offer a high standard of luxury and comfort, tastefully decorated and furnished with country antiques. There is a pleasant lounge with a log fire, and a good English breakfast is served in the cosy dining room, or in the secluded walled garden during summer months. Smoking is not permitted in the dining room or bedrooms.

4 en suite (bth/shr) No smoking in bedrooms No smoking in

dining room CTV in all bedrooms Tea and coffee making facilities Direct dial from bedrooms No dogs Cen ht No children 10yrs 8P No coaches
PRICE GUIDE
ROOMS: s £45-£55; d £55-£66; wkly b&b fr £189∗
CARDS:

TEWKESBURY Gloucestershire Map 03 SO83

GH Ⓠ Ⓠ *The Abbey Hotel* 67 Church St GL20 5RX
☎01684 294247 FAX 01684 297208
Closed 24 Dec-New Year
Meals at this hotel (available on weekdays) are served in a cosy Edwardian-style restaurant which was added a few years ago. The bedrooms which occupy most of the Tudor framed building are, by contrast, modestly furnished in a variety of styles.
16 rms (7 bth 7 shr) (3 fmly) No smoking in 8 bedrooms CTV in all bedrooms Tea and coffee making facilities Licensed Cen ht 11P No coaches Last d 9.30pm
CARDS:

❤ Ⓠ Ⓠ Ⓠ Mrs J Archer **Barn Hill** *(SO929391)* Bredons Norton GL20 7HB (from Bredon take B4080 to Pershore. After 1m take right turn signed Bredons Norton and then take second right. Farmhouse on left after 200 yds)
☎01684 772704 FAX 01684 772704
This Grade II farmhouse is peacefully located on the edge of the Cotswolds, parts of it dating back to 1611. The bedrooms are attractively decorated and furnished with thoughtful extras such as sherry, a sewing kit and toiletries. Imaginative and innovative dinners are served by arrangement, cooked on an Aga in the large farmhouse kitchen. These include home-produced vegetables and lamb and mouth-watering puddings. Jane and Jim Archer are friendly, relaxed hosts who enjoy welcoming guests to their home.
2 rms (1 bth/shr) No smoking CTV in all bedrooms Tea and coffee making facilities Cen ht CTV No children 12yrs 6P 12 acres sheep free range hens Last d 4pm
PRICE GUIDE
ROOMS: s £20-£28; d £34-£40; wkly b&b £112-£126; wkly hlf-bd £161-£175

THAME Oxfordshire Map 04 SP70

GH Ⓠ Ⓠ **Essex House** Chinnor Rd OX9 3LS
☎01844 217567 FAX 01844 216420
rs 23 Dec-2 Jan
Prominently situated in a residential area of the town and dating back to 1870, this detached red brick property with a walled garden and large rear car park is especially well equipped and suited to the needs of the business traveller. Public areas include a cosy bar and a dining room where a choice of dishes is offered. Smoking is not permitted in the annexe or the second floor bedrooms.
7 rms (5 shr) 6 annexe en suite (bth/shr) (1 fmly) No smoking in 11 bedrooms No smoking in dining room No smoking in lounges CTV in all bedrooms Tea and coffee making facilities Direct dial from bedrooms No dogs (ex guide dogs) Licensed Cen ht 20P No coaches Last d 5pm
PRICE GUIDE
ROOMS: s fr £41; d fr £56∗
CARDS:

Premier Selected

❤ Ⓠ Ⓠ Ⓠ Ⓠ Ⓠ Mrs M Aitken **Upper Green** *(SP736053)* Manor Rd, Towersey OX9 3QR (1.5m E unclass rd)
☎01844 212496
FAX 01844 260399
There is a picture postcard perfection about this immaculately kept farmhouse located in a quiet hamlet near Thame. The main building, which houses two bedrooms, is full of 15th-century character. The other bedrooms and a breakfast room are housed in a barn with a high vaulted roof. Additional comforts include a video recorder with a library of films in the lounge - and fed through to the bedrooms if required - and the recently introduced 6-hole pitch and putt circuit. A 'royalty' theme runs through the decoration of the bedrooms. By the end of 1995 there should be two additional bedrooms especially adapted for disabled guests.
2 en suite (bth/shr) 8 annexe en suite (bth/shr) No smoking CTV in 9 bedrooms Tea and coffee making facilities No dogs Cen ht CTV No children 13yrs 11P 6 hole pitch & putt croquet lawn 7 acres poultry sheep
PRICE GUIDE
ROOMS: s £32; d £40-£50

THAXTED Essex Map 05 TL63

GH Ⓠ Ⓠ Ⓠ *Folly House* Watling Ln CM6 2QY
☎01371 830618
Folly House is located close to the heart of the village, yet has pleasing rural views from the rear. Proprietors Jackie and Gerald King pride themselves on personal service, a good example of which is the courtesy car service to and from Stansted Airport. Guests have the use of a comfortable lounge and complimentary tea-making facilities in the dining room. Evening meals are served by prior arrangement and breakfast is available from 3am! New this year is a ground-floor annexe bedroom, furnished in pine with a good en suite shower.
3 rms (1 shr) (3 fmly) CTV in all bedrooms Tea and coffee making facilities No dogs Cen ht CTV No children 3yrs 6P No coaches Last d 9.30pm

---

Selected

❤ Ⓠ Ⓠ Ⓠ Ⓠ Mr & Mrs Hingston **Piggot's Mill** *(TL608314)* Watling Ln CM6 2QY ☎01371 830379
rs Xmas
Great care has been taken to preserve the character of this converted barn and stable which forms the attractive and welcoming nucleus of an 850-acre arable farm run by Richard and Gillian Hingston. The bedrooms are well equipped and furnished, and the large lounge has comfortable seating, a log-burning stove, a piano, and good views, shared with the bedrooms, over the neat garden. Good breakfasts are served at a shared table in the airy breakfast room which has a heated flagstone floor and timbered roof.
2 en suite (bth/shr) No smoking in bedrooms No smoking in dining room CTV in all bedrooms Tea and coffee making

facilities No dogs Cen ht No children 12yrs 6P 800 acres arable
PRICE GUIDE
ROOMS: s £30-£32; d £45-£48; wkly b&b £135-£192

THIRLMERE Cumbria Map **11** NY31

♥ 🔽🔽 Mr & Mrs J Hodgson **Stybeck** *(NY319188)* CA12 4TN (on A591 near junct B5322) ☎017687 73232
Closed 25 Dec
A Victorian Lakeland stone farmhouse, on a dairy cattle, beef and sheep farm, Stybeck is set back from the A591 Ambleside to Keswick road with an impressive backdrop of fells and crags. Bedrooms are comfortably furnished and attractively decorated, and a guests' lounge is provided. Smoking is not permitted.
3 rms (1 shr) (1 fmly) No smoking Tea and coffee making facilities No dogs Cen ht CTV No children 5yrs 4P 200 acres dairy mixed sheep working Last d 3.30pm
PRICE GUIDE
ROOMS: s £15-£16; d £30-£32✱

THIRSK North Yorkshire Map **08** SE48

Selected

GH 🔽🔽🔽🔽 **Spital Hill** York Rd YO7 3AE
☎01845 522273 FAX 01845 524970
Spital Hill is a graceful Victorian house set in one-and-a-half acres of peaceful gardens just off the A19 south of Thirsk. The bedrooms - two of them contained in the Groom's Cottage to the rear - are well furnished and have telephones but no TV sets. A delightful lounge is provided, and home-cooked dinners are served at a large communal table.
3 rms (2 bth/shr) 2 annexe en suite (bth/shr) No smoking Direct dial from bedrooms No dogs (ex guide dogs) Licensed Cen ht CTV No children 12yrs 6P No coaches Croquet Last d 4pm
PRICE GUIDE
ROOMS: s £37.50-£41; d £55-£62; wkly b&b £185-£200; wkly hlf-bd £290-£305
CARDS: 🔲 🔲 🔲

♥ 🔽🔽🔽 Mrs T Williamson **Thornborough House** *(SE427847)* South Kilvington YO7 2NP (through village of South Kilvington to roundabout. Go straight across, entrance 100yds on left.) ☎01845 522103 FAX 01845 522103
3 rms (2 shr) (1 fmly) No smoking in bedrooms No smoking in dining room CTV in all bedrooms Tea and coffee making facilities Cen ht CTV 6P 210 acres arable sheep Last d 3pm
PRICE GUIDE
ROOMS: s £14-£18; d £28-£36; ✱
CARDS: 🔲 🔲

Prices quoted in the Guide are based on information supplied by the establishments themselves.

THORNTON Lancashire Map **07** SD34

Premier Selected

GH 🔽🔽🔽🔽🔽 **The Victorian House** Trunnah Rd FY5 4HF (take A585 in direction of Fleetwood and exit at Thornton. Pass the Gardener's Arms on right and turn right at church) ☎01253 860619
FAX 01253 865350

Standing in its own pleasant garden close to the B5268, this delightful house is, as its name suggests, full of Victorian charm and character. Essentially a restaurant with rooms, it has been decorated and furnished with care by the proprietors Louise and Didier Guerin, and offers high standards throughout. There is an authentic period parlour crammed with objects d'art, prints, paintings and fresh flowers, together with a selection of comfortable chairs and a cosy fire. Aperitifs are available in the snug bar, and dinner is served by long-skirted waitresses in the elegant, well appointed restaurant (lunches are taken in the attractive modern conservatory) where chef patron Didier Guerin offers a French menu with a wide choice of dishes. The three individual bedrooms are most comfortable and equipped with modern facilities and thoughtful extras; one has a four-poster bed, and they are all sumptuously furnished and decorated in Victorian style.
3 en suite (bth/shr) CTV in all bedrooms Tea and coffee making facilities Direct dial from bedrooms Licensed Cen ht No children 6yrs 20P No coaches Last d 9.30pm
PRICE GUIDE
ROOMS: s £35; d £40
CARDS: 🔲 🔲 🔲 🔲

THORNTON DALE North Yorkshire Map **08** SE88

◀ 🔽 **The New Inn** YO18 7LF (on A177 in centre of Thornton le Dale) ☎01751 474226
This Georgian inn dates back to 1720 and prides itself on its home cooked food and warm and friendly service. The bedrooms are simply furnished and a small lounge is provided for residents.
6 rms (1 bth/shr) (1 fmly) No smoking in dining room Tea and coffee making facilities No dogs (ex guide dogs) CTV 9P Last d 8.30pm
PRICE GUIDE
ROOMS: s £21; d £34-£40
MEALS: Lunch £5-£10alc Dinner £5-£10alc

THORPE BAY Essex

See **Southend-on-Sea**

THURNING Norfolk Map **09** TG02

🔁🔽 ♥ 🔽🔽 Mrs A M Fisher **Rookery** *(TG078307)* NR24 2JP ☎01263 860357
Closed Dec-Jan
This idyllic rural retreat is quite hard to find, as the old redbrick house hides behind a flint wall and is surrounded by outbuildings and lawns. The lounge doubles as a breakfast room and, if an

evening meal has been requested, it is also served here.
2 rms (1 shr) (1 fmly) Tea and coffee making facilities No dogs
CTV P 400 acres arable
PRICE GUIDE
ROOMS: s £15-£16; d £30-£32

THURSBY Cumbria Map **11** NY35

♥ Q Q Q Mrs M G Swainson **How End** *(NY316497)* CA5 6PX
(7m W of Carlisle) ☎016973 42487
Dating from 1764, this farmhouse offers attractively decorated
accommodation overlooking meadowland towards the Lakeland
hills. None of the rooms has en suite facilities, but there are two
separate bathrooms. The beamed lounge leads out to the garden,
and in the dining room breakfast is served at one large table. How
End is a working dairy farm of 200 acres.
2 rms (1 fmly) No smoking in bedrooms No smoking in dining
room Tea and coffee making facilities No dogs (ex guide dogs)
Cen ht CTV 4P 200 acres dairy mixed
PRICE GUIDE
ROOMS: s £15-£16; d £30-£32✻

THWAITE North Yorkshire Map **07** SD89

GH Q Q Kearton DL11 6DR
☎01748 886277 FAX 01748 886590
Mar-Dec
Standing amidst beautiful scenery in the heart of the lovely hamlet
of Thwaite, this attractive guesthouse, tea room and restaurant is
well maintained by its resident owners. Bedrooms are modern and
there are a comfortable lounge, a snug bar and a large dining room
where good old-fashioned Yorkshire home cooking is offered.
13 rms (2 fmly) No smoking in dining room Tea and coffee
making facilities No dogs (ex guide dogs) Licensed Cen ht 50P
Last d 6.30pm
PRICE GUIDE
ROOMS: (incl. dinner) s £25; d £50; wkly b&b £133; wkly hlf-
bd £168
CARDS: 🟦 🟦

TIDEFORD Cornwall & Isles of Scilly Map **02** SX35

♥ Q Q Mrs B A Turner *Kilna House* *(SX353600)* PL12 5AD
(on A38, 5m W of Tamar Bridge) ☎01752 851236
Closed Xmas & New Year
This small, stone-built farmhouse is set in a large pleasant garden
and overlooks the River Tiddy Valley; it is situated between
Liskeard and Plymouth, just outside the village. Bedrooms are
well appointed and comfortable and the public areas simple but
neat, with a relaxed atmosphere. The proprietors have run it for
the past twenty years and, having made gradual improvments, now
enjoy a returning clientele.
5 rms (2 fmly) No smoking in dining room CTV in all bedrooms
Tea and coffee making facilities Cen ht CTV 6P 12 acres arable
pasture

TIMSBURY Avon Map **03** ST65

GH Q Q Q Old Malt House Hotel & Licensed Restaurant
Radford BA3 1QF (from A367 turn onto B3115 & follow signs
for Radford Farm) (MIN)
☎01761 470106 FAX 01761 472726
This former malting house on the outskirts of the village has been
renovated to provide spacious public areas and well equipped
bedrooms which all have en suite facilities. The Horler family also
operate a shire horse stud adjacent to the house.
10 en suite (bth/shr) (2 fmly) No smoking in dining room CTV
in all bedrooms Tea and coffee making facilities Direct dial from
bedrooms Licensed Cen ht 40P Shire horse stables & children's

farm adjacent Last d 8.30pm
PRICE GUIDE
ROOMS: s £38; d £66; wkly b&b £192.50-£227.50; wkly hlf-bd
£281.75-£316.75
CARDS: 🟦 🟦 🟦 🟦

TINTAGEL Cornwall & Isles of Scilly Map **02** SX08

🛏🟦 **GH Q Q Q Castle Villa** Molesworth St PL34 0BZ (on
entering Tintagel on B3263 turn left by Nat. West Bank
signposted Camelford/Trebarwith, Castle Villa is 150yds on
left) ☎01840 770373 & 770203
This attractive Cornish stone guest house is close to the village
centre, the 11th-century church and King Arthur's Castle.
Accommodation is in five pretty bedrooms, one of which has en
suite facilities, and there are a comfortable television lounge and a
small bar serving snacks. A choice of evening meals is offered in
the dining room-cum-conservatory which overlooks the garden.
5 rms (1 shr) No smoking in bedrooms No smoking in area of
dining room CTV in all bedrooms Tea and coffee making
facilities Licensed Cen ht CTV 6P No coaches
PRICE GUIDE
ROOMS: s £14.50-£16.50; d £29-£38; wkly b&b
£91.35-£119.70
CARDS: 🟦 🟦 🟦 🟦 🟦

GH Q Q Q Trewarmett Lodge PL34 0ET (from A39 take
B3314 then B3263 to centre of village) ☎01840 770460
Closed 20 Mar-24 Oct
This restaurant with rooms is a former inn, located between
Tintagel and Trebarwith Strand. Most of the five comfortable
bedrooms have delightful views, and public rooms include a cellar
bar and inviting lounge. The restaurant offers both a carte and a
fixed-price menu, and daily specials and snacks are served at ➡

lunch time - on the terrace in fine weather.

5 rms (1 shr) (2 fmly) No smoking in bedrooms No smoking in dining room Tea and coffee making facilities Licensed Cen ht CTV 10P No coaches Last d 9pm

PRICE GUIDE

ROOMS: s £16.50-£19.50; d £33-£40; wkly b&b fr £109; wkly hlf-bd £175-£195

CARDS: 🔲 🔲 (£)

◀ 🔲🔲🔲 **Tintagel Arms Hotel** Fore St PL34 0DB
☎01840 770780

The Tintagel Arms is a well-known meeting place, set in the heart of this historic village. Margaret and George Hunter extend a warm welcome to their guests and offer well-decorated accommodation with a high level of comfort and many useful extras. A wide choice of dishes - including several of Greek origin - is served in the restaurant/bistro, and there are also a lounge area and a main bar. There is a large private car park.

7 en suite (bth/shr) No smoking in bedrooms No smoking in area of dining room CTV in all bedrooms Tea and coffee making facilities No dogs (ex guide dogs) Cen ht 8P Last d 9.30pm

PRICE GUIDE

ROOMS: s £30; d £40-£50✱

MEALS: Bar Lunch £1.50-£10.50 Dinner £5.50-£10.50✱

CARDS: 🔲 🔲 (£)

TISSINGTON Derbyshire Map **07** SK15

❤ 🔲🔲🔲 Mrs B Herridge **Bent** (SK187523) DE6 1RD
☎01335 390214

Etr-Oct

This charming, low, 16th-century cottage-style farmhouse forms part of the Tissington Estate. Surrounded by rolling hills, streams and pasture for the dairy herd and a few sheep, its setting is idyllic. The three bedrooms are traditionally furnished in the character of the house.The breakfast room has linen-clothed tables and there is also a very comfortable sitting room.

3 rms (2 bth) (1 fmly) Tea and coffee making facilities No dogs (ex guide dogs) Cen ht CTV No children 5yrs 6P 280 acres beef dairy mixed sheep

PRICE GUIDE

ROOMS: d £30-£35✱

TIVERTON Devon Map **03** SS91

GH 🔲🔲🔲 **Bridge** 23 Angel Hill EX16 6PE (in centre of Tiverton, beside river Exe) ☎01884 252804

A family-run guesthouse near the centre of town enjoys an enviable position beside the river with its own small garden. The bedrooms are well decorated and some now have en suite showers. There is a cosy guests' lounge and home-cooked dinners are served in the dining room.

9 rms (5 shr) (2 fmly) No smoking in dining room CTV in all bedrooms Tea and coffee making facilities Licensed Cen ht CTV 7P No coaches Fishing Last d 7pm

PRICE GUIDE

ROOMS: s £18-£23; d £35-£42; wkly b&b £120-£142; wkly hlf-bd £170-£192✱

(£)

Entries in this Guide are based on reports filed by our team of professionally trained, full-time inspectors.

Premier Selected

❤ 🔲🔲🔲🔲 Mrs B Pugsley **Hornhill** (SS965117) Exeter Hill EX16 4PL (follow signs to Grand Western Canal, take right fork up Exeter Hill farmhouse on left at top of hill)
☎01884 253352

Parts of this farmhouse - the home of the Pugsley family for more than 100 years, though the adjoining land is now farmed by a neighbour - date back to the 18th century, and its hilltop setting allows it to enjoy panoramic views over the beautiful Exe valley. Comfortable bedrooms with co-ordinating soft furnishings are equipped with effective heating, colour TV and tea-making facilities; many thoughtful extras like bottled water, herbal tea and locally produced toiletries are also provided. A ground-floor bedroom suitable for the partially disabled has an en suite shower room, while the rest have private bathrooms across the corridor. Breakfast is served round one large table and a home-cooked set dinner which makes good use of fresh local produce is available by arrangement. Hospitality is warm and natural, but guests are asked not to smoke in the house.

3 rms (1 shr) No smoking CTV in all bedrooms Tea and coffee making facilities No dogs No children 12yrs 5P 75 acres beef sheep Last d 24hr in advance

PRICE GUIDE

ROOMS: s fr £18.50; d £34-£40; wkly hlf-bd fr £180

❤ 🔲 Rita & Brian Reader **Lodge Hill** (SS945112) EX16 5PA
☎01884 252907 FAX 01884 242090

Just one mile south of the town on the road to Bickleigh, the farmhouse occupies a quiet and elevated rural location set back from the road. It is popular with people touring the area and cyclists, children and pets are all made welcome. As no evening meal is provided, there is a small kitchen available to guests to prepare drinks and snacks.

7 en suite (shr) (2 fmly) No smoking in dining room CTV in all bedrooms Tea and coffee making facilities Licensed Cen ht CTV 14P 10 acres poultry sheep horses

CARDS: 🔲 🔲 🔲

Selected

❤ 🔲🔲🔲🔲 Mrs R Olive **Lower Collipriest** (SS953117) EX16 4PT (off Great Western Way, approx 1m)
☎01884 252321

Etr-Oct

Mrs Linda Olive welcomes guests to her 17th-century farmhouse in the beautiful Exe Valley. The spacious bedrooms have many thoughtful extras, and the bathrooms are also of a good size. In the comfortable lounge a fire burns in the inglenook fireplace on cooler evenings, and there is plenty of tourist information. Guests eat at a communal table and a good set dinner is available.

3 en suite (bth/shr) No smoking Tea and coffee making facilities No dogs (ex guide dogs) Cen ht CTV No children

16yrs 6P Fishing 220 acres beef dairy Last d noon
PRICE GUIDE
ROOMS: s £18.50-£19.50; d £39-£42; wkly b&b £129.50-£134; wkly hlf-bd £190-£196✱

TIVETSHALL ST MARY Norfolk Map **05** TM18

◧ ⓠⓠⓠⓠ **Old Ram Coaching Inn** Ipswich Rd NR15 2DE (on A140) ☎01379 676794 FAX 01379 608399
Closed 25-26 Dec
Located four miles north of Scole, this popular inn draws large crowds of diners and holiday-makers en route to and from the tourist sites further north. A stunning display of gateaux in a chilled cabinet greets guests by the entrance, and a fresh orange juice machine provides a refreshing drink, along with a range of beers and wines. The menu offers a wide choice of staple favourites including grills, and there is a daily menu with fish dishes. Accommodation is sumptuous: each room is individually decorated in plush colour-coordinated style and eqipped with modern amenities.
5 en suite (bth/shr) (1 fmly) CTV in all bedrooms Tea and coffee making facilities Direct dial from bedrooms No dogs (ex guide dogs) Cen ht 120P Last d 10pm
PRICE GUIDE
ROOMS: s £43-£48; d £61-£66; wkly b&b £300; wkly hlf-bd £370
MEALS: Lunch £8.75-£16.75alc Dinner £10-£21.45alc
CARDS: ▨ ▥

TOLLARD ROYAL Wiltshire Map **03** ST91

◧ ⓠⓠⓠ **King John** SP5 5PS (on B3081) ☎01725 516207
3 en suite (bth/shr) No smoking in area of dining room No smoking in 1 lounge CTV in all bedrooms Tea and coffee making facilities No dogs Cen ht CTV No children 10yrs 22P No coaches Golf 9 Last d 9.30pm
PRICE GUIDE
ROOMS: s £30-£35; d £40-£50✱
MEALS. Lunch £7.15-£15.60alc Dinner £7.15-£15.60alc✱
CARDS: ▨ ▥

TONBRIDGE Kent Map **05** TQ54

See also Penshurst & Shipbourne

Premier Selected

GH ⓠⓠⓠⓠⓠ **Goldhill Mill** Golden Green TN11 0BA ☎01732 851626 FAX 01732 851881
Closed 16 Jul-Aug
Holder of the title "Guest House of the Year 1995" for England, this beautiful house offers warm hospitality. The Millhouse was mentioned in the Domesday Book and has been restored by Mr and Mrs Cole. One bedroom has a four-poster bed, another a Louis XVth bed with silk furnishings, and many extras are provided.

Breakfast is served at a large table in the huge kitchen with the mill machinery on display behind glass. There is a sitting room set aside for the guests, furnished with some fine antique furniture.
3 en suite (bth/shr) No smoking CTV in all bedrooms Tea and coffee making facilities Direct dial from bedrooms No dogs (ex guide dogs) Cen ht CTV No children 8yrs 6P No coaches Tennis (hard) Croquet
PRICE GUIDE
ROOMS: s £60-£65; d £70-£75✱
CARDS: ▨ ▥

TORBAY Devon

See **Brixham, Paignton and Torquay**

TORQUAY Devon Map **03** SX96

GH ⓠⓠⓠ *Atlantis Hotel* 68 Belgrave Rd TQ2 5HY ☎01803 292917
A mid-terrace single-fronted Victorian property situated close to the sea front and main shopping areas. The friendly owners Gill and Tom Saunders have furnished and decorated the hotel attractively throughout, and bedrooms are well equipped, complete with satellite TV. There is a comfortable lounge bar leading through double doors to the recently redecorated dining room, where a small set menu including a vegetarian choice is offered each evening.
11 rms (9 bth/shr) (6 fmly) CTV in all bedrooms Tea and coffee making facilities Licensed Cen ht CTV 3P Last d 5pm
CARDS: ▨ ▥

◨ GH ⓠⓠ **Avron Hotel** 70 Windsor Rd TQ1 1SZ (from A3022 follow signs to Plainmoor for Windsor Road) ☎01803 294182
May-Sep
Friendly proprietors go out of their way to make each guest feel at home in their cheerful establishment, which is situated in a quiet residential area close to both Torquay town centre and Babbacombe village. The simply furnished bedrooms, some with en suite facilities, offer modern comforts in a traditional setting. Substantial breakfasts and a four-course evening meal are served in the attractive dining room, both including home baked bread. A guests' lounge is also provided.
14 rms (6 shr) (1 fmly) CTV in 6 bedrooms Tea and coffee making facilities CTV 8P No coaches
PRICE GUIDE
ROOMS: s £13-£18; d £28-£36; wkly b&b £90-£120; wkly hlf-bd £115-£160

GH ⓠⓠⓠ **Bahamas Hotel** 17 Avenue Rd TQ2 5LB ☎01803 296005
The bedrooms are furnished in the modern style and are bright and fresh. Mr and Mrs Cooper are friendly hosts and have a loyal following of regular guests. Mr Cooper is a trained chef and enjoys preparing an interesting selection of wholesome food which has a classical leaning. There is a comfortable bar which is "open all hours" to residents and a well-appointed lounge on the ground floor.
12 en suite (bth/shr) (2 fmly) No smoking in bedrooms No smoking in dining room CTV in all bedrooms Tea and coffee making facilities Licensed 12P Last d 6.30pm
PRICE GUIDE
ROOMS: s £19-£23; d £38-£46; wkly b&b £130-£155; wkly hlf-bd £185-£210
CARDS: ▨ ▥ ▥ ▣

Selected

GH QQQQ **Barn Hayes Country Hotel** Brim Hill,
Maidencombe TQ1 4TR ☎01803 327980
rs Nov-Feb
There are stunning views out to sea from this 1920s country-house hotel and the well kept gardens, outdoor swimming pool and terrace are added attractions. The bedrooms in the house are very attractively coordinated and provide many extras, and the two garden chalet suites are ideal for families. Good public rooms include a large sun-lounge, a separate bar for pre-dinner drinks, a television snug and a main drawing room. A choice of menus is available in the dining room where a collection of local Watcombe pottery takes pride of place on the dresser.
10 rms (8 shr) 2 annexe en suite (bth) (4 fmly) No smoking in dining room No smoking in 1 lounge CTV in all bedrooms Tea and coffee making facilities Licensed Cen ht CTV 16P No coaches Outdoor swimming pool Last d 7pm
PRICE GUIDE
ROOMS: s £24-£27; d £48-£54; wkly b&b £154-£175;
wkly hlf-bd £224-£252
CARDS: £

GH QQ **Beauly** 503 Babbacombe Rd TQ1 1HL
☎01803 296993 FAX 01803 296993
This small personally run guest house is a frequent competitor in the 'Torbay in Bloom' competition, and the recently redecorated exterior is decked with colourful tubs, window boxes and hanging baskets. Inside there are five comfortable bedrooms individually decorated with co-ordinating fabrics. The lounge is combined with the breakfast room, where friendly proprietor Mrs Wilma Farrell provides breakfast; although no evening meals are available, she is happy to recommend various local establishments.
5 en suite (bth/shr) (3 fmly) No smoking in dining room No smoking in lounges CTV in all bedrooms Tea and coffee making facilities Cen ht CTV No parking No coaches
PRICE GUIDE
ROOMS: s £15-£20; d £30-£40; wkly b&b £100-£135✳ £

Selected

GH QQQQ **The Berburry Hotel** 64 Bampfylde Rd
TQ2 5AY (at Torre Railway Station bear right into Avenue Rd signposted Seafront hotel 50yds before 2nd set of lights) ☎01803 297494 FAX 01803 215902
Closed 3 wks during Dec-Jan
The Berburry stands just above the Avenue Road in pleasant terraced gardens. Comprehensively equipped bedrooms are tastefully decorated and well furnished, while the comfortable drawing room is elegantly furnished and the dining room attractive. Rosemary Sellick has a reputation for fine cuisine; a four-course dinner includes several choices to please all tastes. Service is cheerful and efficient at this non-smoking establishment.
10 en suite (bth/shr) (2 fmly) No smoking CTV in all bedrooms Tea and coffee making facilities No dogs Licensed Cen ht CTV No children 8yrs 10P Last d 5pm
PRICE GUIDE
ROOMS: s £21-£27; d £42-£54; wkly b&b £147.60-£175;
wkly hlf-bd £182-£234✳
CARDS: £

Selected

GH QQQQ **Blue Haze Hotel** Seaway Ln TQ2 6PS
(MIN) ☎01803 607186 & 606205 FAX 01803 607186
Apr-Oct rs Wed
This small hotel stands in an elevated position surrounded by a well tended garden, just a short walk from the sea and all the local amenities. Guests are assured a warm welcome and will receive a cup of tea on arrival. The ten en suite bedrooms have been equipped with modern comforts and thoughtful extras such as fridges with fresh milk. Public areas comprise a spacious lounge, a cosy bar lounge overlooking the gardens, and a dining room offering a set four-course meal featuring good home cooking. Dinner is not available on Wednesdays, but there is a selection of places to eat within the vicinity.
9 en suite (bth/shr) (3 fmly) No smoking in dining room CTV in all bedrooms Tea and coffee making facilities No dogs Licensed Cen ht CTV 20P No coaches
PRICE GUIDE
ROOMS: d £52-£56; wkly b&b £167-£182; wkly hlf-bd £222-£232
CARDS: £

⛽🚻 GH QQQ **Braddon Hall Hotel** Braddons Hill Rd
East TQ1 1HF ☎01803 293908
Facing south, this elevated hotel is conveniently located for easy access to the town centre and harbour. Personally run by owners Peter and Carol White, good standards of service and facilities are offered. The bedrooms are comfortably furnished, with one on the ground floor. A good choice of dished is offered for the evening meal, which is served in an attractive dining room , which has an adjacent bar. There is also a small sun lounge.
12 en suite (bth/shr) (2 fmly) No smoking in dining room CTV in all bedrooms Tea and coffee making facilities No dogs Licensed Cen ht No children 5yrs 8P No coaches Last d 5pm
PRICE GUIDE
ROOMS: s £16-£20; d £32-£40; wkly b&b £110-£129; wkly hlf-bd £150-£178
CARDS: £

GH QQQ *Buckingham Lodge* Falkland Rd TQ2 5JP
☎01803 293538
This informal establishment, set back from Falkland Road in a peaceful situation, is owned and personally run by Bernard and Rosemary Sellick who live across the road at the Berburry Hotel. Buckingham Lodge prides itself on flexibility - self contained suites and en-suite bedrooms are available and guests can book on room and breakfast, or room only terms. The No Smoking accommodation is comfortable and equipped with modern facilities. There is a cosy bar lounge and on site parking.
7 en suite (bth/shr) P

GH QQQ *Burleigh House* 25 Newton Rd TQ2 5DB
☎01803 291557
Closed Xmas & New Year
A Tudor-style guest house situated on the main route into Torquay is within walking distance of the town centre. The bedrooms are pleasantly decorated with matching fabrics and there is pine furniture throughout the house. There is a beamed dining room where breakfast and dinner are served, plus a combined lounge and entrance hall.
9 rms (4 bth/shr) CTV in all bedrooms Tea and coffee making facilities No dogs (ex guide dogs) Cen ht CTV 10P No coaches Last d 5pm

GH Q Q Q *Burley Court Hotel* Wheatridge Lane, Livermead TQ2 6RA ☎01803 607879
mid Mar-mid Nov
Quietly situated in an acre of grounds, Burley Court offers traditional style accommodation in well equipped bedrooms. There is a bar in the dining room, where a four-course dinner menu is offered, and the lounge overlooks the swimming pool.
11 en suite (shr) (5 fmly) No smoking in dining room CTV in all bedrooms Tea and coffee making facilities Direct dial from bedrooms No dogs (ex guide dogs) Licensed Cen ht 25P Indoor swimming pool (heated) Outdoor swimming pool (heated) Solarium Gymnasium Table tennis Pool table Darts Last d 6.30pm
CARDS: 🔲

GH Q Q Q Chesterfield Hotel 62 Belgrave Rd TQ2 5HY
☎01803 292318 FAX 01803 293676
In a popular road close to the main shopping areas and the seafront, this Victorian terraced hotel offers neat, en suite accommodation. Rooms vary in size and some are suitable for family occupation. The sitting room has floor to ceiling windows and ample comfortable seating. Traditional set evening meals are served in the attractive dining room.
12 rms (11 shr) (5 fmly) No smoking in dining room CTV in all bedrooms Tea and coffee making facilities Licensed Cen ht CTV 3P Last d 4pm
PRICE GUIDE
ROOMS: s £14-£20; d £28-£40; wkly b&b £88-£129; wkly hlf-bd £118-£175✳
CARDS: 🔲 💳   (£)

GH Q Q Q *Clevedon Hotel* Meadfoot Sea Rd TQ1 2LQ
☎01803 294260
Situated only 300 yards from the Meadfoot beach, this detached Victorian villa has a relaxed atmosphere. Comfortable bedrooms are well equipped and an evening meal is served at 6pm.
12 en suite (bth/shr) (4 fmly) CTV in all bedrooms Tea and coffee making facilities Licensed CTV ch fac 9P No coaches Table tennis Last d 5.30pm
CARDS: 🔲 💳

GH Q Q *Clovelly* 91 Avenue Rd TQ2 5LH (at Torre Station take right hand lane into Avenue Rd guesthouse 100yds on left) ☎01803 292286
This friendly small guest house has a home from home atmosphere and many guests return year after year. Public areas include a spacious TV lounge full of plants and a separate dining room offering a choice at breakfast and an evening meal. The bedrooms are simply decorated and furnished; all are provided with colour and satellite TV and tea making facilities.
6 rms (1 shr) (2 fmly) No smoking in 3 bedrooms No smoking in dining room CTV in all bedrooms Tea and coffee making facilities Cen ht CTV 4P No coaches Last d 5pm
PRICE GUIDE
ROOMS: s £12-£14; d £24-£28; wkly b&b £84-£98; wkly hlf-bd £126-£140
CARDS: 🔲 💳   (£)

GH Q Q Q *Hotel Concorde* 26 Newton Rd TQ2 5BZ
☎01803 292330
Standing on the outskirts of town, this guesthouse has been well modernised and offers spacious public areas, well equipped bedrooms and a sheltered sun-trap garden area with an outdoor heated pool.
22 rms (14 bth/shr) (7 fmly) CTV in all bedrooms Tea and coffee making facilities Licensed Cen ht CTV 18P Outdoor swimming pool (heated) Last d 6pm
CARDS: 🔲 💳

GH Q Q Q *Craig Court Hotel* 10 Ash Hill Rd, Castle Circus TQ1 3HZ (from Castle Circus (town hall) take St Mary Church Road (left by Baptist Church) first on right is Ash Hill Road)
☎01803 294400
Etr-Oct
Craig Court is a large detached Victorian house in a residential area of Torquay, with splendid views over the town to the sea. Bedrooms are well proportioned and carefully maintained, and several have en suite shower rooms. A choice is offered at breakfast and dinner in the spacious dining room. There is a comfortable sitting room and separate bar overlooking the neat garden, where David Anning's model narrow gauge railway is laid out. Visitors are invited to bring their own models to run on the line.
10 rms (5 shr) (2 fmly) No smoking in dining room Tea and coffee making facilities No dogs (ex guide dogs) Licensed CTV 8P No coaches Model railway in garden Last d noon

📖 📺 **GH** Q Q Q *Cranborne Hotel* 58 Belgrave Rd TQ2 5HY ☎01803 298046
Closed Xmas & New Year
A Victorian mid-terrace house in a convenient location within easy walking distance of the sea front, shopping centre, conference halls, Torre Abbey Gardens and marina. The bedrooms are all nicely furnished, and guests have the use of a comfortable sitting room with full length picture windows looking out over the busy street. Traditional meals are served in the cosy dining room by the cheerful Dawkins family.
12 rms (11 bth/shr) (6 fmly) No smoking in dining room CTV in all bedrooms Tea and coffee making facilities No dogs Licensed ➡

Braddons Hill Road East, Torquay TQ1 1HF
Telephone: 01803 293908

A warm welcome awaits you at this delightful personally run hotel. Situated in a peaceful yet convenient position, close to the harbour, shopping centre and all entertainments. All en-suite rooms are individual in character with satellite colour TV and tea-makers. Romantic fourposter bed for that special occasion. Attractive well stocked bar. Superb traditional food with varied menus. Friendly relaxed atmosphere. Parking.

Cen ht CTV 3P Last d 3pm
PRICE GUIDE
ROOMS: s £14-£21; d £30-£46; wkly b&b £90-£152; wkly hlf-bd £125-£177
CARDS: £

GH ⓠⓠⓠ Cranmore 89 Avenue Rd TQ2 5LH (on A3022)
☎01803 298488
Cranmore stands in one of the main residential streets of Torquay, close to the town centre, seafront and beaches. All eight bedrooms have either private or en suite facilities and are attractively decorated and comfortably furnished. Watercolours painted by owner Ken Silver hang in both the relaxing lounge and Tudor-style dining room.
8 en suite (bth/shr) (2 fmly) No smoking in dining room No smoking in lounges CTV in all bedrooms Tea and coffee making facilities No dogs (ex guide dogs) Cen ht CTV 4P No coaches Last d 3.30pm
PRICE GUIDE
ROOMS: wkly b&b £98-£112; wkly hlf-bd £143.50-£157.50
CARDS: ⬛ ⬛ ⬛ ⬛ £

GH ⓠⓠ Devon Court Hotel Croft Rd TQ2 5UE
☎01803 293603
Etr-Oct
A large south-facing house set in a quiet residential street close to the town's main attractions and within easy walking distance of Abbey Sands and Torre Abbey Gardens. The outdoor heated swimming pool set in sheltered gardens is a great attraction to many of the families who stay here, together with the imaginative home cooking.
13 rms (8 shr) (3 fmly) CTV in all bedrooms Tea and coffee making facilities No dogs Licensed Cen ht CTV 14P No coaches Outdoor swimming pool (heated)
CARDS: ⬛ ⬛

GH ⓠⓠⓠ Elmdene Hotel Rathmore Rd TQ2 6NZ
☎01803 294940
Mar-Oct
This small, family-run establishment stands close to the seafront and convenient for the railway station. Bedrooms vary in size, but all offer television sets and tea trays; some have en suite facilities and one is situated on the ground floor. Guests also have access to a large bar/lounge, a sun lounge and a sunny dining room serving a set menu supplemented by extras. Off-road parking is available.
11 rms (2 bth 5 shr) (3 fmly) No smoking in dining room CTV in all bedrooms Tea and coffee making facilities Licensed Cen ht CTV 12P No coaches Last d 5pm
PRICE GUIDE
ROOMS: s £16-£21; d £32-£42; wkly b&b £112-£147; wkly hlf-bd £164.50-£199.50✳
CARDS: ⬛ ⬛ £

GH ⓠⓠⓠ Exmouth View Hotel St Albans Rd, Babbacombe Down TQ1 3LG (from St Marychurch town centre follow Babbacombe Rd towards Torquay after 500yds turn left into St Albans Rd) ☎01803 327307 FAX 01803 329967
Live entertainment, including party nights and dancing, is provided every evening at this friendly and informal hotel. The accommodation is gradually being upgraded and some bedrooms have sea views. There is a popular bar and a large dining room where chef/proprietor John Larkin offers a daily four-course set menu. There is a small TV lounge and facilities include a chair lift on the stairs.
30 rms (24 bth/shr) (8 fmly) No smoking in dining room No smoking in 1 lounge CTV in all bedrooms Tea and coffee making facilities No dogs (ex guide dogs) Licensed Cen ht CTV 25P Last d 6.30pm
CARDS: ⬛ ⬛ ⬛

GH ⓠⓠ Fircroft 69 Avenue Rd TQ2 5LG (turn off A380 onto A3022. At Torre railway station take right fork and establishment 300/400 yds on left) ☎01803 211634
Situated about half a mile from the seafront, this small family-run guesthouse offers comfortable bedrooms, the majority with en suite facilities. Predominantly home-made traditional set menus are served in the attractive blue-and-white painted dining room. There is a comfortable guests' lounge with TV.
6 rms (5 shr) (2 fmly) No smoking in dining room CTV in all bedrooms Tea and coffee making facilities No dogs Cen ht CTV 4P No coaches Last d 10am
PRICE GUIDE
ROOMS: s £14-£17.50; d £27-£33; wkly b&b £85-£106; wkly hlf-bd £119-£141✳
CARDS: ⬛ ⬛ ⬛ £

GH ⓠⓠ Gainsboro Hotel 22 Rathmore Rd TQ2 6NY
☎01803 292032 FAX 01803 292032
Mar-Oct
The Gainsboro is an attractive terraced property a short level stroll from the seafront, railway station and Torre Abbey Gardens. The freshly decorated bedrooms which provide simple but comfortable accommodation include a family room and several with en suite facilities. There are a spacious lounge and a sunny breakfast room where traditional English breakfasts are served (unless otherwise advised), and guests are requested not to smoke in the public rooms. The pretty garden offers plenty of space in which to relax.
7 rms (3 shr) (1 fmly) No smoking in dining room No smoking in lounges CTV in 6 bedrooms Tea and coffee making facilities No dogs Cen ht CTV No children 6yrs 4P No coaches
PRICE GUIDE
ROOMS: s £12-£14; d £30; wkly b&b £72-£102✳
CARDS: ⬛ ⬛ £

 Selected

🔲🔲 GH ⓠⓠⓠⓠ Glenorleigh Hotel 26 Cleveland Rd TQ2 5BE (follow A3022 Newton Abbot/Torquay road until traffic lights at Torre Station, bear right into Avenue Road A379 and Cleveland Road is first left)
☎01803 292135 FAX 01803 292135
6 Jan-14 Oct
Plenty of holiday facilities are provided at this special family hotel, including a beautiful outdoor pool, games room, solarium, darts and video games, plus live entertainment two evenings a week. It is quietly situated in a residential area away from the bustle of the town and seafront, and has a Spanish-style patio overlooking the lovely garden - a frequent winner of the Torbay in Bloom award. Bedrooms are very attractive and there is an elegant lounge with TV. A choice of menus is available in the dining room, and there is a bar-lounge complete with a small dance floor.
16 rms (9 shr) (5 fmly) No smoking in dining room Tea and coffee making facilities No dogs (ex guide dogs) Licensed Cen ht CTV 10P Outdoor swimming pool (heated) Solarium Pool table Last d 6pm
PRICE GUIDE
ROOMS: s £16-£22; d £32-£44; wkly b&b £110-£150; wkly hlf-bd £160-£245
CARDS: ⬛ ⬛
See advertisement inside Front Cover

GH ⓠⓠⓠ Glenross Hotel 25 Avenue Rd TQ2 5LB
☎01803 297517
The Glenross is located on one of the main routes into Torquay from Newton Abbot. Personally managed by owners Mr and Mrs

Ashman, guests are assured of a warm welcome. The en suite rooms are bright, airy and comfortable, while the attractive ground floor restaurant serves a variety of traditional dishes to residents and non-resident alike. Ample car parking is also available.

13 en suite (shr) (2 fmly) No smoking in bedrooms No smoking in dining room CTV in all bedrooms Tea and coffee making facilities Licensed Cen ht CTV 13P Last d 9pm
PRICE GUIDE
ROOMS: s £18.50-£22.50; d £37-£45; wkly b&b £129.50-£157.50∗
CARDS: 🂠 ▆

GH 🆀🆀🆀 *Grosvenor House Hotel* Falkland Rd TQ2 5JP
☎01803 294110
A well placed property close to the seafront and the main shopping area. Ten bedrooms provide good facilities, including satellite television. Guests can relax in the friendly bar or the large lounge, which is a no-smoking room, and breakfast and dinner are served in the dining room. Lighter snacks are available from the bar.

10 en suite (shr) (4 fmly) CTV in all bedrooms Tea and coffee making facilities No dogs (ex guide dogs) Licensed Cen ht CTV 7P Last d 4.30pm
CARDS: 🂠 ▆

GH 🆀🆀🆀 **Hotel Trelawney** 48 Belgrave Rd TQ2 5HS
☎01803 296049 FAX 01803 296049
Positioned within easy walking distance of most of Torquay's main attractions, this family-run hotel provides bedrooms which are all en suite. There are a comfortable sitting room, a separate bar and a dining room where traditional cooking is served.

14 rms (13 bth/shr) (2 fmly) CTV in all bedrooms Tea and coffee making facilities Direct dial from bedrooms No dogs (ex guide dogs) Licensed Cen ht CTV 3P Use of facilities at nearby hotel Last d 2pm
PRICE GUIDE
ROOMS: d £30-£45∗
CARDS: 🂠 ▆

GH 🆀🆀🆀 **Ingoldsby Hotel** 1 Chelston Rd TQ2 6PT
☎01803 607497
The Ingoldsby is a family-run establishment situated in a quiet residential area only 200 yards from the beach and within easy walking distance of the town centre. Its simply furnished bedrooms, most of which have en suite facilities, include several ground-floor rooms, while ample public areas feature a spacious bar overlooking the sun terrace and attractive gardens. A five-course dinner menu is offered each evening in the pretty apricot and white dining room, and the proprietors take special pride in the quality and freshness of the food served.

15 rms (3 bth 9 shr) (3 fmly) CTV in all bedrooms Tea and coffee making facilities No dogs (ex guide dogs) Licensed Cen ht CTV 12P No coaches Last d 7pm
PRICE GUIDE
ROOMS: s £19-£27; d £38-£54; wkly b&b £90-£140; wkly hlf-bd £130-£180∗
CARDS: 🂠 ▆

🏨 GH 🆀 **Jesmond Dene Private Hotel** 85 Abbey Rd TQ2 5NN (take last exit from rdbt at bottom of Union Street, hotel opposite R.C church) ☎01803 293062
An attractive listed building with a balustrade balcony stands within walking distance of the town centre. Bedrooms are adequately furnished and there is a sunny breakfast room where a full breakfast is served, as well as a TV lounge.

10 rms (3 fmly) No smoking in dining room Tea and coffee

making facilities Cen ht CTV 3P No coaches
PRICE GUIDE
ROOMS: s £13-£16; d £26-£32; wkly b&b £82-£92

Selected

🏨 GH 🆀🆀🆀🆀 Kingston House 75 Avenue Rd TQ2 5LL (from A3022 to Torquay turn right at Torre Station down Avenue Road, Kingston House approx a quarter of a mile on left) ☎01803 212760
Apr-Oct
Guests are assured of a warm welcome from resident proprietors Mr and Mrs Sexon who take great care to make their guests feel at home. Bedrooms are all prettily decorated with quality fabrics and furnishings and an excellent range of facilities. Mrs Sexon takes pride in the dinners she prepares and a choice of menus is offered. The cosy lounge with its comfortable sofas and piano contributes to the warm and friendly atmosphere.

6 en suite (bth/shr) (3 fmly) No smoking in dining room CTV in all bedrooms Tea and coffee making facilities No dogs Cen ht No children 8yrs 6P No coaches Last d noon
PRICE GUIDE
ROOMS: s £15.50-£22; d £28-£35; wkly b&b £89-£119; wkly hlf-bd £135-£165
CARDS: 🂠 ▆ 🆔

GH 🆀🆀 **Lindum** Abbey Rd TQ2 5NP ☎01803 292795
Etr-Oct
A long-established family-run hotel centrally situated within easy access of the main shopping centre and the Abbey sands. Bedrooms are well equipped and include some on the ground floor. There is a comfortable lounge, a cosy bar, and a variety of interesting dishes is served in the dining room, which is supervised by the resident proprietor.

20 rms (14 bth/shr) (2 fmly) CTV in all bedrooms Tea and coffee making facilities Licensed Cen ht CTV 14P No coaches Last d 7.15pm

---

Selected

GH 🆀🆀🆀🆀 **Millbrook House** Old Mill Rd, Chelston TQ2 6AP (800yds from seafront)
☎01803 297394 FAX 01803 297394
A small, neatly furnished hotel personally run by Lesley and Brian James is located a level 800-yard walk from the seafront. Bedrooms are well equipped, with de luxe rooms featuring dramatic soft furnishings and mini bars. The lounge has a small conservatory extension, and guests can meet in the White Rose Cellar Bar for a drink and a game of pool or darts. A three-course set dinner is served every day except Sunday. Smoking is not permitted in the hotel except in the Cellar Bar.

9 rms (8 bth/shr) No smoking in bedrooms No smoking in dining room No smoking in lounges CTV in all bedrooms Tea and coffee making facilities No dogs Licensed Cen ht 10P No coaches Mini-gym Pool table Last d 7pm
PRICE GUIDE
ROOMS: s £20-£24.50; d £45-£59; wkly b&b £138-£186∗
CARDS: 🂠 ▆

Selected

GH ▣▣▣▣ **Mulberry House** 1 Scarborough Rd
TQ2 5UJ ☎01803 213639
This attractive Victorian house is conveniently situated for
easy access to the town centre, seafront and the Riviera
Centre. It has built up a good reputation for comfortable,
understated accommodation and the interesting food served in
the Mulberry room. The short menu features the use of fresh
local ingredients; lunches represent exceptional value for
money.
3 en suite (bth/shr) No smoking CTV in all bedrooms No
dogs Licensed Cen ht No parking Last d 9.30pm
PRICE GUIDE
ROOMS: s £25-£35; d £42-£50; wkly b&b £142; wkly hlf-
bd £230

GH ▣▣▣ **Newton House** 31 Newton Rd, Torre TQ2 5DB
☎01803 297520
Closed 21 Dec-1 Jan
On the main route into Torquay, this detached Tudor-style house
has ample private parking and is only a few minutes' stroll from
the seafront and shops. The attractively decorated bedrooms offer
many little extras, such as ironing facilities, sweets and hot water
bottles. There is a large sitting room with family photos, and a
separate dining room for breakfast. Guests are asked to refrain
from smoking in the bedrooms and dining room.
8 rms (6 shr) (2 fmly) CTV in all bedrooms Tea and coffee
making facilities No dogs Cen ht No children 5yrs 12P No
coaches

Selected

GH ▣▣▣▣ **Olivia Court** Upper Braddons Hill Rd
TQ1 1HD ☎01803 292595
A Grade II listed Victorian villa is set in a quiet residential
area close to the town centre, with a secluded garden. The
owners Malcolm and Althea Carr took over in 1991 and have
made improvements to the hotel, creating a new reception
area, lounge and small dispense bar. The bedrooms are
furnished to a high standard and are attractively co-ordinated;
most are en suite. A four-course fixed-price menu is served in
the attractive dining room.
13 rms (12 bth/shr) (2 fmly) No smoking in 4 bedrooms No
smoking in dining room No smoking in 1 lounge CTV in all
bedrooms Tea and coffee making facilities Licensed Cen ht
CTV 4P No coaches Last d 4pm
CARDS: ▣▣ ▣▣ ▣▣

GH ▣▣ **The Porthcressa Hotel** 28 Perinville
Road,Babbacombe TQ1 3NZ (follow A380 turn let at Torbay
Hospital & follow signs to Babbacombe, hotel 200yds from
Babbacombe Theatre) ☎01803 327268
In a quiet residential part of the town, this family-run, licensed
hotel with a terrace provides attractive bedrooms plus a popular
bar and dining room. A three-course evening is served at 6pm if
required.
13 rms (2 shr) (3 fmly) Tea and coffee making facilities
Licensed Cen ht CTV 6P

GH ▣▣▣ **Seaway Hotel** Chelston Rd TQ2 6PU
☎01803 605320
A large Victorian residence is quietly situated in its own garden
with glimpses of the sea. Bedrooms have recently been improved
and the lounge, dining room and bar are all bright and well

furnished. Dinner is available.
14 rms (1 bth 6 shr) (3 fmly) Tea and coffee making facilities
Licensed Cen ht CTV 18P Last d 6.30pm
CARDS: ▣▣ ▣▣

GH ▣▣▣ **Silverlands Hotel** 27 Newton Rd TQ2 5DB (on
A3022 after Torre Station traffic lights) ☎01803 292013
A well maintained Tudor-style house stands close to the centre of
town and the seafront. There are prettily decorated bedrooms and
breakfast is served at pine tables in the airy dining room. Lots of
tourist information is available in the entrance hall-cum-sitting
room
11 rms (7 shr) (2 fmly) No smoking in dining room CTV in all
bedrooms Tea and coffee making facilities Cen ht 13P

GH ▣▣ **Skerries Private Hotel** 25 Morgan Av TQ2 5RR
☎01803 293618
The Skerries is situated in a residential area not far from the town
centre. All the bedrooms are comfortably furnished and have
videos as well as televisions. Breakfast and dinner are served in
the dining room and there is a licensed bar where snacks are
available, plus a homely sitting room.
12 rms (3 shr) (3 fmly) No smoking in dining room CTV in all
bedrooms Tea and coffee making facilities Licensed Cen ht
CTV 7P Last d 2pm
CARDS: ▣

Selected

GH ▣▣▣▣ **Suite Dreams** Steep Hill, Maidencombe
TQ1 4TS (2m from St Marychurch on B3199, turn right at
Maidencombe garage)
☎01803 313900 FAX 01803 313841
A delightful purpose built hotel, Suite Dreams provides
spacious and elegantly furnished bedrooms, each with its own
modern bathroom and range of equipment, including ironing
facilities and fridges. Half the rooms face the sea and many
others overlook lovely countryside. An extensive breakfast
menu is offered in the functional but well decorated breakfast
room, and John and Stella Rothwell extend a warm welcome
to guests. Dinner can be arranged in the Thatched Cottage Inn
next door.
14 en suite (bth/shr) (3 fmly) No smoking in 4 bedrooms No
smoking in dining room CTV in all bedrooms Tea and coffee
making facilities Direct dial from bedrooms Cen ht 12P No
coaches Golfing tuition breaks
PRICE GUIDE
ROOMS: s £29.50-£40; d £39-£60; wkly b&b
£136.50-£280
CARDS: ▣▣ ▣▣ ▣▣ ▣▣ ▣▣   ⓔ

▣▣ **GH** ▣▣ **Sunnymead** 501 Babbacombe Rd TQ1 1HL
☎01803 296938
A single-fronted period property, situated some 600 yards from the
town centre and Torquay's unique harbour, offers a relaxed
atmosphere and comfortable accommodation in soundly furnished
and decorated bedrooms equipped with tea-making facilities and
television. An evening meal can be served in the combined
lounge/dining room by prior arrangement.
5 rms (2 shr) (3 fmly) CTV in all bedrooms Tea and coffee
making facilities Cen ht CTV No parking Last d 6pm
PRICE GUIDE
ROOMS: s £12-£16; d £24-£36; wkly b&b £85-£119; wkly hlf-
bd £129-£161
                                ⓔ

GH ◗◗ *Torbay Rise* Old Mill Rd, Chelston TQ2 6HL
☎01803 605541
Apr-Oct
There are stunning views out across Torbay from this guest house, which is set well above the town. The bedrooms vary in size but all have en suite shower or bathrooms, and one room has a four-poster bed. Public rooms include a games room with a pool table and darts board, a comfortable lounge bar and a dining room, while the garden offers a large heated swimming pool and a sun terrace.
15 en suite (bth/shr) (3 fmly) No smoking in dining room CTV in all bedrooms Tea and coffee making facilities Licensed No children 5yrs 8P No coaches Outdoor swimming pool (heated) Last d noon
CARDS: 🖾 🚾

Selected

GH ◗◗◗◗ *Westgate Hotel* Falkland Rd TQ2 5JP
☎01803 295350
The Westgate is a large semidetached house in a tree-lined road. The bedrooms all have en suite showers or bathrooms, and there is a lounge with bay windows and comfortable seating as well as a large separate bar. A choice of meals is available at breakfast and dinner in the dining room, which extends into a sun room with french doors, and special diets can be catered for by arrangement. A huge games room, with darts, table tennis and a pool table, opens onto the terrace.
13 en suite (shr) (2 fmly) No smoking in 3 bedrooms No smoking in dining room No smoking in lounges CTV in all bedrooms Tea and coffee making facilities No dogs Licensed CTV No children 5yrs 14P Games room Pool table Last d 8pm
CARDS: 🖾 🚾

TOTLAND BAY See **WIGHT, ISLE OF**

TOTNES Devon Map **03** SX86

Selected

GH ◗◗◗◗ **Askew Cottage** Ashprington TQ9 7UP
☎01803 732417
Ashprington is a picturesque village some two and a half miles from Totnes, in the South Hams. Askew Cottage - formerly the baillif's cottage to the Sharpham Estate - is the home of Sheena Lumley, who welcomes guests to her delightful home, the ideal venue for exploring the wonderful walks around the Dart Valley. One bedroom is located on the ground floor, a cosy room with ensuite shower, while the other room on the first floor has an exclusive use bathroom adjacent to the room. In the beamed dining room, guests take a hearty breakfast around one table. By arrangement, Mrs Lumley will provided packed lunches, cream teas and light suppers; the majority of guests preferring to stroll to the Durant Arms, within a minutes walk, which is renowned for good value meals and real ales.
2 rms (1 shr) No smoking CTV in all bedrooms Tea and coffee making facilities No dogs (ex guide dogs) Cen ht CTV No children 3P Last d noon
PRICE GUIDE
ROOMS: s £20-£25; d £36-£40; wkly b&b fr £126✳

Selected

GH ◗◗◗◗ **The Old Forge** Seymour Place TQ9 5AY
☎01803 862174 FAX 01803 865385
rs Xmas wk
The Old Forge dates back to the 14th century and is unusual in that it still has a working forge, complete with its own prison cell. The bedrooms are individually decorated and furnished in a cottage style. Some rooms have direct access on to the garden, and the most recent, self-contained unit is suitable for disabled guests. Breakfast is special, with a wide choice including a vegetarian option. This is served in the Tudor-style dining room, where cream teas, home-made cakes and jams can also be enjoyed. This is a no smoking house.
10 rms (8 bth/shr) (4 fmly) No smoking CTV in all bedrooms Tea and coffee making facilities Direct dial from bedrooms No dogs (ex guide dogs) Licensed Cen ht CTV ch fac 10P Putting
PRICE GUIDE
ROOMS: s £30-£46; d £42-£64✳
CARDS: 🖾 🚾

Selected

GH ◗◗◗◗ **Red Slipper** Stoke Gabriel TQ9 6RU
☎01803 782315 FAX 01803 782315
mid Mar-Oct
Situated in the heart of Stoke Gabriel, a picturesque and unspoilt village right beside the River Dart. Bedrooms are neatly furnished and decorated, mostly located on the ground floor with excellent facilities. Thoughtful extras such as flowers, fruit and home-made biscuits are also included. John and Elizabeth Watts are friendly, attentive owners, who take pride in their small establishment. Imaginative homemade food is another key note. Morning coffee, tasty lunches and cream teas with a tempting array of cakes is served in the sheltered tea garden, when the weather allows. Dinner is provided by arrangement and diets catered for with warning. Smoking is not permitted in the restaurant or bedrooms.
5 rms (3 shr) (1 fmly) No smoking in bedrooms No smoking in dining room CTV in 4 bedrooms Tea and coffee making facilities Licensed Cen ht CTV 7P No coaches Last d 8.30pm
PRICE GUIDE
ROOMS: s £27.50; d £40-£45; wkly b&b £139-£145✳

◀ ◗◗ **Steam Packet** St Peter's Quay TQ9 5EW
☎01803 863880 FAX 01803 868484
The Steam Packet Inn is an imposing Georgian building on the edge of town, its lawn leading down to a private quay on the River Dart. An attractive open-plan bar has exposed brickwork, stone walls and beams, and a dining area offers a blackboard menu of special dishes in addition to the usual meals and sandwiches. The majority of the bedrooms have en suite facilities and all have colour TV and tea-making equipment.
9 rms (6 shr) (1 fmly) CTV in all bedrooms Tea and coffee making facilities Cen ht 30P Tennis (grass) Fishing Squash
PRICE GUIDE
ROOMS: s £14-£32; d £32-£46✳
MEALS: Lunch £7-£15alc Dinner £7-£22alc✳
CARDS: 🖾 🚾

Premier Selected

◀ ◻◻◻◻◻ The **Watermans Arms** Bow Bridge, Ashprington TQ9 7EG (CON)
☎01803 732214
FAX 01803 732214

Situated by the River Dart, next to Bow Bridge, this famous country inn has a long and colourful history. The character bars, with exposed beams and open fires, offer an extensive selection of dishes, while a more sophisticated fixed-price menu is available in the informal restaurant. Bedrooms are tastefully decorated and furnished, and each has an en suite shower room and a range of modern facilities.

15 en suite (bth/shr) (2 fmly) No smoking in area of dining room No smoking in 1 lounge CTV in all bedrooms Tea and coffee making facilities Direct dial from bedrooms Cen ht 60P Last d 9.30pm

PRICE GUIDE
ROOMS: s £34-£42; d £54-£70; wkly b&b £168-£210; wkly hlf-bd £273-£315✱
MEALS: Lunch £4.95-£11alc Dinner £9.25-£15.75alc✱
CARDS: 🅰 🈁

TOTTENHILL Norfolk Map **09** TF61

GH ◻◻ *Oakwood House Private Hotel* PE33 0RH (6m S on A10) ☎01553 810256

This large Georgian house is located on the A10, about five miles south of King's Lynn. In addition to the seven spacious, brightly decorated bedrooms in the main building, there are three separate bedrooms in a modern annexe. The owner displays some of his hand-crafted wooden toys in the comfortable guests' lounge, and dinner is readily provided in the restaurant.

7 rms (5 bth/shr) 3 annexe en suite (bth/shr) CTV in all bedrooms Tea and coffee making facilities Licensed Cen ht 20P Last d 8.30pm
CARDS: 🅰 🈁

TROON Cornwall & Isles of Scilly Map **02** SW63

GH ◻◻ *Sea View* TR14 9JH ☎01209 831260
Closed Dec

This spacious farmhouse on the southern outskirts of the village is in an invigoratingly open position, surrounded by farm land with distant views of the sea. The bedrooms are modern in style, and there is a large and comfortable feature lounge. Dinner is available by prior arrangement, the atmosphere is very relaxed and friendly, service being provided by Sue and Shirley Leonard. There is an outdoor heated pool and well kept gardens.

7 rms (3 fmly) Tea and coffee making facilities Licensed Cen ht CTV 8P Outdoor swimming pool (heated) Last d 6pm

---

TROUTBECK (NEAR KESWICK) Cumbria Map **11** NY32

GH ◻◻◻ **Lane Head Farm** CA11 0SY (midway between Penrith and Keswick on A66) ☎017687 79220
Closed 6 Jan-15 Mar

Formerly a working farm and now a country guest house, Lane Head lies off the A66 west of its junction with the A5091, midway between Penrith and Keswick. Dating from the mid 1700s, the house is full of character, with low beamed ceiling and an open

---

fire in the spacious dining room, cosy bedrooms, some with four-poster beds and a comfortable lounge and sun lounge. Two-course home-cooked dinners are offered, along with a short wine and drinks list.

9 rms (3 bth 2 shr) (1 fmly) No smoking in bedrooms No smoking in dining room No smoking in 1 lounge CTV in 6 bedrooms Tea and coffee making facilities No dogs (ex guide dogs) Cen ht CTV 9P No coaches

PRICE GUIDE
ROOMS: s £16-£25; d £32-£40; wkly b&b fr £112; wkly hlf-bd fr £167✱

GH ◻◻◻ **Netherdene** CA11 0SJ (off A66, on A5091) ☎017684 83475
Closed 25 Dec

This country guest house sits in well tended gardens on the A5091, just off the A66 between Penrith and Keswick. Immaculately maintained, it is attractively decorated throughout, with bright bedrooms, a cosy lounge and a neat little dining room.

5 en suite (shr) (1 fmly) No smoking in bedrooms CTV in all bedrooms Tea and coffee making facilities No dogs Cen ht CTV No children 7yrs 6P No coaches Last d 4pm

PRICE GUIDE
ROOMS: s £20-£23; d £33-£38; wkly b&b £115-£130; wkly hlf-bd £174-£190

£

TROUTBECK (NEAR WINDERMERE) Cumbria Map **07** NY40

GH ◻◻◻ **High Green Lodge** High Green LA23 1PN ☎015394 33005

Luxurious accommodation is offered at this recently built Lakeland lodge beautifully located at Troutbeck, two miles from Windermere, surrounded by fells and mountains. Bedrooms are furnished to a high standard with Belgian pine and all have modern en suite facilities

3 en suite (bth/shr) No smoking in bedrooms CTV in all bedrooms Tea and coffee making facilities Cen ht No children 6P No coaches Fishing Use of nearby leisure centre

PRICE GUIDE
ROOMS: s £30-£35; d £40-£55

TROWBRIDGE Wiltshire Map **03** ST85

Selected

GH ◻◻◻◻ **Old Manor Hotel** Trowle BA14 9BL (S of Bath on A363) (Logis)
☎01225 777393 FAX 01225 765443
rs Xmas/New Year

A delightful property constructed of mellow Bath stone, this hotel is set in over four acres of gardens and grounds on the edge of the town. Many of the bedrooms are located in converted stable blocks around the main house, and all of them have been tastefully decorated and furnished with beautiful antique pieces. Dinner is served in a spacious no-smoking dining room, and drinks can be served in any of the elegant lounges.

3 en suite (bth) 11 annexe en suite (bth/shr) No smoking in 6 bedrooms No smoking in dining room No smoking in lounges CTV in all bedrooms Tea and coffee making facilities Direct dial from bedrooms No dogs (ex guide dogs) Licensed Cen ht ch fac 25P No coaches Last d 8pm

PRICE GUIDE
ROOMS: s £40-£48; d £50-£80✱
CARDS: 🅰 🈁 🈁 🔵 🟢

TRURO Cornwall & Isles of Scilly Map **02** SW84

Selected

GH QQQQ **Bissick Old Mill** Ladock TR2 4PG (7m NE on A39) ☎01726 882557 FAX 01726 884057
Closed 16 Dec-1 Jan
Owners of some three years' standing have carefully refurbished Blissick Old Mill without sacrificing its original character and charm - but beware low beams and doorways if you are tall! Neatly furnished and well decorated bedrooms are equipped with a good range of facilities, and real fires burn in the spacious lounge's large fireplace in winter. Fresh local produce is the basis of set dinner menus which include many French dishes, kitchen staff also creating the home-made cakes and pastries served in a tearoom open to the public.
5 rms (3 shr) No smoking in bedrooms No smoking in dining room CTV in all bedrooms Tea and coffee making facilities Licensed Cen ht No children 10yrs 9P No coaches Last d 5pm
PRICE GUIDE
ROOMS: s £27-£35; d £50-£60; wkly b&b £161-£245; wkly hlf-bd £245-£350*
CARDS: £

GH QQQ **Conifers** 36 Tregolls Rd TR1 1LA (on A39) ☎01872 79925
Set in an elevated position off the A39 St Austell Road, this guest house is within easy walking distance of the city centre. The property dates from the Victorian era and offers a tastefully decorated breakfast room and lounge. Bedrooms are individually styled and equipped with colour TV and tea-making facilities.
4 rms No smoking in dining room CTV in all bedrooms Tea and coffee making facilities No dogs (ex guide dogs) Cen ht CTV 3P No coaches
PRICE GUIDE
ROOMS: s £17.50-£18; d £34-£35; wkly b&b £122.50-£126 £

Selected

GH QQQQ **Lands Vue** Lands Vue, Three Burrows TR4 8JA ☎01872 560242
Closed Xmas & New Year
Lands Vue is a country home set in two acres of peaceful gardens with croquet and a swimming pool. Home cooked food using home grown produce and free range eggs is served in the large dining room, which has panoramic views over the Cornish countryside, and there is a cosy lounge with TV and an open fire.
2 rms (1 shr) 1 annexe en suite (shr) No smoking in bedrooms No smoking in dining room CTV in 2 bedrooms Tea and coffee making facilities No dogs (ex guide dogs) Cen ht CTV No children 12yrs 6P No coaches Outdoor swimming pool Croquet Last d 4pm
PRICE GUIDE
ROOMS: d £30-£38* £

GH ◗◗◗ **Manor Cottage** 3 Tresillian TR2 4BN
☎01872 520212
Closed 24-26 Dec

It is pleasing to see this attractive period cottage with blue shutters being brought back to life by new owners, Gillian Jackson and her partner Carlton Moyle. The cosy bedrooms are comfortable. well equipped and furnished with thoughtful touches. The conservatory dining room is open as a restaurant on Fridays and Saturdays, with talented chef Carlton cooking an imaginative fixed price menu, which is gaining a regular following from the local clientele. It is hoped that soon the restaurant will be opened for additional evenings From the dining room, French windows lead on to a terrace where on sunny mornings, it is possible to have breakfast. A comfortable sitting room is also available for guests.
5 rms (1 fmly) No smoking in dining room CTV in all bedrooms Tea and coffee making facilities No dogs (ex guide dogs) Licensed Cen ht 9P No coaches Last d 9pm
PRICE GUIDE
ROOMS: s £17; d £32-£34; wkly b&b £105-£112✳
CARDS: 🔲 🔲

Selected

GH ◗◗◗◗ **Rock Cottage** Blackwater TR4 8EU
☎01872 560252 FAX 01872 560252
Closed Xmas & New Year

Describing itself as a haven for non-smokers, this 18th-century cob and stone cottage stands in the village of Blackwater. The bedrooms are pleasantly furnished in pine and cane with continental quilts. Although small, they have all modern facilities, and one is located on the ground floor. Two charming sitting rooms with original stone walls and beams are available to guests and dinner can be served - by prior arrangement from a varied carte or with less notice from a no-choice menu. Guests are encouraged to bring their own wine as the house is unlicensed.
3 en suite (shr) No smoking CTV in all bedrooms Tea and coffee making facilities No dogs Cen ht CTV No children 18yrs 3P No coaches Last d 5pm
PRICE GUIDE
ROOMS: d fr £39

Selected

❤ ◗◗◗◗ Mr & Mrs E Dymond **Trevispian Vean**
(SW850502) St Erme TR4 9BL (from A30 take A3076 for Truro, in 2.5m in Trispen village take 2nd left in 0.5m bear sharp left farm entrance 500yds on left)
☎01872 79514
Mar-Oct

This establishment manages to combine life as a working farm and a guesthouse, the Dymonds attending to all guests' needs. There are several sitting rooms, one no-smoking, and a bright dining room with individual tables where, as well as breakfast, a four-course dinner is served. Bedrooms are all attractively decorated and a small kitchen with a fridge is provided for guests wishing to make up picnics or extra tea or coffee.
12 rms (2 bth 8 shr) (7 fmly) No smoking in dining room No smoking in 1 lounge Tea and coffee making facilities No dogs (ex guide dogs) Licensed Cen ht CTV 20P Fishing Pool table Table tennis 300 acres arable pigs sheep Last d 4.30pm
PRICE GUIDE
ROOMS: s £18-£20; d £32-£36; wkly b&b £96-£110; wkly hlf-bd £132-£146✳

TUNBRIDGE WELLS (ROYAL) Kent Map **05** TQ53

Premier Selected

GH ◗◗◗◗◗ **Danehurst House** 41 Lower Green Rd, Rusthall TN4 8TW
☎01892 527739
FAX 01892 514804

This delightful large Victorian house is quietly situated a short distance from Tunbridge Wells. The accommodation is strictly non-smoking, and has been individually furnished to provide a range of spacious, well equipped bedrooms. There is an elegant, candlelit dining room, where a gourmet dinner, including a good selection of wines, is available by arrangement. Service is attentive and friendly. The comfortable drawing room is augmented by a separate conservatory breakfast room.
4 en suite (bth/shr) CTV in all bedrooms Tea and coffee making facilities No dogs Licensed Cen ht CTV No children 8yrs 6P No coaches Last d 6pm
PRICE GUIDE
ROOMS: s £32.50-£45; d £49.50-£60; wkly b&b £227.50-£315; wkly hlf-bd £339.15-£475.65
CARDS: 🔲 🔲 🔲

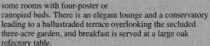
Premier Selected

GH ◗◗◗◗◗ **The Old Parsonage** Frant TN3 9DX (3m S, off A267 in Frant, East Sussex)
☎01892 750773
FAX 01892 750773

Charming proprietors Tony and Mary Dakin are the first non-clerics to live at this delightful Georgian rectory. They offer luxurious accommodation, and some rooms with four-poster or canopied beds. There is an elegant lounge and a conservatory leading to a ballustraded terrace overlooking the secluded three-acre garden, and breakfast is served at a large oak refectory table.
3 en suite (bth/shr) No smoking in bedrooms No smoking in dining room No smoking in lounges CTV in all bedrooms Tea and coffee making facilities Cen ht CTV 12P
PRICE GUIDE
ROOMS: s £34-£39; d £54-£59; wkly b&b fr £184
CARDS: 🔲 🔲

TWO BRIDGES Devon Map **02** SX67

GH ◗◗◗ **Cherrybrook Hotel** PL20 6SP (on B3212)
☎01822 880260 FAX 01822 880260
Closed 24 Dec-2 Jan

Originally a farmhouse, this small family run hotel is located in the heart of Dartmoor, set in three and a half acres of grounds. Bedrooms are comfortable and decorated in attractive colours. The cosy lounge/bar features beams and a slate floor. The fixed-price dinner menus offer fresh local produce, and owners Andy and Margaret Duncan are members of Taste of the West, ensuring standards are high.

7 rms (6 shr) (2 fmly) No smoking in dining room CTV in all bedrooms Tea and coffee making facilities Licensed Cen ht 12P No coaches Last d 7.15pm

PRICE GUIDE

ROOMS: s fr £25; d fr £50; wkly b&b fr £165; wkly hlf-bd fr £240

TYNEMOUTH Tyne & Wear Map **12** NZ36

Selected

GH QQQQ *Hope House* 47 Percy Gardens NE30 4HH
☎0191 257 1989 FAX 0191 257 1989

Hope House is part of an impressive Victorian terrace facing the sea. Two of the bedrooms are very spacious with lovely bay windows , attractive furnishings and shower en suites whilst the third is smaller, simpler and has its own bathroom directly opposite. Day rooms include an ornately furnished drawing room where guest can enjoy a quiet read or a drink and the dining room is equally elegant with a fine Georgian dining table and lovely paintings. Candlelit dinners are available and there is a short, well chosen wine list.

3 en suite (bth/shr) (1 fmly) CTV in all bedrooms Tea and coffee making facilities No dogs (ex guide dogs) Licensed Cen ht 6P No coaches Last d 9pm

CARDS: 🔼 📰 🚾 ⓄⒹ

TYWARDREATH Cornwall & Isles of Scilly Map **02** SX05

Selected

GH QQQQ *Elmswood* Tehidy Rd PL24 2QD (situated in village centre , opposite St Marys church)
☎01726 814221

A very attractive hotel set in a quiet village close to both Mevagissey and Fowey. The accommodation offered is of a high standard, with individually decorated bedrooms furnished with pretty coordinating fabrics, and modern en suite facilities. Pubic rooms are well decorated and furnished and include a sunny dining room overlooking the well tended garden. A set meal of enjoyable home-cooked fare is served in the evenings.

7 rms (1 bth 4 shr) (1 fmly) No smoking in dining room CTV in all bedrooms Tea and coffee making facilities No dogs (ex guide dogs) Licensed Cen ht CTV 8P No coaches Last d noon

UCKFIELD East Sussex Map **05** TQ42

Selected

GH QQQQ *Hooke Hall* 250 High St TN22 1EN
☎01825 761578 FAX 01825 768025
Closed 25-31 Dec

This elegant Queen Anne house stands at the top of the High Street of this small Sussex town and has been transformed by owners Mr and Mrs Percy into a tastefully appointed, yet friendly and relaxing place to stay. Bedrooms are named after historic pairs of lovers, and all have en suite bathrooms and are individually furnished and decorated to offer a high standard of comfort. In the attractive restaurant, the short carte

may include dishes such as the marinated herrings, roast rack of lamb and chocolate marquise enjoyed by our inspector. Although the restaurant is open to non-residents, the atmosphere here is that of a family home, with rooms full of comfortable sofas, antique furniture and open fires.

9 rms (7 bth 1 shr) No smoking in dining room CTV in all bedrooms Tea and coffee making facilities Direct dial from bedrooms No dogs Licensed Cen ht No children 10yrs 8P No coaches Last d 9pm

PRICE GUIDE

ROOMS: s £37.50-£60; d £55-£110
CARDS: 🔼 📰 🚾

Selected

GH QQQQ **South Paddock** Maresfield Park TN22 2HA
☎01825 762335

This delightful country house is set in 3.5 acres of landscaped gardens, found down a peaceful private road opposite the church in the centre of Maresfield village. There are two bedrooms, both facing south, attractively furnished and decorated, and sharing the large bathroom across the hall. They are twin-bedded rooms, but other beds are available to accommodate families. There is a comfortable lounge with a real log fire, and breakfasts, featuring home-made preserves, are taken around the large antique dining table. Major and Mrs Allt are friendly hosts and always available to provide local information and anything else guests might need.

3 rms No smoking in bedrooms No smoking in 1 lounge CTV in all bedrooms Tea and coffee making facilities No ➥

CHERRYBROOK HOTEL
TWO BRIDGES
YELVERTON
DEVON PL20 6SP
Telephone: (01822) 880260

Set in the heart of the National Park, this early 19th century, family run hotel has a splendidly central position for a Dartmoor holiday. All bedrooms have own private facilities and the views from the front are magnificent.
There is good quality home cooked food, where possible using fresh local produce, including fresh herbs from the garden. There is always a choice on the menu.

dogs (ex guide dogs) Cen ht CTV No children 5yrs 7P No coaches Croquet
PRICE GUIDE
ROOMS: s £34-£38; d £50-£55; wkly b&b £160-£210 £

♥ Q Q Q Mr & Mrs D Salmon **Sliders Farm** *(TQ404257)*
Furners Green TN22 3RT (1m S of Danehill village on A275, signposted at small crossroads)
☎01825 790258 FAX 01825 790125
Closed 21 Dec-1 Jan
There are plenty of outdoor pursuits at this quiet farmhouse, located south of the small village of Danehill. The building is surrounded by 30 acres of land with some animals and a trout lake. The accommodation and public areas are spacious and the hosts are keen to make their guests feel at home.
3 en suite (bth/shr) (1 fmly) No smoking in bedrooms No smoking in dining room CTV in all bedrooms Tea and coffee making facilities No dogs Cen ht 12P Outdoor swimming pool (heated) Tennis (hard) Fishing 30 acres non working Last d 24hrs prior
PRICE GUIDE
ROOMS: s £28-£46; d £38-£56

UFFCULME Devon Map **03** ST01

♥ Q Q Mrs S R Farley **Houndaller** *(ST058138)* EX15 3ET
(0.25m from junct 27 of M5) ☎01884 840246
This 16th-century Devonshire longhouse is situated only a quarter of a mile from the M5 at junction 27, and is part of a 600-acre mixed farm. There are two spacious family bedrooms and a lounge/dining room where guests can enjoy their home-cooked breakfasts seated around the large communal table, well looked after by the Farleys.
3 rms (2 fmly) CTV in 2 bedrooms Tea and coffee making facilities Cen ht CTV 3P 176 acres arable beef sheep
CARDS: 🔳 🔳

ULVERSTON Cumbria Map **07** SD27

🛇🌁 **GH** Q Q Q **Church Walk House** Church Walk
LA12 7EW (turn right by Trinity House Hotel, house on corner facing Stables Furniture Shop) ☎01229 582211
This elegant 18th-century gentleman's residence stands in the town centre, opposite the King's Arms and next to Staples furniture shop. Public areas furnished and decorated in period style include a bright dining room and a particularly charming guests' lounge. Equally attractively decorated bedrooms are furnished with antique and pine pieces; two have full en suite facilities and the other has a private bathroom. There is free public car parking only 200 yards away.
3 en suite (bth/shr) (2 fmly) No smoking Tea and coffee making facilities Cen ht CTV No parking No coaches
PRICE GUIDE
ROOMS: s £15-£25; d £35-£40 £

UNDERBARROW Cumbria Map **07** SD49

Selected

♥ Q Q Q Q Mrs D M Swindlehurst **Tranthwaite Hall**
(SD469930) LA8 8HG ☎015395 68285
A charming stone farmhouse - dating back in part to the 11th century and situated on a 250-acre dairy farm in undulating part-wooded countryside - offers accommodation in two traditionally furnished bedrooms. An impressive guests'

lounge retaining its original heavy beams and a very old cooking range offers comfortable chairs, television and books, while meals are taken in a dining room furnished with antiques. Tranthwaite Hall stands on the Kendal side of the village, at the end of a farm lane off the main road.
2 en suite (bth/shr) (1 fmly) No smoking Tea and coffee making facilities No dogs (ex guide dogs) Cen ht CTV 2P 200 acres dairy sheep £

UPPINGHAM Leicestershire Map **04** SP89

Selected

GH Q Q Q Q **Rutland House** 61 High St East LE15 9PY
☎01572 822497 FAX 01572 822497
This comfortable house is located at the quieter end of High Street East, with a small car parking area to the rear. The spacious bedrooms, including one ground floor room, have been carefully furnished to compensate for the lack of lounge area. Each room has en suite facilities, most now with showers over the baths. Breakfast is taken in the strictly no-smoking dining room.
4 en suite (bth/shr) (1 fmly) No smoking in 1 bedrooms No smoking in dining room CTV in all bedrooms Tea and coffee making facilities Cen ht 3P No coaches
PRICE GUIDE
ROOMS: s £29; d £39
CARDS: 🔳 🔳 £

UTTOXETER Staffordshire Map **07** SK03

GH Q Q Q **Hillcrest** 3 Leighton Rd ST14 8BL
☎01889 564627
Closed Xmas Day
A considerably modernised, well maintained detached Victorian house with very friendly proprietors who are regularly making improvements. It is located in a residential area close to the town centre, and offers attractively decorated bedrooms with modern equipment and facilities; family rooms are available, and one room is located on the ground floor; all bedrooms are no smoking. There is a spacious lounge, and separate tables are provided in the dining room.
7 en suite (bth/shr) (6 fmly) No smoking in bedrooms No smoking in dining room CTV in all bedrooms Tea and coffee making facilities No dogs (ex guide dogs) Licensed Cen ht CTV 12P No coaches Last d 7pm
PRICE GUIDE
ROOMS: s £26-£28; d £36✳
CARDS: 🔳 🔳 £

VENN OTTERY Devon Map **03** SY09

GH Q Q Q **Venn Ottery Barton Country Hotel** EX11 1RZ
☎01404 812733
Dating from 1530, this listed building has many period features, such as inglenook fireplaces, beamed ceilings, bible attics and a bread oven in one of the ground-floor bedrooms. It also has two and a half acres of grounds and several cobbled courtyards. The majority of the rooms have their own bath or shower and all are tastefully decorated. There are a comfortable lounge and an airy dining room where both breakfast and dinner are served.
16 rms (5 bth 6 shr) (3 fmly) No smoking in dining room Tea and coffee making facilities Licensed Cen ht CTV 20P No

coaches Large games room Last d 7.30pm
PRICE GUIDE
ROOMS: s £24-£28; d £44-£52; wkly hlf-bd £224-£252✳
CARDS: ▨ ▩ (£)

VENTNOR See **WIGHT, ISLE OF**

WADEBRIDGE Cornwall & Isles of Scilly Map **02** SW97

◢ Q Q Q **Swan Hotel** Molesworth St PL27 7DD (St Austell
Brewery) ☎01208 812526
A character inn at the centre of this riverside town extends a
traditional Cornish welcome to guests. Modern bedrooms are well
equipped, meals are served in bars as well as the restaurant, and
there is a spacious function room on the first floor.
6 en suite (bth) (1 fmly) CTV in all bedrooms Tea and coffee
making facilities No dogs (ex guide dogs) Cen ht 6P Last d
9pm
PRICE GUIDE
ROOMS: s fr £26; d fr £46; wkly b&b fr £140✳
MEALS: Bar Lunch £7-£11alc Dinner £9.50-£15alc✳
CARDS: ▨ ▩ ▩ ⑥

WADHURST East Sussex Map **05** TQ63

◢ Q Q Q **Four Keys** Station Rd TN5 6RZ
☎01892 782252 FAX 01892 784113
Located on the B2099 Frant to Hastings Road and only five
minutes from the main line British Rail station makes this an ideal
base for exploring the local countryside or for quick and direct
access to central London. The accommodation has been designed
to motel standards, all rooms with bath tub showers and TV. Open
all day the bar features a good range of real ale and home-cooked
bar meals, and there is a separate dining room which features a
three-course fixed price menu. Families with children are
especially welcome, and service is personally provided by Peter
and Jean Keys. Other facilities include a coin operated laundry,
children's bar room access, large garden and ample free parking.
7 annexe en suite (bth/shr) (1 fmly) CTV in all bedrooms Tea
and coffee making facilities Direct dial from bedrooms Cen ht
24P Last d 10pm
PRICE GUIDE
ROOMS: d £33-£40
MEALS: Bar Lunch £2-£4 Dinner £3.50-£10
CARDS: ▨ ▩ ▩

WAKEFIELD West Yorkshire Map **08** SE32

Selected

GH Q Q Q Q **Stanley View** 226 / 228 Stanley Rd
WF1 4AE ☎01924 376803 FAX 01924 369123
Stanley View is situated on the main A642 and is an attractive
mid-terrace house and has the benefit of a rear car park. The
house is very well furnished and the bedrooms are well
equipped and even include telephones and Sky television.
There is a cosy lounge and bar and friendly and warm
Yorkshire hospitality is provided by the resident owners Julie
& Bernard Heppinstall.
10 rms (8 shr) (6 fmly) No smoking in bedrooms CTV in all
bedrooms Tea and coffee making facilities Direct dial from
bedrooms No dogs (ex guide dogs) Licensed Cen ht CTV
8P Last d 8.30pm
PRICE GUIDE
ROOMS: s £18-£34; d £30-£34
CARDS: ▨ ▩

WAREHAM Dorset Map **03** SY98

♥ Q Q L S Barnes **Luckford Wood** *(SY873865)* East Stoke
BH20 6AW (turn left off A352 at East Stoke Church, over
level crossing follow lane for approx 0.25m large house on
right) ☎01929 463098 FAX 01929 463098
This modern farmhouse stands in a field, just across from the
original farmhouse and yard. There is a friendly, informal
atmosphere and the Barnes family welcome guests to their home.
Bedrooms are neat and comfortable, with bright coordinating
decor. Telephone reservations are adviseable in order to ensure a
booking. To find the hotel; take the A352 from Wareham, after
two miles turn left at the church, cross the manually-operated level
crossing, and the house is half-a-mile along the lane on the right
hand side. The farm, predominantly dairy, still belongs to the
Barns family, and trips are easily arranged.
4 rms (1 bth 2 shr) (3 fmly) No smoking in dining room No
smoking in lounges CTV in all bedrooms Tea and coffee making
facilities Cen ht CTV 5P 167 acres dairy
PRICE GUIDE
ROOMS: s £20-£25; d £30-£46; wkly b&b £105-£140✳

Selected

♥ Q Q Q Q Mrs J Barnes **Redcliffe** *(SY932866)*
BH20 5BE ☎01929 552225
Closed Xmas
Enjoying an attractive location on the bank of the river Frome,
next to Wareham Yacht Club, this modern farmhouse offers
guests a peaceful and relaxed atmosphere together with a
warm welcome from Mr and Mrs Barnes. The bedrooms are
fresh and bright and although they lack many modern
facilities they are all very comfortable; two of the rooms have
balconies. Breakfast is served at a communal table and is the
only meal available, but Mrs Barnes can suggest local places
to eat in the historic town of Wareham nearby.
4 rms (1 bth 1 shr) No smoking in bedrooms No smoking in
dining room No smoking in lounges No dogs (ex guide
dogs) Cen ht CTV 4P 250 acres dairy mixed

WARKWORTH Northumberland Map **12** NU20

GH Q Q Q **North Cottage** Birling NE65 0XS
☎01665 711263
Closed Xmas & 2wks Nov
Situated on the northern side of the village, this single storey
cottage features an award-winning flower gardens which makes a
magnificent summer spectacle. The cottage itself is spotlessly
clean and well maintained and one can relax in the very attractive
lounge or outside, given the weather. Bedrooms are well equipped
and breakfast is taken round the one table in the dining room.
4 rms (3 shr) No smoking CTV in all bedrooms Tea and coffee
making facilities No dogs Cen ht CTV No children 14yrs 4P
No coaches
PRICE GUIDE
ROOMS: s £17-£17.50; d £34-£35; wkly b&b £112-£115✳

WARREN STREET (NEAR LENHAM) Kent Map **05** TQ95

◢ Q Q Q *Harrow* Hubbards Hill ME17 2ED
☎01622 858727 FAX 01622 850026
Closed 25 & 26 Dec
Originally the forge and resthouse for travellers on the Pilgrims'
Way to Canterbury, this is now an inn, high on the North Downs.
It has modern, spacious bedrooms furnished in cottage style. The
restaurant is in a conservatory and there is a large choice of bar ➟

meals. In summer, guests can sit on the patio that is complete with wishing well and fish pond.

15 en suite (bth/shr) (6 fmly) CTV in all bedrooms Tea and coffee making facilities Direct dial from bedrooms No dogs (ex guide dogs) Cen ht CTV 80P No coaches Last d 10pm
CARDS: ◪ ■ ▨

WARSASH Hampshire Map **04** SU40

Selected

GH Q Q Q Q **Solent View Private Hotel** 33-35 Newtown Rd SO31 9FY ☎01489 572300 FAX 01489 572300
This modern guesthouse is located close to the village centre and the River Hamble. It is personally run by Mrs Anne Mills who maintains a high standard, the rooms are bright and prettily decorated, all have colour television and most have en suite facilities. There are a comfortable lounge and a well stocked bar which overlook the garden. Evening meals are available, and there is off-street parking.

8 en suite (bth/shr) (1 fmly) No smoking in 2 bedrooms No smoking in dining room CTV in all bedrooms Tea and coffee making facilities Direct dial from bedrooms Licensed Cen ht CTV 12P No coaches Last d noon
PRICE GUIDE
ROOMS: s £35; d £45✳
CARDS: ◪ ▨   (£)

WARWICK Warwickshire Map **04** SP26

See also Kineton & Lighthorne

GH Q Q **Austin House** 96 Emscote Rd CV34 5QJ (on A445 Warwick to Leamington Spa) ☎01926 493583
A new lease of life has been brought to this turn-of-the-century house by the new owners, Mr and Mrs Winter. It is gradually being updated but retains its original charm. Breakfast is served in the small dining room, and a large sitting room is also provided.

6 rms (4 shr) (4 fmly) No smoking in 2 bedrooms No smoking in dining room No smoking in lounges CTV in all bedrooms Tea and coffee making facilities No dogs Cen ht CTV 8P
PRICE GUIDE
ROOMS: d £30-£37; wkly b&b £98-£129.50
CARDS: ◪ ▨ ▨ ▨   (£)

GH Q Q **Avon** 7 Emscote Rd CV34 4PH (on A445 opposite entrance to St Nicholas Park)
☎01926 491367 FAX 01926 491367
This early Victorian house is located on the main road to Leamington, east of the centre. Three modern bedrooms in the coach-house annexe have en suite showers, and at the time of the last visit there were plans to install en suite facilities to the bedrooms in the main building.

5 rms (3 shr) 3 annexe rms (4 fmly) No smoking in 6 bedrooms No smoking in dining room CTV in all bedrooms Tea and coffee making facilities No dogs Cen ht CTV 7P No coaches Last d 6pm
PRICE GUIDE
ROOMS: s £17-£18; d £34-£36✳

Selected

GH Q Q Q Q **Croft** CV35 7NL
☎01926 484447 FAX 01926 484447
(For full entry see Haseley Knob)

Selected

GH Q Q Q Q **The Old Rectory** Vicarage Ln, Sherbourne CV35 8AB (off A46 2m SW)
☎01926 624562 FAX 01926 624562
This 17th-century house is conveniently located for both the A46 and the M40 but manages to retain an atmosphere of quiet friendliness and the feeling that the workaday world has been left behind. New proprietors Ian and Dawn Kitchen have a wealth of experience in making guests feel at home and they are warm and thoughtful hosts. Seven rooms are located in the main house and the remainder are in a pretty coach house in the garden. The garden itself is a real delight with an old water pump as the centrepiece. There is an honesty bar where guests can help themselves to refreshments and the attractive dining room with its oak floors and exposed beams serves hearty breakfasts and well prepared traditional dinners.

14 annexe en suite (bth/shr) (2 fmly) No smoking in dining room CTV in all bedrooms Tea and coffee making facilities Licensed Cen ht 14P No coaches Last d 8.30pm
PRICE GUIDE
ROOMS: s £33-£37; d £43-£58; wkly b&b £120-£200; wkly hlf-bd £190-£270✳
CARDS: ◪ ▨
See advertisement on p.421.

Premier Selected

GH Q Q Q Q Q **Shrewley House** Shrewley CV35 7AT (5m NW of Warwick on B4439) ☎01926 842549 FAX 01926 842216

Quietly situated by the village of Shrewley, this charming listed Georgian farmhouse is a welcoming retreat. Mr and Mrs Green provide an exceptionally wide range of services together with some thoughtful extras. In the main house there are three beautifully decorated rooms in Victorian pine, two with king sized, draped, four-poster beds, sumptuous en suites, fluffy towels and excellent linen. Smaller self-catering rooms are offered in the converted stables. There is a cosy sitting room with a piano, and an elegant drawing room opening onto the garden. Generous breakfasts are served in the dining room, and suppers by arrangement. This is a no-smoking establishment.

4 en suite (bth/shr) (1 fmly) No smoking CTV in all bedrooms Tea and coffee making facilities Direct dial from bedrooms Cen ht CTV 17P
PRICE GUIDE
ROOMS: d £60-£72
CARDS: ◪ ▨

◪ Q Q Q **Tudor House** West St CV34 6AW (on A46, opposite entrance to castle)
☎01926 495447 FAX 01926 492948
Built in 1472, this is one of the few buildings to survive the Great Fire of Warwick in 1694. It has a wealth of character with exposed timbers and an abundance of bric-à-brac in both the bars. The style of bedrooms furniture varies, but the rooms are all equipped with direct-dial telephones, TV and radio. A variety of menus is offered, including freshly cooked bar meals and a carte served in

the small restaurant.

11 rms (8 bth/shr) (1 fmly) CTV in all bedrooms Tea and coffee making facilities Direct dial from bedrooms No dogs (ex guide dogs) Cen ht 5P Last d 10.30pm

CARDS: ■ ■ ■ ■

WASHFORD Somerset Map **03** ST04

Selected

◄ QQQQ *Washford* TA23 0PP (on A359 Taunton-Minehead road) ☎01984 640256 FAX 01984 641288

This popular inn backs onto the West Somerset Steam Railway and is ideally situated for an overnight stop or as a base for touring the West Country. The en suite bedrooms are well maintained and equipped, a spacious and convivial bar serves an extensive range of meals and snacks and there is an adjacent patio for summer use.

8 en suite (shr) No smoking in area of dining room CTV in all bedrooms Tea and coffee making facilities Direct dial from bedrooms No dogs (ex guide dogs) Cen ht CTV 40P Last d 9.30pm

CARDS: ■ ■ ■ ■

WASHINGTON Tyne & Wear Map **12** NZ35

GH QQQ **Ye Olde Coppe Shop** 6 The Green, Washington Village NA38 7AB ☎0191 4165333

A friendly welcome is assured at this former police station - think about the name! Bedrooms are compact but well equipped, with two having shower cubicles. The cosy little lounge and separate dining room are attractively decorated and there is good parking ➤

space within the rear garden. Its setting, within the original village, is so different from that of its approach, but access from the A1 is easy if one follows signs to District 4 and then for Washington Village and Old Hall; do not be deterred by the plethora of roundabouts.

4 rms (1 fmly) No smoking in dining room No smoking in lounges CTV in all bedrooms Tea and coffee making facilities No dogs (ex guide dogs) Cen ht CTV 8P No coaches

PRICE GUIDE
ROOMS: s £20; d £30; wkly b&b £95-£126✳

WATCHET Somerset Map **03** ST04

Premier Selected

♥ Ⓠ Ⓠ Ⓠ Ⓠ Ⓠ Mrs L C Lewis **Chidgley Hill** *(ST047365)* Chidgley TA23 0LS ☎01984 640403 Closed 21 Dec-1 Jan

Surrounded by rolling Somerset hills, on the edge of Exmoor, this 15th-century thatched cottage has been lovingly restored to retain its original character. Guests are welcomed into a charming family home where good quality fabrics and attractive furnishings add to the charming atmosphere. A country breakfast is served at a large table in the dining room overlooking the garden.

2 rms (1 bth/shr) No smoking in bedrooms No smoking in lounges CTV in 1 bedroom Tea and coffee making facilities No dogs Cen ht CTV 5P 8 acres non-working

PRICE GUIDE
ROOMS: s £18.50-£19.50; d £39; wkly b&b fr £120

WATERGATE BAY Cornwall & Isles of Scilly Map **02** SW86

🖼🛇 GH Ⓠ Ⓠ **Rosemere Hotel** TR8 4AB (off B3276, 3.5m N of Newquay) ☎01637 860238 FAX 01637 860238

The hotel is situated just one hundred yards from the mile long, sandy Watergate beach. Rosemere Hotel has been run for the last nine years by John and Trish Wharry who have created a happy, relaxed atmosphere, where children and pets are most welcome! The bedrooms are functionally furnished and decorated, but it is in the comfortable public areas where guests spend most of their time. The dining room benefits from excellent seaviews. A varied choice is offered from the fixed price menu of home cooked dishes.

42 rms (35 bth/shr) (18 fmly) No smoking in dining room No smoking in 1 lounge CTV in 33 bedrooms Direct dial from bedrooms Licensed CTV ch fac 36P Outdoor swimming pool (heated) Last d 7.30pm

PRICE GUIDE
ROOMS: s £12-£26; d £24-£64; wkly b&b £112-£168; wkly hlf-bd £190-£236
CARDS: 🔳 🔳

WATERHOUSES Staffordshire Map **07** SK05

🔳 Ⓠ Ⓠ **Ye Olde Crown** ST10 3HL (in centre of village, on A523) ☎01538 308204

This old stone-built inn is situated in the centre of the village, beside the main Leek-Ashbourne road. It offers simple accommodation, and four of the rooms - including one suitable for family occupation, are situated in a cottage adjacent to the main

building. There are two cosy, character bars with low beamed ceilings, and a good choice of popular dishes is available.

7 rms (5 bth/shr) (1 fmly) CTV in all bedrooms Tea and coffee making facilities No dogs (ex guide dogs) Cen ht 50P Last d 10pm

PRICE GUIDE
ROOMS: s £15-£22.50; d £30-£35✳

WATERMILLOCK Cumbria Map **12** NY42

GH Ⓠ Ⓠ Ⓠ **Waterside House** CA11 0JH (on A592) ☎017684 86038
Closed 25-26 Dec

Formerly a Statesman's house, set in ten acres of gardens and grounds leading down to the shore of Lake Ullswater, this charming property was rebuilt and extended in 1771. Bright, fresh bedrooms are individually furnished with a mixture of traditional and antique furniture, one of them also being equipped to meet the needs of disabled visitors. There are two beamed lounge areas - and guests may, if they wish, play the piano contained in one of them. Owner Mrs Jenner provides a good Cumbrian breakfast. Smoking is not permitted.

7 rms (3 bth/shr) (1 fmly) No smoking Tea and coffee making facilities Licensed Cen ht CTV P No coaches Fishing by arrangement Last d 8.30pm

PRICE GUIDE
ROOMS: d £40-£70

£

WATERROW Somerset Map **03** ST02

Selected

GH Ⓠ Ⓠ Ⓠ **Manor Mill** TA4 2AY ☎01984 623317
Closed 24-26 Dec

Dating from the 17th century, this beautiful water mill is set in three acres of gardens in a sheltered position beside the River Tone. The comfortable bedrooms are furnished in a country style, similar to the cosy sitting and breakfast room. Also on the site are six well designed self-catering cottages and apartments, and an indoor heated swimming pool (available to guests staying more than one night). A leisurely 10-minute walk takes guests to the Rock Inn where they can have their evening meal.

3 rms (1 shr) (1 fmly) No smoking No dogs (ex guide dogs) Cen ht CTV 10P No coaches Indoor swimming pool (heated) Fishing

PRICE GUIDE
ROOMS: s £17-£21; d £36-£40; wkly b&b £105-£115

£

🔳 Ⓠ Ⓠ Ⓠ **The Rock** TA4 2AX (on B3227 14m W of Taunton) ☎01984 623293 FAX 01984 623293
Closed 24-26 Dec

An attractive roadside pub built on a rock face in the delightful Tone Valley. Accommodation is in pleasant bedrooms provided with thoughtful extras such as fresh fruit, telephone, radio and TV. On the first floor there is a cosy residents' lounge. The recently refurbished bar retains much of its original charm and a welcoming log fire burns on chilly days. An interesting menu is offered and the restaurant looks out over the valley.

7 en suite (bth/shr) (1 fmly) No smoking in 2 bedrooms CTV in

all bedrooms Direct dial from bedrooms Cen ht CTV 25P Last d 10pm
PRICE GUIDE
ROOMS: s £20-£22; d £40-£44✱
MEALS: Lunch £2.50-£6alc Dinner £8-£12.50alc✱
CARDS: (£)
See advertisement under TAUNTON

WATFORD Hertfordshire Map **04** TQ19

GH 🆀🆀🆀 **Upton Lodge** 26-28 Upton Rd WD1 2EL (Logis)
☎01923 237316 FAX 01923 233109
rs Xmas
Although Upton Lodge is located close to the centre, it is advisable to ask for directions at the time of booking. Accommodation is housed in two buildings, each bedroom offers a good range of amenities which includes direct dial telephones and en suite facilities. Meals are takin in the affiliated 3-star White House Hotel opposite. This hotel also serves as the point of contact.
26 annexe en suite (bth/shr) (1 fmly) No smoking in 5 bedrooms No smoking in 1 lounge CTV in all bedrooms Tea and coffee making facilities Direct dial from bedrooms Licensed Cen ht CTV 35P Last d 9.45pm
PRICE GUIDE
ROOMS: s £39-£49; d £59
CARDS: (£)

WEETON Lancashire Map **07** SD33

💚🆀 Mr & Mrs J Colligan **High Moor** *(SD388365)* PR4 3JJ
☎01253 836273 FAX 01253 836273
Closed mid Jan-mid Feb, Xmas & New Year
This traditional farmhouse on the B5260 is situated in open countryside near the old Weeton barracks. It provides modestly furnished bedrooms, and guests are made to feel very much at home by friendly owners John and Joan Colligan.
2 rms (1 fmly) CTV in all bedrooms Tea and coffee making facilities No dogs Cen ht CTV 10P 7 acres non-working
PRICE GUIDE
ROOMS: d fr £25✱

WELLINGBOROUGH Northamptonshire Map **04** SP86

GH 🆀🆀🆀 **Oak House Private Hotel** 8-11 Broad Green NN8 4LE (turn off A45 & head towards Kettering on A509, hotel on edge of town near cenotaph)
☎01933 271133 FAX 01933 271133
Closed Xmas
Comfortable accommodation is provided at this well run guest house, which has been created from four adjoining buildings. Particular features are its large car park and small bar. Meals can be served by prior arrangement.
16 rms (15 shr) (1 fmly) CTV in all bedrooms Tea and coffee making facilities Licensed Cen ht CTV 12P No coaches Last d noon
PRICE GUIDE
ROOMS: s £28-£32; d £38-£42✱
CARDS: (£)

WELLINGTON Shropshire Map 07 SJ61

See also Telford

Selected

GH Q Q Q Q **Shray Hill** Shray Hill, Crudgington
TF6 6JR (Turn off A442 at Crudgington cross roads onto
B5062 towards Newport. Shray Hill House on left)
☎01952 541260 FAX 01952 541512
Closed 24-31 Dec
This delightful 19th-century house is set in several acres of
well maintained gardens and wooded grounds, just off the
B5062 near Crudgington. There are three pretty bedrooms
with modern en suite shower rooms and an elegantly
furnished lounge with an open fire looking out onto the
grounds. The friendly owners offer a warm welcome to their
guests.
3 en suite (shr) (1 fmly) No smoking CTV in all bedrooms
Tea and coffee making facilities No dogs Cen ht CTV 6P
No coaches Last d 9pm
PRICE GUIDE
ROOMS: s £28-£34; d £38-£45; wkly b&b fr £150

WELLINGTON Somerset Map 03 ST12

Selected

❤ Q Q Q Q Mrs N Ash **Pinksmoor Mill House**
(ST109198) Pinksmoor TA21 0HD (3m S of Wellington on
A38, turn left at Bear Bridge Hotel)
☎01823 672361 FAX 01823 672361
Closed 23-29 Dec
Pinksmoor Farm has been worked by members of the Ash
family since the turn of the century. It is rich in wildlife and
offers the rare chance to see heron, mallard, kingfisher and
snipe. The farm is believed to date back to the 13th century;
and though the mill stones have not been used since the 1940s
the mill leat and pond remain. There is a spacious lounge with
a log burning fire and colour TV and a separate no smoking
lounge. A good value four-course dinner is served, by
arrangement, at a communal table.
3 rms (2 bth/shr) (1 fmly) No smoking CTV in all bedrooms
Tea and coffee making facilities No dogs (ex guide dogs)
Cen ht CTV 6P 98 acres dairy sheep Last d 4pm
PRICE GUIDE
ROOMS: s £21-£21.50; d £37-£38; wkly b&b £114.50-£136;
wkly hlf-bd £185-£216

WELLS Somerset Map 03 ST54

Selected

GH Q Q Q Q **Bekynton House** 7 St Thomas St BA5 2UU
(on B3139) ☎01749 672061 FAX 01749 672222
Closed 24-26 Dec
Well positioned for the cathedral and bishop's palace, this
period house, furnished in keeping with its style of the house,
has good sized bedrooms, all well equipped. There is also a
comfortable lounge and dining room with separate tables.
8 rms (6 bth/shr) (2 fmly) No smoking CTV in all bedrooms

Tea and coffee making facilities No dogs Cen ht No
children 5yrs 6P No coaches
PRICE GUIDE
ROOMS: s £22-£32; d £38-£46
CARDS: 🔲 🔲

Selected

GH Q Q Q Q **Box Tree House** Westbury-sub-Mendip
BA5 1HA (on A371 between Wells & Cheddar next to
Westbury Inn) ☎01749 870777
Westbury-sub-Mendip is situated mid-way between Wells and
Cheddar, Carolyn White's 17th-century former farmhouse
being located in the centre of the village. The bedrooms are
understated and comfortable, two of them having private
bathrooms, literally just outside. A cosy first-floor sitting
room is available for guests. Breakfast is served in the dining
room, and features muffins, croissants and local preserves in
addition to the hearty cooked breakfast. The adjacent hostelry
is a popular venue for both locals and tourists, providing a
good range of value for money meals. In the grounds, Mrs
White has a stained glass workshop, where she is only too
happy to show guests what she makes, some items being for
sale.
3 en suite (bth/shr) No smoking in bedrooms No smoking in
dining room Tea and coffee making facilities No dogs (ex
guide dogs) Cen ht CTV 4P No coaches
PRICE GUIDE
ROOMS: s £22-£25; d £34-£36

Premier Selected

GH Q Q Q Q Q **Infield
House** 36 Portway BA5 2BN
(from city centre, on right
hand side of A371)
☎01749 670989
FAX 01749 679093
American hospitality and
attention to detail combined
with English elegance make
this Victorian property well
worth a visit. Julie and
Maurice Ingerfield offer a

high level of unobtrusive service with genuine warmth and
friendliness. The house is beautifully decorated, and has
superb en suites, excellent beds and crisp linen. The three
bedrooms are individually styled, featuring the original
fireplaces and antique and period furniture. There is a bright
breakfast room where a good range of tempting fresh fruit is
available, in the Californian tradition, followed by a worthy
cooked English breakfast and as much tea or coffee as
required.
3 en suite (bth/shr) No smoking CTV in all bedrooms Tea
and coffee making facilities No dogs (ex guide dogs) Cen ht
No children 16yrs 3P No coaches
PRICE GUIDE
ROOMS: s £31-£33; d £38-£46; wkly b&b £126-£133
CARDS: 🔲 🔲

Premier Selected

GH Q Q Q Q Q **Littlewell Farm** Coxley BA5 1QP (1m from centre on A39 towards Glastonbury)
☎01749 677914

Nestled in a pretty garden just off the A39, only a mile from the famous city of Wells with its beautiful cathedral and bishop's palace, this most attractive 18th-century Somerset farmhouse provides an ideal base from which to explore the area. Charming, individually styled bedrooms are well equipped and beautifully furnished, and an excellent three-course dinner - which must be booked in advance - makes good use of fresh local produce in a range of traditional and original dishes.
5 en suite (bth/shr) No smoking CTV in all bedrooms Tea and coffee making facilities No dogs (ex guide dogs) Licensed Cen ht No children 10yrs 10P No coaches Riding Last d 3pm
PRICE GUIDE
ROOMS: s £21-£23; d £39-£44*

Selected

GH Q Q Q Q *Tor* 20 Tor St BA5 2US
☎01749 672322 FAX 01749 672322
The Tor is a charming 17th-century family home set in attractive grounds overlooking the bishop's palace and the cathedral, and bordering on National Trust land. It offers beautifully furnished and well equipped bedrooms and a comfortable lounge with a selection of books. There are two spacious dining rooms where Mrs Horne offers traditional, continental or vegetarian breakfasts, and a delightful garden with a patio area is available to guests. This is a no-smoking household.
8 rms (2 bth 3 shr) (2 fmly) No smoking CTV in all bedrooms Tea and coffee making facilities No dogs Cen ht CTV No children 5yrs 12P
CARDS: 🔲 🔲
See advertisement on p.425.

✦ Q Q Q Mrs H Millard **Double-Gate Farm** *(ST484424)*
Godney BA5 1RZ (from Wells take A39 towards Glastonbury, at Polsham turn right signposted "Godney/Fenny Castle", continue approx 2m to cross roads, left after inn)
☎01458 832217 & 0585 443333
Feb-Nov
This listed Georgian farmhouse stands on a mixed farm in the village of Godney, about five miles from Wells with fine views of the Mendips. The bedrooms are pleasingly appointed and are equipped with modern facilities. A spacious games room with a full size snooker and table tennis tables are available for guests' use; beware the resident table tennis playing cat!
3 en suite (bth/shr) (1 fmly) No smoking CTV in all bedrooms Tea and coffee making facilities No dogs (ex guide dogs) Cen ht CTV 4P Snooker Table tennis 200 acres beef
PRICE GUIDE
ROOMS: s £17-£18; d £34-£36; wkly b&b £115-£120

❣ QQ Mrs P Higgs **Home** *(ST538442)* Stoppers Ln, Upper Coxley BA5 1QS (2m SW off A39) ☎01749 672434
Closed 1wk Xmas
You are assured of a warm welcome at this Somerset farmhouse only a short drive from the city of Wells, for proprietor Mrs Higgs thoroughly enjoys the company of her guests - many of them "regulars" who return year after year. Bright bedrooms offer wonderful views of rolling countryside, there is a cosy lounge, and breakfast is served in a pleasant dining room with a coal fire.
7 rms (2 bth/shr) (1 fmly) CTV in all bedrooms Tea and coffee making facilities Licensed Cen ht CTV No children 5yrs 12P 15 acres
PRICE GUIDE
ROOMS: s £17-£17.50; d £34-£38✳

❣ QQQ Mrs J Gould **Milton Manor** *(ST546474)* Old Bristol Rd, Upper Milton BA5 3AH (1m W A39 towards Bristol, turn left 200 yds beyond rdbt) ☎01749 673394
Closed 24-27 Dec
In the hamlet of Upper Milton, this gracious Elizabethan farmhouse is set on a 130-acre farm with glorious views to Brent Knoll, and the whole surrounding area is one of outstanding natural beauty. The three cosy guest rooms are pleasantly furnished and breakfast is taken in the panelled dining room, which also serves as a lounge. The garden is a delight, and guests are welcome to sit out and enjoy its tranquillity.
3 rms (1 fmly) No smoking Tea and coffee making facilities No dogs (ex guide dogs) Cen ht CTV 6P 130 acres beef
PRICE GUIDE
ROOMS: s £16.50-£17.50; d £29-£30; wkly b&b £95-£100

Selected

❣ QQQQ Mr & Mrs Frost **Southway** *(ST516423)* Polsham BA5 1RW (3m SW off A39) ☎01749 673396
Feb-Nov
A pleasant farmhouse where bedrooms, with views over the Pennard hills, are a good size and thoughtfully furnished. There is a garden and the interest of a working farm. Breakfast is served round a large mahogany table.
3 rms (1 shr) No smoking in bedrooms No smoking in dining room CTV in 2 bedrooms Tea and coffee making facilities No dogs (ex guide dogs) Cen ht CTV 3P 170 acres dairy
PRICE GUIDE
ROOMS: s £21-£26; d £34-£38

WEM Shropshire Map **07** SJ52

Selected

GH QQQQ **Foxleigh House** Foxleigh Dr SY4 5BP (turn off A49 onto B5063 to Wem, take B5476 towards Whitchurch and second turning right after Hawkstone public house. Then left onto Foxleigh Drive) ☎01939 233528
Closed Xmas
This fine old country mansion lies in pretty grounds on the northern outskirts of the town. The sitting and dining rooms are furnished in keeping with the style of the house and retain their original Victorian ceiling mouldings. One spacious bedroom has its own private bathroom; the others form a suite suitable for families. Croquet can be played on the lawn and the atmosphere is relaxed and peaceful.
2 en suite (bth) No smoking in dining room CTV in all

bedrooms Tea and coffee making facilities No dogs Cen ht No children 10yrs 4P No coaches Croquet lawn Last d previous day
PRICE GUIDE
ROOMS: d £34-£40; wkly b&b fr £119; wkly hlf-bd fr £192.50

Selected

❣ QQQQ Mrs A P Ashton **Soulton Hall** *(SJ543303)* Soulton SY4 5RS ☎01939 232786
This historic manor house retains great character in its exposed timbers, uneven floors and original fireplaces, and it provides large and well furnished bedrooms. Guests are invited to join in the farming activities, and there are ponies available for riding. Fifty acres of oak woodland and miles of riverside will tempt walkers.
3 rms (2 bth) 2 annexe en suite (bth/shr) (2 fmly) CTV in all bedrooms Tea and coffee making facilities Licensed Cen ht ch fac 12P Fishing Riding 560 acres mixed Last d 9pm
CARDS: 🔲 🔲
See advertisement under Colour Section

WEMBLEY Greater London Map **04** TQ18

GH QQQ **Adelphi Hotel** 4 Forty Ln HA9 9EB ☎0181 904 5629 FAX 0181 908 5314
There is the advantage of off-street parking at this modestly run guest house. It shows signs of a boisterous week-end trade but is useful for the commercial market during the week. There is limited space in the lounge/breakfast room but there are plans to create more room.
11 rms (7 shr) (2 fmly) No smoking in dining room CTV in all bedrooms Tea and coffee making facilities No dogs CTV 12P No coaches Last d 8pm
PRICE GUIDE
ROOMS: s £25-£35; d £38-£45; wkly b&b £164-£196✳
CARDS: 🔲 🔲 🔲 🔲   ⓔ

GH QQQ **Arena Hotel** 6 Forty Ln HA9 9EB ☎0181 908 0670 & 0181 908 0019 FAX 0181 908 2007
Conveniently situated for Wembley Stadium and having its own parking facilities, this friendly guest house offers bedroom with modern amenities - some of them on the ground floor; it also has a separate lounge and bright, comfortable dining room.
13 en suite (bth/shr) (1 fmly) No smoking in dining room CTV in all bedrooms Tea and coffee making facilities No dogs (ex guide dogs) Cen ht CTV 15P Last d 10.30pm
PRICE GUIDE
ROOMS: s £28-£35; d £38-£45
CARDS: 🔲 🔲 🔲 🔲 🔲   ⓔ

WEST BAGBOROUGH Somerset Map **03** ST13

Selected

GH QQQQ **Higher House** TA4 3EF ☎01823 432996 FAX 01823 433568
Closed 24-26 Dec
Higher House stands at the far edge of the village, 650 feet up on the southern slopes of the Quantock Hills. The views from the house, gardens and tennis court are spectacular, across the Vale of Taunton to the Brendon Hills and Exmoor beyond. The principal part of the house is 17th-century and is built around two courtyards, one of which contains a heated

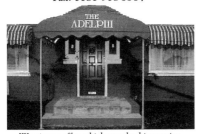

outdoor swimming pool. The bedrooms are attractively decorated and exceedingly well equipped. Imaginative three-course dinners are available by special arrangement, and on other occasions a simple, two-course supper can be provided, complemented by a reasonably priced wine list and drinks from the honesty bar.

3 en suite (bth) (1 fmly) CTV in all bedrooms Tea and coffee making facilities Direct dial from bedrooms No dogs Licensed Cen ht No children 13yrs 13P No coaches Outdoor swimming pool (heated) Tennis (hard) Tennis coaching available

PRICE GUIDE
ROOMS: s fr £25; d fr £40; wkly b&b fr £150✱

WESTCLIFF-ON-SEA Essex

See **Southend-on-Sea**

WEST DOWN Devon Map **02** SS54

Premier Selected

GH 🔲🔲🔲🔲🔲 **The Long House** The Square EX34 8NF
☎01271 863242
FAX 01271 863242
early Mar-early Nov
Formerly the local smithy, this gem of a guest house has been tastefully converted to offer four individually decorated bedrooms with many extras. The quaint tea shop, which is part of the house, is transformed into an attractive dining room in the evening. Pauline Hart offers inspired home cooking accompanied by husband Rob's impeccable wine list. The cosy lounge is a comfortable venue for after dinner coffee and chat.
4 en suite (bth/shr) No smoking in 1 bedrooms No smoking in dining room No smoking in 1 lounge CTV in all bedrooms Tea and coffee making facilities No dogs (ex guide dogs) Licensed Cen ht CTV 4P No coaches Last d 8pm
PRICE GUIDE
ROOMS: d £84; wkly hlf-bd £269.50
CARDS: £

GH 🔲🔲🔲 **Sunnymeade Country House Hotel** Dean Cross EX34 8NT (1m W on A361) ☎01271 863668
A friendly and informal atmosphere, ideal for families, awaits guests at this family-run guest house on the main Ilfracombe-Barnstaple road. Mr Hunt is a trained chef and he offers Devon cream teas in addition to a range of traditional dishes at both lunch and dinner.
10 rms (8 shr) (2 fmly) No smoking in dining room No smoking in 1 lounge CTV in all bedrooms Tea and coffee making facilities Direct dial from bedrooms Licensed Cen ht CTV 14P Last d 7.30pm
PRICE GUIDE
ROOMS: s £16.50-£22.50; d £35-£41; wkly b&b £115-£125; wkly hlf-bd £155-£179
CARDS: £

WEST DRAYTON Greater London

For accommodation details see **Heathrow Airport**

WESTGATE ON SEA Kent Map **05** TR37

GH 🔲🔲 **White Lodge** 12 Domneva Rd CT8 8PE
☎01843 831828
White Lodge is a friendly guesthouse located close to the beach and just a five-minute walk from the railway station. Most of the bedrooms have their own facilities. There is a wood-panelled lounge with an honesty bar and a bright breakfast room.
5 en suite (bth/shr) (2 fmly) No smoking in 3 bedrooms No smoking in dining room No smoking in lounges CTV in all bedrooms Tea and coffee making facilities Licensed Cen ht CTV 3P No coaches
PRICE GUIDE
ROOMS: s £26-£28; d £36-£40; wkly b&b £126-£176✱
CARDS: £

WEST GRAFTON Wiltshire Map **04** SU26

Premier Selected

♥ 🔲🔲🔲🔲🔲 Mrs A Orssich **Mayfield** (*SU246598*)
SN8 3BY ☎01672 810339
FAX 01672 811158
Closed Xmas
This delightful red brick thatched farmhouse is surrounded by well tended gardens and grounds in a rural area close to the village of Burbage. The property has been carefully extended by the present owners, Chris and Angie Orssich, to provide three comfortable rooms and two bathrooms. There is a choice of attractive lounges, and the house is tastefully decorated - with an emphasis on quality and comfort - and furnished with antiques.
3 en suite (bth) No smoking in bedrooms CTV in all bedrooms Tea and coffee making facilities Direct dial from bedrooms Cen ht CTV 6P Outdoor swimming pool (heated) Tennis (hard) Table tennis Play area 8 acres non-working
PRICE GUIDE
ROOMS: s £27-£30; d £40-£42 £

WEST LULWORTH Dorset Map **03** SY88

GH 🔲🔲🔲 **Gatton House Hotel** BH20 5RU (on B3071, left hand side after entering village, 300yds after Castle Inn on right) ☎01929 400252 FAX 01929 400252
Mar-Oct
An attractive property is situated just minutes from the Cove with lovely views over the rolling countryside. The bedrooms feature modern en suite facilities and pretty coordinated fabrics. Public rooms comprise a comfortable guest lounge and a sunny breakfast room overlooking the village church. The house has a private car park and stands at the top of a steep path.
8 en suite (bth/shr) (2 fmly) No smoking in dining room CTV in all bedrooms Tea and coffee making facilities Licensed Cen ht 12P No coaches
PRICE GUIDE
ROOMS: s £29.50-£37; d £41-£55; wkly b&b £129.50-£178.50✱
CARDS:

WEST MALLING Kent Map **05** TQ65

GH ⛟⛟⛟⛟ **Scott House** High St ME19 6QH (on A228) ☎01732 841380 FAX 01732 870025
Closed Xmas
This attractive Georgian building in the village centre now doubles as a guesthouse and an antique and furniture restoration shop. Individually and well furnished bedrooms are all on the first floor. Breakfast is served in a large, bright room overlooking the street and there is a lounge area with comfortable seating.
3 en suite (shr) No smoking CTV in all bedrooms Tea and coffee making facilities No dogs (ex guide dogs) Cen ht No children No parking No coaches
PRICE GUIDE
ROOMS: s £39; d £49✱
CARDS: £

GH ⛟⛟⛟⛟ **Woodgate** Birling Rd, Leybourne ME19 5HT ☎01732 843201
This attractive 18th-century cottage stands in well kept gardens in peaceful rural surroundings. Bedrooms are individually furnished and decorated and there is a comfortable lounge. Breakfasts are served in the dining room round an unusual table made from railway sleepers.
3 rms (2 bth/shr) (1 fmly) No smoking CTV in 2 bedrooms Tea and coffee making facilities Cen ht CTV 5P No coaches Last d 9.30pm
PRICE GUIDE
ROOMS: s £19-£21; d £38-£42; wkly b&b £133-£147; wkly hlf-bd £210.50-£254.50✱ £

WEST MERSEA Essex Map **05** TM01

GH ⛟⛟⛟ **Blackwater Hotel** 20-22 Church Rd CO5 8QH ☎01206 383338 & 383038
Closed first 3 wks Jan
Situated in the heart of the village and close to West Mersea beach, this late-Victorian building with its attractive ivy-clad façade was previously a coaching inn. Comfortable bedrooms are simply furnished but freshly decorated, and most have private bathrooms adjacent. The Champenois restaurant offers genuine French cooking in an authentic and friendly atmosphere, and there is a cosy bar and a comfortable lounge. Ample car parking is available at the rear.
7 rms (2 shr) CTV in all bedrooms Tea and coffee making facilities No dogs (ex guide dogs) Licensed Cen ht 20P No coaches Last d 10pm
PRICE GUIDE
ROOMS: s £29-£445; d £45-£65
CARDS: £

WESTON-SUPER-MARE Avon Map **03** ST36

GH ⛟⛟⛟⛟ **Ashcombe Court** 17 Milton Rd BS23 2SH (follow signs for 'Seafront North' and 'Milton') ☎01934 625104
Tom and Sian Bisdee warmly welcome visitors to their delightful Victorian house, which is ideally situated for the seafront, parks and shopping centre. The beautiful lounge is the perfect place to relax after a delicious dinner cooked by Sian, and the tastefully furnished bedrooms are particularly comfortable, with lots of thoughtful extras to enhance one's stay.
6 en suite (bth/shr) (1 fmly) No smoking in bedrooms No smoking in dining room CTV in all bedrooms Tea and coffee making facilities No dogs Cen ht CTV 9P No coaches Last d 6pm
PRICE GUIDE
ROOMS: s £21-£29; d £32-£38; wkly b&b £115-£123.50; wkly hlf-bd £145.50-£155.50✱ £

▨▨ **GH** ⛟⛟⛟ **Baymead Hotel** Longton Grove Rd BS23 1LS ☎01934 622951 FAX 01934 628110
Closed Jan & Feb
A popular, family-run holiday hotel stands in a central location close to the town centre and all amenities. It offers bright, well equipped bedrooms with private bathrooms and modern facilities. The lively bars provide entertainment three nights a week.
33 rms (30 bth/shr) (3 fmly) No smoking in dining room CTV ➡

in all bedrooms Tea and coffee making facilities Licensed Lift
Cen ht CTV 9P Half size snooker table Last d 7pm
PRICE GUIDE
ROOMS: s £15-£22.50; d £35-£40; wkly b&b £125-£155; wkly
hlf-bd £150-£195

GH QQQ **Beverley** 11 Whitecross Rd BS23 1EP
☎01934 622956
This terraced family home is situated in a quiet residential area of
the town but only a short, level walk from the seafront. Bedrooms
are modern, bright and adequately equipped. Set home-cooked
dinners are available by arrangement, and breakfast is served in
the pleasant dining room.
5 en suite (shr) (3 fmly) No smoking in dining room CTV in all
bedrooms Tea and coffee making facilities No dogs (ex guide
dogs) Cen ht No parking No coaches Last d 4pm
PRICE GUIDE
ROOMS: s £18-£19; d £30-£34; wkly b&b £95-£105; wkly hlf-
bd £125-£140✱

Selected

GH QQQQ **Braeside** 2 Victoria Park BS23 2HZ (with
sea to the left drive along front, 1st right after Winter
Gardens then 1st left into lower Church Rd, Victoria Park
on right) ☎01934 626642 FAX 01934 626642
Braeside, a house of great character and charm, stands in an
elevated position with views over Weston Bay to beautiful
Brean Down; guests are made to feel very welcome and the
emphasis is on warmth and hospitality. The nine guest rooms
all have en suite facilities and some enjoy sea views. A
traditional home-cooked dinner is served in the pleasant
dining room and, as this is a licensed establishment, guests
can enjoy a drink before dinner on the patio and a glass of
wine with the meal. Unrestricted parking is available nearby.
9 en suite (bth/shr) (3 fmly) No smoking in dining room
CTV in all bedrooms Tea and coffee making facilities
Licensed Cen ht No coaches Last d 6pm
PRICE GUIDE
ROOMS: s £22.50; d £45; wkly b&b £135; wkly hlf-bd
£186✱

GH QQQ **Clifton Lodge** 48 Clifton Rd BS23 1BN (follow
main road to sea front, Clifton Rd is 1st turning on left past
the Tropicana) ☎01934 629357
Comfortable accommodation is offered at this hospitable little
guest house close to the seafront. A traditional evening meal
features English roasts with fresh vegetables, and new owners Mr
and Mrs Smith are making extensive improvements which will
include a cosy new guests' lounge.
6 rms (2 shr) (4 fmly) No smoking in dining room No smoking
in lounges CTV in all bedrooms Tea and coffee making facilities
No dogs (ex guide dogs) Cen ht CTV 2P No coaches Last d
breakfast
PRICE GUIDE
ROOMS: s £13-£15.50; d £26-£35; wkly b&b £84-£115; wkly
hlf-bd £126-£157✱
CARDS: 🔲 🔲

GH QQ **Conifers** 63 Milton Rd BS23 2SP (turn off M5 at
junct 21 and follow A370 towards Weston turn right into Bay
Tree Rd left turn at lights into Milton Rd) ☎01934 624404
Closed 22-3 Jan
An immaculately maintained and bright little bed and breakfast
guesthouse close to the town centre and all amenities. Bedrooms

---

are comfortable and well decorated, and there is a small cosy
breakfast room. There is a pretty garden adjacent, and the house is
located with good access to the M5.
3 rms (1 bth/shr) No smoking in dining room CTV in all
bedrooms Tea and coffee making facilities No dogs Cen ht No
children 14yrs 4P
PRICE GUIDE
ROOMS: s £17-£20; d £30-£36; wkly b&b £95-£115

GH QQQ *Lewinsdale Lodge Hotel* 5-7 Clevedon Rd
BS23 1DA ☎01934 632501
May-Sep rs Mar-Apr & Oct-Nov
Well positioned close to the seafront and opposite the Tropicana
leisure centre, this small hotel provides comfortable
accommodation. The original building dates back 150 years and
retains much of its former character, and its facilities have recently
been enhanced by the addition of new bedrooms and a function
suite. Owners Valerie and Thomas Farmer are conscientious
hoteliers and the hotel provides good value for money.
10 en suite (shr) CTV in all bedrooms Tea and coffee making
facilities No dogs (ex guide dogs) Licensed Cen ht No children
12yrs 4P No coaches Last d noon

Selected

GH QQQQ **Milton Lodge** 15 Milton Rd BS23 2SH
(leave M5 follow "Accommodation" sign, after 1m take
right turn at rdbt towards Milton & sea front north, left at
traffic lights continue appox 1m) ☎01934 623161
Mar-Sep
Husband and wife team Adrienne and Les Cox warmly
welcome visitors to their pleasant Victorian villa, providing
warm, comfortable accommodation in spacious, well
equipped bedrooms which are attractively decorated and
furnished to a high standard. Good traditional home cooking
is one of the reasons that guests return year after year, but
there is also a good selection of restaurants in the centre of
Weston, just a pleasant level stroll away.
6 en suite (bth/shr) No smoking in dining room CTV in all
bedrooms Tea and coffee making facilities No dogs Cen ht
CTV No children 6P No coaches Last d 10am
PRICE GUIDE
ROOMS: s £18-£20; d £30-£36; wkly b&b £110-£119; wkly
hlf-bd £130-£159✱

GH QQQ **Saxonia** 95 Locking Rd BS23 3EW (at Hutton
More Sports Centre turn right then left at next lights, Saxonia
half a mile on right at lights)
☎01934 633856 FAX 01934 623141
Well equipped bedrooms are offered at this small guesthouse,
which is in a central location with limited but useful car parking.
A cosy dining room and a bar are provided.
9 en suite (bth/shr) (4 fmly) No smoking in dining room CTV in
all bedrooms Tea and coffee making facilities No dogs Licensed
Cen ht CTV 4P Last d 2pm
PRICE GUIDE
ROOMS: s £18-£25; d £35-£50✱
CARDS: 🔲 🔲 🔲 🔲 🔲 🔲 🔲

GH 🇶🇶🇶🇶 **Wychwood Hotel** 148 Milton Rd
BS23 2UZ ☎01934 627793
Closed Xmas & annual holiday
Owned and enthusiastically run by experienced hoteliers, Mr
and Mrs Whitehouse, this spacious Victorian house is
conveniently positioned on the outskirts of the town, with
good access to the M5 and the town centre. Immaculately
maintained and bright throughout, it provides comfortable and
well furnished bedrooms with modern facilities. There is a
pleasant dining room and a cosy little bar lounge.
9 en suite (bth/shr) (3 fmly) CTV in all bedrooms Tea and
coffee making facilities No dogs (ex guide dogs) Licensed
Cen ht 14P No coaches Outdoor swimming pool (heated)
Last d 6.30pm
PRICE GUIDE
ROOMS: s fr £25; d fr £42; wkly b&b £126-£150; wkly hlf-
bd £182-£206✳
CARDS: 🔳 🔳   (£)

♥ 🇶🇶🇶 Mrs T G Moore *Purn House (ST331571)* Bleadon
BS24 0QE ☎01934 812324
Feb-Nov
An attractive creeper-clad 17th-century farmhouse, situated three
miles from the town and close to the A370 in the peaceful village
of Bleadon, provides comfortable and well equipped
accommodation which nevertheless retains something of the
building's original character and charm. Very much part of a
typical Somerset working farm, it offers a traditional English
breakfast, and the pub - a short stroll from the house - can provide
a tasty supper to suit all pockets. The stable block has been
converted into interesting craft shops and there is ample parking
space for visitors.
6 rms (4 bth/shr) (3 fmly) No smoking in bedrooms No smoking
in dining room CTV in 4 bedrooms Tea and coffee making
facilities No dogs (ex guide dogs) Cen ht CTV 10P Fishing
Childrens playroom Snooker Table tennis 700 acres arable dairy
Last d 10am

WESTON UNDERWOOD Derbyshire Map 08 SK24

♥ 🇶🇶🇶🇶 Mrs L Adams **Parkview Farm** *(SK293425)*
DE6 4PA (6m NW of Derby, 0.5m from Kedleston Hall
National Trust property) ☎01335 360352
Closed 24 & 25 Dec
Parkview Farmhouse is a delightful Victorian property
overlooking the parkland of the National Trust Kedleston Hall
estate. Linda and Michael Adams are enthusiastic hosts who
offer splendid accommodation in beautifully furnished
bedrooms, including two with antique four-poster beds. Each
room has its own wash basin and there are two general
bathrooms. There is a good choice at breakfast, which is
served in the small dining room at polished wood tables. This
is a no-smoking establishment.
3 rms (1 shr) Tea and coffee making facilities No dogs Cen
ht CTV No children 2yrs 10P 375 acres mixed
PRICE GUIDE
ROOMS: s £20-£25; d £38-£44✳   (£)

WEST STOUR Dorset Map 03 ST72

◀ 🇶🇶🇶 **The Ship** SP8 5RP (on A30 between Shaftesbury
& Sherborne) ☎01747 838640
A family run, cosy inn offers accommodation of a very good
standard. The bedrooms are thoughtfully and comfortably
appointed; all are of a good size and well equipped. In the two
small dining rooms guests can choose from either a dinner or bar
menu. The cooking is good, honest and uncomplicated.
6 en suite (bth/shr) (2 fmly) No smoking in area of dining room
CTV in all bedrooms Tea and coffee making facilities No dogs
(ex guide dogs) Cen ht CTV 50P Fishing Last d 9.30pm
PRICE GUIDE
ROOMS: s £28; d £38-£42; wkly b&b £114-£168✳
MEALS: Lunch £6.30-£24.70alc Dinner £6.30-£24.70alc✳
CARDS: 🔳 🔳   (£)

WESTWARD HO! Devon Map 02 SS42

GH 🇶🇶🇶 **The Buckleigh Lodge** 135 Bayview Rd EX39 1BJ
(0.75m W of rdbt near Torridge Bridge, Bideford turn off
A39 onto B3236 signed Westward Ho!, Buckleigh Lodge
approx 0.75m on right) ☎01237 475988
An elegant Victorian property in its own well kept gardens,
Buckleigh Lodge is just a few minutes' steep walk from the sea
and a beautiful sandy beach. It offers a choice of attractive lounges
and a dining room where a set menu is available for dinner.
Bedrooms vary in size and several have en suite facilities.
6 rms (3 bth/shr) (1 fmly) No smoking in bedrooms No smoking
in dining room CTV in all bedrooms Tea and coffee making
facilities No dogs (ex guide dogs) Licensed Cen ht CTV ch fac
➡

8P No coaches Last d 4pm
PRICE GUIDE
ROOMS: s £17-£18; d £34-£36; wkly b&b £112-£120; wkly hlf-bd £165-£172

WETHERBY West Yorkshire Map **08** SE44

GH 🅀🅀 **Prospect House** 8 Caxton St LS22 6RU
☎01937 582428
Standing close to the town centre and in a side road, this friendly guest house offers bright bedrooms together with personal service from the resident owners, Mr and Mrs Watkin. There is a combined breakfast room and lounge area provided for guests to use.
6 rms (1 fmly) CTV in 1 bedroom Tea and coffee making facilities Cen ht CTV 6P No coaches
PRICE GUIDE
ROOMS: s £16.50-£17; d £33-£34✻

WEYBRIDGE Surrey Map **04** TQ06

GH 🅀🅀 *Warbeck House Hotel* 46 Queens Rd KT13 0AR
☎01932 848764 FAX 01932 847290
This attractive Edwardian house is situated on the A317, close to the town centre. Attractive bedrooms offer good facilities; all have TVs and beverage-making facilities and some also have modular en suite showers. Breakfast is taken in the Barclay Room, which has a conservatory extension and a patio overlooking the secluded rear garden. Service is friendly and there is ample forecourt parking.
10 rms (5 shr) (1 fmly) No smoking in dining room CTV in all bedrooms Tea and coffee making facilities Licensed Cen ht CTV 20P

WEYMOUTH Dorset Map **03** SY67

See also Portland

Selected

GH 🅀🅀🅀🅀 **Bay Lodge** 27 Greenhill DT4 7SW (on A353, near Lodmoor Country Park, Park Bay Lodge is 200yds town centre side of entrance)
☎01305 782419 FAX 01305 782828
Closed Nov
This delightful property is set in an elevated position on the edge of the town, and commands superb views over the bay. Proprietors Graham and Barbara Dubben create a warm and friendly atmosphere and are continually making improvements. The bedrooms have are individually decorated, most have king size beds, and deluxe bathrooms. The relaxing public areas include a popular lounge bar, a cosy no-smoking study and an bright dining room where Barbara prepares an interesting menu of good home-cooked dishes.
7 en suite (bth/shr) 5 annexe en suite (bth/shr) No smoking in bedrooms No smoking in dining room No smoking in 1 lounge CTV in all bedrooms Tea and coffee making facilities Direct dial from bedrooms Licensed Cen ht CTV No children 2yrs 15P No coaches Last d 5pm
PRICE GUIDE
ROOMS: s £55; d £44-£67; wkly b&b £154-£234; wkly hlf-bd £220-£345
CARDS: 🅰 ▆ ▆ 🄳 🄾

GH 🅀🅀 **Birchfields** 22 Abbotsbury Rd DT4 0AE (from Jubilee Clock on Esplanade turn into King St 2nd exit continue over bridge, 2nd exit from rdbt into Abbotsbury Rd, hotel 50yds on right) ☎01305 773255
Mar-Oct
Situated on the main Bridport to Weymouth road, this personally run guest house is close to the town centre. The rooms are bright and some have en suite facilities. There is a comfortable lounge with a bar, and a varied menu is served in the evenings.
9 rms (3 shr) (4 fmly) No smoking in dining room CTV in all bedrooms Tea and coffee making facilities Licensed Cen ht CTV 3P Last d 3pm
PRICE GUIDE
ROOMS: s £15-£21; d £30-£42; wkly b&b £73-£115; wkly hlf-bd £120-£156

Selected

GH 🅀🅀🅀🅀 **Channel View** 10 Brunswick Ter, The Esplanade DT4 7RW (at Manor rdbt by Safeway go straight on, at St John's Church follow signs to sea front, pass the church then double back left at pedestrian crossing) ☎01305 782527
A delightful, immaculate small guesthouse situated yards from the promenade and beach, along a 'no through road' where parking is restricted. Bedrooms are thoughtfully decorated with extra personal touches, and front rooms have sea views. The dining room also looks out to sea and there is a very well stocked bar. Home-cooked five-course evening meals feature meat, fish and vegetables in season, delivered fresh daily. Car parking from June 1st - September 30th can be arranged at a reasonable charge.
7 rms (5 shr) (2 fmly) No smoking CTV in all bedrooms Tea and coffee making facilities No dogs (ex guide dogs) Licensed Cen ht CTV No children 12yrs Last d 4pm
PRICE GUIDE
ROOMS: s £17-£22; d £34-£44; wkly b&b £119-£154; wkly hlf-bd £175-£210✻
CARDS: 🅰 ▆

Selected

GH 🅀🅀🅀🅀 *Cumberland Hotel* 95 Esplanade DT4 7BA
☎01305 785644
Valerie and Will Hampshire have been running this small friendly hotel for over twenty years, and it goes from strength to strength. The bedrooms are bright and comfortable with en suite facilities and pretty co-ordinated decor. The attractive dining room is situated on the lower ground floor, and offers a cost atmosphere in which to enjoy the varied home cooked meals.
12 en suite (bth/shr) (4 fmly) CTV in all bedrooms Tea and coffee making facilities No dogs Licensed No children 8yrs 2P

GH 🅀🅀🅀 *Ferndown* 47 Walpole St DT4 7HQ
☎01305 775228
Closed 25 Dec-9 Jan
A neat little guesthouse situated in a quiet residential area, close to the seafront and town centre. It offers pretty, individually decorated bedrooms with some welcoming extra touches. Public areas are compact, but offer a comfortable and friendly atmosphere. A home-cooked evening meal is provided by Mrs

Waddell using good quality fresh produce. The whole Waddell family are involved in running this guesthouse, and the atmosphere is friendly and relaxed.

8 rms No smoking in area of dining room CTV in 6 bedrooms Tea and coffee making facilities CTV

PRICE GUIDE
ROOMS: s £13-£15; d £26-£30; wkly b&b £82-£90; wkly hlf-bd £115-£120✶

GH ⓆⓆ **Hazeldene** 16 Abbotsbury Rd, Westham DT4 0AE (300yds from Westham Roundabout)
☎01305 782579 FAX 01305 761022
rs (evening meal by arrangement only)

Located in a residential area away from the bustle of the town centre, this friendly guesthouse has flourished under new ownership. The simply furnished bedrooms are freshly decorated and have good, firm beds, while public areas have a homely feel. Dinner is only served in the summer months (and then by prior arrangement), but there are plenty of eating places nearby.

6 rms (3 fmly) No smoking in dining room CTV in 5 bedrooms Tea and coffee making facilities No dogs (ex guide dogs) Cen ht CTV 6P Last d noon

PRICE GUIDE
ROOMS: s £13-£16; d £26-£32; wkly b&b £90-£100✶

GH ⓆⓆⓆ **Hotel Malta** 141 The Esplanade DT4 7NJ (eastern end of esplanade, opposite pier bandstand) ☎01305 783129
May-Sep rs Apr & Oct

This friendly, family-owned hotel stands on the seafront with lovely views far out to sea. Pretty bedrooms with co-ordinating decor, like the attractive public areas, are subject to constant improvement and home-cooked meals are served in the front-facing dining room. There is parking space at the rear of the hotel.

12 rms (4 fmly) No smoking in dining room CTV in all bedrooms Tea and coffee making facilities No dogs Licensed CTV 9P Last d 5pm

PRICE GUIDE
ROOMS: s £16.50-£19; d £33-£38; wkly b&b £105-£125; wkly hlf-bd £150-£170

GH ⓆⓆⓆ **Kenora** 5 Stavordale Rd DT4 0AB (from Esplanade left at Jubilee Clock into King St, 2nd exit off rdbt over bridge to next rdbt 2nd exit into Abbotsbury Rd left & then right) ☎01305 771215
Etr & 11 May-28 Sep

This handsome property, quietly located in a residential area, enjoys views across the town towards the harbour. The bedrooms are freshly decorated, well furnished and comfortable, with smart en suite facilities in most rooms. Public areas are also very attractive and the garden recently won a Britain-in-Bloom award.

15 rms (4 bth 9 shr) (5 fmly) No smoking in dining room CTV in all bedrooms Tea and coffee making facilities No dogs (ex guide dogs) Licensed Cen ht 20P Last d 4.30pm

PRICE GUIDE
ROOMS: s £27-£36; d £44-£62; wkly b&b £142-£168; wkly hlf-bd £172-£199✶
CARDS: 🔲 🔲 🔲

GH ⓆⓆⓆ *Kings Acre Hotel* 140 The Esplanade DT4 7NH
☎01305 782534
Closed 15 Dec-5 Jan rs Oct, Nov & Dec

This family run guest house is located on the sea front and enjoys lovely views of the bay. The bedrooms, several with ensuite facilities are bright and spacious. There is a pleasant dining room overlooking the sea, and Mrs Mears prepares traditional home cooking and is happy to cater for special diets. There is some private parking at the rear of the building.

➡

12 rms (8 shr) (4 fmly) No smoking in dining room CTV in all bedrooms Tea and coffee making facilities No dogs Licensed Cen ht CTV 9P Last d 4.30pm
CARDS: ■■ ■■

GH ⓠⓠⓠ **New Salsudas Hotel** 22 Lennox St DT4 7HE (left of clock on Esplanade and turn left at traffic lights, 300yds down Lennox Street) ☎01305 771903
Dating back to 1901, this was originally a public house and is now a friendly and comfortable guest house. Bedrooms vary in size, but all are en suite with a high standard in furnishings. Two are located on the ground floor. There is an airy dining room where breakfast and dinner are served.
7 en suite (bth/shr) (3 fmly) No smoking in dining room CTV in 6 bedrooms Tea and coffee making facilities Licensed Cen ht 3P No coaches Last d 3.30pm
PRICE GUIDE
ROOMS: d £28-£40; wkly b&b £90-£112; wkly hlf-bd £138-£160✱
CARDS: ■■ ■■ (£)

GH ⓠⓠⓠ **Sou'west Lodge Hotel** Rodwell Rd DT4 8QT ☎01305 783749
Closed 22 Dec-1 Jan
This well presented private hotel is located away from the town centre, above the Old Quay on one of the main road routes to Portland. Personally managed by Mrs Moxham, the accommodation is freshly decorated and well appointed, with nicely equipped bedrooms. There are a comfortable lounge bar, a traditionally furnished dining room where home-cooked meals are served and a sunny patio area. Car parking is provided and the hotel offers both a friendly welcome and good value for money.
8 en suite (bth/shr) (2 fmly) No smoking in dining room CTV in all bedrooms Tea and coffee making facilities Licensed Cen ht CTV 12P No coaches Last d 3pm
PRICE GUIDE
ROOMS: s £22-£23; d £44-£47; wkly b&b £110-£155; wkly hlf-bd £165-£195 (£)

GH ⓠⓠⓠ **Sunningdale Private Hotel** 52 Preston Rd, Overcombe DT3 6QD (on A353 near Overcombe Corner beach, 2m E of town centre)
☎01305 832179 FAX 01305 832179
Mar-Oct
Families are made especially welcome at this private hotel, where good, comfortable accommodation is provided. The bedrooms, which are in various sizes, are well equipped. Public areas include a spacious lounge, a dining room, a small bar and a games room.
18 rms (11 bth 2 shr) (8 fmly) No smoking in dining room CTV in all bedrooms Tea and coffee making facilities Licensed CTV 20P Outdoor swimming pool Putting green table tennis games room Last d 6.45pm
PRICE GUIDE
ROOMS: s £20.25-£26; d £40.50-£52; wkly b&b £130-£163; wkly hlf-bd £160-£206
CARDS: ■■ ■■ ■■ ⓪ (£)

GH ⓠⓠⓠ **Tamarisk Hotel** 12 Stavordale Rd, Westham DT4 0AB (follow A354 to Westham Rdbt, take 3rd exit left to Bridport & then immediately left into Stavordale Rd)
☎01305 786514
Mar-Oct
Located in a quiet cul-de-sac close to the town and beach, this family run hotel offers comfortable well equipped rooms. There is a well stocked residents bar and a comfortable lounge. Home cooked evening meals are served in the attractive dining room. There is a private car park at the rear of the building.
16 rms (4 bth 8 shr) (7 fmly) No smoking in dining room CTV

in all bedrooms Tea and coffee making facilities No dogs Licensed Cen ht CTV 19P Last d 2pm
PRICE GUIDE
ROOMS: s £19-£22; d £38-£44; wkly b&b £135-£145

GH ⓠⓠ **Trelawney Hotel** 1 Old Castle Rd DT4 8QB (follow signs Portland on leaving Harbourside for hotel in 700yds on left) ☎01305 783188
Nov-Mar
A small, family-run hotel close to the town centre offers basic but adequate accomodation. There is a comfortable lounge with a small bar and a bright, attractive dining room serving plain English cooking made with fresh produce.
10 en suite (bth/shr) CTV in all bedrooms Tea and coffee making facilities Licensed Cen ht CTV 13P No coaches Putting green Last d 7pm
PRICE GUIDE
ROOMS: s £22-£28; d £44-£49; wkly hlf-bd £185-£210✱
CARDS: ■■ ■■

GH ⓠⓠ *The Westwey* 62 Abbotsbury Rd DT4 0BJ
☎01305 784564
This semi detatched property is situated about half a mile from the centre of the town and the Esplanade. Bedrooms tend to be compact but are equipped with modern facilities. There is a small guests lounge, a separate bar, and meals are served in a bright dining room.
11 rms (1 bth 8 shr) (2 fmly) CTV in all bedrooms Tea and coffee making facilities No dogs Licensed Cen ht CTV No children 6yrs 10P Last d 6.30pm

WHALEY BRIDGE Derbyshire Map 07 SK08

GH ⓠⓠ *Old Bakery* 80 Buxton Rd SK12 7JE (on A5004, N of junction with A5470) ☎01663 732359
Originally the village bakery, this establishment now offers guest house accommodation and a café. The owners - who still rise early to bake fresh bread and muffins for breakfast - provide light meals and refreshments in the café during the day; home-cooked meals can be provided in the evening by prior arrangement. The pine-furnished bedrooms are generally of comfortable proportions and guests have the use of two general bathrooms across the landing. Bedrooms are equipped with TV but guests are welcome to use the shared lounge.
3 rms CTV in all bedrooms Tea and coffee making facilities No dogs (ex guide dogs) Cen ht CTV 3P No coaches Last d 10pm

WHEATLEY Oxfordshire Map 04 SP50

◀ ⓠⓠⓠ **Bat & Ball** 28 High St, Cuddesdon OX44 9HJ
☎01865 874379
This is a lovely upmarket character inn with old wooden tables and floors, stone walls, and a cricketing theme. The bedrooms are beamed,and though on the smaller side, they all have bathrooms. Food is readily available from the blackboard menu. A full cooked breakfast is available at extra charge.
6 en suite (shr) CTV in all bedrooms Tea and coffee making facilities No dogs (ex guide dogs) Cen ht 12P Last d 9.30pm
PRICE GUIDE
ROOMS: s £30-£35; d £40; wkly b&b fr £150; wkly hlf-bd fr £210✱
MEALS: Lunch £10.75-£15.50alc Dinner £10.75-£15.50alc✱
CARDS: ■■ ■■

WHEDDON CROSS Somerset Map 03 SS93

GH ⓠⓠⓠ **Exmoor House** TA24 7DU (at junct of A396/B3224) ☎01643 841432 FAX 01643 841432
Closed 18 Dec-29 Feb rs Nov- 17 Dec
Wheddon Cross lies near the centre of Exmoor National Park, just

six miles from Dunster. Exmoor House is a spacious Edwardian building with distant views over Dunkery Beacon from the dining room. The majority of bedrooms are en suite, all are neatly furnished and decorated with exemplary standards of housekeeping. The lounge is comfortably furnished in keeping with the character of the house, with an open fire for the colder evenings. Each evening a set three-course dinner is served using fresh local produce. At the rear of the property is a private car park, plus secure storage for bicycles, rambling clothes and boots. This is a no smoking establishment.

6 rms (4 bth) (1 fmly) No smoking Tea and coffee making facilities No dogs Licensed Cen ht CTV No children 10yrs 8P No coaches Last d 6pm

PRICE GUIDE
ROOMS: s £28.50-£30; d £38-£40; wkly b&b £135; wkly hlf-bd £215
CARDS: 🟦 ▦ £

 Selected

◀ 🅀🅀🅀🅀 **Rest and be Thankful Inn** Wheddon Cross TA24 7DR (set on the cross roads of the A396 and B3220, 5m S of Dunster) ☎01643 841222 FAX 01643 841222
Closed 24-26 Dec

Situated in one of the highest villages on Exmoor, The Rest and Be Thankful Inn is a former coaching inn. Great care and thought have been given to the furnishing of the bedrooms, and all rooms are exceedingly well equipped, including fully stocked 'mini bars', phones and hair dryers. Rooms are soundproofed, centrally heated and double glazed and those at the rear have views of Dunkery Beacon. A separate lounge is available for guests, with a log fire for colder evenings, while other may prefer to join the locals in the bar. A wide range of meals is offered from both the menu and daily special blackboard dishes, either served in the bar or the no-smoking restaurant. Michael Weaver and Joan Hockin pride themselves on providing high standards of service while retaining old world charm and friendly hospitality.

5 en suite (shr) No smoking in bedrooms No smoking in dining room CTV in all bedrooms Tea and coffee making facilities Direct dial from bedrooms No dogs (ex guide dogs) Cen ht No children 11yrs 35P Pool Darts Skittle alley Last d 10pm

PRICE GUIDE
ROOMS: s £27; d £54; wkly b&b £168; wkly hlf-bd £238✳
MEALS: Lunch £6-£15alc Dinner £6-£15alc✳
CARDS: 🟦 ▦ ▦ £

WHIMPLE Devon Map 03 SY09

 Selected

GH 🅀🅀🅀🅀 **Down House** EX5 2QR ☎01404 822860
An elegant Edwardian farmhouse stands in five acres of gardens and paddocks on the edge of the village of Whimple. Well equipped bedrooms have been tastefully decorated and attractively furnished, the lounge is comfortable and spacious, and breakfast is served around one large table in the dining room. The pleasant proprietors offer a warm welcome to a house which is full of character and charm.

6 rms (2 bth 1 shr) (1 fmly) No smoking CTV in all bedrooms Tea and coffee making facilities Cen ht CTV 12P

PRICE GUIDE
ROOMS: s £18-£22; d £36-£44✳

WHITBY North Yorkshire Map **08** NZ81

GH ◨◨◨ **Corra Lynn Hotel** 28 Crescent Av YO21 3EW
(corner of A174 & Crescent Avenue) ☎01947 602214
Mar-Oct rs Nov-Apr
A small, friendly hotel on a corner site convenient for the West
Cliff, the harbour and the town. Bedrooms are bright and fresh and
there is a pleasant lounge.
5 en suite (bth/shr) (1 fmly) No smoking in dining room CTV in
all bedrooms Tea and coffee making facilities Licensed Cen ht
CTV No children 5yrs 4P No coaches Last d 1pm
PRICE GUIDE
ROOMS: d £40-£50; wkly b&b £130-£144✱

Premier Selected

GH ◨◨◨◨◨ *Dunsley*
Hall Dunsley YO21 3TL (3m
N, off A171. Turn right
signposted Dunsley and 1m
on right) ☎01947 893437
FAX 01947 893505
Closed 25-26 Dec
This lovely old house was
built around the turn of the
century, and is set in four
acres of grounds. The oak-
panelled hall leads to the lounges and to the bright dining
room where well prepared dinners are served. Most of the
bedrooms are spacious and all are very well equipped, having
radios, colour televisions, telephones and hairdryers. There
are also a full-sized snooker table, and, for the more energetic,
a heated indoor pool.
7 en suite (bth/shr) (2 fmly) No smoking in dining room
CTV in all bedrooms Tea and coffee making facilities Direct
dial from bedrooms Licensed Cen ht 10P No coaches
Indoor swimming pool (heated) Tennis (hard) Snooker
Gymnasium Croquet Putting Last d 6.30pm
CARDS: ▆▆ ▆▆

GH ◨◨◨ **Europa Private Hotel** 20 Hudson St YO21 3EP
(A169 from Pickering to Whitby, turn right at A171 follow
signs to West Cliff, turn right at Royal Crescent then first left
Hudson Street) ☎01947 602251
Feb-Oct
A warm and friendly welcome awaits guests at this immaculately
maintained and very well furnished hotel. The charming owners
are excellent hosts, and they offer pretty bedrooms with good
facilities, together with a cosy lounge on the first floor. Good
home cooking is served in the pleasant dining room.
10 rms (2 shr) (1 fmly) No smoking in bedrooms No smoking in
dining room CTV in 9 bedrooms Tea and coffee making facilities
No dogs Cen ht CTV No children 3yrs No coaches Last d 11am
PRICE GUIDE
ROOMS: s fr £18.50; d fr £31; wkly b&b fr £108.50; wkly hlf-
bd fr £168✱

[✉️▆] **GH** ◨◨◨ **Glendale** 16 Crescent Av YO21 3ED (off
Upgang Lane Rd) ☎01947 604242
Apr-Oct
This family-run guest house offers very good value for money,
providing pleasant modern bedrooms, a comfortable first-floor
lounge and an attractive dining room; improvements continue to
be carried out on the whole building.
6 rms (5 shr) (3 fmly) No smoking in dining room CTV in all

bedrooms Tea and coffee making facilities Licensed CTV 6P
No coaches Last d 4.15pm
PRICE GUIDE
ROOMS: s £15-£16; d £36-£38; wkly b&b fr £122; wkly hlf-bd
£160-£165

GH ◨◨◨ **Grantley House** 26 Hudson St YO21 3EP
☎01947 600895
Feb-Nov
This terraced house is very attractive with flower tubs and window
boxes. It's only a few minutes walk from the town centre and the
seafront. Bedrooms are prettily decorated and there is a first-floor
lounge. Good home cooking is provided at separate tables. The
owners are caring hosts.
8 rms (4 shr) (1 fmly) CTV in all bedrooms Tea and coffee
making facilities No dogs (ex guide dogs) Licensed Cen ht
CTV
PRICE GUIDE
ROOMS: d fr £36✱

GH ◨◨◨ **Haven** 4 East Crescent YO21 3HD (West Cliff at
top of Khyber Pass) ☎01947 603842
rs Nov-Mar
Situated in a Victorian crescent, with fine views over the harbour
and sea, this family owned and run hotel offers good all-round
standards of accommodation and service. There is a comfortable
lounge, and the dining room is attractively furnished and
decorated.
8 rms (5 bth/shr) (1 fmly) No smoking in dining room CTV in
all bedrooms Tea and coffee making facilities No dogs (ex guide
dogs) Licensed Cen ht CTV No children 5yrs No coaches
PRICE GUIDE
ROOMS: s £18-£20; d £34-£42; wkly b&b £115-£143

GH ◨◨◨ *Sandbeck Hotel* 2 Crescent Ter, Westcliff
YO21 3EL ☎01947 604012
Etr-Oct
Overlooking the sea, this large guest house has undergone many
improvements over the past year, and now provides a good
standard of accommodation. Bedrooms are well equipped and
mainly quite spacious, and there are a comfortable lounge and bar.
15 en suite (bth/shr) (5 fmly) CTV in all bedrooms Tea and
coffee making facilities No dogs (ex guide dogs) Licensed Cen
ht CTV No children 6yrs No coaches
CARDS: ▆▆ ▆▆

Selected

GH ◨◨◨◨ **Seacliffe Hotel** North Promenade,West Cliff
YO21 3JX (follow signs for West Cliff & West Cliff car
park, hotel on sea front)
☎01947 603139 FAX 01947 603139
A friendly, family-run private hotel is situated in a prime
location high on Whitby's West Cliff overlooking the sea, yet
within easy reach of the town and golf course. Bedrooms are
well equipped, with every modern facility, and many have
fine sea views. Downstairs there is a comfortable lounge and a
cosy bar, with a patio at the rear. The Candlelight Restaurant
offers an extensive menu including a very good choice of
vegetarian dishes.
19 en suite (bth/shr) (4 fmly) No smoking in 1 bedrooms No
smoking in dining room CTV in all bedrooms Tea and coffee
making facilities Direct dial from bedrooms Licensed Cen

ht CTV 8P Last d 8.45pm
PRICE GUIDE
ROOMS: s £29.50-£37.50; d £55.50-£59; wkly b&b £192-£206; wkly hlf-bd £245-£255
CARDS: £

Selected

GH QQQQ **Waverley Private Hotel** 17 Crescent Av
YO21 3ED (follow signs to West Cliff, hotel 200yds from
Crescent Gardens) ☎01947 604389
Mar-Oct
Attentive and friendly service is provided by the resident
owner of this well cared for house set in a side road only a
few minutes' walk from both the sea and town centre.
Spacious, comfortably furnished bedrooms are attractively
decorated and a first-floor lounge invites relaxation.
6 rms (5 shr) (4 fmly) No smoking in dining room CTV in
all bedrooms Tea and coffee making facilities No dogs
Licensed Cen ht CTV No children 3yrs No coaches Last d
5pm
PRICE GUIDE
ROOMS: s £16.50-£25; d £37-£54; wkly b&b £107-£122;
wkly hlf-bd £145-£160✳
£

WHITCHURCH Hereford & Worcester Map 03 SO51

◀ QQ **Crown Hotel** HR9 6DB (A40 to Symonds Yat West,
then B4164) ☎01600 890234
This 16th-century inn stands on the A40, close to Symonds Yat
West. New landlords Graham and Dawn Hodges took over at the
beginning of 1995, and at the time of our last inspection they had
already started to make improvements. The inn is full of character,
enhanced by exposed stone walls, ceiling beams and stone flagged
floors. Public areas include a large lounge bar, a small quiet
residents' lounge and a games room with a pool table and skittle
alley. A range of grills is served in the traditionally furnished
dining area. The bedrooms have period-style furniture, and rooms
with 4-poster beds and family rooms are available.
5 en suite (bth/shr) (3 fmly) No smoking in dining room CTV in
all bedrooms Tea and coffee making facilities No dogs (ex guide
dogs) Cen ht CTV P Skittle alley Pool room Last d 9pm
PRICE GUIDE
ROOMS: s fr £25; d fr £35; wkly b&b fr £130; wkly hlf-bd fr
£170✳
MEALS: Lunch fr £8alc Dinner fr £8alc✳
CARDS: £

WHITCHURCH Shropshire Map 07 SJ54

♥ QQQ Mrs M H Mulliner **Bradeley Green** *(SJ537449)*
Waterfowl Sanctuary, Tarporley Rd SY13 4HD (2m N on A49)
☎01948 663442
Closed Xmas
This spacious farmhouse is part of a working dairy farm two miles
from Tarporley, in an unusual setting in water gardens where there
is a waterfowl collection and a farm nature trail. A feature of the
large bedrooms is their exposed timbers and all are comfortably
furnished. There is a TV lounge with a fine tiled fireplace burning
logs in colder weather. Guests receive a warm welcome from Mrs.
Ruth Mulliner, who provides evening meals with advance notice.
3 rms (2 bth/shr) No smoking Tea and coffee making facilities
No dogs (ex guide dogs) Cen ht CTV 6P Water gardens nature
➡

trails waterfowl sanctuary 180 acres dairy waterfowl fish farming Last d 9am
PRICE GUIDE
ROOMS: s £21-£24; d £36-£40; wkly b&b fr £140; wkly hlf-bd fr £190✱

WHITEPARISH Wiltshire Map **04** SU22

GH Q Q Q **Newton Farmhouse** Southampton Rd SP5 2QL
☎01794 884416
Newton Farmhouse, which was once a gift to Lord Nelson and part of the Trafalgar Estate, is conveniently situated beside the A36 in two and a half acres of garden which includes an outdoor swimming pool for guests' use. Bedrooms, some of which are situated in a more modern annexe immediately adjacent to the main house, are all en suite, attractively appointed, and well equipped, with televisions, tea and coffee making facilities, and many personal extras. Suzi Lanham, helped by her husband and mother, provides an excellent breakfast; dinner is served in the attractive beamed dining room with its stone flagged floor and restored bread oven. The farmhouse is no-smoking throughout.
8 en suite (bth/shr) No smoking CTV in all bedrooms Tea and coffee making facilities Cen ht CTV 10P Outdoor swimming pool Last d noon
PRICE GUIDE
ROOMS: d £35-£40✱

See advertisement under SALISBURY

Selected

♥ Q Q Q Q Mrs S Barry **Brickworth** *(SU218240)*
Brickworth Ln SP5 2QE (on A36 travelling S from Salisbury, Brickworth Ln is on left by bus stop, just before junction with A27 to Romsey and Whiteparish.)
☎01794 884663 FAX 01794 884581
Closed 23 Dec-2 Jan
This charming listed farmhouse dates back to 1725 and once belonged to Admiral Lord Nelson. Midway between Romsey and Salisbury, the house is set in five acres of land in which the family's rare breed chickens roam free. The bedroom's are delightful, bright, spacious and full of character with attractive furnishings, antique beds and patchwork quilts. There is evidence of owner Sue Barry's skilful handicrafts everywhere in the stencilled walls and furniture, soft furnishings and pressed flower pictures. A traditional breakfast is served in the dining room and comprises such treats as home made bread and preserves, in addition to the home produce eggs and honey.
4 rms (2 shr) (1 fmly) No smoking in bedrooms CTV in all bedrooms Tea and coffee making facilities No dogs Cen ht CTV 20P 5 acres
PRICE GUIDE
ROOMS: s £18-£20; d £30-£34✱

WHITESTONE Devon Map **03** SX89

⟦≈≈⟧ ♥ Q Q Mrs S K Lee **Rowhorne House** *(SX880948)*
EX4 2LQ (A30 to Tedburn-St-Mary follow sign to Whitestone after 2m pass Royal Oak pub go to top of hill, sharp left continue for 2m house on left) ☎01392 74675
Rowhorne House is a real away-from-it-all farmhouse. Mrs Lee has a naturally welcoming manner. Bedrooms are large with marvellous views from every window to the Exe estuary. Dinner is available if arranged beforehand.

---

3 rms (2 fmly) CTV in 1 bedroom No dogs CTV 6P 103 acres dairy
PRICE GUIDE
ROOMS: s £14; d £28; wkly b&b £98
CARDS: 🔲 ■ ▦ 🔘

WHITEWELL Lancashire Map **07** SD64

Selected

🟦 Q Q Q Q *The Inn at Whitewell* BB7 3AT
☎01200 448222 FAX 01200 448298
This charming and slightly eccentric inn, which has been personally run by its enthusiastic owner Richard Bowman and family for the last nineteen years, is situated in the beautiful countryside of the Forest of Bowland. There is a very warm welcome as guests enter the stone-flagged hall where there are open fires, magazines, books and bowls of fresh flowers. The reception area also doubles up as an art gallery; a large number of wines are also on display and can be purchased. A good range of traditional dishes is available in the spacious restaurant which overlooks the River Hodder and excellent bar meals are also available. The generally spacious bedrooms are sumptuously decorated and furnished with rich fabrics, paintings and antiques; the many extras including full hi-fi and video systems. Many of the bathrooms have genuine antique fittings including huge baths and shining brass. In winter some rooms are warmed by real peat fires.
10 en suite (bth/shr) (4 fmly) CTV in all bedrooms Direct dial from bedrooms Cen ht CTV 60P Fishing Clay pigeon shooting by arrangement Last d 9.30pm
CARDS: 🔲 ■ ▦ 🔘

WHITLEY BAY Tyne & Wear Map **12** NZ37

GH Q Q Q **Cherrytree House** 35 Brook St NE26 1AF
☎0191 251 4306
This large, double-fronted Edwardian town house is situated in a quiet street between the town centre and seafront. Traditionally furnished bedrooms are cosy and appealing, and Mr and Mrs Coleman are happy to offer the use of their comfortable lounge to guests. Enjoyable home-cooked meals are served in the pleasant dining room, and there is unrestricted parking on the road outside the guest house.
4 rms (3 shr) No smoking in dining room CTV in all bedrooms Tea and coffee making facilities Cen ht CTV Last d 9.30am
PRICE GUIDE
ROOMS: s £15-£28; d £30-£38; wkly b&b £98-£155; wkly hlf-bd £143.50-£197✱

GH Q Q Q **Marlborough Hotel** 20-21 East Pde, Central Promenade NE26 1AP ☎0191 251 3628 FAX 0191 251 3628
This very well positioned hotel overlooks the bay from its setting at the centre of the Promenade. Several bedrooms enjoy fine views out to sea and all are particularly well equipped, having colour televisions, telephones and radio alarms. Downstairs there are two comfortable lounges as well as an attractive dining room. Private parking is provided at the front of the building.
15 rms (11 bth/shr) (4 fmly) No smoking in bedrooms No smoking in dining room CTV in all bedrooms Tea and coffee making facilities Direct dial from bedrooms No dogs (ex guide dogs) Licensed CTV 7P No coaches Last d noon
PRICE GUIDE
ROOMS: s £20-£32; d £40-£48; wkly b&b £140-£190✱
CARDS: 🔲 ■ ▦

GH 🅀🅀🅀 *York House Hotel* 30 Park Pde NE26 1DX
☎0191 252 8313 & 0191 251 3953
Conveniently placed for all amenities, this attractive terraced
house has a small patio at the front and secure parking to the rear.
Bedrooms are all well equipped and parents will appreciate that
children stay free when sharing their room. There is a choice of
meals at both breakfast and dinner and two self catering
apartments are currently being converted from the house next
door.
8 rms (7 bth/shr) (3 fmly) No smoking in dining room CTV in
all bedrooms Tea and coffee making facilities Direct dial from
bedrooms Licensed Cen ht CTV 2P Last d 8pm
CARDS: 🅰 🔳 🔳

WHITNEY-ON-WYE Hereford & Worcester Map 03 SO24

Premier Selected

◀ 🅀🅀🅀🅀🅀 **The
Rhydspence** HR3 6EU (2m W
A438) ☎01497 831262
This attractive black and
white timbered inn - parts of
which date back to the 14th
century - stands beside the
A438 a mile west of the
village. Much of its original
charm survives in the beamed
ceilings and stone walls of
the cosy public areas, while
bedrooms offer a high standard of modern facilities as well as
comfort and a rich decor with coordinating soft furnishings;
guests are welcomed by roaring fires in winter, and in summer
they can enjoy a delightful garden running down to the stream
that forms the English/Welsh border. The bar's range of real
ales and interesting dishes provides an alternative to equally
good but more formal restaurant meals.
7 en suite (bth/shr) No smoking in area of dining room CTV
in all bedrooms Tea and coffee making facilities No dogs (ex
guide dogs) Cen ht 60P No coaches Last d 9.30pm
PRICE GUIDE
ROOMS: s £27.50-£32.50; d £35-£75; wkly b&b £192.50-
£227.50; wkly hlf-bd £355-£420
MEALS: Lunch £18-£25alc Dinner £18-£25alc
CARDS: 🅰 🔳 🔳

WHITSTABLE Kent Map 05 TR16

GH 🅀🅀🅀 **Windy Ridge** Wraik Hill CT5 3BY
☎01227 263506
Great views are afforded by the position of this guest house, which
overlooks the sea and surrounding countryside. Bedrooms are
decorated in a modern style and the owners are keen to upgrade
the bathroom facilities. There is one ground floor bedroom, and
dinner is available if required.
8 rms (4 shr) (1 fmly) No smoking in area of dining room CTV
in all bedrooms Tea and coffee making facilities Direct dial from
bedrooms Licensed Cen ht CTV 8P No coaches Last d 8pm
PRICE GUIDE
ROOMS: s £20-£25; d £38-£45; wkly b&b £140-£175; wkly hlf-
bd £224-£260
CARDS: 🅰 🔳   £

WHIXLEY North Yorkshire Map 08 SE45

GH 🅀🅀🅀 **Princes Lodge** YO5 8EE (leave A1 & follow
A59 York road for 2m, Princes Lodge on left near Whixley
road junct) ☎01423 330168 FAX 01423 331458
A family-run guest house, situated on the A59 between York and
Harrogate, Princess Lodge provides good all-round standards of
comfo:t and service. Bedrooms are bright and fresh and the
comfortable lounge is a delightful feature of the house. Outside,
there are a heated swimming pool and several self-catering units.
3 en suite (bth/shr) No smoking in dining room No smoking in
lounges CTV in all bedrooms Tea and coffee making facilities
No dogs (ex guide dogs) Licensed Cen ht CTV 20P No
coaches Outdoor swimming pool (heated)
                                                            £

WIGAN Greater Manchester Map 07 SD50

GH 🅀🅀 **Aalton Court** 23 Upper Dicconson St WN1 2AG
☎01942 322220 FAX 01942 322220
Aalton Court is a Victorian terraced property located conveniently
close to both the town centre and the rugby league ground.
Catering mainly for commercial visitors, it provides bedrooms
which are modern and well equipped though in some cases rather
small. There is a traditionally furnished dining room where
breakast is served and an evening meal can be provided by prior
arrangement. The guest house also has a small lounge bar.
15 rms (10 bth/shr) (5 fmly) No smoking in 2 bedrooms CTV in
all bedrooms Tea and coffee making facilities No dogs Licensed
Cen ht CTV 6P Last d 2pm
PRICE GUIDE
ROOMS: s £23-£30✳
CARDS: 🅰 🔳

WIGHT, ISLE OF Map 04

BRADING Map 04 SZ68

◀ 🅀🅀🅀 *Red Lion* 10 High St ☎01983 407307
3 en suite (bth/shr) CTV in all bedrooms Tea and coffee making
facilities Cen ht 14P Last d 10.30pm
CARDS: 🅰 🔳 🔳

FRESHWATER Map 04 SZ38

GH 🅀🅀🅀 **Blenheim House Hotel** Gate Ln PO40 9QD (on
main road out of Freshwater & 3m from Yarmouth Ferry
Terminal) ☎01983 752858
May-Sep
This friendly attractive house is located in Freshwater Bay, just
minutes from the sea, and offers a warm welcome. The bright
rooms are comfortably furnished; some have pretty window
boxes. There are a cosy well stocked bar and a good sized heated
swimming pool. Private parking is available at the rear of the
building.
8 en suite (shr) (3 fmly) No smoking in 1 bedrooms No smoking
in dining room CTV in all bedrooms Tea and coffee making
facilities No dogs Licensed Cen ht No children 10yrs 6P No
coaches Outdoor swimming pool (heated) Snooker Table tennis
Billiards Darts Last d noon
PRICE GUIDE
ROOMS: s £22; d £42; wkly b&b £147; wkly hlf-bd £210

NITON Map 04 SZ57

GH 🅀🅀🅀 *Pine Ridge Country House* Niton Undercliff
PO38 2LY ☎01983 730802 FAX 01983 731001
Quietly situated in three and a half acres of mature, well kept
grounds, this extended country house has an established air and
this is borne out inside: large bedrooms are made even more
➡

comfortable by a generous provision of facilities; the public rooms are attractive, and the lounge bar is warmed by an open fire on chillier evenings. There are wonderful views from all sides of the building.

9 rms (6 bth/shr) (2 fmly) No smoking in 2 bedrooms No smoking in dining room CTV in all bedrooms Tea and coffee making facilities Direct dial from bedrooms Licensed Cen ht CTV 10P No coaches Last d 9pm
CARDS: 🔳 🈹

RYDE Map 04 SZ59

GH 🇶🇶🇶 *Teneriffe Hotel* 36 The Strand PO33 1JF
☎01983 563841 FAX 01983 615692
Closed Dec-Feb
This popular hotel is situated near the seafront, and has been run by the Brown family for over thirty years. The bedrooms have modern en suite facilities and are well equipped, and a lift serves most floors. There is a comfortable television lounge, and good home-cooked food is served in the dining room. During the season there is regular live entertainment in the attractive ballroom. Coach parties are welcome.
50 en suite (bth/shr) (7 fmly) No smoking in dining room CTV in all bedrooms Tea and coffee making facilities No dogs (ex guide dogs) Licensed Lift Cen ht CTV 9P Last d 7pm
PRICE GUIDE
ROOMS: s £17.65-£18.50; d £35.30-£37; wkly b&b £123.55-£129.50; wkly hlf-bd £164.50-£173.90✷
CARDS: 🔳 🈹 🈹

SANDOWN Map 04 SZ58

GH 🇶🇶🇶 *Bertram Lodge* 3 Leed St PO36 9DA
☎01983 402551
Closed Xmas
Bertram Lodge is an attractive Victorian property in a quiet residential area of the town. Prettily decorated and well equipped bedrooms have modern en suite shower facilities, while downstairs there are a cosy lounge area and a sunny, recently re-decorated dining room where hearty English breakfasts and home-cooked evening meals are served.
9 rms (8 shr) (3 fmly) No smoking in 5 bedrooms No smoking in dining room No smoking in 1 lounge CTV in all bedrooms Tea and coffee making facilities No dogs Cen ht CTV No children 3yrs 4P No coaches Last d 3.30pm
PRICE GUIDE
ROOMS: s £14-£19.50; d £28.50-£38; wkly b&b £98-£130; wkly hlf-bd £115-£145✷
£

GH 🇶🇶 *Chester Lodge Hotel* Beachfield Rd PO36 8NA
☎01983 402773
mid Mar-mid Oct
The Hayward family have run this guesthouse for many years and continue to make it a cosy and relaxing place to stay. The bedrooms are furnished in a bright and homely style and they all have modern facilities; the majority of them are en suite. The spacious public areas have a happy, relaxed atmosphere about them. Guests are offered a choice of evening meal and the hotel is busy and popular.
18 rms (2 bth 12 shr) (5 fmly) CTV in all bedrooms Tea and coffee making facilities Licensed Cen ht CTV 19P
CARDS: 🔳 🈹

GH 🇶🇶🇶 *Culver Lodge Hotel* Albert Rd PO36 8AW
☎01983 403819 & 402902
Mar-Nov
A large Victorian property a short walk from the centre of town, Culver Lodge offers attractively presented bedrooms in a bright modern style. Public rooms include a smart dining room, where a

---

home-cooked evening meal is served, a comfortable lounge and a well stocked bar.
21 en suite (bth/shr) (4 fmly) No smoking in dining room CTV in all bedrooms Tea and coffee making facilities No dogs Licensed Cen ht CTV 20P Pool room Darts Video games Last d 10pm
PRICE GUIDE
ROOMS: s £16-£23; d £32-£46; wkly b&b £104-£150; wkly hlf-bd £150-£196✷
CARDS: 🔳 🈹 🈹 ⓪

£

GH 🇶🇶🇶 *Cygnet Hotel* 58 Carter St PO36 8DQ
☎01983 402930 FAX 01983 405112
This popular, value-for-money hotel provides plenty of leisure facilities for holiday makers as well as accommodation in bright, freshly decorated bedrooms, most of which have en suite facilities. Spacious public areas with a lively atmosphere include an extensive indoor leisure facility but there are quiet places to relax too. A daily-changing menu is offered in the pretty dining room.
50 rms (36 bth/shr) (8 fmly) No smoking in dining room CTV in 30 bedrooms Tea and coffee making facilities No dogs (ex guide dogs) Licensed Lift Cen ht CTV 30P Indoor swimming pool (heated) Outdoor swimming pool (heated) Sauna Solarium Gymnasium Spa pool Last d 6.30pm
CARDS: 🔳 🈹 🈹

GH 🇶🇶🇶 *Norton Lodge* 22 Victoria Rd PO36 8AL
☎01983 402423
Mar-Oct
An attractive Edwardian property close to the centre of town, Norton Lodge retains many of its original characteristics and offers a welcoming atmosphere. Accommodation is well presented and there are a cosy no-smoking lounge and a newly created smoking area. The dining room, where home-cooked fare is served at dinner, has also been extended.
9 rms (5 shr) (4 fmly) CTV in all bedrooms Tea and coffee making facilities No dogs (ex guide dogs) Licensed Cen ht CTV No children 5yrs 5P

Selected

GH 🇶🇶🇶🇶 *St Catherine's Hotel* 1 Winchester Park Rd PO36 8HJ ☎01983 402392 FAX 01983 402392
Closed 21 Dec-2 Jan
St Catherine's is an attractive Victorian property which continues to be improved every year. Recently some bedrooms have been upgraded with new decor, furnishings and carpets, and the cosy bar area has been redecorated. All of the bedrooms are en suite, and some ground floor rooms are available. A comfortable lounge is provided, and home-cooked meals are served in the dining room.
19 rms (bth/shr) (4 fmly) No smoking in dining room CTV in all bedrooms Tea and coffee making facilities Direct dial from bedrooms Licensed Cen ht CTV 8P No coaches Last d 7pm
PRICE GUIDE
ROOMS: (incl. dinner) s £24.50-£29; d £49-£58; wkly b&b £113.75-£136.50; wkly hlf-bd £159.25-£188.50
CARDS: 🔳 🈹

£

SEAVIEW Map 04 SZ69

GH 🇶 *Northbank Hotel* Circular Rd PO34 5ET
☎01983 612227
Etr-Sep
Northbank is an old Victorian house with a garden sloping down to the seashore. Splendid views are enjoyed from the traditional

lounge, the cosy bar crammed with memorabilia, and many of the bedrooms. The latter vary in size, some have fine old furniture, but most are fairly simple.
18 rms (6 fmly) No smoking in dining room CTV in 2 bedrooms Tea and coffee making facilities Licensed CTV ch fac 12P Fishing Snooker Last d 8pm
PRICE GUIDE
ROOMS: s fr £25; d fr £50; wkly hlf-bd fr £235*

(£)

SHANKLIN Map **04** SZ58

GH QQQ ***Aqua Hotel*** The Esplanade PO37 6BN
☎01983 863024 FAX 01983 864841
Etr-5 Nov
Personally managed by Mr and Mrs Blanchett, this good-value hotel continues to be improved. It stands on the esplanade offering fine sea views, and there is a terrace where guests can sit and enjoy the sunshine. A good choice of dishes is offered in Boaters restaurant, and lunches are also available in the smartly refurbished bar. Bedrooms vary in size but all have comfortable modern furniture and en suite facilities.
22 en suite (bth/shr) (4 fmly) No smoking in dining room CTV in all bedrooms Tea and coffee making facilities No dogs Licensed Cen ht 2P Darts Pool table Last d 4.30pm
CARDS:

Selected

GH QQQQ **The Bondi Hotel** Clarence Rd PO37 7BH (on entering town on A3055 from Ryde, take third turning on right after Texaco garage)
☎01983 862507 FAX 01983 862326
Brian and Hilary Norton extend a warm welcome to their attractive property. The bedrooms are individually decorated and offer ensuite shower rooms and nice personal touches. To relax there is a choce of the comfortably furnished lounge or the bright conservatory style bar. A tempting five course evening meal is served in the pretty dining room overlooking the garden.
8 en suite (shr) (1 fmly) CTV in all bedrooms Tea and coffee making facilities Licensed Cen ht 3P No coaches Last d 6pm
PRICE GUIDE
ROOMS: s £18-£25; d £36-£50; wkly b&b £125-£150; wkly hlf-bd £170-£190
CARDS:

(£)

GH QQQ **Culham Lodge** 31 Landguard Manor Rd PO37 7HZ ☎01983 862880 FAX 01983 862880
Closed Xmas
Away from the bustle of the town centre, this attractive Victorian property offers comfortable, bright accommodation. Some of the bedrooms are on the ground floor and the majority have en suite facilities. There is a well furnished lounge and a dining room leading into another conservatory-style lounge, which overlooks the garden and outdoor swimming pool. A choice of dishes is offered each evening from the fixed-price menu.
10 rms (1 bth 7 shr) No smoking in dining room No smoking in lounges CTV in all bedrooms Tea and coffee making facilities No dogs (ex guide dogs) Cen ht CTV No children 12yrs 8P Outdoor swimming pool (heated) Solarium Last d 4pm
PRICE GUIDE
ROOMS: s £16-£20; d £32-£40; wkly b&b £104-£135; wkly hlf-bd £139-£175*
CARDS:

(£)

GH ⓆⓆ *Curraghmore Hotel* 22 Hope Rd PO37 6EA
☎01983 862605
Mar-Oct
Good value for money is offered at the Curraghmore, which is situated in an elevated position close to the beach and promenade. Recently upgraded, the hotel now provides en suite facilities in every bedroom. Spacious public areas include a bar and ballroom where entertainment is provided during the season. The Andrews' sons are chefs, and they present a daily-changing choice of dishes.
24 en suite (bth/shr) (9 fmly) CTV in all bedrooms Tea and coffee making facilities Licensed 20P Putting Last d 6pm

[▸▪] **GH** ⓆⓆⓆ **Edgecliffe Hotel** Clarence Gardens PO37 6HA (first left down Arthurs Hill, opposite Nursing Home) ☎01983 866199 FAX 01983 404812
A quietly located establishment just off Arthur's Hill, this hotel is a haven for non-smokers and has recently received a no-smoking award from the Isle of Wight authorities. Public areas offer a comfortable lounge and a bright dining room where home-cooked evening meals are served, including vegetarian fare. Bedrooms are comfortably furnished and traditionally styled.
10 rms (6 bth/shr) (2 fmly) No smoking CTV in all bedrooms Tea and coffee making facilities No dogs (ex guide dogs) Licensed Cen ht CTV 3P No coaches Cycles for hire Last d 8.30pm
PRICE GUIDE
ROOMS: s £15-£18.50; d £30-£49; wkly b&b £95-£145; wkly hlf-bd £140-£194
CARDS: ◩ ▬ ▥ ⓄⒹ ▦ ▨ ▨ (£)

GH ⓆⓆⓆ **Hambledon Hotel** Queens Rd PO37 6AW (off A3055) ☎01983 862403 & 863651 FAX 01983 867894
Personally run by cheery proprietors Norman and Beryl Birch, this private hotel offers comfortable bedrooms, a smart dining room, two lounges, one no smoking, and a cosy bar with a host of teddies and cuddly toys which are donated to charity at the end of every season.
11 en suite (shr) (4 fmly) No smoking in dining room No smoking in 1 lounge CTV in all bedrooms Tea and coffee making facilities Direct dial from bedrooms No dogs (ex guide dogs) Licensed Cen ht CTV ch fac 8P Last d 6pm
PRICE GUIDE
ROOMS: s £17-£22; d £34-£44; wkly b&b £100-£150; wkly hlf-bd £146-£192✶
CARDS: ◩ ▥ (£)

GH ⓆⓆⓆ **Kenbury Private Hotel** Clarence Rd PO37 7BH ☎01983 862085
Etr-Oct
Personally run by Mr and Mrs Perez, this handsome Victorian property set in a residential area close to the centre of town, provides well presented, freshly decorated bedrooms with smart en suite showers and bathrooms. Public areas have a comfortable, a short-choice evening meal is served and the establishment offers good value for money.
18 rms (16 bth/shr) (3 fmly) CTV in all bedrooms Tea and coffee making facilities No dogs (ex guide dogs) Licensed Cen ht CTV No children 3yrs 8P Last d 6.30pm
PRICE GUIDE
ROOMS: s £18.50-£20; d £37-£40; wkly b&b £124-£136; wkly hlf-bd £160-£173✶
CARDS: ◩ ▥ (£)

GH ⓆⓆⓆ *Mount House Hotel* 20 Arthurs Hill PO37 6EE ☎01983 862556
Mount House is a family owned hotel on Arthur's Hill, convenient for the sea and shops. The bedrooms are nicely decorated and all but one have modern en suite shower rooms. The traditionally styled public areas are comfortably furnished and include a small,

well stocked bar. A home cooked evening meal is available.
10 en suite (shr) (2 fmly) CTV in all bedrooms Tea and coffee making facilities No dogs (ex guide dogs) Licensed Cen ht CTV 8P Last d 4pm
CARDS: ◩ ▥

Selected

GH ⓆⓆⓆⓆ **Osborne House** Esplanade PO37 6BN (on Seafront opposite Clock Tower)
☎01983 862501 FAX 01983 862501
Jan-18 Oct
Osborne House is an attractive property in a slightly elevated position with lovely sea views, and it has a pretty garden where guests may sit and watch the world go by. The bedrooms are fresh and bright and well equipped with plenty of extras. There are two comfortable lounges, one serving snacks and meals in addition to the restaurant's enjoyable home-cooked dishes.
12 en suite (bth/shr) No smoking in dining room CTV in all bedrooms Tea and coffee making facilities No dogs Licensed Cen ht No children 13yrs No coaches Last d 8pm
PRICE GUIDE
ROOMS: s fr £30; d fr £60✶
CARDS: ◩ ▥

GH ⓆⓆⓆ **Rowborough Hotel** 32 Arthurs Hill PO37 6EX (1m S of Lake at junct of A3055/A3056)
☎01983 866072 FAX 01983 864000
Mar-28 Oct
A well presented establishment, the Rowborough is personally managed by charming proprietors who take good care of their guests. The bedrooms are neat, fresh and pleasantly decorated, all but one small single room having en suite facilities, and the standard of housekeeping is excellent throughout. Friendly public areas include a comfortable sitting room and an additional front-facing lounge area overlooking the gardens. Home-cooked fare is offered in a dining room with a well stocked bar at one end.
8 rms (3 bth 4 shr) (3 fmly) CTV in all bedrooms Tea and coffee making facilities No dogs Licensed Cen ht CTV No children 5yrs 5P No coaches Last d 8pm
PRICE GUIDE
ROOMS: s £18-£22.50; d £36-£45; wkly b&b £108-£135; wkly hlf-bd £156-£184
CARDS: ◩ ▥ Ⓓ (£)

GH ⓆⓆⓆ *Soraba Private Hotel* 2 Paddock Rd PO37 6NZ ☎01983 862367
Mar-Nov
Centrally located in a quiet area of town, this friendly hotel offers bright, freshly decorated accommodation. Many of the bedrooms have en suite facilities and there is a useful ground floor room. A comfortable guests' lounge is provided in addition to the pretty dining room where home-cooked fare is served.
7 rms (4 bth/shr) No smoking in 1 bedroom No smoking in dining room CTV in 4 bedrooms Licensed Cen ht CTV No children 3yrs 4P No coaches Last d 3pm
CARDS: ◩ ▥

GH ⓆⓆⓆ *White House Hotel* Eastcliff Promenade PO37 6AY ☎01983 862776 & 867904 FAX 01983 865980
6 Jan-Oct & Xmas
11 en suite (bth/shr) (1 fmly) No smoking in 9 bedrooms CTV in all bedrooms Tea and coffee making facilities Direct dial from bedrooms No dogs (ex guide dogs) Licensed Cen ht CTV 12P No coaches Last d 7pm
CARDS: ◩ ▥ ▥ Ⓓ

TOTLAND BAY Map **04** SZ38

GH 🇶🇶 *Frenchman's Cove Country Hotel* Alum Bay Old Rd
PO39 0HZ (off B3322, signposted to Freshwater Bay). Hotel
500yds on right) ☎01983 752227 FAX 01983 755125
This hotel is located in a country lane with glorious views across
fields and meadows. The bedrooms vary in size and shape, and
those on the ground and first floors offer more comfort than the
few at the top of the house. Public rooms include a cosy bar,
spacious dining room and a small lounge. This is a no-smoking
establishment.
13 rms (2 bth 7 shr) (9 fmly) No smoking in bedrooms No
smoking in dining room CTV in all bedrooms Tea and coffee
making facilities No dogs (ex guide dogs) Licensed Cen ht
CTV ch fac 15P Badminton Play equipment Table tennis Last d
4pm
CARDS: 🔵 ⬛ 🔳

GH 🇶🇶🇶 **Littledene Lodge** Granville Rd PO39 0AX
☎01983 752411
Mar-Oct
A very well presented friendly guesthouse is located in a quiet
residential area, conveniently close to the Yarmouth ferry.
Bedrooms are well equipped and very attractive, with well
coordinated, fresh, bright decor and pretty soft fabrics; the en suite
facilities are smart and well maintained. The house is efficiently
run by the charming Mrs Wright, who enjoys cooking the fresh
five-course evening meal and who will also offer advice on places
of interest. Public rooms are comfortable and cosy and include a
TV lounge and a spacious dining room with a small bar.
6 rms (2 bth 3 shr) (3 fmly) No smoking in dining room Tea and
coffee making facilities Licensed Cen ht CTV No children 3yrs
5P No coaches Last d 4.30pm
PRICE GUIDE
ROOMS: d £37-£41; wkly b&b £139; wkly hlf-bd
£183-£189✷
CARDS: 🔵 🔳 🔳 🔵 🔘

GH 🇶🇶🇶 **The Nodes Country Hotel** Alum Bay Old Rd
PO39 0HZ ☎01983 752859 FAX 01705 201621
In rural surroundings along a country lane, yet fairly close to both
Alum Bay and Totland, this well managed establishment offers a
good standard of accommodation with brightly decorated, mostly
en suite bedrooms, some in an annexe building. There is a
comfortable, traditionally furnished lounge, and in the dining
room guests are offered home-cooked meals prepared by the
amiable host, Mr Sanchis.
11 rms (3 bth 6 shr) (5 fmly) No smoking in bedrooms No
smoking in dining room CTV in all bedrooms Tea and coffee
making facilities Licensed Cen ht CTV ch fac 15P Badminton
Table tennis Last d 3pm
PRICE GUIDE
ROOMS: (incl. dinner) s £33.50-£41.50; d £59-£75; wkly b&b
£143.50-£190.50; wkly hlf-bd £192-£243.50✷
CARDS: 🔵 🔳

GH 🇶🇶🇶 **Sandford Lodge Hotel** 61 The Avenue PO39 0DN
☎01983 753478
Mar-Oct rs Jan-Feb
Attractive accommodation is offered at this family-run
establishment in a residential area of Totland Bay. A comfortable
lounge is provided and a pretty dining room where home cooked
meals are available. Smoking is not permitted anywhere in the
hotel.
6 rms (3 bth 2 shr) (2 fmly) No smoking CTV in 4 bedrooms
Tea and coffee making facilities No dogs (ex guide dogs)

Licensed Cen ht CTV 6P No coaches Last d 4pm
PRICE GUIDE
ROOMS: s £18-£21; d £32-£45; wkly b&b £98-£140; wkly hlf-
bd £160-£199
CARDS: 🔳

VENTNOR Map **04** SZ57

GH 🇶🇶 **Channel View Hotel** Hambrough Rd PO38 1SQ
☎01983 852230
Apr-19 Oct rs Mar
Set in an elevated position overlooking the promenade, this
family-owned hotel offers simply appointed and freshly decorated
accommodation. Public areas take advantage of the hotel's
location, and in addition to the cosy bar there is a front-facing
dining room where evening meals are served.
14 rms (2 shr) (6 fmly) CTV in 2 bedrooms Tea and coffee
making facilities No dogs (ex guide dogs) Licensed CTV No
parking Last d 8pm
PRICE GUIDE
ROOMS: s £13-£18; d £26-£36; wkly b&b £85-£115; wkly hlf-
bd £135-£165✷
CARDS: 🔵 🔳

GH 🇶🇶🇶 **Glen Islay Hotel** St Boniface Rd PO38 1NP
☎01983 854095
Mar-Oct
In a quiet residential area with views towards St Boniface Downs,
the Glen Islay offers pleasant, mostly en suite bedrooms. Public
rooms include an attractive dining room, where evening meals are
available, a comfortable lounge, and a spacious bar complete with
pool, darts and books. The dining room and bar lead out onto a
sunny patio area, which is popular in summer.
10 rms (1 bth 7 shr) (8 fmly) CTV in all bedrooms Tea and
coffee making facilities No dogs (ex guide dogs) Licensed Cen
ht CTV 6P No coaches
PRICE GUIDE
ROOMS: s £16-£17.50; d £32-£35; wkly b&b £112-£122.50;
wkly hlf-bd £160-£175✷

GH 🇶🇶🇶 *Hillside Private Hotel* Mitchell Av PO38 1DR
☎01983 852271
An attractive 18th-century three-storey thatched house is set in
three acres of mature grounds and garden, with glorious views.
Bedrooms are pretty and well equipped with attractive soft fabrics;
some have recently been redecorated, others enjoy sea views over
the garden and one room is conveniently located on the ground
floor. Public rooms include a comfortable no-smoking lounge and
a separate bar with a sunny conservatory. Meals are served in the
pleasant dining room, and light refreshments are available
throughout the day.
11 en suite (bth/shr) (2 fmly) No smoking in dining room No
smoking in lounges CTV in all bedrooms Tea and coffee making
facilities Licensed Cen ht No children 5yrs 16P Last d 6.30pm
CARDS: 🔵 ⬛ 🔳

GH 🇶🇶🇶 *Lake Hotel* Shore Rd, Bonchurch PO38 1RF
☎01983 852613 FAX 01983 852613
Mar-Oct
This very attractive Victorian house stands in mature and well-
tended gardens in the village of Bonchurch. Most of the
comfortably furnished bedrooms have en suite facilities and are
well decorated, with co-ordinating fabrics and furnishings.
Recently redecorated public rooms include two bright and sunny
conservatory lounges, a drawing room and dining room where
home-cooked food is served in the evenings. Mr and Mrs Wyatt
and their staff are relaxed and friendly.

➡

11 rms (10 bth/shr) 10 annexe en suite (bth/shr) (7 fmly) No smoking in dining room No smoking in 1 lounge Tea and coffee making facilities Licensed Cen ht CTV No children 3yrs 20P Last d 6.30pm

GH **Llynfi Hotel** 23 Spring Hill PO38 1PF
☎01983 852202
Etr-Oct
Many guests return to this small private hotel year after year and have become good friends with owners Mr and Mrs Fisher. Most of the bright, neat bedrooms offer en suite facilities, and there is a choice of lounges and seating areas (including some reserved for non-smokers). A home-cooked evening meal is served in the attractive dining room. The hotel is set in a residential area a short distance from the town centre.
10 rms (7 shr) (2 fmly) No smoking in dining room CTV in all bedrooms Tea and coffee making facilities No dogs (ex guide dogs) Licensed CTV 7P Last d 7pm
CARDS: ■■ ■■ £

GH ■■ **Medina House Hotel** Alma Rd PO38 1JU
☎01983 852424
Close to the esplanade at the top of a steep hill, this personally managed small hotel offers freshly decorated accommodation. Some of the front-facing bedrooms have sunny balconies and a number of the rooms enjoy sea views. There is a cosy TV lounge and a bar area with TV and a pool table. A good choice is offered at breakfast and an extensive range of bar meals is available. The patio, leading out from the bar is a new addition.
10 rms (2 bth 3 shr) No smoking in dining room No smoking in lounges CTV in 8 bedrooms Tea and coffee making facilities No dogs (ex guide dogs) Licensed CTV No children 10yrs 4P Pool table Last d 12am
PRICE GUIDE
ROOMS: s £15-£16; d £30-£38; wkly b&b £105-£129.50; wkly hlf-bd £157.50-£182✱
CARDS: ■■ ■■ ■■ £

GH ■■■ *Hotel Picardie* Esplanade PO38 1JX
☎01983 852647
Mar-Oct
Situated on the esplanade, just yards from the beach, this well kept hotel is personally run by friendly proprietors, Mr and Mrs Sparkes, who create a warm and cheerful atmosphere. Bedrooms vary in size but all have en suite or private facilities. There is a comfortable lounge and an attractive dining room where home cooked food is served, including delicious home-baked bread. The bar is a sunny room at the front of the hotel, where guests can enjoy a drink and watch the world go by.
10 en suite (bth/shr) (3 fmly) No smoking CTV in all bedrooms Tea and coffee making facilities Licensed CTV Last d 4.30pm
CARDS: ■■ ■■

GH ■■■ **St Maur Hotel** Castle Rd PO38 1LG
☎01983 852570 FAX 01983 852306
Closed Dec-Jan
An attractive building in an elevated position, this small private hotel offers a friendly atmosphere and freshly decorated accommodation. All but one of the bedrooms have en suite facilities and recent improvements include the redecoration and carpeting of some of the rooms plus the purchase of some very comfortable beds. Public areas include a smart bar with a cosy style of decor. The home-cooked fare served in the dining room is accompanied by a reasonably priced wine list.
14 rms (13 bth/shr) (4 fmly) No smoking in dining room Tea and coffee making facilities No dogs Licensed Cen ht CTV No

children 3yrs 12P No coaches Last d 7pm
PRICE GUIDE
ROOMS: (incl. dinner) s £20-£25; d £50-£52; wkly b&b £175-£182; wkly hlf-bd £217-£224✱
CARDS: ■■ ■■ ■■ ■■ £

WIGMORE Hereford & Worcester Map **07** SO46

◾ ■ **Compasses Hotel** HR6 9UN
☎01568 770203 FAX 01568 770705
This small, privately owned village inn - once a bakery and farm house - dates back in part to the 16th century. Accommodation is soundly maintained, though not luxurious, two bars feature an abundance of beams and wall timbers, and a pleasant dining room offers separate tables.
4 rms (1 fmly) No smoking in 1 bedrooms No smoking in dining room CTV in 3 bedrooms Tea and coffee making facilities Cen ht 70P Last d 9.30pm
PRICE GUIDE
ROOMS: s fr £18; d fr £36; wkly b&b fr £113.40✱
CARDS: ■■ ■■ ■■ ■■

WIGTON Cumbria Map **11** NY24

♥ ■■■ Mr D Knight **Fiddleback Farm Tea Rooms** *(NY487493)* Fiddleback Farm, West Woodside CA7 8BA (on A595, 7m W of Carlisle, in direction of Cockermouth and lakes) ☎016973 42653
This unique and very interesting establishment, a white-painted Cumbrian round house which incorporates an old barn with cow stalls beneath, is situated off the A595 about seven miles west of Carlisle. Inside, a spiral staircase leads to three spacious bedrooms characteristically furnished with antiques, and morning coffees as well as lunches and dinners are served in two charming dining rooms. Though not a working farm, Fiddleback is still surrounded by meadowland where cattle and sheep graze.
3 rms (1 shr) (2 fmly) No smoking in bedrooms No smoking in dining room No smoking in 1 lounge CTV in all bedrooms Tea and coffee making facilities Licensed Cen ht CTV 26P 9 acres horses beef sheep Last d 8pm
PRICE GUIDE
ROOMS: s £18-£20; d £30-£36; wkly b&b £100-£130✱ £

WILBERFOSS Humberside Map **08** SE75

♥ ■■ Mrs J M Liversidge **Cuckoo Nest** *(SE717510)* YO4 5NL ☎01759 380365
Closed 24-26 Dec
A traditional red-brick farmhouse dating back over 200 years, Cuckoo Nest Farm is surrounded by attractive gardens. The spacious lounge offers comfortable seating, a selection of board games and TV, while a small, traditionally-styled dining room is the setting for communal breakfasts. Smoking is not permitted in the neat, fresh bedrooms.
3 rms (1 fmly) No smoking in bedrooms Tea and coffee making facilities No dogs Cen ht CTV No children 2yrs P 150 acres arable beef dairy mixed sheep
PRICE GUIDE
ROOMS: s £18-£20; d £32-£34✱ £

WILMCOTE Warwickshire Map **04** SP15

GH ■■■ **Dosthill Cottage** The Green CV37 9XJ (turn off A3400 to Wilmcote, Dosthill Cottage in centre of village) ☎01789 266480 FAX 01789 266480
This small house is situated in the centre of the village opposite Mary Arden's house and it dates from the late 17th century. There

are many charming period features such as the thick walls and flagstone floors. The house abounds with books and other personal items which add to its character. Accommodation is comfortable and well equipped and there is a real sense of hospitality.

2 en suite (shr) 1 annexe en suite (shr) No smoking in dining room No smoking in lounges CTV in all bedrooms Tea and coffee making facilities No dogs (ex guide dogs) Cen ht CTV 5P No coaches
PRICE GUIDE
ROOMS: s £25-£28; d £38-£40✱

(£)

See advertisement under STRATFORD-UPON-AVON

WILMINGTON East Sussex Map **05** TQ50

Selected

GH Ⓠ Ⓠ Ⓠ Ⓠ **Crossways Hotel** Lewes Rd BN26 5SG (on A27 between Lewes and Polegate, 2m E of Alfriston roundabout) ☎01323 482455 FAX 01323 487811
Closed 24 Dec-23 Jan
This delightful restaurant with rooms, set in two acres of attractive grounds beside the A27 some seven miles from Eastbourne, provides well appointed accommodation, each of its bright, modern, individually styled bedrooms being equipped with thoughtful extras as well as a mini-bar, TV set, telephone and hairdryer. Some rooms overlook the lawned garden, and one of the best has its own balcony. The restaurant offers lunches and dinners of a high enough quality to have earned it two rosettes and locally produced, organically grown ingredients are also used to create the excellent breakfast - including home-made bread rolls and marmalades - which is served in a bright, sunny breakfast room. Service is particularly attentive and helpful.
7 en suite (bth/shr) CTV in all bedrooms Tea and coffee making facilities Direct dial from bedrooms No dogs (ex guide dogs) Licensed Cen ht No children 12yrs 30P No coaches Last d 8.45pm
CARDS:

WILMSLOW Cheshire Map **07** SJ88

See also Manchester Airport

GH Ⓠ Ⓠ Ⓠ **Fernbank** 188 Wilmslow Rd, Handforth SK9 3JX (2m N on A34) ☎01625 523729
Closed 24 Dec-2 Jan rs Limited reception times
A large detached house in an ideal location for the airport. Rooms are spacious and well equipped and residential ceramic courses are held periodically.
3 en suite (bth/shr) (1 fmly) CTV in all bedrooms Tea and coffee making facilities Cen ht CTV 4P No coaches China restoration and weekend leisure courses
PRICE GUIDE
ROOMS: s £28-£33; d £39-£44

(£)

GH Ⓠ Ⓠ Ⓠ **Grove** 16 Grove Av SK9 5EG (from A34 turn onto A538 turn right into Grove Way 50yds from junct, Grove Way leads to Grove Ave) ☎01625 548484 FAX 01625 548640
Conveniently situated just off the main street, this family owned and run small guest house provides well equipped bedrooms which include radios, televisions and telphones, whilst there is the added convenience of its own car parking at the front.
3 en suite (bth/shr) (1 fmly) No smoking in dining room CTV in all bedrooms Tea and coffee making facilities Direct dial from

bedrooms Cen ht P No coaches
PRICE GUIDE
ROOMS: s £28.50; d £38.50✱

WIMBORNE MINSTER Dorset Map **04** SZ09

GH Ⓠ **Riversdale** 33 Poole Rd BH21 1QB (on A349)
☎01202 884528
Closed Xmas rs Nov-Feb
Mr and Mrs Topham have been running this popular guesthouse for nearly 20 years, and they enjoy a loyal following of regular returning guests. Parts of the house date back 350 years, and some of the bedrooms at the top of the house have quaint features including sloping ceilings and winding staircases; though simply furnished, they are attractively presented, with bright decor. Public areas include a pleasant breakfast room and cosy lounge area, and the house features a collection of antique artefacts and utensils from a bygone era.
8 rms (1 bth) (3 fmly) No smoking in bedrooms No smoking in dining room CTV in all bedrooms Tea and coffee making facilities Cen ht CTV No children 3yrs 3P No coaches Last d 10am
PRICE GUIDE
ROOMS: s £15-£20✱

(£)

 GH Ⓠ Ⓠ Ⓠ **Twynham** 67 Poole Rd BH21 1QB
☎01202 887310
This property has been in the Rendell family for over thirty seven years, and has been recently restored to provide attractive and comfortable accommodation. The bedrooms are bright and prettily decorated, all have colour television, hairdryer and radio alarm. There is off street parking, and although on the main road the house has lovely views of the water meadows.
➡

3 rms No smoking in bedrooms No smoking in lounges CTV in all bedrooms Tea and coffee making facilities No dogs (ex guide dogs) Cen ht 3P No coaches
PRICE GUIDE
ROOMS: s £15-£18; d £25-£36

WIMPSTONE Warwickshire Map **04** SP24

♥ QQ Mrs J E James **Whitchurch** *(SP222485)* CV37 8NS (take A3400 out of Stratford towards Oxford,in 4m turn right to Wimpstone, at telephone box bear left and keep straight on for 0.25m to farm) ☎01789 450275
A modestly appointed family farmhouse offers reasonably spacious bedrooms and a relaxing lounge and dining room. Views are good and access to the Cotswolds easy.
3 en suite (shr) (2 fmly) CTV in all bedrooms Tea and coffee making facilities No dogs Cen ht CTV 6P 220 acres arable beef sheep Last d 6.30pm
PRICE GUIDE
ROOMS: s £17-£18; d £34-£36✱

WINCANTON Somerset Map **03** ST72

Selected

♥ QQQQ Mrs A Teague **Lower Church** *(ST721302)* Rectory Ln, Charlton Musgrove BA9 8ES (from Wincanton take B3081 Bruton Rd, 1m turn right into Rectory Lane opposite the racecourse, first farm on left) ☎01963 32307
Closed Xmas & New Year
A tranquil rural setting and a beautiful garden are offered by this 18th-century farmhouse, where warm hospitality is assured. There are three bedrooms, all full of character and comfort; many of the building's original features have been retained, including red brick interior walls and beams. Breakfast is served at a large family table in a cosy room with plenty of books and magazines for visitors to enjoy
3 rms (2 shr) No smoking Tea and coffee making facilities Cen ht CTV No children 6yrs 3P 60 acres beef sheep
PRICE GUIDE
ROOMS: d £30; wkly b&b £95✱

WINCHCOMBE Gloucestershire Map **04** SP02

GH QQQ **The Homestead** Footbridge, Broadway Rd GL54 5JG (9m form M5 junct5 on the B4632) ☎01242 602536 FAX 01242 602127
Closed 24 Dec-3 Jan
A farmhouse of 1750s construction, Alan and Maureen Brooker's delightful house provides particularly well looked after accommodation. An attractive flagstoned entrance leads into a comfortable lounge and pretty breakfast room, where the hearty meal is taken at a communal table. The boldly decorated bedrooms have good divans and linen. One room is en suite and the other two share a large, well appointed bathroom. This is a no-smoking establishment.
3 rms (1 shr) No smoking CTV in all bedrooms Tea and coffee making facilities Cen ht CTV ch fac 4P No coaches
PRICE GUIDE
ROOMS: d £36-£40

Selected

GH QQQQ **Wesley House** High St GL54 5LJ ☎01242 602366 FAX 01242 602405
Closed 14 Jan-10 Feb rs Sun evenings except BH Sun
A quaint half-timbered building in the centre of the village, Wesley House boasts a fleeting association with the renowned Methodist of that name. The entrance leads to an open lounge with an inglenook fireplace, and it is here that morning coffee and afternoon tea are served. One of the co-owners is an accomplished chef and the ground-floor restaurant is acclaimed in its own right. Sumptuously furnished bedrooms with modern shower rooms offer extras such as fresh flowers and mineral water.
5 en suite (shr) No smoking in bedrooms No smoking in area of dining room CTV in all bedrooms Tea and coffee making facilities Direct dial from bedrooms No dogs (ex guide dogs) Licensed Cen ht No parking Last d 9.30pm
PRICE GUIDE
ROOMS: s £42-£55; d £50-£70✱
CARDS: £

WINCHELSEA East Sussex Map **05** TQ91

Selected

GH QQQQ **The Country House at Winchelsea** Hastings Rd TN36 4AD (set back from A259, Hastings side of town) ☎01797 226669
Closed Xmas
This delightful former farmhouse dating from about 1690, its well kept two-acre grounds surrounded by National Trust land, stands only five minutes' drive from Rye. Personally run by its proprietor, it provides a relaxed, friendly atmosphere and accommodation in individually styled, well equipped bedrooms overlooking the gardens and countryside beyond. Public areas include a drawing room as well as the dining room which serves speciality breakfasts and an evening meal featuring locally caught fish and home-made ice cream and desserts - the crepes Suzette being particularly noteworthy; a good wine list complements the food. Levels of comfort and service are good, and ample car parking facilities are available.
4 rms (3 bth/shr) No smoking in dining room CTV in all bedrooms Tea and coffee making facilities Direct dial from bedrooms No dogs Licensed Cen ht No children 9yrs 6P No coaches Last d 7.30pm
PRICE GUIDE
ROOMS: d £60-£68✱
CARDS:

WINCHESTER Hampshire Map **04** SU52

Selected

GH QQQQ **Leckhampton** 62 Kilham Ln SO22 5QD (follow all routes signs towards A3090 Romsey pass County Hospital over rdbt right at 2nd set of traffic lights) ☎01962 852831
Feb-Nov
Leckhampton is an attractive property located in a rural lane one and a half miles from the centre of town. It has the feel of a comfortable home, with family photographs and ornaments about the house. Mrs Regan takes great care of her guests,

many of whom return regularly. Breakfast is the only meal served (and very good it is too), but menus for local restaurants are to hand. Bedrooms, including two ground-floor rooms, are pretty and bright, and there is a sunny conservatory, breakfast room and a comfortable lounge.

3 rms (1 bth/shr) No smoking CTV in all bedrooms Tea and coffee making facilities No dogs Cen ht 4P No coaches

PRICE GUIDE

ROOMS: d £36-£40; wkly b&b £130✻

GH Q Q Q **Markland** 44 St Cross St SO23 9PS
☎01962 854901

The Markland is a pretty Victorian property situated in the residential area of St Cross on the south side of the city. The neat bedrooms offer good quality beds and modern en suite shower rooms, and there is also a ground floor room suitable for disabled guests. In sunny weather guests can sit out in the garden.

4 en suite (shr) (1 fmly) No smoking in dining room No smoking in lounges CTV in all bedrooms Tea and coffee making facilities Cen ht 4P No coaches

PRICE GUIDE

ROOMS: s £35; d £45

CARDS: 🔳 🔳

Selected

GH Q Q Q Q **Shawlands** 46 Kilham Ln SO22 5QD (take A3090 from Winchester, straight over roundabout and turn right at second set of traffic lights)
☎01962 861166 FAX 01962 861166

Standing in a peaceful rural setting on the Eastern side of town, Shawlands offers comfortable bedrooms, attractively decorated and well-equipped. There is a cosy sitting room with modern furnishings and a dining room with one large table for communal dining.

5 rms (1 bth/shr) (2 fmly) No smoking CTV in 4 bedrooms Tea and coffee making facilities Cen ht CTV 4P No coaches

PRICE GUIDE

ROOMS: s £22-£25; d £34-£38; wkly b&b £126-£144

Premier Selected

◀ Q Q Q Q Q The **Wykeham Arms** 73 Kingsgate St SO23 9PE (immediately south of the Cathedral, by Kingsgate and opposite Winchester College)
☎01962 853834 FAX 01962 854411

Centrally located in the oldest part of the city between the cathedral and the college, this 250-year-old inn is one of the most popular in Winchester and the surrounding area, so booking for its above-average meals is definitely to be recommended. Full of character, the bars are divided into a series of small eating and drinking areas, some of them no-smoking. The attractive bedrooms are all en suite and well equipped for comfort. Breakfast is served to residents in the first-floor breakfast room. ➡

NORTHILL HOUSE

Horton • Wimborne • Dorset • BH21 7HL
Telephone Witchampton (01258) 840407

AA Premier Selected QQQQQ

Six miles north of Wimborne. Peaceful rural situation, mid-19th century farmhouse providing spacious reception rooms and all bedrooms en-suite with TV and tea/coffee making facilities. Within easy reach of Kingston Lacy, Cranborne Chase, Blackmore Vale, New Forest and Salisbury. Traditional English breakfasts with home-made bread and preserves. Excellent evening meals from local produce. One room equipped for disabled guests (Category 1)

Recommended in "The Good Hotel Guide 1995"

SHAWLANDS

46 Kilham Lane, Winchester,
Hampshire SO22 5QD
Tel and Fax: 01962 861166
Proprietor: Mrs E. K. Pollock

Shawlands is situated off the Romsey Road in a quiet residential area overlooking open farmland, just a short walk from a regular bus service to the city centre.

It is a detached family house with a large garden, offering very comfortable bedrooms, including one on the ground floor, with quality beds and modern well tiled bathrooms. All rooms have colour TV, radio, tea/coffee making facilities and hair dryer. There is also a Guest lounge, pay phone and private parking.

7 en suite (bth/shr) CTV in all bedrooms Tea and coffee
making facilities Direct dial from bedrooms Cen ht No
children 14yrs 14P No coaches Sauna Last d 8.45pm
PRICE GUIDE
ROOMS: s £65-£67.50; d £75-£77.50✱
MEALS: Lunch £9-£11alc Dinner £18-£20alc✱
CARDS:

WINDERMERE Cumbria Map 07 SD49

 GH ⓆⓆ **Aaron Slack** 48 Ellerthwaite Rd LA23 2BS
(from the main road between Windermere & Bowness, turn
east into Brook Rd at end of road turn left, Aaron Slack on
left) ☎015394 44649
Part of a Victorian terrace, this small friendly guesthouse provides
freshly decorated accommodation combined with personal service.
The three bedrooms are prettily furnished, each with TV and tea-
making facilities, and two are now en suite. There is a small
lounge and a separate breakfast room. Smoking is not permitted
and pets are not accepted.
3 en suite (bth/shr) No smoking CTV in all bedrooms Tea and
coffee making facilities No dogs Cen ht No children 12yrs No
parking No coaches
PRICE GUIDE
ROOMS: s £15-£22; d £30-£40; wkly b&b £98-£133
CARDS: £

Selected

GH ⓆⓆⓆⓆ **Archway** College Rd LA23 1BU
☎015394 45613
Situated in an attractive terrace close to the village centre this
small Victoiran guesthouse is full of charm and character.
There are open fires, fresh flowers and lots of books and
paintings; the bedrooms have patchwork quilts, direct dial
telephones and homemade biscuits are provided for guests.
The fine English cooking uses the best available produce and
breakfast is also very special.
4 en suite (shr) No smoking CTV in all bedrooms Tea and
coffee making facilities Direct dial from bedrooms No dogs
Licensed Cen ht No children 10yrs 2P No coaches Last d
3pm
PRICE GUIDE
ROOMS: d £42-£52; wkly b&b £150-£154
CARDS: £

Selected

GH ⓆⓆⓆⓆ **The Beaumont Hotel** Holly Rd LA23 2AF
(follow town centre signs through one-way system then
2nd left into Ellerthwaite Rd then 1st left into Holly Rd)
☎015394 47075 FAX 01539 447075
Closed Dec-Jan
A delightfully furnished Victorian house close to the village
centre, the Beaumont prohibits smoking and has been
beautifully redecorated and offers pretty, en suite bedrooms.
Home-cooked dinners are served in the charming dining room.
10 en suite (bth/shr) (4 fmly) No smoking CTV in all
bedrooms Tea and coffee making facilities No dogs (ex
guide dogs) Cen ht CTV No children 6yrs 10P
PRICE GUIDE
ROOMS: s £25-£50; d £44-£60; wkly b&b £140-£189✱
CARDS: £

GH ⓆⓆ **Beech House** 11 Woodland Rd LA23 2AE
☎015394 88983
Attractive public rooms - both the lounge and dining room have
beautiful fire places - are features of this cosy little guest house in
a terraced row close to the town centre. Apart from the large attic
family room, others are compact, but well equipped to include
clock radios.
5 rms (2 bth/shr) (1 fmly) No smoking CTV in all bedrooms
Tea and coffee making facilities Cen ht CTV No parking No
coaches Last d 3pm
PRICE GUIDE
ROOMS: s £18-£19; d £30-£38
CARDS:

GH ⓆⓆⓆ *Belgrave* 2 Ellerthwaite Rd LA23 2AH
☎015394 43335
Situated just off the main road from Windermere to Bowness, a
few minutes' walk from the village shops, this Victorian house
offers fresh, bright accommodation. Two bedrooms have en suite
facilities and all have colour TV. A comfortable guests' lounge is
provided, along with a separate dining room.
3 rms (2 shr) No smoking in bedrooms CTV in all bedrooms Tea
and coffee making facilities No dogs (ex guide dogs) No children
5P No coaches
CARDS:

GH ⓆⓆⓆ **Belsfield House** 4 Belsfield Ter LA23 3EQ (from
A592 in Bowness, take first left after mini-roundabout onto
Kendal road) ☎015394 45823
This is a charming, friendly black and white Victorian house in the
centre of Bowness. Bedrooms are attractively furnished and some
are large enough for families. The sitting room and dining room
have lovely, original fireplaces.
9 en suite (shr) (4 fmly) No smoking in dining room CTV in all
bedrooms No dogs (ex guide dogs) Cen ht 9P No coaches
PRICE GUIDE
ROOMS: s £20-£26; d £36-£48   £

Selected

GH ⓆⓆⓆⓆ *Blenheim Lodge* Brantfell Rd, Bowness on
Windermere LA23 3AE (A592 to Bowness village, across
mini-roundabout, turn first left and left again)
☎015394 43440 FAX 015394 43440
This very comfortable small hotel occupies an elevated
position high above Lake Windermere and Old Bowness,
commanding fine views of both the lake and the mountains
beyond. Television sets and tea/coffee making facilities are
provided in all the individually styled en suite bedrooms -
some of which feature four-poster or half tester beds.
Downstairs there are a very comfortable lounge and the
delightful dining room where Mrs Sanderson's excellent
dinners include home-made soups and such typically English
dishes as topside of beef cooked in brown ale and sticky
toffee pudding.
11 en suite (bth/shr) (1 fmly) No smoking in bedrooms No
smoking in dining room CTV in all bedrooms Tea and coffee
making facilities No dogs Licensed Cen ht CTV No
children 6yrs 13P No coaches Membership of country club
Last d 7pm
CARDS:
See advertisement also in Colour Section

GH Ⓠ Ⓠ Ⓠ **Boston House** The Terrace LA23 1AJ (turn off A591, 50yds S of main junction to Windermere) ☎015394 43654 FAX 015394 43654
Mar-Oct rs Nov & Feb
Now a friendly guest house, this historic building backs on to the A591 Kendal road, a few minutes' walk from the station and town centre. Bedrooms are mostly spacious, and several have four-poster or canopied beds. There are a cosy lounge with plenty of books and board games and a separate dining room with individual tables.
5 en suite (shr) (2 fmly) No smoking CTV in all bedrooms Tea and coffee making facilities Licensed Cen ht CTV 5P No coaches Last d 5pm
PRICE GUIDE
ROOMS: d £39-£50; wkly b&b £120-£160; wkly hlf-bd £185-£225
CARDS: ▥ ▦

⟦♿⟧ GH Ⓠ Ⓠ Ⓠ **Brendan Chase** 1 & 3 College Rd LA23 1BU ☎015394 45638 FAX 015394 45638
A delightful Edwardian house, close to Windermere village with attractively decorated bedrooms, sitting room and dining room. It also has a games room with full-sized snooker table.
8 rms (4 shr) (4 fmly) No smoking in bedrooms No smoking in dining room No smoking in 1 lounge CTV in all bedrooms Tea and coffee making facilities Cen ht CTV ch fac 8P No coaches
PRICE GUIDE
ROOMS: s £15-£30; d £25-£50

(£)

BLENHEIM LODGE
Welcome to our beautiful Lakeland Guest House

Set amongst idyllic countryside yet close to the local attractions. Visitors may expect an extra treat with wonderful, traditional Old English dishes made with local or home-grown fresh produce. The most popular recipes have been produced into an award winning cookbook. All eleven en suite bedrooms have colour TV and tea/coffee facilities most have lake views, Four poster and half testers available. Ideal for a relaxing holiday. All in the most beautiful scenery.
Jackie & Frank Sanderson
Brantfell Road, Bowness-on-Windermere, Cumbria LA23 3AE
Telephone & Fax: (0153 94) 43440

𝕿𝖍𝖊 𝕭𝖊𝖆𝖚𝖒𝖔𝖓𝖙
Holly Rd. Windermere, Cumbria LA23 2AF
Telephone: (015394) 47075   Fax: (015394) 47075

QQQQ
Selected

♛♛
HIGHLY COMMENDED

FHG – Readers Diploma Award 1996

Opened Easter 1992
The Beaumont has very quickly gained a reputation for quality.
Ideally situated for Windermere and Bowness and a perfect central location for touring the lakes. This elegant Victorian house lends itself to all the grace and charm of this era combined with all the comforts of today.
All 10 luxury bedrooms are en-suite with tea making facilities, TV and hair dryer. Four poster rooms are available for that special occasion and a 'Romantic Presentation' of wine, chocolates, fruit and flowers may be ordered. The breakfasts are hearty, the standards are high and the hospitality is warm and sincere. Private parking and some ground floor rooms. Prices from £22.00 per person.
Leisure facilities available nearby

GH 🅠🅠 **Broadlands** 19 Broad St LA23 2AB (from A591 to town centre follow one way system for 300 metres to pelican crossing, Broad Street is next turning on the left) ☎015394 46532 FAX 015394 46532

An attractive little guest house situated in a side road just a short distance from the village centre, Broadlands offers freshly decorated bedrooms, a cosy lounge and a separate dining room where good English breakfasts are served.

5 rms (3 shr) (1 fmly) No smoking in dining room No smoking in lounges CTV in all bedrooms Tea and coffee making facilities Cen ht CTV No parking No coaches Mountain bike hire
PRICE GUIDE
ROOMS: d £26-£40
CARDS: (£)

GH 🅠🅠🅠 **Brooklands** Ferry View, Bowness LA23 3JB (from Windermere enter Bowness, follow Kendal/Lancaster road A5074 in 0.75m establishment on left) ☎015394 42344

This delightful end-of-terrace guesthouse overlooks Lake Windermere and the surrounding hills from its elevated position at the junction of the A5074 and B5284 south of Bowness. The individually decorated rooms are mostly en suite and a comfortable lounge adjoins the attractive breakfast room in which home-cooked breakfasts are served. There is private parking alongside the house.

6 rms (5 shr) (3 fmly) CTV in all bedrooms Tea and coffee making facilities Cen ht CTV 6P
PRICE GUIDE
ROOMS: s £16-£20; d £32-£40; wkly b&b £112-£140* (£)

GH 🅠🅠🅠 **Eastbourne Hotel** Biskey Howe Rd LA23 2JR (from A591 turn left into town and proceed towards Bowness and lake. Take 2nd left after police station) ☎015394 43525

Immaculate and well maintained throughout, this friendly guest house is located in a quiet residential area within walking distance of the centre of Bowness. Bedrooms, some of which are quite spacious, are furnished in pine and attractively decorated. There is an honesty bar stocked with beer, canned wine and soft drinks in the comfortable lounge, and the attractive dining room has individual tables.

8 rms (5 shr) (1 fmly) No smoking in 4 bedrooms No smoking in dining room CTV in all bedrooms Tea and coffee making facilities No dogs Licensed Cen ht 6P No coaches
PRICE GUIDE
ROOMS: s £17-£27; d £34-£52; wkly b&b £113-£140
CARDS: (£)

GH 🅠🅠🅠 **Fairfield Country House Hotel** Brantfell Road, Bowness LA23 3AE (follow signs to Bowness at mini rdbt take road to lake, turn left opposite church & left again in front of Spinney Restaurant) ☎015394 46565 FAX 015394 46565

Set in an elevated position above Bowness yet only a short walk from the village shops and Lake Windermere, this comfortable country house hotel offers a friendly atmosphere under the personal supervision of its resident owners. All the attractively decorated bedrooms have private facilities, television sets and tea/coffee making equipment, while downstairs there are both a cosy bar and a very relaxing lounge; the secluded, colourful garden includes a patio where guests can enjoy their drinks on fine days.

9 rms (8 bth/shr) (2 fmly) No smoking CTV in all bedrooms Tea and coffee making facilities No dogs Licensed Cen ht CTV 12P Last d breakfast
PRICE GUIDE
ROOMS: s £22-£28; d £44-£56; wkly b&b £150-£180; wkly hlf-bd £255-£285*
CARDS:

GH 🅠🅠🅠🅠 **Fayrer Garden House** Lythe Valley Rd, Bowness on Windermere LA23 3JP (on A5074, 1m S of Bowness) (Logis) ☎015394 88195 FAX 015394 45986

Standing in five acres of gardens off the Lythe Valley road, south-east of Bowness, this hotel was built in 1904 as a private residence and enjoys splendid views out across the lake from its elevated position. The panelled lobby leads to two elegant lounges, one with a bar, and the house has been extended to provide additional bedrooms and a smart restaurant.

14 en suite (bth/shr) (3 fmly) No smoking in 4 bedrooms No smoking in dining room CTV in all bedrooms Tea and coffee making facilities Direct dial from bedrooms Licensed Cen ht 20P Fishing Last d 8pm
PRICE GUIDE
ROOMS: s £39.50-£65; d £70-£130*
CARDS: (£)

GH 🅠🅠🅠 **Firgarth** Ambleside Rd LA23 1EU (situated on the A591, Windermere to Ambleside road, opposite Wynlass Beck Riding Stables) ☎015394 46974

A Victorian house with well maintained, comfortable accommodation. All rooms are en suite, with colour TV and tea trays. There is an attractive dining room and a pleasant lounge.

8 en suite (shr) (3 fmly) No smoking in 4 bedrooms No smoking in CTV in all bedrooms Tea and coffee making facilities Cen ht 8P No coaches
PRICE GUIDE
ROOMS: s £17-£21.50; d £32-£40
CARDS: (£)

GH 🅠🅠🅠🅠 **Fir Trees** Lake Rd LA23 2EQ (one and a half miles below town centre on left going toward lake) ☎015394 42272 FAX 015394 42272

Fir Trees is an elegant late Victorian house situated between Windermere and Bowness. Filled with antiques, fine prints and fresh flowers, it is regarded as one of the best bed and breakfast establishments in the area. The bedrooms are warmly decorated and well equipped, and some are suitable for families. Although there is no lounge, seating is provided beneath the stairs, and here guests can plan their day from the informative compendium compiled by the proprietors. Hearty breakfasts are served at individual tables in the attractive dining room.

7 en suite (bth/shr) (2 fmly) No smoking CTV in all bedrooms Tea and coffee making facilities No dogs Cen ht 8P No coaches
PRICE GUIDE
ROOMS: s £24.50-£31; d £39-£52; wkly b&b £130-£170
CARDS: (£)

Entries in this Guide are based on reports filed by our team of professionally trained, full-time inspectors.

GH QQQQ **Glencree Private Hotel** Lake Rd LA23 2EQ (0.5m from town centre after leaving one way system keeping stone clock tower on left at junct of New Rd & Lake Rd, Glencree is on right) ☎015394 45822
Mar-Nov rs Feb

A substantial house built of Lakeland stone stands in a quiet location high above a stream and woodland valley, midway between Windermere and Bowness. Several of the bedrooms enjoy this picturesque view, including one of the two on the top floor (reached by way of a wrought iron spiral staircase). The accommodation is immaculately maintained throughout, and most of the bedrooms are spacious. Downstairs there are a comfortable lounge and an attractive dining room with individual tables.

5 en suite (bth/shr) (1 fmly) No smoking in 2 bedrooms No smoking in dining room No smoking in lounges CTV in all bedrooms Tea and coffee making facilities No dogs (ex guide dogs) Licensed Cen ht No children 9yrs 8P No coaches
PRICE GUIDE
ROOMS: s £35-£45; d £37-£60✳
CARDS: £

GH QQQ **Glenville Hotel** Lake Rd LA23 2EQ (turn left off A591 into Windermere Village, follow main road for 0.5m, Glenville is on the right next to St Johns Church) ☎015394 43371
Xmas day

A Lakeland stone house standing in its own grounds close to St John's church on the main road between Windermere and

Bowness, the Glenville offers predominantly en suite bedrooms which include one situated on the ground floor; all are brightly decorated and well furnished. Downstairs there are a comfortable lounge and an attractive dining room. Ample car parking space is available.

9 en suite (bth/shr) (1 fmly) CTV in all bedrooms Tea and coffee making facilities No dogs Licensed Cen ht CTV 12P Last d 2pm
PRICE GUIDE
ROOMS: s £18-£25; d £35-£48; wkly b&b £110-£140✳
CARDS: £

GH QQQ **Green Gables** 37 Broad St LA23 2AB
☎015394 43886
Closed Xmas & New Year

Green Gables is an attractive double-fronted house in a Victorian terrace facing Elleray Gardens, a short walk from the village centre. Recently considerably refurbished, the house offers comfortable and reasonably priced accommodation. Guests will appreciate the tastefully decorated lounge and the bright bedrooms.

7 rms (3 shr) (2 fmly) No smoking in bedrooms No smoking in dining room CTV in all bedrooms Tea and coffee making facilities No dogs (ex guide dogs) Cen ht CTV 2P No coaches Golf can be arranged
PRICE GUIDE
ROOMS: s £14-£20; d £28-£40; wkly b&b £98-£130✳ £

GH Ⓠ Ⓠ Ⓠ **Haisthorpe** Holly Rd LA23 2AF (turn off A591, onto A5074 and after 0.25m turn left into Ellerthwaite Road and then 1st left) ☎015394 43445

Family owned and run, this semidetached guest house is located in a residential area within walking distance of the town centre. Attractively decorated throughout, it has a very pleasant lounge and a dining room serving popular home-cooked dinners. Bedrooms are thoughtfully equipped.

6 rms (4 shr) (2 fmly) No smoking in bedrooms No smoking in dining room CTV in all bedrooms Tea and coffee making facilities Cen ht CTV 3P No coaches Last d 5pm

PRICE GUIDE

ROOMS: s £15-£20; d £26-£36; wkly b&b £78-£126; wkly hlf-bd £120-£168

CARDS: 🔲 🔲 🔲

GH Ⓠ *The Haven* 10 Birch St LA23 1EG (on A5074, take 3rd left after entering one way system into Birch Street, post office on corner) ☎015394 44017

This Victorian house built of Lakeland stone stands on the corner of a quiet road, just off the main street of the village. Traditionally furnished bedrooms, which include some suitable for families, are equipped with TVs and beverage-making facilities, and there is a large breakfast room downstairs. Parking space is available.

4 rms (3 fmly) CTV in all bedrooms Tea and coffee making facilities No dogs (ex guide dogs) Cen ht No children 3yrs 4P

Selected

GH Ⓠ Ⓠ Ⓠ Ⓠ *The Hawksmoor* Lake Rd LA23 2EQ (follow Windermere town centre one-way system for approximately half a mile and establishment can be found opposite the church) ☎015394 42110

11 Feb-24 Nov & 27 Dec-7 Jan

A family-run guest house in its own well tended gardens, conveniently situated midway between Windermere village and Bowness, Hawksmoor is tastefully furnished and decorated throughout - the co-ordinated modern fabrics which make the bedrooms attractive being echoed in those of an elegant lounge and dining room. Twin, double and family rooms are available, all en suite and some with four-poster beds. The atmosphere is welcoming and good private parking facilities are available.

10 en suite (bth/shr) (3 fmly) No smoking in 5 bedrooms No smoking in dining room CTV in all bedrooms Tea and coffee making facilities No dogs (ex guide dogs) Licensed Cen ht No children 6yrs 12P No coaches Last d 5pm

CARDS: 🔲 🔲

See advertisement also in Colour Section

GH Ⓠ Ⓠ Ⓠ **Hazel Bank** Hazel St LA23 1EL (off A591 opposite Windermere Hotel, turn left into Oak St at Walter Willsons supermarket, 2nd on left into Hazel St) ☎015394 45486

This substantial Victorian house with a mature walled garden and ample private parking is set in a quiet cul-de-sac close to the centre of the village. Spacious en suite bedrooms are tastefully furnished and decorated, and the owners' enthusiasm for walking is reflected in the wealth of information available in the comfortable lounge. Smoking is not permitted anywhere in the house.

2 en suite (shr) No smoking Tea and coffee making facilities No dogs Cen ht CTV No children 7yrs 4P No coaches

PRICE GUIDE

ROOMS: d £32-£40; wkly b&b £115-£122

GH Ⓠ Ⓠ Ⓠ **Holly Lodge** 6 College Rd LA23 1BX (from the A591 opposite Windermere Hotel follow the road downhill towards Bowness through the village turn right into College Rd) ☎015394 43873 FAX 015394 43873

This attractive Victorian house stands in a quiet side road close to the village centre. Individually furnished and decorated bedrooms all have colour television and tea-making facilities. Guests can relax in a comfortable lounge, and the well-appointed dining room has a small bar. Private parking facilities are available.

10 rms (6 shr) (3 fmly) No smoking in bedrooms No smoking in dining room CTV in all bedrooms Tea and coffee making facilities No dogs (ex guide dogs) Licensed Cen ht 7P No coaches Last d 10am

PRICE GUIDE

ROOMS: s £17-£20; d £34-£40; wkly b&b £119-£140; wkly hlf-bd £189-£210

GH Ⓠ Ⓠ Ⓠ **Holly Park House** 1 Park Rd LA23 2AW (from A591 through town centre one way system beyond shops turn left along Broad St continue to end then turn right) ☎015394 42107

Mar-5 Jan

Large, comfortable and very well maintained en suite bedrooms rank high among the attractions of a Lakeland stone house quietly situated on a corner site within easy walking distance of the village shops; guests are also provided with a relaxing lounge and a pleasantly appointed dining room with individual tables.

6 en suite (bth/shr) (4 fmly) No smoking in 4 bedrooms No smoking in dining room CTV in all bedrooms Tea and coffee making facilities Licensed Cen ht CTV 4P No coaches Last d 5pm

PRICE GUIDE

ROOMS: s £24-£27; d £34-£40; wkly b&b fr £119✱

CARDS: 🔲 🔲 🔲 🔲

Selected

GH Ⓠ Ⓠ Ⓠ Ⓠ *Howbeck* New Rd LA23 2LA ☎015394 44739

Closed 25-26 Dec & Jan

Lying in its own gardens on the main road just south of the town centre, this fine period house has been completely refurbished to a high standard. Impressively furnished bedrooms are well proportioned, to compensate for the absence of a guests lounge, and have smart en-suite bathrooms. The dining room is stylishly attractive with well spaced tables offering a good level of comfort.

10 en suite (bth/shr) (1 fmly) No smoking in 8 bedrooms No smoking in dining room No smoking in lounges CTV in all bedrooms Tea and coffee making facilities Cen ht 12P No coaches

---

 GH Ⓠ Ⓠ Ⓠ **Kenilworth** Holly Rd LA23 2AF (drive through one way system, take 2nd left, Ellerthwaite Rd then 1st left into Holly Rd) ☎015394 44004

This semidetached Victorian property lies in a residential area close to the town centre. Well maintained and comfortably furnished, it offers a spacious lounge and attractively decorated dining room. Three of the bedrooms have smart modern en suite shower rooms, the other three being served by a bathroom which also has a separate shower cubicle.

6 rms (3 shr) (1 fmly) No smoking Tea and coffee making

facilities No dogs (ex guide dogs) Cen ht CTV 3P No coaches
PRICE GUIDE
ROOMS: s fr £15; d £30-£40; wkly b&b £102-£125

Selected

GH QQQQ **Kirkwood** Prince's Rd LA23 2DD
☎015394 43907
Kirkwood is an attractive Victorian house situated on a quiet corner between Windermere and Bowness, with colourful floral displays outside in summer. The bedrooms have been attractively furnished and all have en suite facilities. Three rooms have four-poster beds and there is one room on the ground floor. A comfortable residents' lounge and a pleasant dining room are provided.
7 en suite (bth/shr) (4 fmly) CTV in all bedrooms Tea and coffee making facilities Cen ht CTV 1P No coaches
PRICE GUIDE
ROOMS: d £38-£50; wkly b&b £130-£170∗
CARDS: 🔳 💳

GH QQ **Latimer House** Lake Rd LA23 2JJ (on left of main road between Windermere & Bowness village centre on entering Bowness) ☎015394 46888
Built in 1850 and conveniently situated within easy walking distance of Lake Windermere and village amenities, this Victorian house offers bedrooms which are both attractively decorated - some with coronets above the beds and matching fabrics - and so furnished that breakfast may be eaten in comfort, there being no dining room. A private car park is available for guests' use.

Kirkwood

Guest House
**Prince's Road, Windermere
Cumbria LA23 2DD
Tel: (0153 94) 43907)
2 Crown Commended**

AA QQQQ
Recommended

Kirkwood is a large Victorian stone house, ideally positioned for exploring the lakeland area, situated on a quiet corner betwixt Windermere and Bowness. All our rooms are en-suite with radio, TV and tea/coffee making facilities. Some rooms have four poster beds, ideal as honeymoon, anniversary, or just a special treat, and our lounge is cosy and comfortable in which to relax. For breakfast there is a large choice of menu including vegetarian or special diets with prior notice. Help with planning your walk, drive or choosing your mini-bus tour is all part of our individual personal service, all to help make your stay in the most beautiful part of England one to remember.

HAWKSMOOR
**Lake Road, Windermere, Cumbria LA23 2EQ
Telephone: (015394) 42110**

Large ivy-clad house with every modern facility and superb private car park. Ideally situated between Windermere and Bowness. All rooms en-suite, some ground floor rooms. All rooms have colour TV and tea/coffee facilities.

See colour advertisement in colour section.

Latimer House
~ Exclusively for Non-Smokers ~

*To quote our Visitors Book . . .
'We couldn't have chosen a better hotel – fantastic breakfast, a wonderful room & great service.*

AA
LISTED

*For reservations or for our brochure
**Phone Richard or Margaret on (015394) 46888
Lake Road • Bowness on Windermere
Cumbria • LA23 2JJ***

Smoking is not permitted anywhere in the house.
6 rms (4 shr) (1 fmly) No smoking CTV in all bedrooms Tea and coffee making facilities No dogs Cen ht CTV No children 8yrs 6P No coaches
PRICE GUIDE
ROOMS: s £25-£39; d £32-£60; wkly b&b £105-£190
CARDS:

GH QQQ **Laurel Cottage** Saint Martins Square LA23 3EF (from A592 turn right at St Martins church onto A5074 then first cottage on left) ☎015394 45594 FAX 015394 45594
This interesting 17th-century house - originally a grammar school and now a charming cottage with a neat front garden - stands right in the centre of Bowness, offering a choice of well maintained accommodation. The bedrooms in the cottage are full of character but small, with stools or window seats and fitted furniture; the more spacious rooms located in the adjoining building have pine furniture and wicker chairs. There is a cosy lounge, and the dining room has a low oak-beamed ceiling.
15 rms (10 shr) (2 fmly) No smoking in dining room No smoking in lounges CTV in 13 bedrooms Tea and coffee making facilities No dogs (ex guide dogs) Cen ht CTV 14P No coaches
PRICE GUIDE
ROOMS: s £21-£23; d £34-£52; wkly b&b £100-£160

GH QQQ *Little Beck House* 3 Park Av LA23 2AR
☎015394 88014 & 43335
Closed 2 Jan-28 Feb
This small, pleasantly decorated guest house in a quiet residential area offers bright, modern accommodation, the two rooms without en suite facilities having their own private bathrooms. Downstairs there is a small but attractive lounge which also doubles as the dining room.
4 rms (2 shr) (3 fmly) No smoking in dining room No smoking in 1 lounge CTV in all bedrooms Tea and coffee making facilities Cen ht No children 7yrs No parking

---

GH QQQ *Lynwood* Broad St LA23 2AB
☎015394 42550 FAX 015394 42550
All the individually and charmingly decorated bedrooms are equipped with en suite facilities at this friendly guest house positioned at the end of a Victorian terrace within easy walking distance of the village centre. Both the dining rooms are attractively appointed, and there is a cosy, relaxing lounge.
9 en suite (shr) (4 fmly) No smoking CTV in all bedrooms Tea and coffee making facilities No dogs (ex guide dogs) Cen ht No children 5yrs 4P No coaches

---

GH QQQ *Meadfoot* New Rd LA23 2LA ☎015394 42610
Feb-Nov & Xmas
Shielded from traffic noise by being built below the level of the main road, this late sixties house has comfortably furnished bedrooms, some of which look over secluded gardens. The spacious and pleasantly furnished guest lounge has similar views and patio doors leading onto a balcony. There is private parking on the premises.
8 rms (4 shr) (1 fmly) CTV in all bedrooms Tea and coffee making facilities No dogs (ex guide dogs) Cen ht No children 3yrs 9P No coaches

---

GH QQQ **Mylne Bridge House** Brookside, Lake Rd LA23 2BX (at the top of Lake Road behind New Road adjacent to the Carver Church) ☎015394 43314
A Victorian lakeland house situated at the side of Mill Beck, only five minutes' walk from Windermere village, offers accommodation in centrally heated bedrooms (one on the ground floor); most of them are south-facing, comfortably spacious and equipped with en suite amenities. There is a combined

lounge/breakfast room, and good private parking facilities are available.
8 rms (7 shr) (2 fmly) No smoking in dining room No smoking in lounges CTV in all bedrooms Tea and coffee making facilities Licensed Cen ht No children 1yr 10P No coaches
PRICE GUIDE
ROOMS: s £18-£22; d £36-£44; wkly b&b £120-£140
CARDS:

GH QQQQ **Newstead** New Rd LA23 2EE (0.5m from A591 between Windermere/Bowness) ☎015394 44485
A substantial and well presented detached dwelling which offers a superior standard of accommodation and reception rooms. The lounge furnished with deep winged armchairs is most attractive, the dining room bright and cheerful is laid with willow pattern china and furnished with solid polished furniture in keeping with the house's period character. The bedrooms are mostly fitted with solid pine and decorated with Country Diary wall coverings and fabrics to match.
7 en suite (bth/shr) (1 fmly) No smoking CTV in all bedrooms Tea and coffee making facilities No dogs Cen ht No children 7yrs 10P No coaches
PRICE GUIDE
ROOMS: s £20-£25; d £36-£44; wkly b&b £126-£139✳

GH QQQ **Oldfield House** Oldfield Rd LA23 2BY (from A591 continue through Windermere village beyond village turn left into Ellerthwaite Road then 2nd right & 1st left) ☎015394 88445 FAX 015394 43250
Closed Jan
This lovely Lakeland house is located in a quiet residential area south of the town centre, with a pub right across the road. It offers particularly well appointed accommodation featuring pretty co-ordinating fabrics, each of the bedrooms having its own individuality and appeal. The comfortable lounge is provided with books and magazines, and there are individual tables in the pleasant dining room.
8 en suite (bth/shr) (2 fmly) No smoking CTV in all bedrooms Tea and coffee making facilities Direct dial from bedrooms No dogs (ex guide dogs) Cen ht No children 2yrs 7P No coaches Free membership to leisure club
PRICE GUIDE
ROOMS: s £20-£29.50; d £36-£55; wkly b&b £113.40-£173.25✳
CARDS:

GH QQQ **Orrest Close** 3 The Terrace LA23 1AJ (turn off A591, 300yds beyond the Windermere town sign entering from the south) ☎015394 43325 FAX 015394 43325
Conveniently situated near the railway and bus stations as well as other village amenities, this attractive Victorian cottage offers comfortable, predominantly en suite accommodation in well decorated and furnished bedrooms; downstairs there are a relaxing lounge and a pleasant dining room with large separate tables for each guest or party. A private car park adjoins the house.
6 rms (4 shr) (2 fmly) No smoking CTV in all bedrooms Tea and coffee making facilities No dogs (ex guide dogs) Cen ht CTV 7P No coaches Last d 3.30pm
PRICE GUIDE
ROOMS: s fr £20; d £36-£44; wkly b&b £115-£140; wkly hlf-bd £180-£200✳
CARDS:

GH ⓠⓠⓠⓠ **Parson Wyke Country House** Glebe Rd LA23 3GZ (500yds beyond steamer piers & Bowness Bay Tourist Information Centre on the one way system) ☎015394 42837

The former rectory to St Martin's church, this building dates back to the 15th century and is the oldest inhabited house in the area. It stands in 1.5 acres of grounds overlooking the lake and offers three fully en suite bedrooms, two of which are huge and furnished with antiques. There is also a spacious guests' lounge and a beamed dining room where breakfast is served. Although the location is that of a country house, it is only a short walk to the centre of Bowness.

3 en suite (bth/shr) (1 fmly) No smoking in 1 bedrooms No smoking in dining room CTV in all bedrooms Tea and coffee making facilities No dogs (ex guide dogs) Cen ht CTV No children 4yrs 9P No coaches

PRICE GUIDE
ROOMS: s £30-£40; d £45-£60

GH ⓠⓠⓠ **Rocklea** Brookside, Lake Rd LA23 2BX (proceed through village towards Bowness and after approx 0.5m turn sharp left at monument into Lake Road) ☎015394 45326

This Lakeland stone house, located in a residential area south of the town, has a brook flowing beside it. The accommodation is very well looked after, with bright modern bedrooms of various sizes and a pleasant combined lounge/dining room where plenty of magazines are provided.

7 en suite (shr) (1 fmly) CTV in all bedrooms Tea and coffee making facilities Cen ht No children 3yrs 5P No coaches

PRICE GUIDE
ROOMS: s £15-£20; d £30-£40✳
CARDS: 🆑 🆑

GH ⓠⓠⓠ **Rosemount** Lake Rd LA23 2EQ (turn off A591 continue through village on left side of road just beyond modern Catholic church)
☎015394 43739 FAX 015394 43739
Feb-Nov

A well maintained and fresh looking semidetached house, Rosemount stands beside the main road on the northern outskirts of Bowness. Public areas are made up of a small lounge and a dining room with dispense bar, modern bedrooms are thoughtfully furnished, and the whole establishment is no-smoking.

8 rms (5 shr) No smoking CTV in all bedrooms Tea and coffee making facilities No dogs Licensed Cen ht No children 8yrs 8P

PRICE GUIDE
ROOMS: s £17.50-£24; d £35-£48; wkly b&b £115-£160✳
CARDS: 🆑 🆑

GH ⓠⓠⓠ *St Johns Lodge* Lake Rd LA23 2EQ
☎015394 43078
Feb-Nov

This semidetached Lakeland stone house stands on the main road between Windermere and Bowness. Bedrooms, including several with four-posters, are attractively furnished and decorated, and all have private facilities. There are a comfortable lounge, a bar and a cosy dining room which serves four course evening meals and a full English breakfast. Private car parking is available.

14 en suite (bth/shr) (3 fmly) CTV in all bedrooms Tea and coffee making facilities No dogs (ex guide dogs) Licensed Cen ht No children 3yrs 11P No coaches Last d 6pm
CARDS: 🆑 🆑
See advertisement on p.455.

GH Q Q **Southview** Cross St LA23 1AE ☎015394 42951

This Georgian style house lies at the end of a cul-de-sac within two minutes' walk of the town centre. Bedrooms are not large but they are well equipped and include radios, hair dryers and bath robes. There are a lounge with a wood-burning stove, a small sun lounge and a good-sized heated indoor swimming pool. One may have to share a table at breakfast, but the continental version is also served to bedrooms.

6 rms (5 bth/shr) (1 fmly) No smoking in bedrooms No smoking in dining room CTV in all bedrooms Tea and coffee making facilities Cen ht CTV 6P No coaches Indoor swimming pool (heated)

PRICE GUIDE

ROOMS: s £15-£22; d £30-£44; wkly b&b £119-£140✶

CARDS: ▬

GH Q Q Q *Thornleigh* Thornbarrow Rd LA23 2EW (turn off A591 into Windermere, approx 1m down main road to Bowness, Thornburrow Road is on left) ☎015394 44203

Feb-Nov

Thornleigh is an attractive small guest house in a quiet, mainly residential area between Windermere and Bowness. The prettily decorated bedrooms provide a good standard of accommodation, and there is a sizeable lounge/dining room downstairs. Private car parking is available to the rear of the property.

6 rms (2 shr) (4 fmly) No smoking in dining room CTV in 5 bedrooms Tea and coffee making facilities No dogs Cen ht CTV 5P

CARDS: ▣ ▦

🖪 ▦ **GH** Q Q Q **Villa Lodge** Cross St LA23 1AE ☎015394 43318 FAX 015394 43318

This house lies in a cul-de-sac within walking distance of the town centre. Well maintained throughout, it offers attractive public areas which include a cosy lounge and sun room as well as the dining room with its individual tables and fine display of plates adorning the walls. Most bedrooms have modern en suite shower rooms, and those facing the front enjoy fine panoramic views over the rooftops to the distant mountains.

7 rms (5 shr) (3 fmly) No smoking in dining room No smoking in 1 lounge CTV in all bedrooms Tea and coffee making facilities No dogs (ex guide dogs) Cen ht ch fac 8P No coaches

PRICE GUIDE

ROOMS: s £16-£18; d £30-£50; wkly b&b £116-£144

CARDS: ▣ ▦

GH Q Q Q **Westbury House** 27 Broad St LA23 2AB (through village turn left after traffic lights) ☎015394 46839 & 44575 FAX 015394 44575

This small guest house is part of a terraced row close to the town centre. It has modern bedrooms, a small lounge and a cosy attractive dining room with individual tables.

4 rms (2 shr) (2 fmly) No smoking in dining room CTV in all bedrooms Tea and coffee making facilities No dogs (ex guide dogs) Cen ht No children 2yrs No parking Last d 9am

PRICE GUIDE

ROOMS: d £26-£40; wkly hlf-bd £158-£207✶

CARDS: ▦   £

GH Q Q Q **Westlake** Lake Rd LA23 2EQ ☎015394 43020

Comfortable and nicely coordinated bedrooms are a feature of this friendly family-run guesthouse, situated midway between Windermere and Bowness. All the rooms have en suite facilities and colour TV and one has a four-poster bed. Downstairs there is a lounge and dining room.

7 en suite (bth/shr) (2 fmly) No smoking in 2 bedrooms No smoking in dining room CTV in all bedrooms Tea and coffee

making facilities No dogs Licensed Cen ht CTV No children 5yrs 8P Last d 3.30am

CARDS: ▣ ▦

GH Q Q Q *Westwood* 4 Ellerthwaite Rd LA23 2AH ☎015394 43514

A semi-detatched Victorian house situated just a few minutes from the village shops. All bedrooms have en-suite facilities and are comfortably furnished. The guests' lounge and dining room are pleasantly appointed and there is a private car park at the side of the property.

5 en suite (shr) CTV in all bedrooms Tea and coffee making facilities No dogs (ex guide dogs) Cen ht CTV No children 12yrs 4P No coaches

GH Q Q Q **White Lodge Hotel** Lake Rd LA23 2JJ (on main lake road, on right) ☎015394 43624

Mar-Nov

This Victorian country house stands on the main road into Bowness, within easy walking distance of Bowness Bay. Bedrooms are attractively and comfortably furnished; several have four-poster beds, those on the ground floor offer both direct car park access and facilities for the disabled, and all have a colour TV and tea-making equipment. Public areas include a cosy guest lounge, a dining room with antique tables and a separate breakfast room.

12 en suite (bth/shr) (3 fmly) CTV in all bedrooms Tea and coffee making facilities No dogs (ex guide dogs) Licensed Cen ht CTV 14P No coaches Membership of leisure club Last d 6.30pm

PRICE GUIDE

ROOMS: s £24-£28; d £46-£55; wkly b&b £160-£179; wkly hlf-bd £240-£255

CARDS: ▣ ▦   £

South View

Cross Street,
Windermere,
Cumbria
LA23 1AE
Telephone:
015394 42951

AA QQ

South View is only 200 yards off the A591, yet is a world away from the bustle and noise of the busy main roads. We are in a quiet, sunny spot, yet only 3 minutes away from all the facilities of Windermere town. The en-suite rooms all have tea/coffee, hair dryer, bath robes and TV. The in-house swimming pool and spa are always warm and open 12 hours a day, all year. Our freshly cooked breakfasts are justly famous and suit practically every diet. Family run for 23 years, we wait to welcome you!

Villa Lodge

Friendliness and Cleanliness Guaranteed. Extremely comfortable accommodation in quiet peaceful area overlooking Windermere village – 2 mins walk from Rail station. All 7 bedrooms mostly en suite (some 4-posters) have colour TV, tea/coffee making facilities. Full central heating. Magnificent views of lake and mountains. Hearty English breakfast – special diets catered for. Excellent base for exploring the whole of the Lake District. Open all year. Safe private parking.

**John and Liz Christopherson
Villa Lodge, Cross Street,
Windermere, Cumbria LA23 1AE
Telephone and Fax:
015394 43318**

AA QQQ   English Tourist Board COMMENDED

WHITE LODGE HOTEL

Lake Road, Bowness-on-Windermere, Cumbria LA23 2JJ
Tel: Windermere (015394) 43624

☙ ☙ ☙
COMMENDED

'Welcome'
'Welkon'
'Willkommen'
'Bienvenido'
'Bienvenue'
'Benvenuti'

White Lodge Hotel, a Victorian country house, is situated on the road to the Lake and only a short walk from Bowness Bay. Its spacious rooms are all centrally heated and have their own private bathroom and colour television. Four posters and lake views on request. All have complimentary tea and coffee making facilities.
Membership to Lakeland's premier leisure club.
We are a small, friendly, family owned hotel with high standards and good home cooked cuisine. We serve a traditional full English breakfast.
In addition to our licensed residents dining room we also run a small coffee house 'Plants'.
The residents lounge has a colour television. We have our own car park.
Featured on TV holiday programme 'Wish you were here.'

Selected

GH ◙◙◙◙ **Woodlands** New Rd LA23 2EE (from railway station turn left through village, Woodlands about half a mile from station) ☎015394 43915

Closed telephone for details

Attractive floral displays outside this family-run hotel highlight it delightfully in the summer months. Located mid-way between Windermere and Bowness, it offers modern bedrooms which are prettily decorated in colourfully co-ordinated fabrics. There are a comfortable, spacious lounge, a smartly furnished dining room and a small bar. Good parking facilities are available for resident guests.

14 en suite (bth/shr) No smoking in 9 bedrooms No smoking in dining room CTV in all bedrooms Tea and coffee making facilities No dogs (ex guide dogs) Licensed Cen ht No children 5yrs 14P No coaches Last d 4pm

PRICE GUIDE

ROOMS: s £19-£27; d £38-£54; wkly b&b £126-£182; wkly hlf-bd £216-£268✱

CARDS: ◙ ◙ ◙ ◙ ◙

◙ ◙ *Oakthorpe Hotel* High St LA23 1HF ☎015394 43547

Closed 25 Dec-24 Jan

The good home-cooked meals served in the Lamplighter bar are a speciality of this Victorian hotel, and the adjoining restaurant also offers fixed-price and carte menus. Bedrooms are modest, but some have en suite facilities. The hotel is well placed for the village centre and for both railway and coach stations, and there is a small private car park.

16 rms (4 bth 3 shr) (3 fmly) CTV in all bedrooms Tea and coffee making facilities Cen ht 18P Fishing Last d 8.30pm

CARDS: ◙ ◙ ◙ ◙ ◙

WINDSOR Berkshire Map 04 SU97

GH ◙◙ **Clarence Hotel** 9 Clarence Rd SL4 5AE (from M4junct6 follow dual carrriageway to Windsor, turn left at 1st rdbt into Clarence Rd)

☎01753 864436 FAX 01753 857060

An attractive detached Victorian villa situated within walking distance of the town centre and castle. Professionally run, it continues to benefit from improvements, and although some of the bedrooms are compact, they are regularly upgraded and some are smartly decorated. There is a comfortable bar/lounge well stocked with draught lager, and limited car parking is available.

21 en suite (bth/shr) (6 fmly) CTV in all bedrooms Tea and coffee making facilities Licensed Cen ht CTV 4P Steam room

PRICE GUIDE

ROOMS: s £37-£39; d £45-£52

CARDS: ◙ ◙ ◙ ◙ ◙ ◙   £

Selected

GH ◙◙◙◙ **Melrose House** 53 Frances Rd SL4 3AQ ☎01753 865328 FAX 01753 865328

This elegant detached Victorian house, situated in a residential street within a short walk of the town centre, benefits from ample parking space to the rear of the building. Owners Mr and Mrs Mellor have moved back into their home and look after their guests personally. Bedrooms are brightly decorated and well equipped; downstairs there are a spacious breakfast room and cosy TV lounge, and Mrs Mellor has recently started producing supper trays.

9 en suite (bth/shr) (2 fmly) No smoking in 3 bedrooms No smoking in dining room CTV in all bedrooms Tea and coffee

making facilities Direct dial from bedrooms Cen ht CTV 10P No coaches

PRICE GUIDE

ROOMS: s £35-£40; d £45-£50✱

CARDS: ◙ ◙   £

GH ◙◙◙ *Netherton Hotel* 96 Leonards Rd SL4 5DA ☎01753 855508

This newly-converted Edwardian villa close to the town centre offers good-sized bedrooms which have been well decorated and furnished to offer simple and practical accommodation. Bathrooms are smart and modern, and there is car parking space at the rear of the building.

11 en suite (bth/shr) (5 fmly) CTV in all bedrooms Tea and coffee making facilities No dogs Cen ht CTV 9P

CARDS: ◙ ◙

WINSFORD Somerset Map 03 SS93

GH ◙◙◙ **Karslake House Hotel** Halse Ln TA24 7JE (leave A396 signposted Winsford into village turn left beyond village stores signed Tarr Steps continue around corner just beyond Royal Oak) ☎01643 851242 FAX 01643 851242

Closed Jan-mid Mar

This personally run "No Smoking" country hotel, situated in a delightful Exmoor village, with its own pretty garden dates from the 15th-century. The public areas are comfortable and include a quiet lounge and a small bar lounge in part of the dining room. Home cooking is a speciality and guests are offered a choice of interesting dishes. The bedrooms have been equipped with modern comforts and several are en-suite.

7 rms (4 bth/shr) (1 fmly) No smoking CTV in all bedrooms Tea and coffee making facilities Licensed Cen ht 8P No coaches Last d 6pm

PRICE GUIDE

ROOMS: s £25-£35.50; d £38-£59; wkly b&b £133-£206.50; wkly hlf-bd £220.50-£294

WINSTER Derbyshire Map 08 SK26

Selected

GH ◙◙◙◙ **The Dower House** Main St DE4 2DH (from A6 turn onto B5057 to Winster, The Dower House is large house at end of main street)

☎01629 650213 FAX 01629 650894

Mar-Oct

The Dower House, situated at the heart of this small historic village in the Derbyshire Peak National Park, is a fine Grade II Elizabethan country house, furnished in complete harmony with its period. The front door opens into a stone-flagged hallway and oak-floored sitting room complete with comfortable seating around a stone-lintelled open fire. Breakfasts are eaten en famille around a highly polished oak table; jams and preserves are all home-made. The bedrooms, two of which have private bathrooms, are very spacious and cosily decorated. Mrs Bastin is an expert on the history of the county and willingly provides information about the area.

3 rms (1 shr) No smoking in bedrooms No smoking in dining room CTV in all bedrooms Tea and coffee making facilities No dogs Cen ht No children 10yrs 4P No coaches

PRICE GUIDE

ROOMS: d £36-£55; wkly b&b £114-£173✱   £

WINTERBOURNE ABBAS Dorset Map **03** SY69

GH **QQQ** Churchview DT2 9LS (approach Winterbourne Abbas on A35, Church View is in centre of village opposite the church) ☎01305 889296

rs Nov-Feb

This delightful 17th century house is situated five miles west of Dorchester, and makes an ideal base for touring the beautiful local countryside. Michael and Jane Deller offer a warm welcome and are making continual improvements, the bedrooms have pretty co-ordinated decor and most have modern ensuite facilities. Jane prepares an interesting range of good home cooked evening meals which are served in the attractive dining room. There are two comfortable television lounges, one non-smoking.

9 rms (7 bth/shr) (1 fmly) No smoking in bedrooms No smoking in dining room No smoking in 1 lounge Tea and coffee making facilities Licensed Cen ht CTV No children 3yrs 10P No coaches Last d 7pm

PRICE GUIDE

ROOMS: s £18-£27; d £36-£48; wkly b&b £122-£155; wkly hlf-bd £210-£225

CARDS: ■■■

See advertisement under DORCHESTER

WINTERBOURNE STOKE Wiltshire Map **04** SU04

Selected

GH **QQQQ** Scotland Lodge SP3 4TF (on A303 0.25m W of village beyond turning to Berwick St James) ☎01980 620943 FAX 01980 620943

This family home is set in its own grounds and offers three tastefully furnished bedrooms. Breakfast is served around a large table in the dining room and there is a comfortable sitting room for guests. Jane Armfelt and John Singleton make guests very welcome.

3 en suite (bth/shr) (1 fmly) No smoking CTV in all bedrooms Tea and coffee making facilities No dogs (ex guide dogs) Cen ht 5P No coaches

PRICE GUIDE

ROOMS: s £25-£30; d £35-£45; wkly b&b £90-£120✱

WISBECH Cambridgeshire Map **05** TF40

♥ **QQQ** Mrs S M King Stratton *(TF495144)* West Drove North, Walton Highway PE14 7DP (leave A47 at Little Chef onto B198, then right into Walton Highway. After 1m turn left into West Drove North and continue for 0.5m) ☎01945 880162

Stratton Farm is located approximately four miles north-east of Wisbech in 22 acres of peaceful countryside. Mrs King is an enthusiastic and caring hostess who maintains high standards throughout the superior accommodation. The bedrooms (all non-smoking) are well appointed and comfortable, with a thoughtful range of extras and modern en suite bath or shower rooms. Tasty breakfasts, which are taken at a communal dining table, include home produced bacon, sausages, eggs and marmalades. Guests are welcome to use the heated outdoor swimming pool in season and to fish in a small lake which is stocked with carp.

3 en suite (bth/shr) No smoking CTV in all bedrooms Tea and coffee making facilities No dogs (ex guide dogs) Cen ht CTV No children 7yrs 6P outdoor swimming pool (heated) Fishing 22 acres beef

PRICE GUIDE

ROOMS: s £23; d £46; wkly b&b £144.90

WITHERIDGE Devon Map **03** SS81

Selected

♥ **QQQQ** Mrs A Webber Marchweeke *(SS797115)* Thelbridge EX16 8NY (on B3042 towards Thelbridge) ☎01884 860418

Feb-Nov

A delightful Devon longhouse, Marchweeke Farm is set in a peaceful position overlooking its own land and beautiful countryside. One bedroom is en suite, the other has sole use of a bathroom, and both are well equipped. A comfortable lounge offers views of the pretty garden, and home-cooked evening meals and hearty breakfasts are served in the spacious dining room.

2 rms (1 bth) No smoking Tea and coffee making facilities No dogs (ex guide dogs) Cen ht CTV No children 5yrs 2P Small snooker table 112 acres beef sheep cereal

PRICE GUIDE

ROOMS: d £32-£34; wkly b&b £108; wkly hlf-bd £154

■ **QQQ** Thelbridge Cross Thelbridge, Witheridge EX17 4SQ (2m W on the B3042) (Logis) ☎01884 860316 FAX 01884 860316

rs 25 & 26 Dec

Thelbridge Inn, recently renovated, welcomes guests to stay in freshly decorated, comfortable bedrooms. Log fires burn in lounge/bar areas where guests can select their meals either from an extensive menu or from the blackboard with its range of house specials.

8 en suite (bth/shr) (1 fmly) CTV in all bedrooms Tea and coffee making facilities No dogs (ex guide dogs) Cen ht 40P No coaches Last d 9pm

PRICE GUIDE

ROOMS: d £50-£60; wkly b&b £175; wkly hlf-bd fr £350✱ MEALS: Lunch £12-£25alc Dinner £12-£25alc✱

CARDS: ■■■

WITNEY Oxfordshire Map **04** SP30

GH **QQQ** The Close Witney Rd, Long Hanborough OX8 8HF ☎01993 882485 FAX 01993 883819

This detached 1920's pebble-dashed house, protected from the main road by a mature conifer hedge. The house has been extended on one side, providing a suite of purpose built bedrooms, attractively furnished in pine and with great facilities. The breakfast room is light and spacious, and overlooks the gardens to the rear. Dinner is not served, but there are plenty of local inns and restaurants.

3 annexe en suite (shr) (3 fmly) No smoking CTV in all bedrooms Tea and coffee making facilities Cen ht 8P No coaches

---

Factual details of establishments in this Guide are from questionnaires we send to all establishments that feature in the book.

GH 🔲🔲🔲 **Greystones Lodge Hotel** 34 Tower Hill OX8 5ES
☎01993 771898 FAX 01993 771898
Closed 24 Dec-1 Jan
Gradual improvements are being made to this large, friendly
house. Four of the bedrooms are now fully en suite, and all are
brightly decorated and well maintained. A popular set dinner is
provided for residents, served in the dining area overlooking the
outdoor yard and swimming pool.
12 en suite (shr) (1 fmly) No smoking in 4 bedrooms No
smoking in dining room CTV in all bedrooms Tea and coffee
making facilities Licensed Cen ht CTV 15P No coaches
Outdoor swimming pool (heated) Last d 8.30pm
PRICE GUIDE
ROOMS: s £25-£29.50; d £38.55-£44✶
CARDS: 🔲 🔲 🔲 🔲

GH 🔲🔲🔲 **Hawthorn House** 79 Burford Rd OX8 5DR (on
A4095 towards Burford, by Mobil garage) ☎01993 772768
3 en suite (bth/shr) (1 fmly) No smoking CTV in all bedrooms
Tea and coffee making facilities No dogs (ex guide dogs) Cen ht
4P No coaches
PRICE GUIDE
ROOMS: s £20-£22.50; d £40-£45; wkly b&b £120-£140
CARDS: 🔲 🔲 🔲

WIVELISCOMBE Somerset Map 03 ST02

Selected

GH 🔲🔲🔲🔲 **Alpine House** 10 West Rd TA4 2TF (on
B3227, opposite cricket ground, at western edge of
village) ☎01984 623526
Alpine House is the home of Indrani and Neville Hewitt, who
have recently totally upgraded the property. It is an imposing
Victorian house on the edge of Wiveliscombe, overlooking
the town's recreation ground with its tennis courts and open
air swimming pool. Bedrooms are individually furnished and
well equipped, and one is located on the ground floor. A
varied choice is offered at breakfast time, but dinner is
provided by special arrangement only. A set Sri Lankan meal
is the speciality of the house, and guests can bring their own
wine, though corkage is charged. From the terraced garden
there are spectacular views of the Brendon and Blackdown
Hills.
4 en suite (bth/shr) No smoking CTV in all bedrooms Tea
and coffee making facilities No dogs Cen ht No children
15yrs No parking No coaches
PRICE GUIDE
ROOMS: s £26.50-£27.50; d £48-£50; wkly b&b £157-£173
CARDS: 🔲 🔲 🔲

WIX Essex Map 05 TM12

Selected

✌ 🔲🔲🔲🔲 Mrs B Whitworth **Dairy House** *(TM148293)*
Bradfield Rd CO11 2SR (between Colchester and Harwich,
turn off A120 into Wix village. At crossroads take road
signposted Bradfield and farm is 1m on left)
☎01255 870322 FAX 01255 870186
Cake and a cup of tea await visitors on arrival at this large red
brick mid-Victorian house surrounded by 700 acres of arable
land. Bright bedrooms are particularly spacious - the addition
of en suite facilities, together with a new style of decor,

creating a comfortable setting. There is a small lounge, and
breakfast is served around a large oval mahogany table.
Dinner is provided by special arrangement only.
(1 fmly) No smoking in bedrooms No smoking in dining
room CTV in 2 bedrooms Tea and coffee making facilities
No dogs (ex guide dogs) Cen ht CTV 6P Games room Pool
table Croquet 700 acres arable fruit
PRICE GUIDE
ROOMS: s £21-£23; d £31-£33; wkly b&b £100-£107

✌ 🔲🔲🔲 Mrs H P Mitchell **New Farm House** *(TM165289)*
Spinnel's Ln CO11 2UJ (turn off A120 into Wix, at village
crossroads take Bradfield road, under A120 to top of hill turn
right guesthouse 200yds on left)
☎01255 870365 FAX 01255 870837
A modern farmhouse in a peaceful rural location with attractive
lawns and a children's play area. Bedrooms are all maintained to a
very high standard, regular improvements being made; rooms in
the ground-floor annexe all have private bathrooms and two are
equipped for disabled guests. Most rooms are reserved for non-
smokers. Run in a friendly but professional manner, the farmhouse
welcomes children - providing free baby-sitting - and can cater for
the partially disabled and those with special dietary requirements.
There are two lounges and a residential alcohol licence has now
been obtained. An evening meal is available if requested, and the
breakfast menu is translated into seven different languages!
6 rms (1 shr) 6 annexe en suite (shr) (5 fmly) No smoking in 10
bedrooms No smoking in dining room No smoking in 1 lounge
CTV in all bedrooms Tea and coffee making facilities Licensed
Cen ht CTV ch fac 20P Last d 5.30pm
PRICE GUIDE
ROOMS: s £20.50-£25; d £39-£44; wkly hlf-bd £213.15-£228.90
CARDS: 🔲 🔲 🔲 🔲

WOKING Surrey Map 04 TQ05

GH 🔲🔲🔲 **Glen Court** St Johns Hill Rd GU21 1RQ
☎01483 764154 FAX 01483 755737
An attractive Edwardian house set in over an acre of secluded,
well maintained mature woodland and garden. Bedrooms in the
main house are spacious and furnished in very comfortable style,
and those in the house next door are modern and well equipped. In
addition to the breakfast room which overlooks the rear garden, is
the separate, well appointed La Fuente Tapas Bar and Ristaurante
adjoining the hotel, which is now under separate management.
Service is very friendly and helpful, personally supervised by the
proprietor Zelda Lewes.
9 en suite (bth/shr) 3 annexe en suite (bth/shr) (2 fmly) CTV in
all bedrooms Tea and coffee making facilities Direct dial from
bedrooms Licensed Cen ht 29P No coaches Table tennis Last d
10.30pm
PRICE GUIDE
ROOMS: s £47; d £63.45✶
CARDS: 🔲 🔲 🔲

WOLVERHAMPTON West Midlands Map 07 SO99

GH 🔲🔲🔲 *Westdale Lodge* 144 Compton Rd WV3 9QB
☎01902 772399
10 rms (3 shr) (1 fmly) No smoking in dining room CTV in all
bedrooms Tea and coffee making facilities Licensed Cen ht
CTV No parking Last d 8pm
CARDS: 🔲 🔲

WOMENSWOLD Kent Map 05 TR25

GH 🅀🅀 **Woodpeckers Country Hotel** CT4 6HB (from Canterbury A2 to Dover, turn left at B2046 then 1st right) ☎01227 831319 FAX 01227 831319
rs 25-26 Dec
Woodpeckers, a large privately owned hotel, is located in a rural setting five miles from Canterbury. Local popularity means that the restaurant is generally busy, and the meals served here are supplemented by a full range of bar snacks. For entertainment there are a games room with pool table and - during the summer months - an outdoor heated swimming pool. Spacious, individually decorated bedrooms include a few which are readily adaptable to family use.
10 en suite (bth/shr) 1 annexe en suite (bth/shr) (4 fmly) No smoking in bedrooms No smoking in area of dining room CTV in all bedrooms Tea and coffee making facilities Licensed Ccn ht CTV ch fac 40P Outdoor swimming pool (heated) Adventure play area Last d 10pm
PRICE GUIDE
ROOMS: s fr £28; d fr £56; wkly b&b fr £175; wkly hlf-bd fr £224✱
CARDS: 🔳 🔳
See advertisement under CANTERBURY

WOODBRIDGE Suffolk Map 05 TM24

GH 🅀🅀 **Grove House** 39 Grove Rd IP12 4LG (on A12, 400yds beyond junct with B1079) ☎01394 382202
A modern bungalow is located on the northbound section of the A12 on the outskirts of town. Bedrooms are well maintained and adequately equipped, with rooms on the ground floor suitable for partially disabled guests. There is a lounge with an honesty bar, and small business parties and meetings can be accommodated. Reasonably priced evening meals can be served in the small breakfast room, cooked by the cheerful owner Mrs Kelly.
9 rms (5 shr) (1 fmly) No smoking in dining room CTV in all bedrooms Tea and coffee making facilities Licensed Cen ht CTV 12P No coaches Last d 6pm
PRICE GUIDE
ROOMS: s £19.50-£27.50; d £38-£44; wkly b&b £125-£175; wkly hlf-bd £185-£235✱
CARDS: 🔳 🔳 £

WOODFALLS Hampshire Map 04 SU12

Premier Selected

◀ 🅀🅀🅀🅀🅀 **Woodfalls**
The Ridge, Fordingbridge
SP5 2LN (on B3080)
☎01725 513222
FAX 01725 513220
A perfect "off the beaten track" stopping point between Salisbury and Southampton, this inn stands in a village on the northern edge of the New Forest. Bedrooms have been attractively decorated and provided with modern en suite facilities; some also have four-poster beds. Public rooms include bar areas which are full of character, a cosy lounge with an open fire and an intimate restaurant which offers an excellent range of good traditional dishes; there is also a conservatory where guests may choose to breakfast, and a picnic lunch can be provided.

---

10 en suite (bth/shr) (2 fmly) No smoking in 5 bedrooms No smoking in dining room No smoking in 1 lounge CTV in all bedrooms Tea and coffee making facilities Direct dial from bedrooms Cen ht CTV ch fac 30P Fishing Bike hire Last d 9.30pm
PRICE GUIDE
ROOMS: s £28-£42; d £50-£80; wkly b&b £175-£235; wkly hlf-bd £210-£325✱
MEALS: Lunch £9.95-£14.95 Dinner £12.95-£14.95&alc✱
CARDS: 🔳 🔳 £

WOODHALL SPA Lincolnshire Map 08 TF16

GH 🅀🅀 **Claremont** 9/11 Witham Rd LN10 6RW ☎01526 352000
A large detached late Victorian residence stands in the centre of this pretty and popular Spa town. A couple of the rooms are en suite and all are attractively furnished and homely. Mrs Brennan serves a tasty English breakfast with home made jams and marmalade in a cheerful room.
8 rms (2 shr) (1 fmly) No smoking in dining room CTV in all bedrooms Tea and coffee making facilities 4P No coaches
PRICE GUIDE
ROOMS: s £15-£20; d £30-£35✱ £

🔳🔳 **GH** 🅀🅀 **Pitchaway** The Broadway LN10 6SQ (follow B1192 toward Woodhall Spa then turn right onro B1191 Pitchaway is on right) ☎01526 352969
The enthusiastic new owner of this Victorian period guest house has brightened the decor of the bedrooms. The lounge features a stone fireplace and dinners are served on request.
7 rms (2 bth/shr) (2 fmly) No smoking in 3 bedrooms No smoking in dining room CTV in all bedrooms Tea and coffee making facilities No dogs (ex guide dogs) Cen ht CTV 8P Last d 8pm
PRICE GUIDE
ROOMS: s £16-£18; d £32-£36; wkly b&b £100; wkly hlf-bd £140 £

◀ 🅀🅀🅀 *Village Limits Motel* Stixwould Rd LN10 6UJ ☎01526 353312
Set in its own landscaped grounds beside a particularly quiet country lane, this collection of old farm cottages provides really modern, comfortable cottage rooms and fully tiled en suites in an brick and pan tile annexe to the rear. Home-cooked lunches and dinners are served in the dining room and drinks are available in the cosy bar.
8 annexe en suite (bth/shr) (1 fmly) No smoking in dining room CTV in all bedrooms Tea and coffee making facilities Cen ht 30P Last d 10pm
CARDS: 🔳 🔳

WOODSTOCK Oxfordshire Map 04 SP41

Selected

GH 🅀🅀🅀🅀 **The Laurels** Hensington Rd OX20 1JL (from A44 turn into Hensington Rd by the Punchbowl PH, The Laurels is approx 500yds on right opposite a small Catholic church)
☎01993 812583 FAX 01993 812583
Closed Xmas
The Laurels, a Victorian family house, is popular with both ➡

British and overseas visitors as an ideal touring centre. Bedrooms are freshly decorated and furnished in keeping with the house, retaining original features. A choice of dishes is offered at breakfast, and Nikki Lloyd is only too happy to recommend places to dine.

3 en suite (bth/shr) (1 fmly) No smoking CTV in all bedrooms Tea and coffee making facilities No dogs Cen ht No children 7yrs 3P No coaches

PRICE GUIDE
ROOMS: s £30-£40; d £40-£46✱
CARDS: £

GH ⓆⓆⓆ **The Ridings** 32 Banbury Rd OX20 1LQ (on entering Woodstock follow sign to Infromation Centre the take 4th turning left into Banbury Rd) ☎01993 811269
rs Dec-31 Mar

A 1930s detached house with stained-glass windows is situated on the outskirts of the town, edged by pasture and farmlands yet only a few minutes' walk from the centre and Palace Park. Three spacious, light and freshly decorated first-floor bedrooms overlook a large, colourful rear garden and enjoyable breakfasts are served around a communal table in the combined sitting/dining room..

3 rms (1 bth/shr) (1 fmly) No smoking CTV in all bedrooms Tea and coffee making facilities No dogs (ex guide dogs) Cen ht CTV 6P No coaches

PRICE GUIDE
ROOMS: s £20-£25; d £38-£42; wkly b&b £140

£

WOOL Dorset Map **03** SY88

GH ⓆⓆ *Fingle Bridge* Duck St BH20 6DE ☎01929 462739
Convenient for many of Dorset's beauty spots, this family house, alongside a stream, offers good value for money. Guests are very much en famille here, and there is a relaxed and cheery atmosphere about the house. Breakfast is served at a communal table.

3 rms (1 bth/shr) (1 fmly) No smoking CTV in all bedrooms Tea and coffee making facilities No dogs (ex guide dogs) Cen ht CTV 3P No coaches

---

WOOLACOMBE Devon Map **02** SS44

See also Mortehoe

GH ⓆⓆⓆ **Camberley Hotel** Beach Rd EX34 7AA (from A361 Barnstaple to Ilfracombe, turn left at Mullacott roundabout, after 3m establishment is on right) ☎01271 870231 FAX 01271 870231

The Camberley is a small family-run hotel located on the edge of town, commanding fine views across the valley to the sea. The totally en suite bedrooms offer good family accommodation, and there are a cosy bar with a darts board and a comfortable TV lounge.

6 en suite (bth/shr) (2 fmly) No smoking in dining room CTV in all bedrooms Tea and coffee making facilities Licensed Cen ht CTV 6P No coaches Guest have use of nearby heated swimming pool Last d 5.30pm

PRICE GUIDE
ROOMS: s fr £16; d £32-£42✱
CARDS:

GH ⓆⓆⓆ *The Castle* The Esplanade EX34 7DJ ☎01271 870788
Apr-Oct

Built by a Colonel Pickering as his summer retreat, this Victorian folly dates from 1897. Its walls are crenellated in true castle style and the building commands stunning views over Woolacombe Sands. The lounge features a carved cedar wood ceiling and

---

dramatic brass wall panels. Bedrooms are comfortable, and guests are assured of relaxed and friendly service.

8 en suite (shr) (2 fmly) No smoking in dining room CTV in all bedrooms Tea and coffee making facilities No dogs (ex guide dogs) Licensed Cen ht CTV No children 5yrs 8P No coaches Last d 6pm

---

GH ⓆⓆⓆ **Holmesdale Hotel** Bay View Rd EX34 7DQ ☎01271 870335 FAX 01271 870088
Closed Feb

The Oyarzabal family run a welcoming guest house centred around the Gema Restaurant. Carlos Oyarzabal, a professional chef, offers an extensive menu featuring many Spanish and Basque specialities including not only the predictable paella but also such dishes as saddle of lamb with garlic, sherry, artichokes and pimentos. The bedrooms are bright and airy and each room has its own bathroom, either en suite or adjacent to the room.

15 en suite (shr) (10 fmly) No smoking in bedrooms No smoking in dining room No smoking in 1 lounge CTV in all bedrooms Tea and coffee making facilities Licensed Cen ht CTV 14P Last d 8.30pm

PRICE GUIDE
ROOMS: s £18-£20; d £36-£40✱
CARDS: £

WOOLHOPE Hereford & Worcester Map **03** SO63

◾ ⓆⓆⓆ **Butchers Arms** HR1 4RF (from the village of Fownhope on the B4224, turn towards Woolhope, inn is approx 3m on right hand side) ☎01432 860281

This half-timbered building dating back to the 14th century lies on the Ross-on-Wye side of the village. Its rooms are modestly furnished but provide a good range of facilities. The inn has a good reputation for its food, which is served in the informal atmosphere of the bar.

3 rms CTV in all bedrooms Tea and coffee making facilities Direct dial from bedrooms No dogs (ex guide dogs) Cen ht 80P No coaches Last d 9.30pm

---

WOOLSTONE Oxfordshire Map **04** SU28

Selected

◾ ⓆⓆⓆⓆ **The White Horse** SN7 7QL ☎01367 820566 & 820726 FAX 01367 7820566

Warm and charming, a delightful picture-book village pub dating from the sixteenth century holds special appeal for visitors to this attractive area. Comfortable and immaculate en suite bedrooms are equipped with remote control TV, 'phones, radios and tea/coffee making facilities, while the spacious bar offers good service and an extensive menu of well cooked dishes. Just minutes away are a wealth of places to explore - Kingston Lyle House Park and Gardens, The Wayland Smithy and the famous White Horse Hill, to name but a few.

6 annexe en suite (bth/shr) No smoking in 2 bedrooms No smoking in area of dining room CTV in all bedrooms Tea and coffee making facilities Direct dial from bedrooms No dogs (ex guide dogs) Cen ht 60P Last d 10pm

PRICE GUIDE
ROOMS: s £35-£40; d £50-£60; wkly b&b £175-£210; wkly hlf-bd £287-£322✱
MEALS: Lunch £9.96-£15.95&alc✱
CARDS: £

WORCESTER Hereford & Worcester Map **03** SO85

GH Q Q *Wyatt* 40 Barbourne Rd WR1 1HU (im N on A38)
☎01905 26311
Modern, well equipped accommodation is provided at this small,
personally run guest house situated in a terraced row just north of
the city centre. A ground-floor bedroom and several family rooms
are available. There are also a comfortable lounge and a dining
room with separate tables.
8 rms (4 shr) (4 fmly) No smoking in dining room CTV in all
bedrooms Tea and coffee making facilities Cen ht CTV No
parking Last d 5pm
CARDS: 🔲 🔳

WORKINGTON Cumbria Map **11** NX92

GH Q Q Q **Morven Hotel** Siddick Rd CA14 1LE (on A596)
☎01900 602118 & 602002
The Morven is a large Victorian house offering a good all round
standard of accommodation and service. Bedrooms are modern
and well equipped and there are two lounges, one of which is no
smoking.
6 rms (4 bth) (1 fmly) No smoking in dining room No smoking
in 1 lounge CTV in all bedrooms Tea and coffee making facilities
Licensed Cen ht CTV 20P No coaches Last d 4pm
PRICE GUIDE
ROOMS: s £20-£29; d £34-£46; wkly b&b fr £120; wkly hlf-bd
fr £175

WORSTEAD Norfolk Map **09** TG32

GH Q Q Q **Hall Farm** Sloley Rd NR28 9RS (take B1150
signed to North Walsham and take first turn to Worstead. At
crossroads in village, turn right past post office and follow
road for 0.74m) ☎01692 536124
2 rms (1 bth) (1 fmly) No smoking CTV in 1 bedroom Tea and
coffee making facilities No dogs Cen ht CTV 4P No coaches
Reduced rates for guests at the Oasis Leisure Club
PRICE GUIDE
ROOMS: s fr £18; d fr £36; wkly b&b fr £105; wkly hlf-bd fr
£140✱

WORTHING West Sussex Map **04** TQ10

Selected

GH Q Q Q Q **Aspen House** 13 Winchester Rd BN11 4DJ
(from pier travel west along sea front for about half a
mile, turn right into Heene Rd 3rd on right is Winchester
Rd) ☎01903 230584
Closed 21 Dec-5 Jan
An elegant Edwardian house dating back to 1902 but
modernised to a high standard offers particularly bright and
comfortable bedrooms, all individually furnished and
equipped with a good range of extras. Breakfast is taken in the
lounge/dining room, and there are a wide variety of
restaurants within walking distance for dinner; both town
centre and seafront are also just a short walk away. Extra car
parking is now being provided on the forecourt.
3 en suite (bth/shr) No smoking in dining room No smoking
in lounges CTV in all bedrooms Tea and coffee making
facilities No dogs Cen ht No children 13yrs 3P No coaches
PRICE GUIDE
ROOMS: s £22-£23; d £44-£46; wkly b&b
£140-£155✱

GH ⓆⒶⒶ **Blair House** 11 St Georges Rd BN11 2DS (half a mile E of town centre on A259) ☎01903 234071
A long-established, family-run guesthouse is located near the seafront and town centre. There is a good choice of attractive bedrooms, most with private bathrooms and all having TV and tea trays. There is a comfortable lounge with a bar, and service is personally supervised by Mrs Grace Taylor. Chef/proprietor Malcolm Taylor provides a good choice of dishes which are served at separate tables in the dining room. Car parking is generally available at the roadside.
7 en suite (bth/shr) No smoking in dining room CTV in all bedrooms Tea and coffee making facilities No dogs (ex guide dogs) Licensed Cen ht 4P Last d 4.30pm
PRICE GUIDE
ROOMS: s £19.50-£25; d £35-£44; wkly b&b £130-£150; wkly hlf-bd £189.50-£205
CARDS: 🅰 🈺 £

GH ⒶⒶⒶⒶ **Delmar Hotel** 1-2 New Pde BN11 2BQ (off A259 adjoining Aquarena Swimming Pool) ☎01903 211834 FAX 01903 219052
A perfect location facing the sea close to the theatres and shops this delightful small private hotel is home to Norman and Jenny Elms, who provide a very friendly and relaxing atmosphere for their gusts to enjoy. The accommodation is very homely and bedrooms have been well equipped with TV and video, hair dryer, self dial telephone, radio, mini bar and tea tray. There is a very comfortable traditional front facing lounge and double sided dining room, which features a daily menu and home cooking using fresh quality ingredients and all meals served by uniformed staff. There are two car parks, and a furnished roof terrace with an aviary.
13 en suite (bth/shr) (4 fmly) No smoking in bedrooms No smoking in dining room No smoking in 1 lounge CTV in all bedrooms Tea and coffee making facilities Direct dial from bedrooms No dogs (ex guide dogs) Licensed Cen ht CTV 6P Roof garden & sun deck Last d noon
PRICE GUIDE
ROOMS: s £23-£28; d £46-£52.50; wkly b&b £144.90-£170.45; wkly hlf-bd £267.75-£270.90
CARDS: 🅰 🈺 🈺 🔘 🈺 🈺 🈺 £

GH ⒶⒶⒶⒶ **Moorings** 4 Selden Rd BN11 2LL (on A259 towards Brighton, pass indoor swimming pool on right and hotel opposite garage) ☎01903 208882 & 236878
Close to the seafront and within walking distance of the town centre, this cosy Victorian villa with a friendly, welcoming atmosphere offers accommodation in bedrooms which have been individually furnished and equipped to a high standard, each having self-dial telephone, TV and tea tray; the small first-floor lounge has a mini bar and there is a very attractive and well appointed dining room. Guests requiring dinner are asked to make their choice from the interesting daily three-course menu (which could well include locally caught fish) during the course of the morning as everything is freshly home-cooked. A good selection of house wine is also available. On-street car parking is unrestricted.
9 en suite (bth/shr) (3 fmly) CTV in all bedrooms Tea and

coffee making facilities Direct dial from bedrooms Licensed Cen ht 3P Last d 6.30pm
PRICE GUIDE
ROOMS: s £18-£23; d £37-£44; wkly b&b £186-£224; wkly hlf-bd £196-£231
CARDS: 🅰 🈺 🈺 £

GH ⒶⒶ **Wolsey Hotel** 179-181 Brighton Rd BN11 2EX (on A259, facing sea, three quarters of a mile E of town Centre) ☎01903 236149 & 234255
Closed Xmas/New Year
This long-established family-run guesthouse is ideally located on the seafront, convenient for all local leisure facilities and town centre shopping precincts. Run by proprietor Mrs Brenda Price for over 30 years, many reguular guests return to enjoy reliable and consistent standards of comfort and cooking. All bedrooms have satellite TV, radio and tea trays, and some rooms have en suite showers. There is a comfortable lounge, residents' bar and an attractive dining room.
13 rms (5 bth/shr) (2 fmly) CTV in all bedrooms Tea and coffee making facilities Licensed Cen ht CTV No parking Last d 10am
PRICE GUIDE
ROOMS: s £19.50-£27.50; d £39-£55; wkly b&b £130-£182.50; wkly hlf-bd £182.50-£235✻
CARDS: 🅰 🈺 🈺 £

GH ⒶⒶⒶ **Woodlands** 20-22 Warwick Gardens BN11 1PF (from A27/A24 follow town centre signs after railway bridge at 3rd rdbt take 1st exit, take 1st left after Safeways then turn right into Warwick Gdns) ☎01903 233557
Woodlands is located in an Edwardian conservation area, a few minutes from the town centre and seafront. There are bright bedrooms with modern furnishings and a comfortable lounge for guests' use. A freshly prepared set four-course evening meal is served every day, and the breads, desserts, pies and preserves are all home made. Vegetarian dishes are also available.
11 rms (6 bth/shr) (3 fmly) No smoking in 6 bedrooms No smoking in dining room CTV in all bedrooms Tea and coffee making facilities Licensed Cen ht CTV 8P No coaches Last d 6pm
PRICE GUIDE
ROOMS: s £17-£20.50; d £34-£46; wkly b&b £119-£158; wkly hlf-bd £159-£210
CARDS: 🅰 🈺 🈺 🈺 £

WROTHAM Kent Map 05 TQ65

◀ ⒶⒶⒶ **The Bull Hotel** Bull Ln TN15 7RF (off A20) ☎01732 885522 FAX 01732 886288
A 14th-century former coaching inn situated in the centre of the village, the Bull is full of character, with oak beams in the restaurant and bar and a feature inglenook fireplace. Chef Peter Drenowski offers a range of freshly prepared bar food as well as meals in the more formal surroundings of the à la carte restaurant, which also has a good-value fixed-price menu. Bedrooms are sympathetically furnished and well equipped, and there is a function and meeting room which can hold up to 65 people.
10 rms (6 bth/shr) (1 fmly) CTV in all bedrooms Tea and coffee making facilities Direct dial from bedrooms Cen ht 50P Last d 10pm
PRICE GUIDE
ROOMS: s £35-£40; d £45-£50✻
MEALS: Lunch £12.50&alc Dinner £12.50&alc✻
CARDS: 🅰 🈺 🈺 🔘 🈺 🈺 £

WYBUNBURY Cheshire Map **07** SJ64

💙 Q Q Mrs Jean E Callwood **Lea** *(SJ717489)* Wrinehill Rd CW5 7NS (A500 towards Nantwich over 2 rdbts over split railway bridge take 1st road on left to t-junction, turn left 2nd farm on right) ☎01270 841429

Peacocks roam in the attractive gardens which surround this large house situated on a dairy farm between Wybunbury village and Wrinehill. Three bedrooms (two of them suitable for family occupation) are furnished in a mixture of styles, a large modern bathroom serving the only one that does not have en suite facilities. The spacious lounge contains a small snooker table, and an evening meal can be provided, by prior arrangement, round the single table of a traditionally furnished breakfast room overlooking the garden.

3 rms (2 shr) (1 fmly) No smoking in bedrooms No smoking in area of dining room CTV in all bedrooms Tea and coffee making facilities CTV 24P Fishing Pool table 150 acres dairy Last d 5pm

PRICE GUIDE

ROOMS: s fr £18; d fr £29; wkly b&b fr £100; wkly hlf-bd fr £150*

(£)

WYLAM Northumberland Map **12** NZ16

GH Q Q Q **Laburnum House** Main Rd NE41 8AJ (drive downhill beyond church turn left Laburnam House on right) ☎01661 852185

A highly acclaimed restaurant situated in the village of Wylam, six miles west of Newcastle, offers four roomy modern bedrooms, all of which have en suite facilities. There is no lounge, but a cosy cocktail bar adjoins the comfortable and attractively appointed dining room in which both fixed-price and à la carte meals are served.

4 en suite (bth/shr) (1 fmly) CTV in all bedrooms Tea and coffee making facilities Licensed Cen ht 3P No coaches Last d 10pm

PRICE GUIDE

ROOMS: s £30-£40; d £40-£50

CARDS: 🔳 ■ ▩ (£)

YARNTON Oxfordshire Map **04** SP41

GH Q Q Q **Eltham Villa** 148 Woodstock Rd OX5 1PW (on A44) ☎01865 376037 FAX 01865 376037

An attractive cottage set in its own gardens on the A44 midway between Oxford and Woodstock. The owner Mrs Willoughby takes great care to ensure that high standards of housekeeping are maintained throughout. Comfortable bedrooms are named after local rivers and are all well equipped. Breakfast is served in a pine-furnished breakfast room, where set evening meals are available by prior arrangement.

7 en suite (bth/shr) (2 fmly) No smoking in bedrooms No smoking in dining room CTV in all bedrooms Tea and coffee making facilities Direct dial from bedrooms No dogs Cen ht CTV 7P No coaches Last d 10am

See advertisement under WOODSTOCK

YATTON Avon Map **03** ST46

◀ Q Q **Prince of Orange** High St BS19 4JD (on B3133) ☎01934 832193

Situated in Yatton's busy High Street, only five miles from the city of Bristol, this hospitable olde worlde pub offers accommodation in eight bedrooms - five of them in a purpose-built ground-floor extension at the rear of the building. An extensive menu of meals is served by friendly staff in the warm, welcoming bar areas, and new managers are embarking on an extensive refurbishment plan.

8 rms (5 shr) No smoking in bedrooms CTV in 7 bedrooms Tea and coffee making facilities No dogs (ex guide dogs) Cen ht 40P Skittle alley Pool table Last d 9pm

CARDS: 🔳 ▩

YEALAND CONYERS Lancashire Map **07** SD57

Selected

GH Q Q Q Q **The Bower** LA5 9SF (follow A6 towards Milnthorpe for 0.75m, after passing under narrow bridge, take next left and bear left at end) ☎01524 734585

This delightful Georgian country house is set in pretty and mature grounds. It was built as a farmhouse in 1745, and a family home until recently, when it was bought by the Rothwells. They have converted it into a very comfortable guest house, with just two rooms, one with a modern en-suite shower room and the other with private facilities. The lounge is elegantly furnished, and guests dine communally in the dining room. Bridge players are especially welcome! It is a no smoking house.

2 en suite (bth/shr) (1 fmly) No smoking CTV in all bedrooms Tea and coffee making facilities No dogs (ex guide dogs) Cen ht CTV No children 12yrs 6P No coaches Croquet lawn Last d noon

PRICE GUIDE

ROOMS: s £30.50-£35.50; d £46-£56; wkly b&b £145-£175; wkly hlf-bd £250-£280

(£)

DELMAR HOTEL

1/2 New Parade, Worthing
West Sussex BN11 2BQ
Tel: (01903) 211834 Fax: (01903) 219052

Licensed family hotel in quiet location overlooking sea and gardens, convenient for all local amenities. Bedrooms have colour TV/video, telephone/radio, tea making facilities/mini bar, hair dryer/iron. En suite facilities, sun balconies, ground floor rooms and four poster beds. Lounge/bar, 40 channel TV. Roof garden and conservatory. Car parking. Full central heating. Open all year.

YELVERTON Devon Map 02 SX56

GH Q Q Q **Harrabeer Country House Hotel** Harrowbeer Ln
PL20 6EA (at roundabout stay on A386, after 200yds turn right
into Grange rd, at bottom of hill turn right to hotel)
☎01822 853302
Closed 22-31 Dec
Mr and Mrs Back welcome guests to their home which stands on a
quiet, winding country lane (request directions when booking).
Public areas are cosy, with blazing log fires to keep the nip out of
the air. In the dining room, Patsy Back serves wholesome and
enjoyable home cooked food, with a small choice of starter and
dessert and a set main course (though she is always flexible).
Bedrooms are well presented, with good-quality, comfortable beds
and a good range of facilities.
7 rms (4 bth/shr) (1 fmly) No smoking in 2 bedrooms No
smoking in dining room CTV in all bedrooms Tea and coffee
making facilities Direct dial from bedrooms Licensed Cen ht
CTV 6P No coaches Last d 7.30pm
PRICE GUIDE
ROOMS: s £20-£22; d £44-£53; wkly b&b £126-£154; wkly hlf-
bd £196-£234.50
CARDS: 🔴 🔲 🔲 🔲   £
See advertisement under PLYMOUTH

♥ Q Q Q Mrs B Cole **Greenwell** (SX536659) Meavy
PL20 6PY (from Yelverton rbt take A386 signed Plymouth,
then immediately left , signed Cadover Bridge and in 2m over
cattle grid, farm lane in 100yds)
☎01822 853563 FAX 01822 853563
Closed Xmas
Greenwell Farm is situated two miles from Yelverton on the
Cadover Bridge road on the edge of Dartmoor and has parts dating
from the 15th century. The bedrooms are attractively coordinated
and there are books and games for children on the landing.
Traditional farmhouse cooking is provided and a set menu is
served by arrangement only.
3 en suite (bth/shr) (1 fmly) No smoking in bedrooms CTV in 2
bedrooms Tea and coffee making facilities No dogs Licensed
Cen ht CTV 10P Stabling for guests horses Clay shooting 220
acres beef sheep Last d 4pm
PRICE GUIDE
ROOMS: d £38-£44; wkly b&b £130-£140; wkly hlf-bd £195-
£210
                                                                £

YEOVIL Somerset Map 03 ST51

See also Cary Fitzpaine, Crewkerne & Halstock

Premier Selected

GH Q Q Q Q Q **Holywell**
House Holywell, East Coker
BA22 9NQ (leave Yeovil on
A30 Crewkerne road, turn
left in 2m past Yeovil Court
Hotel signed East Coker,
continue down lane Holywell
House is on right).
☎01935 862612
FAX 01935 863035
Closed Xmas & New Year
This charming 18th-century Hamstone house stands in three
acres of delightful gardens which include spring and autumn
flower beds, an interesting water garden and a herb garden

which supplies the kitchen. Bedrooms are individually designed
- the Masters Suite, for example, has fine antique furniture and
a fitted panelled bathroom - but all are very well equipped. An
imaginative dinner is served in the elegantly furnished dining
room; this might include green-lipped mussels with pesto,
guinea fowl marinated in red wine and juniper berries and a
home-made pudding such as steamed syrup sponge. Sherry is
taken before dinner in the drawing room and guests are invited
to retire here after the meal for coffee and mints.
3 en suite (bth/shr) (1 fmly) No smoking in bedrooms No
smoking in dining room No smoking in lounges CTV in all
bedrooms Tea and coffee making facilities No dogs (ex
guide dogs) Cen ht ch fac 12P No coaches Tennis (hard)
Croquet Garden games Last d 24hrs prior
PRICE GUIDE
ROOMS: s £35-£45; d £60-£70; wkly b&b £220-£250;
wkly hlf-bd £350-£400✱
                                                                £

♥ Q Q Q Mrs M Tucker **Carents** (ST546188) Yeovil Marsh
BA21 3QE 2m N of Yeovil off A37 Half a mile into village on
left) ☎01935 76622
Feb-Nov
Only two miles from the centre of Yeovil, this beautiful Somerset
farmhouse enjoys a peaceful location. Most of the house dates
from the 17th century, but there is evidence of an earlier building.
A sitting room is provided for guests, with deep easy chairs and a
superb fireplace, and tasty breakfasts served at a communal table
in the attractive breakfast room. Bedrooms are furnished to
provide adequate standards of comfort.
3 rms No smoking in bedrooms Tea and coffee making facilities
No dogs CTV 6P 350 acres arable beef
PRICE GUIDE
ROOMS: s £15-£16; d £30-£32✱

◀ Q Q Q **The Half Moon** Main St, Mudford BA21 5TF (leave
A303 at Sparkford, onto A359 continus for approx 4 miles)
(MIN) ☎01935 850289 FAX 01935 850842
Situated three miles north of the town, this 17th-century inn offers
two bar areas and two no-smoking restaurant areas. The well
organised ground-floor bedrooms are located at the side of the inn,
and each has its own front door.
11 annexe en suite (bth/shr) No smoking in 6 bedrooms No
smoking in dining room CTV in all bedrooms Tea and coffee
making facilities Direct dial from bedrooms Cen ht 40P Last d
9.30pm
CARDS: 🔴 🔲 🔲 🔲

YORK North Yorkshire Map 08 SE65

See also Acaster Malbis, Copmanthorpe & Rufforth

GH Q Q Q **Abbeyfields** 19 Bootham Ter YO3 7DH (3rd
turning on left of A19 from city walls) ☎01904 636471
This beautiful Georgian house situated in the High Street is owned
and run by Erik and Karen Michel. They first met at design school
in France, and the decor is tasteful and attractive. The short but
interesting menu changes regularly and displays Erik's skill with
flavours together with his love of colour, featured in such dishes
as langoustine tails nestling on a bed of red cabbage with a
coriander sauce, or succulent monkfish tails with a red wine sauce
and cheese-flavoured hollandaise. Prices are fairly high, but offset
by the quality of the cooking. An inviting, reasonably priced wine
list includes some New World labels.
9 rms (8 shr) No smoking CTV in all bedrooms Tea and coffee
making facilities No dogs Cen ht No children 6P No coaches
PRICE GUIDE
ROOMS: s £16 £26; d £36-£44✱

GH QQQ **Acorn** 1 Southlands Rd, Bishopthorpe Rd
YO2 1NP (follow A1036 into City Centre and in .6m turn right
into Scarcroft Rd then right again into Scott St)
☎01904 620081 FAX 01904 613331
The Acorn Guest House, a late 19th-century property about ten
minutes' walk from the city centre, provides accommodation in
pleasantly decorated bedrooms with good facilities which now
include telephones as well as colour TVs. There are also an
attractive small dining room and a cosy lounge.
6 rms (3 shr) (3 fmly) CTV in all bedrooms Tea and coffee
making facilities Direct dial from bedrooms No dogs Cen ht
CTV Last d 10am
PRICE GUIDE
ROOMS: s £13-£18.50; d £26-£35✱
CARDS: £

GH QQQ *Adams House Hotel* 5 Main Street, Fulford
YO1 4HJ ☎01904 655413
A Tudor-style house on the A19 to the south of the city, this
establishment offers a good standard of accommodation and
service. The bedrooms are well equipped and comfortable, and a
large dining room is provided.
7 rms (2 bth 4 shr) (2 fmly) No smoking in dining room CTV in
all bedrooms Tea and coffee making facilities Licensed Cen ht
8P No coaches Last d 6.30pm

GH QQQ **Alcuin Lodge** 15 Sycamore Place, Bootham
YO3 7DW (behind Museum Gardens) ☎01904 632222
Closed 1-9 Nov & 11-31 Jan
Situated in a quiet cul-de-sac and only a short walk from the city
centre, this attractive Edwardian house has been carefully
furnished and decorated throughout and provides a good standard
of both service and accommodation. This is a no smoking house.
5 rms (4 shr) (1 fmly) No smoking CTV in all bedrooms Tea
and coffee making facilities No dogs (ex guide dogs) Cen ht No
children 8yrs 2P No coaches
PRICE GUIDE
ROOMS: d £30-£45
CARDS: £

GH QQQ **Alfreda** 61 Heslington Ln, Fulford YO1 4HN
(approach city centre from A19 and at 1st traffic lights turn
right for house 200yds on left) ☎01904 631698
A large Edwardian house set in its own grounds, the Afreda Guest
House is pleasantly furnished and decorated throughout. It is
situated south of the city, close to the university and the Fulford
Golf Course. Bedrooms are spacious and offer good facilities.
Meals are taken around a large communal table in an attractive
dining room featuring an impressive antique dresser.
10 rms (8 bth/shr) (4 fmly) No smoking in dining room CTV in
all bedrooms Tea and coffee making facilities Direct dial from
bedrooms Cen ht CTV 22P No coaches Play area
PRICE GUIDE
ROOMS: s £20-£35; d £35-£50; wkly b&b £125-£175
CARDS: £

GH QQQ *Ambleside* 62 Bootham Crescent YO3 7AH
☎01904 637165
Closed Jan
A friendly guest house with good standards a short walk from the
city walls. The lounge is comfortable with an attractive fireplace
and television with Sky channels and video. Bedrooms are fresh
and vary in size.
8 rms (6 shr) (1 fmly) No smoking CTV in all bedrooms Tea
and coffee making facilities No dogs Cen ht CTV No children
9yrs No parking No coaches

Premier Selected

GH Q Q Q Q Q **Arndale Hotel** 290 Tadcaster Rd YO2 2ET (turn off A64 on to A1036 towards city centre for 2m, on left overlooking racecourse) ☎01904 702424

Closed Xmas & New Year

David & Gillian Reynard are the proud and very friendly owners of this elegantly furnished house which stands opposite the racecourse and within its own well cared for gardens. The house has a delightful lounge where guests can relax whilst the bedrooms are furnished with many antiques and some have four poster beds and whirlpool baths. Dried and fresh flowers are in abundance and many thoughtful extras have been sited in the bedrooms. An excellent breakfast is provide with plenty of choice being available. Car parking is found through the arch to the rear of the hotel.

10 en suite (bth/shr) (1 fmly) No smoking in dining room CTV in all bedrooms Tea and coffee making facilities No dogs (ex guide dogs) Licensed Cen ht No children 5yrs 20P No coaches

PRICE GUIDE

ROOMS: s £35-£49; d £39-£59; wkly b&b £129.50-£168 (£)

GH Q Q **Arnot House** 17 Grosvenor Ter, Bootham YO3 7AG (from Bootham Bar drive along Bootham the A19 towards Thirsk, Grosvenor terrace is second on right) ☎01904 641966

Closed 20 Dec-Jan

Situated on a quiet side road, within easy walking distance of the city centre, Arnot House offers a warm, friendly welcome. Pleasantly decorated bedrooms are well equipped and stocked with a good selection of books; the wide choice of dishes available for breakfast includes kippers and poached haddock.

4 rms (2 shr) (1 fmly) No smoking CTV in all bedrooms Tea and coffee making facilities No dogs Licensed Cen ht No children 5yrs 2P No coaches Last d 4pm

PRICE GUIDE

ROOMS: s £18; d £36

GH Q Q Q **Ascot House** 80 East Pde, Heworth YO3 7YH (take A1079 into city and at traffic lights turn right into Melrose Gate and at next lights turn left) ☎01904 426826 FAX 01904 431077

A delightful feature of this large Victorian house is the pine staircase and the rare oriel stained glass window on the half landing. The house offers several bedrooms with four-poster beds, and all rooms have colour television and tea trays. The house has a comfortable lounge and is located in a residential area only a short walk from the city centre. There is a private car park.

15 rms (5 bth 7 shr) (3 fmly) No smoking in dining room CTV in all bedrooms Tea and coffee making facilities Licensed Cen ht CTV 14P Sauna

PRICE GUIDE

ROOMS: s £18-£20; d £36-£40; wkly b&b £125-£140

CARDS: 🔲 🔲 (£)

Selected

GH Q Q Q Q **Ashbourne House** 139 Fulford Rd YO1 4HG (on A19) ☎01904 639912 FAX 01904 631332

Aileen and David Minns are the enthusiastic owners of this beautifully furnished small hotel. The bedrooms are well equipped and public areas include a cosy lounge and an attractive dining room where carefully produced home cooking is served.

6 en suite (bth/shr) (1 fmly) No smoking in 3 bedrooms No smoking in dining room No smoking in lounges CTV in all bedrooms Tea and coffee making facilities Direct dial from bedrooms Licensed Cen ht CTV 6P No coaches Last d 6pm

PRICE GUIDE

ROOMS: s £34-£38; d £40-£50; wkly b&b £140-£175.20; wkly hlf-bd £245-£280✳

CARDS: 🔲 🔲 🔲 🔲 🔲

Selected

GH Q Q Q Q **Ashbury Hotel** 103 The Mount YO2 2AX (from A64 take A1036 signposted 'York West') ☎01904 647339

Closed Xmas & January

This very well cared for Victorian house is situated close to the racecourse and is only a short walk from the city centre. Bright, fresh and well equipped bedrooms are provided whilst guests have the use a most delightfully comfortable and inviting lounge. Warm and friendly service is provided by the resident owners Len & Stella Pickles who are always on hand to ensure that their guests are well cared for.

5 en suite (shr) No smoking in 3 bedrooms No smoking in dining room CTV in all bedrooms Tea and coffee making facilities No dogs Licensed Cen ht CTV No parking

PRICE GUIDE

ROOMS: s £30-£40; d £45-£55; wkly b&b £157.50-£175 (£)

See advertisement on p.469.

GH Q Q Q **Barclay Lodge** 19/21 Gillygate YO3 7EA (Gillygate is part of the Inner Ring Rd closest to the Minster entrance to the city) ☎01904 633274

An attractive Georgian town house, retaining much of its original character, is situated close to the Minster and only a short walk from York's many other attractions. Some of the attractive, cosy bedrooms have their original fireplaces and, although only two have en suite facilities, there are modern bathrooms close to all the other rooms. The pretty dining room has individual tables and there is also a comfortable guest lounge.

10 rms (2 bth/shr) (3 fmly) No smoking in dining room CTV in all bedrooms Tea and coffee making facilities No dogs (ex guide dogs) Licensed Cen ht CTV No parking No coaches

PRICE GUIDE

ROOMS: s fr £20; d fr £38✳

CARDS: 🔲 🔲 🔲 (£)

See advertisement on p.469.

GH Q Q Q **The Beckett** 58 Bootham Crescent YO3 7AH (take A19 past traffic lights at Clifton) ☎01904 644728

A terraced house is situated in a residential road at Bootham just a few minutes' walk from the city centre. The attractively decorated bedrooms have many modern features and most have en suite

➡

facilities. There is a comfortable guest lounge and also a small breakfast room at the rear.

7 rms (5 shr) (2 fmly) No smoking in 2 bedrooms No smoking in dining room CTV in all bedrooms Tea and coffee making facilities No dogs (ex guide dogs) Cen ht CTV 3P

PRICE GUIDE

ROOMS: s £16-£17; d £34-£38; wkly b&b £119-£126✱

GH 🇶🇶🇶 **Bedford** 108/110 Bootham YO3 7DG (a few hundred yards N of the Minster) ☎01904 624412

In this private hotel a short walk from the railway museum and the city centre, everything is kept in good order. Bedrooms are fresh and light and the lounge has local information, Sky channels, a video of the Minster fire, and a bar. Guests can have dinner by arrangement.

14 en suite (bth/shr) (3 fmly) No smoking in dining room CTV in all bedrooms Tea and coffee making facilities No dogs (ex guide dogs) Licensed Cen ht CTV 14P No coaches

PRICE GUIDE

ROOMS: s £28-£34; d £40-£50

CARDS: 🔳 🔳

GH 🇶🇶🇶 **Beech House** 6-7 Longfield Terrace, Bootham YO3 7DJ (from A19 follow City Centre signs and in 1.5m under pedestrian flyover and take 2nd right)
☎01904 634581 & 630951

Closed Xmas & New Year

This cosy guest house near the city centre offers bright, well equipped bedrooms, a pleasant lounge and adequate parking facilities.

9 en suite (shr) No smoking in dining room No smoking in lounges CTV in all bedrooms Tea and coffee making facilities Direct dial from bedrooms No dogs Cen ht No children 10yrs 5P No coaches Last d breakfast

PRICE GUIDE

ROOMS: s £20-£28; d £34-£48✱

GH 🇶🇶🇶 **Bentley Hotel** 25 Grosvenor Ter, Bootham YO3 7AG ☎01904 644313 FAX 01904 644313

Closed Xmas

This attractive terraced house with its summer floral display in the small front garden is found in a quiet side road and is within easy walking distance of the city. The house has been carefully furnished and many thoughtful extras have been provide within the bedrooms. The walls throughout the house are adorned with some delightful prints and paintings and the service is very natural and pleasantly friendly. A good hearty breakfast is provided and offers a wide choice.

6 rms (3 shr) (2 fmly) No smoking CTV in all bedrooms Tea and coffee making facilities No dogs (ex guide dogs) Cen ht No children 10yrs No parking

PRICE GUIDE

ROOMS: s £16-£24; d £32-£48✱

GH 🇶🇶🇶 **Bloomsbury Hotel** 127 Clifton YO3 6BL (from By-Pass take A19 to City centre and Clifton, hotel in 1M on right opposite Parish Church) ☎01904 634031

Located beside the A19 at Clifton Green and only 15 minutes walk from the city, this family owned small hotel offers completely refurbished bedrooms and has the benefit of car parking to the rear. There is a well furnished breakfast room and service has a very personal touch and it also provides good value for money.

8 en suite (shr) (3 fmly) No smoking CTV in all bedrooms Tea

and coffee making facilities No dogs (ex guide dogs) Cen ht 10P Last d noon

PRICE GUIDE

ROOMS: s £20-£38; d £30-£48; wkly b&b £105-£168✱

CARDS: 🔳 🔳 🔳 🔳

GH 🇶🇶🇶 **Bootham Bar Hotel** 4 High Petergate YO1 2EH (100yds from Minster) (CON) ☎01904 658516

Closed 24-26 Dec & 3-18 Jan

Situated just inside the city walls, in a narrow lane, this pleasantly furnished house provides attractive, well equipped accommodation. Yorkshire breakfasts and light snacks are served. Secure parking can be arranged with prior notice.

9 en suite (bth/shr) (2 fmly) No smoking in area of dining room CTV in all bedrooms Tea and coffee making facilities No dogs (ex guide dogs) Licensed Cen ht 6P No coaches

PRICE GUIDE

ROOMS: d £40-£65✱

CARDS: 🔳 🔳

GH 🇶🇶 **Brönte House** 22 Grosvenor Terrace, Bootham YO3 7AG (from A1036 turn left signed Railway Station and follow signs for Thirsk then first right as you leave city)
☎01904 621066

This pleasant Victorian house can be found in a quiet side road just off the A19 to the north of town. Bedrooms are cheerful and tidy, and guests have the use of a combined breakfast room/lounge.

6 rms (4 shr) (1 fmly) No smoking in dining room No smoking in lounges CTV in all bedrooms Tea and coffee making facilities No dogs (ex guide dogs) Cen ht CTV 3P

PRICE GUIDE

ROOMS: s £14-£17; d £30-£40; wkly b&b £84-£112✱

CARDS: 🔳 🔳

GH 🇶🇶🇶 **Burswood** 68 Tadcaster Rd, Dringhouses YO2 2LR ☎01904 708377 FAX 01904 708377

Closed 2wks Xmas/New Year

This modern dormer bungalow offers three well equipped ground floor bedrooms and a combined breakfast room/lounge with comfortable seating. There is car parking to the front of the house and delightful gardens to the rear. Burswood is close to the racecourse and within easy reach of the city.

3 en suite (bth/shr) (1 fmly) CTV in all bedrooms Tea and coffee making facilities No dogs (ex guide dogs) Cen ht CTV 3P

PRICE GUIDE

ROOMS: d £37-£39✱

🔳🔳 **GH** 🇶🇶🇶 **Burton Villa** 22 Haxby Rd YO3 7JX (take ring road A1237, leave on B1363, pass hospital then sharp left) ☎01904 626364

Only a short walk from the city walls, and close to the Minster, this Victorian end-of-terrace house has individually furnished rooms which include some family rooms. The breakfast room is well appointed, with individual tables and attractive place settings. Off-street parking is available.

11 rms (1 bth 7 shr) (3 fmly) No smoking in dining room CTV in all bedrooms Tea and coffee making facilities Cen ht 7P

PRICE GUIDE

ROOMS: s £15-£20; d £32-£45

See advertisement on p.471.

GH 🇶🇶🇶 **Byron House Hotel** 7 Driffield Ter, The Mount YO2 2DD ☎01904 632525 FAX 01904 638904

Closed 24-26 Dec

An elegant property in late Regency style, Byron House offers spacious and very well furnished bedrooms which will please the ➡

tourist and business traveller alike. There are a comfortable bar-lounge with dralon upholstered chesterfields and a well proportioned dining room with French windows overlooking the terrace. The hotel has its own car park and is located close to the race course.

10 rms (7 bth/shr) (4 fmly) No smoking in 4 bedrooms No smoking in dining room CTV in all bedrooms Tea and coffee making facilities Direct dial from bedrooms No dogs (ex guide dogs) Licensed Cen ht 6P No coaches Last d noon

PRICE GUIDE
ROOMS: s £24-£42; d £50-£72
CARDS: £

GH Q Q **Carousel** 83 Eldon St, off Stanley St, Haxby Rd YO3 7NH ☎01904 646709
Pleasant accommodation and friendly service are offered at this former dairy, which is best approached by Haxby Road then Stanley Street. There are a small lounge and an attractive panelled dining room where full English breakfast is served.

9 en suite (shr) (2 fmly) No smoking in dining room No smoking in lounges CTV in all bedrooms Tea and coffee making facilities No dogs Licensed Cen ht CTV 9P Last d 9.30am
PRICE GUIDE
ROOMS: s £15-£18; d £30-£34; wkly b&b £100-£110; wkly hlf-bd £156-£166✶

GH Q Q Q **Cavalier Private Hotel** 39 Monkgate YO3 7PB (situated on the A1036 (A64) York to Malton Road, 250mtrs from York Inner Ring road and City Wall (Monkgate)) ☎01904 636615
This early Georgian building, located within easy walking distance of the city, has been carefully refurbished by the present owners, Mr and Mrs Potts. It is a well kept establishment with beautifully decorated bedrooms and a cosy breakfast room. Service is helpful and friendly, and car parking can be arranged.

10 rms (2 bth 5 shr) (4 fmly) No smoking in dining room CTV in all bedrooms Tea and coffee making facilities No dogs (ex guide dogs) Licensed Cen ht CTV 5P No coaches Sauna
PRICE GUIDE
ROOMS: s £21-£22; d £40-£45✶
CARDS: £

GH Q Q Q **City** 68 Monkgate YO3 7PF (take A1036 to City Centre) ☎01904 622483
Pleasant, well furnished accommodation is offered at this family-run guest house, which is located within easy walking distance of the city centre. The en suite bedrooms are modern in style, and public areas include a small lounge and a dining room.

7 rms (1 bth 4 shr) (2 fmly) No smoking CTV in all bedrooms Tea and coffee making facilities No dogs Cen ht 6P No coaches
PRICE GUIDE
ROOMS: s £15-£20; d £30-£44✶
CARDS: £

GH Q Q Q **Collingwood Hotel** 163 Holgate Rd YO2 4DF (Holgate Rd is a continuation of the A59, approx 2m from Outer Ring Rd) ☎01904 783333
This listed Georgian house within walking distance of the city, set in its own grounds beside the A59, provides very good standards of both accommodation and service. All its en suite bedrooms are well furnished - one with a four poster bed - whilst public areas are spacious and comfortable.

10 en suite (bth/shr) (2 fmly) No smoking in 1 bedrooms No smoking in dining room CTV in all bedrooms Tea and coffee making facilities No dogs (ex guide dogs) Licensed Cen ht CTV 10P Last d 8.30pm
PRICE GUIDE
ROOMS: s £20-£30; d £38-£48; wkly b&b £120-£150
CARDS: £

GH Q **Coppers Lodge** 15 Alma Ter, Fulford Rd YO1 4DQ ☎01904 639871
Once a police station and now a guest house offering basically furnished accommodation. There is a small breakfast room and a guest lounge, and service is friendly.

8 rms (1 bth/shr) (5 fmly) No smoking in dining room CTV in all bedrooms Tea and coffee making facilities Cen ht CTV 2P Last d 2pm
PRICE GUIDE
ROOMS: s £16-£18; d £26-£30✶ £

See advertisement on p.473.

GH Q Q Q **Cornmill Lodge** 120 Haxby Rd YO3 7JP (.5m north of the Minster, follow signs for District Hospital) ☎01904 620566
Closed 1 Dec-31 Jan
Conveniently situated about ten minutes' walk from the city centre, this pleasantly appointed Victorian terraced property provides friendly service and accommodation in bright, fresh bedrooms equipped with colour television sets and tea-making facilities. There is car parking space at the rear of the house.

5 rms (3 shr) (1 fmly) No smoking CTV in all bedrooms Tea and coffee making facilities No dogs (ex guide dogs) Cen ht CTV No children 4yrs 4P No coaches
PRICE GUIDE
ROOMS: s £16-£19; d £30-£38; wkly b&b £96-£114 £

𝓑𝓾𝓻𝓽𝓸𝓷 𝓥𝓲𝓵𝓵𝓪

22 Haxby Road, York YO3 7JX
Telephone: (01904) 626364

Experience English home comforts in our Victorian villa with car parking. 5 minutes walk from the old city. We will gladly help you plan your holiday and enjoy your stay.

* AA rating QQQ
* English Tourist Board Commended
* Family & Ensuite rooms
* Excellent full English breakfast

GH Ⓠ Ⓠ Ⓠ **Crescent** 77 Bootham YO3 7DQ (approach city on A19 city centre road, hotel 5mins for centre) ☎01904 623216 FAX 01904 623216
Situated on the A19 to the north of the city, just a short walk from the minster, this well furnished guest house offers well equipped accommodation and friendly service from the resident owners. A small lounge is provided and evening meals are available on request.
10 rms (8 bth/shr) (5 fmly) No smoking in dining room CTV in all bedrooms Tea and coffee making facilities Direct dial from bedrooms No dogs Licensed Cen ht CTV 4P Last d noon
PRICE GUIDE
ROOMS: s £17.50-£29; d £18.50-£56; wkly b&b £120-£203; wkly hlf-bd £187-£261✱
CARDS: 🔳 ▬ ▦ 🔟 🔟

GH Ⓠ Ⓠ Ⓠ **Crook Lodge** 26 St Marys, Bootham YO3 7DD ☎01904 655614
Closed Dec
This attractive early Victorian house forms the end of a terrace in a very pleasant area of the city only a few minutes' walk from the centre. Bedrooms are attractive, well equipped and furnished in keeping with the character of the house. Private parking is available.
7 en suite (bth/shr) No smoking in 1 bedrooms No smoking in dining room No smoking in lounges CTV in all bedrooms Tea and coffee making facilities No dogs Licensed Cen ht No children 8P No coaches Last d 10am

GH Ⓠ Ⓠ **Crossways** 23 Wiggington Rd YO3 7HJ (opposite York District Hospital) ☎01904 637250
A small Edwardian townhouse with a long narrow front garden, is situated a brisk 15 minutes' walk north of the city centre. Bedrooms are compact but have pretty decor and cheerful soft furnishings; one room is located on the ground floor. There is no lounge, but breakfast is taken in the attractive little dining room at individual tables.
6 en suite (shr) CTV in all bedrooms Tea and coffee making facilities No dogs (ex guide dogs) Cen ht 3P
PRICE GUIDE
ROOMS: d £32-£38; wkly b&b £210-£220✱
CARDS: ▦

GH Ⓠ Ⓠ Ⓠ **Cumbria House** 2 Vyner St, Haxby Rd YO3 7HS ☎01904 636817
Only ten minutes' walk from the city centre, this end of terrace house has bedrooms attractively decorated with modern fabrics. A choice of menu is served at breakfast. Smoking is not permitted.
5 rms (2 shr) (2 fmly) No smoking in dining room No smoking in lounges CTV in all bedrooms Tea and coffee making facilities Licensed Cen ht 5P No coaches
PRICE GUIDE
ROOMS: s £15-£18; d £32-£36; wkly b&b £90-£100✱

Selected

GH Ⓠ Ⓠ Ⓠ Ⓠ **Curzon Lodge and Stable Cottages** 23 Tadcaster Rd, Dringhouses YO2 2QG (follow signs for "park & ride" from A64, between Forte Posthouse & Swallow Hotel) ☎01904 703157
Closed Xmas-New Year
This attractive early 17th-century house is situated in colourful gardens on the A1036, close to the famous Knavesmire racecourse. All bedrooms are of a very high standard; some are in the Lodge and others are in a wisteria-clad former coach house and stable block at the rear. Original

oak beams are a feature of the coach house while antique furniture, Victorian brass bedsteads and a four-poster bed adorn the Lodge which also houses a delightful drawing room and a small dining room. Family-run and welcoming, the guesthouse is within easy reach of the city centre and the A64.
5 en suite (bth/shr) 5 annexe en suite (bth/shr) (1 fmly) No smoking in dining room CTV in all bedrooms Tea and coffee making facilities Direct dial from bedrooms No dogs Cen ht No children 7yrs 16P No coaches
PRICE GUIDE
ROOMS: s £30-£39; d £45-£58
CARDS: 🔳 ▦

GH Ⓠ Ⓠ Ⓠ **Field House Hotel** 2 St George's Place, Tadcaster Rd YO2 2DR (turn off A64 onto A1036, 1m on left) ☎01904 639572
Closed 25 & 26 Dec
Field House is located close to the racecourse and is only short walk from the city. Bedrooms are generally spacious and there is a comfortable bar and lounge whilst substantial breakfasts are served in the pleasant lower ground floor dining room. There is parking available at the side of the house.
17 en suite (bth/shr) No smoking in bedrooms No smoking in dining room CTV in all bedrooms Tea and coffee making facilities Direct dial from bedrooms No dogs (ex guide dogs) Licensed Cen ht 20P No coaches Last d 7pm
PRICE GUIDE
ROOMS: s £23-£31; d £40-£59✱
CARDS: 🔳 ▦ ▦ ▦ ▦ 🔟

GH Ⓠ Ⓠ Ⓠ **Four Poster Lodge Hotel** 68-70 Heslington Rd, off Barbican Rd YO1 5AU (follow signs Barbican Leisure Centre and turn right at x-rds) ☎01904 651170
Closed 25-26 Dec
A Victorian villa has been carefully restored to form a pleasantly furnished guest house situated within easy walking distance of the city. As its name suggests, all bedrooms have four-poster beds; they are also well equipped. Public areas include a comfortable lounge and an attractive dining room serving well produced home cooking.
10 en suite (bth/shr) (2 fmly) No smoking in 5 bedrooms No smoking in dining room No smoking in lounges CTV in all bedrooms Tea and coffee making facilities Licensed Cen ht 8P Last d 6pm
PRICE GUIDE
ROOMS: s £35-£37; d £49-£52✱
CARDS: 🔳 ▦ ▦

Selected

GH Ⓠ Ⓠ Ⓠ Ⓠ **Four Seasons Hotel** 7 St Peters Grove, Bootham YO3 6AQ (leave Ring Rd at A19 signed York Centre for St Peters Grove in 2m by pedestrian bridge) ☎01904 622621 FAX 01904 430565
Closed 24 Dec-16 Jan
Quietly situated in a leafy side-road, this attractive detached Victorian house provides a good standard of accommodation. There is an inviting lounge and the fresh en suite bedrooms are prettily decorated and well equipped. On-site car parking is available.
5 en suite (bth/shr) (2 fmly) No smoking in 2 bedrooms No smoking in dining room CTV in all bedrooms Tea and coffee making facilities Licensed Cen ht CTV 8P No coaches
PRICE GUIDE
ROOMS: d £50✱
CARDS: 🔳 ▦

GH 🄠🄠 **Galtres Lodge Hotel** 54 Low Petergate YO1 2HZ
(from Ring road take B1034 ito city via Heworth Green and
Monkgate) ☎01904 622478 FAX 01904 426931
This attractive Georgian building is not only a small hotel but also
a restaurant open seven days a week. Here, snacks and full meals
are served virtually throughout the day and evening. Several of the
cosy bedrooms are fully en suite; two have antique half tester beds
and one a four-poster.
10 rms (5 shr) (1 fmly) No smoking in dining room CTV in all
bedrooms Tea and coffee making facilities Direct dial from
bedrooms Licensed Cen ht 9P Last d 9.30pm
PRICE GUIDE
ROOMS: s £23-£25; d £40-£58✳
CARDS: 🆇 🔤 🔤 🔤 💷 (£)

GH 🄠 **Georgian** 35 Bootham YO3 7BT ☎01904 622874
This family owned and run guest house which dates back in part
to 1668 is within easy walking distance of the city and provides
simple but very adequate accommodation. There is a comfortable
lounge and there is also the benefit of a rear car park.
14 rms (3 bth/shr) (1 fmly) CTV in all bedrooms Tea and coffee
making facilities No dogs (ex guide dogs) Cen ht TV 8P
PRICE GUIDE
ROOMS: s fr £18; d £36-£40
CARDS: 🆇 🔤

Coppers Lodge Guest House

15 Alma Terrace, Fulford Road, York YO1 4DQ
Telephone: (01904) 639871

Quietly situated off the main road just two minutes walk from the River Ouse and five minutes to the City Walls. Coppers Lodge is open all year round offering bed & breakfast with evening meal available on request.

All rooms are tastefully decorated and have colour TV, tea & coffee facilities, hot & cold and central heating. Comfortable lounge with TV is also available.

Curzon Lodge & Stable Cottages
23 Tadcaster Road, Dringhouses, York, North Yorkshire YO2 2QG
 Tel: 01904 703157

A charming 17th century listed house and former stables, in a conservation area overlooking York Racecourse, once a home of the Terry 'chocolate' family. Stay in a unique atmosphere with antiques, beams, cottage style bedrooms, pretty lounge and hearty breakfasts in 'Farmhouse Kitchen' dining room. All rooms en-suite with colour TV and tea/coffee facilities. AA awards. Large car park within grounds. Please ask for our colour brochure.

Four Poster Lodge Hotel
A Victorian villa lovingly restored and furnished, situated between the University and York's historic centre. Enjoy our relaxing atmosphere, good food, (English breakfast a speciality) and quality service.

Our amenities include a residents licence and private car park. The four poster bedrooms have private facilities and are fully equipped for your comfort.

Your hosts, Peter & Judith Jones.
70 Heslington Road, off Barbican Road, York, YO1 5AU.
Telephone: 01904 651170

Selected

GH ⓠⓠⓠⓠ **Grasmead House Hotel** 1 Scarcroft Hill, The Mount YO2 1DF (follow York West signs into city and after Racecourse cross at traffic lights and immediately turn right after) ☎01904 629996 FAX 01904 629996
This impressive house stands just outside the city walls and provides the unusual feature of having antique four posters in all of its well furnished bedrooms. One of the beds dates back to 1730. There is also a very inviting and comfortable lounge available whilst Mr & Mrs Long are delightfully friendly hosts and are always on hand to ensure their guests are well cared for.
6 en suite (bth/shr) (2 fmly) No smoking in bedrooms No smoking in dining room CTV in all bedrooms Tea and coffee making facilities No dogs (ex guide dogs) Licensed Cen ht CTV 1P No coaches
PRICE GUIDE
ROOMS: d £50-£58
CARDS: 🅰 ➖ 🔲 £

🚗 📺 **GH** ⓠⓠ **Greenside** 124 Clifton YO3 6BQ (approach City Centre on A19 and at traffic lights straight on for Greenside opposite Clifton Green) ☎01904 623631
This attractive detached house overlooks the green and is within easy walking distance of the city. Accommodation is provided in pleasantly furnished bedrooms, there is a comfortable lounge, and a hearty breakfast is served in the cosy dining room. There is car parking to the rear of the house.
6 rms (3 shr) (2 fmly) No smoking in dining room No smoking in lounges CTV in all bedrooms Tea and coffee making facilities Licensed Cen ht CTV ch fac 6P Last d 6pm
PRICE GUIDE
ROOMS: s fr £16; d fr £24 £

Selected

GH ⓠⓠⓠⓠ **Hazelwood** 24-25 Portland St, Gillygate YO3 7EH (from A19 turn left before City Gate and take 1st turning left) ☎01904 626548 FAX 01904 628032
Extensively upgraded by its current owners, this attractive Victorian house offers modern, well equipped bedrooms, a comfortable lounge and an inviting breakfast room. Guests should note that this is a no-smoking establishment.
14 rms (11 bth/shr) (4 fmly) No smoking CTV in all bedrooms Tea and coffee making facilities Licensed Cen ht 8P No coaches
PRICE GUIDE
ROOMS: s £19.50-£21.50; d £32-£52; wkly b&b £107-£173✱
CARDS: 🅰 ➖🔲

Selected

GH ⓠⓠⓠⓠ **The Heathers** 54 Shipton Rd, Clifton - Without YO3 6RQ (mid-way between A1237 and town centre) ☎01904 640989
Closed Xmas
A 1930s house standing in a large garden beside the A19 to the north of the city has been expensively and carefully furnished by its caring owners. One of the bedrooms is on the ground floor, where there is also a combined lounge/breakfast

---

room. Adequate car parking facilities are provided.
8 rms (5 shr) (2 fmly) No smoking CTV in all bedrooms Tea and coffee making facilities No dogs Cen ht CTV No children 8yrs 9P No coaches
PRICE GUIDE
ROOMS: d £28-£70✱
CARDS: 🔲

GH ⓠⓠ **Heworth** 126 East Pde, Heworth YO3 7YG (from Outer Ring Rd take East turning towards City Centre and at traffic lights turn right into Melrose Gate then at next lights turn left) ☎01904 426384 FAX 01904 426384
Fresh, bright bedrooms are a feature of this small, pleasantly furnished guest house which is conveniently situated for the city centre. There is a combined lounge/dining room, and informal service is very friendly.
6 rms (3 shr) No smoking in dining room No smoking in lounges CTV in all bedrooms Tea and coffee making facilities Cen ht 4P No coaches
PRICE GUIDE
ROOMS: s £14.50-£16.50; d £29-£44✱ £

GH ⓠⓠⓠ **Hillcrest** 110 Bishopthorpe Rd YO2 1JX (follow signs A1036 for City centre and take 1st right after Swallow Hotel and at t-junct turn left) ☎01904 653160
Hillcrest, a pleasant Victorian house close to the city centre, has been extensively improved by the present owner; bedrooms are attractive and well equipped, and an inviting lounge is provided.
13 rms (7 shr) (4 fmly) No smoking in 9 bedrooms No smoking in dining room CTV in all bedrooms Tea and coffee making facilities Cen ht CTV 9P Last d noon
PRICE GUIDE
ROOMS: s £14-£18; d £28-£38; wkly b&b £91-£126; wkly hlf-bd £150.50-£185.50✱
CARDS: 🅰 ➖🔲 £

Selected

GH ⓠⓠⓠⓠ **Holmwood House Hotel** 112-114 Holgate Rd YO2 4BB (on A59. Harrogate road) ☎01904 626183 FAX 01904 670899
A delightful small hotel created from two early Victorian houses, Holmwood House offers attractive accommodation with lots of thoughtful extras. There are a cosy lounge and a pretty dining room where excellent breakfasts are served. Mr and Mrs Gramellini are pleasant hosts, caring greatly for their guests' comfort.
12 en suite (bth/shr) (1 fmly) No smoking in bedrooms No smoking in dining room CTV in all bedrooms Tea and coffee making facilities Direct dial from bedrooms No dogs (ex guide dogs) Licensed Cen ht No children 8yrs 9P No coaches
PRICE GUIDE
ROOMS: s £40-£50; d £52-£70; wkly b&b £175-£235✱
CARDS: 🅰 ➖🔲

GH ⓠⓠⓠ *Linden Lodge Hotel* Nunthorpe Avenue, Scarcroft Rd YO2 1PF ☎01904 620107
Closed 23 Dec-9 Jan
A well furnished and comfortable Victorian town house which is only a short walk from the city centre. Most of the bedrooms are en-suite, and all have colour TV and tea trays. There are two comfortable lounges, and the resident owners provide friendly and attentive service.

12 rms (9 shr) (2 fmly) No smoking in bedrooms No smoking in dining room CTV in 9 bedrooms Tea and coffee making facilities No dogs Licensed Cen ht CTV
CARDS:

Selected

GH 🇶🇶🇶🇶 **Midway House Hotel** 145 Fulford Rd YO1 4HG (S side on A19)
☎01904 659272 FAX 01904 621799
Good-sized, well equipped bedrooms are offered at this delightfully furnished Victorian house. Public rooms are comfortable and inviting, and there is a walled garden to the rear. Service is friendly and helpful at all times.
12 rms (11 shr) (2 fmly) No smoking CTV in all bedrooms Tea and coffee making facilities No dogs (ex guide dogs) Licensed Cen ht 14P Last d 5pm
PRICE GUIDE
ROOMS: d £36-£45
CARDS: £

GH 🇶🇶🇶 **Minster View** 2 Grosvenor Ter YO3 7AG
☎01904 655034
With the advantage of its own car park, this tall Victorian terrace house faces Bootham Park towards the Minster. Bedrooms are mostly of a good size - some have striking wallpaper. Breakfast is served in a pleasant dining room.
9 rms (5 bth/shr) (4 fmly) No smoking in dining room No smoking in lounges CTV in all bedrooms Tea and coffee making facilities Direct dial from bedrooms Licensed Cen ht CTV 6P Last d 10am
PRICE GUIDE
ROOMS: s £14-£17; d £28-£38; wkly b&b fr £98✱ £

GH 🇶🇶 **Moat Hotel** Nunnery Ln YO2 1AA
☎01904 652926 FAX 01904 652926
Situated beside the city walls and on the inner ring road, this hotel has the advantage of its own car park. Satisfactory all-round standards are maintained, and friendly service is provided by the resident owners. The house is fully no-smoking.
8 en suite (bth/shr) (1 fmly) No smoking CTV in all bedrooms Tea and coffee making facilities No dogs (ex guide dogs) Licensed Cen ht CTV 10P No coaches Fishing
PRICE GUIDE
ROOMS: d fr £40✱
CARDS: £

GH 🇶🇶🇶 **Nunmill House** 85 Bishopthorpe Rd YO2 1NX (400yds inside City Wall at south eastern corner)
☎01904 634047
Closed Dec-Jan
This elegant Victorian house is being lovingly restored by the Hammond family and offers bedrooms of various styles, from the imposing four poster rooms to the cheery but simpler ones. The public rooms feature marble fireplaces.
8 en suite (bth/shr) (1 fmly) No smoking CTV in all bedrooms Tea and coffee making facilities No dogs Cen ht CTV 3P No coaches
PRICE GUIDE
ROOMS: s £18-£22; d £36-£44✱ £

GH 🇶🇶🇶 **Orchard Court Hotel** 4 St Peters Grove YO3 6AQ
☎01904 653964 FAX 01904 653964
This very well cared for Victorian house is found in a quiet side

---

road just off the A19 to the north of the city centre. There is a delightful lounge, together with a well furnished dining room, and the bedrooms are very well equipped. Friendly and attentive service is provided by Mr and Mrs Noble, the resident owners.
14 rms (11 bth/shr) (4 fmly) No smoking in 8 bedrooms No smoking in dining room CTV in all bedrooms Tea and coffee making facilities No dogs (ex guide dogs) Licensed Cen ht CTV 14P No coaches Last d 6pm
PRICE GUIDE
ROOMS: s £22-£35; d £46-£60
CARDS: £

Selected

GH 🇶🇶🇶🇶 *Priory Hotel* 126 Fulford Rd YO1 4BE (on A19) ☎01904 625280 FAX 01904 625280
Closed Xmas
A pleasant, family-run hotel, the Priory provides comfortable, if compact, bedrooms which are currently undergoing refurbishment. Public rooms are also inviting, and the restaurant offers a good range of food. The hotel has its own car park and a garden with gothic arches and a patio.
20 en suite (bth/shr) (5 fmly) CTV in all bedrooms Tea and coffee making facilities No dogs (ex guide dogs) Licensed Cen ht CTV 25P Last d 9.15pm
CARDS:
See advertisement on p.478.

GH 🇶🇶🇶 **Riverside Walk Hotel** 9 Earlsborough Ter, Marygate YO3 7BQ ☎01904 646249
This small and very friendly hotel stands just a short walk from the city and in a delightful riverside location. The bedrooms are pleasantly furnished and an open-plan lounge bar and dining room is the setting for really special breakfasts. Private car parking is available.
10 rms (8 bth/shr) (1 fmly) CTV in all bedrooms Tea and coffee making facilities Direct dial from bedrooms No dogs (ex guide dogs) Licensed Cen ht 14P No coaches Last d 9pm
PRICE GUIDE
ROOMS: s £24-£25; d £30-£52✱
CARDS:

Selected

GH 🇶🇶🇶🇶 **St Denys Hotel** St Denys Rd YO1 1QD (near city centre) ☎01904 622207 FAX 01904 624800
Closed 2wks Xmas
This former vicarage near the city centre is now a comfortable and spacious hotel offering well-equipped modern bedrooms with direct dial telephones and en suite facilities. Friendly, attentive service is provided by resident owners Ruth and Keith Marsh. The lounge and bar are comfortable, and there is a car park to the side of the house.
10 en suite (bth/shr) (4 fmly) CTV in all bedrooms Tea and coffee making facilities Licensed Cen ht CTV 9P Last d noon
PRICE GUIDE
ROOMS: s £25-£35; d £40-£50✱
CARDS: £

GH 🇶🇶🇶 **St Georges House Hotel** 6 St Georges Place, Tadcaster Rd YO2 2DR (enter from A1036 past Racecourse)
☎01904 625056
This large and attractive Victorian house stands in a quiet side road just off the A64, close to the racecourse. Well furnished

throughout, it offers a cosy lounge and a restaurant (now open to the public) featuring a short but interesting carte.

10 en suite (bth/shr) (5 fmly) No smoking in dining room CTV in all bedrooms Tea and coffee making facilities Licensed Cen ht 7P No coaches Last d 7pm

PRICE GUIDE

ROOMS: s £20-£30; d £30-£45; wkly b&b £110-£160∗

CARDS: £

GH QQ **St Raphael** 44 Queen Anne's Rd, Bootham YO3 7AF (A19 north road to City Centre) ☎01904 645028

Limited kerbside parking is available outside this semidetached house which stands in a quiet side road not far from the city centre, just off Bootham. Friendly service is provided by the resident owner and, though there is no lounge, bedrooms are comfortably furnished and adequately equipped.

8 rms (5 shr) (1 fmly) No smoking in dining room CTV in all bedrooms Tea and coffee making facilities Cen ht No parking No coaches Last d 4pm

PRICE GUIDE

ROOMS: s £15-£19; d £28-£34

CARDS:

GH QQQ **Staymor** 2 Southlands Rd YO2 1NP (off A6 through Bishopthorpe to City Centre, pass Terry's factory then turn left) ☎01904 626935

Feb-Nov

This well furnished Victorian house stands in a quiet side road close to the city centre. Non-smoking en suite bedrooms are attractively decorated and have good facilities, hearty breakfasts are served in the pleasant dining room and there is a cosy lounge.

4 en suite (bth/shr) (2 fmly) No smoking in bedrooms No smoking in dining room CTV in all bedrooms Tea and coffee making facilities Cen ht CTV

PRICE GUIDE

ROOMS: s £15-£20; d £24-£35; wkly b&b £160-£245

£

GH QQQ **Sycamore** 19 Sycamore Place, Bootham YO3 7DW (approach from A19 and at Churchill Hotel turn right into Bootham Terrace then in 200yds turn right) ☎01904 624712

Closed 19-27 Dec

Only a short walk from the city centre, an attractive front garden with an old street gas lamp fronts this delightful little guest house situated in a quiet cul-de-sac. Bedrooms have been totally redecorated and new carpets fitted. There is no lounge, but guests may use their rooms at all times. The breakfast room has individual tables.

7 rms (3 shr) (1 fmly) No smoking in dining room No smoking in lounges CTV in all bedrooms Tea and coffee making facilities No dogs Cen ht No children 5yrs 2P No coaches

PRICE GUIDE

ROOMS: d £30-£40; wkly b&b £105-£140∗

See advertisement on p.479.

GH QQQ **Tower** 2 Feversham Crescent, Wigginton Rd YO3 7HQ (on B1363 adjacent to district hospital) ☎01904 655571 & 635924

Distinguished by its blue window canopies, this Edwardian house is within easy walking distance of the city centre. The bedrooms provide contemporary comforts and have been tastefully modernised with white furniture, bright wall coverings and attractive curtains. A spacious dining room is provided, enhanced by small flower arrangements and paintings. Private parking is available at the front of the hotel.

➡

The Priory Hotel, York

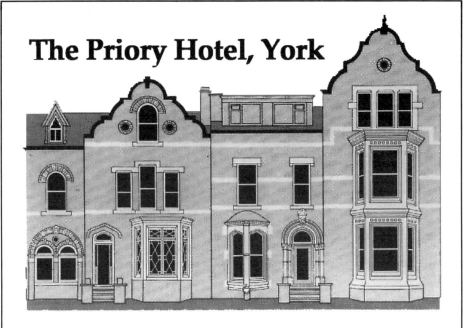

The Priory offers comfortable accommodation with full English breakfast, and is situated 600 yards south of York's medieval city walls, within easy direct reach of the nearby inner and outer ring roads. The city centre can be reached by a pleasant riverside walk.

The 20 bedrooms, all equipped with colour TV and tea/coffee making facilities, include single, double and family accommodation, all with en suite shower and toilet facilities.

The hotel is AA listed, and has full central heating, a licensed bar and restaurant. The pleasant garden leads to the large private car-park. Reductions are available for children sharing accommodation with their parents. Please send for brochure and tariff.

Proprietors:
George and Barbara Jackson
The Priory Hotel
Fulford Road
York YO1 4BE
Telephone York (01904) 625280

5 en suite (bth/shr) (3 fmly) CTV in all bedrooms Tea and coffee making facilities No dogs Cen ht 5P No coaches
PRICE GUIDE
ROOMS: d £32-£40✳
CARDS: (£)

GH **Q Q Q** **Turnberry House** 143 Fulford Rd YO1 4HG (on A19 Selby rd) ☎01904 658435
Closed 25 Dec
Turnberry House is an attractive Edwardian property offering good all-round facilities and friendly service from the resident owners. It is situated on the A19 to the south of the city and has the benefit of its own car park.
4 en suite (shr) (2 fmly) No smoking CTV in all bedrooms Tea and coffee making facilities No dogs (ex guide dogs) Cen ht 6P
PRICE GUIDE
ROOMS: s £25-£32; d £32-£42; wkly b&b £112-£140; wkly hlf-bd £175-£210✳
(£)

◀ Q Q Q **Jacobean Lodge Hotel** Plainville Ln YO3 8RG (take B1363 from York towards Helmsley for approx 3m and turn left after the right turn for Wigginton. After 1.5m turn right at crossroads) ☎01904 762749 FAX 01904 768403
This converted 17th-century farmhouse surrounded by pleasant gardens stands in open countryside between the A19 and the B1363. Well equipped modern bedrooms offer en suite facilities and a good range of food is served in both bar and restaurant.
14 en suite (bth/shr) (2 fmly) No smoking in area of dining room CTV in all bedrooms Tea and coffee making facilities Direct dial from bedrooms Cen ht CTV ch fac 70P Last d 9.30pm
PRICE GUIDE
ROOMS: s £25-£34; d £41-£60
MEALS: Lunch £6-£16alc Dinner £8.65-£21alc
CARDS: (£)

ZEALS Wiltshire Map **3** ST73

GH **Q Q Q** **Zeals Green House** Zeals, Warminster BA12 6NH ☎01747 840171
This 1930s family home, set in its own grounds down a private lane from the village of Zeals is just 1 mile from the A303 at Mere. The beauties of Wiltshire are all within easy reach and day trips to places of interest can be arranged. Three spacious bedrooms have private bathrooms and have been equipped with modern comforts and thoughtful extras like fresh flowers. Breakfast is served at a shared table in the dining room and guests are welcome to enjoy the gardens and the company of the Flowers family and their friendly pets.
2 en suite (bth/shr) (1 fmly) No smoking CTV in all bedrooms Tea and coffee making facilities No dogs (ex guide dogs) Cen ht No children 7yrs P
PRICE GUIDE
ROOMS: s £17.50; d £35; wkly b&b £105✳

CHANNEL ISLANDS Map **16**

ALDERNEY Map **16**

GH **Q Q Q Q** **The Georgian House** Victoria St, St Anne ☎01481 822471 FAX 01481 822471
This elegant Georgian property (one of St Anne's old town houses) is situated on Victoria Street, adjacent to the shops and other amenities; it provides an ideal base from which to explore the delights of the island. The top-floor bedrooms have been tastefully decorated and equipped with en suite

facilities and such comforts as televisions and telephones. There are a small first floor lounge and breakfast room (available for private dining), a friendly bar and character restaurant serving an extensive choice of dishes and snacks. On warmer evenings the bar and barbecue in the garden also proves popular.
3 en suite (bth) (1 fmly) CTV in all bedrooms Tea and coffee making facilities Direct dial from bedrooms No dogs (ex guide dogs) Licensed Cen ht CTV No children 8yrs Last d 9.30pm
PRICE GUIDE
ROOMS: s £25-£27.50; d £50-£55✳
CARDS:

GUERNSEY Map **16**

FOREST

GH **Q Q Q** **Mon Plaisir** Rue Des Landes GY8 0DY ☎01481 64498 FAX 01481 63493
This 19th-century farmhouse is situated close to the Petit Bot Valley, within easy reach of delightful cliff walks and convenient for the airport. The freshly decorated bedrooms are spacious and equipped with 'mini-fridges' in addition to the usual amenities. A guests' sitting room is adjoined by a small dining room which serves a range of hearty breakfasts. Guests have access to a well maintained garden and well find a number of restaurants in the vicinity.
5 en suite (bth/shr) No smoking in dining room CTV in all bedrooms Tea and coffee making facilities No dogs (ex guide dogs) Cen ht 5P No coaches
PRICE GUIDE
ROOMS: d £30-£42

ST PETER PORT

Selected

GH **Q Q Q Q** **Farnborough Hotel** Les Damouettes Ln GY1 1ZN (left at Fermain Tavern) ☎01481 37756 FAX 01481 34082
Oct-Mar
Quietly situated away from the main road just a few minutes' walk from Fermain Bay, this comfortable bed and breakfast is personally run by its friendly owner. The double-glazed bedrooms are furnished in a modern style; some are larger than others and many overlook the rear garden. Public areas comprise two comfortable lounges, a small bar and a well appointed dining room. Forecourt parking is available.
11 en suite (shr) CTV in all bedrooms Tea and coffee making facilities No dogs Licensed Cen ht CTV No children 12yrs 11P No coaches
PRICE GUIDE
ROOMS: s £19-£30; d £38-£46; wkly b&b £133-£161
CARDS: (£)

GH **Q Q Q** **Marine Hotel** Well Rd GY1 1WS (situated just off Glatengy Esplanade, opposite Queen Elizabeth II Marina) ☎01481 724978
The Marine Hotel is ideally located only thirty yards from the seafront and the Queen Elizabeth II Marina, a few minutes' walk from St Peter's Port and the picturesque shopping centre. The neatly appointed bedrooms include some rooms suitable for families; other accommodation comprises a comfortable lounge overlooking the harbour and a sunny terrace with a functioning red

telephone box. Meals can be taken at one of many eating places close by.
11 en suite (bth/shr) (3 fmly) No smoking in dining room No smoking in lounges Tea and coffee making facilities No dogs (ex guide dogs) Cen ht CTV No parking No coaches
PRICE GUIDE
ROOMS: s £15.50-£24.50; d £31-£46✶
CARDS: (£)

ST SAMPSON

Selected

GH ⓆⓆⓆⓆ *Ann-Dawn Private Hotel* Route des Capelles GY2 4GQ ☎01481 725606 FAX 01481 725930
Etr-Oct

This traditional Guernsey hotel sits in a quiet residential area, surrounded by neatly maintained gardens. Bedrooms are all well equipped, and include two spacious deluxe bedrooms on the second floor; the other rooms are more compact in comparison. A choice of menu is offered at dinner complemented by a reasonably priced wine list.

11 en suite (bth/shr) No smoking CTV in all bedrooms Tea and coffee making facilities No dogs Licensed Cen ht No children 12yrs 12P No coaches Last d 5pm
CARDS: 🟦 💳

JERSEY Map 16

GREVE DE LECQ BAY

GH ⓆⓆⓆ *Des Pierres* JE3 2DT (on B65 near beach)
☎01534 481858 FAX 01534 485273
Closed 15 Dec-15 Jan

Many of the well equipped bedrooms of this small, family-run hotel enjoy beautiful views of coast and countryside, its dining room offers a blackboard choice of freshly prepared dishes at both breakfast and dinner, and there is a bar on the lower ground floor. Resident proprietors of long standing are continually making improvements in line with guests' needs.

16 en suite (bth/shr) (4 fmly) No smoking in lounges CTV in all bedrooms Tea and coffee making facilities No dogs Licensed Cen ht CTV 13P Gymnasium Last d 8pm
CARDS: 🟦 💳 💳

GROUVILLE

Selected

GH ⓆⓆⓆⓆ *Lavender Villa Hotel* Rue A Don JE3 9DX (approx 3m from St Helier on East Coast Road just off A3) ☎01534 854937 FAX 01534 856147
Mar-Nov

Extremely high standards have been maintained at this delightful small hotel overlooking the Royal Jersey Golf Club, only a short stroll from the beach and within easy reach of both Gorey harbour and St Helier. En suite bedrooms are tastefully decorated and furnished, public areas full of character including a bar lounge and attractive restaurant, and there is an inviting outdoor pool in the gardens. The charming proprietors and their friendly staff provide service which is both attentive and professional.

21 en suite (bth/shr) (3 fmly) No smoking in dining room No smoking in lounges CTV in all bedrooms Tea and coffee making facilities No dogs Licensed Cen ht CTV No children 3yrs 20P No coaches Outdoor swimming pool Last d 7.45pm
CARDS: 🟦 💳

ST AUBIN

GH ⓆⓆ *Bryn-y-Mor Private Hotel* Route de la Haule JE3 8BA (on A1) ☎01534 20295 FAX 01534 24262
This small hotel overlooks St Aubin's Bay so many of the well

equipped bedrooms have lovely sea views. Light refreshments are available throughout the day, either inside or on the garden terrace, and a daily changing set menu is provided in the dining room and bar. Service here is particularly friendly and helpful.

14 rms (11 bth/shr) (4 fmly) No smoking in dining room CTV in all bedrooms Tea and coffee making facilities Direct dial from bedrooms Licensed 6P No coaches Last d 6.30pm
CARDS: 🟦 💳 💳 💳

Selected

GH ⓆⓆⓆⓆ *The Panorama* La Rue du Crocquet JE3 8BR ☎01534 42429 FAX 01534 45940
Etr-Oct

This attractive little hotel standing high above the village of St Aubin boasts some of the finest sea views in the Channel Islands - particularly from its bedrooms, most of which are positioned at the front of the building; all the well furnished rooms have en suite facilities and are equipped with such modern extras as fridges and microwave cookers. Both the comfortable lounge and tea room feature carved oak fireplaces, and the dining room offers a wide choice of breakfast dishes. Morning coffee, light refreshments and an extensive range of teas are served in the terraced tea garden. Overall high standards and a warm welcome ensure that guests return year after year.

17 en suite (bth/shr) (2 fmly) No smoking in dining room No smoking in lounges CTV in all bedrooms Tea and coffee making facilities No dogs Cen ht No children 10yrs No parking No coaches Tea garden
PRICE GUIDE
ROOMS: s £20-£40; d £40-£70
CARDS: 🟦 💳 💳 💳   ⓕ

ST HELIER

GH ⓆⓆⓆ *Cliff Court Hotel* St Andrews Rd, First Tower JE2 3JG ☎01534 34919 FAX 01534 66715
Mar-Oct

A small, family-run hotel enjoying views across to St Aubins Bay from its setting high in the First Tower area offers accommodation in en suite bedrooms, some of which are quite spacious. Public areas include a bar lounge and a separate lounge with colour television as well as the airy dining room where breakfast and dinner are served.

17 en suite (bth/shr) (3 fmly) No smoking in area of dining room Tea and coffee making facilities No dogs (ex guide dogs) Licensed Cen ht CTV 14P No coaches Outdoor swimming pool (heated) Last d 7.30pm
CARDS: 🟦 💳

Selected

GH ⓆⓆⓆⓆ *Kaieteur* 4 Ralegh Ave JE2 3ZG (take A9 to rdbt turn right onto A14, Raleigh Ave 1st turning on left) ☎01534 37004 FAX 01534 67423
This welcoming, family-run guest house in a quiet residential area offers bright, modern bedrooms which new proprietors are gradually improving. All the rooms are centrally heated and provided with colour television and tea trays; nine have en suite facilites and the tenth a private toilet, though its bathroom is on the landing. Downstairs, a comfortable guests' lounge stands next to the dining room where a good choice of breakfast dishes is served.

10 rms (9 shr) (1 fmly) No smoking in dining room No smoking in lounges CTV in all bedrooms Tea and coffee

making facilities No dogs (ex guide dogs) Cen ht CTV 4P
No coaches
PRICE GUIDE
ROOMS: s £16-£24.50; d £32-£49; wkly b&b £112-
£171.50✶
CARDS: (£)

GH QQQ **Millbrook House** Rue de Trachy, Millbrook
JE2 3JN (1.5m W on A1) ☎01534 33036 FAX 01534 24317
10 Oct-8 Apr
Ten acres of mature grounds surround this peaceful, handsome
house which combines the characteristics of Georgian and colonial
architecture. Located not far from the beach and town centre, it
has been skilfully extended to provide comfortable, well-equipped
bedrooms with private bathrooms, a sunny conservatory, relaxing
lounges - one of them non-smoking - and a dining room which
serves a home-cooked evening meal. This hotel offers good value
for money.
24 en suite (bth/shr) (2 fmly) No smoking in 1 lounge CTV in
all bedrooms Tea and coffee making facilities Direct dial from
bedrooms No dogs Licensed Lift CTV 20P No coaches Last d
7pm
PRICE GUIDE
ROOMS: s £22.50-£30.50; d £45-£61; wkly hlf-bd £192.50-
£248.50
CARDS: ▬

SARK

Selected

GH QQQQ **Hotel Petit Champ** GY9 0SF (from the
Methodist Chapel take lane, signposted, towards sea &
turn left) ☎01481 832046 FAX 01481 832469
Etr-Oct
On clear days this delightful family-run hotel, set high on the
west coast of the island, enjoys stunning views across the sea
to the islands of Herm and Jethou. Sark, a beautiful little
island of automobile-free peace and tranquillity, can only be
reached by boat from Guernsey and France; Petit Champ itself
is situated at the end of a private road and - whilst luggage is
taken care of - access is on foot. Resident proprietors Chris
and Caroline Robins extend a warm welcome to their guests,
many of whom return year after year to be in the company of
such caring hosts. Bedrooms are freshly decorated and
furnished in modern style, several having sea views and the
four in the newer wing featuring balconies.
16 en suite (bth/shr) (2 fmly) No smoking in dining room
No smoking in 1 lounge No dogs (ex guide dogs) Licensed
Cen ht No children 7yrs Outdoor swimming pool
(heated) Putting green Last d 8.30pm
PRICE GUIDE
ROOMS: (incl. dinner) s £43-£47; d £82-£100; wkly hlf-bd
£287-£350
CARDS: ▬ ▬ ▬ ◻ (£)

MAN, ISLE OF Map 06

DOUGLAS Map 06 SC37

GH QQQ **Ainsdale Guest House** 2 Empire Terrace,
Central Prom IM2 4LE (50yds off Central Promenade)
☎01624 676695 FAX 01624 676695
Apr-Sep
This friendly and comfortable property is located in a quiet road
just off Central Promenade. Proprietors Les and Margaret
Whitehouse continue to make improvements; they have recently

created a very pleasant lounge at the front of the hotel and moved
the pleasantly appointed dining room to the rear, enlarging it in the
process. The bedrooms are well maintained and attractively
decorated, while en suite bathrooms are of an extremely high
standard.
14 rms (8 bth/shr) (2 fmly) No smoking in 8 bedrooms No
smoking in dining room No smoking in 1 lounge CTV in 8
bedrooms Tea and coffee making facilities Cen ht CTV No
parking Last d 6pm
PRICE GUIDE
ROOMS: s £16-£18.50; d £32-£40

GH QQ **All Seasons** 11 Clifton Ter, Broadway (turn
off Central Prom Villa Marina in 1st row of hotels on left)
☎01624 676323 FAX 01624 676323
The All Seasons is a centrally situated family-run guest house
providing a good standard of accommodation in pleasantly
decorated bedrooms, most of which have en suite facilities. There
are also a pine-furnished dining room, an inviting lounge bar and a
small, quiet lounge (the latter on the first floor).
8 rms (6 shr) No smoking in dining room No smoking in lounges
CTV in all bedrooms Tea and coffee making facilities Licensed
Cen ht No coaches Last d 6pm
PRICE GUIDE
ROOMS: s £14.50-£17.50; d £35; wkly b&b £87-£122.50 (£)

GH QQ *Hydro Hotel* Queen's Promanade IM2 3NF
☎01624 676870 FAX 01624 663883
Closed 24 Dec-1 Jan
A large family run Edwardian hotel sits on the Promenade, at the
end of a row of terraced properties. Bedrooms vary in size and
shape but they all have modern equipment and many have sea
views; family rooms are also available and a lift serves all floors.
Public areas are spacious and include a choice of bars, two
lounges and a large restaurant, which is also available for
functions.
56 rms (46 bth/shr) (12 fmly) CTV in all bedrooms Tea and
coffee making facilities Direct dial from bedrooms Licensed Lift
Cen ht No parking Solarium Pool table Last d 7.30pm
CARDS: ▬ ▬

GH QQQ **The Laurels** 2 Mona Dr, Central Promenade
IM2 4LG (25yds from sea front)
☎01624 674884 FAX 01624 674884
Mar-Oct
Situated just off Central Promenade, The Laurels is a very well
maintained Victorian terraced property, convenient for the town
centre and all local attractions. The bedrooms, though compact,
are all pleasantly furnished and decorated with much use of
modern co-ordinated fabrics. Downstairs, there are a relaxing
lounge with television, a small but well appointed bar and a neat
dining room with individual tables.
14 rms (8 bth/shr) No smoking in dining room Tea and coffee
making facilities No dogs (ex guide dogs) Licensed CTV No
children 5yrs No coaches Last d noon
PRICE GUIDE
ROOMS: s £17-£18.50; d £34-£38; wkly b&b £119-£133; wkly
hlf-bd £168-£182✶ (£)

GH QQ **Rosslyn Guest House** 3 Empire Ter, Central
Promenade IM2 4LE ☎01624 676056 FAX 01624 674122
Closed Dec-1 Jan
Rosslyn Guest House, standing in a sunny terrace just off Central
Promenade, is both welcoming and well maintained. The
attractively decorated bedrooms vary in shape and size those at the
top of the hotel having views of the sea. Only the rooms with en
suite facilities have television, but it is also provided in an

exceptionally comfortable lounge on the first floor. The lounge
and dining room are non-smoking, but it is allowed in the cosy
bar, where late night hot and cold snacks can be served.
16 rms (4 bth/shr) (3 fmly) No smoking in 4 bedrooms No
smoking in dining room No smoking in lounges CTV in 5
bedrooms Tea and coffee making facilities No dogs (ex guide
dogs) Licensed Cen ht CTV No children 5yrs No parking
PRICE GUIDE
ROOMS: s £15-£25; d £30-£40; wkly b&b £105-£140; wkly hlf-
bd £140-£175✳

(£)

SCOTLAND

PREMIER SELECTED
QQQQQ

A quick-reference of establishments in Scotland in this year's guide with a QQQQQ rating for Quality – the AA's highest rating for guest houses, farmhouses and inns.

BORDERS
COLDINGHAM
Dunlaverock House

JEDBURGH
The Spinney

CENTRAL
BRIG O'TURK
Dundarroch

CALLANDER
Arran Lodge

FIFE
ANSTRUTHER
Hermitage

AUCHTERMUCHTY
Ardchoille Farmhouse

CUPAR
Todhall House

GRAMPIAN
ABERDEEN
Ewood House

HIGHLAND
BOAT OF GARTEN
Heathbank The
   Victorian House

CONON BRIDGE
Kinkell House

DORNOCH
Highfield

FORT WILLIAM
Ashburn House

The Grange
Torbeag House

GRANTOWN-ON-
   SPEY
Ardconnel House
Culdearn House

INVERNESS
Ballifeary House
   Hotel
Culduthel Lodge
Moyness House

LOTHIAN
EDINBURGH
Drummond House
Elmview

STRATHCLYDE
BALLANTRAE
Cosses

CONNEL
Ards House

PAISLEY
Myfarrclane

TOBERMORY
Strongarbh House

TAYSIDE
ABERFELDY
Fernbank House

ARBROATH
Farmhouse Kitchen

SELECTED
QQQQ

A quick-reference of establishments in Scotland in this year's guide with a QQQQ rating for Quality – each year more establishments in the guide rise to this very high standard.

BORDERS
Galashiels
Binniemyre
Jedburgh
Hundalee House
Willow Court
Froylehurst

Melrose
Dunfermline House
Little Fordel
Peebles
Venlaw Farm
Selkirk
Hillholm

CENTRAL
Balquhidder
Stronvar House
Callander
Arden House
Brook Linn

Dunblane
Westwood
Strathyre
Creagan House
Thornhill
Corshill Cottage

▶

485

DUMFRIES & GALLOWAY
Beattock
Broomlands Farm
Dalbeattie
Auchenskeoch Lodge
Dumfries
Orchard House
Kirkbean
Cavens House
Kirkcudbright
Gladstone House
MoffatT
Gilbert House
Twynholm
Fresh Fields

FIFE
Aberdour
Hawkcraig House
Anstruther
The Spindrift
Dunfermline
Clarke Cottage
Hopetoun Lodge
St Andrews
Edenside House
Fossil House
Glenderran

GRAMPIAN
Aberdeen
Cedars Private Hotel
Manorville
Ballater
Glen Lui Hotel
Braemar
Callater Lodge Hotel
Drumlithie
Upper Foord Croft
Forres
Mayfield
Parkmount House
Keith
The Haughs Farm

HIGHLAND
Ardgay
Ardgay House
Ballachulish
Fern Villa
Lyn-Leven
Brora
Lynwood
Carrbridge
Carrmoor
Dornoch
Fourpenny Cottage
Drumbeg
Taigh Druimbeag
 House
Drumnadrochit
Borlum Farmhouse
Kilmore Farm
Woodlands
Foyers
Foyers Bay House
Gairloch
Birchwood
Horisdale House
Grantown-on-Spey
Garden Park
Inverness
Ardmuir House
Brae Ness Hotel
Clach Mhuilinn
Dionard
Eden House Hotel
Taransay Lower
Muckovie Farm
The Old Rectory
Kingussie
Avondale House
Kylesku
Newton Lodge
Nairn
Greenlawns
Nethy Bridge
Aultmore House
Portree
Quiraing
Rogart
Rovie Farm
Rosemarkie
Hillview

Spean Bridge
Distant Hills
Tain
Golf View House
Ullapool
Ardvreck
Dromnan
The Sheiling

LOTHIAN
East Calder
Ashcroft Farmhouse
Edinburgh
Adam Hotel
Ashgrove House
Brunswick Hotel
Classic House
Dorstan Private Hotel
Ellesmere House
Grosvenor Gardens
 Hotel
Kildonan Lodge Hotel
Roselea
Stuart House
The International
The Lodge Hotel
The Town House
Gullane
Faussetthill House

STRATHCLYDE
Ayr
Brenalder Lodge
Glenmore
Balloch
Gowanlea
Brodick
Dunvegan House
Cardross
Kirkton House
Connel
Loch Etive House Hotel
Ronebhal
Dunoon
The Anchorage Hotel
Dunure
Dunduff Farm

Gartocharn
Ardoch Cottage
Mardella Farmhouse
Lamlash
Lilybank Hotel
Largs
Lea-Mar
Whin Park
Oban
Drumriggend
Rhumor
Prestwick
Fairways Hotel
Golf View Hotel
Redlands
Skipness
Skipness Castle
St Catherines
Thistle House
Tobermory
Fairways Lodge

TAYSIDE
Alyth
Drumnacree
Blair Atholl
Dalgreine
Brechin
Blibberhill Farm
Dundee
Beach House Hotel
Forfar
Finavon Farmhouse
Killin
Breadalbane House
Perth
Ardfern House
Kinnaird
Pitlochry
Craigroyston House
Dundarave House
Torrdarach Hotel

WESTERN ISLES
Breasclete
Corran View
Eshcol
South Galson
Galson Farm

SCOTLAND

ABERDEEN Grampian *Aberdeenshire* Map **15** NJ90

GH ⓠⓠ **Applewood** 154 Bon-Accord St AB1 2TX
☎01224 580617
This terraced house lies in a residential area south east of the city centre; it offers bright, practical bedrooms and a period vestibule and dining room, but there is no lounge.
8 rms (1 fmly) No smoking in 2 bedrooms CTV in all bedrooms Tea and coffee making facilities No dogs Cen ht CTV 4P
PRICE GUIDE
ROOMS: s £18-£24; d £32; wkly b&b fr £108✱

GH ⓠⓠ **Bimini** 69 Constitution St AB2 1ET
☎01224 646912 FAX 01224 646912
Situated in the east end, this family-run guest house offers practical accommodation in modern bedrooms and has nice touches such as a world map where guests can mark their home town with a pin. A freshly cooked breakfast is served at shared tables in the combined lounge/dining room and parking is available to the rear.
7 rms (1 fmly) No smoking CTV in all bedrooms Tea and coffee making facilities No dogs (ex guide dogs) Cen ht CTV 7P No coaches
PRICE GUIDE
ROOMS: s £17-£24; d £34-£40✱
CARDS: 💳 💳

Selected

GH ⓠⓠⓠⓠ **Cedars Private Hotel** 339 Great Western Rd AB1 6NW ☎01224 583225 FAX 01224 585050
This detached, granite-built house is located in the west end, about one mile from the city centre, and is a popular base for business guests and tourists alike. The thirteen bedrooms vary in size but are comfortable and provide a good range of amenities, all with TV and tea trays. There is a small snooker table in the spacious lounge, and hearty breakfasts are served in the attractive dining room which features a beautiful ornate ceiling. Efficiently run by the friendly owners Mr and Mrs McBeath, a high standard of housekeeping is maintained. Car parking is provided at both the front and rear.
13 rms (10 bth/shr) (2 fmly) No smoking in dining room CTV in all bedrooms Tea and coffee making facilities Direct dial from bedrooms No dogs (ex guide dogs) Cen ht CTV 13P Pool table
PRICE GUIDE
ROOMS: s £38-£45; d £52-£54✱
CARDS: 💳 💳 💳

GH ⓠⓠⓠ **Corner House Hotel** 385 Great Western Rd AB1 6NY (on A93) ☎01224 313063 FAX 01224 313063
Two semidetached granite stone houses have been linked and extended to create this family run hotel, popular with business and holiday guests. Situated in the west end it has a friendly atmosphere and offers comfortable and well equipped accommodation.
17 en suite (bth/shr) (3 fmly) No smoking in dining room CTV

---

in all bedrooms Tea and coffee making facilities Direct dial from bedrooms Licensed Cen ht CTV 12P No coaches Last d 8pm
PRICE GUIDE
ROOMS: s £35-£48; d £46-£56; wkly b&b £160-£260; wkly hlf-bd £230-£320
CARDS: 💳 💳 💳 💳

Premier Selected

GH ⓠⓠⓠⓠⓠ **Ewood House** 12 Kings Gate AB2 6BJ ☎01224 648408
Fred and Sheila Hawkey have lovingly created a top class establishment in this imposing Victorian house set in its own gardens. Located on the west side of the city it is convenient for the ring road and the city centre.

Bedrooms, including one designed for disabled guests, are spacious and have many attractive touches, with fresh fruit and flowers being a feature. Guests can relax in the large garden or the elegant residents' lounge. An excellent breakfast selection is available in the bright dining room, while the friendly, informal atmosphere prevails throughout.
6 en suite (shr) (3 fmly) No smoking CTV in all bedrooms Tea and coffee making facilities No dogs (ex guide dogs) Cen ht CTV ch fac 8P No coaches
PRICE GUIDE
ROOMS: s £38; d £55; wkly b&b fr £162✱
CARDS: 💳 💳

GH ⓠⓠⓠ **Fourways** 435 Great Western Rd AB1 6NJ
☎01224 310218 FAX 01224 310218
A friendly atmosphere prevails at this semi-detached house, conveniently situated at the junction of the ring road and the A93 and offering bedrooms of varying quality together with an attractive dining room which doubles as a lounge. A small car park is reached by was of a rear lane off the south side of the A93.
7 rms (6 bth/shr) (2 fmly) CTV in all bedrooms Tea and coffee making facilities No dogs (ex guide dogs) Cen ht CTV 7P
PRICE GUIDE
ROOMS: s £22-£25; d £40-£44✱
CARDS: 💳 💳 💳

GH ⓠⓠ **Klibreck** 410 Great Western Rd AB1 6NR
☎01224 316115
Closed Xmas & New Year
A family-run guest house is conveniently situated in a west end residential area and offers good value accommodation. The simply decorated bedrooms are well equipped and immaculately maintained. There is a cosy lounge and good breakfasts are served in the small rear dining room.
6 rms (1 fmly) No smoking CTV in all bedrooms Tea and coffee making facilities No dogs Cen ht CTV 3P No coaches
PRICE GUIDE
ROOMS: s fr £19; d fr £30✱

GH ◻◻◻ **Mannofield Hotel** 447 Great Western Rd
AB1 6NL ☎01224 315888 FAX 01224 208971
This detached turreted granite-stone mansion is conveniently
situated west of the city centre. The neat modern bedrooms
include telephones and there is a comfortable lounge and a dining
room where good value home cooked lunches and dinners are
popular.
9 rms (6 shr) (3 fmly) No smoking in dining room CTV in all
bedrooms Tea and coffee making facilities Direct dial from
bedrooms Licensed Cen ht CTV 12P Last d 7pm
PRICE GUIDE
ROOMS: s £30-£40; d £40-£55; wkly b&b £160-£175; wkly hlf-
bd £240-£255
CARDS: ◼ ◼ ◼

Selected

GH ◻◻◻◻ **Manorville** 252 Gt Western Rd AB1 6PJ
☎01224 594190
An attractive granite house stands in the west end of the city
and offers immaculate accommodation. The pleasantly
furnished bedrooms vary in size; the front bedroom is the
largest and has a huge bathroom. A comfortable lounge is
adorned with figurines and family photos, and breakfast is
served in the neat dining room. There is off-street parking to
the rear of the house.
3 en suite (bth/shr) (2 fmly) No smoking in dining room
CTV in all bedrooms Tea and coffee making facilities Cen ht
CTV 4P
PRICE GUIDE
ROOMS: s £25; d £40

GH ◻◻ **Open Hearth** 349 Holburn St AB1 6DQ
☎01224 596888
Located in the west end and convenient for the city centre, this
well kept family-run guest house offers good value bed and
breakfast accommodation to business guests and tourists alike.
The modern bedrooms and bathrooms are freshly decorated while
the public areas include a comfortable lounge and small breakfast
room with a colourful display of dolls and clowns.
11 rms (2 fmly) No smoking in dining room CTV in all
bedrooms Tea and coffee making facilities Cen ht CTV 5P No
coaches
PRICE GUIDE
ROOMS: s £22; d £36✱

GH ◻◻ **Strathboyne** 26 Abergeldie Ter AB1 6EE (0.5m N
from bridge of Dee roundabout on A92) ☎01224 593400
Mrs Gillanders's semidetached granite-built house is situated in a
quiet residential area, just south of the city centre. Bedrooms are
modest but practical and well equipped: two rooms have en suite
facilities. Public areas include a pleasant lounge and small dining
room.
7 rms (4 shr) (1 fmly) No smoking in dining room CTV in all
bedrooms Tea and coffee making facilities Cen ht CTV No
parking No coaches Last d 12.30pm
PRICE GUIDE
ROOMS: s £19-£27; d £31-£42✱

ABERDOUR Fife Map **11** NT18

Selected

GH ◻◻◻◻ **Hawkcraig House** Hawkcraig Point
KY3 0TZ ☎01383 860335
mid Mar-27 Oct
Elma Barrie offers a warm welcome to her small guest house,
which enjoys stunning views across the Firth of Forth to
Edinburgh. Bedrooms, both of which are on the ground floor,
are immaculately kept and have period furniture. Guests can
relax in the conservatory or ground floor lounge/breakfast
room, with another lounge and elegant dining room being
located on the first floor. The four course home cooked dinner
offers 'A Taste of Scotland'.
2 en suite (bth/shr) No smoking CTV in all bedrooms No
dogs (ex guide dogs) Cen ht CTV No children 10yrs 3P No
coaches Last d 24hr notice
PRICE GUIDE
ROOMS: s £24-£30; d £40-£45

◀ ◻◻◻ **The Aberdour Hotel** 38 High St KY3 0SW (on
A921) ☎01383 860325 FAX 01383 860808
Dating from the 17th century, this friendly village hotel, now offers
charming yet modern accommodation. Bedrooms vary in size but all
have excellent facilities including satellite television and direct dial
telephones. Real ales are a feature in the popular bar, while traditional
cooking is served there and in the nautical themed restaurant.
11 en suite (bth/shr) (1 fmly) CTV in all bedrooms Tea and
coffee making facilities Direct dial from bedrooms Cen ht 7P
No coaches Last d 9pm
PRICE GUIDE
ROOMS: s £35-£37.50; d £48-£52; wkly b&b £165; wkly hlf-bd
£220✱
MEALS: Lunch £4.50-£12.50alc Dinner £4.50-£15alc✱
CARDS: ◼ ◼ ◼

ABERFELDY Tayside *Perthshire* Map **14** NN84

Premier Selected

GH ◻◻◻◻◻ **Fernbank
House** Kenmore St PH15 2BL
☎01887 820345
This large Victorian house,
set in its own well kept
gardens, has been completely
refurbished over the past two
years. The hosts, Rob and
Kerry McHardy, have created
attractive, traditional
accommodation, and are
pleased to welcome guests to
stay in their non-smoking guest house. The well equipped,
simply decorated bedrooms vary in size, while the
comfortable lounge has lots of information for sightseeing in
the local area and beyond. Hearty breakfasts are served at
separate tables in the bright dining room.
7 en suite (bth/shr) (2 fmly) No smoking CTV in all
bedrooms Tea and coffee making facilities No dogs Cen ht
No children 8P No coaches
PRICE GUIDE
ROOMS: s £23.50-£33.50; d £45-£51✱

ABINGTON Strathclyde *Lanarkshire* Map **11** NS92

 Mrs M L Hodge **Craighead** (*NS914236*)
ML12 6SQ (turn off M74 at junct 13 follow signs for
Crawfordjohn, approx 2m on right)
☎01864 502356 FAX 01864 502356
May-Oct
This comfortable farm house lies in a moorland valley next to a
stream yet is only minutes from junction 13 of the M74. Guests
are made to feel at home and can relax in the cosy lounge, while
the two bedrooms are well proportioned and served by modern
bathrooms. From the M74 follow signs to Douglas then take first
turning left off old dual-carriageway.
2 rms (1 shr) No smoking in dining room Tea and coffee making
facilities No dogs (ex guide dogs) Cen ht CTV 10P Fishing
600 acres mixed Last d 5pm
PRICE GUIDE
ROOMS: s £15-£16; d £30-£32

(£)

AIRDRIE Strathclyde *Lanarkshire* Map **11** NS76

GH Q Q **Rosslee** 107 Forrest St ML6 7AR (1m E on A89)
☎01236 765865
This sturdy detached house stands in its own grounds beside the
A89 at the east end of town. Good-value accommodation is
provided in variously sized bedrooms with mixed modern
appointments and public areas include a separate dining room as
well as the homely lounge with dispense bar.
6 rms (4 shr) (2 fmly) No smoking in dining room CTV in all
bedrooms Tea and coffee making facilities Licensed Cen ht
CTV 8P No coaches Last d 11am
PRICE GUIDE
ROOMS: s £18-£22; d £36-£45

(£)

ALYTH Tayside *Perthshire* Map **15** NO25

Selected

GH Q Q Q Q **Drumnacree** St Ninians Rd, Alyth by
Blairgowrie PH11 8AP (first turning on left after
Clydesdale Bank, 300yds on right)
☎01828 632194 FAX 01828 632194
1 Apr-20 Dec
Close to the centre of the village, this large Victorian house
stands in its own mature gardens and offer a high standard of
accommodation and cuisine. Most of the carefully maintained
bedrooms are spacious and have en suite facilities, while the
public areas are adorned with interesting pictures collected
from around the world. There is a large lounge with a small,
but well-stocked bar at one end, while the elegant dining room
overlooks the garden and provides an attractive setting for
guests to sample some interesting dishes, including Cajun
specialities. Much of the produce used in the cooking is
home-grown.
6 en suite (bth/shr) (3 fmly) No smoking in bedrooms No
smoking in dining room CTV in all bedrooms Tea and coffee
making facilities Licensed Cen ht CTV 20P No coaches
Last d 9pm
PRICE GUIDE
ROOMS: s fr £35; d fr £65; wkly b&b fr £205; wkly hlf-bd
fr £328✳
CARDS: ▬ ▬

■ Q Q *Losset* Losset Rd PH11 8BT ☎01828 632393
A choice of two cosy lounge bars is offered at this friendly town
centre inn, both with original fireplaces and many polished
brasses. The bedrooms are more modern in style and all have en
suite bathrooms. A good range of bar food is available.
3 en suite (shr) CTV in all bedrooms Tea and coffee making
facilities Cen ht 10P No coaches Last d 9pm

ANSTRUTHER Fife Map **12** NO50

 GH Q Q **Beaumont Lodge** 43 Pittenweem Rd
KY10 3DT (on A917) ☎01333 310315
Situated on the western edge of this pretty harbour town, this
friendly guest house offers comfortable and good value
accommodation. Bedrooms are spacious and includes some on the
ground floor and two family rooms. Guests have the use of the
family's lounge while breakfast and dinner, on request, is served at
separate tables in the cosy dining room.
7 rms (2 fmly) No smoking in 2 bedrooms No smoking in dining
room No smoking in lounges CTV in all bedrooms Tea and
coffee making facilities No dogs Cen ht 10P
PRICE GUIDE
ROOMS: s £15-£17.50; d £30-£40; wkly b&b £105-£140; wkly
hlf-bd £154-£189

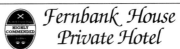

Premier Selected

GH ◨◨◨◨◨ *Hermitage*
Ladywalk KY10 3EX
☎01333 310909
Just a short stroll from the
bustling harbour and
Fisheries Museum, this
interesting historic house,
with its secluded walled
garden, is a haven of peace.
Tastefully restored, it offers a
high standard of well
appointed accommodation.

There are two individually decorated bedrooms on each floor,
and they share their own lounge and bathroom, a particularly
good arrangement for a family or party of four. All enjoy
delightful views. There is also a small, well stocked foyer
library and an attractive dining room where breakfast is
served. Home cooked evening meals are available on request
and the establishment is licensed.
4 rms (2 fmly) No smoking in bedrooms No smoking in
dining room Tea and coffee making facilities Direct dial
from bedrooms No dogs (ex guide dogs) Licensed Cen ht
CTV 6P No coaches Last d 1pm
CARDS: ◼ ◼ ◼

Selected

GH ◨◨◨◨ **The Spindrift** Pittenweem Rd KY10 3DT
(from W first building on left when entering town and
from E last building on right when leaving) (Logis)
☎01333 310573 FAX 01333 310573
Closed 17 Nov-10 Dec & Xmas
Set back from the main road on the west side of this coastal
town, this imposing Victorian house offers attractive
accommodation, which is constantly being improved by the
owners Eric and Moyra McFarlane. The largest bedrooms are
on the first floor, though the timber-lined Captain's Cabin
offers unusual surroundings for those looking for something a
little different. The comfortable lounge has an open fire and
honesty bar, while home-cooking is offered in the bright
dining room.
8 en suite (bth/shr) (3 fmly) No smoking CTV in all
bedrooms Tea and coffee making facilities Direct dial from
bedrooms No dogs Licensed Cen ht CTV 12P No coaches
Last d 7pm
PRICE GUIDE
ROOMS: d £50-£60; wkly b&b £175-£210; wkly hlf-bd
£231-£252
CARDS: ◼ ◼   £

ARBROATH Tayside *Angus* Map **12** NO64

⇄♦ **GH** ◨◨ **Kingsley** 29 Market Gate DD11 1AU (close
to harbour) ☎01241 873933 FAX 01241 873933
A family-run commercial guest house close to the town centre
offers bedrooms with bright, cheerful fabrics, some modern in
style of furnishing. For entertainment there is a games room with
pool and darts and a residents' lounge. In summer evening meals
are provided and a small residents' bar is opened.

14 rms (8 bth/shr) (14 fmly) No smoking in dining room CTV in
all bedrooms Licensed Cen ht CTV 4P Childrens play ground
PRICE GUIDE
ROOMS: s £15-£22; d £26-£34
£

Premier Selected

♦ ◨◨◨◨◨ Mrs S A
Caldwell **Farmhouse Kitchen**
(NO582447) Grange of Conon
DD11 3SD (6m N, signposted
from A933 just beyond
Colliston) ☎01241 860202
FAX 01241 860424

This spacious farmhouse
offers delightful
accommodation in two
stylish twin rooms well
equipped with satellite TV,
music centres, fresh fruit, toiletries, bathrobes and superb
bathrooms. There are an attractive sun lounge overlooking the
gardens and a games room with snooker, table tennis, a sun
bed and an exercise bike. Breakfast is taken communally
around an oval table in the farm's modern kitchen.
2 rms (1 shr) CTV in all bedrooms Tea and coffee making
facilities No dogs (ex guide dogs) Cen ht CTV No children
3yrs 4P Fishing Snooker Solarium Games room 560 acres
arable
PRICE GUIDE
ROOMS: s £30-£40; d £35-£55✱

ARDBRECKNISH Strathclyde *Argyllshire* Map **10** NN02

♦ ◨◨◨ Mrs Whalley **Rockhill** *(NN072219)* PA33 1BH
☎01866 833218
May-Sep
Situated on the picturesque eastern shore of Lach Awe, with views
over the Loch to Ben Cruachan, this comfortable farmhouse has a
friendly atmosphere which makes it a real home-from-home.
Rooms are furnished in both modern and traditional styles. There
is a cosy lounge well-stocked with reading material and enjoyable
home cooking is served in the neat dining room.
5 rms (1 bth/shr) (3 fmly) CTV in all bedrooms Tea and coffee
making facilities Licensed No children 8yrs 8P Fishing 200
acres horses sheep Last d 7pm
PRICE GUIDE
ROOMS: d £32-£38; wkly hlf-bd £200-£245✱

ARDERSIER Highland *Inverness-shire* Map **14** NH85

♦ ◨◨◨ Mrs L E MacBean *Milton-of-Gollanfield* *(NH809534)*
Gollanfield IV1 2QT (just off A96 between Inverness & Nairn)
☎01667 462207
May-Oct
A welcoming homely atmosphere prevails at Mrs MacBean's
comfortable Victorian farmhouse which stands off the A96 mid
way between Nairn and Inverness. There is a relaxing lounge with
CTV and an attractive dining room where hearty farm breakfasts
are served on the communal table. Bedrooms are solidly traditional
in style.
3 rms No smoking Tea and coffee making facilities No dogs (ex
guide dogs) CTV P 365 acres mixed arable

ARDGAY Highland *Sutherland* Map **14** NH58

GH QQQQ *Ardgay House* IV24 3DH (on B9176 or via Tain on A836) ☎01863 766345
Apr-Oct rs Nov-Mar
This grand Victorian house, set in its own pretty gardens, has been lovingly restored by enthusiastic owners Keith and Eileen Denton. Individually styled and well equipped bedrooms have stripped flooring with attractive rugs and period furniture. The elegant dining room displays conch shells from Fiji, and the comfortable lounge features other items collected from around the world.
6 rms (4 bth/shr) (1 fmly) No smoking in dining room No smoking in lounges CTV in all bedrooms Tea and coffee making facilities No dogs (ex guide dogs) Licensed Cen ht No children 8yrs 9P No coaches Last d 7pm

---

ARRAN, ISLE OF Strathclyde *Buteshire* Map **10**

BRODICK Map **10** NS03

GH QQQ *Allandale* KA27 8BJ ☎01770 302278
Closed Jan-Oct
A warm welcome and enjoyable home cooking contribute to the appeal of this comfortable detached house which stands in well tended gardens just south of the town. Bedrooms are furnished in mixed modern styles and offer all the expected amenities. Public areas include a relaxing lounge and a recently refurbished dining room.
4 en suite (bth/shr) 2 annexe en suite (bth/shr) (4 fmly) No smoking in dining room No smoking in 1 lounge CTV in all bedrooms Tea and coffee making facilities Licensed Cen ht P Last d 7pm

GH QQQQ *Dunvegan House* Dunvegan Shore Rd KA27 8AJ (Turn right from ferry terminal, 500yds along Shore Road) ☎01770 302811
This delightful detached sandstone house is situated on the sea front and enjoys splendid views over the bay to Brodick Castle and the impressive mountains beyond. The house has been sympathetically renovated and extended over the years, with bedrooms (which are all non-smoking) decorated to a high standard, with pine and period furniture. There is a relaxing lounge and a dining room where Taste of Scotland dishes are served.
9 en suite (bth/shr) (1 fmly) No smoking in bedrooms CTV in all bedrooms Tea and coffee making facilities No dogs (ex guide dogs) Licensed Cen ht CTV 10P No coaches Last d 4pm
PRICE GUIDE
ROOMS: d £52✳

Factual details of establishments in this Guide are from questionnaires we send to all establishments that feature in the book.

LAMLASH Map **10** NS03

Selected

GH ⓆⓆⓆⓆ **Lilybank Hotel** Shore Rd KA27 8LS
☎01770 600230
Closed 6 Jan-28 Feb
Enthusiastic owners Clive and Carol Berry have tastefully
renovated this small whitewashed hotel in the centre of the
village overlooking the bay and Holy Isle. Bedrooms, though
compact, are bright and cheerful with fresh decor, co-
ordinated fabrics and modern furnishings. Public areas
include a choice of comfortable lounges, one with well filled
bookshelves and a dispense bar. The attractive dining room
which is also open to non residents, offers a range of carefully
prepared Taste of Scotland dishes. With such a relaxed and
friendly atmosphere, this is an ideal base for those wishing to
explore the island.
6 rms (5 shr) (1 fmly) No smoking in bedrooms No smoking
in dining room CTV in all bedrooms Tea and coffee making
facilities Licensed Cen ht 6P No coaches Last d 7.30pm
PRICE GUIDE
ROOMS: s £18-£50; d £36-£50; wkly b&b £126-£175;
wkly hlf-bd £210-£245

LOCHRANZA Map **10** NR95

GH ⓆⓆ *Kincardine Lodge* KA27 8HL ☎01770 830267
Apr-Oct
A sturdy Victorian house, Kincardine Lodge stands in its own well
maintained garden overlooking the bay and castle, close to the
Kintyre ferry terminal. It offers good value holiday
accommodation and a choice of comfortable lounges, one no
smoking.
7 rms (4 fmly) Tea and coffee making facilities CTV 6P

WHITING BAY Map **10** NS02

GH ⓆⓆⓆ **Invermay Hotel** Shore Rd KA27 8PZ
☎01770 700431
Apr-Oct
The Invermay Hotel, a substantial detached house standing in its
own garden beside the main street, commands panoramic views of
the Firth of Clyde. A relaxed atmosphere pervades comfortable
public areas which include a TV lounge, a small bar area and an
attractive dining room where enjoyable home-cooked food is
served. Bedrooms vary in size and are all no-smoking.
7 rms (5 shr) No smoking in bedrooms No smoking in dining
room Tea and coffee making facilities No dogs (ex guide dogs)
Licensed Cen ht CTV 8P No coaches Last d 2pm
PRICE GUIDE
ROOMS: s fr £24; d fr £48; wkly b&b fr £168; wkly hlf-bd fr
£245

£

We endeavour to be as accurate as possible
but changes in personnel and data can occur
in establishments after the Guide has gone to
press.

AUCHTERMUCHTY Fife Map **11** NO21

Premier Selected

♥ ⓆⓆⓆⓆⓆ Mrs I Steven
Ardchoille (NO248096)
Dunshalt KY14 7EY (on
B936) ☎01337 828414
FAX 01337 828414
Over the years the Stevens'
have built up a thriving
business, with many guests
returning on a regular basis.
A more friendly and
hospitable couple would be
hard to find. Donald takes
care of front of house duties, while Isobel is responsible for
the excellent Taste of Scotland dishes and hearty breakfasts
which are served at the communal table in the small neat
dining room. Bedrooms, while not enormous, are bright and
cheery and have all the expected amenities. Smoking is not
permitted.
3 rms (2 shr) (1 fmly) No smoking CTV in all bedrooms
Tea and coffee making facilities No dogs (ex guide dogs)
Cen ht CTV 8P 2 acres Last d 6pm
CARDS: 🔳 🔲

AVIEMORE Highland *Inverness-shire* Map **14** NH81

GH ⓆⓆⓆ *Ravenscraig* Grampian Rd PH22 1RP
☎01479 810278
Robert and Christine Thompson continue to improve standards at
their comfortable home, which stands beside the main road at the
north end of the village. Hearty breakfasts are served at individual
tables in the attractive extended dining room, and there is a lounge
where guests can relax. Bedrooms, including those in a rear
annexe, are modern in style.
6 en suite (shr) 6 annexe en suite (shr) (2 fmly) CTV in all
bedrooms Tea and coffee making facilities Cen ht CTV 15P
CARDS: 🔳

AYR Strathclyde *Ayrshire* Map **10** NS32

See also Dunure

GH ⓆⓆⓆ **Arrandale Hotel** 2-4 Cassillis St KA7 1DW
☎01292 289959
This friendly family-run hotel is situated in a residential area close
to both the beach and town centre. Some bedrooms are spacious;
all have bright cheerful colour schemes and are nicely furnished.
Public areas include a comfortable no-smoking lounge, an open-
plan dining room with a small residents' bar and a games area
with pool table.
12 rms (1 bth 3 shr) (3 fmly) CTV in all bedrooms Tea and
coffee making facilities No dogs (ex guide dogs) Cen ht No
children No parking No coaches
PRICE GUIDE
ROOMS: s £18-£20; d £32-£44; wkly b&b fr £100

GH 🔲🔲🔲🔲 **Brenalder Lodge** 39 Dunure, Doonfoot KA7 4HR (2m S on A719) ☎01292 443939
rs during props holiday

The Taylor family welcome guests warmly to their extended modern detached home which is situated beside the A719 south of town. The compact bedrooms are bright and cheerful, with attractive soft colour schemes and modern appointments - the smart family suite being especially popular. A spacious lounge features an impressive natural stone fireplace and comfortable leather seating, and the attractive dining room provides a suitable setting for Brenda Taylor's delicious home-cooked meals: the four course menu offering a choice at every stage is chalked up on a blackboard each evening. Smoking is only permitted in the lounge.

3 en suite (bth/shr) (1 fmly) No smoking in bedrooms No smoking in dining room CTV in all bedrooms Tea and coffee making facilities Cen ht CTV No children 7yrs 9P No coaches Last d 24hrs prior
£

GH 🔲🔲🔲 **Craggallan** 8 Queens Ter KA7 1DU ☎01292 264998

Hosts Nancy and Bill Hamilton warmly welcome guests to their brightly painted terraced guest house, situated conveniently close to the beach and town centre. Bedrooms, though compact, are tastefully decorated and agreeably furnished in modern style, while public areas include an attractive lounge with a small dining room adjacent.

6 rms (2 shr) (1 fmly) No smoking in 2 bedrooms No smoking in dining room CTV in all bedrooms Tea and coffee making facilities Cen ht CTV 4P No coaches Last d 5pm

PRICE GUIDE
ROOMS: s £16-£18; d £32-£40∗
£

GH 🔲🔲🔲 *Dargill* 7 Queens Ter KA7 1DU ☎01292 261955

This brightly painted terraced house is situated in a residential area overlooking the seafront and close to the town centre. Bedrooms are bright and cheery, with modern appointments and all the expected amenities. Public areas include a comfortable no-smoking lounge and a small dining room where enjoyable home cooking is served at individual tables.

4 rms (1 shr) (2 fmly) No smoking in 1 lounge CTV in all bedrooms Tea and coffee making facilities Cen ht CTV No children 3yrs 5P No coaches Last d 2pm

---

GH 🔲🔲🔲🔲 **Glenmore** 35 Bellevue Crescent KA7 2DP ☎01292 269830 FAX 01292 269830

This charming terraced house is located in a residential, tree-lined crescent just south of the town centre. Attractive decor and fabrics have been used to good effect in the attractive bedrooms, which are individual in style but vary in size. There are a tasteful lounge and small neat dining room, both featuring fine fireplaces, and standards of maintenance and housekeeping are high. Street parking is available, together with permits for areas where restrictions apply.

5 en suite (bth/shr) (2 fmly) No smoking in dining room No smoking in lounges CTV in all bedrooms Tea and coffee making facilities No dogs Cen ht CTV No parking Last d 5pm

PRICE GUIDE
ROOMS: s £17-£20; d £35-£40; wkly b&b £122.50-£140; wkly hlf-bd £178-£196∗
£

♨ 💺 **GH** 🔲🔲🔲 **Langley Bank** 39 Carrick Rd KA7 2RD ☎01292 264246 FAX 01292 282628

Many guests return on a regular basis to Bob and Morna Mitchell's substantial semidetached period house situated in a residential area just south of central amenities. First-floor bedrooms with superb bathrooms are tastefully furnished in period style, and the two ground-floor rooms (which have the use of facilities on the first floor) are more modern in appointment. Hearty breakfasts are served in a smart dining room, but there is no lounge.

6 rms (4 shr) (1 fmly) No smoking in dining room CTV in all bedrooms Tea and coffee making facilities No dogs (ex guide dogs) Cen ht 4P No coaches

PRICE GUIDE
ROOMS: s £15-£35; d £30-£45

CARDS: 🔳 🔳 🔳

GH 🔲🔲 **Windsor Hotel** 6 Alloway Place KA7 2AA (from the centre of Ayr, take the A19 through Wellington Square and establishment is the first guesthouse on the right) ☎01292 264689
Closed Xmas & New Year

Conveniently positioned within walking distance of both the town centre and seafront, Mike and Anne Hamilton's end-of-terrace house is benefiting from ongoing improvements. Bedrooms, which vary in size, include some family rooms and some on the ground floor. There is a spacious first-floor lounge, and both hearty breakfasts and enjoyable home-cooked evening meals are served in an attractively decorated dining room. Picnic lunches can also be provided.

10 rms (7 bth/shr) (4 fmly) No smoking in dining room CTV in all bedrooms Tea and coffee making facilities Cen ht CTV No parking No coaches

PRICE GUIDE
ROOMS: s fr £20; d fr £44; wkly b&b fr £140; wkly hlf-bd fr £195∗

CARDS: 🔳 🔳
£

BALLACHULISH Highland *Argyllshire*   Map **14** NN05

GH 🔲🔲🔲🔲 **Fern Villa** East Laroch PA39 4JE (take left turn on entering village from Glencoe, house 150yds on left) ☎01855 811393

June and Kenneth Chandler's granite-built Victorian villa stands in the centre of the village and is an ideal base from which to explore the surrounding countryside. June is a charming hostess and her love of cooking, combined with careful use of local produce, makes dining at Fern Villa an enjoyable experience. Refreshments are served in the cosy, relaxing lounge, and bedrooms - though small - are well maintained and comfortable. This is a no-smoking establishment.

5 en suite (bth/shr) No smoking Tea and coffee making facilities No dogs (ex guide dogs) Licensed Cen ht CTV No children 10yrs 5P No coaches Last d 7pm

PRICE GUIDE
ROOMS: d £30-£38; wkly b&b £105-£119; wkly hlf-bd £175-£196

Selected

GH ◨◨◨◨ Lyn-Leven White St PA39 4JP (off A82)
☎01855 811392 FAX 01855 811600
Closed Xmas
Many guests return on a regular basis to this friendly and well
maintained guest house situated just off the A82 with fine
views over Loch Leven and the surrounding mountains.
Compact bedrooms, some in an annexe, are decorated to a
high standard and offer mixed modern furnishings and all the
expected amenities. The comfortable lounge looks out onto
the loch while enjoyable home cooking and hearty breakfasts
are served in the attractive dining room.
8 rms (7 shr) 5 annexe en suite (bth/shr) (1 fmly) No
smoking in 1 bedrooms CTV in 8 bedrooms Tea and coffee
making facilities Licensed Cen ht CTV 12P Last d 7.30pm
PRICE GUIDE
ROOMS: s £20-£30; d £32-£38; wkly b&b £112-£133; wkly
hlf-bd £170-£190
CARDS: ◨ ◨

BALLANTRAE Strathclyde *Ayrshire* Map **10** NX08

GH ◨◨◨ Balkissock Lodge KA26 0LP
☎01465 831537 FAX 01465 831537
Situated amongst lovely rolling countryside well inland and North
East of the village is this former shooting lodge with its own
gardens and ample parking. The accommodation is pleasant and
fresh, two rooms being on the ground floor. The cosy dining room,
which has some lounge seating, offers an attractive dinner menu
(if sufficient notice is given) and an innovative breakfast selection.
There is a separate lounge with lots of book, games and
magazines. This is an ideal retreat for lovers of the outdoors, so
the no-smoking policy should not be a surprise.
3 en suite (bth/shr) (1 fmly) No smoking CTV in all bedrooms
Tea and coffee making facilities No dogs (ex guide dogs) Cen ht
30P No coaches Last d 6pm
PRICE GUIDE
ROOMS: s £26.50; d £53; wkly b&b £185.50; wkly hlf-bd
£196-£231
CARDS: ◨ ◨

Premier Selected

GH ◨◨◨◨◨ Cosses
Country House Cosses
KA26 0LR (approach village
on A77 and take turning for
Laggan. Cosses is 2m after
Laggan Caravan Park)
☎01465 831363
FAX 01465 831598
Closed 24 Dec-5 Jan
This converted farm is set at
the end of a tree-lined drive
about two miles east of the village, amidst the gentle
pastureland of Southern Ayrshire. Excellent use has been
made of the old outbuildings; one has become a spacious
games room, another the 'garden suite' containing a family
bedroom together with a separate sitting room and bathroom.
Guests meet in the spacious and comfortable lounge before
taking dinner in the elegant dining room where Cordon Bleu
meals feature produce grown in the farm garden.

3 en suite (bth/shr) (2 fmly) No smoking in bedrooms CTV
in 2 bedrooms Tea and coffee making facilities Licensed
Cen ht ch fac 8P No coaches Games room Last d 7pm
PRICE GUIDE
ROOMS: s £30-£45; d £60-£70✳

BALLATER Grampian *Aberdeenshire* Map **15** NO39

Selected

GH ◨◨◨◨ Glen Lui Hotel Invercauld Rd AB35 5RP
☎013397 55402 FAX 013397 55545
Closed 15 Jan-15 Mar
Located near to the golf course on the west side of the town,
this hotel offers a good level of service and well equipped,
comfortable bedrooms including two suites in the main house
and more spacious annexe rooms. The restaurant and Bistro
offer 'A Taste of Scotland' using fresh ingredients and a great
deal of imagination. There is also a cosy lounge and a
licensed bar.
10 en suite (bth/shr) 9 annexe en suite (bth/shr) (2 fmly) No
smoking in bedrooms No smoking in dining room No
smoking in 1 lounge CTV in all bedrooms Tea and coffee
making facilities Direct dial from bedrooms Licensed Cen
ht CTV ch fac 30P Last d 9pm
PRICE GUIDE
ROOMS: s £28-£38; d £56-£76; wkly b&b £196-£266;
wkly hlf-bd £280-£336
CARDS: ◨ ◨ ◨ ◨

GH ◨◨◨ Green Inn 9 Victoria Rd AB35 5QQ
☎013397 55701 FAX 013397 55701
Closed Sun Oct-Mar & 2 wks in Oct
This restaurant with rooms sits in the square overlooking the
village green and provides bed and breakfast only for residents
taking dinner. Attractive soft furnishings at colour to the
traditional Victorian public rooms, and there is a comfortable
lounge. Bedrooms are more plainly furnished but two in particular
are of a good size.
3 en suite (bth/shr) No smoking in bedrooms No smoking in
dining room CTV in all bedrooms Tea and coffee making
facilities Licensed Cen ht CTV Last d 9pm
PRICE GUIDE
ROOMS: s £30-£40; d £50; wkly b&b £170;
wkly hlf-bd £260
CARDS: ◨ ◨

GH ◨◨◨ Moorside Braemar Rd AB35 5RL (on A93)
☎013397 55492 FAX 013397 55492
Mar-Nov
This extended granite house lies in its own gardens in the centre of
the village. It has a friendly atmosphere and the bright airy
bedrooms offer good value accomodation. There is a comfortable
lounge and hearty breakfasts are served in the separate dining room.
9 en suite (bth/shr) (3 fmly) No smoking in dining room CTV in
all bedrooms Tea and coffee making facilities Licensed Cen ht
10P No coaches
CARDS: ◨ ◨

GH ◨◨◨ Netherley 2 Netherley Place AB35 5QE
☎013397 55792
Closed Nov-Jan rs Feb
Part of a terraced row just off the village green, this guest house is
distinguished by its blue shutters and hanging flower baskets.

Comfortable public rooms include a well proportioned dining room and a lounge with two separate areas. A table with tea and coffee-making equipment is available at all times, and bedrooms vary from large to small.

9 rms (4 bth/shr) (3 fmly) No smoking in dining room No smoking in 1 lounge CTV in 4 bedrooms Tea and coffee making facilities CTV No children 4yrs No parking No coaches
PRICE GUIDE
ROOMS: s £17-£18; d £30-£40

BALLOCH Strathclyde *Dumbartonshire* Map **10** NS38

GH QQQ **Arbor Lodge** Old Luss Rd G83 8QW (400yds from Glasgow to Loch Lomond road)
☎01389 756233 FAX 01389 78988
In a convenient position, this modern house has two large twins and two small double bedrooms, all nicely decorated. There is no lounge and the house is no-smoking.

4 en suite (shr) No smoking CTV in all bedrooms Tea and coffee making facilities No dogs (ex guide dogs) Cen ht 8P No coaches
PRICE GUIDE
ROOMS: d £40-£48✱
CARDS: 🔳 💳

GH QQQ **Beulah** Fisherwood Rd G83 8SW
☎01389 753022
Guests are warmly welcomed to this comfortable house which stands in a well tended garden between the railway station and River Leven. Its two en suite bedrooms are appointed in modern style, and hearty breakfasts are served at individual tables in the combined lounge/dining room.

2 en suite (shr) No smoking CTV in all bedrooms Tea and coffee making facilities Cen ht CTV No children 12yrs 4P No coaches
PRICE GUIDE
ROOMS: s £20-£25; d £32-£40; ✱

Selected

GH QQQQ **Gowanlea** Drymen Rd G83 8HS
☎01389 752456
Closed 24-26 Dec
Many guests return year after year to this delightful semidetached villa situated in a quiet residential area within easy reach of central amenities. Reasonably spacious and attractively coordinated bedrooms are furnished in modern style, television is provided in the comfortable lounge and hearty breakfasts are served in a neat little dining room. Guests are assured of both a warm welcome and a relaxed, friendly atmosphere.

4 en suite (bth/shr) No smoking CTV in all bedrooms Tea and coffee making facilities No dogs (ex guide dogs) Cen ht CTV 4P
PRICE GUIDE
ROOMS: s £18-£25; d £32-£40; wkly b&b £120-£130
CARDS: 🔳 💳 🔳

BALQUHIDDER Central *Perthshire* Map **11** NN52

Selected

GH QQQQ **Stronvar House** FK19 8PB
☎01877 384688 FAX 01877 384230
Mar-Oct
Located in a peaceful setting on the south side of Loch Voil, this Victorian mansion combines a spacious guest house with a 'Bygone Museum', a tea room and a craft shop. Bedrooms all bear the names of famous clans, while two contain four-poster beds; public areas include a drawing room with a pianola and an honesty bar.

4 en suite (bth/shr) No smoking in dining room CTV in all bedrooms Tea and coffee making facilities Licensed Cen ht 60P Last d 7.30pm
PRICE GUIDE
ROOMS: s £39.50; d £59; wkly b&b £185; wkly hlf-bd £295
CARDS: 🔳 💳

BANFF Grampian *Banffshire* Map **15** NJ66

GH QQQ **Morayhill** Bellevue Rd AB45 1BJ (turn off A947 onto A97, direction Aberchirder, second on right and third house on left) ☎01261 815956 FAX 01261 818717
An elegant Victorian house situated close to the centre of this historic coastal town, just off the Huntly road, offers spacious, comfortable and well equipped bedrooms. There is a very attractive lounge with an original marble fireplace, and breakfast

THE GREEN INN
9 Victoria Road, Ballater, Grampian AB35 5QQ
Telephone: 01339 755701 Fax: 01339 755701

This Restaurant with rooms, providing bed and breakfast only for dinner guests, stands in the square looking out on to the village green. Attractive decor in clear pastel shades and pine furniture enhance the traditional Victorian dining room, which has a small dispense bar, and there is also a comfortable lounge. Chef/proprietor Jeff Purves – whose expertise has earned **two rosettes** for the restaurant – produces the best of Scottish meats, game and seafood, and cheese buffs will appreciate the impressive range of local varieties. Bedrooms are plainly furnished, but two of good size. **AA QQQ**

(which is ordered the previous evening) is served at separate tables in the bright dining room. The friendly owners are happy to arrange golfing and fishing on request.
3 rms (2 shr) (2 fmly) CTV in all bedrooms Tea and coffee making facilities Cen ht CTV 5P
PRICE GUIDE
ROOMS: s £17.50; d £30-£35; wkly b&b £90-£105✶

BEATTOCK Dumfries & Galloway *Dumfriesshire*
Map **11** NT00

Selected

♥ **QQQQ** Mrs K Miller **Broomlands** (NT088015)
DG10 9PQ ☎01683 300320 FAX 01683 300320
Etr-Oct
This well kept farmhouse, set in colourful gardens, is about two miles from Moffat, making it an ideal base to explore the Borders, as well as Dumfries and Galloway. The well equipped bedrooms are furnished to a high standard and are immaculately clean, while hearty breakfasts are served in the pretty dining room which features tapestries, hand-made by Kate Miller. There is also a relaxing lounge with an array of books and tourist information.
3 en suite (bth/shr) No smoking CTV in all bedrooms Tea and coffee making facilities No dogs (ex guide dogs) Cen ht CTV No children 12yrs 5P 200 acres beef mixed sheep
PRICE GUIDE
ROOMS: s £20-£20; d £36; wkly b&b fr £116

♥ **QQQ** Mr & Mrs Bell **Cogrie's** *(NY106974)* DG10 9PP (3m S off A74) ☎01576 470320
Mar-Nov
This 18th-century farmhouse is peacefully situated in rural surroundings and offers comfortable bed and breakfast accommodation. The traditionally furnished bedrooms are generally spacious and have modern coordinated fabrics and good beds. Public areas include a comfortable lounge and separate breakfast room.
4 rms (3 fmly) Tea and coffee making facilities No dogs Cen ht CTV 6P 275 acres dairy mixed
PRICE GUIDE
ROOMS: d fr £29

BEAULY Highland *Inverness-shire* Map **14** NH54

GH QQQ Chrialdon Hotel Station Rd IV4 7EH
☎01463 782336
Close to the centre of the village, Anthony and Jennifer Bond's detached Victorian home stands beside the main road in its own well tended garden. Bedrooms are variable in size and offer both modern and traditional appointments, while an attractive lounge invites peaceful relaxation and the tastefully appointed dining room offers an opportunity to sample Jennifer's tempting home cooking. Dinner is a five-course affair based on local produce whenever possible.
8 rms (2 bth 4 shr) (2 fmly) No smoking in bedrooms No smoking in dining room CTV in all bedrooms Tea and coffee making facilities Licensed Cen ht 18P No coaches Last d 7.30pm
PRICE GUIDE
ROOMS: s £18.50-£33; d £44-£53; wkly b&b fr £129
CARDS: █ █

GH QQQ Heathmount Station Rd IV4 7EQ
☎01463 782411
Closed Xmas & New Year
Situated beside the main road close to the village square, this sturdy Victorian villa offers a friendly atmosphere and good-value bed and breakfast accommodation. Bedrooms are bright and airy with attractive decor and modern teak furnishings. Public areas include a spacious lounge and a neat dining room where hearty breakfasts are served at individual tables.
5 rms (2 fmly) No smoking in bedrooms No smoking in dining room CTV in all bedrooms Tea and coffee making facilities Cen ht CTV 5P No coaches
PRICE GUIDE
ROOMS: s £15-£17; d £30-£34; wkly b&b £94-£107✶

BEITH Strathclyde *Renfrewshire* Map **10** NS35

♥ **QQQ** Mrs J Gillan *Shotts Farm (NS363500)* KA15 1LB
☎01505 502273
There is a relaxed and friendly atmosphere at this traditional farmhouse, situated four miles east of Beith and surrounded by rolling countryside. No-smoking bedrooms are bright and cheery, with tasteful modern appointments. There is a residents' lounge, but guests often join the owners in their own lounge, which is where enjoyable breakfasts and home-cooked dinners are served at a communal table.
3 rms (1 fmly) CTV in all bedrooms Tea and coffee making facilities No dogs Cen ht CTV 3P 160 acres dairy Last d 10am

BIGGAR Strathclyde *Lanarkshire* Map **11** NT03

♥ **QQQ** Mrs Margaret Kirby **Walston Mansions Farmhouse** *(NT060456)* ML11 8NF ☎01899 810338
From its elevated position in the village, this farmhouse enjoys sweeping views across open moorland. With its play area, duck pond, aviary, chipmunks and pet rabbits, it will be of particular appeal to families. Guest pets are also welcomed. Of the two comfortable en suite rooms, one has a four-poster and a single bed, and the other a double and a set of full-sized bunks. The smaller twin room has exclusive use of the nearby bathroom.
3 rms (2 bth/shr) (1 fmly) No smoking in bedrooms No smoking in dining room CTV in all bedrooms Tea and coffee making facilities Cen ht CTV ch fac 6P 2000 acres sheep/cattle Last d 3pm

BLACKFORD Tayside *Perthshire* Map **11** NN80

GH QQ Yarrow House Moray St PH4 1PY ☎01764 682358
Attractive flowering baskets adorn the front of this friendly family-run guest house which offers easy access to the A9 from its setting beside the main street. Tastefully decorated bedrooms are equipped with all the expected amenities and a hearty breakfast is served at the open-plan lounge/dining room's communal table.
3 rms (1 shr) No smoking in bedrooms No smoking in dining room CTV in all bedrooms Tea and coffee making facilities Cen ht CTV 3P No coaches
PRICE GUIDE
ROOMS: s £13-£16; d £26-£32; wkly b&b £70-£91; wkly hlf-bd £105-£120✶

Our inspectors never book in the name of the AA. They disclose their identity only after the bill has been paid.

BLAIR ATHOLL Tayside *Perthshire* Map **14** NN86

🛏️ 🍽️ GH QQQQ **Dalgreine** Bridge of Tilt PH18 5SX
☎01796 481276
A beautifully restored detached period house standing in its own sheltered garden offers bedrooms which, though not large, are well furnished and decorated. Downstairs there are a cosy lounge and a dining room with a small snooker table. This is a no-smoking house.
6 rms (2 shr) (1 fmly) No smoking Tea and coffee making facilities CTV 6P No coaches Small snooker table Last d 3pm
PRICE GUIDE
ROOMS: s £14-£17; d £28-£36; wkly b&b £90-£114; wkly hlf-bd £153-£177

GH QQQ *The Firs* Saint Andrews Crescent PH18 5TA
☎01796 481256
Etr-late Oct
This Victorian house is set in its own grounds in a quiet central residential area well away from the main road. Tastefully decorated to reflect the character of the house, some of the bedrooms have retained their original fireplaces, whilst fresh fruit and flowers are a feature in all. The comfortable lounge has an open log fire and overlooks the garden, while the charming owner Mrs Crerar provides home-cooked dinners and hearty breakfasts in the attractive dining room.
4 en suite (bth/shr) (2 fmly) No smoking in bedrooms No smoking in dining room CTV in all bedrooms Tea and coffee making facilities Cen ht 6P Last d 5pm

BLAIRGOWRIE Tayside *Perthshire* Map **15** NO14

GH QQQ **Duncraggan** Perth Rd PH10 6EJ
☎01250 872082
This creeper-clad, turreted house sits in attractive gardens on the southern side of the town. Bedrooms are neat and traditional, there is a large comfortable lounge and a pretty dining room. Christine McClemont is a charming and enthusiastic hostess, committed to an impressive range of evening meal, from high tea to a light snack.
3 rms (2 shr) No smoking in bedrooms CTV in 1 bedroom Tea and coffee making facilities No dogs (ex guide dogs) Cen ht CTV ch fac 6P No coaches 9 hole putting Last d 5pm
PRICE GUIDE
ROOMS: s £18-£18.50; d £37✳

GH QQQ **The Laurels** Golf Course Rd, Rosemount PH10 6LH (S on A93) ☎01250 874920
Closed Dec
This modernised stone house lies off the main road on the south side of the town, close to Rosemount Golf Club. It is well maintained throughout and offers bright contemporary bedrooms with smart en suite shower rooms. There are a comfortable lounge and a small dining room serving breakfast and a good range of food and drink at dinner.
6 rms (4 shr) No smoking CTV in all bedrooms Tea and coffee making facilities No dogs Licensed Cen ht CTV 6P Last d 5.45pm
PRICE GUIDE
ROOMS: s fr £18; d fr £36✳
CARDS: 🔲 🔲 🔲 🔲

🛏️ 🍽️ GH QQQ **Norwood House** Park Dr PH10 6PA
☎01250 874146
This late-Victorian house has been sypathetically modernised to retain many fine features, including beautiful woodwork and corniced ceilings. Well maintained bedrooms have their original fireplaces and contain such thoughtful extras as hair dryers, electric blankets, tissues and face cloths, while the attractive lounge offers a collection of books, games and magazines. Guests also have the use of a cosy little patio dining room with French windows leading to the garden and car park. A peaceful and relaxing atmosphere pervades this non-smoking house.
4 rms (1 fmly) No smoking Tea and coffee making facilities Cen ht CTV 4P No coaches Last d 4.30pm
PRICE GUIDE
ROOMS: s £15-£17; d £30; wkly b&b £94.50-£105; wkly hlf-bd £138.25-£161

> Entries in this Guide are based on reports filed by our team of professionally trained, full-time inspectors.

Morayhill AA QQQ
Bellevue Road, Banff AB45 1BJ
Telephone: 01261 815956

An elegant Victorian house situated in Banff on the Moray Firth coast. Banff has many finely restored 18th Century buildings including Duff House designed by William Adam and recently opened as a country house gallery. There is a fine sandy beach with coastal walks, whisky and castle trails nearby. The town centre is only minutes away. Banff is an ideal centre for a golfing or fishing holiday.

BOAT OF GARTEN Highland *Inverness-shire* Map **14** NH91

Premier Selected

GH QQQQQ **Heathbank**
The Victorian House
PH24 3BD ☎01479 831234
Closed Nov & 1-25 Dec
A welcoming Victorian house
of considerable character and
charm, set in its own garden on
the edge of this Osprey village,
has been restored to its former
splendour over the past few
years by Graham and Lindsay
Burge. Bedrooms vary in size
and are individually furnished with taste and flair; two have
four-poster beds and they all offer good facilities and
thoughtful extra touches. There is a choice of comfortable
lounges with open fires and ample books, games and tourist
information. The new conservatory restaurant provides an
extremely stylish setting for the excellent four-course Taste of
Scotland set dinners for which Graham, a professional chef,
has been awarded an AA rosette.
7 en suite (bth/shr) (1 fmly) No smoking Tea and coffee
making facilities No dogs (ex guide dogs) Licensed Cen ht
CTV No children 5yrs 8P No coaches Last d 6pm
PRICE GUIDE
ROOMS: d £44-£70; wkly b&b £154-£245; wkly hlf-bd
£266-£364

GH QQQ **Moorfield House Hotel** Deshar Rd PH24 3BN
☎01479 831646
A charming detached Victorian house conveniently located in the
centre of the village offers bedrooms which, though not large, are
bright and cheery, with both modern and traditional appointments.
The lounge and bar are comfortable, good home-cooked food is
served at both breakfast and dinner and the atmosphere is relaxing
throughout.
4 en suite (bth/shr) (1 fmly) No smoking CTV in all bedrooms
Tea and coffee making facilities Licensed Cen ht CTV No
children 14yrs 8P No coaches Last d 3pm
PRICE GUIDE
ROOMS: s £22; d £38; wkly b&b fr £133; wkly hlf-bd
fr £203

GH QQQ **Ryvoan** Kinchurdy Rd PH24 3BP (Kinchurdy
Road is directly opposite the Post Office in the main street)
☎01479 831654
The provision of modern facilities has in no way detracted from
the character of this splendid Victorian house which enjoys views
of the Cairngorms from its setting amid mature grounds in a quiet
residential area of the village. Public areas, which have a relaxed
atmosphere, include a comfortable lounge with a log fire and a
traditional dining room where enjoyable home cooking is served
at separate tables. Bedrooms are individually furnished in period
style and vary somewhat in size. This is a no-smoking
establishment.
3 rms (2 bth) (1 fmly) No smoking CTV in all bedrooms Tea
and coffee making facilities No dogs Cen ht 6P No coaches
PRICE GUIDE
ROOMS: d fr £34; wkly b&b fr £119; wkly hlf-bd fr £203

BO'NESS Central *West Lothian* Map **11** NS98

♥ QQQ Mrs B Kirk **Kinglass** *(NT006803)* Borrowstoun Rd
EH51 9RW (off B903) ☎01506 822861 & 824185
FAX 01506 824433
Popular with both business guests and tourists, this welcoming
farmhouse surrounded by fields stands on the south side of town
close to junction 3 of the M9. Bedrooms are well equipped, and a
comfortable lounge and pretty dining room are provided.
6 rms (2 shr) (1 fmly) CTV in all bedrooms Tea and coffee
making facilities Licensed Cen ht CTV 20P 750 acres arable
Last d 5.30pm
PRICE GUIDE
ROOMS: s £18-£25; d £36-£46; wkly b&b £126-£175; wkly hlf-
bd £190-£245

BRAEMAR Grampian *Aberdeenshire* Map **15** NO19

Selected

GH QQQ **Callater Lodge Hotel** 9 Glenshee Rd
AB35 5YQ (beside A93)
☎013397 41275 FAX 013397 41275
Closed Nov-27 Dec
Peter and Mary Nelson are the charming hosts at this detached
Victorian lodge, set in its own gardens on the southern side of
the village. Mary's cooking has earned praise and Peter's
carefully researched selection of malt whiskies deserves
serious investigation. Public rooms are well proportioned and
there is a welcoming open fire in the lounge. Bedrooms are
comfortable and where space permits easy chairs are
provided.
6 en suite (bth/shr) No smoking CTV in all bedrooms Tea
and coffee making facilities Licensed Cen ht 14P No
coaches Last d 7pm
PRICE GUIDE
ROOMS: s £27; d £54; wkly b&b £178;
wkly hlf-bd £297
CARDS: 🔳 🔳 🔳

GH QQQ **Schiehallion House** Glenshee Rd AB35 5YQ
☎013397 41679
Closed Nov
Located on the A93, not far from the village centre, this guest
house offers some ground floor rooms, situated in an annexe,
which have floral decor and some pieces of antique furniture, as
do those in the main house. There are a comfortable lounge and a
bright dining room where good value meals are served.
6 rms (3 shr) 3 annexe en suite (shr) (2 fmly) No smoking in
bedrooms No smoking in dining room No smoking in 1 lounge
Tea and coffee making facilities Licensed Cen ht CTV 8P No
coaches Last d 4.30pm
PRICE GUIDE
ROOMS: s £17; d £32-£36; wkly b&b £112-£126; wkly hlf-bd
£196-£210
CARDS: 🔳 🔳

BREASCLETE See **LEWIS, ISLE OF**

BRECHIN Tayside *Angus* Map **15** NO56

GH QQQ **The Station House** Farnell DD9 6UH (off A92
onto A934 toward Forfar for 5m then turn right, proceed for
0.5m) ☎01674 820208
Quietly situated in this small village, four miles from Brechin and
the A90 trunk road, this well kept guest house offers attractive and

tranquil accommodation. The bedrooms are comfortable with the largest to the front of the house having its own en-suite bathroom. There is a large TV lounge with a window seat looking out over the mature garden, while breakfast and dinner is served, sometimes on shared tables, in the pretty dining room.
3 rms (1 shr) No smoking in dining room Tea and coffee making facilities No dogs (ex guide dogs) Cen ht CTV 6P No coaches Last d noon
PRICE GUIDE
ROOMS: s fr £16; d fr £27✱ (£)

BRIG O'TURK Central *Perthshire* Map **11** NN50

GH Q Q Q Q Q
Dundarroch Country House
Trossachs FK17 8HT (on A821) ☎01877 376200
FAX 01877 376202
rs Nov-19 Dec
Peacefully located near the beautiful Trossachs, this small country house offers a warm welcome, serving tea or sherry on arrival.
Bedrooms are well equipped and attractively furnished; the house also contains a cosy lounge with a wood-burning fire and an elegant dining room commanding spectacular views of Ben Venue. Breakfast is chosen the previous evening from a comprehensive selection, while lunch and dinner can be taken a few minutes' walk away at The Byre.
3 en suite (bth/shr) No smoking CTV in all bedrooms Tea and coffee making facilities Direct dial from bedrooms No dogs Cen ht No children 5yrs 6P No coaches Fishing Last d 7.30pm
PRICE GUIDE
ROOMS: s £33.75-£46.75; d £59.50-£67.50; wkly b&b fr £208✱
CARDS: ⬛ 🟰 (£)

BRODICK See **ARRAN, ISLE OF**

BRORA Highland *Sutherlandshire* Map **14** NC90

GH Q Q Q Q **Lynwood** Golf Rd KW9 6QS (turn off A9 by river bridge onto Golf Rd)
☎01408 621226 FAX 01408 621226
Closed Jan & Feb
A warm welcome is extended to guests at this detached family home which stands in its own walled garden close to the golf course, overlooking the harbour. Mary Cooper's home-cooked dinners and hearty breakfasts are served in a smart dining room with a conservatory extension, and accommodation is provided in tastefully decorated modern rooms - one having external access which makes it suitable for partially disabled guests.
3 en suite (bth/shr) 1 annexe en suite (shr) (1 fmly) No smoking in bedrooms No smoking in 1 lounge CTV in all

bedrooms Tea and coffee making facilities Cen ht CTV 4P No coaches
PRICE GUIDE
ROOMS: s £20-£24; d £34-£40; wkly b&b £110-£130; wkly hlf-bd £176-£198
CARDS: ⬛ 🟰 (£)

BURNMOUTH Borders *Berwickshire* Map **12** NT96

💚 Q Q Q Mrs P Goff **Greystonelees** *(NT958604)*
Greystonelees TD14 5SZ ☎01890 781709
Standing south of the village, just off the A1, this farmhouse is still surrounded by ducks, geese and family pets, though it is no longer part of a working farm. Each of the attractive and well equipped bedrooms contains a cuddly toy and an information pack on the house. A lounge is provided for guests' use, and individual tables are available in the dining room - though the meal can be taken communally.
3 rms (1 bth 1 shr) No smoking CTV in all bedrooms Tea and coffee making facilities Cen ht CTV 10P 140 acres mixed Last d 4pm
PRICE GUIDE
ROOMS: s £15-£22; d £31-£35; wkly b&b £95-£120; wkly hlf-bd £160-£170✱
CARDS: ⬛ 🟰 🔲 (£)

BURRELTON Tayside *Perthshire* Map **11** NO23

⬛ Q Q Q *Burrelton Park* High St PH13 9NX
☎01828 670206 FAX 01828 670676
Colourful hanging baskets adorn the front of this popular village inn which stands on the main road in the centre of the village. Bright, comfortable bedrooms, all en-suite, are offered, and the inn has a good local reputation for its food. An extensive range of menus is available all day in the bar, whilst in the evening, the attractive restaurant has a good value carte menu. The new Charcoal Pit provides a further food option and is gaining in popularity.
6 en suite (bth/shr) (1 fmly) No smoking in 1 bedrooms No smoking in area of dining room CTV in all bedrooms Tea and coffee making facilities Cen ht CTV 28P Last d 10.30pm
CARDS: ⬛ 🟰

CALLANDER Central *Perthshire* Map **11** NN60

GH Q Q Q *Abbotsford Lodge* Stirling Rd FK17 8DA (off A84 eastern approach to town) ☎01877 330066
This extended Victorian house set in its own grounds beside the A84 at the east end of the town provides good-value tourist accommodation in bedrooms - many of them spacious - with a mixture of modern and traditional appointments. Guests have a choice of comfortable lounges (one with a small dispense bar), and meals are served in an attractive candlelit dining room with bright conservatory extension.
18 rms (4 bth 5 shr) (7 fmly) No smoking in dining room Tea and coffee making facilities Licensed Cen ht CTV 20P Last d 7pm

GH Q Q Q **Annfield** 18 North Church St FK17 8EG
☎01877 330204
Closed 20 Dec-5 Jan
A detached Victorian house is set in its own grounds about two minutes' walk from the town centre. The comfortable bedrooms are well maintained and guests have access to an attractive first - floor lounge. Breakfast is served at separate tables and there is ample car parking.

➡

8 rms (4 shr) (2 fmly) Tea and coffee making facilities Cen ht CTV No children 10yrs 9P No coaches
PRICE GUIDE
ROOMS: s fr £17; d fr £34

Selected

GH ◘◘◘◘ **Arden House** Bracklinn Rd FK17 8EQ (from A84 in Callander turn north, opposite Roman Camp Hotel also signposted golf course and Bracklinn Falls) ☎01877 330235
Mar-Oct
Featured in the original television series of Dr Finlay's Casebook - largely filmed in Callander - this sturdy detached stone house with a well tended garden enjoys views over the town to Ben Ledi from its setting in a quiet residential area. Generally spacious bedrooms mingle traditional and modern furnishings, there is a choice of relaxing lounges (one with colour TV) and home-cooked meals are served in an attractive dining room. Please note that this is a non-smoking establishment.
6 en suite (bth/shr) (2 fmly) No smoking Tea and coffee making facilities Cen ht CTV 12P No coaches Putting green Last d 7pm
PRICE GUIDE
ROOMS: s £18-£22; d £36-£44; wkly hlf-bd £185-£195

Premier Selected

GH ◘◘◘◘◘ *Arran Lodge* Leny Rd FK17 8AJ (on W outskirts, on A84)
☎01877 330976
Closed 15 Oct-16 Nov & 10 Jan-1 Mar

Pasqua and Robert Moore's 150-year-old bungalow is situated at the west end of town, with the River Leny flowing past the rear garden. The bedrooms, named after local lochs, are individually styled and two have four-poster beds. The spacious lounge opens onto the verandah, which is a favourite spot for smokers as the house operates a no smoking policy. The Victorian dining room, with period furnishings and highly polished individual tables, is the setting for Robert's carefully prepared dinners and hearty breakfasts.
4 en suite (bth/shr) No smoking CTV in all bedrooms Tea and coffee making facilities No dogs Cen ht CTV No children 12yrs 5P No coaches Fishing Last d 6pm

---

Selected

GH ◘◘◘◘ **Brook Linn Country House** Leny Feus FK17 8AU ☎01877 330103 FAX 01877 330103
Etr-Oct
There are superb views of the surrounding hills from this charming detached house which stands in two acres of terraced lawns in a secluded hillside position above the town.

Tastefully decorated bedrooms are comfortably furnished in traditional style, while public areas include a spacious lounge and an attractive dining room where the short menu is made up of dishes carefully prepared from the best available fresh ingredients.
7 rms (5 shr) (2 fmly) No smoking CTV in all bedrooms Tea and coffee making facilities Licensed Cen ht 10P No coaches Last d 4pm
PRICE GUIDE
ROOMS: s £18-£20; d £42-£48; wkly b&b £126-£147; wkly hlf-bd £210-£231

GH ◘◘◘ **Rock Villa** 1 Bracklinn Rd FK17 8EH
☎01877 330331 FAX 01877 330331
31 Mar-1 Nov
Just off the main road at the eastern end of the town, this compact Victorian villa with its own gardens is cheerfully decorated and well looked after. Bedrooms are comfortable, and there is a pleasant lounge.
6 rms (3 shr) (1 fmly) No smoking in dining room CTV in 3 bedrooms Tea and coffee making facilities Cen ht CTV 7P No coaches
PRICE GUIDE
ROOMS: s £17.50-£18.50; d £32-£38✳

CAMPBELTOWN Strathclyde *Argyllshire* Map **10** NR72

GH ◘◘◘ **Westbank** Dell Rd PA28 6JG (A83 to Campbeltown turn right at T junct follow signs for Southend, B842, through S bend Heritage centre on left, first right Dell Road) ☎01586 553660
This comfortable detached Victorian house is situated in a residential area just off the Machrihanish Road south of the town centre. A programme of bedroom refurbishment has recently been completed and all rooms now offer bright modern appointments. There is also a relaxing lounge and smart dining room where hearty breakfasts and evening meals are served.
8 rms (2 shr) No smoking in dining room CTV in 4 bedrooms Tea and coffee making facilities No dogs (ex guide dogs) Licensed Cen ht CTV No children 3yrs No parking No coaches Last d 5.45pm
PRICE GUIDE
ROOMS: s £22-£25; d £33-£44
CARDS: ◼ ▆

CARDROSS Strathclyde *Dunbartonshire* Map **10** NS37

Selected

GH ◘◘◘◘ **Kirkton House** Darleith Rd G82 5EZ (0.5m N of village) (Logis)
☎01389 841951 FAX 01389 841868
Closed 15 Dec-15 Jan
From its elevated position above the village, this delightful guest house offers fine views of the River Clyde and gentle rolling countryside. Enthusiastic owners Stewart and Gillian MacDonald have worked hard over the years to restore the farmhouse, which is built around a courtyard. The public areas have a rustic feel, and guests can relax with a drink in the lounge before sitting down in the dining room to sample Gillian's home cooking.
6 en suite (bth/shr) (4 fmly) CTV in all bedrooms Tea and

coffee making facilities Direct dial from bedrooms Licensed Cen ht ch fac 12P No coaches Riding Last d 7.30pm
PRICE GUIDE
ROOMS: s £32.50-£37.50; d £54-£59; wkly b&b £147-£182; wkly hlf-bd £269.50-£304.50✳
CARDS: 🅰 ▤ ▥ 🅰
See advertisement under HELENSBURGH

CARRADALE Strathclyde *Argyllshire* Map **10** NR83

GH 🆀🆀🆀 *Dunvalanree* Portrigh Bay PA28 6SE
☎01583 431226 FAX 01583 431339
Etr-Oct
The welcoming atmosphere together with enjoyable home cooking are all part of the appeal of Sue Pryor's comfortable detached home which enjoys glorious views over the bay to the isle of Arran beyond. The spotless bedrooms are bright and airy with both modern and traditional appointments and there is also a relaxing lounge and separate dining room.
14 rms (3 fmly) No smoking in dining room Tea and coffee making facilities Licensed CTV 19P Golf 9 Fishing Squash

---

CARRBRIDGE Highland *Inverness-shire* Map **14** NH92

Selected

GH 🆀🆀🆀🆀 **Carrmoor** Carr Rd PH23 3AD (first right after bistro) ☎01479 841244 FAX 01479 841244
This charming cottage stands in a residential area just off the main street. Bedrooms, though compact, are bright, cheery and well maintained, while public areas include a relaxing TV lounge and an attractive dining room serving carefully prepared home-cooked meals. The daily-changing fixed-price menu is now augmented by a new carte, and non-residents can eat by prior arrangement. Smoking is not allowed in either the bedrooms or the dining room.
5 en suite (shr) (1 fmly) No smoking in bedrooms No smoking in dining room Tea and coffee making facilities Licensed Cen ht CTV 5P No coaches Last d 8pm
PRICE GUIDE
ROOMS: s £19-£23.50; d £33-£37; wkly b&b £101.50-£115.50; wkly hlf-bd £178.50-£193.50
CARDS: 🅰 ▤ £

GH 🆀🆀🆀 **Feith Mhor Country House** Station Rd PH23 3AP (1.25m W) ☎01479 841621
Closed 16 Nov-26 Dec
This sturdy 19th-century house stands in its own well tended grounds amid peaceful countryside just over a mile west of the village. Bedrooms vary in size and have both modern and traditional appointments. Refreshments are available between 6 and 7pm in the relaxing lounge, and wholesome food, carefully prepared from fresh ingredients, is served in the attractive dining room.
6 en suite (bth/shr) (1 fmly) No smoking in dining room No smoking in lounges CTV in all bedrooms Tea and coffee making facilities Licensed Cen ht No children 12yrs 8P No coaches Last d 6pm
PRICE GUIDE
ROOMS: s £22-£23; d £44-£46; wkly hlf-bd £220-£228✳ £

CASTLE DOUGLAS Dumfries & Galloway *Kirkcudbrightshire* Map **11** NX76

⌗ ▦ **GH** 🆀🆀🆀 **Rose Cottage** Gelston DG7 1SH (beside B727, 2m S) ☎01556 502513
Feb-Oct
An attractive house surrounded by neat gardens with a stream running along one side, Rose Cottage offers comfortable, individually styled, ground-floor bedrooms, a relaxing lounge and a conservatory dining room with pine furniture. This friendly and welcoming rural guest house stands in the unspoilt village of Gelston, on the B727 two-and-a-half miles from Castle Douglas.
3 rms (1 bth/shr) 2 annexe rms (1 fmly) No smoking in dining room Tea and coffee making facilities Cen ht CTV 15P No coaches Last d 5pm
PRICE GUIDE
ROOMS: s £16-£19; d £32-£37; wkly b&b £110-£130; wkly hlf-bd £170-£191 £

COATBRIDGE Strathclyde *Lanarkshire* Map **11** NS76

GH 🆀🆀🆀 **Auchenlea** 153 Langmuir Rd, Bargeddie, Baillieston G69 7RS ☎0141 771 6870
Good-value bed and breakfast accommodation is offered at this semidetached cottage on the A752, about a quarter of a mile south of the junction with the A79. Bedrooms vary in size but are all en suite. Hearty breakfasts are served in the combined lounge/dining room. This is a no-smoking establishment.
2 en suite (bth/shr) (1 fmly) No smoking CTV in all bedrooms Tea and coffee making facilities No dogs (ex guide dogs) 8P
PRICE GUIDE
ROOMS: s £15-£18✳ £

COLDINGHAM Borders *Berwickshire* Map **12** NT96

Premier Selected

GH 🆀🆀🆀🆀🆀
Dunlaverock House
TD14 5PA ☎018907 71450
FAX 018907 71450

A fine late-Victorian house and gardens stand in a cliff-top position with splendid views across the bay and out to sea, a little path giving direct access to the beach below. The owners have restored the house and combined stylish modern decor with antique furniture. The bedrooms also retain a period feel with original fireplaces and other items such as a claw-legged bath tub; front-facing rooms are most popular. The relaxed drawing and dining rooms have lovely picture windows, and excellent four-course dinners and filling breakfasts are served. The atmosphere is friendly and service efficient.
6 en suite (bth/shr) (1 fmly) No smoking in 3 bedrooms No smoking in dining room CTV in all bedrooms Tea and coffee making facilities Licensed Cen ht No children 9yrs 8P No coaches Last d 7.30pm
PRICE GUIDE
ROOMS: s £35-£42.50; d £50-£65; wkly b&b £155-£235; wkly hlf-bd £277.50-£357.50✳
CARDS: 🅰 ▤ £
See advertisement on p.503.

COMRIE Tayside *Perthshire* Map **11** NN72

GH 🅀🅀 **Mossgiel** Burrell St PH6 2JP (on A85 opposite parish church) ☎01764 670567
A detached, whitewashed guest house with bright window boxes, standing beside the A85 at the west end of the town, offers accommodation in compact bedrooms which are gradually being upgraded with smart pine furniture and modern fabrics. A hearty breakfast is served in the timber-clad dining room, and there is a cosy little lounge in which guests can relax. Special golf packages are available: details of these are available on direct application.
5 rms (1 fmly) No smoking in bedrooms No smoking in dining room Tea and coffee making facilities No dogs Licensed Cen ht CTV No children 5yrs 6P No coaches Golf packages Last d 6pm
PRICE GUIDE
ROOMS: s £15-£17; d £30; wkly b&b £94.50; wkly hlf-bd £150.50✳

CONNEL Strathclyde *Argyllshire* Map **10** NM93

Premier Selected

GH 🅀🅀🅀🅀🅀 **Ards House** PA37 1PT (on A85, 4m N of Oban) ☎01631 710255 Closed Dec-Jan rs 1-23 Dec
Many guests return year after year to Jean and John Bowman's delightful house, which is on the western edge of the village with views over the Firth of Lorn to Lismore and the hills of Morvern beyond. Bedrooms are individually decorated and vary in style, and the public areas include a spacious drawing room with a real fire on cool evenings. The high point of the day is John's carefully prepared five-course dinner, featuring the best available fresh local produce. This is a no-smoking establishment.
6 rms (5 bth/shr) No smoking CTV in 1 bedroom Tea and coffee making facilities No dogs Licensed Cen ht CTV No children 12yrs 12P No coaches Last d 6pm
PRICE GUIDE
ROOMS: s £23-£37; d £42-£54; wkly b&b £132.30-£170.10; wkly hlf-bd £240.80-£278.60✳
CARDS:
See advertisement under OBAN

Selected

GH 🅀🅀🅀🅀 **Loch Etive House Hotel** Main St PA37 1PH (200yds from A85 road) ☎01631 710400 FAX 01631 710680 Etr-28 Oct
A comfortable private hotel stands in a well tended garden beside a small river in the centre of the village, just off the A85. Bedrooms vary in size, but all offer modern and traditional appointments; two top-floor rooms have most character, one with stone walls and a beamed ceiling, the other substantially clad in pine. Some rooms are non-smoking as is the lounge/dining room which serves a choice of food at dinner.

6 rms (4 bth/shr) (2 fmly) No smoking in 3 bedrooms No smoking in dining room No smoking in lounges CTV in all bedrooms Tea and coffee making facilities Licensed Cen ht 7P No coaches Last d 6.30pm
PRICE GUIDE
ROOMS: s £20-£40; d £38-£50; wkly b&b £126-£167; wkly hlf-bd £190-£230✳
CARDS:

Selected

GH 🅀🅀🅀🅀 **Ronebhal** PA37 1PJ (on A85) ☎01631 710310
Apr-Oct
Ronebhal is a sturdy Victorian house on the A85 with a superb outlook over Loch Etive. Bedrooms are well decorated, bright and airy, and public rooms include an attractive TV lounge and a smart dining room where hearty breakfasts are served at individual tables. The house is maintained to a high standard, the atmosphere is relaxed; smoking is prohibited.
6 rms (4 shr) (1 fmly) No smoking CTV in all bedrooms Tea and coffee making facilities No dogs Cen ht No children 5yrs 6P No coaches Last d 7.30pm
PRICE GUIDE
ROOMS: s £17-£23; d £34-£54; wkly b&b £119-£182
CARDS:

CONON BRIDGE Highland *Ross & Cromarty* Map **14** NH55

Premier Selected

GH 🅀🅀🅀🅀 **Kinkell House** Easter Kinkell IV7 8HY (on B9169) ☎01349 861270 Closed Jan-Feb
Steve and Marsha Fraser have restored this 19th-century farmhouse set in its own grounds with views of Ben Wyvis, the Cromarty Firth and the Wester Ross hills.

Bedrooms are non smoking and are individually decorated and furnished in period style. One lounge has a log-burning stove and the other is a sun lounge. The restaurant, with small patio, is open to non residents, and Marsha is responsible for the daily changing menu of honest, home-cooked food using local produce.
3 en suite (bth/shr) No smoking in bedrooms No smoking in dining room No smoking in 1 lounge CTV in all bedrooms Tea and coffee making facilities Licensed Cen ht CTV 15P No coaches Last d 9pm
PRICE GUIDE
ROOMS: s £38.50-£48.50; d £57-£67✳
CARDS:

COUPAR ANGUS Tayside *Perthshire* Map **11** NO23

🛌🛇 **GH** 🅀🅀 **Eastwood** Forfar Rd PH13 9AN ☎01828 627485
This sturdy, semi detached villa stands beside the main road and

offers good value accommodation. The bedrooms are reasonably sized and modern, and there is a relaxing lounge and a small dining room where hearty breakfasts are served.

3 rms (1 fmly) No smoking in 3 bedrooms No smoking in dining room Tea and coffee making facilities Cen ht CTV 3P No coaches

PRICE GUIDE
ROOMS: s £15; d £28; wkly b&b fr £98

COWDENBEATH Fife Map 11 NT19

GH [Q][Q] **Struan Bank Hotel** 74 Perth Rd KY4 9BG (turn E at junct3 M90 to Cowdenbeath, drive through town centre & up hill) ☎01383 511057

Improvements continue at this family-run commercial hotel. The dining room has recently been redecorated, and there are plans to add en suite bathrooms to all the bedrooms. The rooms are small and the furniture varies from quite modest to more recent smart pine. There is a comfortable lounge bar, and separate tables are provided in the dining room.

9 rms (6 shr) (2 fmly) No smoking in dining room CTV in all bedrooms Tea and coffee making facilities Licensed Cen ht CTV 8P No coaches Last d 6pm

PRICE GUIDE
ROOMS: s £18-£22; d £34-£42✳
CARDS: 🟦 ▬ 🟫

CRAIL Fife Map 12 NO60

GH [Q][Q][Q] *Caiplie* 51-53 High St KY10 3RA ☎01333 450564

Mar-Oct Closed Dec-Jan rs Nov & Feb-1 Mar

A warm welcome is assured at this popular licensed guesthouse situated in the centre of this picturesque coastal village, within easy walking distance of the attractive harbour. Bedrooms vary in shape and size and all are clean and comfortably furnished, with colourful fabrics and thoughtful extras. There is a cosy lounge on the first floor, and the bright, cheerful dining room overlooks the main road and offers daily changing menus which include a choice of Scottish and continental dishes.

7 rms (1 fmly) Tea and coffee making facilities Licensed Cen ht CTV No parking No coaches Last d 4pm

GH [Q][Q] *Selcraig House* 47 Nethergate KY10 3TX ☎01333 450697

A stone-built property dating from the 1700s, Selcraig House is located in a quiet street between the village centre and harbour. The welcoming owner, Margaret Carstairs, has furnished the public areas in appropriate style and included some fascinating family memorabilia. There is an inviting first-floor lounge and a dining room with a conservatory extension. Bedrooms vary in size, one having a stunning pine four-poster bed.

5 rms (2 fmly) No smoking CTV in all bedrooms Tea and coffee making facilities CTV 2P No coaches Last d noon

◀ [Q][Q][Q] *Golf Hotel* 4 High St KY10 3TB ☎01333 450206 & 450500 FAX 01333 450795

rs 26 Dec & 1 Jan

It is reputed that there has been an inn on this town centre site since the 14th century. The current owners have upgraded the bedrooms to a good standard while inevitably retaining the curves and slopes of the historic building; all have en suite shower rooms and are attractively furnished in new pine. There is a comfortable first-floor lounge, and an extensive range of dishes is served in either the large dining room or the bars.

5 en suite (shr) (1 fmly) CTV in all bedrooms Tea and coffee making facilities Cen ht CTV 15P Last d 9pm

CARDS: 🟦 🟫

CRAWFORD Strathclyde *Lanarkshire* Map 11 NS92

GH 🅀🅀 **Field End** ML12 6TN ☎01864 502276
Closed Xmas & New Year
This family-run guest house is situated at the end of a steep
narrow drive off the main street at the north end of the village; it
enjoys an open outlook over the surrounding countryside. There
are a spacious upstairs bedroom and a small one on the ground
floor, both of them well maintained and offering mixed practical
appointments. A cosy TV lounge and pleasant dining room are
also provided. Smoking is not permitted.
3 rms (2 shr) (1 fmly) No smoking CTV in all bedrooms Tea
and coffee making facilities No dogs (ex guide dogs) Cen ht
CTV 7P No coaches Last d 5pm
PRICE GUIDE
ROOMS: s £20-£25; d £30-£36; wkly b&b £120-£150; wkly hlf-
bd £150-£180✳
CARDS: 🄰 🃏

CRIANLARICH Central *Perthshire* Map 10 NN32

GH 🅀🅀🅀 **Glenardran Guest House** FK20 8QS (beside A85
on eastern approach to village) ☎01838 300236
Good-value bed and breakfast accommodation is available at this
friendly family-run guest house which stands beside the A85 at the
eastern end of the village. Well maintained and spacious bedrooms
offer mixed modern appointments, while public areas include a
comfortable quiet lounge and neat dining room. Smoking is not
permitted anywhere within the house.
6 rms (1 shr) (1 fmly) No smoking CTV in all bedrooms Tea
and coffee making facilities Licensed Cen ht 6P No coaches
Last d 6pm
PRICE GUIDE
ROOMS: s £17.50-£19.50; d £35-£39; wkly b&b £122.50-
£136.50; wkly hlf-bd £192.50-£206.50
CARDS: 🄰 🃏

GH 🅀🅀🅀 **The Lodge House** FK20 8RU (on A82, 0.75m N)
☎01838 300276
Mar-Dec
There are beautiful views of the surrounding hills from this
friendly, family-run, licensed establishment which stands just off
the A82 north of the village. Smartly decorated though compact
bedrooms offer mixed modern furnishings and all the expected
amenities, while public areas include a choice of lounges - the one
with a dispense bar being the only place that smoking is allowed -
and a neat little dining room where, at peak times, it may be
necessary to share a table.
5 en suite (shr) 1 annexe en suite (shr) No smoking in bedrooms
No smoking in dining room No smoking in lounges CTV in all
bedrooms Tea and coffee making facilities No dogs (ex guide
dogs) Licensed Cen ht CTV 20P Fishing Last d 8pm
PRICE GUIDE
ROOMS: s £26-£34; d £52; wkly b&b £164; wkly hlf-bd £252✳
CARDS: 🄰 🃏

CRIEFF Tayside *Perthshire* Map 11 NN82

GH 🅀🅀🅀 **Comeley Bank** 32 Burrell St PH7 4DT (on A822)
☎01764 653409
Part of a terraced row, this licensed family-run guest house is
situated on the main road just south of the town centre.
Attractively decorated bedrooms - all of them non-smoking - are
furnished predominantly in pine, there is a relaxing lounge, and
enjoyable home-cooked meals are served at the dining room's
individual tables.

5 rms (2 shr) (2 fmly) No smoking in bedrooms No smoking in
dining room CTV in all bedrooms Tea and coffee making
facilities Licensed Cen ht CTV No coaches Last d 5pm
PRICE GUIDE
ROOMS: s £16-£25; d £34-£38✳

CRUDEN BAY Grampian *Aberdeenshire* Map 15 NK03

◀ 🅀🅀🅀 **Red House Hotel** Aulton Rd AB42 7NJ (in middle
of village, opposite golf course)
☎01779 812215 FAX 01779 812320
Situated in this tranquil village, the hotel overlooks the golf course
and has fabulous seaviews over the Bay. The bedrooms are
spacious and all have large beds and good facilities. There is a
comfortable cocktail bar and a large restaurant which offers local
fare and a children's menu. Continental breakfast is included and a
full cooked beakfast can be supplied at extra charge.
6 rms (3 bth/shr) (1 fmly) CTV in all bedrooms Tea and coffee
making facilities Direct dial from bedrooms Cen ht 28P No
coaches Snooker Pool Last d 9pm
PRICE GUIDE
ROOMS: s £20-£25; d £60-£70
MEALS: Lunch £2-£7.50&alc Dinner £5-£16alc
CARDS: 🄰 🃏 🃏

CULLODEN MOOR Highland *Inverness-shire* Map 14 NH74

💗 🅀🅀 Mrs E M C Alexander **Culdoich** *(NH755435)* Culloden
Moor IV1 2EP ☎01463 790268
May-Oct
This homely farmhouse stands southeast of Inverness, near
Culloden battlefield and Clava Cairns. There are two large
bedrooms (one with a bunk bed - ideal for families), and
comfortable lounge and dining areas. Mrs Alexander is a careful
hostess and retains the tradition of offering complimentary tea and
shortbread in the evening. Leave the A9 at Daviot to join the B851
Croy Road and after 2.5m turn right at crossroads then right again
at the next junction.
2 rms (1 fmly) No smoking in dining room Tea and coffee
making facilities No dogs CTV P 200 acres mixed Last d 5pm
PRICE GUIDE
ROOMS: d fr £30✳

CUPAR Fife Map 11 NO31

GH 🅀🅀🅀🅀🅀 *Todhall*
House Dairsie KY15 4RQ (2m
E, off A91) ☎01334 656344
FAX 01334 656344
rs Nov-Feb
This large period country
house lies in two acres, with
colourful mature gardens
surrounding it. Its elevated
position affords it fine
panoramic views over the
Eden valley. John and Gill

Donald delight in welcoming guests to their family home
which is adorned with family heirlooms and beautiful
paintings. There is a spacious and comfortable guest lounge
with a choice of books and local information, while the
elegant dining room has one large table where breakfast and
dinner, on request, are served. Bedrooms are attractively

furnished and decorated with many thoughtful touches, all serving to create a peaceful haven in the heart of Fife. 3 en suite (bth/shr) No smoking CTV in all bedrooms Tea and coffee making facilities No dogs Cen ht No children 10yrs 5P No coaches Outdoor swimming pool Golf net putting green Last d noon

DALBEATTIE Dumfries & Galloway *Kirkcudbrightshire* Map **11** NX86

Selected

GH ◨◨◨◨ **Auchenskeoch Lodge** DG5 4PG (5m E off B793) ☎01387 780277 FAX 01387 780277
Etr-Oct
Set in 20 acres of beautiful grounds and gardens, this Victorian shooting lodge offers spacious, comfortable and traditionally furnished bedrooms with private facilities. One room on the ground floor is suitable for disabled guests. Public areas include a comfortable sitting room and a television lounge as well as a billiard room with a full-size table. Much emphasis is placed on the quality and freshness of the food served in the elegant dining room, and many of the vegetables, fresh fruits and herbs come from the hotel garden. Guests can play croquet on the lawn or walk in the gardens and woodland.
3 en suite (bth/shr) No smoking in dining room Tea and coffee making facilities Licensed CTV 22P No coaches Tennis (grass) Fishing Snooker Croquet lawn Last d 8pm
PRICE GUIDE
ROOMS: s £30-£37.50; d £50-£60
CARDS: ◨ ◨

◨ ◨◨◨ *Anchor Hotel* Kippford (off A710) ☎01556 620205 FAX 01556 620205
This totally refurbished inn is found in the tiny and picturesque village of Kippford. It offers modern, well equipped bedrooms, most with views over the estuary and yachting marina. The comfortable bars provide a wide range of food.
5 rms (3 shr) (1 fmly) No smoking in area of dining room No smoking in 1 lounge CTV in all bedrooms Tea and coffee making facilities No dogs 6P Golf 12 Children's games room Last d 9pm
CARDS: ◨ ◨

◨ ◨◨ **Pheasant Hotel** 1 Maxwell St DG5 4AH
☎01556 610345 FAX 01557 331513
Families are made especially welcome at this lively town-centre inn, which offers a great-value buffet lunch in the first-floor restaurant. A public bar serving real ale is popular with locals as well as passing tourists. Bedrooms enhanced by the use of bright fabrics all have private bathrooms.
7 rms (6 bth/shr) (3 fmly) CTV in all bedrooms Tea and coffee making facilities Direct dial from bedrooms No dogs (ex guide dogs) Cen ht No parking Last d 9pm
PRICE GUIDE
ROOMS: s £14-£25; d £28-£45✱
MEALS: Lunch £3.95&alc Dinner £3-£5&alc✱
CARDS: ◨ ◨   (£)

DALCROSS Highland *Iverness-shire* Map **14** NH75

♥ ◨◨◨ Mrs M Pottie *Easter Dalziel Farmhouse (NH755509)* Easter Dalziel Farm, Dalcross IV1 2JL
☎01667 462213 FAX 01667 462213
Closed 20 Dec-20Jan rs 1-20 Dec & 20 Jan-28 Feb
Many visitors return year after year to this delightful early Victorian farmhouse, which is set amid gentle wooded countryside, and is convenient for Inverness airport. The spacious bedrooms are tastefully decorated and comfortably furnished with both traditional and period pieces, though they lack facilities such as en suite bathrooms and telephones. There is a cosy lounge and a dining room furnished with antiques where hearty breakfasts are served at a sturdy oak table. Evening meals are available by arrangement.
3 rms Tea and coffee making facilities CTV P 210 acres arable/beef/sheep Last d 10am
CARDS: ◨ ◨

DALMALLY Strathclyde *Argyllshire*

See **Ardbrecknish**

DENNY Central *Stirlingshire* Map **11** NS88

♥ ◨◨◨ Mr & Mrs Steel *The Topps (NS757843)* Fintry Rd FK6 5JF (just off B818, 4m W) ☎01324 822471
Standing at the centre of a working farm specialising in sheep and cashmere goats, this modern farmhouse is located four miles west of Denny on the B818, with splendid views towards the Ochil Hills. Well equipped en suite bedrooms are decorated with cheerful fabrics and pine furnishings. Taste of Scotland dishes are served in a locally popular dining room, and breakfast is prepared by the farmer himself!
8 en suite (bth/shr) (1 fmly) CTV in all bedrooms Tea and coffee making facilities Licensed Cen ht CTV 12P Fishing 300 acres cashmere goats sheep Last d 5pm
CARDS: ◨ ◨

DERVAIG See **MULL, ISLE OF**

DIRLETON Lothian *East Lothian* Map **12** NT58

◨ ◨ *Castle* EH39 5EP (off A198) ☎01620 850221
Closed 21 Dec-5 Jan rs Nov-Apr
This family-run inn lies beside the village green opposite the ruins of Dirleton Castle. It is in the throes of being upgraded, but at the time of our visit provided plain bedrooms, a no-frills dining room and two bars - the public bar offering the greater character. An attractive rear garden is popular in good weather.
4 en suite (bth/shr) 4 annexe rms CTV in 4 bedrooms Tea and coffee making facilities Cen ht CTV 20P Pool table Last d 8.30pm
CARDS: ◨ ◨
See advertisement on p.507.

DORNOCH Highland *Sutherland* Map **14** NH78

Selected

GH ◨◨◨◨ **Fourpenny Cottage** Skelbo IV25 3QF
☎01862 810727 FAX 01862 810727
20 Feb-20 Dec
This renovated and extended Highland croft and byre have become a charming guest house overlooking the Dornoch Firth. Bedrooms are attractively decorated and well equipped, and the comfortable lounge on the first floor has been extended to provide a separate dining room with panoramic

➡

views - a very pleasant place in which to enjoy hearty home-cooked meals. Sheila Board is a mine of local information and is pleased to join guests for an after dinner chat.

3 en suite (bth/shr) 2 annexe en suite (shr) (1 fmly) No smoking in bedrooms No smoking in dining room No smoking in 1 lounge CTV in all bedrooms Tea and coffee making facilities No dogs (ex guide dogs) Cen ht CTV ch fac 6P No coaches Last d 7pm

PRICE GUIDE

ROOMS: d fr £45; wkly b&b fr £157.50; wkly hlf-bd fr £231

Premier Selected

GH ◙◙◙◙◙ **Highfield**
Evelix Rd IV25 3HR (take A9
N over Dornoch Bridge.
After 2m turn right onto
A949. After 1.5m, pass
schools onleft, Highfield
500yds on left)
☎01862 810909
FAX 01862 810909

Convenient for the town centre, a modern guest house in its own mature gardens provides comfortable bedrooms which are maintained to a very high standard. Stephen and Jane Dooley offer a warm welcome, together with extensive information on scenic drives in the area. Bedrooms have fine oak furniture and good facilities, one featuring a jacuzzi bath. An excellent range of breakfast dishes includes home-made jams and herbal teas, and some special diets can be catered for (with prior notice).

3 en suite (bth/shr) No smoking CTV in all bedrooms Tea and coffee making facilities Cen ht No children 12yrs 6P No coaches

PRICE GUIDE

ROOMS: s £28; d £43-£45✱

DRUMBEG Highland *Sutherland* Map **14** NC13

Selected

GH ◙◙◙◙ **Taigh Druimbeg** IV27 4NW
☎01571 833209
Closed Xmas & New Year
A warm welcome from owners Ron and Margaret Wauld awaits guests at Taigh Druimbeag. The Waulds moved to deepest Sutherland from Yorkshire and have made a lot of friends here with their humour, hospitality and good food. The house is Edwardian and has been furnished with bric-à-brac and antiques in keeping with its period. Bedrooms are rather compact but are comfortable and well equipped with lots of personal touches. Margaret serves wholesome dishes based around local produce and has begun to welcome non-residents. Please note that this is a no-smoking establishment.

3 en suite (shr) No smoking Tea and coffee making facilities No dogs (ex guide dogs) Cen ht CTV No children 14yrs 6P No coaches Last d 6pm

PRICE GUIDE

ROOMS: s fr £22.50; d fr £45; wkly b&b fr £157.50; wkly hlf-bd fr £245

DRUMLITHIE Grampian *Kincardineshire* Map **15** NO78

Selected

GH ◙◙◙◙ **Upper Foord Croft** AB3 2XA (2m off A90) ☎01569 740463
This once derelict hill farm cottage was transformed into a delightful home in 1993. Attractive and stylish, but retaining a cosy cottage atmosphere, it offers two pretty first floor bedrooms with modern en-suite shower rooms. There is a neat little dining room where Olga Lawson's cooking and baking are proving irresistible and guests are freely encouraged to use the beautiful lounge. Upper Foord's isolated position affords spectacular panoramic views across open country side, yet it is only 2 miles from the A90 near the village of Drumlithie, 4 miles south of Stonehaven. When approaiching from the south, turn off A90 at second Drumlithie sign and follow signs from village. The cottage lies at the end of a mile long track and is well worth seeking out.

2 en suite (bth/shr) CTV in all bedrooms Tea and coffee making facilities Cen ht CTV No children 12yrs 3P No coaches Last d noon

---

DRUMNADROCHIT Highland *Inverness-shire* Map **14** NH52

GH ◙◙◙ **Enrick Cottage** Lower Milton IV3 6TZ (on A831) ☎01456 450423 FAX 01456 450423
Mar-Oct
This homely cottage stands about half a mile west of the village beside the Cannich Road and offers a warm welcome together with excellent value bed and breakfast accommodation. Bedrooms have private bathrooms and are comfortable if somewhat compact; most of the furnishings are made by Mr Raper in his workshop behind the house. Hearty breakfasts are served at sturdy pine tables in the small combined lounge/dining room. This is a non smoking establishment.

2 en suite (shr) No smoking Tea and coffee making facilities Cen ht CTV No children 15yrs 3P No coaches Chair making course (Windsor chairs)

PRICE GUIDE

ROOMS: s £21-£25; d £34-£36✱
CARDS: 🔲 🔲

Selected

GH ◙◙◙◙ **Kilmore Farm** IV3 6UH ☎01456 450524
A modern, detached house near Loch Ness with smart ground floor bedrooms. Good home cooking and a sauna make it special.
3 en suite (shr) (1 fmly) No smoking CTV in all bedrooms Tea and coffee making facilities Cen ht CTV 6P No coaches Sauna Last d 6pm
CARDS: 🔲 🔲

Selected

GH ◙◙◙◙ **Woodlands** East Lewiston IV3 6UL
☎01456 450356
This modern villa lies just off the A82 to the south of Drumnadrochit. Bright and cheery throughout, the bedrooms are spacious, very comfortable, and thoughtfully equipped. The room without washbasin has sole use of the bathroom just along the corridor. As well as her home cooking, Janette Drysdale bakes her own bread and makes her own jam.

3 rms (1 bth 1 shr) No smoking in bedrooms No smoking in dining room CTV in all bedrooms Tea and coffee making facilities No dogs (ex guide dogs) Cen ht CTV 3P No coaches

PRICE GUIDE

ROOMS: d fr £28✳

CARDS: ▨ ▨

See advertisement under INVERNESS

Selected

♥ ⬤⬤⬤⬤ Mr A D Macdonald-Hair *Borlum Farmhouse* *(NH518291)* IV3 6XN ☎01456 450358
Set off the A82 on a hillside a mile south of the village, this charming 18th-century farmhouse enjoys a splendid outlook over Loch Ness and the surrounding wooded hills. The spacious bedrooms have attractive modern decor, though amenities such as TV and tea trays are provided in only one. Public rooms include a sun lounge overlooking the loch and a delightful breakfast room with a log-burning stove and individual tables. Riding is available, including facilities for disabled riders. This is a no-smoking establishment.
5 rms

DRYMEN Central *Stirlingshire* Map 11 NS48

GH ⬤⬤⬤ Croftburn Cottage Croftamie G63 0HA (2m S on A809) ☎01360 660796
This former keeper's cottage, parts of which date back over two centuries, has a relaxed atmosphere and is particularly popular ➥

The Castle Inn

Dirleton, East Lothian
Telephone: (01620) 850221

Overlooking the green of one of Scotland's most beautiful 'heirloom' villages and situated in an area surrounded by many well known golf courses — North Berwick, Muirfield, Gullane and Luffness.
The Castle Inn offers golfing parties of up to 14 accommodation in a *warm*, friendly atmosphere. *There are 4 en suite rooms in the hotel and four rooms sharing a bathroom in the annexe.* All rooms are centrally heated. Relax in the small lounge in front of the television or enjoy a glass of real ale with a bar lunch or supper.

For further information please contact Robin Stewart

Croftburn Cottage

Croftamie, Drymen,
Loch Lomond G63 0HA
Tel: 01360 660796

Situated 2 miles south of Drymen village in 1 acre of beautiful gardens overlooking the Endrick Valley and Campsie Fells. Ideal touring and walking base. Superior accommodation providing en suite facilities. Rooms have colour TV, clock radio and tea/coffee making facilities. Centrally heated throughout. Guests sitting room. Private parking. Putting and croquet.
We make your stay so memorable that you will want to come back.

Enrick Cottage

Drumnadrochit by Loch Ness,
Inverness-Shire, IV3 6TZ
Tel/Fax: 01456 450423

QQQ   Access/Visa/Mastercard

Avis and Alan invite you to stay at Enrick Cottage and enjoy friendly hospitality in the comfort of their home where every effort will be made to make your visit an enjoyable experience. The cottage is entirely furnished with pieces from our own workshop where we specialise in producing furniture from native woods. Guests are welcome to look around our workshop and see work in progress. Instruction in chair making, wood turning and steam bending is available by arrangement.

with walkers (for whom special packages are available). The no-smoking bedrooms are bright and cheery, with comfortable mixed appointments; the ground-floor room lacks a wash basin but has sole use of a bathroom. Public areas include a comfortable lounge with a pine-clad ceiling and French windows as well as the small, neat dining room where home-cooked evening meals are served (by prior arrangement) round a communal table.

3 rms (1 fmly) No smoking in bedrooms No smoking in area of dining room CTV in all bedrooms Tea and coffee making facilities Cen ht CTV 20P No coaches Croquet Putting Last d 10am

PRICE GUIDE
ROOMS: s £18-£20; d £32-£34; wkly b&b £110-£115; wkly hlf-bd £185-£215✳

£

DUFFTOWN Grampian *Banffshire* Map **15** NJ34

 **Fife Arms Hotel** 2 The Square AB55 4AD
☎01340 820220 FAX 01340 820220

6 annexe en suite (shr) (2 fmly) No smoking in lounges CTV in all bedrooms Tea and coffee making facilities Cen ht 8P Children's play area Last d 8pm

PRICE GUIDE
ROOMS: s £22-£25; d £36-£40✳
MEALS: Lunch £3.50-£20alc Dinner £3.50-£20alc✳
CARDS: ▨ ▤

DUMBARTON Strathclyde

See **Cardross**

DUMFRIES Dumfries & Galloway *Dumfriesshire*
Map **11** NX97

Selected

GH Q Q Q Q **Orchard House** 298 Annan Rd DG1 3JE
☎01387 255099

Orchard House is a former farm standing in an acre of neat and attractive gardens on the main approach to town. Converted stables house prettily decorated ground-floor bedrooms which are well equipped with modern facilities and suitable for disabled people. The lounge and dining room in the main house are spacious and comfortable, and there is a private car park. A total smoking ban is operated here.

3 annexe en suite (bth/shr) (1 fmly) No smoking CTV in all bedrooms Tea and coffee making facilities No dogs Cen ht CTV 10P No coaches

PRICE GUIDE
ROOMS: d £37; wkly b&b £119✳

£

GH Q Q Q **South Park** Quarry Rd, Locharbriggs DG1 1QR
☎01387 710191 FAX 01387 710191

Located just off the A701, this recently renovated guest house enjoys superb country views, while still being convenient for the town. Comfortable bedrooms, attractively decorated with brightly coloured fabrics and furnished with some fine pieces, all have private facilities. The large lounge/dining room is sunny with, an open outlook, and evening meals are available if requested in advance. There is a no-smoking policy throughout the house.

3 en suite (bth/shr) (1 fmly) No smoking CTV in all bedrooms Tea and coffee making facilities No dogs Cen ht CTV 15P No coaches

PRICE GUIDE
ROOMS: d £30
CARDS: ▨ ▤ ▧

DUNBAR Lothian *East Lothian* Map **12** NT67

GH Q Q *Marine* 7 Marine Rd EH42 1AR ☎01368 863315
Mar-Oct

An enthusiastic Italian couple are the owners of this terraced guest house close to the sea. It offers bright, good value accommodation and a first floor lounge with baby snooker table.

10 rms (3 fmly) Cen ht CTV No parking No coaches

GH Q Q Q *Overcliffe* 11 Bayswell Park EH42 1AE (off A1, opposite Lauderdale Park) ☎01368 864004

The red, sandstone semi-detached villa is within reach of the seafront and the town centre. Although compact, it is nicely decorated and has an attractive lounge. All bedrooms have a mini-bar selection.

6 rms (3 shr) (3 fmly) No smoking in dining room CTV in all bedrooms Tea and coffee making facilities Licensed Cen ht CTV 2P No coaches Last d 5pm

---

GH Q Q *St Beys* 2 Bayswell Rd EH42 1AB ☎01368 863571
Feb-Dec

Just off the High Street, this traditional guest house has fine sea views from the first floor lounge. Bedrooms are thoughtfully appointed.

6 rms (3 fmly) CTV in all bedrooms Tea and coffee making facilities Cen ht CTV No parking Last d 6pm

CARDS: ▤

GH Q Q *St Helens* Queens Rd EH42 1LN ☎01368 863716
Closed Nov-Feb

A red sandstone house lying on the main road leading into the town. Bedrooms vary in size with the larger ones being particularly comfortable. St Helens is a totally no-smoking establishment.

7 rms (2 bth/shr) (1 fmly) No smoking CTV in 1 bedroom Tea and coffee making facilities Cen ht CTV 4P

PRICE GUIDE
ROOMS: s £17; d £30-£36

£

GH Q Q Q *Springfield* Edinburgh Rd EH42 1NH (turn off A1 onto Dunbar Loop, establishment is on main road west side of Dunbar near Belhven Church) ☎01368 862502
Feb-Nov

A substantial Victorian villa, this guest house set in its own gardens beside the main road on the western side of town is popular with golfers. It has some well proportioned bedrooms, including a ground floor room with its own private bathroom adjacent. There are also an attractive dining room and a relaxing first-floor lounge, both of which reflect the period of the house.

5 rms (1 bth/shr) (2 fmly) CTV in all bedrooms Tea and coffee making facilities Licensed Cen ht CTV 7P Last d 5pm

PRICE GUIDE
ROOMS: s £17.50; d £33; wkly b&b £115.50-£122.50; wkly hlf-bd £166.95-£179.55
CARDS: ▨ ▤

DUNBLANE Central *Perthshire* Map **11** NN70

GH Q Q *Schiehallian House Hotel* 31 Doune Rd FK15 9AT (from A9 bypass, take A820 slip road in direction of Dunblane. Hotel 0.5m on right)
☎01786 823141 FAX 01786 824604
Closed Feb

A small family-run hotel, Shiehallion House lies in a residential area on the Doune road, close to the bypass. It has a cosy little residents' bar and a restaurant serving good-value meals. Bedrooms vary considerably in quality but all are well equipped.

6 rms (5 bth/shr) (2 fmly) No smoking in bedrooms No smoking

in dining room CTV in all bedrooms Tea and coffee making facilities Direct dial from bedrooms Licensed Cen ht ch fac 12P Last d 8.45pm
CARDS: ◼ ◼ ◼

Selected

GH ⓠⓠⓠⓠ **Westwood** Doune Rd FK15 9ND (leave A9 on A820, turn towards Doune 0.5m on left)
☎01786 822579
Mar-Nov
Set back form the main road in an acre of mature grounds, this modern house has been tastefully decorated and is immaculately kept. The comfortable bedrooms have many thoughtful extras, while the spacious TV lounge is bright and full of local information. Liz and Bob Duncan attend to every detail and many guests come back time and again, using the house as a base to explore the region or a convenient stopover on the way north. Hearty breakfasts are served at separate tables in the dining room, and smoking is not permitted in any area.
3 rms (2 bth/shr) No smoking Tea and coffee making facilities No dogs (ex guide dogs) Cen ht CTV No children 6P No coaches
PRICE GUIDE
ROOMS: s £25; d £34-£37; wkly b&b £228-£256✱

DUNDEE Tayside *Angus* Map **11** NO43

Selected

GH ⓠⓠⓠⓠ **Beach House Hotel** 22 Esplanade, Broughty Ferry DD5 2EN
☎01382 775537 FAX 01382 480241
Mrs Glennie manages to combine the cosiness of a guest house with all the benefits of a larger establishment at this friendly private hotel. It offers unspoilt views over the Tay estuary, and there are facilities for both tourists and business guests. Dinners are provided and drinks are served in the spacious lounge, while snacks and continental breakfast are available through room service. Bedrooms vary in size but are all well equipped.
5 en suite (bth/shr) (1 fmly) No smoking in dining room CTV in all bedrooms Tea and coffee making facilities Direct dial from bedrooms No dogs Licensed Cen ht 1P No coaches Last d 6pm
PRICE GUIDE
ROOMS: s £32-£38; d £44-£50✱
CARDS: ◼ ◼

GH ⓠⓠⓠ **Invermark Hotel** 23 Monifeith Rd, Broughty Ferry DD5 2RN (3m E A930)
☎01382 739430 FAX 01382 739430
This immaculate house lies in its own gardens off the main road to the east side of Broughty Ferry. The modern en suite bedrooms are mostly well proportioned and feature such thoughtful extras as tourist information and tissues. There is a comfortable lounge, and guests from afar can mark their homes on a wall map of the world.
4 rms (3 shr) (1 fmly) No smoking CTV in all bedrooms Tea and coffee making facilities No dogs (ex guide dogs) Licensed Cen ht 14P No coaches Last d by arrangement
PRICE GUIDE
ROOMS: d £40
CARDS: ◼

The Bobbin
Guest House
36 High Street, Gatehouse of Fleet,
Castle Douglas, Scotland DG7 2HP
Telephone: (01557) 814229

Situated in the attractive town of Gatehouse of Fleet, originally planned as an industrial settlement in the 1760's. Now the town has a quiet charm, providing a refuge from the stress and strains of everyday life and work. This is also reflected in Bobbin Guest House, all the bedrooms are comfortable with en suite rooms available. Food is home made with vegetarian and special diets catered for. The Coffee Shop open daily for morning coffee, lunches and afternoon teas. There are many activities and places of interest nearby making Bobbin an ideal base from which to explore.

SOUTHPARK

Southpark's peaceful edge of town location is ideal for touring etc., with easy access to all major routes yet only 5 minutes drive from the town centre. Ample secure parking.
1 double room en suite, 1 twin room en suite, 1 family room with private bathroom adjoining, residents lounge including Sky TV, video, music centre, open log fire.
Proprietor: Mrs. Sheena Maxwell
Tel/Fax: (01387) 710191

DUNFERMLINE Fife Map **11** NT08

Selected

GH QQQQ *Clarke Cottage* 139 Halbeath Rd KY11 4LA
☎01383 735935
Though not large, the stylish guest rooms of this Victorian
cottage - all of which are contained in a modern extension
designed in keeping with the original building - are both
tastefully furnished and comfortable. Smoking is not
permitted on the premises.
4 en suite (shr) No smoking CTV in all bedrooms Tea and
coffee making facilities No dogs (ex guide dogs) Cen ht 5P

Selected

GH QQQQ **Hopetoun Lodge** 141 Halbeath Rd
KY11 4LA (exit M90 at junct 3 and travel 1.5m through
Halbeath, past retail park on right, over the roundabout
and two sets of lights. On left after garage)
☎01383 620906 & 624252
Hopetoun Lodge is a detached house which lies on the A907
between the town and the M90. Attractively decorated
throughout, it offers a superb new en suite twin room, a
spacious family room and a smaller twin, all thoughtfully
equipped. A relaxing lounge with comfortable sofas also
contains the large table around which breakfast is taken.
3 rms (1 shr) (1 fmly) No smoking CTV in all bedrooms
Tea and coffee making facilities No dogs (ex guide dogs)
Cen ht CTV 4P No coaches
PRICE GUIDE
ROOMS: s £23.50-£28.50; d £37-£50✱

DUNKELD Tayside *Perthshire* Map **11** NO04

GH QQQ *Waterbury* Murthly Ter PH8 0BG (next to church
and post office) ☎01350 727324
Traditionally furnished and offering very well looked after, this
three-storey guesthouse is in the main street and all but one of the
bedrooms are on the second floor. They are well proportioned and
four have retained their Victorian features. There is a lounge and
a dining room with sensible sized, well spaced tables.
5 rms (1 fmly) No smoking in bedrooms No smoking in dining
room Tea and coffee making facilities Licensed Cen ht CTV 6P
No coaches Last d 5.30pm
CARDS: 🔳 💳 💳

DUNLOP Strathclyde *Ayrshire* Map **10** NS44

GH QQQ *Struther Farmhouse* Newmill Rd KA3 4BA
(within village approx 200yds from railway station)
☎01560 484946
Closed 2wks spring & autumn rs Sun & Mon
Good-value accommodation is offered at this stone-built house on
the edge of the village north of the railway line. The bedrooms are
spacious and comfortably traditional in style. Public areas include
a lounge and two dining areas where enjoyable Taste of Scotland
dishes are served to residents and non-residents alike.
4 rms (2 fmly) Tea and coffee making facilities Cen ht CTV
16P Last d 8.30pm

DUNOON Strathclyde *Argyllshire* Map **10** NS17

Selected

GH QQQQ **The Anchorage** Lazaretto Point, Shore Rd,
Ardnadam, Holy Loch PA23 8QG (3m N on A815)
☎01369 705108 FAX 01369 705108
About three miles north of Dunoon, with views over the Holy
Loch, this detached period house has been completely
renovated by enthusiastic owners Tony and Dee Hancock.
Bedrooms, including one with a four poster bed, are furnished
in pine with pretty lace and ornaments further enhancing
them. There is a large comfortable lounge with an array of
books and games, and a real fire which burns in cool weather.
Honest home-cooking is provided in the attractive dining
room with its colourful linen and cheeky cherubs creating a
pleasant surrounding for Dee's cuisine. The atmosphere
created is informal and friendly.
5 en suite (bth/shr) (1 fmly) No smoking CTV in all
bedrooms Tea and coffee making facilities No dogs (ex
guide dogs) Licensed Cen ht 10P No coaches Discount on
membership of country club Last d 9.30pm
PRICE GUIDE
ROOMS: d £39-£49; wkly b&b £136.50-£171.50; wkly hlf-
bd £224-£259✱
CARDS: 🔳 💳 🔲 (£)

GH QQQ **The Cedars** 51 Alexandra Pde, East Bay
PA23 8AF ☎01369 702425 FAX 01369 702964
Good value bed and breakfast accommodation is offered at this
friendly family run hotel which enjoys a lovely outlook over the
Firth of Clyde from its position on the seafront. The tastefully
decorated bedrooms are bright and cheerful with modern
amenities; the larger rooms have tables and comfortable chairs,
and non smoking rooms are available on the top floor. There is a
small lounge with sea views , and an attractive dining room where
hearty breakfasts are served.
11 en suite (bth/shr) (1 fmly) No smoking in 4 bedrooms No
smoking in dining room No smoking in lounges CTV in all
bedrooms Tea and coffee making facilities Direct dial from
bedrooms No dogs Licensed Cen ht No parking
PRICE GUIDE
ROOMS: s £19-£25; d £38-£55
CARDS: 🔳 💳 💳 🔘 (£)

DUNURE Strathclyde *Ayrshire* Map **10** NS21

Selected

♥ QQQQ Mrs A Gemmell **Dunduff** *(NS265160)*
Dunure KA7 4LH (on A719, 400yds past village school on
left) ☎01292 500225 FAX 01292 500225
Mar-Oct
A stay in Agnes Gemmell's comfortable family home - which
dates in part from the 15th century - provides excellent value
for money and its setting high above the A719 offers fine
views across gently rolling countryside to the Firth of Clyde.
Two spacious, comfortably furnished bedrooms are equipped
with en suite facilities, while the smaller, plainer third room
has exclusive use of a bathroom. There is an inviting lounge,
and hearty breakfasts are served in the smart dining room.
This is a no-smoking house.
3 rms (2 shr) (2 fmly) No smoking CTV in 2 bedrooms Tea

and coffee making facilities No dogs (ex guide dogs) Cen ht
CTV 10P 600 acres beef sheep
PRICE GUIDE
ROOMS: s £26; d £40-£45; wkly b&b fr £126

DUNVEGAN See **SKYE, ISLE OF**

EAST CALDER Lothian *Midlothian* Map **11** NT06

♥ Ⓠ Ⓠ Ⓠ Ⓠ Mr & Mrs Scott **Ashcroft Farmhouse**
(NT095682) EH53 0ET (on B7015, off A71)
☎01506 881810 FAX 01506 884327
This smart new house stands in five acres of small holding
with lovely views across landscaped gardens to the north, and
offers comfortable modern ground floor bedrooms including
one with a four-poster bed. There is a residents lounge and a
neat dining room. This is a no-smoking establishment.
6 en suite (shr) (2 fmly) No smoking CTV in all bedrooms
Tea and coffee making facilities No dogs (ex guide dogs)
Cen ht 7P 5 acres cattle sheep
PRICE GUIDE
ROOMS: d fr £46; wkly b&b fr £171✳
CARDS: 🔳 ▨ 🔳 🖸

♥ Ⓠ Ⓠ Ⓠ Mrs J Dick **Overshiel** *(NT099689)* EH53 0HT (0.5m
NE off B7015) ☎01506 880469 FAX 01506 883006
This charming 19th century farmhouse is located to the east of the
village within easy reach of Edinburgh by train, car or bus. Two
bedrooms are contained in a converted building and have their
own entrance, while a spacious family room is found in the main
house. Breakfast is served at a communal table and there is a
comfortable guest lounge.
1 rms 2 annexe en suite (shr) No smoking CTV in all bedrooms
Tea and coffee making facilities No dogs (ex guide dogs) Cen ht
6P 340 acres mixed
PRICE GUIDE
ROOMS: s £20-£25; d £32-£36

EDINBURGH Lothian *Midlothian* Map **11** NT27

GH Ⓠ Ⓠ Ⓠ **Abbey Lodge** 137 Drum St, Gilmerton EH17 8RJ
☎0131 664 9548 FAX 0131 664 3965
Situated beside the A7 on the southern outskirts of the city, just a
couple of minutes from the bypass, this purpose-built guest house
will appeal to business guests as well as tourists. Bedrooms (all of
them on the ground floor) are practically furnished and well
equipped, providing radio, hair dryer, satellite TV and plug for
direct dial telephone. Guests have the use of a small sun lounge
off the owners' lounge and there is a cheerful dining room which
shares the friendly and informal atmosphere of the whole
establishment.
5 en suite (bth/shr) (5 fmly) No smoking in 2 bedrooms No
smoking in dining room CTV in all bedrooms Tea and coffee
making facilities Licensed Cen ht CTV 10P Last d noon
PRICE GUIDE
ROOMS: d £40-£50✳
CARDS: 🔳 ▨ 🔳 🖸
See advertisement under Colour Section

GH Ⓠ Ⓠ *The Adria Hotel* 11-12 Royal Ter EH7 5AB
☎0131 556 7875
Closed Nov-Dec
Set in an elegant Georgian terrace this long-established guest
house enjoys magnificent views towards Leith and the Forth. All
the bedrooms are well decorated and some are equipped with TVs
➡

and en suite facilities. Public areas include a breakfast room with separate tables and a spacious lounge which retains its original marble fireplace.
24 rms (6 bth/shr) (7 fmly) Tea and coffee making facilities No dogs Cen ht CTV No parking

GH 🛇🛇 **Anvilla** 1a Granville Ter EH10 4PG
☎0131 228 3381
Set in a residential area, this well maintained detached Victorian house is located just southwest of the city centre. The comfortable bedrooms are freshly decorated and electric blankets are provided. Many original features have been preserved, such as the beautiful ornate ceiling in the first floor lounge and cornicing in the bedrooms and the attractive breakfast room. The latter also contains a tiled fireplace and a collection of wall plates from holidays around the world.
6 rms (2 fmly) No smoking in dining room CTV in all bedrooms Tea and coffee making facilities Cen ht CTV 5P No coaches
PRICE GUIDE
ROOMS: s £19-£21; d £36-£40

GH 🛇🛇🛇 **Ashdene House** 23 Fountainhall Rd EH9 2LN
☎0131 667 6026
Closed 2 wks in winter
High standards of housekeeping and maintenance are assured at this family-run holiday and business guest house, situated in a desirable conservation area on the south side of the city. The comfortable bedrooms vary in size and provide a good range of amenities. Breakfast is served at individual tables in the attractive dining room which also has a small lounge area. This is a no-smoking establishment.
5 rms (4 shr) (2 fmly) No smoking CTV in all bedrooms Tea and coffee making facilities Direct dial from bedrooms No dogs Cen ht 3P No coaches
PRICE GUIDE
ROOMS: d £36-£50; wkly b&b £126-£175✱

Selected

GH 🛇🛇🛇🛇 **Ashgrove House** 12 Osborne Ter
EH12 5HG ☎0131 337 5014 FAX 0131 337 5043
Smart bedrooms, with plenty of extras such as hairdryers, trouser presses, radios and magazines, are offered at this well kept period house which is situated on the Glasgow road just west of the city centre. There is a spacious breakfast room adjoining the sun lounge, and evening meals can be provided by prior arrangement.
7 en suite (shr) (2 fmly) No smoking CTV in all bedrooms Tea and coffee making facilities No dogs (ex guide dogs) Cen ht CTV 10P No coaches Last d 10am
PRICE GUIDE
ROOMS: s £25-£30; d £48-£60

 GH 🛇 **Averon** 44 Gilmore Place EH3 9NQ
☎0131 229 9932
10 rms (3 fmly) No smoking in dining room CTV in all bedrooms Tea and coffee making facilities No dogs Cen ht 9P
PRICE GUIDE
ROOMS: s £16-£25; d £28-£46
CARDS: 🔲 💳 💳 (£)

GH 🛇🛇🛇 **Ben Cruachan** 17 McDonald Rd EH7 4LX
☎0131 556 3709
Etr-Oct
This attractive guest house is located to the east of the city, about five minutes from Princes Street. It offers comfortable accommodation in variously sized bedrooms with good facilities

and bright floral fabrics. A lounge contains a wide range of local information and the dining room serves breakfast at separate tables.
3 en suite (bth/shr) (1 fmly) No smoking CTV in all bedrooms Tea and coffee making facilities No dogs Cen ht No parking
PRICE GUIDE
ROOMS: s £25-£35; d £40-£55; wkly b&b £140-£192.50✱ (£)

GH 🛇🛇 **Ben Doran** 11 Mayfield Gardens EH9 2AX
☎0131 667 8488
Closed 20-27 Dec
This friendly bed and breakfast establishment is situated on the south side of the city - with convenient bus links to the centre - and close to many of the University buildings. The practical bedrooms, some of which have en suite facilities, are approached by way of a sweeping staircase. A small parking area is available at the front of the house.
9 rms (1 bth 3 shr) (5 fmly) CTV in all bedrooms Tea and coffee making facilities Cen ht 8P
PRICE GUIDE
ROOMS: s £18-£25; d £32-£50 (£)

GH 🛇🛇🛇 **Beverley Hotel** 40 Murrayfield Ave EH12 6AY
☎0131 337 1128 FAX 0131 445 1994
Closed 20-27 Dec
This well-kept house forms part of a Victorian terrace in a quiet, leafy area to the west of the city. Bedrooms have been enhanced with fresh decor and bright fabrics, while the comfortable first floor TV lounge is an ideal place for meeting fellow guests over tea or coffee. Hearty breakfasts are served at separate tables in the cosy dining room, and parking is usually available at the front of the hotel.
8 rms (4 bth/shr) (2 fmly) Licensed Cen ht CTV No parking
PRICE GUIDE
ROOMS: s £19-£35; d £40-£60✱

GH 🛇🛇 *Boisdale Hotel* 9 Coates Gardens EH12 5LG
☎0131 337 1134 FAX 0131 313 0048
Conveniently located close to the city centre, this attractive terraced house offers bedrooms of varying sizes, all with en suite facilities. There is a small guest lounge as well as the pleasant dining room where hearty Scottish breakfasts are served at separate tables.
11 en suite (bth/shr) (6 fmly) CTV in all bedrooms Tea and coffee making facilities Licensed Cen ht CTV No parking Last d 7pm

GH 🛇🛇🛇 **Bonnington** 202 Ferry Rd EH6 4NW
☎0131 554 7610
This semidetached Victorian house lies on the north side of the city with views over its well tended garden to the local bowling green and park. The well equipped bedrooms are attractively decorated with tasteful fabrics and have up-to-date bathrooms. There are also a smart modern lounge and a dining room full of heirlooms.
6 rms (2 bth 3 shr) (3 fmly) No smoking in bedrooms No smoking in dining room CTV in all bedrooms Tea and coffee making facilities Cen ht CTV 9P No coaches Last d 10am
PRICE GUIDE
ROOMS: s £20-£30; d £40-£50✱ (£)

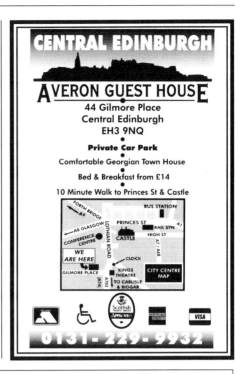

Selected

GH Q Q Q Q **Brunswick Hotel** 7 Brunswick St EH7 5JB
☎0131 556 1238 FAX 0131 557 1404
Closed Xmas
This stylish guest house forms part of a Georgian terrace
within easy walking distance of the city centre. The sitting
room has an ornate ceiling and black marble fireplace, while
bedrooms in a variety of sizes are well furnished and provided
with comfortable seating. Breakfasts are excellent.
11 en suite (shr) (1 fmly) No smoking CTV in all bedrooms
Tea and coffee making facilities No dogs Cen ht No
children 2yrs No parking No coaches
PRICE GUIDE
ROOMS: s £30-£45; d £50-£80
CARDS: ▨ ▬ ▧

GH Q Q Q **Buchan Hotel** 3 Coates Gardens EH12 5LG
(W along A8) ☎0131 337 1045 FAX 0131 538 7055
This family-run bed and breakfast hotel is conveniently situated in
a quiet terrace near Haymarket station. Bedrooms vary in size
from large, airy family rooms to some smaller singles, but all are
equipped with en suite shower rooms. Breakfast is served at
separate tables in the bright dining room and early risers can be
catered for.
12 en suite (shr) (5 fmly) No smoking in dining room CTV in all
bedrooms Tea and coffee making facilities Cen ht CTV No
parking
PRICE GUIDE
ROOMS: s £28-£37.50; d £44-£62✳
CARDS: ▨ ▬ ▧

GH Q **Chalumna** 5 Granville Ter EH10 4PQ
☎0131 229 2086
This guest house lies at the end of a terrace south west of the city
centre. Bedrooms are a good size but modest standards, with
mixed furnishing. There is one single room with private bathroom,
and the dining room also acts as lounge.
8 rms (5 bth/shr) (1 fmly) No smoking in dining room CTV in
all bedrooms Tea and coffee making facilities Cen ht CTV 4P
PRICE GUIDE
ROOMS: s £25-£45; d £36-£60

Selected

GH Q Q Q Q **Classic House** 50 Mayfield Rd EH9 2NH
☎0131 667 5847 FAX 0131 662 1016
A popular 16th century inn stands at the crossroads in the
centre of this charming village. It has been carefully restored
to retain its original character with exposed brickwork, beams,
open fireplaces and a gallery overlooking the high-ceilinged
restaurant. The en suite bedrooms are individually decorated,
comfortably appointed and well equipped. A good range of
interesting cooking is served in both the restaurant and the
bar.
4 rms (3 bth/shr) No smoking CTV in all bedrooms Tea and
coffee making facilities No dogs Cen ht CTV No parking
Last d 8pm
PRICE GUIDE
ROOMS: s £20-£30; d £40-£60✳
CARDS: ▨ ▬ ▨

GH Q Q **Clifton Private Hotel** 1 Clifton Ter, Haymarket
EH12 5DR ☎0131 337 1002 FAX 0131 337 1002
Good value bed and breakfast accommodation is offered at this
friendly private hotel situated in the west end close to Haymarket
railway station. Bedrooms vary in size, and public areas include a
spacious first-floor lounge, due for refurbishment at the time of
our visit. There is a pleasant, ground-floor breakfast room.
11 rms (4 shr) No smoking in dining room CTV in all bedrooms
Tea and coffee making facilities Direct dial from bedrooms Cen
ht CTV No parking No coaches
PRICE GUIDE
ROOMS: s £23-£30; d £40-£60
CARDS: ▨ ▬

GH Q Q Q **Crion** 33 Minto St EH9 2BT
☎0131 667 2708 FAX 0131 662 1946
Constant improvements are being made to this delightful Victorian
house, which is in a desirable south-side residential area, a short
drive from the city centre and bypass. The well decorated
bedrooms, though compact, are tastefully furnished and
comfortable. Well cooked breakfasts are served in the attractive
lounge/dining room.
6 rms (3 shr) (1 fmly) No smoking in dining room No smoking
in lounges CTV in all bedrooms Tea and coffee making facilities
No dogs (ex guide dogs) Cen ht CTV 1P
PRICE GUIDE
ROOMS: s £18-£25; d £15-£30✳

GH Q Q Q **Daisy Park** 41 Abercorn Ter, Joppa EH15 2DG
☎0131 669 2503 FAX 0131 669 0189
An end-of-terrace Victorian house, Daisy Park is situated three
miles east of Edinburgh, within walking distance of Portobello
Promenade. The bedrooms, including a spacious family room, are
pleasantly decorated and have some good en suite facilities;
breakfast is taken in an attractive dining room which can also be
used as a lounge.
6 rms (4 shr) (2 fmly) No smoking in dining room No smoking
in lounges CTV in all bedrooms Tea and coffee making facilities
No dogs (ex guide dogs) Cen ht CTV No parking
PRICE GUIDE
ROOMS: s £20-£25; d £40-£50
CARDS: ▨ ▧

GH Q Q *Dalwin Lodge & Restaurant* 75 Mayfield Rd
EH9 3AA ☎0131 667 2294 FAX 0131 667 2294
Closed 24-27 Dec rs Sun
This small, family-run guest house and restaurant forms part of a
terraced row and is on the city's south side, within a short drive of
the centre. Bedrooms are adequately equipped. The small
restaurant, open to non-residents, offers an excellent value, fixed-
price lunch menu, with a more extensive choice available in the
evening.
5 rms (1 fmly) CTV in all bedrooms Tea and coffee making
facilities No dogs (ex guide dogs) Licensed Cen ht No parking
No coaches Last d 8pm

Selected

GH Q Q Q Q **Dorstan Private Hotel** 7 Priestfield Rd
EH16 5HJ ☎0131 667 6721 & 667 5138
FAX 0131 668 4644
Guests return time and again to sample the high standards of
hospitality from Mairae Campbell, who maintains her guest
house to a high standard. The bedrooms, in this large
Victorian house on the south side of the city, vary in size, but
are attractively furnished and many are enhanced by bold,
bright colours. There is a comfortable lounge with a small

---

aquarium, while good value dinners are served in the dining room which has booth seating and tasteful tartan plaids hung on the ceiling.
14 rms (12 bth/shr) (2 fmly) No smoking in dining room No smoking in lounges CTV in all bedrooms Tea and coffee making facilities Direct dial from bedrooms No dogs (ex guide dogs) Cen ht 8P No coaches Last d 3pm
PRICE GUIDE
ROOMS: s £29-£34; d £35-£45✳
CARDS: 🔳 🔳

Premier Selected

GH 🔲🔲🔲🔲🔲
Drummond House 17 Drummond Place EH3 6PL
☎0131 557 9189
FAX 0131 557 9189

Drummond House is one of the few complete houses left in the elegant Georgian New Town, and is convenient for the city centre sights whilst being set in a tranquil, residential square with pretty gardens. The splendour of the house has been enhanced by a combination of imaginative colour selection, period antiques and swathes of sumptuous fabrics. Many artefacts and rugs from round the world have also been used to create a warm and welcoming atmosphere. The comfortable lounge offers a peaceful setting for planning a day out, while freshly cooked breakfasts are served at one table in the bow-ended dining room. Josephine and Alan Dougall have managed to create the impression that guests are in a private house rather than a hotel.
3 rms (2 bth/shr) No smoking No dogs Cen ht CTV No children 12yrs No parking No coaches
PRICE GUIDE
ROOMS: d £70-£90
CARDS: 🔳 🔳

GH 🔲🔲 **Dunstane House** 4 West Coates EH12 5JQ
☎0131 337 6169 FAX 0131 337 6169
Standing in its own garden, this large Victorian mansion has a relaxed atmosphere. Comfortable bedrooms are of a good size and the lounge has a small bar.
15 rms (9 shr) (5 fmly) No smoking in dining room CTV in all bedrooms Tea and coffee making facilities Licensed Cen ht CTV 10P No coaches
PRICE GUIDE
ROOMS: s £25-£35; d £50-£72✳
CARDS: 🔳 🔳 🔳 🔳

GH 🔲🔲🔲 **Ecosse International** 15 McDonald Rd EH7 4LX
☎0131 556 4967 FAX 0131 556 7394
A neat, cosy guesthouse offering well maintained accommodation and delightful service from the resident proprietress.
5 en suite (bth/shr) (3 fmly) No smoking in bedrooms No smoking in dining room CTV in all bedrooms Tea and coffee making facilities Cen ht
PRICE GUIDE
ROOMS: s £35; d £20-£25✳
CARDS: 🔳 🔳 🔳

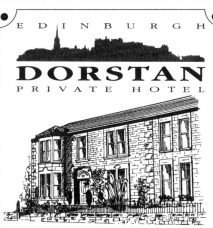

GH Ⓠ Ⓠ Ⓠ *Elder York* 38 Elder St EH1 3OX
☎0131 556 1926
In this city centre guest house near the bus station, the third and
fourth floors of a Victorian tenement have been transformed into
bright, airy bedrooms - some with full en suite facilities and
several with shower units - and an attractive breakfast room with
well spaced tables. There is no lounge.
13 rms (3 shr) (3 fmly) CTV in all bedrooms Tea and coffee
making facilities No dogs (ex guide dogs) Cen ht

Selected

GH Ⓠ Ⓠ Ⓠ Ⓠ *Ellesmere House* 11 Glengyle Ter
EH3 9LN ☎0131 229 4823 FAX 0131 229 5285
Celia and Tommy Leishman offer warm hospitality at their
terraced guesthouse overlooking Bruntsfield Links. The
bedrooms are well proportioned and comfortable, with
bathrooms fitted to a high standard. The lounge also doubles
as a breakfast room, where guests are under no obligation to
share tables.
6 en suite (bth/shr) (2 fmly) No smoking in dining room
CTV in all bedrooms Tea and coffee making facilities No
dogs (ex guide dogs) Cen ht CTV No parking
PRICE GUIDE
ROOMS: d £38-£60; wkly b&b £133-£210*

Premier Selected

GH Ⓠ Ⓠ Ⓠ Ⓠ Ⓠ *Elmview*
15 Glengyle Ter EH3 9LN
☎0131 228 1973
FAX 0131 228 1973
Situated on the edge of the
meadows, about ten minutes'
walk from the city centre,
this friendly Victorian
terraced house has been
steadily upgraded. The
bedrooms are located on the
lower ground floor; all are

attractively decorated and have facilities which would not be
out of place in a four star hotel. Fresh flowers, delicate
figurines and floral fabrics enhance the comfortable rooms
and make this small guest house an ideal base for exploring
the beauty of Edinburgh. Breakfast is served at one large table
and there is a good range of hot and cold items to start the
day, while the walled garden at the rear is a pleasant sun trap.
3 en suite (bth/shr) No smoking CTV in all bedrooms Tea
and coffee making facilities Direct dial from bedrooms No
dogs Cen ht No children 15yrs No parking No coaches
PRICE GUIDE
ROOMS: s £40-£50; d £50-£70*
CARDS: 🔲 🔳

GH Ⓠ Ⓠ Ⓠ *Galloway* 22 Dean Park Crescent EH4 1PH (W on
A9) ☎0131 332 3672
Forming part of a Victorian terrace, this guest house lies little
more than a stroll from the west end of Princes Street. Bedrooms
are mostly a good size. Guests will share tables at breakfast unless
they request otherwise.

10 rms (6 bth/shr) (6 fmly) CTV in all bedrooms Tea and coffee
making facilities Cen ht No parking
PRICE GUIDE
ROOMS: s £22-£38; d £34-£50; wkly b&b £102-£228

🚭 📺 **GH** Ⓠ Ⓠ Ⓠ *Glendale Hotel* 5 Lady Rd EH16 5PA
☎0131 667 6588
Located close to the Cameron Toll shopping centre, this family-
run guest house is conveniently situated for both the city centre
and by-pass. Accommodation is comfortable and well equipped,
the welcoming lounge contains a large fish tank and models of
classic cars, and breakfast is served at separate tables in the
adjacent dining room. Ample car parking is available.
8 rms (4 shr) (1 fmly) No smoking in dining room CTV in all
bedrooms Tea and coffee making facilities Direct dial from
bedrooms No dogs (ex guide dogs) Cen ht CTV 8P No coaches
Last d noon
PRICE GUIDE
ROOMS: s £15-£20; d £32-£58
CARDS: 🔲 🔳

GH Ⓠ Ⓠ *Glenisla Hotel* 12 Lygon Rd EH16 5QB
☎0131 667 4877 FAX 0131 667 4098
This attractive semidetached sandstone house is situated in a quiet
residential area on the south side of the city, and is gradually being
improved by the friendly owners. There is a spacious and
comfortable first floor TV lounge, and good home cooking is
served in the dining room. Bedrooms vary in size.
8 rms (5 shr) (1 fmly) No smoking in dining room Tea and
coffee making facilities Licensed Cen ht CTV 6P No coaches
Last d 8pm
CARDS: 🔲 🔳

GH Ⓠ Ⓠ Ⓠ *Glenora Hotel* 14 Rosebery Crescent EH12 5JY
☎0131 337 1186 FAX 0131 337 1186
Personally run by the resident proprietors, this comfortable private
hotel is situated in the west end close to Haymarket station. The
well kept bedrooms are mostly spacious and offer modern
appointments. Public areas include a comfortable TV lounge and
spacious breakfast room. Smoking is not allowed in any of the
bedrooms or in the breakfast room.
10 en suite (shr) (2 fmly) CTV in all bedrooms Tea and coffee
making facilities No dogs Licensed Cen ht CTV No parking
CARDS: 🔲 🔳

GH Ⓠ Ⓠ *Glenorchy Hotel* 22 Glenorchy Ter EH9 2DH
☎0131 667 5708
Good value commercial and tourist accommodation is offered at
this family run guesthouse quietly situated in a south side
residential area, only ten minutes from the city centre. Bedrooms
are well equipped and spacious, and there is a pleasant first floor
lounge with TV. Enjoyable home cooking is available by
arrangement, and snacks are served in the lounge.
9 en suite (bth/shr) (2 fmly) CTV in all bedrooms Tea and coffee
making facilities Cen ht CTV No parking No coaches
CARDS: 🔲 🔳 🔳

GH Ⓠ Ⓠ Ⓠ *Greenside Hotel* 9 Royal Ter EH7 5AB
☎0131 557 0022 & 557 0121 FAX 0131 557 0022
This private hotel is quietly situated in an impressive Georgian
terrace overlooking Calton Hill, near the east end of Princes
Street. It offers fine panoramic views northwards across the Firth
of Forth from upper front-facing bedrooms, whilst those at the rear
overlook terraced gardens. Bedrooms vary in size, the original
master rooms being particularly spacious, but they are all
particularly well maintained, individually decorated and
comfortably furnished.

14 en suite (bth/shr) (5 fmly) No smoking in dining room CTV in all bedrooms Tea and coffee making facilities No dogs (ex guide dogs) Licensed Cen ht CTV No parking Last d 4pm
PRICE GUIDE
ROOMS: s £25-£45; d £40-£70; wkly b&b £140-£245; wkly hlf-bd £210-£315
CARDS: 🟦 📷 🔲 ⓪

Selected

GH Ⓠ Ⓠ Ⓠ Ⓠ *Grosvenor Gardens Hotel* 1 Grosvenor Gardens EH12 5JU ☎0131 313 3415 FAX 0131 346 8732
Quietly situated in a cul-de-sac in the city's west end, this Victorian town house has been tastefully refurbished to provide an elegant little bed and breakfast establishment; its character has been sympathetically developed, and decorative touches add to the 'country house in town' atmosphere. Bedrooms are individually styled and many are spacious. For relaxation there is the delightful sitting room, with its grand piano and periodicals.
8 en suite (bth/shr) (3 fmly) No smoking in dining room No smoking in lounges CTV in all bedrooms Tea and coffee making facilities No dogs (ex guide dogs) Cen ht CTV No children 5yrs No parking No coaches
CARDS: 🟦 📷 🔲

GH Ⓠ *Halcyon Hotel* 8 Royal Ter EH7 5AB
☎0131 556 1033 & 031-556 1032
Forming part of a Georgian terrace, just east of the city centre, this family-run guesthouse offers good value, practical accommodation. Bedrooms are simply furnished and the standard ➡

Glenisla Hotel

12 Lygon Road, Edinburgh EH16 5QB.
Telephone: 0131-667 4877
Fax: 0131-667 4098

A small family run hotel situated in quiet area of the city, ten minutes from Princes Street and on main bus route. Surrounded by golf courses and within easy reach of Commonwealth Pool and Holyrood Palace. Full central heating, all bedrooms with shower & toilet, tea, coffee and hair dryers. Licensed restaurant for residents and non residents. Residents' TV lounge. Ample parking. Open all year.
Please send for brochure.

CENTRAL EDINBURGH

Ellesmere House

11 Glengyle Terrace
Edinburgh EH3 9LN
Telephone: 0131-229 4823
Fax: 0131-229 5285

A warm welcome is extended to all visitors to this attractive and comfortable Victorian home overlooking the meadows. 6 bedrooms, decorated and furnished to a high standard, all bedrooms en-suite, and equipped with every comfort in mind. Delicious breakfasts and special diets are provided. Cosy lounge available throughout the day. Good local restaurants and convenient for the Castle, Princes Street and the Royal Mile.

AA Selected QQQQ

GREENSIDE HOTEL
9 ROYAL TERRACE,
EDINBURGH EH7 5AB
Tel: 0131-557 0022/0121
Fax: 0131-557 0022
QQQ
Recommended

Ideally situated in the City Centre, surrounded by peaceful garden settings, walking distance to all major tourist attractions.
The Greenside Hotel has all facilities and offers a warm welcome and a comfortable stay.

A full Scottish breakfast is cooked to order.

An oasis of calm in the centre of the city.

of housekeeping is high. There is a comfortable TV lounge on the first floor and generous breakfasts are served in the pleasant dining room.
16 rms (2 shr) (6 fmly) Tea and coffee making facilities Cen ht CTV No parking Tennis (hard)

GH Q Q Q **A Haven** 180 Ferry Rd EH6 4NS (Logis)
☎0131 554 6559 FAX 0131 554 5252
The charming owners, Moira and Ronnie Murdoch, have steadily improved this detached Victorian house, situated on the northern side of the city. Bedrooms vary in size, with the larger rooms on the first floor, though all offer good facilities for both business guests and tourists. The attractive dining room and lounge are hung with some impressive oil paintings by the proprietors' daughter. Secure parking is available to the rear of the house.
12 en suite (shr) (2 fmly) CTV in all bedrooms Tea and coffee making facilities Direct dial from bedrooms No dogs (ex guide dogs) Licensed Cen ht CTV 6P Last d 8pm
PRICE GUIDE
ROOMS: s £30-£47; d £54-£78
CARDS: 🟥 🟥

GH Q Q *Heriott Park* 256 Ferry Rd EH5 3AN
☎0131 552 6628
Set in a terraced row a mile north of the city centre, this neat guest house enjoys unrestricted views across the city to the castle and the distant Pentland Hills.
6 rms (2 shr) (4 fmly) No smoking in dining room No smoking in lounges CTV in all bedrooms Tea and coffee making facilities Cen ht CTV

GH Q Q **Hopetoun** 15 Mayfield Rd EH9 2NG
☎0131 667 7691
This small, friendly, family-run guest house is located to the south side of the city, close to convenient transport to the city centre. There is a strict no smoking rule in all areas of the house. Bedrooms are a good size and include two family rooms, with original shutters a feature. Breakfast is served at separate tables in the cosy dining room, with flexible times and a wide choice of dishes available.
3 rms (2 fmly) No smoking CTV in all bedrooms Tea and coffee making facilities No dogs Cen ht CTV 2P No coaches
PRICE GUIDE
ROOMS: s £25-£30; d £32-£44✳

Selected

GH Q Q Q Q *International* 37 Mayfield Gardens
EH9 2BX ☎0131 667 2511 FAX 0131 667 1109
Attractive floral decor and luxurious bathrooms are the hallmarks of this family run guest house on the southern side of the city. With the exception of two small singles the bedrooms are spacious and solidly furnished; several family rooms and a ground floor room are also available. The combined lounge/dining room has a huge TV and lots of videos, while breakfast is served at individual tables.
7 en suite (bth/shr) (3 fmly) No smoking in dining room No smoking in lounges CTV in all bedrooms Tea and coffee making facilities No dogs (ex guide dogs) Cen ht 3P

GH Q Q Q **Ivy House** 7 Mayfield Gardens EH9 2AX
☎0131 667 3411
Improvements continue at this fine Victorian terraced house situated on the south side of the city. Well proportioned bedrooms have tasteful decor and fabrics; most have a double and a single bed and some can accommodate a family of four. There is no lounge, but the dining room (which features a fine original

fireplace) is bright and cheery. Parking is to the rear, off a narrow lane.
8 rms (6 shr) (4 fmly) No smoking in dining room CTV in all bedrooms Tea and coffee making facilities Cen ht 9P
PRICE GUIDE
ROOMS: s £20-£54; d £30-£58

GH Q Q **Kariba** 10 Granville Ter EH10 4PQ
☎0131 229 3773
Set in a residential area, this terraced guest house is located about five minutes' drive from the city centre. The compact bedrooms all have attractive patchwork quilts and some also contain combined shower/hand basins which fold away. A separate TV lounge now adjoins the dining room.
9 rms (8 bth/shr) (3 fmly) No smoking in dining room No smoking in lounges CTV in all bedrooms Tea and coffee making facilities Cen ht CTV 4P No coaches
PRICE GUIDE
ROOMS: s £20-£30; d £36-£40✳

GH Q Q Q **Kew** 1 Kew Ter, Murrayfield EH12 5JE
☎0131 313 0700 & 313 4407 FAX 0131 313 0747
A period property, located about a mile and a half west of the city on the main A8 Glasgow road, this guest house was completely renovated in 1993. It offers well equipped modern bedrooms, a residents' lounge with large, comfortable sofas, and a small but cheerfully decorated breakfast room.
6 en suite (shr) (2 fmly) No smoking in dining room No smoking in lounges CTV in all bedrooms Tea and coffee making facilities Cen ht 6P No coaches
PRICE GUIDE
ROOMS: s £30-£45; d £55-£65
CARDS: 🟥 🟥 🟥 🟥

Selected

GH Q Q Q Q **Kildonan Lodge Hotel** 27 Craigmillar Park
EH16 5PE ☎0131 667 2793 FAX 0131 667 9777
Enthusiastic owners Bruce and Maggie Urquhart have upgraded this large Victorian house on the south side of the city. Bedrooms have been stylishly refurbished and offer good facilities for business guests and tourists alike. The elegant lounge has retained its original fireplace and there is a small honesty bar. Hearty breakfasts are served at separate tables in the bright dining room and there is ample car parking to the rear of the hotel.
10 en suite (shr) (3 fmly) No smoking in bedrooms No smoking in dining room CTV in 11 bedrooms Tea and coffee making facilities Direct dial from bedrooms No dogs (ex guide dogs) Licensed Cen ht 16P
PRICE GUIDE
ROOMS: s £18-£45; d £44-£70; wkly b&b £150-£240
CARDS: 🟥 🟥 🟥

GH Q Q Q **Kilmaurs** 9 Kilmaurs Rd EH16 5DA
☎0131 667 8315
This well maintained bed and breakfast establishment is situated in a south side residential area. The comfortable bedrooms are equipped with fully tiled en suite shower rooms and include hot water bottles and controllable heating. Breakfast is served at separate tables in the combined lounge/dining room.
5 en suite (shr) (3 fmly) No smoking in dining room No

smoking in lounges CTV in all bedrooms Tea and coffee making facilities Cen ht No children 3yrs No parking
PRICE GUIDE
ROOMS: s £20-£25; d £40-£50

GH 🅀🅀 **Kingsley** 30 Craigmillar Park, Newington EH16 5PS (S on A701) ☎0131 667 8439 FAX 0131 667 8439
With good transport links in to the city centre, this family run guesthouse on the south side offers good value bed and breakfast accommodation. Several family rooms are available and there is a large lounge as well as an airy dining room where breakfast is served at separate tables. Car parking is provided at the rear of the house.
6 rms (4 shr) (3 fmly) No smoking in bedrooms No smoking in dining room CTV in all bedrooms Tea and coffee making facilities No dogs Cen ht CTV No children 6yrs 6P
PRICE GUIDE
ROOMS: d £32-£46✱
CARDS: 🔲 🔲

GH 🅀🅀 **Kirklea** 11 Harrison Rd EH11 1EG (off A70, behind St Michael's church, at junct with A71)
☎0131 337 1129 FAX 0131 337 1129
This guesthouse stands in a terraced row on the west side of the city. Bedrooms vary in size, with a large family room on the first floor. The combined lounge/dining room is adorned with tapestries which are hand-stitched by the owner. The breakfast menus are helpfully translated into French.
6 rms (1 shr) (1 fmly) No smoking in dining room No smoking in lounges CTV in all bedrooms Tea and coffee making facilities Cen ht 1P
PRICE GUIDE
ROOMS: s £19-£24; d £32-£48; wkly b&b £96-£144✱
CARDS: 🔲 🔲 🔲

GH 🅀🅀 **The Lairg** 11 Coates Gardens EH12 5LG
☎0131 337 1050 FAX 0131 346 2167
The bright modern bedrooms (several very large with good en suites) contrast with the more subdued style of the lounge and dining room at this family guest house. The house is part of a terraced row just off the Glasgow road on the western side of the city.
10 en suite (shr) (3 fmly) No smoking in dining room No smoking in lounges CTV in all bedrooms Tea and coffee making facilities Direct dial from bedrooms Licensed Cen ht CTV No parking
PRICE GUIDE
ROOMS: s £18-£30; d £36-£60; wkly b&b £120-£200
CARDS: 🔲 🔲 🔲 🔲

GH 🅀🅀 **Leamington** 57 Leamington Ter EH10 4JS
☎0131 228 3879 FAX 0131 221 1022
Situated in a quiet residential street in the Bruntsfield area of the city, this attractive guest house has been transformed with the stylish redecoration and upgrading of most of the bedrooms. First-floor rooms are large and good views are available from those on the second floor. Hearty breakfasts, including vegetarian options and weekend specials, are served in a cosy dining room where guests are sometimes required to share tables.
8 rms (2 shr) (3 fmly) No smoking CTV in all bedrooms Tea and coffee making facilities Cen ht No parking No coaches
PRICE GUIDE
ROOMS: s £18-£22; d £36-£48; wkly b&b £126-£154✱
CARDS: 🔲 🔲

GH 🔲🔲 *Lindsay* 108 Polwarth Ter EH11 1NN
☎0131 337 1580 FAX 0131 337 9174
Situated in a leafy residential area on the western side of the city,
this guest house is continually upgraded with bedrooms and public
areas being redecorated regularly. There is no lounge but the
bedrooms are a good size and have comfortable armchairs.
Breakfast is served at separate tables in the bright dining room.
8 rms (3 shr) (2 fmly) No smoking in dining room No smoking
in lounges CTV in all bedrooms Tea and coffee making facilities
Cen ht 6P No coaches
CARDS: 💳 💳 💳

```
┌─────────────────────────────────┐
│          Selected               │
└─────────────────────────────────┘
```

GH 🔲🔲🔲🔲 **The Lodge Hotel** 6 Hampton Ter, West
Coates EH12 5JD (on main A8, 1 mile west of city centre)
☎0131 337 3682 FAX 0131 313 1700
Dedicated hosts Linda and George Jarron keep this converted
Georgian house in immaculate order throughout. Most of the
bedrooms are spacious, some have original cornices and all
have splendid, fully tiled modern bathrooms. Extras such as
fresh fruit and flowers provide a welcoming touch. There are
a comfortable lounge and a cosy residents' bar, and George's
home cooking is served in the well appointed dining room.
10 en suite (shr) No smoking in bedrooms No smoking in
dining room CTV in all bedrooms Tea and coffee making
facilities Direct dial from bedrooms No dogs Licensed Cen
ht CTV 10P Last d 7.30pm
PRICE GUIDE
ROOMS: s £38-£48; d £52-£80
CARDS: 💳 💳   £

GH 🔲🔲 *Lugton* 29 Leamington Ter EH10 4JS
☎0131 229 7033 FAX 0131 228 9483
A small terraced house in a residential area of the city. There is no
lounge, but bedrooms are of a good size and very well equipped,
with modern en-suite bathrooms. There is also a smaller single
room with a separate bathroom.
4 en suite (shr) (1 fmly) CTV in all bedrooms Tea and coffee
making facilities No dogs Cen ht

GH 🔲🔲 **Marchhall Hotel** 14-16 Marchhall Crescent
EH16 5HL ☎0131 667 2743 FAX 0131 662 0777
Good value accommodation is offered at this friendly family run
business and tourist hotel in a quiet south-side residential area.
Bedrooms vary in size but most have en suite facilities and all are
well equipped. There is a timber-clad bar serving evening meals as
an alternative to the bright dining room and its short à la carte.
14 rms (10 bth/shr) (4 fmly) No smoking in 4 bedrooms CTV in
all bedrooms Tea and coffee making facilities Direct dial from
bedrooms Licensed Cen ht CTV No parking Last d 9pm
PRICE GUIDE
ROOMS: s £19-£35; d £38-£54; wkly b&b £126-£210; wkly hlf-
bd £182-£287✱
CARDS: 💳 💳   £

GH 🔲🔲🔲 **Mardale** 11 Hartington Place EH10 4LF
☎0131 229 2693
Good-value bed and breakfast accommodation is offered at this
friendly family-run guest house in a residential cul-de-sac on the
south side. Bedrooms, though compact, are well decorated and
attractive fabrics have been used to good effect. Nicely cooked
breakfasts are served in the attractive first-floor dining room,
which incorporates a lounge area.
6 rms (3 shr) (2 fmly) No smoking in dining room No smoking

in lounges CTV in all bedrooms Tea and coffee making facilities
Direct dial from bedrooms Cen ht No parking No coaches
PRICE GUIDE
ROOMS: s £17-£21; d £34-£55✱
CARDS: 💳 💳 💳   £

GH 🔲🔲🔲 **Meadows** 17 Glengyle Ter EH3 9LN (E of A702,
between the Kings Theatre and Bruntsfield Links)
☎0131 229 9559 FAX 0131 229 2226
Closed 18-28 Dec
Comfortable, well proportioned bedrooms are offered at this
efficiently run guest house overlooking the links. The rooms are
sensibly furnished to meet the needs of both the tourist and the
business traveller. A useful map of local amenities is given to each
guest, and breakfast is served refectory-style at two tables.
6 rms (4 shr) (3 fmly) No smoking in dining room CTV in all
bedrooms Tea and coffee making facilities Cen ht No parking
No coaches
CARDS: 💳 💳 💳   £

GH 🔲🔲 **Murrayfield Park** 89 Corstorphine Rd EH12 5QE
☎0131 337 5370 FAX 0131 337 3772
Closed Xmas & New Year
Situated about two miles from the city centre, on the main A8
Glasgow road, this well kept guest house has car parking space to
the front and a pretty garden to the rear. The compact bedrooms
are located on both the ground and lower ground floors and some
have en suite shower rooms, the rest sharing a luxurious public
bathroom. Breakfast is served at separate tables with a view of the
garden, and there is a comfortable TV lounge for residents' use.
6 rms (5 shr) No smoking in dining room No smoking in lounges
CTV in all bedrooms Tea and coffee making facilities No dogs
(ex guide dogs) Cen ht CTV 8P
PRICE GUIDE
ROOMS: s £20-£25; d £40-£50✱   £

GH 🔲🔲🔲 *The Newington* 18 Newington Rd EH9 1QS
☎0131 667 3356
Bedrooms vary in size and character at this solidly traditional
guest house on the south side of the city, one having a four poster
bed. The comfortable lounge is awash with momentoes from the
Far East, while giant pot plants create a tropical feel in the elegant
dining room.
8 rms (3 shr) (1 fmly) CTV in all bedrooms Tea and coffee
making facilities Licensed Cen ht 3P

GH 🔲🔲🔲 **Parklands** 20 Mayfield Gardens EH9 2BZ
(0.5m S) ☎0131 667 7184
A carefully maintained terraced house is situated on the south side
of the city, convenient for the city centre. There is no lounge but
the comfortable bedrooms are spacious and have private facilities.
Well cooked breakfasts are served at separate tables in the bright
dining room.
6 rms (5 shr) (1 fmly) No smoking in 1 bedrooms No smoking
in dining room No smoking in lounges CTV in all bedrooms Tea
and coffee making facilities No dogs (ex guide dogs) Cen ht 1P
No coaches
PRICE GUIDE
ROOMS: d £36-£52
See advertisement on p.523.

GH 🔲🔲 *Park View Villa* 254 Ferry Rd EH5 3AN
☎0131 552 3456
Part of a terraced block on the north side, this family-run
guesthouse offers good value bed and breakfast accommodation.
Bedrooms are neatly furnished and comfortable. Views of the
castle are enjoyed from the lounge, and breakfast is served,
occasionally at shared tables, in the smart dining room.

7 rms (4 shr) (3 fmly) No smoking in dining room CTV in all bedrooms Tea and coffee making facilities No dogs (ex guide dogs) Cen ht CTV No parking
CARDS: ▤ ▨

GH ⓆⓆ **Ravensdown** 248 Ferry Rd EH5 3AN
☎0131 552 5438
This friendly, family-run guest house is situated on the north side and enjoys a fine outlook over the city. Bedrooms, some non-smoking, are tastefully decorated and comfortably furnished. Public areas include a cosy TV lounge and a bright, spacious dining room where hearty breakfasts are served.
6 rms (5 fmly) No smoking CTV in all bedrooms Tea and coffee making facilities No dogs Licensed Cen ht CTV 4P
PRICE GUIDE
ROOMS: s £22-£38; d £32-£42

GH ⓆⓆⓆ *Ravensnuek* 11 Blacket Av EH9 1RR
☎0131 667 5347
Friendly owners have lovingly restored a Victorian house which lies in a quiet leafy lane just off the A68 to the south of the city. Smoking and non-smoking bedrooms are individually furnished and have cast iron fireplaces in character with the rest of the house. A comfortable lounge doubles as a dining room where hearty Scottish breakfasts are served.
6 rms (1 fmly) No smoking in 4 bedrooms No smoking in dining room Tea and coffee making facilities No dogs Cen ht CTV 4P No coaches

Selected

GH ⓆⓆⓆⓆ **Roselea** 11 Mayfield Rd EH9 2NG (on A701, 1m N of the Royal Observatory)
☎0131 667 6115 FAX 0131 667 3556
Closed 1 wedek Xmas
Maureen Invernizzi's flair for interior design is evident in her delightful terraced guest house on the south side of the city. Colourful floral decor and elegant fabrics enhance its period style, while the smart shower rooms would grace a top hotel; bedrooms without en suites each have a private bathroom. There are a small, comfortable lounge and a spacious dining room where speciality teas and freshly baked breakfast rolls are served.
7 rms (5 shr) (3 fmly) No smoking in dining room No smoking in lounges CTV in all bedrooms Tea and coffee making facilities No dogs (ex guide dogs) Cen ht 4P
PRICE GUIDE
ROOMS: s £28-£36; d £50-£64; wkly b&b £175-£224
CARDS: ▤ ▨ ▨ £

GH ⓆⓆ **Rowan** 13 Glenorchy Ter EH9 2DQ
☎0131 667 2463
This sturdy, stone-built Victorian house is situated in a quiet residential area on the south side of the city close to Cameron Toll. Efficiently run by a friendly owner, it offers good-value accommodation in well maintained bedrooms. Breakfast is served in the lounge/dining room.
9 rms (2 shr) (2 fmly) No smoking in dining room No smoking in lounges CTV in all bedrooms Tea and coffee making facilities Cen ht CTV P
PRICE GUIDE
ROOMS: s £18-£22; d £36-£50
CARDS: ▤ ▨ £

GH ⓆⓆⓆ **St Margaret's** 18 Craigmillar Park EH16 5PS
☎0131 667 2202 FAX 0131 667 2202
Feb-Dec
Some of the bedrooms at St Margaret's are very large and all are enhanced by tasteful soft furnishings and coordinated fabrics; there is also an attractive lounge. The guesthouse is on the A7 on the south side of the city centre.
7 rms (4 shr) (3 fmly) No smoking CTV in all bedrooms Tea and coffee making facilities No dogs Cen ht CTV 7P No coaches
PRICE GUIDE
ROOMS: s £25-£30; d £32-£50✳
CARDS: ▤ ▨ £

GH ⓆⓆⓆ **Salisbury Hotel** 45 Salisbury Rd EH16 5AA (left off A7) ☎0131 667 1264 FAX 0131 667 1264
Closed Xmas-New Year
This family run hotel has been converted from two imposing Georgian houses, and is quietly situated between two of the main roads leading in to the city from the south. Except for two single rooms, the bedrooms are spacious and bright and include some on the ground floor. There is also a residents' lounge with a bar and breakfast is served at separate tables in the pleasant dining room. Smoking is not permitted in the hotel.
12 rms (9 bth/shr) (3 fmly) No smoking CTV in all bedrooms Tea and coffee making facilities Licensed Cen ht 12P No coaches
PRICE GUIDE
ROOMS: s £24-£26; d £44-£50✳ £

GH ⓆⓆⓆ **Salisbury View Hotel** 64 Dalkeith Rd EH16 5AE (on A7/A68, 5 mins from city centre, adjacent to Holyrood Park) ☎0131 667 1133 FAX 0131 667 1133
rs 23-28 Dec
Salisbury View is a detached sandstone house on the south side of the city, close to the Commonwealth Swimming Pool and Salisbury Crags. The dining room has recently been refurbished to a high standard, and complements the attractive residents' lounge which also has a small bar. Bedrooms offer good facilities and are popular with tourists and business guests. Ample parking is available to the rear of the hotel.
8 en suite (shr) (1 fmly) No smoking in dining room CTV in all bedrooms Tea and coffee making facilities Direct dial from bedrooms Licensed Cen ht 8P No coaches Last d noon
PRICE GUIDE
ROOMS: s £27-£37; d £52-£64; wkly b&b £182-£224; wkly hlf-bd £276.50-£318.50✳
CARDS: ▤ ▨ ⓞ ▨ ▨ £

GH ⓆⓆ **Sherwood** 42 Minto St EH9 2BR ☎0131 667 1200
Closed 20-29 Dec
This small, friendly guest house on the south side of the city, has been transformed by the new owners who have upgraded the decor and facilities in both the bedrooms and the cosy breakfast room/lounge. The bedrooms are compact but offer good value for money. This is a non-smoking establishment.
6 en suite (shr) (3 fmly) No smoking CTV in all bedrooms Tea and coffee making facilities No dogs Cen ht CTV 3P No coaches
PRICE GUIDE
ROOMS: s £25-£38; d £40-£60; wkly b&b £125-£195
CARDS: ▤ ▨ £

GH ⓆⓆ *Southdown* 20 Craigmillar Park EH16 5PS (off A701) ☎0131 667 2410
Feb-Nov
Located on the southern side of the city, there is a relaxed and friendly atmosphere created by the resident owners. Bedrooms are

practically furnished and include a large family room. A cosy lounge with games is available to guests, while breakfast offers a good range of fresh items from the buffet.
6 rms (4 shr) (2 fmly) No smoking in bedrooms No smoking in dining room CTV in all bedrooms Tea and coffee making facilities Direct dial from bedrooms No dogs (ex guide dogs) Cen ht CTV 7P

GH QQQ *Strathmohr* 23 Mayfield Gardens EH9 2BX
☎0131 667 8475
There are good-sized bedrooms in this family-run property, and its one large public room is split into sitting and dining areas. This is a no-smoking house.
7 en suite (shr) (4 fmly) No smoking CTV in all bedrooms Tea and coffee making facilities No dogs (ex guide dogs) Cen ht CTV 8P

GH QQQ *Stra'ven* 3 Brunstane Rd North, Joppa EH15 2DL
☎0131 669 5580
Set in a residential area three miles east of the city, just off the main road and only yards from Portobello promenade, this detached Victorian house offers accommodation in bedrooms which, though plainly decorated and practically furnished, are warm, comfortable and provided with good showers. There is also a relaxing lounge.
7 en suite (bth/shr) No smoking CTV in all bedrooms Tea and coffee making facilities No dogs (ex guide dogs) Cen ht CTV No parking No coaches

Selected

GH Q Q Q Q **Stuart House** 12 East Claremont St
EH7 4JP ☎0131 557 9030 FAX 0131 557 0563
Closed 18-27 Dec
Convenient for both the centre and the Leith area of the city,
this attractive Georgian terraced house continues to offer a
high standard of accommodation. Bedrooms are stylishly
decorated and well equipped with some thoughtful extra
touches such as books, magazines and useful toiletries. There
is a huge family room on the first floor with two double beds
and elegant chairs. Breakfast is taken at two long tables, in a
room containing a comfortable sofa and armchair.
7 rms (6 bth/shr) (1 fmly) No smoking CTV in all bedrooms
Tea and coffee making facilities Direct dial from bedrooms
No dogs Cen ht No children 2yrs No parking No coaches
PRICE GUIDE
ROOMS: s £32-£35; d £60-£78✱
CARDS: 🃏 💳 💳 💳

GH Q Q Q **Terrace Hotel** 37 Royal Ter EH7 5AH
☎0131 556 3423 FAX 0131 556 2520
Fine views of the River Forth are enjoyed from the upper floors of
this comfortable town house, which forms part of a fashionable
Georgian terrace within easy reach of the east end of Princes
Street. Bedrooms are mostly spacious with lofty ceilings, and the
public rooms comprise an elegant lounge and a neat dining room
where hearty breakfasts are served.
14 rms (11 bth/shr) (7 fmly) CTV in 12 bedrooms Tea and
coffee making facilities No dogs CTV No parking
CARDS: 🃏 💳

🚭 📺 **GH** Q Q **Tiree** 26 Craigmillar Park EH16 5PS
☎0131 667 7477 FAX 0131 662 1608
This stone-built family run guesthouse forms part of a terraced
row in the southside and offers good value, practical
accommodation. Bedrooms vary in size but provide adequate
facilities, and hearty breakfasts are served at individual tables in
the rear dining room. This is a no-smoking establishment.
7 rms (5 shr) (2 fmly) No smoking in dining room No smoking
in lounges CTV in all bedrooms Tea and coffee making facilities
Cen ht 7P
PRICE GUIDE
ROOMS: s £16-£18; d £32-£54

Selected

GH Q Q Q Q **The Town House** 65 Gilmore Place
EH3 9NU (city centre location, access from A1, A8 and
A702, entrance to Gilmore Place opposite the Kings
Theatre) ☎0131 229 1985
This stylish Victorian house excudes charm and character and
is enthusiastically run by Susan Virtue. Bedrooms are
decorated with quality fabrics and furnishings. The dining
room is small but smart, and guests are welcome to use the
owners elegant lounge.
5 en suite (bth/shr) (1 fmly) No smoking CTV in all
bedrooms Tea and coffee making facilities No dogs (ex
guide dogs) Cen ht CTV 3P No coaches
PRICE GUIDE
ROOMS: s £22-£30; d £44-£60

GH Q Q **Villa Nina** 39 Leamington Ter EH10 4JS
☎0131 229 2644 FAX 0131 229 2644
Welcoming owners Bruno and Rosi Cecco run their guest house
with enthusiasm. There is no lounge, but the size of the rooms, all
of which have modern shower cubicles and comfortable seating,
compensates for this.
4 en suite (shr) (1 fmly) CTV in all bedrooms No dogs Cen ht
No children 12yrs No coaches

ELIE Fife Map **12** NO40

GH Q Q Q **The Elms** 14 Park Place KY9 1DH
☎01333 330404 FAX 01333 330404
Apr-Sep
This fine listed house dates from 1880, and is centrally located in
this attractive coastal village which boasts a temperate climate.
The walled garden incorporates a Victorian conservatory which
guests are welcome to use, though there is also a comfortable first
floor lounge. Bedrooms vary in size and include several on the
ground floor, while the spacious dining room has an interesting
aquatic frieze.
7 rms (1 bth 3 shr) (2 fmly) No smoking in dining room CTV in
4 bedrooms Tea and coffee making facilities Licensed Cen ht
CTV No children 6yrs No parking No coaches Last d 6.30pm
PRICE GUIDE
ROOMS: s £20-£39; d £36-£49; wkly hlf-bd £185-£228✱

FORFAR Tayside *Angus* Map **15** NO45

Selected

GH Q Q Q Q **Finavon Farmhouse** Finavon DD8 3PX
(turn off A 90 at Milton of Finavon exit, approximately
5m N of Forfar) ☎01307 850269
Closed Dec & Jan
Finavon is a modern house set in three acres of grounds which
include a pitch and putt course and the vegetable plots that
provide many of the ingredients for Lindsey Rome's cooking.
En suite bedrooms are comfortably furnished in light, floral
fabrics and there are many thoughtful touches. Meals are
served at one table in a cosy dining room hung with hand-
painted plates, and the spacious lounge offers the opportunity
to chat with the friendly proprietors and find out about local
attractions.
3 en suite (bth/shr) CTV in all bedrooms Tea and coffee
making facilities Cen ht CTV 7P No coaches Badminton
Putting green Pitch & putt Last d 6.30pm
PRICE GUIDE
ROOMS: s £15.50-£20.50; d £31-£33; wkly b&b £108.50-
£143.50; wkly hlf-bd £168-£203✱

FORGANDENNY Tayside *Perthshire* Map **11** NO01

💚 Q Q Mrs M Fotheringham *Craighall (NO081176)* PH2 9DF
(0.5m W off B935 Bridge of Earn-Forteviot Rd)
☎01738 812415 FAX 01738 812415
This peaceful bungalow stands near a farm in peaceful countryside
yet only a fifteen minute drive from Perth. Two compact twin
rooms overlook the gardens to the rear; the third room to the front
is larger and able to accommodate an extra bed. A pleasant lounge
is available for guests' use.
3 rms (2 shr) (1 fmly) Tea and coffee making facilities No dogs
Cen ht CTV 4P Fishing 1000 acres beef mixed sheep Last d
9pm

Selected

GH ◻◻◻◻ **Mayfield** Victoria Rd IV36 0BN (opposite
Grant Park car park on main road through town)
☎01309 676931
Quietly situated in its own well kept, colourful gardens, this
fine Victorian house is reached down a short drive leading off
the main road on the east side of town. Bedrooms are spacious
and offer good levels of comfort and modern facilities, while
the public areas include stylishly decorated dining room and a
small first floor lounge with a useful display of tourist
information. Breakfast, served at a communal table, includes a
vegetarian choice, and smoking is not permitted in the
bedrooms.
3 rms (2 shr) (1 fmly) No smoking in bedrooms No smoking
in dining room CTV in all bedrooms Tea and coffee making
facilities No dogs Cen ht CTV 4P No coaches
PRICE GUIDE
ROOMS: s £18-£25; d £30-£40; wkly b&b £105-£175✳
CARDS: 🂠 💳   (£)

Selected

GH ◻◻◻◻ *Parkmount House* St Leonards Rd
IV36 0DW ☎01309 673312 FAX 01309 673312
Mar-Oct
Set in its own grounds in a residential area of the town, this
establishment provides many of the facilities of a hotel - but
in a less formal atmosphere. Bedrooms are bright,
comfortable and well equipped and the beautiful lounge is full
of family heirlooms. The interesting dining room offers a
good choice at both breakfast and dinner.
6 en suite (bth/shr) (2 fmly) No smoking CTV in all
bedrooms Tea and coffee making facilities Direct dial from
bedrooms Licensed Cen ht ch fac 25P Last d 5pm
CARDS: 🂠 💳

Premier Selected

GH ◻◻◻◻◻ *Ashburn*
House Achintore Rd
PH33 6RQ (junc A82 and
Ashburn Ln 500yds from
large rbt at south end of Fort
William High St)
☎01397 706000
FAX 01397 706000
Jan-Oct
This beautifully maintained
house occupies a superb
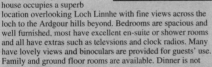
location overlooking Loch Linnhe with fine views across the
loch to the Ardgour hills beyond. Bedrooms are spacious and
well furnished, most have excellent en-suite or shower rooms
and all have extras such as televsions and clock radios. Many
have lovely views and binoculars are provided for guests' use.
Family and ground floor rooms are available. Dinner is not ➡

served, but breakfast is enjoyable, with generous portions and a good choice of dishes. This is a no smoking establishment.
6 en suite (bth/shr) No smoking CTV in all bedrooms Tea and coffee making facilities No dogs (ex guide dogs) Cen ht ch fac 8P
CARDS: ☒ ☷

GH ◗◗◗ **Benview** Belford Rd PH33 6ER ☎01397 702966
Mar-Nov
Conveniently situated beside the A82 at the north end of town this extended detached house has a friendly atmosphere and offers good value bed and breakfast accommodation. The non smoking bedrooms offer pretty decor and comfortable modern appointments. Public areas include a choice of lounges and breakfast is served at individual tables in the spacious dining room.
12 rms (8 bth/shr) No smoking in bedrooms No smoking in dining room CTV in all bedrooms Tea and coffee making facilities No dogs (ex guide dogs) Cen ht CTV 20P
PRICE GUIDE
ROOMS: s £15-£21; d £32-£45✱

GH ◗◗◗ **Distillery House** Nevis Bridge, North Rd PH33 6LH ☎01397 700103 & 702980 FAX 01397 702980
Good value accommodation is offered at this comfortable guest house which is located in the grounds of the former Glenlochy Distillery bedside the A82 just north of the town centre. Tastefully decorated bedrooms offer modern fitted furnishings together with a wide range of facilities, although they do vary in size. There is also an attractive lounge, and hearty breakfasts are served at individual tables in the adjoining dining room.
7 en suite (bth/shr) (1 fmly) No smoking in bedrooms No smoking in dining room CTV in all bedrooms Tea and coffee making facilities Direct dial from bedrooms Cen ht 7P Fishing
PRICE GUIDE
ROOMS: s £18-£30; d £36-£60✱
CARDS: ☒ ☷

GH ◗◗◗ **Glenlochy** Nevis Bridge PH33 6PF (0.5m N on A82) ☎01397 702909
This friendly guest house stands in its own well tended garden at the north end of town, beside the A82 and close to the Glen Nevis access road. Bedrooms are smartly decorated and comfortably furnished in traditional style, and, while some are compact, all benefit from commendable standards of housekeeping. Public areas include a relaxing first-floor lounge and an extended dining room serving hearty breakfasts at individual tables.
10 rms (8 shr) (2 fmly) No smoking in 4 bedrooms No smoking in dining room CTV in all bedrooms Tea and coffee making facilities No dogs (ex guide dogs) Cen ht CTV 12P No coaches
PRICE GUIDE
ROOMS: d £30-£44; wkly b&b £98-£147✱
CARDS: ☒ ☷ ☒

Our inspectors never book in the name of the AA. They disclose their identity only after the bill has been paid.

GH ◗◗◗◗◗ **The Grange** Grange Rd PH33 6JF ☎01397 705516
Mar-mid Nov
This charming detached Victorian home stands in landscaped gardens just off the A82 south of the town. An elegant dining room overlooking Loch Linnhe has been created by the sympathetic conversion of a

private lounge and serves an extensive breakfast menu; the adjacent lounge is the perfect place in which to relax. The bedrooms feature attractive modern decor and co-ordinated fabrics. Two well proportioned front-facing rooms are en suite while the refurbished rear room has a private bathroom. Dedicated hosts offer a warm welcome which includes tea and cakes on arrival.
3 en suite (bth/shr) No smoking CTV in all bedrooms No dogs (ex guide dogs) Cen ht CTV No children 13yrs 3P
PRICE GUIDE
ROOMS: d £52-£66✱

GH ◗◗◗ **Guisachan House** Alma Rd PH33 6HA (off A82, 100yds past St Marys Church)
☎01397 703797 FAX 01397 703797
A relaxed friendly atmosphere prevails at this comfortable family run guest house which is situated just off the A82 at the north end of town overlooking Loch Linnhe. The spotlessly clean and well maintained non smoking bedrooms are tastefully decorated and offer mixed modern appointments. Public areas include a relaxing lounge part of which contains a dispense bar, and enjoyable home cooking is served at individual tables in the recently extended dining room.
13 en suite (bth/shr) (2 fmly) No smoking in bedrooms No smoking in dining room CTV in all bedrooms Tea and coffee making facilities No dogs (ex guide dogs) Licensed Cen ht CTV 16P Last d 6.30pm
PRICE GUIDE
ROOMS: s £17-£25; d £34-£50✱
CARDS: ☒ ☷

GH ◗◗◗ **Lochview** Heathercroft, Argyll Rd PH33 6RE ☎01397 703149
Etr-Oct
A former croft house has been completely modernised and extended to create this comfortable guest house which stands on a hillside above the town overlooking Loch Linnhe. Bedrooms are tastefully decorated and offer mixed modern furnishings together with the expected amenities. Public areas include a pleasant lounge and small dining room where enjoyable breakfasts are served at individual tables. This is a non smoking establishment.
8 en suite (bth/shr) No smoking CTV in all bedrooms Tea and coffee making facilities No dogs Cen ht 8P No coaches
PRICE GUIDE
ROOMS: s £25-£30; d £36-£42; wkly b&b £126-£140
CARDS: ☷

GH ◗ **Rhu Mhor** Alma Rd PH33 6BP (N on A82, after hospital turn first right then first left) ☎01397 702213
Etr-Oct
Home comforts and genuine hospitality are the attractions of this sturdy detached Victorian guest house which stands on the hill

above the town overlooking Loch Linnhe. Bedrooms tend to be compact and offer simple traditional appointments; teamakers are the only concession to modern day amenities. Characterful public areas include a choice of comfortable lounges (one non smoking) and a traditional dining room serving enjoyable home cooking at shared tables.

7 rms (1 fmly) No smoking in dining room No smoking in 1 lounge Tea and coffee making facilities Cen ht CTV 7P No coaches Last d 4pm

PRICE GUIDE
ROOMS: s £16.50-£17; d £33-£34; wkly b&b £110-£113; wkly hlf-bd £172-£175

£

Premier Selected

GH QQQQQQ **Torbeag House** Muirshearlich, Banavie PH33 7PB (5m N, from the A830 take the B8004 going north from Banavie)
☎01397 772412
Closed Nov-Dec

Torbeag is a modern country house, standing in its own well kept, secluded garden amongst natural woodland about five miles from Fort William. Ken and Gladys Whyte offer a warm welcome and good home-cooking at dinner and breakfast, featuring good Scottish produce. The bedrooms and the lounge enjoy spectacular views over the Great Glen to Ben Nevis, and are both comfortable and homely. There is a roaring log fire and many attractive touches in the bright lounge, while trophies and family history abound in the cosy dining room. This is a great base from which to enjoy what is a multi-activity area with breathtaking scenery.

2 en suite (bth/shr) No smoking in bedrooms No smoking in dining room CTV in all bedrooms Tea and coffee making facilities Cen ht 6P No coaches Tennis (grass) Last d 10am

PRICE GUIDE
ROOMS: d £40-£52; wkly b&b £140-£182; wkly hlf-bd £248-£290

£

FOYERS Highland *Invernesshire* Map **14** NH42

Selected

GH QQQQ *Foyers Bay House* Lochness IV1 2YB
☎01456 486624 FAX 01456 486337

Panoramic views over Loch Ness are enjoyed from this fine Victorian house which has been imaginatively restored and converted to create a comfortable holiday base. The well maintained non smoking bedrooms are variable in size and offer tasteful modern appointments together with a wide range of amenities including telephones. As well as a comfortable lounge there is also an attractive conservatory café/restaurant which offers all day snacks and meals.

3 en suite (bth/shr) No smoking in bedrooms CTV in all bedrooms Tea and coffee making facilities Direct dial from bedrooms No dogs (ex guide dogs) Cen ht CTV 6P No coaches Last d 7.30pm

CARDS: ▨ ▨ ▨

GAIRLOCH Highland *Ross & Cromarty* Map **14** NG87

Selected

GH QQQQ **Birchwood** IV21 2AH (overlooks harbour)
☎01445 712011
Apr-mid Oct

This friendly house is situated on the outskirts of the village at the head of Gairloch overlooking the old harbour. Bedrooms are fresh, bright and airy. Furniture is mostly modern in style and the decor is based around attractive pastel shades. There is a pleasant TV lounge and a small sun lounge which enjoys superb views of the harbour. Hearty breakfasts are served in the tasteful dining room where guests may occasionally be required to share tables.

6 en suite (shr) (1 fmly) No smoking in bedrooms No smoking in dining room Tea and coffee making facilities Cen ht CTV 6P No coaches

PRICE GUIDE
ROOMS: d £36-£46; wkly b&b £126-£161✻
See advertisement on p.529.

Selected

GH QQQQ **Horisdale House** Strath IV21 2DA (turn off A832 onto B8021, establishment 0.9m on right just beyond Strathburn House) ☎01445 712151
May-Sep

This large villa is set back from the main road in the small village of Strath. It has extensive grounds and on our last visit ➡

FORT WILLIAM
Glenlochy Guest House
Nevis Bridge, Fort William
Inverness-shire PH33 6PF
Telephone: 01397 702909

This comfortable and tastefully modernised guest house is situated in its own spacious grounds, ½ mile north of town centre and within walking distance of Ben Nevis. It is an ideal base for touring, hill walking, steam train, boat trips and mountain gondola.
8 of the 10 bedrooms are en-suite.
All rooms have colour TV and teasmade.
Cleanliness and warmth guaranteed.

Private Car Park   AA Listed QQQ

the American owners Amelia Windsor and Patricia Strack were working on a water garden. The ladies are charming hosts, dedicated to the well-being of their guests. The bedrooms lack en suite facilities but are attractively decorated with modern furnishings and quality fabrics. Miss Strack is an enthusiastic cook and serves adventurous dishes in the large dining room, and guests keen on cooking will enjoy talking to Miss Windsor who has an enormous collection of classic cookery books.

6 rms (1 bth) (1 fmly) No smoking Tea and coffee making facilities No dogs Cen ht No children 7yrs 10P No coaches Last d 9am
PRICE GUIDE
ROOMS: s £19; d £36; wkly b&b £120; wkly hlf-bd £190✳

GALASHIELS Borders *Selkirkshire* Map **12** NT43

Selected

GH QQQQ **Binniemyre** Abbotsford Rd TD1 3JB
☎01896 757137 FAX 01896 757137
This fine period house lies in gardens off the main road A7 on the south side of the town. Not only has it been sympathetically restored to retain its character, but much charm has been added by owners Carol Murray and Bill Elliot who have made it a really interesting house. Teddy bears and ducks in all forms adorn the house and could be deemed its signature. The entrance hall is in itself a welcoming lounge and has a wood stove burning in cold winter days. There is also a second lounge as well as an attractive dining room. Bedrooms, some of which make ideal family rooms, are tastefully furbished and well equipped to include trouser presses and complementary biscuits. They have luxury en suite shower rooms or a nearby large private bathroom and bathrobes.

5 rms (3 shr) (3 fmly) No smoking in bedrooms No smoking in dining room No smoking in 1 lounge CTV in all bedrooms Tea and coffee making facilities Cen ht CTV 5P Snooker
PRICE GUIDE
ROOMS: s £25-£50; d £35-£50
CARDS: 💳

GH QQQ **Island House** 65 Island St (opposite B & Q store)
☎01896 752649
3 rms (2 shr) No smoking in bedrooms No smoking in dining room CTV in all bedrooms Tea and coffee making facilities Cen ht CTV 2P
PRICE GUIDE
ROOMS: d £28-£36✳
£

◀ QQQ *Clovenfords Hotel* 1 Vine St, Clovenfords TD1 3LU
☎01896 850203 FAX 01896 850596
rs Jan-Etr
This small hotel has been sympathetically refurbished to retain its traditional character. There is real ale on tap, but the emphasis is on food, with a good range of meals being served both here and in the dining room. Bedrooms are of a good size and have a cheerful atmosphere.

5 en suite (bth/shr) (2 fmly) CTV in all bedrooms Tea and coffee making facilities Cen ht 20P Fishing/shooting can be arranged
CARDS: 💳 💳 💳

GALSTON Strathclyde *Ayrshire* Map **11** NS53

✤ QQQ Mrs J Bone **Auchencloigh** *(NS535320)* KA4 8NP
(5m S on B7037-Sorn Road)
☎01563 820567 FAX 01563 820567
This comfortable 18th-century farmhouse, surrounded by gentle rolling countryside, has views over the coast to the Isle of Arran on clear days. Bright, cheerful bedrooms offer both traditional and modern appointments, while public areas include a relaxing lounge and the owners' personal lounge where hearty farmhouse fare is served round a communal table. This is a non-smoking establishment.

3 rms No smoking CTV in all bedrooms Tea and coffee making facilities No dogs Cen ht CTV 8P Sauna 240 acres beef mixed sheep Last d 4pm
PRICE GUIDE
ROOMS: s £14-£15; d £28-£30; wkly b&b £98-£105✳

GARTOCHARN Strathclyde *Dunbartonshire* Map **10** NS48

Selected

GH QQQQ **Ardoch Cottage** Main St G83 8NE (on A811) ☎01389 830452
Mabel and Paul Lindsay's delightful 200-year-old cottage on the southern edge of this picturesque village has been sympathetically restored and modernised to provide an ideal base for touring. Bedrooms are comfortably furnished and attractively decorated, modern fabrics being used to good effect. Mabel Lindsay offers enjoyable home-cooked fare at a communal table in the lounge/dining room, and guests can relax in the comfortable sun lounge. Standards of housekeeping are impeccable throughout, and this is now a no-smoking establishment.

3 en suite (shr) No smoking Tea and coffee making facilities Cen ht CTV 5P Last d 5pm
£

Selected

✤ QQQQ Mrs S Macdonell **Mardella** *(NS442866)* Old School Rd G83 8SD (off A811) ☎01389 830428
Situated about a mile north of the village, off the A811, this friendly modern house is surrounded by beautiful countryside and has sheep, geese, peacocks, hens and ducks in the field opposite. Comfortable bedrooms vary in size, but all offer a mixture of modern and traditional appointments and the largest room has en suite facilities. Public areas include a relaxing lounge and a semi open plan dining room where hearty breakfasts and, by prior arrangement, evening meals are served around a communal table. Duck ornaments fill the house.

3 rms (1 bth/shr) (2 fmly) No smoking Tea and coffee making facilities Cen ht CTV 4P 9 acres sheep poultry Last d 9am
PRICE GUIDE
ROOMS: s £25-£29; d £36-£42; wkly b&b £114-£133; wkly hlf-bd £189-£208
£

GARVE Highland *Ross & Cromarty* Map **14** NH36

GH QQQ **Old Manse** IV23 2PX (turn off A835 by AA telephone 0.5m W of village) ☎01997 414201
Jean and Pete Hollingdale offer good-value bed and breakfast accommodation at their former manse, situated just west of the

village with splendid views of the surrounding countryside. The bedrooms, all no-smoking, are tastefully decorated while public areas include a cosy lounge with natural stone walls and a welcoming open fire as well as a dining room where good breakfasts are served at a communal table.

3 rms (1 shr) No smoking in bedrooms No smoking in dining room No dogs (ex guide dogs) Cen ht 6P No coaches

PRICE GUIDE
ROOMS: d £28-£30; wkly b&b £98-£105

GATEHOUSE OF FLEET Dumfries & Galloway
Kirkcudbrightshire Map **11** NX55

GH Q Q **Bobbin** 36 High St DG7 2HP (signposted from A75 close to clocktower) ☎01557 814229

This neat guest house on the main street doubles as a tea shop, with home-baking served in the cosy dining room throughout the day. The bedrooms vary in size but are comfortably furnished, and one has a recently revealed fireplace. A lounge is provided for guests' use.

6 rms (2 shr) (3 fmly) No smoking in dining room No smoking in lounges CTV in all bedrooms Tea and coffee making facilities Cen ht CTV 8P No coaches Tennis (hard) Last d 5pm

PRICE GUIDE
ROOMS: s £16-£20.50; d £37-£40; wkly b&b £180-£220; wkly hlf-bd £244-£299✱

CARDS: 💳 🈂

See advertisement under **DUMFRIES**

GLASGOW Strathclyde *Lanarkshire* Map **11** NS56

GH Q Q Q *Botanic Hotel* 1 Alfred Ter, Great Western Rd G12 8RF (off M8 at junct 17, turn right for hotel in 0.75m on left, directly above A625 Great Western Road) ☎0141 339 6955 FAX 0141 339 6955

Situated in the west end of the city, this substantial Victorian terraced house has well proportioned bedrooms which offer comfortable modern appointments and a full range of amenities.

11 rms (3 shr) (4 fmly) No smoking in dining room CTV in all bedrooms Tea and coffee making facilities Cen ht Last d 7.30pm

CARDS: 💳 🈂 🈂

GH Q Q Q *Dalmeny Hotel* 62 St Andrews Dr, Nithsdale Cross G41 5EZ ☎0141 427 1106 & 6288

Situated in a south side residential area, this small hotel also boasts an Indian restaurant which is open to the public for both lunch and dinner. There is an attractive conservatory breakfast room, and bedrooms vary in size, offering mixed practical modern appointments.

8 rms (2 bth 1 shr) CTV in all bedrooms Tea and coffee making facilities Licensed Cen ht CTV 20P No coaches Last d 10.30pm

CARDS: 💳 🈂 🈂

GH Q Q Q **Hotel Enterprise** 144 Renfrew St G3 6RF ☎0141 332 8095 FAX 0141 332 8095

Attractive, well equipped bedrooms are a feature of this small terraced hotel in the centre of the city. There is a comfortable lounge and a small dining room where dinner may be served by arrangement.

6 en suite (bth/shr) (2 fmly) No smoking in 1 bedrooms No smoking in dining room CTV in all bedrooms Tea and coffee making facilities Direct dial from bedrooms Licensed Cen ht CTV No parking No coaches Last d 7.30pm

PRICE GUIDE
ROOMS: s £35-£47.50; d £47.50-£70✱

CARDS: 💳 🈂 🈂

Birchwood

Gairloch, Ross-Shire IV21 2AH
Telephone: (01445) 2011

Beautifully situated in its own grounds amongst mature woodland and enjoying magnificent vistas. Recently refurbished to a very high standard, all six comfortable bedrooms are en suite. Birchwood provides the perfect base from which to explore the many and varied places of interest in the Gairloch area. Close to Inverewe Gardens and the beautiful Loch Maree. Sandy beaches and a 9 hole golf course are within walking distance.

GH **Kelvin Private Hotel** 15 Buckingham Ter, Great Western Rd, Hillhead G12 8EB (leave M8 at junct 17 follow A82 Kelvinside/Dumbarton 1m from motorway on right before Botanic Gardens)
☎0141 339 7143 FAX 0141 339 5215
Good-value bed and breakfast accommodation is offered at this friendly family-run hotel, which has been created by linking two Grade A Victorian terraced houses. Single rooms tend to be small, but the others are generally well proportioned. Public areas include a quiet lounge and breakfast room, both on the first floor.
21 rms (9 bth/shr) (5 fmly) CTV in all bedrooms Tea and coffee making facilities Cen ht 5P
PRICE GUIDE
ROOMS: s £22-£35; d £38-£48✳
CARDS: 🅰 ▅ ▆ 🅰   (£)

GH **Lomond Hotel** 6 Buckingham Ter, Great Western Rd, Hillhead G12 8EB (on A82, right hand side before Botanic Gardens) ☎0141 339 2339 FAX 0141 339 5215
Situated in a tree-lined Victorian terrace in the west end, this friendly family-run hotel offers good-value bed and breakfast accommodation. Bedrooms are mostly spacious, and public areas include a lounge/breakfast room where, at peak times, it may be necessary to share a table with other guests.
17 rms (6 bth/shr) (6 fmly) CTV in all bedrooms Tea and coffee making facilities Cen ht No parking
PRICE GUIDE
ROOMS: s £22-£35; d £38-£48✳
CARDS: 🅰 ▅ ▆   (£)

GLASGOW AIRPORT Strathclyde *Lanarkshire* Map **11** NS46

Premier Selected

GH
Myfarrclan 146 Corsebar Rd PA2 9NA ☎0141 884 8285 FAX 0141 884 8285
Inconspicuously located within a leafy suburb of Scotland's largest town is the home of Brenda and Keith Farr, a lavishly converted bungalow that is just 10 minutes from the airport and also very close to the Royal Alexandra Hospital. The three bedrooms are fully equipped, attractively furnished and provided with a host of thoughtful extras. The small, comfortable lounge is an important focal point for Keith to dispense hospitality and discuss the bespoke tours that guests may have enjoyed or wish to take, based on his individually detailed itineraries. By arrangement, Brenda prepares a hearty three-course dinner, which is served at a communal table in the pretty dining room where guests also gather for a wholesome breakfast. Visitors are asked not to smoke within the house.
3 rms (2 shr) No smoking CTV in all bedrooms Tea and coffee making facilities No dogs Cen ht CTV 2P No coaches Last d 5pm
PRICE GUIDE
ROOMS: s £35-£50; d £50-£60
CARDS: 🅰 ▆

GLENCOE Highland *Argyllshire* Map **14** NN15

 GH **Scorrybreac** PA39 4HT (off A82 just outside village, 500 metres from Bridge of Coe)
☎01855 811354
Closed Nov
Good value accommodation is offered at this friendly non-smoking guest house which stands in a well tended garden on a wooded hillside beside the village hospital. The variously sized bedrooms offer mixed modern appointments together with he expected amenities. Public areas include a small lounge and pleasant dining room, where well cooked breakfasts and evening meals (by prior arrangement) are served at individual tables.
6 rms (5 bth/shr) No smoking CTV in all bedrooms Tea and coffee making facilities Cen ht 8P No coaches Last d 10am
PRICE GUIDE
ROOMS: s £15-£24; d £28-£36

GLENMAVIS Strathclyde *Lanarkshire* Map **11** NS76

♥ 🅠 Mrs M Dunbar **Braidenhill** *(NS742673)* ML6 0PJ (on B803 on outskirts of Airdrie/Coatbridge) ☎01236 872319
This unassuming working farm is set in a semi-rural area just off the B803 between Glenmavis and Coatbridge. It offers good-value bed and breakfast accommodation in compact but well appointed bedrooms with views over the surrounding countryside. Public areas include a comfortable TV lounge and a small dining room where hearty breakfasts are served round a communal table. Smoking is not encouraged.
3 rms (1 shr) (1 fmly) No smoking in bedrooms No smoking in dining room Tea and coffee making facilities No dogs Cen ht CTV 4P 50 acres arable mixed
PRICE GUIDE
ROOMS: d £32-£38

GOLSPIE Highland *Sutherland* Map **14** NC80

 ♥ 🅠🅠 Mrs G Murray **Kirkton Farm** *(NE799989)* KW10 6TA (2m S on A9)
☎01408 633267 FAX 01408 633267
Closed 20 Dec-10 Jan rs 11 Jan-19 May & Oct-19 Dec
This welcoming farmhouse, a listed building, stands beside the A9 south of Golspie and offers good value bed and breakfast accommodation. The bright airy bedrooms offer both modern and traditional appointments and hearty farmhouse breakfasts are served at the communal table in the combined lounge/dining room. This is a non smoking establishment.
2 rms No smoking No dogs (ex guide dogs) Cen ht 2P 900 acres arable beef sheep
PRICE GUIDE
ROOMS: s £14-£20; d £28; wkly b&b fr £90   (£)

Our inspectors never book in the name of the AA. They disclose their identity only after the bill has been paid.

GRANTOWN-ON-SPEY Highland *Morayshire* Map **14** NJ02

Premier Selected

Premier Selected

GH Ⓠ Ⓠ Ⓠ Ⓠ Ⓠ **Ardconnel**
House Woodlands Ter
PH26 3JU ☎01479 872104
FAX 01479 872104
Closed Nov-Dec

Enthusiastic owners Jim and
Barbara Casey have lovingly
restored this fine Victorian
house to provide high
standards of comfort and
appointment for their guests,
all of whom are assured of a
warm personal welcome. Jim looks after the front house while
Barbara is responsible for the delicious Taste of Scotland food
which is carefully prepared from fresh ingredients, and is
served at individual tables in the elegant dining room. There is
also a comfortable lounge which invites complete relaxation
while bedrooms, with attractive colour schemes, are furnished
in antiques or pine and offer all the expected amenities. For
the convenience of all, smoking is not permitted in the house.
6 en suite (shr) (2 fmly) No smoking CTV in all bedrooms
Tea and coffee making facilities No dogs Licensed Cen ht
No children 10yrs 9P No coaches Last d 4.30pm
PRICE GUIDE
ROOMS: s £30; d £50-£64; wkly b&b £175-£210; wkly hlf-
bd £265-£320✳
CARDS: 🅰 🔲 🔲

GH Ⓠ Ⓠ Ⓠ *Ardlarig* Woodlands Ter PH26 3JU (just off A95)
☎01479 873245
Closed 22-27 Dec
Set in its own well tended garden to the south of town, this
comfortable Victorian house offers a friendly welcome to visitors.
Though they lack en suite facilities, the bright, spacious bedrooms
are tastefully appointed and well equipped. The comfortable
lounge has a good supply of books and board games while the
dining room is the setting for hearty breakfasts and 'Taste of
Scotland' cuisine.
7 rms (3 fmly) No smoking in 3 bedrooms No smoking in dining
room CTV in all bedrooms Tea and coffee making facilities
Licensed Cen ht CTV 10P No coaches Golf shooting & fishing
can be arranged Last d 4.30pm

GH Ⓠ **Bydand** Dulnain Bridge PH26 3LU (3m S on A95)
☎01479 851278
Betty and Stewart Crabb's sturdy country house stands in its own
grounds and offers a welcoming atmosphere and two comfortable,
traditionally styled bedrooms. Home cooked dinners and hearty
breakfasts are served at individual tables in the small dining room,
and guests are invited to share the owners' lounge. The house has
been adapted to provide facilities for disabled guests.
2 rms No smoking in bedrooms No smoking in dining room Cen
ht CTV 6P No coaches Last d 8.30pm
PRICE GUIDE
ROOMS: d £28-£30; wkly b&b £91-£97.50; wkly hlf-bd £147-
£153.50✳
CARDS: 🅰 🔲 (£)

GH Ⓠ Ⓠ Ⓠ Ⓠ Ⓠ **Culdearn**
House Woodlands Ter
PH26 3JU (off A95 turn left at
30mph sign) (Logis)
☎01479 872106
FAX 01479 873641
Mar-Oct

Situated on the western
approach to the town with
beautiful manicured gardens,
this splendid granite Victorian
villa has been caringly restored
and modernised to provide comfortable and tastefully
appointed accommodation. Bedrooms are thoughtfully
furnished and carefully maintained, while the traditional
lounge is the relaxed setting for pre and post dinner
refreshment, which includes a choice of 40 malt whiskies.
Dinner itself offers the best of local produce from Aberdeen
Angus beef to fish from the Moray Firth. Many guests return
here year after year not only to enjoy the surroundings and
food, but the genuine hospitality of the owners and their staff.
9 en suite (bth/shr) No smoking in 6 bedrooms No smoking
in dining room CTV in all bedrooms Tea and coffee making
facilities No dogs (ex guide dogs) Licensed Cen ht No
children 5yrs 9P No coaches Last d 6pm
PRICE GUIDE
ROOMS: (incl. dinner) s £49.50; d £99;
wkly hlf-bd £280-£299
CARDS: 🅰 🔲 🔲 🔲 🔲 🔲 🔲 (£)

```
┌─────────────────────────────────────────┐
│              Selected                     │
└─────────────────────────────────────────┘
```

GH ⓆⓆⓆⓆ **Garden Park** Woodside Av PH26 3JN (turn off High Street at Forest Road, Garden Park is at junc of Forest Road & Woodside Avenue) ☎01479 873235
Mar-Oct
A homely atmosphere, genuine hospitality and good home cooking are all provided here, in an attractive Victorian house standing in its own gardens near the golf course. Bedrooms - all but one of which have television sets - range from the compact to the very large, the cosy lounge is warmed by a log fire on cooler days and the neat little dining room offers a useful wine list alongside its dinner menu.
5 en suite (bth/shr) No smoking in dining room CTV in 4 bedrooms Tea and coffee making facilities No dogs (ex guide dogs) Licensed Cen ht CTV No children 12yrs 8P No coaches Last d 5pm
PRICE GUIDE
ROOMS: d £41-£46; wkly b&b £135-£145; wkly hlf-bd £190-£210

GH ⓆⓆⓆ **Pines** Woodside Av PH26 3JR (at traffic lights follow Elgin signs then take first rt)
☎01479 872092 FAX 01479 872092
Jan-Oct
A detached Victorian villa, located beside a pine wood in a residential area at the east end of the town, offers good-value accommodation; most of the bedrooms are spacious, with mixed modern appointments, and public areas include a relaxing first-floor lounge and a bright dining room with sun lounge extension.
9 rms (5 shr) (3 fmly) No smoking in dining room CTV in all bedrooms Tea and coffee making facilities Licensed Cen ht 9P No coaches Last d 3pm
PRICE GUIDE
ROOMS: s £16.50-£21.50; d £33-£43; wkly b&b £105-£135; wkly hlf-bd £160-£195
£

GRETNA (WITH GRETNA GREEN) Dumfries & Galloway
Dumfriesshire   Map **11** NY36

GH ⓆⓆⓆ **The Beeches** Loanwath Rd, Off Sarkfoot Rd DG16 5EP (turn left off B7076 at Crossways Garage down Sarkfoot Road for a qaurter of a mile) ☎01461 337448
Closed Dec-Jan
The Beeches is a former farmhouse, situated on the edge of town and looking out across open countryside towards the Solway Firth and Lakeland hills. Both the bedrooms enjoy those views and are comfortably furnished, with their own en suite shower rooms; downstairs, the charming breakfast room also doubles as a TV lounge in the evenings.
2 en suite (shr) (1 fmly) No smoking CTV in all bedrooms Tea and coffee making facilities No dogs Cen ht CTV No children 10yrs 3P No coaches
PRICE GUIDE
ROOMS: d £34-£36

GH ⓆⓆ **Greenlaw** DG16 5DU (off A74) ☎01461 338361
Opposite the newly reopened railway station, this detached red brick house is within walking distance of the famous old Smithy. The bedrooms vary in size (the most spacious being at the front) and there is a bridal room with a four-poster bed and en suite facilities. A breakfast room and welcoming lounge with a real fire are provided, and there is ample car parking.

10 rms (1 shr) (1 fmly) No smoking in dining room CTV in all bedrooms Tea and coffee making facilities Cen ht CTV 13P
PRICE GUIDE
ROOMS: s £18-£20; d £30-£32
£

GH ⓆⓆⓆ **Surrone House** Annan Rd DG16 5DL
☎01461 338341
Set back from the main road, in the romantic border town of Gretna, this one-time farmhouse, with connections dating back to Viking times, now offers modern accommodation. The bedrooms are generally spacious, nicely equipped and have good bathrooms, while the public areas include two small but comfortable lounges and a steak bar style room open to non residents.
7 rms (6 bth/shr) (4 fmly) CTV in all bedrooms Tea and coffee making facilities No dogs (ex guide dogs) Licensed Cen ht CTV 10P No coaches Last d 8pm
PRICE GUIDE
ROOMS: s £30-£32; d £44-£46✱
CARDS:
£

GULLANE Lothian *East Lothian* Map **12** NT48

```
┌─────────────────────────────────────────┐
│              Selected                     │
└─────────────────────────────────────────┘
```

GH ⓆⓆⓆⓆ **Faussetthill House** 20 Main St EH31 2DR (on A198) ☎01620 842396
Mar-Dec
Situated at the east side of the main street in Gullane, this well kept guest house offers comfortable and attractive accommodation. Bedrooms are tastefully decorated and there are some interesting features, including a Dutch tiled fireplace in one room. The dining room is elegant, and the lounge boasts a collection of cups and saucers. Smoking is not permitted.
3 rms (2 shr) No smoking Tea and coffee making facilities No dogs Cen ht CTV No children 10yrs 4P No coaches
PRICE GUIDE
ROOMS: s £25-£32; d £38-£46; wkly b&b £133-£154
CARDS:
£

HADDINGTON Lothian *East Lothian* Map **12** NT57

♥ ⓆⓆ Mrs K Kerr *Barney Mains Farmhouse* (NT524764)
Barney Mains EH41 3SA (off A1, 1m S of Haddington)
☎01620 880310 FAX 01620 880639
Mar-Nov
Conveniently located off the A1, one mile east of the town, this large Georgian house enjoys an elevated position with fine views over the surrounding countryside and the Firth of Forth. Very much a family home, and furnished as such, with comfortable, spacious bedrooms and a relaxing guest lounge. Hearty breakfasts are served at the communal dining table.
3 rms No smoking in bedrooms No smoking in dining room Tea and coffee making facilities No dogs (ex guide dogs) Cen ht CTV 8P 580 acres arable beef sheep

HAWICK Borders *Roxburghshire* Map **12** NT51

GH ⓆⓆⓆ **Oakwood House** Buccleuch Rd TD9 0EH (S on A7) ☎01450 372896 & 372814
Closed 24 Dec-5 Jan
A sandstone Victorian house set in its own gardens, well back from the main road, stands next door to the local bowling green. Immaculate bedrooms are individually decorated, and there are a comfortable lounge and a cheerful little dining room. Mrs

Kirkpatrick, the welcoming owner, is always ready to provide information about the town's attractions.

3 rms (1 shr) No smoking CTV in all bedrooms Tea and coffee making facilities No dogs Cen ht CTV No children 5yrs 6P No coaches

PRICE GUIDE
ROOMS: s £20-£28; d £32-£40
CARDS: £

HELENSBURGH Strathclyde *Dunbartonshire* Map **10** NS28

See also Cardross

GH 🇶🇶 **Thorndean House** 64 Colquhoun St G84 9JP (W off B832 at Stafford Street and take first right) ☎01436 674922 FAX 01436 679913

Good-value accommodation is offered in this sturdy Victorian villa north of the town centre. Bedrooms are bright and airy and a hearty breakfast is served at a large table in the lounge/dining room. By arrangement, guests can be taken for a trip on the owners' yacht. The house is no-smoking.

3 rms (2 shr) (1 fmly) No smoking CTV in all bedrooms Tea and coffee making facilities No dogs Cen ht CTV 8P No coaches Sailing in yacht

PRICE GUIDE
ROOMS: s £17-£32; d £34-£40; wkly b&b £107-£130 £

HELMSDALE Highland *Sutherland* Map **14** ND01

GH 🇶🇶🇶 **Alderwood** 157 West Helmsdale KW8 6HH ☎01431 821538 FAX 01431 821538

Closed Xmas/New Year

2 en suite (bth/shr) (1 fmly) No smoking in bedrooms No smoking in area of dining room No smoking in 1 lounge Tea and coffee making facilities Cen ht CTV P Cycle hire

PRICE GUIDE
ROOMS: s fr £14.50; d fr £29✳
CARDS: 🔵 🔵 🔵

HUNTLY Grampian *Aberdeenshire* Map **15** NJ53

GH 🇶🇶🇶 **Dunedin** 17 Bogie St AB54 5DX (opposite fish and chip shop) ☎01466 794162

This family run holiday and commercial guesthouse is situated at the east end of the town, a short walk from the town square. The bedrooms are furnished in a modern style and have good facilities. There is a cosy top floor lounge and hearty breakfasts are served in the bright dining room, where tables may have to be shared with other guests on occasions.

6 en suite (shr) (1 fmly) CTV in all bedrooms Tea and coffee making facilities No dogs Cen ht CTV 8P

PRICE GUIDE
ROOMS: s £17.50-£25; d £33-£35 £

♥ 🇶🇶🇶 Mrs M Grant **Faich-Hill Farm** *(NJ532347)* Faich-Hill, Gartly AB54 4RR (farm road behind to Gartly church) ☎01466 720240

This large farm house is located near to the pretty village church, about two miles from the A97. The sun lounge has a fridge and tea making equipment and is the only area where smoking is allowed. There is also a homely lounge full of family photos and trophies, while the dining room has one single table where breakfast and dinner, if requested, are served. Bedrooms are well equipped and nicely kept.

2 rms (1 shr) (1 fmly) No smoking Tea and coffee making

facilities No dogs Cen ht CTV No children 5yrs P 650 acres livestock arable Last d noon

PRICE GUIDE
ROOMS: s fr £17.50; d fr £35✳

INNERLEITHEN Borders *Peeblesshire* Map **11** NT33

◀ 🇶🇶🇶 **Traquair Arms Hotel** Traquair Rd EH44 6PD (from A72 Peebles to Galashiels road take B709 for St Mary's Loch & Traquair) ☎01896 830229 FAX 01896 830260

This small, personally run hotel is set just off the main street and provides well equipped bedrooms, including a two-bedroom family suite on the top floor. Its good-value meals enjoy a deservedly high reputation and are served either in the dining room or in the bar where real ales are on tap, including one brewed at historic Traquair House nearby.

10 en suite (bth/shr) (2 fmly) No smoking in dining room CTV in all bedrooms Tea and coffee making facilities Direct dial from bedrooms Cen ht ch fac 18P No coaches Fishing Last d 9pm

PRICE GUIDE
ROOMS: s fr £42; d fr £64; wkly b&b fr £190; wkly hlf-bd fr £292✳

MEALS: Bar Lunch fr £3.50alc Dinner fr £16✳
CARDS: 🔵 🔵 🔵 🔵 £

INVERGARRY Highland *Inverness-shire* Map **14** NH30

GH 🇶🇶🇶 **Craigard** PH35 4HG (off A82 onto A87 for house 1m on right) ☎01809 501258

21 Mar-Oct

A welcoming atmosphere prevails at this comfortable family run holiday guest house which stands beside the A87 on the western edge of the village. The non smoking bedrooms are mostly

➡

spacious and are comfortably furnished in modern and traditional styles. Public areas include a choice of relaxing traditional lounges (both non-smoking) and a pleasant dining room offering carefully prepared dishes from the daily changing menu.

7 rms (2 bth 1 shr) No smoking Tea and coffee making facilities No dogs (ex guide dogs) Licensed CTV No children 8yrs 10P No coaches Last d 11am

PRICE GUIDE
ROOMS: s fr £16; d fr £32; wkly b&b fr £112; wkly hlf-bd fr £196✱

GH Ｑ Ｑ Ｑ **Forest Lodge** South Laggan PH34 4EA (3m SW on north side of A82) ☎01809 501219
This comfortable purpose-built modern guest house stands in a well tended garden south of the village beside the A82. It offers a friendly atmosphere and good-value accommodation in bright bedrooms furnished in a mix of modern and traditional styles. Guests have a choice of traditional lounges following the recent completion of a sun lounge by the entrance, and enjoyable home-cooked four-course dinners are served at individual tables in the attractive dining room.

7 en suite (shr) (2 fmly) No smoking in dining room No smoking in lounges Tea and coffee making facilities Cen ht CTV 10P No coaches Last d 6.30pm

PRICE GUIDE
ROOMS: d £30-£36; wkly b&b £98-£116; wkly hlf-bd £170-£188

INVERGORDON Highland *Ross & Cromarty* Map **14** NH76

GH Ｑ Ｑ Ｑ **Craigaron** 17 Saltburn IV18 0JX (1.25m N on B817, 200yds beyond traffic lights at Saltburn Pier) ☎01349 853640
Closed Xmas & New Year
Good-value accommodation is offered at this family-run commercial and tourist guest house situated north of the town overlooking the Cromarty Firth. Bedrooms - all contained on the ground floor - are compact, while the first-floor public areas include a spacious lounge and a small dinette adjacent to the kitchen. Breakfast and evening meals are served in either the dinette or lounge, and at peak times tables may be shared.

4 rms (2 shr) No smoking in dining room CTV in all bedrooms Tea and coffee making facilities Cen ht CTV No children 10yrs 6P No coaches Last d 4pm

PRICE GUIDE
ROOMS: s £22-£26; d £32-£36✱
CARDS: █ ▒

INVERKEITHING Fife Map **11** NT18

GH Ｑ Ｑ Ｑ **Forth Craig Private Hotel** 90 Hope St KY11 1LL (off A90 at 1st exit after Fortyh Bridge, signed Inverkeithing, for hotel in .5m on right next to church) ☎01383 418440
Practical, well equipped accommodation is offered at this small purpose built hotel, which is on the southern approach to the town, not far from the Forth Road Bridge. In addition to the well maintained bedrooms, there is a cosy lounge and dining room with a small bar, which has views of the Forth of Forth.

5 en suite (shr) No smoking in bedrooms No smoking in dining room CTV in all bedrooms Tea and coffee making facilities Licensed Cen ht 8P No coaches Last d 6pm

PRICE GUIDE
ROOMS: s £24-£26; d £39-£42
CARDS: █ ▒ ▒

GH Ｑ Ｑ Ｑ **The Roods** 16 Bannerman Av KY11 1NG (off A90/M90 onto B981) ☎01383 415049 FAX 01383 415049
Quietly secluded in its own well kept gardens, this friendly family run guest house is only a couple of minutes' walk from the station and also convenient for the M90. The two bedrooms are attractively decorated and offer excellent facilities including some unique features like a mini-store and mini-office. There is a bright, comfortable lounge and conservatory dining room where well cooked breakfasts are served at separate tables.

2 en suite (shr) No smoking CTV in all bedrooms Tea and coffee making facilities Direct dial from bedrooms No dogs (ex guide dogs) Licensed Cen ht CTV 4P No coaches Last d 9am

PRICE GUIDE
ROOMS: s £19-£25; d £38-£50; wkly b&b £130-£170; wkly hlf-bd £200-£240✱

INVERNESS Highland *Inverness-shire* Map **14** NH64

See also Ardersier, Culloden Moor and Dalcross

GH Ｑ Ｑ Ｑ **Aberfeldy Lodge** 11 Southside Rd IV2 3BG ☎01463 231120
Situated in a residential area within easy reach of central amenities, this friendly family-run guest house offers comfortable bedrooms in a variety of sizes, all with modern facilities; public areas include a choice of relaxing little lounges and a separate dining room. Smoking is not permitted on the ground floor, which includes three bedrooms.

9 en suite (shr) (4 fmly) No smoking in 3 bedrooms No smoking in dining room No smoking in lounges CTV in all bedrooms Tea and coffee making facilities No dogs Cen ht 9P No coaches Last d 4pm

PRICE GUIDE
ROOMS: d £36-£50; wkly hlf-bd £217-£266

Selected

GH Ｑ Ｑ Ｑ Ｑ **Ardmuir House** 16 Ness Bank IV2 4SF (on E bank of river, opposite the cathedral) ☎01463 231151
Situated on the north bank of the River Ness overlooking the cathedral, this friendly family run establishment is an ideal base for the visiting holidaymaker. The bright cheery bedrooms, all now with telephones, have been decorated to a high standard and attractive modern fabrics have been used to good effect. Refreshments are available for house guests in the comfortable lounge overlooking the river and enjoyable home cooking is served in the smart dining room.

11 en suite (shr) (2 fmly) No smoking in dining room CTV in all bedrooms Tea and coffee making facilities Direct dial from bedrooms Licensed Cen ht 4P No coaches Last d 7pm

PRICE GUIDE
ROOMS: s £30.50-£33; d £49-£54; wkly b&b £158-£180✱
CARDS: █ ▒

GH Ｑ Ｑ Ｑ **Ardross House** 18 Ardross St IV3 5NS (first turning on right at St Andrews Cathedral) ☎01463 241740
A detached Victorian house stands in a residential street close to the Cathedral. The bedrooms are comfortably furnished in mixed modern styles and offer all the expected amenities; a new extension will provide more rooms in the future. Hearty breakfasts are served at smartly clothed tables in the dining room.

8 rms (6 bth/shr) (2 fmly) No smoking in 1 bedrooms No smoking in dining room No smoking in lounges CTV in all bedrooms Tea and coffee making facilities Cen ht 2P
PRICE GUIDE
ROOMS: s £18-£20; d £30-£40

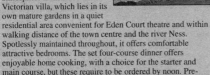

Premier Selected

GH Q Q Q Q Q **Ballifeary House Hotel** 10 Ballifeary Rd IV3 5PJ (off A82, .5m from town centre)
☎01463 235572
FAX 01463 717583
Etr-mid Oct

Margaret and Danny Luscombe have created a friendly atmosphere at their detached Victorian villa, which lies in its own mature gardens in a quiet residential area convenient for Eden Court theatre and within walking distance of the town centre and the river Ness. Spotlessly maintained throughout, it offers comfortable attractive bedrooms. The set four-course dinner offers enjoyable home cooking, with a choice for the starter and main course, but these require to be ordered by noon. Pre-dinner drinks and after dinner coffee are served in the pleasant lounge, but smoking is not permitted.
8 en suite (bth/shr) No smoking CTV in all bedrooms Tea and coffee making facilities No dogs (ex guide dogs)

ARDMUIR HOUSE, INVERNESS

A family run hotel beside the River Ness: close to the town centre.
Our licensed, non-smoking dining-room features home cooking with fresh local produce. All rooms have a private bathroom, colour TV, tea/coffee making, hair dryers and direct dial telephones.
Special discounts are available for stays of 3 days or more. We will be pleased to send our brochure and tariff on request.
Jean and Tony Gatcombe
16 Ness Bank, Inverness IV2 4SF
Tel: (01463) 231151

CRAIGARON
17 Saltburn, Invergordon, Ross-shire IV18 0JX
Tel: Invergordon (01349) 853640

Sunny, seafront accommodation on Cromarty Firth. In comfortable, friendly, family home with good cooking. Pretty en-suite rooms in modernised fisherman's cottage with unique view. 5 minutes drive from town centre, station and all other amenities. On bus route, convenient for airport. One of UK's driest areas, famed for it's naval history, Pictish relics and dolphin/bird watching. 20+ golf courses nearby.

Ardross House
18 Ardross Street, Inverness, Highland IV3 5NS
Tel: 01463 241740

Ardross House is a family run guest house. Built in 1857 this property has recently been converted to a guest house but still retains its original character. Although only 5 mins from the town centre it still enjoys a peaceful location. This guest house has 6 double/ family rooms all with en-suite, colour TV, tea/coffee facilities etc. 3 of the rooms are on the ground floor.

Licensed Cen ht No children 12yrs 8P No coaches Last d 7pm
PRICE GUIDE
ROOMS: s £30-£33; d £60-£66; wkly b&b £210-£224; wkly hlf-bd £322-£336
CARDS:

6 en suite (bth/shr) No smoking in dining room CTV in all bedrooms Tea and coffee making facilities No dogs (ex guide dogs) Cen ht 4P No coaches
PRICE GUIDE
ROOMS: s £16-£20; d £32-£36; wkly b&b £108✱
CARDS:

Selected

GH ◘◘◘◘ **Brae Ness Hotel** 17 Ness Bank IV2 4SF (0.25m along river bank below Inverness Castle in direction of Dores (B862) from town centre)
☎01463 712266 FAX 01463 231732
Etr-Oct
a friendly and efficiently run hotel is pleasantly situated beside the River Ness within a short walk of central amenities. Bedrooms vary in size and range from non-smoking superior rooms to smaller standard rooms which have recently been upgraded. Public areas include a comfortable lounge serving refreshments and an attractive dining room featuring enjoyable home-cooked meals and hearty breakfasts.
10 rms (9 bth/shr) (2 fmly) No smoking in 7 bedrooms No smoking in dining room CTV in all bedrooms Tea and coffee making facilities No dogs (ex guide dogs) Licensed Cen ht 7P No coaches Last d 7pm
PRICE GUIDE
ROOMS: s £25-£33; d £44-£58; wkly b&b £140-£189; wkly hlf-bd £224-£273
CARDS:

Selected

GH ◘◘◘◘ **Clach Mhuilinn** 7 Harris Rd IV2 3LS (off A9 onto B9006 signed Hilton and Culcabock and at rbt follow signs Town Centre then over mini-rbt and take 2nd left) ☎01463 237059
Closed Dec-Jan
This attractive detached house stands in a residential area within a short drive of the town centre. The inviting lounge is comfortable and gives access to the small dining area where wholesome breakfasts are served at a communal table overlooking the patio and well tended garden. Bedrooms, though not expansive, are very comfortable and tastefully modern in appointment. The house is immaculately maintained and smoking is not permitted.
3 rms (1 shr) No smoking Tea and coffee making facilities No dogs Cen ht CTV No children 10yrs 5P No coaches
PRICE GUIDE
ROOMS: s £20-£23; d £40-£45✱
CARDS:

GH ◘◘◘ **Craigside** 4 Gordon Ter IV2 3HD
☎01463 231576 FAX 01463 713409
Efficiently run by Janette and Wilf Skinner, this Victorian lodge is situated in a residential area overlooking the castle and offers good-value bed and breakfast accommodation. The bedrooms, where smoking is not encouraged, vary in size and provide a wide range of amenities, and there is a comfortable lounge with well filled book shelves. Freshly cooked breakfasts are served in the dining room, where at peak times it may be necessary to share a table.

Premier Selected

GH ◘◘◘◘◘ **Culduthel Lodge** 14 Culduthel Rd IV2 4AG (follow Castle St from town centre)
☎01463 240089
FAX 01463 240089

David and Marion Bonsor's finely restored Grade II Georgian residence stands in its own grounds within easy walking distance of the town centre. Deceptively small from the outside it offers spacious, comfortable and elegant accommodation. The well maintained bedrooms offer modern facilities and thoughtful extras such as fruit, mineral water and a small decanter of sherry. Public rooms include a sympathetically furnished drawing room and a well proportioned dining room where a good choice of freshly prepared dishes feature on a daily changing menu. There is also a small patio where guests can enjoy drinks and fine views over the River Ness and the surrounding countryside.
12 en suite (bth/shr) (1 fmly) No smoking in 10 bedrooms No smoking in dining room CTV in all bedrooms Tea and coffee making facilities Direct dial from bedrooms No dogs (ex guide dogs) Licensed Cen ht No children 5yrs 13P No coaches Last d 8.30pm
PRICE GUIDE
ROOMS: s £40-£42.50; d £66-£74; wkly b&b £225-£235; wkly hlf-bd £330-£340
CARDS:

Selected

GH ◘◘◘◘ **Dionard** 39 Old Edinburgh Rd IV2 3HJ
☎01463 233557
This comfortable detached Victorian house which stands in a well tended garden in a residential area close to the town centre. Bedrooms, though not expansive, are comfortable with soft pastel colour schemes and mixed modern furnishings. Public areas include an attractive combined lounge/dining room where hearty breakfasts are served, occasionally at shared tables.
3 en suite (shr) No smoking in 1 bedrooms No smoking in dining room No smoking in 1 lounge CTV in all bedrooms Tea and coffee making facilities Cen ht CTV 6P
PRICE GUIDE
ROOMS: s £20-£30; d £36-£44; wkly b&b £112-£140

GH Q Q Q Q **Eden House Hotel** 8 Ballifeary Rd IV3 5PJ (cross Ness Bridge from High St in town centre. First left and first left again and then second left 200mtrs from Eden Court Theatre)
☎01463 230278 FAX 01463 230278
Situated in a desirable residential area close to the Eden Court Theatre, this charming, semidetatched Victorian villa offers pretty bedrooms which are comfortable and well appointed in a modern style. The dining room is attractive and provides a three-course fixed-price menu. The small conservatory lounge is the only area where smoking is permitted.
5 rms (4 shr) (2 fmly) No smoking CTV in all bedrooms Tea and coffee making facilities No dogs (ex guide dogs) Cen ht No children 3yrs 7P No coaches Last d 4pm
PRICE GUIDE
ROOMS: s £25-£35; d £44-£52; wkly b&b £144.50-£172.50; wkly hlf-bd £249.50-£277.50

◨ ▼ GH Q Q Q **Edinbane** 14 Ballifeary Rd IV3 5PJ (off A82 into Bishops Rd then 1st right) ☎01463 236411 Apr-Sep
3 rms No smoking Tea and coffee making facilities No dogs (ex guide dogs) Cen ht CTV No parking
PRICE GUIDE
ROOMS: s £16-£18; d £28-£30; wkly b&b £98-£112

GH Q Q **Four Winds** 42 Old Edinburgh Rd IV2 3PG (off A9 signed Crown and Kingsmills and past golf course, house opposite Crown Court Hotel) ☎01463 230397
Closed 25 Dec-3 Jan
Good value bed and breakfast accommodation is offered at this friendly family-run establishment, a detached Victorian house set in a residential area within a ten minute walk of the town centre. The variously sized bedrooms offer modern furnishings together with the expected amenities while public areas include an attractive first-floor lounge with well filled book shelves and a separate breakfast room.
5 en suite (shr) (2 fmly) CTV in all bedrooms Tea and coffee making facilities No dogs Cen ht CTV 15P No coaches
PRICE GUIDE
ROOMS: s £18-£19; d £36-£38; wkly b&b £114-£120✱

GH Q Q Q **Greystanes** Greystanes, Daviot West IV1 2EP (turn off A9 at Daviot West, Greystanes signposted) ☎01808 521381
This attractive modern home is peacefully set in landscaped gardens looking out over the Monadhliath Mountains. The well decorated bedrooms have comfortable modern furnishings; one room is en suite but the remainder share a communal bathroom. Public areas include a spacious and attractive lounge/dining room serving breakfasts and, by arrangement, evening meals at a communal table. The establishment is non-smoking and is conveniently placed for access to the A9.
4 rms (1 shr) No smoking CTV in 3 bedrooms Tea and coffee making facilities No dogs Cen ht CTV No children 6yrs 6P No coaches
PRICE GUIDE
ROOMS: s £16-£18; d £35-£38; wkly b&b £105.50-£119; wkly hlf-bd £175.50-£189✱
CARDS: ▨ ▆ ▨

Ballifeary House Hotel

10 Ballifeary Road, Inverness IV3 5PJ
Telephone: 01463 235572 Fax: 01463 717583

This very popular hotel has an excellent reputation and has been awarded the top grade for quality by both the AA and Scottish Tourist Board.
Ideally situated in a desirable area of Inverness, offering a quiet, relaxing atmosphere, and only a 10 minute picturesque walk to town. All rooms have en suite bathrooms, TV, hospitality tray, etc. Excellent home cooking. Table licence. Car park.
No smoking throughout.
Brochure/reservations:
Margaret & Danny Luscombe

BRAE NESS HOTEL

INVERNESS
Ideally situated beside the River Ness. 5 minutes walk from the town centre. Excellent home cooking with fresh produce served in our non-smoking dining room with table licence. All rooms have private bathroom, TV, tea making facilities and most are reserved for non smokers.
John & Margaret Hill,
Ness Bank, Inverness IV2 4SF
Telephone: (01463) 712266
Fax: (01463) 231732

GH 🅀🅀🅀 *Hebrides* 120a Glenurquhart Rd IV3 5TD (on A82 Fort William road) ☎01463 220062

Situated at the south end of town close to the Caledonian canal, this family-run guest house offers good value bed and breakfast accommodation. The two bedrooms are comfortably furnished and well equipped, one with an en suite shower, the other with exclusive use of a bathroom. Enjoyable breakfasts are served at individual tables in the neat dining room. High standards of housekeeping are maintained and smoking is not permitted.

2 rms (1 shr) (1 fmly) No smoking CTV in all bedrooms Tea and coffee making facilities No dogs Cen ht 4P No coaches

CARDS: 🅱 🖭

GH 🅀🅀🅀 *Inverglen* 7 Abertarff Rd IV2 3NW ☎01463 237610

Margaret Bews takes a pride in standards of cleanliness at her comfortable detached home which stands in a residential area within walking distance of central amenities. Bedrooms of variable sizes are bright and airy with comfortable modern appointments. There is also a small relaxing lounge for guests where tea and coffee making facilities are available. Hearty breakfasts are served at individual tables in the adjacent dining room.

5 en suite (shr) (2 fmly) No smoking CTV in all bedrooms Tea and coffee making facilities No dogs Cen ht 6P

PRICE GUIDE

ROOMS: d £34-£40; wkly b&b fr £119✳

GH 🅀🅀🅀 *Laggan View* Ness Castle Fishings, Dores Rd IV1 2DH (3m from town centre on B862) ☎01463 235996 FAX 01463 711552

A welcoming atmosphere prevails at Liz Saggers' comfortable bungalow which stands in its own attractive garden beside the Dores Road some three miles south of town. The non-smoking bedrooms are spacious with mixed modern appointments while public areas include a large, comfortable lounge together with a small dining room where enjoyable home cooked meals are served at individual tables.

3 en suite (bth/shr) (1 fmly) No smoking in bedrooms No smoking in dining room CTV in all bedrooms Tea and coffee making facilities Cen ht CTV 4P No coaches Last d 7.30pm

PRICE GUIDE

ROOMS: s fr £20; d fr £32; wkly b&b fr £110; wkly hlf-bd fr £160✳

CARDS: 🅱 🖭

GH 🅀🅀 *Leinster Lodge* 27 Southside Rd IV2 4XA ☎01463 233311

Closed Xmas & New Year

Leinster Lodge is a friendly family-run house offering good-value bed and breakfast accommodation ten minutes' walk from the central amenities. There are mostly spacious bedrooms, a comfortable lounge and a traditional dining room where substantial breakfasts are served at individual tables.

6 rms (2 shr) (2 fmly) CTV in all bedrooms Tea and coffee making facilities Cen ht CTV 8P No coaches

PRICE GUIDE

ROOMS: s £17; d £32-£36; wkly b&b £112-£126✳

Prices quoted in the Guide are based on information supplied by the establishments themselves.

Premier Selected

GH 🅀🅀🅀🅀🅀 **Moyness House** 6 Bruce Gardens IV3 5EN (leave by A82 Fort William road) ☎01463 233836 FAX 01463 233836 Closed 24 Dec-3 Jan

Once the home of writer Neil M Gunn, this late 19th-century house is in a residential area ten minutes walk from the town centre. It has been Nonna and Michael Jones' home for 11 years and they have built it up into a first-class small hotel. Nonna is an excellent cook, offering a choice of dishes at dinner, and though the house is not licensed you are welcome to bring your own wine. The pine-furnished bedrooms are compact but comfortable.

7 en suite (bth/shr) No smoking in dining room CTV in all bedrooms Tea and coffee making facilities Licensed Cen ht 10P No coaches Last d 7pm

PRICE GUIDE

ROOMS: s £25-£29; d £25-£29; wkly b&b £175-£203; wkly hlf-bd £267-£306✳

CARDS: 🅱 🖭 🖭 🅱 🖾

Selected

GH 🅀🅀🅀 **The Old Rectory** 9 Southside Rd IV2 3BG ☎01463 220969 Closed 21 Dec-5 Jan

Neina and John Lister are constantly striving to improve standards at their detached home. Recent redecoration has enhanced the attractive dining room where good-sized breakfasts are served at individual lace-clothed circular tables. The pleasant lounge is relaxing and bedrooms are comfortably modern and well equipped. Smoking is not encouraged in the house.

4 en suite (shr) (1 fmly) No smoking CTV in all bedrooms Tea and coffee making facilities No dogs (ex guide dogs) Cen ht CTV No children 7yrs 5P

PRICE GUIDE

ROOMS: s £18-£19; d £36-£38

GH 🅀🅀🅀 *Riverside House Hotel* 8 Ness Bank IV2 4SF ☎01463 231052

Situated beside the River Ness close to the town centre, this friendly personally run guest house offers good value holiday accommodation. Public areas include a small but very comfortable lounge and attractive dining room serving enjoyable home cooking; at peak times guests may be asked to share a table. Bedrooms are variable in size with mixed modern appointments.

11 rms (5 bth 5 shr) (3 fmly) CTV in all bedrooms Tea and coffee making facilities Licensed Cen ht CTV No parking Last d 7pm

---

🛌 🖭 **GH** 🅀🅀 *Roseneath* 39 Greig St IV3 5PX (fro A9 turn left at Longman Rbt cross Friars Bridge and take 2nd exit at rbt into Kenneth St then 2nd left) ☎01463 220201

Excellent-value bed and breakfast accommodation is provided at this sturdy sandstone house south of the river. The bedrooms are bright and cheery, and hearty breakfasts are served at individual tables in the combined lounge and dining room.

6 rms (5 shr) (3 fmly) No smoking in dining room CTV in all bedrooms Tea and coffee making facilities Direct dial from bedrooms Cen ht CTV 3P

PRICE GUIDE
ROOMS: s £15-£36; d £30-£36

GH QQQ *St Ann's Hotel* 37 Harrowden Rd IV3 5QN
☎01463 236157 FAX 01463 236157
Situated in a west end residential area, ten minutes' walk from the town centre, this friendly family-run house is now under the ownership of Jim and Betty Gardiner. The bedrooms are bright and airy with modern furniture, and there is a comfortable lounge where guests can relax with a drink from the dispense bar. Evening meals are available with advance notice.
6 rms (5 bth/shr) (3 fmly) No smoking in dining room CTV in all bedrooms Tea and coffee making facilities Licensed Cen ht CTV 3P Last d 9pm

GH QQQ **Sunnyholm** 12 Mayfield Rd IV2 4AE
☎01463 231336
Sunnyholme is an extended modern detached house in a residential area within easy reach of the town centre. It offers good value bed and breakfast accommodation with a relaxed and friendly atmosphere. Bedrooms, though small, are comfortably furnished with predominantly pine pieces and have a good range of amenities. There are a no-smoking TV lounge, a popular sun lounge and a neat dining room where hearty breakfasts are served at individual tables.
4 en suite (shr) No smoking CTV in all bedrooms Tea and coffee making facilities No dogs (ex guide dogs) Cen ht CTV 6P No coaches

PRICE GUIDE
ROOMS: s £20-£22; d £32-£36✳

Selected

♥ ꆛꆛꆛꆛ Mrs A Munro **Taransay Lower Muckovie** *(NH707436)* IV1 2BB (off A9 onto B9177 past Drumossie Hotel) ☎01463 231880

Many guests return year after year to Mrs Munro's comfortable modern bungalow, which stands adjacent to the family farm with panoramic views over the Moray Firth to the Black Isle. In this non-smoking establishment there are two smartly decorated bedrooms, a relaxing lounge, and a dining room where breakfasts are served at a communal table.

2 rms (1 shr) (1 fmly) No smoking CTV in all bedrooms Tea and coffee making facilities No dogs (ex guide dogs) CTV 3P 170 acres dairy

PRICE GUIDE

ROOMS: d £32-£36; wkly b&b £110-£123

◀ ꆛꆛꆛ *Heathmount* Kingsmills Rd IV2 3JU ☎01463 235877 FAX 01463 715749

Closed 31 Dec-2 Jan

Good-value accommodation is offered at this friendly Highland inn, which dates back to 1868 and is situated in a residential area within a reasonable distance of the town centre. Bedrooms - one of them with a four-poster bed - are comfortably modern in style and offer a wide range of amenities. Bars with real ale are popular with locals and a restaurant with a no-smoking area offers a wide range of enjoyable home cooking and char-grills.

5 en suite (bth/shr) (1 fmly) CTV in all bedrooms Tea and coffee making facilities Direct dial from bedrooms Cen ht 20P No coaches Last d 9.15pm

CARDS: ▨ ▨

ISLE OF

Placenames incorporating the words 'Isle' or 'Isle of' will be found under the actual name, eg Isle of Arran is under Arran, Isle of.

JEDBURGH Borders *Roxburghshire* Map **12** NT62

GH ꆛꆛ **Ferniehirst Mill Lodge** TD8 6PQ (2.5m S on A68, at the end of a private track directly off A68) ☎01835 863279

This modern, purpose-built chalet-style lodge in 25 acres of land occupies a secluded position beside the River Jed. The complex - which includes a riding centre - offers small, simply furnished bedrooms and a bright, airy lounge featuring a dispense bar, television and board games. Meals are taken at shared tables in the dining room.

9 en suite (bth/shr) No smoking in dining room Tea and coffee making facilities Direct dial from bedrooms Licensed Cen ht CTV 10P No coaches Fishing Riding Last d 6pm

PRICE GUIDE

ROOMS: s £22; d £44; wkly b&b £140; wkly hlf-bd £224✱

CARDS: ▨ ▨

Selected

GH ꆛꆛꆛꆛ **'Froylehurst'** Friars TD8 6BN (from town centre Market Place leave by Exchange St then 1st right into Friars for 3rd turn on left) ☎01835 862477 FAX 01835 862477

Mar-Nov

This fine late-Victorian house offers very good views from a setting in its own secluded grounds high above the town. Generally spacious bedrooms are very comfortable and

carefully colour co-ordinated; all are thoughtfully equipped with radios, magazines and tissues. The two extremely smart and tasteful bathrooms have double-sized shower cubicles. Guests can relax in the elegant lounge, and there is a charming little dining room with book-lined walls; here breakfast is taken in two sittings around a large communal table.

5 rms (3 fmly) No smoking in bedrooms No smoking in dining room CTV in all bedrooms Tea and coffee making facilities No dogs Cen ht CTV No children 5yrs 5P No coaches

PRICE GUIDE

ROOMS: d £32-£34; wkly b&b fr £100

£

Selected

GH ꆛꆛꆛꆛ **Hundalee House** TD8 6PA (1m S, off A68) ☎01835 863011

Closed Dec-Mar

Located just south of the town of Jedburgh, this large manor house was built in the early 1700's and is set in 10 acres of mature woodlands and well kept gardens. The individually furnished bedrooms offer good facilities, one also has a four poster bed. A hearty breakfast is served at one communal table in the elegant dining room, while guests can relax in the comfort of the drawing room which overlooks the garden.

4 rms (3 bth/shr) (1 fmly) No smoking CTV in all bedrooms Tea and coffee making facilities No dogs (ex guide dogs) Cen ht 6P

PRICE GUIDE

ROOMS: d £32-£40✱

£

GH ꆛꆛꆛ **Kenmore Bank Hotel** Oxnam Rd TD8 6JJ (off A68 entering town from S, take 1st right by church) ☎01835 862369

From its position high above the local river, this family-run guest house enjoys good views over the town and abbey. Friendly, enthusiastic owners offer attractively decorated bedrooms in a range of sizes, both supper and dinner are available, and there is a reasonable wine list. The owner's paintings are displayed in the lounge and dining room, many of them being for sale.

6 en suite (bth/shr) (2 fmly) No smoking in dining room CTV in all bedrooms Tea and coffee making facilities Licensed Cen ht 6P No coaches Fishing Last d 6.30pm

PRICE GUIDE

ROOMS: s £29-£42; d £36-£42; wkly b&b £121-£147; wkly hlf-bd £231-£252✱

CARDS: ▨ ▨

£

Entries in this Guide are based on reports filed by our team of professionally trained, full-time inspectors.

Premier Selected

GH ⬛⬛⬛⬛⬛ **The Spinney** Langlee TD8 6PB (2m S on A68) ☎01835 863525 FAX 01835 863525 Mar-2nd wk Nov

An attractive modern house set in several acres of pleasant landscaped gardens off the A68, two miles south of Jedburgh, offers stylish, well proportioned bedrooms with light colour schemes, tasteful fabrics and comfortable seating. Downstairs there is a relaxing lounge with Chesterfield sofas, a log fire, books and TV. The adjoining dining room has large, individual, well spaced tables at which a good choice of breakfast dishes is served.

3 rms (2 shr) No smoking in bedrooms No smoking in dining room CTV in all bedrooms Tea and coffee making facilities No dogs (ex guide dogs) Cen ht CTV 8P No coaches
PRICE GUIDE
ROOMS: d £40-£42

Selected

GH ⬛⬛⬛⬛ **Willow Court** The Friars TD8 6BN (from Market Sq take Exchange St, Friars 50yds along on the right) ☎01835 863702 FAX 01835 864601

A modern house with most of its accommodation and facilities on the ground floor stands amid two acres of gardens in an elevated position above the town. All but one of the attractively decorated, comfortably furnished bedrooms have en suite facilities (that one having sole use of a shower room nearby) and some of them enjoy views of the town and surrounding countryside; a large room upstairs is available for family use. One of the two lounges offers books and games, the other television, and a conservatory dining room at the front of the house is the setting for both breakfast and an evening meal. A residential drinks licence is held. There is also secure private parking.

4 rms (3 bth/shr) (1 fmly) No smoking in bedrooms No smoking in dining room No smoking in 1 lounge CTV in all bedrooms Tea and coffee making facilities Licensed Cen ht CTV ch fac 6P No coaches Last d 6pm
PRICE GUIDE
ROOMS: s £18-£32; d £28-£40; wkly b&b £98-£133; wkly hlf-bd £168-£203✴

JOHN O'GROATS Highland *Caithness* Map **15** ND37

GH ⬛⬛⬛ **Post Office House** Cannisbay KA1 4YH ☎01955 611213
Situated in the village of Canisbay three miles west of John O' Groats, Jean and Charlie Manson's 100-year-old, stone-built home enjoys views of the Pentland Firth. Jean is a very genuine host and really does go out of her way to ensure that her guests are well cared for. The non smoking bedrooms are of decent size and offer both modern and traditional appointments. There is a cosy sitting room where suppers are served around 10 o'clock and in the morning, superb breakfast including salmon, smoked haddock and

fresh kippers are served in the dining room which forms part of the owners personal lounge.
3 rms (1 shr) CTV in all bedrooms

KEITH Grampian *Banffshire* Map **15** NJ45

Selected

✌ ⬛⬛⬛⬛ Mrs J Jackson **The Haughs** *(NJ416515)* AB55 3QN (1m from Keith off A96, signed Inverness) ☎01542 882238 Apr-Oct
This traditional farmhouse is ideally placed for touring and Mrs Jackson is a most welcoming hostess. Bedrooms are bright and cheery, with all modern comforts; smoking is discouraged. There is an attractive sitting room and a sunny, south-facing dining room where good home cooked meals are served at separate tables.
4 rms (3 bth/shr) (1 fmly) No smoking in bedrooms No smoking in dining room CTV in all bedrooms Tea and coffee making facilities No dogs (ex guide dogs) Cen ht CTV 10P 165 acres beef mixed sheep Last d 3pm
PRICE GUIDE
ROOMS: d £33-£35✴

⬛⬛ ✌ ⬛⬛⬛ Mrs Bain **Saughwells Farm** *(NJ384552)* Forgie AB55 3RJ ☎01343 820409
Lying off the A96 3.5 miles north of Keith, this small cottage-style farm has been modernised and extended to house two attractive, well equipped bedrooms, a cosy lounge and a neat little dining room where hearty meals are taken around a single table.

KENMORE BANK HOTEL JEDBURGH
Oxnam Road, Jedburgh TD8 6JJ
Tel: (01835) 862369
Open all year

A charming, family-run hotel just off the A68 to/from Edinburgh. Situated beside the Jed Water, it enjoys panoramic views of the Abbey and town. Just five minutes' away from shops, restaurants, and pubs. All bedrooms en-suite with colour TV. Central heating. Choice of menu, wines and snacks. Prices from £18.00 B&B.

Proprietors: Charles and Joanne Muller

2 rms No smoking CTV in all bedrooms Tea and coffee making facilities CTV P 200 acres sheep
PRICE GUIDE
ROOMS: s fr £12; d fr £24

KENTALLEN Highland *Argyllshire* Map **14** NN05

♥ Ⓠ Ⓠ Mrs D A Macarthur **Ardsheal Home Farm** *(NN996574)* PA38 4BZ (off A828, 3m south of Ballahulish Bridge)
☎01631 740229
Apr-Oct
Good value holiday accommodation is offered at a comfortable cottage-style farmhouse standing peacefully near the shore of Loch Linnhe. Bedrooms are non smoking; the spacious ground floor room has modern furnishings and has exclusive use of its own bathroom while the upper floor rooms are more compact with traditional furnishings. Public areas include a comfortable TV lounge and a homely dining room serving enjoyable home cooked meals and hearty breakfasts around a communal table. No dogs are admitted apart from guide dogs.
3 rms (1 fmly) No smoking Tea and coffee making facilities No dogs (ex guide dogs) Cen ht CTV 5P 1000 acres beef sheep
PRICE GUIDE
ROOMS: s £18-£20; d £32-£34; wkly hlf-bd £196✱

KILBARCHAN Strathclyde *Renfrewshire* Map **10** NS46

GH Ⓠ Ⓠ **Ashburn** Milliken Park Rd PA10 2DB (follow signs for Johnstone onto B787 and turn right opposite bus garage)
☎01505 705477 FAX 01505 705477
Situated at the south end of the village, this friendly family-run guest house proves a popular stopover for travellers using Glasgow Airport. Bedrooms in a variety of sizes offer mixed modern appointments and the expected facilities, while public areas include a spacious lounge which boasts its own honesty bar. By prior arrangement, hearty home-cooked meals are served at shared tables in the adjacent dining room.
6 rms (2 shr) (3 fmly) CTV in all bedrooms Tea and coffee making facilities Licensed Cen ht CTV 8P No coaches Last d 11am
CARDS: ▨ ▤

KILLIECRANKIE Tayside *Perthshire* Map **14** NN96

GH Ⓠ Ⓠ **Dalnasgadh House** PH16 5LN (turn off A9 N of Pitlochry signposted Killiecrankie B8079) ☎01796 473237
14 Apr-30 Oct
Set in its own grounds, this fine detached house enjoys a lovely secluded location, while remaining convenient for the main A9. A real home from home atmosphere is created by the friendly owner, Mrs McPherson-McDougall, who ensures her guest house is immaculately maintained. Bedrooms are comfortable and traditionally furnished, and stripped woodwork is a feature throughout. Public areas include a bright lounge and attractive breakfast room.
5 rms No smoking TV available Tea and coffee making facilities No dogs (ex guide dogs) Cen ht CTV 10P No coaches

---

KILLIN Central *Perthshire* Map **11** NN53

Selected

GH Ⓠ Ⓠ Ⓠ Ⓠ **Breadalbane House** Main St FK21 8UT
☎01567 820386 FAX 01567 820386
A friendly atmosphere prevails at Dani Grant's tastefully modernised house in the centre of the village. Maintained to a high standard it offers well equipped airy bedrooms which are absolutely up-to-date in style, a relaxing lounge and an

adjacent dining room where Dani's cooking earns well deserved praise. Special diets and vegetarians can be catered for.
5 en suite (bth/shr) (2 fmly) No smoking in bedrooms No smoking in dining room CTV in all bedrooms Tea and coffee making facilities Cen ht CTV 6P Last d 6pm
CARDS: ▨ ▤

KILMARNOCK Strathclyde *Ayrshire* Map **10** NS43

GH Ⓠ Ⓠ Ⓠ **Burnside Hotel** 18 London Rd KA3 7AQ (on main road opposite Dick Institute, Library and Museum)
☎01563 522952 FAX 01563 573381
Enthusiastic owners Judith and David Dye continue to make improvements at their detached sandstone house, including the provision of more en suite bathrooms to the bright bedrooms. Public areas comprise a spacious lounge and a neat dining room where enjoyable home cooking is served. The house has a relaxed atmosphere and high standards of housekeeping are maintained.
10 rms (5 bth/shr) (4 fmly) No smoking in dining room CTV in all bedrooms Tea and coffee making facilities Cen ht CTV 10P No coaches Last d noon
PRICE GUIDE
ROOMS: s £17.50-£26; d £30-£40
CARDS: ▨ ▤ ▤

GH Ⓠ Ⓠ **Eriskay** 2 Dean Ter KA3 1RJ (follow one-way system and right at Railway station and follow Glasgow signs) ☎01563 532061
Eriskay is a detached stone-built house, located north of the town centre, efficiently run by friendly owners Angus and Cathy MacDonald. Bedrooms are bright and airy with modern furnishings, though some of the singles are limited in size. Hearty breakfasts are served at individual tables in the neat dining room, which also has a small lounge area.
7 rms (3 shr) (3 fmly) No smoking in dining room CTV in all bedrooms Tea and coffee making facilities Cen ht CTV 12P
PRICE GUIDE
ROOMS: s £15-£22; d £30-£36✱

KINGHORN Fife Map **11** NT28

◼ Ⓠ Ⓠ Ⓠ **Longboat** 107 Pettycur Rd KY2 9RU (turn off at the 'Scottish Soldier' memorial on A921) ☎01592 890625
Enjoying splendid views over the Firth of Forth to Edinburgh, this friendly family run inn is popular with locals and visitors alike. Bedrooms have modern facilities, with two overlooking the sea and having small terraces. The restaurant and lounge bar have French windows to take advantage of the view, while meals are served all day in the Hideaway Wine Bar, situated on the water's edge.
6 en suite (bth/shr) CTV in all bedrooms Tea and coffee making facilities Cen ht 20P Last d 9.30pm
CARDS: ▨ ▤ ▤ ⓪

KINGUSSIE Highland *Inverness-shire* Map **14** NH70

Selected

GH Ⓠ Ⓠ Ⓠ Ⓠ **Avondale House** Newtonmore Rd
PH21 1HF ☎01540 661731 FAX 01540 661731
A detached Victorian building stands in its own well tended gardens beside the main road just south of the village centre. Though not large, the non-smoking bedrooms are cheery, with mixed modern appointments and attractive co-ordinated fabrics. The lounge invites relaxation, and enjoyable home cooking is served at individual tables in the neat dining room.

Continually improving, the hotel is an ideal base for the touring holidaymaker and many guests return on a regular basis.

7 rms (5 bth/shr) (1 fmly) No smoking CTV in all bedrooms Tea and coffee making facilities Cen ht No children 5yrs 8P No coaches Last d 5pm

PRICE GUIDE
ROOMS: d £34-£42✱

GH QQQ **Homewood Lodge** Newtonmore Rd PH21 1HD (on A86 Newtonmore road on outskirts of village)
☎01540 661507

A relaxed, friendly atmosphere prevails at Shirley Murchie's comfortable house, which stands in an elevated position at the south end of the town, offering fine views over the Spey Valley. Bedrooms are spacious and public areas include a cosy sitting room and a pleasant dining room where enjoyable home cooking is served at individual tables. This is a no-smoking establishment.

4 en suite (shr) (2 fmly) No smoking Tea and coffee making facilities No dogs (ex guide dogs) Cen ht CTV No children 5yrs 6P No coaches Last d 3pm

PRICE GUIDE
ROOMS: s £19.50-£22.50; d £39; wkly b&b £130-£150; wkly hlf-bd £203.50-£223.50

GH QQ **Sonnhalde** East Ter PH21 1JS (exit A9 and turn left into village. Turn right at traffic lights and then first right. Third house on left) ☎01540 661266 FAX 01540 661266
Closed Nov-27 Dec

Fine views over the Spey Valley and Cairngorms are enjoyed from this sturdy Victorian villa set on a hillside close to the clock tower above the town. Owners Bernie and Janis Jones are welcoming hosts, and their special wildlife, walking, fly fishing and photographic packages are increasing in popularity. There is a cosy lounge and enjoyable home cooking is served in the neat dining room. Bedrooms vary in size and are furnished in a comfortably traditional style.

7 rms (3 shr) (2 fmly) No smoking in bedrooms No smoking in dining room Cen ht CTV 10P No coaches Last d 4pm

PRICE GUIDE
ROOMS: d £34-£42; wkly b&b £113-£150.50; wkly hlf-bd £170-£217

KINROSS Tayside *Kinross-shire* Map **11** NO10

◀ QQQ **The Muirs Inn** 49 Muirs KY13 7AU (off M90 junct 6 and follow signs for A922 for inn at T-junct)
☎01577 862270 FAX 01577 862270

Brimming with character, this cottage-style pub and restaurant sits by the main road on the northern side of town. Its bedrooms lie above the bar and are reached by an outside door; while not large, they are well equipped and nicely furnished in pine. The restaurant menus (which include high tea and supper) cater for all tastes and pockets, and the inn is renowned for the range and quality of the real ales which can be enjoyed in both the public bar and the cosy little lounge.

5 en suite (bth/shr) CTV in all bedrooms Tea and coffee making facilities No dogs (ex guide dogs) Cen ht No children 11yrs 8P Last d 9pm

PRICE GUIDE
ROOMS: s £35-£37.50; d £55-£60; wkly b&b £175-£192.50; wkly hlf-bd £245-£262.50
MEALS: Lunch fr £12.95&alc Dinner fr £12.95&alc
CARDS: 🔲 🔲

KIRKBEAN Dumfries & Galloway *Dumfriesshire*
Map **11** NX95

Selected

GH QQQQ **Cavens House** DG2 8AA (on A710)
☎01387 880234 FAX 01387 880234

Reached by way of a long drive through mature grounds and woodland, this country mansion close to the Solway coast has many historical connections. The bedrooms are spacious, one having its own sun lounge; two are located on the ground floor. The large, inviting lounge which overlooks the putting green and garden has an honesty bar and a selection of board games, while the pleasantly appointed dining room makes an attractive setting for home-cooked four-course evening meals.

6 en suite (bth/shr) (1 fmly) No smoking in dining room CTV in all bedrooms Tea and coffee making facilities Licensed Cen ht CTV 10P No coaches Last d 7pm

PRICE GUIDE
ROOMS: s £25-£35; d £44-£56; wkly hlf-bd £252✱
CARDS: 🔲 🔲

THE MUIRS INN KINROSS

A TRADITIONAL SCOTTISH COUNTRY INN
– That's Simply Something Special

Appointed by Taste of Scotland and listed as "One of Scotland's Best Pubs" recommended by CAMRA in their Good Beer Guide, approved by Les Routier and awarded 3 crowns with Commendation by the Scottish Tourist Board and 3Q's by the AA, it is full of character and offers comfort and ambience throughout including its 5 en-suite bedrooms. Award nominated, home cooked Fresh Country Fayre at sensible prices is served from Breakfast to Supper (including Traditional Scottish High Teas) every day of the year in its own popular Maltings & Cellar Restaurant rooms. The Mash Tun & Wee Still Bars serve a connoisseurs choice of a Rare Range of Scottish Fruit Wines & Real Ales plus a superb selection of Malt Whiskies as well as an amazing array of Beers, Wines & Spirits from all over the world. This charming Inn hosts intimate parties of up to 30 guests for all occasions. The ideal venue for business or pleasure and a superb holiday centre with 130 golf courses and all major cities within driving distance. **Write or Ring for Brochure, Tariff & Details to:**
THE INNKEEPER
49 MUIRS, KINROSS, SCOTLAND. Tel: 01577 862270

KIRKCUDBRIGHT Dumfries & Galloway *Kirkcudbrightshire*
Map 11 NX65

GH ◻◻◻◻ **Gladstone House** 48 High St DG6 4JX
(near Historic Tollbooth)
☎01557 331734 FAX 01557 331734
Situated in the High Street, opposite the historic tolbooth, this
beautifully restored Georgian town house offers just three
bedrooms of an exemplary standard, all with modern en suite
facilities. The spacious lounge runs along the entire width of
the building and offers views of the garden to the rear.
Breakfast is served in the attractively appointed little dining
room.
3 en suite (bth/shr) No smoking CTV in all bedrooms Tea
and coffee making facilities No dogs (ex guide dogs) Cen ht
No children 14yrs No coaches
PRICE GUIDE
ROOMS: s £34-£38; d £54-£58
CARDS: 🔳 🎫   £

KIRKMUIRHILL Strathclyde *Lanarkshire* Map 11 NS74

♥ ◻ Mrs I H McInally *Dykecroft (NS776419)* ML11 0JQ (on
A726, 1.5m towards Strathaven) ☎01555 892226
A bungalow-style farmhouse situated north of the village, beside
the A726, offers good-value bed and breakfast accommodation.
The bedrooms, though small, are smartly decorated and
traditionally furnished, while hearty breakfasts are served at
shared tables in the combined lounge/dining room. Smoking is not
encouraged in the bedrooms.
3 rms No smoking in bedrooms No smoking in dining room Tea
and coffee making facilities Cen ht CTV 4P 60 acres sheep

KYLESKU Highland *Sutherland* Map 14 NC23

GH ◻◻◻◻ **Newton Lodge** IV27 4HW (1.5m S on
A894) ☎01971 502070
Etr-mid Oct
This modern purpose built house enjoys a fantastic location
with the Assynt mountains in the background and panoramic
views of Loch Glencoul. Bedrooms are modern and smartly
furnished with extras such as hairdryers, clock radios and
remote control TVs. The spacious lounge is very comfortable
and has a beamed ceiling and leather furniture. Breakfast and
dinner are served in the dining room with its dark wood
furnishings. Local seafood is a frequent menu choice.
7 en suite (bth/shr) No smoking in bedrooms No smoking in
dining room CTV in all bedrooms Tea and coffee making
facilities Licensed Cen ht CTV No children 13yrs 10P No
coaches Last d 7.30pm
PRICE GUIDE
ROOMS: (incl. dinner) d £49*
CARDS: 🔳 🎫   £

◧ ◻◻◻ **Kylesku Hotel** IV27 4HW
☎01971 502231 FAX 01971 502313
Mar-Oct
This informal Highland inn is situated at the meeting place of
several lochs - the Waters of Kylesku, immortalised in song. The
mountain scenery is breathtaking and boat trips can be organised.
The bedrooms are compact but modern and comfortable. The

dining room serves wholesome fare and specialises in quality
seafood from the West Coast. The atmosphere in the bar is
informal and friendly and it is rightly popular with both tourists
and locals alike.
7 en suite (bth/shr) (1 fmly) No smoking in dining room CTV in
all bedrooms Tea and coffee making facilities Cen ht CTV 20P
Fishing Pool table Last d 9pm
PRICE GUIDE
ROOMS: s £25-£27.50; d £42-£50; wkly b&b £160-£180
MEALS: Lunch £9.95-£20 Dinner £9.95-£20
CARDS: 🔳 🎫   £

LADYBANK Fife Map 11 NO30

GH ◻◻◻ **Redlands Country Lodge** KY15 7SH (off M90 at
Tay Bridge/St Andrews exit for Bow of Fife then in 2m turn
right) ☎01337 831091 FAX 01337 831091
Closed 4wks Feb
This converted gamekeeper's cottage about half a mile to the east
of the village offers accommodation in a Norwegian-style pine
lodge. Well equipped bedrooms each have their own entrance, and
there is a comfortable lounge. The dining room is in the orginal
cottage.
4 en suite (shr) (1 fmly) No smoking in bedrooms No smoking
in dining room CTV in all bedrooms Tea and coffee making
facilities No dogs (ex guide dogs) Licensed Cen ht 6P No
coaches Last d 2pm
PRICE GUIDE
ROOMS: s £21-£28; d £42-£46; wkly b&b £133-£147*   £

LAMLASH See **ARRAN, ISLE OF**

LANGHOLM Dumfries & Galloway *Dumfriesshire*
Map 11 NY38

GH ◻◻ **Langholm Guest House & Restaurant** 81 High St
DG13 0DJ (adjacent to Town Hall)
☎01387 381343 FAX 013873 81343
Friendly, young and enthusiastic owners provide warm,
comfortably furnished accommodation at this small guest house
and restaurant. Situated in the centre of town, it has the advantage
of day-long opening, serving breakfast, morning coffee, snacks,
lunches, afternoon tea and a comprehensive dinner.
4 rms (1 shr) (2 fmly) No smoking in bedrooms No smoking in
area of dining room CTV in all bedrooms Tea and coffee making
facilities Licensed Cen ht 6P Golf 9 Tennis (hard) Last d 9pm
PRICE GUIDE
ROOMS: s £19-£22; d £35-£42; wkly b&b fr £100; wkly hlf-bd
fr £150*
                                                                £

LARGS Strathclyde *Ayrshire* Map 10 NS25

GH ◻◻◻◻ **Lea-Mar** 20 Douglas St KA30 8PS (take
A78, on reaching town turn left at sign for Brisbane
Glen/Inverclyde Sports Centre. Lea-mar 100yds on right)
☎01475 672447
Ron and Margo Muir are constantly improving standards at their
welcoming bungalow home, which is situated in a desirable
residential area just off the main road at the north end of town.
Bedrooms, though limited in size, are smartly decorated and
well furnished in pine. The attractive lounge, with its
comfortable chesterfield seating, invites peaceful relaxation, and
hearty breakfasts are served at individual tables in the separate
dining room. This is a non-smoking establishment.

4 en suite (shr) No smoking CTV in all bedrooms Tea and coffee making facilities No dogs (ex guide dogs) Cen ht CTV No children 12yrs 4P No coaches
PRICE GUIDE
ROOMS: d fr £44

£

LERWICK See **SHETLAND**

LEWIS, ISLE OF Western Isles *Ross & Cromarty* Map 13

BREASCLETE Map 13 NB23

Selected

GH QQQ Whin Park 16 Douglas St KA30 8PS (off A78 at Brisbane Glen sign) ☎01475 673437
Closed Feb
A friendly informal atmosphere pervades this comfortable detached bungalow which is situated in a residential area close to the seafront. Attractively furnished bedrooms which have been comfortably furnished in modern style offer quality en suite facilities as well as all the expected amenities, while the spacious, recently upgraded lounge invites peaceful relaxation. Hearty traditional breakfasts are served at individual lace-clothed tables in an adjacent dining room.
4 en suite (shr) (1 fmly) No smoking in bedrooms No smoking in dining room CTV in all bedrooms Tea and coffee making facilities No dogs (ex guide dogs) 4P No coaches
PRICE GUIDE
ROOMS: s fr £22; d fr £44
CARDS:

£

✔ QQQ Mrs M Watson **South Whittlieburn** *(NS218632)*
Brisbane Glen KA30 8SN (2m NE of Largs town centre off the road signed Brisbane Glen) ☎01475 675881
Some two miles northeast of the town, situated in Brisbane Glen and surrounded by gently rolling countryside, this farm offers an ideal base for the touring holidaymaker. Guests are assured of a warm welcome, and improvements are constantly being made; bedrooms, though limited in size, are made cheerful by the use of attractive fabrics and provide thoughtful extras like toiletries as well as all the expected amenities. There is a comfortable lounge (the only area in the house where smoking is permitted), and hearty breakfasts are served - sometimes at shared tables - in the owners' own lounge, which doubles as a breakfast room.
3 rms (1 bth/shr) (1 fmly) No smoking in bedrooms No smoking in dining room CTV in all bedrooms Tea and coffee making facilities No dogs (ex guide dogs) Cen ht CTV 10P 155 acres sheep
PRICE GUIDE
ROOMS: s fr £18.50; d fr £32✳

£

LATHERON Highland *Caithness* Map 15 ND13

🛏🗵 ✔ QQQ Mrs C B Sinclair **Upper Latheron**
(ND195352) KW5 6DT (2m N of Dunbeath off A9, and 2m S of Latherton) ☎01593 741224
May-Sep
This whitewashed cottage style farmhouse enjoys a panoramic outlook over the north sea from its position off the A9 south of the village. Immaculate bedrooms offer both modern and traditional furnishings and substantial breakfasts are served around the communal table in the comfortable lounge/dining room. Pony trekking available. Guests should note this is a non-smoking establishment.
3 rms (1 fmly) No smoking CTV in 1 bedroom No dogs (ex guide dogs) Cen ht CTV 6P Riding 200 acres Cattle Ponies Sheep Last d 6pm
PRICE GUIDE
ROOMS: s £16-£18; d fr £30

£

Selected

GH QQQQ **Eshcol** HS2 9ED ☎01851 621357
mid Mar-mid Oct
This welcoming modern house is a haven of peace of quiet, beautifully situated on a small croft in a west coast weaving village. Bedrooms, though compact, are tastefully decorated and offer comfortable modern amenities. The attractive lounge overlooking Loch Roag and Harris hills beyond is most inviting and enjoyable home cooking is served at individual tables in the small neat dining room. Smoking is permitted in the sun porch but not in any other part of the house.
3 en suite (bth/shr) No smoking in bedrooms No smoking in dining room No smoking in lounges CTV in all bedrooms Tea and coffee making facilities Cen ht No children 8yrs 5P No coaches Last d 6.30pm
PRICE GUIDE
ROOMS: s £20-£23; d £40-£46; wkly b&b £130-£150; wkly hlf-bd £240-£260

£

SOUTH GALSON Map **13** NB45

Selected

GH ⒬⒬⒬⒬ **Galson Farm** HS2 0SH (Off A857)
☎01851 850492
Situated on the north west coast of the island overlooking the
Atlantic Ocean, enthusiastic owners Dorothy and John Russell
have lovingly restored and extended this former croft house to
create a most comfortable and quite charming base for the
visiting holidaymaker. Bedrooms, though variable in size, are
comfortably modern in style and TV's can be provided on
request. There are two inviting lounges, one with well filled
book shelves, where refreshments are willingly served. All
food is traditionally cooked by Dorothy on her trusty Aga and
her carefully prepared set five course dinners are sure to
satisfy the heartiest of appetites. Evening meals are also
available, with prior arrangement, for non residents. For the
comfort of all, the house has adopted a policy of non smoking.
3 en suite (shr) No smoking CTV in all bedrooms Tea and
coffee making facilities Licensed Cen ht CTV 5P No
coaches Last d 6.30pm
PRICE GUIDE
ROOMS: d £48; wkly b&b £151.20; wkly hlf-bd £258.30✱
CARDS: 🖪 🎟

STORNOWAY Map **13** NB43

GH ⒬⒬⒬ **Ardlonan** 29 Francis St HS1 2NF
☎01851 703482
Closed Xmas & New Year
Good-value bed and breakfast accommodation is offered at this
friendly family-run guest house which stands in a residential area
convenient to central amenities. The non-smoking bedrooms are
variable in size with mixed modern appointments, and there is a
relaxing lounge where delicious home-baking is served. A
separate dining room offers a good choice of breakfast dishes.
5 rms (1 fmly) No smoking in bedrooms No smoking in dining
room No smoking in 1 lounge CTV in 3 bedrooms Tea and
coffee making facilities No dogs Cen ht CTV No coaches
PRICE GUIDE
ROOMS: s fr £20; d £36-£40

⒫

LINLITHGOW Lothian *West Lothian* Map **11** NS97

◨🖭 ♥⒬⒬⒬ Mrs A Hay **Belsyde House** *(NS976755)*
Lanark Rd EH49 6QE (1.5m SW on A706, first left after
crossing Union Canal) ☎01506 842098
Closed Xmas
This large period farmhouse stands in mature gardens at the end of
a long drive off the Lanark road two miles south-west of the town.
It offers attractive accommodation for families and business
travellers, featuring a comfortable lounge and a bright dining room
serving hearty breakfasts at separate tables.
4 rms (1 shr) (1 fmly) No smoking CTV in all bedrooms Tea
and coffee making facilities No dogs (ex guide dogs) Cen ht
CTV 10P 246 acres beef sheep Last d noon
PRICE GUIDE
ROOMS: s fr £16; d fr £32
CARDS: 🖪 🎟 🖫

⒫

♥⒬ Mrs W Erskine **Woodcockdale** *(NS974761)* Lanark Rd
EH49 6QE (on A706) ☎01506 842088
This modern farmhouse has lovely views towards the town of
Linlithgow and the surrounding countryside. There is a large
comfortable lounge with a picture window, while breakfast is

served at one communal table. Bedrooms have some fine pieces of
furniture but do not have en suite facilities.
5 rms (1 shr) (3 fmly) No smoking CTV in all bedrooms Tea
and coffee making facilities Cen ht CTV 12P Fishing 700 acres
dairy sheep cattle
PRICE GUIDE
ROOMS: s fr £18; d fr £32; wkly b&b fr £116✱

⒫

LOANHEAD Lothian *Midlothian* Map **11** NT26

GH ⒬⒬⒬ **Aaron Glen** 7 Nivensknowe Rd EH20 9QQ (on
A768) ☎0131 440 1293 FAX 0131 440 1293
5 en suite (shr) (3 fmly) No smoking in dining room CTV in all
bedrooms Tea and coffee making facilities Direct dial from
bedrooms No dogs Licensed Cen ht CTV 15P Last d 9pm
PRICE GUIDE
ROOMS: s £25-£35; d £35-£50✱
CARDS: 🖪 🎟
See advertisement under Colour Section

LOCHEARNHEAD Central *Perthshire* Map **11** NN52

GH ⒬⒬⒬ **Mansewood Country House Hotel** FK19 8NS
☎01567 830213
Set in its own gardens, this comfortable guest house is located off
the main road. The en suite bathrooms are all well equipped and
some have bright new fabrics and rocking chairs. Other
accommodation includes a relaxing lounge with a log burning
stove and a cosy residents' bar. Evening meals prepared from
fresh local produce are served in the pretty dining room.
6 en suite (bth/shr) No smoking in bedrooms No smoking in
dining room No smoking in lounges CTV in all bedrooms Tea
and coffee making facilities No dogs (ex guide dogs) Licensed
Cen ht No children 15yrs 10P Last d 9pm
PRICE GUIDE
ROOMS: s £25-£29; d £40; wkly b&b fr £140; wkly hlf-bd fr
£238✱
CARDS: 🖪 🖭

LOCHRANZA See **ARRAN, ISLE OF**

LOCHWINNOCH Strathclyde *Renfrewshire* Map **10** NS35

♥⒬⒬ Mrs A Mackie **High Belltrees** *(NS377584)* PA12 4JN
(situated 1m off the A737 to Largs road) ☎01505 842376
Enjoying fine views over the surrounding countryside from its
elevated position, this traditional farmhouse is reached by a
narrow single-track road from the south end of the Howwood
bypass. The bedrooms are spacious and comfortable, and hearty
farmhouse breakfasts are served at shared tables in the combined
lounge/dining room. Mrs Mackie is a welcoming hostess and
many guests return on a regular basis.
4 rms (2 fmly) No smoking in area of dining room CTV in all
bedrooms Tea and coffee making facilities No dogs (ex guide
dogs) Cen ht CTV 6P 220 acres dairy mixed sheep
PRICE GUIDE
ROOMS: s £15-£17; d £30-£32; wkly b&b fr £105✱

⒫

LOCKERBIE Dumfries & Galloway *Dumfriesshire*
Map **11** NY18

GH ⒬⒬⒬ **Rosehill** Carlisle Rd DG11 2DR (south end of
town) ☎01576 202378
Dating from 1871, this sandstone house set in an attractive garden
stands beside the B723 just to the south of the town centre. It
offers pleasant bed and breakfast accommodation and the well
proportioned public rooms include a lounge and separate breakfast
room.

5 rms (2 shr) (2 fmly) CTV in all bedrooms Tea and coffee making facilities Cen ht CTV 5P No coaches
PRICE GUIDE
ROOMS: s £18-£20; d £32-£38

LONGNIDDRY Lothian *East Lothian* Map **12** NT47

GH 🅠 **The Spinney** Old School Ln EH32 0NQ
☎01875 853325
Closed Dec-Jan
3 rms (1 shr) (2 fmly) No smoking in bedrooms No smoking in dining room Tea and coffee making facilities No dogs (ex guide dogs) Cen ht CTV 2P No coaches
PRICE GUIDE
ROOMS: s £16-£17; d £30-£34; wkly b&b £105-£110✳

LUNCARTY Tayside *Perthshire* Map **11** NO02

GH 🅠🅠 *Ordie House* PH1 4PR ☎01738 828471
Two crofts have been converted to form this well-kept guest house. All the rooms are on the ground floor, including a large sun lounge and an attractive breakfast room adorned with a variety of clocks. The friendly owners serve tea and biscuits to guests on arrival.
4 rms (2 shr) No smoking in dining room Tea and coffee making facilities Cen ht CTV 4P No coaches Last d 6pm

MACHRIHANISH Strathclyde *Argyllshire* Map **10** NR62

GH 🅠🅠🅠 **Ardell House** PA28 6PT (opposite golf course)
☎01586 810235
Closed Xmas & New Year rs Nov-Feb
Excellent value bed and breakfast accommodation is offered at this comfortable and welcoming family run guest house which stands in it's own garden overlooking with superb views over the golf course to the islands of Islay and Jura beyond. The variable sized bedrooms offer both modern and traditional furnishings and some rooms are located in a converted stable block to the rear. The attractive first floor lounge boasts an honesty bar and guests simple help themselves to refreshments.
7 rms (1 bth 5 shr) 3 annexe en suite (shr) (1 fmly) No smoking in bedrooms No smoking in dining room CTV in all bedrooms Tea and coffee making facilities Licensed Cen ht 12P No coaches
PRICE GUIDE
ROOMS: s £22-£33; d £40-£52✳

MARKINCH Fife Map **11** NO20

◀ 🅠🅠🅠 **Town House Hotel** 1 High St KY7 6DQ
☎01592 758459 FAX 01592 741238
A former coaching inn situated on the main street close to the station, the Town House is popular for its award-winning bar food, served in the pleasant Provost Restaurant. The bedrooms, which have been attractively refurbished with pine units and floral fabrics, offer some thoughtful extras.
4 rms (3 bth/shr) (1 fmly) No smoking in area of dining room No smoking in 1 lounge CTV in all bedrooms Tea and coffee making facilities Cen ht No parking No coaches Last d 9pm
PRICE GUIDE
ROOMS: s £30-£40; d £40-£50
MEALS: Lunch £7.85-£9.85&alc Dinner £11.95-£18.85&alc
CARDS: 🔳 🔳 🔳 🔳

MELROSE Borders *Roxburghshire* Map **12** NT53

Selected

GH 🅠🅠🅠🅠 **Dunfermline House** Buccleuch St TD6 9LB (opposite Abbey car park)
☎01896 822148 FAX 01896 822148
Attractive and beautifully maintained accommodation is offered by Susan and Ian Graham in their delightful Victorian house. Pine-furnished bedrooms provide extras like hairdryers, biscuits, tissues and toiletries, and the single room has exclusive use of a nearby bathroom; those at the front of the house offer glimpses of the abbey, whilst the rear overlooks a lovely garden which is a mass of colour in the summer. There are a cosy little lounge and a tasteful peach dining room where praiseworthy breakfasts are served. This is a no-smoking house.
5 en suite (shr) No smoking CTV in all bedrooms Tea and coffee making facilities No dogs Cen ht CTV No parking No coaches
PRICE GUIDE
ROOMS: s £21-£22; d £42-£44; wkly b&b £140

Selected

GH 🅠🅠🅠🅠 **Little Fordel** Abbey St TD6 9PX (close to Melrose Abbey) ☎01896 822206
Quietly located but still in the centre of the town, this attractively renovated former school house has the advantage of its own parking facilities. Comfortable accommodation comprises one twin and one huge family room, and breakfast is taken at individual tables in the pleasant lounge.
2 en suite (bth/shr) No smoking CTV in all bedrooms Tea and coffee making facilities No dogs Cen ht CTV 4P No coaches
PRICE GUIDE
ROOMS: d £42-£44✳

MELVICH Highland *Sutherland* Map **14** NC86

GH 🅠🅠🅠 **Tigh-na-Clash** Tigh-na-Clash KW14 7YJ (on A836 opposite the Croft Inn)
☎01641 531262 FAX 01641 531262
Mar-Sep
Good value bed and breakfast accommodation is offered at this comfortable detached modern house situated at the east end of the village. The variable sized non smoking bedrooms are furnished in both modern and traditional styles. Hearty breakfasts are served at shared tables in the owner's personal lounge; another small lounge being available for guests. Other meals are offered in the small inn opposite the house, which is owned and run by the same family. This is an ideal base from which to explore the north coast and Orkney.
8 rms (4 shr) No smoking in bedrooms No smoking in dining room CTV in all bedrooms Tea and coffee making facilities No dogs (ex guide dogs) Licensed Cen ht No children 8yrs 8P No coaches Last d 8pm
PRICE GUIDE
ROOMS: s £17-£21; d £34-£42; wkly b&b £112-£140✳
CARDS: 🔳 🔳

MOFFAT Dumfries & Galloway *Dumfriesshire* Map **11** NT00

See also Beattock

GH Q Q **Barnhill Springs Country** DG10 9QS (0.5m E of A74) ☎01683 220580
Standing in its own grounds with fine views of the Annan valley, this early Victorian house is accessible from the southbound carriageway of the A74 immediately to the south of the junction for Moffat. It offers comfortable accommodation, a friendly atmosphere, and dinner by prior arrangement.
5 rms (1 shr) (1 fmly) No smoking in dining room Tea and coffee making facilities Licensed Cen ht CTV 10P No coaches Last d 9am
PRICE GUIDE
ROOMS: s £19-£20; d £38-£40; wkly b&b £133-£140; wkly hlf-bd £217-£224

£

GH Q Q Q **Boleskine** 4 Well Rd DG10 9AS ☎01683 220601
This large Victorian house stands in a side street close to the centre of the town, with easy car parking. The friendly owners Andy and Sheila Armstrong have refurbished the house to high standard, while retaining the character of the house. All rooms are immaculate and offer good facilities. Home-cooked meals and hearty breakfasts are served in the dining room/lounge.
4 rms (2 shr) No smoking in dining room No smoking in lounges CTV in all bedrooms Tea and coffee making facilities Cen ht 2P No coaches Last d 6pm
PRICE GUIDE
ROOMS: s £15-£17.50; d £30-£35; wkly b&b £90-£105; wkly hlf-bd £146-£161✱

Selected

[🛏 💺] **GH** Q Q Q Q **Gilbert House** Beechgrove DG10 9RS (from A74 go through town & turn right after school, for 3rd house on left) ☎01683 220050
This large white stone Victorian house is situated in its own gardens, in a quiet residential area within walking distance of the town centre. Bedrooms, including two family rooms, are spacious and are individually appointed. The comfortable lounge has inviting armchairs, a range of books and a TV. Home-cooked evening meals are served in the dining room.
6 rms (4 shr) (2 fmly) No smoking in dining room No smoking in lounges Tea and coffee making facilities Licensed Cen ht CTV 6P No coaches Last d 5pm
PRICE GUIDE
ROOMS: s £16-£18; d £32-£38; wkly b&b £101-£114; wkly hlf-bd £167-£184
CARDS: 🟦 🔲

GH Q Q **St Olaf** Eastgate, Off Dickson St DG10 9AE ☎01683 220001
Apr-Oct
This comfortable guest house which stands in a quiet side road off the High Street provides accommodation in brightly decorated bedrooms with central heating and tea-making facilities. The guests' lounge on the first floor offers television, and the downstairs dining room is attractively appointed. There is a lock up garage as well as street parking facilities.
7 rms (2 shr) (1 fmly) No smoking in dining room No smoking in lounges Tea and coffee making facilities Cen ht CTV 8P No coaches
PRICE GUIDE
ROOMS: s £18; d £31-£33; wkly b&b fr £108.50

£

MONTROSE Tayside *Angus* Map **15** NO75

GH Q Q Q **Murray Lodge** 2-8 Murray St DD10 8LB ☎01674 678880 FAX 01674 678877
Renovated from an 18th-century linen mill, situated to the north of the town centre, this modern guest house has comfortable and well equipped bedrooms, all of which are smartly furnished. There is a comfortable lounge with some interesting features, including model rockets, a dolls' house and an attractive fireplace. The popular dining room is licensed for residents and serves meals all day.
12 en suite (shr) No smoking in 9 bedrooms No smoking in dining room Tea and coffee making facilities Direct dial from bedrooms No dogs (ex guide dogs) Licensed Cen ht CTV 2P No coaches Last d 6.30pm
PRICE GUIDE
ROOMS: s £22-£45; d £40-£55✱
CARDS: 🟦 🔲

£

GH Q Q Q **Oaklands** 10 Rossie Island Rd DD10 9NN (on A92) ☎01674 672018 FAX 01674 672018
A well kept guest house on the south side of town, just over the bridge, Oaklands offers bedrooms in both the original building and an extension - their sizes varying according to location. There is a bright lounge for guests' use, and breakfast is served at three tables in the dining room.
7 en suite (shr) (1 fmly) No smoking in dining room CTV in all bedrooms Tea and coffee making facilities Cen ht CTV ch fac 8P No coaches
PRICE GUIDE
ROOMS: s fr £18; d fr £33
CARDS: 🟦 🔲

£

MULL, ISLE OF Strathclyde *Argyllshire* Map **10**

DERVAIG Map **13** NM45

GH Q Q **Ardbeg House** PA75 6QT ☎01688 4254
Situated on the main street at the edge of the village, this large white country house is surrounded by its own gardens. Bedrooms and public areas are filled with collectables such as old film posters and plates. Some rooms have four-poster beds, there are two bars and meals are served in the conservatory dining room.
7 rms (3 bth/shr) (1 fmly) No smoking in 1 bedrooms No smoking in dining room Tea and coffee making facilities Licensed Cen ht 12P Fishing Last d 6pm

TOBERMORY Map **13** NM55

Selected

GH Q Q Q Q **Fairways Lodge** PA75 6PS (in Tobermory Follow signposts for golf course) ☎01688 302238 FAX 01688 302238
A purpose-built guest house is situated high above the village of Tobermory looking out over the golf course and the bay. The modern bedrooms have bright co-ordinating fabrics and offer good facilities for the tourist and the business guest. Guests have use of a cosy sun lounge with spectacular views and the owners' gallery lounge. Well cooked breakfasts are available; for dinner guests are encouraged to dine at Strongarbh House which is owned by the same family.
5 en suite (bth/shr) (1 fmly) No smoking in dining room CTV in all bedrooms Tea and coffee making facilities Cen ht CTV 8P No coaches Golf 9
PRICE GUIDE
ROOMS: s £26.50-£31; d £53-£62; wkly b&b £192.50

£

Premier Selected

GH Q Q Q Q Q
Strongarbh House PA75 6PR
☎01688 302328
FAX 01688 302238

This restored Victorian house is located at the top of a steep hill in the upper town overlooking Tobermory Bay. Comfortably furnished bedrooms overlook the Bay or the mature gardens surrounding the house. The hosts are friendly and the elegant restaurant offers fine meals produced using prime local produce, especially seafood.

4 en suite (bth/shr) CTV in all bedrooms Tea and coffee making facilities Licensed Cen ht 7P No coaches Last d 9.45pm

PRICE GUIDE
ROOMS: d £66-£75; wkly hlf-bd £331-£359✱
CARDS: ⬛ ⬛

NAIRN Highland *Nairnshire* Map 14 NH85

Selected

GH Q Q Q Q **Greenlawns** 13 Seafield St IV12 4HG
☎01667 452738

Isabel Caldwell extends a warm welcome at her attractive detached Victorian home which is situated in a west end residential area convenient to the seafront recreational amenities. The well maintained bedrooms offer both modern and traditional furnishings. There is an attractive quiet lounge on the first floor appropriately furnished in period style and substantial breakfasts are served at individual tables in the spacious dining room. Also available is a gallery lounge featuring the work of local artists.

6 rms (4 bth/shr) CTV in all bedrooms Tea and coffee making facilities Cen ht CTV 8P

PRICE GUIDE
ROOMS: s £20-£28; d £34-£50
CARDS: ⬛ ⬛

◀ Q Q Q **Covenanters** High St, Auldearn IV12 5TG (1m E on A96) ☎01667 452456 FAX 01667 453583

This family run village inn was created by the conversion of a former mill and brewhouse dating back to 1645. Bedrooms vary in size but all are prettily decorated, with modern dark wood furnishings. The bar, with its whitewashed walls, beamed ceiling and log burning stove, has a cosy, country atmosphere, and there is a small dining area at one end. Fresh local seafood and game feature extensively on the menu. Guests also have use of a sun lounge.

8 en suite (bth/shr) (2 fmly) No smoking in dining room No smoking in 1 lounge CTV in all bedrooms Tea and coffee making facilities Direct dial from bedrooms Cen ht ch fac 40P Snooker Last d 9pm

PRICE GUIDE
ROOMS: s £35-£48; d £45-£65✱
CARDS: ⬛ ⬛ ⬛

Selected

GH Q Q Q Q **Aultmore House** PH25 3ED (turn right 0.5m N of Nethybridge, off the B970 and then 1st left)
☎01479 821473 FAX 01479 821709
Etr-Oct rs 26 Dec-5 Jan

Built in 1914, this impressive manor house enjoys fine views of the Cairngorms from a setting in 25 acres of secluded, wooded and landscaped grounds about one mile northeast of the village. Charming day rooms include a comfortable lounge with an adjacent sun lounge overlooking the garden, a drawing room with grand piano, a billiard room and a further quiet lounge on the first floor. Hearty home cooking is served at a communal table in the attractive dining room. The atmosphere is that of a private country house rather than a hotel, making this a relaxing base from which to explore the Spey Valley.

3 en suite (bth) No smoking in bedrooms No smoking in dining room No smoking in 1 lounge Tea and coffee making facilities Cen ht No children 12yrs 23P No coaches Fishing Snooker Croquet Last d 11.30pm

PRICE GUIDE
ROOMS: d £37-£50; wkly b&b £111-£150; wkly hlf-bd £170.50-£209.50✱
CARDS: ⬛ ⬛

NEWTONMORE Highland *Inverness-shire* Map 14 NN79

GH Q Q Q **Glenquoich House** Glen Rd PH20 1EB
☎01540 673461 FAX 01540 673461

Christine Watson's comfortable detached house, set in its own garden in a quiet residential area off the main street, offers good-value bed and breakfast accommodation. Bedrooms, some of them quite spacious, are modern in style. Public areas include a relaxing lounge warmed by an open fire and a separate dining room where hearty breakfasts are served at shared tables.

5 rms (1 shr) (1 fmly) No smoking in 1 bedrooms No smoking in dining room CTV in 4 bedrooms Tea and coffee making facilities No dogs Cen ht CTV No children 4yrs 5P No coaches

PRICE GUIDE
ROOMS: s £15-£16; d £32-£34✱

NEWTON STEWART Dumfries & Galloway *Kirkcudbrightshire* Map 10 NX46

◀ Q Q **Stewart Hotel** 62-66 Queen St DG8 6JL
☎01671 402054

4 rms (1 bth/shr) (1 fmly) No smoking in area of dining room CTV in 2 bedrooms Tea and coffee making facilities No dogs (ex guide dogs) Cen ht 8P Last d 9.30pm

PRICE GUIDE
ROOMS: s £17.50-£22.50; d £30-£50; wkly b&b £105-£122.50✱
MEALS: Lunch fr £1.40&alc Dinner £1.40-£13.25✱
CARDS: ⬛ ⬛ ⬛

NORTH BERWICK Lothian *East Lothian* Map 12 NT58

GH Q Q **Craigview** 5 Beach Rd EH39 4AB ☎01620 892257
A white 1920s house stands in the centre of North Beswick with views across the West Bay and the harbour. The rooms feature pretty fabrics and good facilities; one has a four-poster bed and overlooks the seafront. Breakfast is served in the combined lounge/dining room and includes a number of vegetarian choices.

3 rms (1 shr) No smoking CTV in all bedrooms No dogs Cen ht No coaches
PRICE GUIDE
ROOMS: s £16-£25; d £32-£40✱

OBAN Strathclyde *Argyllshire* Map **10** NM83

GH Q Q Q **Ardblair** Dalriach Rd PA34 5JB ☎01631 562668
May-Sep rs Etr
This friendly family-run establishment stands on the hill above the town, close to the bowling green and swimming pool. Bedrooms vary in size and offer modern and traditional appointments. There is a sun lounge with fine views over the bay to the Isle of Mull, and a smaller lounge next to the pleasant dining room.
14 rms (13 bth/shr) (4 fmly) No smoking in bedrooms No smoking in dining room CTV in all bedrooms Tea and coffee making facilities No dogs Cen ht 10P Last d 5.30pm
PRICE GUIDE
ROOMS: s £19-£21; d £38-£42; wkly b&b £136-£147; wkly hlf-bd £185-£200✱

£

GH Q Q Q **Briarbank** Glencruitten Rd PA34 4DN
☎01631 566549
Situated in a residential area close to the town centre, this traditional detatched house has a relaxed friendly atmosphere and offers comfortable accommodation of various sizes and styles. Public areas include a small cosy lounge and a conservatory style dining room where hearty breakfasts and evening meals are served.
4 rms (2 shr) CTV in all bedrooms Tea and coffee making facilities No dogs (ex guide dogs) Cen ht CTV No children 12yrs 3P No coaches Last d 4pm

£

Selected

GH Q Q Q Q **Drumriggend** Drummore Rd PA34 4JL
☎01631 563330
Good-value tourist accommodation is offered at this smartly furnished family-run guesthouse, in compact but tastefully decorated bedrooms. Public areas include a bright lounge and a neat dining room where enjoyable home cooking is served.
3 en suite (bth/shr) (1 fmly) No smoking in dining room CTV in all bedrooms Tea and coffee making facilities Cen ht CTV 6P No coaches
PRICE GUIDE
ROOMS: d £32-£38

£

[symbols] **GH** Q Q Q **Glenbervie House** Dalriach Rd
☎01631 564770 FAX 01631 566723
Excellent value five and seven day breaks are available at Iain and Joan Auld's comfortable house opposite the bowling green and swimming pool. Variably sized bedrooms are bright and airy with a mix of modern and traditional appointments. Beautiful views can be enjoyed from the spacious first floor lounge and in the attractive dining room Joan's home cooking attracts praise.
8 rms (4 shr) (2 fmly) No smoking in dining room CTV in all bedrooms Tea and coffee making facilities No dogs (ex guide dogs) Licensed Cen ht CTV 8P No coaches Last d 4pm
PRICE GUIDE
ROOMS: s £16-£20; d £32-£40; wkly b&b £110-£130; wkly hlf-bd £168-£188

GH Q Q Q **Glenburnie Private Hotel** The Esplanade
PA34 5AQ ☎01631 562089
Apr-Oct
Ongoing improvements are taking place at a comfortable family-run guest house which enjoys a splendid outlook over the bay from its position on the esplanade. The bedrooms have mixed appointments but are scheduled for upgrading; four superior rooms are already of a high standard, including one with a four-poster bed. The refurbished breakfast room is bright and features Laura Ashley designs, while an inviting non-smoking lounge has been created on the ground floor.
17 rms (12 shr) (2 fmly) CTV in all bedrooms Tea and coffee making facilities No dogs (ex guide dogs) Cen ht No children 4yrs 12P No coaches
CARDS: [symbols]

GH Q Q Q **Glenrigh** Esplanade PA34 5AQ ☎01631 562991
Mar-Oct
Immaculate and well maintained throughout, this substantial semidetached Victorian villa sits on the Esplanade and looks out across the bay to the Isle of Mull. Bedrooms of various sizes are all brightly decorated. There is a lounge and a cheerful breakfast room where guests might be asked to share a table.
14 en suite (shr) (6 fmly) No smoking in dining room CTV in all bedrooms Tea and coffee making facilities Cen ht 20P No coaches
PRICE GUIDE
ROOMS: s £20-£25; d £40-£50✱
CARDS: [symbols]

£

GH Q Q **Glenroy** Rockfield Rd PA34 5DQ ☎01631 562585
The Glenroy is a family-run semidetached Victorian villa set on a hillside above the town with views over the bay. It offers good value bed and breakfast accommodation in well decorated bedrooms. A relaxing lounge and a separate breakfast room are provided.
7 rms (5 shr) No smoking in dining room CTV in all bedrooms Tea and coffee making facilities No dogs (ex guide dogs) Cen ht CTV 7P No coaches
PRICE GUIDE
ROOMS: s £16; d £30-£35✱
CARDS: [symbols]

£

Selected

GH Q Q Q Q **Rhumor** Drummore Rd PA34 4JL
☎01631 563544
Closed Dec
This traditionally friendly Highland bungalow stands in its own well tended garden in a residential cul-de-sac off the A816 to the south of town. Compact bedrooms feature attractive fabrics which complement the tasteful decor and modern furnishings. Public areas include a relaxing lounge and a small, neat dining room where hearty breakfasts are served around a communal table. This is a non-smoking establishment.
3 en suite (bth/shr) No smoking in bedrooms CTV in all bedrooms Tea and coffee making facilities Cen ht CTV 4P
PRICE GUIDE
ROOMS: d £32-£36; wkly b&b £112

£

GH Q Q Q **Roseneath** Dalriach Rd PA34 5EQ (turn left off A85 beyond Kings Knoll Hotel and follow signs for Maternity Hospital) ☎01631 562929
Closed 24-26 Dec
This friendly family-run guest house stands in a residential area on the hill above town. It has now undergone significant improvement: bedrooms, though compact, have been refurbished and are bright and cheery, with attractive decor and mixed furnishings. Public areas include a comfortable lounge on the first floor and a more homely ground-floor dining room where table sharing may be necessary at peak times.
10 rms (5 shr) No smoking CTV in 8 bedrooms Tea and coffee making facilities No dogs (ex guide dogs) Cen ht CTV 8P No coaches
PRICE GUIDE
ROOMS: s £15-£18; d £30-£40*

GH Q Q Q *Sgeir Mhaol* Soroba Rd PA34 4JF (on A816) ☎01631 562650
This and well maintained bungalow lies on the southern side of the town. It has a cosy little lounge and an attractive dining room, and while the bedrooms are compact, they are bright and airy.
7 rms (5 shr) (3 fmly) No smoking in dining room CTV in all bedrooms Tea and coffee making facilities No dogs (ex guide dogs) Cen ht CTV 10P No coaches Last d 4pm
PRICE GUIDE
ROOMS: s £16-£24; d £32-£42*

GH Q Q Q **Thornloe** Albert Rd PA34 5JD (from A85, turn left at King's Knoll Hotel and pass swimming pool, last house on right hand side) ☎01631 562879
A house of character, Thornloe has been tastefully refurbished to highlight its period features, with the liberal use of attractive fabrics and objets d'art. Bedrooms vary in size and two have four-poster beds. There is a cosy guests' lounge and attractive dining room. Parking may prove difficult.
8 en suite (shr) (2 fmly) No smoking in 4 bedrooms No smoking in dining room No smoking in lounges CTV in all bedrooms Tea and coffee making facilities No dogs (ex guide dogs) Cen ht CTV 5P
PRICE GUIDE
ROOMS: s £15-£21; d £34-£42; wkly b&b £105-£147*

GH Q Q Q *Verulam* Drummore Rd PA34 4JL ☎01631 566115
Mar-Oct
Good value bed and breakfast accommodation is offered at this friendly family run establishment, a detached bungalow situated in a residential cu-de-sac at the south end of town. The compact bedrooms are bright and cheerful with attractive decor and modern furnishings while public areas include a comfortable lounge and hearty breakfasts are served at individual tables in the recently created dining room.
2 en suite (shr) CTV in all bedrooms Tea and coffee making facilities Cen ht CTV 3P

GH Q Q Q **Wellpark Hotel** Esplanade PA34 5AQ ☎01631 562948 FAX 01631 565808
May-Oct rs Etr
This sturdy semidetached Victorian house enjoys fine views over the bay and offers a friendly atmosphere together with good value holiday accommodation. Bedrooms are mostly well proportioned and smartly decorated with modern furnishings and a good range of amenities such as telephones. Public rooms include a pleasant first-floor lounge overlooking the bay and a separate breakfast room. ➡

17 en suite (shr) No smoking in 8 bedrooms No smoking in dining room No smoking in lounges CTV in all bedrooms Tea and coffee making facilities Direct dial from bedrooms Cen ht 12P No coaches
PRICE GUIDE
ROOMS: s £25.50-£29.50; d £40-£59✻
CARDS: 🔳 🔤 🔳 💲

ONICH Highland *Inverness-shire* Map **14** NN06

GH 🔘🔘🔘 **Cuilcheanna House Hotel** PH33 6SD
☎01855 821226
Apr-Oct
This friendly family-run country house stands in its own well maintained grounds off the A82, close to the shore of Loch Linnhe at the north end of the village. The pleasantly decorated bedrooms are comfortably furnished in traditional style, and public areas include a cosy lounge, an attractive dining room and a modern lounge bar (open to residents) which serves bar food.
7 en suite (bth/shr) No smoking Tea and coffee making facilities Licensed Cen ht CTV No children 10yrs 10P No coaches Last d 5.30pm
PRICE GUIDE
ROOMS: d £69-£75; wkly b&b £147; wkly hlf-bd £241.50
CARDS: 🔳 🔤 🔳

GH 🔘🔘 *Tigh-A-Righ* PH33 6SE ☎01855 821255
Closed 22 Dec-7 Jan
This personally run licensed guest house is situated beside the A82 Fort William road at the north end of the village, and offers genuine Highland hospitality. Compact bedrooms have mixed modern appointments and are bright and cheery. Public areas include a split-level lounge (the lower level non-smoking) and an adjacent dining room offering enjoyable home-cooking to guests and non-residents.
6 rms (1 bth 1 shr) (3 fmly) Tea and coffee making facilities Licensed Cen ht CTV 15P No coaches Last d 9pm

---

ORKNEY

ORPHIR Map **16** HY30

GH 🔘🔘🔘 **Westrow Lodge** On A964 KW17 2RD
☎01856 811360
American owner Kathy Tait has recently taken over this modern purpose-built timber house which stands in its own grounds beside the A964 mid way between Kirkwall and Stromness, and enjoys uninterrupted views over Scappa Flow. At the time of our visit Kathy was busy making the final arrangements for the arrival of her furniture from America. Two of the pine-clad bedrooms are en suite and one can be let in conjunction with a separate room which has no facilities, for family use. Glorious views over Scappa can be enjoyed from the attractive first-floor lounge.
2 en suite (bth/shr) No smoking Tea and coffee making facilities No dogs Cen ht CTV 6P No coaches
PRICE GUIDE
ROOMS: s £18-£20; d £36-£40; wkly b&b £126-£140✻

PEEBLES Borders *Peebleshire* Map **11** NT24

GH 🔘🔘 **Whitestone House** Innerleithen Rd EH45 8BD (on A72, 100yds W of junct with A703) ☎01721 720337
Standing in its own garden on the eastern approach to the town, and enjoying fine views of the hills, this stone-built former manse offers good bed and breakfast accommodation in a friendly atmosphere. The comfortable bedrooms are mostly in traditional style, and hearty breakfasts are served in the lounge/breakfast room.

---

3 rms (1 fmly) No smoking in dining room Tea and coffee making facilities No dogs (ex guide dogs) Cen ht CTV 5P No coaches
PRICE GUIDE
ROOMS: d £30✻

Selected

♥ 🔘🔘🔘🔘 Mrs S Goldstraw **Venlaw Farm** *(NT254416)* EH45 8QG ☎01721 722040
Apr-Oct
A single track off the main Edinburgh road leads to this modern farm bungalow set on a secluded hillside. Bedrooms are traditionally furnished in farmhouse style, and thoughtfully equipped with clock radios and hair dryers. Two double rooms have smart modern en suite bathrooms, while the twin room has sole use of a bath and shower room. The attractive lounge with its coal fire and ticking clocks is a relaxing place, and breakfast is taken communally round a circular table in a separate room.
3 rms (2 bth/shr) (1 fmly) No smoking Tea and coffee making facilities No dogs Cen ht CTV 7P 100 acres beef sheep
PRICE GUIDE
ROOMS: s £20; d £35; wkly b&b £122.50✻
CARDS: 🔳 ■ 🔤

♥ 🔘🔘🔘 Mrs J M Haydock **Winkston** *(NT244433)* Edinburgh Rd EH45 8PH ☎01721 721264
Etr-Oct
This interesting Georgian farm house is set in attractive gardens off the Edinburgh road one and a half miles north of the town. The family bedroom has a modern en suite shower room, whilst the other two bedrooms share a shower room. Downstairs there is comfortable lounge and a neat little dining where home-cooked breakfasts are served. Packed lunches are available and one can buy home-made preserves and baking.
3 rms No smoking in bedrooms No smoking in dining room Tea and coffee making facilities No dogs (ex guide dogs) Cen ht CTV 4P 40 acres sheep

---

PERTH Tayside *Perthshire* Map **11** NO12

See also Luncarty

GH 🔘🔘🔘 **Alpine** 7 Strathview Ter PH2 7HY (on A94, opposite Doo'Cote Park Cricket Ground) ☎01738 637687
A family-run guest house overlooks the cricket ground on the northern edge of the city and offers good value bed and breakfast accommodation. Most of the bedrooms are spacious and all have TVs; there is no lounge. Evening meals are served in an attractive dining room and ample car parking is available.
5 rms (4 shr) (1 fmly) No smoking in dining room No smoking in lounges CTV in 4 bedrooms Tea and coffee making facilities No dogs Cen ht 8P No coaches Last d 7pm
PRICE GUIDE
ROOMS: s £16-£18; d £35-£40; wkly b&b £119-£133; wkly hlf-bd £175-£189✻

Entries in this Guide are based on reports filed by our team of professionally trained, full-time inspectors.

GH 🇶🇶🇶🇶 *Ardfern House* 15 Pitcullen Crescent PH2 7HT ☎01738 637031
This fine Victorian house offers well proportioned bedrooms with extra touches including fresh fruit, flowers and magazines. Two of the single rooms have four foot wide beds. Standards of housekeeping and maintenance are high, and guests are welcome to use the owners' elegant lounge. There is a small nine-hole putting green on the rear lawn of the immaculate garden.
2 rms (1 shr) (1 fmly) No smoking CTV in all bedrooms Tea and coffee making facilities No dogs (ex guide dogs) Cen ht CTV 3P No coaches

GH 🇶🇶🇶 *Castleview* 166 Glasgow Rd PH2 0LY ☎01738 626415
Closed 25th Dec - Feb
Appealing to holiday-makers and business guests alike, this substantial Victorian house is conveniently situated midway between the bypass and the town centre. Bedrooms, though small, are bright and cheerful, with comfortable modern furnishings. Both breakfast and dinner are served at a communal table in the elegant combined lounge/dining room.
3 en suite (bth/shr) (1 fmly) No smoking in 2 bedrooms No smoking in dining room No smoking in lounges CTV in all bedrooms Tea and coffee making facilities No dogs (ex guide dogs) Cen ht 6P No coaches Sauna Solarium Last d 5pm
PRICE GUIDE
ROOMS: s £23-£25; d £36-£38✻

GH 🇶🇶🇶 *Clark Kimberley* 57-59 Dunkeld Rd PH1 5RP (0.5m N on A912) ☎01738 637406 FAX 01738 643983
Situated on the northern side of town, on the main road to Inverness, this friendly guest house has been converted from two adjacent houses with ample parking at the front and rear. Public areas comprise a large lounge and a split dining room. The enthusiastic owners are steadily improving the comfortable bedrooms, and are on hand to provide guests with all the local information they require.
8 rms (6 shr) (4 fmly) No smoking CTV in all bedrooms Tea and coffee making facilities No dogs Cen ht CTV 10P No coaches
PRICE GUIDE
ROOMS: s £17-£19; d £34-£38; wkly b&b £112-£133✻
CARDS: 🔳 🔳

GH 🇶🇶🇶 *Clunie* 12 Pitcullen Crescent PH2 7HT (on A94 opposite side of river from town) ☎01738 623625
A relaxed and friendly atmosphere prevails at this stone-built Victorian house which stands on the A94 on the northern outskirts of the town. Bedrooms, though variable in size, are comfortably modern in style and have a good range of amenities. Public areas include a lounge and a small timber-clad dining room where enjoyable home-cooked meals are served and where it may, on occasions, be necessary to share a table.
7 en suite (bth/shr) (3 fmly) No smoking in dining room CTV in all bedrooms Tea and coffee making facilities Cen ht CTV 8P No coaches Last d noon
PRICE GUIDE
ROOMS: s fr £18; d fr £36✻
CARDS: 🔳 🔳

GH 🇶🇶 *The Gables* 24 Dunkeld Rd PH1 5RW (take A912 towards Perth guesthouse approx one and a half miles on right just beyond 3rd rdbt) ☎01738 624717
This friendly, well kept guest house is close to the junction of the Inverness and Crieff roads on the north side of town. Marjorie

Tucker creates a home from home atmosphere serving up home baking, high teas and tasty hot snacks. There is a small residents' bar in the dining room, while the comfortable lounge has a wide selection of tourist information and board games.
7 rms (5 bth/shr) (2 fmly) No smoking in bedrooms No smoking in dining room CTV in all bedrooms Tea and coffee making facilities Licensed Cen ht CTV 7P No coaches Last d midday
CARDS: 🔳 🔳

🛏 🛆 **GH** 🇶🇶 *The Heidl* 43 York Place PH2 8EH ☎01738 635031
Good-value bed and breakfast accommodation is provided at this family-run commercial and tourist guest house which is situated on the Glasgow road within easy reach of central amenities. Bedrooms are practically furnished and tend to be small, but a hearty breakfast is served in the smart dining room.
10 rms (1 shr) (2 fmly) No smoking in dining room CTV in all bedrooms Tea and coffee making facilities Cen ht 3P
PRICE GUIDE
ROOMS: s £14-£17; d £26-£32
£

GH 🇶🇶🇶 *Iona* 2 Pitcullen Crescent PH2 7HT (approx 300yds along A94 from junct A94/A93) ☎01738 627261
Popular with tourists and business guests alike, this friendly family-run guest house is located on the north side of town beside the A94. The bedrooms - all of which are non-smoking - vary in size and offer comfortable modern appointments, while public areas include a cosy lounge and an attractive dining room with individual tables.
➡

Alpine Guest House
7 Strathview Terrace, Perth PH2 7HY
Telephone: 01738 637687

Our Victorian Guest House, situated on the edge of Perth, yet within a 15 mins walk of the city centre, enjoys spectacular views of Little Glenshee and the surrounding mountains. Good sporting and leisure facilities are locally available as are shopping, theatre, cinema and restaurants.

There is ample private parking ar rear and lawned gardens for your relaxation. Pay phone available.

5 rms (2 shr) (1 fmly) No smoking in bedrooms No smoking in dining room CTV in all bedrooms Tea and coffee making facilities Cen ht CTV 5P No coaches Last d 4.30pm
PRICE GUIDE
ROOMS: s fr £17; d £32-£36; wkly b&b £100-£130; wkly hlf-bd £150-£180✱
CARDS:

G**II** Ⓠ Ⓠ Ⓠ Ⓠ *Kinnaird* 5 Marshall Place PH2 8AH
☎01738 628021 FAX 01738 444056
This friendly family-run guest house, overlooking South Inch Park, has undergone complete refurbishment to offer attractive and good value accommodation. Bedrooms, though compact, are individually styled with pretty floral fabrics and tartans being put to good use, and all have smartly tiled shower-rooms. There is a comfortable first floor lounge and an unusual collection of china pigs and teapots are a feature in the elegant dining room. The proprietors Mr and Mrs Stiell are always on hand to provide information about the local area and beyond.
7 en suite (bth/shr) No smoking in dining room CTV in all bedrooms Tea and coffee making facilities No dogs (ex guide dogs) Cen ht No children 12yrs 7P No coaches Last d 4pm
CARDS: ◪ ▭

GH Ⓠ Ⓠ Ⓠ **Park Lane** 17 Marshall Place PH2 8AG (enter town on A912 and turn left at first set of lights, on right hand side opposite park) ☎01738 637218 FAX 01738 643519
Closed 10 Dec-20 Jan
Part of a Georgian terrace, this guesthouse looks out on to South Inch Park and is within walking distance of the town centre. Bedrooms are individually decorated and several are spacious, including a fine family room. There is a period lounge where breakfast is also taken.
6 en suite (bth/shr) (1 fmly) No smoking in 3 bedrooms No smoking in dining room No smoking in lounges CTV in all bedrooms Tea and coffee making facilities No dogs (ex guide dogs) Cen ht CTV 8P
PRICE GUIDE
ROOMS: s £19-£22; d £38-£44; wkly b&b £130-£140
CARDS: ◪ ▭

GH Ⓠ Ⓠ Ⓠ *Pitcullen* 17 Pitcullen Crescent PH2 7HT (on A94)
☎01738 626506 FAX 01738 628265
This well maintained guest house, a semi detatched villa, is situated on the north side of town and offers good value bed and breakfast accommodation. Bedrooms differ in size with mixed moder appointments, while public areas include a relaxing lounge and a small neat dining room.
6 rms (3 shr) (1 fmly) No smoking in 2 bedrooms No smoking in dining room CTV in all bedrooms Tea and coffee making facilities No dogs Cen ht 6P No coaches Last d 6pm
CARDS: ◪ ▭

GH Ⓠ Ⓠ Ⓠ **Strathcona** 45 Dunkeld Rd PH1 5RP
☎01738 626701 & 628773 FAX 01738 628773
This terraced house conveniently situated on the main road to Inverness, on the north side of the town, offers spacious and well kept accommodation. Bedrooms include a large family room and an attractively furnished double, while breakfast is served in a combined lounge and dining room.

---

3 rms (2 shr) (1 fmly) No smoking in dining room No smoking in lounges CTV in all bedrooms Tea and coffee making facilities No dogs (ex guide dogs) Cen ht No children 3yrs 3P
PRICE GUIDE
ROOMS: s £18-£25; d £36; wkly b&b £114-£120✱
CARDS: ◪ ▭

PITLOCHRY Tayside *Perthshire* Map 14 NN95

[🛌 ♥] GH Ⓠ Ⓠ Ⓠ **Arrandale House** Knockfarrie Rd PH16 5DN ☎01796 472987
Nov-Mar
This friendly, family-run guest house was originally a manse and so has a lofty, spacious feel. It is located in a quiet lane off the main road on the south side of the town, and enjoys fine view across the valley from its elevated position. Comfortable seating is provided in all bedrooms, including the two large family rooms. Ample car parking is provided and smoking is not permitted.
6 rms (4 shr) (2 fmly) No smoking CTV in all bedrooms Tea and coffee making facilities No dogs Cen ht 9P No coaches
PRICE GUIDE
ROOMS: s £15-£19.95; d £30-£39.90; wkly b&b £100-£129

GH Ⓠ Ⓠ Ⓠ **Comar House** Strathview Ter PH16 5AT ☎01796 473531 FAX 01796 473811
Etr-Oct
This imposing stone house with one of the highest vantage points in the town enjoys spectacular views across the valley. Bedrooms are brightly decorated, and the spacious turreted double room is particularly sought after. There is a tasteful lounge with a large bay window and a dining room with well-spaced tables.
6 rms (1 bth 2 shr) No smoking CTV in all bedrooms Tea and coffee making facilities Cen ht CTV 6P
PRICE GUIDE
ROOMS: s £16-£19; d £32-£42; wkly b&b £96-£126✱
CARDS: ◪ ▭

GH Ⓠ Ⓠ Ⓠ Ⓠ **Craigroyston House** 2 Lower Oakfield PH16 5HQ (in town centre just above Information Centre car park) ☎01796 472053
Guests return year after year to this central yet quietly located Victorian House, the character of which has been retained and enhanced by enthusiastic owners, Gretta and Douglas Maxwell. Bedrooms are mostly spacious and furnished with period pieces and co-ordinating Laura Ashley fabrics and wall-coverings. The recently redecorated lounge offers lovely views, while roaring log fires are a feature in the winter. The stylish dining room offers an attractive setting for home-cooked dinners and generous breakfasts.
8 en suite (bth/shr) (1 fmly) No smoking in bedrooms No smoking in dining room CTV in all bedrooms Tea and coffee making facilities No dogs (ex guide dogs) Licensed Cen ht 9P No coaches Last d 6pm
PRICE GUIDE
ROOMS: s £18-£25; d £36-£50; wkly b&b £126-£175; wkly hlf-bd £210-£259

Selected

GH ◖Q◗◖Q◗◖Q◗◖Q◗ *Dundarave House* Strathview Ter
PH16 5AT (from Pitlochry main street turn into West
Moulin Rd second left into Strathview Terrace)
☎01796 473109
Mar-Oct
Enthusiastic owners Mae and Bob Collier provide noteworthy
hospitality in this detached Victorian house which stands in its
own gardens off a quiet lane high above the town. The
spacious front-facing bedrooms enjoy splendid panoramic
views, and all are thoughtfully equipped with fresh fruit and
shortbread or home-made cake. The stylish lounge features
bay windows and a fine black marble fireplace, and Mae
presents an impressive dinner menu in a dining room well
appointed with good china, linen and period furniture.
7 rms (5 bth/shr) (1 fmly) No smoking in dining room CTV
in all bedrooms Tea and coffee making facilities Cen ht 8P
No coaches Last d 5pm

GH ◖Q◗◖Q◗ *Duntrune* 22 East Moulin Rd PH16 5HY
☎01796 472172
Feb-Oct
Set in its own mature gardens, this large Victorian house enjoys
fine views across the town and valley from its elevated position.
The well kept bedrooms provide attractive and good value
accommodation. There is also a comfortable lounge and breakfast
is served at separate tables in the bright dining room.
7 rms (5 shr) (1 fmly) No smoking in bedrooms No smoking in
dining room CTV in all bedrooms Tea and coffee making
facilities No dogs Cen ht No children 5yrs 8P No coaches Last
d 10am

Selected

GH ◖Q◗◖Q◗◖Q◗◖Q◗ *Torrdarach Hotel* Golf Course Rd
PH16 5AU ☎01796 472136
Etr-mid Oct
This impeccably kept house is set in beautiful wooded
gardens close to the golf course, while owners Richard and
Vivienne Cale create a relaxed, friendly atmosphere. Bright
fabrics and pine furnishings enhance the bedrooms, one of
which is on the ground floor. The comfortable lounge offers a
peaceful haven, while the bright dining room is the setting for
'Taste of Scotland' meals.
7 en suite (shr) No smoking CTV in all bedrooms Tea and
coffee making facilities No dogs (ex guide dogs) Licensed
Cen ht No children 12yrs 8P No coaches Last d 5.45pm
PRICE GUIDE
ROOMS: s £25-£28; d £44-£50; wkly b&b £154-£175✻

GH ◖Q◗◖Q◗◖Q◗ *Well House Private Hotel* 11 Toberargan Rd
PH16 5HG ☎01796 472239
Mar-Nov
A small but attractive garden fronts this private hotel within
walking distance of the town centre. Bedrooms are comfortable,
solidly furnished and provided with such thoughtful extras as
biscuits and fresh fruit; a video film is played through the TV each
evening at 9pm. Downstairs there are an attractive lounge and a
spacious dining room.

6 en suite (shr) (1 fmly) No smoking in 1 bedrooms CTV in all
bedrooms Tea and coffee making facilities Licensed Cen ht 8P
No coaches Last d 5.30pm
PRICE GUIDE
ROOMS: d £37-£40; wkly b&b £129.50-£140; wkly hlf-bd
£183.40-£193.20✻
CARDS: ◼◼ ▩▩ ▩▩

PORTNANCON Highland *Sutherland* Map **14** NC46

GH ◖Q◗◖Q◗◖Q◗ *Port-Na-Con House* Loch Eriboll IV27 4UN
(0.25m off A838, on shore of loch)
☎01971 511367 FAX 01971 511367
Mar-Oct
A 200 year old former customs house stands on what used to be
the only landing stage of picturesque Loch Eriboll. The smart
bedrooms are well presented and enjoy superb views over the
Loch. The dining room features local Durness craft work
(available for sale) and serves a good range of cuisine featuring
seafood and with a vegetarian option at all meals. Smoking is not
permitted at the hotel.
4 rms (1 shr) (1 fmly) No smoking Tea and coffee making
facilities Licensed Cen ht 6P No coaches Air available for
divers Last d 5pm
PRICE GUIDE
ROOMS: s £22.50-£24.50; d £33-£36
CARDS: ◼◼ ▩▩ ▩▩ ▩

DUNDARAVE HOUSE
Strathview Terrace, Pitlochry PH16 5AT

For those requiring Quality with Comfort Bed
and Breakfast, with freedom of choice for
evening meal, Dundarave must be your
answer, being situated in one of the most
enviable areas of Pitlochry in its own formal
grounds of ½ acre. All double/twin bedded
rooms with bathrooms en suite, colour TV,
tea/coffee making facilities, fully heated. We
invite you to write or phone for full particulars.

Telephone: 01796 473109

SPECIAL AA QUALITY AWARD
SCOTTISH TOURIST BOARD ♨ ♨ ♨
COMMENDED – ACCOMMODATION AWARD

PORTPATRICK Dumfries & Galloway *Wigtownshire*
Map **10** NX05

GH 🔲🔲🔲 **Blinkbonnie** School Brae DG9 8LG
☎01776 810282
Closed Dec
A large detached bungalow stands in pretty, well kept gardens in
an elevated position overlooking the town and harbour. A
welcoming atmosphere is matched by a good standard of
accomodation; some of the bedrooms have en suite facilities, all
have television and beverage-making facilities and the property is
immaculately maintained. Fine views of the sea are available in
the delightful lounge and a dining room serving good home
cooking every evening.
6 rms (3 shr) No smoking CTV in all bedrooms Tea and coffee
making facilities No dogs Cen ht CTV 10P No coaches Last d
6.30pm
PRICE GUIDE
ROOMS: s £17-£19; d £32-£36; wkly b&b £119-£133✱

PORTREE See **SKYE, ISLE OF**

PORT WILLIAM Dumfries & Galloway *Wigtownshire*
Map **10** NX34

♥ 🔲🔲🔲 Mrs Mary McMuldroch *Jacobs Ladder (NX364502)*
Whauphill DG8 9BD ☎01988 860227
Set in peaceful rural surroundings beside an unclassified road off
the B7054 between Wigton and the village of Mochrum, this
delightful country house surrounded by eight acres of woodland
and gardens offers a friendly and hospitable retreat. Two of its
large, comfortable bedrooms have en suite facilities while the
other has the use of a separate bathroom nearby. Downstairs there
are a relaxing lounge and a spacious dining room where good
home-cooked meals are served.
3 rms (2 shr) (1 fmly) CTV in all bedrooms Tea and coffee
making facilities Cen ht 8P 8 acres beef & sheep Last d 3pm

PRESTWICK Strathclyde *Ayrshire* Map **10** NS32

Selected

GH 🔲🔲🔲🔲 **Fairways Hotel** 19 Links Rd KA9 1QG
☎01292 470396 FAX 01292 470396
This charming semidetached Edwardian house overlooks the
golf course and caters well for devotees of the game; it is also
within easy reach of the seafront. Hearty breakfasts are served
at individual tables in the attractive dining room, and there is
a comfortable lounge upstairs. Immaculately maintained
bedrooms are well equipped and have thoughtful extra
touches.
5 rms (4 shr) (1 fmly) No smoking in dining room CTV in
all bedrooms Tea and coffee making facilities Licensed Cen
ht CTV 8P No coaches
PRICE GUIDE
ROOMS: s £25; d £46✱
CARDS: £

GH 🔲🔲🔲 **Fernbank** 213 Main St KA9 1LH
☎01292 475027
Rachel and Malcolm Connelly's delightful semidetached red
sandstone house is conveniently located on the main street just
south of the town centre. Wood-strip panelling has been used to
great effect throughout, and the accommodation is immaculately
maintained. There is an attractive and spacious lounge, and the
small dining room is tastefully furnished in pine. A no-smoking
policy has recently been introduced.

7 rms (4 shr) (1 fmly) CTV in all bedrooms Tea and coffee
making facilities No dogs Cen ht CTV No children 5yrs 7P No
coaches
PRICE GUIDE
ROOMS: s £16; d £36✱

 £

Selected

GH 🔲🔲🔲🔲 **Golf View Hotel** 17 Links Rd KA9 1QG
(take A77 to Prestwick Airport, turn at Prestwick Cross,
opposite Prestwick golf course)
☎01292 671234 FAX 01292 671244
Graham and Isobel McKerrigan's delightful semidetached red
sandstone house enjoys views over the golf course, home of
the first Open Championship in 1806, and is within a short
walk of both the town centre and seafront. A high standard of
accommodation is offered, comfortable, well appointed
bedrooms being equipped with several extra touches. The
comfortable first-floor lounge overlooks the fourteenth green,
as does an attractive dining room where hearty Scottish
breakfasts are served at individual tables.
6 en suite (bth/shr) (2 fmly) No smoking in bedrooms No
smoking in dining room No smoking in lounges CTV in all
bedrooms Tea and coffee making facilities No dogs (ex
guide dogs) Licensed Cen ht CTV 10P
PRICE GUIDE
ROOMS: s fr £25; d fr £48✱
CARDS: £

GH 🔲🔲🔲 **Kincraig Private Hotel** 39 Ayr Rd KA9 1SY
☎01292 479480
This sturdy red sandstone house standing beside the main road at
the south end of town offers good-value accommodation.
Bedrooms are generally spacious, with modern appointments, and
all have a good range of amenities, while public areas include a
comfortable lounge and a tastefully appointed dining room.
6 rms (3 shr) (1 fmly) No smoking in bedrooms No smoking in
dining room CTV in all bedrooms Tea and coffee making
facilities Licensed Cen ht CTV No children 3yrs 8P No
coaches Last d 5pm
PRICE GUIDE
ROOMS: s £17-£21; d £40✱

 £

Selected

GH 🔲🔲🔲🔲 **Redlands** Redlands, 38 Monkton Rd KA9
1AR (going S on A77 pass airport, take 3rd exit off rdbt
towards Prestwick, Redlands on left in 100yds)
☎01292 479479
Enthusiastic owners Mr and Mrs Jackson take pride in the
standards they offer at their immaculately maintained,
detached, red sandstone house which stands beside the main
road close to the airport. Bedrooms, although not spacious,
are modern and tastefully furnished, with extra welcoming
touches. There are a charming, comfortable lounge and an
attractive dining room where hearty breakfasts are served at
individual tables. Smoking is not permitted.
3 rms (1 shr) (1 fmly) No smoking CTV in all bedrooms
Tea and coffee making facilities No dogs (ex guide dogs)
Cen ht 7P No coaches
PRICE GUIDE
ROOMS: s £16.50-£20; d £31-£37✱

ROGART Highland *Sutherland* Map **14** NC70

Selected

♥ Ⓠ Ⓠ Ⓠ Ⓠ Mrs J S R Moodie **Rovie** *(NC716023)*
IV28 3TZ (A838 into village of Rogart then take first right
over railway crossing and follow sign to guesthouse)
☎01408 641209 FAX 01408 641209
mid Mar-Nov

Christine Moodie has been welcoming guests to her
immaculate farmhouse for over 37 years, and they show their
appreciation of her welcoming hospitality and enjoyable home
cooking by returning year after year. Delicious home baking
is on offer to guests both on arrival and before bed, and hearty
breakfasts and dinners are served. The bedrooms are mostly
spacious, with individual decor and lovely views across the
picturesque Strathfleet valley. The comfortable lounge is
warmed by a peat-burning fire, the pretty dining room has an
attractive collection of wall plates, and there is a sun lounge
with TV. Fishing and shooting can be arranged. There is a real
home-from-home atmosphere here, which resulted in Mrs
Moodie being awarded AA Landlady of the Year in 1994.
6 rms (1 fmly) No smoking in 4 bedrooms No smoking in
dining room No smoking in lounges CTV ch fac 8P Golf 9
Fishing Rough shooting Trout fishing 120 acres beef sheep
Last d 6.30pm
PRICE GUIDE
ROOMS: s £18-£20; d £36-£40; wkly b&b £120-£140;
wkly hlf-bd £210-£224

ROSEMARKIE Highland *Ross & Cromarty* Map **14** NH75

Selected

GH Ⓠ Ⓠ Ⓠ Ⓠ *Hillview* Raddery IV10 8SN (Take A832 to
Cromarty and 1m after Rosemarkie turn left to Raddery
at phone box. Follow road to electric sub-station and turn
left to Hillview) ☎01381 620272 FAX 01381 621178
Good-value bed and breakfast accommodation is offered at
Sandra Gyle's delightful modern bungalow, which is set in
pleasant countryside about two miles north of the village.
Bedrooms, though not large, have modern appointments and
are bright and cheerful. Public areas include a spacious TV
lounge, a sun lounge and an elegant dining area where hearty
breakfasts are served at a communal table. Guests should note
that this is a no-smoking establishment.
2 en suite (bth/shr) No smoking Tea and coffee making
facilities No dogs (ex guide dogs) 4P No coaches

ROSLIN Lothian *Midlothian* Map **11** NT26

◀ Ⓠ Ⓠ *Olde Original Rosslyn* 4 Main St EH25 9LD
☎0131 440 2384
This friendly village inn is just seven miles south of Edinburgh,
conveniently located at the end of the village street. Attractively
furnished bedrooms vary in size and some have four-posters. The
bars have kept their traditional character and there is a delightful
Victorian-style restaurant where prime Scottish steaks are
something of a speciality.
6 en suite (bth/shr) CTV in all bedrooms Tea and coffee making
facilities Cen ht 14P Last d 10pm
CARDS: 🔳 🔳 🔳

ST ANDREWS Fife Map **12** NO51

GH Ⓠ Ⓠ **Albany Private Hotel** 56 North St KY16 9AH
☎01334 477737 FAX 01334 477737
Centrally located, this small hotel is being refurbished. Bedrooms
are pleasant and the quiet lounge has board games and
newspapers. There is also a separate dining room.
12 rms (6 shr) (2 fmly) No smoking CTV in all bedrooms Tea
and coffee making facilities Direct dial from bedrooms No dogs
(ex guide dogs) Licensed Cen ht Last d 5pm
PRICE GUIDE
ROOMS: s £28-£35; d £58-£64; wkly b&b £196-£245; wkly hlf-
bd £300-£350
CARDS: 🔳 🔳
£

GH Ⓠ Ⓠ Ⓠ **Amberside** 4 Murray Pk KY16 9AW
☎01334 474644
Close to the town centre and seafront, this friendly guest house has
undergone considerable improvements in the past year. Bright
floral wall coverings and linens have transformed the bedrooms,
which are now attractive and well equipped. A combined
lounge/dining room offers a good choice of breakfasts.
6 rms (5 shr) (2 fmly) No smoking in dining room No smoking
in lounges CTV in all bedrooms Tea and coffee making facilities
Cen ht CTV No parking
PRICE GUIDE
ROOMS: s £18-£28; d £36-£56; wkly b&b £120-£180✳
CARDS: 🔳 🔳 🔳
£

AA LANDLADY OF THE YEAR 1994

Rovie Farm Guest House
Rogart, Sutherland IV28 3TZ
Telephone: (01408) 641209

*Situated in the picturesque valley of
Strathfleet, just 4 miles off the A9, on the
working farm offering a 'Home from Home'
with good home cooking and baking served.
All the bedrooms are comfortable and have
H & C and heating. Total relaxation or
strenuous exercise is available if desired.
Open Easter until November.
Come to Rovie Farm Guest House for Highland
Hospitality at its best.*

GH **Q Q Q** **Arran House** 5 Murray Park KY16 9AW
☎01334 474724 FAX 01334 472072
Feb-Nov
Situated in a terraced row leading from the town centre to the sea, this small guest house offers bright and cheery accommodation in well equipped bedrooms. There is an attractive, homely breakfast room but no lounge.
4 rms (3 shr) (2 fmly) No smoking CTV in all bedrooms Tea and coffee making facilities No dogs Cen ht CTV No parking
PRICE GUIDE
ROOMS: s £20-£30; d £40-£50; wkly b&b £100-£200
CARDS: 🔲 🔲

GH **Q Q** *Beachway House* 6 Murray Park KY16 9AW
☎01334 473319
Closed Jan
Situated in a side street between the town centre and the seafront, this guesthouse offers practical bed and breakfast accommodation. All bedrooms, including one on the ground floor, have en suite shower rooms. Comfortable seating is provided in the combined lounge/breakfast room.
6 rms (5 shr) (2 fmly) CTV in all bedrooms Tea and coffee making facilities Cen ht No parking

GH **Q Q Q** *Bell Craig* 8 Murray Park KY16 9AW
☎01334 472962 FAX 01334 472962
Conveniently situated between the town centre and the seafront, this improving guest house offers modern accommodation in attractively appointed bedrooms. Hearty breakfasts are served in the lounge/dining room, and all guests receive a friendly welcome.
5 rms (3 shr) (3 fmly) No smoking in dining room CTV in all bedrooms Tea and coffee making facilities Cen ht CTV No parking No coaches
CARDS: 🔲 🔲

GH **Q Q** **Burness House** Murray Park KY16 9AW
☎01334 74314 FAX 01334 74314
Hospitality is a real strength at this guest house, thanks to host Heather McQueen. The house, which occupies a corner site, has recently been tastefully redecorated throughout. Bedrooms are small but all have en suite shower rooms, and there is a combined lounge and breakfast room which offers a good selection of books, games and videos.
5 en suite (shr) (1 fmly) No smoking in 3 bedrooms No smoking in dining room No smoking in lounges CTV in all bedrooms Tea and coffee making facilities Cen ht CTV No parking No coaches
PRICE GUIDE
ROOMS: s £22-£28; d £30-£44

GH **Q Q** **Cleveden House** 3 Murray Place KY16 9AP
☎01334 474212
Located in a small terrace between the town and the seafront, this compact guest house has a relaxing lounge and simply furnished bedrooms.
6 rms (4 shr) (1 fmly) No smoking in bedrooms No smoking in dining room CTV in all bedrooms Tea and coffee making facilities No dogs (ex guide dogs) Cen ht CTV
£

GH **Q Q Q** **Craigmore** 3 Murray Park KY16 9AW
☎01334 472142 FAX 01334 477963
A very well maintained and attractively decorated guests house has modern bedrooms furnished with pine, one ground floor room has recently been added. Hearty Scottish breakfasts are served in the pretty dining room, which also has a lounge area. The friendly owner, Tilda Carruthers, can provide valuable information on the

local golf courses. Craigmore is within minutes of the town centre and the sea front.
5 en suite (bth/shr) (4 fmly) No smoking in 2 bedrooms No smoking in dining room CTV in all bedrooms Tea and coffee making facilities No dogs Cen ht CTV
PRICE GUIDE
ROOMS: d £34-£50; wkly b&b £113-£166
CARDS: 🔲 🔲 £

GH **Q Q Q** *Doune* 5 Murray Place KY16 9AP (A91 into St Andrews, straight over 2 roundabouts and take 2nd road on left) ☎01334 75195
The Doune Guest House, a terraced property set in a side street between the town centre and the sea, has been completely renovated by the present owner. The bright modern bedrooms are small but well equipped, with smart fully tiled en suite bathrooms throughout. The addition of a golf club cupboard at the entrance of the rooms is also a boon. There are a comfortable period-style lounge and a neat dining room with a delightful pine dresser.
4 en suite (shr) CTV in all bedrooms Tea and coffee making facilities No dogs Cen ht CTV No parking

Selected

GH **Q Q Q Q** **Edenside House** Edenside KY16 9SQ (on A91, 2.5m W of St Andrews)
☎01334 838108 FAX 01334 838493
end March-Oct
This modernised 18th Century farmhouse is set back from the A91 about two miles north west of the town overlooking the Eden Estuary nature reserve and bird sanctuary. Pleasant well equipped bedrooms with pretty fabrics and pine furniture are found in the main house and an adjoining extension where they have their own entrances. The lounge in the main house is cosy, and hearty breakfasts are served in the attractive dining room with four pine tables. There is ample car parking and the house is totally non-smoking.
3 en suite (shr) 6 annexe en suite (shr) No smoking CTV in all bedrooms Tea and coffee making facilities Cen ht No children 10yrs 12P No coaches Located on bird sanctuary Stables adjacent
PRICE GUIDE
ROOMS: d £40-£52
CARDS: 🔲 🔲 £

GH **Q Q** **Five Pilmour Place** North St KY16 9HX
☎01334 474001
Part of a Georgian terrace, this sympathetically restored house stands on the A91 which leads to the town centre. The bright en suite bedrooms are named after Scottish flowers and feature attractive fabrics; one first floor room is particularly spacious. A ground-floor lounge/dining room offers a choice of breakfasts.
5 en suite (bth/shr) (2 fmly) No smoking CTV in all bedrooms Tea and coffee making facilities Cen ht No children 5yrs No parking
PRICE GUIDE
ROOMS: s £18-£35; d £36-£50✳

Factual details of establishments in this Guide are from questionnaires we send to all establishments that feature in the book.

GH ◗◗◗◗ **Fossil House** 12-14 Main St, Strathkinness KY16 9RU (Strathkinness signposted, Fossil House at top end of village close to pub)
☎01334 850639 FAX 01334 850639

Situated at the top of a peaceful village two miles from St Andrews, this converted house and cottage is an ideal base from which to explore the East Neuk of Fife. The accommodation is well equipped and split between main house bedrooms and two cottage rooms sharing a conservatory lounge; all are attractively decorated and full of thoughtful extras such as fresh fruit and flowers. Home-made soup is offered on arrival, while breakfast is chosen the previous evening and served farmhouse style at one large table.

2 en suite (bth/shr) 2 annexe en suite (shr) (1 fmly) No smoking in bedrooms No smoking in dining room No smoking in 1 lounge CTV in all bedrooms Tea and coffee making facilities No dogs (ex guide dogs) Cen ht CTV ch fac 4P No coaches Croquet lawn
PRICE GUIDE
ROOMS: d £32-£36
CARDS: 🔲 💳

GH ◗◗◗◗ **Glenderran** 9 Murray Park KY16 9AW
☎01334 477951 FAX 01334 477908

Style is the key attraction of this carefully restored house, with oriental pictures, ornaments and rugs complementing the thoughtfully equipped bedrooms. There is a relaxing lounge and a dining room with a wide selection of music, books and magazines. Guests make their choice from the interesting breakfast menu on the preceding night, to ensure availability and freshness. There is a no-smoking policy throughout the building.

5 rms (3 shr) No smoking CTV in all bedrooms Tea and coffee making facilities No dogs Cen ht No children 12yrs No coaches
PRICE GUIDE
ROOMS: s £20-£26; d £40-£52; wkly b&b £126-£161
CARDS: 🔲 💳

GH ◗◗◗ *Hazlebank Private Hotel* 28 The Scores KY16 9AS
☎01334 472466 FAX 01334 472466

Hazlebank Hotel is situated in a terraced row which overlooks the sea front and is close to the first tee of the Old Course. Bedrooms vary in size, some having superb views of the beach, and all are well equipped and nicely furnished. There is a small lounge, while breakfast and dinner is served in the attractive dining room.

10 en suite (bth/shr) (6 fmly) No smoking in dining room CTV in all bedrooms Tea and coffee making facilities Licensed Cen ht CTV No parking No coaches Last d 6.45pm
CARDS: 🔲 💳

GH ◗◗ **The Larches** 7 River Ter, Guardbridge KY16 0XA (A91 to Guardbridge from St Andrews, turn left before bridge at far end of village by phone and post box, house 50yds on left) ☎01334 838008 FAX 01334 838008

This friendly guest house was converted from a derelict memorial hall and is set in its own mature gardens close to the river. Bedrooms are well kept and have some thoughtful touches.

➡

Edenside House
Edenside, St Andrews, KY16 9SQ

🅰🅰 QQQQ Selected

Pre 1775 former Scottish farmhouse in superb waterfront setting on estuary bird sanctuary. St Andrews and Old Course within 2½ miles (5 mins. by car on A91).
All nine modernised double/twin rooms (some ground floor) have en suite facilities, colour TV, beverage tray and guaranteed parking space.
Golf booking advice and tours arranged.
Exclusively non smoking.
Mobile: 0585 359973   Fax: 01334 838493
Tel: 01334 838108

FOSSIL HOUSE & FOSSIL COTTAGE
12-14 Main Street, Strathkinness, St Andrews, Fife KY16 9RU
Tel: 01334-850639

2 miles from St. Andrews, Deluxe Accommodation. Self-contained Cottage and Family Room, conservatory, lounge, walled garden, parking. All bedrooms en suite, offering Colour TV, Trouser press, tea/coffee/fruit. Games, videos, mini library.
Pub and Restaurant (20 yards)
Peace and tranquillity with Hotel Facilities at B&B prices.
NOT TO BE MISSED!
Access & Visa accepted

Memorabilia from a career in the RAF can be seen in the large combined lounge/dining room, where breakfasts are chosen the previous evening from a wide selection.
3 rms (1 fmly) No smoking in bedrooms No smoking in dining room CTV in all bedrooms Tea and coffee making facilities Cen ht CTV ch fac No parking
PRICE GUIDE
ROOMS: s £17-£23; d £34-£36; wkly b&b £100-£140

GH **Q Q Q** **Lorimer House** 19 Murray Park KY16 9AW
☎01334 476599 FAX 01334 476599
This immaculately maintained guest house is attractively decorated throughout, and is close to both the town centre and the sea front. Bedrooms, including one on the ground floor, vary in size but are well equipped and comfortable. The combined lounge and dining room features an original autumnal themed cornice.
6 rms (5 bth/shr) (2 fmly) No smoking in bedrooms CTV in all bedrooms Tea and coffee making facilities Cen ht CTV No children 15yrs No parking No coaches
PRICE GUIDE
ROOMS: s £16-£25; d £32-£50

⊨ 🖳 GH **Q Q Q** **Romar** 45 Main St, Strathkinness
KY16 9RZ (turn off A91 in Guardbridge, onto unclass road signposted Strathkiness, Romar is last house on left at bottom of hill) ☎01334 850308 FAX 01334 850308
Located at one end of the village, this modern guest house offers a friendly welcome and comfortable accommodation. The two first floor family rooms are the most spacious, though the ground floor bedrooms are also a good size; all are named after Scottish islands. Breakfast, chosen the previous evening, is served in the small dining room, and ample games and tourist information are available in the hall.
4 rms (2 shr) (1 fmly) No smoking in bedrooms No smoking in dining room No smoking in 1 lounge CTV in all bedrooms Tea and coffee making facilities No dogs (ex guide dogs) Cen ht 5P No coaches
PRICE GUIDE
ROOMS: s £16-£20; d £32-£40

GH **Q Q Q** **West Park House** 5 St Mary's Place KY16 9UY
(to the W end of Market St, just beyond Hope Park Church)
☎01334 475933
Closed Jan
Just on the edge of the town centre, this large Georgian house is now a well kept guest house. Bedrooms are comfortable with two on the ground floor and two on the second floor. The quiet residents' lounge overlooks the garden at the rear of the house, while breakfast is served round one large table in the elegant dining room. Smoking is not permitted.
4 rms (1 bth 2 shr) (1 fmly) CTV in all bedrooms Tea and coffee making facilities No dogs (ex guide dogs) Cen ht CTV No parking No coaches
PRICE GUIDE
ROOMS: s £20-£28; d £37-£42
CARDS: 🂠 ⚏

GH **Q Q Q** **Yorkston House Hotel** 68 & 70 Argyle St
KY16 9BU ☎01334 472019 FAX 01334 72019
rs Xmas & New Year
Traditional standards are offered at this long-established guesthouse lying west of the town centre. The bedrooms are spacious and comfortable and there is a pleasant lounge and a large dining room with well spaced tables.
10 rms (1 bth 5 shr) (2 fmly) No smoking in dining room No smoking in lounges CTV in all bedrooms Tea and coffee making

facilities No dogs (ex guide dogs) Licensed Cen ht No parking No coaches Last d 4pm
PRICE GUIDE
ROOMS: s £20-£26; d £36-£60; wkly b&b £126-£210

♥ Q Q Q Mrs A E Duncan **Spinks Town** *(NO541144)*
KY16 8PN (2m E on A917 coast road) ☎01334 473475
This attractive modern house is built on the opposite side of the road to the rest of the farm buildings, and is surrounded by rolling countryside. The bright airy bedrooms are spacious and comfortable, and there is also a very inviting lounge and dining room where breakfast is taken round the one table.
3 en suite (bth/shr) No smoking Tea and coffee making facilities No dogs Cen ht CTV 3P 250 acres arable cattle
PRICE GUIDE
ROOMS: d £34-£36✱

ST CATHERINE'S Strathclyde *Argyllshire* Map **10** NN10

GH **Q Q Q** **Arnish Cottage, Christian Guest House.** Poll Bay
PA25 8BA (on A815) ☎01499 302405
In an idyllic setting beside the shore of Loch Fyne Bill and Maisie Mercer's charming restored stone cottage is an ideal base for exploring the surrounding area. Bedrooms, though compact, are maintained to the highest of standards and offer both modern and traditional furnishings. Maisie's home cooked dinners based on fresh local produce and seafood, are served at the communal table in the attractive dining room which combines an attractive lounge with conservatory extension. This is a non smoking establishment.
4 en suite (shr) No smoking Tea and coffee making facilities No dogs (ex guide dogs) Cen ht CTV No children 16yrs 4P No coaches
PRICE GUIDE
ROOMS: s fr £25; d fr £46; wkly b&b fr £145; wkly hlf-bd fr £250✱

Selected

GH **Q Q Q Q** **Thistle House** PA25 8AZ (on A815)
☎01499 302209
Etr-Oct
This well-proportioned house stands in its own large garden beside the A815 overlooking Loch Fyne to Inveraray. Bedrooms, many with loch views, are spacious with modern comforts but no TVs. Public areas include a comfortable, spacious lounge with ample reading material and a neat dining room serving hearty breakfasts at individual tables.
5 rms (3 shr) (1 fmly) No smoking in dining room Tea and coffee making facilities Cen ht 10P No coaches
PRICE GUIDE
ROOMS: d £37-£44; wkly b&b fr £129.50✱
CARDS: 🂠 ⚏ 🂡

ST MARY'S LOCH Borders *Selkirkshire* Map **11** NT22

◀ Q Q Q **Tibbie Shiels** TD7 5NE (just off A708 between
Moffat/Selkirk) ☎01750 42231
rs Mon Nov-Feb
This historic drovers' and fishermen's inn can be found on the shores of St Mary's Loch, at the western end, between Selkirk and Moffat. The characterful small bar with its low ceiling is known as 'Tibbie's', after its original owner. Bedrooms are housed in a later extension and are currently being upgraded. High teas and evening meals are served in the dining room and bar meals are also available.

5 en suite (shr) (2 fmly) No smoking in area of dining room No smoking in 1 lounge Tea and coffee making facilities No dogs (ex guide dogs) Cen ht CTV 30P Fishing Last d 8.30pm
PRICE GUIDE
ROOMS: s £26; d £46✳
MEALS: Lunch £6-£9.25alc Dinner £11.25-£14.75alc✳
CARDS: 🔳 🔳 🔳

SELKIRK Borders *Selkirkshire* Map **12** NT42

Selected

GH 🅀🅀🅀🅀 **Hillholm** 36 Hillside Ter TD7 4ND (S on A7) ☎01750 21293
Mar-Nov
This semidetached Victorian house stands beside the main road to the south of the town; attractively decorated throughout, it offers a stylish lounge and dining room, breakfasts being taken round the latter's communal table. Bedrooms are furnished in a pleasing blend of period and modern styles.
3 rms (2 shr) No smoking in bedrooms No smoking in dining room Tea and coffee making facilities No dogs Cen ht CTV No children 10yrs No coaches
PRICE GUIDE
ROOMS: s fr £20; d fr £35✳

SHETLAND Map **16**

LERWICK Map **16** HU44

GH 🅀🅀🅀 *Glen Orchy House* 20 Knab Rd ZE1 0AX (adjct to coastguard station) ☎01595 692031
Situated on the south side of town, this comfortable guest house is currently undergoing a major extension and improvement programme. When complete the number of bedrooms will increase and all will be en suite and offer other improved facilities. Also due for enlargement are the cosy lounge and an attractive dining room where home cooking can be enjoyed.
8 rms (1 shr) (2 fmly) No smoking in dining room CTV in all bedrooms Tea and coffee making facilities Licensed Cen ht No coaches Golf 9 Last d 2pm

---

SKIPNESS Strathclyde *Argyllshire* Map **10** NR95

Selected

GH 🅀🅀🅀🅀 **Skipness Castle** PA29 6XU
☎01880 760207 FAX 01880 760208
Closed 15 Dec-10 Jan
Situated beside the ruins of the 13th century castle, Skipness was rebuilt in 1972 following major fire damage and is today the focal point of the James family's private estate. The house commands superb views over the Kilbrannan Sound to the Isle of Arran. Public rooms include the charming first floor drawing room, which features a welcoming log fire and antique furnishings. There is also an honesty bar. A four course dinner is served, many of the ingredients coming from the estate. Co-ordinated fabrics have been used to good effect in the spacious bedrooms, which are comfortably furnished in period style. The atmosphere is relaxed and very much in the style of a private house party.

---

3 rms (2 bth) No smoking in bedrooms Tea and coffee making facilities No dogs (ex guide dogs) Licensed Cen ht CTV P No coaches Last d 4pm
PRICE GUIDE
ROOMS: s £38-£50; d £70-£76✳

SKYE, ISLE OF Highland *Inverness-shire* Map **13**

DUNVEGAN Map **13** NG24

GH 🅀🅀🅀 **Roskhill** Roskhill IV55 8ZD (2m S A863) ☎01470 521317
Mar-Nov
A former croft house has been converted to create this friendly and comfortable family run licensed guest house which is situated south of the village off the A863. Public areas include a small relaxing TV lounge and attractive dining room with beamed ceiling, natural stone walls and welcoming open fire. Bedrooms though compact are bright and cheery with mixed modern appointments. Guests should note this is a non smoking establishment.
5 rms (3 shr) (1 fmly) No smoking Tea and coffee making facilities No dogs Licensed Cen ht CTV 6P No coaches Last d 6pm
PRICE GUIDE
ROOMS: d £31-£40✳
CARDS: 🔳 🔳
See advertisement on p.563.

PORTREE Map **13** NG44

GH ⓆⓆⓆ *Craiglockhart* Beaumont Crescent IV51 9DF
☎01478 612233
Closed Dec
This friendly, homely guest house right on the seafront enjoys a picture postcard setting - front-facing accommodation, as well as the picture windows of the lounge and dining room, looking out over the harbour and Portree Bay. Some of the bedrooms are of marginally superior quality and have en suite facilities.
10 rms (3 shr) CTV in 9 bedrooms Tea and coffee making facilities No dogs Cen ht CTV 4P No coaches

Selected

GH ⓆⓆⓆⓆ *Quiraing* Viewfield Rd IV51 9ES (on A850) ☎01478 612870 FAX 01478 612870
Good value bed and breakfast accommodation is offered at this friendly family run bungalow style guest house which stands beside the main road on the southern edge of town. Completion of a recent extension has created more space in the bright cheerful non smoking bedrooms which offer mixed modern furnishings together with all the expected amenities. Hearty breakfasts are served at individual tables in the attractive dining room which is open plan with the comfortable lounge.
6 en suite (shr) (2 fmly) No smoking in bedrooms No smoking in 1 lounge CTV in all bedrooms Tea and coffee making facilities No dogs (ex guide dogs) Cen ht CTV 8P No coaches
PRICE GUIDE
ROOMS: d fr £40✳

SOUTH GALSON See **LEWIS, ISLE OF**

SPEAN BRIDGE Highland *Inverness-shire* Map **14** NN28

🏨♿️ **GH** ⓆⓆ *Coire Glas* PH34 4EU (on A86, 0.5m from junct of A82) ☎01397 712272
Jan-Oct
Situated in its own grounds at the east end of the village, this friendly family run guest house offers good value holiday accommodation. The well kept non-smoking bedrooms vary in size and offer mixed modern appointments. Public areas include a comfortable lounge with dispense bar and smart dining room offering fresh local produce from the carte.
14 rms (9 shr) (2 fmly) No smoking in bedrooms No smoking in dining room Tea and coffee making facilities No dogs (ex guide dogs) Licensed CTV 20P Last d 8pm
PRICE GUIDE
ROOMS: s £14-£17; d £28-£34; wkly hlf-bd £161-£182

Selected

GH ⓆⓆⓆⓆ *Distant Hills* PH34 4EU (on A86)
☎01397 712452
A relaxed, friendly atmosphere prevails at Meg and Ian McLuskey's modern house which stands in its own garden beside the A86 at the east end of the village. Bright cheerful bedrooms are tastefully decorated and comfortably furnished, although they do vary in size. Public areas include a spacious, comfortable split-level lounge and an attractive dining room

where enjoyable home cooking - with the emphasis on fresh local produce - is served at individual tables.
7 en suite (shr) No smoking in 2 bedrooms No smoking in dining room CTV in all bedrooms Tea and coffee making facilities Cen ht CTV ch fac 10P No coaches Last d 5pm

GH ⓆⓆⓆ *Inverour* PH34 4EU (on A86, before junct with A82) ☎01397 712218
rs Jan
A relaxed friendly atmosphere prevails at this family run guest house which is conveniently situated close to the junction of the A82 and A86. The non smoking bedrooms are variable in size with mixed modern units and offer all the expected amenities. Public areas include a relaxing lounge with conservatory extension and an attractive beamed dining room where, by prior arrangement, a set three course dinner is available.
7 rms (3 shr) (1 fmly) No smoking in bedrooms No smoking in dining room CTV in 1 bedroom Tea and coffee making facilities No dogs Cen ht CTV No children 3yrs 8P Last d 10am
PRICE GUIDE
ROOMS: s £16; d £30-£34✳

STEWARTON Strathclyde *Ayrshire*

See **Dunlop**

STIRLING Central *Stirlingshire* Map **11** NS79

See also **Denny**

GH ⓆⓆⓆ *Castlecroft* Ballengeich Rd FK8 1TN (leave M9 junct10 toward Stirling, turn first right into Raploch Road. Drive to fire station, turn left at Back'O'Hill then immediatley right) ☎01786 474933
Closed Xmas & New Year
Standing in an elevated position in the shadow of the castle, this split-level house offers accommodation on three floors. The well equipped bedrooms all have fully tiled en suite shower rooms and the two on the lower floor have their own patio. Guests can also enjoy a spacious lounge containing its own telescope, and a roof terrace. Breakfast is served at shared tables.
6 en suite (shr) (1 fmly) No smoking in bedrooms No smoking in dining room CTV in all bedrooms Tea and coffee making facilities Lift Cen ht 9P No coaches
PRICE GUIDE
ROOMS: s £30-£37; d £35-£42✳

STORNOWAY See **LEWIS, ISLE OF**

STRATHAVEN Strathclyde *Lanarkshire* Map **11** NS74

GH ⓆⓆ *Springvale Hotel* 18 Letham Rd ML10 6AD
☎01357 21131 FAX 01357 21131
Closed 26-27 Dec & 1-3 Jan
Friendly and family-run, this guest house is situated in a quiet residential area some 300 yards from central amenities. Compact bedrooms with mixed practical appointments offer the expected facilities, while public areas include a homely lounge as well as the large rear dining room where enjoyable high teas are served to residents and non-residents alike. Some long-stay guests are also accommodated.
14 rms (1 bth 10 shr) (1 fmly) CTV in all bedrooms Tea and coffee making facilities Licensed Cen ht CTV 8P Last d 6.45pm

STRATHPEFFER Highland *Ross & Cromarty* Map **14** NH45

GH 🅠🅠🅠 **Inver Lodge** IV14 9DL (from A834 through Strathpeffer Centre, turn beside Spa Pavilion signposted Bowling Green, Inver Lodge on right hand side)
☎01997 421392
Mar-mid Dec
A welcoming atmosphere prevails at this comfortable family run guest-house, a detached Victorian building standing in its own grounds close to the centre of the village. The bright, airy bedrooms are comfortably modern in style and offer the expected amenities; hearty breakfasts and, with prior arrangement, enjoyable home-cooked evening meals can be enjoyed at the communal table in the combined lounge/dining room. This is a non-smoking house.
2 rms (1 fmly) No smoking CTV in all bedrooms Tea and coffee making facilities No dogs Cen ht 2P No coaches Fishing and riding can be arranged Last d 4pm
CARDS: 🔳 🔤 (£)

STRATHTAY Tayside *Perthshire* Map **14** NN95

GH 🅠🅠🅠 *Bendarroch House* PH9 0PG
☎01887 840420 FAX 01887 840438
This imposing Victorian mansion lies in six acres of grounds in a quiet village close to the River Tay. Four of the five bedrooms are elegant twins, well-proportioned and graced with period furniture; the fifth is a more modest single. There are two lounges in which to relax and home-cooked meals are served in the pleasant dining room.
5 en suite (shr) (1 fmly) No smoking in dining room No smoking in 1 lounge CTV in 2 bedrooms Tea and coffee making facilities Direct dial from bedrooms No dogs (ex guide dogs) Licensed Cen ht CTV ch fac 8P No coaches Croquet Last d 5.30pm

STRATHYRE Central *Perthshire* Map **11** NN51

Selected

GH 🅠🅠🅠🅠 **Creagan House** FK18 8ND (0.25m N of Strathyre on A84) (Logis)
☎01877 384638 FAX 01877 384319
Closed 28 Jan-1 Mar
Gordon and Cherry Gunn run their former farmhouse as a restaurant with accommodation, and Gordon's cooking has earned him an AA rosette. The house has been sympathetically restored to retain its period character, with a baronial dining room and cosy lounge. The bedrooms are charming and well equipped. One room has a four poster bed.
5 en suite (bth/shr) (1 fmly) No smoking in bedrooms No smoking in dining room Tea and coffee making facilities Licensed Cen ht 26P Last d 8.30pm
PRICE GUIDE
ROOMS: s fr £42.50; d fr £65; wkly b&b fr £204.50; wkly hlf-bd £320-£351.50
CARDS: 🔳 ◾ 🔤 (£)

GH 🅠🅠 **Dochfour** FK18 8NA
☎01877 384256 FAX 01877 384256
In the centre of this attractive conservation village, this late Victorian house is set back from the main road in its own gardens, with its elevated position ensuring that it enjoys fine views of the area. A friendly welcome awaits with home baking and good value evening meals being a feature. The comfortable bedrooms are nicely decorated and well equipped, while a spacious lounge is also available for guests' use. The dining room has patio door

leading to the garden, with ample car parking provided at the front of the house.
3 en suite (bth/shr) No smoking in 1 bedrooms No smoking in dining room CTV in all bedrooms Tea and coffee making facilities No dogs (ex guide dogs) Cen ht CTV 3P No coaches Last d 8pm
PRICE GUIDE
ROOMS: d £30-£36; wkly b&b £94-£115; wkly hlf-bd £132.50-£185

SWINTON Borders *Berwickshire* Map **12** NT84

◀ 🅠🅠🅠 **Wheatsheaf Hotel** TD11 3JJ (6m N of Duns on A6112) ☎01890 860257 FAX 01890 860257
Closed last wk Oct & last 2 wks Feb rs Mon
Overlooking the village green and with pleasant gardens to the rear, this country inn has built its reputation on a restaurant holding an AA rosette for quality. Bedrooms are pleasantly furnished and three have good en suite bathrooms; there is also a quiet residents' lounge.
4 rms (3 bth/shr) (1 fmly) No smoking in 2 bedrooms No smoking in dining room CTV in all bedrooms Tea and coffee making facilities Cen ht 4P No coaches Last d 9.30pm
PRICE GUIDE
ROOMS: s £28-£42; d £45-£60; wkly b&b £168-£252
MEALS: Lunch £11-£20alc Dinner £14-£25alc
CARDS: 🔳 🔤 (£)

ROSKHILL GUEST HOUSE
Roskhill By Dunvegan Isle of Skye
Telephone: 01470 521317
AA Guest House   STB ♥ ♥
Mr and Mrs Suckling

This traditional Croft house is in an ideal position for touring this lovely island. Dinner is served in the old stone walled dining room with cosy log fires. There is a selection of wines and Malt Whiskies to enjoy with your meal.
A true Highland welcome awaits you

TAIN Highland *Ross & Cromarty* Map **14** NH78

Selected

GH Ⓠ Ⓠ Ⓠ Ⓠ **Golf View House** 13 Knockbreck Rd
IV19 1BN (first right off A9 at Tain (B9174), follow this
road for 0.5m, house signposted on right)
☎01862 892856
Closed 16 Dec-15 Jan
Ian and Kay Ross's impressive Victorian house stands in two
acres of well tended gardens at the south end of town, looking
across the golf course to Dornoch Firth. Maintained to a high
standard throughout, it offers comfortable accommodation in
predominantly spacious no-smoking bedrooms. Public areas
include a relaxing lounge with a bay window overlooking the
golf course and a smart dining room whose French windows
lead on to the patio.
5 rms (3 shr) (1 fmly) No smoking in bedrooms CTV in all
bedrooms Tea and coffee making facilities No dogs (ex
guide dogs) Cen ht CTV 7P No coaches
PRICE GUIDE
ROOMS: s £18-£26; d £30-£37; wkly b&b
£110-£136✱

THORNHILL Central *Stirlingshire* Map **11** NN60

Selected

GH Ⓠ Ⓠ Ⓠ Ⓠ **Corshill** By Thornhill FK8 3QD
☎01786 850270
Apr-Oct
Set in its own immaculately kept garden, this extended
cottage is situated about two miles east of Thornhill. The
comfortable bedrooms are prettily decorated with floral
designs and lace trimmings; many thoughtful extras are
provided. Guests also have use of a sunny split level lounge
and dining room containing a good selection of books and
games. Breakfast is chosen the previous evening from an
extensive menu and dinner can be arranged on request.
3 en suite (shr) No smoking Tea and coffee making facilities
Cen ht CTV 3P No coaches Last d 10am

TOBERMORY See **MULL, ISLE OF**

TWYNHOLM Dumfries & Galloway *Kirkcudbrightshire*
Map **11** NX65

Selected

GH Ⓠ Ⓠ Ⓠ Ⓠ **Fresh Fields** DG6 4PB
☎01557 860221 FAX 01557 860221
Mar-Oct
This three-gabled white house is set in its own colourful
garden amidst fields and meadows just outside the small
village of Twynholm. It has developed quite a following -
caring owners Mr and Mrs Stanley ensuring that guests are
remembered and their requests met. The bedrooms are bright
and attractively furnished, offering private modern facilities.
Downstairs there are a delightful lounge with china miniatures
and a wood-panelled dining room where four-course evening
meals are served.

5 en suite (shr) No smoking in 2 bedrooms No smoking in
dining room No smoking in lounges Tea and coffee making
facilities Licensed Cen ht CTV No children 5yrs 10P No
coaches Last d 5.30pm
PRICE GUIDE
ROOMS: (incl. dinner) s £39-£41; d £78-£82; wkly hlf-bd
£273-£287✱

ULLAPOOL Highland *Ross & Cromarty* Map **14** NH19

Selected

GH Ⓠ Ⓠ Ⓠ Ⓠ *Ardvreck* Morefield Brae IV26 2TH (N on
A835) ☎01854 612028 FAX 01854 612028
Situated on a hillside north of town, with spectacular views
over Loch Broom, this family-run guest house offers excellent
value bed and breakfast accommodation. Bright, airy en suite
bedrooms feature comfortable pine furnishings while public
areas include an open-plan lounge/dining room. In the
interests of guests' comfort, smoking is not permitted.
10 en suite (shr) (2 fmly) No smoking CTV in all bedrooms
Tea and coffee making facilities Cen ht ch fac 14P No
coaches

Selected

GH Ⓠ Ⓠ Ⓠ Ⓠ **Dromnan** Garve Rd IV26 2SX (turn left at
30mph sign as you enter town from A835)
☎01854 6123333
The MacDonald family have recently extended their
comfortable family home to provide quality accommodation.
Standing in its own gardens on the western fringe of the
village, the house enjoys a splendid outlook over Loch
Broom. Bedroom, though varying in size, are all en suite and
offer attractive decor and modern appointments. Public areas
are open plan and include a comfortable lounge and a gright
and ary timber-clad dining room, where enjoyable breakfasts
are served. This is a no-smoking establishment.
7 en suite (bth/shr) (2 fmly) No smoking CTV in all
bedrooms Tea and coffee making facilities No dogs (ex
guide dogs) Cen ht CTV 7P
PRICE GUIDE
ROOMS: d £36-£40; wkly b&b £126-£140✱

Selected

GH Ⓠ Ⓠ Ⓠ Ⓠ **The Sheiling** Garve Rd IV26 2SX (on
A835, at S end of village) ☎01854 612947
Closed Xmas & New Year
This welcoming guest house stands in its own well tended
garden beside the picturesque shore of Loch Broom. Bright,
cheery bedrooms are maintained to the highest standards,
while the split-level dining room offers hearty breakfasts
featuring home-made venison sausages. In the adjacent
Sportsman Lodge facilities include a rod room - brown trout
fishing being available to residents in a selection of hill lochs
- as well as a sauna and laundry/drying room; there is also
secure undercover parking for motor cycles and cycles.
Guests should note this is a non-smoking establishment.

7 en suite (bth/shr) No smoking Tea and coffee making
facilities No dogs (ex guide dogs) Cen ht CTV 7P Fishing
Sauna
PRICE GUIDE
ROOMS: d £36-£42; wkly b&b £114-£132✱

(£)

WHITING BAY See **ARRAN, ISLE OF**

DAYS OUT
IN BRITAIN & IRELAND 1996
HISTORIC HOUSES, CASTLES & GARDENS
MUSEUMS & GALLERIES
INDUSTRIAL HERITAGE & ANCIENT MONUMENTS
WILDLIFE PARKS & NATURE RESERVES
THEME PARKS & CHILDREN'S ATTRACTIONS
COMPLETE WITH LOCATION ATLAS

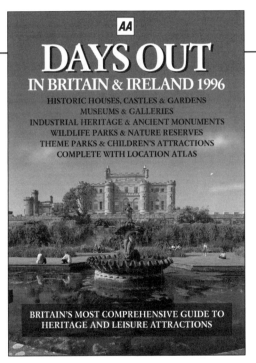

**BRITAIN'S MOST COMPREHENSIVE GUIDE TO
HERITAGE AND LEISURE ATTRACTIONS**

NEW EDITION
PUBLISHED
SPRING 1996

Britain's most comprehensive
Guide to Heritage and
Leisure Attractions. This
Guide is up-dated annually
and is available from all good
bookshops.

Price: £6.99

- HISTORIC HOUSES, CASTLES & GARDENS
- INDUSTRIAL HERITAGE & ANCIENT MONUMENTS
- THEME PARKS & CHILDREN'S ATTRACTIONS
- WILDLIFE PARKS & NATURE RESERVES
- MUSEUMS & GALLERIES
- COMPLETE WITH LOCATION ATLAS

Follow the Country Code

Enjoy the countryside and
respect its life and work.

Guard against all risk of fire.

Fasten all gates.

Keep your dogs under close control.

Keep to public paths across farmland.

Use gates and stiles to cross
fences, hedges and walls.

Leave livestock, crops
and machinery alone.

Take your litter home.

Help to keep all water clean.

Protect wildlife, plants and trees.

Take special care on country roads.

Make no unnecessary noise.

WALES

PREMIER SELECTED
QQQQQ

A quick-reference list of establishments in Wales in this year's guide with a QQQQQ rating for Quality – the AA's highest rating for guest houses, farmhouses and inns.

CLWYD
RUTHIN
Eyarth Station

GWYNEDD
BARMOUTH
Plas Bach

BETWS-Y-COED
Tan-y-Foel

BONTDDU
Borthwnog Hall Hotel

LLANFACHRETH
Ty Isaf Farmhouse

LLANWNDA
Pengwern Farm

POWYS
NEWTOWN
Dyffryn Farmhouse

PENYBONT
Ffaldau

WEST GLAMORGAN
NEATH
Green Lanterns

SELECTED
QQQQ

A quick-reference of establishments in Wales in this year's guide with QQQQ rating for Quality – each year more establishments in the guide rise this very high standard.

CLWYD
Corwen
Powys House Estate
St Asaph
Bach-Y-Graig

DYFED
Aberystwyth
Glyn-Garth
Brechfa
Glasfryn
Carew
Old Stable Cottage
Farm Retreats
Pantgwyn Farm
Fishguard
Erw-Lon Farm
Gwaun Valley
Tregynon Farmhouse
Hotel
Llanrhystud
Pen-Y-Castell Farm
Pembroke
Poyerston Farm
Solva
Lochmeyler Farm
St David's
Ramsey House

GWENT
Abergavenny
Llanwenarth House
Redwick
Brickhouse

GWYNEDD
Aberdovey
Brodawel
Abersoch
Carisbrooke Hotel
Crowrach Isaf
Bala
Abercelyn
Bangor
Country Bumpkin
Nant y Fedw
Betws-Y-Coed
Aberconwy House
The White Horse Inn
Caernarfon
Caer Menai
Cemaes Bay
Haford
Harlech
Castle Cottage Hotel
Gwrach Ynys

Llandudno
Cornerways Hotel
Craiglands Private Hotel
Cranberry House
Hollybank
Hotel Messina
Llanegryn
Bryn Gwyn
Penmachno
Penmachno Hall
Porthmadog
Tyddyn Du Farm
Rowen
Gwern Borter
Tal-Y-Llyn
Dolffanog Fawr

MID GLAMORGAN
Merthyr Tydfil
Llwyn Onn

POWYS
Brecon
Coach Guest House
Brecon
Llandetty Hall Farm

Church Stoke
The Drewin Farm
Llandrindod Wells
Guidfa House
Three Wells
Llangurig
Old Vicarage
Montgomery
Little Brompton Farm
Penybont
Neuadd Farm
Sennybridge
Brynfedwen Farm
Welshpool
Gungrog House
Lower Trelydan
Farmhouse
Moat Farm

WEST GLAMORGAN
Neath
Cwmbach Cottages
Swansea
Cefn Bryn
Tredilion House Hotel

WALES

ABERAERON Dyfed Map **02** SN46

GH 🔲🔲🔲 *Arosfa* 8 Cadwgan Place SA46 0BU
☎01545 570120
This charming little guest house is situated in a row of terraced properties, over 150 years old, standing opposite the harbour. It has a wealth of charm and character, which is enhanced by period and antique furniture and an abundance of bric-⅓-brac. There is a cosy lounge, a bar, and a cottage style dining room. Bedrooms are traditionally furnished and include a family suite. Three rooms are located in a separate cottage, some 100 yards from the main house. These rooms are not en suite, though one has an en suite toilet.
3 en suite (bth/shr) 3 annexe rms (1 fmly) No smoking CTV in 3 bedrooms Tea and coffee making facilities No dogs (ex guide dogs) Licensed Cen ht CTV Last d 6pm

---

GH 🔲🔲🔲 *Fairview* Cadwgan Place SA46 0BU
☎01545 571472
This charming and delightful early 19th century terraced house overlooks the harbour. It has been tastefully restored without any loss of the original character, which is enhanced by the use of period and antique furniture throughout. The three bedrooms are all en-suite with modern facilities and one is a family room. There is a comfortable, cosy lounge and an attractive dining room where guests share one table. This is a non smoking establishment.
3 en suite (bth/shr) (2 fmly) CTV in all bedrooms Tea and coffee making facilities Cen ht CTV No coaches Last d 4pm

---

ABERDOVEY (ABERDYFI) Gwynedd Map **06** SN69

Selected

GH 🔲🔲🔲🔲 *Brodawel* Tywyn Rd, Brodawel LL35 0SA
(on A439) ☎01654 767347
Mar-Oct
This fine Edwardian house is set in pretty lawns and gardens on the western edge of the village, opposite the local championship golf course. Well equipped bedrooms are furnished in pine and decorated with pretty papers and fabrics. There is a comfortably furnished lounge as well as a cosy bar, and several rooms have lovely views. Smoking is not permitted.
6 en suite (bth/shr) No smoking CTV in all bedrooms Tea and coffee making facilities Licensed Cen ht No children 8P No coaches Last d 2pm
PRICE GUIDE
ROOMS: s £22; d £44; wkly b&b £136✱

GH 🔲🔲 *Cartref* LL35 0NR (W on A493) ☎01654 767273
A pleasant family-run guest house, Cartref is situated on the Tywyn side of the village, near the sandy beach and the bowling greens. Bedrooms are equipped with TVs, clock radios and controllable central heating, many also having en suite facilities. A traditional residents' lounge is available and there is a forecourt car park.
7 rms (1 bth 3 shr) (2 fmly) No smoking in dining room CTV in 6 bedrooms Tea and coffee making facilities Cen ht CTV 8P No coaches Last d 5pm
PRICE GUIDE
ROOMS: s £17.50; d £36-£38; wkly b&b £123-£130; wkly hlf-bd £186-£193

GH 🔲🔲 **Rossa** LL35 0NR (W on A493, establishment opposite bowling green and tennis courts) ☎01654 767545
Closed Dec & Jan
The friendly Rowley family run this small, well maintained guest house, which lies on the western side of the village convenient for the bowling green and golf course. All the cosy, brightly decorated bedrooms now have en suite or private bathrooms, a residents' lounge is provided, and there are pretty lawns and gardens.
4 rms (3 shr) (1 fmly) No smoking in dining room CTV in all bedrooms Tea and coffee making facilities Cen ht CTV 3P No coaches Last d 4pm
PRICE GUIDE
ROOMS: d £30-£34; wkly b&b £100-£115; wkly hlf-bd £155-£169✱

ABERGAVENNY Gwent Map **03** SO21

Selected

GH 🔲🔲🔲🔲 **Llanwenarth House** Govilon NP7 9SF (3m W on A465) ☎01873 830289 FAX 01873 832199
rs Jan
Quietly situated within the Brecon Beacons National Park, this large manor house stands in its own extensive grounds. It dates from the 16th century, and was built by the Morgan family, ancestors of the privateer Sir Henry. The present owners, Amanda and Bruce Weatherill, have extensively restored the property, and now offer comfortable and spacious accommodation which has been tastefully furnished in the style of the house. The bedrooms are all decently sized, and come with suite facilities and modern creature comforts. Welcoming log fires burn in the inviting lounge in winter, and there are separate tables in the attractive dining room.
5 en suite (bth/shr) (1 fmly) No smoking in dining room CTV in all bedrooms Tea and coffee making facilities Licensed Cen ht No children 10yrs 6P No coaches Last d 6.30pm
PRICE GUIDE
ROOMS: s £44-£55; d £64-£75✱

♥ 🔲🔲 Mrs D Miles *Great Lwynfranc (SO327193)*
Llanvihangel Crucorney NP7 8EN (off A465 3m N)
☎01873 890418
Apr-Nov
Approached by a bumpy track off the A465 Abergavenny to Hereford road, this friendly little farmhouse offers traditional accommodation. From an elevated position it commands extensive views over the Llanthony Valley.
3 rms (1 shr) (1 fmly) No smoking in bedrooms No smoking in dining room Tea and coffee making facilities Cen ht CTV ch fac 10P 154 acres mixed

---

♥ 🔲🔲🔲 Mrs J Nicholls **Newcourt** *(SO317165)* Mardy NP7 8AU (2m N, on edge of village of Mardy)
☎01873 852300 FAX 01873 852300
Enthusiastically run by a young family, this 17th-century stone-built courthouse offers stylish accommodation in nicely furnished bedrooms. There is a comfortable lounge and dining room with handsome traditional furnishings. The house enjoys fine views of the Sugar Loaf mountain.

3 en suite (bth/shr) No smoking CTV in all bedrooms Tea and coffee making facilities No dogs (ex guide dogs) Cen ht CTV No children 10yrs 10P Snooker 160 acres arable beef
PRICE GUIDE
ROOMS: s £20-£25; d £40✱

♥ Q|Q|Q Mrs A Davies **Penyclawdd** *(SO311201)* Llanvihangel Crucorney NP7 7LB (5m N, off A465) ☎01873 890591
Peacefully situated on a beef and sheep rearing farm in the foothills of the Black Mountains, Penyclawdd Farm is located five miles north of Abergavenny (take the road signed to Pantgelli from the A465). Accommodation consists of two modern family-bedded rooms which share a bathroom, a comfortable lounge and a pleasant breakfast room with separate tables. Smoking is not allowed in the house.
2 rms (2 fmly) No smoking Tea and coffee making facilities Cen ht CTV 6P 160 acres sheep beef
PRICE GUIDE
ROOMS: s £15; d £30; wkly b&b £95✱

ABERPORTH Dyfed Map **02** SN25

GH Q|Q|Q *Ffynonwen Country* SA43 2HT ☎01239 810312
This pleasant family-run, converted farmhouse stands in a lovely rural setting just east of the town. Bedrooms have been mostly modernised; there are several family suites and a ground-floor room adapted for disabled guests. Extensive public rooms include a pleasant lounge-style bar, a conservatory lounge and a small games room.
6 rms (5 bth/shr) (3 fmly) CTV in all bedrooms Tea and coffee making facilities Licensed Cen ht 30P No coaches Fishing

ABERSOCH Gwynedd Map **06** SH32

Selected

GH Q|Q|Q|Q **Carisbrooke Hotel** High St LL53 7DY
☎01758 712526 FAX 01758 712526
8 rms (4 shr) (1 fmly) No smoking in dining room No smoking in lounges No dogs (ex guide dogs) Licensed Cen ht CTV 12P No coaches Last d 6pm
PRICE GUIDE
ROOMS: d £32-£45✱
CARDS: ■ ■

Selected

GH Q|Q|Q|Q **Crowrach Isaf** Bwlchtocyn LL53 7BY (from Abersoch follow road through Sarn Bach, then turn left through Bwlchtocyn. Turn right at 'No Through Road' sign, second on right) ☎01758 712860
This immaculately maintained house is beautifully positioned two miles from Abersoch with magnificent views over Cardigan Bay and the mountains of Snowdonia. Janet and Derek Clark afford their guests a very warm welcome and make every effort to ensure they are comfortable and well looked after. The three no smoking bedrooms, two of which are en suite and one has the exclusive use of a separate bathrooms, are comfortable, attractively decorated and well equipped with televisions, tea and coffee making facilities and fully controllable central heating. A freshly prepared four course dinner and a five-course breakfast are served in the pleasant dining room. Guests have the use of the conservatory

lounge with plenty of books and games, a larger, more formal lounge and the house's beautifully tended gardens.
3 rms (2 bth/shr) No smoking CTV in all bedrooms Tea and coffee making facilities No dogs Cen ht No children 8yrs 7P No coaches Last d 1pm
PRICE GUIDE
ROOMS: s £17-£20; d £34-£40; wkly b&b £110-£125; wkly hlf-bd £189-£210✱

GH Q|Q|Q **Ty Draw** Lon Sarn Bach LL53 7EL (from village centre, take Sarn Bach road, guesthouse 10 metres past Abersoch Fire Station) ☎01758 712647 FAX 01758 712647
May-Sep
Peter and Jean Collins have run this pretty guest house for over twenty years and some of their visitors have come back regularly over this period. They are exceptionally friendly and welcoming, nothing is too much trouble and no guest should forget to try some of Jean's delicious home made bread. Bedrooms are freshly decorated and modern and, by the time this guide is published, all will have ensuite or private bathrooms. There is a cosy lounge, well maintained lawns and gardens and a large car park.
5 en suite (bth/shr) (1 fmly) No smoking in bedrooms No smoking in lounges No dogs (ex guide dogs) CTV ch fac 10P No coaches
PRICE GUIDE
ROOMS: d £32-£40; wkly b&b £108-£136✱

NEW COURT
Mardy, Abergavenny, Gwent.
Telephone: (01873) 852300

17th Century New Court situated 2 miles north of Abergavenny at the base of the Skirrid Mountain. Each room has been tastefully furnished. Double rooms en suite. Twin rooms with private bathroom. All have tea making facilities and colour TV.
An ideal base for touring Wales, offering access to a variety of outdoor activities.
Write or telephone for details to Bryan and Janet Nicholls.

ABERYSTWYTH Dyfed Map **06** SN58

Selected

GH Ⓠ Ⓠ Ⓠ Ⓠ **Glyn-Garth** South Rd SY23 1JS
☎01970 615050
Closed 1 wk Xmas
A very soundly maintained guest house close to the harbour, castle and South Promenade. Bedrooms have modern furnishings and there is one on the ground floor. There is a comfortable lounge and breakfast room with separate tables.
11 rms (6 bth/shr) (2 fmly) No smoking CTV in all bedrooms Tea and coffee making facilities No dogs Cen ht CTV 2P No coaches
PRICE GUIDE
ROOMS: s £17-£36; d £34-£46✱

GH Ⓠ Ⓠ **Llety Gwyn Hotel** Llanbadarn Fawr SY23 3SX (1m E A44) ☎01970 623965
rs 25-26 Dec
This is a family-run hotel has a comfortable lounge, a large bar and a gymnasium. Bedrooms vary in size, with a mix of older and modern furniture. It has family rooms on the ground floor and there are rooms in a separate annexe.
8 rms (4 shr) 6 annexe rms (1 bth 3 shr) CTV in all bedrooms Tea and coffee making facilities Licensed Cen ht CTV 40P Pool table Last d 12.30pm
PRICE GUIDE
ROOMS: s £21-£25; d £40-£48
CARDS: 🔳 💳

GH Ⓠ Ⓠ Ⓠ **Queensbridge Hotel** Promenade, Victoria Ter SY23 2DH (N end of promenade, near Constitution Hill Cliff railway) ☎01970 612343 615025 FAX 01970 617452
Closed 1 wk Xmas
15 en suite (bth/shr) (6 fmly) No smoking in dining room CTV in all bedrooms Tea and coffee making facilities Direct dial from bedrooms No dogs (ex guide dogs) Licensed Lift Cen ht CTV No parking
PRICE GUIDE
ROOMS: s £28-£36; d £44-£50; wkly b&b £150-£165
CARDS: 🔳 💳 💳 💳 💳 💳

GH Ⓠ Ⓠ Ⓠ **Yr Hafod** 1 South Marine Ter SY23 1JX
☎01970 617579
This large house, which stands on the sea front, in a quiet area at the southern end of the town, has been extensively renovated by young proprietor John Evans. It provides very well maintained, modern accommodation, which includes rooms with sea views, rooms with en-suite facilities, no smoking rooms and family bedded rooms. Separate tables are provided in the attractively appointed breakfast room, which enjoys sea views. There is also a cosy lounge.
7 rms (1 bth 1 shr) (2 fmly) No smoking in bedrooms No smoking in dining room No smoking in lounges CTV in all bedrooms Tea and coffee making facilities No dogs Cen ht CTV 1P No coaches
PRICE GUIDE
ROOMS: s £22-£30; d £32-£40; wkly b&b £105-£133

ANGLESEY, ISLE OF Gwynedd Map **06**

BEAUMARIS Map **06** SH67

❚ Ⓠ **Bold Arms Hotel** Church St LL58 8AA ☎01248 810313
5 rms (4 shr) CTV in all bedrooms Tea and coffee making facilities P

CEMAES BAY Map **06** SH39

Selected

GH Ⓠ Ⓠ Ⓠ Ⓠ **Haford Country House** LL67 0DS (off A5025, turning for Llanfechell, opposite renovated windmill) ☎01407 710500
Mar-Oct
Built at the turn of the century, this fine house is set in well maintained and mature grounds. It is located on the outskirts of the village and is best found by taking the Llanfechell road from the A5025 roundabout. Three modern bedrooms are provided and these are attractively decorated and well equipped with such extras as televisions, clock/radios and electric blankets when needed. A spacious lounge is available and tennis and croquet can be played on the lawn. Gina and Tony Hirst are the very friendly owners and Gina has gained a fine reputation for the quality and enjoyment of her food.
3 en suite (shr) No smoking in bedrooms No smoking in dining room CTV in all bedrooms Tea and coffee making facilities No dogs (ex guide dogs) Licensed Cen ht No children 7yrs 5P No coaches Tennis (grass) Croquet Last d 4pm
PRICE GUIDE
ROOMS: d £40; wkly b&b £126; wkly hlf-bd £206.50

HOLYHEAD Map **06** SH28

🛏 🛳 GH Ⓠ Ⓠ **Wavecrest** 93 Newry St LL65 1HU
☎01407 763637
Situated just a short walk from the harbour, this cosy little guest house provides well equipped bedrooms with satellite TV. There is a particularly comfortable residents' lounge, and evening meals are available. There is no car park but street parking is easy. The property is situated near the ferry terminal and consequently is popular with travellers to Ireland.
4 rms (2 shr) (3 fmly) No smoking in dining room No smoking in lounges CTV in all bedrooms Tea and coffee making facilities Cen ht CTV 1P No coaches Last d 3pm
PRICE GUIDE
ROOMS: s £15-£20; d £28-£32; wkly b&b £90-£105; wkly hlf-bd £130-£150

GH Ⓠ Ⓠ **Witchingham** 20 Walthew Av LL65 1AF (A5 to ferry terminal, pass South Stack pub take first left. After passing coast guard station on right, take second left and 50 yds on right) ☎01407 762426
A small, cosy guest house situated just off the harbour and convenient for ferry travellers. The three bedrooms are modern and freshly decorated, and there is a comfortable lounge for residents. Car parking is easily available on the roadside.
5 rms (1 shr) (3 fmly) CTV in all bedrooms Tea and coffee making facilities No dogs (ex guide dogs) Cen ht CTV No parking
PRICE GUIDE
ROOMS: s £12-£15; d £24-£30; wkly b&b £84-£105✱

RHOSCOLYN Map 06 SH27

GH QQQ **The Old Rectory** LL65 2SQ (take B4545 then follow signs Rhoscolyn just after Four Mile Bridge follow rd for 2 miles then rd alongside church) ☎01407 860214
Closed 21 Dec-19 Jan rs 1 wk Oct
This Georgian rectory enjoys superb views over the sea and surrounding countryside. Its grounds are filled with mature trees and shrubs, and the surrounding area is well known for its wild flowers and birdlife. The house itself contains five well decorated en suite bedrooms, one of them situated at ground level and so suitable for less mobile visitors. There is a comfortable sitting room, and guests dine communally in country house style.
5 en suite (bth/shr) (2 fmly) No smoking in 3 bedrooms No smoking in dining room No smoking in lounges CTV in all bedrooms Tea and coffee making facilities Licensed Cen ht CTV 8P No coaches Last d 10 am
PRICE GUIDE
ROOMS: s £31.50; d £48-£51; wkly b&b £160; wkly hlf-bd £260
CARDS: 🔲 💳

TREARDDUR BAY Map 06 SH27

GH QQ **Moranedd** Trearddur Rd LL65 2UE (off A5 in Valley onto B4545 and take 2nd right after Beach Hotel) ☎01407 860324
Quietly situated in its own well tended garden in a residential cul-de-sac within easy reach of the beach, this friendly family-run establishment offers good-value bed and breakfast accommodation. Reasonably spacious, attractively decorated bedrooms are practically furnished while public areas include a choice of comfortable lounges and a separate breakfast room.
6 rms (1 fmly) No smoking in dining room Tea and coffee making facilities No dogs (ex guide dogs) Licensed Cen ht CTV 10P No coaches
PRICE GUIDE
ROOMS: s £14; d £28* £

BALA Gwynedd Map 06 SH93

Selected

GH QQQQ **Abercelyn Country House** Llanycil LL23 7YF (0.5m from outskirts of town on A494 towards Dolgellau) ☎01678 521109 FAX 01678 520556
Closed 21 Dec-4 Jan
For many years this fine house was the local rectory. Dating from 1729 and set in landscaped gardens complete with rushing stream, it offers superb views of the lake. Many original features remain, including a Georgian staircase and marble fireplaces where log fires burn in colder weather. The comfortably furnished sitting room is provided with a large collection of books and tourist brochures. This is a no-smoking establishment.
3 rms (1 bth 1 shr) Tea and coffee making facilities No dogs (ex guide dogs) Cen ht CTV 3P No coaches
PRICE GUIDE
ROOMS: s £20.50-£22.50; d £41-£45
CARDS: 🔲 💳

🏠💷 **GH** QQ **Erw Feurig** Cefnddwysarn LL23 7LL (3m on A494 towards Corwen) ☎01678 530262
This attractive little farmhouse stands in an elevated position just off the A494 3.5 miles east of the town, offering lovely views of the Berwyn mountains. Four pretty rooms are provided, two with

en suite shower rooms and two with private facilities; some rooms are suitable for families. There is a cosy TV lounge for residents, and coarse fishing is available.
4 rms (2 shr) (2 fmly) No smoking in 2 bedrooms No smoking in dining room No smoking in lounges Tea and coffee making facilities No dogs Cen ht CTV 7P Fishing Snooker Pool table Last d 5.30pm
PRICE GUIDE
ROOMS: s £14-£16; d £28-£34; wkly hlf-bd £150-£170 £

GH QQ **Frondderw** Stryd-y-Fron LL23 7YD (down main street north to south pass cinema on left take 1st road on right, up hill 0.25m signposted to Bala golf course, take right fork) ☎01678 520301
Mar-Nov
Superb views over the lake to the Berwyn mountains beyond are offered by this family-run guest house situated above Bala. The bedrooms are attractively decorated and all the beds have woollen covers made by an authentic Welsh mill, while the choice of lounges includes one with TV. The atmosphere is peaceful and relaxing, and honest home-cooked meals are provided.
8 rms (1 bth 3 shr) (3 fmly) No smoking in dining room No smoking in 1 lounge Tea and coffee making facilities No dogs (ex guide dogs) Licensed Cen ht CTV 10P No coaches Last d 5pm
PRICE GUIDE
ROOMS: s £20-£21; d £30-£42; wkly b&b £101.50-£143.50; wkly hlf-bd £168-£204 £

See advertisement on p.573.

QUEENSBRIDGE HOTEL

The Promenade, Aberystwyth SY23 2BX
Dyfed, Wales.
Telephone: 01970 612343

Situated at the quiet north end of Aberystwyth's Promenade, five minutes' walk from town centre and overlooking the panoramic sweep of Cardigan Bay, the Queensbridge offers superior comfort in fifteen spacious en suite bedrooms all with colour TV, hospitality tray and telephone. Comfortable lounge, residents' bar, passenger lift, excellent choice of breakfast.
Our reputation for comfort and service is well-known.

♥ 🔲🔲 Mrs M E Jones **Pen-Y-Bryn** *(SH498723)* Sarnau LL23 7LH (4m N on A494, outskirts of Sarnau village) ☎01678 530297
This 19th-century farmhouse is situated high above the A494, just over 3.5 miles east of Bala, with lovely views towards the Berwyn mountains. Bedrooms are pretty and freshly decorated and residents have a choice of sitting rooms, one having a log fire and TV while the other, which looks out over the countryside, doubles as a dining room.
6 rms (1 fmly) No dogs Cen ht CTV 10P Fishing 200 acres beef mixed sheep Last d 6pm
PRICE GUIDE
ROOMS: s fr £16; d fr £28✳

(£)

BANGOR Gwynedd Map **06** SH57

Selected

GH 🔲🔲🔲🔲 **Country Bumpkin** Cefn Coed, Llandegai LL57 4BG (Bangor side of A5/A55 junct, signposted off A522) ☎01248 370477 FAX 01248 354166
Closed Xmas & Jan
A 200-year-old farmhouse, the Country Bumpkin has been completely modernised in recent years and now provides spacious accommodation; bedrooms all feature Stag furnishings and good en suite bathrooms, some of them also offering views of Penrhyn Castle and the Menai Straits. The modern restaurant - which has gained a fine local reputation - offers a fixed-price menu which makes good use of fresh local produce and fish, and there is an adjacent lounge area for drinks and coffee.
3 en suite (bth/shr) No smoking in dining room CTV in all bedrooms Tea and coffee making facilities Licensed Cen ht CTV No children 16yrs 20P No coaches Last d 8pm
PRICE GUIDE
ROOMS: s £30; d £40✳
CARDS: 🔳 🔳

Selected

GH 🔲🔲🔲🔲 **Nant y Fedw** Trefelin, Llanedgai LL57 4LH ☎01248 351683
This delightful little cottage is quietly situated near Penrhyn Castle, between the villages of Tal-y-Bont and Llandegai. It dates back some 150 years and has a wealth of charm, which is enhanced by original features, such as the exposed ceiling beams in the comfortable lounge and the pleasant dining room. There are two bedrooms, both no smoking, one a twin and the other a double. Both are tastefully furnished and have modern equipment. The twin has an en suite bathroom, whilst the double has a nearby private shower and toilet. There is a lovely mature and spacious garden to the rear of the house.
2 en suite (bth/shr) No smoking in bedrooms No smoking in dining room CTV in all bedrooms Tea and coffee making facilities Cen ht CTV 4P No coaches Last d 8pm
PRICE GUIDE
ROOMS: s £18; d £30

|≕ 🖳| ♥ 🔲🔲🔲 Mr & Mrs Whowell **Goetre Isaf Farmhouse** *(SH557697)* Caernarfon Rd LL57 4DB (2m W on A4087) ☎01248 364541 FAX 01248 364541
Goetre Isaf is a delightful farmhouse situated high above the A5, reached by its own private road. It is set in nine acres of bracken-

covered hills with views of Snowdonia, Anglesey and the Lleyn Peninsula. The house dates from 1780 and there is an impressive inglenook fireplace in the cosy sitting room, complete with a wood burning stove. Bedrooms, one with a canopied bed, are freshly decorated .
3 rms (1 bth/shr) (1 fmly) No smoking in 1 lounge Direct dial from bedrooms Cen ht CTV ch fac P 10 acres sheep horses bees
PRICE GUIDE
ROOMS: s fr £15; d £26-£36; wkly b&b fr £115; wkly hlf-bd fr £153.50

(£)

BARMOUTH Gwynedd Map **06** SH61

GH 🔲🔲 *Endeavour* Marine Pde LL42 1NA ☎01341 280271
Closed mid Dec-mid Jan
A cheerful little guest house on the promenade, a short walk from the shops, the Endeavour has many sea-facing bedrooms. The rooms are all spacious and several are suitable for families.
9 rms (5 shr) CTV in 8 bedrooms Tea and coffee making facilities No dogs (ex guide dogs) Licensed Cen ht CTV Last d 4pm
CARDS: 🔳 🔳

GH 🔲🔲🔲 *Morwendon* Llanaber LL42 1RR (1.5m N on A496 coast road) ☎01341 280566
Mar-Oct
This small guest house is set in two acres of land and overlooks Cardigan Bay, with access to the beach. All bedrooms have sea views, central heating and en-suite shower rooms, and several have tower-shaped sitting areas. Honest home cooking is served in the pretty restaurant, and there is also a bar and a residents lounge.
6 en suite (shr) No smoking in dining room CTV in all bedrooms Tea and coffee making facilities No dogs (ex guide dogs) Licensed Cen ht CTV 7P No coaches Last d 5pm

Premier Selected

GH 🔲🔲🔲🔲🔲 **Plas Bach Country House** Plas Bach, Glandwr, Bontddu LL42 1TG (turn right off A496 onto lane follow signs turning in 2.4m beyond Esso Garage in village, travelling west towards Barmouth) ☎01341 281234
This lovely Georgian house stands in three acres of gardens on the sunny side of the Mawddach estuary with spectacular views of Snowdonia. It has been delightfully refurbished to offer attractive accommodation. The pretty en suite bedrooms are well equipped and have nice personal touches such as fresh fruit and flowers, while a spacious lounge has a log fire on cooler days. An excellent home-cooked dinner uses only the best local produce and service is relaxed and informal. The house is licensed and operates a non-smoking policy.
5 en suite (bth/shr) No smoking CTV in all bedrooms Tea and coffee making facilities Cen ht No children 15yrs 5P No coaches Last d 3pm
PRICE GUIDE
ROOMS: s £27.50-£30; d £55-£60; wkly b&b fr £180; wkly hlf-bd £257-£300✳

(£)

BEAUMARIS See ANGLESEY, ISLE OF

BETWS-Y-COED Gwynedd Map **06** SH75

Selected

GH Q Q Q Q **Aberconwy House** Llanwrst Rd LL24 0HD
(N on A470, half a mile north from A5/A470 junct)
☎01690 710202 FAX 01690 710800
rs Jan-Mar
This large Victorian house is situated just north of the village,
with lovely views of the Conwy and Llugwy valleys and the
surrounding mountains. Maureen and Clive Muskus offer a
warm welcome, and are constantly making improvements
with guests' comfort in mind. Bedrooms are freshly decorated
and furnished with good quality fitted units and several extra
touches; most rooms enjoy magnificent views. There is a
comfortable, modern lounge and pretty dining room, and a
special feature is the large collection of paintings on display,
many of which may be purchased.
8 en suite (bth/shr) (2 fmly) No smoking in dining room
CTV in all bedrooms Tea and coffee making facilities
Licensed Cen ht CTV 10P No coaches
PRICE GUIDE
ROOMS: d £40-£50✱
(£)

GH Q **Bryn Llewelyn** Holyhead Rd LL24 0BN (travelling
west on A5, turn sharp left 100yds beyond "Climber &
Rambler" shop) ☎01690 710601
Good-value accommodation is offered at this stone-built guest
house run by the friendly Naomi and Steve Parker. Bedrooms
include several suitable for families, and these are much in
demand in the tourist season. More en suite shower rooms are
planned over the course of this year and next. A comfortable
lounge is provided for guests.
7 rms (3 shr) (3 fmly) No smoking in 2 bedrooms No smoking
in dining room CTV in 2 bedrooms Tea and coffee making
facilities Cen ht CTV 11P
PRICE GUIDE
ROOMS: s £14.50-£18.50; d £28-£37; wkly b&b £98-£126✱

GH Q Q Q **The Ferns** Holyhead Rd LL24 0AN (on A5 close
to Waterloo Bridge) ☎01690 710587 FAX 01690 710587
A pretty little guest house with a relaxed atmosphere stands in the
middle of the village, with the River Conwy on one side and
beautiful wooded slopes on the other. Seven of its attractively
decorated bedrooms have modern en suite facilities and the other
two share a bathroom. Downstairs there are a comfortable
residents' lounge and separate breakfast room, and good car
parking facilities are provided.
9 rms (7 shr) (2 fmly) No smoking CTV in all bedrooms Tea
and coffee making facilities No dogs Licensed Cen ht CTV No
children 4yrs 10P
PRICE GUIDE
ROOMS: s £18-£20; d £32-£40; wkly b&b £224✱
(£)

See advertisement on p.575.

GH Q Q **Riverside Restaurant** Holyhead Rd LL24 0BN (on
A5) ☎01690 710650 FAX 01690 710650
This small, family run, no smoking guest house is situated on the
A5, close to the village centre. The premises also include a cottage
style restaurant, where a wide range of dishes, plus afternoon teas
and snacks are served. The bedrooms, which include family
rooms, are all situated on the second floor. They are not luxurious,

➡

Frondderw
Bala, Gwynedd LL23 7YD. N. Wales
Tel: Bala (01678) 520301

FRONDDERW is a seventeenth century mansion quietly
situated in its own grounds on the hillside overlooking Bala
town and lake, with magnificent views of the Berwyn
Mountains.

All Bedrooms have hot/cold and tea/coffee making facilities.
Full en-suite facilities are available in 50% of the bedrooms.

There is a large lounge and separate colour TV lounge for
guests' use. No smoking allowed in the dining room.

An excellent evening meal is available on request. Vegetarian
and other diets are catered for, advance notice required.
Supper and residential licence. No garage accommodation.
Outdoor parking free of charge. Sorry no guests' pets allowed
in the house. Ideal centre for sightseeing, touring, walking and
water sports.

Closed December, January and February.

Aberconwy House
S E L E C T E D

Betws-Y-Coed
Llanrwst Road (A470), Gwynedd, LL24 0HD
Tel: 01690 710202 Fax: 01690 710800
This spacious Victorian Guest House overlooks
picturesque village of Betws-Y-Coed and has
beautiful scenic views of the Llugwy Valley. There
are eight bedrooms completely and tastefully
refurnished. Each one has CTV, beverage makers,
central heating, en-suite facilities, etc.
You are assured of a warm welcome by Ann and
Clive Muskus, comfortable accommodation and
robust breakfast.

but are soundly maintained, have modern equipment and represent good value for money. A room with an en suite bathroom is available.

4 rms (1 bth/shr) (2 fmly) No smoking CTV in all bedrooms Tea and coffee making facilities No dogs Licensed Cen ht No children 10yrs No parking Last d 9.30pm

PRICE GUIDE
ROOMS: s £11.95; d £19.90-£23.90; wkly b&b £69.45-£83.45; wkly hlf-bd fr £138.90✻
CARDS: 🔲 🔳 ⓪

GH 🔲🔲 **Summer Hill Non Smokers Guesthouse**
Coedcynhelier Rd LL24 0BL (turn off A5 opposite "Climber & Rambler" shop, gross bridge, turn left go through car park, Summer Hill is 70yds up hill on right) ☎01690 710306
Closed Xmas

Surrounded by trees and looking out over the River Llugwy and Fir Tree Island, this family-run guest house occupies an elevated position above the village. En suite shower rooms have already been added to three bedrooms and there are plans to introduce more over the next year or so. Residents have the use of a comfortable lounge and evening meals can be provided. This is a no-smoking establishment.

7 rms (3 shr) (1 fmly) No smoking CTV in 1 bedroom Tea and coffee making facilities Licensed Cen ht CTV 6P No coaches Last d 5pm

PRICE GUIDE
ROOMS: s fr £18; d £28-£35✻

GH 🔲🔲🔲🔲🔲 **Tan-y-Foel**
Capel Garmon LL26 0RE (take A470 towards Llanrwst right turn up hill signed Capel Garmon & Nebo continue for just over 1m, house on left just before Capel Garmon village) ☎01690 710507 FAX 01690 710681
Closed Xmas rs Jan

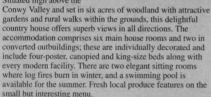

Situated high above the Conwy Valley and set in six acres of woodland with attractive gardens and rural walks within the grounds, this delightful country house offers superb views in all directions. The accommodation comprises six main house rooms and two in converted outbuildings; these are individually decorated and include four-poster, canopied and king-size beds along with every modern facility. There are two elegant sitting rooms where log fires burn in winter, and a swimming pool is available for the summer. Fresh local produce features on the small but interesting menu.

7 en suite (bth/shr) No smoking CTV in all bedrooms Tea and coffee making facilities Direct dial from bedrooms No dogs Licensed Cen ht No children 7yrs 19P No coaches Last d 6pm

PRICE GUIDE
ROOMS: s £69.50-£75; d £99-£110; wkly b&b £245-£329; wkly hlf-bd £378-£403✻
CARDS: 🔲 🔳 🔳 ⓪ 🔲

Selected

🔳 🔲🔲🔲🔲 **White Horse Inn** Capel Garmon LL26 0RW
☎01690 710271 FAX 01690 710271
7 en suite (bth/shr) No smoking in dining room CTV in all bedrooms Tea and coffee making facilities Cen ht No children 7yrs 30P Last d 9pm

PRICE GUIDE
ROOMS: s £30; d £48
MEALS: Lunch £5.25-£9
CARDS: 🔲 🔳 🔳 🔲

BISHOPSTON West Glamorgan

See **Langland Bay & Mumbles**

BLACKWOOD Gwent Map 03 ST19

🔳 🔲🔲 **Plas** Gordon Rd NP2 1D ☎01495 224674
Dating back in parts to the 14th century, this old inn was originally a farmhouse. It is situated next to a large modern housing development, high above the town, with good views of the valley. There is a spacious lounge bar, full of character with stone walls and an open log fire, and a cottage-style restaurant. Half of the bedrooms are located on the ground and first floors of a separate purpose-built annexe across the car park; these have modern furnishings and are more spacious than the rooms in the main building, one of which has a four-poster bed.

6 rms (4 shr) 3 annexe en suite (bth) (1 fmly) CTV in 6 bedrooms Tea and coffee making facilities Cen ht 50P Last d 9.45pm
CARDS: 🔲 🔳 ⓪ 🔲
See advertisement on p.577.

BLAENFFOS Dyfed Map 02 SN13

GH 🔲🔲🔲 **Castellan House** SA37 0HZ (off A478, 6m S of Cardigan) ☎01239 841644
Parts of this stone-built farmhouse date back several hundred years, though it has been much modernised and extended in recent times. It is situated some six miles south of Cardigan, half a mile east of the A478 between the villages of Blaenffos and Crymmych. The house is part of a 34-acre holding which provides a number of facilities, including a riding academy, a tea-room and an antique shop. Three of the bedrooms, on the ground floor of a former dairy, are furnished in a modern style; the others are more traditionally furnished and are in the main house. There is a comfortable lounge and a cottagy dining room, with a conservatory extension, which opens onto the large and very pleasant garden.

6 rms (3 shr) (3 fmly) No smoking in dining room CTV in 4 bedrooms Tea and coffee making facilities Cen ht CTV 12P No coaches Riding Pool table Last d 4pm
PRICE GUIDE
ROOMS: s £19-£24; d £30-£34

Factual details of establishments in this Guide are from questionnaires we send to all establishments that feature in the book.

Fairy Glen Hotel
Betws-y-Coed • Gwynedd • N. Wales
LL24 0SH
Telephone: 01690 710269

A warm and friendly welcome awaits you at our 17th century family run hotel overlooking the River Conwy, amongst mountains and forest. 1 mile from Betws-y-Coed village. Centrally heated en-suite rooms with radio/colour TV and beverage tray. Freshly prepared home cooked food. Residential licence.

B/B en-suite £21pp. D.B.B. £32pp

Colour	Wales Tourist Board
brochure	♛♛♛
available	Highly Commended

The Ferns Guest House
Holyhead Road, Betws-y-Coed,
Gwynedd LL24 0AN
Tel: 01690 710587. Fax 01690 710587

AA
HIGHLY
RECOMMENDED
QQQ

Wales Tourist Board
♛♛

The Ferns Guest House is conveniently situated in the village of Betws-y-Coed in the beautiful Snowdonia National Park. 9 Bedrooms many en-suite, all with TV & beverage trays. Betws is an ideal base for exploring this spectacular region and is within easy reach conway, Caernarfon Portmerrion, Blaenau Ffestiniog. Keith and Teresa Roobottom will make every effort to ensure that your stay is a memorable one.

Tan-y-Foel Country House
Capel Garmon, Nr. Betws-y-Coed, Gwynedd LL26 0RE
Telephone: 01690 710507 Fax: 01690 710681

AA QQQQQ
Premier Selected

WTB ♛ ♛ ♛ ♛
DELUXE

A Roman lookout was situated in what are now the grounds of Tan-y-Foel, such is the view from this delightful Country House set high above the Conwy Valley. The building dates back in part to the 16th Century & Tudor Yeomen also erected the cruck-framed timber barn. Inside the house is attractively decorated and well furnished. There are two elegant sitting rooms in which guests can relax, but it is the bedrooms themselves that are the most impressive feature of the house, some four poster beds canopied with rich fabrics and ensuite modern bathrooms, two bedrooms are reached externally. The house is not just beautiful however it is friendly and unpretentious. Janet and Peter Pitman produce excellent country fare enhanced by a quality Welsh Cheese Board and hold a good well balanced wine list to complement the cuisine. Minimum age 7 years. Totally "no smoking" establishment.

BONTDDU Gwynedd Map **06** SH61

Premier Selected

GH ⚐⚐⚐⚐⚐ *Borthwnog Hall Hotel* LL40 2TT (on A496) ☎01341 430271 FAX 01341 430682
Closed Xmas
This superb Regency country house must have one of the most idyllic settings anywhere in Wales, standing back from the road in beautiful grounds on the Dolgellau side of the village, with views over the lovely Mawddach Estuary to the Arran hills and Cader Idris. Two of the bedrooms have balconies overlooking the estuary, the other a private sitting room; all have large bathrooms and fine furniture. The drawing room features some lovely antiques and fine paintings, and the library is now a gallery displaying paintings (available for sale) by local artists. The restaurant, which offers a carte in addition to its daily fixed-price menu, has gained a good local reputation. Ample parking is provided.
3 en suite (bth/shr) No smoking in dining room No smoking in lounges CTV in all bedrooms Tea and coffee making facilities Licensed Cen ht 6P No coaches Last d 8.15pm
CARDS: 🔲 🔲

BORTH Dyfed Map **06** SN69

GH ⚐⚐⚐ *Glanmor Hotel* Princess St SY24 5JP (turn off A487 onto B4353 signposted Borth, Glanmor is situated at N end of sea front) ☎01970 871689
A small, personally run guest house standing opposite the beach at the northern end of town offers sea views from some rooms. The comfortable lounge contains a bar and there are separate tables in the dining room.
7 rms (2 shr) (3 fmly) CTV in 4 bedrooms Tea and coffee making facilities Licensed CTV 12P No coaches Last d 5pm
PRICE GUIDE
ROOMS: s £19.50; d £39; wkly b&b £136.50; wkly hlf-bd £203✳

BRECHFA Dyfed Map **02** SN53

Selected

GH ⚐⚐⚐⚐ *Glasfryn* SA32 7QY (leave M4 junct49 onto A48 to Cross Hands, towards Carmarthen for approx 1m, turn left onto B4310 cross over A40 continue on B4310) ☎01267 202306
This stone-built detatched house has a car park to the rear and has been considerably improved in recent years. There is a pleasant conservatory extension to the restaurant, and two of the bedrooms are now en suite, whilst the third has a private shower room. The rooms vary in style and furniture ranges from modern to antique pine. There is also a comfortable lounge.
3 en suite (bth/shr) No smoking in bedrooms No smoking in area of dining room Tea and coffee making facilities No

dogs (ex guide dogs) Licensed Cen ht CTV 12P Last d 9pm
PRICE GUIDE
ROOMS: s fr £22; d fr £40; wkly b&b fr £140; wkly hlf-bd fr £200✳

BRECON Powys Map **03** SO02

GH ⚐⚐⚐ *Beacons* 16 Bridge St LD3 8AH (W side of town centre, just across the river) ☎01874 623339
rs 15-27 Dec
Dating back in part to the 18th century, this small privately-owned hotel is situated near the River Usk Bridge to the west of the town centre. Bedrooms, which include family rooms, vary in size and style; all are well equipped and most have en suite facilities. The bright dining room is divided into smoking and non-smoking areas while the lounge and bar are both comfortable. There is a private car park and the hotel is convenient for both the A40 and the A470.
10 rms (7 bth/shr) (2 fmly) No smoking in dining room CTV in all bedrooms Tea and coffee making facilities Licensed Cen ht CTV 12P Mountain bike hire Last d 5.30pm
PRICE GUIDE
ROOMS: s £16.50-£19.50; d £33-£39; wkly b&b £99-£117; wkly hlf-bd £153-£171
CARDS: 🔲 🔲 🔲

GH ⚐⚐ *Borderers* 47 The Watton LD3 7EG (E on A40, opposite barracks of the Welsh Regiment) ☎01874 623559 FAX 01874 623559
This former drovers' inn dates back to the 17th century. It stands close to the town centre, on the road to Abergavenny. The former courtyard is now a secure car park and half of the bedrooms, some of which are on ground floor level, are situated in buildings surrounding the courtyard. No-smoking bedrooms and family rooms are both available. Separate tables are provided in the traditionally furnished breakfast room, which has a low beamed ceiling. New owners in 1995 were, at the time of our last inspection, planning to make extensive improvements to the accommodation.
4 rms (2 shr) 4 annexe en suite (bth/shr) (3 fmly) No smoking in 2 bedrooms No smoking in dining room CTV in all bedrooms Tea and coffee making facilities Cen ht 6P No coaches
PRICE GUIDE
ROOMS: s £19-£22; d £34-£40✳

Selected

GH ⚐⚐⚐⚐ *The Coach* Orchard St, Llanfaes LD3 8AN (town one way system, turn left at traffic lights, over bridge then 300yds on right) ☎01874 623803
Closed 22 Dec-7 Jan
Originally an inn dating back to the early 19th century, this impeccably maintained guesthouse is situated to the west of the town centre at Llanfaes, within easy reach of both the A40 and A470. It provides well equipped, modern accommodation which includes family rooms. There is a cosy residents' lounge with a fine Victorian fireplace, and good home cooking is served at individual tables in the attractive breakfast room. Smoking is not permitted.
6 en suite (bth/shr) (2 fmly) No smoking CTV in all bedrooms Tea and coffee making facilities Direct dial from bedrooms No dogs Licensed Cen ht No children 5P No coaches Last d 7pm

GH 🔲🔲 **Flag & Castle** 11 Orchard St, Llanfaes LD3 8AN (on B460 .5m W) ☎01874 625860
A friendly, cosy little guest house opposite Christ College, west of the town centre. Guests dine together at a communal table in the open-plan lounge and dining room. Bedrooms are freshly decorated.
6 rms (1 shr) (1 fmly) CTV in 1 bedroom Tea and coffee making facilities Licensed Cen ht CTV 2P No coaches
PRICE GUIDE
ROOMS: s fr £16; d fr £30; wkly b&b fr £98✶
CARDS: 💳

GH 🔲🔲🔲 **Pickwick House** ST Johns Rd LD3 9DS
☎01874 624322
Mar-Nov
This well maintained Edwardian house is situated in a quiet residential road, within a short walk of the town centre. It provides modern furnished and equipped accommodation, which includes a family bedded room. Separate tables can be provided in the traditionally furnished dining room, or alternatively guests can have their meals served in an adjacent conservatory. There is also a cosy lounge equipped with a television, books and parlour games.
2 rms (1 shr) (1 fmly) No smoking Tea and coffee making facilities No dogs Cen ht CTV 1P No coaches Last d 6pm
PRICE GUIDE
ROOMS: s £18-£20; d £34-£36

GH 🔲🔲🔲 **Ty Newydd** Cambrian Cruisers Marina, Pencelli LD3 7LJ (off B4558) ☎01874 665315 FAX 01874 665315
Closed Nov-Mar
4 en suite (bth/shr) (1 fmly) No smoking in bedrooms No smoking in dining room CTV in 5 bedrooms Tea and coffee making facilities No dogs (ex guide dogs) Cen ht P No coaches
PRICE GUIDE
ROOMS: s £19; d £35; wkly b&b £105✶

Selected

❤ 🔲🔲🔲🔲 Mrs H E Atkins **Llandetty Hall** *(SO124205)*
Talybont-on-Usk LD3 7YR (7m SE off B4558)
☎01874 676415 FAX 01874 676415
A beautifully preserved 16th-century farmhouse stands on a sheep farm amidst magnificent scenery, just seven miles from Brecon on the B4588. There are two well maintained double-bedded rooms and a twin. All have period-style furniture, soft furnishings and en suite or private bathrooms. Real fires burn in a comfortable lounge and a dining room which has antique furniture and a communal dining table. Guests may not smoke in the house, but may do so in the lovely garden.
3 en suite (bth/shr) No smoking Tea and coffee making facilities Direct dial from bedrooms No dogs (ex guide dogs) Cen ht CTV No children 10yrs 6P 48 acres sheep Last d 6pm
PRICE GUIDE
ROOMS: s £21; d £34-£40; wkly b&b fr £112; wkly hlf-bd fr £175

BUILTH WELLS Powys Map 03 SO05

GH 🔲🔲 **The Owls** 40 High St LD2 3AB
☎01982 552518 FAX 01982 552518
5 rms (3 bth/shr) (1 fmly) No smoking in dining room CTV in

PLAS INN HOTEL & BRASSERIE

Gordon Road, Blackwood, Gwent
Telephone: (01495) 224674
Set on a hill overlooking Blackwood this 14th-C farmhouse offers a varied menu and choice of rooms with private facilities.

Maes-Y-Gwernen
Hotel AA ★
School Road, Abercraf, Swansea Valley SA9 1XD
Tel: 01639 730218 Fax: 01639 730765

A cosy but well appointed hotel set in its own grounds in the village of Abercraf on the southern edge of the Brecon Beacons National Park. Close to Dan-Yr-Ogof Showcaves, the Black Mountains and the Gower Coast with its coves and fine beaches. Past winners of the AA Best Newcomer Wales Award.
Tourist Board 4 Crowns, highly commended.
B&B from £20.00. Major credit cards accepted.
Colour brochure available on request.

all bedrooms Tea and coffee making facilities Licensed Cen ht
CTV 8P Last d 9.30pm
PRICE GUIDE
ROOMS: s fr £13.50; d fr £27✱

BURRY PORT Dyfed Map **02** SN40

◖ Q Q Q **The George** Stepney Rd SA16 0BH (turn off A484
at traffic lights, look for town centre sign, near railway station
at lower end of Stepney Road) ☎01554 832211
This pleasant hostelry is situated in the towncentre, and in addition
to the lounge bar and restaurant, it has a very popular coffee shop.
The modern bedrooms, which include a family room, have good
furniture and equipment. Most even have their own small kitchen.
5 rms (4 bth/shr) (2 fmly) CTV in all bedrooms Tea and coffee
making facilities No dogs (ex guide dogs) Cen ht No children
6yrs No coaches Last d 10.15pm
PRICE GUIDE
ROOMS: s £17-£32; d £33-£42✱
MEALS: Lunch £6.15-£17.75alc Dinner £9.15-£19.75alc✱

CAERNARFON Gwynedd Map **06** SH46

See also Llanwnda

Selected

GH Q Q Q Q **Caer Menai** 15 Church St LL55 1SW
(within Old Town Walls) ☎01286 672612
Apr-Dec
Quietly situated within the town walls, and just a short
distance from both the castle and harbour, this small
guesthouse is meticulously run. Friendly owners Hilary and
Keith Lardner offer fresh, comfortable, modern
accommodation that includes a few family rooms as well as
standard bedrooms. Breakfast only is served in the attractive
dining room, but there is a wide choice of restaurants nearby
for evening meals. The cosy lounge provides a pleasant place
to relax and a solarium is available for guests' use. There is no
car park but street parking is unlimited and there are public
car parks a short walk away.
7 rms (3 shr) (2 fmly) No smoking CTV in all bedrooms
Tea and coffee making facilities No dogs (ex guide dogs)
CTV No parking No coaches Solarium
PRICE GUIDE
ROOMS: s £19-£25; d £31-£38

GH Q Q **Menai View Hotel** North Rd LL55 1BD (N on A487)
☎01286 674602
The Menai View is a modestly appointed, family-run guest house
with modern facilities. The first-floor lounge overlooks the Menai
Straits and some bedrooms also have similar views. TVs and tea
trays are provided, and there is one room at ground level. Car
parking is available nearby and the town centre and castle are only
a short walk away.
8 rms (4 shr) (5 fmly) CTV in all bedrooms Tea and coffee
making facilities No dogs (ex guide dogs) Licensed Cen ht
CTV Last d 6.30pm
PRICE GUIDE
ROOMS: s £16-£19; d £25-£33; wkly b&b £80-£105✱

CARDIFF South Glamorgan Map **03** ST17

GH Q Q **Albany** 191-193 Albany Rd, Roath CF2 3NU
☎01222 494121
Closed Xmas wk
This guest house offers simple, comfortable accommodation in
bright rooms. An attractive dining room serves a full English
breakfast is served. The Albany Road is close to the city centre.
11 rms (7 bth/shr) (4 fmly) No smoking in dining room CTV in
all bedrooms Tea and coffee making facilities No dogs (ex guide
dogs) Cen ht
PRICE GUIDE
ROOMS: s £18; d £36✱

GH Q **Balkan Hotel** 144 Newport Rd CF2 1DJ
☎01222 463673
Conveniently located close to the city centre, this friendly, family
run guest house provides homely public rooms and brigh, simply
styled bedrooms.
14 rms (5 shr) (3 fmly) CTV in 13 bedrooms Tea and coffee
making facilities No dogs Cen ht CTV 18P Last d 7pm
CARDS: ▨ ▨

GH Q Q Q **Clare Court Hotel** 46/48 Clare Rd CF1 7QP
☎01222 344839 FAX 01222 665856
Within walking distance of the city centre this commercial style
hotel offers well equipped bedrooms and a popular bar lounge.
8 en suite (bth/shr) (2 fmly) No smoking in dining room CTV in
all bedrooms Tea and coffee making facilities Direct dial from
bedrooms No dogs (ex guide dogs) Licensed Cen ht CTV ch
fac No parking
PRICE GUIDE
ROOMS: s £25; d £32; wkly b&b £160; wkly hlf-bd £195
CARDS: ▨ ▨ ▨

GH Q Q **Courtfield Hotel** 101 Cathedral Rd CF1 9PH (from
city centre cross bridge over river Taff and turn 1st right into
Cathedral Road) ☎01222 227701 FAX 01222 227701
Closed 24-31 Dec
This popular little hotel is ideally situated close to Cardiff Castle
and the city centre.The accommodation is simply furnished but
well equipped and comfortable. The licensed restaurant is open to
non residents, and a variety of interesting dishes are available.
16 rms (4 shr) (3 fmly) No smoking in lounges CTV in all
bedrooms Tea and coffee making facilities Direct dial from
bedrooms Licensed Cen ht CTV No parking Last d 8.30pm
PRICE GUIDE
ROOMS: s £20-£30; d £35-£45✱
CARDS: ▨ ▨ ▨ ▨ ▨ ▨ ▨

GH Q Q **Domus** 201 Newport Rd CF2 1AJ ☎01222 495785
2 Jan-20 Dec
A small and friendly commercial guest house situated
conveniently close to the city centre offers accommodation in
bedrooms which, though simply styled and compact, are well
equipped; the ground floor houses a homely breakfast room and
congenial little residents' bar.
10 rms (2 shr) (2 fmly) No smoking in dining room CTV in all
bedrooms Tea and coffee making facilities Direct dial from
bedrooms No dogs (ex guide dogs) Licensed Cen ht CTV 10P
No coaches Last d noon
PRICE GUIDE
ROOMS: s £17-£22; d £34-£45✱

GH Ⓠ Ⓠ Ⓠ *Ferrier's (Alva) Hotel* 130/132 Cathedral Rd
CF1 9LQ ☎01222 383413 FAX 01222 383413
Closed 2wks Xmas & New Year
This friendly family run hotel is set in an attractive Victorian
conservation area and just a walk from the city centre. The
accommodation is bright, comfortable and well equipped. Guests
may enjoy light refreshments in the Cane Room, or perhaps a
drink in the relaxed Concorde Bar.
26 rms (6 bth/shr) (4 fmly) CTV in all bedrooms Tea and coffee
making facilities Direct dial from bedrooms Licensed Cen ht
CTV 10P No coaches Last d 7.45pm
CARDS: ▨ ▩ ▨ ⓪

GH Ⓠ Ⓠ *Tane's Hotel* 148 Newport Rd CF2 1DJ
☎01222 491755 & 493898 FAX 01222 491755
Conveniently positioned for access to the city, this friendly family-
run guest house provides value-for-money accommodation and
homely public rooms. High standards are maintained throughout.
9 rms (1 fmly) No smoking in 5 bedrooms CTV in all bedrooms
Tea and coffee making facilities No dogs Licensed Cen ht CTV
No children 2yrs 10P Last d 7pm
CARDS: ▨ £

CARDIGAN Dyfed Map **02** SN14

See also Blaenffos & Pentregat

 GH Ⓠ Ⓠ Ⓠ *Brynhyfryd* Gwbert Rd SA43 1AE (on the
B4548 in Cardigan town)
☎01239 612861 FAX 01239 612861
This impeccably maintained semi-detatched Edwardian house is
situated at the town centre end of the B4548. Improvements are
being constantly made by the long standing owners, Nesta and
Ieuan Davies. Bedrooms, including a family room, provide
modern furnishings and equipment. There is a small but attractive
dining room and a cosy lounge.
7 rms (3 shr) (1 fmly) No smoking in dining room CTV in all
bedrooms Tea and coffee making facilities No dogs (ex guide
dogs) Cen ht CTV No parking No coaches Last d 7.30pm
PRICE GUIDE
ROOMS: s £15-£16; d £30-£36; wkly hlf-bd £140-£175
£

CAREW Dyfed Map **02** SN00

Selected

GH Ⓠ Ⓠ Ⓠ Ⓠ *Old Stable Cottage* 3 Picton Ter SA70 8SL
☎01646 651889
Closed 21 Dec-Jan
This delightful cottage was originally a stable and cart house
for the nearby castle. Sympathetically restored by Lionel and
Joyce Fielder, it is now a charming little retreat in a pretty
location. The trap shed is now the entrance porch, leading into
the spacious sitting room, furnished with deep sofas and
armchairs, with its inglenook fireplace, bread oven and
wrought-iron spiral staircase. Bedrooms feature the original
stable timbers but offer a range of modern creature comforts
and a host of nice little personal touches such as reading
material and dried flowers. Breakfasts, and evening meals by
arrangement, are served at a communal table in the
conservatory which opens onto the sheltered garden.
3 en suite (bth/shr) (1 fmly) CTV in all bedrooms Tea and
coffee making facilities No dogs (ex guide dogs) Cen ht No
children 5yrs 2P No coaches Last d 7pm
PRICE GUIDE
ROOMS: s £35; d £45✳

CARMARTHEN Dyfed Map **02** SN42

See also Cwmduad

♥ Ⓠ Ⓠ Ⓠ Mrs J Willmott **Cwmtwrch Hotel & Four Seasons
Restaurant** *(SN497220)* Nantgaredig SA32 7NY (5m E, off
A40) ☎01267 290238 FAX 01267 290808
This 200 year old farmhouse and buildings has been developed
into a very pleasant hotel, restaurant, restaurant and leisure
complex. It has cosy bedrooms, all with antique furnishings. Three
are located in a separate building. Ground floor bedrooms and
family bedded rooms are available. The main house contains two
breakfast rooms and two lounges. Another former farm building
has been converted into a very pleasant restaurant, which has
sturdy cottage style furniture and a stone flagged floor. There is a
leisure centre, too, with a heated pool, a jacuzzi and a multigym.
6 en suite (bth/shr) (2 fmly) No smoking in bedrooms CTV in 3
bedrooms Tea and coffee making facilities Licensed Cen ht
CTV 20P Indoor swimming pool (heated) Golf 9 Gymnasium
Jacuzzi in swimming pool 30 acres sheep Last d 9pm
PRICE GUIDE
ROOMS: s £34-£40; d £46-£50; wkly b&b £160-£170✳
£

Selected

♥ Ⓠ Ⓠ Ⓠ Ⓠ Mrs F Burns **Farm Retreats** *(SN485203)*
Capel Dewi Uchaf Farm, Capel Dewi SA32 8AY (4m E)
☎01267 290799 FAX 01267 290003
Rustic elegance and modern comforts are the hallmarks of this
unassuming building which has been lovingly restored and is
set in an area of gentle scenic beauty. Guests are encouraged ➡

FERRIER'S HOTEL
132 Cathedral Road, Cardiff, CF1 9LQ
Tel: (01222) 383413

Ferrier's Hotel is a family-managed hotel set in
a Victorian Conservation area and yet within
walking distance of the city centre. 26
bedrooms, including 7 on the ground floor. All
rooms tastefully furnished and have hot and
cold water, central heating, radio, colour TV,
tea & coffee making facilities and direct dial
telephone. Many rooms with private shower
and many en-suite. Bar meals are available
Monday to Thursday. Light refreshments in the
Cane Lounge and well stocked Bar. Resident's
Lounge with colour TV. Full fire certificate. Car
park, locked at night.

to hand feed the nearby herd of deer. The three bedrooms are welcoming and full of character, and there is a large dining room where dinner is provided by the graceful hostess.
3 en suite (bth/shr) No smoking CTV in all bedrooms Tea and coffee making facilities No dogs Licensed Cen ht CTV 8P Fishing 34 acres non-working Last d 10am

Selected

♥ ▣▣▣▣ Mr T Giles **Pantgwyn** *(SN460228)* SA32 7ES (turn off A40 4m E af Carmarthen at Whitemill and follow sign to Pantgwyn Farm)
☎01267 290247 FAX 01267 290880
Closed Xmas
Dating back some 300 years, this beautifully restored house is quietly situated in a picturesque valley five miles east of Carmarthen. There are a double bedded room, a twin and a family, and all have quality furnishings including both antique and modern pine pieces. The twin room is the only one without en suite facilities, but it has a private bathroom. The lounge is attractive and comfortable, with a real fire on colder days. Separate tables are provided in the dining room.
3 en suite (bth/shr) (2 fmly) No smoking CTV in all bedrooms Tea and coffee making facilities No dogs (ex guide dogs) Licensed Cen ht 20P Pool table 12 acres sheep Last d 5pm
PRICE GUIDE
ROOMS: s £28-£35; d £42-£50; wkly b&b £132-£158; wkly hlf-bd £222-£258

◀ ▣▣▣ **Cothi Bridge Hotel** Pontargothi SA32 7NG (6m E on A40 towards Llandeilo)
☎01267 290251 FAX 01267 290251
rs Oct-Mar
A pleasant large public house with modern accommodation and attractive public areas. The restaurant and breakfast room overlook the river.
10 en suite (bth/shr) (1 fmly) No smoking in 5 bedrooms No smoking in lounges CTV in all bedrooms Tea and coffee making facilities Direct dial from bedrooms Cen ht CTV 41P Fishing Last d 9pm
PRICE GUIDE
ROOMS: s fr £33.50; d fr £47.50; wkly b&b fr £160; wkly hlf-bd fr £200✱
MEALS: Bar Lunch £4-£10 Dinner £16.50&alc✱
CARDS: ▨ ▨ ▨

CEMAES BAY See **ANGLESEY, ISLE OF**

CHEPSTOW Gwent

See **Tintern**

CHURCH STOKE Powys Map **07** SO29

Selected

♥ ▣▣▣▣ Mrs C Richards **The Drewin** *(SO261905)* SY15 6TW ☎01588 620325
Apr-Nov rs Etr (if in Mar)
This 17th century farmhouse straddles Offa's Dyke and has lovely views over the border country. Only two bedrooms are available, one with pine furniture and its own en suite shower, the other Stag-furnished and having the use of a nearby bathroom. There are exposed beams throughout the building

and the dining room features an impressive inglenook fireplace where logs burn in winter months. Evening meals are provided if requested and there is a games room (with snooker table) in a converted granary. The Drewin is part of a working sheep and arable farm, and visitors are guaranteed a warm welcome and a peaceful atmosphere. Follow the Pantglas/Cwm signs off the B4385 near Mellington.
2 rms (1 shr) (2 fmly) No smoking CTV in all bedrooms Tea and coffee making facilities No dogs Cen ht CTV 6P Games room 102 acres mixed Last d 7pm

COLWYN BAY Clwyd Map **06** SH87

GH ▣▣ **Crossroads** 15 Coed Pella Rd LL29 7AT
☎01492 530736
Closed 24 Dec-2 Jan
Situated within easy walking distance of the seafront and town centre, this large Victorian house is good value for money. Neat bedrooms have modern facilities, and there is a comfortably spacious residents' lounge. Margaret Owens is a friendly owner.
5 rms (2 shr) (2 fmly) CTV in all bedrooms Tea and coffee making facilities Cen ht CTV No parking No coaches
PRICE GUIDE
ROOMS: s £14; d £28✱

GH ▣ **Grosvenor Hotel** 106-108 Abergele Rd LL29 7PS (on main road through town) ☎01492 530798 & 531586
FAX 01492 531586
This large private hotel near the centre of town has the advantage of its own car park. Bedrooms are modestly furnished but all have TVs and tea trays; several are large and suitable for families. The restaurant offers a good range of inexpensive meals and there are a popular residents' bar and games room.
18 rms (2 shr) (8 fmly) CTV in 15 bedrooms Tea and coffee making facilities Licensed CTV 16P Last d 7pm
PRICE GUIDE
ROOMS: s £17.50-£18.50; d £35-£37; wkly b&b £106.50-£113.50; wkly hlf-bd £151.50-£158.50

GH ▣▣▣ **Northwood Hotel** 47 Rhos Rd, Rhos-on-Sea LL28 4RS ☎01492 549931
The Northwood is a family-run hotel situated in a quiet area just a short walk from the seafront and shops at Rhos-on-Sea. Most of the neat, well decorated bedrooms have en suite shower rooms and there are a comfortable residents' lounge and a restaurant with small bar adjacent.
12 rms (1 bth 10 shr) (3 fmly) No smoking in dining room CTV in all bedrooms Tea and coffee making facilities Licensed Cen ht CTV 11P Last d 6.15pm
PRICE GUIDE
ROOMS: s £18.50; d £37; wkly b&b £120; wkly hlf-bd £140-£149✱
CARDS: ▨ ▨

CONWY Gwynedd Map **06** SH77

See also **Rowen**

GH ▣▣ *Bryn Derwen* Woodlands LL32 8LT (on B5106)
☎01492 596134
Bryn Derwen is a small family-run guest house within walking distance of the castle and town centre. The pretty bedrooms are individually furnished. A small TV lounge and an attractive pine-furnished breakfast room are provided.
4 rms (1 bth/shr) No smoking in dining room CTV in all bedrooms Tea and coffee making facilities No dogs (ex guide dogs) Cen ht 6P

GH ◙◙◙ **Glan Heulog** Llanrwst Rd LL32 8LT (from Conwy Castle take B5106, house approx 0.25m on left side) ☎01492 593845

This pleasant little guest house, the name of which means 'sunny banks', enjoys pleasant views extending as far as the castle from a setting above the town. Well maintained bedrooms equipped with TV sets and tea trays - and, in one instance, boasting a four-poster bed - are steadily being improved by the provision of en suite facilities; there is a modern lounge, and ample car parking space is available.

7 rms (4 bth/shr) (1 fmly) No smoking in dining room No smoking in lounges CTV in all bedrooms Tea and coffee making facilities No dogs (ex guide dogs) Licensed Cen ht 8P No coaches Last d 9.30am

PRICE GUIDE

ROOMS: s £13; d £26-£32; wkly b&b £82-£101; wkly hlf-bd £141-£160✱

GH ◙◙◙ **Pen-y-bryn Tearooms** Lancaster Square LL32 8DE (situated in main town square) ☎01492 596445

Three small but well equipped bedrooms are provided at this popular tea shop which is housed in a building (known, until recently, as The Old Ship) dating back to the sixteenth century and located at the centre of the famous walled town; three car parking spaces are also available nearby. Several daily hot specials, snacks and teas are served between 11am and 5pm.

3 rms (2 shr) (1 fmly) No smoking CTV in all bedrooms Tea and coffee making facilities Cen ht 3P No coaches

PRICE GUIDE

ROOMS: s £17.50-£26; d £30-£36; wkly b&b £105-£124✱

CORWEN Clwyd Map **06** SJ04

GH ◙◙ **Coleg-y-Groes** LL21 0AU ☎01490 412169

Closed 24-27 Dec

A row of six former almshouses for clergy widows, situated between the church and the wooded hillside, has been converted into this quiet Christian retreat. A Grade II listed building, it offers small, cosy bedrooms, several of them suitable for families and some opening on to well maintained lawns and gardens. There are a number of sitting rooms, one with a TV and another featuring a traditional slate fireplace.

6 rms (2 fmly) No smoking Tea and coffee making facilities No dogs (ex guide dogs) Cen ht CTV 6P No coaches Last d previous evening

PRICE GUIDE

ROOMS: s £16-£18; d £32-£36; wkly b&b £105; wkly hlf-bd £157.50✱

🖼🚻 **GH** ◙◙◙ **Corwen Court Private Hotel** London Rd LL21 0DP (on A5) ☎01490 412854

Closed Xmas-New Year rs Dec-Feb

Between 1871 and 1978 this stone-built house was the local police station and court house. The original cells still remain, and have been converted into six single bedrooms furnished with solid period furniture. Four double rooms have also been added and these have en suite bathrooms. Friendly owners Bob and Kit Buckland have created a comfortable lounge and dining room in what was the old court house, and here Kit provides good value evening meals. The hotel lies alongside the A5 near the centre of the village.

10 rms (4 bth/shr) No smoking in dining room Cen ht CTV No parking No coaches Last d 5pm

PRICE GUIDE

ROOMS: s £13-£14; d £28-£30

Selected

GH ◙◙◙◙ **Powys House Estate** Bonwm LL21 9EG (on A5 towards Llangollen) ☎01490 412367

Once a private country residence, this fine house is set in several acres of mature gardens and woodland which include a tennis court and outdoor swimming pool. The three bedrooms are individually and attractively decorated, and each has an en suite shower room. An elegantly furnished sitting room with many original features is warmed by a cheerful wood-burning stove during the winter months and the panelled hall is particularly impressive. The Waite and Quinn families are welcoming owners, and the house is superbly situated for touring North Wales.

3 en suite (shr) (1 fmly) No smoking in bedrooms No smoking in dining room CTV in all bedrooms Tea and coffee making facilities No dogs (ex guide dogs) Cen ht CTV 4P No coaches Outdoor swimming pool Tennis (grass) Last d 6pm

PRICE GUIDE

ROOMS: s £22-£23; d £34-£36; wkly b&b £119-£126; wkly hlf-bd £203-£210

£

CRICCIETH Gwynedd Map **06** SH43

GH ◙◙◙ **Glyn-Y-Coed Private Hotel** Portmadoc Rd LL52 0HL (E on A497) ☎01766 522870 FAX 01766 523341

Closed Xmas & New Year

Glyn-Y-Coed is a friendly family-run hotel situated above the main road into the resort, with fine views over the castle and sea. Bedrooms are fresh and pretty and several have canopied beds. ➡

Farm Retreats

Capel Dewi Uchaf Farm

Capel Dewi, Carmarthen, Dyfed SA32 8AY

Tel: Fredena Burns 01267 290799

Fax: 01267 290003

Beautiful comfortable old house set in the secluded Towy Valley with fishing to the Towy River. Bed & Breakfast at it's best (AA Landlady of the Year finalist 1994). Ideal for touring Wales. Sea, mountains, rivers and views of open countryside. Our aim is to make your holiday memorable. We now have a licensed dining room to compliment our renowned farmhouse fare.

Family rooms are available and one suite. A lounge and small bar is provided for residents, along with a garden and car park. 10 en suite (bth/shr) (5 fmly) No smoking in 2 bedrooms No smoking in area of dining room No smoking in 1 lounge CTV in all bedrooms Tea and coffee making facilities Licensed Cen ht CTV ch fac 14P Last d 4pm
PRICE GUIDE
ROOMS: s £19-£22; d £38-£44; wkly b&b £128-£145; wkly hlf-bd £195-£215✱
CARDS: ◼◼

GH ◘◘◘ **Min y Gaer** Porthmadog Rd LL52 0HP (on A497 400yds E of jct with B4411)
☎01766 522151 FAX 01766 522151
Mar-Oct
Excellent views of the castle and Cardigan Bay are enjoyed from this well maintained hotel which is situated back off the main road into the resort. Bedrooms are bright and fresh, many have sea views and all are well equipped with such amenities as televisions. There is a comfortable lounge and bar for residents and car parking is provided.
10 rms (9 shr) (3 fmly) No smoking in dining room CTV in all bedrooms Tea and coffee making facilities Licensed Cen ht CTV ch fac 12P No coaches Last d 4pm
PRICE GUIDE
ROOMS: s £17.50-£20; d £35-£40; wkly b&b £122.50-£126; wkly hlf-bd £185-£189
CARDS: ◼ ◼ ◼ ◼ ▨

GH ◘◘ **Neptune Hotel** Marine Ter LL52 0EF
☎01766 522794
Apr-Sep
This pair of Victorian houses is situated right on the sea front and has been run by the friendly Williams family for over 27 years. Bedrooms are quite spacious, all now have ensuite facilities and all enjoy views over the castle and Cardigan Bay. There is a choice of two lounges for residents as well as a small bar. Everywhere is fresh and bright and easy car parking is available on the promenade.
8 rms (1 bth 3 shr) (2 fmly) CTV in 4 bedrooms Licensed CTV No parking Last d 5pm

CRICKHOWELL Powys Map **03** SO21

GH ◘◘◘ **Dragon House Hotel** High St NP8 1BE
☎01873 810362 FAX 01873 811868
This friendly family-run 18th-century hotel, situated in the centre of the town, is said to have been built from parts of Alisby's castle ruins. The surrounding beauty of the Brecon Beacons and the Black Mountains makes Crickhowell an ideal touring base but the accommodation at the Dragon Hotel is also suitable for business guests. The bedrooms, in which many original features have been retained, have been equipped with modern creature comforts and the public areas include a cosy residents' lounge and a spacious, beamed restaurant. An interesting selection of dishes is offered from various menus and parking is available.
12 rms (11 bth/shr) 3 annexe en suite (bth/shr) (2 fmly) No smoking in 5 bedrooms No smoking in dining room CTV in all bedrooms Tea and coffee making facilities Direct dial from bedrooms No dogs (ex guide dogs) Licensed Cen ht CTV 15P Last d 8.30pm
PRICE GUIDE
ROOMS: s £35-£40; d £50-£56✱
CARDS: ◼ ◼ ◼ ◼ ▨

GH ◘◘ **The Fir's** Tretower NP8 1RF ☎01874 730780
Mary Eckley extends a warm welcome to visitors to her 300-year-old house, set in attractive lawns and gardens just off the A479 near the mediaeval Tretower Court and Castle. One of the four neat, cosy bedrooms is contained in a converted outbuilding and

the dining room occupies the space where the barn once was; a spacious sitting room, warmed by a wood-burning stove in winter, features some fine exposed timbers.
3 rms (1 bth/shr) 1 annexe en suite (bth/shr) (1 fmly) No smoking in bedrooms CTV in 1 bedroom Tea and coffee making facilities Cen ht CTV 6P No coaches
PRICE GUIDE
ROOMS: d £36-£42✱

CWMDUAD Dyfed Map **02** SN33

GH ◘◘◘ **Neuadd-Wen** SA33 6XJ (alongside A484, 9m N of Carmarthen) ☎01267 281438
This large detatched house stands in the centre of the village and is also the post office. It provides modern furnishings and equipment, and there are ground floor rooms and a family room. Most bedrooms are quite spacious.
7 rms (5 bth/shr) (1 fmly) No smoking in dining room No smoking in 1 lounge CTV in all bedrooms Tea and coffee making facilities Licensed Cen ht CTV 12P Last d 7.30pm
CARDS: ◼ ◼

DENBIGH Clwyd Map **06** SJ06

GH ◘◘ **Cayo** 74 Vale St LL16 3BW ☎01745 812686
Closed Xmas
A red-brick town house close to the town centre has been run by the MacCormack family for nearly 20 years. The bedrooms are pleasantly decorated and there is a television lounge. The dining room offers good home cooking. This is a very friendly place and street parking is easy.
6 rms (1 bth 3 shr) No smoking in bedrooms Licensed Cen ht CTV No parking No coaches Last d 2pm
PRICE GUIDE
ROOMS: s £16; d £32✱
CARDS: ◼ ◼ ◼

DOLGELLAU Gwynedd Map **06** SH71

◙◙ ♥◘◘ Mrs E W Price **Glyn** *(SH704178)* LL40 1YA (1m W) ☎01341 422286
Mar-Nov
This 17th-century farmhouse is set on a working farm high above the town. Bedrooms are cosy and the lounge is comfortable; exposed beams and timbers are evident throughout the building.
4 rms (1 shr) (1 fmly) No smoking in dining room CTV in 2 bedrooms Tea and coffee making facilities Cen ht TV 6P Fishing 150 acres mixed
PRICE GUIDE
ROOMS: s £12-£16; d £28-£30; wkly b&b fr £85

DYLIFE Powys Map **06** SN89

◙ ◘◘ *Star* SY19 7BW (off B4518 9m NW of Llanidloes)
☎01650 521345
The Star is a remote inn set amid wild and rugged scenery. It offers fairly simple but neat accommodation and a good range of food in the character bar or dining room. Service is friendly and a cosy lounge is provided for guests.
7 rms (2 bth/shr) (1 fmly) No smoking in dining room No smoking in 1 lounge Tea and coffee making facilities Cen ht CTV 30P Riding Boat hire Pony trekking Last d 10.30pm
CARDS: ◼ ◼

FELINDRE (NEAR SWANSEA) West Glamorgan
Map **03** SN60

❤ Ⓠ Ⓠ Ⓠ Mr F Jones **Coynant Farm** *(SN648070)* SA5 7PU
(4m N of Felindre off unclass rd linking M4 junct 46 and
Ammanford) ☎01269 595640 & 592064
Coynant Farm is a 200-acre holding, remotely located at the head
of a valley, amidst splendid scenery. It is some nine miles from
Swansea and three miles north of the village of Felindre, via the
road which is signed for Garnswllt. Felindre is signposted from
the A48, near junction 46 of the M4 motorway. The farm is
eventually reached by taking a long, concrete surfaced private
road. Parts of the house date back to the 17th century, but it has
been considerably modernised in recent times to provide well
equipped accommodation, which includes family bedded rooms
and rooms with en suite facilities. Separate tables are provided in
the cottage style dining room. Other facilities include a cosy
lounge, where welcoming log fires burn in the inglenook fireplace,
when the weather is cold. There is also a small bar.
5 rms (3 bth/shr) (2 fmly) No smoking in bedrooms No smoking
in dining room CTV in all bedrooms Tea and coffee making
facilities No dogs (ex guide dogs) Licensed Cen ht 10P Fishing
Riding Games room 200 acres mixed Last d 7pm
PRICE GUIDE
ROOMS: s £19.50-£20.50; d £39-£41

FISHGUARD Dyfed Map **02** SM93

Selected

❤ Ⓠ Ⓠ Ⓠ Ⓠ Mrs Lilwen McAllister **Erw-Lon** *(SN028325)*
Pontfaen SA65 9TS (on B4313 between Fishguard and
Maenclochog) ☎01348 881297
May-Oct
An impeccably maintained farmhouse with rear views over
the Gwaun Valley and is conveniently positioned for the Irish
ferry. Mrs McAllister provides a warm welcome and
comfortable bedrooms for her guests. There is a lounge and
pleasant dining room.
3 rms (1 shr) No smoking CTV in 2 bedrooms Tea and
coffee making facilities No dogs (ex guide dogs) Cen ht
CTV No children 10yrs 5P 128 acres beef sheep
PRICE GUIDE
ROOMS: s £17-£19; d £38; wkly b&b £126; wkly hlf-bd
£189✶

GILWERN Gwent Map **03** SO21

❤ Ⓠ Ⓠ Ⓠ Mr B L Harris **The Wenallt** *(SO245138)* NP7 0HP
(0.75m S of A465 Gilwern by pass) ☎01873 830694
This 16th-century Welsh longhouse has lovely views of the Usk
Valley. Spacious comfortable bedrooms are provided together with
good public rooms.
3 rms (1 bth) 4 annexe en suite (bth/shr) No smoking in 3
bedrooms No smoking in dining room Tea and coffee making
facilities Licensed Cen ht CTV 18P 50 acres sheep Last d 6pm
PRICE GUIDE
ROOMS: s £18-£23.50; d £30-£36; wkly b&b fr £148✶

GLAN-YR-AFON (NEAR CORWEN) Gwynedd Map **06** SJ04

❤ Ⓠ Mr & Mrs D M Jones **Llawr-Bettws** *(SJ016424)* Bala Rd
LL21 0HD (A5 from Corwen to Betws-y-Coed, at 2nd traffic
lights turn onto A494, pass Thomas Motor Mart. Take 1st
right after village) ☎01490 81224
Families are made most welcome at this farmhouse, run by the
friendly Jones family. Guests have the use of two prettily
decorated bedrooms and a TV lounge where an open fire burns in
winter. There is also a caravan and camping park in the grounds.
2 rms (1 fmly) No dogs (ex guide dogs) CTV 12P Table tennis
Swings Climbing frame 20 acres non working Last d 7.30pm

GLASBURY Powys Map **03** SO13

❤ Ⓠ Ⓠ Ⓠ Mrs B Eckley **Fforddfawr** *(SO192398)* HR3 5PT
☎01497 847332
Mar-Nov
This friendly, personally run 17th-century farmhouse is bordered
by the river Wye, just two miles west of Hay-on-Wye on the
B4350. Set back in a pretty garden, it is very much a working farm
with bright, recently decorated, comfortable bedrooms and
spacious lounges.
3 rms (2 shr) No smoking CTV in all bedrooms Tea and coffee
making facilities No dogs Cen ht CTV 4P 280 acres mixed
PRICE GUIDE
ROOMS: s £22; d £36-£38✶

CLIFTON HOUSE
HOTEL AA ★
Smithfield Square, Dolgellau,
Gwynedd LL40 1ES
Telephone: 01341 422554

Centrally situated in the unspoilt market town of
Dolgellau the "Clifton" offers an ideal touring
base for exploring Snowdonia with excellent
walking, cycling, pony trekking and fishing
opportunities nearby. Personal attention from
proprietors Rob and Pauline Dix ensure a
relaxed atmosphere matched by excellent
cuisine from the cellar restaurant which has
consistently achieved AA rosette standard.

GWAUN VALLEY Dyfed Map **02** SN03

Selected

♥ Q Q Q Q Mr P Heard & Mrs M J Heard **Tregynon Country Farmhouse Hotel** *(SN054345)* SA65 9TU (at intersection of B4313/B4329 take B4313 towards Fishguard, then first right and first right again) (Welsh Rarebits) ☎01239 820531 FAX 01239 820808
Closed 2 weeks winter
This 16th-century farmhouse is situated in the scenic Gwaun Valley, in the heart of Pembrokeshire. It has a very attractive lounge with an inglenook fireplace, and features authentic wooden settles in addition to comfortable modern seating. The restaurant is in two parts and wholesome food plus vegetarian dishes are highlighted on the menu. There are a few bedrooms in the main house, which are rather on the small side, although the five bedrooms in the converted outbuilding are larger. All are very well decorated and furnished with mainly pine furniture. Each room has modern en suite facilities and is equipped with a TV and telephone.
3 en suite (shr) 5 annexe en suite (bth) (4 fmly) No smoking in bedrooms No smoking in dining room CTV in all bedrooms Tea and coffee making facilities Direct dial from bedrooms No dogs Licensed Cen ht 20P 10 acres sheep Last d 6pm
PRICE GUIDE
ROOMS: d £46-£67; wkly hlf-bd £250-£330
CARDS: 🔲 🔲

HARLECH Gwynedd Map **06** SH53

Selected

GH Q Q Q Q **Castle Cottage Hotel** Pen Llech LL46 2YL ☎01766 780479
Closed 3 weeks Feb
This guest house dates from 1585, but the warm hospitality from owners Glyn and Jacqueline Roberts is as much a feature as the low ceilings and exposed beams. It offers an equally successful restaurant which is the subject of a separate entry in our restaurant guide. The food is freshly prepared by Glyn, and has justifiably earned our one rosette award. Though compact, the bedrooms are all attractively pine-furnished and decorated with eye-catching papers. There are a warm bar, a separate lounge, and, of course, the cottage-style restaurant.
6 rms (4 bth/shr) No smoking in dining room Tea and coffee making facilities Licensed Cen ht CTV No parking No coaches Last d 9pm
PRICE GUIDE
ROOMS: s £24-£38; d fr £52✻
CARDS: 🔲 🔲 🔲 🔲 🔲 🔲

Selected

GH Q Q Q Q **Gwrach Ynys Country** Ynys, Talsarnau LL47 6TS (2 miles N of Harlech on the A496) ☎01766 780742 FAX 01766 781199
Closed mid Dec-mid Jan
Translated as Dwarf Island, this superbly maintained country guest house lies in a lowland area where the sea once washed up to the walls of Harlech Castle; an acre of pretty lawns and gardens surrounds it, and there is a small paddock for the family's pet ponies. Deborah and Gwynfor Williams epitomise Welsh hospitality: guests are well looked after and children are especially welcome. All the smart modern bedrooms have en suite or private facilities, there is a choice of sitting rooms and Deborah produces honest home-cooked food.
7 rms (1 bth 5 shr) (2 fmly) No smoking in bedrooms No smoking in dining room No smoking in 1 lounge CTV in all bedrooms Tea and coffee making facilities Direct dial from bedrooms Cen ht CTV 10P No coaches Last d noon
PRICE GUIDE
ROOMS: s £17.50-£20; d £35-£40; wkly b&b £115-£135; wkly hlf-bd £175-£190

📺 ♥ Q Mrs E Jones **Tyddyn Gwynt** *(SH601302)* LL46 2TH (2.5m off B4573 (A496)) ☎01766 780298
Fields of sheep enclosed by dry stone walls surround this solid stone-built farmhouse which stands in splendid isolation high on the hills above Harlech. Cosy bedrooms are equipped with television and tea trays, good, honestly cooked meals are provided on request, and the Jones family are very welcoming hosts. Many guests return year after year.
2 rms (1 fmly) No smoking Tea and coffee making facilities CTV 6P 3 acres small holding Last d 7pm
PRICE GUIDE
ROOMS: s fr £15; d fr £27

HAY-ON-WYE Powys Map **03** SO24

See also Glasbury

GH Q Q Q **York House** Hardwick Rd, Cusop HR3 5QX (on B4348) ☎01497 820705
rs Xmas
This large, late Victorian, semi detached house is quietly located on the B4348, at Cusop, half a mile east of the centre of Hay-on-Wye. It has a very extensive and attractive garden in which resides a flock of white doves. The attractively furnished and decorated bedrooms, which include family rooms, have modern equipment and rooms with en-suite facilities are available. Separate tables are provided in the traditionally furnished dining room. There is also a very pleasant, and comfortable lounge, which is attractively and tastefully decorated and furnished. The guest house has its own private car park.
5 rms (4 bth/shr) (2 fmly) No smoking CTV in all bedrooms Tea and coffee making facilities Cen ht No children 8yrs 8P No coaches Last d 5pm
PRICE GUIDE
ROOMS: d £40-£44; wkly b&b £126-£138.60; wkly hlf-bd £201.60-£214.20
CARDS: 🔲 🔲 🔲

HOLYHEAD See ANGLESEY, ISLE OF

HOLYWELL Clwyd Map **07** SJ17

♥ Q Q Mrs M L Williams **Bryn Glas** *(SJ155737)* Babell CH8 7PZ (turn off A55 for Holywell, proceed to traffic lights, turn left uphill to Brynford village pass church to next crossroads turn right for Babell) ☎01352 720493
Apr-Oct
Bryn Glas, a small farm breeding mostly sheep, enjoys lovely views over the Clwydian range of mountains. There are two pretty bedrooms, both of which are suitable for families. The Williams family welcomes guests warmly, and a traditional Welsh breakfast is served; evening meals are not available, but many

establishments nearby offer bar meals - one with a good local reputation being situated at the end of the drive.
2 rms (1 fmly) No smoking Tea and coffee making facilities Cen ht CTV 2P Pony trekking 40 acres beef mixed sheep horses

 ♥ QQQ Mrs M Jones **Greenhill Farm** *(SJ186776)* CH8 7QF (from Holywell follow sign to St Winefrid's Well. 200yds beyond the well, turn left opposite the Royal Oak and follow road uphill to end) ☎01352 713270
Mar-Nov
Dating from the 16th century, this farmhouse has many original beams and timbers in evidence. It stands in an elevated position with panoramic views over the Dee estuary and Hilbre Island. Bedrooms are warm and cosy, one has an en suite bathroom and TVs are now provided. The quaint lounge is comfortable and there is an attractive half-panelled dining room. Friendly owners Mary and John Jones are happy to allow guests to watch the daily milking and roam their 120 acres of farmland.
3 rms (1 bth) (1 fmly) CTV in all bedrooms Tea and coffee making facilities No dogs Cen ht CTV ch fac 6P Snooker Childrens play area 120 acres dairy mixed Last d 9am
PRICE GUIDE
ROOMS: s fr £16; d fr £32 £

ISLE OF

Placenames incorporating the words 'Isle' or 'Isle of' will be found under the actual name, eg Isle of Anglesey is under Anglesey, Isle of.

LANGLAND BAY West Glamorgan Map **02** SS68

See also Bishopston and Mumbles

GH QQQ **Wittemberg Hotel** SA3 4QN
☎01792 369696 FAX 01792 366995
Closed Jan
In a quiet spot just a short walk from the beach, this comfortable hotel has seen many improvements at the hands of its owners, the Thomas family. Bedrooms are well equipped, with pleasant decor and fabrics, and there is a comfortable lounge and bar. On-site car parking is provided.
12 rms (10 shr) (2 fmly) No smoking in bedrooms No smoking in dining room CTV in all bedrooms Tea and coffee making facilities No dogs (ex guide dogs) Licensed Cen ht CTV 11P No coaches Last d 7pm
PRICE GUIDE
ROOMS: s £26-£35; d £42-£55; wkly b&b £100-£160; wkly hlf-bd £130-£210✳
CARDS: 🖃 🖃 🖃 £

LITTLE HAVEN Dyfed Map **02** SM81

GH QQQ *White Gates* Settlelands Hill SA62 3LA (A40 to Haverfordwest, follow signs for Broad Haven and uphill to Little Haven, past bus stop and first on left)
☎01437 781552 FAX 01437 781552
Parts of this charming old former farmhouse date back over 300 years. From its elevated position it commands magnificent views of the bay and islands. Period and antique furnishings have been used throughout, to complement the character of the house. The bedrooms are individually styled and have modern equipement,and many extra touches. There is a family room available. There are separate tables in the pleasant dining room, and also an outdoor heated swimming pool.
4 rms (2 bth/shr) Tea and coffee making facilities Cen ht CTV 6P No coaches Outdoor swimming pool (heated) Fishing Riding Last d 6.30pm
CARDS: 🖃 🖃

LLANBEDR Gwynedd Map **06** SH52

◀ QQQ **Victoria** LL45 2LD ☎01341 23213
In a peaceful village setting, beside the River Artro, this old coaching inn offers pine-furnished bedrooms with en suite bathrooms and modern facilities. There is a choice of bars - one having its original settle bar, flagstone floor and black stove - and a good selection of bar food is available. There are also a large garden, where drinks are served in summer, and a purpose-built children's play area.
5 en suite (bth/shr) No smoking in dining room CTV in all bedrooms Tea and coffee making facilities Cen ht CTV 75P Last d 9.30pm
PRICE GUIDE
ROOMS: s fr £26; d fr £48.50; wkly b&b fr £156✳
CARDS: 🖃 🖃

LLANBERIS Gwynedd Map **06** SH56

GH QQQ **Alpine Lodge Hotel** 1 High St LL55 4EN
☎01286 870294 FAX 01286 870294
Apr-10 Oct rs 10 Oct-Mar
Set in its own grounds this fine Victorian house is situated at the approach to the village from Caernarfon. Several bedrooms enjoy good views over Lake Padarn to the Snowdonian hills beyond and all have ensuite or private ensuite facilities. There is a comfortable lounge for residents and the restaurant has its own small bar. Ample car parking is provided.
6 en suite (bth/shr) (2 fmly) CTV in all bedrooms Tea and coffee making facilities No dogs (ex guide dogs) Licensed Cen ht 10P No coaches Last d 6pm
PRICE GUIDE
ROOMS: d £35-£39✳
CARDS: 🖃 🖃 🖃 🖃 £

Greenhill Farm Guesthouse
Holywell, Clwyd. Tel: Holywell (01352) 713270

A 16th century working dairy farm overlooking the Dee Estuary with beamed and panelled interior retaining old world charm.
Tastefully furnished interior with some bedrooms having bathroom/shower en-suite. We have a childrens play area and utility/games room including washing machine, tumble dryer, snooker table and darts board.
Relax and enjoy typical farmhouse food, within easy reach of both the coastal and mountain areas of N. Wales.

Proprietors: Mary and John Jones

GH Ⓠ Ⓠ Ⓠ **Lake View Hotel** Tan-y-Pant LL55 4EL (on A4086 towards Caernarfon)
☎01286 870422 FAX 01286 872591
This is a cosy roadside hotel and it lies on the Caernarfon side of the village. Many rooms have pretty views over Lake Padarn and the hills of Snowdonia and all have ensuite or private bath/shower rooms. The central part of the hotel is 250 years old and here can be found a character bar and comfortable lounge. There is a modern restaurant facing the mountains and lake and a large selection of snacks and more substantial meals are provided.
10 rms (9 shr) (3 fmly) CTV in all bedrooms Tea and coffee making facilities No dogs (ex guide dogs) Licensed Cen ht CTV 25P Last d 9pm
PRICE GUIDE
ROOMS: s £27.50; d £40✱
CARDS:

LLANDEILO Dyfed Map **03** SN62

GH Ⓠ Ⓠ Ⓠ *Brynawel* 19 New Rd SA19 6DD
☎01558 822925
rs 25 & 26 Dec
Situated on the main road close to the town centre, this small, mid-terrace, family-run hotel provides a cheerful and friendly service. It has a popular café-style restaurant, which serves a selection of hot and cold food throughout the day. The prettily decorated bedrooms are furnished with modern laminated furniture and all have a TV. There is a quiet, modern lounge available for guests.
5 rms (2 bth 1 shr) (1 fmly) CTV in all bedrooms Tea and coffee making facilities No dogs (ex guide dogs) Licensed Cen ht 6P No coaches
CARDS:

LLANDOGO Gwent Map **03** SO50

GH Ⓠ *Brown's Hotel & Restaurant* NP5 4TW
☎01594 530262
Feb-Nov
Positioned in the centre of the village and close to the river, this guesthouse is popular with fishermen. The en-suite bedrooms are modest in furnishings and style. A small cafè, also run by the owners of the guesthouse, provides refreshments all day.
7 rms (1 shr) Licensed CTV No children 20P No coaches Last d 7.30pm

◀ Ⓠ Ⓠ Ⓠ **The Sloop** NP5 4TW (A466)
☎01594 530291 FAX 01594 530935
With lovely views of the Wye valley from its riverside position, this former mill is now a road-side inn offering well equipped modern bedrooms. Its bar is popular, not least for the wide range of food available.
4 en suite (bth/shr) CTV in all bedrooms Tea and coffee making facilities Cen ht No children 9yrs 40P No coaches Last d 10pm
PRICE GUIDE
ROOMS: s £25.50-£35; d £39-£47✱
MEALS: Lunch £6-£16alc Dinner £6-£16alc✱
CARDS: £

LLANDOVERY Dyfed Map **03** SN73

GH Ⓠ Ⓠ Ⓠ **Llwyncelyn** SA20 0EP (on A40, follow signs for Llandeilo, cross railway and river bridge, guest house on left)
☎01550 720566
Closed Xmas
A stone-built Victorian house stands in its own extensive gardens next to the River Tywi just west of the town. Traditionally furnished accommodation includes family and ground-floor

---

rooms, the lounge is relaxing and separate tables are available in the dining room.
6 rms (3 fmly) No smoking in dining room Tea and coffee making facilities No dogs (ex guide dogs) Licensed Cen ht CTV 12P No coaches Fishing Last d 7.30pm
PRICE GUIDE
ROOMS: s £18-£22; d £32-£34; wkly b&b £89.60-£128.80; wkly hlf-bd £171.85-£211✱
£

LLANDRINDOD WELLS Powys Map **03** SO06

See also Penybont

GH Ⓠ Ⓠ Ⓠ **Griffin Lodge Hotel** Temple St LD1 5HF (on A483 in town centre) ☎01597 822432
This detached late-Victorian house stands on the A483, close to the town centre with private car parking to the rear. The modern accommodation is well furnished and comprehensively equipped; family-bedded rooms are available. A spacious lounge contains a bar and separate tables are provided in the pleasant dining room.
8 rms (5 shr) No smoking in dining room CTV in all bedrooms Tea and coffee making facilities Licensed Cen ht CTV 8P Last d 7.30pm
PRICE GUIDE
ROOMS: s £18-£25; d £35-£44; wkly b&b £108-£150; wkly hlf-bd £178-£220
CARDS: £

Selected

GH Ⓠ Ⓠ Ⓠ Ⓠ **Guidfa House** Crossgates LD1 6RF (3m N, at jct of A483/A44) ☎01597 851241 FAX 01597 851875
This very comfortable, family-run guest house, has its own car park as well as well maintained lawns and gardens. Bright, freshly decorated bedrooms are well equipped in modern style, most of them having en suite bath or shower rooms, and there is a comfortable residents' lounge. Small business meetings can now be catered for.
7 rms (5 bth/shr) No smoking in bedrooms No smoking in dining room CTV in all bedrooms Tea and coffee making facilities No dogs (ex guide dogs) Licensed Cen ht No children 10yrs 10P Last d 7pm
PRICE GUIDE
ROOMS: s £21-£31; d fr £44; wkly b&b fr £136; wkly hlf-bd fr £210
CARDS: £

GH Ⓠ Ⓠ *The Kincoed* Temple St LD1 5HF (on A483 50yds beyond the hospital) ☎01597 822656 FAX 01597 824660
This privately-owned guest house stands on the A483, close to the town centre. It provides well equipped accommodation which features family bedded rooms, a small lounge bar and a dining room with separate tables. A rear car park was under construction at the time of our last visit.
10 rms (5 bth/shr) (3 fmly) No smoking in 2 bedrooms CTV in all bedrooms Tea and coffee making facilities Licensed Cen ht No children 2yrs 10P No coaches Last d 9.30pm
CARDS:

♥ Ⓠ Ⓠ Ⓠ Mrs R Jones **Holly** *(SJ045593)* Howey LD1 5PP (2m S A483) ☎01597 822402
Apr-Nov
Well furnished bedrooms are offered at this comfortable, bright family farmhouse. It is set in its own pretty gardens, and a traditional dining room and lounge are also provided.

3 en suite (bth/shr) (1 fmly) Tea and coffee making facilities No dogs Cen ht CTV 4P 70 acres beef sheep Last d 5pm
PRICE GUIDE
ROOMS: d £32-£36; wkly b&b £112-£126; wkly hlf-bd £160-£182✱

£

Selected

💚 ⓠⓠⓠⓠ Mr & Mrs R Bufton *Three Wells* (*SO062586*) Chapel Rd, Howey LD1 5PB (Howey 2m S A483 then unclass rd, E 1m) ☎01597 824427 FAX 01597 822484
The Bufton family has been welcoming guests to this farmhouse for over 27 years. It is still a working farm and pedigree Welsh black ponies are to be seen in the grounds. There is an attractive lake at the front, with fishing available, and ducks and hens roam around. The house has bright modern bedrooms, one with a four-poster bed and several with small lounge areas. Most of the public rooms overlook the lake; there are a spacious bar and a choice of lounges, one of them with a wood-burning stove.
14 en suite (bth/shr) No smoking in dining room No smoking in 1 lounge CTV in all bedrooms Tea and coffee making facilities Direct dial from bedrooms No dogs Licensed Lift Cen ht CTV No children 8yrs 20P Fishing 50 acres beef mixed sheep Last d 6pm

---

LLANDUDNO Gwynedd Map **06** SH78

GH ⓠⓠⓠ Beach Cove 8 Church Walks LL30 2HD (last road on left before pier) ☎01492 879638
Closed Xmas
Karen and Bob Carroll are the friendly owners of this cosy guest house, which is situated just off the promenade at the Great Orme end. The pretty bedrooms include one with a four-poster bed and another on the ground floor, and most of them have modern en suite showers. Public areas offer a residents' lounge, a solarium, and a restaurant adorned with film posters and pictures. There is no car park but street parking is unrestricted.
7 rms (5 shr) (2 fmly) No smoking in 2 bedrooms No smoking in dining room No smoking in lounges CTV in all bedrooms Tea and coffee making facilities No dogs (ex guide dogs) Cen ht CTV No parking No coaches Solarium Last d 5.30pm
PRICE GUIDE
ROOMS: s £13-£15; d £26-£34; wkly b&b £90-£115; wkly hlf-bd £140-£165✱

GH ⓠⓠⓠ Bodnant 39 St Marys Rd LL30 2UE
☎01492 876936
This small Edwardian guest house is situated in a quiet residential area within easy walking distance of the shops and seafront. Owners Peter and Anna Ankers offer guests a truly Welsh welcome, including lessons on the language and its history, and traditional Welsh dishes and folk music. Bedrooms are bright and well maintained, and there is a residents' lounge. Smoking is not permitted.
5 en suite (bth/shr) No smoking CTV in all bedrooms Tea and coffee making facilities No dogs Licensed Cen ht No children 12yrs 3P No coaches Last d 5pm
PRICE GUIDE
ROOMS: s £18-£20; d £34

🛏🔻 **GH** ⓠⓠⓠ Brannock Private Hotel 36 St Davids Rd LL30 2UH (enter town via A470, turn left prior to Holy Trinity Church, through traffic lights then turn right off Trinity Avenue) ☎01492 877483
Apr-Nov
This well established restaurant lies in a residential part of the resort but is within easy walking distance of the sea front and shopping centre. Bedrooms are well equipped with modern amenities; most have en suite shower rooms. Street parking is readily available.
8 rms (5 shr) (1 fmly) No smoking in dining room CTV in all bedrooms Tea and coffee making facilities Cen ht No children 3yrs 5P No coaches Last d 5pm
PRICE GUIDE
ROOMS: s £15-£19; d £30-£38; wkly b&b £95-£109; wkly hlf-bd £125-£139
CARDS: 🃏 💳

£

GH ⓠⓠⓠ Britannia Hotel Promenade, 15 Craig-y-Don Pde LL30 1BG (close to North Wales Theatre & 100yds from Texaco garage) ☎01492 877185
Closed Dec
This well maintained hotel is situated on the Criag-y-Don promenade at the eastern end of the resort. It has been run by the friendly Williams family for over 20 years, and many of its guests visit every year. The bedrooms are attractively decorated, many have en suite facilities and modern amenities are provided. Some rooms have lovely views across the bay and two are at ground floor level. Street parking is unrestricted.
9 rms (7 bth/shr) (5 fmly) No smoking in dining room No smoking in lounges CTV in all bedrooms Tea and coffee making ➡

The Sloop Inn

LLANDOGO, NEAR MONMOUTH
Tel: 01594 530291
Fax: 01594 530935

Llandogo is situated midway between Monmouth and Chepstow on the A466, which follows the River Wye on its Last 16 miles to the Bristol Channel. In the centre of this sleepy village is an award-winning 18th century country inn offering a comfortable mix of tradition and modern facilities. Spotlessly clean en suite character bedrooms, unpretentious food at realistic prices and a cheerful atmosphere make The Sloop Inn a popular place to stay.

facilities No dogs (ex guide dogs) Cen ht No parking No coaches Last d 5pm
PRICE GUIDE
ROOMS: d £28-£36; wkly hlf-bd £135-£162✱

GH 🅀🅀 *Bryn Rosa* 16 Abbey Rd LL30 2EA
☎01492 878215
Brenda and Mick Clay are the friendly hosts at this long established guest house. The bedrooms are on the small side, but are neat and well equipped. Many have en suite shower rooms, and there is a ground-floor room for the less mobile. Both the comfortable lounge and the dining room are attractively decorated and Brenda serves honest home cooking. Easy street parking is available and the seafront and shops are within easy walking distance.
8 rms (4 shr) (2 fmly) No smoking in dining room CTV in all bedrooms Tea and coffee making facilities Cen ht CTV No children 2yrs 4P No coaches Last d 4.30pm
CARDS: 🅂 ▄▄

GH 🅀🅀🅀 **Carmel Private Hotel** 17 Craig-y-Don Pde, Promenade LL30 1BG (on main promenade between the Great and Little Ormes) ☎01492 877643
Etr-Oct rs Apr
This family run private hotel is situated at the eastern end of the promenade, close to the shopping centre and with sweeping views over the bay towards the Great Orme. Bedrooms are bright and fresh with pretty papers and fabrics used to good effect. Family and ground floor rooms are available and all rooms are provided with televisions and tea trays. A comfortable foyer lounge and a rear car park are available for guests.
9 rms (6 shr) (2 fmly) No smoking in dining room No smoking in lounges CTV in all bedrooms Tea and coffee making facilities Cen ht CTV No children 4yrs 6P No coaches Last d noon
PRICE GUIDE
ROOMS: s £15.50-£18.50; d £28-£33; wkly b&b £98-£115.50; wkly hlf-bd £133-£150.50✱

GH 🅀🅀🅀 **Hotel Carmen** Carmen Sylva Rd, Craig-y-Don LL30 1LZ ☎01492 876361
Mar-Nov rs Xmas
This large double fronted hotel is run by the very friendly Newberry family and is situated just off the Craig-y-Don promenade. Bedrooms are modern and well equipped and all except one now have en suite bath or shower rooms. There is a comfortable lounge for residents as well as a bar and entertainment is provided during the season. Easy street parking is available.
18 en suite (bth/shr) (2 fmly) No smoking in 12 bedrooms No smoking in dining room No smoking in 1 lounge CTV in all bedrooms Tea and coffee making facilities No dogs (ex guide dogs) Licensed Cen ht CTV No children 10yrs No parking Last d 5.30pm
PRICE GUIDE
ROOMS: s £25; d £49; wkly b&b £100-£115; wkly hlf-bd £160-£175✱

╭─────────── *Selected* ───────────╮

GH 🅀🅀🅀🅀 **Cornerways Hotel** 2 St Davids Place LL30 2UG ☎01492 877334
Mar-1 Nov
An immaculately maintained private hotel stands in a quiet residential area close to the shops and promenade. Many of the bright, attractively decorated bedrooms have canopied beds and all have en suite facilities; one room has its own

private suite. Guests can relax in either the comfortable lounge or a small seating area in the foyer. A good choice of meals and forecourt parking are also available.
7 en suite (bth/shr) No smoking in bedrooms No smoking in dining room CTV in all bedrooms Tea and coffee making facilities No dogs (ex guide dogs) Licensed Cen ht No children 5P No coaches Last d 3pm
PRICE GUIDE
ROOMS: s £20-£21; d £40-£42; wkly b&b £140-£147; wkly hlf-bd £210-£224✱

╭─────────── *Selected* ───────────╮

GH 🅀🅀🅀🅀 **Craiglands Private Hotel** 7 Carmen Sylva Rd, Craig-y-Don LL30 1LZ ☎01492 875090
Mar-Nov
Blodwen Mullin has been welcoming guests for over a quarter of a century and her smile is as warm as ever. The house is immaculate, and all the bedrooms are equipped with TVs, tea trays and en suite bath or shower rooms; there is also a comfortable lounge for residents. Blodwen is an accomplished cook and everything she produces is fresh. Craiglands is just off Craig-y-Don promenade and easy street parking is available.
6 en suite (bth/shr) (1 fmly) No smoking in dining room No smoking in lounges CTV in all bedrooms Tea and coffee making facilities Cen ht CTV No children 4yrs No parking No coaches Last d 4pm
PRICE GUIDE
ROOMS: d £38; wkly hlf-bd £180-£200✱

╭─────────── *Selected* ───────────╮

GH 🅀🅀🅀🅀 **Cranberry House** 12 Abbey Rd LL30 2EA ☎01492 879760
Mar-Oct
Named after a very attractive collection of Cranberry glassware, this is a delightful family-run guesthouse, strictly for non-smoking guests. The bedrooms have been attractively decorated with coordinating fabrics and wallpaper, and furnished with pine and some fine antiques. The pleasant sitting room has deep sofas and fresh flowers, and meals are served at round lace-covered tables in the dining room. This Victorian house is conveniently situated in a quiet residential area of the town, within easy walking distance of local amenities, with the advantage of its own car park.
6 en suite (bth/shr) No smoking CTV in all bedrooms Tea and coffee making facilities No dogs (ex guide dogs) Cen ht CTV No children 4P No coaches Last d noon
PRICE GUIDE
ROOMS: s £17-£20; d £34-£40; wkly b&b fr £120; wkly hlf-bd fr £170✱
CARDS: 🅂 ▄▄ ▄▄

╭─────────── *Selected* ───────────╮

GH 🅀🅀🅀🅀 **Hollybank** 9 St Davids Place LL30 2UG ☎01492 878521
Etr-Oct
This immaculately maintained establishment operates a strict no-smoking policy. The modern en suite bedrooms (a number of them suitable for family occupation) are freshly decorated

and well equipped, while other facilities include a comfortable lounge, a cottage-style dining room and a small rear car park.
7 en suite (bth/shr) (2 fmly) No smoking CTV in all bedrooms Tea and coffee making facilities Licensed Cen ht 5P No coaches Last d 4pm
PRICE GUIDE
ROOMS: s £21-£24; d £38-£42; wkly b&b £126-£154; wkly hlf-bd £182-£210

Selected

GH Q Q Q Q **Hotel Messina** Hill Ter LL30 2LS
☎01492 875260 FAX 01492 875260
Closed Nov
The Messina is a small family-run hotel situated under the wooded slopes of the Great Orme with excellent views over the promenade. Bedrooms include several suitable for families, and all are attractively decorated and well equipped. A comfortable residents' lounge is provided and the restaurant takes full advantage of the views. The cosy bar features an unusual display of pop records collected by the Astle family over the years.
10 rms (4 bth 3 shr) (5 fmly) No smoking in dining room CTV in all bedrooms Tea and coffee making facilities Licensed Cen ht 3P No coaches Last d 6.30pm
PRICE GUIDE
ROOMS: d £36-£42; wkly b&b £125-£140; wkly hlf-bd £175-£190
CARDS: 🔳 💳 💳

GH Q Q **Minion Private Hotel** 21-23 Carmen Sylva Rd LL30 1EQ ☎01492 877740
8 Apr-23 Oct
The friendly Buet family have been inviting guests to their hotel for no less than 47 years. It is set in a quiet residential area, within easy walking distance of the local shops and the Craig-y-Don promenade. Bedrooms are neat and well decorated, and a cosy bar and a residents' TV lounge are provided.
12 en suite (bth/shr) (1 fmly) No smoking in dining room Tea and coffee making facilities Licensed CTV No children 2yrs 8P Last d 4.30pm

---

GH Q Q Q **Montclare Hotel** North Pde LL30 2LP
☎01492 877061
Mar-Oct
A tall, terraced guesthouse stands almost on the seafront at the pier end of the promenade, conveniently close to the main shopping area. Bedrooms are all neat and modern, with coordinating fabrics and colour schemes; they all have en suite facilities. The comfortable lounge has deep upholstered cane seating and there is a small bar. Enjoyable home cooking using fresh produce is served in the pretty dining room.
15 en suite (bth/shr) (6 fmly) No smoking in 6 bedrooms No smoking in dining room CTV in all bedrooms Tea and coffee making facilities No dogs (ex guide dogs) Licensed Cen ht No parking Last d 3pm
PRICE GUIDE
ROOMS: s £17; d £34; wkly b&b fr £110; wkly hlf-bd fr £150 £

GH Q Q Q **Orotava Private Hotel** 105 Glan-y-Mor Rd, Penrhyn Bay LL30 3PH ☎01492 549780
This family run private hotel enjoys a superb location at Penrhyn Bay with direct access to the beach through pretty lawns and

gardens. The en suite modern bedrooms are smart and have such extras as televisions and tea trays. The lounge is spacious and impressively panelled and this like other rooms has good sea views. Two dining rooms are provided; one serves lunches which have become very popular locally. The hotel has its own forecourt car park.
6 en suite (bth/shr) No smoking in bedrooms No smoking in dining room CTV in all bedrooms Tea and coffee making facilities No dogs Licensed Cen ht CTV No children 15yrs 10P No coaches Last d 6pm
PRICE GUIDE
ROOMS: s £18.50; d £37
CARDS: 🔳 💳

GH Q Q **Rosaire Private Hotel** 2 St Seiriols Rd LL30 2YY
☎01492 877677
Mar-Oct
A small private hotel, run by the friendly Evans family, the Rosaire is situated in a quiet residential part of the resort which is within easy walking distance of the amenities. Many bedrooms have en suite shower rooms and all are equipped with TVs and tea trays. A comfortable residents' lounge is provided.
10 rms (2 bth 6 shr) No smoking in dining room CTV in 9 bedrooms Tea and coffee making facilities Licensed Cen ht No children 3yrs 6P No coaches Last d 4pm

---

GH Q Q Q **St Hilary Hotel** 16 Craig-y-Don Pde, Promenade LL30 1BG (on main promenade close to New Theatre & Conference Centre) ☎01492 875551
Feb-Oct
This family run hotel is situated on the Craig-y-Don promenade and near the local shops. Many bedrooms look out over the bay and these are fresh, bright and well equipped with modern facilities. Three are on the ground floor and suitable for those less mobile guests. There is a welcoming foyer lounge and a further inner lounge for residents. Easy street car parking is available.
11 rms (8 shr) (8 fmly) No smoking in dining room CTV in all bedrooms Tea and coffee making facilities No dogs (ex guide dogs) Cen ht No parking No coaches Last d 5pm
PRICE GUIDE
ROOMS: s £14-£34; d £28-£37; wkly b&b £98-£126; wkly hlf-bd £135-£162*
CARDS: 🔳 💳 💳 💳 💳

GH Q Q Q **Sunnycroft Private Hotel** 4 Claremont Rd LL30 2UF ☎01492 876882
This very friendly private hotel is situated in a residential part of the resort and within easy reach of the shops and seafront. Bedrooms are modern and very well equipped with hairdryers, remote control TVs and adjustable heating. All have en suite shower rooms, and there is a comfortable lounge and bar. A small forecourt car park is available.
9 en suite (shr) (2 fmly) No smoking in dining room CTV in all bedrooms Tea and coffee making facilities Licensed Cen ht CTV No children 4yrs 4P Last d noon
PRICE GUIDE
ROOMS: s £16.45-£20; d £30-£40; wkly b&b £105-£140; wkly hlf-bd £140-£181 £

GH Q Q Q **Sunnyside Private Hotel** Llewelyn Av LL30 2ER
☎01492 877150
Etr-Oct & Xmas
Run by the friendly Bryson family, this large detached house has a patio garden in the front and is only a short walk from the town centre and seafront. The majority of the bedrooms have en suite facilities, and there are some bedrooms on the ground floor. There is a comfortable lounge for residents and a bar complete with its own dance floor where entertainment is provided several times a week. The property has access to the sandy beaches. ➡

26 en suite (bth/shr) (4 fmly) CTV in all bedrooms Tea and coffee making facilities Licensed Cen ht CTV No parking Last d 7.30pm
PRICE GUIDE
ROOMS: s £18; d £36; wkly b&b £115; wkly hlf-bd £150✱

GH Ⓠ Ⓠ Ⓠ **Thorpe House** 3 St Davids Rd LL30 2UL
☎01492 877089 FAX 0161 456 4714
This large semi-detached house stands within easy reach of the town centre and other amenities. It provides soundly maintained, bright, modern furnished and equipped accommodation, which includes family bedded rooms and rooms with en-suite facilities. There is a pleasant and comfortable lounge, a cosy bar and an attractive dining room, where separate tables are provided.
8 rms (1 bth 3 shr) (2 fmly) No smoking in dining room CTV in all bedrooms Tea and coffee making facilities Licensed Cen ht CTV No parking No coaches Last d 6pm £

GH Ⓠ Ⓠ Ⓠ **Warwick Hotel** 56 Church Walks LL30 2HL
☎01492 876823
Set on the lower slopes of the Great Orme this large, detached Victorian house has good views of the town and beyond. The majority of the bedrooms have en suite facilities and satellite television is available. Public areas include a residents' bar, spacious lounge and an attractive restaurant which overlooks lawns where guests can relax in good weather.
16 rms (8 bth 5 shr) (9 fmly) CTV in all bedrooms Tea and coffee making facilities Licensed Cen ht CTV No parking Last d 6.45pm
CARDS: 🔲 ■ 🔳

GH Ⓠ Ⓠ Ⓠ **Wedgwood Hotel** 6 Deganwy Av LL30 2YB
☎01492 878016
Etr-Dec
This family run private hotel is situated within easy walking distance of the shopping centre and seafront. Bedrooms are attractively decorated with pretty papers and fabrics, most have en suite bath or shower rooms and all are well equipped with such extras as televisions, clock/radios and hair dryers. Some are also suitable for families. There is a comfortable lounge for residents and a forecourt car park is provided.
11 rms (2 bth 7 shr) (1 fmly) CTV in all bedrooms Tea and coffee making facilities Licensed Cen ht CTV 7P Last d 3pm

GH Ⓠ Ⓠ Ⓠ **Winston** 5 Church Walks LL30 2HD (guesthouse at the bottom of Church Walks which is opposite the pier on the North Shore) ☎01492 876144
Elaine Healey has run this cosy little guest house for over 20 years. It lies a few yards from the promenade at the Great Orme end, and although there is no car park street parking is unrestricted. Bedrooms are pretty, with many canopied beds and attractive wallpapers, and most have en suite facilities. A comfortable modern lounge is provided and Elaine is justifiably proud of her honest home cooking.
7 en suite (shr) No smoking in dining room CTV in all bedrooms Tea and coffee making facilities No dogs Cen ht CTV No children 2P No coaches Last d 4pm
PRICE GUIDE
ROOMS: s £16.50-£17; d £33-£34; wkly b&b £106-£110; wkly hlf-bd £155-£160✱
CARDS: 🔲 🔳 £

LLANEGRYN Gwynedd Map **06** SH50

GH Ⓠ Ⓠ Ⓠ **Cefn Coch** Llanegryn LL36 9SD (3.5m N of Tywyn, just off A493) ☎01654 712193
This old stone built property was apparently a coaching inn many years ago. It has been extensively renovated in recent times, by proprietors David and Anne Sylvester, who have retained many of

the original feature, such as exposed stone walls, flagged floors and beamed ceilings. Three bedrooms had been completed at the time of our inspection. These are traditionally furnished in a style befitting the character of the house, but they do have modern facilities such as central heating and en suite showers. There is a pleasant cottage style dining room, where separate tables are provided. In addition to the cosy lounge, which has a welcoming wood burning stove, there is a second small area, where drinks can be served. The house, which is no smoking throughout, has extensive gardens and is situated just off the A493, near the village of Llanegryn, three and a half miles north of Tywyn.
3 en suite (shr) No smoking Tea and coffee making facilities No dogs (ex guide dogs) Licensed Cen ht CTV No children 5P No coaches Last d 4.30pm
PRICE GUIDE
ROOMS: s fr £22; d fr £44

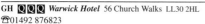

Selected

❤ Ⓠ Ⓠ Ⓠ Ⓠ Mrs Griffiths **Bryn Gwyn Country Farm House** *(SH610060)* LL36 9UF (im inland from A493)
☎01654 711771
Mar-Oct
A stone dower house built in the 18th century stands on the edge of the Dysynni valley, under the Cader Idris range of mountains. Set in four acres of gardens and paddocks and situated within the Snowdonia National Park, it offers neat modern bedrooms, many of them enjoying good views. There are two sitting rooms, one of which has a log fire in winter and opens out on to the grounds during the summer. There are also a lovely dining room with antique furniture and Minton china, and a games room with a large selection of books and guides.
3 rms (1 bth 1 shr) (2 fmly) No smoking CTV in 1 bedroom Tea and coffee making facilities No dogs (ex guide dogs) Cen ht CTV 7P Bicycles 4 acres non-working Last d 2pm
PRICE GUIDE
ROOMS: s fr £20; d £30-£39✱ £

LLANELLI Dyfed Map **02** SN50

GH Ⓠ **Awel Y Mor** 86 Queen Victoria Rd SA15 2TH
☎01554 755357
This detatched house is conveniently located for access to the town centre and has its own private car park at the rear. It provides good value, fairly modern accommodation, and the majority of bedrooms have en suite facilities. Guests have the use of a spacious combined lounge and dining room.
11 rms (4 bth 3 shr) (2 fmly) CTV in 7 bedrooms No dogs (ex guide dogs) Cen ht CTV 13P Last d 4.30pm

We endeavour to be as accurate as possible but changes in personnel and data can occur in establishments after the Guide has gone to press.

LLANFACHRETH Gwynedd Map **06** SH72

Premier Selected

GH ⓠⓠⓠⓠⓠ **Ty Isaf**
LL40 2EA (opposite the
church) ☎01341 423261
Beautifully situated on the
edge of the village and
offering superb views, this
traditional Welsh longhouse
has been lovingly decorated
and furnished by present
owners Graham and Diana
Silverton. There are three
guests' lounges, one with an
open fire and old beams. An excellent evening meal with
some choice is available.
3 en suite (bth/shr) No smoking in bedrooms No smoking in
dining room Tea and coffee making facilities Cen ht CTV
No children 13yrs 4P No coaches Last d 6pm
PRICE GUIDE
ROOMS: s £24; d £48; wkly b&b £168;
wkly hlf-bd £252

LLANFAIR CAEREINION Powys Map **06** SJ10

▣▼ ♥ⓠⓠⓠ Ivernia Watkin **Bryn Penarth** *(SJ101046)*
SY21 0BZ ☎01938 810535
Apr-Oct
This early-Victorian house is situated on a small sheep farm and
surrounded by pleasant gardens. It is about one-and-a-half miles
south of Llanfair Caereinion, and, from its elevated position it
overlooks beautiful countryside. Bedrooms vary in size and style
and the two rooms without en suite facilities have private
bathrooms nearby. There is a comfortable lounge and an attractive
dining room, with exposed beams and period furniture, where
dinner is served at the large table. Breakfast is taken in an adjacent
sun room.
4 rms (3 bth/shr) No smoking in bedrooms No smoking in dining
room CTV in 2 bedrooms Tea and coffee making facilities Cen
ht CTV 6P 37 acres sheep Last d 6pm
PRICE GUIDE
ROOMS: s £15-£18; d £30-£36; wkly b&b £90-£110; wkly hlf-
bd £130-£166

♥ⓠⓠⓠ Mrs J Cornes **Cwmllwynog** *(SJ071065)* SY21 0HF
(turn left off A458 into village pass the church through Milin
y Ddol farm 1m on left) ☎01938 810791
Jan-Nov
This traditional farmhouse, parts of which date back to 1665, is
peacefully situated on a dairy farm in a picturesque area three
miles west of Llanfair Caereinion. Both bedrooms have antique
furniture and good equipment, while one is en suite the other
has a private bathroom nearby. A delightful lounge has a low-
beamed ceiling and an inglenook fireplace, and guests share a
table in the small, traditionally furnished dining room.
2 rms (1 shr) CTV in all bedrooms Tea and coffee making
facilities No dogs Cen ht CTV 3P 105 acres dairy Last d 4pm

◀ⓠⓠ **Goat Hotel** High St SY21 0QS (leave A458 just after
light railway station through town hotel opposite church)
☎01938 810428
This 18th-century hostelry stands opposite the church, close to the
village centre. The well equipped bedrooms have a variety of

furniture and include a family room and another room in an
outbuilding which is accessed from the car park. A quaint bar and
a games room are available, and meals are taken at separate tables
in the traditionally furnished dining room.
6 rms (4 bth/shr) (1 fmly) Tea and coffee making facilities
Direct dial from bedrooms Cen ht 10P No coaches Last d 9pm
PRICE GUIDE
ROOMS: s £20-£25; d £30-£40
MEALS: Lunch £7 Dinner £6.50-£15alc
CARDS: 🅝 ▄▄ ▄▄

LLANGOLLEN Clwyd Map **07** SJ24

GH ⓠⓠⓠ **Hillcrest** Hill St LL20 8EU (leave A5 at traffic
lights up the hill at the side of the Grapes Hotel, Hillcrest 200
metres on left) ☎01978 860208
Though it dates back to the turn of the century, this no-smoking
guest house situated in a quiet area of the town always looks as
though it has been freshly decorated. All the bedrooms have
modern en suite shower facilities and there is a comfortable
lounge. Evening meals and bar snacks are offered, and there is
private parking available.
7 en suite (shr) (2 fmly) No smoking CTV in 3 bedrooms Tea
and coffee making facilities No dogs (ex guide dogs) Licensed
Cen ht CTV 10P Last d noon
PRICE GUIDE
ROOMS: d £38-£40; wkly b&b £133-£140; wkly hlf-bd £192-
£199.50✶

♥ⓠ Mrs A Kenrick **Rhydonnen Ucha** *(SJ177429)* Rhewl
LL20 7AJ ☎01978 860153
Etr-Nov
This farmhouse in the Vale of Llangollen stands near the A5,in an
isolated position beside a minor road. Bedrooms, though modestly
appointed, are brightly decorated, the traditional lounge is made
homely by personal bric-á-brac and the dining room features a fine
Welsh dresser.
4 rms (2 fmly) Cen ht CTV P 125 acres dairy Last d 3pm

LLANGURIG Powys Map **06** SN98

Selected

GH ⓠⓠⓠⓠ **Old Vicarage** SY18 6RN (off A470/A44
trunk road) ☎01686 440280 FAX 01686 440280
Mar-Oct
This well-appointed guest house was built in the late 19th
century as a vicarage and lies amid mature lawns and gardens
in a peaceful cul-de-sac. Neat, comfortable bedrooms all have
en suite bath or shower rooms together with TVs and radios.
There are a small foyer bar and two lounges, one for non-
smokers; a good choice of food is served, with up to twelve
main courses on offer, and afternoon teas are also available
(served on the lawn in fine weather). The proprietors of the
hotel also own the local craft shop and many examples of its
merchandise are on display.
5 rms (2 bth 2 shr) (2 fmly) No smoking in bedrooms No
smoking in dining room No smoking in 1 lounge CTV in 4
bedrooms Tea and coffee making facilities Licensed Cen ht
CTV No children 5yrs 6P Last d 6.30pm
PRICE GUIDE
ROOMS: d £36-£40; wkly b&b £126-£140

LLANIDLOES Powys Map **06** SN98

◼ Ⓠ Ⓠ Ⓠ **Mount** China St SY18 6AB (off A470)
☎01686 412247

A fourteenth-century listed building, this inn at the centre of the busy market town offers smart bars divided into several parts - one of them suitable for children; particularly impressive is what appears to be the original bar, with its polished cobbled floor, wooden settles and black fireplace. Externally accessed bedrooms all have modern en suite shower rooms and are equipped with TV and tea trays. The inn is popular for its wide range of food, and meals are served on the patio in fine weather. On site parking is available.
3 en suite (shr) (1 fmly) CTV in all bedrooms Tea and coffee making facilities No dogs (ex guide dogs) Cen ht CTV 10P Snooker Play area for children Last d 8.45pm

PRICE GUIDE
ROOMS: s fr £26; d fr £37; wkly b&b £117-£163; wkly hlf-bd £180-£250✳
MEALS: Lunch £7.15-£9.60alc Dinner £7.15-£14alc✳

◼ Ⓠ Ⓠ Ⓠ **Red Lion Hotel** Longbridge St SY18 6EE (off A470) ☎01686 412270 & 413120

This friendly family-run inn is located in the centre of the friendly town. Traditional public areas revolve around a large bar, while bedrooms stand out for their brand new appearance, modern bathrooms and contemporary comforts.
6 en suite (shr) 3 annexe en suite (shr) No smoking in bedrooms No smoking in dining room CTV in all bedrooms Tea and coffee making facilities Cen ht 8P Last d 9pm

PRICE GUIDE
ROOMS: s fr £28; d fr £40; wkly b&b fr £150; wkly hlf-bd fr £220
MEALS: Lunch £5.75-£15alc Dinner £5.75-£15alc
CARDS: 🆑 🔳

LLANRHYSTUD Dyfed Map **06** SN56

Selected

♥ Ⓠ Ⓠ Ⓠ Ⓠ Mrs J Vickers **Pen-Y-Castell** (*SN539684*) SY23 5BZ (take B4337 for about 1m climbing steep hill then follow guesthouse signs) ☎01974 272622

High above Cardigan Bay, just 2.5 miles from the village, and commanding beautiful views, this modernised guesthouse sits in pleasant grounds and boasts its own trout lake. Run by the friendly Mizen family, it offers pretty bedrooms with coordinating colour schemes, and a family unit with a separate bunk-bedded room. The cosy lounge has a cheerful wood-burning stove, and there is also a sun lounge with comfortable cushioned cane seating.
6 en suite (bth/shr) (1 fmly) No smoking in bedrooms No smoking in dining room No smoking in 1 lounge CTV in 3 bedrooms Tea and coffee making facilities No dogs (ex guide dogs) Licensed Cen ht CTV 12P Fishing Boating lake 35 acres beef sheep Last d 6pm

LLANSANTFFRAID-YM-MECHAIN Powys Map **07** SJ22

♥ Ⓠ Ⓠ Ⓠ Mrs M E Jones **Glanyrnwy** (*SJ229202*) SY22 6SU (alongside the B4393) ☎01691 828258

This stone-built farmhouse, situated on the edge of the village, dates back some 300 years, and three windows are still bricked up from the time of the window tax. The two neat bedrooms are prettily decorated, and there is a choice of comfortable lounges. Guests also enjoy the well tended gardens and lawns. Mrs Jones

has long extended warm Welsh hospitality, and some guests have been returning regularly for 20 years.
2 rms Tea and coffee making facilities No dogs (ex guide dogs) CTV No children 3yrs 3P 42 acres beef

PRICE GUIDE
ROOMS: s £15; d £29; wkly b&b £105✳

LLANWDDYN Powys Map **06** SJ01

♥ Ⓠ Ⓠ H A Parry **Tynymaes** (*SJ048183*) SY10 0NN (from Shrewsbury take B4393 to Lake Vyrnwy, pass through LLanfyllin, turn left for Lake Vyrnwy in approx 6m Tynymaes is on the right) ☎01691 870216
May-Sep

Situated just a few miles from Lake Vyrnwy this cosy farmhouse, run by the Parry family offers a warm welcome. The lounge is spacious and comfortable and the bedrooms are bright and cheerful.
3 rms (1 fmly) No smoking in bedrooms No smoking in dining room Tea and coffee making facilities No dogs Cen ht CTV 4P 420 acres beef sheep

PRICE GUIDE
ROOMS: s £16; wkly b&b £105✳

LLANWNDA Gwynedd Map **06** SH45

Premier Selected

♥ Ⓠ Ⓠ Ⓠ Ⓠ Ⓠ Mr & Mrs G Rowlands **Pengwern** (*SH459587*) Saron LL54 5UH ☎01286 830717
Closed Dec & Jan

This converted farmhouse - surrounded by lovely countryside and offering views of both Snowdonia and the sea - is reached by turning off the A487 towards Saron then going left at the crossroads. There are three modern en suite bedrooms in the main house, and a family suite in the adjoining annexe building includes a large private sitting room as well as two bedrooms. Guests are offered a warm welcome and honest farmhouse food. Smoking is not permitted in any of the buildings.
3 rms (2 bth/shr) 1 annexe en suite (bth/shr) CTV in all bedrooms Tea and coffee making facilities No dogs Cen ht 4P 130 acres beef sheep

LLANWRTYD WELLS Powys Map **03** SN84

GH Ⓠ Ⓠ Ⓠ **Lasswade Country House Hotel** LD5 4RW (turn off A483 signposted Llangammarch Wells hotel 200yds on right) ☎01591 610515 FAX 01591 610611

A handsome Edwardian house is set in a prime position with commanding views of the surrounding countryside. Owners Jack and Beryl Udall provide a welcoming environment, with spacious well equipped bedrooms, a comfortable traditional lounge and attractive dining room. A choice of plentiful, fresh, home-cooked dishes is offered, making good use of local produce. The hotel also features a sunken garden and south-facing terrace. Many birdwatchers are drawn to the area for the Red Kite, famous in this vicinity.

8 en suite (bth/shr) No smoking in bedrooms No smoking in dining room CTV in all bedrooms Tea and coffee making facilities Direct dial from bedrooms Licensed Cen ht CTV No children 12yrs 9P No coaches Fishing Sauna Solarium 700 acres rough shooting Last d 8.30pm
PRICE GUIDE
ROOMS: s £32.50; d £55; wkly b&b £175; wkly hlf-bd £252
CARDS: £

LLYSWEN Powys Map **03** SO13

GH Q Q Q **Oakfield** Llyswen LD3 0UR (off A470) ☎01874 754301
Mar-Oct
This large detached house dates back to 1914 and is situated close to both the A470 and the village centre. It has pleasant gardens and its own private car park. There are two soundly maintained, traditionally furnished bedrooms, one with an en suite bathroom and the other with a nearby private facility. All guests share one table in the traditionally furnished breakfast room, which also serves as the lounge and contains a TV. The house is no smoking throughout.
2 rms (1 bth) No smoking Tea and coffee making facilities No dogs (ex guide dogs) Cen ht CTV 6P No coaches
PRICE GUIDE
ROOMS: s fr £12; d fr £24✶

MACHYNLLETH Powys Map **06** SH70

GH Q Q Q **Maenllwyd** Newtown Rd SY20 8EY (on A489 opposite the hospital) ☎01654 702928 FAX 01654 702928
Closed 25 & 26 Dec
A large Victorian house standing in a pleasant garden beside the A489 Newtown road has a car park to the rear. Bedrooms, including a number of family rooms, are attractively decorated and well equipped; recent improvements have provided them all with en suite facilities. Public areas consist of a cosy lounge and a traditionally furnished dining room.
8 en suite (bth/shr) (2 fmly) No smoking in bedrooms No smoking in dining room CTV in all bedrooms Tea and coffee making facilities Licensed Cen ht CTV 10P No coaches Last d 1pm
PRICE GUIDE
ROOMS: s £20-£23; d £35; wkly b&b fr £110; wkly hlf-bd fr £167✶
CARDS: £

MARFORD Clwyd Map **07** SJ35

GH Q Q Q **Brackenwood** 67 Wynnstay Ln LL12 8LH (turn off B5445 by Red Lion pub) ☎01978 852866 FAX 01978 852065
This family-run guest house backs on to several acres of woodland, allowing guests to ramble at will. Many of the attractive bedrooms have lovely views, and two are located on the ground floor. There are a very welcoming lounge, a modern conservatory dining room and ample forecourt parking.
7 rms (1 bth 1 shr) (1 fmly) No smoking in bedrooms No smoking in dining room CTV in 3 bedrooms Tea and coffee making facilities Cen ht CTV 6P No coaches Last d at breakfast time
PRICE GUIDE
ROOMS: s £13.50-£21; d £25.50-£30; wkly b&b £105-£125; wkly hlf-bd £180-£195✶

MERTHYR TYDFIL Mid Glamorgan Map **03** SO00

GH Q Q Q Q **Llwyn Onn** Cwmtaf CF48 2HT (4m N off A470, overlooking reservoir) ☎01685 384384
This large, impeccably maintained house stands in attractive gardens on the A470, some four miles north of Merthyr Tydfil. From its elevated position, it overlooks views of the woodland across the Llwyn-Onn Reservoir. It provides well equipped, modern accommodation, which includes rooms with en suite facilities. There is a pleasant and comfortably furnished lounge and separate tables are provided in the attractively appointed dining room.
4 rms (2 bth/shr) No smoking in dining room CTV in all bedrooms Tea and coffee making facilities No dogs (ex guide dogs) Cen ht 4P
PRICE GUIDE
ROOMS: s fr £18; d fr £40✶
CARDS: £

◀ Q Q Q **Tredegar Arms Hotel** 66 High St, Dowlais Top CF48 2YE (off junct of A465 & A470 on the old Merthyr Tydfil road) ☎01685 377467
Conveniently positioned just north of the town close to the junction of the A465/A470, this character inn (under the same ownership as The Little Diner at Dowlais Top) has recently been upgraded to offer accommodation in comfortable, brightly decorated bedrooms well equipped to meet the needs of today's traveller. Popular, friendly bars and a cosily attractive little restaurant make up the public areas, and useful car parking is provided on site.
5 en suite (bth/shr) (1 fmly) CTV in all bedrooms Tea and coffee making facilities Cen ht 6P
CARDS:

MOLD Clwyd Map **07** SJ26

GH Q Q Q **Heulwen** Maes Bodlonfa CH7 1DR ☎01352 758785
Just two rooms are available in this guest house, both are modern and attractively decorated, with use of private bath or shower room. There is a spacious lounge with comfortable seating, and guests dine together in a family atmosphere. There are pretty lawns and gardens, ample car parking space and a sunny conservatory. The house is no smoking.
2 rms (1 fmly) No smoking CTV in all bedrooms Tea and coffee making facilities No dogs (ex guide dogs) Cen ht 3P No coaches Last d 9am
PRICE GUIDE
ROOMS: s £16.50; d £33; wkly b&b £100-£145✶ £

MONMOUTH Gwent Map **03** SO51

GH Q Q **Church Farm** Mitchel Troy NP5 4HZ ☎01600 712176
This spacious 16th century former farmhouse has recently been upgraded. Retaining many original features such as oak beams and inglenook fireplaces, it also provides bright bedrooms and traditional public rooms.
8 rms (6 shr) (2 fmly) No smoking Tea and coffee making facilities Cen ht CTV 12P No coaches Last d noon
PRICE GUIDE
ROOMS: s £17-£19.50; d £34-£39; wkly b&b £112-£129.50; wkly hlf-bd £182-£203

MONTGOMERY Powys Map **07** SO29

Selected

❦ Ⓠ Ⓠ Ⓠ Ⓠ Mrs G M Bright **Little Brompton**
(SO244941) SY15 6HY (2m E on B4385)
☎01686 668371
This pleasant white-painted farmhouse is set in 100 acres of
beef and sheep farmland just off the B4385 two miles east of
the town; near Offa's Dyke, it is popular with walkers. The
house dates back to the early 17th century and features a
wealth of exposed timbers and oak beams. Bedrooms are
decorated with pretty wallpapers and fabrics, and some still
have their original stone fireplaces. Robert and Gaynor Bright
have been the very hospitable owners for over 20 years and
Gaynor serves genuine farm food with an emphasis on
organic produce. There is an impressive inglenook fireplace
in the comfortable lounge and a fine old Welsh dresser in the
dining room.
3 rms (2 shr) (1 fmly) No smoking CTV in all bedrooms
Tea and coffee making facilities Cen ht CTV 4P Shooting
in season 100 acres arable beef mixed sheep Last d 5pm
PRICE GUIDE
ROOMS: s fr £20; d fr £36✱

MUMBLES West Glamorgan Map **03** SS68

See also Bishopston & Langland Bay

GH Ⓠ Ⓠ Ⓠ **The Shoreline Hotel** 648 Mumbles Road,
Southend SA3 4EA ☎01792 366233
Situated directly opposite the pretty harbour with commanding
views over the bay, this small and friendly guest house is
personally run by the resident owners. The clean, compact
bedrooms are equipped to a good standard to suit both the tourist
and business guest, and rooms on the front benefit from the view.
There is an attractive little restaurant with an open-plan bar and
lounge.
14 rms (9 bth/shr) (3 fmly) CTV in all bedrooms Tea and coffee
making facilities Licensed Cen ht CTV No parking Last d
8.30pm

NEATH West Glamorgan Map **03** SS79

Selected

GH Ⓠ Ⓠ Ⓠ Ⓠ **Cwmbach Cottages** Cwmbach Rd,
Cadoxton SA10 8AH ☎01639 639825 & 641436
Although built in the 17th-century, Cwmbach Cottages have
been sympathetically maintained to preserve their character
while still being able to offer modern comforts. The rooms are
equipped with high quality furniture and the whole is
beautifully clean and bright.
5 rms (4 bth/shr) (1 fmly) No smoking in bedrooms No
smoking in dining room CTV in all bedrooms Tea and coffee
making facilities No dogs (ex guide dogs) Cen ht CTV 7P
No coaches Last d 6.30pm
PRICE GUIDE
ROOMS: s £20-£25; d £36-£42; wkly b&b fr £126; wkly
hlf-bd fr £182✱

Premier Selected

GH Ⓠ Ⓠ Ⓠ Ⓠ Ⓠ *Green*
Lanterns Handref Ganol
Farm, Cimla SA12 9SL (exit
M4 at junct 43 in direction
of Neath. Take B4287
signposted Cimla and turn
right for 1m at cross roads
300yds past comprehensive
school) ☎01639 631884
For those who wish to
sample Welsh hospitality at

its best, then a visit to this lovely farmhouse set in a glorious
location is a must. The Green Lantern Guest House is run as a
family affair, with guests enjoying Margaret Brown's warmth
and generosity in this beautifully furnished comfortable
house, and daughter Karen running a thriving Ponytrekking
Centre using the excellent facilities on the farm. There are
four spacious, immaculate bedrooms which enjoy wonderful
views across the rolling countryside, yet the town of Neath is
only a 10 minute drive away. A delicious home cooked
evening meal is offered, and guests may enjoy this and a
super English breakfast round a large dining table. After
dinner there will be an inviting fire in the lounge which is
furnished like the rest of the house ,with beautiful pieces
collected by the Brown family.
3 rms (2 bth/shr) (2 fmly) No smoking in bedrooms No
smoking in dining room CTV in all bedrooms Tea and coffee
making facilities Cen ht CTV 6P Riding Last d 7pm

GH Ⓠ Ⓠ Ⓠ **Tree Tops House** 282 Neath Rd, Briton Ferry
SA11 2SL ☎01639 812419
Closed 23-28 Dec
A large and attractive Victorian house that has benefitted from
recent upgrading, whilst still retaining much of its original charm
and character. Bright and fresh, this friendly, family run
establishment offers comfortable bedrooms and cosy public
rooms.
4 rms (1 shr) No smoking in bedrooms No smoking in dining
room CTV in all bedrooms Tea and coffee making facilities Cen
ht CTV 5P Last d 3pm
PRICE GUIDE
ROOMS: s £18-£22; d £34-£40; wkly b&b £112-£140; wkly hlf-
bd £160-£180
CARDS: 🂱 ▆ ▆ 🂱

NEWPORT Gwent Map **03** ST38

GH Ⓠ Ⓠ **Caerleon House Hotel** 61 Caerau Rd NP9 4HJ (1m
from junct 27 M4, 0.5m from town centre close to Civic
Centre) ☎01633 264869
A friendly guest house in an elevated position with a welcoming
atmosphere, which has undergone recent upgrading.
7 en suite (bth/shr) (1 fmly) No smoking in 1 bedrooms No
smoking in dining room CTV in all bedrooms Tea and coffee
making facilities Licensed Cen ht 8P No coaches Last d
7.30pm
PRICE GUIDE
ROOMS: s fr £25; d fr £36✱

GH Ⓠ Ⓠ Ⓠ **Kepe Lodge** 46a Caerau Rd NP9 4HH
☎01633 262351
Closed 22-31 Dec
Conveniently positioned just a short walk from the town centre
and neatly tucked away in its own grounds, this exceptionally well

maintained guest house offers value-for-money accommodation - equally suited to the needs of businessman or tourist - in comfortable, thoughtfully equipped bedrooms attractively decorated with co-ordinating colours and fabrics.
8 rms (3 shr) No smoking in dining room No smoking in lounges CTV in all bedrooms Tea and coffee making facilities No dogs (ex guide dogs) Cen ht 8P No coaches
PRICE GUIDE
ROOMS: s £19-£22; d £34✳

£

GH QQ *Knoll* 145 Stow Hill NP9 4FZ
☎01633 263557 FAX 01633 212168
This large family-owned Victorian house retaining many of its original features offers cosy public rooms - including a spacious, relaxing guest lounge - and well equipped bedrooms. Set in an elevated position on Stow Hill, it is also conveniently near the main shopping centre.
11 rms (9 bth/shr) (2 fmly) No smoking in 2 bedrooms No smoking in dining room No smoking in lounges CTV in all bedrooms Tea and coffee making facilities Direct dial from bedrooms Licensed Cen ht CTV P No coaches Last d 7pm

---

GH QQ **West Usk Lighthouse** Lighthouse Rd, St Brides Wentlooge NP1 9SF (A48 then B4239 for 2m then turn left)
☎01633 810126 & 815860 FAX 01633 815582
A converted lighthouse, shaped like a wedding cake and perched on reclaimed land overlooking the Bristol Channel, offers bed and breakfast accommodation that is certainly different! Reached by way of a long bumpy lane, it has been restored and converted to provide a cosy retreat with well equipped wedge-shaped bedrooms set round a spiral stone staircase and a gas-lit dining room where a dinner party atmosphere prevails. Smoking is not permitted on the premises.
➡

St.ANNE'S
HOTEL

Western Lane, Mumbles, Swansea SA3 4EY
Tel: (01792) 369147 Fax: (01792) 360537

St. Annes Hotel, set in its own grounds, offers views overlooking the Bay. Most of the 28 bedrooms have en-suite facilities and all have colour TV, tea and coffee facilities, hair dryer and direct dial telephone. Ideally situated for easy access to the Gower Peninsula and also the city of Swansea, the hotel offers a quiet location in the heart of Mumbles, within walking distance of all facilities.

TREE TOPS
Guest House

Wales Tourist Board
👑👑
Highly Commended

TASTE OF WALES

For business or pleasure join us at Tree Tops where a warm welcome and good home cooking awaits. All bedrooms are centrally heated and tastefully furnished while maintaining its original Victorian charm. Each room has colour TV, tea/coffee facilities, radio/alarm clocks and hair dryers. Some rooms have en-suite facilities. There is a comfortable lounge and spacious dining room where home cooked evening meals are available by request. Conveniently situated on the A474 at Briton Ferry 5 mins from Neath and 10 mins from the fine city of Swansea. Why not make Tree Tops your base and explore what this beautiful area has to offer.

282 Neath Road, Briton Ferry, West Glam. SA11 2SL
Telephone: (01639) 812419

CAERLEON HOUSE
——— HOTEL ———
Welsh Tourist Board
👑👑👑   AA QQ

Caerau Road, Newport, Gwent NP9 4HJ
Telephone: 01633 264869

A family run hotel convenient for the M4 and close to the centre of Newport, the ideal base for touring Wales. All bedrooms are en suite and have colour TV and tea & coffee making facilities. Evening meals available. Licensed bar. Ample off-road parking. Whether your visit is for business or pleasure, you are guaranteed a warm and friendly welcome.

3 en suite (shr) No smoking CTV in all bedrooms Tea and coffee making facilities Cen ht CTV 10P No coaches Flotation tank Last d 8pm
PRICE GUIDE
ROOMS: s £30-£45; d £50-£62✱
CARDS: 🔳 ■ ▦

NEW QUAY Dyfed Map **02** SN35

GH 🆀🆀🆀 **Brynarfor Hotel** New Rd SA45 9SB (1m off A487) ☎01545 560358
Mar-Oct
This large detached Victorian house, surrounded by extensive gardens, is situated on the B4342, on the northern outskirts of the town. From its elevated position, it overlooks magnificent views of the sea, the beach and the harbour. It provides well equipped accommodation, which includes family rooms, rooms with sea views, and two bedrooms on the ground floor of an extension to the main house, both of which have entrances from the car park. All the bedrooms have en suite facilities. A wide choice of home cooked dishes is available in the traditionally furnished dining room. Other facilities include a lounge bar, a no smoking lounge and a basement games room.
5 en suite (bth/shr) 2 annexe en suite (bth) (3 fmly) No smoking in dining room No smoking in 1 lounge CTV in all bedrooms Tea and coffee making facilities No dogs (ex guide dogs) Licensed Cen ht CTV ch fac 11P No coaches Games room Last d 8pm
PRICE GUIDE
ROOMS: s £25-£27; d £42-£54; wkly hlf-bd £175-£210✱
CARDS: 🔳 ▦

💘 🆀🆀🆀 Mr M Kelly **Ty Hen** (*SN365553*) Llwyndafydd SA44 6BZ (from Llwyndafydd with phone box on left go up hill for approx 1m, after sharp right bend take 'no thro road' on your right, entrance 100yds) (Logis)
☎01545 560346 FAX 01545 560346
mid Feb-mid Nov
To reach Ty Hen, first locate the village of Llwyndafydd, which is about four miles south of New Quay and some two miles from the A487. With the telephone box on the left, proceed up the hill for about a mile. Turn right after the sharp right hand bend, into the "no through road". The much extended 200-year-old, stone built farmhouse is situated on a 40 acre sheep rearing holding. There are two bedrooms in the main house, plus another two in an adjacent building. There are also a number of self catering cottages. Home cooked meals are served in the cottage style dining room, which has an adjoining conservatory. The house also contains a cosy lounge and a small bar. Other facilities, which have been created by friendly proprietors Veronica and Mike Kelly, include a leisure centre, which has a heated swimming pool. Professional swimming lessons from Veronica can be arranged.
5 en suite (shr) 2 annexe en suite (shr) (2 fmly) No smoking CTV in all bedrooms Tea and coffee making facilities Licensed Cen ht CTV 20P Indoor swimming pool (heated) Sauna Solarium Gymnasium Bowls Skittles Table tennis Pool table 40 acres sheep Last d 6pm
PRICE GUIDE
ROOMS: s £20-£29; d £40-£58; wkly b&b £120-£175; wkly hlf-bd £179.50-£225
CARDS: 🔳 ▦

NEWTOWN Powys Map **06** SO19

Premier Selected

💘 🆀🆀🆀🆀🆀 David & Sue Jones **Dyffryn** (*8OO52954*)
Dyffryn, Aberhafesp SY16 3JD (from town take B4568 to Aberhafesp, turn right to Bwlchyffridd, bear left at next jct, left twice then right at X roads & farm is down hill on right)
☎01686 688817 & 0585 206412
FAX 01686 688324

This delightful family home - originally a 17th-century half-timbered barn - has been carefully restored by owners Dave and Sue Jones to feature an abundance of exposed timbers. Bedrooms are furnished and equipped in modern rustic style and they all have good quality en suite bathrooms. Sue provides traditional farmhouse food and guests dine family style. The house lies in 100 acres of farmland and there are many walks, together with a children's play area. Smoking is not permitted.
3 en suite (bth) (3 fmly) No smoking CTV in all bedrooms Tea and coffee making facilities No dogs (ex guide dogs) Cen ht CTV ch fac 3P 100 acres beef sheep Last d 5pm
PRICE GUIDE
ROOMS: s fr £20; d £40-£46; wkly b&b £140-£160; wkly hlf-bd £210-£230✱ £

PARKMILL (NEAR SWANSEA) West Glamorgan
Map **02** SS58

💘 🆀🆀 Mrs O Edwards **Parc-le-Breos House** (*SS529896*) SA3 2HA (at village turn right 300yds after Shepherds shop, then next left, signposted. Follow private road to end)
☎01792 371636
This 19th Century farmhouse standing in glorious tranquil grounds offers guests who enjoy the country life a chance to relax in a family atmosphere with gracious surroundings. The emphasis at this family home is on comfort and freedom to enjoy the pursuits offered here. It may be riding through the fields and woods, or perhaps group activities, which the Edwards family are happy to help arrange. The accommodation offered is in simply furnished comfortable bedrooms, which are ideal for parties of children or families. Dinner is offered using largely home grown produce. Gower is an area of outstanding beauty, and Parc-le-Breos is the place from which to explore.
10 rms (8 shr) (7 fmly) No dogs (ex guide dogs) Cen ht CTV 12P Riding Games room 65 acres arable horses pigs chickens Last d 3pm
PRICE GUIDE
ROOMS: s £16-£18; d £32-£36; wkly b&b fr £110; wkly hlf-bd £155-£170✱ £

PEMBROKE Dyfed Map **02** SM90

Selected

❤ Ⓠ Ⓠ Ⓠ Ⓠ Mrs S Lewis **Poyerston** *(SM027025)*
Cosheston SA72 4SJ (from Carmarthen take A477
Pembroke road, approx 0.5m past sign for Milton, farm is
on the left just before Vauxhall garage on right)
☎01646 651347
Mar-Oct
This large Victorian house was derelict when bought by the
present owners in 1993. Set well back from the road on a
large dairy, beef and arable holding, the house has been
extensively and tastefully restored and modernised. There are
two bedrooms, a double and a twin, both attractively
decorated, with period style furniture and quality en suite
facilities. There is a cosy lounge, a small conservatory sun
lounge and an attractive dining room with an impressive
original marble fireplace. Dinner is available by arrangement.
2 en suite (bth/shr) (1 fmly) No smoking Tea and coffee
making facilities No dogs (ex guide dogs) Cen ht CTV No
children 4yrs 12P 200 acres arable beef dairy Last d by
arrangement
PRICE GUIDE
ROOMS: d £35-£38; wkly b&b £122.50-£133✱

PENMACHNO Gwynedd Map **06** SH75

Selected

GH Ⓠ Ⓠ Ⓠ Ⓠ **Penmachno Hall** LL24 0PU (turn off A5
2m S of Betws-y-Coed on to B4406. Proceed through
village and turn right at Eagles Hotel, signposted Ty
Mawr) ☎01690 760207
Closed 21 Dec-14 Jan
Modwena and Ian Cutler took over this 19th-century rectory
just four years ago. It has since been transformed into an
elegant country guest house where a house-party atmosphere
is encouraged and guests dine together. All bedrooms have
modern facilities and mostly locally made furniture. Four
sitting rooms are available for guests, including a TV lounge,
library and conservatory. Modwena's cooking has already
achieved local acclaim and she sometimes organises
residential cookery courses. Art exhibitions are also held and
many works are displayed in the house for sale. The house is
set in large gardens, which extend to the river.
4 en suite (bth/shr) No smoking in bedrooms No smoking in
dining room No smoking in 1 lounge No dogs Licensed
Cen ht CTV 30P No coaches Last d 24 hrs prior
PRICE GUIDE
ROOMS: s £30; d £50; wkly b&b £175;
wkly hlf-bd £242
CARDS: 🔳

PENRHYNDEUDRAETH Gwynedd Map **06** SH63

❤ Ⓠ Ⓠ Mrs P Bayley **Y Wern** *(SH620421)* LLanfrothen
LL48 6LX (2m N off B4410)
☎01766 770556 FAX 01766 770556
This attractive, creeper-clad farmhouse dates back at least to the
early 17th century and lies at the foot of the Moelwyn hills,
surrounded by wooded slopes. Bedrooms feature original oak
beams and include several suitable for families. A spacious lounge
is provided and this also has a beamed ceiling as well as an

inglenook fireplace. Outside is a secluded sun terrace and a
mountain stream where guests may try their hand at tickling trout.
Good farmhouse food is provided and the Bayley family really
enjoy welcoming guests to their home.
5 rms (3 shr) (4 fmly) No smoking Tea and coffee making
facilities No dogs Cen ht CTV 6P 110 acres beef sheep
PRICE GUIDE
ROOMS: d £30-£34; wkly b&b £95-£114; wkly hlf-bd £158-
£177✱
Ⓔ

PENTREGAT Dyfed Map **02** SN35

◀ Ⓠ Ⓠ Ⓠ **New Inn** Pentregat SA44 5PT (on A487)
☎01239 654285
This former drover's inn dates back to 1772. It stands on the main
A487, mid-way between New Quay and Cardigan. It provides four
soundly maintained bedrooms, all with en suite facilities and all
no smoking. There is a choice of eating options, including a carte
selection in the quaint and pleasant dining room. Other facilities
include a traditional bar, a room for families, a room with a pool
table and video games, a beer garden and an adventure playground
for children.
4 en suite (bth/shr) No smoking in bedrooms No smoking in
dining room Tea and coffee making facilities No dogs (ex guide
dogs) Cen ht CTV No children 10yrs 35P Pool table Last d
10pm
PRICE GUIDE
ROOMS: s fr £15; d fr £25✱
MEALS: Lunch £9.05-£18.35alc Dinner £9.05-£18.35alc✱

PENYBONT Powys Map **03** SO16

Premier Selected

GH Ⓠ Ⓠ Ⓠ Ⓠ Ⓠ **Ffaldau
Country House & Restaurant**
LD1 5UD (2m E A44)
☎01597 851421
This delightful 16th-century
cruck-built long house has
been lovingly restored over
recent years by owners
Sylvia and Leslie Knott. It is
situated in pleasant grounds
back from the A44 a few

miles east of Crossgates. The
four bedrooms are not spacious but are attractively decorated
and furnished, featuring beams and exposed timbers, period
pieces and an abundance of Victoriana. A landing sitting room
with hundreds of books and a games corner is reserved for
non-smokers. The lounge and bar at the entrance feature a log
fire, and the attractive dining room has a flagstone floor and a
wood-burning stove. Sylvia Knott's commendable cooking
makes innovative use of home-grown vegetables and good
quality local produce.
4 en suite (bth/shr) No smoking in bedrooms No smoking in
dining room No smoking in 1 lounge CTV in 2 bedrooms
Tea and coffee making facilities No dogs (ex guide dogs)
Licensed Cen ht CTV No children 10yrs 25P No coaches
Last d 7.30pm
PRICE GUIDE
ROOMS: s £28-£35; d £40-£45✱
CARDS: 🔳 🔳

Selected

♥ Ⓠ Ⓠ Ⓠ Ⓠ Mrs J Longley *Neuadd (SO091618)*
LD1 5SW (A44 from Kington/Rhayader to Penybont and
take 1st left after Severn Arms, then 1st right and straight
on along 'no through road') ☎01597 822571
Feb-Nov
Splendidly isolated in beautiful countryside near the site of an
ancient castle, this farmhouse dating from the early 17th
century is set in 90 acres of sheep farming country. The house
features exposed beams, and there are inglenook fireplaces in
the sitting room and dining room. The three bedrooms are
attractively decorated with pretty fabrics and furnishings.
3 en suite (bth/shr) (3 fmly) No smoking in bedrooms Tea
and coffee making facilities No dogs (ex guide dogs) Cen ht
CTV No children 12yrs P Fishing 92 acres sheep Last d
noon

PONTYPOOL Gwent Map **03** SO20

♥ Ⓠ Ⓠ Mrs M Price *Ty-Cooke (SO310205)* Mamhilad
NP4 8QZ (turn off A4042 to Mamhilad at the Du Pont factory
and follow road for 2m, first farm on left past Horseshoe Inn)
☎01873 880382
This large house dates back to the early 18th century. It is situated
on a beef and sheep farm, located in a peaceful and picturesque
area, north of the village of Mamhilad, which is north of
Pontypool, via the A4042. It provides soundly maintained,
traditionally furnished accommodation, which includes a family
bedded room. There is a comfortable lounge and a pleasant
breakfast room, with antique furniture, where all guests share one
table.
3 rms (1 fmly) No smoking Tea and coffee making facilities No
dogs (ex guide dogs) CTV P 135 acres beef sheep
PRICE GUIDE
ROOMS: s £18; d £32; wkly b&b fr £112✱

PORTHCAWL Mid Glamorgan Map **03** SS87

[♨ ▼] GH Ⓠ Ⓠ Ⓠ **Heritage** 24 Mary St CF36 3YA
☎01656 771881
Closed 2 wks Jan
Positioned close to the promenade, this friendly little hotel offers
well equipped bedrooms and homely public rooms. The man
strength of the hotel is the cooking of owner James Miller with his
imaginative and well produced menus, making use of quality fresh
ingredients and dishes presented with some flair.
8 rms (6 shr) No smoking in area of dining room CTV in all
bedrooms Tea and coffee making facilities No dogs Licensed
Cen ht No parking Last d 9.30pm
PRICE GUIDE
ROOMS: s fr £16; d fr £30; wkly b&b fr £112; wkly hlf-bd fr
£152
CARDS: ▦ ▦ (£)

GH Ⓠ Ⓠ *Minerva Hotel* 52 Esplanade Av CF36 3YU (turn
right from esplanade at Grand Pavillion) ☎01656 782428
Positioned very close to the promenade, this friendly, family run
hotel offers bright, comfortable public rooms and soundly
furnished bedrooms. The atmosphere is friendly, with the resident
proprietors taking care to create a friendly and welcoming
atmosphere.
9 rms (2 bth 2 shr) (4 fmly) No smoking in dining room CTV in
all bedrooms Tea and coffee making facilities No dogs (ex guide
dogs) Licensed Cen ht CTV No coaches Last d 6.30pm

PORTHMADOG Gwynedd Map **06** SH53

GH Ⓠ **Oakleys** The Harbour LL49 9AS ☎01766 512482
Mar-Oct
This large early 19th-century stone-built house is situated right on
the harbour and within easy walking distance of the local shops.
Bedrooms are rather dated by modern day standards but provide
good value for money; family rooms are available and there is a
bedroom on the ground floor. Guests have the use of a small TV
lounge and there is a large car park.
8 rms (3 fmly) No smoking in dining room Tea and coffee
making facilities No dogs (ex guide dogs) CTV No children 2yrs
12P No coaches Last d 5pm
PRICE GUIDE
ROOMS: s £14-£15; d £26-£30✱

GH Ⓠ Ⓠ *Owen's Hotel* 71 High St LL49 9EU (on A487)
☎01766 512098
A friendly commercial and tourist hotel, conveniently located in
the High Street above the proprietor's café/confectionery
business, provides good-value bed and breakfast accommodation.
Bedrooms in a variety of sizes offer mixed modern appointments
and the expected amenities, while breakfast is served at individual
tables in a ground-floor dining room which forms part of the cafe
during the day.
10 rms (3 bth 4 shr) (3 fmly) No smoking in dining room No
smoking in lounges CTV in all bedrooms Tea and coffee making
facilities Licensed Cen ht CTV 9P
CARDS: ▦ ▦

Selected

♥ Ⓠ Ⓠ Ⓠ Ⓠ Mrs P Williams **Tyddyn Du** *(SH691398)*
Gellilydan, Ffestiniog LL41 4RB (1st farmhouse on left
after junct of A487/A470 near village of Gellilydan)
☎01766 590281 FAX 01766 590281
Closed 24-26 Dec
Dating from the 17th century, this attractive stone-built
farmhouse features oak beams and exposed timbers
throughout. It is set in the heart of the Snowdonia National
Park and is very much a working farm, where guests are
welcome to join in with feeding the ducks or collecting the
eggs. The sitting room has an impressive stone inglenook
fireplace with a wood-burning stove. Bedrooms are modern
and well equipped and include one family suite situated in
converted outbuildings. Good home cooking is offered by
Paula Williams who, together with her family, extends a warm
welcome to visitors.
3 rms (1 shr) 1 annexe en suite (shr) (2 fmly) No smoking
CTV in all bedrooms Tea and coffee making facilities ch fac
P 250 acres sheep
PRICE GUIDE
ROOMS: d £34-£40; wkly b&b £107-£132; wkly hlf-bd
£155-£180 (£)

PRESTATYN Clwyd Map **06** SJ08

GH Ⓠ Ⓠ *Roughsedge House* 26-28 Marine Rd LL19 7HD (on
A548, coast road, opposite fire station & Llys Nant Day Care
Centre) ☎01745 887359 FAX 01745 887359
Value-for-money accommodation is offered at this small guest
house on the eastern side of town. The bedrooms are well
equipped with modern facilities, and public rooms include a cosy
bar, a cottage-style dining room and a comfortable lounge with an
open fire. Four car parking spaces are provided, and street parking
is unrestricted.

10 rms (2 bth 1 shr) (2 fmly) No smoking in 5 bedrooms No smoking in dining room CTV in all bedrooms Tea and coffee making facilities No dogs Licensed Cen ht CTV 3P No coaches Last d 4pm
CARDS: 🔳 ■ ▤ 🔘

◀ Q Q Q **Sophies** 17 Gronant Rd LL19 9DT (leave A548 at Drivers Garage into Nant Dr continue along this road for half a mile) ☎01745 852442
Closed 24 Dec-1 Jan
This fully licensed town-centre restaurant and guest house, just off the Gronant road, has a large car park and a pretty rear garden overlooked by the restaurant. Each of its four bedrooms is equipped with a modern en suite shower as well as such facilities as TV and a hairdryer. The locally popular restaurant serves a wide variety of food, and guests can relax in either an attractive cottage-style bar or the lounge with its wood-burning stove.
5 en suite (shr) (1 fmly) No smoking in bedrooms No smoking in dining room No smoking in 1 lounge CTV in all bedrooms Tea and coffee making facilities Cen ht 24P No coaches Last d 9pm
PRICE GUIDE
ROOMS: s fr £24; d fr £36; wkly b&b fr £140
MEALS: Lunch £7-£10&alc Dinner £8.50-£13&alc
CARDS: 🔳 ▤

REDWICK Gwent Map 03 ST48

Selected

GH Q Q Q Q **Brickhouse** NP6 3DX
☎01633 880230 FAX 01633 880230
Improvements continue at this large and delightful Georgian-style guest house - still part of a working farm, but run quite separately - quietly tucked away on the edge of the village yet only three miles from junction 23 of the M4. Characterised by high standards and genuine, caring hospitality, it offers traditionally furnished bedrooms which are nevertheless equipped with every modern amenity, the majority also having excellent en suite facilities, beds and linen. Public areas include a richly furnished but homely lounge and the dining room where hearty breakfasts and home-cooked evening meals are served.
7 rms (5 bth/shr) (1 fmly) No smoking CTV in all bedrooms No dogs Licensed Cen ht CTV 15P Last d 6pm
PRICE GUIDE
ROOMS: s £30; d £40

RHANDIRMWYN Dyfed Map 03 SN74

◀ Q Q **The Royal Oak** SA20 0NY (follow signs to Rhandirmwyn from A40 at Llandovery)
☎01550 760201 FAX 01550 760332
Reached by a picturesque drive through a wooded valley along the A48 north of Llandovey, this secluded inn has pretty, well equipped bedrooms and a warm, welcoming bar.
5 rms (2 bth 1 shr) (1 fmly) CTV in 3 bedrooms Tea and coffee making facilities 20P Pool table Clay pigeon wknds Last d 9.30pm
PRICE GUIDE
ROOMS: s £18-£20.50; d £40-£50✱
MEALS: Lunch £5-£10alc Dinner £5-£10alc✱
CARDS: 🔳 ▤

THE OAKLEYS GUEST HOUSE
The Harbour, Porthmadog.
Telephone Porthmadog (01766) 512482

Proprietors: Mr & Mrs A. H. Biddle
H&C in bedrooms, electric shaver points. Spacious free car park. No undue restrictions. Informal atmosphere. Personal attention. Comfortable lounge. Interior sprung beds. Tea and snacks obtainable during the day. Excellent facilities for salmon and trout fishing. Also some excellent sea fishing. Comparatively close to an excellent golf course.

TYDDYN DU FARM
Gellilydan, Ffestiniog, Gwynedd LL41 4RB
AA QQQQ
Tel & Fax: 01766 590 281 (Mrs Williams)
Wales Tourist Board ♥♥♥ Highly Commended

*Enchanting old world farmhouse, set amidst spectacular scenery in the **heart of the Snowdonia National Park**, with a friendly, relaxed atmosphere. One superb private ground floor cottage suite. Delicious candle-light dinners with excellent farmhouse cuisine. Working sheep farm – feed the ducks on our mill pond, bottle feed pet lambs and fuss over Polly the pony. Excellent central base. Stamp please for brochure. Weekly Dinner, B&B from £160-£190. B&B from £16-£20*

RHAYADER Powys Map **06** SN96

🔲 🅀 *Lamb & Flag Inn* North St LD6 5BU ☎01597 810819
This old inn is at the heart of the busy market town. The bar, with
exposed timers and an inglenook fireplace, is full of character and
there is a separate restaurant where meals are served. Four
bedrooms are available in the main building and there are two
more in a nearby annexe. One of these is a two-bedroomed family
suite.
4 en suite (shr) 3 annexe en suite (bth/shr) (3 fmly) CTV in 2
bedrooms Tea and coffee making facilities No dogs (ex guide
dogs) Cen ht Last d 9.30pm

RHOSCOLYN See ANGLESEY, ISLE OF

RHOS-ON-SEA Clwyd

See **Colwyn Bay**

RHYL Clwyd Map **06** SJ08

GH 🅀🅀🅀 **Pier Hotel** 23 East Pde LL18 3AL (on promenade
between Sea Life and bowling greens) ☎01745 350280
Closed 22-31 Dec
Robert and Gill Herndlhofer are the friendly owners of this hotel,
which is conveniently located on the promenade near the Sun
Centre. It provides comfortable bedrooms, including one family
suite, all with en suite or private facilities. There is a spacious
residents' lounge as well as a cosy bar. Public parking is available
nearby, though there are a few parking spaces at the rear.
8 rms (3 bth 4 shr) (3 fmly) CTV in all bedrooms Tea and coffee
making facilities Licensed Cen ht CTV 2P No coaches Last d
3pm
PRICE GUIDE
ROOMS: s £14-£16; d £32-£36; wkly b&b £95-£110; wkly hlf-
bd £125-£150✱
CARDS: 🔳 🖃 ⓔ

ROWEN Gwynedd Map **06** SH77

Selected

GH 🅀🅀🅀🅀 **Gwern Borter Country Manor** Barkers Ln
LL32 8YL (from Conwy take B5106 for 2.25m, turn right
onto unclass road towards Rowen for 0.5m then turn right
Gwern Borter approx further 0.5m on left)
☎01492 650360
Closed 23 Dec-2 Jan
A 19th-century manor house and former mink farm, Gwern
Borter is situated in ten acres of landscaped grounds with
farmyard birds, pets and a duck pond. Notable features are the
oak panelled entrance hall and staircase, and the oak fireplace
in the dining room. Bedrooms all have en suite or private
facilities and the beds are attractively canopied. A self-
catering apartment is available in the courtyard.
3 en suite (bth/shr) (1 fmly) No smoking in dining room
CTV in all bedrooms Tea and coffee making facilities
Licensed Cen ht CTV ch fac 14P No coaches Riding
Cycle hire Last d 4pm
PRICE GUIDE
ROOMS: d £36-£48; wkly b&b £120-£160; wkly hlf-bd
£175-£199✱
CARDS: 🔳 🖃 ⓔ

RUTHIN Clwyd Map **06** SJ15

Premier Selected

GH 🅀🅀🅀🅀🅀 **Eyarth
Station** Llanfair Dyffryn
Clwyd LL15 2EE (A525 1m
S) ☎01824 703643
FAX 01824 707464
Until the Beeching axe this
little hotel was a country
railway station. It is set in the
Vale of Clwyd and offers
magnificent views of the
area. An elegant lounge
stands where the railway line
once ran and this is warmed by a cheery wood-burning stove.
Bedrooms, including two in the old station master's house, are
individually styled and most have pretty canopied beds. There
is an attractive garden with a swimming pool for the better
weather.
4 en suite (shr) 2 annexe en suite (shr) (2 fmly) No smoking
in bedrooms No smoking in dining room No smoking in 1
lounge CTV in 1 bedroom Tea and coffee making facilities
Licensed Cen ht CTV 6P No coaches Outdoor swimming
pool (heated) Golf 9 Last d 7pm
PRICE GUIDE
ROOMS: s £27-£30; d £40-£44; wkly b&b £278; wkly hlf-
bd £369✱
CARDS: 🔳 🖃

ST ASAPH Clwyd Map **06** SJ07

Selected

♥ 🅀🅀🅀🅀 Mrs A Roberts **Bach-Y-Graig** *(SJ075713)*
Tremeirchion LL17 0UH (from A55 take A525 to Trefant
and at traffic lights turn right A541 to x-rds with white
railings where turn left) ☎01745 730627
Closed Xmas & New Year
The first brick house to be built in Wales, a carefully
modernised 16th-century farmhouse retaining much of its
original charm provides both a genuine Welsh welcome and
honest home-cooked meals based on fresh produce. Bedrooms
furnished with some fine antique pieces also offer TV sets and
tea-making equipment, while the traditional sitting room with
its impressive inglenook fireplace is supplemented by an
additional lounge for guests' use. The River Clwyd runs
through farmland which also includes 40-acre woods where a
trail has been opened for interested visitors.
3 en suite (bth/shr) (1 fmly) No smoking CTV in all
bedrooms Tea and coffee making facilities No dogs Cen ht
CTV 3P Fishing Woodland trail Games room 200 acres
dairy
PRICE GUIDE
ROOMS: s £24; d £40; wkly b&b £140
 ⓔ

ST DAVID'S Dyfed Map **02** SM72

Selected

GH ⓠⓠⓠⓠ **The Ramsey** Lower Moor SA62 6RP (from A487 bear left in front of Midland bank signposted Porthclais, establishment 0.5m on left)
☎01437 720321 & 720332
Set in pleasant gardens on the outskirts of the own, this friendly guest house within easy walking distance of the Cathedral and shops provides well kept modern bedrooms. Open-plan public areas include a comfortable lounge, dining room and small bar. No smoking is allowed.
7 rms (6 bth/shr) No smoking Tea and coffee making facilities Licensed Cen ht CTV No children 12yrs 9P No coaches Last d 7pm
PRICE GUIDE
ROOMS: (incl. dinner) d £67-£76; wkly hlf-bd £201-£228

☯ ♥ **GH** ⓠⓠⓠ **Y Glennydd** 51 Nun St SA62 6NU
☎01437 720576 FAX 01437 720576
Closed Jan
This very well maintained terraced property dates back to the 1880's and is situated within a few minutes walk of both the city centre and cathedral. The bedrooms vary in size and style, some having period furniture, whilst others are more modern. Many have en suite facilities. Family-bedded rooms and a ground floor room are available. There are a small bar, a cosy lounge and a cottage style restaurant, which is open to non residents during the summer.
10 rms (7 bth/shr) (4 fmly) No smoking in dining room CTV in all bedrooms Tea and coffee making facilities No dogs (ex guide dogs) Licensed Cen ht CTV No parking Last d 9pm
PRICE GUIDE
ROOMS: s £15-£25; d £30-£38
CARDS: ◼ ▆

SAUNDERSFOOT Dyfed Map **02** SN10

GH ⓠⓠⓠ **Jalna Hotel** Stammers Rd SA69 9HH (A478 Kilgetty/Tenby road, first left before rdbt B4316, hotel on left at bottom of hill) ☎01834 812282 FAX 01834 812282
Closed 24 Dec-2 Jan
Located within easy reach of the local amenities, the seafront and the harbour, this privately-owned hotel provides private car parking to the rear. Soundly maintained, well equipped bedrooms include family, ground-floor and non-smoking rooms; a lounge bar, a cosy lounge, a spacious dining room and a solarium are also available.
13 en suite (bth/shr) (8 fmly) No smoking in 7 bedrooms No smoking in dining room No smoking in 1 lounge CTV in all bedrooms Tea and coffee making facilities Licensed Cen ht CTV 14P Solarium Last d 5pm
PRICE GUIDE
ROOMS: s £20-£27; d £40-£50; wkly b&b £139-£150; wkly hlf-bd £160-£195✶
CARDS: ◼ ▆ ▆ ▆

GH ⓠⓠⓠ **The Sandy Hill** Sandy Hill Road/Tenby Rd SA69 9DR ☎01834 813165
Mar-Oct
Parts of this former farmhouse date back to the late 18th century. It stands on the A478, north of Tenby, at its junction with Sandyhill Road, which leads to Saundersfoot. It provides soundly maintained, modern accommodation, which includes family

rooms and a bedroom on ground floor level. Separate tables are provided in the pleasant dining room. There is an attractive and comfortable lounge and a small bar. Other facilities include a large garden, with a swimming pool, and a secure car park.
5 rms (3 bth/shr) (3 fmly) No smoking in dining room CTV in all bedrooms Tea and coffee making facilities Licensed Cen ht No children 3yrs 7P No coaches Outdoor swimming pool
PRICE GUIDE
ROOMS: s £14-£17; d £28-£34; wkly b&b £98-£119; wkly hlf-bd £154-£175✶

GH ⓠⓠⓠ **Vine Farm** The Ridgeway SA69 9LA
☎01834 813543
Apr-Oct
This 200 year old former farmhouse is situated on the outskirts of Saundersfoot. It is set in pleasant and spacious lawned gardens and has its own car park at the rear. The accommodation, which includes a room on the ground floor, which is suitable for disabled guests, has a mix of traditional and modern furnishings. All bedrooms have modern equipment. There is a traditionally furnished dining room, where separate tables are provided, and a comfortable lounge, where a solid fuel stove burns when the weather is cold.
5 en suite (bth/shr) (1 fmly) CTV in all bedrooms Tea and coffee making facilities Licensed Cen ht 10P No coaches Last d 6pm
PRICE GUIDE
ROOMS: s £20-£21.50; d £40-£43; wkly b&b £140-£150.50; wkly hlf-bd £180-£195✶

SENNYBRIDGE Powys Map **03** SN92

Selected

♥ ⓠⓠⓠⓠ Mrs M C Adams **Brynfedwen** (*SN963297*) Trallong Common LD3 8HW (from A40 follow signs Trallong over River Usk to top of hill) ☎01874 636505
With superb views across the Usk Valley and the Brecon Beacons, and set in 150 acres, this establishment is very much a working farm, and during the spring guests are welcome to help bottle feed the numerous lambs. There are two en suite bedrooms in the main house, furnished in pine with pretty duvet covers. The separate annexe flat, ideal for disabled guests, can also be used for self catering and includes a small, private sitting room overlooking the lawn. There is a modern lounge with an open fire, and proprietor Mary Adams offers genuine, warm hospitality as well as good home cooking. Brynfedwen Farm stands high above the A40 in the village of Trallong, which is signposted off the A40 just two miles east of Sennybridge.
3 en suite (bth/shr) 1 annexe en suite (shr) (2 fmly) No smoking CTV in 1 bedroom Tea and coffee making facilities No dogs (ex guide dogs) Cen ht CTV 3P 150 acres mixed Last d 6.30pm
PRICE GUIDE
ROOMS: s fr £17; d fr £34; wkly b&b fr £119; wkly hlf-bd fr £182

Our inspectors never book in the name of the AA. They disclose their identity only after the bill has been paid.

SOLVA Dyfed Map **02** SM82

Selected

♥ Q Q Q Q Mrs M Jones *Lochmeyler (SM855275)*
SA62 6LL (4m N on unclass rd) ☎01348 837724
A 16th-century farmhouse is set in 220 acres of a busy dairy
farm. Six miles from St Davids, near the little hamlet of
Llandeloy, it provides farm trails, duck ponds and an
abundance of wildlife. Bedrooms are large, comfortably
furnished and contain every modern facility including videos
and free films. Two relaxing lounges are available, and good
home cooking is provided by the very hospitable Mrs Jones.
10 en suite (bth/shr) (9 fmly) No smoking in bedrooms No
smoking in dining room No coaches Cen ht CTV No children
bedrooms Tea and coffee making facilities Direct dial from
bedrooms Licensed Cen ht CTV No children 10yrs P 220
acres dairy Last d 6pm
CARDS: 🔲 🔲

STEPASIDE Dyfed Map **02** SN10

🈂️🆖 **GH** Q Q **Bay View Hotel** Pleasant Valley SA67 8LR
(off A477 through village and left by flats then left again
down valley for .5m for hotel behind chapel)
☎01834 813417
Apr-Sep
This fairly modern property is peacefully located in a picturesque
valley, between Stepaside and Wisemans Bridge. Set in its own
extensive gardens, which contain a swimming pool and a putting
green, the house is situated behind the Wesleyan Chapel at
Pleasant Valley. It provides mainly compact, but soundly
maintained accommodation, which includes family bedded rooms
and rooms on ground floor level. Separate tables are provided in
the dining room. Other facilities include a lounge bar and a small
TV lounge.
11 rms (8 shr) (5 fmly) Tea and coffee making facilities No dogs
(ex guide dogs) Licensed Cen ht CTV 14P Outdoor swimming
pool (heated) Last d 5pm
PRICE GUIDE
ROOMS: s £14.50-£18.50; d £29-£37; wkly b&b £101.50-
£129.50; wkly hlf-bd £130-£160

SWANSEA West Glamorgan Map **03** SS69

See also Bishopston, Langland Bay and Mumbles

GH Q Q Q **Alexander Hotel** 3 Sketty Road, Uplands, Sketty
SA2 0EU (on A4118, 1m from city centre on road to Gower
Peninsula) ☎01792 470045 & 476012 FAX 01792 476012
Closed Xmas
This small family run hotel is situated in the popular area known
as the Uplands. There is a range of shops close by and a good
choice of places to eat. Accommodation is comfortable, and some
of the rooms enjoy views to Swansea Bay. A licensed bar, a cosy
lounge and a games room are available and home cooked meals
are served.
7 rms (6 bth/shr) (4 fmly) No smoking in dining room CTV in
all bedrooms Tea and coffee making facilities Direct dial from
bedrooms No dogs (ex guide dogs) Licensed Cen ht CTV No
children 2yrs No parking No coaches Pool table Weights
Exercise bike
PRICE GUIDE
ROOMS: s £30-£32; d £42-£45; wkly b&b £120-£130; wkly hlf-
bd £180-£200*
CARDS: 🔲 🔲 🔲 🔲 🔲   ⓔ

Selected

GH Q Q Q Q **Cefn Bryn** 6 Uplands Crescent SA2 0PB
(on A4118, 1m from Swansea Railway Station)
☎01792 466687
Closed Xmas & New Year
Cefyn Bryn is an attractive late Victorian town house built, it
is believed, by a Master Mariner. Located near the Uplands
shopping area and only a short drive from the city centre, its
makes the ideal base from which to tour the area. The
bedrooms are all very comfortable, well equipped and
immaculate. An attractive dining room has interesting
collections of pictures and china for guests to enjoy.
6 en suite (shr) (2 fmly) No smoking in dining room CTV in
all bedrooms Tea and coffee making facilities No dogs CTV
No parking
PRICE GUIDE
ROOMS: s fr £21; d fr £40; wkly b&b fr £110*

GH Q Q Q **Crescent** 132 Eaton Crescent,Uplands SA1 4QR
(1st left off A4118 after St James Church) ☎01792 466814
Closed 24 Dec-1 Jan
Enjoying a quiet location in a pleasant residential crescent just a
mile from the city centre, this neat guest house offers warm
hospitality and comfortable well equipped rooms. Some of the
bedrooms have wonderful views over Swansea Bay and the roof
tops of this popular seaside town. The dining room is most
attractive with beams and pretty tables with flowers. Parking for
five cars is available.
6 en suite (bth/shr) (1 fmly) No smoking in 2 bedrooms CTV in
all bedrooms Tea and coffee making facilities Cen ht CTV P
No coaches
PRICE GUIDE
ROOMS: s £23-£25; d £38-£40; wkly b&b £133-£168*   ⓔ

GH Q Q Q *The Guest House* 2/4 Bryn Rd SA2 0AR
☎01792 466947
This family run guest house offers value for money
accommodation in immaculate rooms. All are well equipped and
comfortable and the the deluxe style bedrooms have four poster
beds and pretty furnishings. The simpler rooms are well organised
and functional. Two cosy television lounges available for those
who wish to relax and the guest house is conveniently positioned
for the city centre, the beach and the rugby/cricket ground.
14 rms (6 shr) (2 fmly) No smoking in bedrooms No smoking in
dining room No smoking in 1 lounge CTV in 8 bedrooms Tea
and coffee making facilities Licensed Cen ht CTV No children
9yrs No parking No coaches Last d 1pm
CARDS: 🔲 🔲 🔲

Selected

GH Q Q Q Q *Tredilion House Hotel* 26 Uplands
Crescent, Uplands SA2 0PB (on A4118)
☎01792 470766 FAX 01792 456044
rs Xmas
This attractive town house is set back from the road in a
pleasant area close to the city centre with a pretty garden to
the front. The guest lounge, dining room and reception hall
are spacious and have been carefully decorated and furnished
to retain the character and charm of the Victorian era. The
bedrooms are beautifully furnished and offer warmth and
comfort. This is an ideal base from which to enjoy the interest
of the area.

7 en suite (bth/shr) (1 fmly) No smoking in dining room CTV in all bedrooms Tea and coffee making facilities Direct dial from bedrooms Licensed Cen ht CTV 9P No coaches Last d noon
CARDS: 🅴 💳 📧 💷

TALGARTH Powys Map **03** SO13

♥ ◖Q◗◖Q◗◖Q◗ Mrs B Prosser **Upper Genffordd** *(SO171304)* LD3 0EN ☎01874 711360
This charming little single storey cottage was cleverly converted from a stone built barn, some 15 years ago. It is situated just off the A479, in a picturesque area in the heart of the Black Mountains, some three miles south of Talgarth. The two bedrooms, which include a family room, are compact, but are both attractively decorated and furnished. There is a small dining room, where all share one table, and a comfortable and homely lounge.
2 en suite (bth/shr) (1 fmly) No smoking in bedrooms No smoking in lounges CTV in all bedrooms Tea and coffee making facilities Cen ht CTV 4P 200 acres Dairy Mixed Sheep
PRICE GUIDE
ROOMS: s £15-£16; d £30-£32; wkly b&b fr £112✱

◀ ◖Q◗◖Q◗◖Q◗ **Castle Inn** Pengenffordd LD3 0EP (4m S, alongside A479) ☎01874 711353
This pleasant inn is situated in the heart of the Black Mountains, on the A479, at Pengenffordd, some three miles south of Talgarth. It provides attractive, modern furnished and equipped accommodation, which includes a family bedded room and rooms with en suite facilities. There are two pleasant bar areas, one of which is equipped with a darts board and pool table. Separate tables are provided for bar meals and at breakfast.
5 rms (2 bth/shr) (1 fmly) No smoking in bedrooms CTV in all bedrooms Tea and coffee making facilities No dogs (ex guide dogs) Cen ht 50P Last d 9.30pm
PRICE GUIDE
ROOMS: s £18; d £36-£42; wkly b&b £110-£125; wkly hlf-bd £160
MEALS: Lunch £8-£15alc Dinner £8-£15alc
CARDS: 📧

TAL-Y-LLYN Gwynedd Map **06** SH70

Selected

GH ◖Q◗◖Q◗◖Q◗◖Q◗ *Dolffanog Fawr* LL36 9AJ ☎01654 761247
In the short time that they have been in residence, Pam and Alan Coulter have lovingly restored this delightful 17th-century farmhouse set at the foot of Cader Idris and one end of Tal-y-Llyn Lake. The bedrooms are mostly pine-furnished and decorated with pretty papers and rich fabrics; all have modern en suite facilities and TVs and hairdryers are provided. Both the sitting room and the dining room have impressive stone inglenook fireplaces, and the sitting room opens on to the rear gardens which have - like many of the bedrooms - superb views over the lake.
4 rms (3 bth/shr) CTV in all bedrooms Tea and coffee making facilities No dogs (ex guide dogs) Cen ht CTV No children 10yrs 6P No coaches Last d 5pm

TENBY Dyfed Map **02** SN10

GH ◖Q◗◖Q◗◖Q◗ **Buckingham** Esplanade SA70 7DU ☎01834 842622
Apr-Oct
8 en suite (bth/shr) (1 fmly) No smoking in 4 bedrooms No smoking in dining room CTV in all bedrooms Tea and coffee making facilities Licensed Cen ht No children 5yrs No parking Last d 5pm
PRICE GUIDE
ROOMS: s £22-£23; d £35-£39; wkly b&b £109-£123; wkly hlf-bd £168-£185✱
CARDS: 🅴 📧 (£)

GH ◖Q◗◖Q◗ **Castle View Private Hotel** The Norton SA70 8AA (follow sign for Coach Park to Seafront for hotel on right) ☎01834 842666
This small privately owned hotel is situated close to both the town centre and the North Beach It overlooks views of the harbour and the castle. The bedrooms are not luxurious, but are quite soundly maintained. Family bedded rooms and rooms with a sea view are both available. The spacious lounge also enjoys views of the sea and harbour. Separate tables are provided in the traditionally furnished dining room. The hotel also has its own private car park, which is quite an asset in Tenby.
12 rms (7 bth 3 shr) (4 fmly) No smoking in dining room CTV in all bedrooms Tea and coffee making facilities Licensed CTV 7P Last d 6.30pm
PRICE GUIDE
ROOMS: s £16-£21; d £32-£42; wkly b&b £112-£147; wkly hlf-bd £161-£196✱
CARDS: 📧 (£)

GH ◖Q◗◖Q◗◖Q◗ **Clarence House Hotel** Esplanade SA70 7DU (follow South Parade by old town walls to Esplanade and turn right) ☎01834 844371 FAX 01834 844372
Apr-Sep
This large, privately owned hotel, which has been in the same family for over 50 years, stands on The Esplanade, from where it overlooks the South Beach and Caldey Island. It provides well equipped modern accommodation, which includes rooms with a sea view. Public areas include a choice of lounges, a lounge bar which opens onto a pleasant walled garden and terrace, and a large bright dining room. Entertainment is usually provided on at least one night per week. A full cooked breakfast is available at extra charge.
68 en suite (bth/shr) No smoking in 30 bedrooms No smoking in dining room No smoking in 1 lounge CTV in all bedrooms Tea and coffee making facilities Licensed Lift Cen ht CTV No children 3yrs No parking In house entertainment Last d 7.30pm
PRICE GUIDE
ROOMS: s £10-£29; d £14-£64; wkly b&b £91-£266; wkly hlf-bd £147-£322
CARDS: 🅴 📧 💷 💳 (£)
See advertisement on p.605.

GH ◖Q◗◖Q◗ *Gumfreston Private Hotel* Culver Park SA70 7ED ☎01834 842871
Closed Nov
Just a short stroll from the south beach you will find this cosy guesthouse, run by the friendly owners, Bill and Dot Tovey. The individually decorated bedrooms have recently been updated with clever use of bed canopies, satin bed covers and matching fabrics. A comfortable residents' lounge and cosy basement bar provide adequate facilities.
11 en suite (bth/shr) (5 fmly) Tea and coffee making facilities No dogs Licensed Cen ht CTV No parking No coaches Last d 4pm
CARDS: 📧

GH Ⓠ Ⓠ Ⓠ *Hildebrand Hotel* Victoria St SA70 7DY
☎01834 842403
Apr-Oct rs Jan-Mar & Nov
Veronica and Jim Martin have run this small hotel for two decades and make every effort to ensure their guests feel at home. It is situated a short walk from the walled town and just 200yds from the golden South Beach. There is an excellent first-floor lounge, a cosy basement bar and the hotel features award-winning floral displays, which are on show in season.
7 en suite (bth/shr) (4 fmly) No smoking in 4 bedrooms No smoking in dining room CTV in all bedrooms Tea and coffee making facilities Licensed Cen ht CTV No children 3yrs No coaches Last d 4pm
CARDS: 💳 💳 💳 💳

GH Ⓠ Ⓠ Ⓠ *Ripley St Marys Hotel* Saint Mary's St SA70 7HN (take 1st left on entering town signed Harbour/North Beach and turn right at St Marys Church then 2nd left)
☎01834 842837
Apr-Sep rs Feb-Mar & Oct-Nov
This delightful little property dates back to the early 19th century and is situated within the ancient town walls, in a quiet street which is ablaze with colour during the summer, from the numerous floral displays. The town centre, harbour and beach are all within a few minutes walk. Proprietors Alan & Kath Mace have been welcoming guests to their home for over 20 years and they are justifiably proud of their reputation for warm hospitality. The accommodation, which includes family bedded rooms, is soundly maintained and has modern equipment. There is a homely lounge, a small bar and a small dining room, where separate tables are provided. A recent acquisition, which is a great asset in this town, is a secure undercover car park.
14 rms (8 bth/shr) (6 fmly) No smoking in bedrooms No smoking in dining room CTV in all bedrooms Tea and coffee making facilities Licensed Cen ht CTV 9P Last d 5.30pm
PRICE GUIDE
ROOMS: s £17.50-£20; d £34-£40; wkly b&b £114-£130; wkly hlf-bd £170-£190
CARDS: 💳 💳 £

GH Ⓠ Ⓠ *Sea Breezes Hotel* 18 The Norton SA70 8AA
☎01834 842753
Mar-Nov
This small personally run hotel is situated close to the North Beach and is within easy reach of both the town centre and harbour. It provides modern furnished and equipped bedrooms, some of which are compact. There is a small comfortable lounge and separate tables are provided in the traditionally furnished dining room
11 rms (6 bth/shr) (3 fmly) CTV in all bedrooms Tea and coffee making facilities No dogs Licensed Cen ht CTV No children 3yrs No parking

|➧|🔆| **GH** Ⓠ Ⓠ Ⓠ *Tall Ships Hotel* 34 Victoria St SA70 7DY (follow signs Town Centre & South Beach and at Town Hall follow wall to Seafront and turn right into the Esplanade)
☎01834 842055
Mar-Oct
This small and friendly guest house is situated just off The Esplanade, a short distance from the South Beach. It provides well maintained modern furnished and equipped accommodation. Facilities include a quaint bar, with nautical theme bric-a-brac, an attractive lounge and a pleasant dining room, where separate tables are provided.

8 rms (5 shr) (6 fmly) No smoking in dining room CTV in all bedrooms Tea and coffee making facilities No dogs (ex guide dogs) Licensed CTV No parking Last d 5pm
PRICE GUIDE
ROOMS: s £16-£21.50; d £28-£39; wkly b&b £92.50-£130; wkly hlf-bd £135-£175.50
CARDS: 💳 💳 £

THREE COCKS Powys Map 03 SO13

GH Ⓠ Ⓠ Ⓠ *Old Gwernyfed Country Manor* Felindre LD3 0SU
☎01497 4376
mid Mar-mid Nov
This Elizabethan manor house lies in several acres of parkland, and has many notable features including a minstrels' gallery, an oak-panelled banqueting hall, a mast from the Spanish Armada, a secret code carved by Shakespeare and a priest's hole. The accommodation is comfortable, with most of the bedrooms en suite, and there is a good range of home-cooked meals.
11 rms (7 bth 2 shr) (4 fmly) Licensed 15P No coaches Croquet Last d 7.30pm

TINTERN Gwent Map 03 SO50

GH Ⓠ Ⓠ Ⓠ *Valley House* Raglan Rd NP6 6TH (take A466 from Chepstow and turn left at Raglan Road, passing Cherry Tree Inn after 800 yds and Valley House after another 200 yds) ☎01291 689652 FAX 01291 689805
In a lovely position in a wooded valley just above Tintern on the Raglan road, Peter and Ann Howe's stylish, tall, Georgian house offers bright, comfortable bedrooms furnished with antiques, stripped pine and coordinating fabrics. The bedrooms are well equipped and have good en suite facilities.
3 en suite (bth/shr) No smoking CTV in all bedrooms Tea and coffee making facilities Direct dial from bedrooms Cen ht 7P No coaches Last d by arrangement
PRICE GUIDE
ROOMS: s £25-£30; d £35-£38✳
CARDS: 💳 £

|➧|🔆| ◀|Ⓠ| **Fountain** Trellech Grange NP6 6QW (off A466 at Royal George Hotel and in 1m bear right over bridge round pond and right again up hill for 0.5m) ☎01291 689303
In an attractive wooded valley just outside Tintern, on the old Raglan road, this rustic inn offers modest but clean accommodation. The bars are popular with both locals and tourists and there is also a restaurant where good value food is served.
5 rms (1 fmly) (2 fmly) CTV in 4 bedrooms Tea and coffee making facilities Cen ht 40P Last d 10.30pm
PRICE GUIDE
ROOMS: s £15-£18; d £30-£36; wkly b&b £95-£100; wkly hlf-bd £150
CARDS: 💳 💳 💳 £

TREARDDUR BAY See ANGLESEY, ISLE OF

TREGARON Dyfed Map 03 SN65

🔆 Ⓠ Ⓠ Ⓠ Mrs Jacqueline Davies *Neuadd Las Country Guest House (SN663620)* SY25 6LJ (from Tregaron take A485 north towards Aberystwyth, Neuaddlas is in approx 1m on left just over bridge) ☎01974 298905
A dormer bungalow set in a 25-acre holding one mile north of Tregaron, enjoys views of the Cors Caron Nature Reserve and the Cambrian mountains. Bedrooms, including family and ground-floor rooms, vary in style from the traditional to the modern, while public areas include a comfortable lounge with a log fire and a traditionally furnished dining room.
6 rms (3 bth) (2 fmly) No smoking in bedrooms No smoking in dining room No smoking in 1 lounge Tea and coffee making

facilities No dogs (ex guide dogs) Cen ht CTV 10P Fishing 25 acres mixed Last d 9pm
PRICE GUIDE
ROOMS: s £16.50-£19.50; d £33-£39; wkly b&b £110-£130; wkly hlf-bd £169.50-£189.50✷

WELSHPOOL Powys Map **07** SJ20

Selected

✿ ⓆⓆⓆⓆ Mrs E Jones **Gungrog House** *(SJ235089)*
Rhallt SY21 9HS (1m NE off A458)
☎01938 553381 FAX 01938 554612
Apr-Oct
From its elevated position this well-maintained 16th-century house enjoys magnificent views of the Severn Valley and Powis Castle. Quietly located on a 21-acre beef-rearing farm, Gungrog House offers two attractively decorated bedrooms furnished with period pieces, and complete with en suite facilities. Guests are seated around a communal table in the dining room, although separate tables can be provided if preferred. There is also a comfortable lounge.
3 rms (2 shr) No smoking Tea and coffee making facilities No dogs Cen ht CTV 6P 21 acres mixed Last d 5pm
PRICE GUIDE
ROOMS: s £21; d £39; wkly b&b fr £120

✿ ⓆⓆⓆ Mr & Mrs M C Payne **Heath Cottage** *(SJ239023)*
Kingswood, Forden SY21 8LX (next to Forden P.O. on the A490 Welshpool/Churchstoke road) ☎01938 580453
Etr-Oct
This charming old house set on a smallholding dates back to the early 18th century and is located in the village of Forden, just south of Welshpool. Bedrooms are traditionally furnished in the style of the house, and there is a cosy lounge with exposed ceiling beams and a log fire in the inglenook fireplace. Guests share a single table in the attractive dining room.
3 en suite (bth/shr) (1 fmly) No smoking Tea and coffee making facilities No dogs Cen ht CTV 4P 6 acres poultry sheep
PRICE GUIDE
ROOMS: s £17; d £34; wkly b&b £102; wkly hlf-bd £172

Selected

✿ ⓆⓆⓆⓆ Mr & Mrs G Jones **Lower Trelydan**
(SJ225105) Lower Trelydan, Guilsfield SY21 9PH (3.5m N off A490) ☎01938 553105 FAX 01938 553105
This beautifully preserved 16th-century farm is steeped in history, and quietly located on a working farm. The house is full of charm and character, enhanced by exposed wall timbers and ceiling beams in the comfortable lounge and pleasant dining room. Bedrooms in the main house have modern equipment and en suite facilities, and all are non-smoking. A recent barn conversion has resulted in two cottages offering family accommodation which can also be rented on a self-catering basis. Both include a spacious lounge and dining room plus fitted kitchen, and one has two bedrooms. Guests share one table in the old butler's pantry, and there is a tiny bar.
3 en suite (bth/shr) (1 fmly) No smoking in bedrooms No smoking in dining room CTV in 2 bedrooms Tea and coffee

---

making facilities No dogs Licensed Cen ht CTV 10P 108 acres beef dairy sheep Last d 5pm
PRICE GUIDE
ROOMS: s £25; d £38; wkly b&b £133; wkly hlf-bd £217✷

Selected

✿ ⓆⓆⓆⓆ Mr & Mrs W Jones **Moat** *(SJ214042)*
SY21 8SE (on A483, 0.5m from junct with A490)
☎01938 553179
Apr-Oct rs Feb, Mar & Nov
This charming old house which is set in lovely gardens dates back in part about 400 years. Set on a dairy farm in the Severn Valley, it offers attractively decorated bedrooms with antique furniture and colour television; there is also a two-room family suite. The cosy lounge is antique-furnished too, and there is a games room with a pool table. Guests share one large table in the impressive beamed dining room.
3 en suite (bth/shr) (1 fmly) No smoking in 2 bedrooms No smoking in dining room No smoking in lounges CTV in all bedrooms Tea and coffee making facilities No dogs Cen ht 3P Tennis (grass) Pool table 260 acres dairy Last d 2pm
PRICE GUIDE
ROOMS: d £36-£38; wkly b&b £119-£126; wkly hlf-bd £189-£206✷

Clarence House Hotel

ESPLANADE, TENBY, PEMBROKESHIRE SA70 7DU
TEL: 01834 844371 & FAX: 01834 844372
South seafront near old walled town. Superb coastal views to Caldy Island. Residents only bar-patio rose garden. Seaview restaurant, excellent cuisine. Auto-safety Otis lift to all floors. All bedrooms WC/Shower, Col. TV, T/C inc. Groups welcome, Free brochure/Tariff. Quiet old world comfort offering modern amenities at reasonable cost.

 ✔ Q Q Q Mrs F Emberton **Tynllwyn** *(SJ215085)*
SY21 9BW (1m N of town on A490) ☎01938 553175
Providing good comfortable bedrooms and a spacious lounge this
large 18th-century farmhouse is situated off the A490 North of
Welshpool with good rural views.
6 rms (3 fmly) CTV in all bedrooms Tea and coffee making
facilities No dogs Licensed Cen ht CTV 20P 150 acres mixed
Last d 6.30pm
PRICE GUIDE
ROOMS: s £15; d £30; wkly b&b £88

(£)

WHITLAND Dyfed Map **02** SN21

✔ Q Q Q C M & I A Lewis *Cilpost (SN191184)* SA34 0RP
☎01994 240280
Apr-Sep
This tastefully modernised house is quietly situated on a 160 acre
farm north of Whitland (take the A40 into the village centre and
then follow the North Road for about one mile). Bedrooms,
including family rooms, vary in size and style but all are soundly
maintained. There is a homely, comfortable lounge and a very
atractive and traditionally furnished dining room providing
separate tables. The house is surrounded by extensive well tended
gardens, a heated swimming pool is contained in a large
conservatory, and a farm bulding has been converted into a full
size snooker room.
7 rms (3 bth 3 shr) (3 fmly) No dogs Licensed Cen ht 12P
Indoor swimming pool (heated) Fishing Snooker 160 acres dairy
mixed

PREMIER SELECTED
ⓠⓠⓠⓠⓠ

A quick-reference of establishments in Ireland in this year's guide with a ⓠⓠⓠⓠⓠ rating for Quality – the AA's highest rating for guest houses, farmhouses and inns.

NORTHERN IRELAND

TYRONE
DUNGANNON Grange Lodge

THE REPUBLIC OF IRELAND

CORK	DUBLIN	GALWAY
FERMOY	DUBLIN	GALWAY
Ballyvolane House	Aberdeen Lodge	Killeen House
KANTURK	Ariel House	
Assolas	Cedar Lodge	
	The Grey Door	

SELECTED
ⓠⓠⓠⓠ

A quick-reference of establishments in Ireland in this year's guide with a ⓠⓠⓠⓠ rating for Quality – each year more establishments in the guide rise to a very high standard which the AA recognises the award of ⓠⓠⓠⓠ's.

NORTHERN IRELAND	**THE REPUBLIC OF IRELAND**	The Old Rectory **Mallow** Springfort Hall	Glenogra Kingswood Merrion Hall
ANTRIM **Bushmills** White Gables **Lisburn** Brook Lodge Farmhouse	***CARLOW*** **Carlow** Barrowville Town House	**Shanagarry** Ballymaloe House **Youghal** Ahernes	Morehampton Lodge Mount Herbert Ltd No 66 Northumberland Lodge Raglan Lodge
LONDONDERRY **Coleraine** Greenhill House	***CORK*** **Killeagh** Ballymakeigh House **Kinsale** The Moorings **Kinsale** The Old Bank House The Old Presbytery	***DONEGAL*** **Carrigans** Mount Royd ***DUBLIN*** **Dublin** Aaron House Charleville	***GALWAY*** **Clifden** Maldua Mallmore House Sunnybank House **Galway** Ardawn House

KERRY
Camp
Barnagh Bridge
Dingle
Bambury's
Doyles Town House
Greenmount House
Milltown House
Sallyport House

KILLARNEY
Killarney
Foleys Town House
Kathleen's
Tahilla
Tahilla Cove

KILDARE
Straffan
Barberstown House

KILKENNY
Kilkenny
Butler House

Shillogher House
Thomastown
Abbey House

LIMERICK
Adare
Adare Lodge
Coatesland House
Foxhollow House

LOUTH
Drogheda
Tullyesker House

MAYO
Achill Island
Gray's Guest House

MEATH
Dunshaughlin
The Old Workhouse

OFFALY
Tullamore

Pine Lodge

TIPPERARY
Bansha
Bansha House

WATERFORD
Annestown
Annestown House
Cappoquin
Richmond House
Cheekpoint
Three Rivers
Dunmore East
Foxmount Farm
Stradbally
Carrigahilla House &
Gardens

WESTMEATH
Moate
Temple

WEXFORD

Ballyhack
Marsh Mere Lodge
Enniscorthy
Ballinkeele House
Ferns
Clone House
Gorey
Glenbower House
Woodlands Farmhouse
Rosslare Harbour
Churchtown House

WEXFORD
Ardruagh
Clonard House
Slaney Manor

WICKLOW
Glendalough
Laragh Trekking Centre
Rathdrum
Whaley Abbey
Wicklow
The Old Rectory

USEFUL INFORMATION

In most instances, the details for establishments in the Irish Directory are as outlined in the sections at the front of the book headed *AA Inspection and Classification* and *How to Use the Guide*. See also the explanation of *Symbols and Abbreviations*.

Town & Country
In the Republic of Ireland, establishments classified as Town & Country Houses are indicated by the abbreviation T & C. Because of statutory regulations, these properties cannot be officially classified as Guest Houses, although their facilities are similar.

Map References
In the Irish Directory, the six-figure map references shown against establishments have been taken from the Irish National Grid.

Prices
In the Republic, prices are quote in Punts, indicated by the symbol IR£. Please consult your bank or the daily paper for the current

exchange rate.
Hotels must display tariffs, either in the bedrooms or at reception. Application of VAT and service charges varies, but all prices quoted must be inclusive of VAT.

Telephone Numbers
Area codes shown against the numbers in the Republic of Ireland are applicable only within the Republic. If dialling from outside, you will need to check with the telephone directory. The area codes shown for hotels in Britain and Northern Ireland cannot be used directly from the Republic.

Fire Precautions
The Fire Services (NI) Order 1984 covers

establishments accommodating more than 6 persons, and they must have a fire certificate issued by the Northern Ireland Fire Authority. Places accommodating fewer than 6 persons must have adequate exits.

Republic of Ireland:
safety regulations are a matter for local authority regulations, but AA officials inspect emergency notices, fire-fighting equipment and fire exits.
For your own and others' safety, you must read the emergency notices displayed and be sure you understand them.

Licensing Regulations
Northern Ireland: public

houses open from 11.30-23.00, and on Sun 12.30-14.30 and 19.00-22.00. Hotels can serve residents without restriction. Non-residents can be served from 12.30-22.00 on Christmas Day. Children under 18 are not allowed in the bar area and may neither buy nor consume liquor in hotels.

Republic of Ireland:
general licensing hours at present are 10.30-23.00 (23.30 in summer), Mon-Sat. On Sun and St Patrick's Day (17 March), 12.30-14.00 and 16.00-23.00. Hotels can serve residents without restriction. There is no service on Christmas Day or Good Friday.

IRELAND

ACHILL ISLAND Co Mayo Map **01** A4

Selected

GH ⓠⓠⓠⓠ **Gray's** Dugort ☎098 43244 & 43315
Gray's offers comfortable accommodation in a quiet location
with ample lounge space and is especially suitable for family
holidays.
17 rms (6 bth/shr) (4 fmly) No smoking in area of dining
room No smoking in 1 lounge CTV in 3 bedrooms Tea and
coffee making facilities Licensed Cen ht CTV 30P Table
tennis Croquet Pool table Last d 6pm
PRICE GUIDE
ROOMS: s fr IR£20; d fr IR£40; wkly hlf-bd fr IR£200✶

T&C ⓠⓠ **West Coast House** School Rd, Dooagh (turn off N59
onto R319 onto Achill Island continue to Keel & then Dooagh,
West Coast House signed) ☎098 43317 FAX 098 43317
Mar-11 Nov
This smart new house is in an elevated position giving superb
views over Dooagh to the sea. It is furnished to a high standard,
and no effort is spared to make guests comfortable.
4 rms (2 shr) (1 fmly) No smoking No dogs (ex guide dogs)
Cen ht CTV No children 12yrs 4P Last d 6pm
PRICE GUIDE
ROOMS: s IR£19-IR£20; d IR£30-IR£32; wkly b&b IR£100-
IR£105; wkly hlf-bd IR£170✶

ADARE Co Limerick Map **01** B3

Selected

T&C ⓠⓠⓠⓠⓠ **Adare Lodge** Kildimo Rd (in village turn
right at bank) ☎061 396629
A charming modern house, recently extended and suitable for
wheelchair users, stands on a quiet street off the main N21
road in a picturesque village famous for its thatched cottages.
Its comfortable en suite bedrooms are well equipped with TV,
tea/coffee trays and hairdryers. Guests also have the use of a
spacious guest lounge.
6 en suite (shr) (3 fmly) No smoking in bedrooms No
smoking in dining room No smoking in 1 lounge CTV in all
bedrooms Tea and coffee making facilities No dogs Cen ht
CTV 6P
PRICE GUIDE
ROOMS: d IR£34✶
CARDS: ▣ ▤ ▦ ⓪

T&C ⓠⓠⓠ **Avona** Kildimo Rd ☎061 396323
4 rms (3 shr) (1 fmly) No smoking in bedrooms No smoking in
dining room No dogs (ex guide dogs) Cen ht CTV 5P No
coaches
PRICE GUIDE
ROOMS: s IR£18.50; d IR£28; wkly b&b IR£98✶
CARDS: ▣ ▦

GH ⓠⓠⓠ **Carrabawn House** Killarney Rd (on N21)
☎061 396067 FAX 061 396925
This friendly guest house stands on the main Killanney road just a
few minutes from the pretty village of Adare. A dining room and
cosy sun lounge overlook picturesque gardens including a fish

pond. Bedrooms have good-sized en suite showers, are bright and
cheerful and are equipped with TVs and tea/coffee making
facilities. The Lohan family are attentive hosts.
7 en suite (shr) (2 fmly) No smoking in bedrooms No smoking
in dining room CTV in all bedrooms Tea and coffee making
facilities Direct dial from bedrooms Cen ht CTV 12P Last d
noon
PRICE GUIDE
ROOMS: s IR£30-IR£35; d IR£37-IR£45✶
CARDS: ▣ ▦

Selected

T&C ⓠⓠⓠⓠ **Coatesland House** Killarney Rd, Graigue
(from Adare village follow Killarney road N21 for less than
0.5m, Coatesland House is on left)
☎061 396372 FAX 061 396833
Coatesland House, situated on the main Killarney road (N21)
five minutes from Adare village, is a very well appointed
house featuring attractive bedrooms, all with en suite
facilities. Proprietors Florence and Donal Hogan are
welcoming and friendly and give superb attention to detail.
Dinner is available. Nearby activities include hunting, fishing,
golf and there is also an equestrian centre.
6 en suite (shr) (3 fmly) No smoking in 2 bedrooms No
smoking in dining room CTV in 3 bedrooms Tea and coffee
making facilities Direct dial from bedrooms Cen ht CTV
25P
PRICE GUIDE
ROOMS: s IR£20; d IR£33✶
CARDS: ▣ ▦ ▦

Selected

T&C ⓠⓠⓠⓠ **Foxhollow House** Croom Rd (2kms from
village on Route 0542) ☎061 396776
4 rms (3 bth/shr) (1 fmly) No smoking in bedrooms No
smoking in dining room CTV in all bedrooms Tea and coffee
making facilities No dogs (ex guide dogs) Cen ht CTV 6P
PRICE GUIDE
ROOMS: s IR£20; d IR£32; wkly b&b IR£105
CARDS: ▣ ▦

ANNAMOE Co Wicklow Map **01** D3

T&C ⓠⓠ **Carmel's** ☎0404 45297
Etr-Oct
This modern bungalow with nice gardens is situated in a scenic
touring area of Co Wicklow on the R755 giving easy access to all
areas of local interest.
4 rms (3 shr) (2 fmly) No dogs Cen ht CTV No parking No
coaches Last d noon
PRICE GUIDE
ROOMS: s fr IR£16; d fr IR£32✶

ANNESTOWN Co Waterford Map **01** C2

Selected

T&C Ⓠ Ⓠ Ⓠ Ⓠ **Annestown House** ☎051 396160
Closed 24 Dec-1 Jan
This period house stands in an elevated position overlooking a
sandy cove with private access to the beach. The en suite
bedrooms are well equipped and successfully combine period
furnishings and contemporary bathrooms. Public areas
comprise a spacious sitting room, a library, a billiards room
and a dining room serving dinner by arrangement only. The
house has pleasant gardens and is situated 1 hour 20 minutes'
drive from Rosslare.
5 en suite (bth/shr) No smoking in bedrooms Tea and coffee
making facilities Direct dial from bedrooms Cen ht CTV
10P No coaches Tennis (grass) Snooker Croquet lawn
Private beach Last d noon
PRICE GUIDE
ROOMS: s IR£20-IR£30; d IR£36-IR£54; wkly b&b
IR£126-IR£157.50
CARDS: 🔳 🔳 🔳

ARDARA Co Donegal Map **01** B5

T&C Ⓠ Ⓠ Ⓠ **Bay View Country House** Portnoo Rd (half a
mile outside Ardara, on the Portnoo road)
☎075 41145 FAX 075 41145
Mar-5 Nov
This large, modern bungalow, on the outskirts of a small town,
overlooks the sea.
6 en suite (shr) (2 fmly) No smoking in bedrooms No smoking
in dining room No dogs Cen ht CTV 20P Last d noon
PRICE GUIDE
ROOMS: s IR£20; d IR£30; wkly b&b IR£100
CARDS: 🔳

ARDMORE Co Waterford Map **01** C2

💗 Ⓠ Ⓠ Ⓠ Mrs T O'Connor **Newtown View** *(X182818)* Grange
(on N25 Dungarvan to Youghal road, turn left at Flemings public
house) ☎024 94143 & 088 600799 FAX 024 94143
Apr-mid Oct
This comfortable guest house stands in 100 acres of farmland near
the seaside village of Ardmore. The well decorated en suite
bedrooms all have TVs and tea/coffee trays; public areas include a
guest lounge and snooker room. A tennis court, a secure play area
and good car parking are available.
6 annexe en suite (shr) (3 fmly) No smoking in dining room
CTV in all bedrooms Tea and coffee making facilities Cen ht
CTV 12P Tennis (hard) Snooker 110 acres dairy beef Last d
6pm
PRICE GUIDE
ROOMS: s IR£18-IR£20; d IR£28-IR£30; wkly b&b IR£98-
IR£105; wkly hlf-bd IR£172-IR£182✳
CARDS: 🔳 🔳

ATHY Co Kildare Map **01** C3

💗 Ⓠ Ⓠ Mrs V Gorman **Ballindrum** *(S747968)* Ballindrum
(leave N9 at Crookstown onto R415, farm well signed)
☎0507 26294 FAX 0507 26294
Apr-Oct
This white house stands in meticulously-kept farmland at the end
of a tree-lined avenue. Accommodation is comfortable. Hospitable
owners Mary and Vincent Gorman bake their own bread and cook

with fresh farm produce. Golf, fishing, horseriding and forest
walks are available locally.
5 rms (3 shr) (1 fmly) No smoking in bedrooms No smoking in
area of dining room No dogs Cen ht CTV ch fac 20P Guided
farm tours 75 acres dairy & tillage Last d 3pm
PRICE GUIDE
ROOMS: s IR£14; d IR£28-IR£32; wkly b&b IR£93-IR£107;
wkly hlf-bd IR£170-IR£184✳

AVOCA Co Wicklow Map **01** D3

T&C Ⓠ Ⓠ **Ashdene** Knockanree Lower (turn off R752 into
village. House 1m on right beyond Avoca Handweavers on
Avoca/Redcross road) ☎0402 35327
Mar-Oct
Set two miles from Avoca, Ashdene represents an ideal centre for
touring Co Wicklow. Mrs Burne is very enthusiastic in her care of
guests, and takes pride in her breakfast menu.
5 rms (4 shr) (2 fmly) No smoking in bedrooms No smoking in
dining room No dogs (ex guide dogs) Cen ht CTV 5P Tennis
(grass)
PRICE GUIDE
ROOMS: s IR£14-IR£21; d IR£28-IR£32; wkly b&b IR£84-
IR£98✳
CARDS: 🔳 🔳

T&C Ⓠ Ⓠ Ⓠ **Old Coach House** (take road from Rathdrum
follow signs for Avoca, Meetings of the Waters 500yds beyond on
right) ☎0402 35408 FAX 0402 35720
This black and white coaching inn set in the picturesque Vale of
Avoca has been tastefully restored by the friendly Susan and
Aidan Dempsey. A warmly invitng atmosphere pervades the
restful lounge and smart restaurant. Charming en suite bedrooms
feature stripped pine furnishings, pretty decor and tea/coffee
making facilities.
6 en suite (shr) (2 fmly) No smoking in 2 bedrooms No smoking
in area of dining room Tea and coffee making facilities Direct
dial from bedrooms No dogs (ex guide dogs) Licensed Cen ht
CTV ch fac 8P No coaches Last d 9pm
PRICE GUIDE
ROOMS: s IR£18-IR£20; d IR£36-IR£40; wkly b&b IR£115-
IR£126; wkly hlf-bd IR£230-IR£250
CARDS: 🔳 🔳

BALLINADEE Co Cork Map **01** B2

Selected

T&C Ⓠ Ⓠ Ⓠ Ⓠ **Glebe House**
☎021 778294 FAX 021 778456
This lovely old house stands in well kept gardens. Beautifully
furnished rooms have many antiques and the proprietors are
always looking for ways to spoil guests.
4 en suite (bth/shr) (2 fmly) No smoking in area of dining
room No smoking in 1 lounge Tea and coffee making
facilities Direct dial from bedrooms Cen ht CTV ch fac
30P Tennis (grass) Croquet Last d noon
PRICE GUIDE
ROOMS: s IR£30-IR£35; d IR£45-IR£50; wkly b&b
IR£157.50-IR£175✳
CARDS: 🔳 🔳

BALLINHASSIG Co Cork Map **01** B2

T&C Q Q Blanchfield House Rigsdale (main Cork/Bandon Rd N71) ☎021 885167 FAX 021 885167
Mar-Nov
This guesthouse is in a quiet, but convenient location within easy reach of the airport and ferry. Proprietor Patricia Blanchfield offers good home cooking, and private salmon and trout fishing are available.
6 rms (2 bth/shr) (2 fmly) No dogs (ex guide dogs) Licensed Cen ht CTV 20P Last d noon
PRICE GUIDE
ROOMS: s fr IR£20; d fr IR£30; wkly b&b fr IR£95; wkly hlf-bd fr IR£193✱
CARDS: ▨ ▧ ▨ ⑩

BALLYCASTLE Co Antrim Map **01** D6

GH Q Hilsea 28 Quay Hill BT54 6BH ☎01265 762385
Occupying a grand position on the hill overlooking the bay, this hotel offers good-value holiday accommodation. Appetising breakfast with home-baked breads is served in a bright, airy dining room. The well-decorated bedrooms vary in size and there is a cosy lounge.
19 rms (4 fmly) No smoking in dining room Cen ht CTV ch fac 70P Last d 7.30pm
PRICE GUIDE
ROOMS: s £16; d £32✱
CARDS: ▨ ▧ ▨

BALLYHACK Co Wexford Map **01** C2

Selected

T&C Q Q Q Q Marsh Mere Lodge ☎051 389186
This charming shell-pink house is situated a few minutes' walk from the Ballyhack ferry overlooking Waterford harbour. Mrs Mcnamara is a friendly host and the house is full of her personal touches. Bedrooms are delightful and a fine tea is served on the verandah.
5 en suite (bth/shr) No smoking No dogs Cen ht CTV 5P No coaches
PRICE GUIDE
ROOMS: s IR£20-IR£30; d IR£30-IR£35; wkly b&b IR£80-IR£100✱

BALLYHAUNIS Co Mayo Map **01** B4

GH Q Q Q Val's Main St ☎0907 30068 & 30122
This friendly guest house is conveniently located in the centre of Connaught, six miles from Knock and twelve from the airport. Attractively decorated en suite bedrooms are well equipped with TVs and telephones, and while the carte is only available after lunch, the welcoming bar serves food all day. The locality is of interest to archaeologists and geologists, and amenities include an all-year golf course and coarse fishing.
6 en suite (shr) (1 fmly) No smoking in bedrooms CTV in all bedrooms Direct dial from bedrooms No dogs (ex guide dogs) Licensed Cen ht CTV 10P No coaches Last d 8.45pm
PRICE GUIDE
ROOMS: s fr IR£18; d fr IR£32✱
CARDS: ▨ ▨

BALLYMACARBRY Co Waterford Map **01** C2

GH Q Q Q Clonanav Farm Nire Valley
☎052 36141 FAX 052 36141
2 Feb-16 Nov
Lenny and Eileen Ryan have created a friendly atmosphere and comfortable en suite accommodation at this charming hotel. The couple specialise in fishing and walking holidays, their son Andrew offering advice to guests who try the hotel's own salmon and trout fishing.
10 en suite (shr) (1 fmly) No smoking in 4 bedrooms No smoking in dining room Direct dial from bedrooms No dogs (ex guide dogs) Licensed Cen ht CTV 10P No coaches Tennis (hard) Fishing
PRICE GUIDE
ROOMS: s IR£28.50-IR£32; d IR£47-IR£50; wkly b&b IR£165; wkly hlf-bd IR£260
CARDS: ▨ ▧ ▨

BALLYMOTE Co Sligo Map **01** B4

T&C Q Q Q Corran House Sligo Rd (last house on right leaving Ballymote on R293 to Collooney) ☎071 83074
A comfortable, well-maintained house stands in attractive gardens just around the corner from the village. En suite bedrooms have attractive decor and are equipped with televisions and tea/coffee making facilities. The area is well-known as an angling centre.
4 en suite (shr) (1 fmly) No smoking in 2 bedrooms No smoking in dining room CTV in all bedrooms Tea and coffee making facilities No dogs (ex guide dogs) Cen ht CTV 5P No coaches Last d 5pm
PRICE GUIDE
ROOMS: s IR£19; d IR£28✱
CARDS: ▨ ▨

BALLYVAUGHAN Co Clare Map **01** B3

Selected

T&C Q Q Q Q Rusheen Lodge (on N67)
☎065 77092 FAX 065 77152
Closed 17 Dec-Jan
A charming house nestles in the valley of the Burren Limestone mountains, an area famous for its Arctic and Alpine plants in spring and summer. The McGann family were founders of the famous Aillwee Caves and have a fund of local folklore. The bedrooms are excellent, large and well equipped with attractive decor and extras that ensure a comfortable visit. The cosy dining room has patio gardens leading from it. Car parking is available.
6 en suite (bth/shr) (3 fmly) No smoking in 3 bedrooms No smoking in dining room No smoking in lounges CTV in all bedrooms Tea and coffee making facilities Direct dial from bedrooms No dogs (ex guide dogs) Cen ht CTV 12P
PRICE GUIDE
ROOMS: s IR£25-IR£35; d IR£36-IR£50; wkly b&b IR£113-IR£126
CARDS: ▨ ▧ ▨

BALLYVOURNEY Co Cork Map **01** B2

GH Q Q Q The Mills Inn (on main Cork/Killarney road N22)
☎026 45237 FAX 026 45454
Closed 24-25 Dec
This charming inn dates back to the mid 18th century and stands in extensive gardens including a vintage car and folk museum as

➡

well as a shop. Bedrooms are comfortable and licensees Donal and Mary Seannell are welcoming hosts. The bar offers hot food all day and there is also a cosy restaurant. The inn is nine miles from Macroom and twenty miles from Killarney.

9 en suite (bth/shr) 1 annexe en suite (bth/shr) (4 fmly) No smoking in dining room CTV in all bedrooms Tea and coffee making facilities Direct dial from bedrooms Licensed Cen ht CTV 24P Last d 9pm

PRICE GUIDE

ROOMS: s IR£28-IR£30; d IR£44-IR£50✶

CARDS: 🔳 💳 💳 ⑩

BANAGHER Co Offaly Map **01** C3

T&C Ⓠ Ⓠ Ⓠ *Old Forge* Westend ☎0509 51504

4 en suite (bth/shr) (2 fmly) No dogs (ex guide dogs) Cen ht CTV P No coaches

---

BANSHA Co Tipperary Map **01** C3

T&C Ⓠ Ⓠ Ⓠ *Bansha Castle* (5m S of Tipperary on N24) ☎062 54187 FAX 062 54187

Teresa and John Russell have spent the last few years restoring the castle which stands on the edge of the magnificent Glen of Akerlow and was once the residence of the painter Lady Elizabeth Butler. An informal atmosphere pervades the hotel and a genuine warmth is extended to guests. Rooms are spacious, there is a fine walled garden and good car parking. Walking, golf, fishing, hunting and horseriding are all available in the area.

5 rms (3 shr) (3 fmly) No dogs (ex guide dogs) Licensed Cen ht 10P Last d 4pm

CARDS: 🔳 💳 💳

See advertisement under **TIPPERARY**

Selected

♥ Ⓠ Ⓠ Ⓠ Ⓠ J & M Marnane **Bansha House** *(R962320)* (turn off N24 in village opposite Esso filling station) ☎062 54194 FAX 062 54215

Closed 21-31 Dec

Situated in a very scenic area on the N24, this Georgian house is approached along an avenue of beech trees, and has 100 acres of land where visitors can roam. It is comfortable, very well furnished and noted for its home baking.

7 rms (5 fmly) No smoking No dogs (ex guide dogs) Licensed Cen ht CTV 10P Fishing Riding 100 acres mixed Last d 7pm

PRICE GUIDE

ROOMS: s IR£25; d IR£36-IR£40; wkly b&b IR£126-IR£140; wkly hlf-bd IR£215-IR£225✶

CARDS: 🔳 💳

BANTEER Co Cork Map **01** B2

Selected

GH Ⓠ Ⓠ Ⓠ Ⓠ **Clonmeen Lodge** Nr Mallow ☎029 56238 & 56277 FAX 029 56294

This neatly furnished and comfortable house stands a short distance off the N72, beside the River Blackwater and within easy reach of a variety of recreational options which includes fishing, walking, pony trekking, golf and fox hunting; bedrooms are attractively decorated, and a peaceful, hospitable atmosphere pervades the relaxing public areas. Cork airport is within an hour's drive.

6 en suite (bth/shr) (4 fmly) CTV in 4 bedrooms No dogs Licensed Cen ht CTV ch fac 20P Fishing Riding Bicycle hire Last d 9.15pm

PRICE GUIDE

ROOMS: s IR£30-IR£35; d IR£50-IR£60; wkly b&b IR£155-IR£160; wkly hlf-bd IR£260-IR£270

CARDS: 🔳 ⑩

BANTRY Co Cork Map **01** B2

T&C Ⓠ Ⓠ Ⓠ **The Mill** Glenghriff Rd, New Town ☎027 50278 Apr-Oct

Colourful gardens are the setting for this well maintained double bungalow set beside the N71 Bantry/Ballylickey road a few minutes' drive from Bantry. Well appointed bedrooms are equipped with good showers, and a spacious dining/sitting room with TV forms the heart of the house; decor throughout reflects the owner's ebullient personality and enthusiasm. Facilities include laundry service, bicycle hire and ample car parking - and Dutch is spoken here.

6 en suite (bth/shr) No smoking No dogs 15P Bicycle hire

PRICE GUIDE

ROOMS: d IR£30✶

T&C Ⓠ Ⓠ Ⓠ **Shangri-La** Glengarriff Rd (on N71, near Bantry Golf Course) ☎027 50244

Closed Xmas week

This bungalow with spacious gardens ith spacious gardens overlooks Bantry Bay and is an ideal centre for touring Cork and Kerry.

7 rms (4 bth/shr) (1 fmly) No smoking in area of dining room No smoking in 1 lounge Tea and coffee making facilities No dogs Cen ht CTV 12P

PRICE GUIDE

ROOMS: s fr IR£22; d fr IR£32; wkly b&b fr IR£105✶

CARDS: 🔳 💳

BELFAST Map **01** D5

GH Ⓠ Ⓠ **Camera** 44 Wellington Park BT9 6DP ☎01232 660026 & 667856

Situated in a tree-lined avenue close to the University, this end-of-terrace Victorian house offers good-value bed and breakfast. Bedrooms range from singles to large family rooms. There is a comfortable lounge and a breakfast room.

11 rms (2 shr) (2 fmly) No smoking in dining room No smoking in lounges CTV in all bedrooms Tea and coffee making facilities No dogs (ex guide dogs) Cen ht No parking No coaches Last d 9am

PRICE GUIDE

ROOMS: s £18-£35; d £36-£46

CARDS: 🔳 💳 💳

GH Ⓠ Ⓠ Ⓠ **Malone** 79 Malone Rd BT9 6SH ☎01232 669565 Closed 24 Dec-6 Jan

On the south side of the town and close to the University, this detached red brick Victorian villa offers bright and airy bedrooms, a comfortable lounge and breakfast room with separate tables.

8 en suite (shr) CTV in all bedrooms Tea and coffee making facilities No dogs Cen ht No children 12yrs 9P No coaches

PRICE GUIDE

ROOMS: s £25-£32; d £38-£47

BLACKROCK Co Dublin Map **01** D4

T&C 🔲🔲🔲 **Priory Town House** Stillorgan Rd, Mount Nerrion (on N11 Dublin/Wexford road)
☎01 2833715 FAX 01 2835655
Closed 22 Dec-3 Jan
This is a very comfortable place to stay, only two miles from Dun Laoghaire Ferry Port and ten minutes from the city centre. Accommodation has recently been refurbished to a very high standard and rooms are well equipped and attractively decorated. The Priory has off-street parking and is easy to find on the main Stillorgan (N11) road, on the left hand side southbound, beside the Stillorgan Park Hotel.
5 en suite (shr) (2 fmly) No smoking CTV in all bedrooms Tea and coffee making facilities No dogs (ex guide dogs) Cen ht CTV 6P No coaches
PRICE GUIDE
ROOMS: s IR£30-IR£35; d IR£45-IR£55✶
CARDS: 🅰 🔳

BLARNEY Co Cork Map **01** B2

T&C 🔲🔲🔲 **Sylvanmanor** Tower ☎021 381977
Closed 21 Dec-1 Jan
Set on a hilltop in a residential area, this fine red-brick house has been recently purpose-built to be very comfortable throughout. The hospitable owner pays great attention to detail and has established pleasant decor with a number of individual touches. Three of the four en suite bedrooms are on the ground floor; all have colour TVs, radios, trouser presses and tea/coffee making facilities. The TV lounge overlooks a scenic area and a separate breakfast room adjoins. Ample car parking is available.
4 en suite (shr) (1 fmly) No smoking in bedrooms No smoking in dining room CTV in all bedrooms Tea and coffee making facilities No dogs (ex guide dogs) CTV 4P No coaches
PRICE GUIDE
ROOMS: s IR£21; d IR£32; wkly b&b IR£100

T&C 🔲🔲🔲 **White House** Shean Lower (on R617, Cork/Blarney road) ☎021 385338
Conveniently situated close to town in an elevated position with views of Blarney Castle, this attractive well appointed house is dedicated to guests' comfort. There is a lounge, a separate breakfast room and six en suite bedrooms with TVs, hair dryers and clock radios. Spacious shower rooms have power showers and a private car park is available.
6 en suite (shr) (1 fmly) No smoking in bedrooms No smoking in dining room CTV in all bedrooms Tea and coffee making facilities No dogs Cen ht CTV 7P
PRICE GUIDE
ROOMS: s IR£22; d IR£33✶

BUSHMILLS Co Antrim Map **01** C6

Selected

GH 🔲🔲🔲🔲 **White Gables** 83 Dunluce Rd BT57 8SJ (1.8m W on A2 coast road) ☎01265 731611
Mar-Oct
White Gables is an impeccably kept modern property on the A2 Coast Road just west of Portballentrae. It has spacious lawned gardens at the front and from its elevated position commands superb views of the coastline. Bedrooms vary in size and style but all have modern equipment. There is a large lounge and a small but pleasant dining room where guests share two tables.
4 rms (3 bth/shr) No smoking in 2 bedrooms No smoking in dining room No smoking in lounges Tea and coffee making

facilities No dogs Cen ht CTV 12P No coaches Last d 4pm
PRICE GUIDE
ROOMS: s £25; d £45; wkly b&b £150; wkly hlf-bd £255✶

CAHIRCIVEEN Co Kerry Map **01** A2

🔽 🔲🔲🔲 T Sugrue **Valentia View** *(V457773)* ☎066 72227
Mar-Oct
This fine old country farmhouse on The Ring of Kerry has a warm and hospitable atmosphere. Rooms overlook Valentia island and bay.
6 rms (5 shr) (2 fmly) No smoking in dining room Tea and coffee making facilities Cen ht CTV No children 2mths 20P 38 acres beef Last d 7pm
PRICE GUIDE
ROOMS: s IR£20-IR£21; d fr IR£32; wkly b&b fr IR£110; wkly hlf-bd fr IR£180

CAMP Co Kerry Map **01** A2

Selected

GH 🔲🔲🔲🔲 **Barnagh Bridge Country House** (leave N86 Tralee/Dingle road at Camp and follow Conor Pass road for 1 Km) ☎066 30145 FAX 066 30299
Mar-Oct
This is an eyecatching cream-coloured house set back from the road. Its interior is well-designed and offers every comfort. The cosy lounge has an open fire, the dining room overlooks nearby beaches and the well-appointed, en suite bedrooms have scenic views.
5 en suite (shr) No smoking in bedrooms No smoking in dining room CTV in all bedrooms Tea and coffee making facilities Direct dial from bedrooms No dogs (ex guide dogs) Cen ht CTV 7P
PRICE GUIDE
ROOMS: s IR£22-IR£28; d IR£36-IR£44✶
CARDS: 🅰 🔳

CAPPOQUIN Co Waterford Map **01** C2

Selected

GH 🔲🔲🔲🔲 **Richmond House** (on N72, 0.5m from Cappoquin on Dungarvan road) ☎058 54278 FAX 058 54988
Closed 23 Dec-1 Feb
This eighteenth-century Georgian house stands in timbered parkland, about half a mile from the picturesque town of Cappoquin. It is family run and offers tastefully decorated en suite bedrooms with direct dial telephones and central heating. There is also a fully licensed restaurant serving a good standard of food. Located in an area of mountains, woodlands and rivers, the hotel is an obvious base for walkers and anglers, but three golf courses are also within easy reach and there are sandy beaches only half an hour's drive away.
10 en suite (bth/shr) (2 fmly) No smoking in area of dining room CTV in all bedrooms Tea and coffee making facilities ➡

Direct dial from bedrooms No dogs Licensed Cen ht CTV
ch fac 22P Last d 8pm
PRICE GUIDE
ROOMS: s IR£30-IR£37; d IR£50-IR£64✳
CARDS: ▨ ▆ ▨ ◎

CARLOW Co Carlow Map **01** C3

Selected

GH ▢▢▢▢ **Barrowville Town House** Kilkenny Rd (on
N9) ☎0503 43324 FAX 0503 41953
This lovely Georgian house, situated on the edge of town,
offers a high standard of comfort and convenience in well
furnished accommodation.
7 en suite (bth/shr) (2 fmly) No smoking in bedrooms No
smoking in dining room CTV in all bedrooms Tea and coffee
making facilities Direct dial from bedrooms No dogs (ex
guide dogs) Licensed Cen ht CTV No children 12yrs 11P
PRICE GUIDE
ROOMS: s IR£20-IR£25; d IR£37-IR£40
CARDS: ▨ ▨

T&C ▢▢▢ Greenlane House Dublin Rd ☎0503 42670
rs Xmas
Purpose built, family run and very comfortable, this smart dormer-
style house stands on the edge of the town near the N9 route
roundabout, an hour's drive from Rosslare Ferry. Well equipped
en suite bedrooms are provided with TV and guests have their
own sitting room; good car parking facilities are available.
7 en suite (bth/shr) (2 fmly) No smoking CTV in all bedrooms
Tea and coffee making facilities No dogs (ex guide dogs) Cen ht
CTV 35P
PRICE GUIDE
ROOMS: s IR£19-IR£22; d IR£35-IR£38

CARRIGALINE Co Cork Map **01** B2

T&C ▢▢ Beaver Lodge ☎021 372595
Closed Xmas
An old ivy-clad house stands in its own grounds off the main
street.
6 rms (2 bth 2 shr) (5 fmly) CTV in all bedrooms Tea and coffee
making facilities No dogs (ex guide dogs) Cen ht CTV 14P No
coaches Last d 4pm
CARDS: ▨ ▆ ▨

Selected

GH ▢▢▢▢ **Glenwood House** Ballinrea Rd
☎021 373878 FAX 021 373878
Closed 22-31 Dec
8 en suite (bth/shr) No smoking in area of dining room No
smoking in 1 lounge CTV in all bedrooms Tea and coffee
making facilities Direct dial from bedrooms No dogs (ex
guide dogs) Cen ht CTV 12P No coaches
PRICE GUIDE
ROOMS: s IR£30; d IR£50✳
CARDS: ▨ ▨

CARRIGANS Co Donegal Map **01** C5

Selected

T&C ▢▢▢▢ **Mount Royd Country Home** (postal
address is Carrigans, Lifford P.O.) ☎074 40163
Situated off N13, N14 and A40 a large, attractive creeper-clad
house is surrounded by a well tended garden. Very well
appointed bedrooms and excellent home cooking make it
popular with both tourist and business guests. The house was
a Galty Breakfast Award Winner in 1994.
4 en suite (shr) (3 fmly) No smoking in dining room CTV in
all bedrooms Tea and coffee making facilities No dogs (ex
guide dogs) Cen ht CTV 7P Last d noon
PRICE GUIDE
ROOMS: s IR£19-IR£21; d IR£32

CASTLEGREGORY Co Kerry Map **01** A2

❤ ▢ Mrs C Griffin *Griffin's (Q525085)* Goulane ☎066 39147
Apr-Oct
This is a two-storey farmhouse situated on the Dingle Peninsula.
8 en suite (bth/shr) (3 fmly) Cen ht CTV 10P 150 acres dairy
sheep Last d 5pm

CAVAN Co Cavan Map **01** C4

⟷ ▼ **T&C ▢▢ Halcyon** Drumalee (turn right off N3
immediately after the cathedral, signposted 'Cootehill'. Turn right
at X-roads, 'Halcyon' 100yds on left) ☎049 31809
7 Jan-22 Dec
This lovely modern bungalow on the edge of town offers peace
and quiet in attractive, comfortable accommodation. It is very
popular with anglers as there is good coarse fishing in the many
local lakes.
5 rms (4 shr) (4 fmly) No smoking in dining room No dogs (ex
guide dogs) Cen ht CTV No children 2yrs 6P Last d noon
PRICE GUIDE
ROOMS: s IR£15-IR£19; d IR£28-IR£32

CHEEKPOINT Co Waterford Map **01** C2

Selected

GH ▢▢▢▢ **Three Rivers**
☎051 382520 FAX 051 382542
This charming house is superbly located overlooking the
rivers Barrow, Noire and Suir, within sight of the twinkling
lights of passage east where a ferry provides quick access to
Rosslare port. There are well appointed bedrooms, attractive
gardens and a sunny balcony, and the lounge and dining room
are sited to take full advantage of the magnificent views. The
house stands within five minutes of Faithlegg golf course.
14 en suite (shr) (4 fmly) No smoking in bedrooms No
smoking in dining room Direct dial from bedrooms Cen ht
CTV 20P
PRICE GUIDE
ROOMS: s IR£22-IR£30; d IR£40-IR£56✳
CARDS: ▨ ▆ ▨

Co Galway Map **01** A4

 T&C Q Q **Ben View House** Bridge St (entering town on N59, opposite Esso petrol station) ☎095 21256
This town-centre house offers good quality accomodation at a moderate cost making it an ideal touring base.
10 rms (9 shr) (3 fmly) No smoking in 2 bedrooms No smoking in dining room No dogs (ex guide dogs) Cen ht CTV No parking
PRICE GUIDE
ROOMS: s IR£15-IR£30; d IR£30-IR£40; wkly b&b IR£105-IR£140

T&C Q Q Q *Connemara Country Lodge* Westport Rd
☎095 21122
This is a very comfortable house, purpose built to a high standard, on the main Clifden/Westport road. Charming and hospitable owners provide a warm welcome and home cooking. French and German are spoken here.
6 en suite (shr) (4 fmly) CTV in 3 bedrooms Cen ht CTV ch fac 12P Last d noon
CARDS: ■ ■

 T&C Q Q Q **Failte** Ardbear, Ballyconneely Rd
☎095 21159
Apr-Sep
A modern bungalow in scenic location on edge of Clifden features excellent standards of comfort and welcoming hosts and is an ideal touring centre.
5 rms (2 shr) (2 fmly) No smoking in dining room No smoking in 1 lounge No dogs (ex guide dogs) Cen ht CTV 15P
PRICE GUIDE
ROOMS: s IR£14; d IR£28-IR£32; wkly b&b IR£84-IR£91
CARDS: ▲ ■ ■

T&C Q Q **Kingstown House** Bridge St
☎095 21470 FAX 095 21530
Situated just off Clifden's main street and centrally located close to all amenities, this pleasant guesthouse offers a warm welcome from the friendly proprietors Mary and Joe King, who provide comfortable accommodation.
8 rms (6 shr) (3 fmly) No smoking in area of dining room No dogs (ex guide dogs) Cen ht CTV No parking
PRICE GUIDE
ROOMS: d IR£28-IR£32
CARDS: ▲ ■

Selected

GH Q Q Q Q **Maldua** Galway Rd (on N59)
☎095 21171 & 21739 FAX 095 21739
Closed Dec
This guesthouse is situated on the main Galway/Clifden road, just before the entrance to this cosmopolitan village in the heart of Connemara; it is easily distinguished by its conservatory entrance and balcony. The excellent bedrooms are attractive and well appointed, with good facilities. Outside there is a patio, garden and ample car parking.
9 en suite (shr) (2 fmly) No smoking in bedrooms CTV in all bedrooms Tea and coffee making facilities Direct dial from bedrooms No dogs (ex guide dogs) Cen ht 20P
PRICE GUIDE
ROOMS: s IR£18-IR£21; d IR£40-IR£50✱
CARDS: ▲ ■ ■

𝕽𝖎𝖈𝖍𝖒𝖔𝖓𝖉 𝕳𝖔𝖚𝖘𝖊
Cappoquin Co Waterford
Tel: (00 353) 58 54278
Fax: (00 353) 58 54988
Award winning eighteenth century Georgian country house, standing in timbered parkland, ½ mile from the picturesque town of Cappoquin. Old world charm and character, log fires and central heating. All bedrooms en-suite, tea/coffee making facilities, direct dial telephone and Colour T.V. Top class fully licensed restaurant. Listed in most International guides. Ideal centre for golfing, fishing, horse-riding, sightseeing and mountain walking.

Mal Dua Guest House
Galway Road, Clifden, Connemara, Co. Galway.
Tel: 00 353 95 21171/21739
Fax: 00 353 95 21739

Grade A ★★★★
In the heart of Connemara. A high standard of accommodation. All bedrooms individually designed with en-suite facilities, trouser press, hair dryer, direct-dial telephone, Colour TV, radio, tea/coffee making facilities. Iron/board available on request. Local amenities – Golf, Horse Riding, Sea Angling, Cycling, Walk's and Historical Tours.
Rates from £20 per person sharing

Selected

T&C 🔲🔲🔲🔲 **Mallmore House** Ballyconneely Rd
☎095 21460
Mar-1 Nov
A charming Georgian-style house set in 35 acres of woodland overlooking Clifden Bay, is situated one mile from Clifden on the Ballyconneely road, close to the Rock Glen Hotel. Alan and Kathy Hardman have tastefully restored the house, with parquet flooring and some favourite antiques, together with turf fires providing warmth and atmosphere.
6 en suite (shr) (2 fmly) No smoking in dining room No smoking in lounges No dogs (ex guide dogs) Cen ht CTV 15P No coaches Sauna
PRICE GUIDE
ROOMS: d IR£34✳

Selected

GH 🔲🔲🔲🔲 *Sunnybank House* Church Hill
☎095 21437 FAX 095 21976
Mar-Nov
This comfortable period house stands in an elevated position on the N59 a few minutes' walk from town and O'Gradys Restaurant. Spacious en suite bedrooms have attractive decor and are equipped with TVs and telephones; some enjoy fine views of the surrounding countryside. Public areas include a gracious drawing room and breakfast room, while the mature gardens contain a swimming pool (heated from June 1), a sauna and sunbed, tennis courts and a car park.
8 en suite (bth/shr) (4 fmly) No smoking in 1 bedrooms No smoking in 1 lounge CTV in all bedrooms Direct dial from bedrooms No dogs Cen ht CTV No children 7yrs 12P Outdoor swimming pool (heated) Tennis (hard) Sauna Solarium
CARDS: 🔲 🔲

➤ 🔲🔲🔲 Mrs K Conneely **Faul House** *(L650475)*
Ballyconneely Rd (1m from town, turn right at Connemara Pottery and follow signs) ☎095 21239 FAX 095 21998
15 Mar-Oct
A fine modern farmhouse stands on a quiet and secluded road overlooking Clifden Bay. It is smart and comfortable with large en suite bedrooms, all well furnished and with good views on all sides.
6 en suite (shr) (3 fmly) No smoking in 3 bedrooms No smoking in dining room No smoking in 1 lounge No dogs (ex guide dogs) Cen ht CTV 10P 28 acres sheep, ponies
PRICE GUIDE
ROOMS: d fr IR£33✳

CLIFFONY Co Sligo Map **01** B5

🔲🔲 **GH** 🔲🔲 **Villa Rosa** Donegal Rd, Bunduff (1m N)
☎071 66173
May-Oct rs Nov & Mar-Apr
This comfortable house is situated on the main Sligo/Donegal route and has good parking facilities to the rear. The surrounding area is famous for its historic folklore, walks and beautiful scenery.

6 rms (2 shr) (2 fmly) No smoking in 3 bedrooms No smoking in dining room No smoking in lounges No dogs (ex guide dogs) Cen ht CTV 16P Last d noon
PRICE GUIDE
ROOMS: s fr IR£14; d fr IR£29; wkly b&b fr IR£90; wkly hlf-bd fr IR£180
CARDS: 🔲 🔲 🔲

CLONAKILTY Co Cork Map **01** B2

➤ 🔲 D Jennings **Desert House** *(W390411)* Coast Rd (signposted on N71, 1km E of Clonakilty)
☎023 33331 FAX 023 33048
This Georgian farmhouse, overlooking Clonakilty Bay, is an ideal centre for touring West Cork and Kerry.
5 rms (4 shr) (3 fmly) CTV in all bedrooms Tea and coffee making facilities Cen ht CTV 10P 100 acres dairy mixed Last d 5pm
PRICE GUIDE
ROOMS: s IR£19-IR£21; d IR£28-IR£32; wkly b&b IR£91; wkly hlf-bd IR£170-IR£184
CARDS: 🔲 🔲 🔲

➤ 🔲🔲🔲 Mrs N McCarthy **Duvane** *(W349405)* Ballyduvane (2km SW on N71) ☎023 33129
12 Mar-Oct
About a mile from Clonakilty on the R600 - the main West Cork route which curls around the coastal villages - stands this well kept house decorated in cheerful colours. Comfortable throughout, it offers two fully en suite bedrooms and two which, though they only have showers and wash basins, are adjacent to a bathroom. Guests have their own sitting room, and the dining room serves a breakfast which has recently earned a highly commended award; dinner is available by arrangement. Local amenities include beaches, riding and golf (the 18-hole course at Lisselan being memorable for the fact that players raft across the river between the fourth fairway and green). Car parking facilities are good.
4 rms (2 bth) (2 fmly) CTV in 2 bedrooms Tea and coffee making facilities No dogs (ex guide dogs) Cen ht CTV P Fishing 100 acres beef Last d 7pm

CLONBUR Co Galway Map **01** B4

GH 🔲 **Fairhill** ☎092 46176
Owned and run by Mrs Lynch, who offers a most hospitable service, this village guesthouse has recently been refurbished and boasts a cosy bar which serves food throughout the day.
10 rms (3 shr) (2 fmly) No smoking in lounges CTV in 3 bedrooms Tea and coffee making facilities Licensed Cen ht CTV 1P Tennis (hard) Last d 9.30pm
PRICE GUIDE
ROOMS: s IR£13-IR£15; d IR£26-IR£30✳
CARDS: 🔲 🔲 🔲

CLONMEL Co Tipperary Map **01** C2

🔲🔲 **T&C** 🔲🔲🔲 **Farrenwick** Poulmucka, Curranstown
☎052 35130 FAX 052 35130
A modern house stands on the R687 with good parking and an attractive garden to the front. The bedrooms are fully equipped with TVs, phones, courtesy trays and new orthopoedic beds. There are many local beauty spots and the historic towns of Cashel, Clonmel and Kilkeny are all close by.
4 rms (3 shr) (4 fmly) No smoking CTV in all bedrooms Tea and coffee making facilities Direct dial from bedrooms No dogs (ex guide dogs) Cen ht CTV 10P
PRICE GUIDE
ROOMS: s fr IR£15; d fr IR£26; wkly b&b fr IR£70; wkly hlf-bd fr IR£140

COLERAINE Co Londonderry Map **01** C6

Selected

GH ⓆⓆⓆⓆ **Greenhill House** 24 Greenhill Rd,
Aghadowey BT51 4EU (take A29 for 7m turn onto B66 for
approx 300yds house on right) ☎01265 868241
Mar-Oct
This is a lovely Georgian house standing in its own well-
tended garden in the Bann Valley with views of the Antrim
Hills. It is efficiently run by Elizabeth and James Hegarty:
bedrooms are immaculately maintained and there are many
thoughtful extras. There is also a comfortable sitting room and
dining room where good home-cooked meals are served.
6 en suite (bth/shr) (2 fmly) CTV in all bedrooms Tea and
coffee making facilities No dogs (ex guide dogs) Cen ht
CTV 10P Last d noon
PRICE GUIDE
ROOMS: s fr £27; d fr £44
CARDS: ▨ ▧   £

CORK Co Cork Map **01** B2

GH ⓆⓆⓆ *Antoine House* Western Rd (1m from city centre
on the Cork-Macroom-Killarney road)
☎021 273494 FAX 021 273092
This converted four-storey house is close to the University and
caters for both tourist and commercial clientele.
7 en suite (shr) CTV in all bedrooms Tea and coffee making
facilities Direct dial from bedrooms No dogs (ex guide dogs)
Cen ht CTV 8P
CARDS: ▨ ▧ ▣

GH ⓆⓆⓆ **Garnish House** 1 Aldergrove, Western Rd
☎021 275111 FAX 021 273872
This is a three-storey house opposite the University on the main
Cork/Killarney road.
13 en suite (bth/shr) (1 fmly) CTV in all bedrooms Tea and
coffee making facilities Direct dial from bedrooms No dogs (ex
guide dogs) Cen ht CTV 10P
CARDS: ▨ ▬ ▣

GH ⓆⓆⓆ **Killarney House** Western Rd (opposite University
College) ☎021 270290 & 270179 FAX 021 271010
Closed 25-26 Dec
Mrs O'Leary is the welcoming owner of this newly decorated,
well equipped guest house which stands near Cork University on
the N22 road. The 18 en suite bedrooms all have TVs, telephones
and tea/coffee making facilities. A lounge is available to guests
and there is a large car park behind the house.
18 en suite (bth/shr) (3 fmly) No smoking in 10 bedrooms CTV
in all bedrooms Tea and coffee making facilities Direct dial from
bedrooms No dogs (ex guide dogs) Cen ht CTV 15P
PRICE GUIDE
ROOMS: s IR£25-IR£45; d IR£40-IR£55✳
CARDS: ▨ ▬ ▧

GH ⓆⓆⓆ **Roserie Villa** Mardyke Walk, off Western Rd (take
N22 from city centre, pass Jury's hotel on left, turn right at
University College gates, right again and hotel on right)
☎021 272958 FAX 021 274087
This family-run guest house stands just ten minutes' walk from
the city centre. The en suite bedrooms are well appointed and
equipped with TVs, telephones and tea/coffee making facilities.
Off-street parking is available.

16 en suite (shr) (4 fmly) No smoking in dining room CTV in all
bedrooms Tea and coffee making facilities Direct dial from
bedrooms No dogs (ex guide dogs) Cen ht CTV No children
5yrs 8P
PRICE GUIDE
ROOMS: s IR£22.50-IR£30; d IR£35-IR£50; wkly b&b IR£115-
IR£150
CARDS: ▨ ▬ ▧ ▣

GH ⓆⓆⓆ *St Kilda's* Western Rd ☎021 273095 & 275374
FAX 021 275015
A comfortable guest house offers well equipped bedrooms with
TVs, telephones and hair dryers. There is a hospitality trolley in
the guest lounge and a car park in front of the building. Personal
supervision by the owners is attentive and hospitable.
13 rms (12 bth/shr) (1 fmly) CTV in all bedrooms Direct dial
from bedrooms No dogs (ex guide dogs) Cen ht CTV 14P
CARDS: ▨ ▧

COROFIN Co Clare Map **01** B3

♥ ⓆⓆⓆ Mary Kelleher **Fergus View** *(R265919)* Kilnaboy
(2 miles north of Corofin en route to Kilfenora, past the ruins of
Kilnaboy Church) ☎065 37606 FAX 065 37192
Etr-Sep
Sensitively renovated to provide an excellent standard of comfort,
this fourth generation family home is an attractive farmhouse,
centrally located for touring the Burren area. Mary Kelleher
enjoys cooking and wherever possible uses all home-grown
vegetables to prepare the meals.

AA
QQQ

DUVANE FARM

Ballyduvane, Clonakilty
West Cork
Telephone: 00 353 23 33129
Elegant Georgian house situated on a beef farm,
2 km from Clonakilty on N71 on Skibbereen side
of town. Brass and canopy beds, TV, tea/coffee
in bedrooms. Breakfast award winner, all meals
from local and home producers. Leisure activities.
Perfect house and location for touring Cork and
Kerry. Bed & breakfast en suite £18-£20. Dinner
£14. High tea £10. Single supplement £5.

6 rms (5 shr) (4 fmly) No smoking in bedrooms No smoking in dining room No dogs Licensed Cen ht CTV 8P 17 acres non-working Last d noon
PRICE GUIDE
ROOMS: s IR£21-IR£23; d IR£30-IR£34; wkly b&b IR£105-IR£119; wkly hlf-bd IR£203-IR£217

CRATLOE Co Clare Map **01** B3

GH Q Q Q **Bunratty View** Bunratty View (1m from Bunratty Castle, 1st turn left off Shannon/Limerick (N18) as you travel from Bunratty to Limerick) ☎061 357352 FAX 061 357491
6 en suite (bth/shr) (4 fmly) No smoking in bedrooms No smoking in lounges CTV in all bedrooms Tea and coffee making facilities Direct dial from bedrooms No dogs Cen ht CTV 20P
PRICE GUIDE
ROOMS: s IR£22; d IR£30-IR£36✱
CARDS: 💳 💳

CROSSHAVEN Co Cork Map **01** B2

GH Q Q Q *Whispering Pines* ☎021 831843 & 831448 FAX 021 831679
There is something particularly inviting about this comfortable guesthouse with its sun lounge and bar overlooking the river. The Twomey family are most hospitable and cater well for all guests, particularly anglers, for whom a fishing boat and equipment is available for hire. Transfer from Cork Airport can be arranged if required.
15 en suite (bth/shr) (6 fmly) Direct dial from bedrooms No dogs (ex guide dogs) Licensed Cen ht CTV 40P Own angling boats fish daily Last d 9.30pm
CARDS: 💳 💳 💳 💳

CRUSHEEN Co Clare Map **01** B3

♥ Q Q Q Dilly Griffey *Lahardan (R397889)* Lahardan ☎065 27128 FAX 065 27319
rs Nov-Apr
This sensitively restored farmhouse stands on 300 acres of land off the Galway to Limerick road near Ennis. It is a charming old building with spacious rooms that invite relaxation. Guests will experience true hospitality from the welcoming Griffey family, and evening meals are served.
8 en suite (bth/shr) (4 fmly) No smoking in bedrooms No dogs Licensed Cen ht CTV No parking 230 acres beef Last d 3pm
CARDS: 💳 💳

DINGLE Co Kerry Map **01** A2

GH Q Q Q **Alpine** Mail Rd ☎066 51250 FAX 066 51966
On the edge of Dingle, this large, three-storey guesthouse is run by the O'Shea family, who maintain excellent standards.
13 en suite (shr) (4 fmly) No smoking in dining room CTV in all bedrooms No dogs Cen ht CTV 20P No coaches
PRICE GUIDE
ROOMS: s IR£16.50-IR£30; d IR£28-IR£37
CARDS: 💳 💳

T&C Q Q Q **Ard-na-Greine House** Spa Rd
☎066 51113 & 51898 FAX 066 51898
This modern bungalow is situated on the edge of town towards Connor Pass. All the rooms are en suite and offer an unrivalled range of facilities.

---

4 en suite (bth/shr) (2 fmly) No smoking CTV in all bedrooms Tea and coffee making facilities Direct dial from bedrooms No dogs (ex guide dogs) Cen ht CTV No children 7yrs 4P
PRICE GUIDE
ROOMS: d IR£30-IR£34
CARDS: 💳 💳 💳

T&C Q Q Q **Ard-Na-Mara** Ballymore, Ventry ☎066 59072
Etr-Oct
This comfortable country house overlooks Ventry harbour two miles out of Dingle. The bedrooms are en suite with tea/coffee facilities. There is a very good breakfast menu and warm hospitality from the Murphy family.
4 en suite (shr) (1 fmly) No smoking in dining room Tea and coffee making facilities No dogs Cen ht CTV P Last d day before
PRICE GUIDE
ROOMS: s IR£21; d IR£32

T&C Q Q **Ballyegan House** Upper John St ☎066 51702
6 en suite (shr) (4 fmly) No dogs Cen ht CTV P No coaches
PRICE GUIDE
ROOMS: d IR£33✱

Selected

T&C Q Q Q Q **Bambury's** Mail Rd
☎066 51244 FAX 066 51786
Set on the edge of Dingle, this pink house is eyecatching on the outside and attractive on the inside with pretty decor and comfortable appointments. There is a cosy lounge and a spacious dining room. En suite bedrooms are excellent with pine furnishings, pottery lamps, tea/coffee trays and big showers. The friendly Mrs Bambury is very helpful.
12 en suite (shr) CTV in all bedrooms Direct dial from bedrooms Cen ht CTV P
PRICE GUIDE
ROOMS: d IR£32-IR£44✱
CARDS: 💳

T&C Q Q **Dingle Heights** Ballinaboola (proceed up Main Street for 0.5m until hospital, house 3rd on right after further 200yds) ☎066 51543
Set high overlooking Dingle Bay, this house features comfortable, well-appointed accomodation and the hospitality of owner Mrs Fitzgerald.
4 rms (3 bth/shr) (4 fmly) No dogs Cen ht CTV 10P
PRICE GUIDE
ROOMS: s IR£18-IR£21; d IR£30-IR£36; wkly b&b IR£100-IR£120✱

Selected

GH Q Q Q Q **Doyles Town House** 4 John St
☎066 51174 FAX 066 51816
mid Mar-mid Nov
Stella and John Doyle are the warm and friendly owners of this charming town house. Bedrooms are spacious, well equipped and tasteful, with period furnishings and marble tiled bathrooms. Adjoining the house is their award-winning and very popular seafood restaurant, where the chat flows easily as guests make selections from the lobster tank or try the catch of the day specials.

8 en suite (bth/shr) No smoking in area of dining room CTV in all bedrooms Direct dial from bedrooms No dogs (ex guide dogs) Licensed Cen ht Last d 9.30pm
PRICE GUIDE
ROOMS: s IR£42; d IR£65*
CARDS: 🔳 🔳 🔳

Selected

T&C QQQQ *Greenmount House* (on entering town turn right at roundabout & next right at T jct)
☎066 51414 FAX 066 51974
Closed 20-29 Dec
Set on a hillside overlooking Dingle Harbour, Greenmount is run with great dedication and warm hospitality by Mary and John Curran. The accommodation is very comfortable, and Mary's award-winning breakfasts are served in the charming dining room. Car parking facilities are good.
6 en suite (bth/shr) No smoking in bedrooms No smoking in dining room CTV in all bedrooms Direct dial from bedrooms No dogs (ex guide dogs) Cen ht CTV No children 8yrs 6P
CARDS: 🔳 🔳

Selected

GH QQQQ *Milltown House* Milltown (1m W of Dingle on Slea Head road, cross Milltown Bridge and turn left)
☎066 51372 FAX 066 51095
Situated on a sea channel to the west of town, the house has been elegantly refurbished and has a warm inviting atmosphere, Mr and Mrs Gill making guests feel really welcome. Bedrooms are all en suite, have attractive decor and are well equipped. There is also a cosy sitting room leading to a conservatory.
10 en suite (bth/shr) (3 fmly) No smoking in dining room No smoking in 1 lounge CTV in all bedrooms Tea and coffee making facilities Direct dial from bedrooms No dogs (ex guide dogs) Cen ht No children 5yrs 10P No coaches Mini golf Last d 2.30pm
PRICE GUIDE
ROOMS: s IR£40; d IR£50; wkly b&b IR£140-IR£175; wkly hlf-bd IR£245-IR£280*
CARDS: 🔳 🔳

♥ QQQ Mr M Hurley *Hurleys* (Q392080) An Dooneen, Kilcooley ☎066 55112
Etr-Oct
Despite its sombre exterior Hurleys farm is a welcoming and comfortable house featuring relaxing bedrooms, some with large shower rooms. An evening meal is available by arrangement.
4 en suite (shr) No smoking in 1 lounge No dogs (ex guide dogs) Cen ht CTV 32 acres mixed
PRICE GUIDE
ROOMS: s IR£18; d IR£32

DONEGAL Co Donegal Map **01** B5

T&C QQ **Ardeevin** Lough Eske, Barnesmore
☎073 21790 FAX 073 21790
Apr-Oct
This comfortable homely house enjoys a lovely location high above Lough Eske and with superb views of lake and mountain. Well appointed bedrooms have en suite facilities.

---

5 en suite (bth/shr) (2 fmly) No smoking in dining room No smoking in lounges CTV in 1 bedroom Tea and coffee making facilities No dogs Cen ht CTV No children 9yrs 10P No coaches Last d noon
PRICE GUIDE
ROOMS: s IR£19; d IR£32*

DOOLIN Co Clare Map **01** B3

T&C QQQ *Churchfield* (in Doolin village)
☎065 74209 FAX 065 74622
Closed 20-27 Dec
6 rms (5 shr) (3 fmly) Cen ht CTV 12P
CARDS: 🔳 🔳

♥ QQQ J Moloney *Horse Shoe* (R073971) (on N67)
☎065 74006 FAX 065 74421
Closed Nov-Dec
This comfortable farmhouse is the home of the hospitable Moloney family and overlooks a village famous for traditional Irish music. They have a tennis court in the pleasant gardens, and can lend racquets to their guests, and there are bicycles for hire and a bureau de change service.
5 en suite (shr) No dogs (ex guide dogs) Cen ht CTV P Tennis (hard) Boat trips Rent-a-bike 20 acres dairy
CARDS: 🔳

DOWNPATRICK Co Down Map **01** D5

♥ QQ Mrs Macauley *Havine* (J457384) 51 Bally Donnel Rd, Ballykilbeg BT30 8EP ☎01396 851242
Closed Xmas wk
Palm trees grow in the garden of this modernised 18th-century farmhouse. Mrs McAuley is a genial host and many guests return regularly for the genuine home-from-home atmosphere. Bedrooms are small but comfortable, and there is a choice of lounges, one of which has a communal table where enjoyable home cooking is served.
3 rms No smoking in bedrooms No smoking in dining room No smoking in 1 lounge Tea and coffee making facilities No dogs P 125 acres beef sheep

---

DROGHEDA Co Louth Map **01** D4

Selected

T&C QQQQ *Tullyesker House* Monasterboice (3m N on Drogheda/Belfast road N1 on right just past Papal Cross)
☎041 30430 & 32624
Closed 23-30 Dec
This large family-run house occupies a spectacular site on Tullyesker Hill, overlooking the Boyne Valley and Drogheda. Many of the well equipped and beautifully decorated rooms look out over the lovely gardens and wooded grounds. Historic and archaeological sites abound in the area.
5 en suite (shr) (2 fmly) No smoking in dining room CTV in all bedrooms Tea and coffee making facilities No dogs (ex guide dogs) Cen ht CTV No children 7yrs 22P Tennis (hard)
PRICE GUIDE
ROOMS: d IR£36-IR£44

DUBLIN Co Dublin Map **01** D4

Selected

GH QQQQ *Aaron House* 152 Merrion Rd, Ballsbridge
☎01 2601644 & 2601650 FAX 01 2601651
Closed 24-26 Dec
6 en suite (shr) (1 fmly) No smoking in 3 bedrooms No smoking in dining room Tea and coffee making facilities No dogs (ex guide dogs) Cen ht CTV 6P
CARDS: 🔳 🔳

T&C QQQ *Aaronmor House* 1c Sandymount Av, Ballsbridge
☎01 6687972 FAX 01 6682377
This family run house is comfortably furnished and decorated and is situated close to the Royal Dublin Society Showgrounds and Lansdowne rugby ground.
6 en suite (shr) (2 fmly) CTV in 1 bedroom Tea and coffee making facilities No dogs (ex guide dogs) Cen ht CTV No children 5yrs 8P No coaches Last d 10am
CARDS: 🔳 🔳

Premier Selected

GH QQQQQ *Aberdeen Lodge* 53/55 Park Av
☎01 2838155
FAX 01 2837877
This particularly fine early Edwardian house stands on one of Dublin's most prestigious roads near to the main hotel and embassy suburb in Dublin. Bedrooms are fully equipped and there are suites with air spa baths.
It has its own car park and is only minutes away from the centre by DART or bus, as well as being easily accessible from the airport and car ferries. Dinner is served and a Christmas Programme is available.
16 en suite (bth/shr) (8 fmly) CTV in all bedrooms Direct dial from bedrooms No dogs Licensed Cen ht CTV 16P Last d 9pm
CARDS: 🔳 🔳 🔳 🔳

Premier Selected

GH QQQQQ *Ariel House* 52 Lansdowne Rd (turn off at Irish Bank Ballsbridge on left before Lansdowne Rugby Stadium) ☎01 6685512
FAX 01 6685845
Closed 23 Dec-14 Jan
A luxurious Victorian mansion built in 1850 is situated beside Lansdowne Rugby grounds. Charming

proprietors provide guests with every comfort in attractive bedrooms with authentic period antiques. A full cooked breakfast is available at extra charge.

28 en suite (bth/shr) No smoking in bedrooms No smoking in dining room No smoking in 1 lounge CTV in all bedrooms Direct dial from bedrooms No dogs Licensed Cen ht CTV No children 5yrs 40P
PRICE GUIDE
ROOMS: s IR£49.50-IR£120; d IR£70-IR£125; wkly b&b IR£280✱
CARDS: 🔳 🔳 🔳

GH QQQ *Beddington* 181 Rathgar Rd
☎01 4978047 FAX 01 4978275
Closed 23 Dec-13 Jan
At the city end of Rathgar Road, near Rathmines, this comfortable, well maintained house offers beds made up with crisp linen sheets in its attractive bedrooms. There is a residents' lounge, and the premises are licensed. There is secure car parking at the rear, and the hotel stands on a direct bus route to the city centre, three kilometres away.
14 en suite (shr) (1 fmly) No smoking in dining room No smoking in lounges CTV in all bedrooms Tea and coffee making facilities Direct dial from bedrooms Licensed Cen ht CTV No children 7yrs 10P
PRICE GUIDE
ROOMS: s IR£30-IR£35; d IR£55-IR£60✱
CARDS: 🔳 🔳 🔳

GH QQQ *Belgrave* 8-10 Belgrave Square, Rathmines
☎01 4963760 & 4962549 FAX 01 4979243
Closed 23-31 Dec
Interlinked period houses stand in a residential suburb convenient for the city centre and has been recently refurbished to be well appointed throughout. Beedrooms are well decorated and comprehensively equipped with TVs, telephones, tea/coffee making facilities and comfortable semi-orthapoedic beds, while public areas include a comfortable sitting room and a dining room overlooking the gardens. The resident owners are helpful and car parking is available.
18 en suite (shr) (1 fmly) No smoking in area of dining room CTV in all bedrooms Tea and coffee making facilities Direct dial from bedrooms No dogs (ex guide dogs) Cen ht CTV 7P No coaches
PRICE GUIDE
ROOMS: s IR£30-IR£35; d IR£50-IR£60; wkly b&b IR£190-IR£225✱
CARDS: 🔳 🔳 🔳

Premier Selected

GH QQQQQ *Cedar Lodge* 98 Merrion Rd, Ballsbridge (opposite the British Embassy)
☎01 6684410
FAX 01 6684533
A lovely old house with a modern extension is set back from the Dunlaoghaire Road opposite the new British Embassy and offers comfortable, fully equipped

bedrooms. There is ample parking with a secure area to the rear and full access for the disabled.
10 en suite (bth/shr) (3 fmly) No smoking in dining room No smoking in lounges CTV in all bedrooms Tea and coffee

making facilities Direct dial from bedrooms No dogs Cen ht
CTV 18P
PRICE GUIDE
ROOMS: s IR£30-IR£90; d IR£55-IR£90; wkly b&b
IR£210-IR£630∗
CARDS: 🄰 ▆ 🖭

Selected

GH 🅀🅀🅀🅀 **Charleville** 268/272 North Circular Rd
☎01 8386633 FAX 01 8385854
Closed 19-26 Dec
Situated close to the city centre near Phoenix Park, this
elegant terrace of Victorian houses has been tastefully
restored to a high standard. The two interconnecting lounges
are welcoming and the smart dining room offers a choice of
breakfasts. Bedrooms are very comfortable with pleasant
decor and there is a secure car park for guests' use.
20 rms (17 shr) (2 fmly) No smoking in bedrooms CTV in
all bedrooms Direct dial from bedrooms No dogs (ex guide
dogs) Cen ht CTV 30P
PRICE GUIDE
ROOMS: s IR£25-IR£42.50; d IR£40-IR£65; wkly b&b
IR£126-IR£210
CARDS: 🄰 ▆ 🖭

T&C 🅀🅀🅀 **Charlston Manor** 15/16 Charlston Rd, Ranelagh
(on main road between Renalagh & Rathmines)
☎01 4910262 FAX 01 4565140
5 en suite (shr) CTV in all bedrooms Tea and coffee making
facilities No dogs Cen ht 8P No coaches
PRICE GUIDE
ROOMS: s fr IR£30; d fr IR£50∗

T&C 🅀🅀 **Clifden** 32 Gardiner Place (city centre)
☎01 8746364 FAX 01 8746122
10 en suite (shr) (4 fmly) No smoking in dining room No
smoking in lounges CTV in all bedrooms Tea and coffee making
facilities Direct dial from bedrooms No dogs Cen ht CTV 12P
No coaches
PRICE GUIDE
ROOMS: s IR£20-IR£45; d IR£40-IR£80∗
CARDS: 🄰 🖭

GH 🅀🅀🅀 **Egan's** 7/9 Iona Park, Glasnevin
☎01 8303611 & 8305283 FAX 01 8303312
Situated in a quiet suburb on the north side of the city, this
Victorian, red-brick, streetside house has large, comfortable
bedrooms, relaxing lounges and good gardens at the rear. It is a
family-run house renowned for its friendly and cheerful
atmosphere and is conveniently located for the National Botanic
Gardens and airport.
25 en suite (shr) (4 fmly) No smoking in dining room CTV in all
bedrooms Tea and coffee making facilities Direct dial from
bedrooms Licensed Cen ht 8P Last d 8pm
PRICE GUIDE
ROOMS: s IR£32.50-IR£38.50; d IR£57.20-IR£66∗
CARDS: 🄰 🖭

GH 🅀🅀🅀 **The Fitzwilliam** 41 Upper Fitzwilliam St
☎01 6600199 FAX 01 6767488
5 Jan-15 Dec
Situated in the heart of Georgian Dublin, this house has been
newly renovated to a very high standard. Ideal for business people
and tourists it is close to the National Concert Hall. ➡

12 en suite (bth/shr) (1 fmly) CTV in all bedrooms Direct dial from bedrooms Licensed Cen ht CTV 4P Last d 10.30pm
PRICE GUIDE
ROOMS: s IR£33-IR£34.60; d IR£50-IR£75✳
CARDS: 💷 ■ 🔀 ⑩

Selected

GH 🅀🅀🅀🅀 **Glenogra** 64 Merrion Rd, Ballsbridge (opposite Royal Dublin's Showgrounds)
☎01 6683661 & 6683698 FAX 01 6683698
Closed 24 Dec-6 Jan & 2wks in Spring
This fine gabled house run by Cherry and Seamus McNamee is only 2.5 miles from the centre of Dublin and stands in a pleasant suburb opposite the RDS Centre. The house offers comfort with more than a touch of elegance, and the atmosphere is exceptionally welcoming.
9 en suite (bth/shr) (1 fmly) No smoking in dining room CTV in all bedrooms Tea and coffee making facilities Direct dial from bedrooms No dogs (ex guide dogs) Cen ht CTV 10P
PRICE GUIDE
ROOMS: s IR£40-IR£50; d IR£60-IR£80✳
CARDS: 💷 🔀

Premier Selected

GH 🅀🅀🅀🅀🅀 **The Grey Door** 22/23 Upper Pembroke St (city centre, close to St Stephens Green and Grafton Street) ☎01 6763286
FAX 01 6763287
rs Bank Hols
Situated a few minutes from the city centre, this tastefully restored town house is a jewel in the heart of Georgian Dublin. En suite bedrooms are very comfortable with rich fabrics enhancing the gracious atmosphere. Public areas include a charming first-floor sitting room, a spacious private dining room and a choice of two restaurants, the well known 'Grey Door' and the recently redesigned 'Blushers' specialising in seafood. An extra charge is made for cooked breakfast.
7 en suite (bth/shr) (2 fmly) No smoking in 1 bedrooms No smoking in area of dining room No smoking in lounges CTV in all bedrooms Tea and coffee making facilities Direct dial from bedrooms No dogs (ex guide dogs) Licensed Cen ht No parking Last d 11.30pm
PRICE GUIDE
ROOMS: s IR£70; d IR£90✳
CARDS: 💷 ■ 🔀 ⑩

T&C 🅀🅀🅀 **Herbert Lodge** 65 Morehampton Rd, Donnybrook (1.25m from city centre on N11)
☎01 6603403 FAX 01 4730919
Closed 22 Dec-6 Jan

---

6 en suite (shr) (3 fmly) No smoking in 3 bedrooms CTV in all bedrooms Tea and coffee making facilities Direct dial from bedrooms No dogs (ex guide dogs) Cen ht CTV 2P
PRICE GUIDE
ROOMS: s IR£25-IR£40; d IR£50-IR£70; wkly b&b IR£150-IR£280
CARDS: 💷 ■ 🔀

GH 🅀🅀🅀 **Highfield House** 1 Highfield Rd, Rathgar
☎01 4977068 FAX 01 4973991
17 rms (12 bth/shr) (4 fmly) No smoking in 6 bedrooms No smoking in area of dining room No dogs (ex guide dogs) Cen ht CTV 20P
PRICE GUIDE
ROOMS: s IR£25-IR£35; d IR£50-IR£60
CARDS: 💷 🔀

GH 🅀🅀🅀 **Iona House** 5 Iona Park ☎01 8306217 & 8306855 FAX 01 8306742
Closed Dec-Jan
Situated in a quiet residential suburb on the north side of the city, this family-run Victorian red-brick house has large modern bedrooms, a comfortable lounge and a small garden for exclusive use of guests. It is conveniently located for National Botanic Gardens and airport.
12 en suite (shr) (4 fmly) No smoking in area of dining room CTV in 11 bedrooms Direct dial from bedrooms Cen ht No children 3yrs
PRICE GUIDE
ROOMS: s IR£29; d IR£58✳
CARDS: 💷 🔀

Selected

GH 🅀🅀🅀🅀 **Kingswood Country House** Old Kingswood, Naas Rd, Clondalkin D22
☎01 4592428 & 4592207 FAX 01 4592428
Closed 25-28 Dec & Good Fri rs Sat & Sun
Situated off the N7, turn left past Newlands Cross en route from Dublin. This Georgian house offers attractive en suite bedrooms, a cosy sitting room and an intimate restaurant specialising in good home cooking. The proprietors make guests feel very welcome here and there are also well maintained gardens and ample car parking facilities.
7 en suite (bth/shr) (2 fmly) CTV in all bedrooms Direct dial from bedrooms No dogs (ex guide dogs) Licensed Cen ht 60P No coaches Last d 10.30pm
PRICE GUIDE
ROOMS: s IR£45-IR£67; d IR£62-IR£90
CARDS: 💷 ■ 🔀 ⑩

T&C 🅀🅀🅀 **Marelle** 92 Rathfarnham Rd, Terenure
☎01 4904690
This attractive house, recently refurbished, is set back from the road in its own gardens. It has good parking facilities.
6 rms (5 shr) (1 fmly) CTV in all bedrooms No dogs Cen ht CTV No children 5yrs 8P No coaches Last d 10am
PRICE GUIDE
ROOMS: s IR£28-IR£30; d IR£44-IR£50✳
CARDS: 💷 🔀

GH Q Q Q Q **Merrion Hall** 54-56 Merrion Rd, Ballsbridge D4 ☎01 6681426 FAX 01 6684280
Closed 20 Dec-1 Jan
This elegant town house stands right opposite the R.D.S. showgrounds in Ballsbridge. The friendly owners provide a warm welcome and excellent attention to detail. There is a fine sitting room and a separate breakfast room overlooking the attractive gardens; a good choice is available at breakfast. The en suite bedrooms are comfortable and offer a range of facilities.
15 en suite (bth/shr) (4 fmly) CTV in all bedrooms Tea and coffee making facilities Direct dial from bedrooms No dogs Cen ht CTV 10P
PRICE GUIDE
ROOMS: s IR£40-IR£80; d IR£55-IR£90
CARDS: 🔳 🎫

T&C Q Q Q Q **Morehampton Lodge** 113 Morehampton Rd, Donnybrook ☎01 2837499 FAX 01 2837595
Totally restored to a high standard, this Victorian house is very conveniently situated near the city centre and good bus routes. Excellent bedrooms are provided, and off-street parking is available.
5 en suite (bth/shr) (3 fmly) No smoking CTV in all bedrooms Tea and coffee making facilities Direct dial from bedrooms No dogs Cen ht 7P
PRICE GUIDE
ROOMS: s IR£40-IR£50; d IR£55-IR£70✳
CARDS: 🔳 🎫

GH Q Q Q Q **Mount Herbert Ltd** 7 Herbert Rd ☎01 6684321 FAX 01 6607077
Guests return again and again to this guesthouse where the Loughran family and staff provide a welcoming service. Porters are on duty to help the guests with their luggage. The bedrooms are comfortable and well equipped and the pleasant restaurant located at garden level serves good food. There is a children's playground, badminton and good parking. It stands beside the Lansdowne rugby ground and close to the city centre and transport systems.
140 en suite (bth/shr) (9 fmly) No smoking in area of dining room CTV in all bedrooms Direct dial from bedrooms No dogs (ex guide dogs) Licensed Lift Cen ht CTV 120P Sauna Solarium Badminton court Children's playground Last d 9.30pm
PRICE GUIDE
ROOMS: s IR£38-IR£43; d IR£55-IR£65.50✳
CARDS: 🔳 🔳 🎫 💿

Selected

T&C ꆇꆇꆇꆇ **Northumberland Lodge** 68
Northumberland Rd, Ballsbridge (beside US Embassy)
☎01 6605270 FAX 01 6688679
This gracious Georgian house stands in a convenient location,
close to the city centre and the Lansdowne road rugby ground
and a few minutes from the public transport systems. Bridget
and Tony Brady enjoy welcoming guests to their charming
home. The large, well equipped bedrooms are all en suite and
there are attractive gardens.
6 en suite (bth/shr) CTV in all bedrooms Tea and coffee
making facilities Direct dial from bedrooms No dogs (ex
guide dogs) Cen ht CTV 6P
PRICE GUIDE
ROOMS: s IR£30-IR£50; d IR£45-IR£65✱
CARDS: ▨ ▨

Selected

GH ꆇꆇꆇꆇ *Raglan Lodge* 10 Raglan Rd, Ballsbridge
☎01 6606697 FAX 01 6606781
Closed 22-31 Dec
This charming restored Victorian Lodge stands on a tree-lined
road close to the US embassy, the RDS showground and
within easy reach of the city centre. En suite bedrooms are
comfortable with good facilities and antique furnishings, and
a fine dining room serves a breakfast that received the Irish
Breakfast Award for 1993. Guests also have use of a garden
and secure car parking.
7 en suite (bth/shr) (4 fmly) No smoking in 2 bedrooms
CTV in all bedrooms Tea and coffee making facilities Direct
dial from bedrooms Cen ht CTV 12P No coaches
CARDS: ▨ ▨ ▨

Selected

T&C ꆇꆇꆇꆇ **No 66** Northumberland Rd, Ballsbridge
☎01 6600333 & 6600471 FAX 01 6601051
This imposing house has six comfortable bedrooms all fully
equipped to a very high standard. Attractive public areas
include a dining room and two comfortable lounges, one in a
lovely conservatory. It is very convenient for the city,
Landsdowne Road and the RDS showgrounds.
6 en suite (shr) (2 fmly) No smoking in dining room No
smoking in lounges CTV in all bedrooms Tea and coffee
making facilities Direct dial from bedrooms No dogs (ex
guide dogs) Cen ht CTV 4P No coaches
PRICE GUIDE
ROOMS: s IR£35-IR£45; d IR£50-IR£65; wkly b&b
IR£210-IR£315✱
CARDS: ▨ ▨

GH ꆇꆇꆇ **St Aiden's** 32 Brighton Rd, Rathgar
☎01 4902011 & 4906178 FAX 01 4920234
This Victorian house is situated 15 minutes' drive south of the city
centre, near Rathgan village, and has secure off-street parking.
Eight en suite bedrooms are well equipped with TVs telephones
and hair dryers. A restful drawing room with a tea/coffee trolley
and a separate breakfaast room are also available.

10 rms (7 bth/shr) (3 fmly) No smoking in 3 bedrooms No
smoking in dining room CTV in all bedrooms Direct dial from
bedrooms No dogs Licensed Cen ht CTV 8P
PRICE GUIDE
ROOMS: s IR£25-IR£40; d IR£40-IR£66✱
CARDS: ▨ ▨

DUNGANNON Co Tyrone Map **01** C5

Premier Selected

GH ꆇꆇꆇꆇꆇ **Grange**
Lodge 7 Grange Rd BT71 7EJ
(1m from M1 junct 15 on
A29 Armagh)
☎01868 784212
FAX 01868 723891
Closed 21 Dec-9 Jan
Many guests return year after
year to Ralph and Norah
Brown's charming country
house, set in 20 acres of well
laid gardens. Bedrooms are
small, but individually styled and provided with many thoughtful
extras. Fine paintings, fresh flowers and antiques adorn the
drawing room, and the separate small lounge offers a selection of
books and board games as well as TV. Enjoyable home cooking
is served at individual tables in the elegant dining room.
5 en suite (bth/shr) No smoking in bedrooms No smoking in
dining room No smoking in 1 lounge CTV in all bedrooms
Tea and coffee making facilities Direct dial from bedrooms
No dogs (ex guide dogs) Cen ht CTV No children 12yrs
12P No coaches Tennis (hard) Last d 1pm
PRICE GUIDE
ROOMS: s £39-£45; d £59-£65
CARDS: ▨ ▨ £

DUNGARVAN Co Waterford Map **01** C2

♥ ꆇꆇ Miss B Lynch *Killineen House* (X302963) Waterford Rd
(off N25, 4.5m E) ☎051 91294
This attractive house with well-tended gardens and views of
Comeragh mountains is situated four miles east of town on
Waterford road.
5 rms (3 shr) (3 fmly) No smoking in bedrooms Tea and coffee
making facilities Cen ht CTV 10P 50 acres grass Last d 5pm

DUN LAOGHAIRE Co Dublin Map **01** D4

T&C ꆇꆇ **Ferry House** 15 Clarinda Park North ☎01 2808301
FAX 01 2846530
Closed Xmas & holidays
Large Victorian house overlooking People's Park.
6 rms (3 shr) (2 fmly) CTV in all bedrooms No dogs (ex guide
dogs) Cen ht CTV No children 5yrs No parking No coaches
PRICE GUIDE
ROOMS: s IR£20-IR£22; d IR£34-IR£40✱
CARDS: ▨ ▨

T&C ꆇꆇ **Harkins** 7 Claremont Villas, (off Adelaide Road),
Glenageary ☎01 2805346
5 rms (4 bth/shr) (4 fmly) No smoking in bedrooms No smoking
in dining room Cen ht CTV No parking
PRICE GUIDE
ROOMS: d IR£36
CARDS: ▨ ▨ ▨ ▨

T&C Q Q Q Willowmere 39 York Rd
☎01 2844870 FAX 01 2844870
An attractive house stands on a quiet road off Georges Street
Upper, convenient for the buses, trains and car ferry. There is a
comfortable lounge and a range of spacious bedrooms, some with
en suite facilities. Complementary tea/coffee is available in the
evenings.
4 rms (2 shr) No smoking in bedrooms No smoking in dining
room CTV in all bedrooms No dogs (ex guide dogs) Cen ht 5P
No coaches
PRICE GUIDE
ROOMS: d IR£36-IR£45✱
CARDS: 🔳 🎫

DUNLAVIN Co Wicklow Map **01** C3

♥ Q Q Q Mr & Mrs J Lawler Tynte House *(N870015)*
☎045 49561 FAX 045 401586
Closed 23 Dec-2 Jan
A fine 19th-century farmhouse stands in the main street of this
quiet country village with farmland reaching to the back door. The
large bedrooms are very comfortable and look out over Market
House to the front or the farm to the rear. The house is
conveniently positioned for all the tourist attractions of Wicklow.
7 en suite (bth/shr) (2 fmly) No smoking in 2 bedrooms No
smoking in area of dining room Direct dial from bedrooms No
dogs Cen ht CTV ch fac Tennis (hard) Playground 200 acres
arable beef
PRICE GUIDE
ROOMS: s IR£18; d IR£30; wkly b&b IR£105-IR£126; wkly
hlf-bd IR£182-IR£203✱

DUNMORE EAST Co Waterford Map **01** C2

Selected

♥ Q Q Q Q Mrs M Kent Foxmount *(S659091)* Passage
East Rd, Off Dunmore Rd (from Waterford take Dunmore
East road, afetr 3.5m take left fork at Maxol garage towards
Passage East for 0.5m. Right at next Y junct and right befor
☎051 74308
10 Mar-4 Nov
This charming 17th-century country house is set on a busy
dairy farm amidst beautiful lawns and gardens with screening
trees and a hard tennis court. Tastefully modernised, it offers
four en suite bedrooms and attentive service from the
charming hostess. The farm and gardens provide most of the
raw materials for the carefully prepared evening meals.
6 en suite (bth/shr) (2 fmly) No smoking No dogs (ex guide
dogs) Cen ht CTV 6P Tennis (hard) 200 acres dairy Last d
6pm
PRICE GUIDE
ROOMS: s IR£22-IR£25; d IR£34-IR£40; wkly b&b
IR£119-IR£140; wkly hlf-bd IR£210-IR£220✱

DUNSHAUGHLIN Co Meath Map **01** D4

Selected

T&C Q Q Q Q Old Workhouse Ballinlough
☎01 8259251
This striking cut-stone listed building (c1841) was indeed
once a workhouse and has now been tastefully restored. There
are four attractive bedrooms (two en suite and two on the
ground floor sharing a bathroom), and the cosy TV lounge

and the drawing room (formerly the governor's board room)
are filled with antiques. The atmosphere is welcoming and the
cooking is excellent - please reserve dinner. Local tours can
be arranged and fishing, riding and shooting are all available
nearby. Dublin airport is within 45 minutes' drive.
4 rms (2 bth/shr) (1 fmly) No smoking in bedrooms CTV in
all bedrooms Tea and coffee making facilities Cen ht CTV
50P Last d noon
PRICE GUIDE
ROOMS: s fr IR£25; d IR£30-IR£35; wkly b&b IR£44-
IR£50

ENNIS Co Clare Map **01** B3

T&C Q Q Q Carraig Mhuire Barefield
☎065 27106 FAX 065 27375
This attractive and comfortable bungalow is set back from the
main Galway road in well-tended gardens. Well-equipped
bedrooms are welcoming and nothing is too much trouble for
charming hosts Mr and Mrs Morris.
5 rms (3 shr) (1 fmly) No smoking in bedrooms No smoking in
dining room Tea and coffee making facilities No dogs (ex guide
dogs) Cen ht CTV 6P Last d noon
PRICE GUIDE
ROOMS: s IR£18.50-IR£21.50; d IR£30-IR£32; wkly b&b
IR£112; wkly hlf-bd IR£168✱
CARDS: 🔳 🔳 🎫

● 66 ●
T O W N H O U S E

66 Northumberland Road, Ballsbridge,
Dublin 4, Ireland
Tel: 00 3531 6600333
Fax: 00 3531 6601051
Ideally situated in Dublin's most
elegant suburb, 1 mile from the city
centre and 5 miles from Dun Laoghaire
Ferry. Convenient for buses and Dart
rail station. This Victorian residence
has been recently completely
refurbished to provide all rooms with
full facilities including en suite.
Parking available.

Selected

GH ⓆⓆⓆⓆ **Cill Eoin House** Killadysert Cross, Clare Rd (on N18) ☎065 41668 FAX 065 20224
Closed 22 Dec-9 Jan
This smart purpose-built house stands a short distnce from the town centre. It is attractively furnished and comfortable with well-equipped en suite bedrooms. A hospitable owner is always available to attend to guests needs.
14 en suite (shr) (2 fmly) No smoking CTV in all bedrooms Tea and coffee making facilities Direct dial from bedrooms No dogs Cen ht CTV 14P Tennis (hard)
CARDS: 🔳 🔳

ENNISCORTHY Co Wexford Map 01 D3

T&C ⓆⓆⓆ **Lemongrove House** Blackstoops (1km N at roundabout on N11) ☎054 36115
Closed 20-31 Dec
5 en suite (shr) (3 fmly) No smoking in bedrooms No smoking in dining room CTV in all bedrooms Tea and coffee making facilities No dogs (ex guide dogs) Cen ht CTV 8P
PRICE GUIDE
ROOMS: d IR£32-IR£34; wkly b&b IR£96-IR£136✴

Selected

♥ ⓆⓆⓆⓆ Mr & Mrs J Maher **Ballinkeele House** (T030334) Ballymurn ☎053 38105 FAX 053 38468
Mar-12 Nov rs 13 Nov-Feb
Set amid 350 acres of farmland, this classical house - built in 1840 and a good example of the work of Daniel Robertson - has successfully retained its original features while adding modern comforts like central heating and en suite bathrooms. Its fine portico leads to the entrance hall, where a blazing fire helps to create the warm, hospitable atmosphere that pervades throughout. Carefully cooked dinners are served round an elegant table in the fine dining room, and particularly inviting bedrooms welcome guests with a decanter of sherry. Facilities include a billiards room, hard tennis court and easy parking.
5 rms (4 shr) No dogs (ex guide dogs) Licensed Cen ht 20P Tennis (hard) Snooker Croquet 350 acres arable Last d noon
PRICE GUIDE
ROOMS: s IR£38-IR£43; d IR£60-IR£70; wkly b&b IR£189-IR£271; wkly hlf-bd IR£315-IR£397✴
CARDS: 🔳 🔳

ENNISTYMON Co Clare Map 01 B3

Selected

GH ⓆⓆⓆⓆ **Grovemount House** Lahinch Rd
☎065 71431 & 71038 FAX 065 71823
Apr-Oct
A smart purpose-built house enjoys an elevated site on the outskirts of Ennistymon near The Burren and ideally located for touring County Clare. The bedrooms are en suite and well equipped and the atmosphere is hopitable. Friendly owners will recommend local restaurants and traditional pubs, or arrange golf and lake fishing for guests.
8 en suite (shr) (1 fmly) No smoking in 4 bedrooms No smoking in area of dining room CTV in all bedrooms Tea

and coffee making facilities Direct dial from bedrooms No dogs (ex guide dogs) Cen ht CTV 20P
PRICE GUIDE
ROOMS: s IR£25; d IR£33-IR£40; wkly b&b IR£100-IR£120✴
CARDS: 🔳 🔳

FERMOY Co Cork Map 01 B2

Premier Selected

T&C ⓆⓆⓆⓆⓆ
Ballyvolane House
Castlelyons (from N8, turn off onto L188. House signposted) ☎025 36349 FAX 025 36781
This Italianate country house enjoys a magnificent setting in trees, woods and formal gardens which are open to the public in May. The comfortable bedroom all have TVs, tea/coffee making facilities and good bathrooms. Public rooms are filled with antiques and include a pillared reception hall with a baby grand piano and an elegant dining room serving dinner around a fine table. Croquet and private salmon/trout fishing are available and personal attention and a friendly atmosphere are assured.
7 rms (6 bth) No smoking in dining room No smoking in lounges CTV in 4 bedrooms Tea and coffee making facilities No dogs Licensed Cen ht 25P Fishing Croquet Last d noon
PRICE GUIDE
ROOMS: s IR£45-IR£55; d IR£70-IR£90; wkly b&b IR£245-IR£315; wkly hlf-bd IR£402.50-IR£472.50✴
CARDS: 🔳 🔳 🔳

T&C ⓆⓆ **Ghillie Cottage** Kilbarry Stud (take N72 from Fermoy on Fermoy/Tallow road. Take first left turning marked Clondulane. House exactly 3m from Sportsman's Inn, on right hand side) ☎025 32720 FAX 025 33000
This modernised farmhouse - set on a stud that specialises in crossbreeding traditional stallions with thoroughbred mares - stands in the heart of Munster, near the River Blackwater; to reach it, travel five miles east of Fermoy, turning left at Clondulane village. Guests are welcomed hospitably, accommodation is provided in cosy pine-furnished bedrooms and the comfortable sitting room's roaring log fire encourages total relaxation; dinner is available but must be booked in advance. All kinds of fishing can be enjoyed on uncrowded beats and the area also offers the chance to walk the Munster Way as well as golf, hunting and riding
3 rms Tea and coffee making facilities No dogs Cen ht CTV 6P No coaches Last d 4pm
PRICE GUIDE
ROOMS: s IR£17.50; d IR£35✴

Prices quoted in the Guide are based on information supplied by the establishments themselves.

FERNS Co Wexford Map **01** D3

Selected

♥ Ⓠ Ⓠ Ⓠ Ⓠ Mrs B Breen **Clone House** *(T022484)* (2m
SE off N11) ☎054 66113 FAX 054 66113
Mar-Oct
The hospitable Mrs Breen takes great pride in her farmhouse.
Fine furniture from past generations enhances the modern day
comforts and the prize-winning gardens are a delight.
5 rms (4 bth/shr) (4 fmly) No smoking in bedrooms No
smoking in dining room CTV in 3 bedrooms No dogs (ex
guide dogs) Cen ht CTV 37P Tennis (hard) Fishing 280
acres mixed Last d 4pm
PRICE GUIDE
ROOMS: s IR£20-IR£23; d IR£30-IR£36✱

FOULKESMILL Co Wexford Map **01** C2

♥ Ⓠ Ⓠ Ⓠ Ivor Young *Horetown House (S870189)*
☎051 63771 FAX 051 63633
Mar-Jan (ex Xmas day)
This 18th-century manor house stands in 200 acres of parkland 40
minutes' drive from Rosslane. Ongoing refurbishment has added
some en suite bedrooms; other facilities include a drawing room
with a huge log fire, the Cellar Restaurant serving country house
cuisine, and an on-site equestrian centre.
12 rms (10 fmly) Licensed Cen ht CTV 20P Riding All
weather indoor riding arena Outdoor riding 214 acres beef dairy
mixed Last d 9pm
CARDS: 🆇 🆇

GALWAY Co Galway Map **01** B4

Selected

T&C Ⓠ Ⓠ Ⓠ Ⓠ **Ardawn House** 31 College Rd (from N6
into Galway take first left at rdbt at lights take right fork to
city centre, house first guesthouse on right after Galway
Greyhound track) ☎091 568833 & 564551 FAX 091 568833
Closed 21-29 Dec
6 en suite (bth/shr) (2 fmly) No smoking in dining room
CTV in all bedrooms Direct dial from bedrooms No dogs (ex
guide dogs) Cen ht 6P
PRICE GUIDE
ROOMS: s IR£25-IR£40; d IR£34-IR£50; wkly b&b IR£96-
IR£150✱
CARDS: 🆇 🆇 🆇

T&C Ⓠ Ⓠ **Bay View** Gentian Hill, Upper Salthill (follow coast
road in direction of Connemara take 3rd left after Salthill, signed
from main road) ☎091 522116 & 526140
17 Mar-Nov
Modern house situated on edge of Salthill. Ideal touring centre.
6 rms (5 shr) (2 fmly) No smoking CTV in all bedrooms Tea
and coffee making facilities Direct dial from bedrooms No dogs
Cen ht CTV No children 5yrs 6P
PRICE GUIDE
ROOMS: d IR£29; wkly b&b IR£98

T&C Ⓠ Ⓠ Ⓠ **Corrib Haven** 107 Upper Newcastle (on N59)
☎091 524171
A new, purpose-built guesthouse stands on the N9 route to
Connemara, close to the university. The excellent bedrooms all

have private bathrooms, and ample car parking is provided.
6 en suite (shr) (1 fmly) No smoking CTV in all bedrooms No
dogs (ex guide dogs) Cen ht CTV 8P
PRICE GUIDE
ROOMS: s IR£22-IR£40; d IR£34-IR£40; wkly b&b IR£119-
IR£140✱
CARDS: 🆇 🆇

T&C Ⓠ Ⓠ Ⓠ **Flannery's** 54 Dalysfort Rd, Salthill (R338 to
Salthill then first left from Threadneedle Road onto Dr Mannix
Road and second right is Dalysfort Rd)
☎091 522048 FAX 01 6683023
4 rms (3 shr) (2 fmly) No smoking in dining room Cen ht CTV
4P
PRICE GUIDE
ROOMS: s IR£19-IR£21; d IR£28-IR£34; wkly b&b IR£90-
IR£110
CARDS: 🆇 🆇

Factual details of establishments in this Guide
are from questionnaires we send to all
establishments that feature in the book.

• **Lemongrove**
House 🄰🄰 QQQ

Blackstoops, Enniscorthy, Co. Wexford
Telephone: 00 353 54 36115

*Spacious home near roundabout on
Rosslare/Dublin Road N11. 1km north
of Enniscorthy. All rooms en suite with TV,
tea/coffee making facilities.
£16-£18 per person sharing.
Single £21.*

Premier Selected

T&C Ⓠ Ⓠ Ⓠ Ⓠ Ⓠ **Killeen House** Killeen, Bushypark (on N59 Galway/Oughterard road) ☎091 524179 FAX 091 528065
Closed 23-28 Dec
This charming 19th-century house stands in 25 acres of grounds stretching down to the shores of the loch. The interior is beautifully appointed with antique furnishings, hand-woven carpets, fine linen and exquisite crystal. En suite bedrooms reflect the character of the house and are well equipped with TVs, hairdryers and tea/coffee making facilities. Guests have use of two reception rooms and a breakfast room overlooking the garden. The hosts are genuinely hospitable.
4 en suite (bth/shr) (1 fmly) No smoking in dining room CTV in all bedrooms Tea and coffee making facilities Direct dial from bedrooms No dogs Lift Cen ht No children 7yrs 6P No coaches
PRICE GUIDE
ROOMS: s IR£35-IR£50; d IR£50-IR£70
CARDS: 🅰 🔲 ⓪
See advertisement under Colour Section

⊠ ▼ **T&C** Ⓠ Ⓠ Ⓠ **Roncalli House** 24 Whitestrand Av, Lower Salthill (off R336, house on corner opposite Ocean Wave Apartment Complex) ☎091 584159
Mr and Mrs O'Halloran are the hospitable owners of this modern corner house near the beach and in walking distance of the city centre. Bedrooms are all equipped with TV and shower rooms, there is good lounge space and, outside, a patio and well tended garden.
6 en suite (shr) (1 fmly) No smoking in dining room No smoking in 1 lounge CTV in all bedrooms Tea and coffee making facilities No dogs Cen ht CTV 5P No coaches
PRICE GUIDE
ROOMS: s IR£16-IR£22; d IR£30-IR£32

⊠ ▼ **T&C** Ⓠ Ⓠ **Seaview** 7 Beach Court, Gratton Rd, Salthill (on coast road between Galway & Salthill) ☎091 582109 FAX 091 582109
Positioned behind a grassed area near Salthill, this modern house has a balcony overlooking Galway Bay. Its en suite bedrooms have cheerful decor, TVs and tea/coffee making facilities; guests also have the use of the lounge.
4 en suite (bth/shr) (5 fmly) No smoking in area of dining room CTV in all bedrooms Tea and coffee making facilities Cen ht CTV 6P
PRICE GUIDE
ROOMS: s IR£15-IR£25; d IR£26-IR£50
CARDS: 🅰 🔲 🔲 ⓪

GH Ⓠ Ⓠ Ⓠ **Silverseas** Cappagh Rd, Barna ☎091 590575 FAX 091 590575
8 en suite (shr) (3 fmly) CTV in all bedrooms No dogs Cen ht CTV 12P
PRICE GUIDE
ROOMS: s IR£17-IR£25; d IR£30-IR£40; wkly b&b IR£119
CARDS: 🅰 🔲

GH Ⓠ Ⓠ Ⓠ **Summerville** 4 Westbrook, Barna Rd (on coast road drive through Salthill to t-junction, turn left for Barna, then 1st right for Westbrook) ☎091 590424
Mar-1 Dec
5 en suite (bth/shr) (1 fmly) CTV in all bedrooms Tea and coffee making facilities Cen ht CTV 5P
PRICE GUIDE
ROOMS: d IR£30-IR£32✱

T&C Ⓠ Ⓠ Ⓠ **West Point** 87 Threadneedle Rd, Salthill (from N6 N17 & N18, follow signs for Salthill, take R336 through two sets of traffic lights, house is sixth on left from junction) ☎091 521026 FAX 091 521026
Closed 19 Dec-2 Jan
6 en suite (shr) (3 fmly) No smoking in bedrooms No smoking in dining room No smoking in 1 lounge No dogs (ex guide dogs) Cen ht CTV 6P Last d noon
PRICE GUIDE
ROOMS: s IR£21-IR£25; d IR£32-IR£35✱
CARDS: 🅰 🔲

GLENCAR Co Sligo Map 01 B5

T&C Ⓠ Ⓠ Ⓠ **Emara Lodge** Tormore ☎071 41074
Apr-Sep
A modern bungalow is attractively located in a valley between Kings Mountain and Cashelgal within the Sligo region of Yeats Country. The bedrooms are pleasantly co-ordinated; two are en suite and all are on the ground floor. The comfortable sitting room has a TV and video, and the conservatory dining room overlooks Glencar Lake. Guests must book the good home-cooked dinner, and will enjoy the gardens and the fishing and hill-walking available nearby.
4 rms (2 shr) No smoking in bedrooms No smoking in dining room No smoking in lounges No dogs (ex guide dogs) Cen ht CTV 6P No coaches
PRICE GUIDE
ROOMS: d IR£28-IR£32✱

GLENDALOUGH Co Wicklow Map 01 D3

Selected

T&C Ⓠ Ⓠ Ⓠ Ⓠ **Laragh Trekking Centre** (take R755 through Roundwood, Annamoe into Laragh, take 1st right pass Mitchells Restaurant continue for 2 miles centre on right) ☎0404 45282 FAX 0404 45204
This hotel is run by husband and wife team David and Noreen McCallion whose joint skills (Noreen's experience in the hotel industry and David's love and knowledge of horses) combine to make a holiday spent with them a memorable occasion. David personally leads the rides around 600 acres of mountains and forests of Co Wicklow.
6 en suite (shr) (1 fmly) No smoking in 4 bedrooms No smoking in dining room CTV in all bedrooms Tea and coffee making facilities Direct dial from bedrooms Cen ht CTV ch fac 12P No coaches Last d noon
PRICE GUIDE
ROOMS: s IR£20-IR£27.50; d IR£34-IR£37; wkly b&b IR£133.50; wkly hlf-bd IR£190-IR£220✱
CARDS: 🅰 🔲 🔲

GLENEALY Co Wicklow Map **01** D3

♥ Q Q Mrs Mary Byrne *Ballyknocken House (T246925)* (turn right after Jet garage in Ashford) ☎0404 44627 & 44614
FAX 0404 44627
Closed 14 Nov-1 Mar
This comfortable farmhouse stands one mile from Glenealy offering pleasant en suite accomodation. Its hospitable owner Mrs Byrne organizes walking and cycling tours. Dinner is also provided.
7 en suite (shr) (1 fmly) No smoking in bedrooms No smoking in dining room No dogs Licensed Cen ht CTV 8P Tennis (hard) 270 acres beef sheep Last d 6pm

GOREY Co Wexford Map **01** D3

Selected

T&C Q Q Q Q Glenbower House The Avenue
☎055 20514
Closed Dec-Jan
This recently renovated period town house is situated on the Wexford Road. Bedrooms are fully equipped and have new bath/shower rooms; a comfortable guest lounge and well furnished dining room are also available. Local attractions include a championship golf course, the beach and sea angling. The Avenue has its own secure car parking and special arrangements can be made for dogs.
5 en suite (bth/shr) (2 fmly) No smoking in dining room CTV in all bedrooms Tea and coffee making facilities No dogs (ex guide dogs) Cen ht 8P Riding
PRICE GUIDE
ROOMS: s IR£20-IR£25; d IR£40; wkly b&b IR£125✱

Selected

♥ Q Q Q Q P O'Sullivan *Woodlands (T163648)*
Killinierin (signposted from N11) ☎0402 37125 & 37133
Closed Dec-Jan
This Georgian-style residence is tucked back from the main road in a wooded area of farmland. En suite bedrooms are well appointed; three have balconies and all are equipped with TVs. A garden patio stands between the guest lounge and a dining room which serves a good set dinner. Leisure facilities include a tennis court and a games room. Smoking is only allowed in the sitting room.
6 en suite (shr) (3 fmly) No smoking in bedrooms No smoking in dining room CTV in all bedrooms No dogs (ex guide dogs) Licensed Cen ht CTV 6P Tennis (hard) Pool table Pony rides 8 acres beef (non-working) Last d 7pm
PRICE GUIDE
ROOMS: s IR£25-IR£29; d IR£34-IR£38; wkly b&b IR£149-IR£163; wkly hlf-bd IR£195-IR£230✱
CARDS: 💳

GRANARD Co Longford Map **01** C4

♥ Q Q Q Mr & Mrs Smyth *Toberphelim House (N356810)*
☎043 86568
Closed 26 Apr-22 Sep
A large Georgian country house stands at the end of a long driveway. Children are well catered for with a private playground and a chance to see the various farmyard animals and activities. A separate lounge is also available.

3 rms (2 shr) (3 fmly) No smoking in 2 bedrooms No smoking in dining room No dogs (ex guide dogs) Cen ht CTV ch fac 10P Children's playground 200 acres beef sheep Last d 6pm
PRICE GUIDE
ROOMS: s IR£20-IR£23; d IR£36; wkly b&b IR£110; wkly hlf-bd IR£200
CARDS: 💳

KANTURK Co Cork Map **01** B2

Premier Selected

GH Q Q Q Q Q Assolas
Country House (3.5m NE, off
N72) ☎029 50015
FAX 029 50795
Apr-1 Nov
This 17th-century manor house enjoys a sylvan setting on a tributary of the River Blackwater, surrounded by prize-winning gardens, parkland and rolling country. Magnificent public rooms have log fires and fresh garden and local produce is creatively presented in the restaurant.
6 en suite (bth/shr) 3 annexe en suite (bth/shr) (3 fmly) Direct dial from bedrooms No dogs (ex guide dogs) Licensed Cen ht 20P No coaches Tennis (grass) Fishing Croquet Boating Last d 8.30pm
PRICE GUIDE
ROOMS: s IR£51-IR£72; d IR£82-IR£154✱
CARDS: 💳 💳 💳 💳

KENMARE Co Kerry Map **01** B2

GH Q Q Q Foleys Shamrock Henry St
☎064 41361 FAX 064 41799
This is a town-centre guesthouse over a pub/restaurant. All bedrooms have been recently refurbished and are very comfortable. A good food service is available via the bar and restaurant.
10 en suite (bth/shr) CTV in all bedrooms Direct dial from bedrooms No dogs (ex guide dogs) Licensed Cen ht CTV No parking Last d 10pm
PRICE GUIDE
ROOMS: s fr IR£30; d IR£30-IR£44
CARDS: 💳 💳

Selected

T&C Q Q Q Q Sallyport House Glengarriff Rd
☎064 42066 FAX 064 41752
Closed Nov-Mar
This superbly refurbished house - set in its own grounds and luxuriously appointed - stands on the left, near the bridge, as you leave Kenmare for Glengarrif/Castletownbere. Spacious, comfortable and thoughtfully appointed bedrooms are equipped with TV, telephones and excellent bathrooms, while public areas include lounge space round the foyer's large fireplace as well as a separate sitting room and the delightful dining room, overlooking the orchard, where breakfast is served. Good car parking facilities are available.
5 en suite (bth/shr) (2 fmly) No smoking in dining room No

➡

smoking in 1 lounge CTV in all bedrooms Direct dial from bedrooms No dogs Cen ht No children 10yrs 10P
PRICE GUIDE
ROOMS: d IR£40-IR£60✳

✌ Q Q M P O'Sullivan *Sea Shore* *(V899705)* Tubrid
☎064 41270
May-Sep
A modern bungalow stands in its own grounds on the edge of town overlooking Kenmare Bay.
4 en suite (bth/shr) No smoking No dogs Cen ht CTV P Private shore 32 acres dairy

✌ Q Q Mrs R Doran **Templenoe House** *(V840693)* Greenane (on N70) ☎064 41538
Etr-Oct
This two-storey farmhouse reputed to be about 200 years old is situated on the Ring of Kerry about four miles west of Kenmare.
5 rms (2 shr) No smoking in bedrooms No smoking in dining room Tea and coffee making facilities No dogs (ex guide dogs) Cen ht CTV 8P 50 acres mixed
PRICE GUIDE
ROOMS: s IR£20-IR£22; d IR£30-IR£34

KILCULLEN Co Kildare Map **01** C3

T&C Q Q Q *Chapel View Farm* Gormanstown ☎045 81325
May-Dec
6 en suite (shr) (2 fmly) Cen ht CTV 20P Last d 4pm
CARDS: ▨ ▧

KILKENNY Co Kilkenny Map **01** C3

Selected

GH Q Q Q Q **Butler House** Patrick St
☎056 65707 & 22828 FAX 056 65626
Closed 24-29 Dec
13 en suite (bth/shr) (4 fmly) No smoking in area of dining room CTV in all bedrooms Tea and coffee making facilities Direct dial from bedrooms No dogs (ex guide dogs) Cen ht 24P No coaches
PRICE GUIDE
ROOMS: s IR£39.50-IR£49.50; d IR£73-IR£79; wkly b&b IR£226; wkly hlf-bd IR£366-IR£398
CARDS: ▨ ▬ ▧ ⑩

T&C Q Q **Cill Phaoin** off Castlecomer Rd, Greenshill
☎056 22857
Closed 23-31Dec
A modern house run by friendly owners is conveniently situated near the station, five minutes' walk from the city centre. Guests have access to a lounge and dining room on the ground floor, a TV room on the lower ground floor and a private kitchen. The bedrooms are en suite and the patio and gardens overlook the river. Golf and fishing are available nearby.
4 en suite (bth/shr) No smoking in dining room No dogs Cen ht CTV 5P
PRICE GUIDE
ROOMS: s IR£20; d IR£30✳

T&C Q Q Q **Mount Danville** Bennetsbridge Rd ☎056 21521
Apr-Sep
Set in secluded gardens four minutes from the town centre - the first bed and breakfast establishment on the left-hand side past

Kilkenny Castle - Mount Danville House has a sitting room and sun lounge in addition to the attractive dining room where breakfast is served round a communal table; three of the four bedrooms have en suite facilities. Ample car parking space is provided.
4 rms (3 bth/shr) No smoking in bedrooms No smoking in dining room No dogs (ex guide dogs) Cen ht CTV 15P No coaches
PRICE GUIDE
ROOMS: s fr IR£20; d IR£33-IR£40✳

Selected

T&C Q Q Q Q **Shillogher House** Callan Rd ☎056 63249
Closed 24-26 Dec
A lovely new house stands in its own gardens on the road to Clonmel. It is tastefully furnished and decorated and Mrs Kennedy has a keen eye to her guests' comfort.
5 en suite (bth/shr) (1 fmly) No smoking in bedrooms No smoking in dining room CTV in all bedrooms Tea and coffee making facilities Direct dial from bedrooms No dogs (ex guide dogs) Cen ht 10P
PRICE GUIDE
ROOMS: d IR£32-IR£37
CARDS: ▨ ▧

KILLARNEY Co Kerry Map **01** B2

T&C Q Q Q **Avondale House** Tralee Rd (on N22)
☎064 35579
17 Mar-7 Nov
This is a distinctive pink house surrounded by attractive gardens five minutes' drive from Killarney. There is a comfortable lounge and en suite bedrooms equipped with TVs and tea/coffee making facilities. A golf course and riding stables are available nearby.
5 en suite (shr) (4 fmly) No smoking in dining room No smoking in lounges CTV in all bedrooms Tea and coffee making facilities No dogs (ex guide dogs) Cen ht CTV No children 4yrs 8P Last d 3pm
PRICE GUIDE
ROOMS: s IR£19-IR£20; d IR£29-IR£30; wkly b&b IR£100-IR£105

GH Q Q Q **Cois Dara** Rookery Rd ☎064 35567
Mar-Nov
A non-smoking house stands in a quiet area close to town and offers well appointed, comfortable accommodation. Pleasantly decorated bedrooms are all individually styled and feature good beds and fully tiled shower rooms. There is a spacious combined lounge/dining room and off-street car parking is available. Fishing, touring and golf can be arranged.
4 en suite (shr) No smoking No dogs Cen ht CTV P
PRICE GUIDE
ROOMS: s IR£18.50; d IR£30-IR£31; wkly b&b IR£90✳

T&C Q Q Q **Countess House** Countess Rd ☎064 34247
Closed Jan
A cream/red brick house stands a short walk from the town centre in a quiet reidential area. The en suite bedrooms have cheerful decor and good shower rooms have strong water pressure; tea/coffee trays are available on request and there are special rates for the three-bedded room. The lounge is comfortable and the separate dining room serves an extensive breakfast menu which includes vegetarian choices.

5 en suite (shr) (2 fmly) No smoking in dining room No smoking in 1 lounge Tea and coffee making facilities Cen ht CTV 8P
PRICE GUIDE
ROOMS: s IR£20-IR£25; d IR£30-IR£32; wkly b&b IR£180-IR£200✳

T&C 🔲🔲🔲 **Courtmurph House** Muckross Rd
☎064 34586 FAX 064 36630
This modern purpose-built house is situated on Muckross Road, 3kms from Killarney and near the entrance of the Killarney National Park. The en suite bedrooms all have colour TV, and guests have access to two guest lounges, one with facilities for making tea and coffee. Tours, golf and lake fishing can be arranged by the resident proprietor. Good car parking is also available.
5 en suite (shr) No smoking in area of dining room No smoking in 1 lounge CTV in all bedrooms No dogs (ex guide dogs) Cen ht CTV 10P No coaches
PRICE GUIDE
ROOMS: d IR£34-IR£37✳
CARDS: 🔳 💳 💳

T&C 🔲🔲🔲 **Crystal Springs** Ballycasheen
☎064 33272 FAX 064 31188
This spacious, comfortable house stands beside the river bank and offers attractively decorated, very well equipped en suite bedrooms. Mrs Eileen Brosnan has created a welcoming atmosphere and can offer evening meals by arrangement. Her guests can also enjoy free fishing in the spring and there are three golf-courses in the neighbourhood to choose from. There is ample parking space. To reach Crystal Springs, turn off the N22 on the outskirts of Killarney for Ballycasheen, which is also signposted from the N71.
5 en suite (bth/shr) (2 fmly) No smoking in dining room CTV in all bedrooms Tea and coffee making facilities Cen ht CTV 12P Fishing
PRICE GUIDE
ROOMS: s IR£19-IR£22; d IR£30-IR£34✳
CARDS: 🔳 💳

T&C 🔲🔲 **Dirreen House** Tralee Rd (on N22) ☎064 31676
Mar-Nov
This large purpose-built house stands in attractive lawns and flower beds on the Tralee road. The en suite bedrooms are all well-equipped and well-furnished and have good views over the surrounding countryside.
4 en suite (shr) (2 fmly) No smoking in 2 bedrooms No smoking in dining room No smoking in lounges CTV in all bedrooms Tea and coffee making facilities No dogs Cen ht CTV 6P
PRICE GUIDE
ROOMS: s IR£18-IR£20; d IR£28-IR£30; wkly b&b IR£95-IR£99; wkly hlf-bd IR£157.50-IR£164

Selected

GH 🔲🔲🔲🔲 **Foleys Town House** 22/23 High St
☎064 31217 FAX 064 34683
Apr-Oct
Charming bedrooms with stripped pine furniture and coordinated colour schemes are a feature of this delightful town house, which also offers a cosy lounge, a bar and private car park. It is run by Carol Hartnett who is also head chef at her popular adjoining seafood restaurant.
12 en suite (bth/shr) No smoking in 2 bedrooms No smoking in area of dining room CTV in all bedrooms Tea and coffee

making facilities Direct dial from bedrooms No dogs Licensed Cen ht CTV 25P Last d 10.30pm
PRICE GUIDE
ROOMS: s IR£38.50-IR£41.80; d IR£70-IR£77✳
CARDS: 🔳 💳 💳

T&C 🔲🔲🔲 **Friars Glen** Mangerton Rd, Muckross (take N71 towards Kenmare and turn left immediately after Muckross Park Hotel. Entrance 300mtrs on right next to garden centre)
☎064 34044
Mar-Oct
4 en suite (bth/shr) (2 fmly) No smoking in dining room No smoking in lounges Tea and coffee making facilities No dogs (ex guide dogs) Cen ht CTV 6P No coaches
PRICE GUIDE
ROOMS: s IR£20; d IR£32; wkly b&b IR£112✳
CARDS: 🔳 💳

GH 🔲🔲🔲 *Gleann Fia* Deerpark
☎064 35035 FAX 064 35000
14 Mar-Oct
Gleann Fia means 'Glen of the Deer', and it is certainly appropriate, for this guesthouse enjoys a tranquil setting among mature woodlands. The owner, Mora Galvin, takes a real interest in her guests.
8 en suite (shr) (2 fmly) No smoking in 2 bedrooms No smoking in dining room No smoking in 1 lounge Tea and coffee making facilities Direct dial from bedrooms No dogs (ex guide dogs) Cen ht CTV 10P Playground
CARDS: 🔳 💳 💳

GH QQQ *Glena House* Muckross Rd (0.5m from town centre on N71) ☎064 32705 & 34284 FAX 064 35611
A large, comfortable house close to town offers en suite accomodation and on-site parking.
26 en suite (bth/shr) (6 fmly) No smoking in 10 bedrooms No smoking in area of dining room CTV in all bedrooms Tea and coffee making facilities Direct dial from bedrooms No dogs (ex guide dogs) Licensed Cen ht CTV 26P Library Last d 9pm
CARDS: 🔳 📇

T&C QQQ *Gorman's* Tralee Rd ☎064 33149
A large and attractive bungalow is set in well cultivated gardens and 3.5 miles from Killarney on the Tralee road. It offers comfortable en suite bedrooms.
5 en suite (bth/shr) (6 fmly) CTV in all bedrooms Tea and coffee making facilities Cen ht CTV No parking Last d 6pm

T&C QQ *Green Acres* Fossa (2km on T67 Killorglin road) ☎064 31454
Closed Dec-9 Jan
This modern house is situated on the Ring of Kerry 1.5 miles outside town.
8 rms (6 shr) (2 fmly) No smoking in dining room No dogs Cen ht CTV 10P

Selected

GH QQQQ Kathleen's Country House Tralee Rd (on N22 3km N) ☎064 32810 FAX 064 32340
17 Mar-5 Nov
An exclusive, modern, purpose-built guesthouse is set in its own lovely gardens one mile from the town centre on the Tralee road. Family-run, luxury accommodation in scenic countryside makes this an ideal touring centre.
17 en suite (bth/shr) (2 fmly) No smoking in 9 bedrooms No smoking in dining room No smoking in lounges CTV in all bedrooms Tea and coffee making facilities Direct dial from bedrooms No dogs Licensed Cen ht No children 5yrs 20P Croquet Last d 6pm
PRICE GUIDE
ROOMS: s IR£30-IR£60; d IR£50-IR£70✱
CARDS: 🔳 📇

T&C QQQ Killarney Villa Cork-Waterford Rd (N72) ☎064 31878 FAX 064 31878
Apr-Oct
This purpose-built country home run by a family is equipped with all modern comforts and makes an ideal holiday destination.
6 en suite (bth/shr) No smoking in 5 bedrooms No smoking in dining room No smoking in lounges Tea and coffee making facilities No dogs Cen ht CTV No children 6yrs 20P Last d 6.30pm
PRICE GUIDE
ROOMS: s IR£17-IR£21; d IR£31.50-IR£36; wkly b&b IR£104-IR£120; wkly hlf-bd IR£180-IR£197✱
CARDS: 🔳 📇 📇

GH QQQ Lime Court Muckross Rd
☎064 34547 FAX 064 34121
A large modern house has spacious public rooms and well equipped bedrooms with private bathrooms. Many of the rooms have fine views. High standards are maintained throughout, and evening meals can be provided to groups.
12 en suite (bth/shr) (4 fmly) No smoking in 6 bedrooms No smoking in area of dining room No smoking in 1 lounge CTV in

all bedrooms Tea and coffee making facilities Direct dial from bedrooms No dogs (ex guide dogs) Licensed Cen ht CTV 20P
PRICE GUIDE
ROOMS: d IR£42-IR£50; wkly b&b IR£132-IR£152✱
CARDS: 🔳 📇

GH QQQ Lissivigeen House Cork Rd (1m from Killarney, on Cork/Killarney N22) ☎064 35522
May-Oct
This attractive yellow house with its grey slate roof has been purpose-built with the comfort of guests in mind. Bedrooms are attractively furnished in pine and have all modern comforts. The house is on the N22 about a mile from the centre of town. Car parking is good.
8 en suite (shr) No smoking in bedrooms No smoking in dining room CTV in all bedrooms Direct dial from bedrooms No dogs Cen ht CTV 20P
PRICE GUIDE
ROOMS: s IR£20-IR£30; d IR£36-IR£46; wkly b&b IR£125-IR£160✱
CARDS: 🔳 📇 📇 📇

GH QQQ Loch Lein Golf Course Rd, Fossa (on R562) ☎064 31260 FAX 064 36151
17 Mar-Oct
A single-storey bungalow stands in a quiet and peaceful location on the shores of the Lower Lake with well maintained lawns and flower beds.
12 en suite (bth/shr) (7 fmly) No smoking in 8 bedrooms No smoking in dining room No smoking in lounges Direct dial from bedrooms No dogs (ex guide dogs) Cen ht CTV 12P
PRICE GUIDE
ROOMS: s IR£20-IR£30; d IR£32-IR£40; wkly b&b IR£110-IR£126
CARDS: 🔳 📇

T&C QQQ Lohan's Lodge Tralee Rd (on N22) ☎064 33871
Proprietors Cathy and Mike Lohan are hospitable and caring hosts, who keep their house in pristine condition. The bedrooms are cosy and attractive and the comfortable lounge has a turf fire in cooler weather.
5 en suite (shr) (1 fmly) No smoking in 2 bedrooms No smoking in area of dining room No smoking in 1 lounge CTV in all bedrooms Tea and coffee making facilities No dogs Cen ht CTV No children 7yrs 7P Last d noon
PRICE GUIDE
ROOMS: s IR£21; d IR£28-IR£32; wkly b&b IR£92-IR£100; wkly hlf-bd IR£170-IR£180✱

T&C QQ Nashville Tralee Rd (2m from Killarney on main Dublin/Limerick road, N22) ☎064 32924
15 Mar-Nov
This white, double-fronted house on the main N22 road is about two miles from Killarney and very easy to find. The large bedrooms are bright, cheerful, and well equipped. David Nash and his family are very welcoming hosts.
6 en suite (shr) (2 fmly) Tea and coffee making facilities No dogs (ex guide dogs) Cen ht CTV 10P

T&C QQQ Park Lodge Cork Rd
☎064 31539 FAX 064 34892
A large purpose-built double-fronted guesthouse is set on the Cork road beside the Killarney Ryan Hotel. The spacious, well equipped bedrooms overlook the front and rear gardens; ample car parking is available at a hotel just a short walk from the town centre.

20 en suite (shr) (1 fmly) No smoking in 4 bedrooms No smoking in dining room CTV in all bedrooms Tea and coffee making facilities Direct dial from bedrooms Cen ht CTV 24P
PRICE GUIDE
ROOMS: s IR£20-IR£35; d IR£30-IR£44
CARDS: 🔵 🔲

T&C 🔵🔵 The Purple Heather Glencar Rd, Gap of Dunloe
☎064 44266
Mar-Oct
This modern bungalow stands by the roadside among spectacular mountain scenery and is an ideal touring centre.
5 rms (4 shr) (1 fmly) No smoking in bedrooms No smoking in area of dining room No smoking in 1 lounge Tea and coffee making facilities No dogs (ex guide dogs) Cen ht CTV 6P No coaches Tennis (hard) Pool room Last d 7pm
PRICE GUIDE
ROOMS: s IR£19-IR£21; d IR£28-IR£32; wkly b&b IR£98-IR£112; wkly hlf-bd IR£165-IR£170
CARDS: 🔵 🔲

T&C 🔵🔵🔵 River Lodge Ballycasheen ☎064 33163
10 Mar-15 Oct
4 en suite (shr) (1 fmly) No smoking in bedrooms No smoking in dining room No smoking in 1 lounge Cen ht CTV 6P
CARDS: 🔵 ■ 🔲

T&C 🔵🔵🔵 Shillelagh House Aghadoe
☎064 34030 FAX 064 35761
Feb-Oct
6 rms (4 shr) (1 fmly) No smoking No dogs Cen ht CTV 15P Last d 4pm
PRICE GUIDE
ROOMS: s IR£18-IR£21; d IR£28-IR£30; wkly b&b IR£98; wkly hlf-bd IR£180
CARDS: 🔵 ■ 🔲

T&C 🔵🔵🔵 Shraheen House Ballycasheen ☎064 31286
Closed Xmas & New Year
In a peaceful, scenic area, this modern and comfortable house has well equipped bedrooms and a patio lounge.
6 en suite (bth/shr) (2 fmly) No smoking in bedrooms No smoking in dining room CTV in all bedrooms No dogs Cen ht CTV 8P
PRICE GUIDE
ROOMS: s IR£23; d IR£34✱

GH 🔵🔵🔵 Slieve Bloom Manor Muckross Rd
☎064 34237 FAX 064 34237
Closed 16 Dec-Jan
A substantial modern house stands on the edge of the town towards Kenmare, close to Glen River, golf courses and Muckross House. It offers comfortable bedrooms and public rooms; ample car parking is available.
14 rms (13 shr) No smoking in dining room Tea and coffee making facilities No dogs (ex guide dogs) Cen ht CTV 14P
PRICE GUIDE
ROOMS: s IR£15-IR£30; d IR£30-IR£36✱
CARDS: 🔵 🔲

✔🔵 Mrs B O'Connor Glebe (V965965) Off Tralee Rd
☎064 32179
Mar-Dec
In a peaceful location on a side road, but convenient for the N22, this charming guesthouse contains an interesting display of farm memorabilia which has been collected by the owner, Mrs O'Connor.

---

4 en suite (bth/shr) (1 fmly) No smoking in dining room No dogs (ex guide dogs) CTV 10P 80 acres beef sheep horses Last d 1pm
PRICE GUIDE
ROOMS: s IR£17-IR£19; d IR£28-IR£32; wkly b&b fr IR£90; wkly hlf-bd fr IR£170✱

KILLEAGH Co Cork Map 01 C2

T&C 🔵🔵🔵 Tattans (on N8, between Midleton and Youghal)
☎024 95173
Mar-Oct
A town house with its own car park stands on the main N25 Cork-Rosslare road. It offers comfortable bedrooms, a TV room, large attractive gardens and a hard tennis court. Bar snacks are served throughout the day and evening meals are available to residents.
5 rms (4 shr) (3 fmly) No dogs Licensed Cen ht CTV 8P Tennis (hard) Last d 10pm
PRICE GUIDE
ROOMS: s IR£20; d IR£32-IR£34; wkly b&b IR£112-IR£120; wkly hlf-bd IR£220-IR£230✱
CARDS: 🔵 🔲

Selected

✔ 🔵🔵🔵🔵 Mrs Browne Ballymakeigh House (X005765)
☎024 95184 FAX 024 95370
12 Feb-1 Nov
Hospitable Margaret Browne, winner of many awards, makes guests feel very much at home in her delightful, 250-year-old farmhouse. The cheerful bedrooms are attractively decorated and an elegant dining room provides the setting for a five-➡

course dinner served every evening.
5 en suite (bth/shr) (5 fmly) No smoking in dining room No
dogs (ex guide dogs) Licensed Cen ht CTV 10P Tennis
(hard) Snooker Games room 180 acres dairy Last d 6pm
PRICE GUIDE
ROOMS: s IR£25-IR£30; d IR£40-IR£50; wkly b&b
IR£140; wkly hlf-bd IR£280

KILMALLOCK Co Limerick Map **01** B3

❤ 🔘🔘🔘 Mrs Imelda Sheedy-King **Flemingstown House**
(R629255) (on R512) ☎063 98093 FAX 063 98546
Mar-Oct
This 18th-century farmhouse has been modernised to provide
attractive, well equipped accommodation with all the comforts
today's holiday maker expects. Imelda Sheedy-King has good
reason to be proud of her cooking, and much of the produce comes
from her own farm. She will provide dinner for her guests by
arrangement. The farm is on the Limerick/Mitchelstown road, has
good car parking and the countryside is excellent for walkers,
riders, anglers and golfers.
6 rms (5 shr) (2 fmly) No smoking in dining room Tea and
coffee making facilities No dogs (ex guide dogs) Cen ht CTV
40P Riding 102 acres dairy Last d 3pm
PRICE GUIDE
ROOMS: s fr IR£18; d fr IR£36; wkly b&b fr IR£126; wkly hlf-
bd fr IR£225

KILRANE Co Wexford Map **01** D2

[📧💷] ❤ 🔘🔘 K O'Leary **O'Leary's** *(T132101)* Killilane
☎053 33134
rs 24 Dec
This farmhouse is located in a quiet and peaceful setting
overlooking St George's Channel.
10 rms (7 shr) (2 fmly) No smoking in bedrooms No smoking in
dining room Cen ht CTV 14P 100 acres arable Last d noon
PRICE GUIDE
ROOMS: s IR£15-IR£16; d IR£28-IR£32; wkly b&b IR£94.50-
IR£108.50; wkly hlf-bd IR£170-IR£184

KINSALE Co Cork Map **01** B2

Selected

GH 🔘🔘🔘🔘 **The Moorings** Scilly
☎021 772376 FAX 021 772675
This superbly appointed guest house overlooks the harbour
and the yacht marina. Comfortable, individually styled
bedrooms all have en suite facilities and some have balconies.
8 en suite (bth/shr) CTV in all bedrooms Tea and coffee
making facilities Direct dial from bedrooms Cen ht CTV
No children 16yrs 12P No coaches
PRICE GUIDE
ROOMS: d IR£70-IR£90✳
CARDS: 🔳 💷

Selected

GH 🔘🔘🔘🔘 **Old Bank House** 11 Pearse St
☎021 774075 FAX 021 774296
Closed 23-25 Dec
Under the personal supervision of Marie and Michael Riese,
this delightful Georgian house - once a bank house - has been

restored to its former elegance. The en suite bedrooms, with
period furniture and attractive decor, combine charm with
modern comforts. Dinner is offered in the owners' restaurant.
9 en suite (bth/shr) (2 fmly) No smoking in dining room No
smoking in 1 lounge CTV in all bedrooms Tea and coffee
making facilities Direct dial from bedrooms Licensed Cen
ht No children 12yrs No parking No coaches Last d 10pm
PRICE GUIDE
ROOMS: s IR£45-IR£60; d IR£80-IR£120; wkly b&b
IR£210-IR£350✳
CARDS: 🔳 💷 💷

Selected

T&C 🔘🔘🔘🔘 **Old Presbytery** 43 Cork St ☎021 772027
Closed 24-28 Dec
A charming period house stands on a quiet street in the town
centre of this Mediterranean-style seaport. The en suite
bedrooms are traditionally styled with stripped pine
furnishings and brass beds; one has external access via stairs.
Facilities include a comfortable guest lounge, a delightful
breakfast room and an enclosed car park. Excellent sailing
and sea fishing are available locally together with an
abundance of good restaurants. Reservations are advised.
6 en suite (bth/shr) No smoking Tea and coffee making
facilities CTV No children 6P No coaches
PRICE GUIDE
ROOMS: s IR£26-IR£32; d IR£40-IR£52✳

Selected

T&C 🔘🔘🔘🔘 **Old Rectory** Rampart Ln
☎021 772678 FAX 021 772678
Closed 21 Dec-1 Jan
A former rectory stands in an acre of sunny gardens away
from the bustle of the nearby town centre. It has been lovingly
restored to provide luxury guest accommodation with the
emphasis on comfort and relaxation.
4 en suite (bth/shr) No smoking in dining room No dogs
Licensed Cen ht CTV 4P No coaches
PRICE GUIDE
ROOMS: s IR£40-IR£55; d IR£60-IR£80
CARDS: 🔳 💷 💷

T&C 🔘🔘🔘 **Waterlands** Cork Rd
☎021 772318 FAX 021 774873
Mar-Oct
A pink and white house on an elevated site in a slip road is fronted
by boats filled with flowers. A conservatory breakfast room
overlooks the picturesque gardens and serves a good menu
including home-made brown bread and free-range eggs. The TV
lounge has tea/coffee facilities and four comfortable, well
decorated en suite bedrooms have hair dryers and clock radios.
4 en suite (shr) (2 fmly) No smoking in bedrooms No smoking
in dining room No smoking in 1 lounge Tea and coffee making
facilities No dogs Cen ht 10P No coaches
PRICE GUIDE
ROOMS: d IR£32

KNOCK Co Mayo Map **01** B4

T&C 🔘🔘 **Aishling House** Ballyhaunis Rd ☎094 88558
A white house stands in its own grounds with good street parking
and attractive gardens. Four of the bedrooms are en suite and the

fifth is on the ground floor; all are equipped with TVs. Guests have use of two cosy sitting rooms and a separate breakfast room. The friendly owner has information about visits to the famous Knock Shrine, and lake fishing, archaeological sites, golf and riding can all be found locally. Dinner and high tea are available if reserved.
5 rms (4 shr) (2 fmly) CTV in all bedrooms No dogs (ex guide dogs) Cen ht CTV 10P Last d 5pm
PRICE GUIDE
ROOMS: s IR£18; d IR£29

KNOCKFERRY Co Galway Map **01** B4

♥ Q Q D & M Moran **Knockferry Lodge** *(M238412)*
☎091 80122 FAX 091 80328
2 May-1 Oct
Situated on the shores of Lough Corrib, this farmhouse offers good food, cosy turf fires and a welcome that is warm and sincere. Fishing is available outside the door.
10 en suite (bth/shr) (1 fmly) No smoking in dining room No dogs (ex guide dogs) Licensed Cen ht CTV 20P Boats for hire 35 acres mixed Last d 8pm
PRICE GUIDE
ROOMS: s fr IR£25; d fr IR£40; wkly b&b fr IR£140; wkly hlf-bd fr IR£200✱
CARDS: ▨ ▨ ▨ ⓞ

KYLEMORE Co Galway Map **01** C3

GH Q Q Q Kylemore House (turn off N59 from Galway at Recess onto R344) ☎095 411443
May-Oct
6 en suite (bth/shr) (1 fmly) Tea and coffee making facilities No dogs (ex guide dogs) Licensed Cen ht CTV 8P No coaches Fishing Last d 4pm
PRICE GUIDE
ROOMS: s IR£21-IR£25; d IR£33-IR£36; wkly hlf-bd IR£195-IR£200

LARAGH Co Wicklow Map **01** D3

⊨ ▼ ♥ Q Q Mrs M Byrne **Doire Coille** *(T141945)*
Cullentragh, Rathdrum (on R755, 1.5m S of village)
☎0404 45131
Apr-Nov
This fine old farmhouse is set 1.5 miles from Laragh on the Rathdrum Road in the beautiful Vale of Clara. Spacious bedrooms overlook gardens/farmland and offer comfortable beds with electric blankets; the lounge is comfortable and relaxing. The house is surrounded by interesting places to visit.
4 rms (3 shr) (2 fmly) No smoking No dogs (ex guide dogs) 6P Fishing 30 acres dairy sheep
PRICE GUIDE
ROOMS: s fr IR£15; d fr IR£32; wkly b&b fr IR£98

LARNE Co Antrim Map **01** D5

GH Q Q Q Derrin 2 Prince's Gardens BT40 1RQ (access via A2) ☎01574 273269 & 273762 FAX 01574 273269
A substantial property dating from 1912, this guesthouse is just off the A2 Coast Road close to the town centre and within easy reach of the ferry terminal. Impeccably maintained, it provides well equipped accommodation with modern furnishings. There is a spacious lounge and an attractive breakfast room with individual tables.

7 rms (4 shr) (2 fmly) No smoking in dining room CTV in all bedrooms Tea and coffee making facilities Cen ht CTV 5P No coaches
PRICE GUIDE
ROOMS: s £18-£20; d £28-£34
CARDS: ▨ ▨ ▨   ⓔ

LETTERKENNY Co Donegal Map **01** C5

T&C Q Q Q Hill Crest House Lurgybrack, Sligo Rd (take N13 to Derry, at Dryarch roundabout turn right onto N56 to Sligo & proceed for 1m, house at top of hill on right)
☎074 22300 & 25137
rs Xmas wk
6 rms (5 shr) (3 fmly) No smoking in dining room CTV in all bedrooms Tea and coffee making facilities No dogs (ex guide dogs) Cen ht CTV 12P
PRICE GUIDE
ROOMS: s IR£18-IR£21; d IR£30-IR£32
CARDS: ▨ ▨ ▨

LIMERICK Co Limerick Map **01** B3

GH Q Q Q Clifton House Ennis Rd (on direct route to Shannon airport N18, opposite Woodfield House Hotel)
☎061 451166 FAX 061 451224
Closed 18 Dec-4 Jan
Providing well equipped, attractive and very comfortable bedrooms has been the aim of the refurbishment of Michael and Mary Powell's guesthouse. Complimentary tea and coffee are available in the spacious, relaxing lounge and there is an excellent car park.
16 en suite (bth/shr) CTV in all bedrooms Direct dial from bedrooms No dogs (ex guide dogs) Cen ht 22P
PRICE GUIDE
ROOMS: s IR£22-IR£25; d IR£34-IR£36

GH Q Q Q Clonmacken House Clonmacken, off Ennis Rd (on N18, turn left at Ivan's shop) ☎061 327007 FAX 061 369009
Closed 20 Dec-7 Jan
This purpose-built guest house is conveniently situated close to the city centre and has good car parking facilities. The comfortable en suite bedrooms have armchairs, TVs, telephones and tea/coffee trays, and downstairs there are a lounge and dining room.
10 en suite (shr) (2 fmly) No smoking in dining room CTV in all bedrooms Tea and coffee making facilities Direct dial from bedrooms No dogs Cen ht CTV 25P
PRICE GUIDE
ROOMS: s IR£20-IR£22; d IR£34-IR£36; wkly b&b IR£119-IR£126
CARDS: ▨ ▨

LISBURN Co Antrim Map **01** D5

Selected

♥ Q Q Q Q Mrs D Moore **Brook Lodge** *(J3315608)* 79 Old Ballynahinch Rd, Cargacroy BT27 6TH
☎01846 638454
Many guests return on a regular basis to Mrs Moore's delightful modern bungalow which is surrounded by pleasant countryside just off the A49, three miles south of the M1. Bedrooms, although compact, are bright and cheerful with mixed modern appointments. The comfortable lounge has a splendid outlook, and hearty farmhouse fare is served in the small dining room, occasionally at shared tables.

6 rms (4 shr) No smoking in dining room No smoking in lounges CTV in 1 bedroom No dogs (ex guide dogs) Cen ht CTV 10P 65 acres mixed

LISDOONVARNA Co Clare Map **01** B3

T&C QQQ Ore' A Tava House (1km from town on N67, turn left at water pump, 3rd house on left)
☎065 74086 FAX 065 74547
20 Mar-30 Oct
Situated half a mile from Lisdoonvarna, in a quiet area off the Ballyvaughan road, Ore' A Tava House offers attractive public rooms which include a new conservatory lounge; some bedrooms are located on the ground floor and good car parking facilities are available.
6 en suite (bth/shr) (3 fmly) No smoking in 1 lounge CTV in 4 bedrooms Direct dial from bedrooms No dogs (ex guide dogs) Cen ht CTV 6P
PRICE GUIDE
ROOMS: s IR£18-IR£20; d IR£30-IR£32

LISTOWEL Co Kerry Map **01** B3

⌖ ☂ T&C QQ North County 67 Church St (in town centre close to the Square, on the one-way system) ☎068 21238
This comfortable streetside house in the centre of the market town is conveniently situated for Shannon car ferry and all amenities.
8 rms (6 shr) (2 fmly) No smoking in 2 bedrooms No smoking in dining room No dogs (ex guide dogs) Cen ht CTV ch fac No parking Last d noon
PRICE GUIDE
ROOMS: s IR£16-IR£20; d IR£32-IR£40

LUSK Co Dublin Map **01** D4

T&C QQQ Carriage House ☎01 8438857 FAX 01 8438933
This attractive bungalow is set in well tended gardens, just off the N1 main Dublin/Belfast road. The Curtin family are very hospitable and nothing is too much trouble. The well equipped bedrooms are all en suite. The house is convenient for both tourists and business guests with office facilities and an information centre. There is an outdoor heated swimming pool and good car parking.
5 en suite (shr) CTV in all bedrooms Tea and coffee making facilities Direct dial from bedrooms No dogs (ex guide dogs) Cen ht CTV 15P No coaches Indoor swimming pool (heated) Sauna Gymnasium 9 hole putting
CARDS: 🔲 💳 💳 ⊙

MALLOW Co Cork Map **01** B2

Selected

GH QQQQ Springfort Hall (on R581)
☎022 21278 FAX 022 21557
Closed 24 Dec-2 Jan
An 18th-century country house stands in woodlands and landscaped gardens 3.5 miles from Mallow. Bedrooms are split between the main house and a smart new extension, but all have attractive decor, modern equipment and good bathrooms. The restaurant serves a carte at 7pm each evening (except Sundays); local produce such as shellfish and game are used to create enjoyable dishes. Other public areas include an elegant sitting room with an adjoining bar, a banquet hall, a patio and pleasant gardens. Golf and fishing are available nearby.

24 en suite (bth/shr) (3 fmly) No smoking in area of dining room CTV in all bedrooms Direct dial from bedrooms No dogs (ex guide dogs) Licensed Cen ht CTV Last d 9.30pm
PRICE GUIDE
ROOMS: s IR£25-IR£35; d IR£50-IR£70; wkly b&b IR£200-IR£250; wkly hlf-bd IR£300-IR£350✱
CARDS: 🔲 💳 💳 ⊙

MIDLETON Co Cork Map **01** B2

T&C QQQ Ballynona House (turn off N25 opposite Lough Aderra Lake & follow signposts) ☎021 667628 FAX 021 667628
This charming Victorian residence stands in a secluded area two kilometres from Castlemartyr and convenient for Midleton and the N25. Attractively decorated en suite bedrooms, a comfortable guest lounge and a separate dining room have all been restored making good use of period furnishings. A home-cooked dinner can be taken by arrangement and good car parking is provided. Golf, fishing and horse riding are all available nearby.
5 rms (4 bth/shr) (2 fmly) No smoking in bedrooms No smoking in dining room Tea and coffee making facilities No dogs (ex guide dogs) Cen ht CTV No children 12yrs P No coaches Last d noon
PRICE GUIDE
ROOMS: (incl. dinner) s IR£20-IR£22; d IR£36-IR£40; wkly b&b IR£126; wkly hlf-bd IR£224

MILFORD Co Carlow Map **01** C3

Selected

T&C QQQQ Goleen Country House (on N9)
☎0503 46132 FAX 0503 46132
Closed Dec-1 Jan
This is a lovely house, tree-screened from the Carlow/Waterford road (N9) and with substantial well tended gardens to the front. The Mulveys have done everything possible to make guests comfortable and the bedrooms especially reflect this concern - being very fully and comfortably equipped. Mrs Mulvey is a charming hostess.
6 rms (4 shr) No smoking in bedrooms No smoking in dining room CTV in all bedrooms Tea and coffee making facilities Direct dial from bedrooms No dogs Cen ht CTV No children 20P
PRICE GUIDE
ROOMS: d IR£30-IR£34; wkly b&b IR£100-IR£115✱
CARDS: 🔲 💳 💳

MITCHELSTOWN Co Cork Map **01** B2

GH QQQ Clongibbon House New Square
☎025 24116 24288 FAX 025 84065
7 en suite (bth/shr) (3 fmly) CTV in all bedrooms Tea and coffee making facilities Direct dial from bedrooms No dogs (ex guide dogs) Licensed Cen ht Last d 9pm
PRICE GUIDE
ROOMS: s IR£22.50-IR£25; d IR£42-IR£45; wkly b&b IR£140
CARDS: 🔲 💳

Entries in this Guide are based on reports filed by our team of professionally trained, full-time inspectors.

MOATE Co Westmeath Map **01** C4

![Selected banner]

♥ ⬛⬛⬛⬛ Mr & Mrs D Fagan **Temple** *(N267395)*
Horseleap ☎0506 35118 FAX 0506 35118
Mar-1 Dec
A Georgian house with 100 acres, built on the site of an early
monastery, this sympathetically refurbished farmhouse near
the village of Horseleap (midway between Kilbeggan and
Moate and half a mile from the N6) offers accommodation in
very comfortable en suite bedrooms. Dinner - which must be
reserved in advance - is taken round a fine hunting table, then
guests can relax by the sitting room fire and join in chat which
might be about subjects as disparate as the nearby Medieval
site of Clonmacnase or participation in one of the activity
packages (golf, riding, cycling or walking) which can be
arranged here.
4 en suite (bth/shr) (2 fmly) No smoking in dining room No
dogs (ex guide dogs) Licensed Cen ht ch fac P Yoga room
Massage therapy Children's play room 96 acres cattle sheep
Last d 10am
PRICE GUIDE
ROOMS: s IR£30; d IR£45✱
CARDS: ⬛ ⬛

MOUNTRATH Co Laois Map **01** C3

T&C ⬛⬛⬛ **Roundwood House**
☎0502 32120 FAX 0502 32711
Closed 25 Dec
This Palladian villa, in a secluded woodland setting, transports one
back in time to an era of grace and leisure. Excellent hospitality
and good food are offered by hosts Frank and Rosemarie Keenan.
6 en suite (bth) 4 annexe en suite (bth) (2 fmly) No smoking in
bedrooms No dogs (ex guide dogs) Licensed Cen ht ch fac 20P
No coaches Last d 5pm
PRICE GUIDE
ROOMS: s fr IR£41; d fr IR£70
CARDS: ⬛ ⬛ ⬛ ⬛

MOYARD Co Galway Map **01** A4

♥ ⬛⬛⬛ Mrs M O'Toole **Rose Cottage** *(L673565)* Rockfield
☎095 41082
May-Sep
This is a comfortable farm bungalow on the Clifden/Leenane road
(N59), near the new National Park.
6 en suite (2 fmly) Tea and coffee making facilities No
dogs (ex guide dogs) Cen ht CTV 10P 36 acres mixed
PRICE GUIDE
ROOMS: d fr IR£32✱
CARDS: ⬛ ⬛

NAAS Co Kildare Map **01** D4

⬛⬛ ♥ ⬛⬛ Mrs J McLoughlin **Setanta** *(N857230)*
Castlekeely, Caragh (at Caragh Hotel in Naas take Mondello Rd,
Setanta is signposted from this road) ☎045 876481
Mar-Oct
This modern farm bungalow stands in a quiet, peaceful area; from
Naas Town take the Edenderry/Mondells road for 4 miles and the
house is signposted past Canagh village.

5 rms (3 shr) (4 fmly) No smoking in bedrooms No smoking in
dining room Tea and coffee making facilities No dogs (ex guide
dogs) Cen ht CTV 4P 43 acres dry stock Last d noon
PRICE GUIDE
ROOMS: s IR£16; d IR£32

♥ ⬛⬛ M & E Nolan **Westown** *(N921214)* Johnstown (off N7)
☎045 97006
Closed 16 Dec-Jan
Modern two-storey house 0.5m off N7.
5 rms (3 fmly) No dogs Cen ht CTV 9P 92 acres arable mixed
tillage Last d noon

NEWBAWN Co Wexford Map **01** C3

T&C ⬛⬛⬛ **Woodlands House** Carrickbyrne (on N25
Rosslare/New Ross Rd, close to Cedar Lodge Hotel)
☎051 28287 FAX 051 28287
Mar-Nov
Mrs Susan Halpin, the hospitable and charming owner of
Woodlands, is an experienced apiarist and offers guests the
opportunity of seeing the interesting honey-processing tower. The
establishment, which is about twenty miles from Rosslare ferry,
has nearby forest walks, bird watching, horse riding and golf.
4 rms (3 shr) (1 fmly) No smoking in bedrooms No smoking in
dining room CTV in all bedrooms Tea and coffee making
facilities No dogs (ex guide dogs) Cen ht CTV No children 6yrs
8P No coaches Games room
PRICE GUIDE
ROOMS: s IR£15; d IR£28-IR£30✱
CARDS: ⬛ ⬛

NINE MILE HOUSE Co Tipperary Map **01** C3

T&C ⬛⬛ **Grand Inn** (situated on the main Clomnel/Kilkenny
rd, N76) ☎051 647035
This historic, 17th-century historic inn is situated in the scenic
Valley of Slievenamon, on the N76.
5 rms (3 shr) (3 fmly) Cen ht CTV 5P Last d 7pm
PRICE GUIDE
ROOMS: s fr IR£18; d IR£28-IR£32; wkly b&b IR£98-IR£112;
wkly hlf-bd IR£154-IR£168✱

OGONNELLOE Co Clare Map **01** B3

T&C ⬛⬛⬛ **Lantern House** ☎061 923034 & 923123
FAX 061 923139
mid Feb-Oct
Situated overlooking Lough Derg, in a very scenic setting on the
R436 route, this comfortable house offers nicely furnished and
decorated bedrooms, together with a popular restaurant. The well
tended gardens provide a marvellous view of the lake.
6 en suite (shr) (2 fmly) No smoking in bedrooms CTV in all
bedrooms Direct dial from bedrooms No dogs (ex guide dogs)
Licensed Cen ht CTV 25P No coaches Last d 9.30pm
PRICE GUIDE
ROOMS: s IR£20-IR£25; d IR£36-IR£38; wkly b&b IR£119;
wkly hlf-bd IR£224✱
CARDS: ⬛ ⬛ ⬛ ⬛

ORANMORE Co Galway Map **01** B4

T&C ⬛⬛⬛ *Ashbrook House* Dublin Rd ☎091 94196
Closed 22 Dec-1 Jan
Ashbrook House is set in an acre of grounds on the N6 opposite a
yellow water tower, six minutes' drive from Galway. It is
attractively decorated throughout and has cosy, en suite bedrooms
and good car parking.

4 en suite (shr) (4 fmly) No smoking CTV in all bedrooms Tea
and coffee making facilities No dogs (ex guide dogs) Cen ht
CTV 8P

OUGHTERARD Co Galway Map **01** B4

GH Q Q Q **The Boat** The Square (on N59)
☎091 82196 FAX 091 82694
The Boat Inn has recently been refurbished to a very high
standard, with attractive and comfortable bedrooms. Hosts Anne
and Tom Little provide a friendly welcome and are sure to make a
visit a memorable one.
11 en suite (bth/shr) (4 fmly) No smoking in area of dining room
CTV in all bedrooms Tea and coffee making facilities Direct dial
from bedrooms Licensed Cen ht CTV No parking Last d 10pm
PRICE GUIDE
ROOMS: s IR£25-IR£29; d IR£38-IR£46; wkly b&b IR£125-
IR£155; wkly hlf-bd IR£199-IR£239✷
CARDS: 🔳 ■ 🔳 ⃝

T&C Q Q Q **Lakeland Country House** Portacarron (through
Oughterard, pass Gateway Hotel, house on lake shore)
☎091 82121 82146
Closed 20 Dec-3 Jan
9 rms (8 bth/shr) (3 fmly) No smoking in bedrooms No smoking
in dining room Tea and coffee making facilities No dogs
Licensed Cen ht CTV 20P Fishing
PRICE GUIDE
ROOMS: s IR£19-IR£22.50; d IR£33✷

OVENS Co Cork Map **01** B2

T&C Q Q **Milestone** Ballincollig (on N22 west of Ballincollig
on right) ☎021 872562
This large, modern, detached roadside residence enjoys a quiet
and peaceful setting and well-maintained lawns and gardens.
5 en suite (bth/shr) (1 fmly) No smoking in 2 bedrooms No
smoking in dining room No smoking in lounges Tea and coffee
making facilities No dogs Cen ht CTV ch fac 8P Last d noon
PRICE GUIDE
ROOMS: s IR£20-IR£22; d IR£32-IR£36; wkly b&b fr IR£105;
wkly hlf-bd fr IR£175✷

PORTLAOISE Co Laoise Map **01** C3

T&C Q Q **O'Sullivan** 8 Kelly Ville Park (in town centre
600yds from Tourist Office beside town car park) ☎0502 22774
Situated on the outskirts of town, this family-run, two-storey,
semidetached house has a homely atmosphere.
6 en suite (shr) (1 fmly) CTV in all bedrooms No dogs (ex guide
dogs) Cen ht CTV 6P
PRICE GUIDE
ROOMS: s IR£22; d fr IR£33✷
CARDS: 🔳

T&C Q Q **Vicarstown Inn** Vicarstown
☎0502 25189 FAX 0502 25652
Mar-Dec
This 200-year-old roadside village inn, has well appointed
bedrooms and public rooms and is situted on the banks of the
Grand Canal, making it an ideal centre for coarse fishing.
6 rms (2 bth/shr) 3 annexe rms (3 fmly) No smoking in 1
bedrooms No smoking in dining room No dogs (ex guide dogs)
Licensed Cen ht CTV 60P Last d noon
PRICE GUIDE
ROOMS: s IR£20-IR£22.50; d IR£31-IR£35✷
CARDS: ▬

RATHDRUM Co Wicklow Map **01** D3

GH Q Q **Avonbrae House** (200yds on Laragh Road after
leaving village) ☎0404 46198 FAX 0404 46198
31 Mar-12 Nov
This small, exclusively run guesthouse nestles in the Wicklow
Hills amid mountains, rivers and forests. Situated on the
Glendalough road from Rathdrum, it is an ideal touring base, and
walking holidays are a speciality. The Avonbrae has a heated
indoor swimming pool.
7 rms (6 shr) (2 fmly) No smoking in dining room Tea and
coffee making facilities Direct dial from bedrooms Licensed
Cen ht CTV 7P No coaches Indoor swimming pool (heated)
Tennis (grass) Games room Last d noon
PRICE GUIDE
ROOMS: s IR£24-IR£29; d IR£36-IR£46; wkly b&b IR£150;
wkly hlf-bd IR£248✷
CARDS: 🔳 ■ 🔳 ⃝

Selected

T&C Q Q Q Q **Whaley Abbey Country House**
Ballinaclash (between Rathdrum & Aughrim)
☎0404 46529 FAX 0404 46793
Mar-Nov
A fine old country house built in 1760, this was the shooting
lodge of the famous adventurer Buck Whaley. Situated in 200
acres of farm and parkland Whaley Abbey has been
sympathetically restored and offers comfort and hospitality in
beautiful surroundings.
7 en suite (bth/shr) 2 annexe en suite (shr) No dogs (ex guide
dogs) Licensed Cen ht CTV No children 16yrs 50P No
coaches Tennis (hard) Croquet Last d 4pm
PRICE GUIDE
ROOMS: s fr IR£30; d fr IR£50✷
CARDS: 🔳 ■ 🔳

RECESS Co Galway Map **01** A4

♥ Q Q **Terry & Rosie Joyce Glendalough House** (*L835468*)
(signposted 400mtrs off N59) ☎095 34669
Closed May-Sep
This spacious, comfortable bungalow decorated in contemporary
style enjoys superb views of mountains and Glendalough lake
from its setting beside the N59, 20kms from Clifden. Two of the
cosy bedrooms now have en suite facilities and all are provided
with tea/coffee making facilities; guests have a choice of lounges,
one of them with TV. Leisure pursuits include an 18-hole pitch
and putt course in excellent condition and access to mountain
climbing and hill walking. Good private parking is available.
6 rms (2 shr) (2 fmly) No smoking in bedrooms No smoking in
dining room No smoking in 1 lounge Tea and coffee making
facilities No dogs Cen ht CTV 10P Golf 18 100 acres beef
sheep poultry
PRICE GUIDE
ROOMS: d IR£28

ROOSKEY Co Roscommon Map **01** C4

GH Q Q **Mount Carmel** ☎078 38434 38520 FAX 078 38434
This friendly 19th-century house stands in its own grounds beside
the River Shannon. Bedrooms are simply furnished, but equipped
with TVs; two are en suite and one has private use of adjacent
facilities. Public areas comprise a spacious combined lounge and
dining room and a further dining room serving meals to non-
residents. The house has a wine licence and can offer coarse
fishing and cruising.

6 rms (3 shr) No smoking in dining room No smoking in lounges CTV in all bedrooms Tea and coffee making facilities Cen ht CTV ch fac 10P No coaches Fishing Riding Solarium Jacuzzi Massage Holistic healing
PRICE GUIDE
ROOMS: s IR£20; d IR£44; wkly b&b IR£136; wkly hlf-bd IR£206
CARDS: 🖪 ■ ⬛

ROSCREA Co Tipperary Map **01** C3

T&C 🔾🔾🔾 **Cregganbell** Birr Rd ☎0505 21421
4 rms (3 shr) (4 fmly) No smoking 8P
PRICE GUIDE
ROOMS: s IR£18; d IR£29✱

GH 🔾🔾🔾 **Tower Guest House & Restaurant** Church St (On N7 Dublin to Limerick road alongside Round Tower)
☎0505 21774 & 21189 FAX 0505 22425
Closed 25-26 Dec
This comfortable guest house, restaurant and bar is fronted by a smart yellow and green façade. The en suite bedrooms feature locally crafted furniture, attractive decor and a high standard of equipment. The Refectory Restaurant is open for breakfast, lunch and dinner; bar lunches and snacks are available in the West Gable Bar.
10 en suite (bth/shr) (2 fmly) No smoking in area of dining room CTV in all bedrooms Direct dial from bedrooms No dogs (ex guide dogs) Licensed Cen ht 30P Last d 8.45pm
PRICE GUIDE
ROOMS: s IR£20-IR£25; d IR£40-IR£45✱
CARDS: 🖪 ■ ⬛

ROSSLARE HARBOUR Co Wexford Map **01** D2

Selected

GH 🔾🔾🔾🔾 **Churchtown House** Tagoat (take R736 from N25 at Tagoat) ☎053 32555 FAX 053 32555
15 Mar-15 Nov
A charming period house is set in mature grounds on a link road between Rosslare Harbour and Rosslare Strand, just a short distance from the ferry port. Recently refurbished it has spacious, comfortable bedrooms, one of which is suitable for wheelchair users. Dinner is served by arrangement only.
11 en suite (bth/shr) (4 fmly) CTV in 8 bedrooms No dogs (ex guide dogs) Cen ht CTV 16P Last d noon previous day
PRICE GUIDE
ROOMS: s IR£23.50-IR£29.50; d IR£39-IR£71✱
CARDS: 🖪 ⬛

T&C 🔾🔾🔾 **Kilrane House** (on N25 opposite Cullens Pub) ☎053 33135 FAX 053 33739
This period house situated a short distance from Rosslare Harbour in the village of Kilrane, has been restored and all bedrooms now have private bathrooms. There are many original features, open fires and a superb guest lounge. Ample car parking is provided and early breakfasts can be served if required.
(2 fmly) No smoking in dining room CTV in 2 bedrooms Tea and coffee making facilities No dogs (ex guide dogs) Cen ht CTV 10P
PRICE GUIDE
ROOMS: s IR£21-IR£25; d fr IR£32

ROSSNOWLAGH Co Donegal Map **01** B5

T&C 🔾🔾🔾 **Smugglers Creek** ☎072 52366
With probably the best view in Ireland from its hilltop position overlooking Donegal Bay, this delightful inn has been lovingly restored in traditional country style. All the bedrooms are attractive and offer a high standard of comfort; one has a balcony. A bar with superb views serves a wide range of bar food, and the restaurant, open in the evenings, has a good choice of fresh fish.
5 en suite (bth/shr) Direct dial from bedrooms Licensed Cen ht CTV 25P No coaches Last d 9.30pm
CARDS: 🖪 ⬛

SHANAGARRY Co Cork Map **01** C2

Selected

GH 🔾🔾🔾🔾 **Ballymaloe House** ☎021 652531
Telex no 75208 FAX 021 652021
Closed 24-26 Dec
This charming country house stands on a 400-acre farm, part of the old Geraldine Castle estate. Bedrooms are split between the main house and adjacent courtyard buildings such as the 16th-century gatehouse. All of them are comfortable, well furnished and equipped with hairdryers; other facilities include a craft shop and a fine restaurant which uses produce from the farm as the raw material for its dishes.
19 rms (18 bth/shr) 11 annexe en suite (bth/shr) (1 fmly) Direct dial from bedrooms No dogs (ex guide dogs) Licensed Cen ht CTV P Outdoor swimming pool (heated) Golf 7 Tennis (hard) Last d 9pm
CARDS: 🖪 ⬛ 🅓

SKERRIES Co Dublin Map **01** D4

💙 🔾🔾 Mrs M Clinton *Woodview (O220598)* Margaretstown ☎(01) 8491528
This large 1930s farmhouse stands in a quiet location near Ardgillan Park. Most of the rooms have en suite facilities and guests are welcome to join the family in the main lounge.
6 rms (1 shr) (2 fmly) No smoking in dining room CTV in all bedrooms Tea and coffee making facilities Cen ht CTV 8P 5 acres market garden Last d 3pm
CARDS: ⬛

SKIBBEREEN Co Cork Map **01** B2

T&C 🔾🔾🔾 **Fern Lodge** Baltimore Rd ☎028 22327
Feb-Nov
This comfortable modern house stands in its own grounds two kilometres from Skibbereen in West Cork. A range of activities are available in the area including a sailing school, pony trekking, river and sea fishing, walks and ferry trips. The establishment has six attractively furnished en suite bedrooms, a guest lounge and good car parking facilities. Dinner can be provided by arrangement.
6 en suite (bth/shr) No smoking Cen ht CTV 10P
PRICE GUIDE
ROOMS: s fr IR£21; d fr IR£32

T&C 🔾🔾🔾 **Ilenroy House** 10 North St ☎028 22751 & 21711 FAX 028 22552
A three-storey streetside house stands one hundred yards from the main street on the N74 Clonaklity Road. All bedrooms are en suite and equipped to a high standard. This is an excellent base from which to tour South West Cork and the Sherkin Islands.

➠

7 rms (6 bth/shr) (1 fmly) CTV in all bedrooms Tea and coffee making facilities Direct dial from bedrooms No dogs (ex guide dogs) Cen ht CTV P
PRICE GUIDE
ROOMS: s IR£18-IR£20; d IR£36-IR£40✱
CARDS: ⬛ ▪ ▩

SLIGO Co Sligo Map **01** B5

T&C Ⓠ Ⓠ Ⓠ **Aisling** Cairns Hill (approach Sligo on N4 right at 1st set of traffic lights, travelling south from Sligo pass Esso S/Sta turn left at traffic lights) ☎071 60704
Closed 24-28 Dec
A well maintained guest house stands in beautifully tended gardens. Three of the six non-smoking bedrooms are en suite; all have TVs and hair dryers. There is a comfortable combined sitting room/dining room and easy car parking.
6 rms (3 shr) (2 fmly) No smoking No dogs Cen ht CTV No children 6yrs 6P
PRICE GUIDE
ROOMS: s IR£14-IR£16; d IR£28-IR£32✱

T&C Ⓠ Ⓠ Ⓠ **Red Cottage** Donegal Rd ☎071 44283
A friendly establishment with a distinctive red roof stands on the main N15 Donegal road. En suite bedroom all have TVs and tea/coffee making facilities; public areas include a spacious dining room and a split-level lounge with a sunken TV area. Tennis, squash, golf and hill-walking provide an alternative to the local beach.

✸ Ⓠ Ⓠ Mrs E Stuart **Hillside** *(G720394)* Enniskillen Rd (on N16) ☎071 42808
Apr-Oct
Situated in the heart of Yeats Country on the Sligo/Enniskillen road (N16), Hillside offers comfortable accommodation. The pony and donkey will appeal to children.
4 rms (2 shr) (4 fmly) No smoking in bedrooms No smoking in dining room Cen ht CTV 11P 65 acres beef dairy Last d 3pm
PRICE GUIDE
ROOMS: s IR£18-IR£20; d IR£30; wkly b&b IR£90✱
CARDS: ▩

SPIDDAL Co Galway Map **01** B3

T&C Ⓠ Ⓠ **Ard Aoibhinn** Cnocan-Glas (west of Spiddal village on R336 coast road) ☎091 83179
Modern bungalow set back from road in lovely garden. Fine views over Galway Bay and Aran Islands.
6 en suite (3 fmly) No smoking in 3 bedrooms No smoking in area of dining room No smoking in 1 lounge Tea and coffee making facilities Cen ht CTV 6P Last d noon
PRICE GUIDE
ROOMS: s IR£14-IR£16; d IR£28-IR£32; wkly hlf-bd IR£95-IR£110✱
CARDS: ⬛ ▩

T&C Ⓠ Ⓠ Ⓠ **Ardmor Country House** Greenhill ☎091 83145 FAX 091 83596
A luxury, split-level bungalow stands a kilometre from the village, with wonderful views of Galway Bay and the Aran Islands. Attractions include bright, spacious bedrooms, award-winning breakfasts and a relaxing lounge with a well stocked library.
8 en suite (bth/shr) (4 fmly) No smoking in 6 bedrooms No smoking in dining room No smoking in lounges No dogs (ex guide dogs) Cen ht CTV 20P
PRICE GUIDE
ROOMS: s IR£22; d IR£32; wkly b&b IR£105✱
CARDS: ⬛ ▩

T&C Ⓠ Ⓠ Ⓠ **Tuar Beag** Tuar Beag (on R337 west of village) ☎091 83422
Situated five miles west of Spiddal, this large, prominent house incorporates the walls of the thatched cottage where the proprietor grew up. All accommodation is en suite and breakfast is a noteable feature.
6 en suite (shr) (5 fmly) No dogs Cen ht CTV ch fac 20P
PRICE GUIDE
ROOMS: d IR£27-IR£32; wkly b&b IR£95-IR£105

STRADBALLY Co Waterford Map **01** C2

Selected

T&C Ⓠ Ⓠ Ⓠ Ⓠ **Carrigahilla House and Gardens**
Carrighilla ☎051 293127 FAX 051 293127
This unusual building was once a convent and many fine original features remain including heavy wooden doors and wide corridors. These have been renovated and enhanced by modern facilities that have been subtly introduced. The old chapel with its stained glass windows and secret garden is popular with visitors as are the other magnificent gardens. There is also the cheerful Willow room where guests dine (booking is requested), and an elegant sitting room for relaxation. Bedrooms are en suite and are all very comfortable. There is good parking and a sandy beach, a golf course, horse riding and walking are all to be found nearby.
4 en suite (shr) (2 fmly) No smoking in bedrooms No smoking in dining room No smoking in lounges CTV in 2 bedrooms No dogs (ex guide dogs) Licensed Cen ht CTV 15P Over 3 acres of ornamental gardens Last d 7.30pm
PRICE GUIDE
ROOMS: d IR£20-IR£25; wkly b&b IR£140-IR£175; wkly hlf-bd IR£260 IR£300
CARDS: ⬛ ▩

STRAFFAN Co Kildare Map **01** D4

Selected

GH Ⓠ Ⓠ Ⓠ Ⓠ **Barberstown House** Barberstown Cross ☎01 6274007 & 6274018
Closed 21 Dec-5 Jan
This completely refurbished Georgian dwelling standing in three and a half acres of gardens is furnished with antiques throughout; it features tastefully appointed en suite bedrooms complete with power showers, and spacious sitting and dining rooms overlooking the gardens. The house is located 15 miles from Dublin and conveniently near to Geoff's Bloodstock Sales, equestrian centres and a golf course. Good car parking facilities are available.
5 en suite (shr) (2 fmly) No smoking in dining room CTV in all bedrooms Tea and coffee making facilities No dogs Cen ht CTV 15P Tennis (grass)
PRICE GUIDE
ROOMS: s IR£30-IR£40; d fr IR£45✱
CARDS: ⬛ ▩

STREAMSTOWN Co Westmeath Map **01** C4

♥ Q Q Mrs M Maxwell **Woodlands** *(N286426)* Horseleap (from Dublin take N6 and continue through Kilbeggan to Horseleap, turn right at filling station. Farm 2.5m signposted)
☎044 26414
Mar-Oct
Large, attractive house in a sylvan setting off Mullingar/Athlone road.
6 rms (3 bth/shr) (2 fmly) No smoking in 1 lounge Cen ht CTV P 120 acres mixed Last d 5pm
PRICE GUIDE
ROOMS: s fr IR£18; d IR£30-IR£34; wkly b&b fr IR£90; wkly hlf-bd fr IR£165

TAGOAT Co Wexford Map **01** D2

♥ Q Q Mrs E Doyle **Orchard Park** *(T101120)* Rosslare (turn left at Cushens pub in village on to R736) ☎053 32182
This enlarged farm bungalow is in a quiet location, convenient to both the beach and Rosslare car ferry.
8 rms (3 shr) (2 fmly) No smoking in bedrooms No smoking in area of dining room No smoking in 1 lounge CTV 20P Tennis (hard) Fishing Trampoline 80 acres arable Last d noon

TAHILLA Co Kerry Map **01** A2

Selected

GH Q Q Q Q **Tahilla Cove** (just off Ring of Kerry road N70) ☎064 45204 FAX 064 45104
Etr-Oct
Family-run, split-level bungalow in idyllic setting on a sandy cove on Kenmare Bay.
3 en suite (bth/shr) 6 annexe en suite (bth/shr) (4 fmly) No smoking in dining room CTV in all bedrooms Direct dial from bedrooms Licensed Cen ht CTV 20P No coaches Last d 10am
PRICE GUIDE
ROOMS: s IR£33-IR£43; d IR£56-IR£66; wkly hlf-bd IR£280-IR£296
CARDS: 🗴 📷 🗴 ①

THE ROWER Co Kilkenny Map **01** C3

♥ Q Q Mrs J Prendergast **Garranavabby House** *(S708346)* (turn off N79 to R700, proceed for 2m and turn on to R705 for 330metres farmhouse on the right) ☎051 23613
Apr-Sep
A two-storey, old-style farmhouse situated in a scenic setting between Rivers Nore and Barrow.
3 rms (2 fmly) No smoking in bedrooms No smoking in dining room CTV No children 10yrs P 96 acres mixed Last d previous day
PRICE GUIDE
ROOMS: s fr IR£22; d fr IR£36✱

Our inspectors never book in the name of the AA. They disclose their identity only after the bill has been paid.

THOMASTOWN Co Kilkenny Map **01** C3

Selected

T&C Q Q Q Q **Abbey House** Jerpoint Abbey (on the N9 from Dublin directly opposite Jerpoint Abbey)
☎056 24192 FAX 056 24166
Closed 21-30 Dec
This historic house stands on the banks of the Little Argile River and was once part of the Jerpoint Abbey estates. The six en suite bedrooms are well equipped with telephones and radios; tea trays and televisions are available on request. A comfortable sitting room overlooks the river banks, and dinner can be taken by arrangement in a separate dining room. There is trout fishing on the river and golf can be played nearby; the area is also known for its hand crafts.
6 en suite (bth/shr) (3 fmly) No smoking in dining room CTV in 2 bedrooms Direct dial from bedrooms Cen ht CTV ch fac 30P Fishing Last d 9pm
PRICE GUIDE
ROOMS: s IR£18-IR£25; d IR£30-IR£33; wkly b&b fr IR£100; wkly hlf-bd fr IR£210
CARDS: 🗴 📷

TIPPERARY Co Tipperary Map **01** C3

GH Q Q **Ach-na-Sheen** Clonmel Rd ☎062 51298
Closed 23-31 Dec
Large, modern bungalow, five minutes' walk from main street.
➡

Barberstown House

Barberstown Cross,
Straffan, Co. Kildare

AA
QQQQ

Telephone:
00 353 1 6274007
or
00 353 1 6274018

TIPPERARY-WATERFORD

10 rms (5 bth/shr) (2 fmly) No smoking in 8 bedrooms No
smoking in dining room No smoking in 1 lounge Cen ht CTV
10P
PRICE GUIDE
ROOMS: s IR£15-IR£18; d IR£30-IR£32✳
CARDS: 🔳 💳 ⚡ ⓓ

TOBERCURRY Co Sligo Map 01 B4

T&C Q Q Q Cruckawn House Ballymote/Boyle Rd
(signposted on town square) ☎071 85188 FAX 071 85239
Attractively situated next to a golf club - which visitors may use -
on the outskirts of Tubbercurry, and reached by turning into
Ballymote Road from the N17, Cruckawn House offers friendly
hospitality. Five en suite bedrooms are available and there are a
comfortable guest lounge and dining room.
5 en suite (bth/shr) (2 fmly) CTV in all bedrooms Cen ht CTV
8P Golf 9 Tennis (hard) Squash Snooker Sauna Gymnasium
Last d 6pm
PRICE GUIDE
ROOMS: s IR£18-IR£21; d IR£30-IR£32; wkly b&b fr IR£108;
wkly hlf-bd fr IR£185
CARDS: 🔳 ⚡

TRALEE Co Kerry Map 01 A2

T&C Q Q Q Ballingowan House Killarney Rd
☎066 27150 FAX 066 20325
Mar-Nov
4 en suite (shr) (3 fmly) No smoking CTV in all bedrooms Tea
and coffee making facilities No dogs Cen ht CTV 8P
PRICE GUIDE
ROOMS: s IR£21; d IR£32
CARDS: 🔳

T&C Q Cnoc Mhuire Oakpark Rd (on N69) ☎066 26027
Closed Xmas
Modern home on the Listowel road backed by a pleasant park.
Convenient for Shannon car ferry.
4 rms (3 shr) (1 fmly) No smoking in 2 bedrooms No smoking
in area of dining room Tea and coffee making facilities Cen ht
CTV 6P Last d noon
PRICE GUIDE
ROOMS: s IR£15-IR£18; d IR£28-IR£30✳
CARDS: 🔳 💳 ⚡

💙 Q Q Q Mrs H Kerins Heatherville (Q816118) Blennerville
☎066 21054 FAX 066 21054
Mar-Oct
6 en suite (shr) (2 fmly) No smoking CTV in all bedrooms No
dogs Cen ht CTV 8P 40 acres dairy
PRICE GUIDE
ROOMS: d IR£31✳
CARDS: 🔳 ⚡

TRAMORE Co Waterford Map 01 C2

T&C Q Q Rushmere House Branch Rd ☎051 381041
Closed Xmas & New Year
Three-storey, 100-year-old semi-detached house situated on main
road overlooking sea, with well-tended gardens.
6 rms (3 shr) (2 fmly) No smoking in dining room Tea and
coffee making facilities No dogs (ex guide dogs) Cen ht CTV
No parking
PRICE GUIDE
ROOMS: s IR£17.50-IR£19.50; d IR£28-IR£32
CARDS: 🔳 💳 ⚡ ⓓ

T&C Q Q Q Sea View Lodge Seaview Park ☎051 381122
Closed Nov-16 Mar
5 en suite (shr) (2 fmly) No smoking in bedrooms No smoking
in dining room No smoking in 1 lounge CTV in all bedrooms
Tea and coffee making facilities No dogs (ex guide dogs) Cen ht
CTV No children 5yrs 6P
PRICE GUIDE
ROOMS: s fr IR£22; d fr IR£33; wkly b&b fr IR£105✳
CARDS: 🔳 ⚡

TULLAMORE Co Offaly Map 01 C4

T&C Q Q Q Q Pine Lodge Ross, Screggan
☎0506 51927 FAX 0506 51927
Closed 16 Dec-15 Feb
4 en suite (bth/shr) No smoking in bedrooms No smoking in
dining room No dogs (ex guide dogs) Cen ht CTV No
children 12yrs 10P No coaches Indoor swimming pool
(heated) Sauna Solarium Croquet Table tennis Steamroom
PRICE GUIDE
ROOMS: s IR£27; d IR£44; wkly b&b fr IR£140; wkly hlf-
bd fr IR£225✳

WATERFORD Co Waterford Map 01 C2

GH Q Q Q Diamond Hill Diamond Hill, Slieverue
☎051 832855 & 832254 FAX 051 832254
A two-storey house in its own well maintained grounds. Situated
on Waterford/Wexford Road.
10 en suite (bth/shr) (2 fmly) No smoking in 4 bedrooms No
smoking in dining room Tea and coffee making facilities No
dogs (ex guide dogs) Cen ht CTV 20P
PRICE GUIDE
ROOMS: d IR£33-IR£35; wkly b&b fr IR£115✳
CARDS: 🔳 ⚡

T&C Q Q Q Marsuci Country Home Oliver's Hill,
Butlerstown (take N25 towards Cork for 2m to Holy Cross public
house and turn right, signposted. At T junct turn right and house
0.5m on right hand side) ☎051 70429 & 50982 FAX 051 50983
Set in a rural location off the N25 (turn off at the Holy Cross pub),
this attractive stone-built house stands in attractive gardens and
offers comfortable, relaxing accommodation. The pleasant en suite
bedrooms all have telephones and TVs can be suppplied on
request. There is a guest lounge and a separate licensed dining
room serving dinner on request. Country pubs, restaurants, golf
and an equestrian centre can all be found nearby.
6 en suite (bth/shr) (2 fmly) No smoking in 2 bedrooms No
smoking in dining room CTV in 2 bedrooms Tea and coffee
making facilities Direct dial from bedrooms No dogs Licensed
Cen ht CTV 10P No coaches Last d 8.30pm
PRICE GUIDE
ROOMS: s IR£16-IR£20; d IR£32-IR£36✳
CARDS: 🔳 💳 ⚡ ⓓ

T&C Q Q Villa Eildon Belmont Rd, Ferrybank (situated on
N25 2km from Waterford City) ☎051 832174
Jun-Oct
Excellent house situated on New Ross/Waterford road. Beautifully
furnished and decorated with a nice outlook from bedrooms.
4 rms (2 shr) No smoking No dogs Cen ht CTV No children
7yrs 6P No coaches
PRICE GUIDE
ROOMS: d IR£36

642

♥ 🅠🅠 Mrs A Forrest **Ashbourne House** *(S631140)* Slieverue (2.5m E of Waterford, off N25 Waterford/Wexford Rd, signposted) ☎051 832037
Mar-Nov
A comfortable ivy-clad house on the main N25 Waterford/Wexford road. Turn off at the Slieverue sign 2 miles from Waterford. Hospitality is guaranteed from the charming owner Mrs Forrest.
6 en suite (shr) (4 fmly) Tea and coffee making facilities CTV 7P 25 acres beef Last d 2pm
PRICE GUIDE
ROOMS: s IR£20; d IR£32; wkly b&b IR£91✱

WATERVILLE Co Kerry Map **01** A2

T&C 🅠🅠 **Cliffords B & B** Main St (on N70) ☎066 74283
Feb-Oct
6 rms (5 bth/shr) (4 fmly) No smoking in dining room No smoking in 1 lounge No dogs (ex guide dogs) Cen ht CTV 5P
PRICE GUIDE
ROOMS: s IR£14-IR£16; d IR£28-IR£32✱

🔛 ▼ T&C 🅠🅠 **Golf Links View** Murreigh (1km on N side of Waterville village on N70) ☎066 74623 FAX 066 74623
Apr-Oct
A new house stands in developing gardens outside the town. Bedrooms are well appointed and have good views.
4 en suite (bth/shr) (1 fmly) No smoking in bedrooms CTV in all bedrooms Tea and coffee making facilities No dogs (ex guide dogs) Cen ht CTV P Putting green Pitch & put
PRICE GUIDE
ROOMS: s IR£16-IR£19.50; d IR£28-IR£32; wkly b&b IR£95-IR£110; wkly hlf-bd IR£170
CARDS: 🆑 🎫

T&C 🅠🅠🅠 **Klondyke House** New Line Rd (on N70, beside Waterville craft market) ☎066 74119 FAX 066 74666
An attractive house at the western end of the village. Recently extended and refurbished to high standards. A nice sun lounge to the front has views over Waterville Bay. Bedrooms are comfortable with semi-orthopaedic beds and large showers en-suite. Breakfast features an excellent choice including an attractive fruit plate, fresh fruit yoghurts and homebaked breads.
6 en suite (shr) (1 fmly) Tea and coffee making facilities No dogs (ex guide dogs) Cen ht CTV ch fac 10P Tennis (hard)
PRICE GUIDE
ROOMS: s IR£17-IR£21; d IR£26-IR£32✱
CARDS: 🆑 🎫

T&C 🅠🅠🅠 **O'Gradys** Spunkane (off N70 at St Finians Church on northern approach) ☎066 74350
6 en suite (shr) (2 fmly) No smoking in dining room Tea and coffee making facilities No dogs Cen ht CTV P
PRICE GUIDE
ROOMS: s IR£18-IR£20; d IR£28; wkly b&b IR£98✱
CARDS: 🆑 🎫

WESTPORT Co Mayo Map **01** B4

GH 🅠🅠🅠 **Quay West** Quay Rd (on R335 coast road, opposite Westport Woods Hotel) ☎098 27863
6 en suite (shr) (3 fmly) No smoking in bedrooms No smoking in dining room CTV in 1 bedroom No dogs Cen ht CTV No children 3yrs 12P
PRICE GUIDE
ROOMS: s IR£18-IR£25; d IR£32-IR£36; wkly b&b IR£105-IR£112✱
CARDS: 🆑 🎫

♥ 🅠🅠🅠 M O'Malley **Seapoint House** *(L972897)* Kilmeena (signposted on main Westport/Newport road N59, 6km N of Westport turn left and continue straight for 2.5km) ☎098 41254
Apr-Oct
Large and luxurious modern, two-storey farmhouse set in 40 acres on Clew Bay.
6 en suite (bth/shr) (4 fmly) No smoking in bedrooms No smoking in dining room No smoking in lounges CTV in 2 bedrooms Tea and coffee making facilities No dogs Cen ht CTV 8P Sea angling 40 acres mixed Last d 1pm
PRICE GUIDE
ROOMS: d IR£30-IR£32; wkly b&b IR£100-IR£110✱
CARDS: 🆑 🎫 🎫

WEXFORD Co Wexford Map **01** D3

Selected

T&C 🅠🅠🅠🅠 **Ardruagh** Spawell Rd (opposite County Hall on N25) ☎053 23194
Closed 17 Dec-7 Jan
A former Vicarage, this magnificent house on the edge of Wexford looks out over the roofs of houses to the estuary in Wexford. The bedrooms and public rooms are spacious and luxurious and the Corish family take a particular pride in looking after their guests.
5 en suite (shr) (2 fmly) No smoking in dining room CTV in all bedrooms Tea and coffee making facilities No dogs (ex guide dogs) Cen ht CTV 10P No coaches
CARDS: 🆑 🎫

Bansha Castle

Bansha Castle, Bansha, Co. Tipperary, Ireland
Tel: 062-54187 Fax: 062-54294
International: +353-62-54187

Bansha Castle is a lovely old country house, beautifully decorated and featuring large comfortable rooms. It is set in its own private grounds and gardens, with mature trees. Hill-walking, cycling, mountain-climbing, horse riding, fishing, golfing, tennis can all be arranged with ease.
Superb evening meals are available every night. Wine license, full-size snooker/billiards table.
5 miles South of Tipperary Town on the N24.

T&C ⓠⓠⓠ **Auburn House** 2 Auburn Ter, Redmond Rd (opposite railway station) ☎053 23605
Closed 23 Dec-02 Jan
Auburn House is the second in a terrace of three houses near the station and should not be confused with the similarly named house next-door. Bedrooms are attractive and the public rooms are comfortable.
5 rms (4 shr) (4 fmly) No smoking in dining room CTV in all bedrooms Tea and coffee making facilities No dogs (ex guide dogs) Cen ht CTV
PRICE GUIDE
ROOMS: s IR£20; d IR£33✱
CARDS: 🅫 ➿

GH ⓠⓠ **Faythe** Swan View ☎053 22249
Closed 24-27 Dec
This fine old house is centrally situated in a quiet part of the town. A new owner has upgraded the bedrooms which are now very comfortable with new bathrooms. Evening meals are available by arrangement and there is ample car parking.
10 en suite (bth/shr) (4 fmly) CTV in all bedrooms Tea and coffee making facilities Direct dial from bedrooms No dogs (ex guide dogs) Licensed Cen ht CTV No children 6yrs 30P Last d 7.30pm
PRICE GUIDE
ROOMS: s IR£18-IR£20; d IR£32-IR£40; wkly b&b IR£112-IR£133✱
CARDS: 🅫 ➿

T&C ⓠⓠⓠ **Rathaspeck Manor** Rathaspeck (signposted on N25, near Johnstone castle) ☎053 42661 & 45148
May-7 Nov
Standing in its own grounds, which feature an 18-hole par-3 golf course, this 300-year-old restored Georgian country house is situated half a mile from Johnstone Castle. The comfortable, spacious bedrooms are en suite and the public rooms are appointed with period furnishings. Hospitable Mrs Cuddihy will provide dinner by arrangement and the guesthouse holds a wine licence. Good parking is available.
6 en suite (shr) (3 fmly) CTV in all bedrooms Tea and coffee making facilities No dogs Cen ht No children 10yrs 8P Golf 18 Tennis (hard) Last d noon
PRICE GUIDE
ROOMS: d IR£40; wkly b&b IR£130; wkly hlf-bd IR£200✱

Selected

GH ⓠⓠⓠⓠ **Slaney Manor** Ferrycarrig (on N11 400metres W of National Heritage Park) ☎053 20051 & 20144 FAX 053 20510
Closed Dec-Jan
This attractive period manor house stands in 60 acres of woodland overlooking the River Slaney and adjacent to a heritage park. The richly decorated en suite bedrooms are spacious and well equipped with four-poster beds, armchairs, TVs, tea/coffee trays and telephones. The house operates a no-smoking policy and good car parking facilities are available.
8 en suite (bth/shr) (2 fmly) No smoking CTV in all bedrooms Tea and coffee making facilities Direct dial from bedrooms No dogs (ex guide dogs) Lift Cen ht CTV 30P No coaches Last d 3pm
PRICE GUIDE
ROOMS: s IR£37-IR£42; d IR£60-IR£70; wkly b&b IR£189-IR£220; wkly hlf-bd IR£300-IR£332✱
CARDS: 🅫 ➿ ⓪

T&C ⓠⓠⓠ **Tara Villa** Larkins Cross, Barntown (on main Wexford/New Ross route) ☎053 45119 FAX 053 45119
Mar-Nov
Situated on main Wexford/New Ross route (N25) go past the sign for Barntown, continue on main road until a large pink house is reached where a warm welcome awaits the traveller from proprietors Mr and Mrs Whitty.
6 en suite (shr) (3 fmly) No smoking in 1 bedrooms CTV in all bedrooms Tea and coffee making facilities No dogs (ex guide dogs) Licensed Cen ht CTV 10P pool table Last d 8pm
PRICE GUIDE
ROOMS: s IR£25; d IR£32-IR£35✱
CARDS: 🅫 ➿

Selected

💚 ⓠⓠⓠⓠ Mr & Mrs J Hayes **Clonard House** *(T021199)* Clonard Great (signposted on R733/N25 roundabout. Take R733 S for 500mtrs, first road on left and first entrance on left) ☎053 43141 & 47337 FAX 053 43141
Closed Etr-mid Nov
9 en suite (shr) (4 fmly) No smoking in bedrooms No smoking in dining room No smoking in 1 lounge CTV in all bedrooms No dogs (ex guide dogs) Licensed Cen ht CTV 10P 120 acres dairy Last d 6pm
PRICE GUIDE
ROOMS: s IR£22; d IR£34; wkly b&b IR£115; wkly hlf-bd IR£200
CARDS: 🅫 ➿

WICKLOW Co Wicklow Map **01** D3

Selected

GH ⓠⓠⓠⓠ **The Old Rectory Country House & Restaurant** (on R750, 1m S of Rathnew) ☎0404 67048 FAX 0404 69181
Apr-Oct
A charming Victorian rectory has been converted into a very attractive guesthouse on the outskirts of Wicklow town. Paul and Linda Saunders are the hospitable owners, to whom all credit is due for the relaxing atmosphere and the standard of the accommodation. The well equipped bedrooms are all individually styled, with period furniture, while the public rooms have marble fireplaces and high, corniced ceilings. The popular Orangery Restaurant is the showcase for Linda's innovative cooking. It is for these reasons that The Old Rectory has been designated 'Guesthouse of the Year' 1995 for Ireland.
5 en suite (bth/shr) (1 fmly) No smoking in dining room No smoking in 1 lounge CTV in all bedrooms Tea and coffee making facilities Direct dial from bedrooms No dogs Licensed Cen ht 12P No coaches Last d 6pm
PRICE GUIDE
ROOMS: s IR£46-IR£69; d IR£92; wkly b&b IR£242-IR£258; wkly hlf-bd IR£383-IR£409
CARDS: 🅫 ➿ ➿ ⓪

💚 ⓠⓠⓠ Mrs P Klaue **Lissadell House** *(T302925)* Ashtown Ln ☎0404 67458
Mar-Nov
A comfortable two-storey house stands in its own grounds on the outskirts of Wicklow. Bedrooms are neat and well kept; two have en suite facilities and two share a shower room and bathroom.

Other attractions include a guest lounge, a breakfast room and ample parking.
4 rms (1 bth 1 shr) (1 fmly) No smoking in bedrooms No smoking in dining room No dogs (ex guide dogs) Cen ht CTV 285 acres mixed Last d noon
PRICE GUIDE
ROOMS: s IR£19-IR£21; d IR£28-IR£32✱

YOUGHAL Co Cork Map **01** C2

Selected

GH Q Q Q Q **Ahernes** 163 North Main St (on N25)
☎024 92424 FAX 024 93633
Closed 21-31 Dec
Offering accommodation in spacious bedrooms, furnished to the highest standard with antiques and modern facilities, this pleasant guesthouse boasts an award-winning restaurant, well known for its seafood specialities. There is a cosy drawing room provided for guests and parking is available.
10 en suite (bth/shr) No smoking in area of dining room CTV in all bedrooms Direct dial from bedrooms No dogs (ex guide dogs) Licensed Cen ht 10P Last d 9.30pm
PRICE GUIDE
ROOMS: s IR£55-IR£60; d IR£80-IR£100
CARDS: 🔲 🔲 🔲 🔲

♥ Q Mrs E Long **Cherrymount** *(X071823)* ☎024 97110
This 500-year-old farmhouse is situated on high ground off the main N25 road near Youghal. Simple in style, a friendly welcome is offered by owner Mrs Long.
3 rms (1 fmly) Cen ht P 70 acres dairy
PRICE GUIDE
ROOMS: s IR£13; d IR£24; wkly b&b IR£84; wkly hlf-bd IR£126✱

Bed & Breakfast Accommodation offering Leisure Facilities

Many establishments offer a variety of leisure facilities either on site or nearby. These can include tennis, bar billiards, petanque, snooker or riding. Below are lists of Bed & Breakfast establishments with a **Swimming Pool** or with **Fishing** or **Golf** nearby. Enquire from the establishment for further details.

FISHING

The establishments below have fishing available either on the premises or nearby.

ENGLAND

AVON
WESTON-SUPER-MARE
Purn House Farm
01934 812324

BUCKINGHAMSHIRE
DINTON
Wallace Farm
01296 748660
GAYHURST
Mill Farm
01908 611489

CAMBRIDGESHIRE
MAXEY
Abbey House
01778 344642
WISBECH
Stratton Farm
01945 880162

CHESHIRE
CREWE
Clayhanger Hall Farm
01270 583952
WYBUNBURY
Lea Farm
01270 841429

CO DURHAM
DARLINGTON
Clow Beck House
01325 721075

CORNWALL
CONSTANTINE
Trengilly Wartha Inn
01326 340332

BODMIN
Treffry Farm
01208 74405
LAUNCESTON
Lower Dutson Farm
01566 776456
TRURO
Trevispian Vean Farm
01872 79514

CUMBRIA
AMBLESIDE
Drunken Duck Inn
015394 36347
AMBLESIDE
Rydal Lodge Hotel
015394 33208
BRAMPTON
Cracrop Farm
016977 48245
BUTTERMERE
Pickett Howe
01900 85444
HAWKSHEAD
Ivy House
015394 36204
HAWKSHEAD
Kings Arms Hotel
015394 36372
KIRKBY LONSDALE
Cobwebs Country House
015242 72141
KIRKBY THORE
Bridge End Farm
017683 61362

RAVENSTONEDALE
Kings Head
015396 23284
TEBAY
The Cross Keys Inn
015396 24240

TROUTBECK
High Green Lodge
015394 33005
WINDERMERE
Fayrer Garden House
015394 88195
WINDERMERE
Oakthorpe Hotel
015394 43547

DERBYSHIRE
ALFRETON
Oaktree Farm
01773 832957

DEVON
BUCKFASTLEIGH
Dartbridge Manor
01364 643575
BRIDESTOWE
Little Bidlake
01837 861233
CLAWTON
Clawford Vineyard
01409 254177
CLOVELLY
Burnstone Farm
01237 431219
HARTLAND
Fosfelle Guest House
01237 441273
HOLSWORTHY
Leworthy Farm
01409 253488
KINGSBRIDGE
South Allington House
01548 511272
MORETONHAMPSTEAD
Blackaller Hotel & Restaurant
01647 440322
OAKFORD
Newhouse Farm
01398 351347

OTTERY ST MARY
Fluxton Farm Hotel
01404 812818
POUNDSGATE
New Cott Farm
01364 631421
SHILLINGFORD
The Old Mill
01398 331064
TIVERTON
Bridge Guest House
01884 252804
TIVERTON
Lower Collipriest Farm
01884 252321
TOTNES
Steam Packet Inn
01803 863880

DORSET
WEST STOUR
The Ship Inn
01747 838640

EAST SUSSEX
BATTLE
Little Hemingfold Farmhouse
Hotel
01424 774338
PEVENSEY
Napier Guesthouse
01323 768875
UCKFIELD
Sliders Farm
01825 790258

GLOUCESTERSHIRE
CHARFIELD
Huntingford Mill Hotel
01453 843431

GREATER MANCHESTER
ROCHDALE
Leaches Farm
01706 41116

HAMPSHIRE
DIBDEN
Dale Farm Guest House
01703 849632
WOODFALLS
The Woodfalls Inn
01725 513222

HEREFORD & WORCESTER
BROMYARD
Nether Court
01432 820247
RUCKHALL
The Ancient Camp Inn
01981 250449
SYMONDS YAT [EAST]
Garth Cottage Hotel
01600 890364

ISLE OF WIGHT
SEAVIEW
Northbank Hotel
01983 612227

LANCASHIRE
WHITEWELL
The Inn at Whitewell
01200 448222

LEICESTERSHIRE
BRUNTINGTHORPE
Knaptoft House Farm & The
Greenway
0116 247 8388

LINCOLNSHIRE
STAMFORD
The Priory
01780 720215

NORFOLK
BARNEY
The Old Brick Kilns
01328 878305
BLICKLING
Buckinghamshire Arms Hotel
01263 732133
FAKENHAM
Sculthorpe Mill
01328 856161
REEDHAM
Briars
01493 700054

NORTH YORKSHIRE
ACASTER MALBIS
Ship Inn
01904 705609
BOROUGHBRIDGE
The Crown Inn
01423 322578

BURNSALL
Manor House
01756 720231
CLAPHAM
The Flying Horseshoe
01524 251229
HAWNBY
Laskill Farm
01439 798268
HUBY
The New Inn Motel
01347 810219
INGLEBY GREENHOW
Manor House Farm
01642 722384
INGLETON
Springfield Private Hotel
01524 241280
PATRICK BROMPTON
Elmfield House
01677 450558
YORK
Moat Hotel
01904 652926

NORTHUMBERLAND
EMBLETON
Doxford Farmhouse
01665 579235
GREENHEAD
Holmhead Farmhouse
016977 47402
ROCHESTER
Woolaw Farm
01830 520686

SHROPSHIRE
BRIDGNORTH
Severn Arms Hotel
01746 764616
CLUN
Hurst Mill Farm
01588 640224
LUDLOW
Moor Hall
01584 823209
MARKET DRAYTON
Stoke Manor
01630 685222
SHREWSBURY
The Day House
01743 860212

SHREWSBURY
Mytton Hall
01743 850264
WEM
Soulton Hall
01939 232786

SOMERSET
CARY FITZPAINE
Cary Fitzpaine Farm
01458 223250
HENSTRIDGE
Toomer Farm
01963 250237
PAWLETT
Brickyard Farm Guest House
01278 683381
SOMERTON
Church Farm Guest House
01458 272927
WATERROW
Manor Mill
01984 623317

SUFFOLK
HADLEIGH
The Marquis of Cornwallis
01473 822051

STAFFORDSHIRE
STONE
Whitgreave Manor
01785 51767

SUFFOLK
BRANDON
Riverside Lodge
01842 811236
HIGHAM
The Old Vicarage
01206 337248
HITCHAM
Wetherden Hall
01449 740412
NEEDHAM MARKET
Pipps Ford Farm
01449 760208

WARWICKSHIRE
MARTON
Marton Fields Farm
01926 632410

NUNEATON
Leathermill Grange
01827 716094
OXHILL
Nolands Farm
01926 640309
STRATFORD-UPON-AVON
Monk's Barn Farm
01789 293714

WEST MIDLANDS
KNOWLE
Ivy House
01564 770247

WEST SUSSEX
BILLINGSHURST
Old Wharf
01403 784096
LOWER BEEDING
Brookfield Farm Hotel
01403 891568
ROGATE
Trotton Farm
01730 813618

WILTSHIRE
ERLESTOKE
Longwater Park Farm
01380 830095
PEWSEY
Woodbridge Inn
01980 630266
RODBOURNE
Angrove Farm
01666 822982
SALISBURY
Grasmere House
01722 338388

SCOTLAND
BORDERS
INNERLEITHEN
Traquair Arms Hotel
01896 830229
JEDBURGH
Kenmore Bank Hotel
01835 862369

JEDBURGH
Ferniehirst Mill Lodge
01835 863279

ST MARY'S LOCH
Tibbie Shiels Inn
01750 42231

CENTRAL
BRIG O'TURK
Dundarroch Country House
01877 376200
CALLANDER
Arran Lodge
01877 330976
CRIANLARICH
The Lodge House
01838 300276
DENNY
The Topps
01324 822471

DUMFRIES & GALLOWAY
DALBEATTIE
Auchenskeoch Lodge
01387 780277

HIGHLAND
FORT WILLIAM
Distillery House
01397 700103
KYLESKU
Kylesku Hotel
01971 502231
NETHY BRIDGE
Aultmore House
01479 821473
ROGART
Rovie Farm Guesthouse
01408 641209
ULLAPOOL
The Sheiling
01854 612947

LOTHIAN
LINLITHGOW
Woodcockdale Farm
01506 842088

STRATHCLYDE
ABINGTON
Craighead Farm
01864 502356

ARDBRECKNISH
Rockhill Farm
01866 833218

CARRADALE
Dunvalanree Guest House
01583 431226
DERVAIG
Ardbeg House Hotel
01688 4254

TAYSIDE
ARBROATH
Farmhouse Kitchen
01241 860202
FORGANDENNY
Craighall Farm House
01738 812415

WALES
CLWYD
ST ASAPH
Bach-Y-Graig
01745 730627

DYFED
ABERPORTH
Ffynonwen Country Guest House
01239 810312
CARMARTHEN
Cothi Bridge Hotel
01267 290251
CARMARTHEN
Farm Retreats
01267 290799
LITTLE HAVEN
White Gates
01437 781552
LLANDOVERY
Llwyncelyn Guest House
01550 720566
LLANRHYSTUD
Pen-Y-Castell Farm
01974 272622
TREGARON
Neuadd Las Country Guest
House
01974 298905
WHITLAND
Cilpost Farm
01994 240280

GWYNEDD
BALA
Erw Feurig Guest House
01678 530262

BALA
Pen-Y-Bryn
01678 530297
DOLGELLAU
Glyn Farm
01341 422286

POWYS
LLANDRINDOD WELLS
Three Wells
01597 824427
LLANWRTYD WELLS
Lasswade Country House Hotel
01591 610515
PENYBONT
Neuadd Farm
01597 822571

WEST GLAMORGAN
FELINDRE
Coynant Farm
01269 595640

REPUBLIC OF IRELAND
CORK
BANTEER
Clonmeen Lodge
029 56238
FERMOY
Ballyvolane House
025 36349
KANTURK
Assolas Country House
029 50015

GALWAY
KYLEMORE
Kylemore House
095 411443
OUGHTERARD
Lakeland Country House
091 82121

KERRY
KILLARNEY
Crystal Springs
064 33272

KILKENNY
THOMASTOWN
Abbey House
056 24192

ROSCOMMON
ROOSKEY
Mount Carmel
078 38434

WATERFORD
BALLYMACARBRY
Clonanav Farm Guest House
052 36141

CORK
CLONAKILTY
Duvane Farm
023 33129

TIPPERARY
BANSHA
Bansha House
062 54194

WEXFORD
FERNS
Clone House
054 66113
TAGOAT
Orchard Park Farmhouse
053 32182

WICKLOW
LARAGH
Doire Coille
0404 45131

SWIMMING POOLS
Many establishments have swimming
pools, the majority are outdoor but a
number have indoor pools and some
establishments have both.

CHANNEL ISLANDS

JERSEY
GROUVILLE
Lavender Villa Hotel
01534 854937
ST HELIER
Cliff Court Hotel
01534 34919

SARK
SARK
Hotel Petit Champ
01481 832046

ENGLAND

AVON
BATH
Ashley Villa Hotel
01225 421683
BATH
The Lodge Hotel
01225 858467
FARMBOROUGH
Streets Hotel
01761 471452
WESTON-SUPER-MARE
Wychwood Hotel
01934 627793

BERKSHIRE
LAMBOURN
Lodge Down
01672 540304

BUCKINGHAMSHIRE
ASTON CLINTON
West Lodge Hotel
01296 630362
KINGSEY
Foxhill Farm
0184 4291650
MARLOW
Holly Tree House
01628 891110

CAMBRIDGESHIRE
CAMBRIDGE
Old School Hotel & Guest House
01223 861609
WISBECH
Stratton Farm
01945 880162

CORNWALL & ISLES OF SCILLY
BUDE
Cliff Hotel
01288 353110
Court Farm
01288 361494
HELSTON
Nanplough Farm Country House
01326 41088
FOWEY
Carnethic House
01726 833336

LOOE
Coombe Farm Guest House
01503 240223
MEVAGISSEY
Kerryanna Country House
01726 843558
Treleaven Farm House
017268 42413
Tremarne Hotel
017268 42213
NEWQUAY
Arundell Hotel
01637 872481
Kellsboro Hotel
01637 874620
Priory Lodge Hotel
01637 874111
POLMASSICK
Kilbol House Country Hotel
01726 842481
POLPERRO
Lanhael House Guest House
01503 272428
ST BLAZEY
Nanscawen House
01726 814488
ST HILARY
Ennys Farm
01736 740262
ST IVES
Monowai Private Hotel
01736.795733
Tregorran Hotel
01736 795889
ST MARY'S
Carnwethers Country House
01720 422415
SALTASH
The Crooked Inn
017528 48177
TROON
Sea View Farm Guest House
01209 831260
TRURO
Lands Vue
01872 560242
WATERGATE BAY
The Rosemere Hotel
01637 860238

CUMBRIA
LONGTOWN
Bessiestown Farm
012285 77219

KESWICK
Skiddaw Grove Hotel
01768 773324
WINDERMERE
Southview Guest House
01539 442951

DEVON
AVETON GIFFORD
Court Barton Farmhouse
01548 550312
AXMOUTH
Boshill House
01297 553201
BICKINGTON
East Burne Farm
01626 821496
BRIDESTOWE
Week Farm
01837 861221
DODDISCOMBSLEIGH
Whitemoor Farm
016472 52423
HOLNE
Wellpritton Farm
01364 631273
MORCHARD BISHOP
Wigham
01363 877350
MORETONHAMPSTEAD
Gate House
01647 440479
NEWTON ABBOT
Lamorna Hotel
01626 65627
PLYMOUTH
Netton Farm House
01752 873080

TORQUAY
Glenorleigh Hotel
01803 292135
Hotel Concorde
01803 292330
Devon Court Hotel
01803 293603
Barn Hayes Country Hotel
01803 327980
Torbay Rise Hotel
01803 605541
Burley Court Hotel
01803 607879

DORSET
BETTISCOMBE
  Marshwood Manor
  013088 68442
BOURNEMOUTH
  The Boltons Hotel
  01202 751517
PIDDLETRENTHIDE
  Old Bakehouse Hotel
  01300 348305
  The Poachers Inn
  01300 348358
RINGSTEAD
  The Creek
  01305 852251
STURMINSTER NEWTON
  Holebrook Farm
  012588 17348
WEYMOUTH
  Sunningdale Private Hotel
  01305 832179

EAST SUSSEX
HASTINGS & ST LEONARDS
  Bryn-y-Mor
  01424 722744
BATTLE
  Little Hemingfold Farmhouse
  Hotel
  01424 774338
LEWES
  Fairseat House
  01825 722263
RUSHLAKE GREEN
  Great Crouch's
  01435 830145
RYE
  Green Hedges
  01797 222185

UCKFIELD
  Sliders Farm
  01825 790258

ESSEX
CANVEY ISLAND
  Maisonwyck
  012685 10222
FRATING
  Hockley Place
  012062 51703

GLOUCESTERSHIRE
FALFIELD
  Green Farm Guest House
  014542 60319
NORTH NIBLEY
  Burrows Court Hotel
  01453 546230
STOW-ON-THE-WOLD
  Crestow House
  01451 830969

HAMPSHIRE
EMSWORTH
  Jingles Hotel
  012433 73755
HAYLING ISLAND
  Cockle Warren Cottage Hotel
  01705 464961
LYMINGTON
  Our Bench
  01590 673141
STOCKBRIDGE
  Carbery Guest House
  01264 810771

HEREFORD & WORCESTER
BODENHAM
  Maund Court Farm House
  01568 84282

ISLE OF WIGHT
FRESHWATER
  Blenheim House Hotel
  019837 52858
SANDOWN
  Cygnet Hotel
  01983 402930
SHANKLIN
  Culham Lodge Hotel
  01983 862880

KENT
CANTERBURY
  Thanington Hotel
  01227 453227
CANTERBURY
  Ebury Hotel
  01227 768433
HAWKHURST
  Conghurst Farm
  015807 53331
SITTINGBOURNE
  Hempstead House Country Hotel
  01795 428020

WOMENSWOLD
  Woodpeckers Country Hotel
  01227 831319

LEICESTERSHIRE
REDMILE
  Peacock Farm Guest House &
  Restaurant
  01949 842475

LINCOLNSHIRE
SKEGNESS
  Crawford Hotel
  01754 764215

NOTTINGHAMSHIRE
NOTTINGHAM
  Hall Farm House
  01159 663112

NORFOLK
MUNDESLEY
  Manor Hotel
  01263 720309

NORTH YORKSHIRE
WHITBY
  Dunsley Hall
  01947 893437
WHIXLEY
  Princes Lodge
  01423 330168

OXFORDSHIRE
BANBURY
  La Madonette Country Guest
  House
  01295 730212
BRIZE NORTON
  Rookery Farm
  01993 842957
OXFORD
  Conifer Guest House
  01865 63055
  Fallowfields Country House &
  Restaurant
  01865 820416
WITNEY
  Greystones Lodge Hotel
  01993 771898Y

SOMERSET
BEERCROMBE
Frog Street Farm
01823 480430
ROADWATER
Wood Advent Farm
01984 640920
WATERROW
Manor Mill
019846 23317
WEST BAGBOROUGH
Higher House
01823 432996

STAFFORDSHIRE
KINVER
Kinfayre Restaurant
01384 872565
STONE
Whitgreave Manor
01785 51767

SUFFOLK
FRESSINGFIELD
Chippenhall Hall
01379 586733
HIGHAM
The Old Vicarage
01206 337248
HIGHAM
The Bauble
01206 337254
NEEDHAM MARKET
Pipps Ford Farm
01449 760208

SURREY
REDHILL
Ashleigh House Hotel
01737 764763
REIGATE
Cranleigh Hotel
01737 223417

WARWICKSHIRE
LIGHTHORNE
Redlands Farm
01926 651241
STRATFORD-UPON-AVON
The Croft
01789 293419
STUDLEY
Bug In The Blanket
01527 854275

WEST MIDLANDS
BIRMINGHAM
Cape Race Hotel
0121 373 3085

WEST SUSSEX
BEPTON
Park House Hotel
01730 812880
BOSHAM
Kenwood
012435 72727
LOWER BEEDING
Brookfield Farm Hotel
01403 891568
ROGATE
Mizzards Farm
01730 821656
STEYNING
Springwells Hotel
01903 812446
Nash Hotel
01903 814988

WILTSHIRE
BOX
The Hermitage
012257 44187
BRADFORD ON AVON
Widbrook Grange
012258 63173
CALNE
Chilvester Hill House
01249 813981
WEST GRAFTON
Mayfield
01672 810339
SALISBURY
Stratford Lodge
01722 325177
WHITEPARISH
Newton Farmhouse
01794884416

REPUBLIC OF IRELAND
CORK
SHANAGARRY
Ballymaloe House Guest House
021 652531

DUBLIN
LUSK
Carriage House
018 438857

GALWAY
CLIFDEN
Sunnybank House
095 21437

OFFALY
TULLAMORE
Pine Lodge
050 651927

WICKLOW
RATHDRUM
Avonbrae House Guesthouse
040 446198

SCOTLAND
FIFE
CUPAR
Todhall House
01334 656344

WALES
CLWYD
CORWEN
Powys House Estate
01490 412367
RUTHIN
Eyarth Station
01824 703643

DYFED
CARMARTHEN
Cwmtwrch Hotel & Four Seasons
Restaurant
01267 290238
LITTLE HAVEN
White Gates
014377 81552
NEWQUAY
Ty Hen Farm Hotel, Cottages &
Leisure Centre
01545 560346
SAUNDERSFOOT
The Sandy Hill Guest House
01834 813165
STEPASIDE
Bay View Hotel
01834 813417
WHITLAND
Cilpost Farm
01994 240280

GOLF

A number of establishments are close to golf courses, or may even have their own course, and may be able to make special arrangements for their visitors.

ENGLAND

AVON
BATH
Astor House
01225 429134

CORNWALL
BODMIN
Treffry Farm
01208 74405

CUMBRIA
KENDAL
Higher House Farm
015395 61177
WINDERMERE
Green Gables
015394 43886

DEVON
BIDEFORD
The Pines at Eastleigh
01271 860561
TORQUAY
Suite Dreams
01803 313900

DORSET
BOURNEMOUTH
Woodford Court Hotel
01202 764907
Wood Lodge Hotel
01202 290891
SHERBORNE
The Alders
01963 220666

GREATER MANCHESTER
HYDE
Needhams Farm
0161 368

EAST SUSSEX
BRIGHTON
Regency Hotel
01273 202690

GLOUCESTER
LEDBURY
Wall Hills
01531 632833

HAMPSHIRE
LYNDHURST
Whitemoor House Hotel
01703 282186

HEREFORD & WORCESTER
BISHAMPTON
Nightingale Hotel
01386 462521

LINCOLNSHIRE
LINCOLN
Brierley House Hotel
01522 526945

SOMERSET
MINEHEAD
Kildare Lodge
01643 702009

WARWICKSHIRE
STRATFORD-UPON-AVON
Gravelside Barn
01789 750502
LOWER BRAILES
New House Farm
01608 686239

WEST SUSSEX
LOWER BEEDING
Brookfield Farm Hotel
01403 891568

WILTSHIRE
NETTLETON
Fosse Farmhouse Country Hotel
01249 782286
TOLLARD ROYAL
The King John Inn
01725 516207

SCOTLAND
DUMFRIES & GALLOWAY
DALBEATTIE
The Anchor Hotel
01556 620205
LANGHOLM
Langholm Guest House
01387 381343

HIGHLAND
GRANTOWN ON SPEY
Ardlairg
01479 873245

SHETLAND
LERWICK
Glen Orchy House
01595 692031

STRATHCLYDE
CARRADALE
Dunvalanree Guest House
01583 431226
TOBERMORY
Fairways Lodge
01688 302238

TAYSIDE
BLAIRGOWRIE
Duncraggan
01250 872082
COMRIE
Mossgiel
01764 670567

WALES
CLWYD
RUTHIN
Eyarth Station
01824 703643

DYFED
CARMARTHEN
Cwmtwrch Hotel
01267 290238

REPUBLIC OF IRELAND
CORK
SHANAGARRY
Ballymaloe House Guest House
021 652531

GALWAY
RECESS
Glendalough House
095 34669

SLIGO
TOBERCURRY
Cruckawn House
071 85188

WEXFORD
WEXFORD
Rathaspeck Manor
053 42661

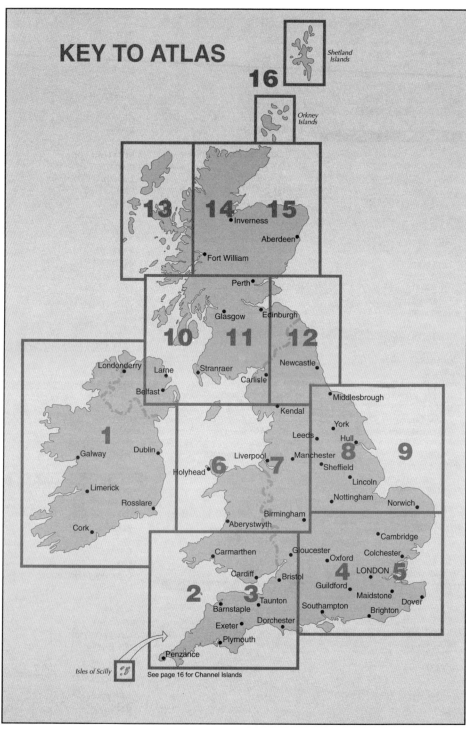

KEY TO ATLAS

Shetland Islands

16

Orkney Islands

13 **14** Inverness **15**

Aberdeen

Fort William

Perth

Glasgow Edinburgh

10 **11** **12**

Londonderry Larne Stranraer Newcastle

Belfast Carlisle Middlesbrough

Kendal

York

Leeds Hull

1 Liverpool Manchester **8** **9**

Galway Dublin **6** **7** Sheffield

Holyhead Lincoln

Limerick Nottingham Norwich

Rosslare Birmingham

Aberystwyth

Cork Cambridge

Carmarthen Gloucester Colchester

Cardiff Oxford

Bristol **4** LONDON **5**

2 **3** Guildford

Taunton Maidstone

Barnstaple Southampton Dover

Exeter Dorchester Brighton

Plymouth

Penzance

Isles of Scilly See page 16 for Channel Islands

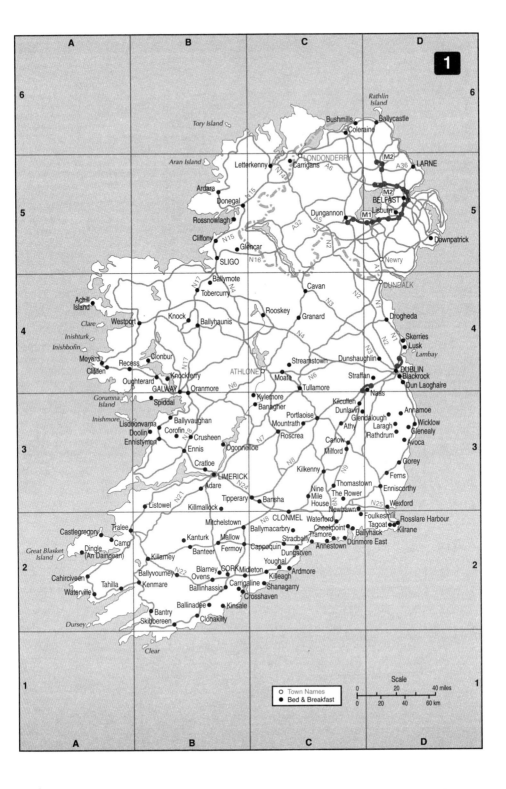

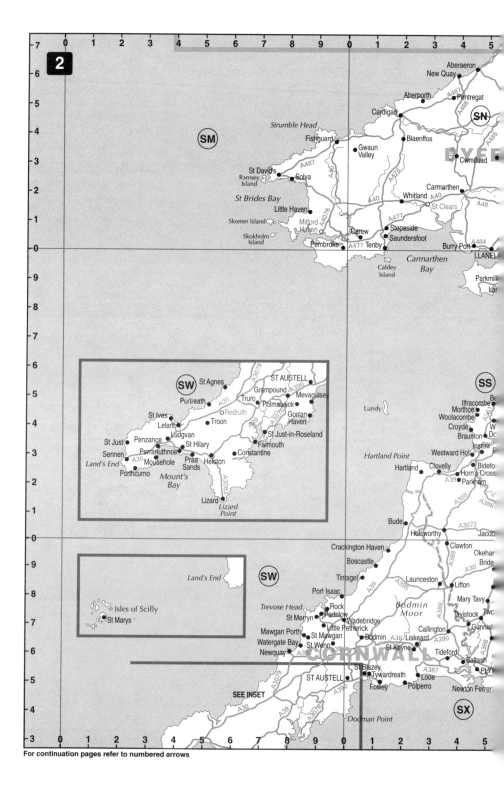

For continuation pages refer to numbered arrows

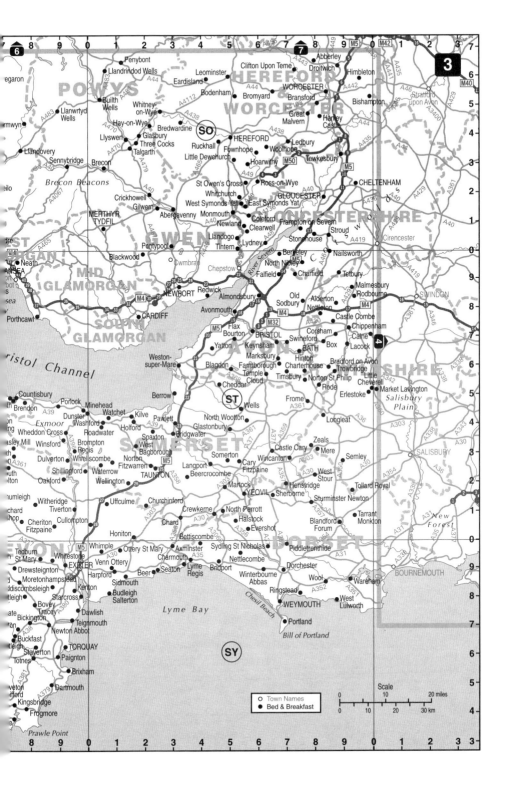

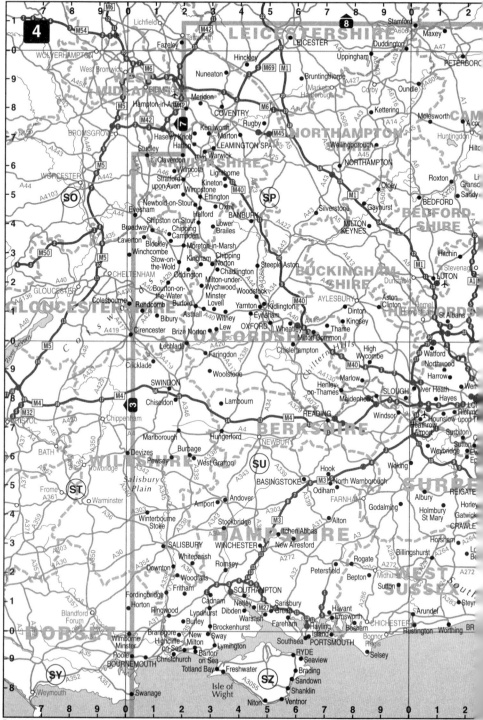

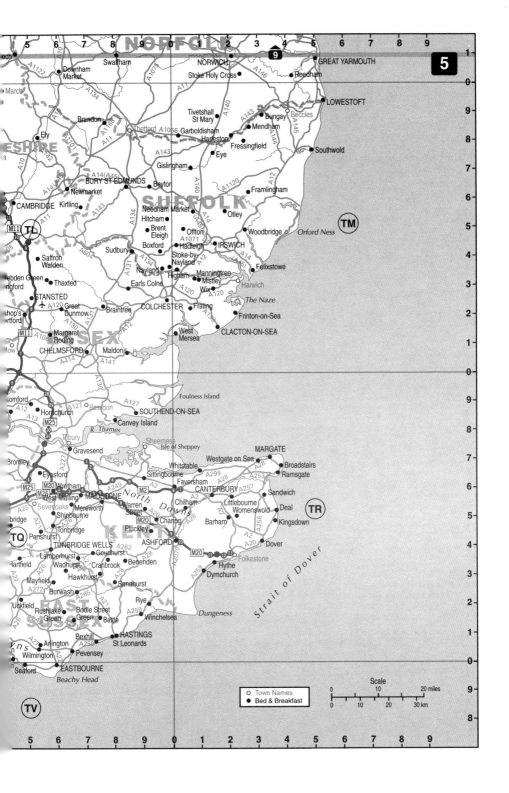

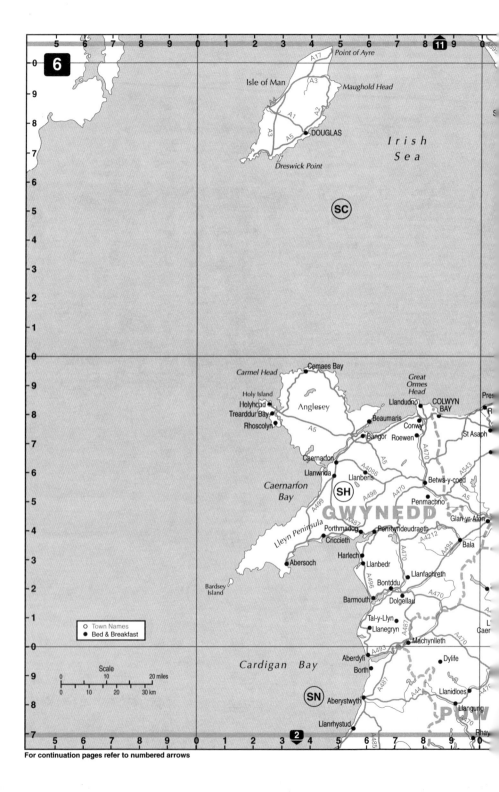

5 6 7 8 9 0 1 2 3 4 5 6 7 8 **11** 9 0

-0
-9
-8
-7
-6
-5
-4
-3
-2
-1
-0
-9
-8
-7
-6
-5
-4
-3
-2
-1
-0
-9
-8
-7

Point of Ayre

A17

Isle of Man

A3

Maughold Head

A4

A1

A2

DOUGLAS

A3   A5

Irish Sea

Dreswick Point

(SC)

Carmel Head

Cemaes Bay

Great Ormes Head

Holy Island

Holyhead

Anglesey

Llandudno

COLWYN BAY

Pres

R

Trearddur Bay

Rhoscolyn

A5

Beaumaris

Conwy

St Asaph

Bangor   Roewen

Caernarfon

A5

A4086

Caernarfon Bay

Llanwnda

Llanberis

Betws-y-coed

A543

(SH)

A498

A470

Penmachno

A5

Glan-yr-Afon

GWYNEDD

Lleyn Peninsula

A499

A487

Porthmadog

Penrhyndeudraeth

A4212

A494

Bala

Criccieth

A470

Abersoch

Harlech

Llanbedr

Llanfachreth

Bardsey Island

A496

Bontddu

A470

Barmouth

Dolgellau

A470

Tal-y-Llyn

L

Caer

Llanegryn

A487

Machynlleth

A470

○	Town Names
●	Bed & Breakfast

Aberdyfi

A493

Dylife

Cardigan Bay

Borth

Scale

0   10   20 miles

0   10   20   30 km

(SN)

A487

A44

Llanidloes

Aberystwyth

Llangurig

P

Llanrhystud

Rhay

5 6 7 8 9 0 1 2 3 **2** 4 5 6 7 8 9 0

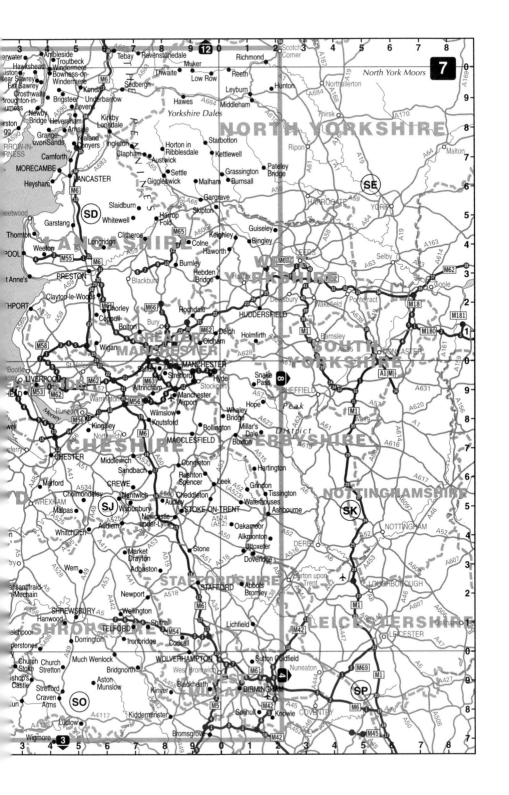

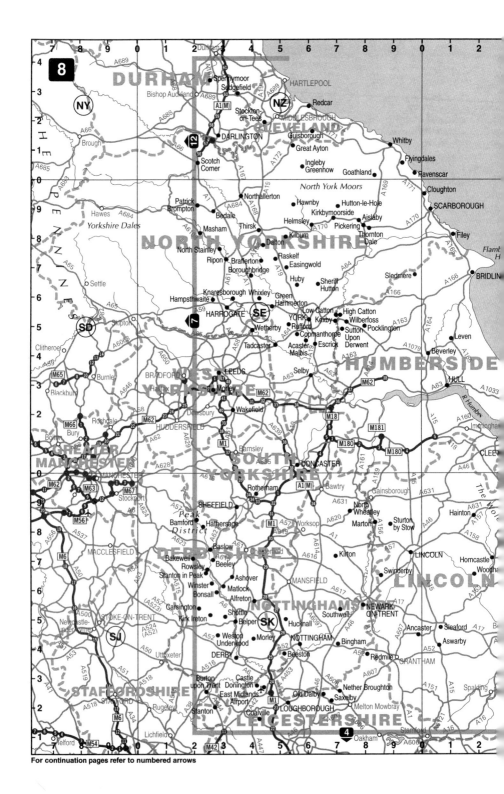

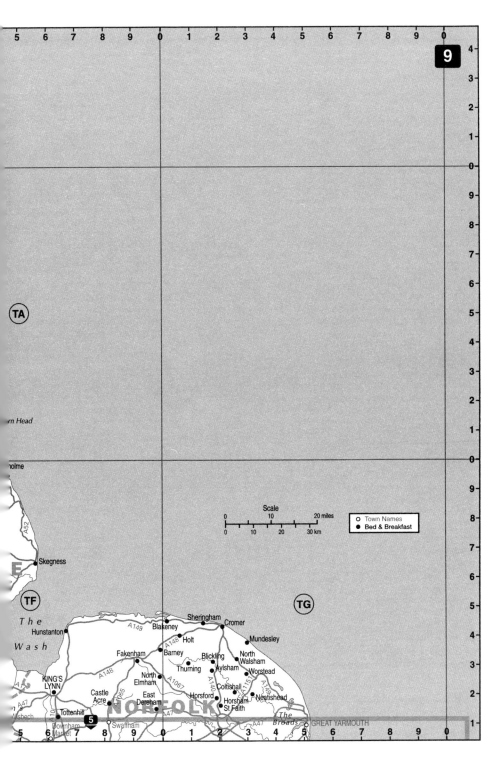

9

TA

rn Head

holme

Scale
0 ____ 10 ____ 20 miles
0 ___ 10 ___ 20 ___ 30 km

○ Town Names
● Bed & Breakfast

Skegness

TF

TG

The
Hunstanton

Wash

A149   Blakeney   Sheringham   Cromer

A148   Holt   Mundesley

Fakenham   Barney   Blickling   North Walsham

Thurning   Aylsham   Worstead

North Elmham   Coltishall   A1151

KING'S LYNN   A1067   Horsford   Neatishead

Castle Acre   East Dereham   Horsham St Faith

A47

NORFOLK

Tottenhill

isbech

Downham Market   5   Swaffham   A47   *The Broads*   GREAT YARMOUTH

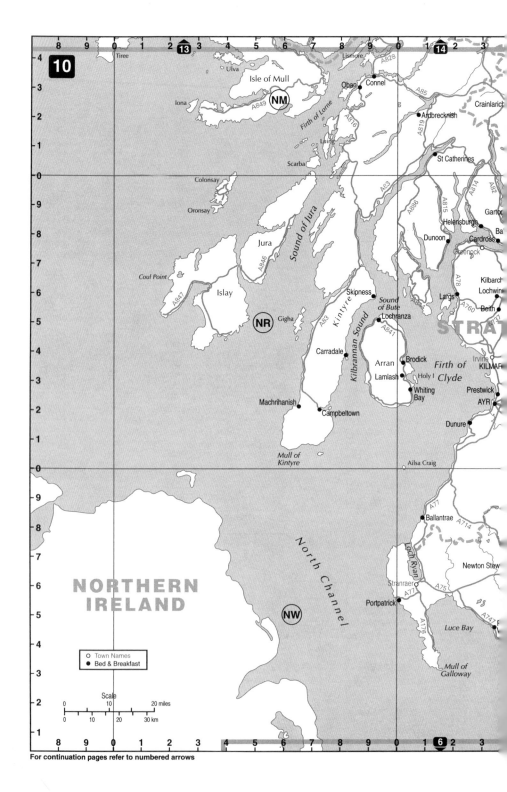

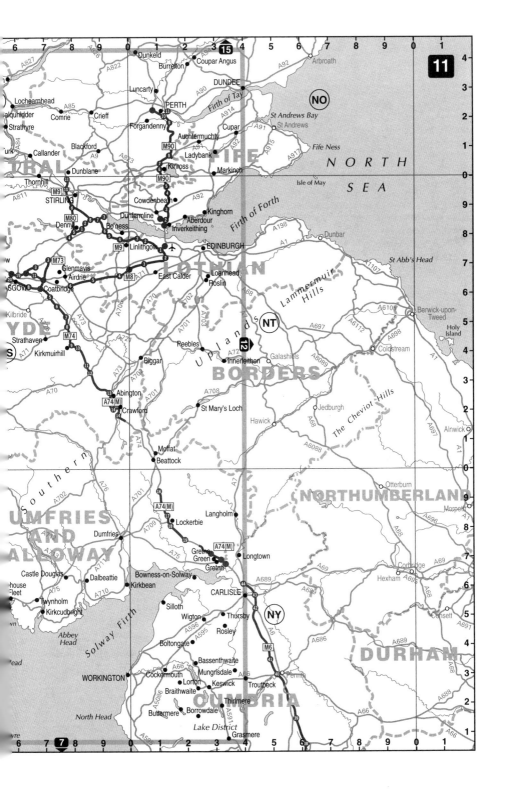

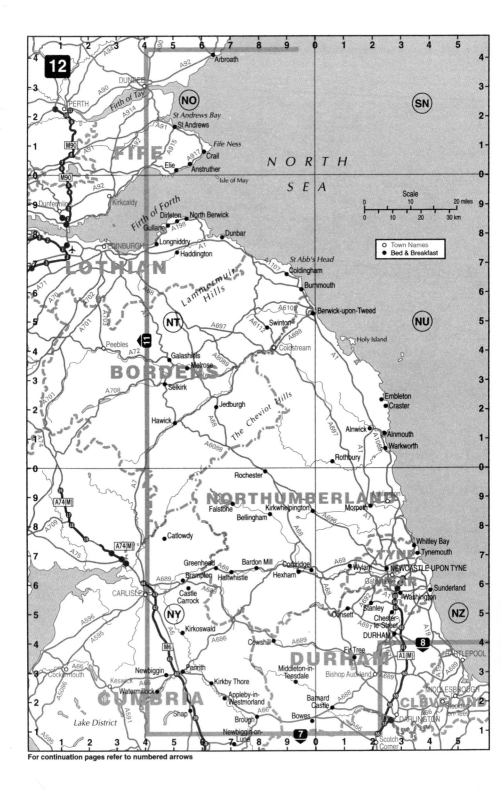

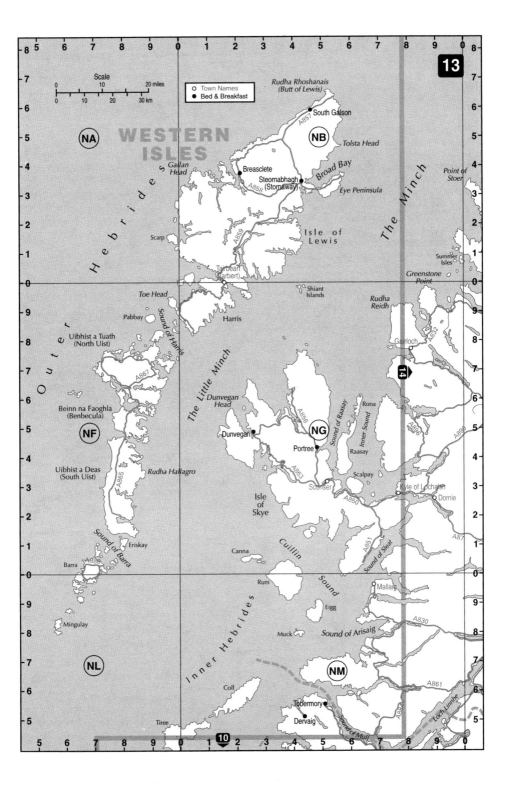

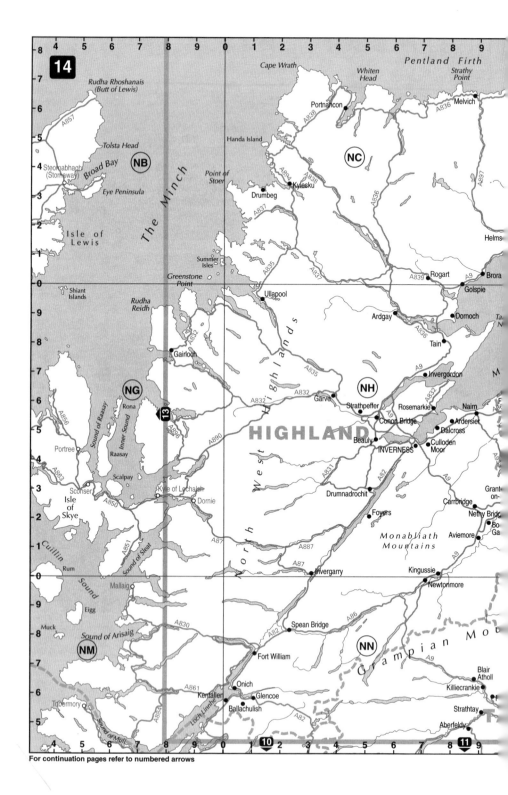

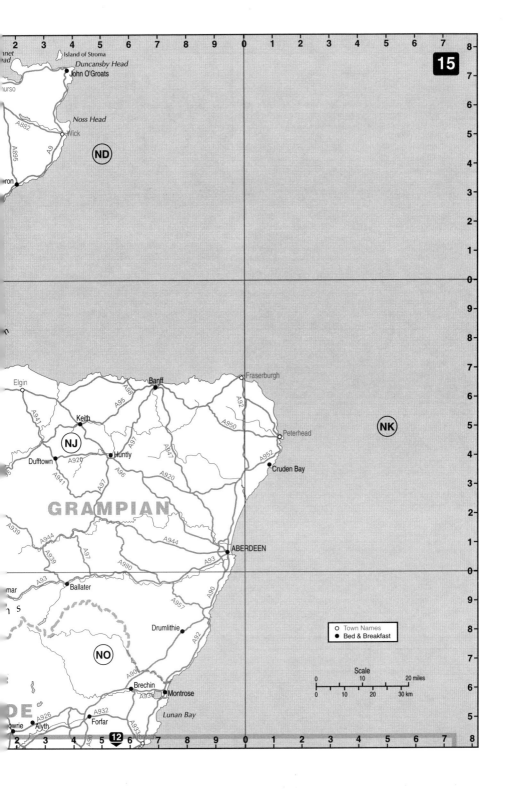

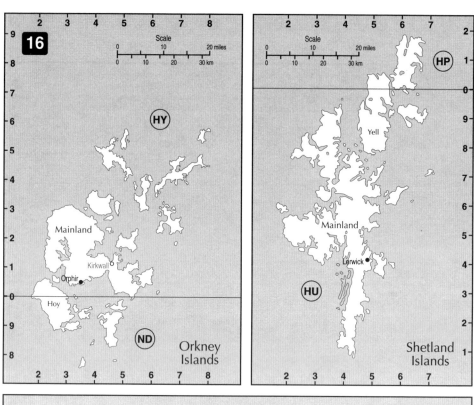
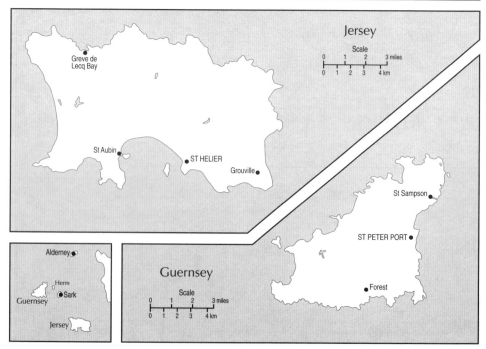

£1 VOUCHER

May be redeemed in accordance with the conditions overleaf at any establishment whose entry displays the £ symbol

£1 VOUCHER

May be redeemed in accordance with the conditions overleaf at any establishment whose entry displays the £ symbol

£1 VOUCHER

May be redeemed in accordance with the conditions overleaf at any establishment whose entry displays the £ symbol

£1 VOUCHER

May be redeemed in accordance with the conditions overleaf at any establishment whose entry displays the £ symbol

£1 VOUCHER

May be redeemed in accordance with the conditions overleaf at any establishment whose entry displays the £ symbol

£1 VOUCHER

May be redeemed in accordance with the conditions overleaf at any establishment whose entry displays the £ symbol

£1 VOUCHER

May be redeemed in accordance with the conditions overleaf at any establishment whose entry displays the £ symbol

£1 VOUCHER

May be redeemed in accordance with the conditions overleaf at any establishment whose entry displays the £ symbol

£1 VOUCHER

May be redeemed in accordance with the conditions overleaf at any establishment whose entry displays the £ symbol

£1 VOUCHER

May be redeemed in accordance with the conditions overleaf at any establishment whose entry displays the £ symbol

CONDITIONS

Voucher and AA Bed and Breakfast 1996 Guide
must be shown on check in. Only one voucher per
person or party per night accepted.
Not redeemable for cash. No change given.
Valid until midnight 31 December 1996.
Only valid against full-tariff accommodation bill.
For full details, see page 9

CONDITIONS

Voucher and AA Bed and Breakfast 1996 Guide
must be shown on check in. Only one voucher per
person or party per night accepted.
Not redeemable for cash. No change given.
Valid until midnight 31 December 1996.
Only valid against full-tariff accommodation bill.
For full details, see page 9

CONDITIONS

Voucher and AA Bed and Breakfast 1996 Guide
must be shown on check in. Only one voucher per
person or party per night accepted.
Not redeemable for cash. No change given.
Valid until midnight 31 December 1996.
Only valid against full-tariff accommodation bill.
For full details, see page 9

CONDITIONS

Voucher and AA Bed and Breakfast 1996 Guide
must be shown on check in. Only one voucher per
person or party per night accepted.
Not redeemable for cash. No change given.
Valid until midnight 31 December 1996.
Only valid against full-tariff accommodation bill.
For full details, see page 9

CONDITIONS

Voucher and AA Bed and Breakfast 1996 Guide
must be shown on check in. Only one voucher per
person or party per night accepted.
Not redeemable for cash. No change given.
Valid until midnight 31 December 1996.
Only valid against full-tariff accommodation bill.
For full details, see page 9

CONDITIONS

Voucher and AA Bed and Breakfast 1996 Guide
must be shown on check in. Only one voucher per
person or party per night accepted.
Not redeemable for cash. No change given.
Valid until midnight 31 December 1996.
Only valid against full-tariff accommodation bill.
For full details, see page 9

CONDITIONS

Voucher and AA Bed and Breakfast 1996 Guide
must be shown on check in. Only one voucher per
person or party per night accepted.
Not redeemable for cash. No change given.
Valid until midnight 31 December 1996.
Only valid against full-tariff accommodation bill.
For full details, see page 9

CONDITIONS

Voucher and AA Bed and Breakfast 1996 Guide
must be shown on check in. Only one voucher per
person or party per night accepted.
Not redeemable for cash. No change given.
Valid until midnight 31 December 1996.
Only valid against full-tariff accommodation bill.
For full details, see page 9

CONDITIONS

Voucher and AA Bed and Breakfast 1996 Guide
must be shown on check in. Only one voucher per
person or party per night accepted.
Not redeemable for cash. No change given.
Valid until midnight 31 December 1996.
Only valid against full-tariff accommodation bill.
For full details, see page 9

CONDITIONS

Voucher and AA Bed and Breakfast 1996 Guide
must be shown on check in. Only one voucher per
person or party per night accepted.
Not redeemable for cash. No change given.
Valid until midnight 31 December 1996.
Only valid against full-tariff accommodation bill.
For full details, see page 9